CNN VIDEO

CNN Video segments bring the "real world" right to your desktop. The accompanying CNN video exercises help to illustrate how finance is an important part of your daily life.

XTRA! QUIZZING

In addition to the open-access chapter-by-chapter quizzes found at the Brigham Web site, Brigham Xtra! offers an opportunity to practice for midterms and finals by taking online quizzes that span multiple chapters.

THE PROBLEM BANK

The Problem Bank: Practice Problems for Financial Management has been revised to fit specifically with this text and contains over 400 multiple-choice finance problems with solutions, divided into seven major categories such as Time Value of Money, Capital Budgeting, Risk and Return, etc. Solving these problems requires the use of a financial calculator (General Calculator Keystrokes also are provided) and is intended to supplement the text's end-of-chapter problems, thereby providing additional practice for students in their preparation of homework assignments and for exams.

The Brigham Xtra! CD also contains spreadsheet models that illustrate how concepts covered in the text are implemented in the real world, giving students a significant advantage in the job market. The models include thorough explanations and serve both as an Excel tutorial and as a template for solving financial problems for each chapter of the book. The CD also includes the PowerPoint slides.

TO USE BRIGHAM XTRA!:

1. Insert the CD into your CD-ROM drive.
2. Select RUN from the start menu.
3. Type D:\start.html (where D is the letter for your CD-ROM drive), then press Enter.

   Internet Connectivity Required for Select Features.

INSTRUCTIONS

FUNDAMENTALS OF FINANCIAL MANAGEMENT

TENTH EDITION

EUGENE F. BRIGHAM
University of Florida

JOEL F. HOUSTON
University of Florida

THOMSON
™
SOUTH-WESTERN

Australia · Canada · Mexico · Singapore · Spain · United Kingdom · United States

THOMSON

SOUTH-WESTERN

Fundamentals of Financial Management, 10e

Eugene F. Brigham and Joel F. Houston

Editor-in-Chief:
Jack W. Calhoun

Vice President/Team Director:
Michael P. Roche

Executive Editor:
Michael R. Reynolds

Developmental Editor:
Elizabeth R. Thomson

Editorial Assistant:
Joe Squance

Senior Marketing Manager:
Charlie Stutesman

Senior Production Editor:
Kara ZumBahlen

Senior Media Technology Editor:
Vicky True

Media Developmental Editor:
John Barans

Senior Media Production Editor:
Mark Sears

Manufacturing Coordinator:
Sandee Milewski

Production House:
Elm Street Publishing Services, Inc.

Compositor:
The Clarinda Company

Printer:
R.R. Donnelley, Willard

Senior Designer:
Chris A. Miller

Cover Illustrator:
Andy Powell, Scott Hull Associates

Photography Manager:
Deanna Ettinger

Photo Researcher:
Terri Miller, E-Visual Communications

Library of Congress Pre-assigned
Control Number: 2002113160

ISBN: 0-324-17829-8 (package, text
and CD)

0-324-17830-1 (text only)

0-324-17831-X (CD only)

ISE ISBN:
0-324-20306-3 (package, text and CD)

The tenth edition continues to offer the most complete and integrated teaching system available.

When *Fundamentals of Financial Management* was first published 25 years ago, our intent was to write an introductory finance text that students would find interesting and could truly understand. *Fundamentals* immediately became the leading undergraduate finance text, and it has maintained that position ever since. Our goal with this tenth edition has been to produce a book and ancillary package that not only maintains its lead but also sets a new standard for finance textbooks. By incorporating the latest developments in the fields of finance, education, and publishing into *Fundamentals* and its related ancillaries, we have made the tenth edition the most clear, complete, and integrated learning package available.

Finance is an exciting, challenging, and ever-changing discipline. New technology and increased globalization are dramatically transforming financial practices and markets. Over the past few years, we have witnessed a dramatic rise and equally dramatic fall in the stock market, along with the collapses of such giants as Enron, WorldCom, and Global Crossing. Investors, regulators, and lawmakers are currently scrutinizing the questionable practices of many leading accounting firms, investment banks, and market analysts. Many of these issues are discussed in this tenth edition of *Fundamentals*, and we explain these events from both a financial and ethical perspective. As the excesses of recent years unwind, it is more important than ever for students to have a solid understanding of basic financial principles.

In developing and improving *Fundamentals*, we tried to convey the excitement and ever-changing nature of finance, and to make students realize its importance and relevance. More often than not, students discover that finance is more interesting and relevant than they had anticipated. Nevertheless, finance remains a challenging subject for many students, and we kept this in mind as we developed the text and its supporting materials. Without sacrificing rigor, we tried to explain each topic as clearly and completely as possible.

One drawback of this approach is that over the years our text has grown ever larger as we added new topics and new features such as spreadsheet presentations, cyberproblems, and boxes that illustrate how the various concepts apply to actual companies. After soliciting the opinions of several instructors and students, we found that many felt that parts of the text should be streamlined to make room for new materials. With this in mind, we took steps to shorten the book and thus make it more readable. In some cases, we shortened the discussion of peripheral topics. In other cases, we moved some of the material to the newly enhanced web site for *Fundamentals*.

We firmly believe that the introductory finance course should be more than just a series of topics—students should understand not only the basic concepts but also how they fit together. With this in mind, *Fundamentals* begins with a discussion of financial objectives, including how managers and investors use financial statements to determine how well a firm is meeting its objectives. We also discuss how incentive compensation, along with the threat of takeovers, can be used to motivate managers and how that can benefit both stockholders and society at large. We also describe early on the financial environment, the trade-off between risk and return, and the time value of money, and we build on these basic concepts to explain how stock and bond prices are determined.

With this background, subsequent chapters explain the financial tools and techniques that are used by managers to help maximize firms' values. Included are capital budgeting techniques, procedures for determining the optimal capital structure, the process firms use to raise capital, and various aspects of working capital management. The final section of the book consists of five chapters that deal with financial forecasting, derivatives and risk management, multinational financial management, hybrid financing vehicles, and mergers.

Our organization has four important advantages:

Four important advantages of the tenth edition's organization.

1. Explaining early on how accounting data are used, how financial markets operate, and how security prices are determined helps students understand how financial management affects stock prices. Also, the early coverage of risk analysis, time value of money, and valuation techniques permits us to use and reinforce those concepts throughout the remainder of the book.

2. Structuring the book around markets and valuation enhances continuity and helps students see how the various topics are related to one another.

3. Most students—even those who do not plan to major in finance—are interested in stock and bond values, rates of return, and the like. Because the ability to learn a topic is a function of individual interest and motivation and because *Fundamentals* covers securities and security markets early, our organization is pedagogically sound.

4. Once the basic concepts have been established, it is easier for students to understand how and why corporations make specific investment and financing decisions and how they develop and execute their working capital policies.

RELATIONSHIP TO OTHER SOUTH-WESTERN BOOKS

The growing body of financial knowledge makes it difficult, if not impossible, to include everything that one might desire in one textbook. This led Gene Brigham to coauthor two other texts that deal with materials that go beyond what can be covered in an introductory course. The first of these books is a comprehensive book aimed primarily at MBAs (*Financial Management: Theory and Practice*, tenth edition, coauthored with Michael C. Ehrhardt). The second is an upper-level undergraduate text (*Intermediate Financial Management*, seventh edition, coauthored with Phillip R. Daves).

Also, some time ago a survey of professors indicated that some preferred a smaller, more streamlined textbook than *Fundamentals*. With that in mind, we created yet another text, *Fundamentals of Financial Management: Concise Fourth Edition*, which is significantly shorter than *Fundamentals*. Most of the *Concise* chapters are quite similar to the corresponding ones in *Fundamentals*, but *Fundamentals* goes further by including additional chapters on capital budgeting, working capital, derivatives and risk management, hybrids, and mergers.

Although *Concise* has been well received, there are two significant advantages to a more complete book such as *Fundamentals*:

1. *Fundamentals* provides professors with more flexibility in designing their courses.
2. *Fundamentals* is a more complete reference book for students after they complete the course. This is important for nonfinance majors, who will not otherwise have access to the materials contained in *Fundamentals* but omitted from *Concise*, and also for finance majors, who need a reference to the omitted materials. In this regard, it should be noted that the chapters in *Fundamentals* are written in a modular, self-contained format that makes it easy for students to read them on their own.

INTENDED MARKET

All chapters are written in a flexible, modular format.

Fundamentals is intended for use in an introductory finance course. The key chapters can be covered in a one-term course but supplemented with cases and perhaps outside readings; the book can also be used for a two-term course. When it is covered in one term, instructors generally assign only selected chapters, leaving the others for students to examine on their own or use for reference purposes in later courses and after graduation. Note also that we made every effort to write all the chapters in a flexible, modular format designed to help instructors cover the material in whatever sequence they choose.

Thomson Analytics — Business School Edition

This is an analytical web-based product that provides seamless access to Thomson Financial content for the purpose of financial analysis.

Thomson Analytics BSE provides data and information on 500 companies and includes most of the same features and functionality found in the full Thomson Analytics product. The 500 companies will encompass entities, spanning from large to small capitalization, from the DJ Global Index. Thomson Analytics — Business School Edition includes the following content sets:

I/B/E/S Consensus Estimates

Includes consensus estimates—averages, means, and medians; analyst-by-analyst earnings coverage; analysts' forecasts based on 15 industry standard measures; current and historic coverage for the selected 500 companies. Current history is five years forward and historic history is from 1976 for U.S companies and 1987 for international companies; current data are updated daily, and historic are updated monthly.

Worldscope

Includes company profiles, financials, and accounting results and market per-share data for the selected 500 companies; annual information and monthly prices going back to 1980, all updated daily.

Disclosure SEC Database

Includes company profiles, annual and quarterly company financials, pricing information, and earnings estimates for selected U.S. and Canadian companies: annually from 1987, quarterly data rolling 10 years, and monthly pricing—all updated weekly.

DataStream Pricing

International Equity and Index pricing provided daily. Provides share price (open, high, low, close, P/E), index and exchange rate data. History is rolling ten years.

ILX Systems Delayed Quotes

Includes 20-minute delayed quotes of equities and indices from U.S. and global tickers covering 130 exchanges in 25 developed countries.

Comtex Real-Time News

Includes current news releases.

SEC Edgar Filings and Global Image Source Filings

Includes regulatory and nonregulatory filings for both corporate and individual entities. Edgar filings are real-time and go back ten years; Image filings are updated daily and go back seven years.

An Ongoing Discussion of Recent Financial Events

The past few years have witnessed great turmoil in the financial markets. We have seen an incredible rise and fall of the stock market and the stunning collapses of Enron, WorldCom, Arthur Andersen, and others. Some of these problems were caused by fraud and by questionable accounting practices, and also by badly designed executive compensation programs. Industry and regulatory groups are working to improve the situation, and in this tenth edition, we discuss these events at relevant spots throughout the text, consider their implications for both investors and corporations, and describe what is being done to improve corporate financial reporting.

Revised Treatment of Financial Statements and Accounting-Related Issues

In the wake of these tumultuous events, we have taken steps to enhance our discussion of financial statements and accounting-related issues. In Chapter 2, we continued our emphasis on cash flow and economic value, and expanded our discussion of the differences between net income, net cash flow, and free cash flow. We also streamlined the discussion of taxes, focusing on the major tax issues facing investors and corporations but leaving many details for the Xtra! CD and a Web Appendix which can be found on the enhanced web site for *Fundamentals*. In Chapter 3, we added a new vignette that discusses the accounting problems with Enron and WorldCom and the lessons we learned from these debacles. We also added a new Industry Practice box that highlights some potential "red flags" investors should consider when they review financial statements.

UPDATED DISCUSSION OF RECENT EVENTS IN THE STOCK AND BOND MARKETS

We updated Chapters 7 and 8 to reflect many of the changes that have occurred in the stock and bond markets since the last edition. We also added a brief discussion of putable bonds, plus information on recent initial public offerings.

REWORKED SECTION ON MARKET EFFICIENCY AND BEHAVIORAL FINANCE

The events surrounding the stock market bubble have led many to reevaluate the efficiency of financial markets, which has generated new academic research in the area of behavioral finance. While most authorities still believe that market efficiency is a cornerstone of finance, it is important to recognize that there are limitations of market efficiency. Consequently, we have added a new discussion about the implications of market efficiency, and we discuss evidence regarding the extent of stock market efficiency. In this section, we also discuss the growing interest in behavioral finance.

NEW XTRA! CD AND WEB APPENDIXES

To make room for important new materials, and also to streamline the book, we moved certain interesting but not critically important material to the Xtra! CD. Also, this same material was placed on the textbook's web site. The Xtra! CD and web site also contain spreadsheet models and other useful information. Much of the information on the Xtra! CD and web site relates to specific chapters,

and when this is the case, it is designated as an Xtra! CD/Web Appendix to the relevant chapter. Finally, note that initially the Xtra! CD and the web site will have virtually identical content, but over time the web site will be updated.

STREAMLINED DISCUSSION OF THE TIME VALUE OF MONEY

We took several steps to increase the readability of this very important chapter. First, because computer and calculator technology have made interest factor tables obsolete for most purposes, we moved the discussion of the tables to the Xtra! CD/Web Appendix. We also moved some of the spreadsheet discussions in the last edition to the Xtra! CD/web site spreadsheet models because our surveys indicated many instructors did not cover this material in the first course, and moving it streamlined the chapter quite a bit. Also, students need to be at a computer to work with spreadsheets, so nothing was lost to those who want to deal with spreadsheets by moving this material to the Xtra! CD/web site. In addition, we streamlined the discussion of multiperiod compounding. We also added several new Self-Test Questions that give students an opportunity to solve a series of quick, focused problems so that they can better gauge their understanding of the material. Finally, because students find it interesting, we expanded and updated the material on personal financial planning issues, including a discussion of partial amortization/balloon loans.

RELOCATION OF CHAPTER ON FINANCIAL FORECASTING

In the last edition of *Fundamentals*, we covered financial forecasting early, in Chapter 4. At the time, we thought this would make it easier for students to see how forecasted cash flows affect stock valuation and capital budgeting analysis. However, this sequence did not work as well in the classroom as we had anticipated, primarily because students needed a broader background before they tackled forecasting. Other instructors expressed similar thoughts. Consequently, we decided to move this chapter back to Chapter 17, where it can be used to summarize and integrate much of the earlier material.

ANALYZING FINANCIAL DECISIONS WITH SPREADSHEETS

Spreadsheet programs are ideally suited for analyzing many financial issues, and a knowledge of spreadsheets is rapidly becoming essential for people in business. Therefore, we "modernized" the book by indicating how spreadsheets are used to deal with the issues discussed in the text.

However, we recognize that students need to understand the basics before they get into computer modeling. Therefore, in the text chapters, we discuss finance concepts, provide examples of the concepts, and explain how the analysis necessary to make optimal financial decisions is done. Where the analysis involves arithmetic, we assume that students are using calculators to do the math. However, if the problem is one that could be solved more efficiently with a computer, we state this and briefly describe how the computer would be used. These explanations are short, easy to follow, and can be skipped without loss of continuity. Thus, students will get an idea of how they could go from calculators to spreadsheets, but they can stop at that point. However, if instructors want to emphasize computers in the course, or if individual students want to learn more about spreadsheets on their own, a spreadsheet ancillary makes that relatively easy.

We developed a spreadsheet model for each chapter in the book except Chapter 1. These models show how the decisions dealt with in the chapter can be analyzed with an *Excel* spreadsheet. Our models include a good bit of explanation, and they were designed to serve both as an *Excel* tutorial and as a template for analyzing the financial issues covered in the particular chapter. Each of these chapter models has been revised for the tenth edition. Also new to the tenth edition, we now provide a spreadsheet model to accompany each of the integrated cases on the Instructor's Resource CD-ROM.

As always, we updated and clarified both the text and the end-of-chapter problems, as well as adding several new problems for most chapters, and we made numerous improvements in the pedagogy. In particular, we updated the real-world examples and pointed out recent developments in the financial environment. We also moved some of the more technical appendixes from the text and placed them in the Xtra! CD/Web Appendix. Finally, we expanded the coverage of certain topics whose importance has increased, and we deleted redundant and less important material to streamline the discussion and improve the flow. Some of the more important changes are noted in the following table:

CONTENTS

- A new "Industry Practice" box discusses socially responsible funds and the fact that some investors are adding social responsibility as a new criterion to their investing goals. Updated "Business Ethics" section to address current accounting scandals.

- Streamlined tax discussion within text; added additional financial analysis web sites in "Technology Matters" box; clarified difference between net cash flow and free cash flow.

- Added a new vignette that discusses accounting scandals and the financial analysis lessons learned from them; streamlined Du Pont discussion; added a new "Industry Practice" box that discusses "red flag" items when looking at a company's financial statements.

- Added a new vignette that discusses how organizations must adapt to changes in the financial environment, regulation, globalization, and technology; updated chapter to reflect current financial environment.

- Updated chapter for recent events in stock market; updated "Industry Practice" box on the market risk premium and its implications for today's market.

- Streamlined discussion to concentrate on solution process, equations, and calculator solutions; updated "Technology Matters" box for financial planning Internet web sites; added discussion of partial amortization/balloon loans.

- Added a new vignette that discusses the risks of the bond market in general, and, more specifically, risk within the current financial environment; added a brief discussion of putable bonds; updated chapter information to reflect today's current financial environment.

- Added a new vignette that discusses stocks' roller coaster ride in recent years; updated recent initial public offering information; added a discussion about the implications of market efficiency and whether the stock market is really efficient (behavioral finance); updated chapter information to reflect today's current financial environment.

- Streamlined chapter to reduce length, clarified sections to improve readability.

- Added a new vignette that illustrates how important the capital budgeting process is to a company's financial and operating performance; streamlined discussion to improve flow of chapter.

- Updated and clarified information presented in the chapter.

- Updated vignette to reflect a recent survey on corporate managers' use and understanding of real option analysis; added a brief discussion of how growth options affect a company's value.

■ Added a new vignette that highlights the difference between a company's market and book debt ratios, and the implications of such differences.

■ Moved a relatively difficult quantitative discussion that illustrated the three dividend theories to the Web, which improved the readability and flow of the chapter; added a discussion of problems encountered in empirical tests of the dividend theories.

■ Added a new vignette discussing working capital management and the implications for inventory levels; positioned the discussion of the cash conversion cycle and concept of zero working capital earlier in the chapter to improve flow; added a new "Industry Practice" box that discusses supply chain management.

■ Changed terminology from "accruals" to "accrued liabilities" to reduce student confusion.

■ Shifted from Chapter 4 to Chapter 17 so that students will be better prepared to deal with the concepts involved. Now, the chapter can be used to summarize and tie together materials covered in earlier chapters. Also, streamlined the chapter to improve information flow and readability; added an illustration on how to calculate growth rates; and provided in an Xtra! CD/Web Appendix a discussion of the differences between arithmetic and geometric averages.

■ Added a new vignette that discusses risk management using derivatives; updated options quotations to reflect decimal pricing; added a new "Industry Practice" box on the accounting treatment of executive stock options; updated chapter information to reflect current financial environment.

■ Updated the discussion of exchange rates and cross currency rates to reflect euro; eliminated fixed monetary system discussion to streamline chapter; updated "Global Perspectives" box on purchasing power parity to reflect euro and recent price information.

■ Added a new "Industry Practice" box on Berkshire Hathaway's convertible security that has a negative coupon to illustrate recent innovations in financial products.

■ Streamlined chapter discussion to improve readability and flow; updated chapter information to reflect current merger environment; revised/updated discussions of "Taxes and the Structure of Takeover Bids" and "Financial Reporting for Mergers" to reflect recent accounting changes.

New! Use your Xtra! CD-ROM to access **Thomson Analytics — Business School Edition.** Students can apply the industry's most reliable financial information to answer discussion questions and work through group projects.

We developed a **Spreadsheet Model** for each chapter in the book except Chapter 1. These models show exactly how the problems dealt with in the chapter can be solved with an *Excel* spreadsheet. In addition, spreadsheet problems that require students to use the spreadsheet model can be found with the end-of-chapter pedagogy. Electronic versions of the models are available on the text's companion web site and are included on the Xtra! CD that is packaged with every copy of the text.

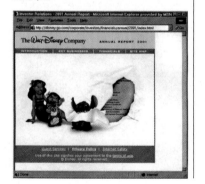

Cyberproblems — These exercises plug students into the Internet, allowing them to hone their web research skills to solve financial problems. Cyberproblems are found on the companion web site for the text at **http://brigham.swlearning.com**. The Cyberproblems were developed by Steven Bouchard and Christopher Buzzard. They have been revised and updated in this edition.

Web addresses are included in each chapter to give students access to additional information about the companies and government agencies discussed in the text. These web addresses will be updated on the text's companion web site, **http://brigham.swlearning.com**.

An excellent site for information on many types of bonds is Bonds Online, which can be found at **http://www.bondsonline.com**. The site has a great deal of information about corporates, municipals, treasuries, and bond funds. It includes free bond searches, through which the user specifies the attributes desired in a bond and then the search returns the publicly traded bonds meeting the criteria. The site also includes a downloadable bond calculator and an excellent glossary of bond terminology.

An enhanced web site with separate resources for students and instructors has updated Web Appendixes, Small Business Boxes, Cyberproblems, and Integrated Case Spreadsheet models. Available at **http://brigham. swlearning.com**.

Each chapter opens with a **vignette** describing how an actual corporation has contended with the issues discussed in the chapter. These vignettes heighten students' interest by pointing out the real-world relevance and applicability of what might otherwise seem to be dry, technical material.

Throughout the book there are **"Industry Practice,"** **"Global Perspectives,"** and **"Technology Matters"** boxes that provide real-world illustrations of how financial concepts are applied in practice.

Throughout the book, key terms are highlighted in the text and defined in the margins. These **marginal glossaries** enable students to quickly find and review the key topics covered in the chapter.

Self-Test Questions, which serve as checkpoints for students to test their understanding, follow each major section of the chapters.

The **end-of-chapter** materials contain a large number of Questions, Self-Test Problems, Starter Problems, Exam-Type Problems, Problems, and Spreadsheet Problems. The problems vary in level of difficulty yet cover all the topics discussed in the chapter. New end-of-chapter problems have been added to this edition.

An **Integrated Case,** which is generally related to the vignette, appears at the end of each chapter. These "mini-cases" both illustrate and tie together the key topics covered in the chapter, hence, provide an ideal platform for lectures that systematically cover the key materials in the chapter. Spreadsheet models that accompany these cases have been developed for instructors and can be found on the companion web site.

THE INSTRUCTIONAL PACKAGE: AN INTEGRATED SYSTEM

Fundamentals now offers an even more innovative, technologically advanced ancillary package to enhance students' learning and to make it easier for instructors to prepare for and conduct classes. The integrated package includes many outstanding resources, all of which have been revised and updated for the new tenth edition.

ESSENTIAL COURSE MANAGEMENT TOOLS FOR THE INSTRUCTOR

- **Spreadsheet Models for Integrated Cases**—These spreadsheet models were designed for instructors to illustrate application of spreadsheets to finance concepts using Integrated Case data.

- **Instructor's Resource CD-ROM**—This innovative instructor's resource system includes electronic versions of the *Instructor's Manual*, *Word Test Bank*, spreadsheet models, solutions to spreadsheet problems, and *PowerPoint* presentations. It is laid out so as to maximize accessibility and minimize search time.

- *Fundamentals of Financial Management* **Online Course**—Delivered via the Web Tutor platform, this integrated web-based learning environment accompanies the textbook and ancillary package with the vast resources of the Internet and the convenience of anytime learning. Extremely user friendly, the powerful customization features of the Web Tutor framework enable instructors to customize this online course to their own unique teaching styles and their students' individual needs. Course features include content keyed to the tenth edition, self-tests and online exams, Internet activities and links to related resources, a suggested course syllabus, student and instructor materials, free technical support for instructors, and much more.

- *Instructor's Manual*—This comprehensive manual contains answers to all text questions and problems, plus detailed solutions to the integrated cases. A computerized version in *Microsoft Word* is also available on the Instructor's Resource CD-ROM and on the text's companion web site. This digital version of the *Instructor's Manual* is available for posting on a secure, instructor's password-protected web site.

- *PowerPoint* **Lecture Presentation**—Prepared in *Microsoft PowerPoint*, this computer graphics slide show covers all the essential issues presented in each chapter. Graphs, tables, lists, and calculations are developed sequentially, much as one might develop them on a blackboard. The new and improved slides are even more crisp, colorful, and professor-friendly. The slides, if used with the student's *Blueprints* supplement, facilitate student note taking. Instructors can, of course, modify or delete our slides, or add some of their own. The PowerPoints can be found on the Xtra! CD, the Instructor's Resource CD-ROM, and the companion web site at **http://brigham.swlearning.com**.

- **Transparencies**—A set of more than 200 transparency acetates is available that is designed to be used with the integrated cases, with the lecture notes from the *Instructor's Manual*, or on a stand-alone basis separate from either of these elements. Designed for maximum flexibility, the transparencies enable instructors to tailor lectures to meet their unique requirements.

- **Test Bank**—This large *Test Bank* contains more than 1,200 class-tested questions and problems and is available both in printed and electronic form. Information regarding the topics, degree of difficulty, and the correct answers, along with complete solutions for all numerical problems, is provided with each question. The *Test Bank* in *Microsoft Word* is also available for download on the text's companion web site.

- **ExamView**—This software has many features that make test preparation, scoring, and grade recording easy. Also, the *ExamView* allows automatic conversion of multiple-choice questions and problems into free-response questions. In addition, questions can be altered to make different versions of a given test, and the software makes it easy to add to or edit the existing test items, or to compile a test that covers specific topics.

- **IMPROVED! Web Site for *Fundamentals*, Tenth Edition**—Designed to be both a teaching and learning tool, the *Fundamentals* web site, at **http://brigham. swlearning.com**, has separate resources for instructors and students. In the instructor's password-protected area, a number of the *Fundamentals* ancillaries can be downloaded, and instructors also have access to Cyberproblems, spreadsheet models that accompany Integrated Cases, NewsWire: Finance in the News articles, chapter-specific finance links, data files for companies featured in opening vignettes, spreadsheet problems, online quizzing, and many more financial resources.

- **Technology Supplement**—The *Technology Supplement* contains tutorials for five commonly used financial calculators, for *Microsoft Excel*, and for *PowerPoint* presentation software. The calculator tutorials cover everything a student needs to know about the calculator to work the problems in the text.

- **Turner Learning/CNN Finance Video with Integration Guide**—Professors can bring the real world into the classroom by using the Turner Learning/CNN Finance Video. This video provides current stories of economic interest. The accompanying integration guide provides a summary and discussion questions for each clip. The video is produced in cooperation with Turner Learning Inc. Contact your South-Western/Thomson Learning sales representative for ordering information.

- **NewsWire: Finance in the News**—Adopters of *Fundamentals* will have access to a password-protected portion of the South-Western Finance web site, where they will be provided with summaries of recent articles in *The Wall Street Journal*, *BusinessWeek*, or other major business publications, along with discussion questions and references to the text. These summaries, written by Emery Trahan and Paul Bolster of Northeastern University, facilitate incorporating late-breaking news into classroom discussions.

SUPERIOR STUDENT ANCILLARY PACKAGE

- **Brigham Xtra! CD-ROM**—Packaged with every new text, the Brigham Xtra! CD-ROM provides students and instructors with complimentary access to the robust set of additional online learning tools found at the Brigham Xtra! Web site. Brigham Xtra! contains
  - **Thomson Analytics—Business School Edition**—Use the Thomson Analytics Academic online database to work a chapter's Thomson Analytics prob-

lems. Thomson Analytics, a product of Thomson Financial's Investment Banking Group, combines a full range of fundamental financials, earnings estimates, market data, and source documents for hundreds of real-world companies. This is your opportunity to access and apply the industry's most reliable information to answer the discussion questions and work through group projects.

- **E-Lectures**—Difficult concepts from each chapter are explained and illustrated via streaming video and animated tutorials. These video clips and tutorials can be extremely helpful review and clarification tools if you have trouble understanding an in-class lecture or if you are more of a visual learner who sometimes has difficulty grasping concepts as they are presented in the text.

- **Introductory Video and Ask the Author Video**—Introductory video pieces, as illustrated by text coauthor Eugene F. Brigham, set the tone for the study of each chapter. These streaming video clips provide context for the forthcoming reading and exercises. Upon finishing a chapter, they may be used as excellent review tools for summarizing key points and major concepts. In the Ask the Author video, difficult concepts and frequently asked questions from each chapter are explained and illustrated by the textbook coauthor, Joel F. Houston. These video clips can be extremely helpful review and clarification tools if you have trouble understanding an in-class lecture or if you are a visual learner.

- **CNN Video**—CNN video segments bring the real world right to your desktop. The accompanying CNN video exercises help to illustrate how finance is an important part of your daily life.

- **Xtra! Quizzing**—In addition to the open-access chapter-by-chapter quizzes found at the Brigham web site, Brigham Xtra! offers an opportunity to practice for midterms and finals by taking online quizzes that span multiple chapters.

- **The Problem Bank**—*The Problem Bank: Practice Problems for Financial Management* has been revised to fit specifically with this text and contains more than 400 multiple-choice finance problems with solutions, divided into seven major categories such as time value of money, capital budgeting, and risk and return. Solving these problems requires the use of a financial calculator (general calculator keystrokes also are provided) and is intended to supplement the text's end-of-chapter problems, thereby providing additional practice for students in their preparation of homework assignments and for exams.

The Brigham Xtra! CD-ROM also contains spreadsheet models that illustrate how concepts covered in the text are implemented in the real world, giving students a significant advantage in the job market. The models include thorough explanations and serve both as an *Excel* tutorial and as a template for solving financial problems for each chapter of the book. The CD-ROM also includes the *PowerPoint* slides.

- **Study Guide**—This supplement lists the key learning objectives for each chapter, outlines the key sections, provides self-test questions, and provides a set of problems similar to those in the text and the *Test Bank*, but with fully worked-out solutions.

- **Blueprints**—This supplement, which is based on the end-of-chapter Integrated Cases and keyed to the *PowerPoint* presentation, was developed (1) to help guide students through the chapter in a systematic manner and (2) to help students listen to lectures and also take good notes. Each chapter of the *Blue-*

prints begins with the case itself and is then followed by copies of each slide, along with space for notes and comments.

- **Finance Interactive**—This supplement is an online interactive tutorial that helps students practice calculations and definitions. *Finance Interactive* provides a chapter-by-chapter review of topics covered in *Fundamentals*, with approximately 500 questions and many straightforward examples.

- **IMPROVED! Student Web Site for *Fundamentals*, Tenth Edition**—This site serves as both a resource and review tool for students taking the introductory finance course. It contains links to relevant finance sites keyed to chapters in the text, and archived news summaries tied to chapters in the text. Students can also test their understanding of material with self-grading chapter quizzes, Cyberproblems, and *Excel* spreadsheet problems. The site can be found at **http://brigham.swlearning.com**.

- **Spreadsheet Books**—South-Western College Publishing has published several books on spreadsheets, including *Financial Analysis with Microsoft Excel*, third edition.

- *Effective Use of a Financial Calculator*—Written by Pamela Hall, this handbook is designed to help increase students' understanding of both finance and financial calculators, enabling them to work problems more quickly and effectively.

- **Finance Online Case Library**—More than 100 cases written by Eugene Brigham and Linda Klein are now available via Thomson in Text Choice. This customized case database allows instructors to select cases and create their own customized casebooks. These cases can be used as supplements to illustrate the various topics covered in the textbook.

ACKNOWLEDGMENTS

This textbook reflects the efforts of a great many people, both those who have worked on *Fundamentals* and our related books over a number of years, as well as those who worked specifically on this tenth edition. First, we would like to thank Dana Aberwald Clark, who worked closely with us at every stage of the revision—her assistance was absolutely invaluable. Second, Christopher Buzzard did an outstanding job helping us develop the *Excel* models, the web site, and the *PowerPoint* presentations.

Our colleagues Lou Gapenski, Andy Naranjo, M. Nimalendran, Jay Ritter, Mike Ryngaert, Craig Tapley, and Carolyn Takeda gave us many useful suggestions regarding the ancillaries and many parts of the book, including the integrated cases. Also, we benefited from the work of Mike Ehrhardt and Phillip Daves of the University of Tennessee, who worked on two companion books. Next, we would like to thank the following professors, who reviewed this edition in detail and provided many useful comments and suggestions: Gary Benesh, Florida State University; Charles Chan, Berkeley College; Brent Dalrymple, University of Central Florida; Morris Danielson, Temple University; Bill Rives, Ohio State University; Travis Sapp, Iowa State University; and Shelton Weeks, Florida Gulf Coast University.

We would also like to thank the following professors, whose reviews and comments on our earlier books have contributed to this edition:

Robert Adams, Mike Adler, Sharif Ahkam, Syed Ahmad, Ed Altman, Bruce Anderson, Ron Anderson, Tom Anderson, John Andrews, Bob Angell, Vince Apilado, Harvey Arbalaez, Kavous Ardalan, Henry Arnold, Bob Aubey, Gil Babcock, Peter Bacon, Kent Baker, Robert Balik, Tom Bankston, Babu Baradwaj, Les Barenbaum, Charles Barngrover, Sam Basu, Greg Bauer, Bill Beedles, Brian Belt, Moshe Ben-Horim, Bill Beranek, Tom Berry, Will Bertin, Scott Besley, Dan Best, Roger Bey, Gilbert W. Bickum, Dalton Bigbee, John Bildersee, Laurence E. Blose, Russ Boisjoly, Bob Boldin, Keith Boles, Michael Bond, Geof Booth, Waldo Born, Rick Boulware, Kenneth Boudreaux, Helen Bowers, Oswald Bowlin, Don Boyd, G. Michael Boyd, Pat Boyer, Joe Brandt, Elizabeth Brannigan, Mary Broske, David T. Brown, Christopher Brown, Kate Brown, Larry Brown, Bill Brueggeman, Paul Bursik, Bill Campsey, Bob Carlson, Severin Carlson, David Cary, Steve Celec, Mary Chaffin, Don Chance, Antony Chang, Susan Chaplinsky, K. C. Chen, Jay Choi, S. K. Choudhary, Lal Chugh, Maclyn Clouse, Bruce Collins, Mitch Conover, Margaret Considine, Phil Cooley, Joe Copeland, David Cordell, Marsha Cornett, M. P. Corrigan, John Cotner, Charles Cox, David Crary, John Crockett, Jr., Roy Crum, Bill Damon, Joel Dauten, Steve Dawson, Sankar De, Fred Dellva, Chad Denson, James Desreumaux, Bodie Dickerson, Bernard Dill, Gregg Dimkoff, Les Dlabay, James D'Mello, Mark Dorfman, Tom Downs, Frank Draper, Gene Drzycimski, Dean Dudley, David Durst, Ed Dyl, Fred J. Ebeid, Daniel Ebels, Richard Edelman, Charles Edwards, U. Elike, John Ellis, George Engler, Suzanne Erickson, Dave Ewert, John Ezzell, L. Franklin Fant, Richard J. Fendler, Michael Ferri, Jim Filkins, John Finnerty, Robert Fiore, Susan Fischer, Peggy Fletcher, Steven Flint, Russ Fogler, Jennifer Frazier, Dan French, Michael Garlington, David Garraty, Sharon Garrison, Jim Garven, Adam Gehr, Jr., Jim Gentry, Wafica Ghoul, Armand Gilinsky, Jr., Philip Glasgo, Rudyard Goode, Raymond Gorman, Walt Goulet, Bernie Grablowsky, Theoharry Grammatikos, Owen Gregory, Ed Grossnickle, John Groth, Alan Grunewald, Manak Gupta, Darryl Gurley, Sam Hadaway, Don Hakala, Gerald Hamsmith, William Hardin, John Harris, Paul Hastings, Bob Haugen, Steve Hawke, Stevenson Hawkey, Del Hawley, Eric M. Haye, Robert Hehre, Kath Henebry, David Heskel, George Hettenhouse, Hans Heymann, Kendall Hill, Roger Hill, Tom Hindelang, Linda Hittle, Ralph Hocking, J. Ronald Hoffmeister, Robert Hollinger, Jim Horrigan, John Houston, John Howe, Keith Howe, Steve Isberg, Jim Jackson, Vahan Janjigian, Narayanan Jayaraman, Zhenhn Jin, Kose John, Craig Johnson, Keith Johnson, Ramon Johnson, Steven Johnson, Ray Jones, Frank Jordan, Manuel Jose, Sally Joyner, Alfred Kahl, Gus Kalogeras, Rajiv Kalra, Ravi Kamath, John Kaminarides, Michael Keenan, Bill Kennedy, Peppi M. Kenny, James Keys, Carol Kiefer, Joe Kiernan, Richard Kish, Robert Kleiman, Erich Knehans, Don Knight, Ladd Kochman, Dorothy Koehl, Jaroslaw Komarynsky, Duncan Kretovich, Harold Krogh, Charles Kroncke, Don Kummer, Robert A. Kunkel, Reinhold Lamb, Joan Lamm, Larry Lang, David Lange, P. Lange, Howard Lanser, Edward Lawrence, Martin Lawrence, Wayne Lee, Jim LePage, David E. LeTourneau, Jules Levine, John Lewis, Jason Lin, Chuck Linke, Bill Lloyd, Susan Long, Judy Maese, Bob Magee, Ileen Malitz, Bob Malko, Phil Malone, Abbas Mamoozadeh, Terry Maness, Chris Manning, Surendra Mansinghka, Timothy Manuel, Brian Maris, Terry Martell, David Martin, D. J. Masson, John Mathys, Ralph May, John McAlhany, Andy McCollough, Ambrose McCoy, Thomas McCue, Bill McDaniel, John McDowell, Charles McKinney, Robyn McLaughlin, James McNulty, Jeanette Medewitz-Diamond, Jamshid Mehran, Larry Merville, Rick Meyer, Jim Millar, Ed Miller, John Miller, John Mitchell, Carol Moerdyk, Bob Moore, Scott Moore, Barry Morris, Gene Morris, Dianne R. Morrison, Chris Muscarella, David Nachman, Tim Nantell, Don Nast, Edward Nelling, Bill Nelson, Bob Nelson, William Nelson, Bob Niendorf, Bruce Niendorf, Ben Nonnally, Jr., Tom O'Brien, William O'Connell, Dennis O'Connor, John O'Donnell, Jim Olsen, Robert Olsen, Dean Olson, Jim Pappas, Stephen Parrish, Helen Pawlowski, Barron Peake, Michael Pescow, Glenn Petry, Jim Pettijohn, Rich Pettit, Dick Pettway, Aaron Phillips, Hugo Phillips, H. R. Pickett, John Pinkerton, Gerald Pogue, Eugene Poindexter, R. Potter, Franklin Potts, R. Powell, Dianna Preece, Chris Prestopino, John Primus, Jerry Prock, Howard Puckett, Herbert Quigley, George Racette, Bob Radcliffe, Allen Rappaport, Bill Rentz, Ken Riener, Charles Rini, John Ritchie, Pietra Rivoli, Antonio Rodriguez, James Rosenfeld, Stuart Rosenstein, E. N. Roussakis, Dexter Rowell, Marjorie Rubash, Bob Ryan, Jim Sachlis, Abdul Sadik, Thomas Scampini, Kevin Scanlon, Frederick Schadeler, Patricia L. Schaeff, David Schalow, Mary Jane Scheuer, David Schirm, Robert Schwebach, Carol Schweser, John Settle, Alan Severn, James Sfiridis, Sol Shalit, Frederic Shipley, Dilip Shome, Ron Shrieves, Neil Sicherman, J. B. Silvers, Clay Singleton, Joe Sinkey, Stacy Sirmans, Jaye Smith, Patricia Smith, Patricia Matisz Smith, Don Sorensen, David Speairs, Ken Stanley, Ed Stendardi, Alan Stephens, Don Stevens, Jerry Stevens, Glen Strasburg, David Suk, Katherine Sullivan, Timothy Sullivan, Philip Swensen, Bruce Swenson, Ernest Swift, Paul Swink, Eugene Swinnerton, Gary Tallman, Dular Talukdar, Dennis Tanner, Craig Tapley, Russ Taussig, Richard Teweles, Ted Teweles, Madeline Thimmes, Francis D. Thomas, Andrew Thompson, John Thompson, Arlene Thurman, Dogan Tirtirogu, Janet Todd, Holland J. Toles, William Tozer, Emery Trahan, George Trivoli, George Tsetsekos, David Upton, Howard Van Auken, Pretorious Van den Dool, Pieter Vandenberg, Paul Vanderheiden, David Vang, JoAnn Vaughan, Jim Verbrugge, Patrick Vincent, Steve Vinson, Susan Visscher, John Wachowicz, Joe Walker, Mike Walker, Sam Weaver, Marsha Weber, Al Webster, Kuo-Chiang Wei, Bill Welch, Fred Weston, Richard Whiston, Norm Williams, Tony Wingler, Ed Wolfe, Criss Woodruff, Don Woods, Robert Wyatt, Steve Wyatt, Michael Yonan, John Zietlow, Dennis Zocco, and Kent Zumwalt.

Special thanks are due to Chris Barry, Texas Christian University, and Shirley Love, Idaho State University, who wrote many of the boxes relating to small-business issues that are on the web; to Steven Bouchard, Goldey Beacom College, who helped develop the cyberproblems; to Emery Trahan and Paul Bolster, Northeastern University, who developed and wrote the summaries and questions for NewsWire; to Dilip Shome, Virginia Polytechnic Institute, who helped greatly with the capital structure chapter; to Dave Brown and Mike Ryngaert, University of Florida, who helped us with the bankruptcy and merger material; to Roy Crum, Andy Naranjo, and Subu Venkataraman, who worked with us on the international materials; to Scott Below, East Carolina University, who developed the web site information and references; to Laurie and Stan Eakins of East Carolina, who developed the materials on *Excel* for the *Technology Supplement*; and to Larry Wolken, Texas A&M University, who offered his hard work and advice for the development of the *Lecture Presentation Software*. Susan Whitman typed and helped proof the various manuscripts. Finally, the South-Western and Elm Street Publishing Services staffs, especially Sue Nodine, Mike Reynolds, Charlie Stutesman, Elizabeth Thomson, Vicky True, John Barans, and Mark Sears, helped greatly with all phases of the textbook's development and production.

ERRORS IN THE TEXTBOOK

At this point, most authors make a statement like this: "We appreciate all the help we received from the people listed above, but any remaining errors are, of course, our own responsibility." And generally there are more than enough remaining errors! Having experienced difficulties with errors ourselves, both as students and instructors, we resolved to avoid this problem in *Fundamentals*. As a result of our detection procedures, we are convinced that this book is relatively free of significant errors, meaning those that either confuse or distract readers.

Partly because of our confidence that few such errors remain, but primarily because we want very much to detect any errors that may have slipped by to correct them in subsequent printings, we decided to offer a reward of $10 per error to the first person who reports it to us. For purpose of this reward, errors are defined as misspelled words, non-rounding numerical errors, incorrect statements, and any other error that inhibits comprehension. Typesetting problems such as irregular spacing and differences of opinion regarding grammatical or punctuation conventions do not qualify for this reward. Given the ever-changing nature of the World Wide Web, changes in web addresses also do not qualify as errors, although we would like to learn about them. Finally, any qualifying error that has follow-through effects is counted as two errors only. Please report any errors to Joel Houston either through e-mail at **http://fundamentals@joelhouston.com** or by regular mail at the address below.

CONCLUSION

Finance is, in a real sense, the cornerstone of the enterprise system—good financial management is vitally important to the economic health of business firms, hence, to the nation and the world. Because of its importance, finance should be widely and thoroughly understood, but this is easier said than done. The field is relatively complex, and it is undergoing constant change in response to shifts in economic conditions. All of this makes finance stimulating and exciting, but also challenging and sometimes perplexing. We sincerely hope that this tenth edition of *Fundamentals* will meet its own challenge by contributing to a better understanding of our financial system.

EUGENE F. BRIGHAM
JOEL F. HOUSTON
4723 N.W. 53rd Ave., Suite A
Gainesville, Florida 32606-4399

January 2003

BRIEF CONTENTS

CONTENTS

Chapter 10   The Basics of Capital Budgeting   388

Chapter 11   Cash Flow Estimation and Risk Analysis   422

Chapter 12   Other Topics in Capital Budgeting   452

Additional Web Materials

Cyberproblems

Small Business Boxes

Additional Problems

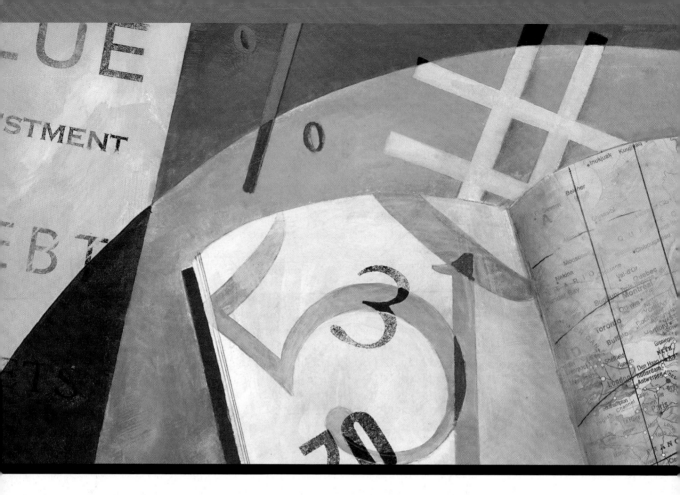

PART 1

INTRODUCTION TO FINANCIAL MANAGEMENT

AN OVERVIEW OF FINANCIAL MANAGEMENT

1

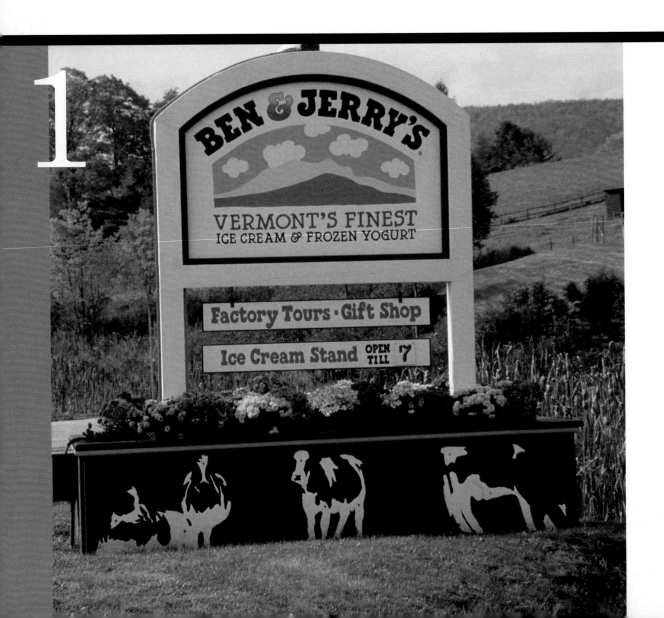

STRIKING THE RIGHT BALANCE

BEN & JERRY'S

For many companies, the decision would have been an easy "yes." However, Ben & Jerry's Homemade Inc. has always taken pride in doing things differently. Its profits had been declining, but in 1995 the company was offered an opportunity to sell its premium ice cream in the lucrative Japanese market. However, Ben & Jerry's turned down the business because the Japanese firm that would have distributed their product had failed to develop a reputation for promoting social causes! Robert Holland Jr., Ben & Jerry's CEO at the time, commented that, "The only reason to take the opportunity was to make money." Clearly, Holland, who resigned from the company in late 1996, thought there was more to running a business than just making money.

The company's cofounders, Ben Cohen and Jerry Greenfield, opened the first Ben & Jerry's ice cream shop in 1978 in a vacant Vermont gas station with just $12,000 of capital plus a commitment to run the business in a manner consistent with their underlying values. Even though it is more expensive, the company only buys milk and cream from small local farms in Vermont. In addition, 7.5 percent of the company's before-tax income is donated to charity, and each of the company's employees receives three free pints of ice cream each day.

Many argue that Ben & Jerry's philosophy and commitment to social causes compromises its ability to make money. For example, in a recent article in *Fortune* magazine, Alex Taylor III commented that, "Operating a business is tough enough. Once you add social goals to the demands of serving customers, making a profit, and returning value to shareholders, you tie yourself up in knots."

Ben & Jerry's financial performance has had its ups and downs. While the company's stock grew by leaps and bounds through the early 1990s, problems began to arise in 1993. These problems included increased competition in the premium ice cream market, along with a leveling off of sales in that market, plus their own inefficiencies and sloppy, haphazard product development strategy.

The company lost money for the first time in 1994, and as a result, Ben Cohen stepped down as CEO. Bob Holland, a former consultant for McKinsey & Co. with a reputation as a turnaround specialist, was tapped as Cohen's replacement. The company's stock price rebounded in 1995, as the market responded positively to the steps made by Holland to right the company. The stock price, however, floundered toward the end of 1996, following Holland's resignation.

Over the last few years, Ben & Jerry's has had a new resurgence. Holland's replacement, Perry Odak, did a number of things to improve the company's financial performance and its reputation among Wall Street's analysts and institutional investors. Odak quickly brought in a new management team to rework the company's production and sales operations, and he aggressively opened new stores and franchises both in the United States and abroad.

In April 2000, Ben & Jerry's took a more dramatic step to benefit its shareholders. It agreed to be acquired by Unilever, a large Anglo-Dutch conglomerate that owns a host of major brands including Dove Soap, Lipton Tea, and Breyers Ice Cream. Unilever agreed to pay $43.60 for each share of Ben & Jerry's stock — a 66 percent increase over the price the stock traded at just before takeover rumors first surfaced in December 1999. The total price tag for Ben & Jerry's was $326 million.

While the deal clearly benefited Ben & Jerry's shareholders, some investors believe that the company "sold out" and abandoned its original mission. To address these concerns, Unilever allowed Ben & Jerry's to retain its Vermont headquarters, and the company agreed to make several sizeable contributions to the Ben and Jerry's Foundation. Others have suggested that Ben & Jerry's philosophy may even induce Unilever to increase its own corporate philanthropy. Despite these assurances, both of the company's founders have expressed concerns about the deal, and it remains to be seen whether Ben & Jerry's vision can be maintained within the confines of a large conglomerate.

As you will see throughout the book, many of today's companies face challenges similar to those of Ben & Jerry's. Every day, corporations struggle with decisions such as these: Is it fair to our labor force to shift production overseas? What is the appropriate level of compensation for senior management? Should we increase, or decrease, our charitable contributions? In general, how do we balance social concerns against the need to create shareholder value?

PUTTING THINGS IN PERSPECTIVE

See **http://www. benjerry.com/ mission.html** for Ben & Jerry's interesting mission statement. It might be a good idea to print it out and take it to class for discussion.

The purpose of this chapter is to give you an idea of what financial management is all about. After you finish the chapter, you should have a reasonably good idea of what finance majors might do after graduation. You should also have a better understanding of (1) some of the forces that will affect financial management in the future; (2) the place of finance in a firm's organization; (3) the relationships between financial managers and their counterparts in the accounting, marketing, production, and personnel departments; (4) the goals of a firm; and (5) the way financial managers can contribute to the attainment of these goals. ■

CAREER OPPORTUNITIES IN FINANCE

Information on finance careers, additional chapter links, and practice quizzes are available on the web site to accompany this text: **http:// brigham.swlearning.com/**.

Finance consists of three interrelated areas: (1) *money and capital markets*, which deals with securities markets and financial institutions; (2) *investments*, which focuses on the decisions made by both individual and institutional investors as they choose securities for their investment portfolios; and (3) *financial management*, or "business finance," which involves decisions within firms. The career opportunities within each field are many and varied, but financial managers must have a knowledge of all three areas if they are to do their jobs well.

MONEY AND CAPITAL MARKETS

Many finance majors go to work for financial institutions, including banks, insurance companies, mutual funds, and investment banking firms. For success here, one needs a knowledge of valuation techniques, the factors that cause interest rates to rise and fall, the regulations to which financial institutions are subject, and the various types of financial instruments (mortgages, auto loans, certificates of deposit, and so on). One also needs a general knowledge of all aspects of business administration, because the management of a financial institution involves accounting, marketing, personnel, and computer systems, as well as financial management. An ability to communicate, both orally and in writing, is important, and "people skills," or the ability to get others to do their jobs well, are critical.

INVESTMENTS

 Consult **http://www. careers-in-business. com** for an excellent site containing information on a variety of business career areas, listings of current jobs, and a variety of other reference materials.

Finance graduates who go into investments often work for a brokerage house such as Merrill Lynch, either in sales or as a security analyst. Others work for banks, mutual funds, or insurance companies in the management of their investment portfolios; for financial consulting firms advising individual investors or pension funds on how to invest their capital; for investment banks whose primary function is to help businesses raise new capital; or as financial planners whose job is to help individuals develop long-term financial goals and portfolios. The three main functions in the investments area are sales, analyzing individual securities, and determining the optimal mix of securities for a given investor.

FINANCIAL MANAGEMENT

Financial management is the broadest of the three areas, and the one with the most job opportunities. Financial management is important in all types of businesses, including banks and other financial institutions, as well as industrial and retail firms. Financial management is also important in governmental operations, from schools to hospitals to highway departments. The job opportunities in financial management range from making decisions regarding plant expansions to choosing what types of securities to issue when financing expansion. Financial managers also have the responsibility for deciding the credit terms under which customers may buy, how much inventory the firm should carry, how much cash to keep on hand, whether to acquire other firms (merger analysis), and how much of the firm's earnings to plow back into the business versus pay out as dividends.

Regardless of which area a finance major enters, he or she will need a knowledge of all three areas. For example, a bank lending officer cannot do his or her job well without a good understanding of financial management, because he or she must be able to judge how well a business is being operated. The same thing holds true for Merrill Lynch's security analysts and stockbrokers, who must have an understanding of general financial principles if they are to give their customers intelligent advice. Similarly, corporate financial managers need to know what their bankers are thinking about, and they also need to know how investors judge a firm's performance and thus determine its stock price. So, if you decide to make finance your career, you will need to know something about all three areas.

But suppose you do not plan to major in finance. Is the subject still important to you? Absolutely, for two reasons: (1) You need a knowledge of finance to make many personal decisions, ranging from investing for your retirement to deciding whether to lease versus buy a car. (2) Virtually all important business decisions have financial implications, so important decisions are generally made by teams from the accounting, finance, legal, marketing, personnel, and production departments. Therefore, if you want to succeed in the business arena, you must be highly competent in your own area, say, marketing, but you must also have a familiarity with the other business disciplines, including finance.

Thus, there are financial implications in virtually all business decisions, and nonfinancial executives simply must know enough finance to work these implications into their own specialized analyses.[1] Because of this, every student of business, regardless of his or her major, should be concerned with financial management.

SELF-TEST QUESTIONS

What are the three main areas of finance?

If you have definite plans to go into one area, why is it necessary that you know something about the other areas?

Why is it necessary for business students who do not plan to major in finance to understand the basics of finance?

FINANCIAL MANAGEMENT IN THE NEW MILLENNIUM

When financial management emerged as a separate field of study in the early 1900s, the emphasis was on the legal aspects of mergers, the formation of new firms, and the various types of securities firms could issue to raise capital. During the Depression of the 1930s, the emphasis shifted to bankruptcy and reorganization, corporate liquidity, and the regulation of security markets. During the 1940s and early 1950s, finance continued to be taught as a descriptive, institutional subject, viewed more from the standpoint of an outsider rather than that of a manager. However, a movement toward theoretical analysis began during the late 1950s, and the focus shifted to managerial decisions designed to maximize the value of the firm.

The focus on value maximization continues as we begin the 21st century. However, two other trends are becoming increasingly important: (1) the globalization of business and (2) the increased use of information technology. Both of these trends provide companies with exciting new opportunities to increase profitability and reduce risks. However, these trends are also leading to increased competition and new risks. To emphasize these points throughout the book, we regularly profile how companies or industries have been affected by increased globalization and changing technology. These profiles are found in the boxes labeled "Global Perspectives" and "Technology Matters."

GLOBALIZATION OF BUSINESS

Many companies today rely to a large and increasing extent on overseas operations. Table 1-1 summarizes the percentage of overseas revenues and profits for 10 well-known corporations. Very clearly, these 10 "American" companies are really international concerns.

---

[1] It is an interesting fact that the course "Financial Management for Nonfinancial Executives" has the highest enrollment in most executive development programs.

TABLE 1-1

Percentage of Revenue and Net Income from Overseas Operations for 10 Well-Known Corporations

COMPANY	PERCENTAGE OF REVENUE ORIGINATED OVERSEAS	PERCENTAGE OF NET INCOME GENERATED OVERSEAS
Coca-Cola	60.8	35.9
Exxon Mobil	69.4	60.2
General Electric	32.6	25.2
General Motors	26.1	60.6
IBM	57.9	48.4
JP Morgan Chase & Co.	35.5	51.7
McDonald's	63.1	61.7
Merck	18.3	58.1
Minn. Mining & Mfg.	52.9	47.0
Sears, Roebuck	10.5	7.8

SOURCE: Adapted from *Forbes* Magazine's 2000 Ranking of the 100 Largest U.S. Multinationals; *Forbes,* July 23, 2001, 136–148.

Four factors have led to the increased globalization of businesses: (1) Improvements in transportation and communications lowered shipping costs and made international trade more feasible. (2) The increasing political clout of consumers, who desire low-cost, high-quality products. This has helped lower trade barriers designed to protect inefficient, high-cost domestic manufacturers and their workers. (3) As technology has become more advanced, the costs of developing new products have increased. These rising costs have led to joint ventures between such companies as Eastman Kodak and SANYO, and to global operations for many firms as they seek to expand markets and thus spread development costs over higher unit sales. (4) In a world populated with multinational firms able to shift production to wherever costs are lowest, a firm whose manufacturing operations are restricted to one country cannot compete unless costs in its home country happen to be low, a condition that does not necessarily exist for many U.S. corporations. As a result of these four factors, survival requires that most manufacturers produce and sell globally.

Service companies, including banks, advertising agencies, and accounting firms, are also being forced to "go global," because these firms can best serve their multinational clients if they have worldwide operations. There will, of course, always be some purely domestic companies, but the most dynamic growth, and the best employment opportunities, are often with companies that operate worldwide.

Even businesses that operate exclusively in the United States are not immune to the effects of globalization. For example, the costs to a homebuilder in rural Nebraska are affected by interest rates and lumber prices—both of which are determined by worldwide supply and demand conditions. Furthermore, demand for the homebuilder's houses is influenced by interest rates and also by conditions in the local farm economy, which depend to a large extent on foreign demand for wheat. To operate efficiently, the Nebraska builder must be able to forecast the demand for houses, and that demand depends on worldwide events. So, at least some knowledge of global economic conditions is important to virtually everyone, not just to those involved with businesses that operate internationally.

COKE RIDES THE GLOBAL ECONOMY WAVE

During the past 20 years, Coca-Cola has created tremendous value for its shareholders. A $10,000 investment in Coke stock in January 1980 would have grown to nearly $600,000 by mid-1998. A large part of that impressive growth was due to Coke's overseas expansion program. Today 60 percent of Coke's revenues come from overseas, and Coke sells roughly half of the world's soft drinks.

More recently, Coke has discovered that there are also risks when investing overseas. Indeed, between mid-1998 and March 2002, Coke's stock fell by roughly 42 percent—which means that the $600,000 stock investment decreased in value to nearly $350,000 in about 3.5 years. Coke's poor performance during this period was due in large part to troubles overseas. Weak economic conditions in Brazil, Germany, Japan, Southeast Asia, Venezuela, Colombia, and Russia, plus a quality scare in Belgium and France, hurt the company's bottom line.

Despite its recent difficulties, Coke remains committed to its global vision. Coke is also striving to learn from these difficulties. The company's leaders have acknowledged that Coke may have become overly centralized. Centralized control enabled Coke to standardize quality and to capture operating efficiencies, both of which initially helped to establish its brand name throughout the world. More recently, however, Coke has become concerned that too much centralized control has made it slow to respond to changing circumstances and insensitive to differences among the various local markets it serves.

Coke's CEO, Douglas N. Daft, reflected these concerns in an editorial that was published in the March 27, 2000, edition of *Financial Times*. Daft's concluding comments appear below:

So overall, we will draw on a long-standing belief that Coca-Cola always flourishes when our people are allowed to use their insight to build the business in ways best suited to their local culture and business conditions.

We will, of course, maintain clear order. Our small corporate team will communicate explicitly the clear strategy, policy, values, and quality standards needed to keep us cohesive and efficient. But just as important, we will also make sure we stay out of the way of our local people and let them do their jobs. That will enhance significantly our ability to unlock growth opportunities, which will enable us to consistently meet our growth expectations.

In our recent past, we succeeded because we understood and appealed to global commonalties. In our future, we'll succeed because we will also understand and appeal to local differences. The 21st century demands nothing less.

For more information about the Coca-Cola Company, go to **http://www2.Coca-Cola.com/ourcompany/aroundworld.html**, where you can find profiles of Coca-Cola's presence in foreign countries.

INFORMATION TECHNOLOGY

As we advance into the new millennium, we will see continued advances in computer and communications technology, and this will continue to revolutionize the way financial decisions are made. Companies are linking networks of personal computers to one another, to the firms' own mainframe computers, to the Internet, and to their customers' and suppliers' computers. Thus, financial managers are increasingly able to share information and to have "face-to-face" meetings with distant colleagues through video teleconferencing. The ability to access and analyze data on a real-time basis also means that quantitative analysis is becoming more important, and "gut feel" less sufficient, in business decisions. As a result, the next generation of financial managers will need stronger computer and quantitative skills than were required in the past.

Changing technology affects not only the risks and opportunities that financial managers face each day, but it has also dramatically transformed the corporate landscape. Table 1-2 shows the top 15 companies in the *Fortune* 500 listing (ranked according to their market capitalization) as of 2000, 1990, and 1980. Oil, automobile, and manufacturing companies dominated the earlier lists, while the 2000 list includes technology-oriented companies such as Microsoft, America Online, Intel, and Cisco

Top 15 *Fortune* 500 Companies for 2000, 1990, and 1980 (Ranked According to Market Capitalization)

2000	1990	1980
General Electric	IBM	Exxon
Exxon Mobil	Exxon	General Motors
Microsoft	General Motors	IBM
Pfizer	Ford Motor	Mobil
Citigroup	General Electric	Texaco
Wal-Mart Stores	Mobil	Standard Oil of California
Intel	DuPont	Gulf Oil
American International Group	Shell Oil	Standard Oil of Indiana
America Online	Chevron	Ford Motor
Merck	Amoco	General Electric
AT&T	Philip Morris	Shell Oil
IBM	Texaco	Atlantic Richfield
Cisco Systems	Dow Chemical	International Telephone & Telegraph
SBC Communications	Digital Equipment	Eastman Kodak
Verizon Communications	Procter & Gamble	DuPont

SOURCES: Adapted from various issues of *Fortune* magazine (April 16, 1981; April 16, 1991; and April 16, 2001), and **http://www.fortune.com**.

Systems. Other more traditional companies such as Wal-Mart and Citigroup, which joined the list in 2000, have grown in large part because of their ability to take advantage of changing technology.

Changing technology provides both opportunities and threats. Improved technology enables businesses to reduce costs and expand markets. At the same time, changing technology can introduce additional competition, which may reduce profitability in existing markets.

The banking industry provides a good example of the double-edged technology sword. Improved technology has allowed banks to process information much more efficiently, which reduces the costs of processing checks, providing credit, and identifying bad credit risks. Technology has also allowed banks to serve customers better. For example, today bank customers use automatic teller machines (ATMs) everywhere, from the supermarket to the local mall. Today, many banks also offer products that allow their customers to use the Internet to manage their accounts and to pay bills. However, changing technology also threatens banks' profitability. Many customers no longer feel compelled to use a local bank, and the Internet allows them to shop worldwide for the best deposit and loan rates. An even greater threat is the continued development of electronic commerce. Electronic commerce allows customers and businesses to transact directly, thus reducing the need for intermediaries such as commercial banks. In the years ahead, financial managers will have to continue to keep abreast of technological developments, and they must be prepared to adapt their businesses to the changing environment.

INTERNET CHANGES THE TOY BUSINESS

The toy market illustrates how electronic commerce is changing the way firms operate. Over the past decade, this market has been dominated by Toys "Я" Us, although Toys "Я" Us has faced increasing competition from retail chains such as Wal-Mart, Kmart, and Target. Then, in 1997, Internet startup eToys Inc. began selling and distributing toys through the Internet.

When eToys first emerged, many analysts believed that the Internet provided toy retailers with a sensational opportunity. This point was made amazingly clear in May 1999 when eToys issued stock to the public in an initial public offering (IPO). The stock immediately rose from its $20 offering price to $76 per share, and the company's market capitalization (calculated by multiplying stock price by the number of shares outstanding) was a mind-blowing $7.8 billion.

To put this valuation in perspective, eToys' market value at the time of the offering ($7.8 billion) was 35 percent greater than that of Toys "Я" Us ($5.7 billion). eToys' valuation was particularly startling given that the company had yet to earn a profit. (It lost $73 million in the year ending March 1999.) Moreover, while Toys "Я" Us had nearly 1,500 stores and revenues in excess of $11 billion, eToys had no stores and revenues of less than $35 million.

Investors were clearly expecting an increasing number of toys to be bought over the Internet. One analyst estimated at the time of the offering that eToys would be worth $10 billion within a decade. His analysis assumed that in 10 years the toy market would total $75 billion, with $20 billion coming from online sales. Indeed, online sales do appear to be here to stay. For many customers, online shopping is quicker and more convenient, particularly for working parents of young children, who purchase the lion's share of toys. From the company's perspective, Internet commerce has a number of other advantages. The costs of maintaining a web site and distributing toys online may be smaller than the costs of maintaining and managing 1,500 retail stores.

Not surprisingly, Toys "Я" Us did not sit idly by — it announced plans to invest $64 million in a separate online subsidiary, Toysrus.com. The company also announced an online partnership with Internet retailer Amazon.com. In addition, Toys "Я" Us is redoubling its efforts to make traditional store shopping more enjoyable and less frustrating.

While the Internet provides toy companies with new and interesting opportunities, these companies also face tremendous risks as they try to respond to the changing technology. Indeed, in the months following eToys' IPO, Toys "Я" Us' stock fell sharply, and by January 2000, its market value was only slightly above $2 billion. Since then, Toys "Я" Us stock has regained only part of its lost value. As of April 2002, its market capitalization was around $3.75 billion. The shareholders of eToys were less fortunate. Concerns about inventory management during the 1999 holiday season and the collapse of many Internet stocks spurred a tremendous collapse in eToys' stock — its stock fell from a post–IPO high of $76 a share to $0.31 a share in January 2001. Two months later, eToys declared bankruptcy.

The recent experience of Toys "Я" Us and eToys dramatically illustrates the striking effects of changing technology. In all likelihood these effects will continue to be felt for years to come.

ALTERNATIVE FORMS OF BUSINESS ORGANIZATION

There are three main forms of business organization: (1) sole proprietorships, (2) partnerships, and (3) corporations. In terms of numbers, about 80 percent of businesses are operated as sole proprietorships, while most of the remainder are divided equally between partnerships and corporations. Based on the dollar value of sales, however, about 80 percent of all business is conducted by corporations, about 13 percent by sole proprietorships, and about 7 percent by partnerships. Because most business is conducted by corporations, we will concentrate on them in this book. However, it is important to understand the differences among the various forms.

SOLE PROPRIETORSHIP

Sole Proprietorship
An unincorporated business owned by one individual.

A **sole proprietorship** is an unincorporated business owned by one individual. Going into business as a sole proprietor is easy—one merely begins business operations. However, even the smallest businesses normally must be licensed by a governmental unit.

The proprietorship has three important advantages: (1) It is easily and inexpensively formed, (2) it is subject to few government regulations, and (3) the business avoids corporate income taxes.

The proprietorship also has three important limitations: (1) It is difficult for a proprietorship to obtain large sums of capital; (2) the proprietor has unlimited personal liability for the business's debts, which can result in losses that exceed the money he or she has invested in the company; and (3) the life of a business organized as a proprietorship is limited to the life of the individual who created it. For these three reasons, sole proprietorships are used primarily for small-business operations. However, businesses are frequently started as proprietorships and then converted to corporations when their growth causes the disadvantages of being a proprietorship to outweigh the advantages.

PARTNERSHIP

Partnership
An unincorporated business owned by two or more persons.

A **partnership** exists whenever two or more persons associate to conduct a noncorporate business. Partnerships may operate under different degrees of formality, ranging from informal, oral understandings to formal agreements filed with the secretary of the state in which the partnership was formed. The major advantage of a partnership is its low cost and ease of formation. Partnerships also avoid corporate income taxes. The disadvantages are similar to those associated with proprietorships: (1) unlimited liability, (2) limited life of the organization, (3) difficulty of transferring ownership, and (4) difficulty of raising large amounts of capital.

Regarding liability, the partners can potentially lose all of their personal assets, even assets not invested in the business, because under partnership law, each partner is liable for the business's debts. Therefore, if any partner is unable to meet his or her pro rata liability in the event the partnership goes bankrupt, the remaining partners must make good on the unsatisfied claims, drawing on their personal assets to the extent necessary. The partners of the national accounting firm Laventhol and Horwath, a huge partnership that went bankrupt as a result of suits filed by investors who relied on faulty audit statements, learned all about the perils of doing business as a partnership. Currently, Arthur Andersen is fighting to avoid a similar fate. Thus, a Texas partner who audits a business that goes under can bring ruin to a millionaire New York partner who never went near the client company.

The first three disadvantages—unlimited liability, impermanence of the organization, and difficulty of transferring ownership—lead to the fourth, the difficulty partnerships have in attracting substantial amounts of capital. This is generally not a problem for a slow-growing business, but if a business's products or services really catch on, and if it needs to raise large amounts of capital to capitalize on its opportunities, the difficulty in attracting capital becomes a real drawback. Thus, growth companies such as Hewlett-Packard and Microsoft generally begin life as a proprietorship or partnership, but at some point their founders find it necessary to convert to a corporation.

CORPORATION

Corporation
A legal entity created by a state, separate and distinct from its owners and managers, having unlimited life, easy transferability of ownership, and limited liability.

A **corporation** is a legal entity created by a state, and it is separate and distinct from its owners and managers. This separateness gives the corporation three major advantages: (1) *Unlimited life*. A corporation can continue after its original owners and managers are deceased. (2) *Easy transferability of ownership interest*. Ownership interests can be divided into shares of stock, which, in turn, can be transferred far more easily than can proprietorship or partnership interests. (3) *Limited liability*. Losses are limited to the actual funds invested. To illustrate limited liability, suppose you invested $10,000 in a partnership that then went bankrupt, owing $1 million. Because the owners are liable for the debts of a partnership, you could be assessed for a share of the company's debt, and you could be held liable for the entire $1 million if your partners could not pay their shares. Thus, an investor in a partnership is exposed to unlimited liability. On the other hand, if you invested $10,000 in the stock of a corporation that then went bankrupt, your potential loss on the investment would be limited to your $10,000 investment.[2] These three factors—unlimited life, easy transferability of ownership interest, and limited liability—make it much easier for corporations than for proprietorships or partnerships to raise money in the capital markets.

The corporate form offers significant advantages over proprietorships and partnerships, but it also has two disadvantages: (1) Corporate earnings may be subject to double taxation—the earnings of the corporation are taxed at the corporate level, and then any earnings paid out as dividends are taxed again as income to the stockholders. (2) Setting up a corporation, and filing the many required state and federal reports, is more complex and time-consuming than for a proprietorship or a partnership.

A proprietorship or a partnership can commence operations without much paperwork, but setting up a corporation requires that the incorporators prepare a charter and a set of bylaws. Although personal computer software that creates charters and bylaws is now available, a lawyer is required if the fledgling corporation has any nonstandard features. The *charter* includes the following information: (1) name of the proposed corporation, (2) types of activities it will pursue, (3) amount of capital stock, (4) number of directors, and (5) names and addresses of directors. The charter is filed with the secretary of the state in which the firm will be incorporated, and when it is approved, the corporation is officially in existence.[3] Then, after the corporation is in

---

[2] In the case of small corporations, the limited liability feature is often a fiction, because bankers and other lenders frequently require personal guarantees from the stockholders of small, weak businesses.

[3] Note that more than 308,000 companies are incorporated in Delaware, including 60 percent of the *Fortune* 500 and 50 percent of the companies listed on the New York Stock Exchange. Over the years, Delaware has provided a favorable legal environment for corporations. It is not necessary for a firm to be headquartered, or even to conduct operations, in its state of incorporation.

operation, quarterly and annual employment, financial, and tax reports must be filed with state and federal authorities.

The *bylaws* are a set of rules drawn up by the founders of the corporation. Included are such points as (1) how directors are to be elected (all elected each year, or perhaps one-third each year for three-year terms); (2) whether the existing stockholders will have the first right to buy any new shares the firm issues; and (3) procedures for changing the bylaws themselves, should conditions require it.

The value of any business other than a very small one will probably be maximized if it is organized as a corporation for the following three reasons:

1. Limited liability reduces the risks borne by investors, and, other things held constant, *the lower the firm's risk, the higher its value.*

2. A firm's value is dependent on its *growth opportunities*, which in turn are dependent on the firm's ability to attract capital. Since corporations can attract capital more easily than can unincorporated businesses, they are better able to take advantage of growth opportunities.

3. The value of an asset also depends on its *liquidity*, which means the ease of selling the asset and converting it to cash at a "fair market value." Since an investment in the stock of a corporation is much more liquid than a similar investment in a proprietorship or partnership, this too enhances the value of a corporation.

As we will see later in the chapter, most firms are managed with value maximization in mind, and this, in turn, has caused most large businesses to be organized as corporations.

SELF-TEST QUESTIONS

What are the key differences between sole proprietorships, partnerships, and corporations?

Why will the value of any business other than a very small one probably be maximized if it is organized as a corporation?

FINANCE IN THE ORGANIZATIONAL STRUCTURE OF THE FIRM

Organizational structures vary from firm to firm, but Figure 1-1 presents a fairly typical picture of the role of finance within a corporation. The chief financial officer (CFO) generally has the title of vice-president: finance, and he or she reports to the president. The financial vice-president's key subordinates are the treasurer and the controller. In most firms the treasurer has direct responsibility for managing the firm's cash and marketable securities, for planning its capital structure, for selling stocks and bonds to raise capital, for overseeing the corporate pension plan, and for managing risk. The treasurer also supervises the credit manager, the inventory manager, and the director of capital budgeting (who analyzes decisions related to investments in fixed assets). The controller is typically responsible for the activities of the accounting and tax departments.

FIGURE 1-1   Role of Finance in a Typical Business Organization

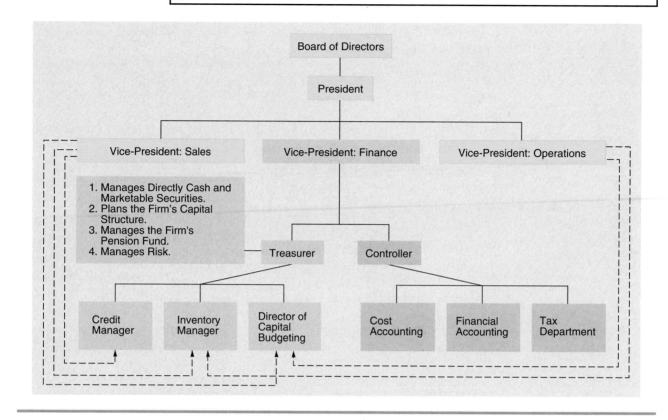

SELF-TEST QUESTION

Identify the two primary subordinates who report to the firm's chief financial officer, and indicate the primary responsibilities of each.

THE FINANCIAL STAFF'S RESPONSIBILITIES

The financial staff's task is to acquire and then help operate resources so as to maximize the value of the firm. Here are some specific activities:

1. **Forecasting and planning.** The financial staff must coordinate the planning process. This means they must interact with people from other departments as they look ahead and lay the plans that will shape the firm's future.

2. **Major investment and financing decisions.** A successful firm usually has rapid growth in sales, which requires investments in plant, equipment, and inventory. The financial staff must help determine the optimal sales growth

rate, help decide what specific assets to acquire, and then choose the best way to finance those assets. For example, should the firm finance with debt, equity, or some combination of the two, and if debt is used, how much should be long term and how much short term?

3. **Coordination and control.** The financial staff must interact with other personnel to ensure that the firm is operated as efficiently as possible. All business decisions have financial implications, and all managers—financial and otherwise—need to take this into account. For example, marketing decisions affect sales growth, which in turn influences investment requirements. Thus, marketing decision makers must take account of how their actions affect and are affected by such factors as the availability of funds, inventory policies, and plant capacity utilization.

4. **Dealing with the financial markets.** The financial staff must deal with the money and capital markets. As we shall see in Chapter 4, each firm affects and is affected by the general financial markets where funds are raised, where the firm's securities are traded, and where investors either make or lose money.

5. **Risk management.** All businesses face risks, including natural disasters such as fires and floods, uncertainties in commodity and security markets, volatile interest rates, and fluctuating foreign exchange rates. However, many of these risks can be reduced by purchasing insurance or by hedging in the derivatives markets. The financial staff is responsible for the firm's overall risk management program, including identifying the risks that should be managed and then managing them in the most efficient manner.

In summary, people working in financial management make decisions regarding which assets their firms should acquire, how those assets should be financed, and how the firm should conduct its operations. If these responsibilities are performed optimally, financial managers will help to maximize the values of their firms, and this will also contribute to the welfare of consumers and employees.

SELF-TEST QUESTION

What are some specific activities with which a firm's finance staff is involved?

THE GOALS OF THE CORPORATION

Stockholder Wealth Maximization
The primary goal for management decisions; considers the risk and timing associated with expected earnings per share in order to maximize the price of the firm's common stock.

Shareholders are the owners of a corporation, and they purchase stocks because they are looking for a financial return. In most cases, shareholders elect directors, who then hire managers to run the corporation on a day-to-day basis. Since managers are working on behalf of shareholders, it follows that they should pursue policies that enhance shareholder value. Consequently, throughout this book we operate on the assumption that management's primary goal is **stockholder wealth maximization,** which translates into *maximizing the price of the firm's common stock*. Firms do, of course, have other objectives—in particular, the managers who make the actual decisions are interested in their own personal satisfaction, in their employees' welfare, and in the good of the community and of society at large. Still, for the reasons set forth in the following sections, *stock price maximization is the most important goal for most corporations.*

MANAGERIAL INCENTIVES TO MAXIMIZE SHAREHOLDER WEALTH

Stockholders own the firm and elect the board of directors, which then selects the management team. Management, in turn, is supposed to operate in the best interests of the stockholders. We know, however, that because the stock of most large firms is widely held, managers of large corporations have a great deal of autonomy. This being the case, might not managers pursue goals other than stock price maximization? For example, some have argued that the managers of large, well-entrenched corporations could work just hard enough to keep stockholder returns at a "reasonable" level and then devote the remainder of their effort and resources to public service activities, to employee benefits, to higher executive salaries, or to golf.

It is almost impossible to determine whether a particular management team is trying to maximize shareholder wealth or is merely attempting to keep stockholders satisfied while managers pursue other goals. For example, how can we tell whether employee or community benefit programs are in the long-run best interests of the stockholders? Similarly, are huge executive salaries really necessary to attract and retain excellent managers, or are they just another example of managers taking advantage of stockholders?

It is impossible to give definitive answers to these questions. However, we do know that the managers of a firm operating in a competitive market will be forced to undertake actions that are reasonably consistent with shareholder wealth maximization. If they depart from that goal, they run the risk of being removed from their jobs, either by the firm's board of directors or by outside forces. We will have more to say about this in a later section.

SOCIAL RESPONSIBILITY

Social Responsibility
The concept that business should be actively concerned with the welfare of society at large.

Another issue that deserves consideration is **social responsibility:** Should businesses operate strictly in their stockholders' best interests, or are firms also responsible for the welfare of their employees, customers, and the communities in which they operate? Certainly firms have an ethical responsibility to provide a safe working environment, to avoid polluting the air or water, and to produce safe products. However, socially responsible actions have costs, and not all businesses would voluntarily incur all such costs. If some firms act in a socially responsible manner while others do not, then the socially responsible firms will be at a disadvantage in attracting capital. To illustrate, suppose all firms in a given industry have close to **"normal" profits** and **rates of return on investment,** that is, close to the average for all firms and just sufficient to attract capital. If one company attempts to exercise social responsibility, it will have to raise prices to cover the added costs. If other firms in its industry do not follow suit, their costs and prices will be lower. The socially responsible firm will not be able to compete, and it will be forced to abandon its efforts. Thus, any voluntary

Normal Profits and Rates of Return
Those profits and rates of return that are close to the average for all firms and are just sufficient to attract capital.

socially responsible acts that raise costs will be difficult, if not impossible, in industries that are subject to keen competition.

What about oligopolistic firms with profits above normal levels—cannot such firms devote resources to social projects? Undoubtedly they can, and many large, successful firms do engage in community projects, employee benefit programs, and the like to a greater degree than would appear to be called for by pure profit or wealth maximization goals.[4] Furthermore, many such firms contribute large sums to charities. Still, publicly owned firms are constrained by capital market forces. To illustrate, suppose a saver who has funds to invest is considering two alternative firms. One devotes a substantial part of its resources to social actions, while the other concentrates on profits and stock prices. Many investors would shun the socially oriented firm, thus putting it at a disadvantage in the capital market. After all, why should the stockholders of one corporation subsidize society to a greater extent than those of other businesses? For this reason, even highly profitable firms (unless they are closely held rather than publicly owned) are generally constrained against taking unilateral cost-increasing social actions.

Does all this mean that firms should not exercise social responsibility? Not at all. But it does mean that most significant cost-increasing actions will have to be put on a *mandatory* rather than a voluntary basis to ensure that the burden falls uniformly on all businesses. Thus, such social benefit programs as fair hiring practices, minority training, product safety, pollution abatement, and antitrust actions are most likely to be effective if realistic rules are established initially and then enforced by government agencies. Of course, it is critical that industry and government cooperate in establishing the rules of corporate behavior, and that the costs as well as the benefits of such actions be estimated accurately and then taken into account.

In spite of the fact that many socially responsible actions must be mandated by government, in recent years numerous firms have voluntarily taken such actions, especially in the area of environmental protection, because they helped sales. For example, many detergent manufacturers now use recycled paper for their containers, and food companies are packaging more and more products in materials that consumers can recycle or that are biodegradable. To illustrate, McDonald's replaced its styrofoam boxes, which take years to break down in landfills, with paper wrappers that are less bulky and decompose more rapidly. Some companies, such as The Body Shop and Ben & Jerry's Ice Cream, go to great lengths to be socially responsible. According to the president of The Body Shop, the role of business is to promote the public good, not just the good of the firm's shareholders. Furthermore, she argues that it is impossible to separate business from social responsibility. For some firms, socially responsible actions may not de facto be costly—the companies heavily advertise their actions, and many consumers prefer to buy from socially responsible companies rather than from those that shun social responsibility.

Go to **http://www. usa.thebodyshop. com/web/tbsus/ values.jsp** to see the corporate values The Body Shop embraces.

STOCK PRICE MAXIMIZATION AND SOCIAL WELFARE

If a firm attempts to maximize its stock price, is this good or bad for society? In general, it is good. Aside from such illegal actions as attempting to form monopolies, violating safety codes, and failing to meet pollution control requirements, *the same*

---

[4] Even firms like these often find it necessary to justify such projects at stockholder meetings by stating that these programs will contribute to long-run profit maximization.

INVESTING IN SOCIALLY RESPONSIBLE FUNDS

The same societal pressures that have encouraged consumers to buy products of companies that they believe to be socially responsible have also led some investors to search for ways to limit their investments to only those firms that they deem to be socially responsible. Indeed, today there are a large number of mutual funds that only invest in companies that meet specified social goals. Each of these socially responsible funds applies different criteria, but typically they consider a company's environmental record, its commitment to social causes, and its employee relations. Many of these funds also avoid investments in companies that are involved with alcohol, tobacco, gambling, and nuclear power. Investment performance varies among funds from year to year, but the accompanying chart, which shows the past performance of a representative socially responsible fund, the Domini Social Equity Fund, suggests that restricting investments may lead to restricted returns.

Recent Performance of Domini Social Equity Fund versus S&P 500

SOURCE: http://www.bigcharts.com, April 29, 2002.

actions that maximize stock prices also benefit society. First, note that stock price maximization requires efficient, low-cost businesses that produce high-quality goods and services at the lowest possible cost. Second, stock price maximization requires the development of products and services that consumers want and need, so the profit motive leads to new technology, to new products, and to new jobs. Finally, stock price maximization necessitates efficient and courteous service, adequate stocks of merchandise, and well-located business establishments—these are the factors that lead to sales, which in turn are necessary for profits. Therefore, most actions that help a firm increase the price of its stock also benefit society at large. This is why profit-motivated, free-enterprise economies have been so much more successful than socialistic and communistic economic systems. Since financial management plays a crucial role in the operations of successful firms, and since successful firms are absolutely necessary for a healthy, productive economy, it is easy to see why finance is important from a social welfare standpoint.[5]

SELF-TEST QUESTIONS

What is management's primary goal?

What actions could be taken to remove a management team if it departs from the goal of maximizing shareholder wealth?

What would happen if one firm attempted to exercise costly socially responsible programs but its competitors did not follow suit?

How does the goal of stock price maximization benefit society at large?

BUSINESS ETHICS

Business Ethics
A company's attitude and conduct toward its employees, customers, community, and stockholders.

The word *ethics* is defined in Webster's dictionary as "standards of conduct or moral behavior." **Business ethics** can be thought of as a company's attitude and conduct toward its employees, customers, community, and stockholders. High standards of ethical behavior demand that a firm treat each party that it deals with in a fair and honest manner. A firm's commitment to business ethics can be measured by the tendency of the firm and its employees to adhere to laws and regulations relating to such factors as product safety and quality, fair employment practices, fair marketing and selling practices, the use of confidential information for personal gain, community involvement, bribery, and illegal payments to obtain business.

Most firms today have in place strong codes of ethical behavior, and they also conduct training programs designed to ensure that employees understand the correct behavior in different business situations. However, it is imperative that top management—the chairman, president, and vice-presidents—be openly committed to ethical behavior, and that they communicate this commitment through their own personal actions as well as through company policies, directives, and punishment/reward systems.

---

[5] People sometimes argue that firms, in their efforts to raise profits and stock prices, increase product prices and gouge the public. In a reasonably competitive economy, which we have, prices are constrained by competition and consumer resistance. If a firm raises its prices beyond reasonable levels, it will simply lose its market share. Even giant firms such as General Motors lose business to the Japanese and German automakers, as well as to Ford, if they set prices above levels necessary to cover production costs plus a "normal" profit. Of course, firms *want* to earn more, and they constantly try to cut costs, to develop new products, and so on, and thereby to earn above-normal profits. Note, though, that if they are indeed successful and do earn above-normal profits, those very profits will attract competition, which will eventually drive prices down, so again the main long-term beneficiary is the consumer.

When conflicts arise between profits and ethics, sometimes the ethical considerations are so strong that they clearly dominate. However, in many cases the choice between ethics and profits is not clear cut. For example, suppose Norfolk Southern's managers know that its coal trains are polluting the air along its routes, but the amount of pollution is within legal limits and preventive actions would be costly. Are the managers ethically bound to reduce pollution? Similarly, suppose a medical products company's own research indicates that one of its new products may cause problems. However, the evidence is relatively weak, other evidence regarding benefits to patients is strong, and independent government tests show no adverse effects. Should the company make the potential problem known to the public? If it does release the negative (but questionable) information, this will hurt sales and profits, and possibly keep some patients who would benefit from the new product from using it. There are no obvious answers to questions such as these, but companies must deal with them on a regular basis, and a failure to handle the situation properly can lead to huge product liability suits, which could push a firm into bankruptcy.

Over the past few years, there have been a number of instances where unethical practices have contributed to or led to bankruptcy. The recent collapse of two once high-flying stocks, Enron and WorldCom, dramatically illustrates how unethical behavior can lead to a firm's rapid decline. In both cases, top executives have come under fire for using misleading accounting practices that led to an overstatement of profitability and financial condition. It has also been alleged that these same executives sold large blocks of stock at the same time they were aggressively promoting the stock to their employees and outside investors. Thus, the executives reaped millions before the stock declined, while the employees and outside investors were left holding the bag. In the months and years ahead, many of these executives will no doubt face the risk of civil lawsuits and perhaps even criminal prosecution. The accounting and law firms that advise companies such as Enron and WorldCom must also be wary of ethics. Indeed, Arthur Andersen, long regarded as perhaps the top accounting firm, is likely to disappear as a result of its involvement with Enron, and several law firms may also be charged with aiding and abetting Enron's fraud.

SELF-TEST QUESTIONS

How would you define "business ethics"?

Is "being ethical" good for profits in the long run? In the short run?

AGENCY RELATIONSHIPS

It has long been recognized that managers may have personal goals that compete with shareholder wealth maximization. Managers are empowered by the owners of the firm—the shareholders—to make decisions, and that creates a potential conflict of interest known as *agency theory*.

An *agency relationship* arises whenever one or more individuals, called *principals*, hire another individual or organization, called an *agent*, to perform some service and delegate decision-making authority to that agent. In financial management, the primary agency relationships are those between (1) stockholders and managers and (2) managers and debtholders.[6]

STOCKHOLDERS VERSUS MANAGERS

Agency Problem
A potential conflict of interests between the agent (manager) and (1) the outside stockholders or (2) the creditors (debtholders).

A potential **agency problem** arises whenever the manager of a firm owns less than 100 percent of the firm's common stock. If the firm is a proprietorship managed by its owner, the owner-manager will presumably operate so as to maximize his or her own welfare, with welfare measured in the form of increased personal wealth, more leisure, or perquisites.[7] However, if the owner-manager incorporates and then sells some of the stock to outsiders, a potential conflict of interests immediately arises. Now the owner-manager may decide to lead a more relaxed lifestyle and not work as strenuously to maximize shareholder wealth, because less of this wealth will accrue to him or her. Also, the owner-manager may decide to consume more perquisites, because some of those costs will be borne by the outside shareholders. In essence, the fact that the owner-manager will neither gain all the benefits of the wealth created by his or her efforts nor bear all of the costs of perquisites will increase the incentive to take actions that are not in the best interests of other shareholders.

In most large corporations, potential agency conflicts are important, because large firms' managers generally own only a small percentage of the stock. In this situation, shareholder wealth maximization could take a back seat to any number of conflicting managerial goals. For example, people have argued that some managers' primary goal seems to be to maximize the size of their firms. By creating a large, rapidly growing firm, managers (1) increase their job security, because a hostile takeover is less likely; (2) increase their own power, status, and salaries; and (3) create more opportunities for their lower- and middle-level managers. Furthermore, since the managers of most large firms own only a small percentage of the stock, it has been argued that they have a voracious appetite for salaries and perquisites, and that they generously contribute corporate dollars to their favorite charities because they get the glory but outside stockholders bear the cost.[8]

Managers can be encouraged to act in stockholders' best interests through incentives that reward them for good performance but punish them for poor performance. Some specific mechanisms used to motivate managers to act in shareholders' best in-

---

[6] The classic work on the application of agency theory to financial management was by Michael C. Jensen and William H. Meckling, "Theory of the Firm, Managerial Behavior, Agency Costs, and Ownership Structure," *Journal of Financial Economics*, October 1976, 305–360.

[7] *Perquisites* are fringe benefits such as luxurious offices, executive assistants, expense accounts, limousines, corporate jets, generous retirement plans, and the like.

[8] An excellent article that reviews the effectiveness of various mechanisms for aligning managerial and shareholder interests is Andrei Shleifer and Robert Vishny, "A Survey of Corporate Governance," *Journal of Finance*, June 1997, 737–783. Another paper that looks at managerial stockholding worldwide is Rafael La Porta, Florencio Lopez-De-Silanes, and Andrei Shleifer, "Corporate Ownership Around the World," *Journal of Finance*, April 1999, 471–517.

ARE CEOS OVERPAID?

BusinessWeek's annual survey of executive compensation recently reported that the average large-company CEO made $11 million in 2001, a 16 percent decline from 2000. The decline can be attributed to a sluggish economy that reduced bonuses and the values of stock options.

Even though average CEO compensation was down, some executives continued to do quite well. Heading the pack on the BusinessWeek list was Oracle's Lawrence Ellison, who in 2001 made $706.1 million, all from stock options. Rounding out the top five were Jozef Straus of JDS Uniphase ($150.8 million), Howard Solomon of Forest Laboratories ($148.5 million), Richard Fairbank of Capital One Financial ($142.2 million), and retired IBM CEO Louis Gerstner ($127.4 million). In most cases, these payouts occurred primarily because the executives exercised stock options granted in earlier years. It is worth noting that the high payouts to these top five executives mask an even larger decline in average CEO compensation. For example, if we remove Lawrence Ellison from the list, average CEO compensation fell more than 30 percent in 2001.

Despite this decline, the average compensation levels are still significantly higher than they were a decade ago, when the average CEO made "only" $2 million. The dramatic increase over the past decade can be attributed to the fact that CEOs increasingly receive most of their compensation in the form of stock and stock options, which skyrocketed in value because of the strong stock market in the 1990s.

The large shifts in CEO compensation over time illustrate the importance of stock options. Once a relatively small part of total compensation, stock options now account for roughly 80 percent of a typical CEO's compensation. Stock options provide CEOs with an incentive to raise their companies' stock prices. Indeed, most observers believe there is a strong causal relationship between CEO compensation procedures and stock price performance.

However, some critics argue that although performance incentives are entirely appropriate as a method of compensation, the overall level of CEO compensation is just too high. The critics ask such questions as these: Would these CEOs have been unwilling to take their jobs if they had been offered only half as many stock options? Would they have put forth less effort, and would their firms' stock prices have not gone up as much? It is hard to say. Other critics lament that the exercise of stock options has dramatically increased the compensation of not only truly excellent CEOs, but it has also dramatically increased the compensation of some pretty average CEOs, who were lucky enough to have had the job during a stock market boom that raised the stock prices of even companies with rather poor performance. Another problem is that the huge CEO salaries are widening the gap between top executives and middle manager salaries. This is leading to employee discontent and a decrease in employee morale and loyalty.

SOURCE: Louis Lavelle, Frederick F. Jespersen, and Michael Arndt, "Executive Pay," *BusinessWeek*, April 15, 2002, 80–86.

---

terests include (1) managerial compensation, (2) direct intervention by shareholders, (3) the threat of firing, and (4) the threat of takeover.

1. **Managerial compensation.** Managers obviously must be compensated, and the structure of the compensation package can and should be designed to meet two primary objectives: (a) to attract and retain able managers and (b) to align managers' actions as closely as possible with the interests of stockholders, who are primarily interested in stock price maximization. Different companies follow different compensation practices, but a typical senior executive's compensation is structured in three parts: (a) a specified annual salary, which is necessary to meet living expenses; (b) a bonus paid at the end of the year, which depends on the company's profitability during the year; and (c) options to buy stock, or actual shares of stock, which reward the executive for long-term performance.

Managers are more likely to focus on maximizing stock prices if they are themselves large shareholders. Often, companies grant senior managers

Performance Shares
Stock that is awarded to executives on the basis of the company's performance.

Executive Stock Option
An option to buy stock at a stated price within a specified time period that is granted to an executive as part of his or her compensation package.

performance shares, where the executive receives a number of shares dependent upon the company's actual performance and the executive's continued service. For example, in 1991 Coca-Cola granted one million shares of stock worth $81 million to its CEO at the time, the late Roberto Goizueta. The award was based on Coke's performance under Goizueta's leadership, but it also stipulated that Goizueta would receive the shares only if he stayed with the company for the remainder of his career.

Boeing Corporation provides a more recent example of how performance shares can be designed to induce managers to increase shareholder wealth. For its managers to receive even a small performance share award, Boeing's stock must show an average annual increase of at least 10 percent, and executives must meet even higher hurdles to receive larger awards. In recent years, this compensation plan has produced wide swings in the total compensation levels of Boeing's top executives. Boeing's stock rose nearly 50 percent in 2000—which triggered the incentive plan to pay out more than $31 million in bonuses to the company's top five executives. One year later, the stock fell sharply and the top executives received nothing from the plan.

Most large corporations also provide **executive stock options,** which allow managers to purchase stock at some future time at a given price. Obviously, a manager who has an option to buy, say, 10,000 shares of stock at a price of $10 during the next five years will have an incentive to help raise the stock's value to an amount greater than $10.

The number of performance shares or options awarded is generally based on objective criteria. Years ago, the primary criteria were accounting measures such as earnings per share (EPS) and return on equity (ROE). Today, though, the focus is more on the market value of the firm's shares or, better yet, on the performance of its shares relative to other stocks in its industry. Various procedures are used to structure compensation programs, and good programs are relatively complicated. Still, it has been thoroughly established that a well-designed compensation program can do wonders to improve a company's financial performance.

2. **Direct intervention by shareholders.** Years ago most stock was owned by individuals, but today the majority is owned by institutional investors such as insurance companies, pension funds, and mutual funds. Therefore, the institutional money managers have the clout, if they choose to use it, to exercise considerable influence over most firms' operations. First, they can talk with a firm's management and make suggestions regarding how the business should be run. In effect, institutional investors act as lobbyists for the body of stockholders. Second, any shareholder who has owned at least $2,000 of a company's stock for one year can sponsor a proposal that must be voted on at the annual stockholders' meeting, even if the proposal is opposed by management. Although shareholder-sponsored proposals are nonbinding and are limited to issues outside of day-to-day operations, the results of such votes are clearly heard by top management.[9]

3. **The threat of firing.** Until recently, the probability of a large firm's management being ousted by its stockholders was so remote that it posed little threat.

---

[9] A recent article that provides a detailed investigation of shareholder proposals during 1997 is Cynthia J. Campbell, Stuart L. Gillan, and Cathy M. Niden, "Current Perspectives on Shareholder Proposals: Lessons from the 1997 Proxy Season," *Financial Management*, Spring 1999, 89–98.

This situation existed because the shares of most firms were so widely distributed, and management's control over the voting mechanism was so strong, that it was almost impossible for dissident stockholders to get the votes needed to overthrow a management team. However, as noted above, that situation is changing.

Indeed, in recent years the top executives at Mattel, Compaq, Coca-Cola, Lucent, Honeywell, Yahoo, UAL, and Xerox have resigned or been fired after serving as CEO only a short period of time. Most of these departures were no doubt due to their companies' poor performance.

Hostile Takeover
The acquisition of a company over the opposition of its management.

4. **The threat of takeovers. Hostile takeovers** (when management does not want the firm to be taken over) are most likely to occur when a firm's stock is undervalued relative to its potential because of poor management. In a hostile takeover, the managers of the acquired firm are generally fired, and any who manage to stay on lose status and authority. Thus, managers have a strong incentive to take actions designed to maximize stock prices. In the words of one company president, "If you want to keep your job, don't let your stock sell at a bargain price."

STOCKHOLDERS (THROUGH MANAGERS) VERSUS CREDITORS

In addition to conflicts between stockholders and managers, there can also be conflicts between creditors and stockholders. Creditors have a claim on part of the firm's earnings stream for payment of interest and principal on the debt, and they have a claim on the firm's assets in the event of bankruptcy. However, stockholders have control (through the managers) of decisions that affect the profitability and risk of the firm. Creditors lend funds at rates that are based on (1) the riskiness of the firm's existing assets, (2) expectations concerning the riskiness of future asset additions, (3) the firm's existing capital structure (that is, the amount of debt financing used), and (4) expectations concerning future capital structure decisions. These are the primary determinants of the riskiness of a firm's cash flows, hence the safety of its debt issues.

Now suppose stockholders, acting through management, cause a firm to take on a large new project that is far riskier than was anticipated by the creditors. This increased risk will cause the required rate of return on the firm's debt to increase, and that will cause the value of the outstanding debt to fall. If the risky project is successful, all the benefits go to the stockholders, because creditors' returns are fixed at the old, low-risk rate. However, if the project is unsuccessful, the bondholders may have to share in the losses. From the stockholders' point of view, this amounts to a game of "heads I win, tails you lose," which is obviously not good for the creditors. Similarly, suppose its managers borrow additional funds and use the proceeds to repurchase some of the firm's outstanding stock in an effort to "leverage up" stockholders' return on equity. The value of the debt will probably decrease, because more debt will have a claim against the firm's cash flows and assets. In both the riskier asset and the increased leverage situations, stockholders tend to gain at the expense of creditors.

Can and should stockholders, through their managers/agents, try to expropriate wealth from creditors? In general, the answer is no, for unethical behavior is penalized in the business world. First, creditors attempt to protect themselves against stockholders by placing restrictive covenants in debt agreements. Moreover, if creditors perceive that a firm's managers are trying to take advantage of them, they will either refuse to deal further with the firm or else will charge a higher-than-normal interest rate to compensate for the risk of possible exploitation. Thus, firms that deal unfairly with creditors either lose access to the debt markets or are saddled with high interest rates and restrictive covenants, all of which are detrimental to shareholders.

In view of these constraints, it follows that to best serve their shareholders in the long run, managers must play fairly with creditors. As agents of both shareholders and creditors, managers must act in a manner that is fairly balanced between the interests of the two classes of security holders. Similarly, because of other constraints and sanctions, management actions that would expropriate wealth from any of the firm's other *stakeholders*, including its employees, customers, suppliers, and community, will ultimately be to the detriment of its shareholders. In our society, stock price maximization requires fair treatment for all parties whose economic positions are affected by managerial decisions.[10]

SELF-TEST QUESTIONS

What are agency costs, and who bears them?

What are some mechanisms that encourage managers to act in the best interests of stockholders? To not take advantage of bondholders?

Why should managers not take actions that are unfair to any of the firm's stakeholders?

MANAGERIAL ACTIONS TO MAXIMIZE SHAREHOLDER WEALTH

What types of actions can managers take to maximize the price of a firm's stock? To answer this question, we first need to ask, "What factors determine the price of a company's stock?" While we will address this issue in detail in Chapter 8, we can lay out three basic facts here. (1) Any financial asset, including a company's stock, is valuable only to the extent that the asset generates cash flows. (2) The timing of the cash flows matters—cash received sooner is better, because it can be reinvested to produce additional income. (3) Investors are generally averse to risk, so all else equal, they will pay more for a stock whose cash flows are relatively certain than for one with relatively risky cash flows. Because of these three factors, managers can enhance their firms' value (and the stock price) by increasing expected cash flows, speeding them up, and reducing their riskiness.

Within the firm, managers make investment decisions regarding the types of products or services produced, as well as the way goods and services are produced and delivered. Also, managers must decide *how to finance the firm*—what mix of debt

---

[10] For an interesting discussion of the interaction between stockholder value and stakeholder value, see Michael C. Jensen, "Value Maximization, Stakeholder Theory, and Corporate Objective Function," *Journal of Applied Corporate Finance*, Fall 2001, 8–21.

Dividend Policy Decision
The decision as to how much of current earnings to pay out as dividends rather than retain for reinvestment in the firm.

and equity should be used, and what specific types of debt and equity securities should be issued? In addition, the financial manager must decide what percentage of current earnings to pay out as dividends rather than retain and reinvest; this is called the **dividend policy decision.** Each of these investment and financing decisions is likely to affect the level, timing, and riskiness of the firm's cash flows, and therefore the price of its stock. Naturally, managers should make investment and financing decisions designed to maximize the firm's stock price.

Although managerial actions affect the value of a firm's stock, stock prices are also affected by such external factors as legal constraints, the general level of economic activity, tax laws, interest rates, and conditions in the stock market. Figure 1-2 diagrams these general relationships. Working within the set of external constraints shown in the box at the extreme left, management makes a set of long-run strategic policy decisions that chart a future course for the firm. These policy decisions, along with the general level of economic activity and the level of corporate income taxes, influence the firm's expected cash flows, their timing, their eventual payment to stockholders as dividends, and their riskiness.

SELF-TEST QUESTION

Identify some factors beyond a firm's control that influence its stock price.

Profit Maximization
The maximization of the firm's net income.

Earnings Per Share (EPS)
Net income available to common divided by the number of shares of common stock outstanding.

DOES IT MAKE SENSE TO TRY TO MAXIMIZE EARNINGS PER SHARE?

In arguing that managers should take steps to maximize the firm's stock price, we have said nothing about the traditional objective, **profit maximization,** or the maximization of **earnings per share (EPS).** However, while a growing number of ana-

---

FIGURE 1-2 **Summary of Major Factors Affecting Stock Prices**

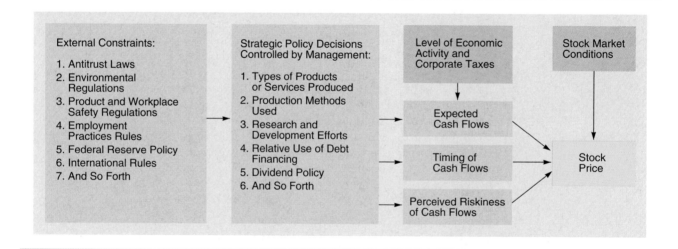

lysts rely on cash flow projections to assess performance, at least as much attention is still paid to accounting measures, especially EPS. The traditional accounting performance measures are appealing because (1) they are easy to use and understand; (2) they are calculated on the basis of more or less standardized accounting practices, which reflect the accounting profession's best efforts to measure financial performance on a consistent basis both across firms and over time; and (3) net income is supposed to be reflective of the firm's potential to produce cash flows over time.

Generally, there is a high correlation between EPS, cash flow, and stock price, and all of them generally rise if a firm's sales rise. Nevertheless, as we will see in subsequent chapters, stock prices depend not just on today's earnings and cash flows—future cash flows and the riskiness of the future earnings stream also affect stock prices. Some actions may increase earnings and yet reduce stock price, while other actions may boost stock price but reduce earnings. For example, consider a company that undertakes large expenditures today that are designed to improve future performance. These expenditures will likely reduce earnings per share, yet the stock market may respond positively if it believes that these expenditures will significantly enhance future earnings. By contrast, a company that undertakes actions today to enhance its earnings may see a drop in its stock price, if the market believes that these actions compromise future earnings and/or dramatically increase the firm's risk.

Even though the level and riskiness of current and future cash flows ultimately determine stockholder value, financial managers cannot ignore the effects of their decisions on reported EPS, because earnings announcements send messages to investors. Say, for example, a manager makes a decision that will ultimately enhance cash flows and stock price, yet the short-run effect is to lower this year's profitability and EPS. Such a decision might be a change in inventory accounting policy that increases reported expenses but also increases cash flow because it reduces current taxes. In this case, it makes sense for the manager to adopt the policy because it generates additional cash, even though it reduces reported profits. Note, though, that management must communicate the reason for the earnings decline, for otherwise the company's stock price will probably decline after the lower earnings are reported.

SELF-TEST QUESTIONS

Is profit maximization an appropriate goal for financial managers?

Should financial managers concentrate strictly on cash flow and ignore the impact of their decisions on EPS?

TYING IT ALL TOGETHER

This chapter has provided an overview of financial management. The key concepts covered are listed below.

- Finance consists of three interrelated areas: (1) **money and capital markets,** (2) **investments,** and (3) **financial management.**

- In recent years the two most important trends in finance have been the **increased globalization of business** and the growing use of **computers and information technology.** These trends are likely to continue in the future.

- The three main forms of business organization are the **sole proprietorship,** the **partnership,** and the **corporation.**

- Although each form of organization offers advantages and disadvantages, **most business is conducted by corporations because this organizational form maximizes larger firms' values.**

- The **financial staff's** task is to **obtain** and **use funds** so as to **maximize the value of the firm.**

- The primary goal of management should be to **maximize stockholders' wealth,** and this means **maximizing the firm's stock price.** Note, though, that actions that maximize stock prices also increase social welfare.

- An **agency problem** is a potential conflict of interests that can arise between a principal and an agent. Two important agency relationships are (1) those between the owners of the firm and its management and (2) those between the managers, acting for stockholders, and the debtholders.

- There are a number of ways to **motivate managers to act in the best interests of stockholders,** including (1) properly structured **managerial compensation,** (2) **direct intervention by stockholders,** (3) the **threat of firing,** and (4) the **threat of takeovers.**

- The **price of a firm's stock** depends on the **cash flows paid to shareholders,** the **timing of the cash flows,** and their **riskiness.** The level and riskiness of cash flows are affected by the **financial environment** as well as by **investment, financing,** and **dividend policy decisions** made by financial managers.

QUESTIONS

1-1 What are the three principal forms of business organization? What are the advantages and disadvantages of each?

1-2 Would the "normal" rate of return on investment be the same in all industries? Would "normal" rates of return change over time? Explain.

1-3 Would the role of a financial manager be likely to increase or decrease in importance relative to other executives if the rate of inflation increased? Explain.

1-4 Should stockholder wealth maximization be thought of as a long-term or a short-term goal— for example, if one action would probably increase the firm's stock price from a current level of $20 to $25 in 6 months and then to $30 in 5 years but another action would probably keep the stock at $20 for several years but then increase it to $40 in 5 years, which action would be better? Can you think of some specific corporate actions that might have these general tendencies?

1-5 Drawing on your background in accounting, can you think of any accounting differences that might make it difficult to compare the relative performance of different firms?

1-6 Would the management of a firm in an oligopolistic or in a competitive industry be more likely to engage in what might be called "socially conscious" practices? Explain your reasoning.

1-7 What's the difference between stock price maximization and profit maximization? Under what conditions might profit maximization *not* lead to stock price maximization?

1-8 If you were the president of a large, publicly owned corporation, would you make decisions to maximize stockholders' welfare or your own personal interests? What are some actions stockholders could take to ensure that management's interests and those of stockholders coincided? What are some other factors that might influence management's actions?

1-9 The president of Southern Semiconductor Corporation (SSC) made this statement in the company's annual report: "SSC's primary goal is to increase the value of the common stockholders' equity over time." Later on in the report, the following announcements were made:
a. The company contributed $1.5 million to the symphony orchestra in Birmingham, Alabama, its headquarters city.
b. The company is spending $500 million to open a new plant in Mexico. No revenues will be produced by the plant for 4 years, so earnings will be depressed during this period versus what they would have been had the decision not been made to open the new plant.
c. The company is increasing its relative use of debt. Whereas assets were formerly financed with 35 percent debt and 65 percent equity, henceforth the financing mix will be 50–50.
d. The company uses a great deal of electricity in its manufacturing operations, and it generates most of this power itself. Plans are to utilize nuclear fuel rather than coal to produce electricity in the future.
e. The company has been paying out half of its earnings as dividends and retaining the other half. Henceforth, it will pay out only 30 percent as dividends.
Discuss how each of these actions would be reacted to by SSC's stockholders and customers, and then how each action might affect SSC's stock price.

1-10 Assume that you are serving on the board of directors of a medium-sized corporation and that you are responsible for establishing the compensation policies of senior management. You believe that the company's CEO is very talented, but your concern is that she is always looking for a better job and may want to boost the company's short-run performance (perhaps at the expense of long-run profitability) to make herself more marketable to other corporations. What effect would these concerns have on the compensation policy you put in place?

1-11 If the overall stock market is extremely volatile, and if many analysts foresee the possibility of a stock market crash, how might these factors influence the way corporations choose to compensate their senior executives?

1-12 Teacher's Insurance and Annuity Association–College Retirement Equity Fund (TIAA–CREF) is the largest institutional shareholder in the United States. Traditionally, TIAA–CREF has acted as a passive investor. However, TIAA–CREF announced a tough new corporate governance policy beginning October 5, 1993.

In a statement mailed to all 1,500 companies in which it invests, TIAA–CREF outlined a policy designed to improve corporate performance, including a goal of higher stock prices for the assets it holds (currently $280 billion), and to encourage corporate boards to have a majority of independent (outside) directors. TIAA–CREF wants to see management more accountable to shareholder interests, as evidenced by its statement that the fund will vote against any director "where companies don't have an effective, independent board which can challenge the CEO."

Historically, TIAA–CREF did not quickly sell poor-performing stocks. In addition, the fund invested a large part of its assets to match performance of the major market indexes locking TIAA–CREF into ownership of certain companies. Further complicating the problem, TIAA–CREF owns stakes of from 1 percent to 10 percent in several companies, and selling such large blocks of stock would depress their prices.

Common stock ownership confers a right to sponsor initiatives to shareholders regarding the corporation. A corresponding voting right exists for shareholders.
a. Is TIAA–CREF an ordinary shareholder?
b. Due to its asset size, TIAA–CREF assumes large positions with which it plans to actively vote. However, who owns TIAA–CREF?
c. Should the investment managers of a fund like TIAA–CREF determine the voting practices of the fund's shares, or should the voting rights be passed on to TIAA–CREF's stakeholders?

1-13 The senior managers of Hancock Oil are evaluating a new oil exploration project. The project requires a large amount of capital and is quite risky, but it has the possibility of being extremely profitable. In a separate action, the company's managers are also considering increasing Hancock's dividend payout ratio. The proposed project and proposed dividend increase are both expected to increase the company's stock price.
a. How would the proposed exploration project affect Hancock's outstanding bondholders?
b. How would the proposed dividend increase affect Hancock's outstanding bondholders?

c. Should Hancock's managers go ahead with the proposed project and dividend increase?

d. What steps can bondholders take to protect themselves against managerial decisions that reduce the value of their bonds?

1-14 Stewart Web Design currently operates an unincorporated partnership with 75 employees. The partners are contemplating organizing as a corporation. How might each of the following actions affect the firm's decision to incorporate?

a. Congress is considering a tax bill that would reduce individual tax rates but increase corporate tax rates.

b. Congress is considering a bill that would extend the coverage of a large number of environmental and labor regulations to now include companies that have more than 50 employees. Presently, companies with fewer than 200 employees are excluded from these regulations.

1-15 Edmund Enterprises recently made a large investment in upgrading its technology. While the technology improvements will not have much of an impact on performance in the short run, they are expected to produce significant cost savings over the next several years. What impact will this investment have on Edmund Enterprises' earnings per share this year? What impact might this investment have on the company's stock price?

SELF-TEST PROBLEM (SOLUTION APPEARS IN APPENDIX B)

ST-1
Key terms
Define each of the following terms:

a. Sole proprietorship; partnership; corporation
b. Stockholder wealth maximization
c. Social responsibility; business ethics
d. Normal profits; normal rate of return
e. Agency problem
f. Performance shares; executive stock options
g. Hostile takeover
h. Profit maximization
i. Earnings per share
j. Dividend policy decision

INTEGRATED CASE

TAKE A DIVE

1-1 Financial Management Overview Kato Summers opened Take A Dive 17 years ago; the store is located in Malibu, California, and sells surfing-related equipment. Today, Take a Dive has 50 employees including Kato and his daughter Amber, who works part time in the store to help pay for her college education.

Kato's business has boomed in recent years, and he is looking for new ways to take advantage of his increasing business opportunities. Although Kato's formal business training is limited, Amber will soon graduate with a degree in finance. Kato has offered her the opportunity to join the business as a full-fledged partner. Amber is interested, but she is also considering other career opportunities in finance.

Right now, Amber is leaning toward staying with the family business, partly because she thinks it faces a number of interesting challenges and opportunities. Amber is particularly interested in further expanding the business and then incorporating it. Kato is intrigued by her ideas, but he is also concerned that her plans might change the way in which he does business. In particular, Kato has a strong commitment to social activism, and he has always tried to strike a balance between work and pleasure. He is worried that these goals will be compromised if the company incorporates and brings in outside shareholders.

Amber and Kato plan to take a long weekend off to sit down and think about all of these issues. Amber, who is highly organized, has outlined a series of questions for them to address:

a. What kinds of career opportunities are open to finance majors?

b. What are the primary responsibilities of a corporate financial staff?

c. What are the most important financial management issues today?
d. (1) What are the alternative forms of business organization?
   (2) What are their advantages and disadvantages?
e. What is the primary goal of the corporation?
   (1) Do firms have any responsibilities to society at large?
   (2) Is stock price maximization good or bad for society?
   (3) Should firms behave ethically?
f. What is an agency relationship?
   (1) What agency relationships exist within a corporation?
   (2) What mechanisms exist to influence managers to act in shareholders' best interests?
   (3) Should shareholders (through managers) take actions that are detrimental to bondholders?
g. Is maximizing stock price the same thing as maximizing profit?
h. What factors affect stock prices?
i. What factors affect the level and riskiness of cash flows?

Please go to our web site **http://brigham.swlearning.com** to access the Cyberproblems.

With your Xtra! CD-ROM, access the Thomson Analytics Problems and use the Thomson Analytics Academic online database to work this chapter's problem.

FINANCIAL STATEMENTS, CASH FLOW, AND TAXES

2

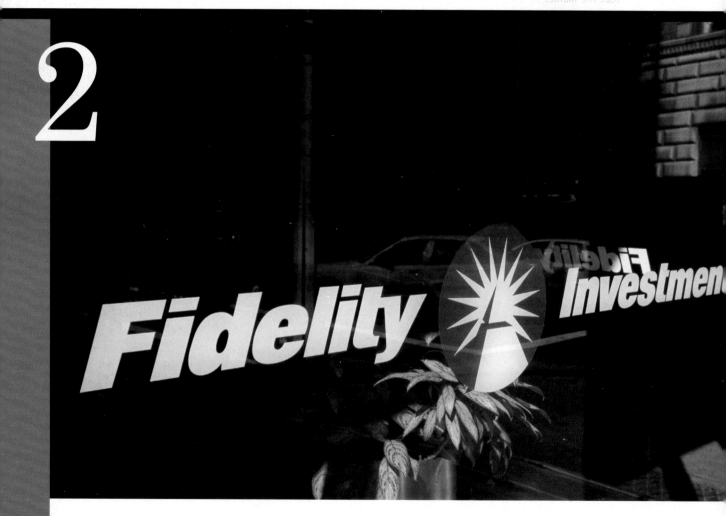

S uppose you are a small investor who knows a little about finance and accounting. Could you compete successfully against large institutional investors with armies of analysts, high-powered computers, and state-of-the-art trading strategies?

The answer, according to one Wall Street legend, is a re-sounding yes! Peter Lynch, who had an outstanding track record as manager of the $10 billion Fidelity Magellan fund and then went on to become the best-selling author of *One Up on Wall Street* and *Beating the Street*, has long argued that small investors can beat the market by using common sense and information available to all of us as we go about our day-to-day lives.

For example, a college student may be more adept at scouting out the new and interesting products that will become tomorrow's success stories than is an investment banker who works 75 hours a week in a New York office. Parents of young children are likely to know which baby foods will succeed, or which diapers are best. Couch potatoes may have the best feel for which tortilla chips have the brightest future, or whether a new remote control is worth its price.

DOING YOUR HOMEWORK
WITH FINANCIAL STATEMENTS

The trick is to find a product that will boom, yet whose manufacturer's stock is undervalued. If this sounds too easy, you are right. Lynch argues that once you have discovered a good product, there is still much homework to be done. This involves combing through the vast amount of financial information that is regularly provided by companies. It also requires taking a closer and more critical look at how the company conducts its business—Lynch refers to this as "kicking the tires."

To illustrate his point, Lynch relates his experience with Dunkin' Donuts. As a consumer, Lynch was impressed with the quality of the product. This impression led him to take a closer look at the company's financial statements and operations. He liked what he saw, and Dunkin' Donuts became one of the best investments in his portfolio.

The next two chapters discuss what financial statements are and how they are analyzed. Once you have identified a good product as a possible investment, the principles discussed in these chapters will help you "kick the tires."

A manager's primary goal is to maximize the value of his or her firm's stock. Value is based on the stream of cash flows the firm will generate in the future. But how does an investor go about estimating future cash flows, and how does a manager decide which actions are most likely to increase cash flows? The answers to both questions lie in a study of the financial statements that publicly traded firms must provide to investors. Here "investors" include both institutions (banks, insurance companies, pension funds, and the like) and individuals. Thus, this chapter begins with a discussion of what the basic financial statements are, how they are used, and what kinds of financial information users need.

The value of any business asset — whether it is a *financial asset* such as a stock or a bond, or a *real (physical) asset* such as land, buildings, and equipment — depends on the usable, after-tax cash flows the asset is expected to produce. Therefore, the chapter also explains the difference between accounting income and cash flow. Finally, since it is *after-tax* cash flow that is important, the chapter provides an overview of the federal income tax system.

Much of the material in this chapter reviews concepts covered in basic accounting courses. However, the information is important enough to go over again. Accounting is used to "keep score," and if a firm's managers do not know the score, they won't know if their actions are appropriate. If you took midterm exams but were not told how you were doing, you would have a difficult time improving your grades. The same thing holds in business. If a firm's managers — whether they are in marketing, personnel, production, or finance — do not understand financial statements, they will not be able to judge the effects of their actions, and the firm will not be successful. Although only accountants need to know how to *make* financial statements, everyone involved with business needs to know how to *interpret* them. ■

A BRIEF HISTORY OF ACCOUNTING
AND FINANCIAL STATEMENTS

www Are you interested in learning more about the history of accounting? If so, take a tour through the "Virtual History of Accounting" organized by the Association of Chartered Accountants in the United States and located at **http://www. acaus.org/acc_his.html**.

Financial statements are pieces of paper with numbers written on them, but it is important to also think about the real assets that underlie the numbers. If you understand how and why accounting began, and how financial statements are used, you can better visualize what is going on, and why accounting information is so important.

Thousands of years ago, individuals (or families) were self-contained in the sense that they gathered their own food, made their own clothes, and built their own shelters. Then specialization began—some people became good at making pots, others at making arrowheads, others at making clothing, and so on.

As specialization began, so did trading, initially in the form of barter. At first, each artisan worked alone, and trade was strictly local. Eventually, though, master craftsmen set up small factories and employed workers, money (in the form of clamshells) began to be used, and trade expanded beyond the local area. As these developments occurred, a primitive form of banking began, with wealthy merchants lending profits from past dealings to enterprising factory owners who needed capital to expand or to young traders who needed money to buy wagons, ships, and merchandise.

When the first loans were made, lenders could physically inspect borrowers' assets and judge the likelihood of the loan's being repaid. Eventually, though, lending became more complex—borrowers were developing larger factories, traders were acquiring fleets of ships and wagons, and loans were being made to develop distant mines and trading posts. At that point, lenders could no longer personally inspect the assets that backed their loans, and they needed some way of summarizing borrowers' assets. Also, some investments were made on a share-of-the-profits basis, and this meant that profits (or income) had to be determined. At the same time, factory owners and large merchants needed reports to see how effectively their own enterprises were being run, and governments needed information for use in assessing taxes. For all these reasons, a need arose for financial statements, for accountants to prepare those statements, and for auditors to verify the accuracy of the accountants' work.

The economic system has grown enormously since its beginning, and accounting has become more complex. However, the original reasons for financial statements still apply: Bankers and other investors need accounting information to make intelligent decisions, managers need it to operate their businesses efficiently, and taxing authorities need it to assess taxes in a reasonable way.

It should be intuitively clear that it is not easy to translate physical assets into numbers, which is what accountants do when they construct financial statements. The numbers shown on balance sheets generally represent the historical costs of assets. However, inventories may be spoiled, obsolete, or even missing; fixed assets such as machinery and buildings may have higher or lower values than their historical costs; and accounts receivable may be uncollectable. Also, some liabilities such as obligations to pay retirees' medical costs may not even show up on the balance sheet. Similarly, some costs reported on the income statement may be understated, as would be true if a plant with a useful life of 10 years were being depreciated over 40 years. When you examine a set of financial statements, you should keep in mind that a physical reality lies behind the numbers, and you should also realize that the translation from physical assets to "correct" numbers is far from precise.

As mentioned previously, it is important for accountants to be able to generate financial statements, while others involved in the business need to know how to interpret them. Particularly, financial managers must have a working knowledge of financial statements and what they reveal to be effective. Spreadsheets provide financial managers with a powerful and reliable tool to conduct financial analysis, and several different types of spreadsheet models are provided with the text. These models demonstrate how financial principles taught in this book are applied in practice. Readers are encouraged to use these models to gain further insights into various concepts and procedures.

FINANCIAL STATEMENTS AND REPORTS

Annual Report
A report issued annually by a corporation to its stockholders. It contains basic financial statements, as well as management's analysis of the past year's operations and opinions about the firm's future prospects.

For an excellent example of a corporate annual report, take a look at 3M's annual report found at **http://www.mmm. com/about3M/index.jhtml**. Then, click on investor relations and annual reports on the left-hand side of your screen. Here you can find several recent annual reports in Adobe Acrobat format. A source for links to the annual reports of many companies is **http://www. annualreportservice.com**.

Of the various reports corporations issue to their stockholders, the **annual report** is probably the most important. Two types of information are given in this report. First, there is a verbal section, often presented as a letter from the chairman, that describes the firm's operating results during the past year and discusses new developments that will affect future operations. Second, the annual report presents four basic financial statements—the *balance sheet*, the *income statement*, the *statement of retained earnings*, and the *statement of cash flows*. Taken together, these statements give an accounting picture of the firm's operations and financial position. Detailed data are provided for the two or three most recent years, along with historical summaries of key operating statistics for the past 5 or 10 years.[1]

The quantitative and verbal materials are equally important. The financial statements report *what has actually happened* to assets, earnings, and dividends over the past few years, whereas the verbal statements attempt to explain why things turned out the way they did.

For illustrative purposes, we shall use data taken from Allied Food Products, a processor and distributor of a wide variety of staple foods, to discuss the basic financial statements. Formed in 1978 when several regional firms merged, Allied has grown steadily, and it has earned a reputation for being one of the best firms in its industry. Allied's earnings dropped a bit in 2002, to $113.5 million versus $117.8 million in 2001. Management reported that the drop resulted from losses associated with a drought and from increased costs due to a three-month strike. However, management then went on to paint a more optimistic picture for the future, stating that full operations had been resumed, that several unprofitable businesses had been eliminated, and that 2003 profits were expected to rise sharply. Of course, an increase in profitability may not occur, and analysts should compare management's past statements with subsequent results. In any event, *the information contained in an annual report is used by investors to help form expectations about future earnings and dividends*. Therefore, the annual report is obviously of great interest to investors.

---

[1] Firms also provide quarterly reports, but these are much less comprehensive. In addition, larger firms file even more detailed statements, giving breakdowns for each major division or subsidiary, with the Securities and Exchange Commission (SEC). These reports, called *10-K reports*, are made available to stockholders upon request to a company's corporate secretary. Finally, many larger firms also publish *statistical supplements*, which give financial statement data and key ratios going back 10 to 20 years, and their reports are available on the World Wide Web.

What is the annual report, and what two types of information are given in it?

What four types of financial statements are typically included in the annual report?

Why is the annual report of great interest to investors?

Are the quantitative and verbal sections of the annual report equally important? Explain.

THE BALANCE SHEET

Balance Sheet
A statement of the firm's financial position at a specific point in time.

The left-hand side of Allied's year-end 2002 and 2001 **balance sheets,** which are given in Table 2-1, shows the firm's assets, while the right-hand side shows the liabilities and equity, or the claims against these assets. The assets are listed in order of their "liquidity," or the length of time it typically takes to convert them to cash. The claims are listed in the order in which they must be paid: Accounts payable must generally be paid within 30 days, notes payable within 90 days, and so on, down to the stockholders' equity accounts, which represent ownership and need never be "paid off."

Some additional points about the balance sheet are worth noting:

1. **Cash versus other assets.** Although the assets are all stated in terms of dollars, only cash represents actual money. (Marketable securities can be converted to cash within a day or two, so they are almost like cash and are reported with cash on the balance sheet.) Receivables are bills others owe Allied. Inventories show the dollars the company has invested in raw materials, work-in-process,

TABLE 2-1	**Allied Food Products: December 31 Balance Sheets (Millions of Dollars)**					
ASSETS	**2002**	**2001**	**LIABILITIES AND EQUITY**		**2002**	**2001**
Cash and marketable securities	$ 10	$ 80	Accounts payable		$ 60	$ 30
Accounts receivable	375	315	Notes payable		110	60
Inventories	615	415	Accruals		140	130
Total current assets	$1,000	$ 810	Total current liabilities		$ 310	$ 220
Net plant and equipment	1,000	870	Long-term bonds		754	580
			Total liabilities		$1,064	$ 800
			Preferred stock (400,000 shares)		40	40
			Common stock (50,000,000 shares)		130	130
			Retained earnings		766	710
			Total common equity		$ 896	$ 840
Total assets	$2,000	$1,680	Total liabilities and equity		$2,000	$1,680

NOTE: The bonds have a sinking fund requirement of $20 million a year. Sinking funds are discussed in Chapter 7, but in brief, a sinking fund simply involves the repayment of long-term debt. Thus, Allied was required to pay off $20 million of its mortgage bonds during 2002. The current portion of the long-term debt is included in notes payable here, although in a more detailed balance sheet it would be shown as a separate item under current liabilities.

and finished goods available for sale. And net plant and equipment reflect the amount of money Allied paid for its fixed assets when it acquired those assets in the past, less accumulated depreciation. Allied can write checks for a total of $10 million (versus current liabilities of $310 million due within a year). The noncash assets should produce cash over time, but they do not represent cash in hand, and the amount of cash they would bring if they were sold today could be higher or lower than the values at which they are carried on the books.

2. **Liabilities versus stockholders' equity.** The claims against assets are of two types—liabilities (or money the company owes) and the stockholders' ownership position.[2] The **common stockholders' equity,** or **net worth,** is a residual. For example, at the end of 2002,

Common Stockholders' Equity (Net Worth)
The capital supplied by common stockholders—common stock, paid-in capital, retained earnings, and, occasionally, certain reserves. *Total equity* is common equity plus preferred stock.

$$\text{Assets} - \text{Liabilities} - \text{Preferred stock} = \text{Common stockholder's equity}$$

$$\$2,000,000,000 - \$1,064,000,000 - \$40,000,000 = \$896,000,000$$

Suppose assets decline in value; for example, suppose some of the accounts receivable are written off as bad debts. Liabilities and preferred stock remain constant, so the value of the common stockholders' equity must decline. Therefore, the risk of asset value fluctuations is borne by the common stockholders. Note, however, that if asset values rise (perhaps because of inflation), these benefits will accrue exclusively to the common stockholders.

3. **Preferred versus common stock.** Preferred stock is a hybrid, or a cross between common stock and debt. In the event of bankruptcy, preferred stock ranks below debt but above common stock. Also, the preferred dividend is fixed, so preferred stockholders do not benefit if the company's earnings grow. Finally, many firms do not use any preferred stock, and those that do generally do not use much of it. Therefore, when the term "equity" is used in finance, we generally mean "common equity" unless the word "total" is included.

4. **Breakdown of the common equity accounts.** The common equity section is divided into two accounts—"common stock" and "retained earnings." The **retained earnings** account is built up over time as the firm "saves" a part of its earnings rather than paying all earnings out as dividends. The common stock account arises from the issuance of stock to raise capital, as discussed in Chapter 8.

Retained Earnings
That portion of the firm's earnings that has been saved rather than paid out as dividends.

The breakdown of the common equity accounts is important for some purposes but not for others. For example, a potential stockholder would want to know whether the company actually earned the funds reported in its equity accounts or whether the funds came mainly from selling stock. A potential creditor, on the other hand, would be more interested in the total equity the owners have in the firm and would be less concerned with the source of the equity. In the remainder of this chapter, we generally aggregate the two common equity accounts and call this sum *common equity* or *net worth.*

---

[2] One could divide liabilities into (1) debts owed to someone and (2) other items, such as deferred taxes, reserves, and so on. Because we do not make this distinction, the terms *debt* and *liabilities* are used synonymously. It should be noted that firms occasionally set up reserves for certain contingencies, such as the potential costs involved in a lawsuit currently in the courts. These reserves represent an accounting transfer from retained earnings to the reserve account. If the company wins the suit, retained earnings will be credited, and the reserve will be eliminated. If it loses, a loss will be recorded, cash will be reduced, and the reserve will be eliminated.

5. **Inventory accounting.** Allied uses the FIFO (first-in, first-out) method to determine the inventory value shown on its balance sheet ($615 million). It could have used the LIFO (last-in, first-out) method. During a period of rising prices, by taking out old, low-cost inventory and leaving in new, high-cost items, FIFO will produce a higher balance sheet inventory value but a lower cost of goods sold on the income statement. (This is strictly accounting; companies actually use older items first.) Since Allied uses FIFO, and since inflation has been occurring, (a) its balance sheet inventories are higher than they would have been had it used LIFO, (b) its cost of goods sold is lower than it would have been under LIFO, and (c) its reported profits are therefore higher. In Allied's case, if the company had elected to switch to LIFO in 2002, its balance sheet figure for inventories would have been $585,000,000 rather than $615,000,000, and its earnings (which will be discussed in the next section) would have been reduced by $18,000,000. Thus, the inventory valuation method can have a significant effect on financial statements. This is important when an analyst is comparing different companies.

6. **Depreciation methods.** Most companies prepare two sets of financial statements—one for tax purposes and one for reporting to stockholders. Generally, they use the most accelerated method permitted under the law to calculate depreciation for tax purposes, but they use straight line, which results in a lower depreciation charge, for stockholder reporting. However, Allied has elected to use rapid depreciation for both stockholder reporting and tax purposes. Had Allied elected to use straight line depreciation for stockholder reporting, its 2002 depreciation expense would have been $25,000,000 less, so the $1 billion shown for "net plant" on its balance sheet would have been $25,000,000 higher. Its net income and its retained earnings would also have been higher.

7. **The time dimension.** The balance sheet may be thought of as a snapshot of the firm's financial position *at a point in time*—for example, on December 31, 2001. Thus, on December 31, 2001, Allied had $80 million of cash and marketable securities, but this account had been reduced to $10 million by the end of 2002. The balance sheet changes every day as inventories are increased or decreased, as fixed assets are added or retired, as bank loans are increased or decreased, and so on. Companies whose businesses are seasonal have especially large changes in their balance sheets. Allied's inventories are low just before the harvest season, but they are high just after the fall crops have been brought in and processed. Similarly, most retailers have large inventories just before Christmas but low inventories and high accounts receivable just after Christmas. Therefore, firms' balance sheets change over the year, depending on when the statement is constructed.

SELF-TEST QUESTIONS

What is the balance sheet, and what information does it provide?

How is the order of the information shown on the balance sheet determined?

Why might a company's December 31 balance sheet differ from its June 30 balance sheet?

Income Statement

A statement summarizing the firm's revenues and expenses over an accounting period, generally a quarter or a year.

Table 2-2 gives the 2002 and 2001 **income statements** for Allied Food Products. Net sales are shown at the top of each statement, after which various costs are subtracted to obtain the net income available to common shareholders, which is generally referred to as net income. These costs include operating costs, interest costs, and taxes. A report on earnings and dividends per share is given at the bottom of the income statement. Earnings per share (EPS) is called "the bottom line," denoting that of all the items on the income statement, EPS is the most important. Allied earned $2.27 per share in 2002, down from $2.36 in 2001, but it still raised the dividend from $1.06 to $1.15.[3]

Taking a closer look at the income statement, we see that depreciation and amortization are important components of total operating costs. Since they are similar, depreciation and amortization are often lumped together on the income statement. Depreciation and amortization both represent allocations of the costs of assets over their useful lives; however, there are some important distinctions. Recall from accounting that **depreciation** is an annual charge against income that reflects the estimated dollar cost of the capital equipment used up in the production process. Depreciation applies to **tangible assets,** such as plant and equipment, whereas **amortization** applies to **intangible assets** such as patents, copyrights, and trademarks. Until a recent change in accounting standards, companies were allowed to amortize goodwill that was recorded when one firm purchased another firm for more than its book value.

Depreciation

The charge to reflect the cost of assets used up in the production process. Depreciation is not a cash outlay.

Tangible Assets

Physical assets such as plant and equipment.

Amortization

A noncash charge similar to depreciation except that it is used to write off the costs of intangible assets.

Managers, security analysts, and bank loan officers often calculate **EBITDA,** which is defined as earnings before interest, taxes, depreciation, and amortization. Allied currently has no amortization charges, so the depreciation and amortization on its income statement comes solely from depreciation. In 2002, Allied's EBITDA was $383.8 million. Subtracting the $100 million of depreciation expense from its EBITDA leaves the company with $283.8 million in operating income (EBIT). After subtracting $88 million in interest expense and $78.3 million in taxes, we obtain net income before preferred dividends of $117.5 million. Finally, we subtract out $4 million in preferred dividends, which leaves Allied with $113.5 million in net income available to common stockholders. When analysts refer to a company's net income, they generally mean net income available to common shareholders. Likewise, throughout this book unless otherwise indicated, net income means net income available to common stockholders.

Intangible Assets

Assets such as patents, copyrights, trademarks, and goodwill.

EBITDA

Earnings before interest, taxes, depreciation, and amortization.

While the balance sheet can be thought of as a snapshot in time, the income statement reports on operations *over a period of time,* for example, during the calendar year 2002. During 2002 Allied had sales of $3 billion, and its net income available to common stockholders was $113.5 million. Income statements can cover any period of time, but they are usually prepared monthly, quarterly, or annually. Of course, sales, costs, and profits will be larger the longer the reporting period, and the sum of the last 12 monthly (or 4 quarterly) income statements should equal the values shown on the annual income statement.

---

[3] Companies must report "comprehensive income" as well as net income. Comprehensive income is equal to net income plus several comprehensive income items, such as the unrealized gain or loss that occurs when a marketable security, classified as available for sale, is marked-to-market. For our purposes, in this introductory finance text, we will assume that there are no comprehensive income items, so we will present only basic income statements throughout the text.

TABLE 2-2

Allied Food Products: Statement of Retained Earnings for Year Ending December 31, 2002 (Millions of Dollars)

	2002	2001
Net sales	$3,000.0	$2,850.0
Operating costs excluding depreciation and amortization	2,616.2	2,497.0
Earnings before interest, taxes, depreciation, and amortization (EBITDA)	$ 383.8	$ 353.0
Depreciation	100.0	90.0
Amortization	0.0	0.0
Depreciation and amortization	$ 100.0	$ 90.0
Earnings before interest and taxes (EBIT, or operating income)	$ 283.8	263.0
Less interest	88.0	60.0
Earnings before taxes (EBT)	$ 195.8	$ 203.0
Taxes (40%)	78.3	81.2
Net income before preferred dividends[a]	$ 117.5	$ 121.8
Preferred dividends	4.0	4.0
Net income	$ 113.5	$ 117.8
Common dividends	$ 57.5	$ 53.0
Addition to retained earnings	$ 56.0	$ 64.8
Per-share data:		
Common stock price	$23.00	$26.00
Earnings per share (EPS)[b]	$ 2.27	$ 2.36
Dividends per share (DPS)[b]	$ 1.15	$ 1.06
Book value per share (BVPS)[b]	$17.92	$16.80
Cash flow per share (CFPS)[b]	$ 4.27	$ 4.16

[a] On a typical firm's income statement, this line would be labeled "net income" rather than "net income before preferred dividends." However, when we use the term net income in this text, we mean net income available to common shareholders. To simplify the terminology, we refer to net income available to common shareholders as simply net income. Students should understand that when they review annual reports, firms use the term net income to mean income after taxes but before preferred and common dividends.

[b] There are 50,000,000 shares of common stock outstanding. Note that EPS is based on earnings after preferred dividends—that is, on net income available to common stockholders. Calculations of EPS, DPS, BVPS, and CFPS for 2002 are as follows:

$$\text{Earnings per share} = \text{EPS} = \frac{\text{Net income}}{\text{Common shares outstanding}} = \frac{\$113,500,000}{50,000,000} = \$2.27.$$

$$\text{Dividends per share} = \text{DPS} = \frac{\text{Dividends paid to common stockholders}}{\text{Common shares outstanding}} = \frac{\$57,500,000}{50,000,000} = \$1.15.$$

$$\text{Book value per share} = \text{BVPS} = \frac{\text{Total common equity}}{\text{Common shares outstanding}} = \frac{\$896,000,000}{50,000,000} = \$17.92.$$

$$\text{Cash flow per share} = \text{CFPS} = \frac{\text{Net income} + \text{Depreciation} + \text{Amortization}}{\text{Common shares outstanding}} = \frac{\$213,500,000}{50,000,000} = \$4.27.$$

For planning and control purposes, management generally forecasts monthly (or perhaps quarterly) income statements, and it then compares actual results to the budgeted statements. If revenues are below and costs above the forecasted levels, then management should take corrective steps before the problem becomes too serious.

What is an income statement, and what information does it provide?

Why is earnings per share called "the bottom line"?

Differentiate between amortization and depreciation.

What is EBITDA?

Regarding the time period reported, how does the income statement differ from the balance sheet?

STATEMENT OF RETAINED EARNINGS

Statement of Retained Earnings
A statement reporting how much of the firm's earnings were retained in the business rather than paid out in dividends. The figure for retained earnings that appears here is the sum of the annual retained earnings for each year of the firm's history.

Changes in retained earnings between balance sheet dates are reported in the **statement of retained earnings.** Table 2-3 shows that Allied earned $113.5 million during 2002, paid out $57.5 million in common dividends, and plowed $56 million back into the business. Thus, the balance sheet item "Retained earnings" increased from $710 million at the end of 2001 to $766 million at the end of 2002.

Note that "Retained earnings" represents a *claim against assets*, not assets per se. Moreover, firms retain earnings primarily to expand the business, and this means investing in plant and equipment, in inventories, and so on, *not* piling up cash in a bank account. Changes in retained earnings occur because common stockholders allow the firm to reinvest funds that otherwise could be distributed as dividends. *Thus, retained earnings as reported on the balance sheet do not represent cash and are not "available" for the payment of dividends or anything else.*[4]

---

[4] The amount reported in the retained earnings account is *not* an indication of the amount of cash the firm has. Cash (as of the balance sheet date) is found in the cash account, an asset account. A positive number in the retained earnings account indicates only that in the past the firm has earned some income, but its dividends have been less than its earnings. Even though a company reports record earnings and shows an increase in the retained earnings account, it still may be short of cash.

The same situation holds for individuals. You might own a new BMW (no loan), lots of clothes, and an expensive stereo, hence have a high net worth, but if you had only 23 cents in your pocket plus $5 in your checking account, you would still be short of cash.

TABLE 2-3	Allied Food Products: Statement of Retained Earnings for Year Ending December 31, 2002 (Millions of Dollars)

Balance of retained earnings, December 31, 2001	$710.0
Add: Net income, 2002	113.5
Less: Dividends to common stockholders	(57.5)[a]
Balance of retained earnings, December 31, 2002	$766.0

[a] Here, and throughout the book, parentheses are used to denote negative numbers.

FINANCIAL ANALYSIS ON THE INTERNET

A wide range of valuable financial information is available on the Internet. With just a couple of clicks, an investor can easily find the key financial statements for most publicly traded companies.

Say, for example, you are thinking about buying Disney stock, and you are looking for financial information regarding the company's recent performance. Here's a partial (but by no means a complete) list of places you can go to get started:

■ One source is Yahoo's finance web site, **finance.yahoo. com**.[a] Here you will find updated market information along with links to a variety of interesting research sites. Enter a stock's ticker symbol, click on Get Quotes, and you will see the stock's current price, along with recent news about the company. Click on Profile and you will find a report on the company's key financial ratios. Links to the company's financials (income statement, balance sheet, and statement of cash flows) can also be found. The Yahoo site also has a list of insider transactions, so you can tell if a company's CEO and other key insiders are buying or selling their company's stock. In addition, there is a message board where investors share opinions about the company, and there is a link to the company's filings with the Securities and Exchange Commission (SEC). Note that, in most cases, a more complete list of the SEC filings can be found at **www.sec.gov** or at **www.edgar-online.com**.

■ Other sources for up-to-date market information are **money.cnn.com** and **cbs.marketwatch.com**. Each also has an area where you can obtain stock quotes along with company financials, links to Wall Street research, and links to SEC filings.

■ Another good source is **www.quicken.com**. Enter the ticker symbol in the area labeled quotes and research. The site will take you to an area where you can find a link to the company's financial statements, along with analysts' earnings estimates and SEC filings. This site also has a section where you can estimate the stock's intrinsic value. (In Chapter 8 we will discuss various methods for calculating intrinsic value.)

■ If you are looking for charts of key accounting variables (for example, sales, inventory, depreciation and amortization, and reported earnings), along with the financial statements, take a look at **www.smartmoney.com**.

■ Another good place to look is **www.marketguide.com**. Here you find links to analysts' research reports along with the key financial statements.

■ Online access to annual reports for thousands of companies is provided at **www.annualreportservice.com**. The user must sign up but membership is free.

■ Mergent Inc., formerly known as Moody's Financial Information Services, provides a subscription-based web site **www.fisonline.com**. Once you click on "Sign-In" on the left side of the computer screen, you can enter either a company name or its ticker symbol and then click submit. When the new screen appears, click on the company name, and a listing of available information appears on the screen. You can obtain the company's highlights, history, and various financial information, including ratio analysis, earnings estimates, and access to Edgar documents.

■ The **www.bloomberg.com** site provides the user with general market and money information. When you input a stock's ticker symbol, you obtain price and return information, earnings estimates, and fundamental data such as shares outstanding, market capitalization, last dividend reported, and so on.

■ The **moneycentral.msn.com/investor/home.asp** site provides the user with general market information as well as stock information. When you enter a stock's ticker symbol, you obtain fundamental data and access to earnings estimates, SEC filings, etc.

■ A market snapshot including the S&P 500 Index, NYSE Composite Index, and Nasdaq Composite Index are provided at **www.spcomstock.com**. When you enter a stock's ticker symbol, you obtain the stock price quote, company profile, and charts of the firm's stock price over time.

■ If you enter a stock's ticker symbol at **money.netscape. cnn.com/money/**, you can then obtain the company's financials, profile, stock charts, and so on.

■ Two other places to consider: **www.hoovers.com** and **my.zacks.com**. Each has free research available along with more detailed information provided to subscribers.

Once you have accumulated all of this information, you may be looking for sites that provide opinions regarding the direction of the overall market and views regarding individual stocks. Two popular sites in this category are The Motley Fool's web site, **www.fool.com**, and the web site for TheStreet.com, **www.thestreet.com**.

Keep in mind that this list is just a small subset of the information available online. You should also realize that a lot of these sites change their content over time, and new and interesting sites are always being added to the Internet.

---

[a] To avoid redundancy, we have intentionally left off **http://** in all web addresses given here. A quick way to change an address is to highlight the portion of the address that is different and type in the appropriate letters of the new address. Once you're finished just press Enter.

ANALYSTS ARE INCREASINGLY RELYING ON CASH FLOW TO VALUE STOCKS

A few years ago, Tokyo-based Softbank acquired several Internet-related businesses, including Ziff-Davis Inc., which publishes more than 80 magazines including *PC Week* and *PC Magazine*. Ziff-Davis also provides training courses in computer technology, and it distributes information through the Internet and computer trade shows.

In an article on Softbank, *Barron's* indicated that Ziff-Davis has been "losing money," and a quick look at the company's recent income statements confirms that it had losses in 1998 and the first quarter of 1999. Despite the company's negative reported earnings, the company's chief financial officer, Timothy O'Brien, took exception with the notion that Ziff-Davis was "losing money." So, he sent *Barron's* the following response:

To the Editor:

In his discussion of Softbank, Neil Martin (*International Trader*, June 14) referred to Ziff-Davis as "losing money." In fact, Ziff-Davis continues to generate significant positive cash flow.

We are a diversified media company. Analysts measure our strength and stability relative to our ability to generate EBITDA (earnings before interest, taxes, depreciation, and amortization). Analysts project that we will generate EBITDA of approximately $220 million in 1999, and that takes into account our substantial investment in ZDTV, the company's 24-hour cable network devoted to computing and the Internet.

Ziff-Davis did report a net loss for 1998 and for the first quarter of 1999. However, this loss was due to noncash expenses, primarily the amortization of approximately $120 million in goodwill per year. Even with continuing investments in our key businesses, Ziff-Davis has the financial flexibility to continue to repay indebtedness with free cash flow.

Timothy C. O'Brien,
Chief Financial Officer, Ziff-Davis

Cash-flow measures such as EBITDA have long been popular with bankers and other short-term lenders, who focus more on borrowers' ability to generate cash to pay off loans than on ac-

---

What is the statement of retained earnings, and what information does it provide?

Why do changes in retained earnings occur?

Explain why the following statement is true: "Retained earnings as reported on the balance sheet do not represent cash and are not 'available' for the payment of dividends or anything else."

NET CASH FLOW

Net Cash Flow

The actual net cash, as opposed to accounting net income, that a firm generates during some specified period.

When you studied income statements in accounting, the emphasis was probably on the firm's net income. In finance, however, we focus on **net cash flow.** The value of an asset (or a whole firm) is determined by the cash flow it generates. The firm's net income is important, but cash flow is even more important because dividends must be paid in cash and because cash is necessary to purchase the assets required to continue operations.

As we discussed in Chapter 1, the firm's goal should be to maximize its stock price. Since the value of any asset, including a share of stock, depends on the cash flow produced by the asset, managers should strive to maximize the cash flow available to investors over the long run. A business's *net cash flow* generally differs from its counting earnings. In the past, these measures were less popular with stock analysts, who focused on reported earnings and price earnings ratios. However, today more and more Wall Street analysts are siding with Tim O'Brien, arguing that cash flow measures such as EBITDA often provide a better indication of true value than do earnings per share.

These analysts note that the DA part of EBITDA reduces reported profits but not cash, so EBITDA reflects the cash available to a firm better than accounting profits. It is logical that credit analysts interested in a company's ability to repay its loans focus heavily on EBITDA, but what about equity analysts, who are seeking to find a firm's value to its stockholders? First, most analysts agree that a firm's value depends on its ability to generate cash flows over the long run. If depreciation and amortization (DA) charges truly reflect a decline in the assets used to produce cash flows, then the DA will have to be reinvested in the business if cash flows are to continue. The DA may reflect "available cash" in the short run, but it is not truly available to investors because it will have to be reinvested if the business is to continue to operate.

So, analysts must consider the nature of the D and A charges. If these charges are related to essential assets then they should be deducted to get an idea of the firm's long-run cash generat-

ing potential. The key question then becomes, "Will the company be required to reinvest the cash flow reflected in the DA part of EBITDA if it is to continue to generate cash flow on into the future?" If the answer is yes, then the DA component is not "free cash flow" that is available to investors, and it should be deducted when determining the firm's long-run earning power. If the answer is no, then DA does represent free cash flow and is available to investors.

As it turns out, Ziff-Davis' performance has been much weaker than expected. In 2000, Softbank split up the company and sold the magazine portion to Willis Stein & Partners, where it now operates under the name Ziff-Davis Media. More recently, Ziff-Davis Media has struggled to meet its large debt obligations in the face of a declining economy and a struggling technology sector. So, it may be the case that the original *Barron's* article was correct and that the company's net loss was an early indicator of troubles to come.

SOURCE: *Barron's*, July 19, 1999, 54.

Accounting Profit
A firm's net income as reported on its income statement.

accounting profit because some of the revenues and expenses listed on the income statement were not paid in cash during the year. The relationship between net cash flow and net income can be expressed as follows:

$$\text{Net cash flow} = \text{Net income} - \text{Noncash revenues} + \text{Noncash charges}. \quad (2\text{-}1)$$

The primary examples of noncash charges are depreciation and amortization. These items reduce net income but are not paid out in cash, so we add them back to net income when calculating net cash flow. Another example of a noncash charge is deferred taxes. In some instances, companies are allowed to defer tax payments to a later date even though the tax payment is reported as an expense on the income statement. Therefore, deferred tax payments would be added to net income when calculating net cash flow.[5] At the same time, some revenues may not be collected in cash during the year, and these items must be subtracted from net income when calculating net cash flow.

Typically, depreciation and amortization are by far the largest noncash items, and in many cases the other noncash items roughly net out to zero. For this reason, many analysts assume that net cash flow equals net income plus depreciation and amortization:

$$\text{Net cash flow} = \text{Net income} + \text{Depreciation and amortization}. \quad (2\text{-}2)$$

---

[5] Deferred taxes may arise, for example, if a company uses accelerated depreciation for tax purposes but straight-line depreciation for reporting its financial statements to investors.

To keep things simple, we will generally assume Equation 2-2 holds. However, you should remember that Equation 2-2 will not accurately reflect net cash flow in those instances where there are significant noncash items beyond depreciation and amortization.

We can illustrate Equation 2-2 with 2002 data for Allied taken from Table 2-2:

$$\text{Net cash flow} = \$113.5 + \$100.0 = \$213.5 \text{ million.}$$

To illustrate depreciation itself, suppose a machine with a life of five years and a zero expected salvage value was purchased in 2001 for $100,000 and placed into service in 2002. This $100,000 cost is not expensed in the purchase year; rather, it is charged against production over the machine's five-year depreciable life. If the depreciation expense were not taken, profits would be overstated, and taxes would be too high. So, the annual depreciation charge is deducted from sales revenues, along with such other costs as labor and raw materials, to determine income. However, because the $100,000 was actually expended back in 2001, the depreciation charged against income in 2002 and subsequent years is not a cash outlay, as are labor or raw materials charges. *Depreciation is a noncash charge, so it must be added back to net income to obtain the net cash flow.* If we assume that all other noncash items (including amortization) sum to zero, then net cash flow is simply equal to net income plus depreciation.

SELF-TEST QUESTIONS

Differentiate between net cash flow and accounting profit.

In accounting, the emphasis is on net income. What is emphasized in finance, and why is that item emphasized?

Assuming that depreciation and amortization are a firm's only noncash costs, how is the firm's net cash flow calculated?

STATEMENT OF CASH FLOWS

Net cash flow represents the amount of cash a business generates for its shareholders in a given year. However, the fact that a company generates high cash flow does not necessarily mean that the *amount of cash* reported on its balance sheet will also be high. The cash flow may be used in a variety of ways. For example, the firm may use its cash flow to pay dividends, to increase inventories, to finance accounts receivable, to invest in fixed assets, to reduce debt, or to buy back common stock. Indeed, the company's cash position as reported on the balance sheet is affected by a great many factors, including the following:

1. **Cash flow.** Other things held constant, a positive net cash flow will lead to more cash in the bank. However, as we discuss below, other things are generally not held constant.

2. **Changes in working capital.** Net working capital, which is discussed in detail in Part 6, is defined as current assets minus current liabilities. Increases in current assets other than cash, such as inventories and accounts receivable, decrease cash, whereas decreases in these accounts increase cash. For example, if

inventories are to increase, the firm must use some of its cash to buy the additional inventory, whereas if inventories decrease, this generally means the firm is selling off inventories and not replacing them, hence generating cash. On the other hand, increases in current liabilities such as accounts payable increase cash, whereas decreases in these accounts reduce it. For example, if payables increase, the firm has received additional credit from its suppliers, which saves cash, but if payables decrease, this means the firm has used cash to pay off its suppliers.

3. **Fixed assets.** If a company invests in fixed assets, this will reduce its cash position. On the other hand, the sale of fixed assets will increase cash.

4. **Security transactions and dividend payments.** If a company issues stock or bonds during the year, the funds raised will enhance its cash position. On the other hand, if it uses cash to buy back outstanding debt or equity, or pays dividends to its shareholders, this will reduce cash.

Statement of Cash Flows
A statement reporting the impact of a firm's operating, investing, and financing activities on cash flows over an accounting period.

Each of the above factors is reflected in the **statement of cash flows,** which summarizes the changes in a company's cash position. The statement separates activities into three categories:

1. *Operating activities,* which includes net income, depreciation, and changes in current assets and current liabilities other than cash and short-term debt.

2. *Investing activities,* which includes investments in or sales of fixed assets.

3. *Financing activities,* which includes cash raised during the year by issuing short-term debt, long-term debt, or stock. Also, since dividends paid or cash used to buy back outstanding stock or bonds reduces the company's cash, such transactions are included here.

Accounting texts explain how to prepare the statement of cash flows, but the statement is used to help answer questions such as these: Is the firm generating enough cash to purchase the additional assets required for growth? Is the firm generating any extra cash that can be used to repay debt or to invest in new products? Will inadequate cash flows force the company to issue more stock? Such information is useful both for managers and investors, so the statement of cash flows is an important part of the annual report. Financial managers generally use this statement, along with the cash budget, when forecasting their companies' cash positions. This issue is considered in more detail in Part 6.

Table 2-4 is Allied's statement of cash flows as it would appear in the company's annual report. The top part of the table shows cash flows generated by and used in operations—for Allied, operations provided net cash flows of *minus* $2.5 million. The operating cash flows are generated in the normal course of business, and this amount is determined by adjusting the net income figure to account for depreciation and amortization plus other cash flows related to operations. Allied's day-to-day operations in 2002 provided $257.5 million; however, the increase in receivables and inventories more than offset this amount, resulting in a *negative* $2.5 million cash flow from operations.

The second section shows long-term fixed-assets investing activities. Allied purchased fixed assets totaling $230 million; this was the only long-term investment it made during 2002.

Allied's financing activities, shown in the third section, include borrowing from banks (notes payable), selling new bonds, and paying dividends on its common and

OPERATING ACTIVITIES	
Net income before preferred dividends	$117.5
Additions (Sources of Cash)	
Depreciation and amortization[a]	100.0
Increase in accounts payable	30.0
Increase in accruals	10.0
Subtractions (Uses of Cash)	
Increase in accounts receivable	(60.0)
Increase in inventories	(200.0)
Net cash provided by operating activities	($ 2.5)
LONG-TERM INVESTING ACTIVITIES	
Cash used to acquire fixed assets[b]	($230.0)
FINANCING ACTIVITIES	
Increase in notes payable	$ 50.0
Increase in bonds	174.0
Payment of common and preferred dividends	(61.5)
Net cash provided by financing activities	$162.5
Net decrease in cash and marketable securities	($ 70.0)
Cash and securities at beginning of year	80.0
Cash and securities at end of year	$ 10.0

[a] Depreciation and amortization are noncash expenses that were deducted when calculating net income. They must be added back to show the actual cash flow from operations.

[b] The net increase in fixed assets is $130 million; however, this net amount is after deducting the year's depreciation expense. Depreciation expense must be added back to find the actual expenditures on fixed assets. From the company's income statement, we see that the 2002 depreciation expense is $100 million; thus, expenditures on fixed assets were actually $230 million.

preferred stock. Allied raised $224 million by borrowing, but it paid $61.5 million in preferred and common dividends, so its net inflow of funds from financing activities was $162.5 million.

When all of the sources and uses of cash are totaled, we see that Allied's cash outflows exceeded its cash inflows by $70 million during 2002. It met that shortfall by drawing down its cash and marketable securities holdings by $70 million, as confirmed by Table 2-1, the firm's balance sheet.

Allied's statement of cash flows should be worrisome to its managers and to outside analysts. The company had a $2.5 million cash shortfall from operations, it spent $230 million on new fixed assets, and it paid out another $61.5 million in dividends. It covered these cash outlays by borrowing heavily and by selling off most of its marketable securities. Obviously, this situation cannot continue year after year, so something will have to be done. In Chapter 3, we will consider some of the actions Allied's financial staff might recommend to ease the cash flow problem.

Does the fact that a company generates high cash flow necessarily mean that the amount of cash reported on its balance sheet will also be high? Briefly explain.

Identify four factors that affect the company's cash position as reported on the balance sheet.

What is the statement of cash flows, and what types of questions does it answer?

Identify and briefly explain the three different categories of activities shown in the statement of cash flows.

MODIFYING ACCOUNTING DATA FOR MANAGERIAL DECISIONS

Thus far in the chapter we have focused on financial statements as they are prepared by accountants and presented in the annual report. However, these statements are designed more for use by creditors and tax collectors than for managers and equity (stock) analysts. Therefore, certain modifications are used for corporate decision making and stock valuation purposes. In the following sections we discuss how financial analysts combine stock prices and accounting data to evaluate and reward managerial performance.

OPERATING ASSETS AND OPERATING CAPITAL

Different firms have different financial structures, different tax situations, and different amounts of nonoperating assets. These differences affect traditional accounting measures such as the rate of return on equity. They can cause two firms, or two divisions within a single firm, that actually have similar operations to appear to be operated with different efficiency. This is important, because if managerial compensation systems are to function properly, operating managers must be judged and compensated for those things that are under their control, not on the basis of things outside their control. Therefore, to judge managerial performance, we need to compare managers' ability to generate *operating income* (or *EBIT*) with the *operating assets* under their control.

Operating Assets
The cash and marketable securities, accounts receivable, inventories, and fixed assets necessary to operate the business.

The first step in modifying the traditional accounting framework is to divide total assets into two categories, **operating assets,** which consist of the cash and marketable securities, accounts receivable, inventories, and fixed assets necessary to operate the business, and **nonoperating assets,** which would include cash and marketable securities above the level required for normal operations, investments in subsidiaries, land held for future use, and the like. Moreover, operating assets are further divided into *working capital* and fixed assets such as plant and equipment. Obviously, if a manager can generate a given amount of profits and cash flows with a relatively small investment in operating assets, that reduces the amount of capital investors must put up and thus increases the rate of return on that capital.

Nonoperating Assets
Cash and marketable securities above the level required for normal operations, investments in subsidiaries, land held for future use, and other nonessential assets.

Notice that our definitions of operating assets and nonoperating assets make no mention of such intangible assets as patents, copyrights, trademarks, and goodwill. Most companies do not report significant levels of intangible assets, so to keep things as simple as possible, we simply assume that intangibles are included in reported fixed operating assets.

The primary source of capital for business is investors—stockholders, bondholders, and lenders such as banks. Investors must be paid for the use of their money, with payment coming as interest in the case of debt and as dividends plus capital gains in the case of stock. So, if a company acquires more assets than it actually needs, and thus raises too much capital, then its capital costs will be unnecessarily high.

Must all of the capital used to acquire assets be obtained from investors? The answer is no, because some of the funds will come from suppliers and be reported as *accounts payable*, while other funds will come as *accrued wages and accrued taxes*, which amount to short-term loans from workers and tax authorities. Generally, both accounts payable and accruals are "free" in the sense that no explicit fee is charged for their use. Therefore, if a firm needs $100 million of current assets, but it has $10 million of accounts payable and another $10 million of accrued wages and taxes, then its *investor-supplied capital* would be only $80 million.

Those current assets used in operations are called **operating working capital,** and operating working capital less accounts payable and accruals is called **net operating working capital.** Therefore, net operating working capital is the working capital acquired with investor-supplied funds.[6] Here is a workable definition in equation form:

Operating Working Capital
Current assets used in operations.

Net Operating Working Capital
Operating working capital less accounts payable and accruals. It is the working capital acquired with investor-supplied funds.

$$\text{Net operating working capital} = \text{All current assets} - \begin{array}{c}\text{All current}\\ \text{liabilities that do}\\ \text{not charge interest.}\end{array} \qquad (2\text{-}3)$$

Now think about how these concepts can be used in practice. First, all companies must carry some cash to "grease the wheels" of their operations. Companies continuously cash checks from customers and write checks to suppliers, employees, and so on. Because inflows and outflows do not coincide perfectly, a company must keep some cash and marketable securities in its bank account. In other words, some cash and marketable securities is required to conduct operations. The same is true for most other current assets, such as inventory and accounts receivable, which are required for normal operations. Our measure of operating working capital assumes that cash and marketable securities on the balance sheet represent the amount that is required under normal operations. However, in some instances companies have large holdings of cash and marketable securities that they are holding as a reserve for some contingency, or as a "parking place" for funds prior to an acquisition, a major capital investment program, or the like. In such instances, the excess cash and marketable securities should not be viewed as part of operating working capital.

---

[6] Note that the term "capital" can be given two meanings. First, when accountants use the term "capital," they typically mean the sum of long-term debt, preferred stock, and common equity, or perhaps those items plus interest-bearing short-term debt. However, when economists use the term, they generally mean assets used in production, as in "labor plus capital." If all funds were raised from long-term sources, and if all assets were operating assets, then money capital would equal operating assets, and the accountants' capital would always equal the economists' capital. When you encounter the term "capital" in the business and financial literature, it can mean either asset capital or money capital. For example, in Coca-Cola's operating manuals, which explain to its employees how Coke wants the company to be operated, capital means "assets financed by investor-supplied capital." However, in most accounting and finance textbooks, and in the traditional finance literature, "capital" means investor-supplied capital, not assets. It might be easier if we picked one meaning and then used it consistently in this book. However, that would be misleading, because both meanings are encountered in practice. Therefore, we shall use the term "capital" in both ways. However, you should be able to figure out which definition is implied from the context in which the term is used.

Looking at the other side of the balance sheet, some current liabilities—especially accounts payable and accruals—arise in the normal course of operations. Moreover, each dollar of these current liabilities is a dollar that the company does not have to raise from investors to acquire current assets. Therefore, when finding the net operating working capital, we deduct these current liabilities from the operating current assets. Other current liabilities that charge interest, such as notes payable to banks, are treated as investor-supplied capital and thus are not deducted when calculating net operating working capital.

We can apply these definitions to Allied, using the balance sheet data given back in Table 2-1. Here is the net operating working capital for 2002:

$$\begin{matrix} \text{Net} \\ \text{operating} \\ \text{working} \\ \text{capital} \end{matrix} = \left(\begin{matrix} \text{Cash and} \\ \text{marketable} + \begin{matrix} \text{Accounts} \\ \text{receivable} \end{matrix} + \text{Inventories} \\ \text{securities} \end{matrix} \right) - \left(\begin{matrix} \text{Accounts} \\ \text{payable} \end{matrix} + \text{Accruals} \right)$$

$$= (\$10 + \$375 + \$615) - (\$60 + \$140)$$

$$= \$800 \text{ million.}$$

Allied's total operating capital for 2002 was

$$\begin{aligned} \text{Total operating capital} &= \text{Net operating working capital} \\ &\quad + \text{Net fixed assets} \end{aligned} \qquad (2\text{-}4)$$

$$= \$800 + \$1,000$$

$$= \$1,800 \text{ million.}$$

Now note that Allied's net operating working capital a year earlier, at year-end 2001, was

$$\text{Net operating working capital} = (\$80 + \$315 + \$415) - (\$30 + \$130)$$

$$= \$650 \text{ million,}$$

and, since it had $870 million of fixed assets, its total operating capital was

$$\text{Total operating capital} = \$650 + \$870$$

$$= \$1,520 \text{ million.}$$

Therefore, Allied increased its operating capital from $1,520 to $1,800 million, or by $280 million, during 2002. Furthermore, most of this increase went into working capital, which rose by $150 million. This 23 percent increase in net operating working capital, when sales only rose 5 percent (from $2,850 to $3,000 million), should set off warning bells in your head: What caused Allied to tie up so much additional cash in working capital? Are inventories not moving? Are receivables not being collected and thus building up? We will address these questions in detail later in the chapter.

NET OPERATING PROFIT AFTER TAXES (NOPAT)

If two companies have different amounts of debt, hence different interest charges, they could have identical operating performances but different net incomes—the one with more debt would have a lower net income. Net income is certainly important, but as the example below shows, net income does not always reflect the true performance of a company's operations or the effectiveness of its operating managers and employees. A better measurement for comparing managers' performance is **net operating profit after taxes,** or **NOPAT,** which is the amount of profit a company would generate if it had no debt and held no nonoperating assets. NOPAT is defined as follows:[7]

Net Operating Profit After Taxes (NOPAT)
The profit a company would generate if it had no debt and held no nonoperating assets.

$$NOPAT = EBIT(1 - \text{Tax rate}). \qquad (2\text{-}5)$$

Using data from the income statement in Table 2-2, Allied's 2002 NOPAT was

$$NOPAT = \$283.8(1 - 0.4) = \$283.8(0.6) = \$170.3 \text{ million.}$$

Thus, Allied generated an after-tax profit of $170.3 million from its operations. This was a little better than the 2001 NOPAT of $263(0.6) = $157.8 million. However, the income statements in Table 2-2 show that Allied's earnings per share declined from 2001 to 2002. This decrease in EPS was caused by an increase in interest expense, not by a decrease in operating profit. See Table 2-2. Moreover, the balance sheets in Table 2-1 show that debt increased from 2001 to 2002. But why did Allied increase its debt? The reason was that Allied's investment in operating capital increased dramatically from 2001 to 2002, and that increase was financed primarily with debt.

FREE CASH FLOW

Free Cash Flow
The cash flow actually available for distribution to all investors (stockholders and debtholders) after the company has made all the investments in fixed assets, new products, and working capital necessary to sustain ongoing operations.

Earlier in the chapter we defined net cash flow as being equal to net income plus noncash adjustments, typically net income plus depreciation and amortization. Note, though, that cash flows cannot be maintained over time unless depreciating fixed assets are replaced and new products are developed, so management is not completely free to use cash flows however it chooses. Therefore, we now define another term, **free cash flow,** which is the cash flow actually available for distribution to all investors (stockholders and debtholders) *after the company has made all the investments in fixed assets, new products, and working capital necessary to sustain ongoing operations.*

To be more specific, the value of a company's operations depends on all the future expected free cash flows (FCF), defined as after-tax operating profit minus the amount of investment in working capital and fixed assets necessary to sustain the business. Thus, free cash flow represents the cash that is actually available for distribution to investors. Therefore, the way for managers to make their companies more valuable is to increase their free cash flow.

Free cash flow differs from net cash flow in two important ways. First, free cash flow represents funds available to all investors, whereas net cash flow represents funds

---

[7] For firms with a more complicated tax situation, it is better to define NOPAT as follows: NOPAT = (Net income before preferred dividends) + (Net interest expense)(1 − Tax rate). Also, if firms are able to defer paying some of their taxes, perhaps by the use of accelerated depreciation, then NOPAT should be adjusted to reflect the taxes that the company actually paid on its operating income. For additional information see Tom Copeland, Tim Koller, and Jack Murrin, *Valuation: Measuring and Managing the Value of Companies,* 3rd edition (New York: John Wiley & Sons, Inc., 2000); and G. Bennett Stewart III, *The Quest for Value* (New York: HarperCollins Publishers, Inc., 1991).

available to common stockholders. Consequently, payments to bondholders and preferred stockholders reduce net cash flow, but they are not subtracted out of free cash flow. Second, free cash flow represents the funds available to all investors after subtracting out the investments that are necessary to sustain the firm's ongoing operations. Thus, investments in fixed assets and net working capital reduce free cash flow, but they are not subtracted out of net cash flow. While analysts often calculate net cash flow to measure the cash generated for shareholders in a given year, we will see in subsequent chapters that free cash flow is often more relevant when estimating the value of a project or firm.

CALCULATING FREE CASH FLOW

Operating Cash Flow
Equal to NOPAT plus any noncash adjustments, calculated on an after-tax basis.

As shown earlier in the chapter, Allied had a 2002 NOPAT of $170.3 million. Its **operating cash flow** is NOPAT plus any noncash adjustments as shown on the statement of cash flows. For Allied, where depreciation is the only noncash charge, the 2002 operating cash flow is

$$\text{Operating cash flow} = \text{NOPAT} + \text{Depreciation and amortization} \qquad (2\text{-}6)$$
$$= \$170.3 + \$100$$
$$= \$270.3 \text{ million.}$$

Please note that this definition of operating cash flow is calculated on an after-tax basis. As shown earlier in the chapter, Allied had $1,520 million of operating assets, or operating capital, at the end of 2001, but $1,800 million at the end of 2002. Therefore, during 2002 it made a *net investment in operating capital* of

$$\text{Net investment in operating capital} = \$1,800 - \$1,520 = \$280 \text{ million.}$$

Fixed assets rose from $870 to $1,000 million, or by $130 million. However, Allied took $100 million of depreciation, so its gross investment in fixed assets was $130 + $100 = $230 million for the year. With this background, we find the *gross investment in operating capital* as follows:

$$\frac{\text{Gross investment}}{\text{in operating capital}} = \frac{\text{Net}}{\text{investment}} + \frac{\text{Depreciation}}{\text{and amortization}}$$
$$= \quad \$280 \quad + \quad \$100 \quad = \$380 \text{ million.}$$

Allied's free cash flow in 2002 was

$$\text{FCF} = \text{Operating cash flow} - \text{Gross investment in operating capital} \qquad (2\text{-}7)$$
$$= \$270.3 - \$380$$
$$= -\$109.7 \text{ million.}$$

If we subtract depreciation and amortization from both operating cash flow and gross investment in operating capital in Equation 2-7, we obtain the following algebraically equivalent expression for free cash flow:

$$\text{FCF} = \text{NOPAT} - \text{Net investment in operating capital} \qquad (2\text{-}7a)$$
$$= \$170.3 - \$280$$
$$= -\$109.7 \text{ million.}$$

Even though Allied had a positive NOPAT, its very high investment in operating capital resulted in a negative free cash flow. Since free cash flow is what is available for distribution to investors, not only was there nothing for investors, but investors actually had to provide *more* money to Allied to keep the business going. Investors provided most of the required new money as debt.

Is a negative free cash flow always bad? The answer is, "Not necessarily. It depends on *why* the free cash flow was negative." If FCF was negative because NOPAT was negative, this is bad, because the company is probably experiencing operating problems. Exceptions to this might be startup companies, or companies that are incurring significant current expenses to launch a new product line. Also, many high-growth companies have positive NOPAT but negative free cash flow due to investments in operating assets needed to support growth. There is nothing wrong with profitable growth, even if it causes negative cash flows in the short term.

SELF-TEST QUESTIONS

What is net operating working capital?

What is total operating capital?

What is NOPAT? Why might it be a better performance measure than net income?

What is free cash flow? Why is free cash flow the most important determinant of a firm's value?

Briefly explain why we need to compare managers' ability to generate operating income with the operating assets under their control to judge their performance.

MVA AND EVA

Neither traditional accounting data nor the modified data discussed in the preceding section bring in stock prices. Since the primary goal of management is to maximize the firm's stock price, we need to bring stock prices into the picture. Financial analysts have therefore developed two performance measures, MVA, or Market Value Added, and EVA, or Economic Value Added. These concepts are discussed in this section.[8]

MARKET VALUE ADDED (MVA)

The primary goal of most firms is to maximize shareholders' wealth. This goal obviously benefits shareholders, but it also helps to ensure that scarce resources are allo-

---

[8] The concepts of EVA and MVA were developed by Joel Stern and Bennett Stewart, co-founders of the consulting firm Stern Stewart & Company. Stern Stewart copyrighted the terms "EVA" and "MVA," so other consulting firms have given other names to these values. Still, EVA and MVA are the terms most commonly used in practice.

cated efficiently, which benefits the economy. Shareholder wealth is maximized by maximizing the *difference* between the market value of the firm's stock and the amount of equity capital that was supplied by shareholders. This difference is called the **Market Value Added (MVA):**

$$\text{MVA} = \text{Market value of stock} - \text{Equity capital supplied by shareholders} \quad (2\text{-}8)$$
$$= (\text{Shares outstanding})(\text{Stock price}) - \text{Total common equity.}$$

To illustrate, consider our illustrative company, Allied Food Products. In 2002, its total market equity value was \$1,150 million, while its balance sheet showed that stockholders had put up only \$896 million. Thus, Allied's MVA was \$1,150 − \$896 = \$254 million. This \$254 million represents the difference between the money that Allied's stockholders have invested in the corporation since its founding—including retained earnings—versus the cash they could get if they sold the business. The higher its MVA, the better the job management is doing for the firm's shareholders.

ECONOMIC VALUE ADDED (EVA)

Whereas MVA measures the effects of managerial actions since the very inception of a company, **Economic Value Added (EVA)** focuses on managerial effectiveness in a given year. The basic formula for EVA is as follows:

$$\text{EVA} = \text{NOPAT} - \text{After-tax dollar cost of operating capital} \quad (2\text{-}9)$$
$$= \text{EBIT}(1 - \text{T}) - [(\text{Total investor-supplied operating capital})$$
$$\times (\text{After-tax percentage cost of capital})].$$

Total investor-supplied operating capital is the sum of the interest-bearing debt, preferred stock, and common equity used to acquire the company's net operating assets, that is, its net operating working capital plus net plant and equipment.

EVA is an estimate of a business's true economic profit for the year, and it differs sharply from accounting profit.[9] EVA represents the residual income that remains after the cost of *all* capital, including equity capital, has been deducted, whereas accounting profit is determined without imposing a charge for equity capital. As we will discuss more completely in Chapter 9, equity capital has a cost, because funds provided by shareholders could have been invested elsewhere where they would have earned a return. Shareholders give up the opportunity to invest funds elsewhere when they provide capital to the firm. The return they could earn elsewhere in investments of equal risk represents the cost of equity capital. This cost is an *opportunity cost* rather than an *accounting cost*, but it is quite real nevertheless.

Note that when calculating EVA we do not add back depreciation. Although it is not a cash expense, depreciation is a cost, and it is therefore deducted when determining both net income and EVA. Our calculation of EVA assumes that the true

---

Market Value Added (MVA)
The difference between the market value of the firm's stock and the amount of equity capital investors have supplied.

Economic Value Added (EVA)
Value added to shareholders by management during a given year.

 If you want to read more about EVA and MVA, surf over to **http://www.sternstewart.com** and hear about it from the people that invented it, Stern Stewart & Co. While you are there, you may like to take a look at a video of executives describing how EVA has helped them, which can be found at **http://www. sternstewart.com/evaabout/ comments.shtml**. To see the video, you will need Real Player, which can be downloaded for free from **http://www.real.com**.

---

[9] The most important reason EVA differs from accounting profit is that the cost of equity capital is deducted when EVA is calculated. Other factors that could lead to differences include adjustments that might be made to depreciation, to research and development costs, to inventory valuations, and so on. See Stewart, *The Quest for Value*.

economic depreciation of the company's fixed assets exactly equals the depreciation used for accounting and tax purposes. If this were not the case, adjustments would have to be made to obtain a more accurate measure of EVA.

EVA provides a good measure of the extent to which the firm has added to shareholder value. Therefore, if managers focus on EVA, this will help to ensure that they operate in a manner that is consistent with maximizing shareholder wealth. Note too that EVA can be determined for divisions as well as for the company as a whole, so it provides a useful basis for determining managerial compensation at all levels.

Table 2-5 shows how Allied's MVA and EVA are calculated. The stock price was $23 per share at year-end 2002, down from $26 per share at the end of 2001; its percentage after-tax cost of capital was 10.3 percent in 2001 and 10.0 percent in 2002, and its tax rate was 40 percent. Other data in Table 2-5 were given in the basic financial statements provided earlier in the chapter.

Note first that the lower stock price and the higher book value of equity (due to retaining earnings during 2002) combined to reduce the MVA. The 2002 MVA is still positive, but $460 − $254 = $206 million of stockholders' value was lost during 2002.

EVA for 2001 was just barely positive, and in 2002 it was negative. Operating income (NOPAT) rose, but EVA still declined, primarily because the amount of capital rose more sharply than NOPAT—by about 18 percent versus 8 percent—and the cost of this increased capital pulled EVA down.

| TABLE 2-5 | MVA and EVA for Allied (Millions of Dollars) | | |

	2002	2001
MVA CALCULATION		
Price per share	$ 23.0	$ 26.0
Number of shares (millions)	× 50	× 50
Market value of equity	$1,150.0	$1,300.0
Book value of equity	− 896.0	− 840.0
MVA	$ 254.0	$ 460.0
EVA CALCULATION		
EBIT	$ 283.8	$ 263.0
1 − Tax rate	× 60%	× 60%
NOPAT = EBIT(1 − T)	$ 170.3	$ 157.8
Total investor-supplied operating capital[a]	$1,800.0	$1,520.0
After-tax cost of capital (%)	× 10.0%	× 10.3%
Dollar cost of capital	$ 180.0	$ 156.6
EVA = NOPAT − Dollar cost of capital	($ 9.7)	$ 1.2

[a]Investor-supplied operating capital equals the sum of notes payable, long-term debt, preferred stock, and common equity. It could also be calculated as total liabilities and equity minus accounts payable and accruals. It is also equal to net operating working capital plus net fixed assets.

Recall also that net income fell somewhat from 2001 to 2002, but not nearly so dramatically as the decline in EVA. Net income does not reflect the amount of equity capital employed, but EVA does. Because of this omission, net income is not as useful as EVA for setting corporate goals and measuring managerial performance.

We will have more to say about both MVA and EVA later in the book, but we can close this section with two observations. First, there is a relationship between MVA and EVA, but it is not a direct one. If a company has a history of negative EVAs, then its MVA will probably be negative, and vice versa if it has a history of positive EVAs. However, the stock price, which is the key ingredient in the MVA calculation, depends more on expected future performance than on historical performance. Therefore, a company with a history of negative EVAs could have a positive MVA, provided investors expect a turnaround in the future.

The second observation is that when EVAs or MVAs are used to evaluate managerial performance as part of an incentive compensation program, EVA is the measure that is typically used. The reasons are (1) EVA shows the value added during a given year, whereas MVA reflects performance over the company's entire life, perhaps even including times before the current managers were born, and (2) EVA can be applied to individual divisions or other units of a large corporation, whereas MVA must be applied to the entire corporation. For these reasons, MVA is used primarily to evaluate top corporate officers over periods of five to 10 years, or longer.

SELF-TEST QUESTIONS

Define the terms "Market Value Added (MVA)" and "Economic Value Added (EVA)." How does EVA differ from accounting profit?

THE FEDERAL INCOME TAX SYSTEM

 A web site of interest concerning federal tax law is **http://www. taxsites.com/federal.html**. From this home page one can visit other sites that provide summaries of recent tax legislation or current information on corporate and individual tax rates. Another useful web site is **http://www.taxplanet.com**. The official government web site is **http://www.irs.gov**.

Corporations must pay a significant portion of their income out as taxes, and individuals are also taxed on their income. We summarize some important points about the U.S. tax system here, based on 2002 provisions. A more detailed discussion is provided in Web Appendix 2A located on the book's web site.

CORPORATE TAXES

Corporate income is generally taxed by the federal government at rates that begin at 15 percent and go up to 35 percent on taxable income of $10 million or more. Thus, the corporate tax structure is *progressive* in the sense that higher rates are imposed on companies with larger incomes. State governments also impose income taxes on corporations, with 5 percent being a typical rate. Therefore, the larger companies generally pay taxes of about 40 percent on their income, and we typically use that rate in our examples. The tax system is incredibly complex, so we will not attempt to cover it in any detail. However, as noted above, we do provide a bit more tax information on the textbook's web site.

PERSONAL TAXES

Individuals are taxed on their taxable income by the federal government at rates that begin at 10 percent and rise to 38.6 percent on incomes of $307,050 or more. Some states also impose a state income tax, with rates varying across states. Note that income on investments held in pension accounts are not taxed until the money is withdrawn, presumably after retirement. Thus, a person might be in the 38.6 percent tax bracket on his or her ordinary income, but the tax rate would be zero on income earned in a 401(k) or other type of retirement account (or certain college savings plans).

INTEREST PAID

Borrowers must pay interest on their debts. For a business, the interest payments are regarded as an expense, and they may be deducted when calculating taxable income. Individuals also incur debts and pay interest, but generally individuals cannot deduct interest payments (the big exception is interest on home loans, which, within limits, is deductible).

INTEREST EARNED

Most interest earned, whether by businesses or individuals, is taxable income, and hence is subject to income taxes. An important exception is that interest on most state and local government debt is exempt from federal taxes. State and local bonds are often called "munis," and individuals in the high tax brackets generally purchase them.

DIVIDENDS PAID

Corporations pay dividends, and dividends paid are generally not deductible for tax purposes. Thus, corporations pay interest out of pre-tax income, but they pay dividends out of after-tax income. Thus, if a company had a combined federal-plus-state tax rate of 40 percent and $10 million of pre-tax cash income, it could pay out $10 million of interest but only $6 million of dividends because it would have to pay $4 million of taxes.[10]

Note that if one company uses a lot of debt financing, whereas another company with similar operations uses only common stock financing, the stock-financed company will have no interest, hence no interest tax deductions, hence a higher income tax bill. The company that uses debt will have a lower tax bill, and thus more of its operating income will be passed on to investors (stockholders and debtholders). Thus, our tax system encourages debt financing. We will discuss this at length in the chapter on capital structure.

---

[10] This is not exactly correct, because the tax bill on $10 million of income would actually be somewhat lower ($3.4 million) because some of the income would be taxed at lower rates.

DIVIDENDS RECEIVED

Dividends received by an individual are taxed as ordinary income. Note that there is a double tax on dividend income—the corporation that paid the dividend is first taxed, and then the individual who receives it is taxed again. For corporate recipients, the situation is somewhat different—the corporation that receives dividend income can exclude some of the dividends from its taxable income. This provision is in the Tax Code to minimize the amount of *triple taxation* that would otherwise occur—one corporation would pay dividends out of after-tax income, the second corporation would be taxed again, and the person who received dividends from the second corporation would be taxed also.

TAX LOSS CARRY-BACK AND CARRY-FORWARD

Corporations' incomes often fluctuate from year to year, so one year a firm might be taxed at a 40 percent rate and it might have a large loss the following year, hence pay no taxes. The Tax Code allows firms to carry losses back to offset profits in prior years, and, if losses haven't been offset by past profits, to carry losses forward to offset profits in the future, which causes taxes over time to reflect average income over time.

CAPITAL GAINS

Capital gains are, generally speaking, defined as profits from the sale of assets that are not normally bought and sold in the course of business. For individuals, capital gains typically arise from the sale of stocks or bonds for more than the purchase price of the security. Thus, if someone buys some Microsoft stock for $10,000 and later sells it for $15,000, then he or she will have a $5,000 capital gain. If the stock was held for less than a year, the $5,000 gain is just added to ordinary income and taxed as such. If the stock had been held for a year or more, then the gain will be taxed at a lower rate. For someone in the top (38.6 percent) federal tax bracket, the long-term capital gains rate is generally 20 percent. Corporations face somewhat different rules, and individual tax rates also vary a bit, but long-term capital gains tax rates are always lower than the tax rate on dividends.

If a company earns, say, $1 million and then pays it out as dividends, its stockholders will have to pay taxes on those dividends at their normal federal tax rates, which go up to 38.6 percent. However, if the company retains and invests the $1 million, and thereby increases the value of the business by $1 million, then presumably the value of the stock will also rise by $1 million. Then, a stockholder who wants cash can sell some of his or her stock (which was held for over a year) and be taxed at the lower capital gains rate, rather than the rate on dividends (20 percent versus 38.6 percent for top bracket investors). As we will see in the dividend chapter, this tax treatment has an effect on corporate dividend policy.

DEPRECIATION

When a business buys an asset with a life greater than one year, for stockholder reporting and internal management use it generally depreciates that asset over the years in which the asset will be used. Generally, the company estimates the actual likely years of use, divides the cost by the number of years, and charges the calculated value as a cost on the income statement each year. (This is called "straight line depreciation.") However, Congress allows companies to use a different method for calculating depreciation used for tax purposes. Congress authorizes depreciation rates for different types of assets, and those rates generally mean that depreciation charges are higher than what the company uses for stockholder reporting. For example, a company might buy a machine for $100,000, estimate that it will be used for 10 years, and thus depreciate it at a rate of $10,000 per year for 10 years. However, Congress might prescribe a depreciable life of 5 years, in which case the annual depreciation charge for tax purposes would be $20,000 per year for 5 years. That would lower the firm's taxable income and thus its taxes in the years immediately after the asset was put into service. The lower taxes would increase the company's cash flow.[11] Congress adjusts depreciation rates periodically as a part of its fiscal policy decisions, recognizing that faster depreciation rates stimulate corporate investment and thus encourage economic growth, but at the cost of lower tax collections in the immediate future. We discuss depreciation in greater detail in the web appendix for Chapter 11 entitled, "Depreciation."

SMALL BUSINESSES

If a business is operated as a proprietorship or partnership, its income is allocated to its owners in proportion to their ownership interests. If the same business is operated as a corporation, with its owners being stockholders rather than proprietors or partners, the business's income is first taxed at the corporate rate and then any dividends the company passes on to its owners are taxed again, at the stockholders' personal tax rates. However, if the business meets certain criteria related to size and number of stockholders, it could elect to be a corporation yet still be taxed as a partnership, thus bypassing the corporate taxes. Such a corporation is called an "S corporation" because it is Subsection S of the Tax Code that allows this procedure. An S corporation can thus enjoy the advantages of the corporate form of organization yet still get the tax advantages of a partnership. Most small business corporations are actually set up as S corporations.

SELF-TEST QUESTIONS

Explain the statement, "Our tax rates are progressive."

What is a "muni" bond, and how are these bonds taxed?

What are long-term capital gains, and how are they taxed relative to dividend income?

How does our tax system influence the use of debt financing by corporations?

How does our tax system influence the use of a corporation's dividend policy, that is, the percentage of a corporation's income it pays out as dividends?

---

[11] Depreciation is not a cash charge, so higher depreciation charges would have no adverse effect on cash flow. Rather, more depreciation would lower taxes and thus increase cash flow. But what about net income—wouldn't more depreciation mean lower reported profits? The answer is no, because in our example the depreciation used for stockholder reporting would probably be only $10,000, not the $20,000 used for tax purposes. Congress sets the tax depreciable life as a part of fiscal policy and politics, and it doesn't necessarily have anything to do with assets' actual useful lives.

COOKING THE BOOKS

Before closing this chapter, we should note that in June 2002 it was discovered that WorldCom Corporation, owner of MCI and the second largest U.S. telecommunications company, had committed the most massive accounting fraud of all time. It had recorded $3.8 billion of ordinary operating costs as capital expenditures. Operating costs are subtracted from revenues during the current year to find net income and cash flow, whereas capital expenditures are shown as an asset and then depreciated in future years. This fraudulent procedure, which clearly violated generally accepted accounting principles, resulted in a massive overstatement of earnings and cash flows.

WorldCom's published financial statements fooled most investors—stockholders bid the stock price up to $64.50, and banks and other lenders provided the company with more than $30 billion of debt capital. Arthur Andersen, the auditor, was faulted for not detecting the fraud. Andersen's defense was that WorldCom's management had lied. However, a number of security analysts went through the type of ratio analysis covered in the next chapter, became suspicious, and got out of the stock before it collapsed. One ought to be able to rely on audited financial statements, but WorldCom demonstrated that this can be dangerous. Still, a careful analysis of financial statements can help disclose problems, including fraud, so pay close attention when you get to Chapter 3.

TYING IT ALL TOGETHER

The primary purposes of this chapter were (1) to describe the basic financial statements, (2) to present some background information on cash flows, and (3) to provide an overview of the federal income tax system. The key concepts covered are listed below.

- The four basic statements contained in the **annual report** are the balance sheet, the income statement, the statement of retained earnings, and the statement of cash flows. Investors use the information provided in these statements to form expectations about the future levels of earnings and dividends, and about the firm's riskiness.

- The **balance sheet** shows assets on the left-hand side and liabilities and equity, or claims against assets, on the right-hand side. The balance sheet may be thought of as a snapshot of the firm's financial position at a particular point in time.

- The **income statement** reports the results of operations over a period of time, and it shows earnings per share as its "bottom line."

- The **statement of retained earnings** shows the change in retained earnings between the balance sheet dates. Retained earnings represent a claim against assets, not assets per se.

- The **statement of cash flows** reports the impact of operating, investing, and financing activities on cash flows over an accounting period.

- **Net cash flow** differs from **accounting profit** because some of the revenues and expenses reflected in accounting profits may not have been received or paid out in cash during the year. Depreciation is typically the largest noncash item, so net cash flow is often expressed as net income plus depreciation. Investors are at least as interested in a firm's projected net cash flow as in reported earnings because it is cash, not paper profit, that is paid out as dividends and plowed back into the business to produce growth.

- **Net operating working capital** is defined as the difference between the current assets necessary to operate the business and those current liabilities on which no interest is charged (generally, accounts payable and accruals). Thus, net operating working capital is the working capital acquired with investor-supplied funds.

- **Operating assets** are the cash and marketable securities, accounts receivable, inventories, and fixed assets necessary to operate the business.

- **NOPAT** is net operating profit after taxes. It is the after-tax profit a company would have if it had no debt and no investments in nonoperating assets. Since it excludes the effects of financial decisions, it is a better measure of operating performance than is net income.

- **Operating cash flow** arises from normal operations, and it is the difference between cash revenues and cash costs, including taxes on operating income. Operating cash flow differs from net cash flow because operating cash flow does not include either interest income or interest expense. It is equal to NOPAT plus any noncash adjustments.

- **Free cash flow (FCF)** is the amount of cash flow remaining after a company makes the asset investments necessary to support operations. In other words, FCF is the amount of cash flow available for distribution to investors, *so the value of a company is directly related to its ability to generate free cash flow*.

- The value of any asset depends on the stream of **after-tax cash flow** it produces.

- **Market Value Added (MVA)** represents the difference between the market value of a firm's stock and the amount of equity its investors have supplied.

- **Economic Value Added (EVA)** is the difference between after-tax operating profit and the total cost of capital, including the cost of equity capital. EVA is an estimate of the value created by management during the year, and it differs substantially from accounting profit because no charge for the use of equity capital is reflected in accounting profit.

- In the United States, tax rates are **progressive**—the higher one's income, the larger the percentage paid in taxes.

- Operating income paid out as dividends is subject to **double taxation:** the income is first taxed at the corporate level, and then shareholders must pay personal taxes on their dividends.

- Interest income received by a corporation is taxed as **ordinary income;** however, some of the dividends received by one corporation from another are excluded from **taxable income.** The reason for this exclusion is that corporate dividend income is ultimately subjected to **triple taxation.**

- Because interest paid by a corporation is a **deductible** expense while dividends are not, our tax system favors debt over equity financing.
- **S corporations** are small businesses that have the limited-liability benefits of the corporate form of organization yet are taxed as a partnership or a proprietorship.

QUESTIONS

2-1 What four financial statements are contained in most annual reports?

2-2 If a "typical" firm reports $20 million of retained earnings on its balance sheet, could its directors declare a $20 million cash dividend without any qualms whatsoever?

2-3 Explain the following statement: "While the balance sheet can be thought of as a snapshot of the firm's financial position *at a point in time*, the income statement reports on operations *over a period of time*."

2-4 Differentiate between accounting income and net cash flow. Why might these two numbers differ?

2-5 Differentiate between operating cash flow and net cash flow. Why might these two numbers differ?

2-6 What do the numbers on financial statements actually represent?

2-7 Who are some of the basic users of financial statements, and how do they use them?

2-8 What is operating capital, and why is it important?

2-9 Explain the difference between NOPAT and net income. Which is a better measure of the performance of a company's operations?

2-10 What is free cash flow? Why is it the most important measure of cash flow?

2-11 What does *double taxation of corporate income* mean?

2-12 Explain how the federal income tax structure affects the choice of financing (use of debt versus equity) of U.S. business firms.

2-13 How might it be possible for a company to generate positive net accounting income yet have a negative EVA?

SELF-TEST PROBLEMS (SOLUTIONS APPEAR IN APPENDIX B)

ST-1
Key terms
Define each of the following terms:
a. Annual report; balance sheet; income statement
b. Common stockholders' equity, or net worth; retained earnings
c. Statement of retained earnings; statement of cash flows
d. Depreciation; tangible assets; amortization; intangible assets; EBITDA
e. Accounting profit; net cash flow
f. Operating assets; nonoperating assets
g. Operating working capital; net operating working capital
h. Net operating profit after taxes (NOPAT); operating cash flow; free cash flow
i. Market Value Added (MVA); Economic Value Added (EVA)
j. Progressive tax
k. Capital gain
l. S corporation

ST-2
Net income, cash flow, and EVA
Last year Rattner Robotics had $5 million in operating income (EBIT). The company had net depreciation expense of $1 million and interest expense of $1 million; its corporate tax rate was 40 percent. The company has $14 million in current assets and $4 million in non-interest-bearing current liabilities; it has $15 million in net plant and equipment. It estimates that it has an after-tax cost of capital of 10 percent. Assume that Rattner's only noncash item was depreciation.
a. What was the company's net income for the year?
b. What was the company's net cash flow?
c. What was the company's net operating profit after taxes (NOPAT)?
d. What was the company's operating cash flow?

e. If operating capital in the previous year was $24 million what was the company's free cash flow (FCF) for the year?

f. What was the company's Economic Value Added (EVA)?

STARTER PROBLEMS

2-1
Income statement

Little Books Inc. recently reported net income of $3 million. Its operating income (EBIT) was $6 million, and the company pays a 40 percent tax rate. What was the company's interest expense for the year? [Hint: Divide $3 million by $(1 - T) = 0.6$ to find taxable income.]

2-2
Net cash flow

Kendall Corners Inc. recently reported net income of $3.1 million. The company's depreciation expense was $500,000. What is the company's approximate net cash flow? Assume the firm has no amortization expense.

2-3
EVA

Kordell Company recently reported $170,000 in operating income (EBIT). The company's total operating capital is $800,000. The company's after-tax cost of that capital is 11.625 percent, and the company is in the 40 percent tax bracket. What is Kordell's EVA?

2-4
Statement of retained earnings

In its most recent financial statements, Newhouse Inc. reported $50 million of net income and $810 million of retained earnings. The previous year, its balance sheet showed $780 million of retained earnings. What were the total dividends paid to shareholders during the most recent year?

2-5
Income statement

Pearson Brothers recently reported an EBITDA of $7.5 million and $1.8 million of net income. The company has $2.0 million of interest expense and the corporate tax rate is 40 percent. What was the company's depreciation and amortization expense?

EXAM-TYPE PROBLEMS

The problems included in this section are set up in such a way that they could be used as multiple-choice exam problems.

2-6
Cash flow

The Klaven Corporation has operating income (EBIT) of $750,000. The company's depreciation expense is $200,000. Klaven is 100 percent equity financed, and it faces a 40 percent tax rate. Assume that the firm has no amortization expense. What are its net income, its net cash flow, and its operating cash flow?

2-7
Balance sheet

Which of the following actions will, all else equal, increase the amount of cash on a company's balance sheet?
a. The company issues $2 million in new common stock.
b. The company invests $3 million in new plant and equipment.
c. The company generates negative net income and negative net cash flow during the year.
d. The company increases the dividend paid on its common stock.

2-8
Cash flow

Bailey Corporation recently reported the following income statement (dollars are in thousands):

Sales	$14,000,000
Operating costs excluding depreciation and amortization	7,000,000
EBITDA	$ 7,000,000
Depreciation and amortization	3,000,000
EBIT	$ 4,000,000
Interest	1,500,000
EBT	$ 2,500,000
Taxes (40%)	1,000,000
Net income	$ 1,500,000

Bailey's total operating capital is $20 billion and its after-tax cost of capital is 10 percent. Therefore, Bailey's total after-tax dollar cost of operating capital is $2 billion. During the past year, Bailey made a $1.3 billion net investment in its operating capital.
a. What is Bailey's NOPAT for the year?
b. What is Bailey's net cash flow for the year?

c. What is Bailey's operating cash flow for the year?
d. What is Bailey's free cash flow for the year?
e. What is Bailey's EVA for the year?

2-9
MVA

Henderson Industries has $500 million of common equity on its balance sheet. The company's current stock price is $60 per share, and its Market Value Added (MVA) is $130 million. How many shares of the company's stock are currently outstanding?

2-10
EVA

The Ronayne Corporation has on its balance sheet $5 million in net operating working capital and $37 million in net fixed assets. The company's weighted average cost of capital is 8.5 percent. The company has the following income statement:

Sales	$25,000,000
Operating costs	18,625,000
EBIT	$ 6,375,000
Interest	2,325,000
EBT	$ 4,050,000
Taxes (40%)	1,620,000
Net income	$ 2,430,000

What is Ronayne's EVA?

2-11
Statement of retained earnings

In its recent income statement ComputerWorld Inc. reported paying out $22.5 million in total dividends to shareholders during the most recent year, and in its year-end balance sheet ComputerWorld reported $278.9 million of retained earnings. Its balance sheet the previous year showed $212.3 million of retained earnings. What was the firm's reported net income for the current year?

2-12
Statement of cash flows

Williams Cycling Company had $55,000 in cash on the balance sheet at the end of 2001. At year-end 2002, the company had $25,000 in cash. We know cash flow from long-term investing activities totaled −$250,000 and cash flow from financing activities totaled $170,000.

a. What was the firm's cash flow from operating activities?
b. If the firm's accruals increased by $25,000, receivables and inventories increased by $100,000, and the firm's depreciation and amortization expense totaled $10,000, what was the firm's net income for the year? Assume that the firm has no preferred stock.

2-13
Income statement

Hermann Industries is forecasting the following income statement for the upcoming year:

Sales	$8,000,000
Operating costs (excluding depreciation and amortization)	4,400,000
EBITDA	$3,600,000
Depreciation and amortization	800,000
EBIT	$2,800,000
Interest	600,000
EBT	$2,200,000
Taxes (40%)	880,000
Net income	$1,320,000

The company's CEO is disappointed with the forecast and would like to see Hermann generate higher sales and a forecasted net income of $2,500,000.

Assume that operating costs (excluding depreciation and amortization) are always 55 percent of sales. Assume that the company's depreciation and amortization and interest expenses will increase by 10 percent from what they are now. The company's tax rate, which is 40 percent, will remain the same. What level of sales would the firm have to obtain to generate $2,500,000 in net income?

PROBLEMS

2-14
Financial statements

The Smythe-Davidson Corporation just issued its annual report. The current year's balance sheet and income statement as they appeared in the annual report are given below. Answer the questions that follow based on information given in the financial statements.

Smythe-Davidson Corporation: Balance Sheet as of December 31, 2002 (Millions of Dollars)

ASSETS		LIABILITIES AND EQUITY	
Cash and marketable securities	$ 15	Accounts payable	$ 120
Accounts receivable	515	Notes payable	220
Inventories	880	Accruals	280
Total current assets	$1,410	Total current liabilities	$ 620
Net plant and equipment	2,590	Long-term bonds	1,520
		Total debt	$2,140
		Preferred stock (800,000 shares)	80
		Common stock (100 million shares)	260
		Retained earnings	1,520
		Common equity	$1,780
Total assets	$4,000	Total liabilities and equity	$4,000

Smythe-Davidson Corporation: Income Statement for Year Ending December 31, 2002 (Millions of Dollars)

Sales	$6,250
Operating costs excluding depreciation and amortization	5,230
EBITDA	$1,020
Depreciation and amortization	220
EBIT	$ 800
Less: Interest	180
EBT	$ 620
Taxes (40 %)	248
Net income before preferred dividends	$ 372
Preferred dividends	8
Net income available to common stockholders	$ 364
Common dividends paid	$ 146
Earnings per share	$ 3.64

a. Assume that all of the firm's revenues were received in cash during the year and that all costs except depreciation and amortization were paid in cash during the year. What is the firm's net cash flow available to common stockholders for the year? How is this number different from the accounting profit reported by the firm?
b. Construct the firm's Statement of Retained Earnings for December 31, 2002.
c. How much money has the firm reinvested in itself over the years instead of paying out dividends?
d. At the present time, how large a check could the firm write without it bouncing?
e. How much money must the firm pay its current creditors within the next year?

2-15
Income and cash flow analysis

The Menendez Corporation expects to have sales of $12 million in 2003. Costs other than depreciation and amortization are expected to be 75 percent of sales, and depreciation and amortization expenses are expected to be $1.5 million. All sales revenues will be collected in cash, and costs other than depreciation and amortization must be paid for during the year. Menendez's federal-plus-state tax rate is 40 percent.
a. Set up an income statement. What is Menendez's expected net cash flow?
b. Suppose Congress changed the tax laws so that Menendez's depreciation and amortization expenses doubled. No changes in operations occurred. What would happen to reported profit and to net cash flow?
c. Now suppose that Congress, instead of doubling Menendez's depreciation and amortization expenses, reduced them by 50 percent. How would profit and net cash flow be affected?
d. If this were your company, would you prefer Congress to cause your depreciation and amortization expenses to be doubled or halved? Why?
e. In the situation in which depreciation and amortization doubled, would this possibly have an adverse effect on the company's stock price and on its ability to borrow money?

2-16
Income statement

Last year Martin Motors reported the following income statement:

Sales	$2,000,000
Cost of goods sold	1,200,000
EBITDA	$ 800,000
Depreciation and amortization	500,000
Operating income (EBIT)	$ 300,000
Interest expense	100,000
Taxable income (EBT)	$ 200,000
Taxes (40%)	80,000
Net income	$ 120,000

The company's CEO, Joe Lawrence, was unhappy with the firm's performance. This year, he would like to see net income doubled to $240,000. Depreciation and amortization, interest expense, and the tax rate will all remain constant, and the cost of goods sold will also remain at 60 percent of sales. How much sales revenue must the company generate to achieve the CEO's net income target?

You have just obtained financial information for the past 2 years for Powell Panther Corporation. Answer the following questions.

**Powell Panther Corporation: Income Statements for Year Ending December 31
(Millions of Dollars)**

	2002	2001
Sales	$1,200.0	$1,000.0
Operating costs excluding depreciation and amortization	1,020.0	850.0
EBITDA	$ 180.0	$ 150.0
Depreciation and amortization	30.0	25.0
Earnings before interest and taxes	$ 150.0	$ 125.0
Less: Interest	21.7	20.2
Earnings before taxes	$ 128.3	$ 104.8
Taxes (40%)	51.3	41.9
Net income available to common stockholders	$ 77.0	$ 62.9
Common dividends	$ 60.5	$ 46.4

Powell Panther Corporation: Balance Sheets as of December 31 (Millions of Dollars)

	2002	2001
ASSETS		
Cash and marketable securities	$ 12.0	$ 10.0
Accounts receivable	180.0	150.0
Inventories	180.0	200.0
Total current assets	$372.0	$360.0
Net plant and equipment	300.0	250.0
Total assets	$672.0	$610.0
LIABILITIES AND EQUITY		
Accounts payable	$108.0	$ 90.0
Notes payable	67.0	51.5
Accruals	72.0	60.0
Total current liabilities	$247.0	$201.5
Long-term bonds	150.0	150.0
Total debt	$397.0	$351.5
Common stock (50 million shares)	50.0	50.0
Retained earnings	225.0	208.5
Common equity	$275.0	$258.5
Total liabilities and equity	$672.0	$610.0

a. What is the net operating profit after taxes (NOPAT) for 2002?
b. What are the amounts of net operating working capital for 2001 and 2002?

c. What are the amounts of total operating capital for 2001 and 2002?
d. What is the free cash flow for 2002?
e. How can you explain the large increase in dividends in 2002?

SPREADSHEET PROBLEM

2-18
Financial statements, EVA, and MVA

Laiho Industries' 2001 and 2002 balance sheets (in thousands of dollars) are shown below:

	2002	2001
Cash	$102,850	$ 89,725
Accounts receivable	103,365	85,527
Inventories	38,444	34,982
Total current assets	$244,659	$210,234
Net fixed assets	67,165	42,436
Total assets	$311,824	$252,670
Accounts payable	$ 30,761	$ 23,109
Accruals	30,477	22,656
Notes payable	16,717	14,217
Total current liabilities	$ 77,955	$ 59,982
Long-term debt	76,264	63,914
Total liabilities	$154,219	$123,896
Common stock	100,000	90,000
Retained earnings	57,605	38,774
Total common equity	$157,605	$128,774
Total liabilities and equity	$311,824	$252,670

a. The company's sales for 2002 were $455,150,000, and EBITDA was 15 percent of sales. Furthermore, depreciation amounted to 11 percent of net fixed assets, interest charges were $8,575,000, the state-plus-federal corporate tax rate was 40 percent, and Laiho pays 40 percent of its net income out in dividends. Assume the firm has no amortization expense. Given this information, construct Laiho's 2002 income statement. (Hint: You might find it easiest to select the balance sheets, then copy them, and then paste them to an *Excel* worksheet. You might have to move the data around some in the worksheet to get things lined up properly.)
b. Next, construct the firm's statement of retained earnings for the year ending December 31, 2002, and then its 2002 statement of cash flows.
c. Calculate net operating working capital, total operating capital, net operating profit after taxes, operating cash flow, and free cash flow for 2002.
d. Calculate the firm's EVA and MVA for 2002. Assume that Laiho had 10 million shares outstanding, that the year-end closing stock price was $17.25 per share, and its after-tax cost of capital was 12 percent.

D'LEON INC., PART I

2-19 Financial Statements and Taxes Donna Jamison, a 1997 graduate of the University of Florida with four years of banking experience, was recently brought in as assistant to the chairman of the board of D'Leon Inc., a small food producer that operates in north Florida and whose specialty is high-quality pecan and other nut products sold in the snack-foods market. D'Leon's president, Al Watkins, decided in 2001 to undertake a major expansion and to "go national" in competition with Frito-Lay, Eagle, and other major snack-food companies. Watkins felt that D'Leon's products were of a higher quality than the competition's, that this quality differential would enable it to charge a premium price, and that the end result would be greatly increased sales, profits, and stock price.

The company doubled its plant capacity, opened new sales offices outside its home territory, and launched an expensive advertising campaign. D'Leon's results were not satisfactory, to put it mildly. Its board of directors, which consisted of its president and vice-president plus its major stockholders (who were all local business people), was most upset when directors learned how the expansion was going. Suppliers were being paid late and were unhappy, and the bank was complaining about the deteriorating situation and threatening to cut off credit. As a result, Watkins was informed that changes would have to be made, and quickly, or he would be fired. Also, at the board's insistence Donna Jamison was brought in and given the job of assistant to Fred Campo, a retired banker who was D'Leon's chairman and largest stockholder. Campo agreed to give up a few of his golfing days and to help nurse the company back to health, with Jamison's help.

Jamison began by gathering the financial statements and other data given in Tables IC2-1, IC2-2, IC2-3, and IC2-4. Assume that you are Jamison's assistant, and you must help her answer the following questions for Campo. (Note: We will continue with this case in Chapter 3, and you will feel more comfortable with the analysis there, but answering these questions will help prepare you for Chapter 3. Provide clear explanations, not just yes or no answers!)

a. What effect did the expansion have on sales, net operating profit after taxes (NOPAT), net operating working capital (NOWC), total investor-supplied operating capital, and net income?

b. What effect did the company's expansion have on its net cash flow, operating cash flow, and free cash flow?

c. Jamison also has asked you to estimate D'Leon's EVA. She estimates that the after-tax cost of capital was 10 percent in 2001 and 13 percent in 2002.

d. Looking at D'Leon's stock price today, would you conclude that the expansion increased or decreased MVA?

e. D'Leon purchases materials on 30-day terms, meaning that it is supposed to pay for purchases within 30 days of receipt. Judging from its 2002 balance sheet, do you think D'Leon pays suppliers on time? Explain. If not, what problems might this lead to?

f. D'Leon spends money for labor, materials, and fixed assets (depreciation) to make products, and still more money to sell those products. Then, it makes sales that result in receivables, which eventually result in cash inflows. Does it appear that D'Leon's sales price exceeds its costs per unit sold? How does this affect the cash balance?

g. Suppose D'Leon's sales manager told the sales staff to start offering 60-day credit terms rather than the 30-day terms now being offered. D'Leon's competitors react by offering similar terms, so sales remain constant. What effect would this have on the cash account? How would the cash account be affected if sales doubled as a result of the credit policy change?

h. Can you imagine a situation in which the sales price exceeds the cost of producing and selling a unit of output, yet a dramatic increase in sales volume causes the cash balance to decline?

i. Did D'Leon finance its expansion program with internally generated funds (additions to retained earnings plus depreciation) or with external capital? How does the choice of financing affect the company's financial strength?

j. Refer to Tables IC2-2 and IC2-4. Suppose D'Leon broke even in 2002 in the sense that sales revenues equaled total operating costs plus interest charges. Would the asset expansion have caused the company to experience a cash shortage that required it to raise external capital?

k. If D'Leon started depreciating fixed assets over 7 years rather than 10 years, would that affect (1) the physical stock of assets, (2) the balance sheet account for fixed assets, (3) the company's reported net income, and (4) its cash position? Assume the same depreciation method is used for stockholder reporting and for tax calculations, and the accounting change has no effect on assets' physical lives.

l. Explain how earnings per share, dividends per share, and book value per share are calculated, and what they mean. Why does the market price per share *not* equal the book value per share?

m. Explain briefly the tax treatment of (1) interest and dividends paid, (2) interest earned and dividends received, (3) capital gains, and (4) tax loss carry-back and carry-forward. How might each of these items affect D'Leon's taxes?

TABLE IC2-1	Balance Sheets		

		2002	2001
ASSETS			
Cash		$ 7,282	$ 57,600
Accounts receivable		632,160	351,200
Inventories		1,287,360	715,200
Total current assets		$1,926,802	$1,124,000
Gross fixed assets		1,202,950	491,000
Less accumulated depreciation		263,160	146,200
Net fixed assets		$ 939,790	$ 344,800
Total assets		$2,866,592	$1,468,800
LIABILITIES AND EQUITY			
Accounts payable		$ 524,160	$ 145,600
Notes payable		636,808	200,000
Accruals		489,600	136,000
Total current liabilities		$1,650,568	$ 481,600
Long-term debt		723,432	323,432
Common stock (100,000 shares)		460,000	460,000
Retained earnings		32,592	203,768
Total equity		$ 492,592	$ 663,768
Total liabilities and equity		$2,866,592	$1,468,800

TABLE IC2-2	Income Statements		

	2002	2001
Sales	$6,034,000	$3,432,000
Cost of goods sold	5,528,000	2,864,000
Other expenses	519,988	358,672
Total operating costs excluding depreciation and amortization	$6,047,988	$3,222,672
EBITDA	($13,988)	$ 209,328
Depreciation and amortization	116,960	18,900
EBIT	($ 130,948)	$ 190,428
Interest expense	136,012	43,828
EBT	($ 266,960)	$ 146,600
Taxes (40%)	(106,784)[a]	58,640
Net income	($ 160,176)	$ 87,960

continued

	2002	2001
EPS	($ 1.602)	$ 0.880
DPS	$ 0.110	$ 0.220
Book value per share	$ 4.926	$ 6.638
Stock price	$ 2.25	$ 8.50
Shares outstanding	100,000	100,000
Tax rate	40.00%	40.00%
Lease payments	40,000	40,000
Sinking fund payments	0	0

[a]The firm had sufficient taxable income in 2000 and 2001 to obtain its full tax refund in 2002.

TABLE IC2-3 | **Statement of Retained Earnings, 2002**

Balance of retained earnings, 12/31/01	$203,768
Add: Net income, 2002	(160,176)
Less: Dividends paid	(11,000)
Balance of retained earnings, 12/31/02	$ 32,592

TABLE IC2-4 | **Statement of Cash Flows, 2002**

OPERATING ACTIVITIES

Net income	($ 160,176)
Additions (Sources of Cash)	
Depreciation and amortization	116,960
Increase in accounts payable	378,560
Increase in accruals	353,600
Subtractions (Uses of Cash)	
Increase in accounts receivable	(280,960)
Increase in inventories	(572,160)
Net cash provided by operating activities	($ 164,176)

LONG-TERM INVESTING ACTIVITIES

Cash used to acquire fixed assets	($ 711,950)

continued

FINANCING ACTIVITIES

Increase in notes payable	$ 436,808
Increase in long-term debt	400,000
Payment of cash dividends	(11,000)
Net cash provided by financing activities	$ 825,808
Sum: net decrease in cash	($ 50,318)
Plus: cash at beginning of year	57,600
Cash at end of year	$ 7,282

CYBER PROBLEM

Please go to our web site **http://brigham.swlearning.com** to access the Cyberproblems.

With your Xtra! CD-ROM, access the Thomson Analytics Problems and use the Thomson Analytics Academic online database to work this chapter's problem.

ANALYSIS OF FINANCIAL STATEMENTS

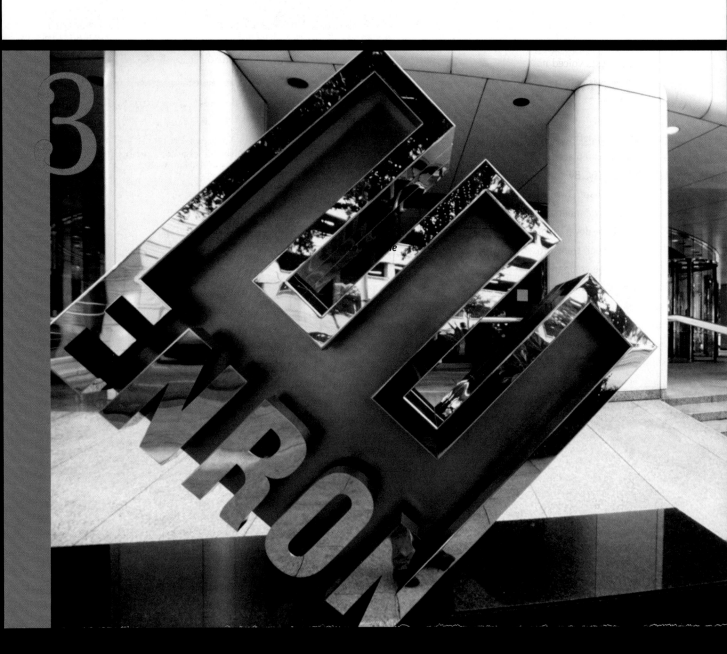

ENRON AND WORLDCOM

In early 2001, Enron appeared to be on top of the world. The high-flying energy firm had a market capitalization of $60 billion, and its stock was trading at $80 a share. Wall Street analysts frequently touted its innovation and management success, and most strongly recommended the stock. Less than a year later, Enron had declared bankruptcy, its stock was basically worthless, and investors had lost billions of dollars. This dramatic and sudden collapse left many wondering how so much value could be destroyed in such a short period of time.

While Enron's stock fell steadily throughout the first part of 2001, most analysts voiced no concerns. The general consensus was that Enron was simply caught up in a sell-off that was affecting the entire stock market, and that the company's long-run prospects remained strong. However, a hint of trouble came when Enron's CEO, Jeffrey Skilling, unexpectedly resigned in August 2001 and was replaced by the company's chairman and previous CEO, Ken Lay. By the end of August, Enron's stock had fallen to $35 a share. Two months later, Enron stunned the financial markets by announcing a $638 million loss, along with a $1.2 billion write-down in its equity value. The write-down, which was later seen to be grossly inadequate, stemmed primarily from losses the company had realized from a series of partnerships set up by the company's CFO, Andrew Fastow. Shortly thereafter it was revealed Enron had guaranteed debt taken on by the partnerships, so its true liabilities were considerably higher than the financial statements indicated. All of these revelations destroyed Enron's credibility, caused its customers to flee, and led directly to its bankruptcy. Not surprisingly, Enron's investors and employees were enraged to learn that its senior executives had realized some $750 million in salaries, bonuses, and profits from stock options in the 12 months before the company went bankrupt. During that year, when the executives were bailing out of the stock as fast as they could, they were putting out misleading statements and touting the stock to their own employees and to outside investors. Lay, Skilling, and Fastow may ultimately face criminal charges for these actions.

After Enron's collapse, critics turned their attention to the company's auditor, Arthur Andersen, and to the Wall Street analysts who had blindly recommended the stock over the years. Critics contend that the auditors and analysts neglected their responsibilities in part because of conflicts of interest. Perhaps Andersen's auditors looked the other way because they didn't want to compromise their lucrative consulting contracts with Enron, and perhaps the analysts kept recommending the stock because they wanted to help their firms to get some of Enron's investment banking business.

As if the Enron debacle was not enough, in June 2002 it was learned that WorldCom, an even larger company, had "cooked its books" and inflated its profits and cash flows by about $3.8 billion. Shortly thereafter, WorldCom collapsed, with many more billions of investor losses and thousands of more thrown out of work. Enron had set up complicated partnerships to deceive investors, but WorldCom simply lied, reporting normal operating costs as capital expenditures and thus boosting its reported profits. Interestingly, Enron and WorldCom used the same auditing firm, Arthur Andersen. It is also interesting to note that Citigroup's investment banking subsidiary, Salomon Smith Barney, earned many millions in

---

NOTE: We have covered this chapter both early in the course and toward the end. Early coverage gives students an overview of how financial decisions affect financial statements and results, and thus of what financial management is all about. Later coverage, after students have an understanding of stock valuation, risk analysis, capital budgeting, capital structure, and working capital management, helps students appreciate why ratios are the way they are, and how they are used for different purposes. Depending on students' backgrounds, instructors may want to cover the chapter early or late.

fees from WorldCom, and that Salomon's lead telecom analyst, Jack Grubman, did not downgrade WorldCom to a sell until the very day it announced the fraud. At that point the stock was selling for less than a dollar, down from its high of $64.50.

The Enron and WorldCom collapses caused investors throughout the world to wonder if these companies' misdeeds were isolated situations or symptomatic of undiscovered problems in a host of other companies. Those fears led to a broad decline in stock prices, and President Bush expressed outrage at executives whose actions were imperiling our financial markets and indeed our entire economic system. All this has led to a series of investigations that will almost certainly result in new guidelines and regulations regarding the construction of financial statements, insider trading, auditor involvement in consulting,

responsibilities of stock analysts, and penalties for officers and directors who participate in or even fail to detect fraud or other deceptive practices. The good news in all this is that financial statements—which in our judgment are generally not improperly constructed—will in the future be better than ever.

Despite recent concerns, the financial statements still provide a wealth of information that can be used by managers, investors, lenders, customers, suppliers, and regulators. As you will see in this chapter, a careful analysis of a company's statements can highlight its strengths and shortcomings. Also, as you will see, financial analysis can be used to predict how such strategic decisions as the sale of a division, a change in credit or inventory policy, or a plant expansion are likely to affect a firm's future performance.

PUTTING THINGS IN PERSPECTIVE

The primary goal of financial management should be to maximize the stock price over the long run, not to maximize accounting measures such as net income or EPS. However, accounting data do influence stock prices, and to understand why a company is performing the way it is and to forecast where it is heading, one needs to evaluate the accounting information reported in the financial statements. Chapter 2 described the key financial statements and showed how they change as a firm's operations undergo change. Now, in Chapter 3, we show how financial statements are used by managers to improve performance, by lenders to evaluate the likelihood of collecting on loans, and by stockholders to forecast earnings, dividends, and stock prices.

If management is to maximize a firm's value, it must take advantage of the firm's strengths and correct its weaknesses. Financial statement analysis involves (1) comparing the firm's performance with that of other firms in the same industry and (2) evaluating trends in the firm's financial position over time. These studies help management identify deficiencies and then take actions to improve performance. In this chapter, we focus on how financial managers (and investors) evaluate a firm's current financial position. Then, in the remaining chapters, we examine the types of actions management can take to improve future performance and thus increase its stock price.

This chapter should, for the most part, be a review of concepts you learned in accounting. However, accounting focuses on how financial statements are *made*, whereas our focus is on how they are *used* by management to improve the firm's performance and by investors when they set values on the firm's stock and bonds. Like Chapter 2, a spreadsheet model accompanies this chapter. You are encouraged to use the model and follow along with the textbook examples. ■

RATIO ANALYSIS

Financial statements report both on a firm's position at a point in time and on its operations over some past period. However, the real value of financial statements lies in the fact that they can be used to help predict future earnings and dividends. From an investor's standpoint, *predicting the future is what financial statement analysis is all about*, while from management's standpoint, *financial statement analysis is useful both to help anticipate future conditions and, more important, as a starting point for planning actions that will improve the firm's future performance.*

Financial ratios are designed to help one evaluate a financial statement. For example, Firm A might have debt of $5,248,760 and interest charges of $419,900, while Firm B might have debt of $52,647,980 and interest charges of $3,948,600. Which company is stronger? The burden of these debts, and the companies' ability to repay them, can best be evaluated (1) by comparing each firm's debt to its assets and (2) by comparing the interest it must pay to the income it has available for payment of interest. Such comparisons are made by *ratio analysis*.

In the paragraphs that follow, we will calculate the Year 2002 financial ratios for Allied Food Products, using data from the balance sheets and income statements given in Tables 2-1 and 2-2 back in Chapter 2. We will also evaluate the ratios in relation to the industry averages.[1] Note that all dollar amounts in the ratio calculations are in millions.

LIQUIDITY RATIOS

Liquid Asset
An asset that can be converted to cash quickly without having to reduce the asset's price very much.

A **liquid asset** is one that trades in an active market and hence can be quickly converted to cash at the going market price, and a firm's "liquidity position" deals with this question: Will the firm be able to pay off its debts as they come due over the next year or so? As shown in Table 2-1 in Chapter 2, Allied has debts totaling $310 million that must be paid off within the coming year. Will it have trouble satisfying those obligations? A full liquidity analysis requires the use of cash budgets, but by

---

[1] In addition to the ratios discussed in this section, financial analysts also employ a tool known as *common size* balance sheets and income statements. To form a common size balance sheet, one simply divides each asset and liability item by total assets and then expresses the result as a percentage. The resultant percentage statement can be compared with statements of larger or smaller firms, or with those of the same firm over time. To form a common size income statement, one simply divides each income statement item by sales. With a spreadsheet, this is trivially easy.

Liquidity Ratios
Ratios that show the relationship of a firm's cash and other current assets to its current liabilities.

Current Ratio
This ratio is calculated by dividing current assets by current liabilities. It indicates the extent to which current liabilities are covered by those assets expected to be converted to cash in the near future.

relating the amount of cash and other current assets to current obligations, ratio analysis provides a quick, easy-to-use measure of liquidity. One of the most commonly used **liquidity ratios** is discussed in this section.

ABILITY TO MEET SHORT-TERM OBLIGATIONS: THE CURRENT RATIO

The **current ratio** is calculated by dividing current assets by current liabilities:

$$\text{Current ratio} = \frac{\text{Current assets}}{\text{Current liabilities}}$$

$$= \frac{\$1,000}{\$310} = 3.2 \text{ times.}$$

$$\text{Industry average} = 4.2 \text{ times.}$$

Current assets normally include cash, marketable securities, accounts receivable, and inventories. Current liabilities consist of accounts payable, short-term notes payable, current maturities of long-term debt, accrued taxes, and other accrued expenses (principally wages).

If a company is getting into financial difficulty, it begins paying its bills (accounts payable) more slowly, borrowing from its bank, and so on. If current liabilities are rising faster than current assets, the current ratio will fall, and this could spell trouble. Because the current ratio provides the best single indicator of the extent to which the claims of short-term creditors are covered by assets that are expected to be converted to cash fairly quickly, it is the most commonly used measure of short-term solvency.

Allied's current ratio is well below the average for its industry, 4.2, so its liquidity position is relatively weak. Still, since current assets are scheduled to be converted to cash in the near future, it is highly probable that they could be liquidated at close to their stated value. With a current ratio of 3.2, Allied could liquidate current assets at only 31 percent of book value and still pay off current creditors in full.[2]

Although industry average figures are discussed later in some detail, it should be noted at this point that an industry average is not a magic number that all firms should strive to maintain—in fact, some very well-managed firms will be above the average while other good firms will be below it. However, if a firm's ratios are far removed from the averages for its industry, an analyst should be concerned about why this variance occurs. Thus, a deviation from the industry average should signal the analyst (or management) to check further.[3]

SELF-TEST QUESTIONS

What are the characteristics of a liquid asset? Give some examples.

Identify the key ratio that is used to analyze a firm's liquidity position, and write out its equation.

Why is the current ratio the most commonly used measure of short-term solvency?

---

[2] 1/3.2 = 0.31, or 31 percent. Note that 0.31($1,000) = $310, the amount of current liabilities.

[3] Another liquidity ratio that is sometimes used is the *quick, or acid test, ratio*, defined as (Current assets − Inventories)/Current liabilities. This ratio is used if there is a fear that inventories cannot be sold at their book value.

Asset Management Ratios
A set of ratios that measure how effectively a firm is managing its assets.

The second group of ratios, the **asset management ratios,** measures how effectively the firm is managing its assets. These ratios are designed to answer this question: Does the total amount of each type of asset as reported on the balance sheet seem reasonable, too high, or too low in view of current and projected sales levels? When they acquire assets, Allied and other companies must borrow or obtain capital from other sources. If a firm has too many assets, its cost of capital will be too high, hence its profits will be depressed. On the other hand, if assets are too low, profitable sales will be lost. Ratios that analyze the different types of assets are described in this section.

EVALUATING INVENTORIES: THE INVENTORY TURNOVER RATIO

Inventory Turnover Ratio
This ratio is calculated by dividing sales by inventories.

The **inventory turnover ratio** is defined as sales divided by inventories:

$$\text{Inventory turnover ratio} = \frac{\text{Sales}}{\text{Inventories}}$$

$$= \frac{\$3,000}{\$615} = 4.9 \text{ times.}$$

$$\text{Industry average} = 9.0 \text{ times.}$$

As a rough approximation, each item of Allied's inventory is sold out and restocked, or "turned over," 4.9 times per year. "Turnover" is a term that originated many years ago with the old Yankee peddler, who would load up his wagon with goods, then go off on his route to peddle his wares. The merchandise was called "working capital" because it was what he actually sold, or "turned over," to produce his profits, whereas his "turnover" was the number of trips he took each year. Annual sales divided by inventory equaled turnover, or trips per year. If he made 10 trips per year, stocked 100 pans, and made a gross profit of $5 per pan, his annual gross profit would be (100)($5)(10) = $5,000. If he went faster and made 20 trips per year, his gross profit would double, other things held constant. So, his turnover directly affected his profits.

Allied's turnover of 4.9 times is much lower than the industry average of 9 times. This suggests that Allied is holding too much inventory. Excess inventory is, of course, unproductive, and it represents an investment with a low or zero rate of return. Allied's low inventory turnover ratio also makes us question the current ratio. With such a low turnover, we must wonder whether the firm is actually holding obsolete goods not worth their stated value.[4]

Note that sales occur over the entire year, whereas the inventory figure is for one point in time. For this reason, it is better to use an average inventory measure.[5] If the

---

[4] A problem arises calculating and analyzing the inventory turnover ratio. Sales are stated at market prices, so if inventories are carried at cost, as they generally are, the calculated turnover overstates the true turnover ratio. Therefore, it would be more appropriate to use cost of goods sold in place of sales in the formula's numerator. However, some established compilers of financial ratio statistics such as Dun & Bradstreet use the ratio of sales to inventories carried at cost. To develop a figure that can be compared with those published by Dun & Bradstreet and similar organizations, it is necessary to measure inventory turnover with sales in the numerator, as we do here.

[5] Preferably, the average inventory value should be calculated by summing the monthly figures during the year and dividing by 12. If monthly data are not available, one can add the beginning and ending figures and divide by 2. Both methods adjust for growth but not for seasonal effects.

firm's business is highly seasonal, or if there has been a strong upward or downward sales trend during the year, it is especially useful to make some such adjustment. To maintain comparability with industry averages, however, we did not use the average inventory figure.

EVALUATING RECEIVABLES: THE DAYS SALES OUTSTANDING

Days Sales Outstanding (DSO)
This ratio is calculated by dividing accounts receivable by average sales per day; it indicates the average length of time the firm must wait after making a sale before it receives cash.

Days sales outstanding (DSO), also called the "average collection period" (ACP), is used to appraise accounts receivable, and it is calculated by dividing accounts receivable by average daily sales to find the number of days' sales that are tied up in receivables. Thus, the DSO represents the average length of time that the firm must wait after making a sale before receiving cash. Allied has 46 days sales outstanding, well above the 36-day industry average:

$$\text{DSO} = \begin{array}{c}\text{Days} \\ \text{sales} \\ \text{outstanding}\end{array} = \frac{\text{Receivables}}{\text{Average sales per day}} = \frac{\text{Receivables}}{\text{Annual sales}/365}$$

$$= \frac{\$375}{\$3,000/365} = \frac{\$375}{\$8.2192} = 45.625 \text{ days} \approx 46 \text{ days}.$$

$$\text{Industry average} = 36 \text{ days}.$$

Note that in this calculation we used a 365-day year. Other analysts use a 360-day year for this calculation. If Allied had calculated its DSO using a 360-day year, its DSO would have been reduced slightly to 45 days.[6]

The DSO can also be evaluated by comparison with the terms on which the firm sells its goods. For example, Allied's sales terms call for payment within 30 days, so the fact that 46 days' sales, not 30 days', are outstanding indicates that customers, on the average, are not paying their bills on time. This deprives Allied of funds that it could use to invest in productive assets. Moreover, in some instances the fact that a customer is paying late may signal that the customer is in financial trouble, in which case Allied may have a hard time ever collecting the receivable. Therefore, if the trend in DSO over the past few years has been rising, but the credit policy has not been changed, this would be strong evidence that steps should be taken to expedite the collection of accounts receivable.

EVALUATING FIXED ASSETS: THE FIXED ASSETS TURNOVER RATIO

Fixed Assets Turnover Ratio
The ratio of sales to net fixed assets.

The **fixed assets turnover ratio** measures how effectively the firm uses its plant and equipment. It is the ratio of sales to net fixed assets:

$$\text{Fixed assets turnover ratio} = \frac{\text{Sales}}{\text{Net fixed assets}}$$

$$= \frac{\$3,000}{\$1,000} = 3.0 \text{ times.}$$

$$\text{Industry average} = 3.0 \text{ times.}$$

---

[6] It would be better to use *average* receivables, either an average of the monthly figures or (Beginning receivables + Ending receivables)/2 = ($315 + $375)/2 = $345 in the formula. Had the annual average receivables been used, Allied's DSO on a 365-day basis would have been $345.00/$8.2192 = 41.975 days, or approximately 42 days. The 42-day figure is the more accurate one, but because the industry average was based on year-end receivables, we used 46 days for our comparison. The DSO is discussed further in Part 6.

Allied's ratio of 3.0 times is equal to the industry average, indicating that the firm is using its fixed assets about as intensively as are other firms in its industry. Therefore, Allied seems to have about the right amount of fixed assets in relation to other firms.

A potential problem can exist when interpreting the fixed assets turnover ratio. Recall from accounting that fixed assets reflect the historical costs of the assets. Inflation has caused the value of many assets that were purchased in the past to be seriously understated. Therefore, if we were comparing an old firm that had acquired many of its fixed assets years ago at low prices with a new company that had acquired its fixed assets only recently, we would probably find that the old firm had the higher fixed assets turnover ratio. However, this would be more reflective of the difficulty accountants have in dealing with inflation than of any inefficiency on the part of the new firm. The accounting profession is trying to devise ways of making financial statements reflect current values rather than historical values. If balance sheets were actually stated on a current value basis, this would help us make better comparisons, but at the moment the problem still exists. Since financial analysts typically do not have the data necessary to make adjustments, they simply recognize that a problem exists and deal with it judgmentally. In Allied's case, the issue is not a serious one because all firms in the industry have been expanding at about the same rate, hence the balance sheets of the comparison firms are reasonably comparable.[7]

EVALUATING TOTAL ASSETS: THE TOTAL ASSETS TURNOVER RATIO

Total Assets Turnover Ratio
This ratio is calculated by dividing sales by total assets.

The final asset management ratio, the **total assets turnover ratio,** measures the turnover of all the firm's assets; it is calculated by dividing sales by total assets:

$$\text{Total assets turnover ratio} = \frac{\text{Sales}}{\text{Total assets}}$$

$$= \frac{\$3,000}{\$2,000} = 1.5 \text{ times.}$$

$$\text{Industry average} = 1.8 \text{ times.}$$

Allied's ratio is somewhat below the industry average, indicating that the company is not generating a sufficient volume of business given its total assets investment. Sales should be increased, some assets should be disposed of, or a combination of these steps should be taken.

SELF-TEST QUESTIONS

Identify four ratios that are used to measure how effectively a firm is managing its assets, and write out their equations.

How might rapid growth distort the inventory turnover ratio?

When evaluating a firm's DSO, with what should it be compared?

What potential problem might arise when comparing different firms' fixed assets turnover ratios?

---

[7] See FASB #89, *Financial Reporting and Changing Prices* (December 1986), for a discussion of the effects of inflation on financial statements.

Financial Leverage
The use of debt financing.

The extent to which a firm uses debt financing, or **financial leverage,** has three important implications: (1) By raising funds through debt, stockholders can maintain control of a firm while limiting their investment. (2) Creditors look to the equity, or owner-supplied funds, to provide a margin of safety, so the higher the proportion of the total capital that was provided by stockholders, the less the risk faced by creditors. (3) If the firm earns more on investments financed with borrowed funds than it pays in interest, the return on the owners' capital is magnified, or "leveraged."

To understand better how financial leverage affects risk and return, consider Table 3-1. Here we analyze two companies that are identical except for the way they are financed. Firm U (for "unleveraged") has no debt, whereas Firm L (for "leveraged") is financed with half equity and half debt that costs 15 percent. Both companies have $100 of assets and $100 of sales, and their expected operating income (also called earnings before interest and taxes, or EBIT) is $30. Thus, both firms *expect* to earn $30, before taxes, on their assets. Of course, things could turn out badly, in which case EBIT would be lower. Thus, in the second column of the table, we show EBIT declining from $30 to $2.50 under bad conditions.

Even though both companies' assets produce the same expected EBIT, under normal conditions Firm L should provide its stockholders with a return on equity of 27 percent versus only 18 percent for Firm U. This difference is caused by Firm L's use of debt, which "leverages up" its expected rate of return to stockholders. There are two reasons for the leveraging effect: (1) Since interest is deductible, the use of debt lowers the tax bill and leaves more of the firm's operating income available to its investors. (2) If operating income as a percentage of assets exceeds the interest rate on debt, as it generally does, then a company can use debt to acquire assets, pay the interest on the debt, and have something left over as a "bonus" for its stockholders. For our hypothetical firms, these two effects combine to push Firm L's expected rate of return on equity up far above that of Firm U. Thus, debt can "leverage up" the rate of return on equity.

However, financial leverage can cut both ways. As we show in Column 2, if sales are lower and costs are higher than were expected, the return on assets will also be lower than was expected. Under these conditions, the leveraged firm's return on equity falls especially sharply, and losses occur. Under the "bad conditions" in Table 3-1, the debt-free firm still shows a profit, but Firm L shows a loss and thus has a negative return on equity. This occurs because Firm L needs cash to service its debt, while Firm U does not. Firm U, because of its strong balance sheet, could ride out the recession and be ready for the next boom. Firm L, on the other hand, must pay interest of $7.50 regardless of its level of sales. Since in the recession its operations do not generate enough income to meet the interest payments, cash would be depleted, and the firm probably would need to raise additional funds. Because it would be running a loss, Firm L would have a hard time selling stock to raise capital, and its losses would cause lenders to raise the interest rate, increasing L's problems still further. As a result, Firm L just might not survive to enjoy the next boom.

We see, then, that firms with relatively high debt ratios have higher expected returns when the economy is normal, but they are exposed to risk of loss when the economy goes into a recession. Therefore, decisions about the use of debt require firms to balance higher expected returns against increased risk. Determining the optimal amount of debt is a complicated process, and we defer a discussion of this topic until the chapter on capital structure and leverage. For now, we simply look at two

FIRM U (UNLEVERAGED)

Current assets	$ 50	Debt	$ 0
Fixed assets	50	Common equity	100
Total assets	$100	Total liabilities and equity	$100

	EXPECTED CONDITIONS (1)	BAD CONDITIONS (2)
Sales	$100.00	$82.50
Operating costs	70.00	80.00
Operating income (EBIT)	$ 30.00	$ 2.50
Interest	0.00	0.00
Earnings before taxes (EBT)	$ 30.00	$ 2.50
Taxes (40%)	12.00	1.00
Net income (NI)	$ 18.00	$ 1.50
$ROE_U = NI/\text{Common equity} = NI/\$100 =$	18.00%	1.50%

FIRM L (LEVERAGED)

Current assets	$ 50	Debt (interest = 15%)	$ 50
Fixed assets	50	Common equity	50
Total assets	$100	Total liabilities and equity	$100

	EXPECTED CONDITIONS (1)	BAD CONDITIONS (2)
Sales	$100.00	$82.50
Operating costs	70.00	80.00
Operating income (EBIT)	$ 30.00	$ 2.50
Interest (15%)	7.50	7.50
Earnings before taxes (EBT)	$ 22.50	($ 5.00)
Taxes (40%)	9.00	(2.00)
Net income (NI)	$ 13.50	($ 3.00)
$ROE_L = NI/\text{Common equity} = NI/\$50 =$	27.00%	(6.00%)

procedures analysts use to examine the firm's debt: (1) They check the balance sheet to determine the proportion of total funds represented by debt, and (2) they review the income statement to see how well fixed charges are covered by operating profits.

HOW THE FIRM IS FINANCED: TOTAL DEBT TO TOTAL ASSETS

Debt Ratio
The ratio of total debt to total assets.

The ratio of total debt to total assets, generally called the **debt ratio**, measures the percentage of funds provided by creditors:

$$\text{Debt ratio} = \frac{\text{Total debt}}{\text{Total assets}}$$

$$= \frac{\$310 + \$754}{\$2,000} = \frac{\$1,064}{\$2,000} = 53.2\%.$$

Industry average = 40.0%.

Total debt includes both current liabilities and long-term debt. Creditors prefer low debt ratios because the lower the ratio, the greater the cushion against creditors' losses in the event of liquidation. Stockholders, on the other hand, may want more leverage because it magnifies expected earnings.

Allied's debt ratio is 53.2 percent, which means that its creditors have supplied more than half the total financing. As we will discuss in the chapter on capital structure and leverage, there are a variety of factors that determine a company's optimal debt ratio. Nevertheless, the fact that Allied's debt ratio exceeds the industry average raises a red flag and may make it costly for Allied to borrow additional funds without first raising more equity capital. Creditors may be reluctant to lend the firm more money, and management would probably be subjecting the firm to the risk of bankruptcy if it sought to increase the debt ratio any further by borrowing additional funds.[8]

ABILITY TO PAY INTEREST: TIMES-INTEREST-EARNED RATIO

Times-Interest-Earned (TIE) Ratio
The ratio of earnings before interest and taxes (EBIT) to interest charges; a measure of the firm's ability to meet its annual interest payments.

The **times-interest-earned (TIE) ratio** is determined by dividing earnings before interest and taxes (EBIT in Table 2-2) by the interest charges:

$$\text{Times-interest-earned (TIE) ratio} = \frac{\text{EBIT}}{\text{Interest charges}}$$

$$= \frac{\$283.8}{\$88} = 3.2 \text{ times.}$$

Industry average = 6.0 times.

The TIE ratio measures the extent to which operating income can decline before the firm is unable to meet its annual interest costs. Failure to meet this obligation can bring legal action by the firm's creditors, possibly resulting in bankruptcy. Note that earnings before interest and taxes, rather than net income, is used in the numerator. Because interest is paid with pre-tax dollars, the firm's ability to pay current interest is not affected by taxes.

Allied's interest is covered 3.2 times. Since the industry average is 6 times, Allied is covering its interest charges by a relatively low margin of safety. Thus, the TIE ratio reinforces the conclusion from our analysis of the debt ratio that Allied would face difficulties if it attempted to borrow additional funds.

ABILITY TO SERVICE DEBT: EBITDA COVERAGE RATIO

The TIE ratio is useful for assessing a company's ability to meet interest charges on its debt, but this ratio has two shortcomings: (1) Interest is not the only fixed finan-

---

[8] The ratio of debt to equity is also used in financial analysis. The debt-to-assets (D/A) and debt-to-equity (D/E) ratios are simply transformations of each other:

$$\text{D/E} = \frac{\text{D/A}}{1 - \text{D/A}} \quad \text{and} \quad \text{D/A} = \frac{\text{D/E}}{1 + \text{D/E}}.$$

cial charge—companies must also reduce debt on schedule, and many firms lease assets and thus must make lease payments. If they fail to repay debt or meet lease payments, they can be forced into bankruptcy. (2) EBIT does not represent all the cash flow available to service debt, especially if a firm has high depreciation and/or amortization charges. To account for these deficiencies, bankers and others have developed the **EBITDA coverage ratio,** defined as follows:[9]

EBITDA Coverage Ratio
A ratio whose numerator includes all cash flows available to meet fixed financial charges and whose denominator includes all fixed financial charges.

$$\text{EBITDA coverage ratio} = \frac{\text{EBITDA} + \text{Lease payments}}{\text{Interest} + \text{Principal payments} + \text{Lease payments}}$$

$$= \frac{\$283.8 + \$100 + \$28}{\$88 + \$20 + \$28} = \frac{\$411.8}{\$136} = 3.0 \text{ times.}$$

$$\text{Industry average} = 4.3 \text{ times.}$$

Allied had $283.8 million of operating income (EBIT), presumably all cash. Non-cash charges of $100 million for depreciation and amortization (the DA part of EBITDA) were deducted in the calculation of EBIT, so they must be added back to find the cash flow available to service debt. Also, lease payments of $28 million were deducted before getting the $283.8 million of EBIT.[10] That $28 million was available to meet financial charges, hence it must be added back, bringing the total available to cover fixed financial charges to $411.8 million. Fixed financial charges consisted of $88 million of interest, $20 million of sinking fund payments, and $28 million for lease payments, for a total of $136 million.[11] Therefore, Allied covered its fixed financial charges by 3.0 times. However, if operating income declines, the coverage will fall, and operating income certainly can decline. Moreover, Allied's ratio is well below the industry average, so again, the company seems to have a relatively high level of debt.

The EBITDA coverage ratio is most useful for relatively short-term lenders such as banks, which rarely make loans (except real estate-backed loans) for longer than about five years. Over a relatively short period, depreciation-generated funds can be used to service debt. Over a longer time, those funds must be reinvested to maintain the plant and equipment or else the company cannot remain in business. Therefore, banks and other relatively short-term lenders focus on the EBITDA coverage ratio, whereas long-term bondholders focus on the TIE ratio.

---

[9] Different analysts define the EBITDA coverage ratio in different ways. For example, some would omit the lease payment information, and others would "gross up" principal payments by dividing them by $(1 - T)$ because these payments are not tax deductions, hence must be made with after-tax cash flows. We included lease payments because, for many firms, they are quite important, and failing to make them can lead to bankruptcy just as surely as can failure to make payments on "regular" debt. We did not gross up principal payments because, if a company is in financial difficulty, its tax rate will probably be zero, hence the gross up is not necessary whenever the ratio is really important.

[10] Lease payments are included in the numerator because, unlike interest, they were deducted when EBITDA was calculated. We want to find *all* the funds that were available to service debt, so lease payments must be added to the EBIT and DA to find the funds that could be used to service debt and meet lease payments. To illustrate this, suppose EBIT before lease payments was $100, lease payments were $100, and DA was zero. After lease payments, EBIT would be $100 − $100 = $0. Yet lease payments of $100 were made, so obviously there was cash to make those payments. The available cash was the reported EBIT of $0 plus the $100 of lease payments.

[11] A sinking fund is a required annual payment designed to reduce the balance of a bond or preferred stock issue. A sinking fund payment is like the principal repayment portion of the payment on an amortized loan, but sinking funds are used for publicly traded bond issues, whereas amortization payments are used for bank loans and other private loans.

SELF-TEST QUESTIONS

Identify three important implications of the extent to which a firm uses financial leverage.

How does the use of financial leverage affect stockholders' control position?

In what way do taxes influence a firm's willingness to finance with debt?

In what way does the decision to use debt involve a risk-versus-return trade-off?

Explain the following statement: "Analysts look at both balance sheet and income statement ratios when appraising a firm's financial condition."

Name three ratios that are used to measure the extent to which a firm uses financial leverage, and write out their equations.

PROFITABILITY RATIOS

Profitability Ratios
A group of ratios that show the combined effects of liquidity, asset management, and debt on operating results.

Profitability is the net result of a number of policies and decisions. The ratios examined thus far provide useful clues as to the effectiveness of a firm's operations, but the **profitability ratios** show the combined effects of liquidity, asset management, and debt on operating results.

PROFIT MARGIN ON SALES

Profit Margin on Sales
This ratio measures net income per dollar of sales; it is calculated by dividing net income by sales.

The **profit margin on sales,** calculated by dividing net income by sales, gives the profit per dollar of sales:

$$\text{Profit margin on sales} = \frac{\text{Net income available to common stockholders}}{\text{Sales}}$$

$$= \frac{\$113.5}{\$3,000} = 3.8\%.$$

$$\text{Industry average} = 5.0\%.$$

Allied's profit margin is below the industry average of 5 percent. This sub-par result occurs because costs are too high. High costs, in turn, generally occur because of inefficient operations. However, Allied's low profit margin is also a result of its heavy use of debt. Recall that net income is income *after interest*. Therefore, if two firms have identical operations in the sense that their sales, operating costs, and EBIT are the same, but if one firm uses more debt than the other, it will have higher interest charges. Those interest charges will pull net income down, and since sales are constant, the result will be a relatively low profit margin. In such a case, the low profit margin would not indicate an operating problem, just a difference in financing strategies. Thus, the firm with the low profit margin might end up with a higher rate of return on its stockholders' investment due to its use of financial leverage. We will see

INTERNATIONAL ACCOUNTING DIFFERENCES CREATE HEADACHES FOR INVESTORS

You must be a good financial detective to analyze financial statements, especially if the company operates overseas. Despite attempts to standardize accounting practices, there are many differences in the way financial information is reported in different countries, and these differences create headaches for investors trying to make cross-border company comparisons.

A study by two Rider College accounting professors demonstrated that huge differences can exist. The professors developed a computer model to evaluate the net income of a hypothetical but typical company operating in different countries. Applying the standard accounting practices of each country, the hypothetical company would have reported net income of $34,600 in the United States, $260,600 in the United Kingdom, and $240,600 in Australia.

Such variances occur for a number of reasons. In most countries, including the United States, an asset's balance sheet value is reported at original cost less any accumulated depreciation. However, in some countries, asset values are adjusted to reflect current market prices. Also, inventory valuation methods vary from country to country, as does the treatment of goodwill. Other differences arise from the treatment of leases, research and development costs, and pension plans.

These differences arise from a variety of legal, historical, cultural, and economic factors. For example, in Germany and Japan large banks are the key source of both debt and equity capital, whereas in the United States public capital markets are most important. As a result, U.S. corporations disclose a great deal of information to the public, while German and Japanese corporations use very conservative accounting practices that appeal to the banks.

The accounting profession has long recognized that international accounting differences exist, and it has taken steps toward making international comparisons easier. The International Accounting Standards Board (IASB) was formed for the purpose of bringing financial accounting and reporting standards into closer conformity on a global basis. This board, whose recognition and acceptance is growing, is currently working on projects to produce the first globally recognized accounting standards. A global accounting structure would enable investors and practitioners around the world to read and understand financial reports produced anywhere in the world. So, as you can see, the IASB's task is a very important one. It remains to be seen whether the IASB's lofty goal will be achieved.

SOURCE: "All Accountants Soon May Speak the Same Language," *The Wall Street Journal*, August 29, 1995, A15.

---

exactly how profit margins and the use of debt interact to affect stockholder returns shortly, when we examine the Du Pont equation.

BASIC EARNING POWER (BEP)

Basic Earning Power (BEP) Ratio
This ratio indicates the ability of the firm's assets to generate operating income; calculated by dividing EBIT by total assets.

The **basic earning power (BEP) ratio** is calculated by dividing earnings before interest and taxes (EBIT) by total assets:

$$\text{Basic earning power ratio (BEP)} = \frac{\text{EBIT}}{\text{Total assets}}$$

$$= \frac{\$283.8}{\$2,000} = 14.2\%.$$

Industry average $= 17.2\%$.

This ratio shows the raw earning power of the firm's assets, before the influence of taxes and leverage, and it is useful for comparing firms with different tax situations and different degrees of financial leverage. Because of its low turnover ratios and low profit margin on sales, Allied is not earning as high a return on its assets as is the average food-processing company.[12]

RETURN ON TOTAL ASSETS

Return on Total Assets (ROA)
The ratio of net income to total assets.

The ratio of net income to total assets measures the **return on total assets (ROA)** after interest and taxes:

$$\text{Return on total assets} = \text{ROA} = \frac{\text{Net income available to common stockholders}}{\text{Total assets}}$$

$$= \frac{\$113.5}{\$2,000} = 5.7\%.$$

Industry average $= 9.0\%$.

Allied's 5.7 percent return is well below the 9 percent average for the industry. This low return results from (1) the company's low basic earning power plus (2) high interest costs resulting from its above-average use of debt, both of which cause its net income to be relatively low.

RETURN ON COMMON EQUITY

Return on Common Equity (ROE)
The ratio of net income to common equity; measures the rate of return on common stockholders' investment.

Ultimately, the most important, or "bottom line," accounting ratio is the ratio of net income to common equity, which measures the **return on common equity (ROE)**:

$$\text{Return on common equity} = \text{ROE} = \frac{\text{Net income available to common stockholders}}{\text{Common equity}}$$

$$= \frac{\$113.5}{\$896} = 12.7\%.$$

Industry average $= 15.0\%$.

Stockholders invest to get a return on their money, and this ratio tells how well they are doing in an accounting sense. Allied's 12.7 percent return is below the 15 percent industry average, but not as far below as the return on total assets. This somewhat better result is due to the company's greater use of debt, a point that is analyzed in detail later in the chapter.

SELF-TEST QUESTIONS

Identify and write out the equations for four ratios that show the combined effects of liquidity, asset management, and debt management on profitability.

Why is the basic earning power ratio useful?

Why does the use of debt lower the ROA?

What does ROE measure? Since interest expense lowers profits, does using debt lower ROE?

---

[12] Notice that EBIT is earned throughout the year, whereas the total assets figure is an end-of-the-year number. Therefore, it would be conceptually better to calculate this ratio as EBIT/Average assets = EBIT/[(Beginning assets + Ending assets)/2]. We have not made this adjustment because the published ratios used for comparative purposes do not include it. However, when we construct our own comparative ratios, we do make the adjustment. Incidentally, the same adjustment would also be appropriate for the next two ratios, ROA and ROE.

Market Value Ratios
A set of ratios that relate the firm's stock price to its earnings, cash flow, and book value per share.

A final group of ratios, the **market value ratios,** relates the firm's stock price to its earnings, cash flow, and book value per share. These ratios give management an indication of what investors think of the company's past performance and future prospects. If the liquidity, asset management, debt management, and profitability ratios all look good, then the market value ratios will be high, and the stock price will probably be as high as can be expected.

PRICE/EARNINGS RATIO

Price/Earnings (P/E) Ratio
The ratio of the price per share to earnings per share; shows the dollar amount investors will pay for $1 of current earnings.

The **price/earnings (P/E) ratio** shows how much investors are willing to pay per dollar of reported profits. Allied's stock sells for $23, so with an EPS of $2.27 its P/E ratio is 10.1:

$$\text{Price/earnings (P/E) ratio} = \frac{\text{Price per share}}{\text{Earnings per share}}$$

$$= \frac{\$23.00}{\$2.27} = 10.1 \text{ times.}$$

Industry average = 12.5 times.

As we will see in Chapter 8, P/E ratios are higher for firms with strong growth prospects, other things held constant, but they are lower for riskier firms. Since Allied's P/E ratio is below the average for other food processors, this suggests that the company is regarded as being somewhat riskier than most, as having poorer growth prospects, or both.

PRICE/CASH FLOW RATIO

Price/Cash Flow Ratio
The ratio of price per share divided by cash flow per share; shows the dollar amount investors will pay for $1 of cash flow.

In some industries, stock price is tied more closely to cash flow rather than net income. Consequently, investors often look at the **price/cash flow ratio:**

$$\text{Price/cash flow} = \frac{\text{Price per share}}{\text{Cash flow per share}}$$

$$= \frac{\$23.00}{\$4.27} = 5.4 \text{ times.}$$

Industry average = 6.8 times.

The calculation for cash flow per share was shown in Chapter 2, but just to refresh your memory, cash flow per share is calculated as net income plus depreciation and amortization divided by common shares outstanding.

Allied's price/cash flow ratio is also below the industry average, once again suggesting that its growth prospects are below average, its risk is above average, or both.

Note that some analysts look at multiples beyond just the price/earnings and the price/cash flow ratios. For example, depending on the industry, some may look at measures such as price/sales, price/customers, or price/EBITDA per share. Ultimately, though, value depends on earnings and cash flows, so if these "exotic" ratios do not forecast future EPS and cash flow, they may turn out to be misleading.

MARKET/BOOK RATIO

The ratio of a stock's market price to its book value gives another indication of how investors regard the company. Companies with relatively high rates of return on equity generally sell at higher multiples of book value than those with low returns. First, we find Allied's book value per share:

$$\text{Book value per share} = \frac{\text{Common equity}}{\text{Shares outstanding}}$$

$$= \frac{\$896}{50} = \$17.92.$$

Market/Book (M/B) Ratio
The ratio of a stock's market price to its book value.

Now we divide the market price per share by the book value to get a **market/book (M/B) ratio** of 1.3 times:

$$\text{Market/book ratio} = \text{M/B} = \frac{\text{Market price per share}}{\text{Book value per share}}$$

$$= \frac{\$23.00}{\$17.92} = 1.3 \text{ times.}$$

$$\text{Industry average} = 1.7 \text{ times.}$$

Investors are willing to pay less for a dollar of Allied's book value than for one of an average food-processing company.

The average company followed by the *Value Line Investment Survey* had a market/book ratio of about 3.99 in March 2002. Since M/B ratios typically exceed 1.0, this means that investors are willing to pay more for stocks than their accounting book values. This situation occurs primarily because asset values, as reported by accountants on corporate balance sheets, do not reflect either inflation or "goodwill." Thus, assets purchased years ago at preinflation prices are carried at their original costs, even though inflation might have caused their actual values to rise substantially, and successful going concerns have a value greater than their historical costs.

If a company earns a low rate of return on its assets, then its M/B ratio will be relatively low versus an average company. Thus, some airlines, which have not fared well in recent years, sell at M/B ratios below 1.0, while very successful firms such as Microsoft (which makes the operating systems for virtually all PCs) achieve high rates of return on their assets, causing their market values to be well in excess of their book values. In March 2002, Microsoft's book value per share was $10.15 versus a market price of $60.45, so its market/book ratio was $60.45/$10.15 = 5.96 times.

SELF-TEST QUESTIONS

Describe three ratios that relate a firm's stock price to its earnings, cash flow, and book value per share, and write out their equations.

How do market value ratios reflect what investors think about a stock's risk and expected rate of return?

What does the price/earnings (P/E) ratio show? If one firm's P/E ratio is lower than that of another, what are some factors that might explain the difference?

How is book value per share calculated? Explain how inflation and "goodwill" could cause book values to deviate from market values.

TREND ANALYSIS

Trend Analysis
An analysis of a firm's financial ratios over time; used to estimate the likelihood of improvement or deterioration in its financial condition.

It is important to analyze trends in ratios as well as their absolute levels, for trends give clues as to whether a firm's financial condition is likely to improve or to deteriorate. To do a **trend analysis,** one simply plots a ratio over time, as shown in Figure 3-1. This graph shows that Allied's rate of return on common equity has been declining since 1999, even though the industry average has been relatively stable. All the other ratios could be analyzed similarly.

SELF-TEST QUESTIONS

How does one do a trend analysis?

What important information does a trend analysis provide?

TYING THE RATIOS TOGETHER: THE DU PONT EQUATION

Du Pont Equation
A formula which shows that the rate of return on assets can be found as the product of the profit margin times the total assets turnover.

Table 3-2 summarizes Allied's ratios. The profit margin times the total assets turnover is called the **Du Pont equation,** and it gives the rate of return on assets (ROA):

$$\text{ROA} = \text{Profit margin} \times \text{Total assets turnover}$$
$$= \frac{\text{Net income}}{\text{Sales}} \times \frac{\text{Sales}}{\text{Total assets}} \quad (3\text{-}1)$$
$$= 3.8\% \times 1.5 = 5.7\%.$$

| FIGURE 3-1 | Rate of Return on Common Equity, 1998–2002 |

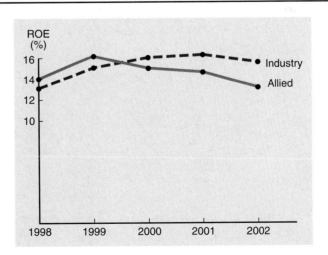

TABLE 3-2

Allied Food Products: Summary of Financial Ratios (Millions of Dollars)

RATIO	FORMULA FOR CALCULATION	CALCULATION	RATIO	INDUSTRY AVERAGE	COMMENT
Liquidity					
Current	$\dfrac{\text{Current assets}}{\text{Current liabilities}}$	$\dfrac{\$1,000}{\$310}$	= 3.2×	4.2×	Poor
Asset Management					
Inventory turnover	$\dfrac{\text{Sales}}{\text{Inventories}}$	$\dfrac{\$3,000}{\$615}$	= 4.9×	9.0×	Poor
Days sales outstanding (DSO)	$\dfrac{\text{Receivables}}{\text{Annual sales}/365}$	$\dfrac{\$375}{\$8.2192}$	= 46 days	36 days	Poor
Fixed assets turnover	$\dfrac{\text{Sales}}{\text{Net fixed assets}}$	$\dfrac{\$3,000}{\$1,000}$	= 3.0×	3.0×	OK
Total assets turnover	$\dfrac{\text{Sales}}{\text{Total assets}}$	$\dfrac{\$3,000}{\$2,000}$	= 1.5×	1.8×	Somewhat low
Debt Management					
Total debt to total assets	$\dfrac{\text{Total debt}}{\text{Total assets}}$	$\dfrac{\$1,064}{\$2,000}$	= 53.2%	40.0%	High (risky)
Times-interest-earned (TIE)	$\dfrac{\text{Earnings before interest and taxes (EBIT)}}{\text{Interest charges}}$	$\dfrac{\$283.8}{\$88}$	= 3.2×	6.0×	Low (risky)
EBITDA coverage	$\dfrac{\text{EBITDA} + \text{Lease payments}}{\text{Interest} + \text{Principal payments} + \text{Lease payments}}$	$\dfrac{\$411.8}{\$136}$	= 3.0×	4.3×	Low (risky)
Profitability					
Profit margin on sales	$\dfrac{\text{Net income available to common stockholders}}{\text{Sales}}$	$\dfrac{\$113.5}{\$3,000}$	= 3.8%	5.0%	Poor
Basic earning power (BEP)	$\dfrac{\text{Earnings before interest and taxes (EBIT)}}{\text{Total assets}}$	$\dfrac{\$283.8}{\$2,000}$	= 14.2%	17.2%	Poor
Return on total assets (ROA)	$\dfrac{\text{Net income available to common stockholders}}{\text{Total assets}}$	$\dfrac{\$113.5}{\$2,000}$	= 5.7%	9.0%	Poor
Return on common equity (ROE)	$\dfrac{\text{Net income available to common stockholders}}{\text{Common equity}}$	$\dfrac{\$113.5}{\$896}$	= 12.7%	15.0%	Poor
Market Value					
Price/earnings (P/E)	$\dfrac{\text{Price per share}}{\text{Earnings per share}}$	$\dfrac{\$23.00}{\$2.27}$	= 10.1×	12.5×	Low
Price/cash flow	$\dfrac{\text{Price per share}}{\text{Cash flow per share}}$	$\dfrac{\$23.00}{\$4.27}$	= 5.4×	6.8×	Low
Market/book (M/B)	$\dfrac{\text{Market price per share}}{\text{Book value per share}}$	$\dfrac{\$23.00}{\$17.92}$	= 1.3×	1.7×	Low

Allied made 3.8 percent, or 3.8 cents, on each dollar of sales, and assets were "turned over" 1.5 times during the year. Therefore, the company earned a return of 5.7 percent on its assets.

If the company were financed only with common equity, the rate of return on assets (ROA) and the return on equity (ROE) would be the same because total assets would equal common equity:

$$\text{ROA} = \frac{\text{Net income}}{\text{Total assets}} = \frac{\text{Net income}}{\text{Common equity}} = \text{ROE}.$$

This equality holds if and only if Total assets = Common equity, that is, if the company uses no debt. Allied does use debt, so its common equity is less than total assets. Therefore, the return to the common stockholders (ROE) must be greater than the ROA of 5.7 percent. Specifically, the rate of return on assets (ROA) can be multiplied by the *equity multiplier*, which is the ratio of total assets to common equity:

$$\text{Equity multiplier} = \frac{\text{Total assets}}{\text{Common equity}}.$$

Firms that use a large amount of debt financing (more leverage) will necessarily have a high equity multiplier—the more the debt, the less the equity, hence the higher the equity multiplier. For example, if a firm has $1,000 of assets and is financed with $800, or 80 percent debt, then its equity will be $200, and its equity multiplier will be $1,000/$200 = 5. Had it used only $200 of debt, then its equity would have been $800, and its equity multiplier would have been only $1,000/$800 = 1.25.[13]

Allied's return on equity (ROE) depends on its ROA and its use of leverage.[14]

$$\text{ROE} = \text{ROA} \times \text{Equity multiplier}$$

$$= \frac{\text{Net income}}{\text{Total assets}} \times \frac{\text{Total assets}}{\text{Common equity}} \quad (3\text{-}2)$$

$$= 5.7\% \times \$2,000/\$896$$

$$= 5.7\% \times 2.23$$

$$= 12.7\%.$$

Now we can combine Equations 3-1 and 3-2 to form the *Extended Du Pont Equation*, which shows how the profit margin, the total assets turnover ratio, and the equity multiplier combine to determine the ROE:

$$\text{ROE} = (\text{Profit margin})(\text{Total assets turnover})(\text{Equity multiplier})$$

$$= \frac{\text{Net income}}{\text{Sales}} \times \frac{\text{Sales}}{\text{Total assets}} \times \frac{\text{Total assets}}{\text{Common equity}}. \quad (3\text{-}3)$$

---

[13] Expressed algebraically,

$$\text{Debt ratio} = \frac{D}{A} = \frac{A - E}{A} = \frac{A}{A} - \frac{E}{A} = 1 - \frac{1}{\text{Equity multiplier}}.$$

Here D is debt, E is equity, A is total assets, and A/E is the equity multiplier. This equation ignores preferred stock.

[14] Note that we could also find the ROE by "grossing up" the ROA, that is, by dividing the ROA by the common equity fraction: ROE = ROA/Equity fraction = 5.7%/0.448 = 12.7%. The two procedures are algebraically equivalent.

For Allied, we have

$$\text{ROE} = (3.8\%)(1.5)(2.23)$$
$$= 12.7\%.$$

The 12.7 percent rate of return could, of course, be calculated directly: both Sales and Total assets cancel, leaving Net income/Common equity = \$113.5/\$896 = 12.7%. However, the Du Pont equation shows how the profit margin, the total assets turnover, and the use of debt interact to determine the return on equity.[15]

Allied's management can use the extended Du Pont equation to analyze ways of improving performance. Focusing on the profit margin, Allied's marketing people can study the effects of raising sales prices (or lowering them to increase volume), of moving into new products or markets with higher margins, and so on. The company's cost accountants can study various expense items and, working with engineers, purchasing agents, and other operating personnel, seek ways to hold down costs. Regarding the "turnover" term, Allied's financial analysts, working with both production and marketing people, can investigate ways to reduce the investment in various types of assets. At the same time, the treasury staff can analyze the effects of alternative financing strategies, seeking to hold down interest expense and the risk of debt while still using leverage to increase the rate of return on equity.

As a result of such an analysis, Ellen Jackson, Allied's president, recently announced a series of moves designed to cut operating costs by more than 20 percent per year. Jackson and Allied's other executives have a strong incentive for improving the company's financial performance, because their compensation is based to a large extent on how well the company does. Allied's executives receive a salary that is sufficient to cover their living costs, but their compensation package also includes stock options that will be awarded if and only if the company meets or exceeds target levels for earnings and the stock price. These target levels are based on Allied's performance relative to other food companies. So, if Allied does well, then Jackson and the other executives—and the stockholders—will also do well. But if things deteriorate, Jackson could be looking for a new job.

SELF-TEST QUESTIONS

Explain how the extended Du Pont equation can be used to reveal the basic determinants of ROE.

What is the equity multiplier?

How can management use the extended Du Pont equation to analyze ways of improving the firm's performance?

---

[15] Another frequently used ratio is the following:

$$\text{Rate of return on investors' capital} = \frac{\text{Net income} + \text{Interest}}{\text{Debt} + \text{Equity}}.$$

The numerator shows the dollar returns to investors, the denominator shows the total amount of money investors have put up, and the ratio itself shows the rate of return on all investors' capital. This ratio is especially important in the public utility industries, where regulators are concerned about the companies' using their monopoly positions to earn excessive returns on investors' capital. In fact, regulators try to set utility prices (service rates) at levels that will force the return on investors' capital to equal a company's cost of capital as defined in Chapter 9.

COMPARATIVE RATIOS AND "BENCHMARKING"

Ratio analysis involves comparisons—a company's ratios are compared with those of other firms in the same industry, that is, to industry average figures. However, like most firms, Allied's managers go one step further—they also compare their ratios with those of a smaller set of leading food companies. This technique is called **benchmarking**, and the companies used for the comparison are called *benchmark companies*. Allied's management benchmarks against Campbell Soup, a leading manufacturer of canned soups; Dean Foods, a processor of canned and frozen vegetables; Dole Food Company, a processor of fruits and vegetables; H.J. Heinz, which makes ketchup and other products; Flowers Industries, a producer of bakery and snack-food goods; Sara Lee, a manufacturer of baked goods; and Hershey Foods Corp., a producer of chocolates, nonchocolate confectionary products, and pasta. Ratios are calculated for each company. Then the ratios are listed in descending order, as shown below for the profit margin on sales (as reported on the firms' latest 12 months' results by *MSN Money* on May 5, 2002):

	PROFIT MARGIN
Sara Lee	9.1%
Campbell Soup	8.5
Hershey Foods	4.8
H. J. Heinz	4.4
Dole Food Company	3.9
Allied Food Products	**3.8**
Dean Foods	1.9
Flowers Industries	−1.1

The benchmarking setup makes it easy for Allied's management to see exactly where the company stands relative to its competition. As the data show, Allied is in the bottom third of its benchmark group with respect to its profit margin, so the company has lots of room for improvement. Other ratios are analyzed similarly.

Comparative ratios are available from a number of sources, including *Value Line*. Table 3-3 presents a list of key ratios for a variety of industries covered by *Value Line*. Useful ratios are also compiled by Dun and Bradstreet (D&B) and the *Annual Statement Studies* published by Robert Morris Associates, which is the national association of bank loan officers. Also, financial statement data for thousands of publicly owned corporations are available on magnetic tapes and diskettes, and since brokerage houses, banks, and other financial institutions have access to these data, security analysts can and do generate comparative ratios tailored to their specific needs.

Each of the data-supplying organizations uses a somewhat different set of ratios designed for its own purposes. For example, D&B deals mainly with small firms, many of which are proprietorships, and it sells its services primarily to banks and other lenders. Therefore, D&B is concerned largely with the creditor's viewpoint, and its ratios emphasize current assets and liabilities, not market value ratios. So, when you select a comparative data source, you should be sure that your emphasis is similar to that of the agency whose ratios you plan to use. Additionally, there are often definitional differences in the ratios presented by different sources, so before using a source, be sure to verify the exact definitions of the ratios to ensure consistency with your own work.

TABLE 3-3   Key Financial Ratios for Selected Industries[a]

INDUSTRY NAME	CURRENT RATIO	INVENTORY TURNOVER[b]	FIXED ASSETS TURNOVER	TOTAL ASSETS TURNOVER	DEBT RATIO[c]	DAYS SALES OUTSTANDING[d]	PROFIT MARGIN	RETURN ON ASSETS	RETURN ON EQUITY
Aerospace/defense	1.58×	7.08×	7.72×	1.00×	57.26%	71.07 days	5.25%	5.22%	17.83%
Apparel	2.50	5.87	11.37	1.71	47.30	45.95	5.23	8.63	18.88
Auto and truck	1.40	14.66	4.62	0.86	64.75	137.12	1.95	1.71	5.45
Beverage (soft drink)	0.99	20.02	3.48	0.96	56.54	35.32	5.94	5.70	17.52
Educational services	1.84	83.09	4.80	1.28	33.81	42.06	11.17	12.90	20.76
Electronics	2.56	9.60	12.13	1.31	41.92	70.02	7.73	7.92	15.11
Environmental	1.36	72.01	3.75	0.67	47.31	69.28	6.00	3.80	13.12
Food processing	1.53	12.04	4.86	1.52	51.94	35.64	5.32	6.64	40.60
Food wholesalers	1.30	18.21	15.75	4.02	63.15	17.26	1.04	4.10	13.91
Grocery	1.32	20.66	5.67	2.67	55.30	6.56	1.53	3.63	17.52
Hotel/gaming	1.53	68.68	1.83	0.64	56.56	29.08	8.30	5.28	21.79
Medical services	1.70	78.91	20.82	1.13	48.23	57.17	6.17	6.07	15.39
Metals and mining	1.52	6.22	1.38	0.66	44.82	52.40	5.90	3.54	5.66
Newspaper	1.44	91.81	3.22	0.65	39.90	51.55	8.42	5.97	24.30
Paper and forest products	1.53	9.47	1.36	0.77	48.68	39.24	6.22	3.51	9.72
Precision instruments	3.43	6.88	6.85	0.90	33.50	81.32	10.41	9.58	15.88
Railroad	0.59	37.05	0.52	0.38	42.45	46.36	8.92	3.45	9.89
Recreation	1.38	28.58	9.12	1.20	49.05	36.00	8.55	8.38	17.90
Restaurant	0.84	73.65	2.14	1.42	39.93	8.75	5.52	8.20	7.05
Retail store	2.00	6.20	5.45	2.04	48.85	35.41	3.02	6.03	13.35
Steel—general	2.12	6.55	3.70	1.31	39.19	50.76	3.68	4.04	8.79
Telecommunications equipment	4.93	8.86	6.87	0.64	25.19	82.62	−13.09	−2.29	−20.12
Textile	2.17	6.02	2.96	1.19	69.06	49.18	1.05	1.34	0.58
Tobacco	1.64	9.56	8.63	1.43	69.78	26.75	9.20	10.98	35.94
Water utilities	0.52	95.73	0.32	0.27	44.76	39.46	12.06	3.03	10.24

[a] The ratios presented are averages for each industry. Ratios for the individual companies are also available.

[b] The inventory turnover ratio in this table is calculated as sales divided by inventory.

[c] The debt ratio in this table is calculated as the sum of all debt (current liabilities, deferred taxes, long-term debt, and preferred stock) divided by total assets.

[d] The days sales outstanding ratio in this table is calculated assuming a 365-day accounting year.

SOURCE: *Value Line*, March 2002.

LOOKING FOR WARNING SIGNS WITHIN THE FINANCIAL STATEMENTS

Enron's decline has spurred a renewed interest in financial accounting, and analysts are once again scouring other companies' financial statements to see if trouble is lurking. This renewed interest has led to a list of "red flags" to consider when reviewing a company's financial statements. For example, after conferring with New York University Accounting Professor Baruch Lev, *Fortune* magazine's Shawn Tully identified the following warning signs:

■ Year after year, a company reports restructuring charges and/or write-downs. This practice raises concerns because companies can use write-downs to mask operating expenses that would lead to lower earnings.
■ A company's earnings have been propped up through a series of acquisitions. Acquisitions can increase earnings if the acquiring company has a higher P/E than the acquired firm, but such "growth" cannot be sustained over the long run.
■ A company depreciates its assets more slowly than the industry average. Lower depreciation will boost earnings, but again, this cannot be sustained because eventually depreciation must be recognized.
■ A company routinely has high earnings but low cash flow. As Tully points out, this warning sign would have exposed Enron's problems. In the second quarter of 2001 (a few months before its problems began to unfold), Enron reported earnings of $423 million versus a cash flow of minus $527 million.

Along similar lines, after consulting with various professionals, Ellen Simon of the *Newark Star Ledger* came up with her list of "red flags":

■ You wouldn't buy the stock at today's price.
■ You don't really understand the company's financial statements.
■ The company is in a business that lends itself to "creative accounting."
■ The company keeps taking nonrecurring charges.
■ Accounts receivable and inventory are increasing faster than sales revenue.
■ The company's insiders are selling their stock.
■ The company is making aggressive acquisitions, especially in unrelated fields.

Note that there is some overlap between these two lists. Note also that none of these items automatically means there is something wrong with the company—instead, the items should be viewed as warning signs that lead you to take a closer look at the company's performance before making an investment.

SELF-TEST QUESTIONS

Differentiate between trend analysis and comparative ratio analysis.

Why is it useful to do a comparative ratio analysis?

What is benchmarking?

USES AND LIMITATIONS OF RATIO ANALYSIS

 www To find quick information about a company, link to http://www.marketguide.com. Here you can find company profiles, stock price and share information, and several key ratios.

As noted earlier, ratio analysis is used by three main groups: (1) *managers*, who employ ratios to help analyze, control, and thus improve their firms' operations; (2) *credit analysts*, including bank loan officers and bond rating analysts, who analyze ratios to help ascertain a company's ability to pay its debts; and (3) *stock analysts*, who are interested in a company's efficiency, risk, and growth prospects. In later chapters we will look more closely at the basic factors that underlie each ratio, which will give you a better idea about how to interpret and use ratios. Note, though, that while ratio analysis can provide useful information concerning a company's operations and financial condition, it does have limitations that necessitate care and judgment. Some potential problems are listed below:

1. Many large firms operate different divisions in different industries, and for such companies it is difficult to develop a meaningful set of industry averages. Therefore, ratio analysis is more useful for small, narrowly focused firms than for large, multidivisional ones.

2. Most firms want to be better than average, so merely attaining average performance is not necessarily good. As a target for high-level performance, it is best to focus on the industry leaders' ratios. Benchmarking helps in this regard.

3. Inflation may have badly distorted firms' balance sheets—recorded values are often substantially different from "true" values. Further, since inflation affects both depreciation charges and inventory costs, profits are also affected. Thus, a ratio analysis for one firm over time, or a comparative analysis of firms of different ages, must be interpreted with judgment.

4. Seasonal factors can also distort a ratio analysis. For example, the inventory turnover ratio for a food processor will be radically different if the balance sheet figure used for inventory is the one just before versus just after the close of the canning season. This problem can be minimized by using monthly averages for inventory (and receivables) when calculating turnover ratios.

"Window Dressing" Techniques
Techniques employed by firms to make their financial statements look better than they really are.

5. Firms can employ **"window dressing" techniques** to make their financial statements look stronger. To illustrate, a Chicago builder borrowed on a two-year basis on December 27, 2002, held the proceeds of the loan as cash for a few days, and then paid off the loan ahead of time on January 2, 2003. This improved his current and quick ratios, and made his year-end 2002 balance sheet look good. However, the improvement was strictly window dressing; a week later the balance sheet was back at the old level.

6. Different accounting practices can distort comparisons. As noted earlier, inventory valuation and depreciation methods can affect financial statements and thus distort comparisons among firms. Also, if one firm leases a substantial amount of its productive equipment, then its assets may appear low relative to sales because leased assets often do not appear on the balance sheet. At the same time, the liability associated with the lease obligation may not be shown as a debt. Therefore, leasing can artificially improve both the turnover and the debt ratios. However, the accounting profession has taken steps to reduce this problem.

7. It is difficult to generalize about whether a particular ratio is "good" or "bad." For example, a high current ratio may indicate a strong liquidity position, which is good, or excessive cash, which is bad (because excess cash in the bank is a nonearning asset). Similarly, a high fixed assets turnover ratio may denote either a firm that uses its assets efficiently or one that is undercapitalized and cannot afford to buy enough assets.

8. A firm may have some ratios that look "good" and others that look "bad," making it difficult to tell whether the company is, on balance, strong or weak. However, statistical procedures can be used to analyze the *net effects* of a set of ratios. Many banks and other lending organizations use such procedures to

analyze firms' financial ratios, and then to classify them according to their probability of getting into financial trouble.[16]

Ratio analysis is useful, but analysts should be aware of these problems and make adjustments as necessary. Ratio analysis conducted in a mechanical, unthinking manner is dangerous, but used intelligently and with good judgment, it can provide useful insights into a firm's operations. Your judgment in interpreting a set of ratios is bound to be weak at this point, but it will improve as you go through the remainder of the book.

PROBLEMS WITH ROE

In Chapter 1 we said that managers should strive to maximize shareholder wealth. If a firm takes steps to improve its ROE, does it mean that shareholder wealth will also increase? Not necessarily, for despite its widespread use and the fact that ROE and shareholder wealth are often highly correlated, some problems can arise when firms use ROE as the sole measure of performance.

First, ROE does not consider risk. While shareholders clearly care about returns, they also care about risk. To illustrate this point, consider two divisions within the same firm. Division S has very stable cash flows and a predictable 15 percent ROE. Division R, on the other hand, has a 16 percent expected ROE, but its cash flows are very risky, so the expected ROE may not materialize. If managers were compensated solely on the basis of ROE, and if the expected ROEs were actually achieved, then Division R's manager would receive a higher bonus than Division S's manager, even though Division S may actually create more value for shareholders as a result of its lower risk.

Second, ROE does not consider the amount of invested capital. To illustrate this point, let's consider a rather extreme example. A large company has $1 invested in Project A, which has an ROE of 50 percent, and $1 million invested in Project B, which has a 40 percent ROE. The projects are equally risky, and the two returns are both well above the cost the company had to pay for the capital invested in the projects. In this example, Project A has a higher ROE, but since it is so small, it does little to enhance shareholder wealth. Project B, on the other hand, has the lower ROE, but it adds much more to shareholder value.

---

[16] The technique used is discriminant analysis. For a detailed discussion, see Edward I. Altman, "Financial Ratios, Discriminant Analysis, and the Prediction of Corporate Bankruptcy," *Journal of Finance*, September 1968, 589–609. For a summary, see Eugene F. Brigham and Philip R. Daves, *Intermediate Financial Management*, 7th ed. (Cincinnati, OH: South-Western College Publishing, 2002), Chapter 24 Extensions.

EVA AND ROE

To better understand the idea behind EVA and how it is connected to ROE, let's look at Keller Electronics. Keller has $100,000 in investor-supplied operating capital, which, in turn, consists of $50,000 of long-term debt and $50,000 of common equity. The company has no preferred stock or notes payable. The long-term debt has a 10 percent interest rate. However, since the company is in the 40 percent tax bracket and interest expense is tax deductible, the after-tax cost of debt is only 6 percent. On the basis of their assessment of the company's risk, shareholders require a 14 percent return. This 14 percent return is what shareholders could expect to earn if they were to take their money elsewhere and invest in stocks that have the same risk as Keller. Keller's overall cost of capital is a weighted average of the cost of debt and equity, and it is 10 percent, found as $0.50(6\%) + 0.50(14\%) = 10\%$. The total dollar cost of capital per year is $0.10(\$100,000) = \$10,000$.

Now let's look at Keller's income statement. Its operating income, EBIT, is $20,000, and its interest expense is $0.10 (\$50,000) = \$5,000$. Therefore, its taxable income is $20,000 − $5,000 = \$15,000$. Taxes equal 40 percent of taxable income, or $0.4(\$15,000) = \$6,000$, so the firm's net income is $9,000, and its return on equity, ROE, is $9,000/\$50,000 = 18\%$.

Now what is Keller's EVA? Recall from Chapter 2 that the basic formula for EVA is:

$$EVA = EBIT\ (1 - Corporate\ tax\ rate) - (Total\ investor\text{-}$$
$$supplied\ operating\ capital)(After\text{-}tax\ percentage$$
$$cost\ of\ capital)$$

$$= \$20,000\ (1 - 0.40) - (\$100,000)(0.10) = \$2,000.$$

This $2,000 EVA indicates that Keller provided its shareholders with $2,000 more than they could have earned elsewhere by investing in other stocks with the same risk as Keller's stock. To see where this $2,000 comes from, let's trace what happens to the money:

- The firm generates $20,000 in operating income.
- $6,000 goes to the government to pay taxes, leaving $14,000.
- $5,000 goes to the bondholders in the form of interest payments, thus leaving $9,000.
- $7,000 is what Keller's shareholders expected to earn: $0.14(\$50,000) = \$7,000$. Note that this $7,000 payment is not a requirement to stay in business—companies can stay in business as long as they pay their bills and their taxes. However, this $7,000 is what shareholders *expected to earn*, and it is the amount the firm *must earn* if it is to avoid reducing shareholder wealth.

- What's left over, the $2,000, is EVA. In this case, Keller's management created wealth because it provided shareholders with a return greater than what they presumably would have earned on alternative investments with the same risk as Keller's stock.

SOME ADDITIONAL POINTS

- In practice, it is often necessary to make several adjustments in order to arrive at a "better" measure of EVA. The adjustments deal with leased assets, depreciation, and other accounting details.
- Shareholders may not immediately receive the $9,000 that Keller made for them this year (the $7,000 that shareholders expected plus the $2,000 of EVA). Keller can either pay its earnings out as dividends or keep them in the firm as retained earnings. In either event, the $9,000 is shareholders' money. The factors influencing the dividend payout decision are discussed in the chapter on dividend policy.

THE CONNECTION BETWEEN ROE AND EVA

We said that EVA is different from the traditional accounting measure of profit in that EVA explicitly considers not just the interest cost of debt but also the cost of equity. Indeed, using the simple example above, we could also express EVA as net income minus the dollar cost of equity:

$$EVA = Net\ income - [(Equity\ capital)$$
$$(Cost\ of\ equity\ capital)]$$

$$= \$9,000 - [(\$50,000)(0.14)]$$

$$= \$2,000.$$

Note that this is the same number we calculated before when we used the other formula for calculating EVA. Note also that the expression above could be rewritten as follows:

$$EVA = (Equity\ capital)[Net\ income/Equity\ capital$$
$$- Cost\ of\ equity\ capital],$$

or simply as:

$$EVA = (Equity\ capital)(ROE - Cost\ of\ equity\ capital).$$

This last expression implies that EVA depends on three factors: rate of return, as reflected in ROE; risk, which affects the cost of equity; and size, which is measured by the amount of equity capital employed. Recall that earlier in this chapter we said that shareholder value depends on risk, return, and the amount of capital invested. This final equation illustrates this point.

Consider one last problem with ROE. Assume that you manage a division of a large firm. The firm uses ROE as the sole measure of performance, and it determines bonuses on the basis of ROE. Toward the end of the fiscal year, your division's ROE is an impressive 45 percent. Now you have an opportunity to invest in a large, low-risk project that has an estimated ROE of 35 percent, which is well above the cost of the capital you need to make the investment. Even though this project is profitable, you might be reluctant to make the investment because it would reduce your division's average ROE, and therefore reduce the size of your year-end bonus.

These three examples suggest that a project's return must be combined with its risk and size to determine its effect on shareholder value. To the extent that ROE focuses only on rate of return, increasing ROE may in some cases be inconsistent with increasing shareholder wealth. With this in mind, academics, practitioners, and consultants have tried to develop alternative measures that overcome ROE's potential problems when it is used as the sole gauge of performance. One such measure is Economic Value Added (EVA). In Chapter 2, we showed how to calculate EVA. For a discussion of the connection between ROE and EVA, see the accompanying box, "EVA and ROE."

SELF-TEST QUESTION

If a firm takes steps to improve its ROE, does this mean that shareholder wealth will also increase? Explain.

LOOKING BEYOND THE NUMBERS

 Students might want to refer to AAII's educational web site at **http://www.aaii.com**. The site provides information on investing basics, financial planning, portfolio management, and the like, so individuals can manage their own assets more effectively.

Hopefully, working through this chapter has helped your understanding of financial statements and improved your ability to interpret accounting numbers. These important and basic skills are necessary when making business decisions, when evaluating performance, and when forecasting likely future developments.

Sound financial analysis involves more than just calculating numbers—good analysis requires that certain qualitative factors be considered when evaluating a company. These factors, as summarized by the American Association of Individual Investors (AAII), include the following:

1. *Are the company's revenues tied to one key customer?* If so, the company's performance may decline dramatically if the customer goes elsewhere. On the other hand, if the relationship is firmly entrenched, this might actually stabilize sales.

2. *To what extent are the company's revenues tied to one key product?* Companies that rely on a single product may be more efficient and focused, but a lack of diversification increases risk. If revenues come from several different products, the overall bottom line will be less affected by a drop in the demand for any one product.

3. *To what extent does the company rely on a single supplier?* Depending on a single supplier may lead to unanticipated shortages, which investors and potential creditors should consider.

4. *What percentage of the company's business is generated overseas?* Companies with a large percentage of overseas business are often able to realize higher growth and larger profit margins. However, firms with large overseas operations find that the value of their operations depends in large part on the value of the local currency. Thus, fluctuations in currency markets create additional risks for firms with large overseas operations. Also, the potential stability of the region is important.

5. *Competition.* Generally, increased competition lowers prices and profit margins. In forecasting future performance, it is important to assess both the likely actions of the current competition and the likelihood of new competitors in the future.

6. *Future prospects.* Does the company invest heavily in research and development? If so, its future prospects may depend critically on the success of new products in the pipeline. For example, the market's assessment of a computer company depends on how next year's products are shaping up. Likewise, investors in pharmaceutical companies are interested in knowing whether the company has developed any potential blockbuster drugs that are doing well in the required tests.

7. *Legal and regulatory environment.* Changes in laws and regulations have important implications for many industries. For example, when forecasting the future of tobacco companies, it is crucial to factor in the effects of proposed regulations and pending or likely lawsuits. Likewise, when assessing banks, telecommunications firms, and electric utilities, analysts need to forecast both the extent to which these industries will be regulated in the future, and the ability of individual firms to respond to changes in regulation.

SELF-TEST QUESTION

What are some qualitative factors analysts should consider when evaluating a company's likely future financial performance?

TYING IT ALL TOGETHER

The primary purpose of this chapter was to discuss techniques used by investors and managers to analyze financial statements. The key concepts covered are listed below.

- **Financial statement analysis** generally begins with a set of **financial ratios** designed to reveal the strengths and weaknesses of a company as compared with other companies in the same industry, and to show whether its financial position has been improving or deteriorating over time.

- **Liquidity ratios** show the relationship of a firm's current assets to its current liabilities, and thus its ability to meet maturing debts. The most commonly used liquidity ratio is the **current ratio.**

- **Asset management ratios** measure how effectively a firm is managing its assets. These ratios include **inventory turnover, days sales outstanding, fixed assets turnover,** and **total assets turnover.**

- **Debt management ratios** reveal (1) the extent to which the firm is financed with debt and (2) its likelihood of defaulting on its debt obligations. They include the **debt ratio, times-interest-earned ratio,** and **EBITDA coverage ratio.**

- **Profitability ratios** show the combined effects of liquidity, asset management, and debt management policies on operating results. They include the **profit margin on sales,** the **basic earning power ratio,** the **return on total assets,** and the **return on common equity.**

- **Market value ratios** relate the firm's stock price to its earnings, cash flow, and book value per share, thus giving management an indication of what investors think of the company's past performance and future prospects. These include the **price/earnings ratio, price/cash flow ratio,** and the **market/book ratio.**

- **Trend analysis,** where one plots a ratio over time, is important, because it reveals whether the firm's condition is improving or deteriorating over time.

- The **extended Du Pont equation** is designed to show how the profit margin on sales, the total assets turnover ratio, and the use of debt interact to determine the rate of return on equity. The firm's management can use the extended Du Pont equation to analyze ways of improving the firm's performance.

- **Benchmarking** is the process of comparing a particular company with a group of "benchmark" companies.

- ROE is important, but it does not take account of either the amount of investment or risk. **Economic Value Added (EVA)** adds these factors to the analysis.

Ratio analysis has limitations, but used with care and judgment, it can be very helpful.

QUESTIONS

3-1 Financial ratio analysis is conducted by four groups of analysts: managers, equity investors, long-term creditors, and short-term creditors. What is the primary emphasis of each of these groups in evaluating ratios?

3-2 Why would the inventory turnover ratio be more important when analyzing a grocery chain than an insurance company?

3-3 Over the past year, M. D. Ryngaert & Co. has realized an increase in its current ratio and a drop in its total assets turnover ratio. However, the company's sales, cash and marketable securities, DSO, and fixed assets turnover ratio have remained constant. What explains these changes?

3-4 Profit margins and turnover ratios vary from one industry to another. What differences would you expect to find between a grocery chain and a steel company? Think particularly about the turnover ratios, the profit margin, and the Du Pont equation.

3-5 How does inflation distort ratio analysis comparisons, both for one company over time (trend analysis) and when different companies are compared? Are only balance sheet items or both balance sheet and income statement items affected?

3-6 If a firm's ROE is low and management wants to improve it, explain how using more debt might help.

3-7 How might (a) seasonal factors and (b) different growth rates distort a comparative ratio analysis? Give some examples. How might these problems be alleviated?

3-8 Why is it sometimes misleading to compare a company's financial ratios with those of other firms that operate in the same industry?

3-9 Indicate the effects of the transactions listed in the following table on total current assets, current ratio, and net income. Use (+) to indicate an increase, (−) to indicate a decrease, and (0) to indicate either no effect or an indeterminate effect. Be prepared to state any necessary assumptions, and assume an initial current ratio of more than 1.0. (Note: A good accounting background is necessary to answer some of these questions; if yours is not strong, just answer the questions you can handle.)

	TOTAL CURRENT ASSETS	CURRENT RATIO	EFFECT ON NET INCOME
a. Cash is acquired through issuance of additional common stock.	___	___	___
b. Merchandise is sold for cash.	___	___	___
c. Federal income tax due for the previous year is paid.	___	___	___
d. A fixed asset is sold for less than book value.	___	___	___
e. A fixed asset is sold for more than book value.	___	___	___
f. Merchandise is sold on credit.	___	___	___
g. Payment is made to trade creditors for previous purchases.	___	___	___
h. A cash dividend is declared and paid.	___	___	___
i. Cash is obtained through short-term bank loans.	___	___	___
j. Short-term notes receivable are sold at a discount.	___	___	___
k. Marketable securities are sold below cost.	___	___	___
l. Advances are made to employees.	___	___	___
m. Current operating expenses are paid.	___	___	___
n. Short-term promissory notes are issued to trade creditors in exchange for past due accounts payable.	___	___	___
o. Ten-year notes are issued to pay off accounts payable.	___	___	___
p. A fully depreciated asset is retired.	___	___	___
q. Accounts receivable are collected.	___	___	___
r. Equipment is purchased with short-term notes.	___	___	___
s. Merchandise is purchased on credit.	___	___	___
t. The estimated taxes payable are increased.	___	___	___

3-10 Johnson Electric doubled its EVA last year, yet its return on equity declined. What could explain these changes?

ST-1
Key terms

Define each of the following terms:

a. Liquidity ratio: current ratio

b. Asset management ratios: inventory turnover ratio; days sales outstanding (DSO); fixed assets turnover ratio; total assets turnover ratio

c. Financial leverage: debt ratio; times-interest-earned (TIE) ratio; EBITDA coverage ratio

d. Profitability ratios: profit margin on sales; basic earning power (BEP) ratio; return on total assets (ROA); return on common equity (ROE)

e. Market value ratios: price/earnings (P/E) ratio; price/cash flow ratio; market/book (M/B) ratio

f. Trend analysis; comparative ratio analysis; benchmarking

g. Du Pont equation; book value per share

h. "Window dressing"; seasonal effects on ratios

ST-2
Debt ratio

K. Billingsworth & Co. had earnings per share of $4 last year, and it paid a $2 dividend. Total retained earnings increased by $12 million during the year, while book value per share at year-end was $40. Billingsworth has no preferred stock, and no new common stock was issued during the year. If Billingsworth's year-end debt (which equals its total liabilities) was $120 million, what was the company's year-end debt/assets ratio?

ST-3
Ratio analysis

The following data apply to A.L. Kaiser & Company (millions of dollars):

Cash and marketable securities	$100.00
Fixed assets	$283.50
Sales	$1,000.00
Net income	$50.00
Current liabilities	$105.50
Current ratio	3.0×
DSO[a]	40.55 days
ROE	12%

[a] Calculation is based on a 365-day year.

Kaiser has no preferred stock—only common equity, current liabilities, and long-term debt.

a. Find Kaiser's (1) accounts receivable (A/R), (2) current assets, (3) total assets, (4) ROA, (5) common equity, and (6) long-term debt.

b. In part a, you should have found Kaiser's accounts receivable (A/R) = $111.1 million. If Kaiser could reduce its DSO from 40.55 days to 30.4 days while holding other things constant, how much cash would it generate? If this cash were used to buy back common stock (at book value), thus reducing the amount of common equity, how would this affect (1) the ROE, (2) the ROA, and (3) the total debt/total assets ratio?

STARTER PROBLEMS

3-1
Days sales outstanding

Baker Brothers has a DSO of 40 days. The company's annual sales are $7,300,000. What is the level of its accounts receivable? Assume there are 365 days in a year.

3-2
Debt ratio

Bartley Barstools has an equity multiplier of 2.4. The company's assets are financed with some combination of long-term debt and common equity. What is the company's debt ratio?

3-3
Du Pont analysis

Doublewide Dealers has an ROA of 10 percent, a 2 percent profit margin, and a return on equity equal to 15 percent. What is the company's total assets turnover? What is the firm's equity multiplier?

3-4
Market/book ratio

Jaster Jets has $10 billion in total assets. The right side of its balance sheet consists of $1 billion in current liabilities, $3 billion in long-term debt, and $6 billion in common equity. The company has 800 million shares of common stock outstanding, and its stock price is $32 per share. What is Jaster's market/book ratio?

EXAM-TYPE PROBLEMS

The problems included in this section are set up in such a way that they could be used as multiple-choice exam problems.

3-5
Ratio calculations

Graser Trucking has $12 billion in assets, and its tax rate is 40 percent. The company's basic earning power (BEP) ratio is 15 percent, and its return on assets (ROA) is 5 percent. What is Graser's times-interest-earned (TIE) ratio?

3-6
Ratio calculations

Assume you are given the following relationships for the Brauer Corporation:

Sales/total assets	1.5×
Return on assets (ROA)	3%
Return on equity (ROE)	5%

Calculate Brauer's profit margin and debt ratio.

3-7
Current ratio

The Petry Company has $1,312,500 in current assets and $525,000 in current liabilities. Its initial inventory level is $375,000, and it will raise funds as additional notes payable and use them to increase inventory. How much can Petry's short-term debt (notes payable) increase without pushing its current ratio below 2.0?

3-8
Times-interest-earned ratio

The H.R. Pickett Corporation has $500,000 of debt outstanding, and it pays an interest rate of 10 percent annually. Pickett's annual sales are $2 million, its average tax rate is 30 percent, and its net profit margin on sales is 5 percent. If the company does not maintain a TIE ratio of at least 5 times, its bank will refuse to renew the loan, and bankruptcy will result. What is Pickett's TIE ratio?

3-9
EBITDA coverage ratio

Willis Publishing has $30 billion in total assets. The company's basic earning power (BEP) ratio is 20 percent, and its times-interest-earned ratio is 8.0. Willis' depreciation and amortization expense totals $3.2 billion. It has $2 billion in lease payments and $1 billion must go toward principal payments on outstanding loans and long-term debt. What is Willis' EBITDA coverage ratio?

3-10
Return on equity

Midwest Packaging's ROE last year was only 3 percent, but its management has developed a new operating plan designed to improve things. The new plan calls for a total debt ratio of 60 percent, which will result in interest charges of $300,000 per year. Management projects an EBIT of $1,000,000 on sales of $10,000,000, and it expects to have a total assets turnover ratio of 2.0. Under these conditions, the tax rate will be 34 percent. If the changes are made, what return on equity will the company earn?

3-11
Return on equity

Central City Construction Company, which is just being formed, needs $1 million of assets, and it expects to have a basic earning power ratio of 20 percent. Central City will own no securities, so all of its income will be operating income. If it chooses to, Central City can finance up to 50 percent of its assets with debt, which will have an 8 percent interest rate. Assuming a 40 percent federal-plus-state tax rate on all taxable income, what is the *difference* between its expected ROE if Central City finances with 50 percent debt versus its expected ROE if it finances entirely with common stock?

3-12
Conceptual: Return on equity

Which of the following statements is most correct? (Hint: Work Problem 3-11 before answering 3-12, and consider the solution setup for 3-11, as you think about 3-12.)
a. If a firm's expected basic earning power (BEP) is constant for all of its assets and exceeds the interest rate on its debt, then adding assets and financing them with debt will raise the firm's expected rate of return on common equity (ROE).
b. The higher its tax rate, the lower a firm's BEP ratio will be, other things held constant.
c. The higher the interest rate on its debt, the lower a firm's BEP ratio will be, other things held constant.
d. The higher its debt ratio, the lower a firm's BEP ratio will be, other things held constant.
e. Statement a is false, but statements b, c, and d are all true.

3-13
Return on equity

Lloyd and Daughters Inc. has sales of $200,000, a net income of $15,000, and the following balance sheet:

Cash	$ 10,000	Accounts payable	$ 30,000
Receivables	50,000	Other current liabilities	20,000
Inventories	150,000	Long-term debt	50,000
Net fixed assets	90,000	Common equity	200,000
Total assets	$300,000	Total liabilities and equity	$300,000

a. The company's new owner thinks that inventories are excessive and can be lowered to the point where the current ratio is equal to the industry average, 2.5×, without affecting either sales or net income. If inventories are sold off and not replaced so as to reduce the current ratio to 2.5×, if the funds generated are used to reduce common equity (stock can be repurchased at book value), and if no other changes occur, by how much will the ROE change?

b. Now suppose we wanted to take this problem and modify it for use on an exam, that is, to create a new problem that you have not seen to test your knowledge of this type of problem. How would your answer change if (1) We doubled all the dollar amounts? (2) We stated that the target current ratio was 3×? (3) We stated that the target was to achieve an inventory turnover ratio of 2× rather than a current ratio of 2.5×? (Hint: Compare the ROE obtained with an inventory turnover ratio of 2× to the original ROE obtained before any changes are considered.) (4) We said that the company had 10,000 shares of common stock outstanding, and we asked how much the change in part a would increase EPS? (5) What would your answer to (4) be if we changed the original problem to state that the stock was selling for twice book value, so common equity would not be reduced on a dollar-for-dollar basis?

c. Now explain how we could have set the problem up to have you focus on changing accounts receivable, or fixed assets, or using the funds generated to retire debt (we would give you the interest rate on outstanding debt), or how the original problem could have stated that the company needed *more* inventories and it would finance them with new common equity or with new debt.

3-14
EBITDA coverage ratio

Harriett Industries has $7.5 billion in total assets. The company's basic earning power (BEP) ratio is 10 percent, and its times-interest-earned ratio is 2.5. Harriett's depreciation and amortization expense totals $1.25 billion. It has $775 million in lease payments and $500 million must go toward principal payments on outstanding loans and long-term debt. What is Harriett's EBITDA coverage ratio?

3-15
TIE ratio

AEI Incorporated has $5 billion in assets, and its tax rate is 40 percent. The company's basic earning power (BEP) ratio is 10 percent, and its return on assets (ROA) is 5 percent. What is AEI's times-interest-earned (TIE) ratio?

3-16
M/B and share price

You are given the following information: Stockholders' equity = $3.75 billion; price/earnings ratio = 3.5; common shares outstanding = 50 million; and market/book ratio = 1.9. Calculate the market price of a share of the company's common stock.

3-17
DSO and accounts receivable

Harrelson Inc. currently has $750,000 in accounts receivable. Its days sales outstanding (DSO) is 55 days. The company wants to reduce its DSO to the industry average of 35 days by pressuring more of its customers to pay their bills on time. The company's CFO estimates that if this policy is adopted the company's average sales will fall by 15 percent. Assuming that the company adopts this change and succeeds in reducing its DSO to 35 days and does lose 15 percent of its sales, what will be the level of accounts receivable (to the nearest dollar) following the change? Assume a 365-day year.

3-18
P/E and stock price

Fontaine & Associates Inc. recently reported net income of $2 million. The company has 500,000 shares of common stock, and it currently trades at $40 a share. The company continues to expand and anticipates that one year from now its net income will be $3.25 million. Over the next year the company also anticipates issuing an additional 150,000 shares of stock, so that one year from now the company will have 650,000 shares of common stock. Assuming the company's price/earnings ratio remains at its current level, what will be the company's stock price 1 year from now?

3-19
Du Pont and net income

Ebersoll Manufacturing Company has $6 million in sales. Its ROE is 12 percent and its total assets turnover is 3.2×. The company is 50 percent equity financed. What is the company's net income?

3-20
Basic earning power

Duval Manufacturing Inc. recently reported the following information:

Net income	$600,000
ROA	8%
Interest expense	$225,000

The company's tax rate is 35 percent. What is the company's basic earning power (BEP)?

3-21
Balance sheet analysis

Complete the balance sheet and sales information in the table that follows for Hoffmeister Industries using the following financial data:

Debt ratio: 50%

Current ratio: 1.8×

Total assets turnover: 1.5×

Days sales outstanding: 36.5 days[a]

Gross profit margin on sales: (Sales − Cost of goods sold)/Sales = 25%

Inventory turnover ratio: 5×

[a]Calculation is based on a 365-day year.

BALANCE SHEET

Cash	_____	Accounts payable	_____
Accounts receivable	_____	Long-term debt	60,000
Inventories	_____	Common stock	_____
Fixed assets	_____	Retained earnings	97,500
Total assets	$300,000	Total liabilities and equity	_____
Sales	_____	Cost of goods sold	_____

3-22
Ratio analysis

Data for Barry Computer Company and its industry averages follow.
a. Calculate the indicated ratios for Barry.
b. Construct the extended Du Pont equation for both Barry and the industry.
c. Outline Barry's strengths and weaknesses as revealed by your analysis.
d. Suppose Barry had doubled its sales as well as its inventories, accounts receivable, and common equity during 2002. How would that information affect the validity of your ratio analysis? (Hint: Think about averages and the effects of rapid growth on ratios if averages are not used. No calculations are needed.)

Barry Computer Company: Balance Sheet as of December 31, 2002 (In Thousands)

Cash	$ 77,500	Accounts payable	$ 129,000
Receivables	336,000	Notes payable	84,000
Inventories	241,500	Other current liabilities	117,000
Total current assets	$ 655,000	Total current liabilities	$ 330,000
Net fixed assets	292,500	Long-term debt	256,500
		Common equity	361,000
Total assets	$ 947,500	Total liabilities and equity	$ 947,500

Barry Computer Company: Income Statement for Year Ended December 31, 2002 (In Thousands)

Sales		$1,607,500
Cost of goods sold		
Materials	$717,000	
Labor	453,000	
Heat, light, and power	68,000	
Indirect labor	113,000	
Depreciation	41,500	1,392,500

Gross profit	$ 215,000
Selling expenses	115,000
General and administrative expenses	30,000
Earnings before interest and taxes (EBIT)	$ 70,000
Interest expense	24,500
Earnings before taxes (EBT)	$ 45,500
Federal and state income taxes (40%)	18,200
Net income	$ 27,300

RATIO	BARRY	INDUSTRY AVERAGE
Current assets/current liabilities	————	2.0×
Days sales outstanding[a]	————	35 days
Sales/inventories	————	6.7×
Sales/total assets	————	3.0×
Net income/sales	————	1.2%
Net income/total assets	————	3.6%
Net income/common equity	————	9.0%
Total debt/total assets	————	60.0%

[a]Calculation is based on a 365-day year.

3-23
Du Pont analysis

The Ferri Furniture Company, a manufacturer and wholesaler of high-quality home furnishings, has been experiencing low profitability in recent years. As a result, the board of directors has replaced the president of the firm with a new president, Helen Adams, who has asked you to make an analysis of the firm's financial position using the extended Du Pont equation. In addition to the information given below, you have been informed by the new president that the firm has no lease payments but has a $2 million sinking fund payment on its debt. The most recent industry average ratios, and Ferri's financial statements, are as follows:

INDUSTRY AVERAGE RATIOS

Current ratio	2×	Sales/fixed assets	6×
Debt/total assets	30%	Sales/total assets	3×
Times interest earned	7×	Profit margin on sales	3%
EBITDA coverage	9×	Return on total assets	9%
Sales/inventory	10×	Return on common equity	12.9%
Days sales outstanding[a]	24 days		

[a]Calculation is based on a 365-day year.

Ferri Furniture Company: Balance Sheet as of December 31, 2002 (Millions of Dollars)

Cash	$ 45	Accounts payable	$ 45
Marketable securities	33	Notes payable	45
Net receivables	66	Other current liabilities	21
Inventories	159	Total current liabilities	$111
Total current assets	$303	Long-term debt	24
		Total liabilities	$135

Gross fixed assets	225
Less depreciation	78
Net fixed assets	$147
Total assets	$450

Common stock	114
Retained earnings	201
Total stockholders' equity	$315
Total liabilities and equity	$450

Ferri Furniture Company: Income Statement for Year Ended December 31, 2002 (Millions of Dollars)

Net sales	$795.0
Cost of goods sold	660.0
Gross profit	$135.0
Selling expenses	73.5
EBITDA	$ 61.5
Depreciation expense	12.0
Earnings before interest and taxes (EBIT)	$ 49.5
Interest expense	4.5
Earnings before taxes (EBT)	$ 45.0
Taxes (40%)	18.0
Net income	$ 27.0

a. Calculate those ratios that you think would be useful in this analysis.
b. Construct an extended Du Pont equation for Ferri, and compare the company's ratios to the industry average ratios.
c. Do the balance sheet accounts or the income statement figures seem to be primarily responsible for the low profits?
d. Which specific accounts seem to be most out of line in relation to other firms in the industry?
e. If Ferri had a pronounced seasonal sales pattern, or if it grew rapidly during the year, how might that affect the validity of your ratio analysis? How might you correct for such potential problems?

3-24
Ratio analysis
The Corrigan Corporation's forecasted 2003 financial statements follow, along with some industry average ratios.
a. Calculate Corrigan's 2003 forecasted ratios, compare them with the industry average data, and comment briefly on Corrigan's projected strengths and weaknesses.
b. What do you think would happen to Corrigan's ratios if the company initiated cost-cutting measures that allowed it to hold lower levels of inventory and substantially decreased the cost of goods sold? No calculations are necessary. Think about which ratios would be affected by changes in these two accounts.

Corrigan Corporation: Forecasted Balance Sheet as of December 31, 2003

Cash	$ 72,000
Accounts receivable	439,000
Inventories	894,000
Total current assets	$1,405,000
Land and building	238,000
Machinery	132,000
Other fixed assets	61,000
Total assets	$1,836,000

Accounts and notes payable	$ 432,000
Accrued liabilities	170,000
Total current liabilities	$ 602,000
Long-term debt	404,290
Common stock	575,000
Retained earnings	254,710
Total liabilities and equity	$1,836,000

Corrigan Corporation: Forecasted Income Statement for Year Ended December 31, 2003

Sales	$4,290,000
Cost of goods sold	3,580,000
Gross operating profit	$ 710,000
General administrative and selling expenses	236,320
Depreciation	159,000
Miscellaneous	134,000
Earnings before taxes (EBT)	$ 180,680
Taxes (40%)	72,272
Net income	$ 108,408

Per-Share Data

EPS	$ 4.71
Cash dividends	$ 0.95
Market price (average)	$23.57
P/E ratio	5×
Number of shares outstanding	23,000

INDUSTRY FINANCIAL RATIOS (2003)[a]

Current ratio	2.7×
Inventory turnover[b]	7.0×
Days sales outstanding[c]	32 days
Fixed assets turnover[b]	13.0×
Total assets turnover[b]	2.6×
Return on assets	9.1%
Return on equity	18.2%
Debt ratio	50.0%
Profit margin on sales	3.5%
P/E ratio	6.0×
Price/cash flow ratio	3.5×

[a]Industry average ratios have been constant for the past 4 years.

[b]Based on year-end balance sheet figures.

[c]Calculation is based on a 365-day year.

3-25
Ratio analysis

This problem requires you to analyze the financial data given back in the spreadsheet problem for Chapter 2.

Laiho Industries' common stock has increased in price from $14.75 to $17.25 from the end of 2001 to the end of 2002, and its common shares outstanding increased from 9 to 10 million shares during that same period. Laiho has annual lease payments of $75,000 (which are included in operating costs on the income statement), but no sinking fund payments are required. Now answer the following questions.

Using Laiho Industries' financial statements as given in the Chapter 2 spreadsheet problem, perform a ratio analysis for 2001 and 2002. Consider its liquidity, asset management, debt management, profitability, and market value ratios. (Hint: If you worked the Chapter 2 problem and saved your file, you can rename that file something like Prob-03 and then perform the necessary calculations with the data generated for Chapter 2. This will save you from having to re-enter data.)

a. Has Laiho's liquidity position improved or worsened? Explain.
b. Has Laiho's ability to manage its assets improved or worsened? Explain.
c. How has Laiho's profitability changed during the last year?
d. Perform an extended Du Pont analysis for Laiho for 2001 and 2002.

INTEGRATED | CASE

D'LEON INC., PART II

3–26 Financial Statement Analysis   Part I of this case, presented in Chapter 2, discussed the situation that D'Leon Inc., a regional snack-foods producer, was in after an expansion program. D'Leon had increased plant capacity and undertaken a major marketing campaign in an attempt to "go national." Thus far, sales have not been up to the forecasted level, costs have been higher than were projected, and a large loss occurred in 2002 rather than the expected profit. As a result, its managers, directors, and investors are concerned about the firm's survival.

Donna Jamison was brought in as assistant to Fred Campo, D'Leon's chairman, who had the task of getting the company back into a sound financial position. D'Leon's 2001 and 2002 balance sheets and income statements, together with projections for 2003, are given in Tables IC3-1 and IC3-2. In addition, Table IC3-3 gives the company's 2001 and 2002 financial ratios, together with industry average data. The 2003 projected financial statement data represent Jamison's and Campo's best guess for 2003 results, assuming that some new financing is arranged to get the company "over the hump."

Jamison examined monthly data for 2002 (not given in the case), and she detected an improving pattern during the year. Monthly sales were rising, costs were falling, and large losses in the early months had turned to a small profit by December. Thus, the annual data look somewhat worse than final monthly data. Also, it appears to be taking longer for the advertising program to get the message across, for the

new sales offices to generate sales, and for the new manufacturing facilities to operate efficiently. In other words, the lags between spending money and deriving benefits were longer than D'Leon's managers had anticipated. For these reasons, Jamison and Campo see hope for the company—provided it can survive in the short run.

Jamison must prepare an analysis of where the company is now, what it must do to regain its financial health, and what actions should be taken. Your assignment is to help her answer the following questions. Provide clear explanations, not yes or no answers.

a. Why are ratios useful? What are the five major categories of ratios?
b. Calculate D'Leon's 2003 current ratio based on the projected balance sheet and income statement data. What can you say about the company's liquidity position in 2001, 2002, and as projected for 2003? We often think of ratios as being useful (1) to managers to help run the business, (2) to bankers for credit analysis, and (3) to stockholders for stock valuation. Would these different types of analysts have an equal interest in this liquidity ratio?
c. Calculate the 2003 inventory turnover, days sales outstanding (DSO), fixed assets turnover, and total assets turnover. How does D'Leon's utilization of assets stack up against other firms in its industry?
d. Calculate the 2003 debt, times-interest-earned, and EBITDA coverage ratios. How does D'Leon compare with the industry with respect to financial leverage? What can you conclude from these ratios?

e. Calculate the 2003 profit margin, basic earning power (BEP), return on assets (ROA), and return on equity (ROE). What can you say about these ratios?
f. Calculate the 2003 price/earnings ratio, price/cash flow ratio, and market/book ratio. Do these ratios indicate that investors are expected to have a high or low opinion of the company?
g. Use the extended Du Pont equation to provide a summary and overview of D'Leon's financial condition as projected for 2003. What are the firm's major strengths and weaknesses?
h. Use the following simplified 2003 balance sheet to show, in general terms, how an improvement in the DSO would tend to affect the stock price. For example, if the company could improve its collection procedures and thereby lower its DSO from 45.6 days to the 32-day industry average without affecting sales, how would that change "ripple through" the financial statements (shown in thousands below) and influence the stock price?

Accounts receivable	$ 878	Debt	$1,545
Other current assets	1,802		
Net fixed assets	817	Equity	1,952
Total assets	$3,497	Liabilities plus equity	$3,497

i. Does it appear that inventories could be adjusted, and, if so, how should that adjustment affect D'Leon's profitability and stock price?
j. In 2002, the company paid its suppliers much later than the due dates, and it was not maintaining financial ratios at levels called for in its bank loan agreements. Therefore, suppliers could cut the company off, and its bank could refuse to renew the loan when it comes due in 90 days. On the basis of data provided, would you, as a credit manager, continue to sell to D'Leon on credit? (You could demand cash on delivery, that is, sell on terms of COD, but that might cause D'Leon to stop buying from your company.) Similarly, if you were the bank loan officer, would you recommend renewing the loan or demand its repayment? Would your actions be influenced if, in early 2003, D'Leon showed you its 2003 projections plus proof that it was going to raise over $1.2 million of new equity capital?
k. In hindsight, what should D'Leon have done back in 2001?
l. What are some potential problems and limitations of financial ratio analysis?
m. What are some qualitative factors analysts should consider when evaluating a company's likely future financial performance?

TABLE IC3-1	Balance Sheets		
	2003E	**2002**	**2001**
Assets			
Cash	$ 85,632	$ 7,282	$ 57,600
Accounts receivable	878,000	632,160	351,200
Inventories	1,716,480	1,287,360	715,200
Total current assets	$2,680,112	$1,926,802	$1,124,000
Gross fixed assets	1,197,160	1,202,950	491,000
Less accumulated depreciation	380,120	263,160	146,200
Net fixed assets	$ 817,040	$ 939,790	$ 344,800
Total assets	$3,497,152	$2,866,592	$1,468,800
Liabilities and Equity			
Accounts payable	$ 436,800	$ 524,160	$ 145,600
Notes payable	300,000	636,808	200,000
Accruals	408,000	489,600	136,000
Total current liabilities	$1,144,800	$1,650,568	$ 481,600
			(continued)

	2003E	2002	2001
Long-term debt	400,000	723,432	323,432
Common stock	1,721,176	460,000	460,000
Retained earnings	231,176	32,592	203,768
Total equity	$1,952,352	$ 492,592	$ 663,768
Total liabilities and equity	$3,497,152	$2,866,592	$1,468,800

NOTE: "E" indicates estimated. The 2003 data are forecasts.

TABLE IC3-2   Income Statements

	2003E	2002	2001
Sales	$7,035,600	$6,034,000	$3,432,000
Cost of goods sold	5,875,992	5,528,000	2,864,000
Other expenses	550,000	519,988	358,672
Total operating costs excluding depreciation	$6,425,992	$6,047,988	$3,222,672
EBITDA	$ 609,608	($ 13,988)	$ 209,328
Depreciation	116,960	116,960	18,900
EBIT	$ 492,648	($ 130,948)	$ 190,428
Interest expense	70,008	136,012	43,828
EBT	$ 422,640	($ 266,960)	$ 146,600
Taxes (40%)	169,056	(106,784)[a]	58,640
Net income	$ 253,584	($ 160,176)	$ 87,960
EPS	$1.014	($ 1.602)	$0.880
DPS	$0.220	$ 0.110	$0.220
Book value per share	$7.809	$ 4.926	$6.638
Stock price	$12.17	$ 2.25	$ 8.50
Shares outstanding	250,000	100,000	100,000
Tax rate	40.00%	40.00%	40.00%
Lease payments	40,000	40,000	40,000
Sinking fund payments	0	0	0

NOTE: "E" indicates estimated. The 2003 data are forecasts.

[a] The firm had sufficient taxable income in 2000 and 2001 to obtain its full tax refund in 2002.

	2003E	2002	2001	INDUSTRY AVERAGE
Current		1.2×	2.3×	2.7×
Inventory turnover		4.7×	4.8×	6.1×
Days sales outstanding (DSO)[a]		38.2	37.4	32.0
Fixed assets turnover		6.4×	10.0×	7.0×
Total assets turnover		2.1×	2.3×	2.6×
Debt ratio		82.8%	54.8%	50.0%
TIE		−1.0×	4.3×	6.2×
EBITDA coverage		0.1×	3.0×	8.0×
Profit margin		−2.7%	2.6%	3.5%
Basic earning power		−4.6%	13.0%	19.1%
ROA		−5.6%	6.0%	9.1%
ROE		−32.5%	13.3%	18.2%
Price/earnings		−1.4×	9.7×	14.2×
Price/cash flow		−5.2×	8.0×	11.0×
Market/book		0.5×	1.3×	2.4×
Book value per share		$4.93	$6.64	n.a.

NOTE: "E" indicates estimated. The 2003 data are forecasts.

[a]Calculation is based on a 365-day year.

CYBER PROBLEM

Please go to our web site **http://brigham.swlearning.com** to access the Cyberproblems.

THOMSON
★
ANALYTICS

With your Xtra! CD-ROM, access the Thomson Analytics Problems and use the Thomson Analytics Academic online database to work this chapter's problems.

THE FINANCIAL ENVIRONMENT: MARKETS, INSTITUTIONS, AND INTEREST RATES

4

CITIGROUP BUILT TO COMPETE IN A CHANGING ENVIRONMENT

CITIGROUP INC.

Financial managers and investors don't operate in a vacuum — they make decisions within a large and complex financial environment. This environment includes financial markets and institutions, tax and regulatory policies, and the state of the economy. The environment both defines the available financial alternatives and affects the outcomes of various decisions. Therefore, it is crucial that financial managers and investors have a good understanding of the environment in which they operate.

Good financial decisions require good estimates of movements in the economy, interest rates, and the stock market, but figuring out what's likely to happen is no trivial matter. Throughout most of the 1990s the financial environment was extraordinarily favorable: The stock market registered impressive gains, the economy was strong, and both interest rates and inflation were low. More recently, though, the economy has slowed and the stock market has declined, and accurately predicting the next moves is difficult.

The underlying financial environment has been undergoing tremendous changes, including breakthroughs in technology, increased globalization, and shifts in the regulatory environment. All of these factors have presented financial managers and investors with opportunities, but opportunities accompanied by substantial risks.

Consider the case of Citigroup Inc. which was created in 1998 when Citicorp and Travelers Group (which included the investment firm Salomon Smith Barney) merged. Citigroup today operates in 100 countries, has roughly 200 million customers and 230,000 employees, and holds more than a trillion dollars (that's a thousand billion!) worth of assets.

Citigroup was created because of three important trends: (1) A regulatory change made it possible for a U.S. corporation to be engaged in commercial banking, investment banking, and insurance. (2) Increased globalization made it desirable to follow their clients and operate in many countries. (3) Changing technology led to increased economies of scale and scope, both of which helped spur a rapid consolidation of the financial services industry.

The same forces that are transforming the financial services industry have affected other industries. In particular, the growth of the Internet has provided many companies with increased opportunities, but it has also created additional competition and additional risk. For example, it has altered the way millions of consumers purchase airline tickets, hotel rooms, books, and automobiles. Consequently, financial managers must understand today's technological environment and be ready to change operations as the environment evolves.

In earlier chapters we discussed financial statements and showed how financial managers and others analyze them to see where their firms have been and are headed. Financial managers also need to understand the environment and markets within which businesses operate. Therefore, this chapter describes the markets where capital is raised, securities are traded, and stock prices are established, as well as the institutions that operate in these markets. In the process, we also explore the principal factors that determine the level of interest rates. ■

THE FINANCIAL MARKETS

Businesses, individuals, and governments often need to raise capital. For example, suppose Carolina Power & Light (CP&L) forecasts an increase in the demand for electricity in North Carolina, and the company decides to build a new power plant. Because CP&L almost certainly will not have the $1 billion or so necessary to pay for the plant, the company will have to raise this capital in the financial markets. Or suppose Mr. Fong, the proprietor of a San Francisco hardware store, decides to expand into appliances. Where will he get the money to buy the initial inventory of TV sets, washers, and freezers? Similarly, if the Johnson family wants to buy a home that costs $100,000, but they have only $20,000 in savings, how can they raise the additional $80,000? If the city of New York wants to borrow $200 million to finance a new sewer plant, or the federal government needs money to meet its needs, they too need access to the capital markets.

On the other hand, some individuals and firms have incomes that are greater than their current expenditures, so they have funds available to invest. For example, Carol Hawk has an income of $36,000, but her expenses are only $30,000, and in 2001 Ford Motor Company had accumulated roughly $18 billion of cash and marketable securities, which it has available for future investments.

TYPES OF MARKETS

People and organizations wanting to borrow money are brought together with those having surplus funds in the *financial markets*. Note that "markets" is plural—there are a great many different financial markets in a developed economy such as ours. Each market deals with a somewhat different type of instrument in terms of the instrument's maturity and the assets backing it. Also, different markets serve different types of customers, or operate in different parts of the country. For these reasons it is often useful to classify markets along various dimensions:

1. **Physical asset vs. Financial asset markets.** *Physical asset markets* (also called "tangible" or "real" asset markets) are those for such products as wheat, autos,

real estate, computers, and machinery. *Financial asset markets*, on the other hand, deal with stocks, bonds, notes, mortgages, and other *claims on real assets*, as well as with *derivative securities* whose values are *derived* from changes in the prices of other assets.

2. **Spot vs. Futures markets. Spot markets** are markets in which assets are bought or sold for "on-the-spot" delivery (literally, within a few days). **Futures markets** are markets in which participants agree today to buy or sell an asset at some future date. For example, a farmer may enter into a futures contract in which he agrees today to sell 5,000 bushels of soybeans six months from now at a price of $5 a bushel. In contrast, an international food producer looking to buy soybeans in the future may enter into a futures contract in which it agrees to buy soybeans three months from now.

3. **Money vs. Capital markets. Money markets** are the markets for short-term, highly liquid debt securities. The New York, London, and Tokyo money markets are among the world's largest. **Capital markets** are the markets for intermediate- or long-term debt and corporate stocks. The New York Stock Exchange, where the stocks of the largest U.S. corporations are traded, is a prime example of a capital market. There is no hard and fast rule on this, but when describing debt markets, "short term" generally means less than one year, "intermediate term" means one to five years, and "long term" means more than five years.

4. **Primary vs. Secondary markets. Primary markets** are the markets in which corporations raise new capital. If Microsoft were to sell a new issue of common stock to raise capital, this would be a primary market transaction. The corporation selling the newly created stock receives the proceeds from the sale in a primary market transaction. **Secondary markets** are markets in which existing, already outstanding, securities are traded among investors. Thus, if Jane Doe decided to buy 1,000 shares of AT&T stock, the purchase would occur in the secondary market. The New York Stock Exchange is a secondary market, since it deals in outstanding, as opposed to newly issued, stocks and bonds. Secondary markets also exist for mortgages, various other types of loans, and other financial assets. The corporation whose securities are being traded is not involved in a secondary market transaction and, thus, does not receive any funds from such a sale.

The **initial public offering (IPO) market** is a subset of the primary market. Here firms "go public" by offering shares to the public for the first time. Microsoft had its IPO in 1986. Previously, Bill Gates and other insiders owned all the shares. In many IPOs, the insiders sell some of their shares plus the company sells new shares to raise additional capital. We discuss IPOs in more detail in Chapter 8.

5. **Private vs. Public markets. Private markets,** where transactions are worked out directly between two parties, are differentiated from **public markets,** where standardized contracts are traded on organized exchanges. Bank loans and private placements of debt with insurance companies are examples of private market transactions. Since these transactions are private, they may be structured in any manner that appeals to the two parties. By contrast, securities that are issued in public markets (e.g., common stock and corporate bonds) are ultimately held by a large number of individuals. Public securities must have fairly standardized contractual features, both to appeal to a broad range of investors and also because public investors cannot afford the time to study

Spot Markets
The markets in which assets are bought or sold for "on-the-spot" delivery.

Futures Markets
The markets in which participants agree today to buy or sell an asset at some future date.

Money Markets
The financial markets in which funds are borrowed or loaned for short periods (less than one year).

Capital Markets
The financial markets for stocks and for intermediate- or long-term debt (one year or longer).

Primary Markets
Markets in which corporations raise capital by issuing new securities.

Secondary Markets
Markets in which securities and other financial assets are traded among investors after they have been issued by corporations.

Initial Public Offering (IPO) Market
The market in which firms "go public" by offering shares to the public.

Private Markets
Markets in which transactions are worked out directly between two parties.

Public Markets
Markets in which standardized contracts are traded on organized exchanges.

INSTRUMENT (1)	MARKET (2)	MAJOR PARTICIPANTS (3)	SECURITY CHARACTERISTICS		
			RISKINESS (4)	ORIGINAL MATURITY (5)	INTEREST RATE ON 4/12/02[a] (6)
U.S. Treasury bills	Money	Sold by U.S. Treasury to finance federal expenditures	Default-free	91 days to 1 year	1.68%
Bankers' acceptances	Money	A firm's promise to pay, guaranteed by a bank	Low degree of risk if guaranteed by a strong bank	Up to 180 days	1.90
Dealer commercial paper	Money	Issued by financially secure firms to large investors	Low default risk	Up to 270 days	1.86
Negotiable certificates of deposit (CDs)	Money	Issued by major money-center commercial banks to large investors	Default risk depends on the strength of the issuing bank	Up to 1 year	1.86
Money market mutual funds	Money	Invest in Treasury bills, CDs, and commercial paper; held by individuals and businesses	Low degree of risk	No specific maturity (instant liquidity)	1.56
Eurodollar market time deposits	Money	Issued by banks outside U.S.	Default risk depends on the strength of the issuing bank	Up to 1 year	1.88
Consumer credit loans	Money	Issued by banks/credit unions/finance companies to individuals	Risk is variable	Variable	Variable
U.S. Treasury notes and bonds	Capital	Issued by U.S. government	No default risk, but price will decline if interest rates rise	2 to 30 years	5.65

[a] The yields reported (except for the corporate and municipal bonds) are from *The Wall Street Journal*. Money market rates assume a 3-month maturity. The corporate and municipal bond rates are for 30-year AAA-rated bonds; quotes are from **http://www.bondsonline.com.**

unique, nonstandardized contracts. Their diverse ownership also ensures that public securities are relatively liquid. Private market securities are, therefore, more tailor-made but less liquid, whereas public market securities are more liquid but subject to greater standardization.

Other classifications could be made, but this breakdown is sufficient to show that there are many types of financial markets. Also, note that the distinctions among markets are often blurred and unimportant, except as a general point of reference. For example, it makes little difference if a firm borrows for 11, 12, or 13 months, hence, whether we have a "money" or "capital" market transaction. You should recognize the big differences among types of markets, but don't get hung up trying to distinguish them at the boundaries.

A healthy economy is dependent on efficient transfers of funds from people who are net savers to firms and individuals who need capital. Without efficient transfers,

| | | TABLE 4-1 | continued | | | |

			SECURITY CHARACTERISTICS		
INSTRUMENT (1)	MARKET (2)	MAJOR PARTICIPANTS (3)	RISKINESS (4)	ORIGINAL MATURITY (5)	INTEREST RATE ON 4/12/02[a] (6)
Mortgages	Capital	Borrowings from commercial banks and S&Ls by individuals and businesses	Risk is variable	Up to 30 years	6.53%
State and local government bonds	Capital	Issued by state and local governments to individuals and institutional investors	Riskier than U.S. government securities, but exempt from most taxes	Up to 30 years	5.22
Corporate bonds	Capital	Issued by corporations to individuals and institutional investors	Riskier than U.S. government securities, but less risky than preferred and common stocks; varying degree of risk within bonds depending on strength of issuer	Up to 40 years[b]	6.79
Leases	Capital	Similar to debt in that firms can lease assets rather than borrow and then buy the assets	Risk similar to corporate bonds	Generally 3 to 20 years	Similar to bond yields
Preferred stocks	Capital	Issued by corporations to individuals and institutional investors	Riskier than corporate bonds, but less risky than common stock	Unlimited	7 to 9%
Common stocks[c]	Capital	Issued by corporations to individuals and institutional investors	Risky	Unlimited	NA

[b] Just recently, a few corporations have issued 100-year bonds; however, the majority have issued bonds with maturities less than 40 years.

[c] While common stocks do not pay interest, they are expected to provide a "return" in the form of dividends and capital gains. As you will see in Chapter 5, historical stock returns have averaged between 10 and 15 percent a year. Of course, if you buy a stock, your *actual* return may be considerably higher or lower than these historical averages.

 Students can access current and historical interest rates and economic data as well as regional economic data for the states of Arkansas, Illinois, Indiana, Kentucky, Mississippi, Missouri, and Tennessee from the Federal Reserve Economic Data (FRED) site at **http://research. stlouisfed.org/fred/**.

the economy simply could not function: Carolina Power & Light could not raise capital, so Raleigh's citizens would have no electricity; the Johnson family would not have adequate housing; Carol Hawk would have no place to invest her savings; and so on. Obviously, the level of employment and productivity, hence our standard of living, would be much lower. Therefore, it is absolutely essential that our financial markets function efficiently — not only quickly, but also at a low cost.[1]

Table 4-1 gives a listing of the most important instruments traded in the various financial markets. The instruments are arranged from top to bottom in ascending order of typical length of maturity. As we go through the book, we will look in much

[1] As the countries of the former Soviet Union and other Eastern European nations move toward capitalism, just as much attention must be paid to the establishment of cost-efficient financial markets as to electrical power, transportation, communications, and other infrastructure systems. Economic efficiency is simply impossible without a good system for allocating capital within the economy.

more detail at many of the instruments listed in Table 4-1. For example, we will see that there are many varieties of corporate bonds, ranging from "plain vanilla" bonds to bonds that are convertible into common stocks to bonds whose interest payments vary depending on the inflation rate. Still, the table gives an idea of the characteristics and costs of the instruments traded in the major financial markets.

RECENT TRENDS

Financial markets have experienced many changes during the last two decades. Technological advances in computers and telecommunications, along with the globalization of banking and commerce, have led to deregulation, and this has increased competition throughout the world. The result is a much more efficient, internationally linked market, but one that is far more complex than existed a few years ago. While these developments have been largely positive, they have also created problems for policy makers. At a recent conference, Federal Reserve Board Chairman Alan Greenspan stated that modern financial markets "expose national economies to shocks from new and unexpected sources, and with little if any lag." He went on to say that central banks must develop new ways to evaluate and limit risks to the financial system. Large amounts of capital move quickly around the world in response to changes in interest and exchange rates, and these movements can disrupt local institutions and economies.

With globalization has come the need for greater cooperation among regulators at the international level. Various committees are currently working to improve coordination, but the task is not easy. Factors that complicate coordination include (1) the differing structures among nations' banking and securities industries, (2) the trend in Europe toward financial service conglomerates, and (3) a reluctance on the part of individual countries to give up control over their national monetary policies. Still, regulators are unanimous about the need to close the gaps in the supervision of worldwide markets.

Derivative
Any financial asset whose value is derived from the value of some other "underlying" asset.

Another important trend in recent years has been the increased use of **derivatives.** A derivative is any security whose value is *derived* from the price of some other "underlying" asset. An option to buy IBM stock is a derivative, as is a contract to buy Japanese yen six months from now. The value of the IBM option depends on the price of IBM's stock, and the value of the Japanese yen "future" depends on the exchange rate between yen and dollars. The market for derivatives has grown faster than any other market in recent years, providing corporations with new opportunities but also exposing them to new risks.

Derivatives can be used either to reduce risks or to speculate. Suppose an importer's net income tends to fall whenever the dollar falls relative to the yen. That company could reduce its risk by purchasing derivatives that increase in value whenever the dollar declines. This would be called a *hedging operation*, and its purpose is to reduce risk exposure. Speculation, on the other hand, is done in the hope of high returns, but it raises risk exposure. For example, in the late 1990s, Procter & Gamble disclosed that it lost $150 million on derivative investments, and Orange County (California) went bankrupt as a result of its treasurer's speculation in derivatives.

The size and complexity of derivatives transactions concern regulators, academics, and members of Congress. Fed Chairman Greenspan noted that, in theory, derivatives should allow companies to manage risk better, but that it is not clear whether recent innovations have "increased or decreased the inherent stability of the financial system."

Distinguish between physical asset and financial asset markets.

What is the difference between spot and futures markets?

Distinguish between money and capital markets.

What is the difference between primary and secondary markets?

Differentiate between private and public markets.

Why are financial markets essential for a healthy economy?

What is a derivative, and how is its value related to that of an "underlying asset"?

FINANCIAL INSTITUTIONS

Transfers of capital between savers and those who need capital take place in the three different ways diagrammed in Figure 4-1:

1. *Direct transfers* of money and securities, as shown in the top section, occur when a business sells its stocks or bonds directly to savers, without going through any type of financial institution. The business delivers its securities to savers, who in turn give the firm the money it needs.

2. As shown in the middle section, transfers may also go through an *investment banking house* such as Merrill Lynch, which *underwrites* the issue. An underwriter

| FIGURE 4-1 | **Diagram of the Capital Formation Process** |

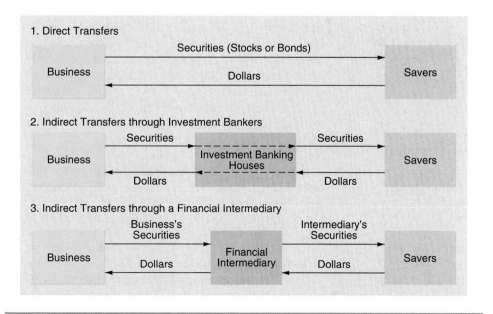

serves as a middleman and facilitates the issuance of securities. The company sells its stocks or bonds to the investment bank, which in turn sells these same securities to savers. The businesses' securities and the savers' money merely "pass through" the investment banking house. However, the investment bank does buy and hold the securities for a period of time, so it is taking a risk — it may not be able to resell them to savers for as much as it paid. Because new securities are involved and the corporation receives the proceeds of the sale, this is a primary market transaction.

3. Transfers can also be made through a *financial intermediary* such as a bank or mutual fund. Here the intermediary obtains funds from savers in exchange for its own securities. The intermediary then uses this money to purchase and then hold businesses' securities. For example, a saver might give dollars to a bank, receiving from it a certificate of deposit, and then the bank might lend the money to a small business in the form of a mortgage loan. Thus, intermediaries literally create new forms of capital — in this case, certificates of deposit, which are both safer and more liquid than mortgages and thus are better securities for most savers to hold. The existence of intermediaries greatly increases the efficiency of money and capital markets.

In our example, we assume that the entity needing capital is a business, and specifically a corporation, but it is easy to visualize the demander of capital as a home purchaser, a government unit, and so on.

Direct transfers of funds from savers to businesses are possible and do occur on occasion, but it is generally more efficient for a business to enlist the services of an **investment banking house** such as Merrill Lynch, Salomon Smith Barney, Morgan Stanley Dean Witter, or Goldman Sachs. Such organizations (1) help corporations design securities with features that are currently attractive to investors, (2) then buy these securities from the corporation, and (3) resell them to savers. Although the securities are sold twice, this process is really one primary market transaction, with the investment banker acting as a facilitator to help transfer capital from savers to businesses.

The **financial intermediaries** shown in the third section of Figure 4-1 do more than simply transfer money and securities between firms and savers—they literally create new financial products. Since the intermediaries are generally large, they gain economies of scale in analyzing the creditworthiness of potential borrowers, in processing and collecting loans, and in pooling risks and thus helping individual savers diversify, that is, "not putting all their financial eggs in one basket." Further, a system of specialized intermediaries can enable savings to do more than just draw interest. For example, individuals can put money into banks and get both interest income and a convenient way of making payments (checking), or put money into life insurance companies and get both interest income and protection for their beneficiaries.

In the United States and other developed nations, a set of specialized, highly efficient financial intermediaries has evolved. The situation is changing rapidly, however, and different types of institutions are performing services that were formerly reserved for others, causing institutional distinctions to become blurred. Still, there is a degree of institutional identity, and here are the major classes of intermediaries:

1. *Commercial banks*, the traditional "department stores of finance," serve a wide variety of savers and borrowers. Historically, commercial banks were the major institutions that handled checking accounts and through which the Federal Reserve System expanded or contracted the money supply. Today, however, several

Investment Banking House
An organization that underwrites and distributes new investment securities and helps businesses obtain financing.

Financial Intermediaries
Specialized financial firms that facilitate the transfer of funds from savers to demanders of capital.

other institutions also provide checking services and significantly influence the money supply. Conversely, commercial banks are providing an ever-widening range of services, including stock brokerage services and insurance.

2. *Savings and loan associations (S&Ls)*, which have traditionally served individual savers and residential and commercial mortgage borrowers, take the funds of many small savers and then lend this money to home buyers and other types of borrowers. In the 1980s, the S&L industry experienced severe problems when (a) short-term interest rates paid on savings accounts rose well above the returns being earned on the existing mortgages held by S&Ls and (b) commercial real estate suffered a severe slump, resulting in high mortgage default rates. Together, these events forced many S&Ls to either merge with stronger institutions or close their doors.

3. *Mutual savings banks*, which are similar to S&Ls, operate primarily in the northeastern states, accept savings primarily from individuals, and lend mainly on a long-term basis to home buyers and consumers.

4. *Credit unions* are cooperative associations whose members are supposed to have a common bond, such as being employees of the same firm. Members' savings are loaned only to other members, generally for auto purchases, home improvement loans, and home mortgages. Credit unions are often the cheapest source of funds available to individual borrowers.

5. *Pension funds* are retirement plans funded by corporations or government agencies for their workers and administered primarily by the trust departments of commercial banks or by life insurance companies. Pension funds invest primarily in bonds, stocks, mortgages, and real estate.

6. *Life insurance companies* take savings in the form of annual premiums; invest these funds in stocks, bonds, real estate, and mortgages; and finally make payments to the beneficiaries of the insured parties. In recent years, life insurance companies have also offered a variety of tax-deferred savings plans designed to provide benefits to the participants when they retire.

7. *Mutual funds* are corporations that accept money from savers and then use these funds to buy stocks, long-term bonds, or short-term debt instruments issued by businesses or government units. These organizations pool funds and thus reduce risks by diversification. They also achieve economies of scale in analyzing securities, managing portfolios, and buying and selling securities. Different funds are designed to meet the objectives of different types of savers. Hence, there are bond funds for those who desire safety, stock funds for savers who are willing to accept significant risks in the hope of higher returns, and still other funds that are used as interest-bearing checking accounts (the **money market funds**). There are literally thousands of different mutual funds with dozens of different goals and purposes.

Money Market Fund
A mutual fund that invests in short-term, low-risk securities and allows investors to write checks against their accounts.

Mutual funds have grown more rapidly than any other institution in recent years, in large part because of a change in the way corporations provide for employees' retirement. Before the 1980s, most corporations said, in effect, "Come work for us, and when you retire, we will give you a retirement income based on the salary you were earning during the last five years before you retired." The company was then responsible for setting aside funds each year to make sure that it had the money available to pay the agreed-upon retirement benefits. That situation is changing rapidly. Today, new employees are likely to be told, "Come work for us, and we will give you some money each payday that you can invest for your future retirement. You can't get the money until you retire (without paying a huge tax penalty), but if you invest wisely, you can retire in comfort." Most workers know they don't know how to invest wisely, so they turn their retirement funds over to a mutual fund. Hence, mutual funds are growing rapidly. Excellent information on the objectives and past performances of the various funds are provided in publications such as *Value Line Investment Survey* and *Morningstar Mutual Funds*, which are available in most libraries.

Financial institutions have historically been heavily regulated, with the primary purpose of this regulation being to ensure the safety of the institutions and thus to protect investors. However, these regulations — which have taken the form of prohibitions on nationwide branch banking, restrictions on the types of assets the institutions can buy, ceilings on the interest rates they can pay, and limitations on the types of services they can provide — have tended to impede the free flow of capital and thus have hurt the efficiency of our capital markets. Recognizing this fact, Congress has authorized some major changes, and more are on the horizon.

The result of the ongoing regulatory changes has been a blurring of the distinctions between the different types of institutions. Indeed, the trend in the United States today is toward huge **financial service corporations,** which own banks, S&Ls, investment banking houses, insurance companies, pension plan operations, and mutual funds, and which have branches across the country and around the world. Examples of financial service corporations, most of which started in one area but have now diversified to cover most of the financial spectrum, include Merrill Lynch, American Express, Citigroup, Fidelity, and Prudential.

Panel a of Table 4-2 lists the 10 largest U.S. bank and thrift holding companies, and Panel b shows the leading world banking companies. Among the world's

Financial Service Corporation
A firm that offers a wide range of financial services, including investment banking, brokerage operations, insurance, and commercial banking.

TABLE 4-2	10 Largest U.S. Bank and Thrift Holding Companies and World Banking Companies and Top 10 Leading Underwriters

PANEL A	PANEL B	PANEL C
U.S. Bank and Thrift Holding Companies[a]	*World Banking Companies[b]*	*Leading Global Underwriters[c]*
Citigroup Inc.	Mizuho Holdings (Tokyo)	Citigroup/Salomon Smith Barney
J. P. Morgan Chase & Co.	Citigroup Inc. (New York)	Merrill Lynch
Bank of America Corp.	Sumitomo Mitsui Banking Corp. (Tokyo)	Credit Suisse First Boston
Wachovia Corp.	Mitsubishi Tokyo Financial Group (Tokyo)	J. P. Morgan Chase & Co.
Wells Fargo & Co.	Deutsche Bank (Frankfurt)	Goldman Sachs
Bank One Corp.	Allianz AG (Munich)	Morgan Stanley Dean Witter
MetLife Inc.	UBS AG (Zurich)	Lehman Brothers
Taunus Corp.	BNP Paribas (Paris)	UBS Warburg
Washington Mutual Inc.	HSBC Holdings PLC (London)	Deutsche Bank
FleetBoston Financial Corp.	J. P. Morgan Chase & Co. (New York)	Banc of America Securities

NOTES:

[a] Ranked by total assets as of December 31, 2001. SOURCE: "Top 150 Bank and SL Holding Companies by Yearend '01 Assets," *AmericanBanker.com*, June 11, 2002.

[b] Ranked by total assets as of December 31, 2001. SOURCE: "World's Top Banking Companies by Assets," *AmericanBanker.com*, July 12, 2002.

[c] Ranked by dollar amount raised through new issues in 2001. For this ranking, the lead underwriter (manager) is given credit for the entire issue. SOURCE: Adapted from *The Wall Street Journal*, January 2, 2002, R19.

10 largest, only two (Citigroup and J. P. Morgan Chase) are from the United States. While U.S. banks have grown dramatically as a result of recent mergers, they are still small by global standards. Panel c of the table lists the 10 leading underwriters in terms of dollar volume of new issues. Six of the top underwriters are also major commercial banks or are part of bank holding companies, which confirms the continued blurring of distinctions among different types of financial institutions.

SELF-TEST QUESTIONS

Identify three different ways capital is transferred between savers and borrowers.

What is the difference between a commercial bank and an investment bank?

Distinguish between investment banking houses and financial intermediaries.

List the major types of intermediaries and briefly describe the primary function of each.

THE STOCK MARKET

As noted earlier, secondary markets are those in which outstanding, previously issued securities are traded. By far the most active secondary market, and the most important one to financial managers, is the *stock market*, where the prices of firms' stocks are established. Since the primary goal of financial management is to maximize the firm's stock price, a knowledge of the stock market is important to anyone involved in managing a business.

While the two leading stock markets today are the New York Stock Exchange and the Nasdaq stock market, stocks are actually traded using a variety of market procedures. However, there are just two basic types of stock markets: (1) *physical location exchanges*, which include the New York Stock Exchange (NYSE), the American Stock Exchange (AMEX), and several regional stock exchanges, and (2) electronic dealer-based markets that include the Nasdaq stock market, the less formal over-the-counter market, and the recently developed electronic communications networks (ECNs). (See the Technology Matters box entitled, "Online Trading Systems.") Because the physical location exchanges are easier to describe and understand, we consider them first.

THE PHYSICAL LOCATION STOCK EXCHANGES

Physical Location Exchanges
Formal organizations having tangible physical locations that conduct auction markets in designated ("listed") securities.

The **physical location exchanges** are tangible physical entities. Each of the larger ones occupies its own building, has a limited number of members, and has an elected governing body — its board of governors. Members are said to have "seats" on the exchange, although everybody stands up. These seats, which are bought and sold, give the holder the right to trade on the exchange. There are currently 1,366 seats on the New York Stock Exchange, and on February 19, 2002, two seats on the NYSE sold for $2.5 million and $2.475 million each, which was down from the previous high of $2.65 million.

Most of the larger investment banking houses operate *brokerage departments*, and they own seats on the exchanges and designate one or more of their officers as members. The exchanges are open on all normal working days, with the members meeting in a large room equipped with telephones and other electronic equipment that enable each member to communicate with his or her firm's offices throughout the country.

Like other markets, security exchanges facilitate communication between buyers and sellers. For example, Merrill Lynch (the second largest brokerage firm) might receive an order in its Atlanta office from a customer who wants to buy shares of AT&T stock. Simultaneously, Morgan Stanley Dean Witter's Denver office might receive an order from a customer wishing to sell shares of AT&T. Each broker communicates electronically with the firm's representative on the NYSE. Other brokers throughout the country are also communicating with their own exchange members. The exchange members with *sell orders* offer the shares for sale, and they are bid for by the members with *buy orders*. Thus, the exchanges operate as *auction markets*.[2]

THE OVER-THE-COUNTER AND THE NASDAQ STOCK MARKETS

While the stocks of most large companies trade on the NYSE, a larger number of stocks trade off the exchange in what has traditionally been referred to as the **over-the-counter market (OTC).** An explanation of the term "over-the-counter" will help clarify how this term arose. As noted earlier, the exchanges operate as auction markets — buy and sell orders come in more or less simultaneously, and exchange members match these orders. If a stock is traded infrequently, perhaps because the firm is new or small, few buy and sell orders come in, and matching them within a reasonable amount of time would be difficult. To avoid this problem, some brokerage firms maintain an inventory of such stocks and stand prepared to make a market for these stocks. These "dealers" buy when individual investors want to sell, and then sell part of their inventory when investors want to buy. At one time, the inventory of securities was kept in a safe, and the stocks, when bought and sold, were literally passed over the counter.

Over-the-Counter Market
A large collection of brokers and dealers, connected electronically by telephones and computers, that provides for trading in unlisted securities.

Today, these markets are often referred to as **dealer markets.** A dealer market is defined to include all facilities that are needed to conduct security transactions not made on the physical location exchanges. These facilities include (1) the relatively few

Dealer Market
Includes all facilities that are needed to conduct security transactions not conducted on the physical location exchanges.

---

[2] The NYSE is actually a modified auction market, wherein people (through their brokers) bid for stocks. Originally — about 200 years ago — brokers would literally shout, "I have 100 shares of Erie for sale; how much am I offered?" and then sell to the highest bidder. If a broker had a buy order, he or she would shout, "I want to buy 100 shares of Erie; who'll sell at the best price?" The same general situation still exists, although the exchanges now have members known as *specialists* who facilitate the trading process by keeping an inventory of shares of the stocks in which they specialize. If a buy order comes in at a time when no sell order arrives, the specialist will sell off some inventory. Similarly, if a sell order comes in, the specialist will buy and add to inventory. The specialist sets a *bid price* (the price the specialist will pay for the stock) and an *asked price* (the price at which shares will be sold out of inventory). The bid and asked prices are set at levels designed to keep the inventory in balance. If many buy orders start coming in because of favorable developments or sell orders come in because of unfavorable events, the specialist will raise or lower prices to keep supply and demand in balance. Bid prices are somewhat lower than asked prices, with the difference, or *spread*, representing the specialist's profit margin.

Special facilities are available to help institutional investors such as mutual funds or pension funds sell large blocks of stock without depressing their prices. In essence, brokerage houses that cater to institutional clients will purchase blocks (defined as 10,000 or more shares) and then resell the stock to other institutions or individuals. Also, when a firm has a major announcement that is likely to cause its stock price to change sharply, it will ask the exchanges to halt trading in its stock until the announcement has been made and digested by investors.

ONLINE TRADING SYSTEMS

The forces described in the vignette that have spurred the consolidation of the financial services industry have also promoted online trading systems that bypass the traditional exchanges. These systems, known as Electronic Communications Networks (ECNs), use technology to bring buyers and sellers together electronically. ECNs have already captured about 30 percent of Nasdaq's trading volume, and the vast majority of these transactions are conducted by three firms: Instinet, Island, and the recently merged firm of Archipelago and Redibook. In mid-2002, Instinet had also begun talks to explore buying Island ECN. If that merger is consumated, the two firms will have about 22 percent of Nasdaq's trading volume, which will provide more liquidity and the ability to spread the cost of new technology over more trades. If this transaction is completed, the combined company would pose an even more significant threat to Nasdaq.

In either event, ECNs will accelerate the move toward 24-hour trading. Large clients who want to trade after the other markets have closed may utilize an ECN, bypassing the NYSE and Nasdaq. The move toward faster, cheaper, and continuous trading obviously benefits investors, but it does present regulators, who try to ensure that all investors have access to a "level playing field," with a number of headaches.

Because of the threat from ECNs and the need to raise capital and increase flexibility, both the NYSE and Nasdaq plan to convert from privately held, member-owned businesses to stockholder-owned, for-profit corporations. This suggests that the financial landscape will continue to undergo dramatic changes in the upcoming years.

SOURCES: Katrina Brooker, "Online Investing: It's Not Just for Geeks Anymore," *Fortune*, December 21, 1998, 89–98; "Fidelity, Schwab Part of Deal to Create Nasdaq Challenger," *The Milwaukee Journal Sentinel*, July 22, 1999, 1; and "Instinet Group Is Holding Talks to Buy Island ECN," *The Wall Street Journal*, May 16, 2002, C1.

dealers who hold inventories of these securities and who are said to "make a market" in these securities; (2) the thousands of brokers who act as *agents* in bringing the dealers together with investors; and (3) the computers, terminals, and electronic networks that provide a communication link between dealers and brokers. The dealers who make a market in a particular stock quote the price at which they will pay for the stock (the *bid price*) and the price at which they will sell shares (the *ask price*). Each dealer's prices, which are adjusted as supply and demand conditions change, can be read off computer screens all across the world. The *bid-ask spread*, which is the difference between bid and ask prices, represents the dealer's markup, or profit. The dealer's risk increases if the stock is more volatile, or if the stock trades infrequently. Generally, we would expect volatile, infrequently traded stocks to have wider spreads in order to compensate the dealers for assuming the risk of holding them in inventory.

Brokers and dealers who participate in the over-the-counter market are members of a self-regulatory body known as the *National Association of Securities Dealers (NASD)*, which licenses brokers and oversees trading practices. The computerized network used by the NASD is known as the NASD Automated Quotation System.

Nasdaq started as just a quotation system, but it has grown to become an organized securities market with its own listing requirements. Over the past decade the competition between the NYSE and Nasdaq has become increasingly fierce. In an effort to become more competitive with the NYSE and with international markets, the Nasdaq and the AMEX merged in 1998 to form the Nasdaq-Amex Market Group, which might best be referred to as an *organized investment network*. This investment network is often referred to as Nasdaq, but stocks continue to be traded and reported separately on the two markets. Increased competition among global stock markets assuredly will result in similar alliances among other exchanges and markets in the future.

Since most of the largest companies trade on the NYSE, the market capitalization of NYSE-traded stocks is much higher than for stocks traded on Nasdaq ($11.7 trillion compared with $2.9 trillion at year-end 2001). However, reported volume (number of shares traded) is often larger on Nasdaq, and more companies are listed on Nasdaq.[3]

Interestingly, many high-tech companies such as Microsoft and Intel have remained on Nasdaq even though they easily meet the listing requirements of the NYSE. At the same time, however, other high-tech companies such as Gateway 2000, America Online, and Iomega have left Nasdaq for the NYSE. Despite these defections, Nasdaq's growth over the past decade has been impressive. In the years ahead, the competition will no doubt remain fierce.

SELF-TEST QUESTIONS

What are the differences between the physical location exchanges and the Nasdaq stock market?

What is the bid-ask spread?

THE COST OF MONEY

Production Opportunities
The returns available within an economy from investments in productive (cash-generating) assets.

Time Preferences for Consumption
The preferences of consumers for current consumption as opposed to saving for future consumption.

Risk
In a financial market context, the chance that an investment will provide a low or negative return.

Inflation
The amount by which prices increase over time.

Capital in a free economy is allocated through the price system. *The interest rate is the price paid to borrow debt capital. With equity capital, investors expect to receive dividends and capital gains, whose sum is the cost of equity money.* The factors that affect supply of and demand for investment capital, hence the cost of money, are discussed in this section.

The four most fundamental factors affecting the cost of money are (1) **production opportunities,** (2) **time preferences for consumption,** (3) **risk,** and (4) **inflation.** To see how these factors operate, visualize an isolated island community where the people live on fish. They have a stock of fishing gear that permits them to survive reasonably well, but they would like to have more fish. Now suppose Mr. Crusoe had a bright idea for a new type of fishnet that would enable him to double his daily catch. However, it would take him a year to perfect his design, to build his net, and to learn how to use it efficiently, and Mr. Crusoe would probably starve before he could put his new net into operation. Therefore, he might suggest to Ms. Robinson, Mr. Friday, and several others that if they would give him one fish each day for a year, he would return two fish a day during all of the next year. If someone accepted the offer, then the fish that Ms. Robinson or one of the others gave to Mr. Crusoe would constitute *savings;* these savings would be *invested* in the fishnet; and the extra fish the net produced would constitute a *return on the investment.*

---

[3]One transaction on Nasdaq generally shows up as two separate trades (the buy and the sell). This "double counting" makes it difficult to compare the volume between stock markets.

Obviously, the more productive Mr. Crusoe thought the new fishnet would be, the more he could afford to offer potential investors for their savings. In this example, we assume that Mr. Crusoe thought he would be able to pay, and thus he offered, a 100 percent rate of return — he offered to give back two fish for every one he received. He might have tried to attract savings for less — for example, he might have decided to offer only 1.5 fish next year for every one he received this year, which would represent a 50 percent rate of return to Ms. Robinson and the other potential savers.

How attractive Mr. Crusoe's offer appeared to a potential saver would depend in large part on the saver's *time preference for consumption*. For example, Ms. Robinson might be thinking of retirement, and she might be willing to trade fish today for fish in the future on a one-for-one basis. On the other hand, Mr. Friday might have a wife and several young children and need his current fish, so he might be unwilling to "lend" a fish today for anything less than three fish next year. Mr. Friday would be said to have a high time preference for current consumption and Ms. Robinson a low time preference. Note also that if the entire population were living right at the subsistence level, time preferences for current consumption would necessarily be high, aggregate savings would be low, interest rates would be high, and capital formation would be difficult.

The *risk* inherent in the fishnet project, and thus in Mr. Crusoe's ability to repay the loan, would also affect the return investors would require: the higher the perceived risk, the higher the required rate of return. Also, in a more complex society there are many businesses like Mr. Crusoe's, many goods other than fish, and many savers like Ms. Robinson and Mr. Friday. Therefore, people use money as a medium of exchange rather than barter with fish. When money is used, its value in the future, which is affected by *inflation*, comes into play: the higher the expected rate of inflation, the larger the required return. We discuss this point in detail later in the chapter.

Thus, we see that the interest rate paid to savers depends in a basic way (1) on the rate of return producers expect to earn on invested capital, (2) on savers' time preferences for current versus future consumption, (3) on the riskiness of the loan, and (4) on the expected future rate of inflation. Producers' expected returns on their business investments set an upper limit on how much they can pay for savings, while consumers' time preferences for consumption establish how much consumption they are willing to defer, hence how much they will save at different rates of interest offered by producers.[4] Higher risk and higher inflation also lead to higher interest rates.

SELF-TEST QUESTIONS

What is the price paid to borrow money called?

What are the two items whose sum is the "price" of equity capital?

What four fundamental factors affect the cost of money?

---

[4] The term "producers" is really too narrow. A better word might be "borrowers," which would include corporations, home purchasers, people borrowing to go to college, or even people borrowing to buy autos or to pay for vacations. Also, the wealth of a society and its demographics influence its people's ability to save and thus their time preferences for current versus future consumption.

MEASURING THE MARKET

A *stock index* is designed to show the performance of the stock market. The problem is that there are many stock indexes, and it is difficult to determine which index best reflects market actions. Some are designed to represent the whole equity market, some to track the returns of certain industry sectors, and others to track the returns of small-cap, mid-cap, or large-cap stocks. We discuss below three of the leading indexes.

DOW JONES INDUSTRIAL AVERAGE

Unveiled in 1896 by Charles H. Dow, the Dow Jones Industrial Average (DJIA) provided a benchmark for comparing individual stocks with the overall market and for comparing the market with other economic indicators. The industrial average began with just 10 stocks, was expanded in 1916 to 20 stocks, and then to 30 in 1928. Also, in 1928 *The Wall Street Journal* editors began adjusting it for stock splits, and making substitutions. Today, the DJIA still includes 30 companies. They represent almost a fifth of the market value of all U.S. stocks, and all are both leading companies in their industries and widely held by individual and institutional investors. Visit **http://www.dowjones.com** and click on "Dow Jones Industrial Average" to get more information about the DJIA. You can find out how it is calculated, the current divisor, the companies that make up the DJIA, more history about the DJIA, and other interesting facts. In addition, "Dow data" charts the performance of the DJIA on a time line annotated with historical events.

S&P 500 INDEX

Created in 1926, the S&P 500 Index is widely regarded as the standard for measuring large-cap U.S. stock market performance. The stocks in the S&P 500 are selected by the Standard & Poor's Index Committee for being the leading companies in the leading industries, and for accurately reflecting the U.S. stock market. It is value weighted, so the largest companies (in terms of value) have the greatest influence. The S&P 500 Index is used by 97 percent of all U.S. money managers and pension plan sponsors, and approximately $700 billion is managed so as to obtain the same performance as this index (that is, in indexed funds).

NASDAQ COMPOSITE INDEX

The Nasdaq Composite Index measures the performance of all common stocks listed on the Nasdaq stock market. Currently, it includes more than 5,000 companies, and because many of the technology-sectored companies are traded on the computer-based Nasdaq exchange, this index is generally regarded as an economic indicator of the high-tech industry. Microsoft, Intel, and Cisco Systems are the three largest Nasdaq companies, and they comprise a high percentage of the index's value-weighted market capitalization. For this reason, substantial movements in the same direction by these three companies can move the entire index.

RECENT PERFORMANCE

The accompanying figure plots the value that an investor would now have if he or she had invested $1.00 in each of the three indexes on January 1, 1992. The returns on the three indexes are compared to an investment strategy that only invests in T-bills. For the returns on T-bills, the one-year Treasury constant maturity rate is used. Looking over the past 10 years, each of these indexes performed quite well through 1999. More recently, each of these indexes has stumbled. During the last 10 years the av-

INTEREST RATE LEVELS

Capital is allocated among borrowers by interest rates: Firms with the most profitable investment opportunities are willing and able to pay the most for capital, so they tend to attract it away from inefficient firms or from those whose products are not in demand. Of course, our economy is not completely free in the sense of being influenced only by market forces. Thus, the federal government has agencies that help designated individuals or groups obtain credit on favorable terms. Among those eligible for this kind of assistance are small businesses, certain minorities, and firms willing to build plants in areas with high unemployment. Still, most capital in the U.S. economy is allocated through the price system.

Figure 4-2 shows how supply and demand interact to determine interest rates in two capital markets. Markets A and B represent two of the many capital markets in erage annualized returns of these indexes ranged from 11.0 percent for the S&P 500 to 12.4 percent for the Dow Jones Industrial Average. The Nasdaq Composite Index experienced a huge bubble in 1999, reflecting overly optimistic valuations of technology companies. However, in 2000 the bubble burst and technology stock valuations spiraled downward, causing the Nasdaq Index to revert back to a level comparable to the S&P 500 and Dow Jones Industrial Average Index.

Growth of a $1 Investment Made on January 1, 1992

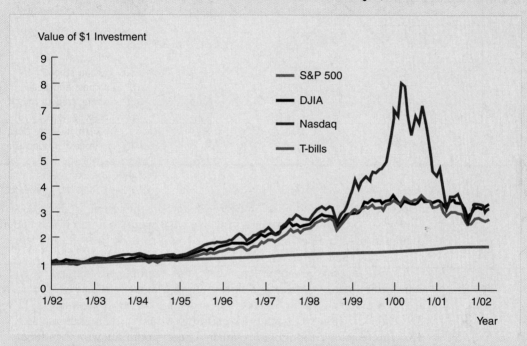

SOURCES: Adapted from Yahoo! Finance, Nasdaq, FRED Database, and **http://www.dowjones.com**.

existence. The going interest rate, which can be designated as either k or i, but for purposes of our discussion is designated as k, is initially 10 percent for the low-risk securities in Market A.[5] Borrowers whose credit is strong enough to borrow in this market can obtain funds at a cost of 10 percent, and investors who want to put their money to work without much risk can obtain a 10 percent return. Riskier borrowers must obtain higher-cost funds in Market B. Investors who are more willing to take risks invest in Market B, expecting to earn a 12 percent return but also realizing that they might actually receive much less.

If the demand for funds declines, as it typically does during business recessions, the demand curves will shift to the left, as shown in Curve D_2 in Market A. The

---

[5] The letter "k" is the traditional symbol for interest rates and the cost of equity, but "i" is used frequently today because this term corresponds to the interest rate key on financial calculators. Therefore, in Chapter 6, when we discuss calculators, the term "i" will be used for the interest rate.

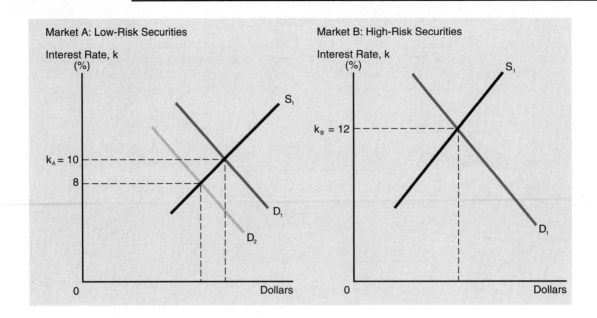

Market A: Low-Risk Securities

Market B: High-Risk Securities

market-clearing, or equilibrium, interest rate in this example declines to 8 percent. Similarly, you should be able to visualize what would happen if the Federal Reserve tightened credit: The supply curve, S_1, would shift to the left, and this would raise interest rates and lower the level of borrowing in the economy.

Capital markets are interdependent. For example, if Markets A and B were in equilibrium before the demand shift to D_2 in Market A, then investors were willing to accept the higher risk in Market B in exchange for a *risk premium* of 12% − 10% = 2%. After the shift to D_2, the risk premium would initially increase to 12% − 8% = 4%. Immediately, though, this much larger premium would induce some of the lenders in Market A to shift to Market B, which would, in turn, cause the supply curve in Market A to shift to the left (or up) and that in Market B to shift to the right. The transfer of capital between markets would raise the interest rate in Market A and lower it in Market B, thus bringing the risk premium back closer to the original 2 percent.

There are many capital markets in the United States. U.S. firms also invest and raise capital throughout the world, and foreigners both borrow and lend in the United States. There are markets for home loans; farm loans; business loans; federal, state, and local government loans; and consumer loans. Within each category, there are regional markets as well as different types of submarkets. For example, in real estate there are separate markets for first and second mortgages and for loans on single-family homes, apartments, office buildings, shopping centers, vacant land, and so on. Within the business sector there are dozens of types of debt and also several different markets for common stocks.

There is a price for each type of capital, and these prices change over time as shifts occur in supply and demand conditions. Figure 4-3 shows how long- and short-term interest rates to business borrowers have varied since the early 1960s. Notice that short-term interest rates are especially prone to rise during booms and then fall

FIGURE 4-3

Long- and Short-Term Interest Rates, 1961–2001

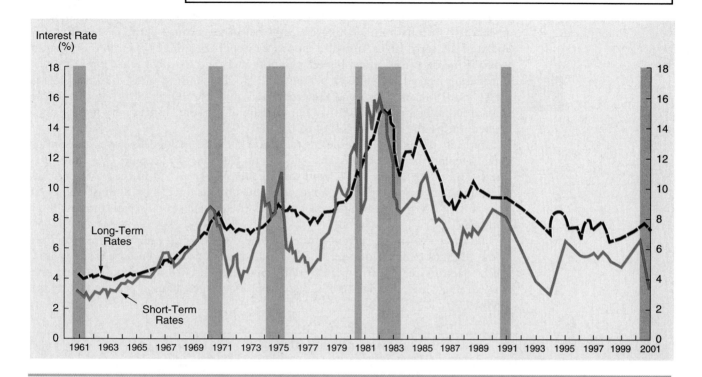

NOTES:
a. The shaded areas designate business recessions.
b. Short-term rates are measured by three- to six-month loans to very large, strong corporations, and long-term rates are measured by AAA corporate bonds.
SOURCE: Adapted from *Federal Reserve Bulletin; Federal Reserve Statistical Release.*

during recessions. (The shaded areas of the chart indicate recessions.) When the economy is expanding, firms need capital, and this demand for capital pushes rates up. Also, inflationary pressures are strongest during business booms, and that also exerts upward pressure on rates. Conditions are reversed during recessions such as the one that began in March 2001. Slack business reduces the demand for credit, the rate of inflation falls, and the result is a drop in interest rates. Furthermore, the Federal Reserve deliberately lowers rates during recessions to help stimulate the economy.

These tendencies do not hold exactly—the period after 1984 is a case in point. The price of oil fell dramatically in 1985 and 1986, reducing inflationary pressures on other prices and easing fears of serious long-term inflation. Earlier, these fears had pushed interest rates to record levels. The economy from 1984 to 1987 was strong, but the declining fears of inflation more than offset the normal tendency of interest rates to rise during good economic times, and the net result was lower interest rates.[6]

_____

[6] Short-term rates are responsive to current economic conditions, whereas long-term rates primarily reflect long-run expectations for inflation. As a result, short-term rates are sometimes above and sometimes below long-term rates. The relationship between long-term and short-term rates is called the *term structure of interest rates*, and it is discussed later in the chapter.

The relationship between inflation and long-term interest rates is highlighted in Figure 4-4, which plots rates of inflation along with long-term interest rates. In the early 1960s, inflation averaged 1 percent per year, and interest rates on high-quality, long-term bonds averaged 4 percent. Then the Vietnam War heated up, leading to an increase in inflation, and interest rates began an upward climb. When the war ended in the early 1970s, inflation dipped a bit, but then the 1973 Arab oil embargo led to rising oil prices, much higher inflation rates, and sharply higher interest rates.

Inflation peaked at about 13 percent in 1980, but interest rates continued to increase into 1981 and 1982, and they remained quite high until 1985, because people were afraid inflation would start to climb again. Thus, the "inflationary psychology" created during the 1970s persisted to the mid-1980s.

Gradually, though, people began to realize that the Federal Reserve was serious about keeping inflation down, that global competition was keeping U.S. auto producers and other corporations from raising prices as they had in the past, and that constraints on corporate price increases were diminishing labor unions' ability to push through cost-increasing wage hikes. As these realizations set in, interest rates declined.

The gap between the current interest rate and the current inflation rate is defined as the "current real rate of interest." It is called the "real rate" because it shows how much investors really earned after taking out the effects of inflation. The real rate was extremely high during the mid-1980s, but it averaged about 4 percent during the 1990s.

| FIGURE 4-4 | Relationship between Annual Inflation Rates and Long-Term Interest Rates, 1961–2001 |

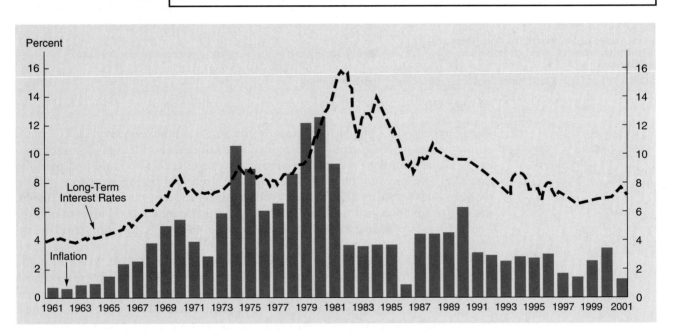

NOTES:
a. Interest rates are those on AAA long-term corporate bonds.
b. Inflation is measured as the annual rate of change in the Consumer Price Index (CPI).

SOURCES: Adapted from *Federal Reserve Bulletin; Federal Reserve Statistical Release.*

In recent years, inflation has been running at about 2.5 percent a year. However, long-term interest rates have been volatile, because investors are not sure if inflation is truly under control or is getting ready to jump back to the higher levels of the 1980s. In the years ahead, we can be sure that the level of interest rates will vary (1) with changes in the current rate of inflation and (2) with changes in expectations about future inflation.

SELF-TEST QUESTIONS

How are interest rates used to allocate capital among firms?

What happens to market-clearing, or equilibrium, interest rates in a capital market when the demand for funds declines? What happens when inflation increases or decreases?

Why does the price of capital change during booms and recessions?

How does risk affect interest rates?

THE DETERMINANTS OF MARKET INTEREST RATES

In general, the quoted (or nominal) interest rate on a debt security, k, is composed of a real risk-free rate of interest, k*, plus several premiums that reflect inflation, the riskiness of the security, and the security's marketability (or liquidity). This relationship can be expressed as follows:

$$\text{Quoted interest rate} = k = k^* + IP + DRP + LP + MRP. \qquad (4\text{-}1)$$

Here

k = the quoted, or nominal, rate of interest on a given security.[7] There are many different securities, hence many different quoted interest rates.

k^* = the real risk-free rate of interest. k^* is pronounced "k-star," and it is the rate that would exist on a riskless security if zero inflation were expected.

k_{RF} = $k^* + IP$, and it is the quoted risk-free rate of interest on a security such as a U.S. Treasury bill, which is very liquid and also free of most risks. Note that k_{RF} includes the premium for expected inflation, because $k_{RF} = k^* + IP$.

IP = inflation premium. IP is equal to the average expected inflation rate over the life of the security. The expected future inflation rate is not necessarily equal to the current inflation rate, so IP is not necessarily equal to current inflation as reported in Figure 4-4.

DRP = default risk premium. This premium reflects the possibility that the issuer will not pay interest or principal at the stated time and in the stated amount. DRP is zero for U.S. Treasury securities, but it rises as the riskiness of issuers increases.

LP = liquidity, or marketability, premium. This is a premium charged by lenders to reflect the fact that some securities cannot be converted to cash on short notice at a "reasonable" price. LP is very low for Treasury securities and for

---

[7] The term *nominal* as it is used here means the *stated* rate as opposed to the *real* rate, which is adjusted to remove inflation effects. If you had bought a 10-year Treasury bond in April 2002, the quoted, or nominal, rate would be about 5.2 percent, but if inflation averages 2.5 percent over the next 10 years, the real rate would be about 5.2% − 2.5% = 2.7%.

securities issued by large, strong firms, but it is relatively high on securities issued by very small firms.

MRP = maturity risk premium. As we will explain later, longer-term bonds, even Treasury bonds, are exposed to a significant risk of price declines, and a maturity risk premium is charged by lenders to reflect this risk.

As noted above, since $k_{RF} = k^* + IP$, we can rewrite Equation 4-1 as follows:

$$\text{Nominal, or quoted, rate} = k = k_{RF} + DRP + LP + MRP.$$

We discuss the components whose sum makes up the quoted, or nominal, rate on a given security in the following sections.

THE REAL RISK-FREE RATE OF INTEREST, k*

Real Risk-Free Rate of Interest, k*
The rate of interest that would exist on default-free U.S. Treasury securities if no inflation were expected.

The **real risk-free rate of interest, k*,** is defined as the interest rate that would exist on a riskless security if no inflation were expected, and it may be thought of as the rate of interest on *short-term* U.S. Treasury securities in an inflation-free world. The real risk-free rate is not static — it changes over time depending on economic conditions, especially (1) on the rate of return corporations and other borrowers expect to earn on productive assets and (2) on people's time preferences for current versus future consumption. Borrowers' expected returns on real asset investments set an upper limit on how much they can afford to pay for borrowed funds, while savers' time preferences for consumption establish how much consumption they are willing to defer, hence the amount of funds they will lend at different interest rates. It is difficult to measure the real risk-free rate precisely, but most experts think that k* has fluctuated in the range of 1 to 5 percent in recent years.[8] The best estimate of k* is the rate of return on indexed Treasury bonds, which are discussed in a box later in the chapter.

THE NOMINAL, OR QUOTED, RISK-FREE RATE OF INTEREST, k_{RF}

Nominal (Quoted) Risk-Free Rate, k_{RF}
The rate of interest on a security that is free of all risk; k_{RF} is proxied by the T-bill rate or the T-bond rate. k_{RF} includes an inflation premium.

The **nominal,** or **quoted, risk-free rate, k_{RF},** is the real risk-free rate plus a premium for expected inflation: $k_{RF} = k^* + IP$. To be strictly correct, the risk-free rate should mean the interest rate on a totally risk-free security — one that has no risk of default, no maturity risk, no liquidity risk, no risk of loss if inflation increases, and no risk of any other type. There is no such security, hence there is no observable truly risk-free rate. However, there is one security that is free of most risks — an indexed

---

[8] The real rate of interest as discussed here is different from the *current* real rate as discussed in connection with Figure 4-4. The current real rate is the current interest rate minus the current (or latest past) inflation rate, while the real rate, without the word "current," is the current interest rate minus the *expected future* inflation rate over the life of the security. For example, suppose the current quoted rate for a one-year Treasury bill is 5 percent, inflation during the latest year was 2 percent, and inflation expected for the coming year is 4 percent. Then the *current* real rate would be 5% − 2% = 3%, but the *expected* real rate would be 5% − 4% = 1%. The rate on a 10-year bond would be related to the expected inflation rate over the next 10 years, and so on. In the press, the term "real rate" generally means the current real rate, but in economics and finance, hence in this book unless otherwise noted, the real rate means the one based on *expected* inflation rates.

U.S. Treasury security. These securities are free of default, maturity, and liquidity risks, and also of risk due to changes in the general level of interest rates.[9]

If the term "risk-free rate" is used without either the modifier "real" or the modifier "nominal," people generally mean the quoted (nominal) rate, and we will follow that convention in this book. Therefore, when we use the term risk-free rate, k_{RF}, we mean the nominal risk-free rate, which includes an inflation premium equal to the average expected inflation rate over the life of the security. In general, we use the T-bill rate to approximate the short-term risk-free rate, and the T-bond rate to approximate the long-term risk-free rate. So, whenever you see the term "risk-free rate," assume that we are referring either to the quoted U.S. T-bill rate or to the quoted T-bond rate.

INFLATION PREMIUM (IP)

Inflation has a major impact on interest rates because it erodes the purchasing power of the dollar and lowers the real rate of return on investments. To illustrate, suppose you saved $1,000 and invested it in a Treasury bill that matures in one year and pays a 5 percent interest rate. At the end of the year, you will receive $1,050 — your original $1,000 plus $50 of interest. Now suppose the inflation rate during the year is 10 percent, and it affects all items equally. If gas had cost $1 per gallon at the beginning of the year, it would cost $1.10 at the end of the year. Therefore, your $1,000 would have bought $1,000/$1 = 1,000 gallons at the beginning of the year, but only $1,050/$1.10 = 955 gallons at the end. In *real terms*, you would be worse off — you would receive $50 of interest, but it would not be sufficient to offset inflation. You would thus be better off buying 1,000 gallons of gas (or some other storable asset such as land, timber, apartment buildings, wheat, or gold) than buying the Treasury bill.

Inflation Premium (IP)
A premium equal to expected inflation that investors add to the real risk-free rate of return.

Investors are well aware of all this, so when they lend money, they build in an **inflation premium (IP)** equal to the average expected inflation rate over the life of the security. As discussed previously, for a short-term, default-free U.S. Treasury bill, the actual interest rate charged, $k_{T\text{-bill}}$, would be the real risk-free rate, k^*, plus the inflation premium (IP):

$$k_{T\text{-bill}} = k_{RF} = k^* + IP.$$

Therefore, if the real risk-free rate of interest were $k^* = 2.8\%$, and if inflation were expected to be 2 percent (and hence IP = 2%) during the next year, then the quoted rate of interest on one-year T-bills would be 2.8% + 2% = 4.8%.

It is important to note that the inflation rate built into interest rates is the *inflation rate expected in the future*, not the rate experienced in the past. Thus, the latest reported figures might show an annual inflation rate of 3.3 percent, but that is for the *past* year. If people on the average expect a 6 percent inflation rate in the future, then 6 percent would be built into the current interest rate. Note also that the inflation rate reflected in the quoted interest rate on any security is the *average rate of inflation expected over the security's life*. Thus, the inflation rate built into a one-year bond is the

---

[9] Indexed Treasury securities are the closest thing we have to a riskless security, but even they are not totally riskless, because k^* itself can change and cause a decline in the prices of these securities. For example, between October 1998 and January 2000, the price of one indexed Treasury security declined from 98 to 89, or by almost 10 percent. The cause was an increase in the real rate on long-term securities from 3.7 percent to 4.4 percent. Two years later, the real rate on long-term securities has dropped to 3.375 percent.

expected inflation rate for the next year, but the inflation rate built into a 30-year bond is the average rate of inflation expected over the next 30 years.[10]

Expectations for future inflation are closely, but not perfectly, correlated with rates experienced in the recent past. Therefore, if the inflation rate reported for last month increased, people would tend to raise their expectations for future inflation, and this change in expectations would cause an increase in interest rates.

Note that Germany, Japan, and Switzerland have over the past several years had lower inflation rates than the United States, hence their interest rates have generally been lower than ours. Italy and most South American countries have experienced high inflation, and that is reflected in their interest rates.

Default Risk Premium (DRP)

The risk that a borrower will *default* on a loan, which means not pay the interest or the principal, also affects the market interest rate on a security: the greater the default risk, the higher the interest rate. Treasury securities have no default risk, hence they carry the lowest interest rates on taxable securities in the United States. For corporate bonds, the higher the bond's rating, the lower its default risk, and, consequently, the lower its interest rate.[11] Here are some representative interest rates on long-term bonds during February 2002:

	RATE	DRP
U.S. Treasury	5.4%	—
AAA	6.5	1.1%
AA	7.0	1.6
A	7.4	2.0
BBB	7.9	2.5

Default Risk Premium (DRP)
The difference between the interest rate on a U.S. Treasury bond and a corporate bond of equal maturity and marketability.

The difference between the quoted interest rate on a T-bond and that on a corporate bond with similar maturity, liquidity, and other features is the **default risk premium (DRP).** Therefore, if the bonds listed above were otherwise similar, the default risk premium would be DRP = 6.5% − 5.4% = 1.1 percentage points for AAA corporate bonds, 7.0% − 5.4% = 1.6 percentage points for AA, 7.4% − 5.4% =

---

[10] To be theoretically precise, we should use a *geometric average*. Also, since millions of investors are active in the market, it is impossible to determine exactly the consensus expected inflation rate. Survey data are available, however, which give us a reasonably good idea of what investors expect over the next few years. For example, in 1980 the University of Michigan's Survey Research Center reported that people expected inflation during the next year to be 11.9 percent and that the average rate of inflation expected over the next 5 to 10 years was 10.5 percent. Those expectations led to record-high interest rates. However, the economy cooled in 1981 and 1982, and, as Figure 4-4 showed, actual inflation dropped sharply after 1980. This led to gradual reductions in the *expected future* inflation rate. As inflationary expectations change, so do quoted market interest rates.

[11] Bond ratings, and bonds' riskiness in general, are discussed in detail in Chapter 7. For now, merely note that bonds rated AAA are judged to have less default risk than bonds rated AA, while AA bonds are less risky than A bonds, and so on. Ratings are designated AAA or Aaa, AA or Aa, and so forth, depending on the rating agency. In this book, the designations are used interchangeably.

2.0 percentage points for A corporate bonds, and so forth. Default risk premiums vary somewhat over time, but the February 2002 figures are representative of levels in recent years.

LIQUIDITY PREMIUM (LP)

Liquidity Premium (LP)
A premium added to the equilibrium interest rate on a security if that security cannot be converted to cash on short notice and at close to "fair market value."

A "liquid" asset can be converted to cash quickly and at a "fair market value." Financial assets are generally more liquid than real assets. Because liquidity is important, investors include **liquidity premiums (LPs)** when market rates of securities are established. Although it is difficult to accurately measure liquidity premiums, a differential of at least two and probably four or five percentage points exists between the least liquid and the most liquid financial assets of similar default risk and maturity.

MATURITY RISK PREMIUM (MRP)

Interest Rate Risk
The risk of capital losses to which investors are exposed because of changing interest rates.

Maturity Risk Premium (MRP)
A premium that reflects interest rate risk.

Reinvestment Rate Risk
The risk that a decline in interest rates will lead to lower income when bonds mature and funds are reinvested.

U.S. Treasury securities are free of default risk in the sense that one can be virtually certain that the federal government will pay interest on its bonds and will also pay them off when they mature. Therefore, the default risk premium on Treasury securities is essentially zero. Further, active markets exist for Treasury securities, so their liquidity premiums are also close to zero. Thus, as a first approximation, the rate of interest on a Treasury bond should be the risk-free rate, k_{RF}, which is equal to the real risk-free rate, k^*, plus an inflation premium, IP. However, an adjustment is needed for long-term Treasury bonds. The prices of long-term bonds decline sharply whenever interest rates rise, and since interest rates can and do occasionally rise, all long-term bonds, even Treasury bonds, have an element of risk called **interest rate risk.** As a general rule, the bonds of any organization, from the U.S. government to Continental Airlines, have more interest rate risk the longer the maturity of the bond.[12] Therefore, a **maturity risk premium (MRP),** which is higher the longer the years to maturity, must be included in the required interest rate.

The effect of maturity risk premiums is to raise interest rates on long-term bonds relative to those on short-term bonds. This premium, like the others, is difficult to measure, but (1) it varies somewhat over time, rising when interest rates are more volatile and uncertain, then falling when interest rates are more stable, and (2) in recent years, the maturity risk premium on 30-year T-bonds appears to have generally been in the range of one or two percentage points.[13]

We should mention that although long-term bonds are heavily exposed to interest rate risk, short-term bills are heavily exposed to **reinvestment rate risk.** When short-term bills mature and the funds are reinvested, or "rolled over," a decline in interest rates would necessitate reinvestment at a lower rate, and this would result in a decline in interest income. To illustrate, suppose you had $100,000 invested in one-year

---

[12] For example, if someone had bought a 30-year Treasury bond for $1,000 in 1998, when the long-term interest rate was 5.25 percent, and held it until April 2002, when long-term T-bond rates were about 5.7 percent, the value of the bond would have declined to about $936. That would represent a loss of 6.4 percent, and it demonstrates that long-term bonds, even U.S. Treasury bonds, are not riskless. However, had the investor purchased short-term T-bills in 1998 and subsequently reinvested the principal each time the bills matured, he or she would still have had $1,000. This point will be discussed in detail in Chapter 7.

[13] The MRP for long-term bonds has averaged 1.3 percent over the last 76 years. See *Stocks, Bonds, Bills, and Inflation: (Valuation Edition) 2002 Yearbook* (Chicago: Ibbotson Associates, 2002).

AN ALMOST RISKLESS TREASURY BOND

Investors who purchase bonds must constantly worry about inflation. If inflation turns out to be greater than expected, bonds will provide a lower-than-expected real return. To protect themselves against expected increases in inflation, investors build an inflation risk premium into their required rate of return. This raises borrowers' costs.

In order to provide investors with an inflation-protected bond, and also to reduce the cost of debt to the government, on January 29, 1997, the U.S. Treasury issued $7 billion of 10-year inflation-indexed bonds. These initial bonds paid an interest rate of 3.375 percent plus an additional amount to offset inflation. At the end of each six-month period, the principal (originally set at par, or $1,000) is adjusted by the inflation rate. For example, during the first six-month interest period, inflation (as measured by the CPI) was 1.085 percent. The inflation-adjusted principal was then calculated as $1,000(1 + inflation) = $1,000 × 1.01085 = $1,010.85. So, on July 15, 1997, each bond paid interest of 0.03375/2 × $1,010.85 = $17.06. Note that the interest rate is divided by two because interest is paid twice a year.

By January 15, 1998, a bit more inflation had occurred, and the inflation-adjusted principal was up to $1,019.69, so on January 15, 1998, each bond paid interest of 0.03375/2 × $1,019.69 = $17.21. Thus, the total return during the first year consisted of $17.06 + $17.21 = $34.27 of interest and $1,019.69 − $1,000.00 = $19.69 of "capital gains," or $34.27 + $19.69 = $53.96 in total. Thus, the total return was $53.96/$1,000 = 5.396%.

This same adjustment process will continue each year until the bonds mature on January 15, 2007, at which time they will pay the adjusted maturity value. Thus, the cash income provided by the bonds rises by exactly enough to cover inflation, producing a real, inflation-adjusted rate of 3.375 percent. Further, since the principal also rises by the inflation rate, it too is protected from inflation. The accompanying table gives the inflation-adjusted principal and interest paid during the life of these 3⅜ percent coupon, 10-year, inflation-indexed bonds:

DATE	INFLATION-ADJUSTED PRINCIPAL	INTEREST PAID
7/15/97	$1,010.85	$17.06
1/15/98	1,019.69	17.21
7/15/98	1,026.51	17.32
1/15/99	1,035.12	17.47
7/15/99	1,049.01	17.70
1/15/00	1,061.92	17.92
7/15/00	1,080.85	18.24
1/15/01	1,098.52	18.54
7/15/01	1,118.82	18.88
1/15/02	1,120.74	18.91

SOURCE: Bureau of the Public Debt's Online, Historical Reference CPI Numbers and Daily Index Ratios for 3⅜%, 10-year note due January 15, 2007, at **http://www.publicdebt.treas.gov/of/ofhiscpi.htm**.

The Treasury regularly conducts auctions to issue indexed bonds. The 3.375 percent rate was based on the relative supply and demand for the issue, and it will remain constant over the

T-bills, and you lived on the income. In 1981, short-term rates were about 15 percent, so your income would have been about $15,000. However, your income would have declined to about $9,000 by 1983, and to just $2,370 by 2002. Had you invested your money in long-term T-bonds, your income (but not the value of the principal) would have been stable.[14] Thus, although "investing short" preserves one's principal, the interest income provided by short-term T-bills is less stable than the interest income on long-term bonds.

---

[14] Long-term bonds also have some reinvestment rate risk. If one is saving and investing for some future purpose, say, to buy a house or for retirement, then to actually earn the quoted rate on a long-term bond, the interest payments must be reinvested at the quoted rate. However, if interest rates fall, the interest payments must be reinvested at a lower rate; thus, the realized return would be less than the quoted rate. Note, though, that reinvestment rate risk is lower on a long-term bond than on a short-term bond because only the interest payments (rather than interest plus principal) on the long-term bond are exposed to reinvestment rate risk. Zero coupon bonds, which are discussed in Chapter 7, are completely free of reinvestment rate risk during their life.

life of the bond. However, new bonds are issued periodically, and their "coupon" real rates depend on the market at the time the bond is auctioned. In January 2002, 10-year indexed securities had a real rate of 3.375 percent.

Federal Reserve Board Chairman Greenspan lobbied in favor of the indexed bonds on the grounds that they would help him and the Fed make better estimates of investors' expectations about inflation. He did not explain his reasoning (to our knowledge), but it might have gone something like this:

- We know that interest rates in general are determined as follows:

$$k = k^* + IP + MRP + DRP + LP.$$

- For Treasury bonds, DRP and LP are essentially zero, so for a 10-year bond the rate is

$$k_{RF} = k^* + IP + MRP.$$

The reason the MRP is not zero is that if inflation increases, interest rates will rise and the price of the bonds will decline. Therefore, "regular" 10-year bonds are exposed to maturity risk, hence a maturity risk premium is built into their market interest rate.

- The indexed bonds are protected against inflation—if inflation increases, then so will their dollar returns, and as a result, their price will not decline in real terms. Therefore, indexed bonds should have no MRP, hence their market return is

$$k_{RF} = k^* + 0 + 0 = k^*.$$

In other words, the market rate on indexed bonds is the real rate.

- The difference between the yield on a regular 10-year bond and that on an indexed bond is the sum of the 10-year bonds' IP and MRP. In 1997, the yield on regular 10-year bonds was 6.80 percent when the first indexed bonds were issued, and the indexed bonds' yield was 3.375 percent. The difference, 3.425 percent, is the average expected inflation rate over the next 10 years plus the MRP for 10-year bonds.
- The 10-year MRP is about 1.0 percent, and it has been relatively stable in recent years. Therefore, the expected rate of inflation in January 1997 was about 2.425 percent (3.425% − 1.00% = 2.425%).

The interest received and the increase in principal are taxed each year as interest income, even though cash from the appreciation will not be received until the bond matures. Therefore, these bonds are especially suitable for individual retirement accounts (IRAs), which are not taxed until funds are withdrawn.

Keep in mind, though, that despite their protection against inflation, indexed bonds are not completely riskless. The real rate of interest can change, and if k* rises, the price of the indexed bonds will decline. This just confirms one more time that there is no such thing as a free lunch or a riskless security!

SOURCES: "Inflation Notes Will Offer Fed Forecast Tool," *The Wall Street Journal*, February 3, 1997, C1; and *The Wall Street Journal*, January 6, 2000, C21.

SELF-TEST QUESTIONS

Write out an equation for the nominal interest rate on any debt security.

Distinguish between the *real* risk-free rate of interest, k*, and the *nominal*, or *quoted*, risk-free rate of interest, k_{RF}.

How is inflation dealt with when interest rates are determined by investors in the financial markets?

Does the interest rate on a T-bond include a default risk premium? Explain.

Distinguish between liquid and illiquid assets, and identify some assets that are liquid and some that are illiquid.

Briefly explain the following statement: "Although long-term bonds are heavily exposed to interest rate risk, short-term bills are heavily exposed to reinvestment rate risk. The maturity risk premium reflects the net effects of these two opposing forces."

THE TERM STRUCTURE OF INTEREST RATES

Term Structure of Interest Rates
The relationship between bond yields and maturities.

Yield Curve
A graph showing the relationship between bond yields and maturities.

 www Students can find current U.S. Treasury yield curve graphs and other global and domestic interest rate information at Bloomberg markets' site at **http://www.bloomberg.com/markets/index.html**.

"Normal" Yield Curve
An upward-sloping yield curve.

Inverted ("Abnormal") Yield Curve
A downward-sloping yield curve.

Humped Yield Curve
A yield curve where interest rates on medium-term maturities are higher than rates on both short- and long-term maturities.

The **term structure of interest rates** describes the relationship between long- and short-term rates. The term structure is important to corporate treasurers who must decide whether to borrow by issuing long- or short-term debt and to investors who must decide whether to buy long- or short-term bonds. Thus, it is important to understand (1) how long- and short-term rates relate to each other and (2) what causes shifts in their relative positions.

Interest rates for bonds with different maturities can be found in a variety of publications, including *The Wall Street Journal* and the *Federal Reserve Bulletin*, and on a number of web sites, including Bloomberg, Yahoo, and CNN Financial. From interest rate data obtained from these sources, we can construct the term structure at a given point in time. For example, the tabular section below Figure 4-5 presents interest rates for different maturities on three different dates. The set of data for a given date, when plotted on a graph such as that in Figure 4-5 is called the **yield curve** for that date.

The yield curve changes both in position and in slope over time. In March 1980, all rates were relatively high, and since short-term rates were higher than long-term rates, the yield curve was *downward sloping*. However, by February 2000, all rates were lower, and the yield curve had become *humped* — medium-term rates were higher than both short- and long-term rates. Roughly two years later, all rates had fallen below the 2000 levels, and because short-term rates were lower than long-term rates, the yield curve was *upward sloping*.

Figure 4-5 shows yield curves for U.S. Treasury securities, but we could have constructed curves for corporate bonds issued by AT&T, IBM, Delta Airlines, or any other company that borrows money over a range of maturities. Had we constructed corporate curves and plotted them on Figure 4-5, they would have been above those for Treasury securities because corporate yields include default risk premiums. However, the corporate yield curves would have had the same general shape as the Treasury curves. Also, the riskier the corporation, the higher its yield curve, so Delta Airlines, which has a lower bond rating than either AT&T or IBM, would have a higher yield curve than those of AT&T and IBM.

Historically, in most years long-term rates have been above short-term rates, so the yield curve usually slopes upward. For this reason, people often call an upward-sloping yield curve a **"normal" yield curve** and a yield curve that slopes downward an **inverted,** or **"abnormal" curve.** Thus, in Figure 4-5 the yield curve for March 1980 was inverted, while the yield curve in April 2002 was normal. However, the February 2000 curve was **humped,** which means that interest rates on medium-term maturities were higher than rates on both short- and long-term maturities. We explain in detail in the next section why an upward slope is the normal situation, but briefly, the reason is that short-term securities have less interest rate risk than longer-term securities, hence smaller MRPs. Therefore, short-term rates are normally lower than long-term rates.

SELF-TEST QUESTIONS

What is a yield curve, and what information would you need to draw this curve?

Distinguish among the shapes of a "normal" yield curve, an "abnormal" curve, and a "humped" curve.

FIGURE 4-5

U.S. Treasury Bond Interest Rates on Different Dates

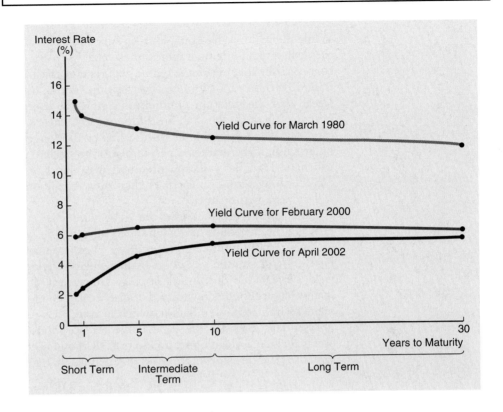

TERM TO MATURITY	INTEREST RATE		
	MARCH 1980	FEBRUARY 2000	APRIL 2002
6 months	15.0%	6.0%	2.0%
1 year	14.0	6.2	2.3
5 years	13.5	6.7	4.5
10 years	12.8	6.7	5.2
30 years	12.3	6.3	5.7

WHAT DETERMINES THE SHAPE OF THE YIELD CURVE?

Since maturity risk premiums are positive, then if other things were held constant, long-term bonds would have higher interest rates than short-term bonds. However, market interest rates also depend on expected inflation, default risk, and liquidity, and each of these factors can vary with maturity.

Expected inflation has an especially important effect on the yield curve's shape. To see why, consider U.S. Treasury securities. Because Treasuries have essentially no default or liquidity risk, the yield on a Treasury bond that matures in t years can be expressed as follows:

$$k^*_t + IP_t + MRP_t.$$

While the real risk-free rate, k^*, may vary somewhat over time because of changes in the economy and demographics, these changes are random rather than predictable, so it is reasonable to assume that k^* will remain constant. However, the inflation premium, IP, does vary significantly over time, and in a somewhat predictable manner. Recall that the inflation premium is simply the average level of expected inflation over the life of the bond. Thus, if the market expects inflation to increase in the future, the inflation premium will be higher the longer the bond's maturity. On the other hand, if the market expects inflation to decline in the future, long-term bonds will have a smaller inflation premium than short-term bonds. Finally, if investors consider long-term bonds riskier than short-term bonds, the maturity risk premium will increase with maturity.

Panel a of Figure 4-6 shows the yield curve when inflation is expected to increase. Here long-term bonds have higher yields for two reasons: (1) Inflation is expected to be higher in the future, and (2) there is a positive maturity risk premium. Panel b of Figure 4-6 shows the yield curve when inflation is expected to decline, causing the yield curve to be downward sloping. Downward sloping yield curves often foreshadow an economic downturn, because weaker economic conditions tend to be correlated with declining inflation, which in turn leads to lower long-term rates.

Now let's consider the yield curve for corporate bonds. Recall that corporate bonds include a default-risk premium (DRP) and a liquidity premium (LP). Therefore, the yield on a corporate bond that matures in t years can be expressed as follows:

$$k^*_t + IP_t + MRP_t + DRP_t + LP_t.$$

A corporate bond's default and liquidity risks are affected by its maturity. For example, the default risk on Coca-Cola's short-term debt is very small, since there is almost no chance that Coca-Cola will go bankrupt over the next few years. However, Coke has some 100-year bonds, and while the odds of Coke defaulting on these bonds still might not be that high, the default risk on these bonds is considerably higher than that on its short-term debt.

Longer-term corporate bonds are also less liquid than shorter-term debt, hence the liquidity premium rises as maturity lengthens. The primary reason for this is that, for the reasons discussed earlier, short-term debt has less default risk, so a buyer can buy short-term debt without having to do as much credit checking as would be necessary for long-term debt. Thus, people can move into and out of short-term corporate debt much more rapidly than long-term debt. The end result is that short-term corporate debt is more liquid, hence has a smaller liquidity premium than the same company's long-term debt.

Figure 4-7 shows yield curves for two hypothetical corporate bonds, an AA-rated bond with minimal default risk and a BBB-rated bond with more default risk, along with the yield curve for Treasury securities as taken from Panel a of Figure 4-6. Here we assume that inflation is expected to increase, so the Treasury yield curve is upward sloping. Because of their additional default and liquidity risk, corporate bonds always trade at a higher yield than Treasury bonds with the same maturity, and BBB-rated bonds trade at higher yields than AA-rated bonds. Finally, note that the yield spread between corporate bonds and Treasury bonds is larger the longer the maturity. This occurs because longer-term corporate bonds have more default and liquidity risk than shorter-term bonds, and both of these premiums are absent in Treasury bonds.

How do maturity risk premiums affect the yield curve?

If the rate of inflation is expected to increase, would this increase or decrease the slope of the yield curve?

If the rate of inflation is expected to remain constant in the future, would the yield curve slope up, down, or be horizontal?

Explain why corporate bonds' default and liquidity premiums are likely to increase with maturity.

Explain why corporate bonds always trade at higher yields than Treasury bonds and why BBB-rated bonds always trade at higher yields than AA-rated bonds.

FIGURE 4-6　　**Illustrative Treasury Yield Curves**

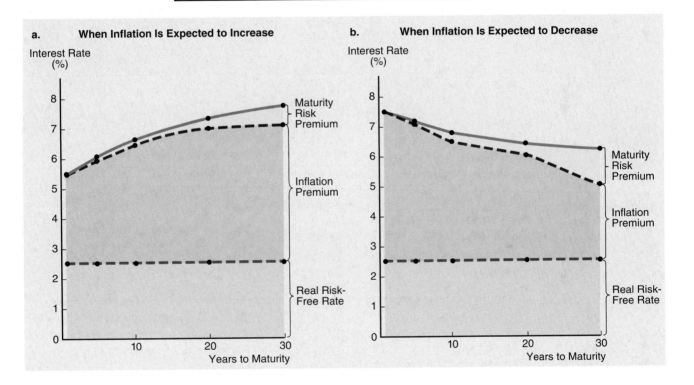

MATURITY	WITH INCREASING EXPECTED INFLATION				MATURITY	WITH DECREASING EXPECTED INFLATION			
	k*	IP	MRP	YIELD		k*	IP	MRP	YIELD
1 year	2.50%	3.00%	0.00%	**5.50%**	1 year	2.50%	5.00%	0.00%	**7.50%**
5 years	2.50	3.40	0.18	**6.08**	5 years	2.50	4.60	0.18	**7.28**
10 years	2.50	4.00	0.28	**6.78**	10 years	2.50	4.00	0.28	**6.78**
20 years	2.50	4.50	0.42	**7.42**	20 years	2.50	3.50	0.42	**6.42**
30 years	2.50	4.67	0.53	**7.70**	30 years	2.50	3.33	0.53	**6.36**

FIGURE 4-7 | Corporate and Treasury Yield Curves

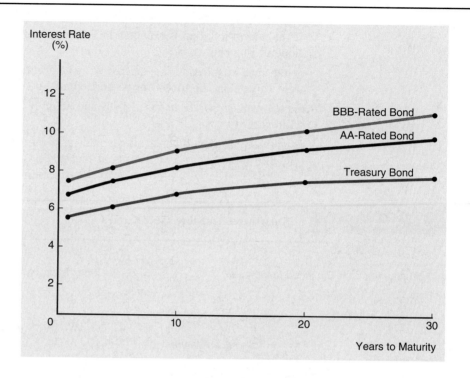

TERM TO MATURITY	INTEREST RATE		
	TREASURY BOND	AA-RATED BOND	BBB-RATED BOND
1 year	5.5%	6.7%	7.4%
5 years	6.1	7.4	8.1
10 years	6.8	8.2	9.1
20 years	7.4	9.2	10.2
30 years	7.7	9.8	11.1

USING THE YIELD CURVE TO ESTIMATE FUTURE INTEREST RATES[15]

In the last section we saw that the shape of the yield curve depends primarily on two factors: (1) expectations about future inflation and (2) the relative riskiness of securities with different maturities. We also saw how to calculate the yield curve, given inflation and maturity-related risks. In practice, this process often works in reverse: Investors and analysts plot the yield curve and then use information embedded in it to estimate the market's expectations regarding future inflation and risk.

---

[15]This section is relatively technical, but instructors can omit it without loss of continuity.

This process of using the yield curve to estimate future expected interest rates is straightforward, provided (1) we focus on Treasury securities, and (2) we assume that all Treasury securities have the same risk; that is, there is no maturity risk premium. Some academics and practitioners contend that this second assumption is reasonable, at least as an approximation. They argue that the market is dominated by large bond traders who buy and sell securities of different maturities each day, that these traders focus only on short-term returns, and that they are not concerned with risk. According to this view, a bond trader is just as willing to buy a 30-year bond to pick up a short-term profit as he would be to buy a three-month security. Strict proponents of this view argue that the shape of the yield curve is therefore determined only by market expectations about future interest rates, thus their position has been called the *pure expectations theory* of the term structure of interest rates.

Expectations Theory
A theory which states that the shape of the yield curve depends on investors' expectations about future interest rates.

The pure **expectations theory** (which is sometimes simply referred to as the "expectations theory") assumes that investors establish bond prices and interest rates strictly on the basis of expectations for interest rates. This means that they are indifferent with respect to maturity in the sense that they do not view long-term bonds as being riskier than short-term bonds. If this were true, then the maturity risk premium (MRP) would be zero, and long-term interest rates would simply be a weighted average of current and expected future short-term interest rates. For example, if 1-year Treasury bills currently yield 7 percent, but 1-year bills were expected to yield 7.5 percent a year from now, investors would expect to earn an average of 7.25 percent over the next two years.[16]

$$\frac{7\% + 7.5\%}{2} = 7.25\%.$$

According to the expectations theory, this implies that a 2-year Treasury note purchased today should also yield 7.25 percent. Similarly, if 10-year bonds yield 9 percent today, and if 5-year bonds are expected to yield 7.5 percent 10 years from now, then investors should expect to earn 9 percent for 10 years and 7.5 percent for 5 years, for an average return of 8.5 percent over the next 15 years:

$$\frac{9\% + 9\% + \cdots + 9\% + 7.5\% + \cdots + 7.5\%}{15} = \frac{10(9\%) + 5(7.5\%)}{15} = 8.5\%.$$

Consequently, a 15-year bond should yield this same return, 8.5 percent.

To understand the logic behind this averaging process, ask yourself what would happen if long-term yields were *not* an average of expected short-term yields. For example, suppose 2-year bonds yielded only 7 percent, not the 7.25 percent calculated above. Bond traders would be able to earn a profit by adopting the following trading strategy:

1. Borrow money for two years at a cost of 7 percent.
2. Invest the money in a series of 1-year bonds. The expected return over the 2-year period would be (7.0 + 7.5)/2 = 7.25%.

In this case, bond traders would rush to borrow money (demand funds) in the 2-year market and invest (or supply funds) in the 1-year market. Recall from Figure 4-2 that

---

[16] Technically, we should be using geometric averages rather than arithmetic averages, but the differences are not material in this example. For a discussion of this point, see Robert C. Radcliffe, *Investment: Concepts, Analysis, and Strategy*, 5th ed. (Reading, MA: Addison-Wesley, 1997), Chapter 5.

an increase in the demand for funds raises interest rates, whereas an increase in the supply of funds reduces interest rates. Therefore, bond traders' actions would push up the 2-year yield but reduce the yield on 1-year bonds. The net effect would be to bring about a market equilibrium in which 2-year rates were a weighted average of expected future 1-year rates.

Under these assumptions, we can "back out" of the yield curve the bond market's best guess about future interest rates. If, for example, you observe that Treasury securities with 1- and 2-year maturities yield 7 percent and 8 percent, respectively, this information can be used to calculate the market's forecast of what 1-year rates will yield one year from now. If the pure expectations theory is correct, the rate on 2-year bonds is the average of the current 1-year rate and the 1-year rate expected a year from now. Since the current 1-year rate is 7 percent, this implies that the 1-year rate one year from now is expected to be 9 percent:

$$\text{2-year yield} = 8\% = \frac{7\% + X\%}{2}$$

$$X = 16\% - 7\% = 9\% = \text{1-year yield expected next year.}$$

The preceding analysis was based on the assumption that the maturity risk premium is zero. However, most evidence suggests that there is a positive maturity risk premium, so the MRP should be taken into account.

For example, assume once again that 1- and 2-year maturities yield 7 percent and 8 percent, respectively, but now assume that the maturity risk premium on the 2-year bond is 0.5 percent. This maturity risk premium implies that the expected return on 2-year bonds (8 percent) is 0.5 percent higher than the expected returns from buying a series of 1-year bonds (7.5 percent). With this background, we can use the following two-step procedure to back out X, the expected 1-year rate one year from now:

Step 1: 2-year yield − MRP on 2-year bond = 8.0% − 0.5% = 7.5%.

Step 2: 7.5% = (7.0% + X%)/2

X = 15.0% − 7.0% = 8.0%.

Therefore, the yield next year on a 1-year T-bond should be 8 percent, up from 7 percent this year.

SELF-TEST QUESTIONS

What key assumption underlies the pure expectations theory?

Assuming that the pure expectations theory is correct, how are long-term interest rates calculated?

According to the pure expectations theory, what would happen if long-term rates were *not* an average of expected short-term rates?

INVESTING OVERSEAS

Country Risk
The risk that arises from investing or doing business in a particular country.

Investors should consider additional risk factors before investing overseas. First there is **country risk,** which refers to the risk that arises from investing or doing business in a particular country. This risk depends on the country's economic, political, and social environment. Countries with stable economic, social, political, and regulatory systems provide a safer climate for investment, and therefore less country risk, than less stable nations. Examples of country risk include the risk associated with changes in tax rates, regulations, currency conversion, and exchange rates. Country risk also includes the risk that property will be expropriated without adequate compensation, as well as new host country stipulations about local production, sourcing or hiring practices, and damage or destruction of facilities due to internal strife.

Exchange Rate Risk
The risk that exchange rate changes will reduce the number of dollars provided by a given amount of a foreign currency.

A second point to keep in mind when investing overseas is that more often than not the security will be denominated in a currency other than the dollar, which means that the value of your investment will depend on what happens to exchange rates. This is known as **exchange rate risk.** For example, if a U.S. investor purchases a Japanese bond, interest will probably be paid in Japanese yen, which must then be converted into dollars if the investor wants to spend his or her money in the United States. If the yen weakens relative to the dollar, then it will buy fewer dollars, hence the investor will receive fewer dollars when it comes time to convert. Alternatively, if the yen strengthens relative to the dollar, the investor will earn higher dollar returns. It therefore follows that the effective rate of return on a foreign investment will depend on both the performance of the foreign security and on what happens to exchange rates over the life of the investment.

SELF-TEST QUESTIONS

What is country risk?

What is exchange rate risk?

OTHER FACTORS THAT INFLUENCE INTEREST RATE LEVELS

In addition to inflationary expectations, other factors also influence both the general level of interest rates and the shape of the yield curve. The four most important factors are (1) Federal Reserve policy; (2) the federal budget deficit or surplus; (3) international factors, including the foreign trade balance and interest rates in other countries; and (4) the level of business activity.

FEDERAL RESERVE POLICY

The home page for the Board of Governors of the Federal Reserve System can be found at **http://www.federalreserve.gov/**. You can access general information about the Federal Reserve, including press releases, speeches, and monetary policy.

As you probably learned in your economics courses, (1) the money supply has a major effect on both the level of economic activity and the inflation rate, and (2) in the United States, the Federal Reserve Board controls the money supply. If the Fed

MEASURING COUNTRY RISK

Various forecasting services measure the level of country risk in different countries and provide indexes that measure factors such as each country's expected economic performance, access to world capital markets, political stability, and level of internal conflict. Country risk analysts use sophisticated models to measure it, thus providing corporate managers and overseas investors with a way to judge both the relative and absolute risk of investing in a given country. A sample of recent country risk estimates compiled by *Institutional Investor* is presented in the following table. The higher the country's score, the lower its estimated country risk. The maximum possible score is 100.

The countries with the least amount of country risk all have strong, market-based economies, ready access to worldwide capital markets, relatively little social unrest, and a stable political climate. Switzerland's top ranking may surprise you, but that country's ranking is the result of its strong economic performance. You may also be surprised that the United States was not ranked in the top five—it is ranked seventh.

Arguably, there are fewer surprises when looking at the bottom five. Each of these countries has considerable social and political unrest, and none has embraced a market-based economic system. Clearly, an investment in any of these countries is a risky proposition.

Top Five Countries (Least Amount of Country Risk)

RANK	COUNTRY	TOTAL SCORE (MAXIMUM POSSIBLE = 100)
1	Switzerland	95.6
2	Luxembourg	94.2
3	Germany	94.1
4	Netherlands	93.8
5	United Kingdom	93.7

Bottom Five Countries (Greatest Amount of Country Risk)

RANK	COUNTRY	TOTAL SCORE (MINIMUM POSSIBLE = 0)
147	North Korea	8.8
148	Democratic Republic of Congo	8.4
149	Sierra Leone	8.3
150	Liberia	8.0
151	Afganistan	4.5

SOURCE: Adapted from Harvey D. Shapiro, "Looking Up," *Institutional Investor*, March 2002, 165–167.

wants to stimulate the economy, as it did in 1995, it increases growth in the money supply. The initial effect of such an action is to cause interest rates to decline. However, a larger money supply may also lead to an increase in the expected inflation rate, which, in turn, could push interest rates up. The reverse holds if the Fed tightens the money supply.

To illustrate, in 1981 inflation was quite high, so the Fed tightened up the money supply. The Fed deals primarily in the short-term end of the market, so this tightening had the direct effect of pushing short-term rates up sharply. At the same time, the very fact that the Fed was taking strong action to reduce inflation led to a decline in expectations for long-run inflation, which led to a decline in long-term bond yields.

In 1991, the situation was just the reverse. To combat the recession, the Fed took steps to reduce interest rates. Short-term rates fell, and long-term rates also dropped, but not as sharply. These lower rates benefited heavily indebted businesses and individual borrowers, and home mortgage refinancings put additional billions of dollars into consumers' pockets. Savers, of course, lost out, but the net effect of lower interest rates was a stronger economy. Lower rates encourage businesses to borrow for investment, stimulate the housing market, and bring down the value of the dollar relative to other currencies, which helps U.S. exporters and thus lowers the trade deficit.

During periods when the Fed is actively intervening in the markets, the yield curve may be temporarily distorted. Short-term rates will be temporarily "too low" if the Fed is easing credit, and "too high" if it is tightening credit. Long-term rates are not affected as much by Fed intervention. For example, the fear of rising inflation led the Federal Reserve to increase short-term interest rates six times during 1994. While short-term rates rose by nearly 4 percentage points, long-term rates increased by only 1.5 percentage points.

BUDGET DEFICITS OR SURPLUSES

If the federal government spends more than it takes in from tax revenues, it runs a deficit, and that deficit must be covered either by borrowing or by printing money (increasing the money supply). If the government borrows, this added demand for funds pushes up interest rates. If it prints money, this increases expectations for future inflation, which also drives up interest rates. Thus, the larger the federal deficit, other things held constant, the higher the level of interest rates. Whether long- or short-term rates are more affected depends on how the deficit is financed, so we cannot state, in general, how deficits will affect the slope of the yield curve.

Over the past several decades, the federal government routinely ran large budget deficits. However, in 1999, for the first time in recent memory, the government had a budget surplus, and further surpluses are projected on into the future. As a result, the government is buying back some of the outstanding Treasury securities. If these surpluses become a reality, the government would become a net supplier of funds rather than a net borrower of funds. All else equal, this would tend to reduce interest rates.

INTERNATIONAL FACTORS

Businesses and individuals in the United States buy from and sell to people and firms in other countries. If we buy more than we sell (that is, if we import more than we export), we are said to be running a *foreign trade deficit*. When trade deficits occur, they must be financed, and the main source of financing is debt. In other words, if we import $200 billion of goods but export only $100 billion, we run a trade deficit of

$100 billion, and we would probably borrow the $100 billion.[17] Therefore, the larger our trade deficit, the more we must borrow, and as we increase our borrowing, this drives up interest rates. Also, foreigners are willing to hold U.S. debt if and only if the rate paid on this debt is competitive with interest rates in other countries. Therefore, if the Federal Reserve attempts to lower interest rates in the United States, causing our rates to fall below rates abroad, then foreigners will sell U.S. bonds, those sales will depress bond prices, and the result will be higher U.S. rates. Thus, if the trade deficit is large relative to the size of the overall economy, it may hinder the Fed's ability to combat a recession by lowering interest rates.

The United States has been running annual trade deficits since the mid-1970s, and the cumulative effect of these deficits is that the United States has become the largest debtor nation of all time. As a result, our interest rates are very much influenced by interest rates in other countries around the world (higher rates abroad lead to higher U.S. rates). Because of all this, U.S. corporate treasurers — and anyone else who is affected by interest rates — must keep up with developments in the world economy.

BUSINESS ACTIVITY

Figure 4-3, presented earlier, can be examined to see how business conditions influence interest rates. Here are the key points revealed by the graph:

1. Because inflation increased from 1961 to 1981, the general tendency during that period was toward higher interest rates. However, since the 1981 peak, the trend has generally been downward.

2. Until 1966, short-term rates were almost always below long-term rates. Thus, in those years the yield curve was almost always "normal" in the sense that it was upward sloping.

3. The shaded areas in the graph represent recessions, during which (1) both the demand for money and the rate of inflation tend to fall and (2) the Federal Reserve tends to increase the money supply in an effort to stimulate the economy. As a result, there is a tendency for interest rates to decline during recessions. For example, the economy began to slow down in 2000, and we entered a mild recession in 2001. In response to this economic weakness, the Federal Reserve cut interest rates. Now, in mid-2002, there are some tentative signs that the economy has begun to rebound, so the Fed has stopped cutting short-term rates, and is poised to raise rates once it is sure the economy has truly regained its strength.

4. During recessions, short-term rates decline more sharply than long-term rates. This occurs because (1) the Fed operates mainly in the short-term sector, so its intervention has the strongest effect there, and (2) long-term rates reflect the average expected inflation rate over the next 20 to 30 years, and this expectation generally does not change much, even when the current inflation rate is low because of a recession or high because of a boom. So, short-term rates are more volatile than long-term rates. Taking another look at Figure 4-3, we indeed see that short-term rates have declined much more than long-term rates have during the most recent economic decline in 2001.

---

[17] The deficit could also be financed by selling assets, including gold, corporate stocks, entire companies, and real estate. The United States has financed its massive trade deficits by all of these means in recent years, but the primary method has been by borrowing from foreigners.

INTEREST RATES AND BUSINESS DECISIONS

The yield curve for April 2002, shown earlier in Figure 4-5, indicates how much the U.S. government had to pay in 2002 to borrow money for one year, five years, ten years, and so on. A business borrower would have had to pay somewhat more, but assume for the moment that we are back in April 2002 and that the yield curve for that year also applies to your company. Now suppose your company has decided (1) to build a new plant with a 30-year life that will cost $1 million and (2) to raise the $1 million by selling an issue of debt (or borrowing) rather than by selling stock. If you borrowed in 2002 on a short-term basis — say, for one year — your interest cost for that year would be only 2.3 percent, or $23,000. On the other hand, if you used long-term (30-year) financing, your cost would be 5.7 percent, or $57,000. Therefore, at first glance, it would seem that you should use short-term debt.

However, this could prove to be a horrible mistake. If you use short-term debt, you will have to renew your loan every year, and the rate charged on each new loan will reflect the then-current short-term rate. Interest rates could return to their previous highs, in which case you would be paying 14 percent, or $140,000, per year. Those high interest payments would cut into, and perhaps eliminate, your profits. Your reduced profitability could easily increase your firm's risk to the point where its bond rating would be lowered, causing lenders to increase the risk premium built into the interest rate they charge. That would force you to pay an even higher rate, which would further reduce your profitability, worrying lenders even more, and making them reluctant to renew your loan. If your lenders refused to renew the loan and demanded its repayment, as they would have every right to do, you might have to sell assets at a loss, which could lead to bankruptcy.

On the other hand, if you used long-term financing in 2002, your interest costs would remain constant at $57,000 per year, so an increase in interest rates in the economy would not hurt you. You might even be able to buy up some of your bankrupt competitors at bargain prices — bankruptcies increase dramatically when interest rates rise, primarily because many firms do use too much short-term debt.

Does all this suggest that firms should always avoid short-term debt? Not necessarily. If inflation falls over the next few years, so will interest rates. If you had borrowed on a long-term basis for 5.7 percent in April 2002, your company would be at a major disadvantage if it were locked into 5.7 percent debt while its competitors (who used short-term debt in 2002 and thus rode interest rates down in subsequent years) had a borrowing cost of only 3 or 4 percent.

Financing decisions would be easy if we could make accurate forecasts of future interest rates. Unfortunately, predicting interest rates with consistent accuracy is somewhere between difficult and impossible — people who make a living by selling interest rate forecasts say it is difficult, but many others say it is impossible.

Even if it is difficult to predict future interest rate *levels*, it is easy to predict that interest rates will *fluctuate* — they always have, and they always will. This being the case, sound financial policy calls for using a mix of long- and short-term debt, as well as equity, to position the firm so that it can survive in any interest rate environment. Further, the optimal financial policy depends in an important way on the nature of the firm's assets — the easier it is to sell off assets to generate cash, the more feasible it is to use large amounts of short-term debt. This makes it more feasible for a firm to finance its current assets such as inventories than its fixed assets such as buildings with short-term debt. We will return to this issue later in the book, when we discuss working capital policy.

Changes in interest rates also have implications for savers. For example, if you had a 401(k) plan — and someday you almost certainly will — you would probably want to invest some of your money in a bond mutual fund. You could choose a fund that had an average maturity of 25 years, 20 years, and so on, down to only a few months (a money market fund). How would your choice affect your investment results, hence your retirement income? First, your annual interest income would be affected. For example, if the yield curve were upward sloping, as it normally is, you would earn more interest if you choose a fund that held long-term bonds. Note, though, that if you choose a long-term fund and interest rates then rose, the market value of the bonds in the fund would decline. For example, as we will see in Chapter 7, if you had $100,000 in a fund whose average bond had a maturity of 25 years and a coupon rate of 6 percent, and if interest rates then rose from 6 percent to 10 percent, the market value of your fund would decline from $100,000 to about $64,000. On the other hand, if rates declined, your fund would increase in value. In any event, your choice of maturity would have a major effect on your investment performance, hence your future income.

SELF-TEST QUESTIONS

If short-term interest rates are lower than long-term rates, why might a borrower still choose to finance with long-term debt?

Explain the following statement: "The optimal financial policy depends in an important way on the nature of the firm's assets."

TYING IT ALL TOGETHER

In this chapter, we discussed the nature of financial markets, the types of institutions that operate in these markets, how interest rates are determined, and some of the ways interest rates affect business decisions. In later chapters we will use this information to help value different investments, and to better understand corporate financing and investing decisions. The key concepts covered are listed below.

- There are many different types of **financial markets.** Each market serves a different region or deals with a different type of security.

- **Physical asset markets,** also called tangible or real asset markets, are those for such products as wheat, autos, and real estate.

- **Financial asset markets** deal with stocks, bonds, notes, mortgages, and other claims on real assets.

- **Spot markets** and **futures markets** are terms that refer to whether the assets are bought or sold for "on-the-spot" delivery or for delivery at some future date.

- **Money markets** are the markets for debt securities with maturities of less than one year.

- **Capital markets** are the markets for long-term debt and corporate stocks.

- **Primary markets** are the markets in which corporations raise new capital.

- **Secondary markets** are markets in which existing, already outstanding, securities are traded among investors.

- A **derivative** is a security whose value is derived from the price of some other "underlying" asset.

- Transfers of capital between borrowers and savers take place (1) by **direct transfers** of money and securities; (2) by transfers through **investment banking houses,** which act as middlemen; and (3) by transfers through **financial intermediaries,** which create new securities.

- Among the major classes of intermediaries are **commercial banks, savings and loan associations, mutual savings banks, credit unions, pension funds, life insurance companies,** and **mutual funds.**

- One result of ongoing regulatory changes has been a blurring of the distinctions between the different financial institutions. The trend in the United States has been toward **financial service corporations** that offer a wide range of financial services, including investment banking, brokerage operations, insurance, and commercial banking.

- The **stock market** is an especially important market because this is where stock prices (which are used to "grade" managers' performances) are established.

- There are two basic types of stock markets — the **physical location exchanges** (like the NYSE) and the **electronic dealer-based markets** (that include the Nasdaq and the over-the-counter market).

- Capital is allocated through the price system — a price must be paid to "rent" money. Lenders charge **interest** on funds they lend, while equity investors receive **dividends and capital gains** in return for letting firms use their money.

- Four fundamental factors affect the cost of money: (1) **production opportunities,** (2) **time preferences for consumption,** (3) **risk,** and (4) **inflation.**

- The **risk-free rate of interest,** k_{RF}, is defined as the real risk-free rate, k^*, plus an inflation premium, IP, hence $k_{RF} = k^* + IP$.

- The **nominal** (or **quoted**) **interest rate** on a debt security, **k,** is composed of the real risk-free rate, k^*, plus premiums that reflect inflation (IP), default risk (DRP), liquidity (LP), and maturity risk (MRP):

$$k = k^* + IP + DRP + LP + MRP.$$

- If the **real risk-free rate of interest and the various premiums were constant over time,** interest rates would be stable. However, both the real rate and the premiums — especially the premium for expected inflation — **do change over time, causing market interest rates to change.** Also, Federal Reserve intervention to increase or decrease the money supply, as well as international currency flows, leads to fluctuations in interest rates.

- The relationship between the yields on securities and the securities' maturities is known as the **term structure of interest rates,** and the **yield curve** is a graph of this relationship.

- The shape of the yield curve depends on two key factors: (1) **expectations about future inflation** and (2) **perceptions about the relative riskiness of securities with different maturities.**

- The yield curve is normally **upward sloping** — this is called a **normal yield curve.** However, the curve can slope downward (an **inverted yield curve**) if the inflation rate is expected to decline. The yield curve can also be **humped,** which means that interest rates on medium-term maturities are higher than rates on both short- and long-term maturities.

- Because interest rate levels are difficult if not impossible to predict, **sound financial policy** calls for using a mix of short- and long-term debt, and also for positioning the firm to survive in any future interest rate environment.

QUESTIONS

4-1 What are financial intermediaries, and what economic functions do they perform?

4-2 Suppose interest rates on residential mortgages of equal risk were 7 percent in California and 9 percent in New York. Could this differential persist? What forces might tend to equalize rates? Would differentials in borrowing costs for businesses of equal risk located in California and New York be more or less likely to exist than differentials in residential mortgage rates? Would differentials in the cost of money for New York and California firms be more likely to exist if the firms being compared were very large or if they were very small? What are the implications of all this with respect to nationwide branching?

4-3 What would happen to the standard of living in the United States if people lost faith in the safety of our financial institutions? Why?

4-4 How does a cost-efficient capital market help to reduce the prices of goods and services?

4-5 Which fluctuate more, long-term or short-term interest rates? Why?

4-6 Suppose you believe that the economy is just entering a recession. Your firm must raise capital immediately, and debt will be used. Should you borrow on a long-term or a short-term basis? Why?

4-7 Suppose the population of Area Y is relatively young while that of Area O is relatively old, but everything else about the two areas is equal.
a. Would interest rates likely be the same or different in the two areas? Explain.
b. Would a trend toward nationwide branching by banks and savings and loans, and the development of nationwide diversified financial corporations, affect your answer to part a?

4-8 Suppose a new process was developed that could be used to make oil out of seawater. The equipment required is quite expensive, but it would, in time, lead to very low prices for gasoline, electricity, and other types of energy. What effect would this have on interest rates?

4-9 Suppose a new and much more liberal Congress and administration were elected, and their first order of business was to take away the independence of the Federal Reserve System, and to force the Fed to greatly expand the money supply. What effect would this have
a. On the level and slope of the yield curve immediately after the announcement?
b. On the level and slope of the yield curve that would exist two or three years in the future?

4-10 It is a fact that the federal government (1) encouraged the development of the savings and loan industry; (2) virtually forced the industry to make long-term, fixed-interest-rate mortgages; and (3) forced the savings and loans to obtain most of their capital as deposits that were withdrawable on demand.

a. Would the savings and loans have higher profits in a world with a "normal" or an inverted yield curve?

b. Would the savings and loan industry be better off if the individual institutions sold their mortgages to federal agencies and then collected servicing fees or if the institutions held the mortgages that they originated?

4-11 Suppose interest rates on Treasury bonds rose from 7 to 14 percent as a result of higher interest rates in Europe. What effect would this have on the price of an average company's common stock?

4-12 What does it mean when it is said that the United States is running a trade deficit? What impact will a trade deficit have on interest rates?

4-13 What are the two leading stock exchanges in the United States today?

4-14 Differentiate between dealer markets and stock markets that have a physical location.

SELF-TEST PROBLEMS (SOLUTIONS APPEAR IN APPENDIX B)

ST-1
Key terms

Define each of the following terms:
a. Money market; capital market
b. Primary market; secondary market; initial public offering (IPO) market
c. Private markets; public markets
d. Spot market; futures market
e. Derivatives
f. Investment banking house; financial service corporation
g. Financial intermediary
h. Mutual fund; money market fund
i. Physical location exchanges; dealer market; over-the-counter market
j. Production opportunities; time preferences for consumption; risk; inflation
k. Real risk-free rate of interest, k*; nominal (quoted) risk-free rate of interest, k_{RF}
l. Inflation premium (IP)
m. Default risk premium (DRP)
n. Liquidity; liquidity premium (LP)
o. Interest rate risk; maturity risk premium (MRP)
p. Reinvestment rate risk; country risk
q. Term structure of interest rates; yield curve
r. "Normal" yield curve; inverted ("abnormal") yield curve; humped yield curve
s. Expectations theory
t. Foreign trade deficit; exchange rate risk

ST-2
Inflation rates

Assume that it is January 1, 2003. The rate of inflation is expected to be 4 percent throughout 2003. However, increased government deficits and renewed vigor in the economy are then expected to push inflation rates higher. Investors expect the inflation rate to be 5 percent in 2004, 6 percent in 2005, and 7 percent in 2006. The real risk-free rate, k*, is expected to remain at 2 percent over the next 5 years. Assume that no maturity risk premiums are required on bonds with 5 years or less to maturity. The current interest rate on 5-year T-bonds is 8 percent.
a. What is the average expected inflation rate over the next 4 years?
b. What should be the prevailing interest rate on 4-year T-bonds?
c. What is the implied expected inflation rate in 2007, or Year 5, given that Treasury bonds which mature in that year yield 8 percent?

STARTER PROBLEMS

4-1
Expected rate of interest

The real risk-free rate of interest is 3 percent. Inflation is expected to be 2 percent this year and 4 percent during the next 2 years. Assume that the maturity risk premium is zero. What is the yield on 2-year Treasury securities? What is the yield on 3-year Treasury securities?

4-2
Default risk premium

A Treasury bond that matures in 10 years has a yield of 6 percent. A 10-year corporate bond has a yield of 8 percent. Assume that the liquidity premium on the corporate bond is 0.5 percent. What is the default risk premium on the corporate bond?

4-3
Expected rate of interest
One-year Treasury securities yield 5 percent. The market anticipates that 1 year from now, 1-year Treasury securities will yield 6 percent. If the pure expectations theory is correct, what should be the yield today for 2-year Treasury securities?

4-4
Maturity risk premium
The real risk-free rate is 3 percent, and inflation is expected to be 3 percent for the next 2 years. A 2-year Treasury security yields 6.2 percent. What is the maturity risk premium for the 2-year security?

EXAM-TYPE PROBLEMS

The problems included in this section are set up in such a way that they could be used as multiple-choice exam problems.

4-5
Expected rate of interest
Interest rates on 4-year Treasury securities are currently 7 percent, while interest rates on 6-year Treasury securities are currently 7.5 percent. If the pure expectations theory is correct, what does the market believe that 2-year securities will be yielding 4 years from now?

4-6
Expected rate of interest
The real risk-free rate is 3 percent. Inflation is expected to be 3 percent this year, 4 percent next year, and then 3.5 percent thereafter. The maturity risk premium is estimated to be $0.0005 \times (t - 1)$, where t = number of years to maturity. What is the nominal interest rate on a 7-year Treasury note?

4-7
Expected rate of interest
Suppose the annual yield on a 2-year Treasury bond is 4.5 percent, while that on a 1-year bond is 3 percent. k* is 1 percent, and the maturity risk premium is zero.
a. Using the expectations theory, forecast the interest rate on a 1-year bond during the second year. (Hint: Under the expectations theory, the yield on a 2-year bond is equal to the average yield on 1-year bonds in Years 1 and 2.)
b. What is the expected inflation rate in Year 1? Year 2?

4-8
Expected rate of interest
Assume that the real risk-free rate is 2 percent and that the maturity risk premium is zero. If the nominal rate of interest on 1-year bonds is 5 percent and that on comparable-risk 2-year bonds is 7 percent, what is the 1-year interest rate that is expected for Year 2? What inflation rate is expected during Year 2? Comment on why the average interest rate during the 2-year period differs from the 1-year interest rate expected for Year 2.

4-9
Interest rates
Due to a recession, the inflation rate expected for the coming year is only 3 percent. However, the inflation rate in Year 2 and thereafter is expected to be constant at some level above 3 percent. Assume that the real risk-free rate is k* = 2% for all maturities and that the expectations theory fully explains the yield curve, so there are no maturity risk premiums. If 3-year Treasury bonds yield 2 percentage points more than 1-year bonds, what inflation rate is expected after Year 1?

4-10
Default risk premium
The real risk-free rate, k*, is 2.5 percent. Inflation is expected to average 2.8 percent a year for the next 4 years, after which time inflation is expected to average 3.75 percent a year. Assume that there is no maturity risk premium. An 8-year corporate bond has a yield of 8.3 percent. Assume that the liquidity premium on the corporate bond is 0.75 percent. What is the default risk premium on the corporate bond?

4-11
Real risk-free rate
You read in *The Wall Street Journal* that 30-day T-bills are currently yielding 5.5 percent. Your brother-in-law, a broker at Safe and Sound Securities, has given you the following estimates of current interest rate premiums:

- Inflation premium = 3.25%.
- Liquidity premium = 0.6%.
- Maturity risk premium = 1.8%.
- Default risk premium = 2.15%.

On the basis of these data, what is the real risk-free rate of return?

4-12
Default risk premium
The 5-year bonds of Cartwright Enterprises are yielding 7.75 percent per year. Treasury bonds with the same maturity are yielding 5.2 percent per year. The real risk-free rate (k*) has not changed in recent years and is 2.3 percent. The average inflation premium is 2.5 percent, and the maturity risk premium takes the form: MRP = 0.1%(t − 1), where t = number of years to maturity. If the liquidity premium is 1 percent, what is the default risk premium on Cartwright's corporate bonds?

4-13

Maturity risk premium

An investor in Treasury securities expects inflation to be 2.5 percent in Year 1, 3.2 percent in Year 2, and 3.6 percent each year thereafter. Assume that the real risk-free rate is 2.75 percent, and that this rate will remain constant over time. Three-year Treasury securities yield 6.25 percent, while 5-year Treasury securities yield 6.80 percent. What is the difference in the maturity risk premiums (MRPs) on the two securities; that is, what is $MRP_5 - MRP_3$?

PROBLEMS

4-14

Yield curves

Suppose you and most other investors expect the inflation rate to be 7 percent next year, to fall to 5 percent during the following year, and then to remain at a rate of 3 percent thereafter. Assume that the real risk-free rate, k^*, will remain at 2 percent and that maturity risk premiums on Treasury securities rise from zero on very short-term bonds (those that mature in a few days) to a level of 0.2 percentage point for 1-year securities. Furthermore, maturity risk premiums increase 0.2 percentage point for each year to maturity, up to a limit of 1.0 percentage point on 5-year or longer-term T-bonds.

a. Calculate the interest rate on 1-, 2-, 3-, 4-, 5-, 10-, and 20-year Treasury securities, and plot the yield curve.

b. Now suppose Exxon Mobil, an AAA-rated company, had bonds with the same maturities as the Treasury bonds. As an approximation, plot an Exxon Mobil yield curve on the same graph with the Treasury bond yield curve. (Hint: Think about the default risk premium on Exxon Mobil's long-term versus its short-term bonds.)

c. Now plot the approximate yield curve of Exelon Corp., a risky nuclear utility.

4-15

Yield curves

The following yields on U.S. Treasury securities were taken from a recent financial publication:

TERM	RATE
6 months	5.1%
1 year	5.5
2 years	5.6
3 years	5.7
4 years	5.8
5 years	6.0
10 years	6.1
20 years	6.5
30 years	6.3

Plot a yield curve based on these data.

4-16

Inflation and interest rates

In late 1980, the U.S. Commerce Department released new figures that showed that inflation was running at an annual rate of close to 15 percent. At the time, the prime rate of interest was 21 percent, a record high. However, many investors expected the new Reagan administration to be more effective in controlling inflation than the Carter administration had been. Moreover, many observers believed that the extremely high interest rates and generally tight credit, which resulted from the Federal Reserve System's attempts to curb the inflation rate, would shortly bring about a recession, which, in turn, would lead to a decline in the inflation rate and also in the interest rate. Assume that at the beginning of 1981, the expected inflation rate for 1981 was 13 percent; for 1982, 9 percent; for 1983, 7 percent; and for 1984 and thereafter, 6 percent.

a. What was the average expected inflation rate over the 5-year period 1981–1985? (Use the arithmetic average.)

b. What average *nominal* interest rate would, over the 5-year period, be expected to produce a 2 percent real risk-free rate of return on 5-year Treasury securities?

c. Assuming a real risk-free rate of 2 percent and a maturity risk premium that starts at 0.1 percent and increases by 0.1 percent each year, estimate the interest rate in January

1981 on bonds that mature in 1, 2, 5, 10, and 20 years, and draw a yield curve based on these data.

d. Describe the general economic conditions that could be expected to produce an upward-sloping yield curve.

e. If the consensus among investors in early 1981 had been that the expected inflation rate for every future year was 10 percent (that is, $I_t = I_{t+1} = 10\%$ for $t = 1$ to ∞), what do you think the yield curve would have looked like? Consider all the factors that are likely to affect the curve. Does your answer here make you question the yield curve you drew in part c?

SPREADSHEET PROBLEM

4-17
Analyzing interest rates

a. Suppose you are considering two possible investment opportunities: a 12-year Treasury bond and a 7-year, A-rated corporate bond. The current real risk-free rate is 4 percent, and inflation is expected to be 2 percent for the next two years, 3 percent for the following four years, and 4 percent thereafter. The maturity risk premium is estimated by this formula: MRP = 0.1%(t − 1). The liquidity premium for the corporate bond is estimated to be 0.7 percent. Finally, you may determine the default risk premium, given the company's bond rating, from the default risk premium table in the text. What yield would you predict for each of these two investments?

b. Given the following Treasury bond yield information from a recent financial publication, construct a graph of the yield curve.

MATURITY	YIELD
1 year	5.37%
2 years	5.47
3 years	5.65
4 years	5.71
5 years	5.64
10 years	5.75
20 years	6.33
30 years	5.94

c. Based on the information about the corporate bond that was given in part a, calculate yields and then construct a new yield curve graph that shows both the Treasury and the corporate bonds.

d. Using the Treasury yield information above, calculate the following forward rates:
(1) The 1-year rate, 1 year from now.
(2) The 5-year rate, 5 years from now.
(3) The 10-year rate, 10 years from now.
(4) The 10-year rate, 20 years from now.

INTEGRATED CASE

SMYTH BARRY & COMPANY

4-18 Financial Markets, Institutions, and Interest Rates
Assume that you recently graduated with a degree in finance and have just reported to work as an investment advisor at the brokerage firm of Smyth Barry & Co. Your first assignment is to explain the nature of the U.S. financial markets to Michelle Varga, a professional tennis player who has just come to the United States from Mexico. Varga is a

highly ranked tennis player who expects to invest substantial amounts of money through Smyth Barry. She is also very bright, and, therefore, she would like to understand in general terms what will happen to her money. Your boss has developed the following set of questions that you must ask and answer to explain the U.S. financial system to Varga.

a. What is a market? Differentiate between the following types of markets: physical asset vs. financial markets, spot vs. futures markets, money vs. capital markets, primary vs. secondary markets, and public vs. private markets.

b. What is an initial public offering (IPO) market?

c. If Apple Computer decided to issue additional common stock, and Varga purchased 100 shares of this stock from Merrill Lynch, the underwriter, would this transaction be a primary market transaction or a secondary market transaction? Would it make a difference if Varga purchased previously outstanding Apple stock in the dealer market?

d. Describe the three primary ways in which capital is transferred between savers and borrowers.

e. What are the two leading stock markets? Describe the two basic types of stock markets.

f. What do we call the price that a borrower must pay for debt capital? What is the price of equity capital? What are the four most fundamental factors that affect the cost of money, or the general level of interest rates, in the economy?

g. What is the real risk-free rate of interest (k*) and the nominal risk-free rate (k$_{RF}$)? How are these two rates measured?

h. Define the terms inflation premium (IP), default risk premium (DRP), liquidity premium (LP), and maturity risk premium (MRP). Which of these premiums is included when determining the interest rate on (1) short-term U.S. Treasury securities, (2) long-term U.S. Treasury securities, (3) short-term corporate securities, and (4) long-term corporate securities? Explain how the premiums would vary over time and among the different securities listed above.

i. What is the term structure of interest rates? What is a yield curve?

j. Suppose most investors expect the inflation rate to be 5 percent next year, 6 percent the following year, and 8 percent thereafter. The real risk-free rate is 3 percent. The maturity risk premium is zero for bonds that mature in 1 year or less, 0.1 percent for 2-year bonds, and then the MRP increases by 0.1 percent per year thereafter for 20 years, after which it is stable. What is the interest rate on 1-year, 10-year, and 20-year Treasury bonds? Draw a yield curve with these data. What factors can explain why this constructed yield curve is upward sloping?

k. At any given time, how would the yield curve facing an AAA-rated company compare with the yield curve for U.S. Treasury securities? At any given time, how would the yield curve facing a BB-rated company compare with the yield curve for U.S. Treasury securities? Draw a graph to illustrate your answer.

l. What is the pure expectations theory? What does the pure expectations theory imply about the term structure of interest rates?

m. Suppose that you observe the following term structure for Treasury securities:

MATURITY	YIELD
1 year	6.0%
2 years	6.2
3 years	6.4
4 years	6.5
5 years	6.5

Assume that the pure expectations theory of the term structure is correct. (This implies that you can use the yield curve given above to "back out" the market's expectations about future interest rates.) What does the market expect will be the interest rate on 1-year securities one year from now? What does the market expect will be the interest rate on 3-year securities two years from now?

n. Finally, Varga is also interested in investing in countries other than the United States. Describe the various types of risks that arise when investing overseas.

CYBER PROBLEM

Please go to our web site **http://brigham.swlearning.com** to access the Cyberproblems.

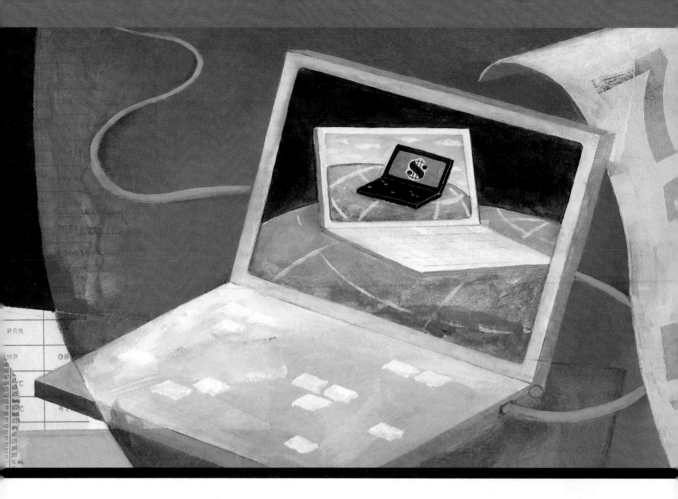

PART 2

FUNDAMENTAL CONCEPTS IN FINANCIAL MANAGEMENT

Risk and
Rates of Return 5

Time Value
of Money 6

RISK AND RATES OF RETURN

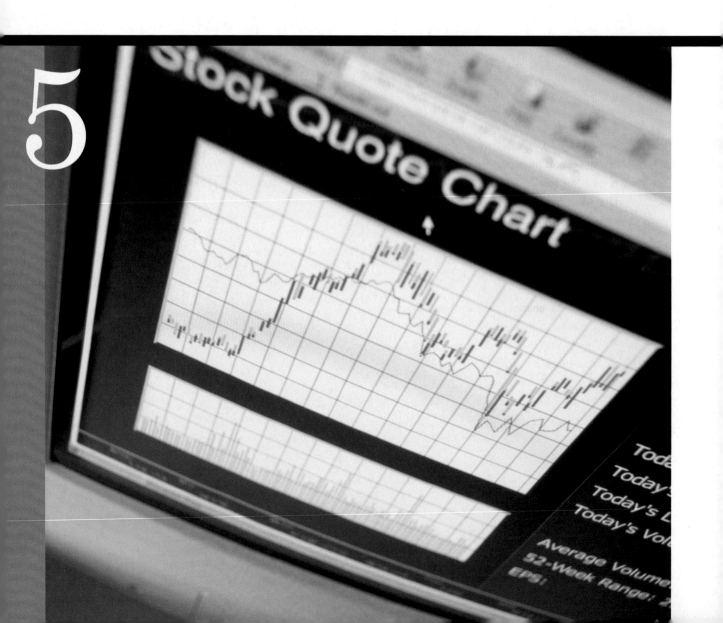

NO PAIN NO GAIN

Throughout most of the 1990s, the market soared, and investors became accustomed to great stock market returns. More recently, they have had to suffer through the pain of a declining market, leading to a reassessment of the risks inherent in the stock market. This point is underscored by a *Wall Street Journal* article written shortly after the terrorist attacks of September 2001:

Investing in the stock market can be risky, sometimes very risky. While that may seem obvious after the Dow Jones Industrial Average posted its worst weekly percentage loss in 61 years and its worst-ever weekly point loss, it wasn't something that most investors spent enough time thinking about during the bull market of the 1990s.

Now, with the Bush administration warning of a lengthy battle against terrorism, investment advisors say that the risks associated with owning stocks — as opposed to safer securities with more predictable returns, such as bonds — are poised to rise. This is what analysts call a "risk premium," and as it gets higher, investors require a greater return from stocks compared to bonds.

For most analysts, it is not a question of whether stocks are riskier today than they have been in recent years. Rather, they are asking how much riskier? And for how long will this period of heightened risk continue?

It is also important to understand that some stocks are riskier than others, and even in years when the overall stock market goes up, many individual stocks go down. Therefore, putting all your money into one stock is extremely risky. According to a *Business Week* article, the single best weapon against risk is diversification: "By spreading your money around, you're not tied to the fickleness of a given market, stock, or industry. . . . Correlation, in portfolio-manager speak, helps you diversify properly because it describes how

closely two investments track each other. If they move in tandem, they're likely to suffer from the same bad news. So, you should combine assets with low correlations."

U.S. investors tend to think of "the stock market" as the U.S. stock market. However, U.S. stocks amount to only 35 percent of the value of all stocks. Foreign markets have been quite profitable, and they are not perfectly correlated with U.S. markets. Therefore, global diversification offers U.S. investors an opportunity to raise returns and at the same time reduce risk. However, foreign investing brings some risks of its own, most notably "exchange rate risk," which is the danger that exchange rate shifts will decrease the number of dollars a foreign currency will buy.

Although the central thrust of the *Business Week* article was on ways to measure and then reduce risk, it did point out that some recently created instruments that are actually extremely risky have been marketed as low-risk investments to naive investors. For example, several mutual funds have advertised that their portfolios "contain only securities backed by the U.S. government" but then failed to highlight that the funds themselves are using financial leverage, are investing in "derivatives," or are taking some other action that boosts current yields but exposes investors to huge risks.

When you finish this chapter, you should understand what risk is, how it is measured, and what actions can be taken to minimize it, or at least to ensure that you are adequately compensated for bearing it.

Sources: "Figuring Risk: It's Not So Scary," *BusinessWeek*, November 1, 1993, 154–155; "T-Bill Trauma and the Meaning of Risk," *The Wall Street Journal*, February 12, 1993, C1; and "Stock Risks Poised to Rise in Changed Postattack World," *The Wall Street Journal*, September 24, 2001, C1.

In this chapter, we start from the basic premise that investors like returns and dislike risk. Therefore, people will invest in risky assets only if they expect to receive higher returns. We define precisely what the term risk means as it relates to investments, we examine procedures managers use to measure risk, and we discuss the relationship between risk and return. Then, in Chapters 6, 7, and 8, we extend these relationships to show how risk and return interact to determine security prices. Managers must understand these concepts and think about them as they plan the actions that will shape their firms' futures.

As you will see, risk can be measured in different ways, and different conclusions about an asset's riskiness can be reached depending on the measure used. Risk analysis can be confusing, but it will help if you remember the following:

1. All financial assets are expected to produce *cash flows,* and the riskiness of an asset is judged in terms of the riskiness of its cash flows.

2. The riskiness of an asset can be considered in two ways: (1) on a *stand-alone basis,* where the asset's cash flows are analyzed by themselves, or (2) in a *portfolio context,* where the cash flows from a number of assets are combined, and then the consolidated cash flows are analyzed.[1] There is an important difference between stand-alone and portfolio risk, and an asset that has a great deal of risk if held by itself may be much less risky if it is held as part of a larger portfolio.

3. In a portfolio context, an asset's risk can be divided into two components: (a) *diversifiable risk,* which can be diversified away and thus is of little concern to diversified investors, and (b) *market risk,* which reflects the risk of a general stock market decline and which cannot be eliminated by diversification, hence *does* concern investors. Only market risk is *relevant* — diversifiable risk is *irrelevant* to rational investors because it can be eliminated.

4. An asset with a high degree of relevant (market) risk must provide a relatively high expected rate of return to attract investors. Investors in general are *averse to risk,* so they will not buy risky assets unless those assets have high expected returns.

5. In this chapter, we focus on *financial assets* such as stocks and bonds, but the concepts discussed here also apply to *physical assets* such as computers, trucks, or even whole plants. ■

---

[1] A *portfolio* is a collection of investment securities. If you owned some General Motors stock, some Exxon Mobil stock, and some IBM stock, you would be holding a three-stock portfolio. Because diversification lowers risk, most stocks are held in portfolios.

INVESTMENT RETURNS

With most investments, an individual or business spends money today with the expectation of earning even more money in the future. The concept of *return* provides investors with a convenient way of expressing the financial performance of an investment. To illustrate, suppose you buy 10 shares of a stock for $1,000. The stock pays no dividends, but at the end of one year, you sell the stock for $1,100. What is the return on your $1,000 investment?

One way of expressing an investment return is in *dollar terms*. The dollar return is simply the total dollars received from the investment less the amount invested:

$$\text{Dollar return} = \text{Amount received} - \text{Amount invested}$$
$$= \$1,100 - \$1,000$$
$$= \$100.$$

If at the end of the year you had sold the stock for only $900, your dollar return would have been −$100.

Although expressing returns in dollars is easy, two problems arise: (1) To make a meaningful judgment about the return, you need to know the scale (size) of the investment; a $100 return on a $100 investment is a good return (assuming the investment is held for one year), but a $100 return on a $10,000 investment would be a poor return. (2) You also need to know the timing of the return; a $100 return on a $100 investment is a very good return if it occurs after one year, but the same dollar return after 20 years would not be very good.

The solution to the scale and timing problems is to express investment results as *rates of return*, or *percentage returns*. For example, the rate of return on the 1-year stock investment, when $1,100 is received after one year, is 10 percent:

$$\text{Rate of return} = \frac{\text{Amount received} - \text{Amount invested}}{\text{Amount invested}}$$
$$= \frac{\text{Dollar return}}{\text{Amount invested}} = \frac{\$100}{\$1,000}$$
$$= 0.10 = 10\%.$$

The rate of return calculation "standardizes" the return by considering the return per unit of investment. In this example, the return of 0.10, or 10 percent, indicates that each dollar invested will earn 0.10($1.00) = $0.10. If the rate of return had been negative, this would indicate that the original investment was not even recovered. For example, selling the stock for only $900 results in a −10 percent rate of return, which means that each dollar invested lost 10 cents.

Note also that a $10 return on a $100 investment produces a 10 percent rate of return, while a $10 return on a $1,000 investment results in a rate of return of only 1 percent. Thus, the percentage return takes account of the size of the investment.

Expressing rates of return on an annual basis, which is typically done in practice, solves the timing problem. A $10 return after one year on a $100 investment results in a 10 percent annual rate of return, while a $10 return after five years yields only a 1.9 percent annual rate of return. We will discuss all this in detail in Chapter 6, which deals with the time value of money.

Although we illustrated return concepts with one outflow and one inflow, in later chapters we demonstrate that rate of return concepts can easily be applied in situations where multiple cash flows occur over time. For example, when Intel makes an investment in new chip-making technology, the investment is made over several years and the resulting inflows occur over even more years. For now, it is sufficient to recognize that the rate of return solves the two major problems associated with dollar returns, size and timing. Therefore, the rate of return is the most common measure of investment performance.

SELF-TEST QUESTIONS

Differentiate between dollar return and rate of return.

Why is the rate of return superior to the dollar return in terms of accounting for the size of investment and the timing of cash flows?

STAND-ALONE RISK

Risk
The chance that some unfavorable event will occur.

Risk is defined in *Webster's* as "a hazard; a peril; exposure to loss or injury." Thus, risk refers to the chance that some unfavorable event will occur. If you engage in skydiving, you are taking a chance with your life — skydiving is risky. If you bet on the horses, you are risking your money. If you invest in speculative stocks (or, really, *any* stock), you are taking a risk in the hope of making an appreciable return.

An asset's risk can be analyzed in two ways: (1) on a stand-alone basis, where the asset is considered in isolation, and (2) on a portfolio basis, where the asset is held as one of a number of assets in a portfolio. Thus, an asset's **stand-alone risk** is the risk an investor would face if he or she held only this one asset. Obviously, most assets are held in portfolios, but it is necessary to understand stand-alone risk in order to understand risk in a portfolio context.

Stand-Alone Risk
The risk an investor would face if he or she held only one asset.

To illustrate the riskiness of financial assets, suppose an investor buys $100,000 of short-term Treasury bills with an expected return of 5 percent. In this case, the rate of return on the investment, 5 percent, can be estimated quite precisely, and the investment is defined as being essentially *risk free*. However, if the $100,000 were invested in the stock of a company just being organized to prospect for oil in the mid-Atlantic, then the investment's return could not be estimated precisely. One might analyze the situation and conclude that the *expected* rate of return, in a statistical sense, is 20 percent, but the investor should also recognize that the *actual* rate of return could range from, say, +1,000 percent to −100 percent. Because there is a significant danger of actually earning much less than the expected return, the stock would be relatively risky.

No investment will be undertaken unless the expected rate of return is high enough to compensate the investor for the perceived risk of the investment. In our example, it is clear that few if any investors would be willing to buy the oil company's stock if its expected return were the same as that of the T-bill.

Risky assets rarely produce their expected rates of return — generally, risky assets earn either more or less than was originally expected. Indeed, if assets always produced their expected returns, they would not be risky. Investment risk, then, is related to the probability of actually earning a low or negative return — the greater the chance of a low or negative return, the riskier the investment. However, risk can be defined more precisely, and we do so in the next section.

PROBABILITY DISTRIBUTIONS

Probability Distribution
A listing of all possible outcomes, or events, with a probability (chance of occurrence) assigned to each outcome.

An event's *probability* is defined as the chance that the event will occur. For example, a weather forecaster might state, "There is a 40 percent chance of rain today and a 60 percent chance that it will not rain." If all possible events, or outcomes, are listed, and if a probability is assigned to each event, the listing is called a **probability distribution.** For our weather forecast, we could set up the following probability distribution:

OUTCOME (1)	PROBABILITY (2)
Rain	0.4 = 40%
No rain	0.6 = 60
	1.0 = 100%

The possible outcomes are listed in Column 1, while the probabilities of these outcomes, expressed both as decimals and as percentages, are given in Column 2. Notice that the probabilities must sum to 1.0, or 100 percent.

Probabilities can also be assigned to the possible outcomes (or returns) from an investment. If you buy a bond, you expect to receive interest on the bond plus a return of your original investment, and those payments will provide you with a rate of return on your investment. The possible outcomes from this investment are (1) that the issuer will make the required payments or (2) that the issuer will default on the payments. The higher the probability of default, the riskier the bond, and the higher the risk, the higher the required rate of return. If you invest in a stock instead of buying a bond, you will again expect to earn a return on your money. A stock's return will come from dividends plus capital gains. Again, the riskier the stock — which means the higher the probability that the firm will fail to perform as you expected — the higher the expected return must be to induce you to invest in the stock.

With this in mind, consider the possible rates of return (dividend yield plus capital gain or loss) that you might earn next year on a $10,000 investment in the stock of either Martin Products Inc. or U.S. Water Company. Martin manufactures and distributes computer terminals and equipment for the rapidly growing data transmission industry. Because it faces intense competition, its new products may or may not be competitive in the marketplace, so its future earnings cannot be predicted very well. Indeed, some new company could develop better products and literally bankrupt Martin. U.S. Water, on the other hand, supplies an essential service, and because it has city franchises that protect it from competition, its sales and profits are relatively stable and predictable.

The rate-of-return probability distributions for the two companies are shown in Table 5-1. There is a 30 percent chance of strong demand, in which case both companies will have high earnings, pay high dividends, and enjoy capital gains. There is a 40 percent probability of normal demand and moderate returns, and there is a 30 percent probability of weak demand, which will mean low earnings and dividends as well as capital losses. Notice, however, that Martin Products' rate of return could vary far more widely than that of U.S. Water. There is a fairly high probability that the value of Martin's stock will drop substantially, resulting in a 70 percent loss, while there is no chance of a loss for U.S. Water.[2]

---

[2] It is, of course, completely unrealistic to think that any stock has no chance of a loss. Only in hypothetical examples could this occur. To illustrate, the price of Columbia Gas's stock dropped from $34.50 to $20.00 in just three hours a few years ago. All investors were reminded that any stock is exposed to some risk of loss, and those investors who bought Columbia Gas learned that lesson the hard way.

TABLE 5-1

Probability Distributions for Martin Products and U.S. Water

DEMAND FOR THE COMPANY'S PRODUCTS	PROBABILITY OF THIS DEMAND OCCURRING	RATE OF RETURN ON STOCK IF THIS DEMAND OCCURS	
		MARTIN PRODUCTS	U.S. WATER
Strong	0.3	100%	20%
Normal	0.4	15	15
Weak	0.3	(70)	10
	1.0		

EXPECTED RATE OF RETURN

Expected Rate of Return, $\hat{k}$
The rate of return expected to be realized from an investment; the weighted average of the probability distribution of possible results.

If we multiply each possible outcome by its probability of occurrence and then sum these products, as in Table 5-2, we have a *weighted average* of outcomes. The weights are the probabilities, and the weighted average is the **expected rate of return, $\hat{k}$,** called "k-hat."[3] The expected rates of return for both Martin Products and U.S. Water are shown in Table 5-2 to be 15 percent. This type of table is known as a *payoff matrix.*

The expected rate of return calculation can also be expressed as an equation that does the same thing as the payoff matrix table:[4]

$$\text{Expected rate of return} = \hat{k} = P_1 k_1 + P_2 k_2 + \cdots + P_n k_n$$

$$= \sum_{i=1}^{n} P_i k_i. \tag{5-1}$$

Here k_i is the *i*th possible outcome, P_i is the probability of the *i*th outcome, and n is the number of possible outcomes. Thus, $\hat{k}$ is a weighted average of the possible outcomes (the k_i values), with each outcome's weight being its probability of occurrence. Using the data for Martin Products, we obtain its expected rate of return as follows:

$$\hat{k} = P_1(k_1) + P_2(k_2) + P_3(k_3)$$
$$= 0.3(100\%) + 0.4(15\%) + 0.3(-70\%)$$
$$= 15\%.$$

U.S. Water's expected rate of return is also 15 percent:

$$\hat{k} = 0.3(20\%) + 0.4(15\%) + 0.3(10\%)$$
$$= 15\%.$$

---

[3] In Chapters 7 and 8, we will use k_d and k_s to signify the returns on bonds and stocks, respectively. However, this distinction is unnecessary in this chapter, so we just use the general term, k, to signify the expected return on an investment.

[4] The second form of the equation is simply a shorthand expression in which sigma (Σ) means "sum up," or add the values of n factors. If i = 1, then $P_i k_i = P_1 k_1$; if i = 2, then $P_i k_i = P_2 k_2$; and so on until i = n, the last possible outcome. The symbol $\sum_{i=1}^{n}$ simply says, "Go through the following process: First, let i = 1 and find the first product; then let i = 2 and find the second product; then continue until each individual product up to i = n has been found, and then add these individual products to find the expected rate of return."

TABLE 5-2

Calculation of Expected Rates of Return: Payoff Matrix

DEMAND FOR THE COMPANY'S PRODUCTS (1)	PROBABILITY OF THIS DEMAND OCCURRING (2)	MARTIN PRODUCTS		U.S. WATER	
		RATE OF RETURN IF THIS DEMAND OCCURS (3)	PRODUCT: (2) × (3) = (4)	RATE OF RETURN IF THIS DEMAND OCCURS (5)	PRODUCT: (2) × (5) = (6)
Strong	0.3	100%	30%	20%	6%
Normal	0.4	15	6	15	6
Weak	0.3	(70)	(21)	10	k 3
	1.0		$\hat{k} = 15\%$		$\hat{k} = 15\%$

We can graph the rates of return to obtain a picture of the variability of possible outcomes; this is shown in the Figure 5-1 bar charts. The height of each bar signifies the probability that a given outcome will occur. The range of probable returns for Martin Products is from −70 to +100 percent, with an expected return of 15 percent. The expected return for U.S. Water is also 15 percent, but its range is much narrower.

FIGURE 5-1

Probability Distributions of Martin Products' and U.S. Water's Rates of Return

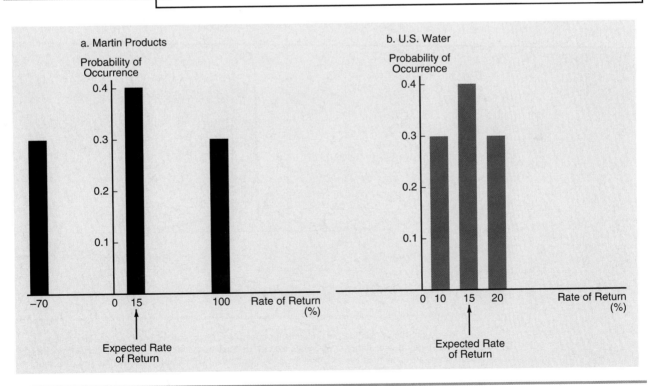

Thus far, we have assumed that only three situations can exist: strong, normal, and weak demand. Actually, of course, demand could range from a deep depression to a fantastic boom, and there are an unlimited number of possibilities in between. Suppose we had the time and patience to assign a probability to each possible level of demand (with the sum of the probabilities still equaling 1.0) and to assign a rate of return to each stock for each level of demand. We would have a table similar to Table 5-1, except that it would have many more entries in each column. This table could be used to calculate expected rates of return as shown previously, and the probabilities and outcomes could be approximated by continuous curves such as those presented in Figure 5-2. Here we have changed the assumptions so that there is essentially a zero probability that Martin Products' return will be less than −70 percent or more than 100 percent, or that U.S. Water's return will be less than 10 percent or more than 20 percent, but virtually any return within these limits is possible.

The tighter, or more peaked, the probability distribution, the more likely it is that the actual outcome will be close to the expected value, and, consequently, the less likely it is that the actual return will end up far below the expected return. Thus, the tighter the probability distribution, the lower the risk assigned to a stock. Since U.S. Water has a relatively tight probability distribution, its *actual return* is likely to be closer to its 15 percent *expected return* than is that of Martin Products.

FIGURE 5-2 | **Continuous Probability Distributions of Martin Products' and U.S. Water's Rates of Return**

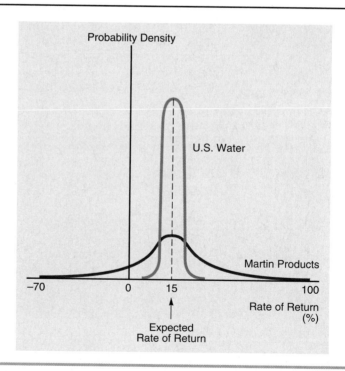

NOTE: The assumptions regarding the probabilities of various outcomes have been changed from those in Figure 5-1. There the probability of obtaining exactly 15 percent was 40 percent; here it is *much smaller* because there are many possible outcomes instead of just three. With continuous distributions, it is more appropriate to ask what the probability is of obtaining at least some specified rate of return than to ask what the probability is of obtaining exactly that rate. This topic is covered in detail in statistics courses.

MEASURING STAND-ALONE RISK: THE STANDARD DEVIATION

Risk is a difficult concept to grasp, and a great deal of controversy has surrounded attempts to define and measure it. However, a common definition, and one that is satisfactory for many purposes, is stated in terms of probability distributions such as those presented in Figure 5-2: *The tighter the probability distribution of expected future returns, the smaller the risk of a given investment.* According to this definition, U.S. Water is less risky than Martin Products because there is a smaller chance that its actual return will end up far below its expected return.

To be most useful, any measure of risk should have a definite value — we need a measure of the tightness of the probability distribution. One such measure is the **standard deviation**, the symbol for which is **σ**, pronounced "sigma." The smaller the standard deviation, the tighter the probability distribution, and, accordingly, the lower the riskiness of the stock. To calculate the standard deviation, we proceed as shown in Table 5-3, taking the following steps:

Standard Deviation, σ
A statistical measure of the variability of a set of observations.

1. Calculate the expected rate of return:

$$\text{Expected rate of return} = \hat{k} = \sum_{i=1}^{n} P_i k_i.$$

For Martin, we previously found $\hat{k} = 15\%$.

2. Subtract the expected rate of return ($\hat{k}$) from each possible outcome (k_i) to obtain a set of deviations about $\hat{k}$ as shown in Column 1 of Table 5-3:

$$\text{Deviation}_i = k_i - \hat{k}.$$

Variance, σ^2
The square of the standard deviation.

3. Square each deviation, then multiply the result by the probability of occurrence for its related outcome, and then sum these products to obtain the **variance** of the probability distribution as shown in Columns 2 and 3 of the table:

$$\text{Variance} = \sigma^2 = \sum_{i=1}^{n} (k_i - \hat{k})^2 P_i. \tag{5-2}$$

4. Finally, find the square root of the variance to obtain the standard deviation:

$$\text{Standard deviation} = \sigma = \sqrt{\sum_{i=1}^{n} (k_i - \hat{k})^2 P_i.} \tag{5-3}$$

TABLE 5-3	Calculating Martin Products' Standard Deviation

$k_i - \hat{k}$ (1)	$(k_i - \hat{k})^2$ (2)	$(k_i - \hat{k})^2 P_i$ (3)
$100 - 15 = \quad 85$	7,225	$(7,225)(0.3) = 2,167.5$
$15 - 15 = \quad 0$	0	$(0)(0.4) = \quad 0.0$
$-70 - 15 = -85$	7,225	$(7,225)(0.3) = \underline{2,167.5}$
		Variance $= \sigma^2 = \underline{4,335.0}$
		Standard deviation $= \sigma = \sqrt{\sigma^2} = \sqrt{4,335} = 65.84\%.$

Thus, the standard deviation is essentially a weighted average of the deviations from the expected value, and it provides an idea of how far above or below the expected value the actual value is likely to be. Martin's standard deviation is seen in Table 5-3 to be $\sigma = 65.84\%$. Using these same procedures, we find U.S. Water's standard deviation to be 3.87 percent. Martin Products has the larger standard deviation, which indicates a greater variation of returns and thus a greater chance that the expected return will not be realized. Therefore, Martin Products is a riskier investment than U.S. Water when held alone.

If a probability distribution is normal, the *actual* return will be within ±1 standard deviation of the *expected* return 68.26 percent of the time. Figure 5-3 illustrates this point, and it also shows the situation for ±2σ and ±3σ. For Martin Products, $\hat{k} = 15\%$ and $\sigma = 65.84\%$, whereas $\hat{k} = 15\%$ and $\sigma = 3.87\%$ for U.S. Water. Thus, if the two distributions were normal, there would be a 68.26 percent probability that Martin's actual return would be in the range of 15 ± 65.84 percent, or from −50.84 to 80.84 percent. For U.S. Water, the 68.26 percent range is 15 ± 3.87 percent, or

| FIGURE 5-3 | **Probability Ranges for a Normal Distribution** |

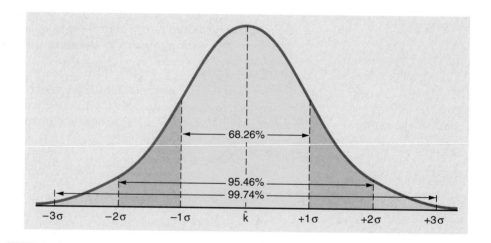

NOTES:
a. The area under the normal curve always equals 1.0, or 100 percent. *Thus, the areas under any pair of normal curves drawn on the same scale, whether they are peaked or flat, must be equal.*
b. Half of the area under a normal curve is to the left of the mean, indicating that there is a 50 percent probability that the actual outcome will be less than the mean, and half is to the right of k, indicating a 50 percent probability that it will be greater than the mean.
c. Of the area under the curve, 68.26 percent is within ±1σ of the mean, indicating that the probability is 68.26 percent that the actual outcome will be within the range $\hat{k} - 1\sigma$ to $\hat{k} + 1\sigma$.
d. Procedures exist for finding the probability of other ranges. These procedures are covered in statistics courses.
e. For a normal distribution, the larger the value of σ, the greater the probability that the actual outcome will vary widely from, and hence perhaps be far below, the expected, or most likely, outcome. *Since the probability of having the actual result turn out to be far below the expected result is one definition of risk, and since σ measures this probability, we can use σ as a measure of risk.* This definition may not be a good one, however, if we are dealing with an asset held in a diversified portfolio. This point is covered later in the chapter.

from 11.13 to 18.87 percent. With such a small σ, there is only a small probability that U.S. Water's return would be significantly less than expected, so the stock is not very risky. For the average firm listed on the New York Stock Exchange, σ has generally been in the range of 35 to 40 percent in recent years.[5]

MEASURING STAND-ALONE RISK: THE COEFFICIENT OF VARIATION

If a choice has to be made between two investments that have the same expected returns but different standard deviations, most people would choose the one with the lower standard deviation and, therefore, the lower risk. Similarly, given a choice between two investments with the same risk (standard deviation) but different expected returns, investors would generally prefer the investment with the higher expected return. To most people, this is common sense — return is "good," risk is "bad," and,

---

[5] In the example, we described the procedure for finding the mean and standard deviation when the data are in the form of a known probability distribution. If only sample returns data over some past period are available, the standard deviation of returns can be estimated using this formula:

$$\text{Estimated } \sigma = S = \sqrt{\frac{\sum_{t=1}^{n} (\bar{k}_t - \bar{k}_{Avg})^2}{n - 1}}. \tag{5-3a}$$

Here $\bar{k}_t$ ("k bar t") denotes the past realized rate of return in Period t, and $\bar{k}_{Avg}$ is the average annual return earned during the last n years. Here is an example:

YEAR	$\bar{k}_t$
2000	15%
2001	−5
2002	20

$$\bar{k}_{Avg} = \frac{(15 - 5 + 20)}{3} = 10.0\%.$$

$$\text{Estimated } \sigma \text{ (or S)} = \sqrt{\frac{(15 - 10)^2 + (-5 - 10)^2 + (20 - 10)^2}{3 - 1}}$$

$$= \sqrt{\frac{350}{2}} = 13.2\%.$$

The historical σ is often used as an estimate of the future σ. Much less often, and generally incorrectly, $\bar{k}_{Avg}$ for some past period is used as an estimate of k, the expected future return. Because past variability is likely to be repeated, σ may be a good estimate of future risk, but it is much less reasonable to expect that the past *level* of return (which could have been as high as +100% or as low as −50%) is the best expectation of what investors think will happen in the future.

Equation 5-3a is built into all financial calculators, and it is very easy to use. We simply enter the rates of return and press the key marked S (or S_x) to get the standard deviation. Note, though, that calculators have no built-in formula for finding σ where probabilistic data are involved; there you must go through the process outlined in Table 5-3 and Equation 5-3. The same situation holds for computer spreadsheet programs.

consequently, investors want as much return and as little risk as possible. But how do we choose between two investments if one has the higher expected return but the other the lower standard deviation? To help answer this question, we use another measure of risk, the **coefficient of variation (CV)**, which is the standard deviation divided by the expected return:

Coefficient of Variation (CV)

Standardized measure of the risk per unit of return; calculated as the standard deviation divided by the expected return.

$$\text{Coefficient of variation} = \text{CV} = \frac{\sigma}{\hat{k}} \qquad (5\text{-}4)$$

The coefficient of variation shows the risk per unit of return, and it provides a more meaningful basis for comparison when the expected returns on two alternatives are not the same. Since U.S. Water and Martin Products have the same expected return, the coefficient of variation is not necessary in this case. The firm with the larger standard deviation, Martin, must have the larger coefficient of variation when the means are equal. In fact, the coefficient of variation for Martin is 65.84/15 = 4.39 and that for U.S. Water is 3.87/15 = 0.26. Thus, Martin is almost 17 times riskier than U.S. Water on the basis of this criterion.

For a case where the coefficient of variation is necessary, consider Projects X and Y in Figure 5-4. These projects have different expected rates of return and different standard deviations. Project X has a 60 percent expected rate of return and a 15 percent standard deviation, while Project Y has an 8 percent expected return but only a 3 percent standard deviation. Is Project X riskier, on a relative basis, because it has the larger standard deviation? If we calculate the coefficients of variation for these two projects, we find that Project X has a coefficient of variation of 15/60 = 0.25, and Project Y has a coefficient of variation of 3/8 = 0.375. Thus, we see that Project Y actually has more risk per unit of return than Project X, in spite of the fact that X's standard deviation is larger. Therefore, even though Project Y has the lower standard deviation, according to the coefficient of variation it is riskier than Project X.

FIGURE 5-4   **Comparison of Probability Distributions and Rates of Return for Projects X and Y**

Project Y has the smaller standard deviation, hence the more peaked probability distribution, but it is clear from the graph that the chances of a really low return are higher for Y than for X because X's expected return is so high. Because the coefficient of variation captures the effects of both risk and return, it is a better measure for evaluating risk in situations where investments have substantially different expected returns.

RISK AVERSION AND REQUIRED RETURNS

Suppose you have worked hard and saved $1 million, which you now plan to invest. You can buy a 5 percent U.S. Treasury note, and at the end of one year you will have a sure $1.05 million, which is your original investment plus $50,000 in interest. Alternatively, you can buy stock in R&D Enterprises. If R&D's research programs are successful, your stock will increase in value to $2.1 million. However, if the research is a failure, the value of your stock will go to zero, and you will be penniless. You regard R&D's chances of success or failure as being 50-50, so the expected value of the stock investment is 0.5($0) + 0.5($2,100,000) = $1,050,000. Subtracting the $1 million cost of the stock leaves an expected profit of $50,000, or an expected (but risky) 5 percent rate of return:

$$\text{Expected rate of return} = \frac{\text{Expected ending value} - \text{Cost}}{\text{Cost}}$$

$$= \frac{\$1,050,000 - \$1,000,000}{\$1,000,000}$$

$$= \frac{\$50,000}{\$1,000,000} = 5\%.$$

Thus, you have a choice between a sure $50,000 profit (representing a 5 percent rate of return) on the Treasury note and a risky expected $50,000 profit (also representing a 5 percent expected rate of return) on the R&D Enterprises stock. Which one would you choose? *If you choose the less risky investment, you are risk averse. Most investors are indeed risk averse, and certainly the average investor is risk averse with regard to his or her "serious money." Because this is a well-documented fact, we shall assume* **risk aversion** *throughout the remainder of the book.*

Risk Aversion
Risk-averse investors dislike risk and require higher rates of return as an inducement to buy riskier securities.

What are the implications of risk aversion for security prices and rates of return? *The answer is that, other things held constant, the higher a security's risk the lower its price and the higher its required return.* To see how risk aversion affects security prices, look back at Figure 5-2 and consider again U.S. Water and Martin Products stocks. Suppose each stock sold for $100 per share and each had an expected rate of return of 15 percent. Investors are averse to risk, so under these conditions there would be a general preference for U.S. Water. People with money to invest would bid for U.S. Water rather than Martin stock, and Martin's stockholders would start selling their stock and using the money to buy U.S. Water. Buying pressure would drive up U.S. Water's stock, and selling pressure would simultaneously cause Martin's price to decline.

These price changes, in turn, would cause changes in the expected returns of the two securities. In general, if expected future cash flows remain the same, your expected

THE TRADE-OFF BETWEEN RISK AND RETURN

The table accompanying this box summarizes the historical trade-off between risk and return for different classes of investments from 1926 through 2001. As the table shows, those assets that produced the highest average returns also had the highest standard deviations and the widest ranges of returns. For example, small-company stocks had the highest average annual return, 17.3 percent, but their standard deviation of returns, 33.2 percent, was also the highest. By contrast, U.S. Treasury bills had the lowest standard deviation, 3.2 percent, but they also had the lowest average return, 3.9 percent.

When deciding among alternative investments, one needs to be aware of the trade-off between risk and return. While there is certainly no guarantee that history will repeat itself, returns observed in the past are a good starting point for estimating investments' returns in the future. Likewise, the standard deviations of past returns provide useful insights into the risks of different investments. For T-bills, however, the standard deviation needs to be interpreted carefully. Note that the table shows that Treasury bills have a positive standard deviation, which indicates some risk. However, if you invested in a one-year Treasury bill and held it for the full year, your realized return would be the same regardless of what happened to the economy that year, and thus the standard deviation of your return would be zero. So, why does the table show a 3.2 percent standard deviation for T-bills, which indicates some risk? In fact, a T-bill is riskless *if you hold it for one year*, but if you invest in a rolling portfolio of one-year T-bills and hold the portfolio for a number of years, your investment income will vary depending on what happens to the level of interest rates in each year. So, while you can be sure of the return you will earn on a T-bill in a given year, you cannot be sure of the return you will earn on a portfolio of T-bills over a period of time.

Selected Realized Returns, 1926–2001

	AVERAGE RETURN	STANDARD DEVIATION
Small-company stocks	17.3%	33.2%
Large-company stocks	12.7	20.2
Long-term corporate bonds	6.1	8.6
Long-term goverment bonds	5.7	9.4
U.S. Treasury bills	3.9	3.2

SOURCE: Based on *Stocks, Bonds, Bills, and Inflation: (Valuation Edition) 2002 Yearbook* (Chicago: Ibbotson Associates, 2002), 28.

Risk Premium, RP
The difference between the expected rate of return on a given risky asset and that on a less risky asset.

return is higher if you are able to purchase the stock at a lower price. Suppose, for example, that U.S. Water's stock price was bid up from $100 to $150, whereas Martin's stock price declined from $100 to $75. Also assume that these price changes cause U.S. Water's expected return to fall to 10 percent, and Martin's expected return to rise to 20 percent.[6] The difference in returns, $20\% - 10\% = 10\%$, is a **risk premium, RP,** which represents the additional compensation investors require for assuming the additional risk of Martin stock.

---

[6] To understand how we might arrive at these numbers, assume that each stock is expected to pay shareholders $15 a year in perpetuity. As you will see in Chapter 6, the price of this perpetuity can be found by dividing the annual cash flow by the stock's return. Thus, in this example, if the stock's expected return is 15 percent, the price of the stock would be $100 ($15/0.15). Likewise, a 10 percent expected return would be consistent with a $150 stock price ($15/0.10), and a 20 percent expected return would be consistent with a $75 stock price ($15/0.20).

This example demonstrates a very important principle: *In a market dominated by risk-averse investors, riskier securities must have higher expected returns, as estimated by the marginal investor, than less risky securities. If this situation does not exist, buying and selling in the market will force it to occur.* We will consider the question of how much higher the returns on risky securities must be later in the chapter, after we see how diversification affects the way risk should be measured. Then, in Chapters 7 and 8, we will see how risk-adjusted rates of return affect the prices investors are willing to pay for different securities.

SELF-TEST QUESTIONS

What does "investment risk" mean?

Set up an illustrative probability distribution for an investment.

What is a payoff matrix?

Which of the two stocks graphed in Figure 5-2 is less risky? Why?

How does one calculate the standard deviation?

Which is a better measure of risk if assets have different expected returns: (1) the standard deviation or (2) the coefficient of variation? Why?

Explain the following statement: "Most investors are risk averse."

How does risk aversion affect rates of return?

RISK IN A PORTFOLIO CONTEXT

In the preceding section, we considered the riskiness of assets held in isolation. Now we analyze the riskiness of assets held in portfolios. As we shall see, an asset held as part of a portfolio is less risky than the same asset held in isolation. Accordingly, most financial assets are held as parts of portfolios. Banks, pension funds, insurance companies, mutual funds, and other financial institutions are required by law to hold diversified portfolios. Even individual investors — at least those whose security holdings constitute a significant part of their total wealth — generally hold portfolios, not the stock of only one firm. This being the case, from an investor's standpoint the fact that a particular stock goes up or down is not very important; *what is important is the return on his or her portfolio, and the portfolio's risk. Logically, then, the risk and return of an individual security should be analyzed in terms of how that security affects the risk and return of the portfolio in which it is held.*

To illustrate, Pay Up Inc. is a collection agency company that operates nationwide through 37 offices. The company is not well known, its stock is not very liquid, its earnings have fluctuated quite a bit in the past, and it doesn't pay a dividend. All this suggests that Pay Up is risky and that its required rate of return, k, should be relatively high. However, Pay Up's required rate of return in 2002, and all other years, was quite low in comparison to those of most other companies. This indicates that investors regard Pay Up as being a low-risk company in spite of its uncertain profits. The reason for this counterintuitive fact has to do with diversification and its effect on risk. Pay Up's earnings rise during recessions, whereas most other companies' earnings tend to decline when the economy slumps. It's like fire insurance — it pays off when other things go bad. Therefore, adding Pay Up to a portfolio of "normal" stocks tends to stabilize returns on the entire portfolio, thus making the portfolio less risky.

PORTFOLIO RETURNS

Expected Return on a Portfolio, $\hat{k}_p$
The weighted average of the expected returns on the assets held in the portfolio.

The **expected return on a portfolio, $\hat{k}_p$,** is simply the weighted average of the expected returns on the individual assets in the portfolio, with the weights being the fraction of the total portfolio invested in each asset:

$$\hat{k}_p = w_1\hat{k}_1 + w_2\hat{k}_2 + \cdots + w_n\hat{k}_n$$

$$= \sum_{i=1}^{n} w_i\hat{k}_i. \qquad (5\text{-}5)$$

Here the $\hat{k}_i$'s are the expected returns on the individual stocks, the w_i's are the weights, and there are n stocks in the portfolio. Note (1) that w_i is the fraction of the portfolio's dollar value invested in Stock i (that is, the value of the investment in Stock i divided by the total value of the portfolio) and (2) that the w_i's must sum to 1.0.

Assume that in May 2002, a security analyst estimated that the following returns could be expected on the stocks of four large companies:

	EXPECTED RETURN, $\hat{k}$
Microsoft	12.0%
General Electric	11.5
Pfizer	10.0
Coca-Cola	9.5

If we formed a $100,000 portfolio, investing $25,000 in each stock, the expected portfolio return would be 10.75%:

$$\hat{k}_p = w_1\hat{k}_1 + w_2\hat{k}_2 + w_3\hat{k}_3 + w_4\hat{k}_4$$

$$= 0.25(12\%) + 0.25(11.5\%) + 0.25(10\%) + 0.25(9.5\%)$$

$$= 10.75\%.$$

Realized Rate of Return, $\bar{k}$
The return that was actually earned during some past period. The actual return ($\bar{k}$) usually turns out to be different from the expected return ($\hat{k}$) except for riskless assets.

Of course, after the fact and a year later, the actual **realized rates of return, $\bar{k}$,** on the individual stocks — the $\bar{k}_i$, or "k-bar," values — will almost certainly be different from their expected values, so $\bar{k}_p$ will be different from $\hat{k}_p = 10.75\%$. For example, Coca-Cola stock might double in price and provide a return of +100%, whereas Microsoft stock might have a terrible year, fall sharply, and have a return of −75%. Note, though, that those two events would be somewhat offsetting, so the portfolio's return might still be close to its expected return, even though the individual stocks' actual returns were far from their expected returns.

PORTFOLIO RISK

As we just saw, the expected return on a portfolio is simply the weighted average of the expected returns on the individual assets in the portfolio. However, unlike returns, the riskiness of a portfolio, σ_p, is generally *not* the weighted average of the standard deviations of the individual assets in the portfolio; the portfolio's risk will be *smaller* than the weighted average of the assets' σ's. In fact, it is theoretically possible to combine stocks that are individually quite risky as measured by their standard deviations and to form a portfolio that is completely riskless, with $\sigma_p = 0$.

Correlation

The tendency of two variables to move together.

Correlation Coefficient, r

A measure of the degree of relationship between two variables.

To illustrate the effect of combining assets, consider the situation in Figure 5-5. The bottom section gives data on rates of return for Stocks W and M individually, and also for a portfolio invested 50 percent in each stock. The three top graphs show plots of the data in a time series format, and the lower graphs show the probability distributions of returns, assuming that the future is expected to be like the past. The two stocks would be quite risky if they were held in isolation, but when they are combined to form Portfolio WM, they are not risky at all. (Note: These stocks are called W and M because the graphs of their returns in Figure 5-5 resemble a W and an M.)

The reason Stocks W and M can be combined to form a riskless portfolio is that their returns move countercyclically to each other — when W's returns fall, those of M rise, and vice versa. The tendency of two variables to move together is called **correlation,** and the **correlation coefficient, r,** measures this tendency.[7] In statistical terms, we say that the returns on Stocks W and M are *perfectly negatively correlated*, with r = −1.0.

The opposite of perfect negative correlation, with r = −1.0, is *perfect positive correlation*, with r = +1.0. Returns on two perfectly positively correlated stocks (M and M′) would move up and down together, and a portfolio consisting of two such stocks would be exactly as risky as the individual stocks. This point is illustrated in Figure 5-6, where we see that the portfolio's standard deviation is equal to that of the individual stocks. *Thus, diversification does nothing to reduce risk if the portfolio consists of perfectly positively correlated stocks.*

Figures 5-5 and 5-6 demonstrate that when stocks are perfectly negatively correlated (r = −1.0), all risk can be diversified away, but when stocks are perfectly positively correlated (r = +1.0), diversification does no good whatsoever. In reality, most stocks are positively correlated, but not perfectly so. On average, the correlation coefficient for the returns on two randomly selected stocks would be about +0.6, and for most pairs of stocks, r would lie in the range of +0.5 to +0.7. *Under such conditions, combining stocks into portfolios reduces risk but does not eliminate it completely.* Figure 5-7 illustrates this point with two stocks whose correlation coefficient is r = +0.67. The portfolio's average return is 15 percent, which is exactly the same as the average return for each of the two stocks, but its standard deviation is 20.6 percent, which is less than the standard deviation of either stock. Thus, the portfolio's risk is *not* an average of the risks of its individual stocks — diversification has reduced, but not eliminated, risk.

From these two-stock portfolio examples, we have seen that in one extreme case (r = −1.0), risk can be completely eliminated, while in the other extreme case (r = +1.0), diversification does nothing to limit risk. The real world lies between these extremes, so in general combining two stocks into a portfolio reduces, but does not eliminate, the riskiness inherent in the individual stocks.

What would happen if we included more than two stocks in the portfolio? *As a rule, the riskiness of a portfolio will decline as the number of stocks in the portfolio increases.* If we added enough partially correlated stocks, could we completely eliminate risk? In general, the answer is no, but the extent to which adding stocks to a portfolio reduces its risk depends on the *degree of correlation* among the stocks: The smaller the positive correlation coefficients, the lower the risk in a large portfolio. If we could find a set of

---

[7] The *correlation coefficient, r,* can range from +1.0, denoting that the two variables move up and down in perfect synchronization, to −1.0, denoting that the variables always move in exactly opposite directions. A correlation coefficient of zero indicates that the two variables are not related to each other — that is, changes in one variable are *independent* of changes in the other.

It is easy to calculate correlation coefficients with a financial calculator. Simply enter the returns on the two stocks and then press a key labeled "r." For W and M, r = −1.0.

FIGURE 5-5

Rate of Return Distributions for Two Perfectly Negatively Correlated Stocks (r = −1.0) and for Portfolio WM

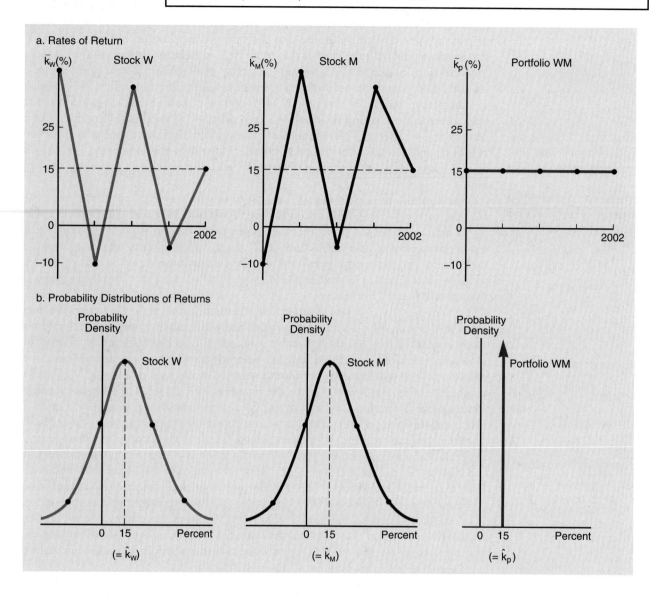

a. Rates of Return

b. Probability Distributions of Returns

YEAR	STOCK W ($\bar{k}_W$)	STOCK M ($\bar{k}_M$)	PORTFOLIO WM ($\bar{k}_P$)
1998	40.0%	(10.0%)	15.0%
1999	(10.0)	40.0	15.0
2000	35.0	(5.0)	15.0
2001	(5.0)	35.0	15.0
2002	15.0	15.0	15.0
Average return	15.0%	15.0%	15.0%
Standard deviation	22.6%	22.6%	0.0%

FIGURE 5-6

Rate of Return Distributions for Two Perfectly Positively Correlated Stocks (r = +1.0) and for Portfolio MM'

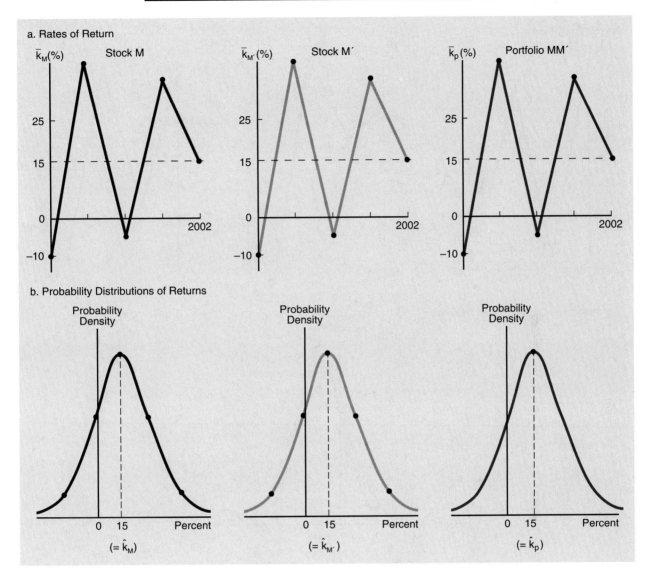

a. Rates of Return

b. Probability Distributions of Returns

YEAR	STOCK M ($\bar{k}_M$)	STOCK M' ($\bar{k}_{M'}$)	PORTFOLIO MM' ($\bar{k}_p$)
1998	(10.0%)	(10.0%)	(10.0%)
1999	40.0	40.0	40.0
2000	(5.0)	(5.0)	(5.0)
2001	35.0	35.0	35.0
2002	15.0	15.0	15.0
Average return	15.0%	15.0%	15.0%
Standard deviation	22.6%	22.6%	22.6%

FIGURE 5-7

Rate of Return Distributions for Two Partially Correlated Stocks (r = +0.67) and for Portfolio WY

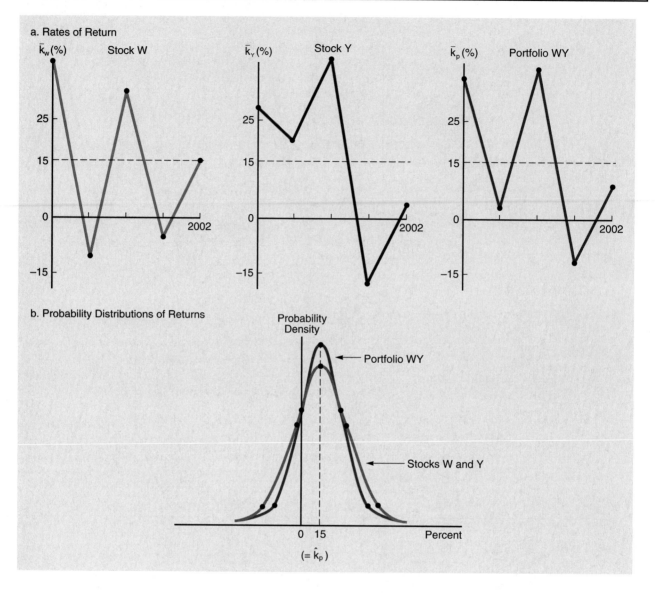

a. Rates of Return

b. Probability Distributions of Returns

YEAR	STOCK W $(\bar{k}_W)$	STOCK Y $(\bar{k}_Y)$	PORTFOLIO WY $(\bar{k}_p)$
1998	40.0%	28.0%	34.0%
1999	(10.0)	20.0	5.0
2000	35.0	41.0	38.0
2001	(5.0)	(17.0)	(11.0)
2002	15.0	3.0	9.0
Average return	15.0%	15.0%	15.0%
Standard deviation	22.6%	22.6%	20.6%

stocks whose correlations were zero or negative, all risk could be eliminated. *In the real world, where the correlations among the individual stocks are generally positive but less than +1.0, some, but not all, risk can be eliminated.*

To test your understanding, would you expect to find higher correlations between the returns on two companies in the same or in different industries? For example, would the correlation of returns on Ford's and General Motors' stocks be higher, or would the correlation coefficient be higher between either Ford or GM and AT&T, and how would those correlations affect the risk of portfolios containing them?

Answer: Ford's and GM's returns have a correlation coefficient of about 0.9 with one another because both are affected by auto sales, but their correlation is only about 0.6 with AT&T.

Implications: A two-stock portfolio consisting of Ford and GM would be less well diversified than a two-stock portfolio consisting of Ford or GM, plus AT&T. Thus, to minimize risk, portfolios should be diversified across industries.

Before leaving this section we should issue a warning — in the real world, it is *impossible* to find stocks like W and M, whose returns are expected to be perfectly negatively correlated. *Therefore, it is impossible to form completely riskless stock portfolios.* Diversification can reduce risk, but it cannot eliminate it. The real world is closer to the situation depicted in Figure 5-7.

DIVERSIFIABLE RISK VERSUS MARKET RISK

As noted above, it is difficult if not impossible to find stocks whose expected returns are negatively correlated — most stocks tend to do well when the national economy is strong and badly when it is weak.[8] Thus, even very large portfolios end up with a substantial amount of risk, but not as much risk as if all the money were invested in only one stock.

To see more precisely how portfolio size affects portfolio risk, consider Figure 5-8, which shows how portfolio risk is affected by forming larger and larger portfolios of randomly selected New York Stock Exchange (NYSE) stocks. Standard deviations are plotted for an average one-stock portfolio, a two-stock portfolio, and so on, up to a portfolio consisting of all 2,000-plus common stocks that were listed on the NYSE at the time the data were graphed. The graph illustrates that, in general, the riskiness of a portfolio consisting of large-company stocks tends to decline and to approach some limit as the size of the portfolio increases. According to data accumulated in recent years, σ_1, the standard deviation of a one-stock portfolio (or an average stock), is approximately 35 percent. A portfolio consisting of all stocks, which is called the **market portfolio,** would have a standard deviation, σ_M, of about 20.4 percent, which is shown as the horizontal dashed line in Figure 5-8.

Thus, almost half of the riskiness inherent in an average individual stock can be eliminated if the stock is held in a reasonably well-diversified portfolio, which is one containing 40 or more stocks. Some risk always remains, however, so it is virtually impossible to diversify away the effects of broad stock market movements that affect almost all stocks.

The part of a stock's risk that *can* be eliminated is called *diversifiable risk*, while the part that *cannot* be eliminated is called *market risk*.[9] The fact that a large part of the

Market Portfolio
A portfolio consisting of all stocks.

---

[8] It is not too hard to find a few stocks that happened to have risen because of a particular set of circumstances in the past while most other stocks were declining, but it is much harder to find stocks that could logically be *expected* to go up in the future when other stocks are falling.

[9] Diversifiable risk is also known as *company-specific*, or *unsystematic*, risk. Market risk is also known as *nondiversifiable*, or *systematic*, or *beta*, risk; it is the risk that remains after diversification.

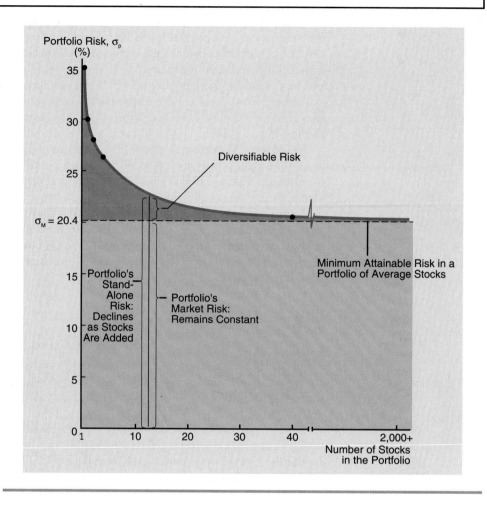

riskiness of any individual stock can be eliminated is vitally important, because rational investors *will* eliminate it and thus render it irrelevant.

Diversifiable Risk
That part of a security's risk associated with random events; it *can* be eliminated by proper diversification.

Market Risk
That part of a security's risk that *cannot* be eliminated by diversification.

Diversifiable risk is caused by such random events as lawsuits, strikes, successful and unsuccessful marketing programs, winning or losing a major contract, and other events that are unique to a particular firm. Since these events are random, their effects on a portfolio can be eliminated by diversification — bad events in one firm will be offset by good events in another. **Market risk,** on the other hand, stems from factors that systematically affect most firms: war, inflation, recessions, and high interest rates. Since most stocks are negatively affected by these factors, market risk cannot be eliminated by diversification.

We know that investors demand a premium for bearing risk; that is, the higher the riskiness of a security, the higher its expected return must be to induce investors to buy (or to hold) it. However, if investors are primarily concerned with the riskiness of their *portfolios* rather than the riskiness of the individual securities in the portfolio, how should the riskiness of an individual stock be measured? One answer is provided by the **Capital Asset Pricing Model (CAPM),** an important tool used to analyze the relationship between risk and rates of return.[10] The primary conclusion of the CAPM is this: *The relevant riskiness of an individual stock is its contribution to the riskiness of a well-diversified portfolio.* In other words, the riskiness of General Electric's stock to a doctor who has a portfolio of 40 stocks or to a trust officer managing a 150-stock portfolio is the contribution the GE stock makes to the portfolio's riskiness. The stock might be quite risky if held by itself, but if half of its risk can be eliminated by diversification, then its **relevant risk,** which is its *contribution to the portfolio's risk*, is much smaller than its stand-alone risk.

A simple example will help make this point clear. Suppose you are offered the chance to flip a coin once. If a head comes up, you win $20,000, but if a tail comes up, you lose $16,000. This is a good bet — the expected return is 0.5($20,000) + 0.5(−$16,000) = $2,000. However, it is a highly risky proposition, because you have a 50 percent chance of losing $16,000. Thus, you might well refuse to make the bet. Alternatively, suppose you were offered the chance to flip a coin 100 times, and you would win $200 for each head but lose $160 for each tail. It is possible that you would flip all heads and win $20,000, and it is also possible that you would flip all tails and lose $16,000, but the chances are very high that you would actually flip about 50 heads and about 50 tails, winning a net of about $2,000. Although each individual flip is a risky bet, collectively you have a low-risk proposition because most of the risk has been diversified away. This is the idea behind holding portfolios of stocks rather than just one stock, except that with stocks all of the risk cannot be eliminated by diversification — those risks related to broad, systematic changes in the stock market will remain.

Are all stocks equally risky in the sense that adding them to a well-diversified portfolio would have the same effect on the portfolio's riskiness? The answer is no. Different stocks will affect the portfolio differently, so different securities have different degrees of relevant risk. How can the relevant risk of an individual stock be measured? As we have seen, all risk except that related to broad market movements can, and presumably will, be diversified away. After all, why accept risk that can be easily eliminated? *The risk that remains after diversifying is market risk, or the risk that is inherent in the market, and it can be measured by the degree to which a given stock tends to move up or down with the market.* In the next section, we develop a measure of a stock's market risk, and then, in a later section, we introduce an equation for determining the required rate of return on a stock, given its market risk.

THE CONCEPT OF BETA

The tendency of a stock to move up and down with the market is reflected in its **beta coefficient, b.** Beta is a key element of the CAPM. An *average-risk stock* is *defined* as one that tends to move up and down in step with the general market as measured by some index such as the Dow Jones Industrials, the S&P 500, or the New York Stock Exchange Index. Such a stock will, *by definition*, be assigned a beta, b, of 1.0, which indicates that, in general, if the market moves up by 10 percent, the stock will also

---

[10] Indeed, the 1990 Nobel Prize was awarded to the developers of the CAPM, Professors Harry Markowitz and William F. Sharpe. The CAPM is a relatively complex subject, and only its basic elements are presented in this text. For a more detailed discussion, see any standard investments textbook.

The basic concepts of the CAPM were developed specifically for common stocks, and, therefore, the theory is examined first in this context. However, it has become common practice to extend CAPM concepts to capital budgeting and to speak of firms having "portfolios of tangible assets and projects." Capital budgeting is discussed in Part 4.

move up by 10 percent, while if the market falls by 10 percent, the stock will likewise fall by 10 percent. A portfolio of such b = 1.0 stocks will move up and down with the broad market averages, and it will be just as risky as the averages. If b = 0.5, the stock is only half as volatile as the market — it will rise and fall only half as much — and a portfolio of such stocks will be half as risky as a portfolio of b = 1.0 stocks. On the other hand, if b = 2.0, the stock is twice as volatile as an average stock, so a portfolio of such stocks will be twice as risky as an average portfolio. The value of such a port-

FIGURE 5-9   Relative Volatility of Stocks H, A, and L

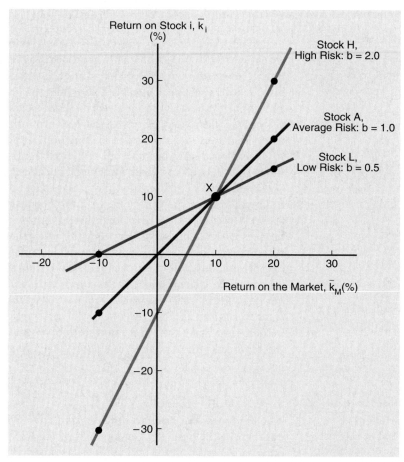

YEAR	$\bar{k}_H$	$\bar{k}_A$	$\bar{k}_L$	$\bar{k}_M$
1	10%	10%	10%	10%
2	30	20	15	20
3	(30)	(10)	0	(10)

NOTE: These three stocks plot exactly on their regression lines. This indicates that they are exposed only to market risk. Mutual funds that concentrate on stocks with betas of 2, 1, and 0.5 would have patterns similar to those shown in the graph.

folio could double — or halve — in a short time, and if you held such a portfolio, you could quickly go from millionaire to pauper.

Figure 5-9 graphs the relative volatility of three stocks. The illustrative data below the graph assume that in Year 1, the "market," defined as a portfolio consisting of all stocks, had a total return (dividend yield plus capital gains yield) of $k_M = 10\%$, and Stocks H, A, and L (for High, Average, and Low risk) also all had returns of 10 percent. In Year 2, the market went up sharply, and the return on the market portfolio was $\bar{k}_M = 20\%$. Returns on the three stocks also went up: H soared to 30 percent; A went up to 20 percent, the same as the market; and L only went up to 15 percent. Now suppose the market dropped in Year 3, and the market return was $\bar{k}_M = -10\%$. The three stocks' returns also fell, H plunging to -30 percent, A falling to -10 percent, and L going down only to $\bar{k}_L = 0\%$. Thus, the three stocks all moved in the same direction as the market, but H was by far the most volatile; A was just as volatile as the market; and L was less volatile.

Beta measures a stock's volatility relative to an average stock, which by definition has b = 1.0, and a stock's beta can be calculated by plotting a line like those in Figure 5-9. The slopes of the lines show how each stock moves in response to a movement in the general market — *indeed, the slope coefficient of such a "regression line" is defined as a beta coefficient*. (Procedures for actually calculating betas are described in Web Appendix 5A, which can be found on the textbook's web site, **http://brigham.swlearning. com**.) Betas for literally thousands of companies are calculated and published by Merrill Lynch, Value Line, and numerous other organizations, and the beta coefficients of some well-known companies are shown in Table 5-4. Most stocks have betas in the range of 0.50 to 1.50, and the average for all stocks is 1.0 by definition.

Theoretically, it is possible for a stock to have a negative beta. In this case, the stock's returns would tend to rise whenever the returns on other stocks fall. Keep in mind, though, that a stock in a given year may move counter to the overall market, even though the stock's beta is positive. If a stock has a positive beta, we would *expect*

TABLE 5-4	Illustrative List of Beta Coefficients

STOCK	BETA
Merrill Lynch	1.85
AOL Time Warner	1.65
General Electric	1.30
Microsoft Corp.	1.20
IBM	1.05
Coca-Cola	0.85
Energen Corp.[a]	0.75
Procter & Gamble	0.65
Heinz	0.55
FPL Group	0.45

[a] Energen is a gas distribution company. It has a monopoly in much of Alabama, and its prices are adjusted every three months so as to keep its profits relatively constant.
SOURCE: Adapted from *Value Line*, May 2002.

THE BENEFITS OF DIVERSIFYING OVERSEAS

The size of the global stock market has grown steadily over the last several decades, and it passed the $15 trillion mark during 1995. U.S. stocks account for approximately 41 percent of this total, whereas the Japanese and European markets constitute roughly 25 and 26 percent, respectively. The rest of the world makes up the remaining 8 percent. Although the U.S. equity market has long been the world's biggest, its share of the world total has decreased over time.

The expanding universe of securities available internationally suggests the possibility of achieving a better risk-return trade-off than could be obtained by investing solely in U.S. securities. So, investing overseas might lower risk and simultaneously increase expected returns. The potential benefits of diversification are due to the facts that the correlation between the returns on U.S. and international securities is fairly low, and returns in developing nations are often quite high.

Figure 5-8, presented earlier, demonstrated that an investor can significantly reduce the risk of his or her portfolio by holding a large number of stocks. The figure accompanying this box suggests that investors may be able to reduce risk even further by holding a large portfolio of stocks from all around the world, given the fact that the returns of domestic and international stocks are not perfectly correlated.

Despite the apparent benefits from investing overseas, the typical U.S. investor still dedicates less than 10 percent of his or her portfolio to foreign stocks — even though foreign stocks represent roughly 60 percent of the worldwide equity market. Researchers and practitioners alike have struggled to understand this reluctance to invest overseas. One explanation is that investors prefer domestic stocks because they have lower transaction costs. However, this explanation is not completely convincing, given that recent studies have found that investors buy and sell their overseas stocks more frequently than they trade their domestic stocks. Other explanations for the domestic bias focus on the additional risks from investing overseas (for example, exchange rate risk) or suggest that the typical U.S. investor is uninformed about international investments and/or views international investments as being extremely risky or uncertain. More recently, other analysts have argued that as world capital markets have become more integrated, the correlation of returns between different countries has increased, and hence the benefits from international diversification have declined. A third explanation is that U.S. corporations are themselves investing more internationally, hence U.S. investors are de facto obtaining international diversification.

Whatever the reason for the general reluctance to hold international assets, it is a safe bet that in the future U.S. investors will shift more and more of their assets to overseas investments.

SOURCE: Kenneth Kasa, "Measuring the Gains from International Portfolio Diversification," *Federal Reserve Bank of San Francisco Weekly Letter*, Number 94–14, April 8, 1994.

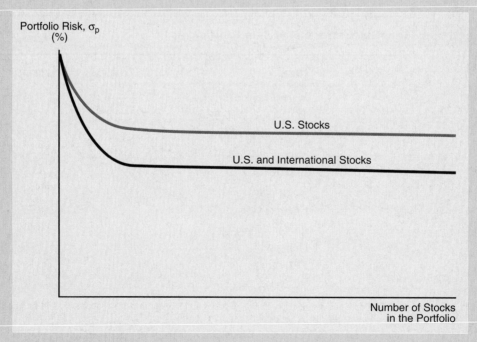

its return to increase whenever the overall stock market rises. However, company-specific factors may cause the stock's realized return to decline, even though the market's return is positive.

If a stock whose beta is greater than 1.0 is added to a b = 1.0 portfolio, then the portfolio's beta, and consequently its riskiness, will increase. Conversely, if a stock whose beta is less than 1.0 is added to a b = 1.0 portfolio, the portfolio's beta and risk will decline. *Thus, since a stock's beta measures its contribution to the riskiness of a portfolio, beta is the theoretically correct measure of the stock's riskiness.*

The preceding analysis of risk in a portfolio context is part of the Capital Asset Pricing Model (CAPM), and we can summarize our discussion to this point as follows:

1. A stock's risk consists of two components, market risk and diversifiable risk.

2. Diversifiable risk can be eliminated by diversification, and most investors do indeed diversify, either by holding large portfolios or by purchasing shares in a mutual fund. We are left, then, with market risk, which is caused by general movements in the stock market and which reflects the fact that most stocks are systematically affected by events like war, recessions, and inflation. Market risk is the only relevant risk to a rational, diversified investor because such an investor would eliminate diversifiable risk.

3. Investors must be compensated for bearing risk — the greater the riskiness of a stock, the higher its required return. However, compensation is required only for risk that cannot be eliminated by diversification. If risk premiums existed on stocks due to diversifiable risk, well-diversified investors would start buying those securities (which would not be especially risky to such investors) and bidding up their prices, and the stocks' final (equilibrium) expected returns would reflect only nondiversifiable market risk.

    If this point is not clear, an example may help clarify it. Suppose half of Stock A's risk is market risk (it occurs because Stock A moves up and down with the market), while the other half of A's risk is diversifiable. You hold only Stock A, so you are exposed to all of its risk. As compensation for bearing so much risk, you want a risk premium of 8 percent over the 10 percent T-bond rate. Thus, your required return is k_A = 10% + 8% = 18%. But suppose other investors, including your professor, are well diversified; they also hold Stock A, but they have eliminated its diversifiable risk and thus are exposed to only half as much risk as you. Therefore, their risk premium will be only half as large as yours, and their required rate of return will be k_A = 10% + 4% = 14%.

    If the stock were yielding more than 14 percent in the market, diversified investors, including your professor, would buy it. If it were yielding 18 percent, you would be willing to buy it, but well-diversified investors would bid its price up and its yield down, hence you could not buy it at a price low enough to provide you with an 18 percent return. In the end, you would have to accept a 14 percent return or else keep your money in the bank. Thus, risk premiums in a market populated by rational, diversified investors can reflect only market risk.

4. The market risk of a stock is measured by its beta coefficient, which is an index of the stock's relative volatility. Some benchmark betas follow:

    b = 0.5: Stock is only half as volatile, or risky, as an average stock.

    b = 1.0: Stock is of average risk.

    b = 2.0: Stock is twice as risky as an average stock.

5. A portfolio consisting of low-beta securities will itself have a low beta, because the beta of a portfolio is a weighted average of its individual securities' betas:

$$b_p = w_1 b_1 + w_2 b_2 + \cdots + w_n b_n$$

$$= \sum_{i=1}^{n} w_i b_i. \tag{5-6}$$

Here b_p is the beta of the portfolio, and it shows how volatile the portfolio is in relation to the market; w_i is the fraction of the portfolio invested in the ith stock; and b_i is the beta coefficient of the ith stock. For example, if an investor holds a $100,000 portfolio consisting of $33,333.33 invested in each of three stocks, and if each of the stocks has a beta of 0.7, then the portfolio's beta will be $b_p = 0.7$:

$$b_p = 0.3333(0.7) + 0.3333(0.7) + 0.3333(0.7) = 0.7.$$

Such a portfolio will be less risky than the market, so it should experience relatively narrow price swings and have relatively small rate-of-return fluctuations. In terms of Figure 5-9, the slope of its regression line would be 0.7, which is less than that for a portfolio of average stocks.

Now suppose one of the existing stocks is sold and replaced by a stock with $b_i = 2.0$. This action will increase the beta of the portfolio from $b_{p1} = 0.7$ to $b_{p2} = 1.13$:

$$b_{p2} = 0.3333(0.7) + 0.3333(0.7) + 0.3333(2.0)$$

$$= 1.13.$$

Had a stock with $b_i = 0.2$ been added, the portfolio beta would have declined from 0.7 to 0.53. Adding a low-beta stock, therefore, would reduce the riskiness of the portfolio. Consequently, adding new stocks to a portfolio can change the riskiness of that portfolio.

6. *Since a stock's beta coefficient determines how the stock affects the riskiness of a diversified portfolio, beta is the most relevant measure of any stock's risk.*

SELF-TEST QUESTIONS

Explain the following statement: "An asset held as part of a portfolio is generally less risky than the same asset held in isolation."

What is meant by *perfect positive correlation, perfect negative correlation,* and *zero correlation?*

In general, can the riskiness of a portfolio be reduced to zero by increasing the number of stocks in the portfolio? Explain.

What is an average-risk stock? What will be its beta?

Why is beta the theoretically correct measure of a stock's riskiness?

If you plotted the returns on a particular stock versus those on the Dow Jones Index over the past five years, what would the slope of the regression line you obtained indicate about the stock's market risk?

THE RELATIONSHIP BETWEEN RISK AND RATES OF RETURN

In the preceding section, we saw that under the CAPM theory, beta is the appropriate measure of a stock's relevant risk. Now we must specify the relationship between risk and return: For a given level of risk as measured by beta, what rate of return will investors require to compensate them for bearing that risk? To begin, let us define the following terms:

$\hat{k}_i$ = *expected* rate of return on the ith stock.

k_i = *required* rate of return on the ith stock. Note that if $\hat{k}_i$ is less than k_i, you would not purchase this stock, or you would sell it if you owned it. If $\hat{k}_i$ were greater than k_i, you would want to buy the stock, because it looks like a bargain. You would be indifferent if $\hat{k}_i = k_i$.

$\bar{k}$ = realized, after-that-fact return. One obviously does not know $\bar{k}$ at the time he or she is considering the purchase of a stock.

k_{RF} = risk-free rate of return. In this context, k_{RF} is generally measured by the return on long-term U.S. Treasury bonds.

b_i = beta coefficient of the ith stock. The beta of an average stock is $b_A = 1.0$.

k_M = required rate of return on a portfolio consisting of all stocks, which is called the *market portfolio*. k_M is also the required rate of return on an average ($b_A = 1.0$) stock.

$RP_M = (k_M - k_{RF})$ = risk premium on "the market," and also on an average ($b = 1.0$) stock. This is the additional return over the risk-free rate required to compensate an average investor for assuming an average amount of risk. Average risk means a stock whose $b_i = b_A = 1.0$.

$RP_i = (k_M - k_{RF})b_i = (RP_M)b_i$ = risk premium on the ith stock. The stock's risk premium will be less than, equal to, or greater than the premium on an average stock, RP_M, depending on whether its beta is less than, equal to, or greater than 1.0. If $b_i = b_A = 1.0$, then $RP_i = RP_M$.

Market Risk Premium, RP_M
The additional return over the risk-free rate needed to compensate investors for assuming an average amount of risk.

The **market risk premium, RP_M,** shows the premium investors require for bearing the risk of an average stock. The size of this premium depends on the perceived risk of the stock market and investors' degree of risk aversion. Let us assume that at the current time Treasury bonds yield $k_{RF} = 6\%$ and an average share of stock has a required rate of return of $k_M = 11\%$. Therefore, the market risk premium is 5 percent calculated as:

$$RP_M = k_M - k_{RF} = 11\% - 6\% = 5\%.$$

It should be noted that the risk premium of an average stock, $k_M - k_{RF}$, is hard to measure because it is impossible to obtain precise estimates of the expected future

HAS THERE BEEN A SHIFT IN THE MARKET RISK PREMIUM?

In the 18-year period between 1982 and 1999, the Dow Jones Industrial Average rose from 777 to over 10,526, or an increase of approximately 1,255 percent! Although millions of investors profited from this increase, many analysts believed at the time that stocks were overvalued. These analysts pointed to record P/E ratios as an indication that stock prices were too high. Federal Reserve Chairman Alan Greenspan made the same point, warning about the dangers of "irrational exuberance."

In sharp contrast to this bearish perspective, James Glassman and Kevin Hassett, co-authors of a book, *Dow 36,000*, made the following argument in March 1999:

> Using sensible assumptions, we are comfortable with stock prices rising to three or four times their current levels. Our calculations show that with earnings growing at the same rate as the gross domestic product and Treasury bond yields below 6 percent, a perfectly reasonable level for the Dow would be 36,000 — tomorrow, not 10 or 20 years from now.

How did Glassman and Hassett reach this conclusion? They claimed that the market risk premium ($k_M - k_{RF}$) had declined, and that it would continue to decline in the future. Investors require a risk premium for bearing risk, and the size of that premium depends on the average investor's degree of risk aversion. From 1926 through 1999, large-company stocks produced average annual returns of 13.3 percent, while the returns on long-term government bonds averaged 5.5 percent, suggesting a risk premium of $13.3\% - 5.5\% = 7.8\%$. However, Glassman and Hassett made the following assertion in March 1999:

> What has happened since 1982, and especially during the past four years, is that investors have become calmer and smarter. They are requiring a much smaller extra return, or "risk premium," from stocks to compensate for their fear. That premium, which has averaged about 7 percent in modern history, is now around 3 percent. We believe that it is headed for its proper level: zero. That means that stock prices should rise accordingly.

A declining risk premium leads to a lower required return on stocks. This, in turn, implies that stock prices should rise because the same cash flows will then be discounted at a lower rate. To support their argument, Glassman and Hassett cite research by Jeremy Siegel of the University of Pennsylvania's Wharton School. In his best-selling book, *Stocks for the Long Run*, Siegel documents that over the long run stocks have not been riskier than bonds. Indeed, based on his research, Siegel concludes that, "The safest long-term investment for the preservation of purchasing power has clearly been stocks, not bonds."

Siegel acknowledges that stocks are riskier for short-term investors. This point is confirmed when we compare the average annual standard deviation of stock market returns (20 percent)

return of the market, k_M.[11] Given the difficulty of estimating future market returns, analysts often look to historical data to estimate the market risk premium. Historical data suggest that the market risk premium varies somewhat from year to year, and it has generally ranged from 4 to 8 percent.

While historical estimates might be a good starting point for estimating the market risk premium, historical estimates may be misleading if investors' attitudes toward risk change considerably over time. (See the Industry Practice Box entitled "Estimating the Market Risk Premium.") Indeed, many analysts have argued that the market risk premium has fallen in recent years because an increasing number of investors have been willing to bear the risks of the stock market. If this claim is correct, the market risk premium may be considerably lower than what would be implied using historical data. (See the Industry Practice Box entitled "Has There Been a Shift

---

[11] This concept, as well as other aspects of the CAPM, is discussed in more detail in Chapter 3 of Eugene F. Brigham and Phillip R. Daves, *Intermediate Financial Management*, 7th ed. (Cincinnati, OH: South-Western College Publishing, 2002). Chapter 3 of *Intermediate Financial Management* also discusses the assumptions embodied in the CAPM framework. Some of these are unrealistic, and because of this the theory does not hold exactly.

with that of bonds (9 percent). The higher volatility of stocks occurs because stocks get hit harder than bonds in the short run when the economy weakens or inflation increases. However, stocks have always eventually recovered, and over longer periods they have outperformed bonds.

To put all of this in perspective, we need to address three important points. First, the relevant market risk premium is forward looking — it is based on investors' perceptions of the relative riskiness of stocks versus bonds in the future, and it will change over time. Most analysts acknowledge that the risk premium has fallen, but few agree with Glassman and Hassett that it is or should be zero. Most believe that investors require a premium in the neighborhood of at least 3 to 5 percent as an inducement for holding stocks. Moreover, the risk premium would probably rise sharply if something led to a sustained market decline.

Second, if the risk premium were to stabilize at a relatively low level, then investors would receive low stock returns in the future. For example, if the T-bond yield were 5 percent and the market risk premium were 3 percent, then the required return on the market would be 8 percent. In this situation, it would be unreasonable to expect stock returns of 12 to 13 percent in the future.

Third, investors should be concerned with real returns, which take inflation into account. For example, suppose the risk-free nominal rate of return were 5.5 percent and the market risk premium were 3 percent. Here, the expected nominal return on an average stock would be 8.5 percent. If inflation were 3.5 percent, the real return would be only 5.0 percent. Correctly looking at things in terms of real returns suggests that with low market risk premiums, stocks will have a hard time competing with inflation-indexed Treasury securities, which currently provide investors with only a slightly lower real return with considerably less risk.

Glassman and Hassett raise some interesting points, and there are reasons to believe that the market risk premium is lower today than it was a generation ago. Nevertheless, we can also make the case that the authors of *Dow 36,000* exaggerated the shift in investor attitudes, and that their book reflects the overheated euphoria that existed at the height of the stock market boom. Indeed, it is worth noting that in the three years since Glassman and Hassett published *Dow 36,000*, many investors have experienced large declines in the values of their portfolios, especially after the September 11, 2001, terrorist attacks. It remains an open question how much all this has affected investors' perceptions of the market's risk. In the midst of this declining market and terrorist fears, James Glassman recently acknowledged that things may have changed since the book was written: "We're having our theory put to the test. Can the economy continue to grow at its historic rate of 2.5 percent? And have investors been so spooked by terrorism that it permanently changed their view about the future? The problem is that it's too soon to tell if either of these is happening."

SOURCES: James K. Glassman and Kevin A. Hassett, "Stock Prices Are Still Far Too Low," *The Wall Street Journal*, March 17, 1999, A26; and "Stock Risks Poised to Rise in Changed Postattack World," *The Wall Street Journal*, September 24, 2001, C1.

in the Market Risk Premium?" for a discussion of how changes in investor risk aversion may have influenced the market risk premium and stock returns in recent years.)

While the market risk premium represents the risk premium for the entire stock market, the risk premium on individual stocks will vary. For example, if one stock were twice as risky as another, its risk premium would be twice as high, while if its risk were only half as much, its risk premium would be half as large. Further, we can measure a stock's relative riskiness by its beta coefficient. If we know the market risk premium, RP_M, and the stock's risk as measured by its beta coefficient, b_i, we can find the stock's risk premium as the product $(RP_M)b_i$. For example, if $b_i = 0.5$ and $RP_M = 5\%$, then RP_i is 2.5 percent:

$$\text{Risk premium for Stock i} = RP_i = (RP_M)b_i \qquad (5\text{-}7)$$
$$= (5\%)(0.5)$$
$$= 2.5\%.$$

As the discussion in Chapter 4 implied, the required return for any investment can be expressed in general terms as

$$\text{Required return} = \text{Risk-free return} + \text{Premium for risk.}$$

Here the risk-free return includes a premium for expected inflation, and we assume that the assets under consideration have similar maturities and liquidity. Under these conditions, the required return for Stock i can be written as follows:

SML Equation:
$$\text{Required return on Stock i} = \text{Risk-free rate} + \left(\text{Market risk premium}\right)\left(\text{Stock i's beta}\right)$$

$$k_i = k_{RF} + (k_M - k_{RF})b_i \qquad (5\text{-}8)$$
$$= k_{RF} + (RP_M)b_i$$
$$= 6\% + (11\% - 6\%)(0.5)$$
$$= 6\% + 5\%(0.5)$$
$$= 8.5\%.$$

Equation 5-8 is called the Security Market Line (SML).

If some other Stock j were riskier than Stock i and had $b_j = 2.0$, then its required rate of return would be 16 percent:

$$k_j = 6\% + (5\%)2.0 = 16\%.$$

An average stock, with $b = 1.0$, would have a required return of 11 percent, the same as the market return:

$$k_A = 6\% + (5\%)1.0 = 11\% = k_M.$$

Security Market Line (SML)
The line on a graph that shows the relationship between risk as measured by beta and the required rate of return for individual securities. Equation 5-8 is the equation for the SML.

As noted above, Equation 5-8 is called the **Security Market Line (SML)** equation, and it is often expressed in graph form, as in Figure 5-10 which shows the SML when $k_{RF} = 6\%$ and $k_M = 11\%$. Note the following points:

1. Required rates of return are shown on the vertical axis, while risk as measured by beta is shown on the horizontal axis. This graph is quite different from the one shown in Figure 5-9, where the returns on individual stocks were plotted on the vertical axis and returns on the market index were shown on the horizontal axis. The slopes of the three lines in Figure 5-9 were used to calculate the three stocks' betas, and those betas were then plotted as points on the horizontal axis of Figure 5-10.

2. Riskless securities have $b_i = 0$; therefore, k_{RF} appears as the vertical axis intercept in Figure 5-10. If we could construct a portfolio that had a beta of zero, it would have an expected return equal to the risk-free rate.

3. The slope of the SML (5% in Figure 5-10) reflects the degree of risk aversion in the economy — the greater the average investor's aversion to risk, then (a) the steeper the slope of the line, (b) the greater the risk premium for all stocks, and (c) the higher the required rate of return on all stocks.[12] These points are discussed further in a later section.

4. The values we worked out for stocks with $b_i = 0.5$, $b_i = 1.0$, and $b_i = 2.0$ agree with the values shown on the graph for k_{Low}, k_A, and k_{High}.

---

[12] Students sometimes confuse beta with the slope of the SML. This is a mistake. The slope of any straight line is equal to the "rise" divided by the "run," or $(Y_1 - Y_0)/(X_1 - X_0)$. Consider Figure 5-10. If we let $Y = k$ and $X = $ beta, and we go from the origin to $b = 1.0$, we see that the slope is $(k_M - k_{RF})/(b_M - b_{RF}) = (11\% - 6\%)/(1 - 0) = 5\%$. Thus, the slope of the SML is equal to $(k_M - k_{RF})$, the market risk premium. In Figure 5-10, $k_i = 6\% + 5\%b_i$, so a doubling of beta (for example, from 1.0 to 2.0) would produce a 5 percentage point increase in k_i.

FIGURE 5-10   The Security Market Line (SML)

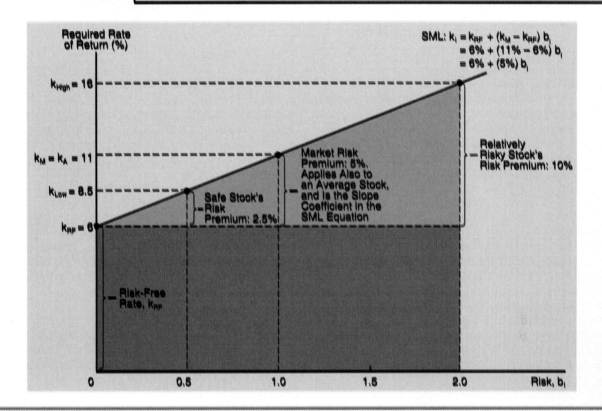

Both the Security Market Line and a company's position on it change over time due to changes in interest rates, investors' aversion to risk, and individual companies' betas. Such changes are discussed in the following sections.

THE IMPACT OF INFLATION

As we learned in Chapter 4, interest amounts to "rent" on borrowed money, or the price of money. Thus, k_{RF} is the price of money to a riskless borrower. We also learned that the risk-free rate as measured by the rate on U.S. Treasury securities is called the *nominal*, or *quoted*, *rate*, and it consists of two elements: (1) a *real inflation-free rate of return*, k^*, and (2) an *inflation premium*, IP, equal to the anticipated rate of inflation.[13] Thus, $k_{RF} = k^* + IP$. The real rate on long-term Treasury bonds has historically ranged from 2 to 4 percent, with a mean of about 3 percent. Therefore, if no inflation were expected, long-term Treasury bonds would yield about 3 percent. However, as the expected rate of inflation increases, a premium must be added to the real risk-free rate of return to compensate investors for the loss of purchasing power that results from inflation. Therefore, the 6 percent k_{RF} shown in Figure 5-10 might

---

[13] Long-term Treasury bonds also contain a maturity risk premium, MRP. Here we include the MRP in k^* to simplify the discussion.

ESTIMATING THE MARKET RISK PREMIUM

The Capital Asset Pricing Model (CAPM) is more than just a theory describing the trade-off between risk and return. The CAPM is also widely used in practice. As we will see in Chapter 8, investors use the CAPM to determine the discount rate for valuing stocks. Later, in Chapter 9, we will also see that corporate managers use the CAPM to estimate the cost of equity financing.

The market risk premium is an important component of the CAPM. In practice, what we would ideally like to use in the CAPM is the *expected* market risk premium, which gives an indication of investors' future returns. Unfortunately, we cannot directly observe investors' expectations. Instead, academicians and practitioners often use an historical estimate of the market risk premium as a proxy for the expected risk premium.

Historical premiums are found by taking the differences between actual returns of the overall stock market and the risk-free rate. Ibbotson Associates provide perhaps the most comprehensive estimates of historical risk premiums. Their estimates indicate that the equity risk premium has averaged about 8 percent a year over the past 76 years.

Analysts have pointed out some of the shortcomings of using an historical estimate as a proxy for the expected risk premium. First, historical estimates may be very misleading at times when the market risk premium is changing. As we mentioned in an earlier box entitled "Has There Been a Shift in the Market Risk Premium?," many analysts believe that the expected risk premium has fallen in recent years. It is important to recognize that a sharp drop in the expected risk premium (perhaps because of lower perceived risk and/or declining risk aversion) pushes up stock prices, and that ironically *increases* the observed (historical) risk premium. In this situation, an analyst would be seriously missing the boat if he used the historical risk premium to approximate the expected risk premium. To further illustrate this point, the strong performance in the stock market over the past several years has produced high historical premiums — indeed, Ibbotson Associates estimate that the market risk premium averaged 22.3 percent a year during the period between 1995 and 1999. Nobody would seriously suggest that future investors require a 22.3 percent premium to invest in the stock market! Given these concerns, Ibbotson and others suggest that historical estimates are more reliable if estimated over longer time intervals.

A second concern is that historical estimates may be biased upward because they only include the returns of firms that have survived and do not take into account the performances of failing firms. Stephen Brown, William Goetzmann, and Stephen Ross discussed the implications of this "survivorship bias" in a 1995 *Journal of Finance* article. Putting these ideas into practice, Tom Copeland, Tim Koller, and Jack Murrin have recently suggested that this "survivorship bias" increases historical returns by 1½ to 2 percent a year. For that reason, they suggest that practitioners trying to estimate a forward-looking expected risk premium subtract 1½ to 2 percent from their historical risk premium estimates.

SOURCES: *Stocks, Bonds, Bills, and Inflation: (Valuation Edition) 2002 Yearbook* (Chicago: Ibbotson Associates, 2002); Stephen J. Brown, William N. Goetzmann, and Stephen A. Ross, "Survival," *Journal of Finance*, Vol. 50, No. 3, July 1995, 853–873; and Tom Copeland, Tim Koller, and Jack Murrin, *Valuation: Measuring and Managing the Value of Companies*, 3rd edition (New York: McKinsey & Company, 2000).

be thought of as consisting of a 3 percent real risk-free rate of return plus a 3 percent inflation premium: $k_{RF} = k^* + IP = 3\% + 3\% = 6\%$.

If the expected inflation rate rose by 2 percent, to $3\% + 2\% = 5\%$, this would cause k_{RF} to rise to 8 percent. Such a change is shown in Figure 5-11. Notice that under the CAPM, the increase in k_{RF} leads to an *equal* increase in the rate of return on all risky assets, because the same inflation premium is built into the required rate of return of both riskless and risky assets.[14] For example, the rate of return on an

---

[14] Recall that the inflation premium for any asset is equal to the average expected rate of inflation over the asset's life. Thus, in this analysis we must assume either that all securities plotted on the SML graph have the same life or else that the expected rate of future inflation is constant.

It should also be noted that k_{RF} in a CAPM analysis can be proxied by either a long-term rate (the T-bond rate) or a short-term rate (the T-bill rate). Traditionally, the T-bill rate was used, but in recent years there has been a movement toward use of the T-bond rate because there is a closer relationship between T-bond yields and stocks than between T-bill yields and stocks. See *Stocks, Bonds, Bills, and Inflation: (Valuation Edition) 2002 Yearbook* (Chicago: Ibbotson Associates, 2002) for a discussion.

FIGURE 5-11 Shift in the SML Caused by an Increase in Inflation

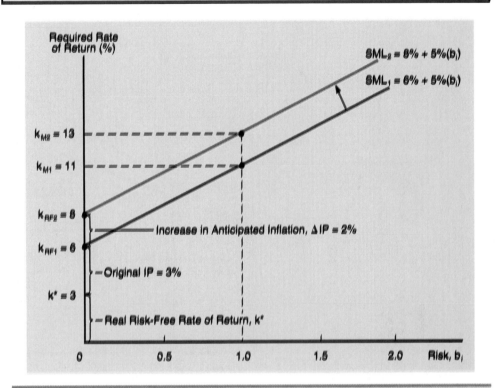

average stock, k_M, increases from 11 to 13 percent. Other risky securities' returns also rise by two percentage points.

CHANGES IN RISK AVERSION

The slope of the Security Market Line reflects the extent to which investors are averse to risk — the steeper the slope of the line, the greater the average investor's risk aversion. Suppose investors were indifferent to risk; that is, they were not risk averse. If k_{RF} were 6 percent, then risky assets would also provide an expected return of 6 percent, because if there were no risk aversion, there would be no risk premium, and the SML would graph as a horizontal line. As risk aversion increases, so does the risk premium, and this causes the slope of the SML to become steeper.

Figure 5-12 illustrates an increase in risk aversion. The market risk premium rises from 5 to 7.5 percent, causing k_M to rise from $k_{M1} = 11\%$ to $k_{M2} = 13.5\%$. The returns on other risky assets also rise, and the effect of this shift in risk aversion is more pronounced on riskier securities. For example, the required return on a stock with $b_i = 0.5$ increases by only 1.25 percentage points, from 8.5 to 9.75 percent, whereas that on a stock with $b_i = 1.5$ increases by 3.75 percentage points, from 13.5 to 17.25 percent.

CHANGES IN A STOCK'S BETA COEFFICIENT

As we shall see later in the book, a firm can influence its market risk, hence its beta, through changes in the composition of its assets and also through its use of debt. A

FIGURE 5-12

Shift in the SML Caused by Increased Risk Aversion

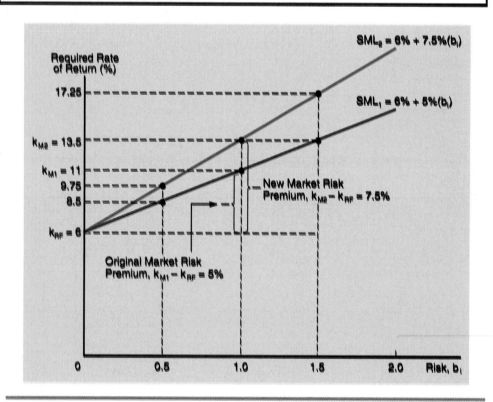

company's beta can also change as a result of external factors such as increased competition in its industry, the expiration of basic patents, and the like. When such changes occur, the required rate of return also changes, and, as we shall see in Chapter 8, this will affect the firm's stock price. For example, consider Allied Food Products, with a beta of 1.40. Now suppose some action occurred that caused Allied's beta to increase from 1.40 to 2.00. If the conditions depicted in Figure 5-10 held, Allied's required rate of return would increase from 13 to 16 percent:

$$k_1 = k_{RF} + (k_M - k_{RF})b_i$$
$$= 6\% + (11\% - 6\%)1.40$$
$$= 13\%$$

to

$$k_2 = 6\% + (11\% - 6\%)2.0$$
$$= 16\%.$$

As we shall see in Chapter 8, this change would have a dramatic impact on Allied's stock price.

Differentiate among the expected rate of return ($\hat{k}$), the required rate of return (k), and the realized, after-the-fact return ($\bar{k}$) on a stock. Which would have to be larger to get you to buy the stock, $\hat{k}$ or k? Would $\hat{k}$, k, and $\bar{k}$ typically be the same or different? Explain.

What are the differences between the relative volatility graph (Figure 5-9), where "betas are made," and the SML graph (Figure 5-10), where "betas are used"? Discuss both how the graphs are constructed and the information they convey.

What happens to the SML graph in Figure 5-10 when inflation increases or decreases?

What happens to the SML graph when risk aversion increases or decreases?

What would the SML look like if investors were indifferent to risk, that is, if they had zero risk aversion?

How can a firm influence its market risk as reflected in its beta?

PHYSICAL ASSETS VERSUS SECURITIES

In a book on financial management for business firms, why do we spend so much time discussing the riskiness of stocks? Why not begin by looking at the riskiness of such business assets as plant and equipment? *The reason is that, for a management whose primary goal is stock price maximization, the overriding consideration is the riskiness of the firm's stock, and the relevant risk of any physical asset must be measured in terms of its effect on the stock's risk as seen by investors.* For example, suppose Goodyear Tire Company is considering a major investment in a new product, recapped tires. Sales of recaps, hence earnings on the new operation, are highly uncertain, so on a stand-alone basis the new venture appears to be quite risky. However, suppose returns in the recap business are negatively correlated with Goodyear's regular operations — when times are good and people have plenty of money, they buy new tires, but when times are bad, they tend to buy more recaps. Therefore, returns would be high on regular operations and low on the recap division during good times, but the opposite would occur during recessions. The result might be a pattern like that shown earlier in Figure 5-5 for Stocks W and M. Thus, what appears to be a risky investment when viewed on a stand-alone basis might not be very risky when viewed within the context of the company as a whole.

This analysis can be extended to the corporation's stockholders. Because Goodyear's stock is owned by diversified stockholders, the real issue each time management makes an asset investment is this: How will this investment affect the risk of our stockholders? Again, the stand-alone risk of an individual project may look quite high, but viewed in the context of the project's effect on stockholders' risk, it may not be very large. We will address this issue again in Chapter 9, where we examine the effects of capital budgeting on companies' beta coefficients and thus on stockholders' risks.

SOME CONCERNS ABOUT BETA AND THE CAPM

www Kenneth French's web site http://mba.tuck. dartmouth.edu/pages/faculty/ ken.french/index.html is an excellent resource for data and information regarding factors related to stock returns.

The Capital Asset Pricing Model (CAPM) is more than just an abstract theory described in textbooks — it is also widely used by analysts, investors, and corporations. However, despite the CAPM's intuitive appeal, a number of recent studies have raised concerns about its validity. In particular, a recent study by Eugene Fama of the University of Chicago and Kenneth French of Yale found no historical relationship between stocks' returns and their market betas, confirming a position long held by a number of professors and stock market analysts.[15]

If beta does not determine returns, what does? Fama and French found two variables that are consistently related to stock returns: (1) the firm's size and (2) its market/book ratio. After adjusting for other factors, they found that smaller firms have provided relatively high returns, and that returns are higher on stocks with low market/book ratios. By contrast, they found no relationship between a stock's beta and its return.

As an alternative to the traditional CAPM, researchers and practitioners have begun to look to more general multi-beta models that encompass the CAPM and address its shortcomings. The multi-beta model is an attractive generalization of the traditional CAPM model's insight that market risk — risk that cannot be diversified away — underlies the pricing of assets. In the multi-beta model, market risk is measured relative to a set of risk factors that determine the behavior of asset returns, whereas the CAPM gauges risk only relative to the market return. It is important to note that the risk factors in the multi-beta model are all nondiversifiable sources of risk. Empirical research investigating the relationship between economic risk factors and security returns is ongoing, but it has discovered several systematic empirical risk factors, including the bond default premium, the bond term structure premium, and inflation.

Practitioners and academicians have long recognized the limitations of the CAPM, and they are constantly looking for ways to improve it. The multi-beta model is a potential step in that direction. Although the CAPM represents a significant step forward in security pricing theory, it does have some deficiencies when applied in practice, hence estimates of k_i found through use of the SML may be subject to considerable error.

---

[15] See Eugene F. Fama and Kenneth R. French, "The Cross-Section of Expected Stock Returns," *Journal of Finance*, Vol. 47, 1992, 427–465; and Eugene F. Fama and Kenneth R. French, "Common Risk Factors in the Returns on Stocks and Bonds," *Journal of Financial Economics*, Vol. 33, 1993, 3–56.

Are there any reasons to question the validity of the CAPM? Explain.

VOLATILITY VERSUS RISK

Before closing this chapter, we should note that volatility does not necessarily imply risk. For example, suppose a company's sales and earnings fluctuate widely from month to month, from year to year, or in some other manner. Does this imply that the company is risky in either the stand-alone or portfolio sense? If the fluctuations follow seasonal or cyclical patterns, as for an ice cream distributor or a steel company, they can be predicted, hence volatility would not signify much in the way of risk. If the ice cream company's earnings dropped about as much as they normally did in the winter, this would not concern investors, so the company's stock price would not be affected. Similarly, if the steel company's earnings fell during a recession, this would not be a surprise, so the company's stock price would not fall nearly as much as its earnings. Therefore, earnings volatility does not necessarily imply investment risk.

Now consider some other company, say, Wal-Mart. In 1995 Wal-Mart's earnings declined for the first time in its history. That decline worried investors — they were concerned that Wal-Mart's era of rapid growth had ended. The result was that Wal-Mart's stock price declined more than its earnings. Again, we conclude that while a downturn in earnings does not necessarily imply risk, it could, depending on conditions.

Now let's consider stock price volatility as opposed to earnings volatility. Is stock price volatility more likely to imply risk than earnings volatility? The answer is a loud yes! Stock prices vary because investors are uncertain about the future, especially about future earnings. So, if you see a company whose stock price fluctuates relatively widely (which will result in a high beta), you can bet that its future earnings are relatively unpredictable. Thus, biotech companies have less predictable earnings than utilities, biotechs' stock prices are volatile, and they have relatively high betas.

To conclude, keep two points in mind: (1) Earnings volatility does not necessarily signify risk — you have to think about the cause of the volatility before reaching any conclusion as to whether earnings volatility indicates risk. (2) Stock price volatility *does* signify risk.

Does earnings volatility necessarily imply risk? Explain.

Why is stock price volatility more likely to imply risk than earnings volatility?

In this chapter, we described the trade-off between risk and return. We began by discussing how to calculate risk and return for both individual assets and portfolios. In particular, we differentiated between stand-alone risk and risk in a portfolio context, and we explained the benefits of diversification. Finally, we developed the CAPM, which explains how risk affects rates of return. In the chapters that follow, we will give you the tools to estimate the required rates of return for bonds, preferred stock, and common stock, and we will explain how firms use these returns to develop their costs of capital. As you will see, the cost of capital is an important element in the firm's capital budgeting process. The key concepts covered in this chapter are listed below.

- **Risk** can be defined as the chance that some unfavorable event will occur.
- The riskiness of an asset's cash flows can be considered on a **stand-alone basis** (each asset by itself) or in a **portfolio context,** where the investment is combined with other assets and its risk is reduced through **diversification.**
- Most rational investors hold **portfolios of assets,** and they are more concerned with the riskiness of their portfolios than with the riskiness of individual assets.
- The **expected return** on an investment is the mean value of its probability distribution of returns.
- The **greater the probability** that the actual return will be far below the expected return, the **greater the stand-alone risk** associated with an asset. Two measures of stand-alone risk are the **standard deviation** and the **coefficient of variation.**
- The average investor is **risk averse,** which means that he or she must be compensated for holding risky assets. Therefore, riskier assets have higher required returns than less risky assets.
- An asset's risk consists of (1) **diversifiable risk,** which can be eliminated by diversification, plus (2) **market risk,** which cannot be eliminated by diversification.
- The **relevant risk** of an individual asset is its contribution to the riskiness of a well-diversified **portfolio,** which is the asset's **market risk.** Since market risk cannot be eliminated by diversification, investors must be compensated for bearing it.
- The **Capital Asset Pricing Model** is a model based on the proposition that any stock's required rate of return is equal to the risk-free rate of return plus a risk premium that reflects only the risk remaining after diversification.
- A stock's **beta coefficient, b,** is a measure of its market risk. Beta measures the extent to which the stock's returns move relative to the market.
- A **high-beta stock** is more volatile than an average stock, while a **low-beta stock** is less volatile than an average stock. An average stock has b = 1.0.
- The **beta of a portfolio** is a **weighted average** of the betas of the individual securities in the portfolio.
- The **Security Market Line (SML)** equation shows the relationship between a security's market risk and its required rate of return. The return required for any security i is equal to the **risk-free rate** plus the **market risk premium** times the security's beta: $k_i = k_{RF} + (k_M - k_{RF})b_i$.

- Even though the expected rate of return on a stock is generally equal to its required return, a number of things can happen to cause the required rate of return to change: (1) **the risk-free rate can change** because of changes in either real rates or anticipated inflation, (2) **a stock's beta can change,** and (3) **investors' aversion to risk can change.**

- Because returns on assets in different countries are not perfectly correlated, **global diversification** may result in lower risk for multinational companies and globally diversified portfolios.

In the next three chapters, we will see how a security's rate of return affects its value. Then, in the remainder of the book, we will examine the ways in which a firm's management can influence a stock's riskiness and hence its price.

QUESTIONS

5-1 The probability distribution of a less risky expected return is more peaked than that of a riskier return. What shape would the probability distribution have for (a) completely certain returns and (b) completely uncertain returns?

5-2 Security A has an expected return of 7 percent, a standard deviation of expected returns of 35 percent, a correlation coefficient with the market of −0.3, and a beta coefficient of −0.5. Security B has an expected return of 12 percent, a standard deviation of returns of 10 percent, a correlation with the market of 0.7, and a beta coefficient of 1.0. Which security is riskier? Why?

5-3 Suppose you owned a portfolio consisting of $250,000 worth of long-term U.S. government bonds.
   a. Would your portfolio be riskless?
   b. Now suppose you hold a portfolio consisting of $250,000 worth of 30-day Treasury bills. Every 30 days your bills mature, and you reinvest the principal ($250,000) in a new batch of bills. Assume that you live on the investment income from your portfolio and that you want to maintain a constant standard of living. Is your portfolio truly riskless?
   c. Can you think of any asset that would be completely riskless? Could someone develop such an asset? Explain.

5-4 A life insurance policy is a financial asset. The premiums paid represent the investment's cost.
   a. How would you calculate the expected return on a life insurance policy?
   b. Suppose the owner of a life insurance policy has no other financial assets — the person's only other asset is "human capital," or lifetime earnings capacity. What is the correlation coefficient between returns on the insurance policy and returns on the policyholder's human capital?
   c. Life insurance companies have to pay administrative costs and sales representatives' commissions; hence, the expected rate of return on insurance premiums is generally low, or even negative. Use the portfolio concept to explain why people buy life insurance in spite of negative expected returns.

5-5 If investors' aversion to risk increased, would the risk premium on a high-beta stock increase more or less than that on a low-beta stock? Explain.

5-6 If a company's beta were to double, would its expected return double?

5-7 Is it possible to construct a portfolio of stocks that has an expected return equal to the risk-free rate?

5-8 A stock had a 12 percent return last year, a year in which the overall stock market declined in value. Does this mean that the stock has a negative beta?

SELF-TEST PROBLEMS (SOLUTIONS APPEAR IN APPENDIX B)

ST-1
Key terms
Define the following terms, using graphs or equations to illustrate your answers wherever feasible:
   a. Stand-alone risk; risk; probability distribution
   b. Expected rate of return, k
   c. Continuous probability distribution

d. Standard deviation, σ; variance, σ^2; coefficient of variation, CV
e. Risk aversion; realized rate of return, $\bar{k}$
f. Risk premium for Stock i, RP_i; market risk premium, RP_M
g. Capital Asset Pricing Model (CAPM)
h. Expected return on a portfolio, $\hat{k}_p$; market portfolio
i. Correlation coefficient, r; correlation
j. Market risk; diversifiable risk; relevant risk
k. Beta coefficient, b; average stock's beta, b_A
l. Security Market Line (SML); SML equation
m. Slope of SML as a measure of risk aversion

ST-2
Realized rates of return

Stocks A and B have the following historical returns:

YEAR	STOCK A'S RETURNS, k_A	STOCK B'S RETURNS, k_B
1998	(10.00%)	(3.00%)
1999	18.50	21.29
2000	38.67	44.25
2001	14.33	3.67
2002	33.00	28.30

a. Calculate the average rate of return for each stock during the period 1998 through 2002. Assume that someone held a portfolio consisting of 50 percent of Stock A and 50 percent of Stock B. What would have been the realized rate of return on the portfolio in each year from 1998 through 2002? What would have been the average return on the portfolio during this period?
b. Now calculate the standard deviation of returns for each stock and for the portfolio. Use Equation 5-3a in Footnote 5.
c. Looking at the annual returns data on the two stocks, would you guess that the correlation coefficient between returns on the two stocks is closer to 0.9 or to −0.9?
d. If you added more stocks at random to the portfolio, which of the following is the most accurate statement of what would happen to σ_p?
   (1) σ_p would remain constant.
   (2) σ_p would decline to somewhere in the vicinity of 21 percent.
   (3) σ_p would decline to zero if enough stocks were included.

ST-3
Beta and required rate of return

ECRI Corporation is a holding company with four main subsidiaries. The percentage of its business coming from each of the subsidiaries, and their respective betas, are as follows:

SUBSIDIARY	PERCENTAGE OF BUSINESS	BETA
Electric utility	60%	0.70
Cable company	25	0.90
Real estate	10	1.30
International/special projects	5	1.50

a. What is the holding company's beta?
b. Assume that the risk-free rate is 6 percent and the market risk premium is 5 percent. What is the holding company's required rate of return?
c. ECRI is considering a change in its strategic focus; it will reduce its reliance on the electric utility subsidiary, so the percentage of its business from this subsidiary will be 50 percent. At the same time, ECRI will increase its reliance on the international/special projects division, so the percentage of its business from that subsidiary will rise to 15 percent. What will be the shareholders' required rate of return if ECRI adopts these changes?

5-1
Expected return

A stock's expected return has the following distribution:

DEMAND FOR THE COMPANY'S PRODUCTS	PROBABILITY OF THIS DEMAND OCCURRING	RATE OF RETURN IF THIS DEMAND OCCURS
Weak	0.1	(50%)
Below average	0.2	(5)
Average	0.4	16
Above average	0.2	25
Strong	0.1	60
	1.0	

Calculate the stock's expected return, standard deviation, and coefficient of variation.

5-2
Portfolio beta

An individual has $35,000 invested in a stock that has a beta of 0.8 and $40,000 invested in a stock with a beta of 1.4. If these are the only two investments in her portfolio, what is her portfolio's beta?

5-3
Expected and required rates of return

Assume that the risk-free rate is 5 percent and the market risk premium is 6 percent. What is the expected return for the overall stock market? What is the required rate of return on a stock that has a beta of 1.2?

5-4
Required rate of return

Assume that the risk-free rate is 6 percent and the expected return on the market is 13 percent. What is the required rate of return on a stock that has a beta of 0.7?

5-5
Beta and required rate of return

A stock has a required return of 11 percent. The risk-free rate is 7 percent, and the market risk premium is 4 percent.
a. What is the stock's beta?
b. If the market risk premium increases to 6 percent, what will happen to the stock's required rate of return? Assume the risk-free rate and the stock's beta remain unchanged.

The problems included in this section are set up in such a way that they could be used as multiple-choice exam problems.

5-6
Expected returns

Stocks X and Y have the following probability distributions of expected future returns:

PROBABILITY	X	Y
0.1	(10%)	(35%)
0.2	2	0
0.4	12	20
0.2	20	25
0.1	38	45

a. Calculate the expected rate of return, $\hat{k}$, for Stock Y. ($\hat{k}_x = 12\%$.)
b. Calculate the standard deviation of expected returns for Stock X. (That for Stock Y is 20.35 percent.) Now calculate the coefficient of variation for Stock Y. Is it possible that most investors might regard Stock Y as being *less* risky than Stock X? Explain.

5-7
Required rate of return

Suppose $k_{RF} = 9\%$, $k_M = 14\%$, and $b_i = 1.3$.
a. What is k_i, the required rate of return on Stock i?
b. Now suppose k_{RF} (1) increases to 10 percent or (2) decreases to 8 percent. The slope of the SML remains constant. How would this affect k_M and k_i?

c. Now assume k_{RF} remains at 9 percent but k_M (1) increases to 16 percent or (2) falls to 13 percent. The slope of the SML does not remain constant. How would these changes affect k_i?

5-8
Portfolio beta
Suppose you hold a diversified portfolio consisting of a $7,500 investment in each of 20 different common stocks. The portfolio beta is equal to 1.12. Now, suppose you have decided to sell one of the stocks in your portfolio with a beta equal to 1.0 for $7,500 and to use these proceeds to buy another stock for your portfolio. Assume the new stock's beta is equal to 1.75. Calculate your portfolio's new beta.

5-9
Portfolio required return
Suppose you are the money manager of a $4 million investment fund. The fund consists of 4 stocks with the following investments and betas:

STOCK	INVESTMENT	BETA
A	$ 400,000	1.50
B	600,000	(0.50)
C	1,000,000	1.25
D	2,000,000	0.75

If the market's required rate of return is 14 percent and the risk-free rate is 6 percent, what is the fund's required rate of return?

5-10
Required rate of return
Stock R has a beta of 1.5, Stock S has a beta of 0.75, the expected rate of return on an average stock is 13 percent, and the risk-free rate of return is 7 percent. By how much does the required return on the riskier stock exceed the required return on the less risky stock?

5-11
Evaluating risk and return
Stock X has an expected return of 10 percent, a beta coefficient of 0.9, and a standard deviation of expected returns of 35 percent. Stock Y has an expected return of 12.5 percent, a beta coefficient of 1.2, and a standard deviation of expected returns of 25 percent. The risk-free rate is 6 percent, and the market risk premium is 5 percent.
a. Calculate each stock's coefficient of variation.
b. Which stock is riskier for diversified investors?
c. Calculate each stock's required rate of return.
d. On the basis of the two stocks' expected and required returns, which stock would be most attractive to a diversified investor?
e. Calculate the required return of a portfolio that has $7,500 invested in Stock X and $2,500 invested in Stock Y.
f. If the market risk premium increased to 6 percent, which of the two stocks would have the largest increase in their required return?

5-12
CAPM and required return
Calculate the required rate of return for Manning Enterprises, assuming that investors expect a 3.5 percent rate of inflation in the future. The real risk-free rate is equal to 2.5 percent and the market risk premium is 6.5 percent. Manning has a beta of 1.7, and its realized rate of return has averaged 13.5 percent over the last 5 years.

5-13
CAPM and market risk premium
Consider the following information for three stocks, Stock X, Stock Y, and Stock Z. The returns on each of the three stocks are positively correlated, but they are not perfectly correlated. (That is, all of the correlation coefficients are between 0 and 1.)

STOCK	EXPECTED RETURN	STANDARD DEVIATION	BETA
X	9.00%	15%	0.8
Y	10.75	15	1.2
Z	12.50	15	1.6

Portfolio P has half of its funds invested in Stock X and half invested in Stock Y. Portfolio Q has one-third of its funds invested in each of the three stocks. The risk-free rate is 5.5 percent, and the market is in equilibrium. (That is, required returns equal expected returns.) What is the market risk premium ($k_M - k_{RF}$)?

5-14
Beta coefficient

Given the following information, determine which beta coefficient for Stock J is consistent with equilibrium:

$$\hat{k}_J = 12.5\%; \ k_{RF} = 4.5\%; \ k_M = 10.5\%.$$

5-15
CAPM and required return

HR Industries (HRI) has a beta of 1.8, while LR Industries' beta is 0.6. The risk-free rate is 6 percent, and the required rate of return on an average stock is 13 percent. Now the expected rate of inflation built into k_{RF} falls by 1.5 percentage points, the real risk-free rate remains constant, the required return on the market falls to 10.5 percent, and the betas remain constant. When all of these changes are made, what will be the difference in the required returns on HRI's and LRI's stocks?

5-16
CAPM and required return

Bradford Manufacturing Company has a beta of 1.45, while Farley Industries has a beta of 0.85. The required return on an index fund that holds the entire stock market is 12.5 percent. The risk-free rate of interest is 5 percent. By how much does Bradford's required return exceed Farley's required return?

5-17
CAPM and portfolio return

You have been managing a $5 million portfolio. The portfolio has a beta of 1.25 and a required rate of return of 12 percent. The current risk-free rate is 5.25 percent. Assume that you receive another $500,000. If you invest the money in a stock that has a beta of 0.75, what will be the required return on your $5.5 million portfolio?

5-18
Portfolio beta

A mutual fund manager has a $20,000,000 portfolio with a beta of 1.5. Assume that the risk-free rate is 4.5 percent and that the market risk premium is 5.5 percent. The manager expects to receive an additional $5,000,000 in funds soon. She wants to invest these funds in a variety of stocks. After making these additional investments, she wants the fund's expected return to be 13 percent. What should be the average beta of the new stocks added to the portfolio?

PROBLEMS

5-19
Expected returns

Suppose you won the Florida lottery and were offered (1) $0.5 million or (2) a gamble in which you would receive $1 million if a head were flipped but zero if a tail came up.
a. What is the expected value of the gamble?
b. Would you take the sure $0.5 million or the gamble?
c. If you choose the sure $0.5 million, are you a risk averter or a risk seeker?
d. Suppose you actually take the sure $0.5 million. You can invest it in either a U.S. Treasury bond that will return $537,500 at the end of a year or a common stock that has a 50-50 chance of being either worthless or worth $1,150,000 at the end of the year.
   (1) What is the expected dollar profit on the stock investment? (The expected profit on the T-bond investment is $37,500.)
   (2) What is the expected rate of return on the stock investment? (The expected rate of return on the T-bond investment is 7.5 percent.)
   (3) Would you invest in the bond or the stock?
   (4) Exactly how large would the expected profit (or the expected rate of return) have to be on the stock investment to make you invest in the stock, given the 7.5 percent return on the bond?
   (5) How might your decision be affected if, rather than buying one stock for $0.5 million, you could construct a portfolio consisting of 100 stocks with $5,000 invested in each? Each of these stocks has the same return characteristics as the one stock — that is, a 50-50 chance of being worth either zero or $11,500 at year-end. Would the correlation between returns on these stocks matter?

5-20
Security market line

The Kish Investment Fund, in which you plan to invest some money, has total capital of $500 million invested in five stocks:

STOCK	INVESTMENT	STOCK'S BETA COEFFICIENT
A	$160 million	0.5
B	120 million	2.0
C	80 million	4.0
D	80 million	1.0
E	60 million	3.0

The beta coefficient for a fund like Kish Investment can be found as a weighted average of the fund's investments. The current risk-free rate is 6 percent, whereas market returns have the following estimated probability distribution for the next period:

PROBABILITY	MARKET RETURN
0.1	7%
0.2	9
0.4	11
0.2	13
0.1	15

a. What is the estimated equation for the Security Market Line (SML)? (Hint: First determine the expected market return.)
b. Calculate the fund's required rate of return for the next period.
c. Suppose Bridget Nelson, the president, receives a proposal for a new stock. The investment needed to take a position in the stock is $50 million, it will have an expected return of 15 percent, and its estimated beta coefficient is 2.0. Should the new stock be purchased? At what expected rate of return should the fund be indifferent to purchasing the stock?

5-21
Realized rates of return

Stocks A and B have the following historical returns:

YEAR	STOCK A'S RETURNS, k_A	STOCK B'S RETURNS, k_B
1998	(18.00%)	(14.50%)
1999	33.00	21.80
2000	15.00	30.50
2001	(0.50)	(7.60)
2002	27.00	26.30

a. Calculate the average rate of return for each stock during the period 1998 through 2002.
b. Assume that someone held a portfolio consisting of 50 percent of Stock A and 50 percent of Stock B. What would have been the realized rate of return on the portfolio in each year from 1998 through 2002? What would have been the average return on the portfolio during this period?
c. Calculate the standard deviation of returns for each stock and for the portfolio.
d. Calculate the coefficient of variation for each stock and for the portfolio.
e. If you are a risk-averse investor, would you prefer to hold Stock A, Stock B, or the portfolio? Why?

SPREADSHEET PROBLEM

5-22
Evaluating risk and return

Bartman Industries' and Reynolds Inc.'s stock prices and dividends, along with the Wilton 5000 Index, are shown below for the period 1996–2001. The Wilton 5000 data are adjusted to include dividends.

| | BARTMAN INDUSTRIES | | REYNOLDS INCORPORATED | | WILTON 5000 |
YEAR	STOCK PRICE	DIVIDEND	STOCK PRICE	DIVIDEND	INCLUDES DIVS.
2001	$17.250	$1.15	$48.750	$3.00	11,663.98
2000	14.750	1.06	52.300	2.90	8,785.70
1999	16.500	1.00	48.750	2.75	8,679.98
1998	10.750	0.95	57.250	2.50	6,434.03
1997	11.375	0.90	60.000	2.25	5,602.28
1996	7.625	0.85	55.750	2.00	4,705.97

a. Use the data given to calculate annual returns for Bartman, Reynolds, and the Wilton 5000 Index, and then calculate average returns over the 5-year period. (Hint: Remember, returns are calculated by subtracting the beginning price from the ending price to get the capital gain or loss, adding the dividend to the capital gain or loss, and dividing the result by the beginning price. Assume that dividends are already included in the index. Also, you cannot calculate the rate of return for 1996 because you do not have 1995 data.)

b. Calculate the standard deviations of the returns for Bartman, Reynolds, and the Wilton 5000. (Hint: Use the sample standard deviation formula given in Footnote 5 to this chapter, which corresponds to the STDEV function in *Excel*.)

c. Now calculate the coefficients of variation for Bartman, Reynolds, and the Wilton 5000.

d. Construct a scatter diagram graph that shows Bartman's and Reynolds' returns on the vertical axis and the market index's returns on the horizontal axis.

e. Estimate Bartman's and Reynolds' betas by running regressions of their returns against the Wilton 5000's returns. Are these betas consistent with your graph?

f. The risk-free rate on long-term Treasury bonds is 6.04 percent. Assume that the average annual return on the Wilton 5000 is *not* a good estimate of the market's required return — it is too high, so use 11 percent as the expected return on the market. Now use the SML equation to calculate the two companies' required returns.

g. If you formed a portfolio that consisted of 50 percent of Bartman stock and 50 percent of Reynolds stock, what would be the beta and the required return for the portfolio?

h. Suppose an investor wants to include Bartman Industries' stock in his or her portfolio. Stocks A, B, and C are currently in the portfolio, and their betas are 0.769, 0.985, and 1.423, respectively. Calculate the new portfolio's required return if it consists of 25 percent of Bartman, 15 percent of Stock A, 40 percent of Stock B, and 20 percent of Stock C.

INTEGRATED CASE

MERRILL FINCH INC.

5-23 Risk and return Assume that you recently graduated with a major in finance, and you just landed a job as a financial planner with Merrill Finch Inc., a large financial services corporation. Your first assignment is to invest $100,000 for a client. Because the funds are to be invested in a business at the end of 1 year, you have been instructed to plan for a 1-year holding period. Further, your boss has restricted you to the following investment alternatives in the table below, shown with their probabilities and associated outcomes. (Disregard for now the items at the bottom of the data; you will fill in the blanks later.)

Merrill Finch's economic forecasting staff has developed probability estimates for the state of the economy, and its security analysts have developed a sophisticated computer program, which was used to estimate the rate of return on each alternative under each state of the economy. High Tech Inc. is an electronics firm; Collections Inc. collects past-due debts; and U.S. Rubber manufactures tires and various other rubber and plastics products. Merrill Finch also maintains a "market portfolio" that owns a market-weighted fraction of all publicly traded stocks; you can invest in that portfolio, and thus obtain average stock market

results. Given the situation as described, answer the following questions.

a. (1) Why is the T-bill's return independent of the state of the economy? Do T-bills promise a completely risk-free return? (2) Why are High Tech's returns expected to move with the economy whereas Collections' are expected to move counter to the economy?

b. Calculate the expected rate of return on each alternative and fill in the blanks on the row for k in the table below.

c. You should recognize that basing a decision solely on expected returns is only appropriate for risk-neutral individuals. Since your client, like virtually everyone, is risk averse, the riskiness of each alternative is an important aspect of the decision. One possible measure of risk is the standard deviation of returns. (1) Calculate this value for each alternative, and fill in the blank on the row for σ in the table below. (2) What type of risk is measured by the standard deviation? (3) Draw a graph that shows *roughly* the shape of the probability distributions for High Tech, U.S. Rubber, and T-bills.

d. Suppose you suddenly remembered that the coefficient of variation (CV) is generally regarded as being a better measure of stand-alone risk than the standard deviation when the alternatives being considered have widely dif-

STATE OF THE ECONOMY	PROBABILITY	T-BILLS	HIGH TECH	COLLECTIONS	U.S. RUBBER	MARKET PORTFOLIO	2-STOCK PORTFOLIO
				ESTIMATED RATE OF RETURN			
Recession	0.1	8.0%	(22.0%)	28.0%	10.0%*	(13.0%)	3.0%
Below average	0.2	8.0	(2.0)	14.7	(10.0)	1.0	
Average	0.4	8.0	20.0	0.0	7.0	15.0	10.0
Above average	0.2	8.0	35.0	(10.0)	45.0	29.0	
Boom	0.1	8.0	50.0	(20.0)	30.0	43.0	15.0
$\hat{k}$				1.7%	13.8%	15.0%	
σ		0.0		13.4	18.8	15.3	3.3
CV				7.9	1.4	1.0	0.3
b				−0.87	0.89		

* Note that the estimated returns of U.S. Rubber do not always move in the same direction as the overall economy. For example, when the economy is below average, consumers purchase fewer tires than they would if the economy was stronger. However, if the economy is in a flat-out recession, a large number of consumers who were planning to purchase a new car may choose to wait and instead purchase new tires for the car they currently own. Under these circumstances, we would expect U.S. Rubber's stock price to be higher if there is a recession than if the economy was just below average.

fering expected returns. Calculate the missing CVs, and fill in the blanks on the row for CV in the table above. Does the CV produce the same risk rankings as the standard deviation?

e. Suppose you created a 2-stock portfolio by investing $50,000 in High Tech and $50,000 in Collections. (1) Calculate the expected return ($\hat{k}_p$), the standard deviation (σ_p), and the coefficient of variation (CV_p) for this portfolio and fill in the appropriate blanks in the table above. (2) How does the riskiness of this 2-stock portfolio compare with the riskiness of the individual stocks if they were held in isolation?

f. Suppose an investor starts with a portfolio consisting of one randomly selected stock. What would happen (1) to the riskiness and (2) to the expected return of the portfolio as more and more randomly selected stocks were added to the portfolio? What is the implication for investors? Draw a graph of the two portfolios to illustrate your answer.

g. (1) Should portfolio effects impact the way investors think about the riskiness of individual stocks? (2) If you decided to hold a 1-stock portfolio, and consequently were exposed to more risk than diversified investors, could you expect to be compensated for all of your risk; that is, could you earn a risk premium on that part of your risk that you could have eliminated by diversifying?

h. The expected rates of return and the beta coefficients of the alternatives as supplied by Merrill Finch's computer program are as follows:

SECURITY	RETURN ($\hat{k}$)	RISK (BETA)
High Tech	17.4%	1.30
Market	15.0	1.00
U.S. Rubber	13.8	0.89
T-bills	8.0	0.00
Collections	1.7	(0.87)

(1) What is a beta coefficient, and how are betas used in risk analysis? (2) Do the expected returns appear to be related to each alternative's market risk? (3) Is it possible to choose among the alternatives on the basis of the information developed thus far? Use the data given at the start of the problem to construct a graph that shows how the T-bill's, High Tech's, and the market's beta coefficients are calculated. Then discuss what betas measure and how they are used in risk analysis.

i. The yield curve is currently flat, that is, long-term Treasury bonds also have an 8 percent yield. Consequently, Merrill Finch assumes that the risk-free rate is 8 percent. (1) Write out the Security Market Line (SML) equation, use it to calculate the required rate of return on each alternative, and then graph the relationship between the expected and required rates of return. (2) How do the expected rates of return compare with the required rates of return? (3) Does the fact that Collections has an expected return that is less than the T-bill rate make any sense?

(4) What would be the market risk and the required return of a 50-50 portfolio of High Tech and Collections? Of High Tech and U.S. Rubber?

j. (1) Suppose investors raised their inflation expectations by 3 percentage points over current estimates as reflected in the 8 percent risk-free rate. What effect would higher inflation have on the SML and on the returns required on high- and low-risk securities? (2) Suppose instead that investors' risk aversion increased enough to cause the market risk premium to increase by 3 percentage points. (Inflation remains constant.) What effect would this have on the SML and on returns of high- and low-risk securities?

Please go to our web site **http://brigham.swlearning.com** to access the Cyberproblems.

With your Xtra! CD-ROM, access the Thomson Analytics Problems and use the Thomson Analytics Academic online database to work this chapter's problems.

TIME VALUE OF MONEY[1]

6

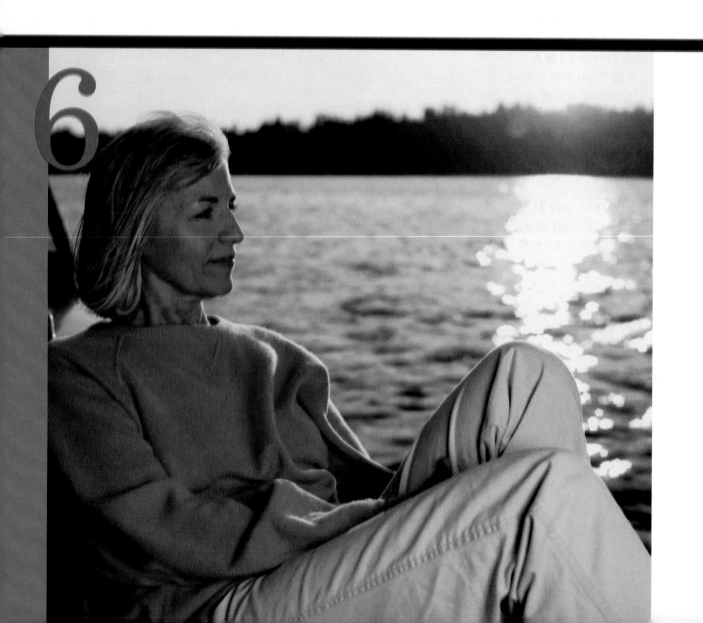

Your reaction to the question in the title of this vignette is probably, "First things first! I'm worried about getting a job, not retiring!" However, an awareness of the retirement situation could help you land a job because (1) this is an important issue today, (2) employers prefer to hire people who know the issues, and (3) professors often test students on time value of money with problems related to saving for some future purpose, including retirement. So read on.

A recent *Fortune* article began with some interesting facts: (1) The U.S. savings rate is the lowest of any industrial nation. (2) The ratio of U.S. workers to retirees, which was 17 to 1 in 1950, is now down to 3.2 to 1, and it will decline to less than 2 to 1 after 2020. (3) With so few people paying into the Social Security System, and so many drawing funds out, Social Security may soon be in serious trouble. The article concluded that even people making $85,000 per year will have trouble maintaining a reasonable standard of living after they retire, and many of today's college students will have to support their parents.

If Ms. Jones, who earns $85,000, retires in 2002, expects to live for another 20 years after retirement, and needs 80 percent of her pre-retirement income, she would require $68,000 during 2002. However, if inflation amounts to 5 percent per year, her income requirement would increase to $110,765 in 10 years and to $180,424 in 20 years. If inflation were 7 percent, her Year 20 requirement would jump to $263,139! How much wealth would Ms. Jones need at retirement to maintain her standard of living, and how much would she have had to save during each working year to accumulate that wealth?

The answer depends on a number of factors, including the rate she could earn on her savings, the inflation rate, and when her savings program began. Also, the answer would depend on how much she will receive from Social Security and from her corporate retirement plan, if she has one. (She might not receive much from Social Security unless she is really down and out.) Note, too, that her plans could be upset if the inflation rate increased, if the return on her savings changed, or if she lived beyond 20 years.

Fortune and other organizations have done studies relating to the retirement issue, using the tools and techniques described in this chapter. The general conclusion is that most Americans have been putting their heads in the sand—many of us have been ignoring what is almost certainly going to be a huge personal and social problem. But if you study this chapter carefully, you can avoid the trap that seems to be catching so many people.

---

[1] This chapter was written on the assumption that most students will be using a financial calculator. Calculators are relatively inexpensive, and business students who cannot use them are often deemed obsolete and uncompetitive before they even graduate. We originally planned to explain in the chapter how *Excel* spreadsheets can be used to solve time value problems. Spreadsheets are actually better for many time value analyses than calculators. However, it is more efficient to discuss spreadsheets within actual spreadsheet models, where students can read our explanations and immediately go through the steps required for the analysis. Also, many students in the introductory finance course have not yet covered the basics of spreadsheets, and the models would not be useful for those students. Therefore, we moved our discussion of spreadsheets to the chapter models, which may be obtained from the text's web site and from the CD-ROM accompanying this text.

We highly recommend that students who have a basic knowledge of *Excel* work through the *Excel* models, proceeding as follows: First, read the chapter and work through the calculator solutions. This will give you a good idea of the concepts. Then, access the chapter model and work through it. You will soon see the power of spreadsheets and understand why they are the dominant tool used for financial analysis. The sensitivity analysis performed within the spreadsheet models will also increase your understanding of various time value issues.

Note too that in past editions we discussed compound interest tables. However, calculators and computers have rendered the tables obsolete—no one in practice uses them any more. Therefore, we moved our discussion of the tabular approach to Web Appendix 6A, which can be found on the text's web site: **http//brigham.swlearning.com**.

Note also that tutorials on how to use both *Excel* and several Hewlett-Packard, Texas Instruments, and Sharp calculators are provided in the *Technology Supplement* to this book, which is available to adopting instructors. For this chapter, a more complete discussion of spreadsheets is contained in the file 06MODEL.xls.

In Chapter 1, we saw that the primary objective of financial management is to maximize the value of the firm's stock. We also saw that stock values depend in part on the timing of the cash flows investors expect to receive from an investment—a dollar expected soon is worth more than a dollar expected in the distant future. Therefore, it is essential for financial managers to have a clear understanding of the time value of money and its impact on stock prices. These concepts are discussed in this chapter, where we show how the timing of cash flows affects asset values and rates of return.

The principles of time value analysis have many applications, ranging from setting up schedules for paying off loans to decisions about whether to acquire new equipment. *In fact, of all the concepts used in finance, none is more important than the time value of money, also called discounted cash flow (DCF) analysis.* Since this concept is used throughout the remainder of the book, it is vital that you understand the material in this chapter before you move on to other topics. ■

TIME LINES

Time Line
An important tool used in time value of money analysis; it is a graphical representation used to show the timing of cash flows.

One of the most important tools in time value analysis is the **time line**, which is used by analysts to help visualize what is happening in a particular problem and then to help set up the problem for solution. To illustrate the time line concept, consider the following diagram:

Time: 0   1   2   3   4   5

Time 0 is today; Time 1 is one period from today, or the end of Period 1; Time 2 is two periods from today, or the end of Period 2; and so on. Thus, the numbers above the tick marks represent end-of-period values. Often the periods are years, but other time intervals such as semiannual periods, quarters, months, or even days can be used. If each period on the time line represents a year, the interval from the tick mark corresponding to 0 to the tick mark corresponding to 1 would be Year 1, the interval from 1 to 2 would be Year 2, and so on. Note that each tick mark corresponds to the end of one period as well as the beginning of the next period. In other words, the tick mark at Time 1 represents the *end* of Year 1, and it also represents the *beginning* of Year 2 because Year 1 has just passed.

Cash flows are placed directly below the tick marks, and interest rates are shown directly above the time line. Unknown cash flows, which you are trying to find in the analysis, are indicated by question marks. Now consider the following time line:

Time: 0   5%   1   2   3
         |----------|---------|---------|
Cash flows: −100   ?

Outflow
A cash deposit, cost, or amount paid. It has a minus sign.

Inflow
A cash receipt.

Here the interest rate for each of the three periods is 5 percent; a single amount (or lump sum) cash **outflow** is made at Time 0; and the Time 3 value is an unknown **inflow**. Since the initial $100 is an outflow (an investment), it has a minus sign. Since the Period 3 amount is an inflow, it does not have a minus sign, which implies a plus sign. In this example, no cash flows occur at Time 1 or 2. Note also that to reduce clutter we generally do not show dollar signs on time lines.

Now consider a different situation, where a $100 cash outflow is made today, and we will receive an unknown amount at the end of Time 2:

    0   5%   1   10%   2
    |----------|----------|
  −100   ?

Here the interest rate is 5 percent during the first period, but it rises to 10 percent during the second period. If the interest rate is constant in all periods, we show it only in the first period, but if it changes, we show all the relevant rates on the time line.

Time lines are essential when you are first learning time value concepts, but even experts use time lines to analyze complex finance problems. We will be using time lines throughout the book, and you should get into the habit of using them when you work problems.

SELF-TEST QUESTION

Set up a time line to illustrate the following situation: You currently have $2,000 on hand and would like to invest it in a three-year certificate of deposit that pays 4 percent annually.

FUTURE VALUE

A dollar in hand today is worth more than a dollar to be received in the future because, if you had it now, you could invest it, earn interest, and end up with more than one dollar in the future. The process of going from today's values, or present values (PVs), to future values (FVs) is called **compounding**. To illustrate, suppose you deposit $100 in a bank that pays 5 percent interest each year. How much would you have at the end of one year? To begin, we define the following terms:

Compounding
The arithmetic process of determining the final value of a cash flow or series of cash flows when compound interest is applied.

PV = present value, or beginning amount, in your account. Here PV = $100.
 i = interest rate the bank pays on the account per year. The interest earned is based on the balance at the beginning of each year, and we assume that it is paid at the end of the year. Here i = 5%, or, expressed as a decimal, i = 0.05.

Throughout this chapter, we designate the interest rate as i (or I) because that symbol is used on most financial calculators. Note, though, that in later chapters we use the symbol k to denote interest rates because k is used more often in the financial literature.

INT = dollars of interest you earn during the year = Beginning amount × i. Here INT = $100(0.05) = $5.

FV_n = future value, or ending amount, of your account at the end of n years. Whereas PV is the value now, or the *present value*, FV_n is the value n years into the *future*, after the interest earned has been added to the account.

n = number of periods involved in the analysis. Here n = 1.

In our example, n = 1, so FV_n can be calculated as follows:

$$FV_n = FV_1 = PV + INT$$
$$= PV + PV(i)$$
$$= PV(1 + i)$$
$$= \$100(1 + 0.05) = \$100(1.05) = \$105.$$

Future Value (FV)
The amount to which a cash flow or series of cash flows will grow over a given period of time when compounded at a given interest rate.

Thus, the **future value (FV)** at the end of one year, FV_1, equals the present value multiplied by 1 plus the interest rate, so you will have $105 after one year.

What would you end up with if you left your $100 in the account for five years? Here is a time line set up to show the amount at the end of each year:

	0	5%	1	2	3	4	5
Initial deposit:	−100		$FV_1 = ?$	$FV_2 = ?$	$FV_3 = ?$	$FV_4 = ?$	$FV_5 = ?$
Interest earned:			5.00	5.25	5.51	5.79	6.08
Amount at the end of each period = FV_n:			105.00	110.25	115.76	121.55	**127.63**

Note the following points: (1) You start by depositing $100 in the account — this is shown as an outflow at t = 0. (2) You earn $100(0.05) = $5 of interest during the first year, so the amount at the end of Year 1 (or t = 1) is $100 + $5 = $105. (3) You start the second year with $105, earn $5.25 on the now larger amount, and end the second year with $110.25. Your interest during Year 2, $5.25, is higher than the first year's interest, $5, because you earned $5(0.05) = $0.25 interest on the first year's interest. (4) This process continues, and because the beginning balance is higher in each succeeding year, the annual interest earned increases. (5) The total interest earned, $27.63, is reflected in the final balance at t = 5, $127.63.

Note that the value at the end of Year 2, $110.25, is equal to

$$FV_2 = FV_1(1 + i)$$
$$= PV(1 + i)(1 + i)$$
$$= PV(1 + i)^2$$
$$= \$100(1.05)^2 = \$110.25.$$

Continuing, the balance at the end of Year 3 is

$$FV_3 = FV_2(1 + i)$$
$$= PV(1 + i)^3$$
$$= \$100(1.05)^3 = \$115.76,$$

and

$$FV_5 = \$100(1.05)^5 = \$127.63.$$

In general, the future value of an initial lump sum at the end of n years can be found by applying Equation 6-1:

$$FV_n = PV(1 + i)^n. \tag{6-1}$$

Equation 6-1 and most other time value of money equations can be solved with a financial calculator or with a computer spreadsheet.

As shown above, we can use Equation 6-1 to find the future value. Simply multiply $(1 + i) = (1.05)$ by itself $n = 5$ times and then multiply that result by $PV = \$100$ to get the future value, $FV = \$127.63$. That's easy enough, but as we go through the chapter, you will see that some formulas would involve a lot more arithmetic. Therefore, financial calculators (and computer spreadsheets) have been programmed to simplify the process. For our first example, you may think calculators are more trouble than they are worth, but before you finish the chapter you will realize that they are worth their weight in gold when dealing with most real-world problems.

To use the calculator, first note that calculators have five keys that correspond to the five most commonly used time value of money variables:

Here

    N = the number of periods. Some calculators use n rather than N.
     I = interest rate per period. Some calculators use i or I/YR rather than I.
  PV = present value.
PMT = payment. This key is used only if the cash flows involve a series of equal, or constant, payments (an annuity). If there are no periodic payments in a particular problem, then PMT = 0.
  FV = future value.

On some financial calculators, these keys are actually buttons on the face of the calculator, while on others they are shown on a screen after going into the time value of money (TVM) menu.

In this chapter, we deal with equations involving only four of the variables at any one time—three of the variables are known, and the calculator then solves for the fourth (unknown) variable. In the next chapter, when we deal with bonds, we will use all five variables in the bond valuation equation.[2]

To find the future value of \$100 after five years at 5 percent most financial calculators solve Equation 6-1:

$$FV_n = PV(1 + i)^n. \tag{6-1}$$

The equation has four variables, FV_n, PV, i, and n. If we know any three, we can solve for the fourth. In our example, we enter $N = 5$, $I = 5$, $PV = 100$, and $PMT = 0$,

[2] The equation programmed into the calculators actually has five variables, one for each key. In this chapter, the value of one of the variables is always zero. It is a good idea to get into the habit of inputting a zero for the unused variable (whose value is automatically set equal to zero when you clear the calculator's memory); if you forget to clear your calculator, inputting a zero will help you avoid trouble.

Then, when we press the FV key, we get the answer, FV = 127.63 (rounded to two decimal places).[3]

Notice that either PV or FV_n in Equation 6-1 must be negative to make the equation true, assuming nonnegative interest rates. Thus, most financial calculators require that all cash flows be designated as either inflows or outflows, with outflows being entered as negative numbers. In our illustration, you deposit, or put in, the initial amount (which is an outflow to you) and you take out, or receive, the ending amount (which is an inflow to you). Here the PV would be entered as -100 by keying in 100 and then pressing the "change sign" or +/- key. (If you entered 100, then the FV would appear as -127.63.) Also, on some calculators you are required to press a "Compute" key before pressing the FV key.

Sometimes the convention of changing signs can be confusing. For example, if you have $100 in the bank now and want to find out how much you will have after five years if your account pays 5 percent interest, the calculator will give you a negative answer, in this case -127.63, because the calculator assumes you are going to withdraw the funds. This sign convention should cause you no problem if you think about what you are doing.

Financial calculators also permit you to specify the number of decimal places that are displayed. Twelve significant digits are actually used in the calculations, but we generally use two places for answers when working with dollars or percentages and four places when working with decimals. The nature of the problem dictates how many decimal places should be displayed.

PROBLEM FORMAT

To help you understand the various types of time value problems, we generally use a standard format. First, we state the problem in words. Next, we diagram the problem on a time line. Then, beneath the time line, we show the equation that must be solved. Finally, we explain how to find the answer using a financial calculator. Separately, in the chapter model, we explain how to solve the same problem using an *Excel* spreadsheet.[4]

To illustrate the format, consider again our five-year, 5 percent example:

```
0    5%    1         2         3         4         5
|----------|---------|---------|---------|---------|
-100                                              FV=?
```

$$FV_n = PV(1 + i)^n = \$100(1.05)^5.$$

---

[3] Here we assume that compounding occurs once each year. Most calculators have a setting that can be used to designate the number of compounding periods per year. For example, the HP-10BII comes preset with payments at 12 per year. You would need to change it to 1 per year to get FV = 127.63. With the HP-10BII, you would do this by typing 1, pressing the gold key, and then pressing the P/YR key.

[4] If you plan to go through the spreadsheet material, you could cover it immediately after going through the calculator solution. However, our students tell us that they prefer to finish the chapter using the calculator, then turn on the computer and access the chapter model, and then go through the spreadsheet analysis. Regardless of how you approach it, we strongly recommend that students who have a basic knowledge of *Excel* go through the spreadsheet material.

Here is the calculator setup:

Inputs: 5   5   −100   0

| N | I | PV | PMT | FV |

Output: = 127.63

The calculator diagram tells you to input N = 5, I = 5, PV = −100, and PMT = 0, and then to press the FV key to get the answer, 127.63. Interest rates are entered as percentages (5), not decimals (0.05). Also, in this particular problem, the PMT key does not come into play, as no constant series of payments are involved.[5]

GRAPHIC VIEW OF THE COMPOUNDING PROCESS: GROWTH

Figure 6-1 shows how $1 (or any other lump sum) grows over time at various interest rates. The data used to plot the curves could be obtained by solving Equation 6-1 with different inputs, but we actually generated the data and then made the graph with a spreadsheet model. See 06MODEL.xls. The higher the rate of interest, the faster the rate of growth. The interest rate is, in fact, a growth rate: If a sum is de-

---

[5] We input PMT = 0, but if you cleared the calculator before you started, the PMT register would already have been set to 0.

FIGURE 6-1   **Relationships among Future Value, Growth, Interest Rates, and Time**

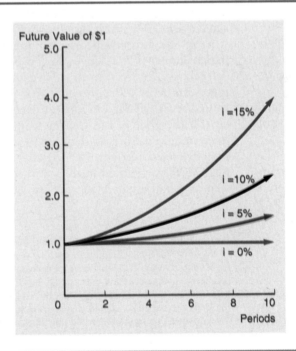

posited and earns 5 percent interest, then the funds on deposit will grow at a rate of 5 percent per period. Note also that time value concepts can be applied to anything that is growing—sales, population, earnings per share, or your future salary.

SELF-TEST QUESTIONS

Explain what is meant by the following statement: "A dollar in hand today is worth more than a dollar to be received next year."

What is compounding? Explain why earning "interest on interest" is called "compound interest."

You currently have $2,000 on hand that you plan to use to purchase a three-year bank certificate of deposit (CD). The CD pays 4 percent interest annually. How much money will you have when the CD matures? ($2,249.73)

How would your answer change if the CD matured in five years rather than three years? What if the interest rate increased from 4 percent to 6 percent, but the CD maturity was still three years? ($2,433.31; $2,382.03)

PRESENT VALUE

Opportunity Cost Rate
The rate of return on the best available alternative investment of equal risk.

Present Value (PV)
The value today of a future cash flow or series of cash flows.

Suppose you have some extra cash, and you have a chance to buy a low-risk security that will pay $127.63 at the end of five years. Your local bank is currently offering 5 percent interest on five-year certificates of deposit (CDs), and you regard the security as being exactly as safe as a CD. The 5 percent rate is defined as your **opportunity cost rate,** or the rate of return you could earn on an alternative investment of similar risk. How much should you be willing to pay for the security?

From the future value example presented in the previous section, we saw that an initial amount of $100 invested at 5 percent per year would be worth $127.63 at the end of five years. As we will see in a moment, you should be indifferent between $100 today and $127.63 at the end of five years.[6] The $100 is defined as the **present value,** or **PV,** of $127.63 due in five years when the opportunity cost rate is 5 percent. If the price of the security were less than $100, you should buy it, because its price would then be less than the $100 you would have to spend on a similar-risk alternative to end up with $127.63 after five years. Conversely, if the security cost more than $100, you should not buy it, because you would have to invest only $100 in a similar-risk alternative to end up with $127.63 after five years. If the price were

---

[6] It would be more correct to use the term "an average investor" rather than "you" in this sentence. You, or any other individual, might have a strong reason for wanting the $100 to spend today, hence would prefer $100 today to $127.63 in five years. Some other person, who would just save the $100 even if it would earn less than 5 percent and thus grow to less than $127.63, would much prefer the $127.63. However, by definition an average (or marginal) investor would be indifferent, for if he or she were not indifferent, then the "going interest rate" would change from the stated 5 percent. For example, if most investors were in a saving mode, more money would flow into banks than they could invest profitably while paying 5 percent, so they would cut the rate on CDs. That would reduce the inflow of funds and establish a new equilibrium rate for CDs.

THE POWER OF COMPOUND INTEREST

You are 21 years old and have just graduated from college. After reading the introduction to this chapter, you decide to start investing in the stock market for your retirement. Your goal is to have $1 million when you retire at age 65. Assuming you earn a 10 percent annual rate on your stock investments, how much must you invest at the end of each year in order to reach your goal?

The answer is $1,532.24, but this amount depends critically on the return earned on your investments. If returns drop to 8 percent, your required annual contributions would rise to $2,801.52, while if returns rise to 12 percent, you would only need to put away $825.21 per year.

What if you are like most of us and wait until later to worry about retirement? If you wait until age 40, you will need to save $10,168 per year to reach your $1 million goal, assuming you earn 10 percent, and $13,679 per year if you earn only 8 percent. If you wait until age 50 and then earn 8 percent, the required amount will be $36,830 per year.

While $1 million may seem like a lot of money, it won't be when you get ready to retire. If inflation averages 5 percent a year over the next 44 years, your $1 million nest egg will be worth only $116,861 in today's dollars. At an 8 percent rate of return, and assuming you live for 20 years after retirement, your annual retirement income in today's dollars would be only $11,903 before taxes. So, after celebrating graduation and your new job, start saving!

Fair (Equilibrium) Value
The price at which investors are indifferent between buying or selling a security.

Discounting
The process of finding the present value of a cash flow or a series of cash flows; discounting is the reverse of compounding.

exactly $100, then you should be indifferent — you could either buy the security or turn it down. Therefore, $100 is defined as the security's **fair, or equilibrium, value.**

In general, *the present value of a cash flow due n years in the future is the amount which, if it were on hand today, would grow to equal the future amount.* Since $100 would grow to $127.63 in five years at a 5 percent interest rate, $100 is the present value of $127.63 due in five years when the opportunity cost rate is 5 percent.

Finding present values is called **discounting,** and it is simply the reverse of compounding — if you know the PV, you can compound to find the FV, while if you know the FV, you can discount to find the PV. Here is the time line used to visualize the present value:

```
    0    5%    1        2        3        4        5
    |----------|--------|--------|--------|--------|
  PV = ?                                        127.63
```

To develop the discounting equation, we begin with the future value equation, Equation 6-1:

$$FV_n = PV(1 + i)^n. \tag{6-1}$$

Next, we solve it for PV:

$$PV = \frac{FV_n}{(1 + i)^n}. \tag{6-2}$$

We could divide $127.63 by 1.05 five times, or by $(1.05)^5$, to find PV = $100 as shown below:

```
    0    5%    1         2         3         4         5
    |----------|---------|---------|---------|---------|
 -100 =   ← 105.00  ← 110.25  ← 115.76  ← 121.55  ← 127.63
          ÷ 1.05    ÷ 1.05    ÷ 1.05    ÷ 1.05    ÷ 1.05
```

However, financial calculators are programmed to do this arithmetic for us. Here is the procedure:

Inputs: 5   5   0   127.63

| N | I | PV | PMT | FV |

Output: = −100

Enter N = 5, I = 5, PMT = 0, and FV = 127.63, and then press PV to get PV = −100.

GRAPHIC VIEW OF THE DISCOUNTING PROCESS

Figure 6-2 shows how the present value of $1 (or any other sum) to be received in the future diminishes as the years to receipt and the interest rate increase. The data used to plot the curves could be obtained with a calculator, but we used a spreadsheet, 06MODEL.xls, to calculate the data and make the graph. The graph shows (1) that the present value of a sum to be received at some future date decreases and approaches zero as the payment date is extended further into the future, and (2) that the rate of decrease is greater the higher the interest (discount) rate. At relatively high interest rates, funds due in the future are worth very little today, and even at a relatively low discount rate, the present value of a sum due in the very distant future is quite small. For example, at a 20 percent discount rate, $1 million due in 100 years is worth approximately 1 cent today. (However, 1 cent would grow to almost $1 million in 100 years at 20 percent.)

FIGURE 6-2   **Relationships among Present Value, Interest Rates, and Time**

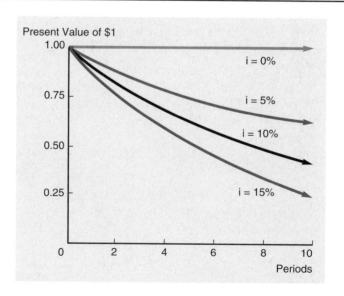

What is meant by the term "opportunity cost rate"?

What is discounting? How is it related to compounding?

How does the present value of an amount to be received in the future change as the time is extended and as the interest rate increases?

What amount must you deposit today in a three-year CD paying 4 percent interest annually to provide you with $2,249.73 at the end of the CD's maturity? ($2,000.00)

How would your answer to the preceding question change if the CD matured in five years rather than three years? What if the interest rate increased from 4 percent to 6 percent but the CD's maturity was still three years? ($1,849.11; $1,888.92)

SOLVING FOR INTEREST RATE AND TIME

At this point, you should realize that compounding and discounting are related, and that we have been dealing with one equation that can be solved for either the FV or the PV.

FV Form:

$$FV_n = PV(1 + i)^n. \tag{6-1}$$

PV Form:

$$PV = \frac{FV_n}{(1 + i)^n}. \tag{6-2}$$

There are four variables in these equations—PV, FV, i, and n—and if you know the values of any three, you can find the value of the fourth. Thus far, we have always given you the interest rate (i) and the number of years (n), plus either the PV or the FV. In many situations, though, you will need to solve for either i or n, as we discuss below.

SOLVING FOR i

Suppose you can buy a security at a price of $78.35, and it will pay you $100 after five years. Here you know PV, FV, and n, and you want to find i, the interest rate you would earn if you bought the security. Here is the time line and the equation:

$$FV_n = PV(1 + i)^n \tag{6-1}$$

$$\$100 = \$78.35(1 + i)^5. \text{ Solve for i.}$$

You could go through a trial-and-error process in which you insert different values of i into Equation 6-1 until you find a value that "works" in the sense that the right-hand side of the equation equals $100. The solution value is i = 0.05, or 5 percent. The trial-and-error procedure is extremely tedious and inefficient, but it is easy to solve the equation with a calculator or spreadsheet. Here is the calculator setup:

Inputs: 5   −78.35   0   100

| N | I | PV | PMT | FV |

Output: = 5.0

Enter N = 5, PV = −78.35, PMT = 0, and FV = 100, and then press I to get I = 5%. This procedure is easy, and it can be used for any interest rate or for any value of n, including fractional values.

SOLVING FOR n

Suppose you invest $78.35 at an interest rate of 5 percent per year. How long will it take your investment to grow to $100? Here you know PV, FV, and i, but you do not know n, the number of periods. Here is the situation:

```
0    5%    1         2              n − 1      n = ?
+----------+---------+- - - - - - - -+----------+
−78.35                                          100
```

$$FV_n = PV(1 + i)^n \tag{6-1}$$

$100 = $78.35(1.05)^n$. Solve for n.

You could go through a trial-and-error process wherein you substitute different values for n into the equation. You would find (eventually) that n = 5 "works," so 5 is the number of years it takes for $78.35 to grow to $100 if the interest rate is 5 percent. Again, though, it is easy to find n with a financial calculator or spreadsheet. Here is the calculator setup:

Inputs: 5   −78.35   0   100

| N | I | PV | PMT | FV |

Output: = 5.0

Enter I = 5, PV = −78.35, PMT = 0, and FV = 100, and then press N to get N = 5.

SELF-TEST QUESTIONS

You invest $5,000 today in a CD that pays 5 percent interest annually. If you leave your money invested in the CD for its entire maturity period, you will have $6,077.53. What is the CD's term to maturity? (4 years)

You invested $10,000 10 years ago in a 10-year CD. You just received word from your bank that the CD has matured and that you now have $18,771.37 in your account. What was the annual rate of interest earned on the 10-year CD? (6.5 percent)

Annuity
A series of payments of an equal amount at fixed intervals for a specified number of periods.

Ordinary (Deferred) Annuity
An annuity whose payments occur at the *end* of each period.

Annuity Due
An annuity whose payments occur at the *beginning* of each period.

FVA_n
The future value of an annuity over n periods.

An **annuity** is a series of equal payments made at fixed intervals for a specified number of periods. For example, $100 at the end of each of the next three years is a three-year annuity. The fixed payments are given the symbol PMT, and they can occur at either the beginning or the end of each period. If the payments occur at the *end* of each period, as they typically do, the annuity is called an **ordinary, or deferred, annuity.** Payments on mortgages, car loans, and student loans are typically set up as ordinary annuities. If payments are made at the *beginning* of each period, the annuity is an **annuity due.** Rental payments for an apartment, life insurance premiums, and lottery payoffs are typically set up as annuities due. Since ordinary annuities are more common in finance, when the term "annuity" is used in this book, you should assume that the payments occur at the end of each period unless otherwise noted.

ORDINARY ANNUITIES

An ordinary, or deferred, annuity consists of a series of equal payments made at the *end* of each period. If you deposit $100 at the end of each year for three years in a savings account that pays 5 percent interest per year, how much will you have at the end of three years? To answer this question, we must find the future value of the annuity, **FVA_n**. Each payment is compounded out to the end of Period n, and the sum of the compounded payments is the future value of the annuity, FVA_n.

Here we show the regular time line as the top portion of the diagram, but we also show how each cash flow is compounded to produce the value FVA_n in the lower portion of the diagram.

$$FVA_n = PMT(1 + i)^{n-1} + PMT(1 + i)^{n-2} + PMT(1 + i)^{n-3} + \cdots$$
$$+ PMT(1 + i)^0$$

$$= PMT \sum_{t=1}^{n} (1 + i)^{n-t}. \qquad (6\text{-}3)$$

The first line of Equation 6-3 represents the application of Equation 6-1 to each individual payment of the annuity. In other words, each term is the compounded amount of a single payment, with the superscript in each term indicating the number of periods during which the payment earns interest. For example, because the first annuity payment was made at the *end* of Period 1, interest would be earned in Periods 2 through n only, so compounding would be for $n - 1$ periods rather than n periods. Compounding for the second annuity payment would be for Period 3 through Period n, or $n - 2$ periods, and so on. The last annuity payment is made at the end of the annuity's life, so there is no time for interest to be earned. The second form of Equation 6-3 is just a shorthand version of the first.

We could find the FV by going through the arithmetic as shown below the annuity's time line, but if there were a lot of payments, say, 30, that would be a tedious process. However, financial calculators and spreadsheets are programmed to solve annuity problems. Here is the calculator setup for our three-year, $100 annuity problem:

In annuity problems the PMT key is used in conjunction with the N and I keys, plus either the PV or the FV key, depending on whether you are trying to find the PV or the FV of the annuity. In our example, you are solving for FV, so press the FV key to get the answer, $315.25. Since there is no initial payment, we input PV = 0.

ANNUITIES DUE

Had the three $100 payments in the previous example been made at the *beginning* of each year, the annuity would have been an *annuity due*. On the time line, each payment would be shifted to the left one year, so each payment would be compounded for one extra year:

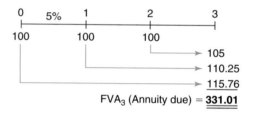

Here we show the regular time line as the top portion of the diagram, and we also show how each cash flow is compounded to produce the value FVA_n (Annuity due) in the lower portion of the diagram. Here the payments occur earlier, so more interest is earned. Therefore, the future value of the annuity due is larger: $331.01 versus $315.25 for the ordinary annuity.

Annuity due problems can also be solved with a calculator. Most financial calculators have a switch, or key, marked "DUE" or "BEG" that permits you to switch from end-of-period payments (ordinary annuity) to beginning-of-period payments (annuity due). When the beginning mode is activated, the display will normally show the word "BEGIN." Thus, to deal with annuities due, switch your calculator to "BEGIN" and proceed as before:

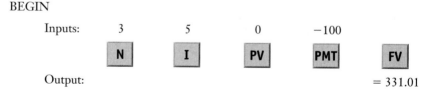

Enter N = 3, I = 5, PV = 0, PMT = −100, and then press FV to get the answer, $331.01. *Since most problems specify end-of-period cash flows, you should always switch your calculator back to "END" mode after you work an annuity due problem.*

What is the difference between an ordinary annuity and an annuity due?

Other things held constant, which annuity has the greater *future* value: an ordinary annuity or an annuity due? Why?

You deposit $7,500 at the *end* of each of the next three years in a bank account that pays 3 percent interest. How much will you have in your account at the end of the three-year period? ($23,181.75)

How would your answer to the preceding question change if you only deposited $3,750? What if you still deposited $7,500 for three years, but instead of earning 3 percent interest you now earn 6 percent interest? ($11,590.88; $23,877.00)

You deposit $7,500 at the *beginning* of each of the next three years in a bank account that pays 3 percent interest. How much will you have in your account at the end of the three-year period? What is the difference in the future values of the $7,500 annuity due and the $7,500 ordinary annuity at a 3 percent interest rate? Why does the difference occur? ($23,877.20; $695.45)

PRESENT VALUE OF AN ANNUITY

Suppose you were offered the following alternatives: (1) a three-year annuity with payments of $100 or (2) a lump sum payment today. You have no need for the money during the next three years, so if you accept the annuity, you would deposit the payments in a bank account that pays 5 percent interest per year. Similarly, the lump sum payment would be deposited into a bank account. How large must the lump sum payment today be to make it equivalent to the annuity?

ORDINARY ANNUITIES

If the payments come at the end of each year, then the annuity is an ordinary annuity, and it is set up as follows:

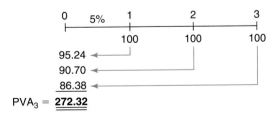

PVA_n
The present value of an annuity of n periods.

The time line is shown at the top of the diagram, and the discounted values are shown in the left column. The PV of the annuity, PVA_n, is $272.32.

The general equation used to find the PV of an ordinary annuity is shown below:

$$PVA_n = \frac{PMT}{(1+i)^1} + \frac{PMT}{(1+i)^2} + \cdots + \frac{PMT}{(1+i)^n}$$

$$= \sum_{t=1}^{n} \frac{PMT}{(1+i)^t}. \tag{6-4}$$

The present value of each cash flow is found and then summed to find the PV of the annuity. This procedure is simple enough, and easy for a three-year annuity, but it would be tedious for a long annuity. Again, though, financial calculators and spreadsheets are programmed to make the process easy. Here is the calculator setup:

Enter N = 3, I = 5, PMT = −100, and FV = 0, and then press the PV key to find the PV, $272.32.

ANNUITIES DUE

Had the three $100 payments in the preceding example been made at the beginning of each year, the annuity would have been an *annuity due*. Each payment would be shifted to the left one year, so each payment would be discounted for one less year. Here is the time line and the general equation:

Again, we can find the PV of each cash flow and then sum these PVs to find the PV of the annuity due.

$$PVA_n \text{ (Annuity due)} = \frac{PMT}{(1+i)^0} + \frac{PMT}{(1+i)^1} + \cdots + \frac{PMT}{(1+i)^{n-1}}$$

$$= \sum_{t=1}^{n} \frac{PMT}{(1+i)^{t-1}}. \tag{6-4a}$$

However, it is easier to use a financial calculator, especially if the annuity has a long life. Here is the calculator setup:

BEGIN

Inputs: 3 [N] 5 [I] [PV] −100 [PMT] 0 [FV]

Output: = 285.94

Switch to the beginning-of-period mode, then enter N = 3, I = 5, PMT = −100, and FV = 0, and then press PV to get the answer, $285.94. *Again, since most problems deal with end-of-period cash flows, don't forget to switch your calculator back to the "END" mode.*

SELF-TEST QUESTIONS

Which annuity has the greater present value: an ordinary annuity or an annuity due? Why?

Explain how financial calculators can be used to find the present value of annuities.

What amount today deposited in a bank account paying 3 percent annually would allow you to withdraw $7,500 at the end of each of the next three years? ($21,214.59)

How would your answer to the preceding question change if now you only wanted to withdraw $3,750 at the *end* of each of the next three years? What if you still wanted to withdraw $7,500 at the end of each of the next three years, but instead of earning 3 percent interest you now earn 6 percent on the account? ($10,607.29; $20,047.59)

What is the value today of an annuity of $7,500 received at the *beginning* of each of the next three years that earns 3 percent interest annually? What is the difference in the present values of the annuity due calculated here and the $7,500 ordinary annuity earning 3 percent calculated above? Why is this so? ($21,851.02; $636.43)

PERPETUITIES

Perpetuity
A stream of equal payments expected to continue forever.

Most annuities call for payments to be made over some finite period of time—for example, $100 per year for three years. However, some annuities go on indefinitely, or perpetually, and these are called **perpetuities.** The present value of a perpetuity is found by applying Equation 6-5.[7]

$$PV \text{ (Perpetuity)} = \frac{\text{Payment}}{\text{Interest rate}} = \frac{PMT}{i}. \tag{6-5}$$

---

[7] The derivation of Equation 6-5 is given in the Web/CD Extension to Chapter 5 of Eugene F. Brigham and Phillip R. Daves, *Intermediate Financial Management*, 7th ed. (Cincinnati, OH: South-Western College Publishing, 2002).

Perpetuities can be illustrated by some British securities issued after the Napoleonic Wars. In 1815, the British government sold a huge bond issue and used the proceeds to pay off many smaller issues that had been floated in prior years to pay for the wars. Since the purpose of the bonds was to consolidate past debts, the bonds were called **consols.** Suppose each consol promised to pay $100 per year in perpetuity. (Actually, interest was stated in pounds.) What would each bond be worth if the opportunity cost rate, or discount rate, was 5 percent? The answer is $2,000:

Consol
A perpetual bond issued by the British government to consolidate past debts; in general, any perpetual bond.

$$PV\,(\text{Perpetuity}) = \frac{\$100}{0.05} = \$2,000 \text{ if } i = 5\%.$$

Suppose the interest rate rose to 10 percent; what would happen to the consol's value? The value would drop to $1,000:

$$PV\,(\text{Perpetuity}) = \frac{\$100}{0.10} = \$1,000 \text{ at } i = 10\%.$$

Thus, we see that the value of a perpetuity changes dramatically when interest rates change. Perpetuities are discussed further in Chapter 8.

SELF-TEST QUESTIONS

What happens to the value of a perpetuity when interest rates increase?

What happens when interest rates decrease?

What is today's value of a perpetuity of $150 per year at an interest rate of 10 percent? How does that value compare with the value of a 100-year, $150 ordinary annuity at the 10 percent interest rate? What does that tell you about the present value of distant cash flows; that is, how much are the cash flows from Year 101 to infinity worth today? ($1,500.00; $1,499.89; $0.11)

If the value of a perpetuity today is $6,000 and the current interest rate is 6 percent, what payment would you receive in perpetuity? ($360.00)

UNEVEN CASH FLOW STREAMS

Uneven Cash Flow Stream
A series of cash flows in which the amount varies from one period to the next.

Payment (PMT)
This term designates *equal* cash flows coming at regular intervals.

Cash Flow (CF)
This term designates *uneven* cash flows.

The definition of an annuity includes the words *constant payment*—in other words, annuities involve payments that are equal in every period. Although many financial decisions do involve constant payments, other important decisions involve uneven, or nonconstant, cash flows; for example, common stocks typically pay an increasing stream of dividends over time, and fixed asset investments such as new equipment normally do not generate constant cash flows. Consequently, it is necessary to extend our time value discussion to include **uneven cash flow streams.**

Throughout the book, we will follow convention and reserve the term **payment (PMT)** for annuity situations where the cash flows are equal amounts, and we will use the term **cash flow (CF)** to denote uneven cash flows. Financial calculators are set up to follow this convention, so if you are dealing with uneven cash flows, you will need to use the "cash flow register."

PRESENT VALUE OF AN UNEVEN CASH FLOW STREAM

The PV of an uneven cash flow stream is found as the sum of the PVs of the individual cash flows of the stream. For example, suppose we must find the PV of the following cash flow stream, discounted at 6 percent:

The PV will be found by applying this general present value equation:

$$PV = \frac{CF_1}{(1+i)^1} + \frac{CF_2}{(1+i)^2} + \cdots + \frac{CF_n}{(1+i)^n}$$

$$= \sum_{t=1}^{n} \frac{CF_t}{(1+i)^t}. \tag{6-6}$$

We could find the PV of each individual cash flow and then sum these values to find the present value of the stream. Here is what the process would look like:

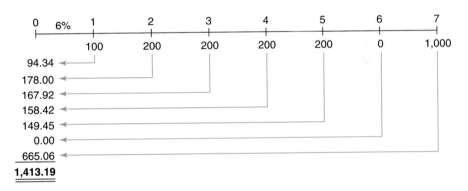

All we did was to apply Equation 6-6, show the individual PVs in the left column of the diagram, and then sum these individual PVs to find the PV of the entire stream.[8]

---

[8] The present value of a cash flow stream can always be found as shown above, but cash flow regularities within the stream may allow the use of shortcuts. For example, notice that the cash flows in periods 2 through 5 represent an annuity. We can use that fact to solve the problem in a slightly different manner:

Cash flows during Years 2 to 5 represent an ordinary annuity, and we find its PV at Year 1 (one period before the first payment). This PV ($693.02) must then be discounted back one more period to get its Year 0 value, $653.79.

Problems involving uneven cash flows can be solved easily with a financial calculator or spreadsheet. With a calculator, you first input the individual cash flows, in chronological order, into the cash flow register. Cash flows are usually designated CF_0, CF_1, CF_2, CF_3, and so on. Next, you enter the interest rate, I. At this point, you have substituted in all the known values of Equation 6-6, so you only need to press the NPV key to find the present value of the stream. Calculators are programmed to find the PV of each cash flow and then to sum these values to find the PV of the entire stream. To input the cash flows for this problem, enter 0 (because $CF_0 = 0$), 100, 200, 200, 200, 200, 0, 1000 in that order into the cash flow register, enter I = 6, and then press NPV to obtain the answer, $1,413.19.

Two points should be noted. First, when dealing with the cash flow register, the calculator uses the term "NPV" rather than "PV." The N stands for "net," so NPV is the abbreviation for "Net Present Value," which is simply the net present value of a series of positive and negative cash flows, including the cash flow at time zero. Our example has no negative cash flows, but if it did, we would simply input them with negative signs.[9]

The second point to note is that annuities can be entered into the cash flow register more efficiently by using the N_j key.[10] In this illustration, you would enter $CF_0 = 0$, $CF_1 = 100$, $CF_2 = 200$, $N_j = 4$ (which tells the calculator that the 200 occurs 4 times), $CF_6 = 0$, and $CF_7 = 1000$. Then enter I = 6 and press the NPV key, and 1,413.19 will appear in the display. Also, note that amounts entered into the cash flow register remain in the register until they are cleared. Thus, if you had previously worked a problem with eight cash flows, and then you moved to a problem with only four cash flows, the calculator would simply add the cash flows from the second problem to those of the first problem. Therefore, you must be sure to clear the cash flow register before starting a new problem.

FUTURE VALUE OF AN UNEVEN CASH FLOW STREAM

Terminal Value
The future value of an uneven cash flow stream.

The future value of an uneven cash flow stream (sometimes called the **terminal value**) is found by compounding each payment to the end of the stream and then summing the future values:

$$FV_n = CF_1(1 + i)^{n-1} + CF_2(1 + i)^{n-2} + \cdots + CF_n$$

$$= \sum_{t=1}^{n} CF_t(1 + i)^{n-t}. \tag{6-7}$$

---

[9] To input a negative number, type in the positive number, then press the +/− key to change the sign to negative. If you begin by typing the minus sign, you make the mistake of subtracting the negative number from the last number that was entered in the calculator.

[10] On some calculators, you are prompted to enter the number of times the cash flow occurs, and on still other calculators, the procedures for inputting data may be different. You should consult your calculator manual or our *Technology Supplement* to determine the appropriate steps for your specific calculator.

The future value of our illustrative uneven cash flow stream is $2,124.92:

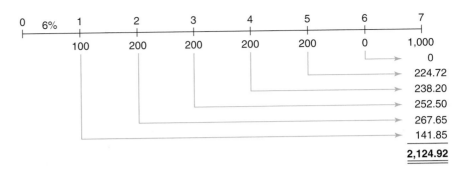

Some financial calculators have a net future value (NFV) key which, after the cash flows and interest rate have been entered, can be used to obtain the future value of an uneven cash flow stream. Even if your calculator doesn't have the NFV feature, you can use the cash flow stream's net present value to find its net future value: NFV = $NPV(1 + i)^n$. Thus, in our example, you could find the PV of the stream, then find the FV of that PV, compounded for n periods at i percent. In the illustrative problem, find PV = 1,413.19 using the cash flow register and I = 6. Then enter N = 7, I = 6, PV = −1413.19, and PMT = 0, and then press FV to find FV = 2,124.92, which equals the NFV shown on the time line above.

SOLVING FOR i WITH UNEVEN CASH FLOW STREAMS

Before calculators and spreadsheets existed, it was *extremely difficult* to solve for i if the cash flows were uneven, because then we had to go through many tedious trial-and-error calculations. With a spreadsheet program or a financial calculator, though, it is easy to find the value of i. Simply input the CF values into the cash flow register and then press the IRR key. IRR stands for "internal rate of return," which is the percentage return on an investment. We will defer further discussion of this calculation for now, but we will take it up later, in our discussion of capital budgeting methods in Chapter 10.[11]

---

[11] To obtain an IRR solution, at least one of the cash flows must have a negative sign, indicating that it is an investment. Since none of the CFs in our example were negative, the cash flow stream has no IRR. However, had we input a cost for CF_0, say, −$1,000, we could have obtained an IRR, which would be the rate of return earned on the $1,000 investment. Here IRR would be 13.96 percent.

YEAR	CASH FLOWS
0	0
1	250
2	500
3	500
4	0
5	2,500

What is the *future value* of the cash flow stream? ($3,933.94)

SEMIANNUAL AND OTHER COMPOUNDING PERIODS

Annual Compounding
The arithmetic process of determining the final value of a cash flow or series of cash flows when interest is added *once* a year.

Semiannual Compounding
The arithmetic process of determining the final value of a cash flow or series of cash flows when interest is added *twice* a year.

In all of our examples thus far, we have assumed that interest is compounded once a year, or annually. This is called **annual compounding.** Suppose, however, that you put $100 into a bank which states that it pays a 6 percent annual interest rate, but interest is credited each six months. This is called **semiannual compounding.** How much would you have accumulated at the end of one year, two years, or some other period under semiannual compounding? Note that virtually all bonds pay interest semiannually, most stocks pay dividends quarterly, and most mortgages, student loans, and auto loans require monthly payments. Therefore, it is essential that you understand how to deal with nonannual compounding.

To illustrate semiannual compounding, assume that $100 is placed into an account that pays 6 percent, and it is left there for three years. First, consider again what would happen under *annual* compounding:

$$FV_n = PV(1 + i)^n = \$100(1.06)^3$$
$$= \$119.10.$$

We would, of course, get this same answer using a financial calculator or a spreadsheet.

How would things change if interest were paid semiannually rather than annually? First, whenever payments occur more frequently than once a year, or when interest is stated to be compounded more than once a year, then you must (1) convert the stated interest rate to a "periodic rate," and (2) convert the number of years to "number of periods," as follows:

    (1) Periodic rate = Stated rate/Number of payments per year.
    (2) Number of periods = Number of years × Periods per year.

USING THE INTERNET FOR PERSONAL FINANCIAL PLANNING

People continually face important financial decisions that require an understanding of the time value of money. Should we buy or lease a car? How much and how soon do we need to save for our children's education? What size house can we afford? Should we refinance our home mortgage? How much must we save in order to retire comfortably?

The answers to these questions are often complicated, and they depend on a number of factors, such as housing and education costs, interest rates, inflation, expected family income, and stock market returns. Hopefully, after completing this chapter, you will have a better idea of how to answer such questions. Moreover, there are a number of online resources available to help with financial planning.

A good place to start is **http://www.smartmoney.com**. *Smartmoney* is a personal finance magazine produced by the publishers of *The Wall Street Journal*. If you go to *Smartmoney*'s

web site you will find a tab titled "Personal Finance." This section has a number of financial calculators, spreadsheets, and descriptive materials that cover a wide range of personal finance issues.

Another good place to look is Quicken's web site, **http://www.quicken.com**. Here you will find several interesting sections that deal with a variety of personal finance issues. Within these sections you will find background articles plus spreadsheets and calculators that you can use to analyze your own situation.

Finally, **http://investormap.com/personal-calc.htm** provides a list of personal finance–financial calculator web sites that you can access. The financial calculators listed range from retirement savings to education savings to home mortgage calculators. Some of the financial calculators listed here are fairly detailed, while others are fairly simplistic.

In our example, where we must find the value of $100 after three years when the stated interest rate is 6 percent, compounded semiannually (or twice a year), you would begin by making the following conversions:

$$\text{Periodic rate} = 6\%/2 = 3\% \text{ per 6-month period.}$$

$$\text{Periods} = N = 3 \times 2 = 6 \text{ semiannual periods.}$$

In this situation, the investment will earn 3 percent every six months for six semiannual periods, not 6 percent per year for three years. As we shall see, there is a significant difference between these two procedures.

You should make the conversions as your first step when working on such a problem *because calculations must be done using the appropriate number of periods and the periodic rate, not the number of years and stated rate*. Periodic rates and number of periods, not yearly rates and number of years, should normally be shown on time lines and entered into the calculator whenever you are dealing with nonannual compounding.[12]

With this background, we can now find the value of $100 after three years if it is held in an account that pays a stated rate of 6 percent, but with semiannual compounding. Here is the time line:

---

[12] With some financial calculators, you can enter the annual (nominal) rate and the number of compounding periods rather than make the conversion we recommend. We prefer making the conversion because it is easier to see the problem setup in a time line, and also because it is easy to forget to readjust your calculator after you change its settings and then to make an error on the next problem because of the incorrect setting.

$$FV_n = PV(1+i)^n = \$100(1.03)^6$$
$$= \$100(1.1941) = \$119.41.$$

Here i = rate per period = annual rate/compounding periods per year = 6%/2 = 3%, and n = the total number of periods = years × periods per year = 3 × 2 = 6.

Inputs:

	6	3	−100	0	
	N	**I**	**PV**	**PMT**	**FV**

Output: = 119.41

Enter N = years × periods per year = 3 × 2 = 6, I = annual rate/periods per year = 6/2 = 3, PV = −100, and PMT = 0. Then press FV to find the answer, $119.41.

Throughout the world economy, different compounding periods are used for different types of investments. For example, bank accounts generally pay interest daily; most bonds pay interest semiannually; and stocks generally pay dividends quarterly.[13] If we are to properly compare securities with different compounding periods, we need to put them on a common basis. This requires us to distinguish between nominal and effective annual rates.[14]

Also, in practice people use several different terms when discussing the nominal and effective rates, so you need to be aware of these different definitions:

Nominal (Quoted, or Stated, or APR) Interest Rate

The contracted, or quoted, or stated, interest rate.

- The **Nominal Rate** is also called the *Annual Percentage Rate* (or **APR**), or the **Stated** or **Quoted** Rate. This is the rate that banks, credit card companies, student loan officers, auto dealers, and so on tell you that they are charging on loans. It is also the rate banks say they are paying on deposits. Note that if two banks offer loans with an APR rate of 8 percent, but payments must be made at different times, then they are not necessarily charging the same rate—one could really be charging a lot more than the other. So, to compare loans across lenders, or interest earned across different institutions, you must use effective rates as described below.

Effective (Equivalent) Annual Rate (EFF% or EAR)

The annual rate of interest actually being earned, as opposed to the quoted rate. Also called the "equivalent annual rate."

- The **Effective Rate**, abbreviated as **EFF%** is also called the **Equivalent Annual Rate** (or **EAR**). This is the rate that would produce the same ending (or future) value under annual compounding as would more frequent compounding at a given nominal rate. You can convert any nominal rate to an equivalent annual rate, or EFF%. When comparing loans or investments that make payments at different intervals, you should focus on the EFF%.

In our example, we saw that with semiannual compounding at a nominal rate of 6 percent, a $100 lump sum would have a future value of $119.41. Thus, the effective

---

[13] Some banks and savings and loans even pay interest compounded *continuously*. Continuous compounding is discussed in Web Appendix 6B.

[14] The term *nominal rate* as it is used here has a different meaning than the way it was used in Chapter 4. There, nominal interest rates referred to stated market rates as opposed to real (zero inflation) rates. In this chapter, the term *nominal rate* means the stated, or quoted, annual rate as opposed to the effective annual rate. In both cases, though, *nominal* means *stated*, or *quoted*, as opposed to some adjusted rate.

annual rate is the once-a-year rate that would produce an FV of $119.41 at the end of Year 3. Here is a time line of the situation:

Our task now is to find the effective annual rate, EAR or EFF%, that is equivalent to 6 percent with semiannual compounding.

We can determine the effective annual rate, given the nominal rate and the number of compounding periods per year, by solving this equation:

$$\text{Effective annual rate} = \text{EAR (or EFF\%)} = \left(1 + \frac{i_{\text{Nom}}}{m}\right)^m - 1.0. \qquad (6\text{-}8)$$

Here i_{Nom} is the nominal, or quoted, interest rate, and m is the number of compounding periods per year. For example, to find the effective annual rate if the nominal rate is 6 percent and semiannual compounding is used, we have[15]

$$\text{Effective annual rate} = \text{EAR (or EFF\%)} = \left(1 + \frac{0.06}{2}\right)^2 - 1.0.$$
$$= (1.03)^2 - 1.0$$
$$= 1.0609 - 1.0 = 0.0609 = 6.09\%.$$

The points made about semiannual compounding can be generalized as follows. When compounding occurs more frequently than once a year, we can use a modified version of Equation 6-1 to find the future value of any lump sum:

$$\text{Annual compounding: } FV_n = PV(1 + i)^n. \qquad \textbf{(6-1)}$$

$$\text{More frequent compounding: } FV_n = PV\left(1 + \frac{i_{\text{Nom}}}{m}\right)^{mn}. \qquad (6\text{-}9)$$

Here i_{Nom} is the nominal, or quoted, rate, m is the number of times compounding occurs per year, and n is the number of years. For example, when banks pay daily interest, the value of m is set at 365 and Equation 6-9 is applied.[16]

To illustrate further the effect of compounding monthly rather than annually, consider the interest rate charged on credit cards. Many banks charge 1.5 percent per month, and, in their advertising, they state that the **Annual Percentage Rate (APR)** is 1.5% × 12 = 18%. However, the effective annual rate is 19.6 percent:

$$\text{Effective annual rate} = \text{EAR (or EFF\%)} = \left(1 + \frac{0.18}{12}\right)^{12} - 1.0.$$
$$= (1.015)^{12} - 1.0$$
$$= 0.196 = 19.6\%.$$

Annual Percentage Rate (APR)
The periodic rate × the number of periods per year.

---

[15] Most financial calculators are programmed to find the EFF% or, given the EFF%, to find the nominal rate. This is called "interest rate conversion," and you simply enter the nominal rate and the number of compounding periods per year and then press the EFF% key to find the effective annual rate.

[16] To illustrate, the future value of $1 invested at 10 percent for 1 year under daily compounding is $1.1052:

$$FV_n = \$1\left(1 + \frac{0.10}{365}\right)^{365(1)} = \$1(1.105156) = \$1.1052.$$

Note also that banks sometimes use 360 as the number of days per year for this and other calculations.

Semiannual and other compounding periods can also be used for discounting, and for both lump sums and annuities. First, consider the case where we want to find the PV of an ordinary annuity of $100 per year for three years when the interest rate is 8 percent, *compounded annually*:

Here we could simply find the PV of each cash flow and sum them, obtaining a PV of $257.71. With a financial calculator we would proceed as follows:

Now let's change the situation to *semiannual compounding*, where the annuity calls for payments of $50 each six months rather than $100 per year. The quoted rate is still 8 percent, but now it is compounded semiannually. Here is the time line:

We could find the PV of each cash flow by discounting at 4 percent. Treat each tick mark on the time line as a period, so there are six periods. The PV of the annuity is $262.11 versus $257.71 under annual compounding.

We could also use a financial calculator, proceeding as follows:

Inputs: 6   4   50   0

          [N]   [I]   [PV]   [PMT]   [FV]

Output: = −262.11

The annuity value with semiannual compounding is $262.11, which is greater than the annual annuity value. The reason is that the semiannual payments come in sooner and thus earn interest over a longer period.

SELF-TEST QUESTIONS

What changes must you make in your calculations to determine the future value of an amount that is being compounded at 8 percent semiannually versus one being compounded annually at 8 percent?

Why is semiannual compounding better than annual compounding from a saver's standpoint? What about a borrower's standpoint?

Define the terms "Annual Percentage Rate," or "APR," "Effective (or Equivalent) Annual Rate," and "Nominal Interest Rate."

How does the term "nominal rate" as used in this chapter differ from the term as it was used in Chapter 4?

What is the future value of $2,000 deposited today and left in a bank account for three years if it earns 6 percent annually? What if the interest rate is 6 percent compounded semiannually? What if the interest rate is 6 percent compounded quarterly? ($2,382.03; $2,388.10; $2,391.24)

COMPARISON OF DIFFERENT TYPES OF INTEREST RATES

Finance deals with three main types of interest rates: nominal rates, i_{Nom}; periodic rates, i_{PER}; and effective annual rates, EAR or EFF%. Therefore, it is essential that you understand what each one is and when it should be used.

1. **Nominal, or quoted, or APR rate.** This is the rate that is quoted by banks, brokers, and other financial institutions. So, if you talk with a banker, broker, mortgage lender, auto finance company, or student loan officer about rates, the nominal rate is the one he or she will normally quote you. However, to be meaningful, the quoted nominal rate must also include the number of compounding periods per year. For example, a bank might offer 6 percent, compounded quarterly, on CDs, or a mutual fund might offer 5 percent, compounded monthly, on its money market account.

   The nominal rate on loans to consumers is also called the Annual Percentage Rate (APR). If a credit card issuer quotes an APR of 18 percent, monthly, this means an interest rate of 18%/12 = 1.5 percent per month.

   Nominal rates can be compared with one another, *but this should be done only if the instruments being compared use the same number of compounding periods per year.* Thus, you could compare the quoted yields on two bonds if they both pay interest semiannually. However, to compare a 6 percent, semiannual payment bond with a 5 percent, daily payment money market fund, we would need to put both instruments on an *effective (or equivalent) annual rate (EFF%)* basis as discussed later in this section.

   Note that the nominal rate is never shown on a time line, and it is never used as an input in a financial calculator (unless compounding occurs only once a year, in which case i_{Nom} = periodic rate = EAR). If more frequent compounding occurs, you must use the periodic rate as discussed below for calculations.

2. **Periodic rate, i_{PER}.** This is the rate charged by a lender or paid by a borrower *each period.* It can be a rate per year, per six-month period, per quarter, per month, per day, or per any other time interval. For example, a bank might charge an APR rate of 18 percent, or 1.5 percent per month on its credit card loans, or a finance company might charge 3 percent per quarter on installment loans. We find the periodic rate as follows:

$$\text{Periodic rate, } i_{PER} = i_{Nom}/m, \tag{6-10}$$

which implies that

$$\text{Nominal annual (APR) rate} = i_{Nom} = (\text{Periodic rate})(m). \tag{6-11}$$

Here i_{Nom} is the nominal annual rate and m is the number of compounding periods per year. To illustrate, consider a finance company loan at 3 percent per quarter:

$$\text{Nominal annual (APR) rate} = i_{Nom} = (\text{Periodic rate})(m) = (3\%)(4) = 12\%,$$

or

$$\text{Periodic rate} = i_{Nom}/m = 12\%/4 = 3\% \text{ per quarter.}$$

If there is only one payment per year, or if interest is added only once a year, then m = 1, and the periodic rate is equal to the nominal rate.

The periodic rate is the rate that is generally shown on time lines and used in calculations.[17] To illustrate use of the periodic rate, suppose you make the following eight quarterly payments of $100 each into an account that pays a nominal rate of 12 percent, compounded quarterly. How much would you have after two years?

0	3%	1	2	3	4	5	6	7	8 Quarters
		−100	−100	−100	−100	−100	−100	−100	−100

FV = ?

$$FVA_n = \sum_{t=1}^{n} PMT(1 + i)^{n-t} = \sum_{t=1}^{8} \$100(1.03)^{8-t}.$$

You could compound each $100 payment at 12/4 = 3 percent for the appropriate number of periods, and then sum these individual FVs to find the FV of the payment stream, $889.23. You could also solve the problem with a calculator:

Inputs:	8	3	0	−100	
	N	I	PV	PMT	FV
Output:					= 889.23

Input N = 2 × 4 = 8, I = 12/4 = 3, PV = 0, and PMT = −100, and then press the FV key to get FV = $889.23.

3. **Effective (or equivalent) annual rate (EAR).** This is the annual rate that produces the same result as if we had compounded at a given periodic rate m times per year. The EAR is found as follows:

$$\text{EFF\% (or EAR)} = \left(1 + \frac{i_{Nom}}{m}\right)^m - 1.0. \tag{6-8}$$

You could also use the interest conversion feature of a financial calculator.

In the EFF% equation, i_{Nom}/m is the periodic rate, and m is the number of periods per year. For example, suppose you could borrow using either a credit card that charges 1 percent per month or a bank loan with a 12 percent quoted nominal (APR) rate that is compounded quarterly. Which should you choose? To answer this question, the cost rate of each alternative must be expressed as an EAR:

---

[17] The only exception is in situations where (1) annuities are involved and (2) the payment periods do not correspond to the compounding periods. If an annuity is involved and if its payment periods do not correspond to the compounding periods—for example, if you are making quarterly payments into a bank account to build up a specified future sum, but the bank pays interest on a daily basis—then the calculations are more complicated. For such problems, we would determine the periodic (daily) interest rate by dividing the nominal rate by 360 (or 365 if the bank uses a 365-day year), then compound each payment over the exact number of days from the payment date to the terminal point, and then sum the compounded payments to find the future value of the annuity. With a computer, this is a simple process. We could also calculate the EAR based on daily compounding, then find the corresponding nominal rate based on quarterly compounding (because the annuity payments are made quarterly), then find the quarterly periodic rate, and then use that rate with standard annuity procedures. The second procedure is hard to explain and generally not used in practice given the ready availability of computers.

Credit card loan: EFF% = $(1 + 0.01)^{12} - 1.0 = (1.01)^{12} - 1.0$

$$= 1.126825 - 1.0 = 0.126825 = 12.6825\%.$$

Bank loan: EFF% = $(1 + 0.03)^{4} - 1.0 = (1.03)^{4} - 1.0$

$$= 1.125509 - 1.0 = 0.125509 = 12.5509\%.$$

Thus, the credit card loan is slightly more costly than the bank loan. This result should have been intuitive to you — both loans have the same 12 percent nominal rate, yet you would have to make monthly payments on the credit card versus quarterly payments under the bank loan.

The EFF% rate is not used in calculations. However, it should be used to compare the effective cost or rate of return on loans or investments when payment periods differ, as in the credit card versus bank loan example.

SELF-TEST QUESTIONS

Define the nominal (or quoted, or APR) rate, the periodic rate, and the effective annual rate.

How are the nominal rate, the periodic rate, and the effective annual rate related?

What is the one situation where all three of these rates will be the same?

Which rate should be shown on time lines and used in calculations?

FRACTIONAL TIME PERIODS[18]

In all the examples used thus far in the chapter, we have assumed that payments occur at either the beginning or the end of periods, but not at some date *within* a period. However, we often encounter situations that require compounding or discounting over fractional periods. For example, suppose you deposited $100 in a bank that adds interest to your account daily, that is, uses daily compounding, and pays a nominal rate of 10 percent with a 365-day year. How much will be in your account after nine months? The answer is $107.79:[19]

Periodic rate = i_{PER} = 0.10/365 = 0.000273973 per day.

Number of days = 0.75(365) = 273.75 rounded to 274.

Ending amount = $100(1.000273973)^{274}$ = $107.79.

Now suppose you borrow $100 from a bank that charges 10 percent per year "simple interest," which means annual rather than daily compounding, but you borrow the $100 for only 274 days. How much interest would you have to pay for the use of $100 for 274 days? Here we would calculate a daily interest rate, i_{PER}, as above, but multiply by 274 rather than use it as an exponent:

Interest owed = $100(0.000273973)(274)$ = $7.51 interest charged.

---

[18] This section is relatively technical, but it can be omitted without loss of continuity.

[19] Here we assumed a 365-day year. In real-world calculations, the bank's computer (and many financial calculators) has a built-in calendar, and if you input the beginning and ending dates, the computer or calculator would tell you the exact number of days, taking account of 30-day months, 31-day months, and 28- or 29-day months.

You would owe the bank a total of $107.51 after 274 days. This is the procedure most banks actually use to calculate interest on loans, except that they generally require you to pay the interest on a monthly basis rather than after 274 days.

Finally, let's consider a somewhat different situation. Say an Internet access firm had 100 customers at the end of 2002, and its customer base is expected to grow steadily at the rate of 10 percent per year. What is the estimated customer base nine months into the new year? This problem would be set up exactly like the bank account with daily compounding, and the estimate would be 107.79 customers, rounded to 108.

The most important thing in problems like these, as in all time value problems, is to be careful! Think about what is involved in a logical, systematic manner, draw a time line if it would help you visualize the situation, and then apply the appropriate equations.

AMORTIZED LOANS

Amortized Loan
A loan that is repaid in equal payments over its life.

One of the most important applications of compound interest involves loans that are paid off in installments over time. Included are automobile loans, home mortgage loans, student loans, and most business loans other than very short-term loans and long-term bonds. If a loan is to be repaid in equal periodic amounts (monthly, quarterly, or annually), it is said to be an **amortized loan.**[20]

Table 6-1 illustrates the amortization process. A firm borrows $1,000, and the loan is to be repaid in three equal payments at the end of each of the next three years. (In this case, there is only one payment per year, so years = periods and the stated rate = periodic rate.) The lender charges a 6 percent interest rate on the loan balance that is outstanding at the beginning of each year. The first task is to determine the amount the firm must repay each year, or the constant annual payment. To find this amount, recognize that the $1,000 represents the present value of an annuity of PMT dollars per year for three years, discounted at 6 percent:

```
0    6%    1         2         3
|----------|---------|---------|
1,000     PMT       PMT       PMT
```

[20] The word *amortized* comes from the Latin *mors*, meaning "death," so an amortized loan is one that is "killed off" over time.

	BEGINNING AMOUNT (1)	PAYMENT (2)	INTEREST[a] (3)	REPAYMENT OF PRINCIPAL[b] (2) − (3) = (4)	REMAINING BALANCE (1) − (4) = (5)
TABLE 6-1	**Loan Amortization Schedule, 6 Percent Interest Rate**				
YEAR					
1	$1,000.00	$ 374.11	$ 60.00	$ 314.11	$685.89
2	685.89	374.11	41.15	332.96	352.93
3	352.93	374.11	21.18	352.93	0.00
		$1,122.33	$122.33	$1,000.00	

[a] Interest is calculated by multiplying the loan balance at the beginning of the year by the interest rate. Therefore, interest in Year 1 is $1,000(0.06) = $60; in Year 2 it is $685.89(0.06) = $41.15; and in Year 3 it is $352.93(0.06) = $21.18.
[b] Repayment of principal is equal to the payment of $374.11 minus the interest charge for each year.

$$PVA_3 = \frac{PMT}{(1 + i)^1} + \frac{PMT}{(1 + i)^2} + \frac{PMT}{(1 + i)^3} = \sum_{t=1}^{3} \frac{PMT}{(1 + i)^t}$$

$$\$1{,}000 = \sum_{t=1}^{3} \frac{PMT}{(1.06)^t}.$$

Here we know everything except PMT, so we can solve the equation for PMT. You could follow the trial-and-error procedure, inserting values for PMT in the equation until you found a value that "worked" and caused the right side of the equation to equal $1,000. This would be a tedious process, but you would eventually find PMT = $374.11. The easy way would be to use a calculator, set up as follows:

Inputs:	3	6	1000		0
	N	**I**	**PV**	**PMT**	**FV**
Output:				= −374.11	

Enter N = 3, I = 6, PV = 1000, and FV = 0, and then press the PMT key to find PMT = −$374.11.

Therefore, the firm must pay the lender $374.11 at the end of each of the next three years, and the percentage cost to the borrower, which is also the rate of return to the lender, will be 6 percent. Each payment consists partly of interest and partly of repayment of principal. This breakdown is given in the **amortization schedule** shown in Table 6-1. The interest component is largest in the first year, and it declines as the outstanding balance of the loan decreases. For tax purposes, a business borrower or homeowner reports the interest component shown in Column 3 as a deductible cost each year, while the lender reports this same amount as taxable income.

Financial calculators are programmed to calculate amortization tables—you simply enter the input data, and then press one key to get each entry in Table 6-1. It would be worthwhile to read the appropriate section of the calculator manual and learn how to use its amortization feature. However, as we show in the model for this chapter, with a spreadsheet such as *Excel*, it is easy to set up and print out a full amortization schedule.

Amortization Schedule
A table showing precisely how a loan will be repaid. It gives the required payment on each payment date and a breakdown of the payment, showing how much is interest and how much is repayment of principal.

PARTIAL AMORTIZATION: BALLOON LOANS

In the preceding section we discussed fully amortized loans. However, many loans are set up on a *partial amortization basis*, with a *"balloon payment"* coming due at some date before the loan has been fully amortized. For example, home buyers sometimes do not have enough cash to make the required down payment, and the seller of the home agrees to take a note rather than cash to enable the sale to go through. To illustrate, suppose a house is on the market for $200,000, and a bank agrees to lend the potential home buyer $175,000 secured by a mortgage on the house. Thus, the buyer must come up with $25,000 (plus assorted closing costs) to complete the transaction. Now suppose the buyer has only $5,000, and the seller really, really wants to sell the house. The seller may then agree to take a note with the following terms: a face value of $20,000, an 8 percent interest rate, and payments at the end of the year based on a 20-year amortization schedule, but with the loan maturing at the end of the 10th year.

In our example, the annual payments could be found with a calculator by inputting N = 20, I = 8, PV = 20000, and FV = 0. The annual payment would be PMT = –$2,037.04, and an amortization schedule similar to Table 6-1 could be set up. It would begin with 20 years of data, and we would see that the remaining balance at the end of the 10th year is $13,668.73. This amount, along with the regular annual payment of $2,037.04, or a total of $15,705.78, would be due at the end of the 10th year. The note would be called a "balloon note," and the $13,668.73 is the "balloon."

Note that if the $20,000 loan had been set up as a fully amortized note at 8 percent for 10 years, the annual payments would have been $2,980.59, with no balloon payment. In that case, though, the potential buyer might have felt unable to pay the extra $943.55 per year, and thus might have been unwilling to go ahead with the purchase. Thus, setting up a balloon note often enables a transaction to go through.

SELF-TEST QUESTION

Why are the payments under a partially amortized loan smaller than those under an otherwise similar fully amortized loan?

TYING IT ALL TOGETHER

Financial decisions often involve situations in which someone pays money at one point in time and receives money at some later time. Dollars paid or received at two different points in time are different, and this difference is recognized and accounted for by *time value of money (TVM) analysis*. We summarize below the types of TVM analysis and the key concepts covered in this chapter, using the data shown in Figure 6-3 to illustrate the various points. Refer to the figure constantly, and try to find in it an example of the points covered as you go through this summary.

- **Compounding** is the process of determining the **future value (FV)** of a cash flow or a series of cash flows. The compounded amount, or future value, is equal to the beginning amount plus the interest earned.

FIGURE 6-3

Illustration for Chapter Summary
(i = 4%, Annual Compounding)

- Future value: $FV_n = PV(1 + i)^n$.
  (single payment)

  Example: $1,000 compounded for 1 year at 4 percent:
  $$FV_1 = \$1,000(1.04)^1 = \$1,040.$$

- **Discounting** is the process of finding the **present value (PV)** of a future cash flow or a series of cash flows; discounting is the reciprocal, or reverse, of compounding.

- Present value: $PV = \dfrac{FV_n}{(1 + i)^n}$.
  (single payment)

  Example: $1,000 discounted back for 2 years at 4 percent:
  $$PV = \frac{\$1,000}{(1.04)^2} = \$1,000(0.92456) = \$924.56.$$

- An **annuity** is defined as a series of equal periodic payments (PMT) for a specified number of periods.

- Future value:
  (annuity)

$$FVA_n = PMT(1 + i)^{n-1} + PMT(1 + i)^{n-2} + PMT(1 + i)^{n-3} + \cdots + PMT(1 + i)^0$$
$$= \sum_{t=1}^{n} PMT(1 + i)^{n-t}.$$

  Example: FVA of 3 payments of $1,000 when i = 4%:
  $$FVA_3 = \$1,000(1.04)^2 + \$1,000(1.04)^1 + \$1,000(1.04)^0$$
  $$= \$3,121.60.$$

- Present value: $PVA_n = \dfrac{PMT}{(1 + i)^1} + \dfrac{PMT}{(1 + i)^2} + \cdots + \dfrac{PMT}{(1 + i)^n}$
  (annuity)
  $$= \sum_{t=1}^{n} \frac{PMT}{(1 + i)^t}.$$

  Example: PVA of 3 payments of $1,000 when i = 4% per period:
  $$PVA_3 = \frac{\$1,000}{(1.04)^1} + \frac{\$1,000}{(1.04)^2} + \frac{\$1,000}{(1.04)^3}$$
  $$= \$2,775.10.$$

- An annuity whose payments occur at the *end* of each period is called an **ordinary annuity.** The formulas above are for ordinary annuities.

- If each payment occurs at the beginning of the period rather than at the end, then we have an **annuity due.** In Figure 6-3, the payments would be shown at Years 0, 1, and 2 rather than at Years 1, 2, and 3. The PV of each payment would be larger, because each payment would be discounted back one year less, so the PV of the annuity would also be larger. Similarly, the FV of the annuity due would also be larger because each payment would be compounded for an extra year.

- If the time line in Figure 6-3 were extended out forever so that the $1,000 payments went on forever, we would have a **perpetuity** whose value could be found as follows:

$$\text{Value of perpetuity} = \frac{\text{PMT}}{i} = \frac{\$1,000}{0.04} = \$25,000.$$

- If the cash flows in Figure 6-3 were unequal, we could not use the annuity formulas. To find the PV or FV of an uneven series, find the PV or FV of each individual cash flow and then sum them. Note, though, that if some of the cash flows constitute an annuity, then the annuity formula can be used to calculate the present or future value of that part of the cash flow stream.

- **Financial calculators** have built-in programs that perform all of the operations discussed in this chapter. It would be useful for you to buy such a calculator and to learn how to use it.

- **Spreadsheet programs** are especially useful for problems with many uneven cash flows. They are also very useful if you want to solve a problem repeatedly with different inputs. See 06MODEL.xls, which is available on the web site for the book and on the CD-ROM accompanying this text, for spreadsheet models of the topics covered in this chapter.

- TVM calculations generally involve equations that have four variables, and if you know three of the values, you (or your calculator) can solve for the fourth.

- If you know the cash flows and the PV (or FV) of a cash flow stream, you can **determine the interest rate.** For example, in the Figure 6-3 illustration, if you were given the information that a loan called for 3 payments of $1,000 each, and that the loan had a value today of PV = $2,775.10, then you could find the interest rate that caused the sum of the PVs of the payments to equal $2,775.10. Since we are dealing with an annuity, you could proceed as follows: With a financial calculator, enter N = 3, PV = 2775.10, PMT = −1000, FV = 0, and then press the I key to find I = 4%.

- Thus far in this section we have assumed that payments are made, and interest is earned, annually. However, many contracts call for more frequent payments; for example, mortgage and auto loans call for monthly payments, and most bonds pay interest semiannually. Similarly, most banks compute interest daily. When compounding occurs more frequently than once a year, this fact must be recognized. We can use the Figure 6-3 example to illustrate semiannual compounding. First, recognize that the 4 percent stated rate is a nominal rate that must be converted to a periodic rate, and the number of years must be converted to periods:

$$i_{\text{PER}} = \text{Stated rate/Periods per year} = 4\%/2 = 2\%.$$
$$\text{Periods} = \text{Years} \times \text{Periods per year} = 3 \times 2 = 6.$$

The periodic rate and number of periods would be used for calculations and shown on time lines.

If the $1,000 per-year payments were actually payable as $500 each 6 months, you would simply redraw Figure 6-3 to show 6 payments of $500 each, but you would also use a **periodic interest rate** of 4%/2 = 2% for determining the PV or FV of the payments.

- If we are comparing the costs of loans that require payments more than once a year, or the rates of return on investments that pay interest more frequently, then the comparisons should be based on **equivalent** (or **effective**) **rates of return** using this formula:

$$\text{Effective annual rate} = \text{EAR (or EFF\%)} = \left(1 + \frac{i_{Nom}}{m}\right)^m - 1.0.$$

For semiannual compounding, the effective annual rate is 4.04 percent:

$$\left(1 + \frac{0.04}{2}\right)^2 - 1.0 = (1.02)^2 - 1.0 = 1.0404 - 1.0 = 0.0404 = 4.04\%.$$

- The general equation for finding the future value for any number of compounding periods per year is:

$$FV_n = PV\left(1 + \frac{i_{Nom}}{m}\right)^{mn},$$

where

$$i_{Nom} = \text{quoted interest rate.}$$
$$m = \text{number of compounding periods per year.}$$
$$n = \text{number of years.}$$

- An **amortized loan** is one that is paid off in equal payments over a specified period. An **amortization schedule** shows how much of each payment constitutes interest, how much is used to reduce the principal, and the unpaid balance at each point in time.

- A loan can also call for **partial amortization** with a **balloon payment.** Here we would set up a regular amortization schedule, but at a designated point the full unpaid balance (the balloon) would have to be repaid.

The concepts covered in this chapter will be used throughout the remainder of the book. For example, in Chapters 7 and 8, we apply present value concepts to find the values of bonds and stocks, and we see that the market prices of securities are established by determining the present values of the cash flows they are expected to provide. In later chapters, the same basic concepts are applied to corporate decisions involving expenditures on capital assets, to the types of capital that should be used to pay for assets, and so forth.

QUESTIONS

6-1 What is an *opportunity cost rate*? How is this rate used in time value analysis, and where is it shown on a time line? Is the opportunity rate a single number that is used in all situations?

6-2 An *annuity* is defined as a series of payments of a fixed amount for a specific number of periods. Thus, $100 a year for 10 years is an annuity, but $100 in Year 1, $200 in Year 2, and $400 in Years 3 through 10 does *not* constitute an annuity. However, the second series *contains* an annuity. Is this statement true or false?

6-3 If a firm's earnings per share grew from $1 to $2 over a 10-year period, the *total growth* would be 100 percent, but the *annual growth rate* would be *less than* 10 percent. True or false? Explain.

6-4 Would you rather have a savings account that pays 5 percent interest compounded semi-annually or one that pays 5 percent interest compounded daily? Explain.

6-5 To find the present value of an uneven series of cash flows, you must find the PVs of the individual cash flows and then sum them. Annuity procedures can never be of use, even if some of the cash flows constitute an annuity (for example, $100 each for Years 3, 4, 5, and 6), because the entire series is not an annuity. Is this statement true or false? Explain.

6-6 The present value of a perpetuity is equal to the payment on the annuity, PMT, divided by the interest rate, i: $PV = PMT/i$. What is the *sum*, or future value, of a perpetuity of PMT dollars per year? (Hint: The answer is infinity, but explain why.)

SELF-TEST PROBLEMS (SOLUTIONS APPEAR IN APPENDIX B)

ST-1
Key terms
Define each of the following terms:
a. PV; i; INT; FV_n; n; PVA_n; FVA_n; PMT; m; i_{Nom}
b. Opportunity cost rate; fair (equilibrium) value
c. Annuity; lump sum payment; cash flow; uneven cash flow stream
d. Ordinary (deferred) annuity; annuity due
e. Perpetuity; consol
f. Outflow; inflow; time line
g. Compounding; discounting
h. Annual, semiannual, quarterly, monthly, and daily compounding
i. Effective (equivalent) annual rate (EAR); nominal (quoted) interest rate; Annual Percentage Rate (APR); periodic rate
j. Amortization schedule; principal component versus interest component of a payment; amortized loan
k. Terminal value
l. Partial amortization; balloon payment

ST-2
Future value
Assume that it is now January 1, 2003. On January 1, 2004, you will deposit $1,000 into a savings account that pays 8 percent.
a. If the bank compounds interest annually, how much will you have in your account on January 1, 2007?
b. What would your January 1, 2007, balance be if the bank used quarterly compounding rather than annual compounding?
c. Suppose you deposited the $1,000 in 4 payments of $250 each on January 1 of 2004, 2005, 2006, and 2007. How much would you have in your account on January 1, 2007, based on 8 percent annual compounding?
d. Suppose you deposited 4 equal payments in your account on January 1 of 2004, 2005, 2006, and 2007. Assuming an 8 percent interest rate, how large would each of your payments have to be for you to obtain the same ending balance as you calculated in part a?

ST-3
Time value of money
Assume that it is now January 1, 2003, and you will need $1,000 on January 1, 2007. Your bank compounds interest at an 8 percent annual rate.
a. How much must you deposit on January 1, 2004, to have a balance of $1,000 on January 1, 2007?
b. If you want to make equal payments on each January 1 from 2004 through 2007 to accumulate the $1,000, how large must each of the 4 payments be?
c. If your father were to offer either to make the payments calculated in part b ($221.92) or to give you a lump sum of $750 on January 1, 2004, which would you choose?
d. If you have only $750 on January 1, 2004, what interest rate, compounded annually, would you have to earn to have the necessary $1,000 on January 1, 2007?
e. Suppose you can deposit only $186.29 each January 1 from 2004 through 2007 but you still need $1,000 on January 1, 2007. What interest rate, with annual compounding, must you seek out to achieve your goal?
f. To help you reach your $1,000 goal, your father offers to give you $400 on January 1, 2004. You will get a part-time job and make 6 additional payments of equal amounts each 6 months thereafter. If all of this money is deposited in a bank that pays 8 percent, compounded semiannually, how large must each of the 6 payments be?

g. What is the effective annual rate being paid by the bank in part f?

h. *Reinvestment rate risk* was defined in Chapter 4 as being the risk that maturing securities (and coupon payments on bonds) will have to be reinvested at a lower rate of interest than they were previously earning. Is there a reinvestment rate risk involved in the preceding analysis? If so, how might this risk be eliminated?

ST-4
Effective annual rates

Bank A pays 8 percent interest, compounded quarterly, on its money market account. The managers of Bank B want its money market account to equal Bank A's effective annual rate, but interest is to be compounded on a monthly basis. What nominal, or quoted, or APR rate must Bank B set?

STARTER PROBLEMS

6-1
Future value

If you deposit $10,000 in a bank account that pays 10 percent interest annually, how much money will be in your account after 5 years?

6-2
Present value

What is the present value of a security that promises to pay you $5,000 in 20 years? Assume that you can earn 7 percent if you were to invest in other securities of equal risk.

6-3
Time for a lump sum to double

If you deposit money today into an account that pays 6.5 percent interest, how long will it take for you to double your money?

6-4
Reaching a financial goal

John Roberts has $42,180.53 in a brokerage account, and he plans to contribute an additional $5,000 to the account at the end of every year. The brokerage account has an expected annual return of 12 percent. If John's goal is to accumulate $250,000 in the account, how many years will it take for John to reach his goal?

6-5
Effective rate of interest

Your parents are planning to retire in 18 years. They currently have $250,000, and they would like to have $1,000,000 when they retire. What annual rate of interest would they have to earn on their $250,000 in order to reach their goal, assuming they save no more money?

6-6
Future value of an annuity

What is the future value of a 5-year ordinary annuity that promises to pay you $300 each year? The rate of interest is 7 percent.

6-7
Future value of an annuity due

What is the future value of a 5-year annuity due that promises to pay you $300 each year? Assume that all payments are reinvested at 7 percent a year, until Year 5.

6-8
Present and future value of a cash flow stream

An investment pays you $100 at the end of each of the next 3 years. The investment will then pay you $200 at the end of Year 4, $300 at the end of Year 5, and $500 at the end of Year 6. If the interest rate earned on the investment is 8 percent, what is its present value? What is its future value?

6-9
Loan amortization and effective interest rate

You are thinking about buying a car, and a local bank is willing to lend you $20,000 to buy the car. Under the terms of the loan, it will be fully amortized over 5 years (60 months), and the nominal rate of interest will be 12 percent, with interest paid monthly. What would be the monthly payment on the loan? What would be the effective rate of interest on the loan?

EXAM-TYPE PROBLEMS

The problems included in this section are set up in such a way that they could be used as multiple-choice exam problems.

6-10
Growth rates

Shalit Corporation's 2002 sales were $12 million. Sales were $6 million 5 years earlier (in 1997).
a. To the nearest percentage point, at what rate have sales been growing?
b. Suppose someone calculated the sales growth for Shalit Corporation in part a as follows: "Sales doubled in 5 years. This represents a growth of 100 percent in 5 years, so, dividing 100 percent by 5, we find the growth rate to be 20 percent per year." Explain what is wrong with this calculation.

6-11
Expected rate of return

Washington-Atlantic invests $4 million to clear a tract of land and to set out some young pine trees. The trees will mature in 10 years, at which time Washington-Atlantic plans to sell the forest at an expected price of $8 million. What is Washington-Atlantic's expected rate of return?

6-12
Effective rate of interest

A mortgage company offers to lend you $85,000; the loan calls for payments of $8,273.59 per year for 30 years. What interest rate is the mortgage company charging you?

6-13
Required lump sum payment

To complete your last year in business school and then go through law school, you will need $10,000 per year for 4 years, starting next year (that is, you will need to withdraw the first

$10,000 one year from today). Your rich uncle offers to put you through school, and he will deposit in a bank paying 7 percent interest, compounded annually, a sum of money that is sufficient to provide the 4 payments of $10,000 each. His deposit will be made today.

a. How large must the deposit be?

b. How much will be in the account immediately after you make the first withdrawal?

6-14
Reaching a financial goal

You need to accumulate $10,000. To do so, you plan to make deposits of $1,250 per year, with the first payment being made a year from today, in a bank account that pays 12 percent interest, compounded annually. Your last deposit will be less than $1,250 if less is needed to round out to $10,000. How many years will it take you to reach your $10,000 goal, and how large will the last deposit be?

6-15
Present value of a cash flow stream

A rookie quarterback is in the process of negotiating his first contract. The team's general manager has offered him three possible contracts. Each of the contracts lasts for 4 years. All of the money is guaranteed and is paid at the end of each year. The terms of each of the contracts are listed below:

	CONTRACT 1 PAYMENTS	CONTRACT 2 PAYMENTS	CONTRACT 3 PAYMENTS
Year 1	$3 million	$2 million	$7 million
Year 2	3 million	3 million	1 million
Year 3	3 million	4 million	1 million
Year 4	3 million	5 million	1 million

The quarterback discounts all cash flows at 10 percent. Which of the three contracts offers him the most value?

6-16
Present value of a perpetuity

What is the present value of a perpetuity of $100 per year if the appropriate discount rate is 7 percent? If interest rates in general were to double and the appropriate discount rate rose to 14 percent, what would happen to the present value of the perpetuity?

6-17
PV and effective annual rate

Assume that you inherited some money. A friend of yours is working as an unpaid intern at a local brokerage firm, and her boss is selling some securities that call for 4 payments, $50 at the end of each of the next 3 years, plus a payment of $1,050 at the end of Year 4. Your friend says she can get you some of these securities at a cost of $900 each. Your money is now invested in a bank that pays an 8 percent nominal (quoted) interest rate, but with quarterly compounding. You regard the securities as being just as safe, and as liquid, as your bank deposit, so your required effective annual rate of return on the securities is the same as that on your bank deposit. You must calculate the value of the securities to decide whether they are a good investment. What is their present value to you?

6-18
Loan amortization

Assume that your aunt sold her house on December 31, and that she took a mortgage in the amount of $10,000 as part of the payment. The mortgage has a quoted (or nominal) interest rate of 10 percent, but it calls for payments every 6 months, beginning on June 30, and the mortgage is to be amortized over 10 years. Now, one year later, your aunt must file Schedule B of her tax return with the IRS, informing them of the interest that was included in the 2 payments made during the year. (This interest will be income to your aunt and a deduction to the buyer of the house.) To the closest dollar, what is the total amount of interest that was paid during the first year?

6-19
Loan amortization

Your company is planning to borrow $1,000,000 on a 5-year, 15%, annual payment, fully amortized term loan. What fraction of the payment made at the end of the second year will represent repayment of principal?

6-20
Nonannual compounding

a. It is now January 1, 2003. You plan to make 5 deposits of $100 each, one every 6 months, with the first payment being made *today*. If the bank pays a nominal interest rate of 12 percent, but uses semiannual compounding, how much will be in your account after 10 years?

b. Ten years from today you must make a payment of $1,432.02. To prepare for this payment, you will make 5 equal deposits, beginning today and for the next 4 quarters, in a bank that pays a nominal interest rate of 12 percent, quarterly compounding. How large must each of the 5 payments be?

6-21
Nominal rate of return

As the manager of Oaks Mall Jewelry, you want to sell on credit, giving customers 3 months in which to pay. However, you will have to borrow from the bank to carry the accounts receivable. The bank will charge a nominal 15 percent, but with monthly compounding. You want to quote a nominal rate to your customers (all of whom are expected to pay on time) that will exactly cover your financing costs. What nominal annual rate should you quote to your credit customers?

6-22
Required annuity payments

Assume that your father is now 50 years old, that he plans to retire in 10 years, and that he expects to live for 25 years after he retires, that is, until he is 85. He wants a fixed retirement income that has the same purchasing power at the time he retires as $40,000 has today (he realizes that the real value of his retirement income will decline year by year after he retires). His retirement income will begin the day he retires, 10 years from today, and he will then get 24 additional annual payments. Inflation is expected to be 5 percent per year from today forward; he currently has $100,000 saved up; and he expects to earn a return on his savings of 8 percent per year, annual compounding. To the nearest dollar, how much must he save during each of the next 10 years (with deposits being made at the end of each year) to meet his retirement goal?

6-23
Value of an annuity

The prize in last week's Florida lottery was estimated to be worth $35 million. If you were lucky enough to win, the state will pay you $1.75 million per year over the next 20 years. Assume that the first installment is received immediately.
a. If interest rates are 8 percent, what is the present value of the prize?
b. If interest rates are 8 percent, what is the future value after 20 years?
c. How would your answers change if the payments were received at the end of each year?

6-24
Future value of an annuity

Your client is 40 years old and wants to begin saving for retirement. You advise the client to put $5,000 a year into the stock market. You estimate that the market's return will be, on average, 12 percent a year. Assume the investment will be made at the end of the year.
a. If the client follows your advice, how much money will she have by age 65?
b. How much will she have by age 70?

6-25
Present value

You are serving on a jury. A plaintiff is suing the city for injuries sustained after falling down an uncovered manhole. In the trial, doctors testified that it will be 5 years before the plaintiff is able to return to work. The jury has already decided in favor of the plaintiff, and has decided to grant the plaintiff an award to cover the following items:
(1) Recovery of 2 years of back-pay ($34,000 in 2001, and $36,000 in 2002). Assume that it is December 31, 2002, and that all salary is received at year end. This recovery should include the time value of money.
(2) The present value of 5 years of future salary (2003–2007). Assume that the plaintiff's salary would increase at a rate of 3 percent a year.
(3) $100,000 for pain and suffering.
(4) $20,000 for court costs.
Assume an interest rate of 7 percent. What should be the size of the settlement?

6-26
Future value

You just started your first job, and you want to buy a house within 3 years. You are currently saving for the down payment. You plan to save $5,000 the first year. You also anticipate that the amount you save each year will rise by 10 percent a year as your salary increases over time. Interest rates are assumed to be 7 percent, and all savings occur at year end. How much money will you have for a down payment in 3 years?

6-27
Required annuity payment

A 15-year security has a price of $340.4689. The security pays $50 at the end of each of the next 5 years, and then it pays a different fixed cash flow amount at the end of each of the following 10 years. Interest rates are 9 percent. What is the annual cash flow amount between Years 6 and 15?

6-28
Nonannual compounding

An investment pays $20 semiannually for the next 2 years. The investment has a 7 percent nominal interest rate, and interest is compounded quarterly. What is the future value of the investment?

6-29
Reaching a financial goal

Erika and Katherine have both been given $30,000 by their grandparents today on their 25th birthdays. They want to save for their future and have aspirations of one day being millionaires. Each woman plans to make annual contributions on her birthday, beginning next year. Erika and Katherine have each opened investment accounts at the First National Bank and Second National Bank, respectively, and they expect to earn nominal returns of 8 and 9 percent, respectively. Erika has already decided to deposit $5,000 each year into her investment account, while Katherine is unsure of the amount she will deposit annually.
a. How long will it take Erika before she reaches her investment goal of $1 million?
b. If Katherine decides to make the same annual contributions as Erika, how much sooner would she reach the investment goal?

c. Suppose Katherine was interested in reaching the investment goal at the same time as Erika. What is the minimum monthly contribution she could make in order to reach $1 million at the same time as Erika?

6-30
Evaluating lump sum amounts and annuities

Crissie has just won the state lottery and has three award options to choose from. She can elect to receive a lump sum payment today of $61 million, 10 annual end-of-year payments of $9.5 million, or 30 annual end-of-year payments of $5.5 million.
a. If she expects to earn a 7 percent annual return on her investments, which option should she choose?
b. If she expects to earn an 8 percent annual return on her investments, which option should she choose?
c. If she expects to earn a 9 percent annual return on her investments, which option should she choose?

6-31
Present value

Jarrett has saved $4,000 and intends to use his savings as a down payment on a new car. After careful examination of his income and expenses, Jarrett has concluded that the most he can afford to spend every month on his car payment is $350. The car loan that Jarrett uses to buy the car will have an APR of 12 percent. What is the price of the most expensive car that Jarrett can afford if he finances his new car for 48 months? 60 months?

6-32
Reaching a financial goal

Simon, like many college students, recently filled out a credit card application. Not surprisingly, his application was accepted at a nominal interest rate of 24 percent. Upon receiving the credit card, Simon purchased a new stereo, which cost him $305.44, with the card. Upon receiving his first bill, Simon was delighted to learn that the credit card company only requires a minimum payment of $10 per month.
a. If Simon makes the minimum payment (and makes no other charges) every month, how many months will it be before the account is completely paid off?
b. If Simon continues to make the minimum monthly payment, how much will the final payment be? Assume that the last payment occurs at the end of the month, rather than in the middle of a billing period.
c. On the advice of a friend majoring in finance, Simon is considering making monthly payments of $30. How long will it take him to pay off the debt now?
d. How much more in total payments will Simon make under the $10-a-month plan than under the $30-a-month plan? Again, assume that the last payment occurs at the end of the month, rather than in the middle of a billing period.

6-33
Expected rate of return

A 5-year security has a price of $1,300. The security pays $400 at the end of each of the next 5 years. What is the expected return of this investment to that investor?

PROBLEMS

6-34
Present and future values for different periods

Find the following values, *using the equations*, and then work the problems using a financial calculator. (Hint: When using a financial calculator, you can enter the known values, and then press the appropriate key to find the unknown variable. Then, without clearing the TVM register, you can "override" the variable that changes by simply entering a new value for it and then pressing the key for the unknown variable to obtain the second answer. This procedure can be used in parts b and d, and in many other situations, to see how changes in input variables affect the output variable.) Assume that compounding/discounting occurs once a year.
a. An initial $500 compounded for 1 year at 6 percent.
b. An initial $500 compounded for 2 years at 6 percent.
c. The present value of $500 due in 1 year at a discount rate of 6 percent.
d. The present value of $500 due in 2 years at a discount rate of 6 percent.

6-35
Present and future values for different interest rates

Use a financial calculator to find the following values. See the hint for Problem 6-34. Assume that compounding/discounting occurs once a year.
a. An initial $500 compounded for 10 years at 6 percent.
b. An initial $500 compounded for 10 years at 12 percent.
c. The present value of $500 due in 10 years at a 6 percent discount rate.
d. The present value of $1,552.90 due in 10 years at a 12 percent discount rate and at a 6 percent rate. Give a verbal definition of the term *present value*, and illustrate it using a time line

with data from this problem. As a part of your answer, explain why present values are dependent upon interest rates.

6-36
Time for a lump sum to double

To the closest year, how long will it take $200 to double if it is deposited and earns the following rates? [Notes: (1) See the hint for Problem 6-34. (2) This problem cannot be solved exactly with some financial calculators. For example, if you enter PV = −200, FV = 400, and I = 7 in an HP-12C, and then press the N key, you will get 11 years for part a. The correct answer is 10.2448 years, which rounds to 10, but the calculator rounds up. However, the HP-10BII and HP-17B give the correct answer.] Assume that compounding occurs once a year.
a. 7 percent.
b. 10 percent.
c. 18 percent.
d. 100 percent.

6-37
Future value of an annuity

Find the *future value* of the following annuities. The first payment in these annuities is made at the *end* of Year 1; that is, they are *ordinary annuities*. (Note: See the hint to Problem 6-34. Also, note that you can leave values in the TVM register, switch to "BEG," press FV, and find the FV of the annuity due.) Assume that compounding occurs once a year.
a. $400 per year for 10 years at 10 percent.
b. $200 per year for 5 years at 5 percent.
c. $400 per year for 5 years at 0 percent.
d. Now rework parts a, b, and c assuming that payments are made at the *beginning* of each year; that is, they are *annuities due*.

6-38
Present value of an annuity

Find the *present value* of the following *ordinary annuities* (see note to Problem 6-37). Assume that discounting occurs once a year.
a. $400 per year for 10 years at 10 percent.
b. $200 per year for 5 years at 5 percent.
c. $400 per year for 5 years at 0 percent.
d. Now rework parts a, b, and c assuming that payments are made at the beginning of each year; that is, they are *annuities due*.

6-39
Uneven cash flow stream

a. Find the present values of the following cash flow streams. The appropriate interest rate is 8 percent, compounded annually. (Hint: It is fairly easy to work this problem dealing with the individual cash flows. However, if you have a financial calculator, read the section of the manual that describes how to enter cash flows such as the ones in this problem. This will take a little time, but the investment will pay huge dividends throughout the course. Note that if you do work with the cash flow register, you must enter $CF_0 = 0$.)

YEAR	CASH STREAM A	CASH STREAM B
1	$100	$300
2	400	400
3	400	400
4	400	400
5	300	100

b. What is the value of each cash flow stream at a 0 percent interest rate, compounded annually?

6-40
Effective rate of interest

Find the interest rates, or rates of return, on each of the following:
a. You *borrow* $700 and promise to pay back $749 at the end of 1 year.
b. You *lend* $700 and receive a promise to be paid $749 at the end of 1 year.
c. You borrow $85,000 and promise to pay back $201,229 at the end of 10 years.
d. You borrow $9,000 and promise to make payments of $2,684.80 per year for 5 years.

6-41
Future value for various compounding periods

Find the amount to which $500 will grow under each of the following conditions:
a. 12 percent compounded annually for 5 years.
b. 12 percent compounded semiannually for 5 years.
c. 12 percent compounded quarterly for 5 years.
d. 12 percent compounded monthly for 5 years.

6-42

Present value for various compounding periods

Find the present value of $500 due in the future under each of the following conditions:
a. 12 percent nominal rate, semiannual compounding, discounted back 5 years.
b. 12 percent nominal rate, quarterly compounding, discounted back 5 years.
c. 12 percent nominal rate, monthly compounding, discounted back 1 year.

6-43

Future value of an annuity for various compounding periods

Find the future values of the following ordinary annuities:
a. FV of $400 each 6 months for 5 years at a nominal rate of 12 percent, compounded semi-annually.
b. FV of $200 each 3 months for 5 years at a nominal rate of 12 percent, compounded quarterly.
c. The annuities described in parts a and b have the same amount of money paid into them during the 5-year period, and both earn interest at the same nominal rate, yet the annuity in part b earns $101.75 more than the one in part a over the 5 years. Why does this occur?

6-44

Effective versus nominal interest rates

The First City Bank pays 7 percent interest, compounded annually, on time deposits. The Second City Bank pays 6 percent interest, compounded quarterly.
a. Based on effective, or equivalent, interest rates, in which bank would you prefer to deposit your money?
b. Could your choice of banks be influenced by the fact that you might want to withdraw your funds during the year as opposed to at the end of the year? In answering this question, assume that funds must be left on deposit during the entire compounding period in order for you to receive any interest.

6-45

Amortization schedule

a. Set up an amortization schedule for a $25,000 loan to be repaid in equal installments at the end of each of the next 5 years. The interest rate is 10 percent, compounded annually.
b. How large must each annual payment be if the loan is for $50,000? Assume that the interest rate remains at 10 percent, compounded annually, and that the loan is paid off over 5 years.
c. How large must each payment be if the loan is for $50,000, the interest rate is 10 percent, compounded annually, and the loan is paid off in equal installments at the end of each of the next 10 years? This loan is for the same amount as the loan in part b, but the payments are spread out over twice as many periods. Why are these payments not half as large as the payments on the loan in part b?

6-46

Amortization schedule

The Jackson family is interested in buying a home. The family is applying for a $125,000, 30-year mortgage. Under the terms of the mortgage, they will receive $125,000 today to help purchase their home. The loan will be fully amortized over the next 30 years. Current mortgage rates are 8 percent. Interest is compounded monthly and all payments are due at the end of the month.
a. What is the monthly mortgage payment?
b. What portion of the mortgage payments made during the first year will go toward interest?
c. What will be the remaining balance on the mortgage after 5 years?
d. How much could the Jacksons borrow today if they were willing to have a $1,200 monthly mortgage payment? (Assume that the interest rate and the length of the loan remain the same.)

6-47

Effective rates of return

Assume that AT&T's pension fund managers are considering two alternative securities as investments: (1) Security Z (for zero intermediate year cash flows), which costs $422.41 today, pays nothing during its 10-year life, and then pays $1,000 after 10 years or (2) Security B, which has a cost today of $1,000 and which pays $80 at the end of each of the next 9 years and then $1,080 at the end of Year 10.
a. What is the rate of return on each security?
b. Assume that the interest rate AT&T's pension fund managers can earn on the fund's money falls to 6 percent, compounded annually, immediately after the securities are purchased and is expected to remain at that level for the next 10 years. What would the price of each security change to, what would the fund's profit be on each security, and what would be the percentage profit (profit divided by cost) for each security?
c. Assuming that the cash flows for each security had to be reinvested at the new 6 percent market interest rate, (1) what would be the value attributable to each security at the end of 10 years and (2) what "actual, after-the-fact" rate of return would the fund have earned on each security? (Hint: The "actual" rate of return is found as the interest rate that causes the PV of the compounded Year 10 amount to equal the original cost of the security.)
d. Now assume all the facts as given in parts b and c, except assume that the interest rate *rose* to 12 percent rather than fell to 6 percent. What would happen to the profit figures as de-

veloped in part b and to the "actual" rates of return as determined in part c? Explain your results.

6-48
Required annuity payments

A father is planning a savings program to put his daughter through college. His daughter is now 13 years old. She plans to enroll at the university in 5 years, and it should take her 4 years to complete her education. Currently, the cost per year (for everything—food, clothing, tuition, books, transportation, and so forth) is $12,500, but a 5 percent annual inflation rate in these costs is forecasted. The daughter recently received $7,500 from her grandfather's estate; this money, which is invested in a bank account paying 8 percent interest, compounded annually, will be used to help meet the costs of the daughter's education. The remaining costs will be met by money the father will deposit in the savings account. He will make 6 equal deposits to the account, one deposit in each year from now until his daughter starts college. These deposits will begin today and will also earn 8 percent interest, compounded annually.

a. What will be the present value of the cost of 4 years of education at the time the daughter becomes 18? [Hint: Calculate the future value of the cost (at 5%) for each year of her education, then discount 3 of these costs back (at 8%) to the year in which she turns 18, then sum the 4 costs.]

b. What will be the value of the $7,500 that the daughter received from her grandfather's estate when she starts college at age 18? (Hint: Compound for 5 years at an 8 percent annual rate.)

c. If the father is planning to make the first of 6 deposits today, how large must each deposit be for him to be able to put his daughter through college? (Hint: An annuity due assumes interest is earned on all deposits; however, the 6th deposit earns no interest—therefore, the deposits are an ordinary annuity.)

SPREADSHEET PROBLEM

6-49
Time value of money

Answer the following questions, using a spreadsheet model to do the calculations.

a. Find the FV of $1,000 invested to earn 10 percent after 5 years. Answer this question by using a math formula and also by using the *Excel* function wizard.

b. Now create a table that shows the FV at 0 percent, 5 percent, and 20 percent for 0, 1, 2, 3, 4, and 5 years. Then create a graph with years on the horizontal axis and FV on the vertical axis to display your results.

c. Find the PV of $1,000 due in 5 years if the discount rate is 10 percent. Again, work the problem with a formula and also by using the function wizard.

d. A security has a cost of $1,000 and will return $2,000 after 5 years. What rate of return does the security provide?

e. Suppose California's population is 30 million people, and its population is expected to grow by 2 percent per year. How long would it take for the population to double?

f. Find the PV of an annuity that pays $1,000 at the end of each of the next 5 years if the interest rate is 15 percent. Then find the FV of that same annuity.

g. How would the PV and FV of the annuity change if it were an annuity due rather than an ordinary annuity?

h. What would the FV and the PV for parts a and c be if the interest rate were 10 percent with semiannual compounding rather than 10 percent with annual compounding?

i. Find the PV and the FV of an investment that makes the following end-of-year payments. The interest rate is 8 percent.

YEAR	PAYMENT
1	$100
2	200
3	400

j. Suppose you bought a house and took out a mortgage for $50,000. The interest rate is 8 percent, and you must amortize the loan over 10 years with equal end-of-year payments.

Set up an amortization schedule that shows the annual payments and the amount of each payment that goes to pay off the principal and the amount that constitutes interest expense to the borrower and interest income to the lender.

  (1) Create a graph that shows how the payments are divided between interest and principal repayment over time.
  (2) Suppose the loan called for 10 years of monthly payments, with the same original amount and the same nominal interest rate. What would the amortization schedule show now?

  k. Refer to Problem 6-48. Solve this problem using a spreadsheet model.

INTEGRATED CASE

FIRST NATIONAL BANK

6-50 Time Value of Money Analysis Assume that you are nearing graduation and that you have applied for a job with a local bank, First National Bank. As part of the bank's evaluation process, you have been asked to take an examination that covers several financial analysis techniques. The first section of the test addresses time value of money analysis. See how you would do by answering the following questions.

a. Draw time lines for (1) a $100 lump sum cash flow at the end of Year 2, (2) an ordinary annuity of $100 per year for 3 years, and (3) an uneven cash flow stream of −$50, $100, $75, and $50 at the end of Years 0 through 3.

b. (1) What is the future value of an initial $100 after 3 years if it is invested in an account paying 10 percent, annual compounding?
   (2) What is the present value of $100 to be received in 3 years if the appropriate interest rate is 10 percent, annual compounding?

c. We sometimes need to find how long it will take a sum of money (or anything else) to grow to some specified amount. For example, if a company's sales are growing at a rate of 20 percent per year, how long will it take sales to double?

d. What is the difference between an ordinary annuity and an annuity due? What type of annuity is shown below? How would you change it to the other type of annuity?

e. (1) What is the future value of a 3-year ordinary annuity of $100 if the appropriate interest rate is 10 percent, annual compounding?
   (2) What is the present value of the annuity?
   (3) What would the future and present values be if the annuity were an annuity due?

f. What is the present value of the following uneven cash flow stream? The appropriate interest rate is 10 percent, compounded annually.

g. What annual interest rate will cause $100 to grow to $125.97 in 3 years?

h. A 20-year-old student wants to begin saving for her retirement. Her plan is to save $3 a day. Every day she places $3 in a drawer. At the end of each year, she invests the accumulated savings ($1,095) in an online stock account that has an expected annual return of 12 percent.
   (1) If she keeps saving in this manner, how much will she have accumulated by age 65?
   (2) If a 40-year-old investor began saving in this manner, how much would he have by age 65?
   (3) How much would the 40-year-old investor have to save each year to accumulate the same amount at age 65 as the 20-year-old investor described above?

i. (1) Will the future value be larger or smaller if we compound an initial amount more often than annually, for example, every 6 months, or *semiannually*, holding the stated interest rate constant? Why?
   (2) Define (a) the stated, or quoted, or nominal, rate, (b) the periodic rate, and (c) the effective annual rate (EAR).
   (3) What is the effective annual rate corresponding to a nominal rate of 10 percent, compounded semiannually? Compounded quarterly? Compounded daily?
   (4) What is the future value of $100 after 3 years under 10 percent semiannual compounding? Quarterly compounding?

j. When will the effective annual rate be equal to the nominal (quoted) rate?

k. (1) What is the value at the end of Year 3 of the following cash flow stream if the quoted interest rate is 10 percent, compounded semiannually?

(2) What is the PV of the same stream?

(3) Is the stream an annuity?

(4) An important rule is that you should *never* show a nominal rate on a time line or use it in calculations unless what condition holds? (Hint: Think of annual compounding, when i_{Nom} = EAR = i_{PER}.) What would be wrong with your answer to parts k(1) and k(2) if you used the nominal rate, 10 percent, rather than the periodic rate, $i_{Nom}/2$ = 10%/2 = 5%?

l. (1) Construct an amortization schedule for a $1,000, 10 percent, annual compounding loan with 3 equal installments.

(2) What is the annual interest expense for the borrower, and the annual interest income for the lender, during Year 2?

m. Suppose a house is on the market for $250,000, and a bank agrees to lend the potential home buyer $220,000 secured by a mortgage on the house. Thus, the buyer must come up with $30,000 to complete the transaction. For purposes of this question, ignore any additional closing costs. Suppose the buyer has only $7,500 cash, and the seller agrees to take a note with the following terms: a face value of $22,500, a 7.5 percent annual interest rate, and payments at the end of the year based on a 20-year amortization schedule, but with the loan maturing at the end of the 10th year.

(1) What is the balloon portion of the payment due at the end of the 10th year?

(2) What is the total payment that will be due at the end of the 10th year?

CYBER PROBLEM

Please go to our web site **http://brigham.swlearning.com** to access the Cyberproblems.

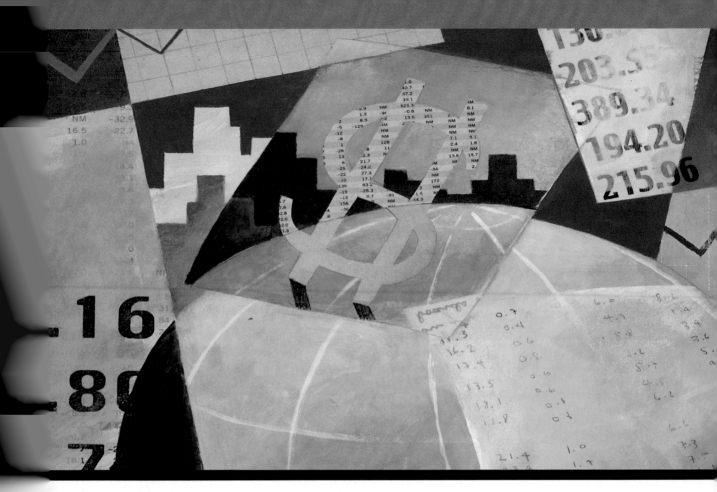

PART 3

FINANCIAL ASSETS

BONDS AND THEIR VALUATION

7

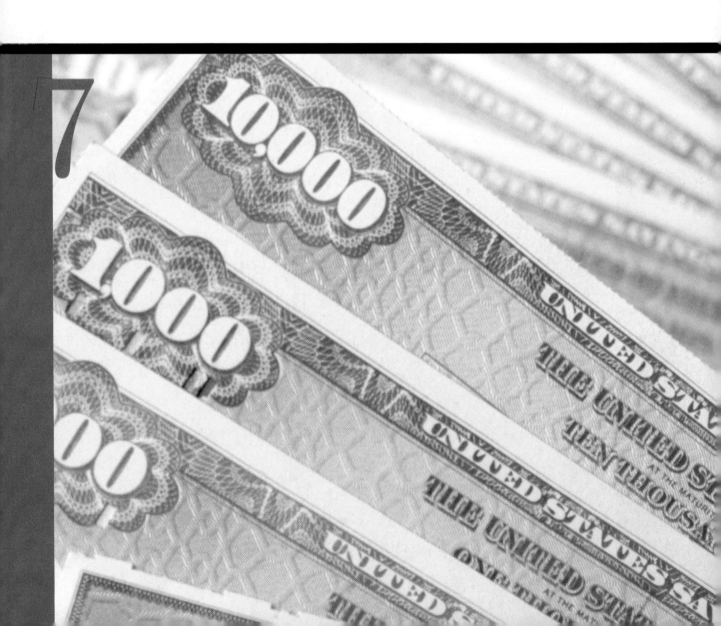

SIZING UP THE RISKS OF THE BOND MARKET

Many investors view Treasury securities as a safe but boring place to invest their funds. To be sure, Treasury securities are among the safest investments. Nevertheless, in any given year, changes in interest rates can lead to significant changes in bond values, particularly for long-term bonds. For example, Treasury bond prices fell nearly 9 percent in 1999. More recently, the Treasury market has done quite well—between mid-2001 and mid-2002, long-term Treasuries were up nearly 9 percent versus a 10 percent decline for the S&P 500 index and more than a 20 percent decline for the Nasdaq index.

A variety of factors led to the recent rise in Treasury prices. First, low inflation and a slow economy helped keep interest rates low. Moreover, a number of investors have been moving their money from the stock market to U.S. Treasuries. This "flight to quality" resulted from continuing uncertainty following the recent terrorist attacks plus the series of accounting scandals that brought into question the level and quality of reported corporate earnings.

Note that bonds don't all move in the same direction. Because of call and default risks, corporate bonds trade at higher yields than Treasury bonds. When all goes well, corporate bonds out-perform Treasury securities. But when concerns about default accelerate, corporate bonds do worse than Treasuries. For example, the recent accounting scandals have increased corporate bond defaults, and that has pushed up the spreads between corporate and Treasury bonds. According to a recent article in the *Financial Times*, 2001 was a record year for defaults with companies defaulting on $116 billion worth of debt, and during the first quarter of 2002 there were defaults on another $34 billion.

As a result of concerns about credit quality, spreads between low-rated "junk" bonds and Treasury bonds averaged nearly 9 percent in mid-2002 versus about 5 percent in more normal times. Some analysts have argued that these low-rated bonds, given their generous spreads, have become attractive investments. Others point to the recent collapse of Enron and warn that investors can sometimes get badly burned by investing in the bonds of risky companies, even among familiar companies that were once well respected. For example, amidst concerns about WorldCom's long-term survival, its five-year bonds that once yielded just 1.67 percent more than Treasuries with the same maturity were trading at a spread of over 20 percent in mid-2002.

In the face of these concerns, a recent *BusinessWeek Online* article gave investors the following useful advice:

> Take the same diversified approach to bonds as you do with stocks. Blend in U.S. government, corporate—both high-quality and high yield—and perhaps even foreign government debt. If you're investing taxable dollars, consider tax-exempt municipal bonds. And it doesn't hurt to layer in some inflation-indexed bonds.

Sources: Vincent Boland and Stephen Fidler, "Where the Risk Falls," *Financial Times*, May 31, 2002, 26; Susan Scherreik, "Getting the Most Bang Out of Your Bonds," *BusinessWeek Online*, November 12, 2001; and "Markets Data: Major Bond Indexes," *The Wall Street Journal Online*, June 17, 2002.

Bonds are one of the most important types of securities. If you skim through *The Wall Street Journal*, you will see references to a wide variety of these securities. This variety may seem confusing, but in actuality just a few characteristics distinguish the various types of bonds.

While bonds are often viewed as relatively safe investments, one can certainly lose money on them. Indeed, "riskless" long-term U.S. Treasury bonds have declined in value three of the last eight years. Note, though, that it is also possible to rack up impressive gains in the bond market. Long-term government bonds provided a total return of nearly 22 percent in 2000 and more than 30 percent in 1995.

In this chapter, we will discuss the types of bonds companies and government agencies issue, the terms that are contained in bond contracts, the types of risks to which both bond investors and issuers are exposed, and procedures for determining the values of and rates of return on bonds. ■

WHO ISSUES BONDS?

Bond
A long-term debt instrument.

A **bond** is a long-term contract under which a borrower agrees to make payments of interest and principal, on specific dates, to the holders of the bond. For example, on January 3, 2003, Allied Food Products borrowed $50 million by issuing $50 million of bonds. For convenience, we assume that Allied sold 50,000 individual bonds for $1,000 each. Actually, it could have sold one $50 million bond, 10 bonds with a $5 million face value, or any other combination that totals to $50 million. In any event, Allied received the $50 million, and in exchange it promised to make annual interest payments and to repay the $50 million on a specified maturity date.

Investors have many choices when investing in bonds, but bonds are classified into four main types: Treasury, corporate, municipal, and foreign. Each type differs with respect to expected return and degree of risk.

Treasury Bonds
Bonds issued by the federal government, sometimes referred to as government bonds.

Treasury bonds, sometimes referred to as government bonds, are issued by the federal government.[1] It is reasonable to assume that the federal government will make good on its promised payments, so these bonds have no default risk. However, Treasury bond prices decline when interest rates rise, so they are not free of all risks.

---

[1] The U.S. Treasury actually calls its debt issues "bills," "notes," or "bonds." T-bills generally have maturities of 1 year or less at the time of issue, notes generally have original maturities of 2 to 7 years, and bond maturities extend out to 30 years. There are technical differences between bills, notes, and bonds, but they are not important for our purposes, so we generally call all Treasury securities "bonds." Note too that a 30-year T-bond at the time of issue becomes a 1-year bond 29 years later.

Corporate Bonds
Bonds issued by corporations.

Municipal Bonds
Bonds issued by state and local governments.

Foreign Bonds
Bonds issued by either foreign governments or foreign corporations.

Corporate bonds, as the name implies, are issued by corporations. Unlike Treasury bonds, corporate bonds are exposed to default risk—if the issuing company gets into trouble, it may be unable to make the promised interest and principal payments. Different corporate bonds have different levels of default risk, depending on the issuing company's characteristics and on the terms of the specific bond. Default risk is often referred to as "credit risk," and, as we saw in Chapter 4, the larger the default or credit risk, the higher the interest rate the issuer must pay.

Municipal bonds, or "munis," are issued by state and local governments. Like corporate bonds, munis have default risk. However, munis offer one major advantage over all other bonds: As we discussed in Chapter 2, the interest earned on most municipal bonds is exempt from federal taxes and also from state taxes if the holder is a resident of the issuing state. Consequently, municipal bonds carry interest rates that are considerably lower than those on corporate bonds with the same default risk.

Foreign bonds, are issued by foreign governments or foreign corporations. Foreign corporate bonds are, of course, exposed to default risk, and so are some foreign government bonds. An additional risk exists if the bonds are denominated in a currency other than that of the investor's home currency. For example, if you purchase corporate bonds denominated in Japanese yen, you will lose money—even if the company does not default on its bonds—if the Japanese yen falls relative to the dollar.

An excellent site for information on many types of bonds is Bonds Online, which can be found at **http://www.bondsonline.com**. The site has a great deal of information about corporates, municipals, treasuries, and bond funds. It includes free bond searches, through which the user specifies the attributes desired in a bond and then the search returns the publicly traded bonds meeting the criteria. The site also includes a downloadable bond calculator and an excellent glossary of bond terminology.

SELF-TEST QUESTIONS

What is a bond?

What are the four main types of bonds?

Why are U.S. Treasury bonds not riskless?

To what types of risk are investors of foreign bonds exposed?

KEY CHARACTERISTICS OF BONDS

Although all bonds have some common characteristics, they do not always have the same contractual features. For example, most corporate bonds have provisions for early repayment (call features), but these provisions can be quite different for different bonds. Differences in contractual provisions, and in the underlying strength of the companies backing the bonds, lead to major differences in bonds' risks, prices, and expected returns. To understand bonds, it is important that you understand the following terms.

PAR VALUE

Par Value
The face value of a bond.

The **par value** is the stated face value of the bond; for illustrative purposes we generally assume a par value of $1,000, although any multiple of $1,000 (for example, $5,000 or $5 million) can be used. The par value generally represents the amount of money the firm borrows and promises to repay on the maturity date.

COUPON INTEREST RATE

Coupon Payment
The specified number of dollars of interest paid each period, generally each six months.

Allied's bonds require the company to pay a fixed number of dollars of interest each year (or, more typically, each six months). When this **coupon payment,** as it is called, is divided by the par value, the result is the **coupon interest rate.** For example, Allied's bonds have a $1,000 par value, and they pay $100 in interest each year. The bond's coupon interest is $100, so its coupon interest rate is $100/$1,000 = 10 percent. The $100 is the yearly "rent" on the $1,000 loan. This payment, which is fixed at the time the bond is issued, remains in force during the life of the bond.[2] Typically, at the time a bond is issued, its coupon payment is set at a level that will enable the bond to be issued at or near its par value. Consequently, most of our examples and problems throughout this text will focus on bonds with fixed coupon rates.

Coupon Interest Rate
The stated annual interest rate on a bond.

Floating Rate Bond
A bond whose interest rate fluctuates with shifts in the general level of interest rates.

In some cases, however, a bond's coupon payment will vary over time. These **floating rate bonds** work as follows. The coupon rate is set for, say, the initial six-month period, after which it is adjusted every six months based on some market rate. Some corporate issues are tied to the Treasury bond rate, while other issues are tied to other rates. Many additional provisions can be included in floating rate issues. For example, some are convertible to fixed rate debt, whereas others have upper and lower limits ("caps" and "floors") on how high or low the rate can go.

Some bonds pay no coupons at all, but are offered at a substantial discount below their par values and hence provide capital appreciation rather than interest income. These securities are called **zero coupon bonds** *("zeros").* Other bonds pay some coupon interest, but not enough to be issued at par. In general, any bond originally offered at a price significantly below its par value is called an **original issue discount (OID) bond.** Some of the details associated with issuing or investing in zero coupon bonds are discussed more fully in Web Appendix 7A.

Zero Coupon Bond
A bond that pays no annual interest but is sold at a discount below par, thus providing compensation to investors in the form of capital appreciation.

Original Issue Discount (OID) Bond
Any bond originally offered at a price below its par value.

MATURITY DATE

Maturity Date
A specified date on which the par value of a bond must be repaid.

Bonds generally have a specified **maturity date** on which the par value must be repaid. Allied's bonds, which were issued on January 3, 2003, will mature on January 2, 2018; thus, they had a 15-year maturity at the time they were issued. Most bonds have **original maturities** (the maturity at the time the bond is issued) ranging from 10 to 40 years, but any maturity is legally permissible.[3] Of course, the effective maturity of a bond declines each year after it has been issued. Thus, Allied's bonds had a 15-year original maturity, but in 2004, a year later, they will have a 14-year maturity, and so on.

Original Maturity
The number of years to maturity at the time a bond is issued.

---

[2] Incidentally, some time ago bonds literally had a number of small (1/2- by 2-inch), dated coupons attached to them, and on each interest payment date, the owner would clip off the coupon for that date and either cash it at his or her bank or mail it to the company's paying agent, who would then mail back a check for the interest. A 30-year, semiannual bond would start with 60 coupons, whereas a 5-year annual payment bond would start with only 5 coupons. Today, new bonds must be *registered*—no physical coupons are involved, and interest checks are mailed automatically to the registered owners of the bonds. Even so, people continue to use the terms *coupon* and *coupon interest rate* when discussing registered bonds.

[3] In July 1993, Walt Disney Co., attempting to lock in a low interest rate, issued the first 100-year bonds to be sold by any borrower in modern times. Soon after, Coca-Cola became the second company to stretch the meaning of "long-term bond" by selling $150 million worth of 100-year bonds.

CALL PROVISIONS

Call Provision
A provision in a bond contract that gives the issuer the right to redeem the bonds under specified terms prior to the normal maturity date.

Many corporate bonds contain a **call provision,** which gives the issuing corporation the right to call the bonds for redemption.[4] The call provision generally states that the company must pay the bondholders an amount greater than the par value if they are called. The additional sum, which is termed a *call premium*, is often set equal to one year's interest if the bonds are called during the first year, and the premium declines at a constant rate of INT/N each year thereafter, where INT = annual interest and N = original maturity in years. For example, the call premium on a $1,000 par value, 10-year, 10 percent bond would generally be $100 if it were called during the first year, $90 during the second year (calculated by reducing the $100, or 10 percent, premium by one-tenth), and so on. However, bonds are often not callable until several years (generally 5 to 10) after they were issued. This is known as a *deferred call*, and the bonds are said to have *call protection*.

Suppose a company sold bonds when interest rates were relatively high. Provided the issue is callable, the company could sell a new issue of low-yielding securities if and when interest rates drop. It could then use the proceeds of the new issue to retire the high-rate issue and thus reduce its interest expense. This process is called a *refunding operation*.

The call privilege is valuable to the firm but potentially detrimental to the investor, especially if the bonds were issued in a period when interest rates were cyclically high. Accordingly, the interest rate on a new issue of callable bonds will exceed that on a new issue of noncallable bonds. For example, on August 30, 2002, Pacific Timber Company sold a bond issue yielding 9.5 percent; these bonds were callable immediately. On the same day, Northwest Milling Company sold an issue of similar risk and maturity yielding 9.2 percent; its bonds were noncallable for 10 years. Investors were willing to accept a 0.3 percent lower interest rate on Northwest's bonds for the assurance that the 9.2 percent interest rate would be earned for at least 10 years. Pacific, on the other hand, had to incur a 0.3 percent higher annual interest rate to obtain the option of calling the bonds in the event of a decline in rates.

SINKING FUNDS

Sinking Fund Provision
A provision in a bond contract that requires the issuer to retire a portion of the bond issue each year.

Some bonds also include a **sinking fund provision** that facilitates the orderly retirement of the bond issue. On rare occasions the firm may be required to deposit money with a trustee, which invests the funds and then uses the accumulated sum to retire the bonds when they mature. Usually, though, the sinking fund is used to buy back a certain percentage of the issue each year. A failure to meet the sinking fund requirement causes the bond to be thrown into default, which may force the company into bankruptcy. Obviously, a sinking fund can constitute a significant cash drain on the firm.

---

[4] The number of new corporate issues with call provisions attached has declined somewhat in recent years. In the 1980s, nearly 80 percent of new issues contained call provisions; however, in recent years this number has fallen to about 35 percent. The use of call provisions also varies with credit quality. Roughly 25 percent of investment grade bonds issued in recent years have call provisions. By contrast, about 75 percent of recent non-investment-grade bond issues include a call provision. For more information on the use of callable bonds, see Levent Güntay, N.R. Prabhala, and Haluk Unal, "Callable Bonds and Hedging," a Wharton Financial Institutions Center working paper.

In most cases, the firm is given the right to handle the sinking fund in either of two ways:

1. The company can call in for redemption (at par value) a certain percentage of the bonds each year; for example, it might be able to call 5 percent of the total original amount of the issue at a price of $1,000 per bond. The bonds are numbered serially, and those called for redemption are determined by a lottery administered by the trustee.

2. The company may buy the required number of bonds on the open market.

The firm will choose the least-cost method. If interest rates have risen, causing bond prices to fall, it will buy bonds in the open market at a discount; if interest rates have fallen, it will call the bonds. Note that a call for sinking fund purposes is quite different from a refunding call as discussed above. A sinking fund call typically requires no call premium, but only a small percentage of the issue is normally callable in any one year.[5]

Although sinking funds are designed to protect bondholders by ensuring that an issue is retired in an orderly fashion, you should recognize that sinking funds can work to the detriment of bondholders. For example, suppose the bond carries a 10 percent interest rate, but yields on similar bonds have fallen to 7.5 percent. A sinking fund call at par would require an investor to give up a bond that pays $100 of interest and then to reinvest in a bond that pays only $75 per year. This is an obvious disadvantage to those bondholders whose bonds are called. On balance, however, bonds that have a sinking fund are regarded as being safer than those without such a provision, so at the time they are issued sinking fund bonds have lower coupon rates than otherwise similar bonds without sinking funds.

OTHER FEATURES

Convertible Bond
A bond that is exchangeable, at the option of the holder, for common stock of the issuing firm.

Warrant
A long-term option to buy a stated number of shares of common stock at a specified price.

Putable Bond
A bond with provisions that allow the bond's investor to sell the bond back to the company prior to maturity at a prearranged price.

Income Bond
A bond that pays interest only if the interest is earned.

Indexed (Purchasing Power) Bond
A bond that has interest payments based on an inflation index so as to protect the holder from inflation.

Several other types of bonds are used sufficiently often to warrant mention.[6] First, **convertible bonds** are bonds that are convertible into shares of common stock, at a fixed price, at the option of the bondholder. Convertibles have a lower coupon rate than nonconvertible debt, but they offer investors a chance for capital gains in exchange for the lower coupon rate. Bonds issued with **warrants** are similar to convertibles. Warrants are options that permit the holder to buy stock for a stated price, thereby providing a capital gain if the price of the stock rises. Bonds that are issued with warrants, like convertibles, carry lower coupon rates than straight bonds.

Unlike callable bonds that give the issuer the option to buy back their debt prior to maturity, **putable bonds** contain provisions that allow the bonds' investors to sell the bonds back to the company prior to maturity at a prearranged price. Another type of bond is an **income bond,** which pays interest only if the interest is earned. Thus, these securities cannot bankrupt a company, but from an investor's standpoint they are riskier than "regular" bonds. Yet another bond is the **indexed,** or **purchasing power, bond,** which first became popular in Brazil, Israel, and a few other countries plagued by high inflation rates. The interest rate paid on these bonds is based on an inflation index such as the consumer price index, so the interest paid

---

[5] Some sinking funds require the issuer to pay a call premium.

[6] A recent article by John D. Finnerty and Douglas R. Emery reviews new types of debt (and other) securities that have been created in recent years. See "Corporate Securities Innovation: An Update," *Journal of Applied Finance: Theory, Practice, Education*, Vol. 12, No. 1, Spring/Summer 2002, 21–47.

rises automatically when the inflation rate rises, thus protecting the bondholders against inflation. In January 1997, the U.S. Treasury began issuing indexed bonds, and 10-year indexed bonds currently (2002) pay a real rate that is 3.375 percent plus the rate of inflation.

BOND VALUATION

The value of any financial asset—a stock, a bond, a lease, or even a physical asset such as an apartment building or a piece of machinery—is simply the present value of the cash flows the asset is expected to produce.

The cash flows from a specific bond depend on its contractual features as described above. For a standard coupon-bearing bond such as the one issued by Allied Foods, the cash flows consist of interest payments during the 15-year life of the bond, plus the amount borrowed (generally the $1,000 par value) when the bond matures. In the case of a floating rate bond, the interest payments vary over time. In the case of a zero coupon bond, there are no interest payments, only the face amount when the bond matures. For a "regular" bond with a fixed coupon rate, here is the situation:

Here

k_d = the bond's market rate of interest = 10%. This is the discount rate that is used to calculate the present value of the bond's cash flows. Note that k_d is *not* the coupon interest rate, and it is equal to the coupon rate only if (as in this case) the bond is selling at par. Generally, most coupon bonds are issued at par, which implies that the coupon rate is set at k_d. Thereafter, interest rates as measured by k_d will fluctuate, but the coupon rate is fixed, so k_d will equal the coupon rate only by chance. We used the term "i" or "I" to designate the interest rate in Chapter 6 because those terms are used on financial calculators, but "k," with the subscript "d" to designate the rate on a debt security, is normally used in finance.[7]

N = the number of years before the bond matures = 15. Note that N declines each year after the bond has been issued, so a bond that had a maturity of 15 years when it was issued (original maturity = 15) will have N = 14 after one year, N = 13 after two years, and so on. Note also that at this point we assume that the bond pays interest once a year, or annually, so N is measured in years. Later on, we will deal with semiannual payment bonds, which pay interest each six months.

INT = dollars of interest paid each year = Coupon rate × Par value = 0.10($1,000) = $100. In calculator terminology, INT = PMT = 100. If the bond had been a semiannual payment bond, the payment would have been $50 each six months. The payment would be zero if Allied had issued zero coupon bonds, and it would vary if the bond was a "floater."

M = the par, or maturity, value of the bond = $1,000. This amount must be paid off at maturity.

We can now redraw the time line to show the numerical values for all variables except the bond's value:

The following general equation can be solved to find the value of any bond:

$$\text{Bond's value} = V_B = \frac{INT}{(1 + k_d)^1} + \frac{INT}{(1 + k_d)^2} + \cdots + \frac{INT}{(1 + k_d)^N} + \frac{M}{(1 + k_d)^N}$$

$$= \sum_{t=1}^{N} \frac{INT}{(1 + k_d)^t} + \frac{M}{(1 + k_d)^N} . \tag{7-1}$$

Inserting values for our particular bond, we have

$$V_B = \sum_{t=1}^{15} \frac{\$100}{(1.10)^t} + \frac{\$1,000}{(1.10)^{15}} .$$

Note that the cash flows consist of an annuity of N years plus a lump sum payment at the end of Year N, and this fact is reflected in Equation 7-1.

We could simply discount each cash flow back to the present and sum these PVs to find the bond's value; see Figure 7-1 for an example. This procedure is not very efficient, especially if the bond has many years to maturity. Therefore, we use a fi-

---

[7] The appropriate interest rate on debt securities was discussed in Chapter 4. The bond's riskiness, liquidity, and years to maturity, as well as supply and demand conditions in the capital markets, all influence the interest rate on bonds. Note also that the term "r" for return is also used in the finance literature as an alternative to "k."

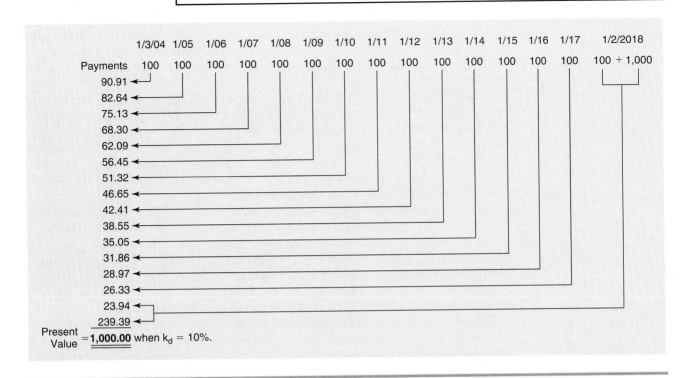

nancial calculator to solve the problem. In Chapter 6, we worked problems where only four of the five time value of money (TVM) keys were used. However, all five keys are used with bonds. Here is the setup:

Simply input N = 15, I = k = 10, INT = PMT = 100, M = FV = 1000, and then press the PV key to find the value of the bond, $1,000. Since the PV is an outflow to the investor, it is shown with a negative sign. The calculator is programmed to solve Equation 7-1: It finds the PV of an annuity of $100 per year for 15 years, discounted at 10 percent, then it finds the PV of the $1,000 maturity payment, and then it adds these two PVs to find the value of the bond.

CHANGES IN BOND VALUES OVER TIME

At the time a coupon bond is issued, the coupon is generally set at a level that will cause the market price of the bond to equal its par value. If a lower coupon were set, investors would not be willing to pay $1,000 for the bond, while if a higher coupon were set, investors would clamor for the bond and bid its price up over $1,000. Investment bankers can judge quite precisely the coupon rate that will cause a bond to sell at its $1,000 par value.

A bond that has just been issued is known as a *new issue*. (Investment bankers classify a bond as a new issue for about one month after it has first been issued.) Once the bond has been on the market for a while, it is classified as an *outstanding bond*, also called a *seasoned issue*. Newly issued bonds generally sell very close to par, but the prices of seasoned bonds vary widely from par. Except for floating rate bonds, coupon payments are constant, so when economic conditions change, a bond with a $100 coupon that sold at par when it was issued will sell for more or less than $1,000 thereafter.

Allied's bonds with a 10 percent coupon rate were originally issued at par. If k_d remained constant at 10 percent, what would the value of the bond be one year after it was issued? Now the term to maturity is only 14 years—that is, N = 14. With a financial calculator, just override N = 15 with N = 14, press the PV key, and you find a value of $1,000. If we continued, setting N = 13, N = 12, and so forth, we would see that the value of the bond will remain at $1,000 as long as the going interest rate remains constant at the coupon rate, 10 percent.[8]

Now suppose interest rates in the economy fell after the Allied bonds were issued, and, as a result, k_d *fell below the coupon rate*, decreasing from 10 to 5 percent. Both the coupon interest payments and the maturity value remain constant, but the going interest rate, k_d, is now 5 percent and N, the number of years remaining to maturity, is 14. With a financial calculator, just change k_d = I from 10 to 5 (N should already be set at 14), and then press the PV key to get the answer, $1,494.93. Thus, if k_d fell *below* the coupon rate, the bond would sell above par, or at a *premium*.

The arithmetic of the bond value increase should be clear, but what is the logic behind it? The fact that k_d has fallen to 5 percent means that if you had $1,000 to invest, you could buy new bonds like Allied's (every day some 10 to 12 companies sell new bonds), except that these new bonds would pay $50 of interest each year rather than $100. Naturally, you would prefer $100 to $50, so you would be willing to pay more than $1,000 for an Allied bond to obtain its higher coupons. All investors would react similarly, and as a result, the Allied bonds would be bid up in price to $1,494.93, at which point they would provide the same rate of return to a potential investor as the new bonds, 5 percent.

Assuming that interest rates remain constant at 5 percent for the next 14 years, what would happen to the value of an Allied bond? It would fall gradually from $1,494.93 at present to $1,000 at maturity, when Allied will redeem each bond for $1,000. This point can be illustrated by calculating the value of the bond 1 year later, when it has 13 years remaining to maturity. With a financial calculator, merely input the values for N, I, PMT, and FV, now using N = 13, and press the PV key to find the value of the bond, $1,469.68. Thus, the value of the bond will have fallen from $1,494.93 to $1,469.68, or by $25.25. If you were to calculate the value of the

---

[8] The bond prices quoted by brokers are calculated as described. However, if you bought a bond between interest payment dates, you would have to pay the basic price plus accrued interest. Thus, if you purchased an Allied bond six months after it was issued, your broker would send you an invoice stating that you must pay $1,000 as the basic price of the bond plus $50 interest, representing one-half the annual interest of $100. The seller of the bond would receive $1,050. If you bought the bond the day before its interest payment date, you would pay $1,000 + (364/365)($100) = $1,099.73. Of course, you would receive an interest payment of $100 at the end of the next day. See Self-Test Problem 2 for a detailed discussion of bond quotations between interest payment dates.

Throughout the chapter, we assume that bonds are being evaluated immediately after an interest payment date. The more expensive financial calculators such as the HP-17B have a built-in calendar that permits the calculation of exact values between interest payment dates, as do spreadsheet programs.

bond at other future dates, the price would continue to fall as the maturity date approached.

Notice that if you purchased the bond at a price of $1,494.93 and then sold it one year later with k_d still at 5 percent, you would have a capital loss of $25.25, or a total return of $100.00 − $25.25 = $74.75. Your percentage rate of return would consist of an *interest yield* (also called a *current yield*) plus a *capital gains yield*, calculated as follows:

$$\text{Interest, or current, yield} = \$100/\$1,494.93 = 0.0669 = 6.69\%$$
$$\text{Capital gains yield} = -\$25.25/\$1,494.93 = -0.0169 = -1.69\%$$
$$\text{Total rate of return, or yield} = \$74.75/\$1,494.93 = 0.0500 = 5.00\%$$

Had interest rates risen from 10 to 15 percent during the first year after issue rather than fallen from 10 to 5 percent, then you would enter $N = 14$, $I = 15$, PMT = 100, and FV = 1000, and then press the PV key to find the value of the bond, $713.78. In this case, the bond would sell at a *discount* of $286.22 below its par value:

$$\text{Discount} = \text{Price} - \text{Par value} = \$713.78 - \$1,000.00$$
$$= -\$286.22.$$

The total expected future return on the bond would again consist of a current yield and a capital gains yield, but now the capital gains yield would be *positive*. The total return would be 15 percent. To see this, calculate the price of the bond with 13 years left to maturity, assuming that interest rates remain at 15 percent. With a calculator, enter $N = 13$, $I = 15$, PMT = 100, and FV = 1000, and then press PV to obtain the bond's value, $720.84.

Notice that the capital gain for the year is the difference between the bond's value at Year 2 (with 13 years remaining) and the bond's value at Year 1 (with 14 years remaining), or $720.84 − $713.78 = $7.06. The interest yield, capital gains yield, and total yield are calculated as follows:

$$\text{Interest, or current, yield} = \$100/\$713.78 = 0.1401 = 14.01\%$$
$$\text{Capital gains yield} = \$7.06/\$713.78 = 0.0099 = 0.99\%$$
$$\text{Total rate of return, or yield} = \$107.06/\$713.78 = 0.1500 = 15.00\%$$

Figure 7-2 graphs the value of the bond over time, assuming that interest rates in the economy (1) remain constant at 10 percent, (2) fall to 5 percent and then remain constant at that level, or (3) rise to 15 percent and remain constant at that level. Of course, if interest rates do *not* remain constant, then the price of the bond will fluctuate. However, regardless of what future interest rates do, the bond's price will approach $1,000 as it nears the maturity date (barring bankruptcy, in which case the bond's value might fall dramatically).

Figure 7-2 illustrates the following key points:

1. Whenever the going rate of interest, k_d, is equal to the coupon rate, a *fixed-rate* bond will sell at its par value. Normally, the coupon rate is set equal to the going rate when a bond is issued, causing it to sell at par initially.

2. Interest rates do change over time, but the coupon rate remains fixed after the bond has been issued. Whenever the going rate of interest *rises above* the coupon

FIGURE 7-2

Time Path of the Value of a 10% Coupon, $1,000 Par Value Bond When Interest Rates Are 5%, 10%, and 15%

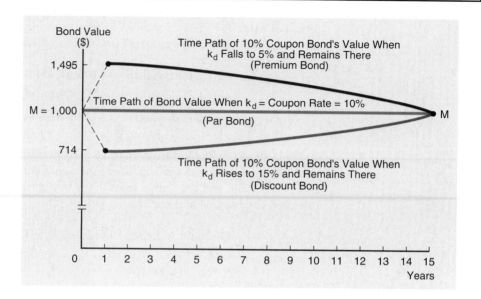

YEAR	$k_d = 5\%$	$k_d = 10\%$	$k_d = 15\%$
0	—	$1,000	—
1	$1,494.93	1,000	$713.78
.	.	.	.
.	.	.	.
.	.	.	.
15	1,000	1,000	1,000

NOTE: The curves for 5% and 15% have a slight bow.

Discount Bond
A bond that sells below its par value; occurs whenever the going rate of interest is *above* the coupon rate.

Premium Bond
A bond that sells above its par value; occurs whenever the going rate of interest is *below* the coupon rate.

rate, a fixed-rate bond's price will fall *below* its par value. Such a bond is called a **discount bond.**

3. Whenever the going rate of interest *falls below* the coupon rate, a fixed-rate bond's price will rise *above* its par value. Such a bond is called a **premium bond.**

4. Thus, an *increase* in interest rates will cause the prices of outstanding bonds to *fall*, whereas a *decrease* in rates will cause bond prices to *rise*.

5. The market value of a bond will always approach its par value as its maturity date approaches, provided the firm does not go bankrupt.

These points are very important, for they show that bondholders may suffer capital losses or make capital gains, depending on whether interest rates rise or fall after the bond was purchased. And, as we saw in Chapter 4, interest rates do indeed change over time.

Explain, verbally, the following equation:

$$V_B = \sum_{t=1}^{N} \frac{INT}{(1 + k_d)^t} + \frac{M}{(1 + k_d)^N}.$$

What is meant by the terms "new issue" and "seasoned issue"?

Last year a firm issued 20-year, 8 percent annual coupon bonds that sold at a par value of $1,000. (1) Suppose that one year after issue the going interest rate for these bonds was 6 percent. What is the price of the bonds, assuming that the bonds now have 19 years to maturity? (2) Suppose that one year after issue the going interest rate for these bonds was 10 percent (rather than 6 percent). What is the price of the bonds, assuming that the bonds now have 19 years to maturity?   ($1,223.16; $832.70)

Why do the prices of fixed-rate bonds fall if expectations for inflation rise?

What is a "discount bond"? A "premium bond"?

BOND YIELDS

If you examine the bond market table of *The Wall Street Journal* or a price sheet put out by a bond dealer, you will typically see information regarding each bond's maturity date, price, and coupon interest rate. You will also see the bond's reported yield. Unlike the coupon interest rate, which is fixed, the bond's yield varies from day to day depending on current market conditions. Moreover, the yield can be calculated in three different ways, and three "answers" can be obtained. These different yields are described in the following sections.

YIELD TO MATURITY

Yield to Maturity (YTM)
The rate of return earned on a bond if it is held to maturity.

Suppose you were offered a 14-year, 10 percent annual coupon, $1,000 par value bond at a price of $1,494.93. What rate of interest would you earn on your investment if you bought the bond and held it to maturity? This rate is called the bond's **yield to maturity (YTM),** and it is the interest rate generally discussed by investors when they talk about rates of return. The yield to maturity is generally the same as the market rate of interest, k_d, and to find it, all you need to do is solve Equation 7-1 for k_d:

$$V_B = \$1,494.93 = \frac{\$100}{(1 + k_d)^1} + \cdots + \frac{\$100}{(1 + k_d)^{14}} + \frac{\$1,000}{(1 + k_d)^{14}}.$$

You could substitute values for k_d until you find a value that "works" and forces the sum of the PVs on the right side of the equation to equal $1,494.93.

Finding k_d = YTM by trial-and-error would be a tedious, time-consuming process, but as you might guess, it is easy with a financial calculator.[9] Here is the setup:

Inputs:
	14			−1494.93	100	1000
	N	**I**	**PV**		**PMT**	**FV**

Output: = 5

Simply enter N = 14, PV = −1494.93, PMT = 100, and FV = 1000, and then press the I key. The answer, 5 percent, will then appear.

The yield to maturity is identical to the total rate of return discussed in the preceding section. The yield to maturity can also be viewed as the bond's *promised rate of return*, which is the return that investors will receive if all the promised payments are made. However, the yield to maturity equals the *expected rate of return* only if (1) the probability of default is zero and (2) the bond cannot be called. If there is some default risk, or if the bond may be called, then there is some probability that the promised payments to maturity will not be received, in which case the calculated yield to maturity will differ from the expected return.

The YTM for a bond that sells at par consists entirely of an interest yield, but if the bond sells at a price other than its par value, the YTM will consist of the interest yield plus a positive or negative capital gains yield. Note also that a bond's yield to maturity changes whenever interest rates in the economy change, and this is almost daily. An investor who purchases a bond and holds it until it matures will receive the YTM that existed on the purchase date, but the bond's calculated YTM will change frequently between the purchase date and the maturity date.

YIELD TO CALL

If you purchased a bond that was callable and the company called it, you would not have the option of holding the bond until it matured. Therefore, the yield to maturity would not be earned. For example, if Allied's 10 percent coupon bonds were callable, and if interest rates fell from 10 percent to 5 percent, then the company could call in the 10 percent bonds, replace them with 5 percent bonds, and save $100 − $50 = $50 interest per bond per year. This would be beneficial to the company, but not to its bondholders.

Yield to Call (YTC)
The rate of return earned on a bond if it is called before its maturity date.

If current interest rates are well below an outstanding bond's coupon rate, then a callable bond is likely to be called, and investors will estimate its expected rate of return as the **yield to call (YTC)** rather than as the yield to maturity. To calculate the YTC, solve this equation for k_d:

$$\text{Price of bond} = \sum_{t=1}^{N} \frac{\text{INT}}{(1 + k_d)^t} + \frac{\text{Call price}}{(1 + k_d)^N}. \qquad (7\text{-}2)$$

Here N is the number of years until the company can call the bond; call price is the price the company must pay in order to call the bond (it is often set equal to the par value plus one year's interest); and k_d is the YTC.

---

[9] You could also find the YTM with a spreadsheet. In *Excel*, you would use the Rate function, inputting Nper = 14, Pmt = 100, Pv = −1494.93, Fv = 1000, 0 for Type, and leave Guess blank.

To illustrate, suppose Allied's bonds had a provision that permitted the company, if it desired, to call the bonds 10 years after the issue date at a price of $1,100. Suppose further that interest rates had fallen, and one year after issuance the going interest rate had declined, causing the price of the bonds to rise to $1,494.93. Here is the time line and the setup for finding the bond's YTC with a financial calculator:

The YTC is 4.21 percent—this is the return you would earn if you bought the bond at a price of $1,494.93 and it was called nine years from today. (The bond could not be called until 10 years after issuance, and one year has gone by, so there are nine years left until the first call date.)

Do you think Allied *will* call the bonds when they become callable? Allied's action would depend on what the going interest rate is when the bonds become callable. If the going rate remains at $k_d = 5\%$, then Allied could save $10\% - 5\% = 5\%$, or $50 per bond per year, by calling them and replacing the 10 percent bonds with a new 5 percent issue. There would be costs to the company to refund the issue, but the interest savings would probably be worth the cost, so Allied would probably refund the bonds. Therefore, you would probably earn YTC = 4.21% rather than YTM = 5% if you bought the bonds under the indicated conditions.

In the balance of this chapter, we assume that bonds are not callable unless otherwise noted, but some of the end-of-chapter problems deal with yield to call.

CURRENT YIELD

Current Yield
The annual interest payment on a bond divided by the bond's current price.

If you examine brokerage house reports on bonds, you will often see reference to a bond's **current yield.** The current yield is the annual interest payment divided by the bond's current price. For example, if Allied's bonds with a 10 percent coupon were currently selling for $985, the bond's current yield would be 10.15 percent ($100/$985).

Unlike the yield to maturity, the current yield does not represent the return that investors should expect to receive from holding the bond. The current yield provides information regarding the amount of cash income that a bond will generate in a given year, but since it does not take account of capital gains or losses that will be realized if the bond is held until maturity (or call), it does not provide an accurate measure of the bond's total expected return.

The fact that the current yield does not provide an accurate measure of a bond's total return can be illustrated with a zero coupon bond. Since zeros pay no annual income, they always have a current yield of zero. This indicates that the bond will not provide any cash interest income, but since the bond will appreciate in value over time, its total rate of return clearly exceeds zero.

DRINKING YOUR COUPONS

Chateau Teyssier, an English vineyard, was looking for some cash to purchase some additional vines and to modernize its production facilities. Their solution? With the assistance of a leading underwriter, Matrix Securities, the vineyard issued 375 bonds, each costing 2,650 British pounds. The issue raised nearly 1 million pounds, which, at the time, was worth roughly $1.5 million.

What made these bonds interesting is that, instead of getting paid with something boring like money, these bonds paid their investors back with wine. Each June until 2002, when the bond matured, investors received their "coupons." Between 1997 and 2001, each bond provided six cases of the vineyard's rose or claret. Starting in 1998 and continuing through maturity in 2002, investors also received four cases of its prestigious Saint Emilion Grand Cru. Then, in 2002, they received their money back.

The bonds were not without risk. The vineyard's owner, Jonathan Malthus, acknowledges that the quality of the wine, "is at the mercy of the gods."

SOURCE: Steven Irvine, "My Wine Is My Bond, and I Drink My Coupons," *Euromoney,* July 1996, 7. Used with permission.

SELF-TEST QUESTIONS

Describe the difference between the yield to maturity and the yield to call.

How does a bond's current yield differ from its total return?

Could the current yield exceed the total return?

Halley Enterprises' bonds currently sell for $975. The bonds have a seven-year maturity, pay an annual coupon of $90, and have a par value of $1,000. What is their yield to maturity? What is their current yield? (9.51%; 9.23%)

Henderson Company bonds currently sell for $1,275. These bonds can be called in five years at a call price of $1,120 and pay an annual coupon of $120. What is their yield to call? (7.31%)

BONDS WITH SEMIANNUAL COUPONS

Although some bonds pay interest annually, the vast majority actually pay interest semiannually. To evaluate semiannual payment bonds, we must modify the valuation model (Equation 7-1) as follows:

1. Divide the annual coupon interest payment by 2 to determine the dollars of interest paid each six months.

2. Multiply the years to maturity, N, by 2 to determine the number of semiannual periods.

3. Divide the nominal (quoted) interest rate, k_d, by 2 to determine the periodic (semiannual) interest rate.

By making these changes, we obtain the following equation for finding the value of a bond that pays interest semiannually:

$$V_B = \sum_{t=1}^{2N} \frac{INT/2}{\left(1 + k_d/2\right)^t} + \frac{M}{\left(1 + k_d/2\right)^{2N}}. \qquad (7\text{-}1a)$$

To illustrate, assume now that Allied Food Products' bonds pay $50 interest each six months rather than $100 at the end of each year. Thus, each interest payment is only half as large, but there are twice as many of them. The coupon rate is thus "10 percent, semiannual payments." This is the nominal, or quoted, rate.[10]

When the going (nominal) rate of interest is 5 percent with semiannual compounding, the value of this 15-year bond is found as follows:

Inputs:	30	2.5		50	1000
	N	**I**	**PV**	**PMT**	**FV**
Output:			= −1,523.26		

Enter N = 30, k = I = 2.5, PMT = 50, FV = 1000, and then press the PV key to obtain the bond's value, $1,523.26. The value with semiannual interest payments is slightly larger than $1,518.98, the value when interest is paid annually. This higher value occurs because interest payments are received somewhat faster under semiannual compounding.

SELF-TEST QUESTIONS

Describe how the annual bond valuation formula is changed to evaluate semiannual coupon bonds. Then, write out the revised formula.

Hartwell Corporation bonds have a 20-year maturity, an 8 percent semiannual coupon, and a face value of $1,000. If the going interest rate is currently 7 percent, what is the current price of these bonds? ($1,106.78)

---

[10] In this situation, the nominal coupon rate of "10 percent, semiannually," is the rate that bond dealers, corporate treasurers, and investors generally would discuss. Of course, the *effective annual rate* would be higher than 10 percent at the time the bond was issued:

$$EAR = EFF\% = \left(1 + \frac{k_{Nom}}{m}\right)^m - 1 = \left(1 + \frac{0.10}{2}\right)^2 - 1 = (1.05)^2 - 1 = 10.25\%.$$

Note also that 10 percent with annual payments is different than 10 percent with semiannual payments. Thus, we have assumed a change in effective rates in this section from the situation in the preceding section, where we assumed 10 percent with annual payments.

INTEREST RATE RISK

Interest Rate Risk
The risk of a decline in a bond's price due to an increase in interest rates.

As we saw in Chapter 4, interest rates go up and down over time, and an increase in interest rates leads to a decline in the value of outstanding bonds. This risk of a decline in bond values due to rising interest rates is called **interest rate risk.** To illustrate, suppose you bought some 10 percent Allied (annual coupon) bonds at a price of $1,000, and interest rates in the following year rose to 15 percent. As we saw before, the price of the bonds would fall to $713.78, so you would have a loss of $286.22 per bond.[11] Interest rates can and do rise, and rising rates cause a loss of value for bondholders. Thus, people or firms who invest in bonds are exposed to risk from changing interest rates.

One's exposure to interest rate risk is higher on bonds with long maturities than on those maturing in the near future.[12] This point can be demonstrated by showing how the value of a 1-year bond with a 10 percent annual coupon fluctuates with changes in k_d, and then comparing these changes with those on a 14-year bond as calculated previously. The 1-year bond's values at different interest rates are shown below:

Value at k_d = 5%:

Inputs:

1	5		100	1000
N	**I**	**PV**	**PMT**	**FV**

Output: $-1,047.62$ = 1-year bond's value at k_d = 5%.

Value at k_d = 10%:

Inputs:

1	10		100	1000
N	**I**	**PV**	**PMT**	**FV**

Output: $-1,000.00$ = 1-year bond's value at k_d = 10%.

---

[11] You would have an *accounting* (and tax) loss only if you sold the bond; if you held it to maturity, you would not have such a loss. However, even if you did not sell, you would still have suffered a *real economic loss in an opportunity cost sense* because you would have lost the opportunity to invest at 15 percent and would be stuck with a 10 percent bond in a 15 percent market. In an economic sense, "paper losses" are just as bad as realized accounting losses.

[12] Actually, a bond's maturity and coupon rate both affect interest rate risk. Low coupons mean that most of the bond's return will come from repayment of principal, whereas on a high coupon bond with the same maturity, more of the cash flows will come in during the early years due to the relatively large coupon payments. A measurement called "duration," which finds the average number of years the bond's PV of cash flows remain outstanding, has been developed to combine maturity and coupons. A zero coupon bond, which has no interest payments and whose payments all come at maturity, has a duration equal to the bond's maturity. Coupon bonds all have durations that are shorter than maturity, and the higher the coupon rate, the shorter the duration. Bonds with longer duration are exposed to more interest rate risk. A discussion of duration would go beyond the scope of this book, but see any investments text for a discussion of the concept.

Value at $k_d = 15\%$:

Inputs:	1	15		100	1000
	N	**I**	**PV**	**PMT**	**FV**

Output: $-956.52 = $ 1-year bond's
value at $k_d = 15\%$.

You would obtain the first value with a financial calculator by entering N = 1, I = 5, PMT = 100, and FV = 1000, and then pressing PV to get \$1,047.62. With everything still in your calculator, enter I = 10 to override the old I = 5, and press PV to find the bond's value at $k_d = I = 10$; it is \$1,000. Then enter I = 15 and press the PV key to find the last bond value, \$956.52.

The values of the 1-year and 14-year bonds at several current market interest rates are summarized and plotted in Figure 7-3. Note how much more sensitive the price of the 14-year bond is to changes in interest rates. At a 10 percent interest rate, both the 14-year and the 1-year bonds are valued at \$1,000. When rates rise to 15 percent, the 14-year bond falls to \$713.78, but the 1-year bond only falls to \$956.52.

For bonds with similar coupons, this differential sensitivity to changes in interest rates always holds true—the longer the maturity of the bond, the more its price changes in response to a given change in interest rates. Thus, even if the risk of default on two bonds is exactly the same, the one with the longer maturity is typically exposed to more risk from a rise in interest rates.[13]

The logical explanation for this difference in interest rate risk is simple. Suppose you bought a 14-year bond that yielded 10 percent, or \$100 a year. Now suppose interest rates on comparable-risk bonds rose to 15 percent. You would be stuck with only \$100 of interest for the next 14 years. On the other hand, had you bought a 1-year bond, you would have a low return for only 1 year. At the end of the year, you would get your \$1,000 back, and you could then reinvest it and receive 15 percent, or \$150 per year, for the next 13 years. Thus, interest rate risk reflects the length of time one is committed to a given investment.

REINVESTMENT RATE RISK

As we saw in the preceding section, an *increase* in interest rates will hurt bondholders because it will lead to a decline in the value of a bond portfolio. But can a *decrease* in interest rates also hurt bondholders? The answer is yes, because if interest rates fall, a bondholder will probably suffer a reduction in his or her income. For example, consider a retiree who has a portfolio of bonds and lives off the income they produce. The bonds, on average, have a coupon rate of 10 percent. Now suppose interest rates decline to 5 percent. Many of the bonds will be called, and as calls occur, the bondholder will have to replace 10 percent bonds with 5 percent bonds. Even bonds that

---

[13] If a 10-year bond were plotted in Figure 7-3, its curve would lie between those of the 14-year bond and the 1-year bond. The curve of a 1-month bond would be almost horizontal, indicating that its price would change very little in response to an interest rate change, but a 100-year bond (or a perpetuity) would have a very steep slope. Also, zero coupon bond prices are quite sensitive to interest rate changes, and the longer the maturity of the zero, the greater its price sensitivity. Therefore, 30-year zero coupon bonds have a huge amount of interest rate risk.

FIGURE 7-3

Value of Long- and Short-Term 10% Annual Coupon Bonds at Different Market Interest Rates

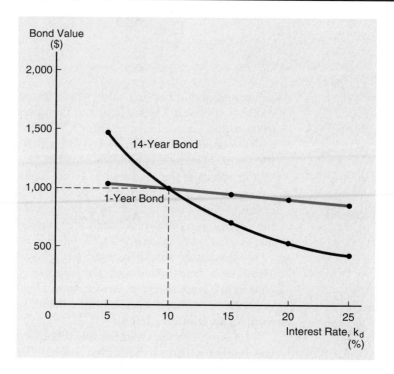

CURRENT MARKET INTEREST RATE, k_d	VALUE OF	
	1-YEAR BOND	14-YEAR BOND
5%	$1,047.62	$1,494.93
10	1,000.00	1,000.00
15	956.52	713.78
20	916.67	538.94
25	880.00	426.39

NOTE: Bond values were calculated using a financial calculator assuming annual, or once-a-year, compounding.

are not callable will mature, and when they do, they will have to be replaced with lower-yielding bonds. Thus, our retiree will suffer a reduction of income.

Reinvestment Rate Risk
The risk that a decline in interest rates will lead to a decline in income from a bond portfolio.

The risk of an income decline due to a drop in interest rates is called **reinvestment rate risk,** and its importance has been demonstrated to all bondholders in recent years as a result of the sharp drop in rates since the mid-1980s. Reinvestment rate risk is obviously high on callable bonds. It is also high on short maturity bonds, because the shorter the maturity of a bond, the fewer the years when the relatively high old interest rate will be earned, and the sooner the funds will have to be reinvested at the new low rate. Thus, retirees whose primary holdings are short-term securities, such as bank CDs and short-term bonds, are hurt badly by a decline in rates, but holders of long-term bonds continue to enjoy their old high rates.

COMPARING INTEREST RATE AND REINVESTMENT RATE RISK

Investment Horizon
The period of time an investor plans to hold a particular investment.

Note that interest rate risk relates to the *value* of the bonds in a portfolio, while reinvestment rate risk relates to the *income* the portfolio produces. If you hold long-term bonds, you will face interest rate risk, that is, the value of your bonds will decline if interest rates rise, but you will not face much reinvestment rate risk, so your income will be stable. On the other hand, if you hold short-term bonds, you will not be exposed to much interest rate risk, so the value of your portfolio will be stable, but you will be exposed to reinvestment rate risk, and your income will fluctuate with changes in interest rates.

It is important to recognize that a bond's risk depends critically on how long the investor plans to hold the bond—this is often referred to as the **investment horizon.** To illustrate the connection between risk and the investment horizon, consider first an investor that has a relatively short, one-year investment horizon. Reinvestment rate risk is of minimal concern to this investor, since there is little time for reinvestment. This investor could also eliminate his interest rate risk by buying a one-year Treasury security, since he is assured that he will receive the face value of the bond one year from now (which is also his investment horizon). However, if this investor were to buy a long-term Treasury security, he would bear a considerable amount of interest rate risk. Since the investor plans to hold the security for only one year, he will have to sell the security one year from now, and the price he will receive will depend on what happens to interest rates during the next year. As we demonstrated earlier, even a small change in interest rates can have a large effect on the prices of long-term securities. Consequently, investors with shorter investment horizons view long-term bonds as risky investments.

By contrast, short-term bonds tend to be riskier than long-term bonds for investors who have longer investment horizons. Consider an investor who is saving to accumulate a large amount of money by the date of her retirement, which is anticipated to be in 25 years. If she buys a series of short-term bonds over the next 25 years, all of the coupons and principal payments must be reinvested until the date of her planned retirement. Since there is uncertainty today about the rates that will be earned on these reinvested cash flows, long-term investors who buy a series of short-term bonds face a substantial amount of reinvestment rate risk. If she instead buys a longer-term bond today, this reinvestment rate risk will be smaller because there will be fewer maturity payments to reinvest.

One simple way to minimize interest rate and reinvestment rate risk is to buy a zero coupon Treasury security with a maturity that equals your investment horizon. For example, assume your investment horizon is 10 years. If you buy a 10-year zero, you will receive a guaranteed payment in 10 years that equals the bond's face value. Moreover, since there are no coupons to reinvest, there is no reinvestment rate risk. This feature explains why many investors find zero coupon bonds so attractive.

Nevertheless, two words of caution are in order. First, as we show in Web Appendix 7A, investors in zeros have to pay taxes each year on their amortized gain in value, even though the bonds don't produce any cash until the bonds mature or are sold—a feature that some investors find unattractive. Second, buying a zero coupon with a maturity equal to your investment horizon enables you to lock in nominal cash flow, but the value of that cash flow will still depend on what happens to inflation during your investment horizon.

The connection between investment horizon and risk also has implications for the maturity risk premium. While the maturity risk premium cannot be directly observed, most estimates indicate that there is a positive maturity risk premium.[14] Recall from Chapter 4 that a positive maturity risk premium suggests that investors believe that long-term bonds are riskier than short-term bonds. A positive maturity risk premium would suggest that a majority of bond investors have short-term investment horizons.

SELF-TEST QUESTIONS

Differentiate between interest rate risk and reinvestment rate risk.

To which type of risk are holders of long-term bonds more exposed? Short-term bondholders?

Identify one way to minimize both interest rate and reinvestment rate risk for an investor with a fixed investment horizon.

DEFAULT RISK

Another important risk associated with bonds is default risk. If the issuer defaults, investors receive less than the promised return on the bond. Therefore, investors need to assess a bond's default risk before making a purchase. Recall from Chapter 4 that the quoted interest rate includes a default risk premium—the greater the default risk, the higher the bond's yield to maturity. The default risk on Treasury securities is zero, but default risk can be substantial for corporate and municipal bonds.

Suppose two bonds have the same promised cash flows, coupon rate, maturity, liquidity, and inflation exposure, but one bond has more default risk than the other. Investors will naturally pay less for the bond with the greater chance of default. As a result, bonds with higher default risk will have higher interest rates: $k_d = k^* + IP + DRP + LP + MRP$.

If its default risk changes, this will affect the price of a bond. For example, if the default risk of the Allied bonds increases, the bonds' price will fall and the yield to maturity (YTM = k_d) will increase.

In this section we consider some issues related to default risk. First, we show that corporations can influence the default risk of their bonds by changing the types of bonds they issue. Second, we discuss bond ratings, which are used to measure default risk. Finally, we consider bankruptcy and reorganization, which affect how much an investor will recover if a default occurs.

VARIOUS TYPES OF CORPORATE BONDS

Default risk is influenced by both the financial strength of the issuer and the terms of the bond contract, especially whether collateral has been pledged to secure the bond. Some types of bonds are described below.

---

[14] The maturity risk premium for long-term bonds has averaged 1.4 percent over the last 76 years. See *Stocks, Bonds, Bills, and Inflation: (Valuation Edition) 2002 Yearbook* (Chicago: Ibbotson Associates, 2002).

Mortgage Bonds

Mortgage Bond
A bond backed by fixed assets. *First mortgage bonds* are senior in priority to claims of *second mortgage bonds*.

Under a **mortgage bond,** the corporation pledges certain assets as security for the bond. To illustrate, in 2002, Billingham Corporation needed $10 million to build a major regional distribution center. Bonds in the amount of $4 million, secured by a *first mortgage* on the property, were issued. (The remaining $6 million was financed with equity capital.) If Billingham defaults on the bonds, the bondholders can foreclose on the property and sell it to satisfy their claims.

If Billingham chose to, it could issue *second mortgage bonds* secured by the same $10 million of assets. In the event of liquidation, the holders of these second mortgage bonds would have a claim against the property, but only after the first mortgage bondholders had been paid off in full. Thus, second mortgages are sometimes called *junior mortgages,* because they are junior in priority to the claims of *senior mortgages,* or *first mortgage bonds.*

Indenture
A formal agreement between the issuer of a bond and the bondholders.

All mortgage bonds are subject to an **indenture,** which is a legal document that spells out in detail the rights of both the bondholders and the corporation. The indentures of many major corporations were written 20, 30, 40, or more years ago. These indentures are generally "open ended," meaning that new bonds can be issued from time to time under the same indenture. However, the amount of new bonds that can be issued is virtually always limited to a specified percentage of the firm's total "bondable property," which generally includes all land, plant, and equipment.

For example, in the past Savannah Electric Company had provisions in its bond indenture that allowed it to issue first mortgage bonds totaling up to 60 percent of its net fixed assets. If its fixed assets totaled $1 billion, and if it had $500 million of first mortgage bonds outstanding, it could, by the property test, issue another $100 million of bonds (60% of $1 billion = $600 million).

At times, Savannah Electric was unable to issue any new first mortgage bonds because of another indenture provision: its times-interest-earned (TIE) ratio was below 2.5, the minimum coverage that it must have in order to sell new bonds. Thus, although Savannah Electric passed the property test, it failed the coverage test, so it could not issue any more first mortgage bonds. Savannah Electric then had to finance with junior bonds. Since first mortgage bonds carried lower rates of interest than junior long-term debt, this restriction was a costly one.

Savannah Electric's neighbor, Georgia Power Company, had more flexibility under its indenture—its interest coverage requirement was only 2.0. In hearings before the Georgia Public Service Commission, it was suggested that Savannah Electric should change its indenture coverage to 2.0 so that it could issue more first mortgage bonds. However, this was simply not possible—the holders of the outstanding bonds would have to approve the change, and it is inconceivable that they would vote for a change that would seriously weaken their position.

Debentures

Debenture
A long-term bond that is not secured by a mortgage on specific property.

A **debenture** is an unsecured bond, and as such it provides no lien against specific property as security for the obligation. Debenture holders are, therefore, general creditors whose claims are protected by property not otherwise pledged. In practice, the use of debentures depends both on the nature of the firm's assets and on its general credit strength. Extremely strong companies such as Exxon Mobil often use debentures; they simply do not need to put up property as security for their debt. Debentures are also issued by weak companies that have already pledged most of their assets as collateral for mortgage loans. In this latter case, the debentures are quite risky, and they will bear a high interest rate.

Subordinated Debentures

Subordinated Debentures
A bond having a claim on assets only after the senior debt has been paid off in the event of liquidation.

The term *subordinate* means "below," or "inferior to," and, in the event of bankruptcy, subordinated debt has claims on assets only after senior debt has been paid off. **Subordinated debentures** may be subordinated either to designated notes payable (usually bank loans) or to all other debt. In the event of liquidation or reorganization, holders of subordinated debentures cannot be paid until all senior debt, as named in the debentures' indenture, has been paid. Precisely how subordination works, and how it strengthens the position of senior debtholders, is explained in detail in Web Appendix 7B.

BOND RATINGS

Since the early 1900s, bonds have been assigned quality ratings that reflect their probability of going into default. The three major rating agencies are Moody's Investors Service (Moody's), Standard & Poor's Corporation (S&P), and Fitch Investors Service. Moody's and S&P's rating designations are shown in Table 7-1.[15] The triple- and double-A bonds are extremely safe. Single-A and triple-B bonds are also strong enough to be called **investment-grade bonds,** and they are the lowest-rated bonds that many banks and other institutional investors are permitted by law to hold. Double-B and lower bonds are speculative, or **junk bonds.** These bonds have a significant probability of going into default.

Investment-Grade Bonds
Bonds rated triple-B or higher; many banks and other institutional investors are permitted by law to hold only investment-grade bonds.

Junk Bond
A high-risk, high-yield bond.

Bond Rating Criteria

Bond ratings are based on both qualitative and quantitative factors, some of which are listed below:

1. Various ratios, including the debt ratio and the times-interest-earned ratio. The better the ratios, the higher the rating.
2. Mortgage provisions: Is the bond secured by a mortgage? If it is, and if the property has a high value in relation to the amount of bonded debt, the bond's rating is enhanced.

---

[15] In the discussion to follow, reference to the S&P rating is intended to imply the Moody's and Fitch's ratings as well. Thus, triple-B bonds mean both BBB and Baa bonds; double-B bonds mean both BB and Ba bonds; and so on.

TABLE 7-1 | **Moody's and S&P Bond Ratings**

	INVESTMENT GRADE				JUNK BONDS			
Moody's	Aaa	Aa	A	Baa	Ba	B	Caa	C
S&P	AAA	AA	A	BBB	BB	B	CCC	D

NOTE: Both Moody's and S&P use "modifiers" for bonds rated below triple-A. S&P uses a plus and minus system; thus, A+ designates the strongest A-rated bonds and A— the weakest. Moody's uses a 1, 2, or 3 designation, with 1 denoting the strongest and 3 the weakest; thus, within the double-A category, Aa1 is the best, Aa2 is average, and Aa3 is the weakest.

3. Subordination provisions: Is the bond subordinated to other debt? If so, it will be rated at least one notch below the rating it would have if it were not subordinated. Conversely, a bond with other debt subordinated to it will have a somewhat higher rating.

4. Guarantee provisions: Some bonds are guaranteed by other firms. If a weak company's debt is guaranteed by a strong company (usually the weak company's parent), the bond will be given the strong company's rating.

5. Sinking fund: Does the bond have a sinking fund to ensure systematic repayment? This feature is a plus factor to the rating agencies.

6. Maturity: Other things the same, a bond with a shorter maturity will be judged less risky than a longer-term bond, and this will be reflected in the ratings.

7. Stability: Are the issuer's sales and earnings stable?

8. Regulation: Is the issuer regulated, and could an adverse regulatory climate cause the company's economic position to decline? Regulation is especially important for utilities and telephone companies.

9. Antitrust: Are any antitrust actions pending against the firm that could erode its position?

10. Overseas operations: What percentage of the firm's sales, assets, and profits are from overseas operations, and what is the political climate in the host countries?

11. Environmental factors: Is the firm likely to face heavy expenditures for pollution control equipment?

12. Product liability: Are the firm's products safe? The tobacco companies today are under pressure, and so are their bond ratings.

13. Pension liabilities: Does the firm have unfunded pension liabilities that could pose a future problem?

14. Labor unrest: Are there potential labor problems on the horizon that could weaken the firm's position? As this is written, a number of airlines face this problem, and it has caused their ratings to be lowered.

15. Accounting policies: If a firm uses relatively conservative accounting policies, its reported earnings will be of "higher quality" than if it uses less conservative procedures. Thus, conservative accounting policies are a plus factor in bond ratings.

Representatives of the rating agencies have consistently stated that no precise formula is used to set a firm's rating; all the factors listed, plus others, are taken into account, but not in a mathematically precise manner. Statistical studies have borne out this contention, for researchers who have tried to predict bond ratings on the basis of quantitative data have had only limited success, indicating that the agencies use subjective judgment when establishing a firm's rating.[16]

Nevertheless, as we see in Table 7-2, there is a strong correlation between bond ratings and many of the ratios that we described in Chapter 3. Not surprisingly, companies with lower debt ratios, higher free cash flow to debt, higher returns on invested capital, higher EBITDA coverage ratios, and higher times-interest-earned (TIE) ratios typically have higher bond ratings.

---

[16] See Ahmed Belkaoui, *Industrial Bonds and the Rating Process* (London: Quorum Books, 1983).

TABLE 7-2	Bond Rating Criteria; Three-Year (1998–2000) Median Financial Ratios for Different Bond Rating Classifications						
	AAA	AA	A	BBB	BB	B	CCC
Times-interest-earned (EBIT/Interest)	21.4×	10.1×	6.1×	3.7×	2.1×	0.8×	0.1×
EBITDA interest coverage (EBITDA/Interest)	26.5	12.9	9.1	5.8	3.4	1.8	1.3
Net cash flow/Total debt	128.8%	55.4%	43.2%	30.8%	18.8%	7.8%	1.6%
Free cash flow/Total debt	84.2	25.2	15.0	8.5	2.6	(3.2)	(12.9)
Return on capital	34.9	21.7	19.4	13.6	11.6	6.6	1.0
Operating income/Sales[a]	27.0	22.1	18.6	15.4	15.9	11.9	11.9
Long-term debt/Total capital	13.3	28.2	33.9	42.5	57.2	69.7	68.8
Total debt/Total capital	22.9	37.7	42.5	48.2	62.6	74.8	87.7

NOTE:

[a]Operating income here is defined as sales minus cost of goods manufactured (before depreciation and amortization), selling, general and administrative, and research and development costs.

SOURCE: Adapted from "Adjusted Key U.S. Industrial Financial Ratios," *Standard & Poor's CreditWeek*, August 29, 2001, 30–35.

Importance of Bond Ratings

Bond ratings are important both to firms and to investors. First, because a bond's rating is an indicator of its default risk, the rating has a direct, measurable influence on the bond's interest rate and the firm's cost of debt. Second, most bonds are purchased by institutional investors rather than individuals, and many institutions are restricted to investment-grade securities. Thus, if a firm's bonds fall below BBB, it will have a difficult time selling new bonds because many potential purchasers will not be allowed to buy them.

As a result of their higher risk and more restricted market, lower-grade bonds have higher required rates of return, k_d, than high-grade bonds. Figure 7-4 illustrates this point. In each of the years shown on the graph, U.S. government bonds have had the lowest yields, AAAs have been next, and BBB bonds have had the highest yields. The figure also shows that the gaps between yields on the three types of bonds vary over time, indicating that the cost differentials, or risk premiums, fluctuate from year to year. This point is highlighted in Figure 7-5, which gives the yields on the three types of bonds and the risk premiums for AAA and BBB bonds in June 1963 and May 2002.[17] Note first that the risk-free rate, or vertical axis intercept, rose 1.8 percentage

---

[17] The term *risk premium* ought to reflect only the difference in expected (and required) returns between two securities that results from differences in their risk. However, the differences between *yields to maturity* on different types of bonds consist of (1) a true risk premium; (2) a liquidity premium, which reflects the fact that U.S. Treasury bonds are more readily marketable than most corporate bonds; (3) a call premium, because most Treasury bonds are not callable whereas corporate bonds are; and (4) an expected loss differential, which reflects the probability of loss on the corporate bonds. As an example of the last point, suppose the yield to maturity on a BBB bond was 8.1 percent versus 5.8 percent on government bonds, but there was a 5 percent probability of total default loss on the corporate bond. In this case, the expected return on the BBB bond would be 0.95(8.1%) + 0.05(0%) = 7.7%, and the risk premium would be 1.9 percent, not the full 2.3 percentage points difference in "promised" yields to maturity. Because of all these points, the risk premiums given in Figure 7-5 overstate somewhat the true (but unmeasurable) theoretical risk premiums.

FIGURE 7-4 **Yields on Selected Long-Term Bonds, 1960–2001**

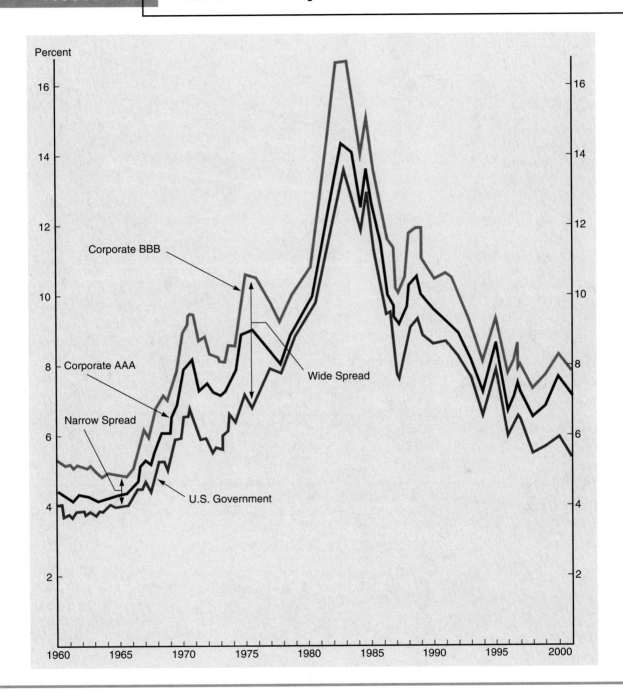

SOURCES: Federal Reserve Board, *Historical Chart Book*, 1983; *Federal Reserve Bulletin,* various issues; and *Federal Reserve Statistical Release,* Selected Interest Rates (Historical Data), **http://www.federalreserve.gov/releases/H15/data.htm**.

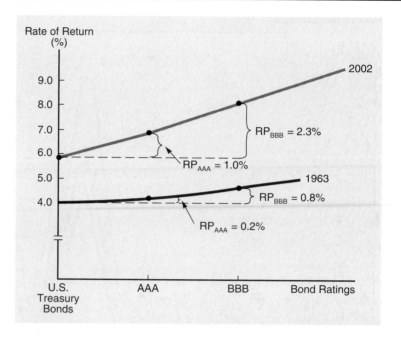

	LONG-TERM GOVERNMENT BONDS (DEFAULT-FREE) (1)	AAA CORPORATE BONDS (2)	BBB CORPORATE BONDS (3)	RISK PREMIUMS	
				AAA (4) = (2) − (1)	BBB (5) = (3) − (1)
June 1963	4.0%	4.2%	4.8%	0.2%	0.8%
May 2002	5.8	6.8	8.1	1.0	2.3

RP$_{AAA}$ = risk premium on AAA bonds.
RP$_{BBB}$ = risk premium on BBB bonds.

SOURCES: *Federal Reserve Bulletin*, December 1963; Federal Reserve Bank of St. Louis, Selected Interest Rates and U.S. Financial Data; and *Federal Reserve Statistical Release*, Selected Interest Rates (Historical Data), **http://www.federalreserve.gov/releases/H15/data.htm**.

points from 1963 to 2002, primarily reflecting the increase in realized and anticipated inflation. Second, the slope of the line has increased since 1963, indicating an increase in investors' risk aversion. Thus, the penalty for having a low credit rating varies over time. Occasionally, as in 1963, the penalty is quite small, but at other times it is large. These slope differences reflect investors' aversion to risk.

Changes in Ratings

Changes in a firm's bond rating affect both its ability to borrow long-term capital and the cost of that capital. Rating agencies review outstanding bonds on a periodic basis, occasionally upgrading or downgrading a bond as a result of its issuer's changed circumstances. For example, the June 12, 2002, issue of *Standard & Poor's CreditWeek* reported that America West Holdings' and America West Airlines' corporate credit ratings were upgraded from CCC− to B−. The firm's unsecured debt ratings were also raised. America West Holdings' major subsidiary is America West Airlines, the eighth-largest airline in the United States. The firm's rating upgrade reflected its improved liquidity and expected improvement in its financial performance after receiving proceeds from a $429 million federal government loan and $600 million in concessions from its labor unions. America West's low rating reflects the risk of the airline industry, a weak balance sheet, and limited financial flexibility. However, these risks were offset to some extent by the company's relatively low operating costs, which are among the lowest in the industry.

The June 12, 2002, *CreditWeek* also reported that Briggs & Stratton's corporate credit rating had been downgraded from BBB− to BB+, which put it in the junk bond category. The firm's senior unsecured debt and bank loan ratings were also lowered. Briggs & Stratton is the world's largest producer of air-cooled gasoline engines, which are used primarily for lawn and garden power equipment. The firm's rating downgrade reflects the increased volatility of engine sales, the effect of weather conditions on its products, its high debt ratio, and its weaker-than-expected sales and earnings after acquiring Generac Portable Products Inc., which manufactures generators and power washers.

On balance, it is fair to say that bond ratings generally do a good job of measuring the average credit risk of bonds, and that the bond rating agencies do their best to change ratings whenever they perceive a change in credit quality. At the same time, it is important to understand that bond ratings do not immediately adjust to changes in credit quality, and in some cases there can be a considerable lag between a change in credit quality and a change in bond rating. For example, like many investors, the rating agencies were caught off guard by Enron's rapid decline. Enron declared bankruptcy on a Sunday in December 2001, and the preceding Friday its bonds still had an investment-grade rating.

BANKRUPTCY AND REORGANIZATION

When a business becomes *insolvent*, it does not have enough cash to meet its interest and principal payments. A decision must then be made whether to dissolve the firm through *liquidation* or to permit it to *reorganize* and thus stay alive. These issues are addressed in Chapters 7 and 11 of the federal bankruptcy statutes, and the final decision is made by a federal bankruptcy court judge.

The decision to force a firm to liquidate versus permit it to reorganize depends on whether the value of the reorganized firm is likely to be greater than the value of the firm's assets if they are sold off piecemeal. In a reorganization, the firm's creditors negotiate with management on the terms of a potential reorganization. The reorganization plan may call for a *restructuring* of the firm's debt, in which case the interest rate may be reduced, the term to maturity lengthened, or some of the debt may be exchanged for equity. The point of the restructuring is to reduce the financial charges to a level that the firm's cash flows can support. Of course, the common stockholders also have to give up something—they often see their position diluted as a result of additional shares being given to debtholders in exchange for accepting a reduced amount of debt principal and interest. A trustee may be appointed by the court to oversee the reorganization, but generally the existing management is allowed to retain control.

Liquidation occurs if the company is deemed to be too far gone to be saved—if it is worth more dead than alive. If the bankruptcy court orders a liquidation, assets are sold off and the cash obtained is distributed as specified in Chapter 7 of the Bankruptcy Act. Here is the priority of claims:

1. Secured creditors are entitled to the proceeds from the sale of the specific property that was used to support their loans.
2. The trustee's costs of administering and operating the bankrupt firm are next in line.
3. Expenses incurred after bankruptcy was filed come next.
4. Wages due workers, up to a limit of $2,000 per worker, follow.
5. Claims for unpaid contributions to employee benefit plans are next. This amount, together with wages, cannot exceed $2,000 per worker.
6. Unsecured claims for customer deposits up to $900 per customer are sixth in line.
7. Federal, state, and local taxes due come next.
8. Unfunded pension plan liabilities are next. (Limitations exist as specified in Web Appendix 7B.)
9. General unsecured creditors are ninth on the list.
10. Preferred stockholders come next, up to the par value of their stock.
11. Common stockholders are finally paid, if anything is left, which is rare.

Web Appendix 7B provides an illustration of how a firm's assets are distributed after it has been liquidated. For now, you should know (1) that the federal bankruptcy statutes govern both reorganization and liquidation, (2) that bankruptcies occur frequently, and (3) that a priority of the specified claims must be followed when distributing the assets of a liquidated firm.

SELF-TEST QUESTIONS

Differentiate between mortgage bonds and debentures.

Name the major rating agencies, and list some factors that affect bond ratings.

Why are bond ratings important both to firms and to investors?

Differentiate between a Chapter 7 liquidation and a Chapter 11 reorganization. When would each be used?

List the priority of claims for the distribution of a liquidated firm's assets.

BOND MARKETS

Corporate bonds are traded primarily in the over-the-counter market. Most bonds are owned by and traded among the large financial institutions (for example, life insurance companies, mutual funds, and pension funds, all of which deal in very large blocks of securities), and it is relatively easy for the over-the-counter bond dealers to arrange the transfer of large blocks of bonds among the relatively few holders of the bonds. It would be much more difficult to conduct similar operations in the stock market among the literally millions of large and small stockholders, so a higher percentage of stock trades occur on the exchanges.

Information on bond trades in the over-the-counter market is not published, but a representative group of bonds is listed and traded on the bond division of the NYSE. Figure 7-6 gives a section of the bond market page of *The Wall Street Journal* for trading on June 14, 2002. We show only the bonds of BellSouth Telecommunications. Note that BellSouth Telecommunications had eight different bonds that were traded on June 14. The company actually had more than 10 bond issues outstanding, but several of them did not trade on that date.

The bonds of BellSouth and other companies can have various denominations, but for convenience we generally think of each bond as having a par value of $1,000—this is how much per bond the company borrowed and how much it must someday repay. However, since other denominations are possible, for trading and reporting purposes bonds are quoted as percentages of par. Looking at the fourth bond listed in the data in Figure 7-6, we see that there is a 7 just after the company's name; this indicates that the bond is of the series that pays 7 percent interest, or 0.07($1,000) = $70.00 of interest per year. The 7 percent is the bond's *coupon rate*. The BellSouth Telecommunications bonds, and all the others listed in the *Journal*, pay interest semiannually, so all rates are nominal, not EAR rates. The 25 which comes next indicates that this bond matures and must be repaid in the year 2025; it is not shown in the figure, but this bond was issued in 1995, so it had a 30-year original maturity. The 6.8 in the second column is the bond's current yield: Current yield = $70/$1,030 = 6.80%. The 32 in the third column indicates that 32 of these bonds were traded on June 14, 2002. Since the price shown in the fourth column is expressed as a percentage of par, the bond closed at 103 percent, which translates to $1,030, up 0.38 percent from the previous close.

Coupon rates are generally set at levels that reflect the "going rate of interest" on the day a bond is issued. If the rates were set lower, investors simply would not buy

---

FIGURE 7-6   NYSE Bond Market Transactions, June 14, 2002

CORPORATION BONDS				
BONDS	CUR YLD	VOL	CLOSE	NET CHG.
BellsoT 6¼03	6.1	25	102.63	−0.16
BellsoT 6½05	6.2	10	105.38	0.25
BellsoT 5⅞09	5.8	7	102.25	0.38
BellsoT 7s25	6.8	32	103	0.38
BellsoT 7⅞32	7.6	50	103	−0.13
BellsoT 7½33	7.3	25	103.38	0.75
BellsoT 6¾33	7.0	13	96.63	1.50
BellsoT 7⅝35	7.5	168	102.38	−1.13

SOURCE: Adapted from *The Wall Street Journal*, June 17, 2002, C14.

FIGURE 7-7

BellSouth Telecommunications 7%, 30-Year Bond: Market Value as Interest Rates Change

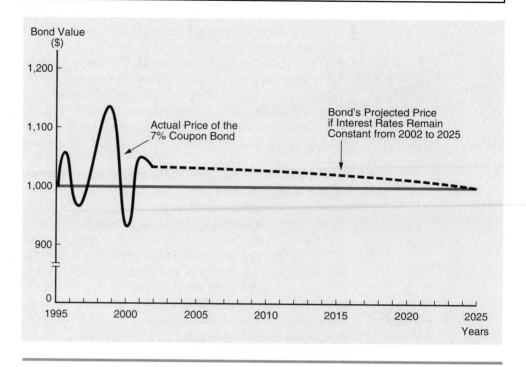

NOTE: The line from 2002 to 2025 appears linear, but it actually has a slight upward curve.

the bonds at the $1,000 par value, so the company could not borrow the money it needed. Thus, bonds generally sell at their par values on the day they are issued, but their prices fluctuate thereafter as interest rates change.

As shown in Figure 7-7, the BellSouth Telecommunications bonds initially sold at par. The bonds rose above par in 1995 when interest rates dipped below 7 percent, but then fell below par in 1996 when interest rates rose. Over the next four years this pattern was repeated: The price rose above par in 1997 and 1998 when interest rates fell, but the price fell again in 1999 and 2000 after another increase in interest rates. Interest rates declined again in 2001 and 2002, so the price rose above par during this time period. The dashed line in Figure 7-7 shows the projected price of the bonds, in the unlikely event that interest rates remain constant from 2002 to 2025. Looking at the actual and projected price history of these bonds, we see (1) the inverse relationship between interest rates and bond values and (2) the fact that bond values approach their par values as their maturity date approaches.

SELF-TEST QUESTIONS

Why do most bond trades occur in the over-the-counter market?

If a bond issue is to be sold at par, how will its coupon rate be determined?

This chapter described the different types of bonds governments and corporations issue, explained how bond prices are established, and discussed how investors estimate the rates of return they can expect to earn. We also discussed the various types of risks that investors face when they buy bonds.

It is important to remember that when an investor purchases a company's bonds, that investor is providing the company with capital. Therefore, when a firm issues bonds, *the return that investors receive represents the cost of debt financing for the issuing company*. This point is emphasized in Chapter 9, where the ideas developed in this chapter are used to help determine a company's overall cost of capital, which is a basic component in the capital budgeting process.

The key concepts covered in this chapter are listed below.

- A **bond** is a long-term promissory note issued by a business or governmental unit. The issuer receives money in exchange for promising to make interest payments and to repay the principal on a specified future date.

- Some recent innovations in long-term financing include **zero coupon bonds,** which pay no annual interest but which are issued at a discount; **floating rate debt,** whose interest payments fluctuate with changes in the general level of interest rates; and **junk bonds,** which are high-risk, high-yield instruments issued by firms with very high debt ratios.

- A **call provision** gives the issuing corporation the right to redeem the bonds prior to maturity under specified terms, usually at a price greater than the maturity value (the difference is a **call premium**). A firm will typically call a bond if interest rates fall substantially below the coupon rate.

- A **sinking fund** is a provision that requires the corporation to retire a portion of the bond issue each year. The purpose of the sinking fund is to provide for the orderly retirement of the issue. A sinking fund typically requires no call premium.

- The **value of a bond** is found as the present value of an **annuity** (the interest payments) plus the present value of a lump sum (the **principal**). The bond is evaluated at the appropriate periodic interest rate over the number of periods for which interest payments are made.

- The equation used to find the value of an annual coupon bond is:

$$V_B = \sum_{t=1}^{N} \frac{INT}{(1 + k_d)^t} + \frac{M}{(1 + k_d)^N}.$$

  An adjustment to the formula must be made if the bond pays interest **semiannually:** divide INT and k_d by 2, and multiply N by 2.

- The return earned on a bond held to maturity is defined as the bond's **yield to maturity (YTM).** If the bond can be redeemed before maturity, it is **callable,** and the return investors receive if it is called is defined as the **yield to call (YTC).** The YTC is found as the present value of the interest payments received while the bond is outstanding plus the present value of the call price (the par value plus a call premium).

- The longer the maturity of a bond, the more its price will change in response to a given change in interest rates; this is called **interest rate risk.** However, bonds with short maturities expose investors to high **reinvestment rate risk,** which is the risk that income will decline because cash flows received from a bond will be rolled over at a lower interest rate.

- Corporate and municipal bonds have **default risk.** If an issuer defaults, investors receive less than the promised return on the bond. Therefore, investors should evaluate a bond's default risk before making a purchase.

- There are many different types of bonds. They include **mortgage bonds, debentures, convertibles, bonds with warrants, putable bonds, income bonds,** and **purchasing power (indexed) bonds.** The return required on each type of bond is determined by the bond's riskiness.

- Bonds are assigned **ratings** that reflect the probability of their going into default. The highest rating is AAA, and they go down to D. The higher a bond's rating, the lower its risk and its interest rate.

Two related issues are discussed in detail in Web Appendixes 7A and 7B: zero coupon bonds and bankruptcy. (See **http://brigham.swlearning.com.**) In recent years many companies have used zeros to raise billions of dollars, while bankruptcy is an important consideration for both companies that issue debt and investors.

QUESTIONS

7-1 Is it true that the following equation can be used to find the value of an N-year bond that pays interest once a year?

$$V_B = \sum_{t=1}^{N} \frac{\text{Annual interest}}{(1+k_d)^t} + \frac{\text{Par value}}{(1+k_d)^N}.$$

7-2 "The values of outstanding bonds change whenever the going rate of interest changes. In general, short-term interest rates are more volatile than long-term interest rates. Therefore, short-term bond prices are more sensitive to interest rate changes than are long-term bond prices." Is this statement true or false? Explain.

7-3 The rate of return you would get if you bought a bond and held it to its maturity date is called the bond's yield to maturity. If interest rates in the economy rise after a bond has been issued, what will happen to the bond's price and to its YTM? Does the length of time to maturity affect the extent to which a given change in interest rates will affect the bond's price?

7-4 If you buy a *callable* bond and interest rates decline, will the value of your bond rise by as much as it would have risen if the bond had not been callable? Explain.

7-5 A sinking fund can be set up in one of two ways:
(1) The corporation makes annual payments to the trustee, who invests the proceeds in securities (frequently government bonds) and uses the accumulated total to retire the bond issue at maturity.
(2) The trustee uses the annual payments to retire a portion of the issue each year, either calling a given percentage of the issue by a lottery and paying a specified price per bond or buying bonds on the open market, whichever is cheaper.
Discuss the advantages and disadvantages of each procedure from the viewpoint of both the firm and its bondholders.

7-6 Indicate whether each of the following actions will increase or decrease a bond's yield to maturity:
a. A bond's price increases.
b. The company's bonds are downgraded by the rating agencies.

c. A change in the bankruptcy code makes it more difficult for bondholders to receive payments in the event a firm declares bankruptcy.

d. The economy enters a recession.

e. The bonds become subordinated to another debt issue.

7-7 Assume that you have a short investment horizon (that is, less than one year). You are considering two investments: a 1-year Treasury security and a 20-year Treasury security. Which of the two investments would you view as being more risky?

SELF-TEST PROBLEMS (SOLUTIONS APPEAR IN APPENDIX B)

ST-1
Key terms

Define each of the following terms:

a. Bond; Treasury bond; corporate bond; municipal bond; foreign bond

b. Par value; maturity date; original maturity

c. Coupon payment; coupon interest rate

d. Floating rate bond

e. Premium bond; discount bond

f. Current yield (on a bond); yield to maturity (YTM); yield to call (YTC)

g. Reinvestment rate risk; interest rate risk; investment horizon

h. Default risk

i. Mortgage bond

j. Debenture; subordinated debenture

k. Convertible bond; warrant; putable bond; income bond; indexed, or purchasing power, bond

l. Call provision; sinking fund provision; indenture

m. Zero coupon bond; original issue discount (OID) bond

n. Junk bond; investment grade bonds

ST-2
Bond valuation

The Pennington Corporation issued a new series of bonds on January 1, 1979. The bonds were sold at par ($1,000), have a 12 percent coupon, and mature in 30 years, on December 31, 2008. Coupon payments are made semiannually (on June 30 and December 31).

a. What was the YTM of Pennington's bonds on January 1, 1979?

b. What was the price of the bond on January 1, 1984, 5 years later, assuming that the level of interest rates had fallen to 10 percent?

c. Find the current yield and capital gains yield on the bond on January 1, 1984, given the price as determined in part b.

d. On July 1, 2002, Pennington's bonds sold for $916.42. What was the YTM at that date?

e. What were the current yield and capital gains yield on July 1, 2002?

f. Now, assume that you purchased an outstanding Pennington bond on March 1, 2002, when the going rate of interest was 15.5 percent. How large a check must you have written to complete the transaction? This is a hard question!

ST-3
Sinking fund

The Vancouver Development Company has just sold a $100 million, 10-year, 12 percent bond issue. A sinking fund will retire the issue over its life. Sinking fund payments are of equal amounts and will be made *semiannually*, and the proceeds will be used to retire bonds as the payments are made. Bonds can be called at par for sinking fund purposes, or the funds paid into the sinking fund can be used to buy bonds in the open market.

a. How large must each semiannual sinking fund payment be?

b. What will happen, under the conditions of the problem thus far, to the company's debt service requirements per year for this issue over time?

c. Now suppose Vancouver Development set up its sinking fund so that *equal annual amounts*, payable at the end of each year, are paid into a sinking fund trust held by a bank, with the proceeds being used to buy government bonds that pay 9 percent interest. The payments, plus accumulated interest, must total $100 million at the end of 10 years, and the proceeds will be used to retire the bonds at that time. How large must the annual sinking fund payment be now?

d. What are the annual cash requirements for covering bond service costs under the trusteeship arrangement described in part c? (Note: Interest must be paid on Vancouver's outstanding bonds but not on bonds that have been retired.)

e. What would have to happen to interest rates to cause the company to buy bonds on the open market rather than call them under the original sinking fund plan?

7-1
Bond valuation

Callaghan Motors' bonds have 10 years remaining to maturity. Interest is paid annually, the bonds have a $1,000 par value, and the coupon interest rate is 8 percent. The bonds have a yield to maturity of 9 percent. What is the current market price of these bonds?

7-2
Yield to maturity and call

Thatcher Corporation's bonds will mature in 10 years. The bonds have a face value of $1,000 and an 8 percent coupon rate, paid semiannually. The price of the bonds is $1,100. The bonds are callable in 5 years at a call price of $1,050. What is the yield to maturity? What is the yield to call?

7-3
Bond valuation

Nungesser Corporation has issued bonds that have a 9 percent coupon rate, payable semiannually. The bonds mature in 8 years, have a face value of $1,000, and a yield to maturity of 8.5 percent. What is the price of the bonds?

7-4
Current yield and yield to maturity

A bond that matures in 10 years sells for $985. The bond has a face value of $1,000 and a 7 percent annual coupon.
a. What is the bond's current yield?
b. What is the bond's yield to maturity (YTM)?
c. Assume that the yield to maturity remains constant for the next 3 years. What will be the price of the bond 3 years from today?

EXAM-TYPE PROBLEMS

The problems included in this section are set up in such a way that they could be converted to multiple-choice exam problems.

7-5
Bond valuation

The Garraty Company has two bond issues outstanding. Both bonds pay $100 annual interest plus $1,000 at maturity. Bond L has a maturity of 15 years, and Bond S a maturity of 1 year.
a. What will be the value of each of these bonds when the going rate of interest is (1) 5 percent, (2) 8 percent, and (3) 12 percent? Assume that there is only one more interest payment to be made on Bond S.
b. Why does the longer-term (15-year) bond fluctuate more when interest rates change than does the shorter-term bond (1-year)?

7-6
Yield to maturity

The Heymann Company's bonds have 4 years remaining to maturity. Interest is paid annually; the bonds have a $1,000 par value; and the coupon interest rate is 9 percent.
a. What is the yield to maturity at a current market price of (1) $829 or (2) $1,104?
b. Would you pay $829 for one of these bonds if you thought that the appropriate rate of interest was 12 percent—that is, if $k_d = 12\%$? Explain your answer.

7-7
Yield to call

Six years ago, The Singleton Company sold a 20-year bond issue with a 14 percent annual coupon rate and a 9 percent call premium. Today, Singleton called the bonds. The bonds originally were sold at their face value of $1,000. Compute the realized rate of return for investors who purchased the bonds when they were issued and who surrender them today in exchange for the call price.

7-8
Bond yields

A 10-year, 12 percent semiannual coupon bond, with a par value of $1,000, may be called in 4 years at a call price of $1,060. The bond sells for $1,100. (Assume that the bond has just been issued.)
a. What is the bond's yield to maturity?
b. What is the bond's current yield?
c. What is the bond's capital gain or loss yield?
d. What is the bond's yield to call?

7-9
Yield to maturity

You just purchased a bond that matures in 5 years. The bond has a face value of $1,000, an 8 percent annual coupon, and has a current yield of 8.21 percent. What is the bond's yield to maturity (YTM)?

7-10
Current yield

A bond that matures in 7 years sells for $1,020. The bond has a face value of $1,000 and a yield to maturity of 10.5883 percent. The bond pays coupons semiannually. What is the bond's current yield?

7-11
Nominal interest rate

Lloyd Corporation's 14 percent coupon rate, semiannual payment, $1,000 par value bonds, which mature in 30 years, are callable 5 years from now at a price of $1,050. The bonds sell at a price of $1,353.54, and the yield curve is flat. Assuming that interest rates in the economy are expected to remain at their current level, what is the best estimate of Lloyd's nominal interest rate on new bonds?

7-12
Yield to maturity and yield to call

Kaufman Enterprises has bonds outstanding with a $1,000 face value and 10 years left until maturity. The bonds have an 11 percent annual coupon payment. The current price of these bonds is $1,175. The bonds may be called in 5 years at 109 percent of face value (Call price = $1,090).
a. What is the yield to maturity of these bonds?
b. What is the yield to call for these bonds, if called in 5 years?
c. Which yield might investors expect to earn on these bonds, and why?
d. Further inspection of Kaufman Enterprises' bond indenture reveals that the call provision on Kaufman's bonds allows the firm the option to call the bonds at the end of each year beginning in Year 5. Recall that in Year 5, the bonds may be called, but each year the call percentage will decline by 1 percent. Hence, in Year 6 the bonds may be called at 108 percent of face value, in Year 7 the bonds may be called at 107 percent of face value, etc. If interest rates remain the same, when is the latest that investors might expect the firm to call the bonds?

7-13
Bond valuation

A 20-year corporate bond has a par value of $1,000 and a 9 percent annual coupon rate. Assume that your required rate of return is 10 percent and that you plan to hold on to this bond for 5 years. You, and the market, have expectations that in 5 years the yield to maturity for this bond (or another bond with similar risk and maturity) will be 8.5 percent. How much are you willing to pay for this bond today? (Hint: You will need to know how much you can sell the bond for at the end of 5 years.)

7-14
Bond valuation

You have just purchased a 10-year, $1,000 par value bond. The coupon rate on this bond is 9 percent and interest is paid semiannually. If you require an "effective" annual interest rate of 8.16 percent, then how much should you have paid for this bond?

7-15
Current yield and yield to maturity

Hooper Printing Inc. has bonds outstanding with 9 years left to maturity. The bonds have an 8 percent annual coupon rate and, were issued last year at par value of $1,000, but due to changes in interest rates, each bond's value has fallen to $901.40. The capital gains yield earned by investors over the last year was −9.86 percent.
a. What is the expected current yield for the next year?
b. What is the yield to maturity?
c. What is the expected capital gains yield for the next year if interest rates do not change?

7-16
Bond covenants

Heekin Industries currently has $140 million in long-term bonds outstanding at an average cost of 7.5 percent. Therefore, the firm has an interest expense of $10.5 million on its income statement. The firm currently has a times-interest-earned (TIE) ratio of 3.2×. Heekin's bond covenants prohibit it from issuing new bonds when the TIE ratio falls below 2.5×. Heekin's board of directors have elected to raise funds for expansion through a new bond issue. The firm may raise up to $25 million at a cost of 8 percent, another $25 million at 10 percent, and an additional $25 million at a cost of 13 percent. How much money, in new bonds, can Heekin raise before it violates its bond covenant?

7-17
Bond returns

Last year, Baili purchased a $1,000 face value corporate bond with an 11 percent annual coupon rate and a 10-year maturity. At the time of the purchase, the bonds had an expected yield to maturity of 9.79 percent, and today she sold the bond for $1,060.49. What is the one-period return that Baili earned on this investment?

PROBLEMS

7-18
Bond reporting

Look up the prices of American Telephone & Telegraph's (AT&T) bonds in *The Wall Street Journal* (or some other newspaper that provides this information).
a. If AT&T were to sell a new issue of $1,000 par value long-term bonds, approximately what coupon interest rate would it have to set on the bonds if it wanted to bring them out at par?
b. If you had $10,000 and wanted to invest it in AT&T, what return would you expect to get if you bought AT&T's bonds?

7-19
Yield to call

It is now January 1, 2003, and you are considering the purchase of an outstanding Racette Corporation bond that was issued on January 1, 2001. The Racette bond has a 9.5 percent annual coupon and a 30-year original maturity (it matures on December 31, 2030). There is a 5-year call protection (until December 31, 2005), after which time the bond can be called at 109 (that is, at 109 percent of par, or $1,090). Interest rates have declined since the bond was issued, and the bond is now selling at 116.575 percent of par, or $1,165.75. You want to determine both the yield to maturity and the yield to call for this bond.

   a. What is the yield to maturity in 2003 for the Racette bond? What is its yield to call?

   b. If you bought this bond, which return do you think you would actually earn? Explain your reasoning.

   c. Suppose the bond had sold at a discount. Would the yield to maturity or the yield to call have been more relevant?

7-20
Interest rate sensitivity

A bond trader purchased each of the following bonds at a yield to maturity of 8 percent. Immediately after she purchased the bonds interest rates fell to 7 percent. What is the percentage change in the price of each bond after the decline in interest rates? Fill in the following table:

	PRICE @ 8%	PRICE @ 7%	PERCENTAGE CHANGE
10-year, 10% annual coupon	_____	_____	_____
10-year zero	_____	_____	_____
5-year zero	_____	_____	_____
30-year zero	_____	_____	_____
$100 perpetuity	_____	_____	_____

7-21
Bond valuation

An investor has two bonds in his portfolio. Each bond matures in 4 years, has a face value of $1,000, and has a yield to maturity equal to 9.6 percent. One bond, Bond C, pays an annual coupon of 10 percent; the other bond, Bond Z, is a zero coupon bond.

   a. Assuming that the yield to maturity of each bond remains at 9.6 percent over the next 4 years, what will be the price of each of the bonds at the following time periods? Fill in the following table:

t	PRICE OF BOND C	PRICE OF BOND Z
0	_____	_____
1	_____	_____
2	_____	_____
3	_____	_____
4	_____	_____

   b. Plot the time path of the prices for each of the two bonds.

SPREADSHEET PROBLEM

7-22
Bond valuation

Rework Problem 7-8 using a spreadsheet model. After completing parts a through d, answer the following related questions.

   e. How would the price of the bond be affected by changing interest rates? (Hint: Conduct a sensitivity analysis of price to changes in the yield to maturity, which is also the going market interest rate for the bond. Assume that the bond will be called if and only if the going rate of interest *falls below* the coupon rate. That is an oversimplification, but assume it anyway for purposes of this problem.)

   f. Now assume that the date is 10/25/2002. Assume further that our 12 percent, 10-year bond was issued on 7/1/2002, is callable on 7/1/2006 at $1,060, will mature on 6/30/2012, pays interest semiannually (January 1 and July 1), and sells for $1,100. Use your spreadsheet to find (1) the bond's yield to maturity and (2) its yield to call.

WESTERN MONEY MANAGEMENT INC.

7-23 Bond Valuation Robert Black and Carol Alvarez are vice-presidents of Western Money Management and codirectors of the company's pension fund management division. A major new client, the California League of Cities, has requested that Western present an investment seminar to the mayors of the represented cities, and Black and Alvarez, who will make the actual presentation, have asked you to help them by answering the following questions.

a. What are the key features of a bond?

b. What are call provisions and sinking fund provisions? Do these provisions make bonds more or less risky?

c. How is the value of any asset whose value is based on expected future cash flows determined?

d. How is the value of a bond determined? What is the value of a 10-year, $1,000 par value bond with a 10 percent annual coupon if its required rate of return is 10 percent?

e. (1) What would be the value of the bond described in part d if, just after it had been issued, the expected inflation rate rose by 3 percentage points, causing investors to require a 13 percent return? Would we now have a discount or a premium bond?

(2) What would happen to the bond's value if inflation fell, and k_d declined to 7 percent? Would we now have a premium or a discount bond?

(3) What would happen to the value of the 10-year bond over time if the required rate of return remained at 13 percent, or if it remained at 7 percent? (Hint: With a financial calculator, enter PMT, I, FV, and N, and then change (override) N to see what happens to the PV as the bond approaches maturity.)

f. (1) What is the yield to maturity on a 10-year, 9 percent, annual coupon, $1,000 par value bond that sells for $887.00? That sells for $1,134.20? What does the fact that a bond sells at a discount or at a premium tell you about the relationship between k_d and the bond's coupon rate?

(2) What are the total return, the current yield, and the capital gains yield for the discount bond? (Assume the bond is held to maturity and the company does not default on the bond.)

g. What is *interest rate (or price) risk*? Which bond has more interest rate risk, an annual payment 1-year bond or a 10-year bond? Why?

h. What is *reinvestment rate risk*? Which has more reinvestment rate risk, a 1-year bond or a 10-year bond?

i. How does the equation for valuing a bond change if semiannual payments are made? Find the value of a 10-year, semiannual payment, 10 percent coupon bond if nominal $k_d = 13\%$.

j. Suppose you could buy, for $1,000, either a 10 percent, 10-year, annual payment bond or a 10 percent, 10-year, semiannual payment bond. They are equally risky. Which would you prefer? If $1,000 is the proper price for the semiannual bond, what is the equilibrium price for the annual payment bond?

k. Suppose a 10-year, 10 percent, semiannual coupon bond with a par value of $1,000 is currently selling for $1,135.90, producing a nominal yield to maturity of 8 percent. However, the bond can be called after 4 years for a price of $1,050.

(1) What is the bond's *nominal yield to call (YTC)*?

(2) If you bought this bond, do you think you would be more likely to earn the YTM or the YTC? Why?

l. Does the yield to maturity represent the promised or expected return on the bond?

m. These bonds were rated AA– by S&P. Would you consider these bonds investment grade or junk bonds?

n. What factors determine a company's bond rating?

o. If this firm were to default on the bonds, would the company be immediately liquidated? Would the bondholders be assured of receiving all of their promised payments?

Please go to our web site **http://brigham.swlearning.com** to access the Cyberproblems.

STOCKS AND THEIR VALUATION

8

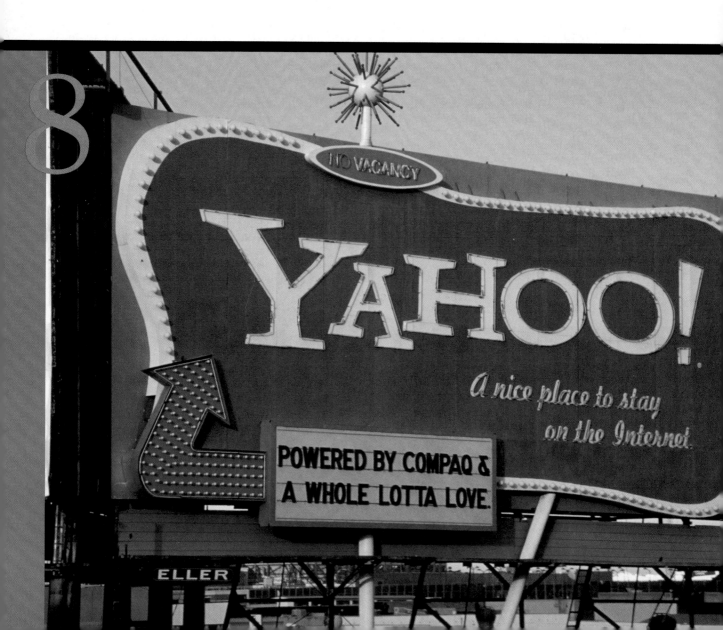

THE BUBBLE BURSTS FOR

YAHOO'S INVESTORS

A $10,000 investment in Yahoo! Inc. when it went public in 1996 would have grown to nearly $1 million by the end of 1999. Since then, Yahoo's stock has declined steadily, from $200 a share in March 2000 to $13 a share in July 2002.

Yahoo's dramatic rise and fall was far from unusual. The stock market, as measured by the Dow, performed extraordinarily well up to 2000, rising from below 4,000 in early 1995 to over 11,000 in 1999. To put this remarkable 7,000-point rise in perspective, consider that the Dow first reached 1,000 in 1965, took another 22 years to hit 2,000, then four more years to reach 3,000, and another four to get to 4,000 (in 1995). Then, in just five years, it soared over 11,000. Thus, in that one 5-year period investors made almost twice as much in the stock market as in the previous 70 years!

The strong bull market of the 1990s made it possible for many people to take early retirement, buy expensive homes, and afford high college tuitions. Encouraged by this performance, more and more investors flocked to the market, pushing prices up and up. However, some astute observers were becoming concerned that investors did not realize just how risky stocks actually are. Most notably, Federal Reserve Chairman Alan Greenspan expressed concerns that "irrational exuberance" was pushing stock prices to unsustainable heights.

Greenspan's concerns turned out to be warranted. Indeed, after nearing the 12,000 mark in early 2000, the Dow dropped

YAHOO! INC.

later in the year to below 10,000, and in 2002 it fell below 8,000 due to investors' concerns about the economy, future terrorist attacks, and accounting scandals that threatened to destroy a number of the nation's largest firms. The drop in the once high-flying Nasdaq was even more dramatic. After topping 5,000 in March 2000, the Nasdaq plunged below 1,400 in July 2002, a decline of more than 70 percent.

Note too that while all boats rise equally with the tide, the same thing does not hold for stocks—in any given period, some make huge gains while others suffer tremendous losses. For example, 2002 witnessed the stunning collapse of once high-flying stocks such as Enron, WorldCom, and Global Crossing, even while other stocks such as Lockheed Martin, Aetna, and AutoZone were gaining more than 70 percent.

While it is difficult to predict future stock prices, we are not completely in the dark, and after studying this chapter, you should have a reasonably good understanding of the factors that influence stock prices. With that knowledge—and a little luck—you should be able to successfully navigate the stock market's often-treacherous ups and downs.

In Chapter 7 we examined bonds. We now turn to common and preferred stock, beginning with some important background material that helps establish a framework for valuing these securities.

While it is generally easy to predict the cash flows received from bonds, forecasting the cash flows on common stocks is much more difficult. However, two fairly straightforward models can be used to help estimate the "true," or intrinsic, value of a common stock: (1) the dividend growth model and (2) the total corporate value model. A stock should be bought if its intrinsic value exceeds its market price but sold if its price exceeds the intrinsic value.

The concepts and models developed here will also be used when we estimate the cost of capital in Chapter 9. In subsequent chapters, we demonstrate how the cost of capital is used to help make many important decisions, especially the decision to invest or not invest in new assets. Consequently, it is critically important that you understand the basics of stock valuation. ■

LEGAL RIGHTS AND PRIVILEGES OF COMMON STOCKHOLDERS

The common stockholders are the *owners* of a corporation, and as such they have certain rights and privileges as discussed in this section.

CONTROL OF THE FIRM

Its common stockholders have the right to elect a firm's directors, who, in turn, elect the officers who manage the business. In a small firm, the major stockholder typically assumes the positions of president and chairperson of the board of directors. In a large, publicly owned firm, the managers typically have some stock, but their personal holdings are generally insufficient to give them voting control. Thus, the managements of most publicly owned firms can be removed by the stockholders if the management team is not effective.

State and federal laws stipulate how stockholder control is to be exercised. First, corporations must hold an election of directors periodically, usually once a year, with the vote taken at the annual meeting. Frequently, one-third of the directors are elected each year for a three-year term. Each share of stock has one vote; thus, the owner of 1,000 shares has 1,000 votes for each director.[1] Stockholders can appear at the annual meeting and vote in person, but typically they transfer their right to vote to a second party by means of a **proxy.** Management always solicits stockholders' proxies and usually gets them. However, if earnings are poor and stockholders are dissatisfied, an outside group may solicit the proxies in an effort to overthrow management and take control of the business. This is known as a **proxy fight.**

The question of control has become a central issue in finance in recent years. The frequency of proxy fights has increased, as have attempts by one corporation to take over another by purchasing a majority of the outstanding stock. These actions are called **takeovers.** Some well-known examples of takeover battles include KKR's acquisition of RJR Nabisco, Chevron's acquisition of Gulf Oil, and the QVC/Viacom fight to take over Paramount.

Managers who do not have majority control (more than 50 percent of their firms' stock) are very much concerned about proxy fights and takeovers, and many of them are attempting to get stockholder approval for changes in their corporate charters that would make takeovers more difficult. For example, a number of companies have gotten their stockholders to agree (1) to elect only one-third of the directors each year (rather than electing all directors each year), (2) to require 75 percent of the stockholders (rather than 50 percent) to approve a merger, and (3) to vote in a "poison pill" provision that would allow the stockholders of a firm that is taken over by another firm to buy shares in the second firm at a reduced price. The poison pill makes the acquisition unattractive and, thus, wards off hostile takeover attempts. Managements seeking such changes generally cite a fear that the firm will be picked up at a bargain price, but it often appears that managers' concerns about their own positions might be an even more important consideration.

Management's moves to make takeovers more difficult have been countered by stockholders, especially large institutional stockholders, who do not want to see barriers erected to protect incompetent managers. To illustrate, the California Public Employees Retirement System (Calpers), which is one of the largest institutional investors, announced plans in early 1994 to conduct a proxy fight with several corporations whose financial performances were poor in Calpers' judgment. Calpers wants companies to give outside (nonmanagement) directors more clout and to force managers to be more responsive to stockholder complaints.

Prior to 1993, SEC rules prohibited large investors such as Calpers from getting together to force corporate managers to institute policy changes. However, the SEC changed its rules in 1993, and now large investors can work together to force management changes. This ruling has served to keep managers focused on stockholder concerns, which means the maximization of stock prices.

THE PREEMPTIVE RIGHT

Common stockholders often have the right, called the **preemptive right,** to purchase any additional shares sold by the firm. In some states, the preemptive right is automatically included in every corporate charter; in others, it is necessary to insert it specifically into the charter.

Proxy
A document giving one person the authority to act for another, typically the power to vote shares of common stock.

Proxy Fight
An attempt by a person or group to gain control of a firm by getting its stockholders to grant that person or group the authority to vote their shares to replace the current management.

Takeover
An action whereby a person or group succeeds in ousting a firm's management and taking control of the company.

Preemptive Right
A provision in the corporate charter or bylaws that gives common stockholders the right to purchase on a pro rata basis new issues of common stock (or convertible securities).

---

[1] In the situation described, a 1,000-share stockholder could cast 1,000 votes for each of three directors if there were three contested seats on the board. An alternative procedure that may be prescribed in the corporate charter calls for *cumulative voting.* Here the 1,000-share stockholder would get 3,000 votes if there were three vacancies, and he or she could cast all of them for one director. Cumulative voting helps small groups to get representation on the board.

The purpose of the preemptive right is twofold. First, it enables current stockholders to maintain control. If it were not for this safeguard, the management of a corporation could issue a large number of additional shares and purchase these shares itself. Management could thereby seize control of the corporation and frustrate the will of the current stockholders.

The second, and by far the more important, reason for the preemptive right is to protect stockholders against a dilution of value. For example, suppose 1,000 shares of common stock, each with a price of $100, were outstanding, making the total market value of the firm $100,000. If an additional 1,000 shares were sold at $50 a share, or for $50,000, this would raise the total market value to $150,000. When total market value is divided by new total shares outstanding, a value of $75 a share is obtained. The old stockholders thus lose $25 per share, and the new stockholders have an instant profit of $25 per share. Thus, selling common stock at a price below the market value would dilute its price and transfer wealth from the present stockholders to those who were allowed to purchase the new shares. The preemptive right prevents such occurrences.

SELF-TEST QUESTIONS

Identify some actions that companies have taken to make takeovers more difficult.

What are the two primary reasons for the existence of the preemptive right?

TYPES OF COMMON STOCK

Classified Stock
Common stock that is given a special designation, such as Class A, Class B, and so forth, to meet special needs of the company.

Although most firms have only one type of common stock, in some instances **classified stock** is used to meet the special needs of the company. Generally, when special classifications are used, one type is designated *Class A*, another *Class B*, and so on. Small, new companies seeking funds from outside sources frequently use different types of common stock. For example, when Genetic Concepts went public recently, its Class A stock was sold to the public and paid a dividend, but this stock had no voting rights for five years. Its Class B stock, which was retained by the organizers of the company, had full voting rights for five years, but the legal terms stated that dividends could not be paid on the Class B stock until the company had established its earning power by building up retained earnings to a designated level. The use of classified stock thus enabled the public to take a position in a conservatively financed growth company without sacrificing income, while the founders retained absolute control during the crucial early stages of the firm's development. At the same time, outside investors were protected against excessive withdrawals of funds by the original owners. As is often the case in such situations, the Class B stock was called **founders' shares.**

Founders' Shares
Stock owned by the firm's founders that has sole voting rights but restricted dividends for a specified number of years.

Note that "Class A," "Class B," and so on, have no standard meanings. Most firms have no classified shares, but a firm that does could designate its Class B shares as founders' shares and its Class A shares as those sold to the public, while another could reverse these designations. Still other firms could use stock classifications for entirely different purposes. For example, when General Motors acquired Hughes Aircraft for $5 billion, it paid in part with a new Class H common, GMH, which had limited voting rights and whose dividends are tied to Hughes's performance as a GM subsidiary. The reasons for the new stock were reported to be (1) that GM wanted to limit voting privileges on the new classified stock because of management's concern about a possible takeover and (2) that Hughes employees wanted to be rewarded more directly on Hughes's own performance than would have been possible through regular GM stock.

GM's deal posed a problem for the NYSE, which had a rule against listing a company's common stock if the company had any nonvoting common stock outstanding. GM made it clear that it was willing to delist if the NYSE did not change its rules. The NYSE concluded that such arrangements as GM had made were logical and were likely to be made by other companies in the future, so it changed its rules to accommodate GM. In reality, though, the NYSE had little choice. In recent years, the Nasdaq market has proven that it can provide a deep, liquid market for common stocks, and the defection of GM would have hurt the NYSE much more than GM.

> ### SELF-TEST QUESTION
>
> What are some reasons why a company might use classified stock?

THE MARKET FOR COMMON STOCK

Closely Held Corporation
A corporation that is owned by a few individuals who are typically associated with the firm's management.

Publicly Owned Corporation
A corporation that is owned by a relatively large number of individuals who are not actively involved in its management.

Some companies are so small that their common stocks are not actively traded; they are owned by only a few people, usually the companies' managers. Such firms are said to be *privately owned*, or **closely held, corporations,** and their stock is called *closely held stock*. In contrast, the stocks of most larger companies are owned by a large number of investors, most of whom are not active in management. Such companies are called **publicly owned corporations,** and their stock is called *publicly held stock*.

As we saw in Chapter 4, the stocks of smaller publicly owned firms are not listed on an exchange; they trade in the over-the-counter (OTC) market, and the companies and their stocks are said to be *unlisted*. However, larger publicly owned companies generally apply for listing on physical location exchanges, and they and their stocks are said to be *listed*. Many companies are first listed on Nasdaq or on a regional exchange, such as the Pacific Coast or Midwest exchanges. Once they become large enough to be listed on the "Big Board," many, but by no means all, choose to move to the NYSE. The largest company in the world in terms of market value, Microsoft, trades on the Nasdaq market, as do most other high-tech firms.

A recent study found that institutional investors owned about 46 percent of all publicly held common stocks. Included are pension plans (26 percent), mutual funds (10 percent), foreign investors (6 percent), insurance companies (3 percent), and brokerage firms (1 percent). These institutions buy and sell relatively actively, however, so they account for about 75 percent of all transactions. Thus, institutional investors have a heavy influence on the prices of individual stocks.

TYPES OF STOCK MARKET TRANSACTIONS

We can classify stock market transactions into three distinct types:

Secondary Market
The market in which "used" stocks are traded after they have been issued by corporations.

1. *Trading in the outstanding shares of established, publicly owned companies: the secondary market.* Allied Food Products, the company we analyzed in earlier chapters, has 50 million shares of stock outstanding. If the owner of 100 shares sells his or her stock, the trade is said to have occurred in the **secondary market.**

Thus, the market for outstanding shares, or *used shares*, is the secondary market. The company receives no new money when sales occur in this market.

2. *Additional shares sold by established, publicly owned companies: the primary market.* If Allied decides to sell (or issue) an additional 1 million shares to raise new equity capital, this transaction is said to occur in the **primary market.**[2]

3. *Initial public offerings by privately held firms: the IPO market.* Several years ago, the Coors Brewing Company, which was owned by the Coors family at the time, decided to sell some stock to raise capital needed for a major expansion program.[3] This type of transaction is called **going public**— whenever stock in a closely held corporation is offered to the public for the first time, the company is said to be going public. The market for stock that is just being offered to the public is called the **initial public offering (IPO) market.**

IPOs have received a lot of attention in recent years, primarily because a number of "hot" issues have realized spectacular gains—often in the first few minutes of trading. Consider the 1999 IPO of Red Hat Inc., the open-source provider of software products and services. The company's underwriters set an offering price of $14 per share. However, because of intense demand for the issue, the stock's price rose more than 270 percent the first day of trading.

With the recent decline in the stock market, we have also seen a decline in the number of new IPOs. Table 8-1 lists the largest, the best performing, and the worst performing IPOs of 2001, and it shows how they performed from their offering dates through year-end 2001. As the table shows, not all IPOs are as well received as Red Hat's. Moreover, even if you are able to identify a "hot" issue, it is often difficult to purchase shares in the initial offering. These deals are generally *oversubscribed*, which means that the demand for shares at the offering price exceeds the number of shares issued. In such instances, investment bankers favor large institutional investors (who are their best customers), and small investors find it hard, if not impossible, to get in on the ground floor. They can buy the stock in the after-market, but evidence suggests that if you do not get in on the ground floor the average IPO underperforms the overall market over the long run.[4]

Indeed, the subsequent performance of Red Hat illustrates the risks that arise when investing in new issues. After its dramatic first day run-up, Red Hat's stock closed just above $54 per share. Demand for the stock continued to surge, and the stock's price reached a high of just over $300 in December 1999. Soon afterward, the company announced a two-for-one stock split. The split effectively cut the stock's price in half but it doubled the number of shares held by each shareholder. After adjusting for the split, the stock's price stood at $132 per share in early January 2000. However, from that point forward, Red Hat's stock

Primary Market
The market in which firms issue new securities to raise corporate capital.

Going Public
The act of selling stock to the public at large by a closely held corporation or its principal stockholders.

Initial Public Offering (IPO) Market
The market for stocks of companies that are in the process of going public.

---

[2] Allied has 60 million shares authorized but only 50 million outstanding; thus, it has 10 million authorized but unissued shares. If it had no authorized but unissued shares, management could increase the authorized shares by obtaining stockholders' approval, which would generally be granted without any arguments.

[3] The stock Coors offered to the public was designated Class B, and it was nonvoting. The Coors family retained the founders' shares, called Class A stock, which carried full voting privileges. The company was large enough to obtain an NYSE listing, but at that time the Exchange had a requirement that listed common stocks must have full voting rights, which precluded Coors from obtaining an NYSE listing.

[4] See Jay R. Ritter, "The Long-Run Performance of Initial Public Offerings," *Journal of Finance*, March 1991, Vol. 46, No. 1, 3–27.

TABLE 8-1   Initial Public Offerings in 2001

| ISSUER | ISSUE DATE | U.S. PROCEEDS (BILLIONS) | PERCENT CHANGE FROM OFFER | |
			FIRST DAY TRADING	THROUGH 12/31/01
THE BIGGEST IPOs				
Kraft Foods	6/12/01	$8.68	+0.8%	+9.0%
Agere Systems (Lucent)	3/27/01	4.14	+0.3	−6.8
Prudential Financial	12/12/01	3.48	+6.6	+19.8
KPMG Consulting	2/7/01	2.33	+30.5	−8.6
Principal Financial Group	10/22/01	2.13	+13.5	+27.1
Anthem	10/29/01	1.99	+13.6	+34.7
Accenture	7/18/01	1.90	+4.6	+83.1
Reliant Resources	4/30/01	1.79	+10.0	−45.3
Converium Holding	12/10/01	1.72	0.0	−1.7
CNOOC (China National Offshore Oil)	2/27/01	1.43	+4.7	+24.4

| ISSUER | ISSUE DATE | OFFER PRICE | U.S. PROCEEDS (MILLIONS) | PERCENT CHANGE FROM OFFER | |
				FIRST DAY TRADING	THROUGH 12/31/01
THE BEST PERFORMERS					
Verisity	3/21/01	$ 7.00	$ 26.8	+14.3%	+170.7%
Magma Design Automation	11/19/01	13.00	63.1	+46.1	+129.2
Monolithic System Technology	6/27/01	10.00	50.0	+12.2	+108.0
Williams Energy Partners	2/5/01	21.50	98.9	+11.6	+91.2
Nassda	12/12/01	11.00	55.0	+40.5	+85.6
Accenture	7/18/01	14.50	1,900.2	+4.6	+83.1
PDF Solutions	7/26/01	12.00	62.1	+26.3	+77.9
Willis Group Holdings	6/11/01	13.50	310.5	+23.0	+73.3
Select Medical	4/4/01	9.50	98.3	+6.6	+71.3
Odyssey Healthcare	10/30/01	15.00	62.1	+15.0	+68.3

| ISSUER | ISSUE DATE | OFFER PRICE | U.S. PROCEEDS (MILLIONS) | PERCENT CHANGE FROM OFFER | |
				FIRST DAY TRADING	THROUGH 12/31/01
THE WORST PERFORMERS					
Briazz	5/2/01	$ 8.00	$ 16.0	+0.4%	−88.9%
ATP Oil & Gas	2/5/01	14.00	84.0	0.0	−79.9
Investors Capital Holdings	2/8/01	8.00	8.0	−6.1	−64.9
Align Technology	1/25/01	13.00	149.5	+33.2	−64.6
Torch Offshore	6/7/01	16.00	80.0	+0.4	−62.8
Enterra (Westlinks)	1/10/01	4.50	5.2	−4.2	−60.4
Tellium	5/17/01	15.00	155.3	+39.5	−57.5
Smith & Wollensky Restaurant	5/22/01	8.50	45.0	−8.6	−55.3
General Maritime	6/12/01	18.00	144.0	−6.9	−47.2
GMX Resources	3/15/01	8.00	10.0	0.0	−46.9

SOURCE: Kate Kelly, "For IPOs, Market Conditions Go from Decent to Downright Inhospitable," *The Wall Street Journal*, January 2, 2002, R8. Reprinted by permission of *The Wall Street Journal*, Copyright © 2002 Dow Jones & Company, Inc. All Rights Reserved Worldwide.

MARTHA STEWART TAKES ON THE WWF

During the week of October 18, 1999, both Martha Stewart Living Omnimedia Inc. and the World Wrestling Federation (WWF) went public in IPOs. This created a lot of public interest, and it led to media reports comparing the two companies. Both deals attracted strong investor demand, and both were well received. In its first day of trading, WWF's stock closed above $25, an increase of nearly 49 percent above its $17 offering price. Martha Stewart did even better—it closed a little above $37, which was 105 percent above its $18 offering price. This performance led CBS MarketWatch reporter Steve Gelsi to write an online report entitled, "Martha Bodyslams the WWF!"

Both stocks generated a lot of interest, but when the hype died down, astute investors recognized that both stocks have risk. Indeed, since its IPO, WWF's stock has steadily fallen, and its price traded at $12.66 per share in July 2002. During this same time period, Martha Stewart's stock has fallen even more, hitting an all-time low of $9.60 a share in late June 2002, when federal prosecutors announced that they were investigating Martha Stewart for potential insider trading violations. So, while both stocks have stumbled, Round 2 clearly belongs to the WWF.

SOURCE: Steve Gelsi, "Martha Bodyslams the WWF," http://cbs.marketwatch.com, October 19, 1999.

has tumbled. Note that at mid-year 2002, Red Hat's price was $5.50 per share, which is equivalent to $11 per share before the split.

Lawmakers and regulators have recently begun to take a much closer look at the IPO market. They are particularly concerned about Wall Street's practice of allocating hot IPOs to the personal accounts of officers and directors of companies, in the hopes of securing these companies' investment banking business at a later date. While it is not clear if this practice is illegal, it has tarnished the reputations of several of Wall Street's leading firms including Goldman Sachs, Salomon Smith Barney, and Credit Suisse First Boston, and it may ultimately lead to additional regulations in this market.

Finally, it is important to recognize that firms can go public without raising any additional capital. For example, the Ford Motor Company was once owned exclusively by the Ford family. When Henry Ford died, he left a substantial part of his stock to the Ford Foundation. When the Foundation later sold some of this stock to the general public, the Ford Motor Company went public, even though the company raised no capital in the transaction.

SELF-TEST QUESTIONS

Differentiate between a closely held corporation and a publicly owned corporation.

Differentiate between a listed stock and an unlisted stock.

Differentiate between primary and secondary markets.

What is an IPO?

COMMON STOCK VALUATION

Common stock represents an ownership interest in a corporation, but to the typical investor, a share of common stock is simply a piece of paper characterized by two features:

1. It entitles its owner to dividends, but only if the company has earnings out of which dividends can be paid, and only if management chooses to pay dividends rather than retaining and reinvesting all the earnings. Whereas a bond contains a *promise* to pay interest, common stock provides no such promise—if you own a stock, you may *expect* a dividend, but your expectations may not in fact be met. To illustrate, Long Island Lighting Company (LILCO) had paid dividends on its common stock for more than 50 years, and people expected those dividends to continue. However, when the company encountered severe problems a few years ago, it stopped paying dividends. Note, though, that LILCO continued to pay interest on its bonds; if it had not, then it would have been declared bankrupt, and the bondholders could potentially have taken over the company.

2. Stock can be sold at some future date, hopefully at a price greater than the purchase price. If the stock is actually sold at a price above its purchase price, the investor will receive a *capital gain*. Generally, at the time people buy common stocks, they do expect to receive capital gains; otherwise, they would not purchase the stocks. However, after the fact, one can end up with capital losses rather than capital gains. LILCO's stock price dropped from $17.50 to $3.75 in one year, so the *expected* capital gain on that stock turned out to be a huge *actual* capital loss.

DEFINITIONS OF TERMS USED IN STOCK VALUATION MODELS

Common stocks provide an expected future cash flow stream, and a stock's value is found in the same manner as the values of other financial assets—namely, as the present value of the expected future cash flow stream. The expected cash flows consist of two elements: (1) the dividends expected in each year and (2) the price investors expect to receive when they sell the stock. The expected final stock price includes the return of the original investment plus an expected capital gain.

We saw in Chapter 1 that managers seek to maximize the values of their firms' stocks. A manager's actions affect both the stream of income to investors and the riskiness of that stream. Therefore, managers need to know how alternative actions are likely to affect stock prices. At this point we develop some models to help show how the value of a share of stock is determined. We begin by defining the following terms:

D_t = dividend the stockholder *expects* to receive at the end of Year t. D_0 is the most recent dividend, which has already been paid; D_1 is the first dividend expected, and it will be paid at the end of this year; D_2 is the dividend expected at the end of two years; and so forth. D_1 represents the first cash flow a

Market Price, P_0
The price at which a stock sells in the market.

Intrinsic Value, $\hat{P}_0$
The value of an asset that, in the mind of a particular investor, is justified by the facts; $\hat{P}_0$ may be different from the asset's current market price.

Growth Rate, g
The expected rate of growth in dividends per share.

Required Rate of Return, k_s
The minimum rate of return on a common stock that a stockholder considers acceptable.

Expected Rate of Return, $\hat{k}_s$
The rate of return on a common stock that a stockholder expects to receive in the future.

Actual Realized Rate of Return, $\bar{k}_s$
The rate of return on a common stock actually received by stockholders in some past period. $\bar{k}_s$ may be greater or less than $\hat{k}_s$ and/or k_s.

new purchaser of the stock will receive. Note that D_0, the dividend that has just been paid, is known with certainty. However, all future dividends are expected values, so the estimate of D_t may differ among investors.[5]

P_0 = actual **market price** of the stock today.

$\hat{P}_t$ = expected price of the stock at the end of each Year t (pronounced "P hat t"). $\hat{P}_0$ is the **intrinsic,** or *theoretical*, **value** of the stock today as seen by the particular investor doing the analysis; $\hat{P}_1$ is the price expected at the end of one year; and so on. Note that $\hat{P}_0$ is the intrinsic value of the stock today based on a particular investor's estimate of the stock's expected dividend stream and the riskiness of that stream. Hence, whereas the market price P_0 is fixed and is identical for all investors, $\hat{P}_0$ could differ among investors depending on how optimistic they are regarding the company. The caret, or "hat," is used to indicate that $\hat{P}_t$ is an estimated value. $\hat{P}_0$, the individual investor's estimate of the intrinsic value today, could be above or below P_0, the current stock price, but an investor would buy the stock only if his or her estimate of $\hat{P}_0$ were equal to or greater than P_0.

Since there are many investors in the market, there can be many values for $\hat{P}_0$. However, we can think of a group of "average," or "marginal," investors whose actions actually determine the market price. For these marginal investors, P_0 must equal $\hat{P}_0$; otherwise, a disequilibrium would exist, and buying and selling in the market would change P_0 until $P_0 = \hat{P}_0$ for the marginal investor.

g = expected **growth rate** in dividends as predicted by a marginal investor. If dividends are expected to grow at a constant rate, g is also equal to the expected rate of growth in earnings and in the stock's price. Different investors may use different g's to evaluate a firm's stock, but the market price, P_0, is set on the basis of the g estimated by marginal investors.

k_s = minimum acceptable, or **required, rate of return** on the stock, considering both its riskiness and the returns available on other investments. Again, this term generally relates to marginal investors. The determinants of k_s include the real rate of return, expected inflation, and risk, as discussed in Chapter 5.

$\hat{k}_s$ = **expected rate of return** that an investor who buys the stock expects to receive in the future. $\hat{k}_s$ (pronounced "k hat s") could be above or below k_s, but one would buy the stock only if $\hat{k}_s$ were equal to or greater than k_s.

$\bar{k}_s$ = **actual,** or **realized,** *after-the-fact* **rate of return,** pronounced "k bar s." You may *expect* to obtain a return of $\bar{k}_s =$

---

[5] Stocks generally pay dividends quarterly, so theoretically we should evaluate them on a quarterly basis. However, in stock valuation, most analysts work on an annual basis because the data generally are not precise enough to warrant refinement to a quarterly model. For additional information on the quarterly model, see Charles M. Linke and J. Kenton Zumwalt, "Estimation Biases in Discounted Cash Flow Analysis of Equity Capital Cost in Rate Regulation," *Financial Management*, Autumn 1984, 15–21.

Dividend Yield
The expected dividend divided by the current price of a share of stock.

Capital Gains Yield
The capital gain during a given year divided by the beginning price.

Expected Total Return
The sum of the expected dividend yield and the expected capital gains yield.

15 percent if you buy Exxon Mobil stock today, but if the market goes down, you may end up next year with an actual realized return that is much lower, perhaps even negative.

D_1/P_0 = expected **dividend yield** on the stock during the coming year. If the stock is expected to pay a dividend of $D_1 = \$1$ during the next 12 months, and if its current price is $P_0 = \$10$, then the expected dividend yield is $\$1/\$10 = 0.10 = 10\%$.

$\dfrac{\hat{P}_1 - P_0}{P_0}$ = expected **capital gains yield** on the stock during the coming year. If the stock sells for $10 today, and if it is expected to rise to $10.50 at the end of one year, then the expected capital gain is $\hat{P}_1 - P_0 = \$10.50 - \$10.00 = \$0.50$, and the expected capital gains yield is $\$0.50/\$10 = 0.05 = 5\%$.

Expected total return = $\hat{k}_s$ = expected dividend yield (D_1/P_0) plus expected capital gains yield $[(\hat{P}_1 - P_0)/P_0]$. In our example, the **expected total return** = $\hat{k}_s = 10\% + 5\% = 15\%$.

EXPECTED DIVIDENDS AS THE BASIS FOR STOCK VALUES

In our discussion of bonds, we found the value of a bond as the present value of interest payments over the life of the bond plus the present value of the bond's maturity (or par) value:

$$V_B = \frac{INT}{(1 + k_d)^1} + \frac{INT}{(1 + k_d)^2} + \cdots + \frac{INT}{(1 + k_d)^N} + \frac{M}{(1 + k_d)^N}.$$

Stock prices are likewise determined as the present value of a stream of cash flows, and the basic stock valuation equation is similar to the bond valuation equation. What are the cash flows that corporations provide to their stockholders? First, think of yourself as an investor who buys a stock with the intention of holding it (in your family) forever. In this case, all that you (and your heirs) will receive is a stream of dividends, and the value of the stock today is calculated as the present value of an infinite stream of dividends:

Value of stock = $\hat{P}_0$ = PV of expected future dividends

$$= \frac{D_1}{(1 + k_s)^1} + \frac{D_2}{(1 + k_s)^2} + \cdots + \frac{D_\infty}{(1 + k_s)^\infty}$$

$$= \sum_{t=1}^{\infty} \frac{D_t}{(1 + k_s)^t}. \tag{8-1}$$

What about the more typical case, where you expect to hold the stock for a finite period and then sell it—what will be the value of $\hat{P}_0$ in this case? Unless the company is likely to be liquidated or sold and thus to disappear, *the value of the stock is again determined by Equation 8-1.* To see this, recognize that for any individual investor, the expected cash flows consist of expected dividends plus the expected sale price of the stock. However, the sale price the current investor receives will depend on the dividends some future investor expects. Therefore, for all present and future investors in total, expected cash flows must be based on expected future dividends. Put another way, unless a firm is liquidated or sold to another concern, the cash flows it provides to its stockholders will consist only of a stream of dividends; therefore, the value of a share of its stock must be established as the present value of that expected dividend stream.

The general validity of Equation 8-1 can also be confirmed by asking the following question: Suppose I buy a stock and expect to hold it for one year. I will receive dividends during the year plus the value $\hat{P}_1$ when I sell out at the end of the year. But what will determine the value of $\hat{P}_1$? The answer is that it will be determined as the present value of the dividends expected during Year 2 plus the stock price at the end of that year, which, in turn, will be determined as the present value of another set of future dividends and an even more distant stock price. This process can be continued ad infinitum, and the ultimate result is Equation 8-1.[6]

SELF-TEST QUESTIONS

Explain the following statement: "Whereas a bond contains a promise to pay interest, a share of common stock typically provides an expectation of, but no promise of, dividends plus capital gains."

What are the two parts of most stocks' expected total return?

How does one calculate the capital gains yield and the dividend yield of a stock?

CONSTANT GROWTH STOCKS

Equation 8-1 is a generalized stock valuation model in the sense that the time pattern of D_t can be anything: D_t can be rising, falling, fluctuating randomly, or it can even be zero for several years and Equation 8-1 will still hold. With a computer spreadsheet we can easily use this equation to find a stock's intrinsic value for any pattern of dividends. In practice, the hard part is getting an accurate forecast of the future dividends.

In many cases, the stream of dividends is expected to grow at a constant rate. If this is the case, Equation 8-1 may be rewritten as follows:[7]

$$\hat{P}_0 = \frac{D_0(1 + g)^1}{(1 + k_s)^1} + \frac{D_0(1 + g)^2}{(1 + k_s)^2} + \cdots + \frac{D_0(1 + g)^\infty}{(1 + k_s)^\infty}$$

$$= \frac{D_0(1 + g)}{k_s - g} = \frac{D_1}{k_s - g}. \tag{8-2}$$

---

[6] We should note that investors periodically lose sight of the long-run nature of stocks as investments and forget that in order to sell a stock at a profit, one must find a buyer who will pay the higher price. If you analyze a stock's value in accordance with Equation 8-1, conclude that the stock's market price exceeds a reasonable value, and then buy the stock anyway, then you would be following the "bigger fool" theory of investment—you think that you may be a fool to buy the stock at its excessive price, but you also think that when you get ready to sell it, you can find someone who is an even bigger fool. The bigger fool theory was widely followed in the summer of 1987, just before the stock market lost more than one-third of its value in the October 1987 crash. Many people think it is back in vogue now, in 2002.

[7] The last term in Equation 8-2 is derived in the Web/CD Extension to Chapter 5 of Eugene F. Brigham and Phillip R. Daves, *Intermediate Financial Management*, 7th ed. (Cincinnati, OH: South-Western College Publishing, 2002). In essence, Equation 8-2 is the sum of a geometric progression, and the final result is the solution value of the progression.

The last term of Equation 8-2 is called the **constant growth model,** or the **Gordon model** after Myron J. Gordon, who did much to develop and popularize it.

ILLUSTRATION OF A CONSTANT GROWTH STOCK

Assume that Allied Food Products just paid a dividend of $1.15 (that is, $D_0 = \$1.15$). Its stock has a required rate of return, k_s, of 13.4 percent, and investors expect the dividend to grow at a constant 8 percent rate in the future. The estimated dividend one year hence would be $D_1 = \$1.15(1.08) = \$1.24$; D_2 would be $1.34; and the estimated dividend five years hence would be $1.69:

$$D_5 = D_0(1 + g)^5 = \$1.15(1.08)^5 = \$1.69.$$

We could use this procedure to estimate all future dividends, then use Equation 8-1 to determine the current stock value, $\hat{P}_0$. In other words, we could find each expected future dividend, calculate its present value, and then sum all the present values to find the intrinsic value of the stock.

Such a process would be time consuming, but we can take a short cut—just insert the illustrative data into Equation 8-2 to find the stock's intrinsic value, $23:

$$\hat{P}_0 = \frac{\$1.15(1.08)}{0.134 - 0.08} = \frac{\$1.242}{0.054} = \$23.00.$$

Note that a necessary condition for the derivation of Equation 8-2 is that $k_s > g$. If the equation is used in situations where k_s is not greater than g, the results will be both wrong and meaningless.

The concept underlying the valuation process for a constant growth stock is graphed in Figure 8-1. Dividends are growing at the rate g = 8%, but because $k_s > g$, the present value of each future dividend is declining. For example, the dividend in Year 1 is $D_1 = D_0(1 + g)^1 = \$1.15(1.08) = \$1.242$. However, the present value of this dividend, discounted at 13.4 percent, is $PV(D_1) = \$1.242/(1.134)^1 = \$1.095$. The dividend expected in Year 2 grows to $1.242(1.08) = $1.341, but the present value of this dividend falls to $1.043. Continuing, $D_3 = \$1.449$ and $PV(D_3) = \$0.993$, and so on. Thus, the expected dividends are growing, but the present value of each successive dividend is declining, because the dividend growth rate (8%) is less than the rate used for discounting the dividends to the present (13.4%).

If we summed the present values of each future dividend, this summation would be the value of the stock, $\hat{P}_0$. When g is a constant, this summation is equal to $D_1/(k_s - g)$, as shown in Equation 8-2. Therefore, if we extended the lower step function curve in Figure 8-1 on out to infinity and added up the present values of each future dividend, the summation would be identical to the value given by Equation 8-2, $23.00.

DIVIDEND AND EARNINGS GROWTH

Growth in dividends occurs primarily as a result of growth in *earnings per share (EPS)*. Earnings growth, in turn, results from a number of factors, including (1) inflation, (2) the amount of earnings the company retains and reinvests, and (3) the rate of return the company earns on its equity (ROE). Regarding inflation, if output (in

FIGURE 8-1

Present Values of Dividends of a Constant Growth Stock where $D_0 = \$1.15$, $g = 8\%$, $k_s = 13.4\%$

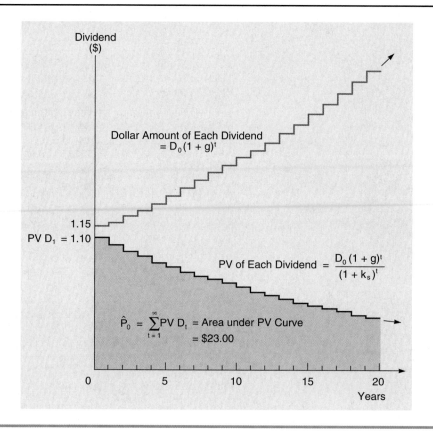

Dividend ($)

Dollar Amount of Each Dividend
$= D_0(1 + g)^t$

1.15

$PV\ D_1 = 1.10$

PV of Each Dividend $= \dfrac{D_0(1 + g)^t}{(1 + k_s)^t}$

$\hat{P}_0 = \displaystyle\sum_{t=1}^{\infty} PV\ D_t = $ Area under PV Curve
$= \$23.00$

0   5   10   15   20

Years

units) is stable, but both sales prices and input costs rise at the inflation rate, then EPS will also grow at the inflation rate. Even without inflation, EPS will also grow as a result of the reinvestment, or plowback, of earnings. If the firm's earnings are not all paid out as dividends (that is, if some fraction of earnings is retained), the dollars of investment behind each share will rise over time, which should lead to growth in earnings and dividends.

Even though a stock's value is derived from expected dividends, this does not necessarily mean that corporations can increase their stock prices by simply raising the current dividend. Shareholders care about *all* dividends, both current and those expected in the future. Moreover, there is a trade-off between current dividends and future dividends. Companies that pay high current dividends necessarily retain and reinvest less of their earnings in the business, and that reduces future earnings and dividends. So, the issue is this: Do shareholders prefer higher current dividends at the cost of lower future dividends, the reverse, or are stockholders indifferent? As we will see in the chapter on distributions to shareholders, there is no simple answer to this question. Shareholders prefer to have the company retain earnings, hence pay less current dividends, if it has highly profitable investment opportunities, but they want the company to pay earnings out if investment opportunities are poor. Taxes also play a role—since dividends and capital gains are taxed differently, dividend policy affects investors' taxes. We will consider dividend policy in detail later in Part 5 of this text.

WHEN CAN THE CONSTANT GROWTH MODEL BE USED?

The constant growth model is often appropriate for mature companies with a stable history of growth. Expected growth rates vary somewhat among companies, but dividend growth for most mature firms is generally expected to continue in the future at about the same rate as nominal gross domestic product (real GDP plus inflation). On this basis, one might expect the dividends of an average, or "normal," company to grow at a rate of 5 to 8 percent a year.

Zero Growth Stock
A common stock whose future dividends are not expected to grow at all; that is, g = 0.

Note too that Equation 8-2 is sufficiently general to handle the case of a **zero growth stock,** where the dividend is expected to remain constant over time. If g = 0, Equation 8-2 reduces to Equation 8-3:

$$\hat{P}_0 = \frac{D}{k_s}. \tag{8-3}$$

This is essentially the same equation as the one we developed in Chapter 6 for a perpetuity, and it is simply the dividend divided by the discount rate.

SELF-TEST QUESTIONS

Write out and explain the valuation formula for a constant growth stock.

Explain how the formula for a zero growth stock is related to that for a constant growth stock.

EXPECTED RATE OF RETURN ON A CONSTANT GROWTH STOCK

We can solve Equation 8-2 for k_s, again using the hat to indicate that we are dealing with an expected rate of return:[8]

$$
\begin{array}{ccc}
\text{Expected rate} & \text{Expected} & \text{Expected growth} \\
\text{of return} & = \text{dividend} + & \text{rate, or capital} \\
 & \text{yield} & \text{gains yield}
\end{array}
$$

$$\hat{k}_s = \frac{D_1}{P_0} + g. \tag{8-4}$$

---

[8] The k_s value in Equation 8-2 is a *required* rate of return, but when we transform to obtain Equation 8-4, we are finding an *expected* rate of return. Obviously, the transformation requires that $k_s = \hat{k}_s$. This equality holds if the stock market is in equilibrium, a condition that will be discussed later in the chapter.

OTHER APPROACHES TO VALUING COMMON STOCKS

While the dividend growth and the corporate value models presented in this chapter are the most widely used methods for valuing common stocks, they are by no means the only approaches. Analysts often use a number of different techniques to value stocks. Two of these alternative approaches are described below.

THE P/E MULTIPLE APPROACH

Investors have long looked for simple rules of thumb to determine whether a stock is fairly valued. One such approach is to look at the stock's price-to-earnings (P/E) ratio. Recall from Chapter 3 that a company's P/E ratio shows how much investors are willing to pay for each dollar of reported earnings. As a starting point, you might conclude that stocks with low P/E ratios are undervalued, since their price is "low" given current earnings, while stocks with high P/E ratios are overvalued.

Unfortunately, however, valuing stocks is not that simple. We should not expect all companies to have the same P/E ratio. P/E ratios are affected by risk — investors discount the earnings of riskier stocks at a higher rate. Thus, all else equal, riskier stocks should have lower P/E ratios. In addition, when you buy a stock, you not only have a claim on current earnings — you

also have a claim on all future earnings. All else equal, companies with stronger growth opportunities will generate larger future earnings and thus should trade at higher P/E ratios. Therefore, Microsoft is not necessarily overvalued just because its P/E ratio is 36 at a time when the median firm has a P/E of 18. Investors believe that Microsoft's growth potential is well above average. Whether the stock's future prospects justify its P/E ratio remains to be seen, but in and of itself a high P/E ratio does not mean that a stock is overvalued.

Nevertheless, P/E ratios can provide a useful starting point in stock valuation. If a stock's P/E ratio is well above its industry average, and if the stock's growth potential and risk are similar to other firms in the industry, this may indicate that the stock's price is too high. Likewise, if a company's P/E ratio falls well below its historical average, this may signal that the stock is undervalued — particularly if the company's growth prospects and risk are unchanged, and if the overall P/E for the market has remained constant or increased.

One obvious drawback of the P/E approach is that it depends on reported accounting earnings. For this reason, some analysts choose to rely on other multiples to value stocks. For example, some analysts look at a company's price-to-cash-flow ratio, while others look at the price-to-sales ratio.

Thus, if you buy a stock for a price $P_0 = \$23$, and if you expect the stock to pay a dividend $D_1 = \$1.242$ one year from now and to grow at a constant rate $g = 8\%$ in the future, then your expected rate of return will be 13.4 percent:

$$\hat{k}_s = \frac{\$1.242}{\$23} + 8\% = 5.4\% + 8\% = 13.4\%.$$

In this form, we see that $\hat{k}_s$ is the *expected total return* and that it consists of an *expected dividend yield*, $D_1/P_0 = 5.4\%$, plus an *expected growth rate or capital gains yield*, $g = 8\%$.

Suppose this analysis had been conducted on January 1, 2003, so $P_0 = \$23$ is the January 1, 2003, stock price, and $D_1 = \$1.242$ is the dividend expected at the end of 2003. What is the expected stock price at the end of 2003? We would again apply Equation 8-2, but this time we would use the year-end dividend, $D_2 = D_1 (1 + g) = \$1.242(1.08) = \$1.3414$:

$$\hat{P}_{12/31/03} = \frac{D_{2004}}{k_s - g} = \frac{\$1.3414}{0.134 - 0.08} = \$24.84.$$

Now, notice that $24.84 is 8 percent greater than P_0, the $23 price on January 1, 2003:

$$\$23(1.08) = \$24.84.$$

THE EVA APPROACH

In recent years, analysts have looked for more rigorous alternatives to the dividend growth model. More than a quarter of all stocks listed on the NYSE pay no dividends. This proportion is even higher on Nasdaq. While the dividend growth model can still be used for these stocks (see additional Industry Practice box, "Evaluating Stocks That Don't Pay Dividends"), this approach requires that analysts forecast when the stock will begin paying dividends, what the dividend will be once it is established, and the future dividend growth rate. In many cases, these forecasts contain considerable errors.

An alternative approach is based on the concept of economic value added (EVA), which we discussed back in Chapter 2. Also, recall from the Industry Practice box in Chapter 3 entitled, "EVA and ROE," that EVA can be written as:

$$\left(\frac{\text{Equity}}{\text{Capital}}\right)\left(\text{ROE} - \frac{\text{Cost of}}{\text{Equity Capital}}\right).$$

This equation suggests that companies can increase their EVA by investing in projects that provide shareholders with returns that are above their cost of capital, which is the return they could expect to earn on alternative investments with the same level of risk. When you buy stock in a company, you receive more than just the book value of equity—you also receive a claim on all future value that is created by the firm's managers (the present value of all future EVAs). It follows that a company's market value of equity can be written as:

$$\frac{\text{Market Value}}{\text{of Equity}} = \frac{\text{Book}}{\text{Value}} + \frac{\text{PV of all}}{\text{future EVAs}}.$$

We can find the "fundamental" value of the stock, P_0, by simply dividing the above expression by the number of shares outstanding.

As is the case with the dividend growth model, we can simplify the above expression by assuming that at some point in time annual EVA becomes a perpetuity, or grows at some constant rate over time.[a]

---

[a] What we have presented here is a simplified version of what is often referred to as the Edwards-Bell-Ohlson (EBO) model. For a more complete description of this technique and an excellent summary of how it can be used in practice, take a look at the article, "Measuring Wealth," by Charles M.C. Lee in *CA Magazine*, April 1996, 32–37.

Thus, we would expect to make a capital gain of $24.84 - $23.00 = 1.84 during 2003, which would provide a capital gains yield of 8 percent:

$$\text{Capital gains yield}_{2003} = \frac{\text{Capital gain}}{\text{Beginning price}} = \frac{\$1.84}{\$23.00} = 0.08 = 8\%.$$

We could extend the analysis on out, and in each future year the expected capital gains yield would always equal g, the expected dividend growth rate.

Continuing, the dividend yield in 2004 could be estimated as follows:

$$\text{Dividend yield}_{2004} = \frac{\text{D}_{2004}}{\hat{\text{P}}_{12/31/03}} = \frac{\$1.3414}{\$24.84} = 0.054 = 5.4\%.$$

The dividend yield for 2005 could also be calculated, and again it would be 5.4 percent. Thus, *for a constant growth stock*, the following conditions must hold:

 The popular Motley Fool web site **http:// www.fool.com/ school/introductiontovaluation. htm** provides a good description of some of the benefits and drawbacks of a few of the more commonly used valuation procedures.

1. The dividend is expected to grow forever at a constant rate, g.
2. The stock price is expected to grow at this same rate.
3. The expected dividend yield is a constant.
4. The expected capital gains yield is also a constant, and it is equal to g.
5. The expected total rate of return, $\hat{\text{k}}$, is equal to the expected dividend yield plus the expected growth rate: $\hat{\text{k}} = $ dividend yield $+$ g.

The term *expected* should be clarified — it means expected in a probabilistic sense, as the "statistically expected" outcome. Thus, if we say the growth rate is expected to remain constant at 8 percent, we mean that the best prediction for the growth rate in any future year is 8 percent, not that we literally expect the growth rate to be exactly 8 percent in each future year. In this sense, the constant growth assumption is a reasonable one for many large, mature companies.

SELF-TEST QUESTIONS

What conditions must hold if a stock is to be evaluated using the constant growth model?

What does the term "expected" mean when we say expected growth rate?

VALUING STOCKS THAT HAVE A NONCONSTANT GROWTH RATE

Supernormal (Nonconstant) Growth
The part of the firm's life cycle in which it grows much faster than the economy as a whole.

For many companies, it is inappropriate to assume that dividends will grow at a constant rate. Firms typically go through *life cycles*. During the early part of their lives, their growth is much faster than that of the economy as a whole; then they match the economy's growth; and finally their growth is slower than that of the economy.[9] Automobile manufacturers in the 1920s, computer software firms such as Microsoft in the 1990s, and Internet firms such as AOL in the late 1990s are examples of firms in the early part of the cycle; these firms are called **supernormal**, or **nonconstant, growth** firms. Figure 8-2 illustrates nonconstant growth and also compares it with normal growth, zero growth, and negative growth.[10]

In the figure, the dividends of the supernormal growth firm are expected to grow at a 30 percent rate for three years, after which the growth rate is expected to fall to 8 percent, the assumed average for the economy. The value of this firm, like any other, is the present value of its expected future dividends as determined by Equation 8-1. In the case in which D_t is growing at a constant rate, we simplified Equation 8-1 to $\hat{P}_0 = D_1/(k_s - g)$. In the supernormal case, however, the expected growth rate is not a constant — it declines at the end of the period of supernormal growth.

---

[9] The concept of life cycles could be broadened to *product cycle*, which would include both small startup companies and large companies like Procter & Gamble, which periodically introduce new products that give sales and earnings a boost. We should also mention *business cycles*, which alternately depress and boost sales and profits. The growth rate just after a major new product has been introduced, or just after a firm emerges from the depths of a recession, is likely to be much higher than the "expected long-run average growth rate," which is the proper number for a DCF analysis.

[10] A negative growth rate indicates a declining company. A mining company whose profits are falling because of a declining ore body is an example. Someone buying such a company would expect its earnings, and consequently its dividends and stock price, to decline each year, and this would lead to capital losses rather than capital gains. Obviously, a declining company's stock price will be relatively low, and its dividend yield must be high enough to offset the expected capital loss and still produce a competitive total return. Students sometimes argue that they would never be willing to buy a stock whose price was expected to decline. However, if the annual dividends are large enough to *more than offset* the falling stock price, the stock could still provide a good return.

FIGURE 8-2   Illustrative Dividend Growth Rates

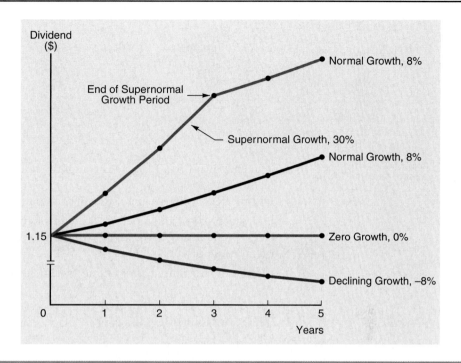

Because Equation 8-2 requires a constant growth rate, we obviously cannot use it to value stocks that have nonconstant growth. However, assuming that a company currently enjoying supernormal growth will eventually slow down and become a constant growth stock, we can combine Equations 8-1 and 8-2 to form a new formula, Equation 8-5, for valuing it. First, we assume that the dividend will grow at a nonconstant rate (generally a relatively high rate) for N periods, after which it will grow at a constant rate, g. N is often called the **terminal date,** or **horizon date.**

Terminal Date (Horizon Date)
The date when the growth rate becomes constant. At this date it is no longer necessary to forecast the individual dividends.

We can use the constant growth formula, Equation 8-2, to determine what the stock's **horizon,** or **terminal, value** will be N periods from today:

$$\text{Horizon value} = \hat{P}_N = \frac{D_{N+1}}{k_s - g}.$$

Horizon (Terminal) Value
The value at the horizon date of all dividends expected thereafter.

The stock's intrinsic value today, $\hat{P}_0$, is the present value of the dividends during the nonconstant growth period plus the present value of the horizon value:

$$\hat{P}_0 = \frac{D_1}{(1+k_s)^1} + \frac{D_2}{(1+k_s)^2} + \cdots + \frac{D_N}{(1+k_s)^N} + \frac{D_{N+1}}{(1+k_s)^{N+1}} + \cdots + \frac{D_\infty}{(1+k_s)^\infty}.$$

PV of dividends during the nonconstant growth period
$t = 1, \cdots N$

PV of dividends during the nonconstant growth period
$t = N + 1, \cdots \infty$

$$\hat{P}_0 = \underbrace{\frac{D_1}{(1 + k_s)^1} + \frac{D_2}{(1 + k_s)^2} + \cdots + \frac{D_N}{(1 + k_s)^N}}_{\substack{\text{PV of dividends during the} \\ \text{nonconstant growth period} \\ t = 1, \ldots N}} + \underbrace{\frac{\hat{P}_N}{(1 + k_s)^N}}_{\substack{\text{PV of horizon} \\ \text{value, } \hat{P}_N: \\ \frac{[(D_{N+1})/(k_s - g)]}{(1 + k_s)^N}}}. \qquad (8\text{-}5)$$

To implement Equation 8-5, we go through the following three steps:

1. Find the PV of the dividends during the period of nonconstant growth.
2. Find the price of the stock at the end of the nonconstant growth period, at which point it has become a constant growth stock, and discount this price back to the present.
3. Add these two components to find the intrinsic value of the stock, $\hat{P}_0$.

Figure 8-3 can be used to illustrate the process for valuing nonconstant growth stocks. Here we assume the following five facts exist:

k_s = stockholders' required rate of return = 13.4%. This rate is used to discount the cash flows.

N = years of supernormal growth = 3.

g_s = rate of growth in both earnings and dividends during the supernormal growth period = 30%. This rate is shown directly on the time line. (Note: The growth rate during the supernormal growth period could vary from year to year. Also, there could be several different supernormal growth periods, e.g., 30% for three years, then 20% for three years, and then a constant 8%.)

g_n = rate of normal, constant growth after the supernormal period = 8%. This rate is also shown on the time line, between Periods 3 and 4.

D_0 = last dividend the company paid = $1.15.

The valuation process as diagrammed in Figure 8-3 is explained in the steps set forth below the time line. The value of the supernormal growth stock is calculated to be $39.21.

SELF-TEST QUESTIONS

Explain how one would find the value of a supernormal growth stock.

Explain what is meant by "terminal (horizon) date" and "horizon (terminal) value."

FIGURE 8-3

Process for Finding the Value of a Supernormal Growth Stock

NOTES TO FIGURE 8-3:

Step 1. Calculate the dividends expected at the end of each year during the supernormal growth period. Calculate the first dividend, $D_1 = D_0(1 + g_s) = \$1.15(1.30) = \$1.4950$. Here g_s is the growth rate during the three-year supernormal growth period, 30 percent. Show the $1.4950 on the time line as the cash flow at Time 1. Then, calculate $D_2 = D_1(1 + g_s) = \$1.4950(1.30) = \$1.9435$, and then $D_3 = D_2(1 + g_s) = \$1.9435(1.30) = \$2.5266$. Show these values on the time line as the cash flows at Time 2 and Time 3. Note that D_0 is used only to calculate D_1.

Step 2. The price of the stock is the PV of dividends from Time 1 to infinity, so in theory we could project each future dividend, with the normal growth rate, $g_n = 8\%$, used to calculate D_4 and subsequent dividends. However, we know that after D_3 has been paid, which is at Time 3, the stock becomes a constant growth stock. Therefore, we can use the constant growth formula to find $\hat{P}_3$, which is the PV of the dividends from Time 4 to infinity as evaluated at Time 3.

First, we determine $D_4 = \$2.5266(1.08) = \$2.7287$ for use in the formula, and then we calculate $\hat{P}_3$ as follows:

$$\hat{P}_3 = \frac{D_4}{k_s - g_n} = \frac{\$2.7287}{0.134 - 0.08} = \$50.5310.$$

We show this $50.5310 on the time line as a second cash flow at Time 3. The $50.5310 is a Time 3 cash flow in the sense that the owner of the stock could sell it for $50.5310 at Time 3 and also in the sense that $50.5310 is the present value of the dividend cash flows from Time 4 to infinity. Note that the total cash flow at Time 3 consists of the sum of $D_3 + \hat{P}_3 = \$2.5266 + \$50.5310 = \$53.0576$.

Step 3. Now that the cash flows have been placed on the time line, we can discount each cash flow at the required rate of return, $k_s = 13.4\%$. We could discount each cash flow by dividing by $(1.134)^t$, where $t = 1$ for Time 1, $t = 2$ for Time 2, and $t = 3$ for Time 3. This produces the PVs shown to the left below the time line, and the sum of the PVs is the value of the supernormal growth stock, $39.21.

With a financial calculator, you can find the PV of the cash flows as shown on the time line with the cash flow (CFLO) register of your calculator. Enter 0 for CF_0 because you get no cash flow at Time 0, $CF_1 = 1.495$, $CF_2 = 1.9435$, and $CF_3 = 2.5266 + 50.5310 = 53.0576$. Then enter I = 13.4, and press the NPV key to find the value of the stock, $39.21.

VALUING THE ENTIRE CORPORATION

In the previous sections, we presented several equations for valuing a firm's common stock. These equations had one common element: They all assumed that the firm is currently paying a dividend. But consider the situation of a startup company formed to develop and market a new product. Such a company generally expects to have low sales during its first few years as it develops and begins to market its product. Then, if the product catches on, sales will grow rapidly for several years. For example, Compaq Computer had just three employees when it was founded in 1982. Its first year was devoted to product development, so 1982 sales were zero. In early 1983, however, Compaq introduced its personal computer, and its 1983 sales hit $111 million, a record first-year volume for any new firm. Two years later, Compaq was included in *Fortune*'s 500 largest U.S. industrial firms. Obviously, Compaq was more successful than most new businesses, but growth rates of 100, 500, or even 1,000 percent are not uncommon during a firm's early years.

Growing sales require additional assets—Compaq could not have grown as it did without increasing its assets. Moreover, asset growth must be financed by increasing some liability and/or equity account. Small firms can often obtain some bank credit, but they must maintain a reasonable balance between debt and equity. Thus, additional bank borrowings require increases in equity, but small firms have limited access to the stock market. Moreover, even if they can sell stock, their owners are often reluctant to do so for fear of losing voting control. Therefore, the best source of equity for most small businesses is from retaining earnings, so most small firms pay no dividends during their rapid growth years. Eventually, most successful firms do pay dividends, with dividends growing rapidly at first but then slowing down as the firm approaches maturity.

Although most larger firms do pay a dividend, some firms, even highly profitable ones such as Microsoft, have never paid a dividend. How can the value of such a company be determined? Similarly, suppose you start a business, and someone offers to buy it from you. How could you determine its value, or that of any privately held business? Or suppose you work for a company with a number of divisions. How could you determine the value of one particular division that the company wants to sell? In none of these cases could you use the dividend growth model. However, you could use the **total company,** or **corporate value, model.**

Total Company (Corporate Value) Model
A valuation model used as an alternative to the dividend growth model to determine the value of a firm, especially one that does not pay dividends or is privately held. This model discounts a firm's free cash flows at the WACC to determine its value.

Note too that the value of its stock is directly linked to a firm's total value. In the next section, we find the total value of the firm and then subtract the market value of the debt and preferred stock. We are then left with the total value of the common equity. We then divide by the number of shares outstanding to obtain an estimate of the value per share. That estimate should, in theory, be identical to the share value found using the discounted dividend model described earlier in the chapter.

While the total company model generally requires more data than the discounted dividend model, these data are often more reliable, particularly for companies that do not pay dividends and where future dividends are especially difficult to predict.

THE CORPORATE VALUE MODEL

In Chapter 2 we explained that a firm's value is determined by its ability to generate cash flow, both now and in the future. Therefore, the market value of any company can be expressed as follows:

Market value of company $= V_{Company} =$ PV of expected future free cash flows

$$= \frac{FCF_1}{(1 + WACC)^1} + \frac{FCF_2}{(1 + WACC)^2} + \cdots + \frac{FCF_\infty}{(1 + WACC)^\infty}. \quad (8\text{-}6)$$

Now recall from Chapter 2 that free cash flow represents the cash generated in a given year minus the cash needed to finance the capital expenditures and operating working capital needed to support future growth. More specifically, we showed that free cash flow (FCF) can be expressed as follows:

$$FCF = NOPAT - \text{Net new investment in operating capital.}$$

The value of the firm is the present value of its future FCF. This question arises: Given the projected FCF, at what rate should those flows be discounted to find the value of the firm? Note first that free cash flow is the cash generated *before making any payments to common or preferred stockholders, or to bondholders, so it is the cash flow that is available to all investors.* Therefore, the FCF should be discounted at the company's weighted average cost of debt, preferred stock, and common stock, or the WACC.

To find a firm's value, we proceed as follows:

1. Assume that the firm will experience nonconstant growth for N years, after which it will grow at some constant rate.
2. Calculate the expected free cash flow (FCF) for each of the N nonconstant growth years, and find the PV of these cash flows.
3. Recognize that after Year N growth will be constant. Therefore, we can use the constant growth formula to find the firm's value at Year N. This "terminal value" is the sum of the PVs of the FCFs for N + 1 and all subsequent years, discounted back to Year N. Then, the Year N value must be discounted back to the present to find its PV at Year 0.
4. Now sum all the PVs, those of the annual free cash flows during the nonconstant period plus the PV of the terminal value, to find the firm's value.

Table 8-2 illustrates the free cash flow approach to estimating Allied Food's total corporate value. The figures represented in this valuation model are the product of an independent stock analyst. This analyst has reviewed Allied's financial statements, visited Allied's facilities, spoken to Allied's key personnel, and spoken to key figures outside the firm. On the basis of all the information gathered by this analyst, she has constructed the valuation model for Allied Food Products that is outlined in Table 8-2.

In her model, the analyst assumes that Allied's free cash flow will grow at a nonconstant rate for five years, after which time the company's free cash flow will grow at a constant rate of 7 percent a year. To construct her estimates of free cash flow for the first five years, she begins by forecasting the annual growth rate in sales. In its own internal forecast, Allied's managers expect Allied's sales to grow 10 percent in 2003 to $3.3 billion. We see in Table 8-2 that this independent analyst also expects sales to increase by 10 percent in 2003. Looking further ahead, this analyst believes that Allied's sales will continue to grow, but at a slower rate—more specifically, she forecasts that annual sales growth will fall to 9 percent in 2004 through 2006 and then decline to 8 percent in 2007.

In addition to her sales forecast, the analyst has also forecasted that Allied's after-tax operating margin (NOPAT/Sales) will be 6.5 percent for 2004 through 2007. This forecasted margin exceeds the current operating margin, but the analyst believes that this is sustainable because of anticipated improvements in operating efficiency and favorable market conditions. The forecasted level of NOPAT for each year is obtained by simply multiplying the forecasted sales level by the forecasted after-tax operating margin. Note that while the analyst has assumed a constant operating margin for 2004 through 2007, the valuation model is flexible enough to allow for annual variations.

Next the analyst considers Allied's use of operating capital. Recall the free cash flow formula requires net capital expenditures and changes in operating working capital to be subtracted from NOPAT. The analyst has lumped these two variables into one category called net operating capital expenditures. In her valuation, the analyst assumes that operating capital will grow at 5 percent annually through 2005

	A	B	C	D	E	F	G	H
263								
264	(Time Line of Annual Free Cash Flows - millions of dollars)							
265					Years			
266				1	2	3	4	5
267	Key Input Data			2003	2004	2005	2006	2007
268	Sales growth rate			10.0%	9.0%	9.0%	9.0%	8.0%
269	After-tax operating margin				6.5%	6.5%	6.5%	6.5%
270	Operating capital growth rate				5.0%	5.0%	4.0%	4.0%
271	WACC			10%				
272	Tax rate			40%				
273	Long-run FCF growth rate			7.0%				
274								
275	*Free Cash Flows (Years 1-5)*							
276	Sales			$3,300.0	$3,597.0	$3,920.7	$4,273.6	$4,615.5
277	NOPAT			187.3	233.8	254.8	277.8	300.0
278	Net operating capital expenditures			180.0	189.0	198.5	206.4	214.6
279	FCF			$7.3	$44.8	$56.4	$71.4	$85.4
280	PV of FCFs			$6.6	$37.0	$42.4	$48.8	$53.0
281								
282	*Terminal Year Firm Value*							
283	Free Cash Flow - Year 6			$91.3		$TV_5 =$	FCF_6	
284	TV of Firm - Year 5			$3,044.6			WACC - g	
285	PV of Firm Terminal Value			$1,890.5				
286								
287	*Calculation of Firm Intrinsic Value*							
288	PV of FCFs (Years 1-5)			$187.8				
289	PV of Firm TV			$1,890.5				
290	Total corporate value			$2,078.3				
291	Less: MV of debt and pref			$904.0				
292	Value of common equity			$1,174.3				
293	Shares outstanding (millions)			50.0				
294	ESTIMATE OF STOCK PRICE			$23.49				
295								

and then will decline to 4 percent in 2006 and 2007. After 2007, the analyst believes that Allied's nonconstant growth pattern will cease and will be replaced by a long-run constant growth pattern that will enable free cash flow to grow by 7 percent per year.

In order to estimate the present value of the free cash flows, the analyst also needs to estimate the company's weighted average cost of capital (WACC). In Chapter 9, we will explain how to calculate the WACC, but for now just assume that Allied's WACC is 10 percent.

When we discount the first five free cash flows at 10 percent and sum them, we see that the present value of the free cash flows during the nonconstant growth period is $187.8 million. Next, we find the value of all the free cash flows beyond the nonconstant growth period, using a constant growth formula, just as we did with the supernormal growth stock in the previous section. This is the firm's value at Year N. It is called the terminal value, and it is calculated as follows:

$$\text{Terminal value} = V_{\text{Company at } t = N} = FCF_{N+1}/(WACC - g_{FCF}). \quad (8\text{-}7)$$

Here g_{FCF} is the constant rate at which free cash flows are expected to grow after Year N. For Allied, the nonconstant growth period is five years, so $N = 5$, and the constant growth rate for Year 6 and thereafter is 7 percent. As we see in Table 8-2, Allied's terminal value is \$3,044.6 million. Note, though, that this is the value at the end of Year 5, so to find its value today we must discount this terminal value back for five years at the WACC. As Table 8-2 shows, the present value of the terminal value is \$1,890.5 million. When we add this number to the \$187.8 million calculated earlier for the present value of the free cash flows during the nonconstant growth period, we find Allied's total corporate value to be \$2,078.3 million.

If Allied's total value on December 31, 2002, is \$2,078.3 million, what is the value of its common equity? First, note that notes payable and long-term debt total \$110 + \$754 = \$864 million, and these securities have first claim on assets and income. (Accounts payable and accruals were netted out earlier in the calculation of free cash flow.) Next, the preferred stock has a claim of \$40 million, and it also ranks above common stock.[11] Therefore, the value left for common stockholders is \$2,078.3 − \$864 − \$40 = \$1,174.3 million. As a final step, we divide the value of the common equity by the 50 million shares outstanding to obtain the value per share: \$1,174.3/50 = \$23.49.

COMPARING THE TOTAL COMPANY AND DIVIDEND GROWTH MODELS

In principle, we should find the same intrinsic value for a stock using the total company model or the dividend growth model. In our Allied example, the estimates were close but not exactly the same—the dividend growth model predicted a price of \$23.00 per share versus \$23.49 using the total company model. Note too that both models' estimates were close to Allied's actual \$23 stock price.

It is important to realize that stock value estimates are very sensitive to the assumptions used to generate them. This valuation model is very sensitive to the inputs used. For example, if the long-run constant growth rate for free cash flow was determined to be 6 percent (instead of 7 percent), the stock price estimate would change to \$13.77. By contrast, if the long-run growth rate was 8 percent, the predicted stock price would be \$42.92. (Note: You can use the spreadsheet model, 08MODEL.xls, that accompanies this chapter to verify all of these numbers.) For this reason, stock price valuations are heavily dependent on the analyst's inputs. Moreover, opinions about the value of a firm's stock price can vary widely amongst analysts.

In practice, the estimates of intrinsic value will often deviate considerably from the actual stock price. Such deviations occur because the forecaster's assumptions are different from those of the marginal investor in the marketplace. If the assumptions we used—about the initial cash flows, the long-term growth rate, the years before normal growth begins, and the WACC—differ from those of "the market," then the forecasted value will be above or below the actual price. The calculated value will be above the market price if the forecaster is more optimistic and below if he or she is less optimistic. If the forecaster has made the better assumptions, then eventually the market price will move toward the calculated value. If the analyst is wrong, convergence will not occur. It is dangerous to bet against the market, because "the market"

---

[11] For our purposes here, we are assuming that the market and book values are the same for both long-term debt and preferred stock. If market conditions significantly changed after these securities were originally issued, the market and book values would be different. In that situation, we would use the market value of long-term debt and preferred stock.

reflects the judgments of millions of investors, some of whom may have better information than we do. However, if the analyst really can make a better-than-average forecast, then he or she can do well in the market.

Given all of this, does it matter whether you use the total company model or the dividend growth model to value stocks? Generally it does. For example, if you were a financial analyst estimating the values of mature companies whose dividends are expected to grow steadily in the future, it would probably be more efficient to use the dividend growth model. Here you would only need to estimate the growth rate in dividends, not the entire set of pro forma financial statements.

However, if a company is paying a dividend but is still in the high-growth stage of its life cycle, you would need to project the future financial statements before you could make a reasonable estimate of future dividends. Then, since you would have already estimated future financial statements, it would be a toss-up as to whether the total company model or the dividend growth model would be easier to apply. Intel, which pays a dividend of 8 cents versus earnings of about $0.65, is an example of a company where either model could be used.

Now suppose you were trying to estimate the value of a company that has never paid a dividend, such as Microsoft, or a new firm that is about to go public, or a division that GE or some other large company is planning to sell. In all of these situations, you would have no choice: You would have to estimate future financial statements and use the total company value model.

Actually, even if a company is paying steady dividends, much can be learned from the corporate value model, so analysts today use it for all types of valuations. The process of projecting future financial statements can reveal quite a bit about the company's operations and financing needs. Also, such an analysis can provide insights into actions that might be taken to increase the company's value, as we discuss later in the financial planning and forecasting chapter.

SELF-TEST QUESTIONS

Write out the equation for the corporate value model, and explain what it does.

Why might someone use the corporate model even though the dividend model could be used?

What are the steps for finding a firm's total value?

Why might the calculated intrinsic stock value differ from the stock's current market price? Which would be "correct"? What does "correct" mean?

STOCK MARKET EQUILIBRIUM

Recall that k_X, the required return on Stock X, can be found using the Security Market Line (SML) equation as it was developed in our discussion of the Capital Asset Pricing Model (CAPM) back in Chapter 5:

$$k_X = k_{RF} + (k_M - k_{RF}) b_X.$$

EVALUATING STOCKS THAT DON'T PAY DIVIDENDS

The dividend growth model presented in the chapter assumed that the firm is currently paying a dividend. However, many firms, even highly profitable ones, such as Microsoft, have never paid a dividend. If a firm is expected to begin paying dividends in the future, we can modify the equations presented in the chapter and use them to determine the value of the stock.

A new business often expects to have low sales during its first few years of operation as it develops its product. Then, if the product catches on, sales will grow rapidly for several years. Sales growth brings with it the need for additional assets—a firm cannot increase sales without also increasing its assets, and asset growth requires an increase in liability and/or equity accounts. Small firms can generally obtain some bank credit, but they must maintain a reasonable balance between debt and equity. Thus, additional bank borrowings require increases in equity, and getting the equity capital needed to support growth can be difficult for small firms. They have limited access to the capital markets, and, even when they can sell common stock, their owners are reluctant to do so for fear of losing voting control. Therefore, the best source of equity for most small businesses is retained earnings, and for this reason most small firms pay no dividends during their rapid growth years. Eventually, though, successful small firms do pay dividends, and those dividends generally grow rapidly at first but slow down to a sustainable constant rate once the firm reaches maturity.

If a firm currently pays no dividend but is expected to pay dividends in the future, the value of its stock can be found as follows:

1. Estimate when dividends will be paid, the amount of the first dividend, the growth rate during the supernormal growth period, the length of the supernormal period, the long-run (constant) growth rate, and the rate of return required by investors.
2. Use the constant growth model to determine the price of the stock after the firm reaches a stable growth situation.
3. Set out on a time line the cash flows (dividends during the supernormal growth period and the stock price once the constant growth state is reached), and then find the present value of these cash flows. That present value represents the value of the stock today.

To illustrate this process, consider the situation for Marvel-Lure Inc., a company that was set up in 2001 to produce and market a new high-tech fishing lure. MarvelLure's sales are currently growing at a rate of 200 percent per year. The company expects to experience a high but declining rate of growth in sales and earnings during the next 10 years, after which analysts estimate that it will grow at a steady 10 percent per year. The firm's management has announced that it will pay no dividends for five years, but if earnings materialize as forecasted, it will pay a dividend of $0.20 per share at the end of Year 6, $0.30 in Year 7, $0.40 in Year 8, $0.45 in Year 9, and $0.50 in Year 10. After Year 10, current plans are to increase the dividend by 10 percent per year.

MarvelLure's investment bankers estimate that investors require a 15 percent return on similar stocks. Therefore, we find the value of a share of MarvelLure's stock as follows:

$$P_0 = \frac{\$0}{(1.15)^1} + \cdots + \frac{\$0}{(1.15)^5}$$
$$+ \frac{\$0.20}{(1.15)^6} + \frac{\$0.30}{(1.15)^7}$$
$$+ \frac{\$0.40}{(1.15)^8} + \frac{\$0.45}{(1.15)^9} + \frac{\$0.50}{(1.15)^{10}}$$
$$+ \left(\frac{\$0.50(1.10)}{0.15 - 0.10}\right)\left(\frac{1}{(1.15)^{10}}\right)$$
$$= \$3.30.$$

The last term finds the expected price of the stock in Year 10 and then finds the present value of that price. Thus, we see that the dividend growth model can be applied to firms that currently pay no dividends, provided we can estimate future dividends with a fair degree of confidence. However, in many cases one can have more confidence in the forecasts of free cash flows, and in these situations it is better to use the corporate model.

If the risk-free rate of return is 8 percent, the required return on an average stock is 12 percent, and Stock X has a beta of 2, then the marginal investor will require a return of 16 percent on Stock X:

$$k_X = 8\% + (12\% - 8\%)\,2.0$$
$$= 16\%.$$

This 16 percent required return is shown as the point on the SML in Figure 8-4 associated with beta = 2.0.

Marginal Investor
A representative investor whose actions reflect the beliefs of those people who are currently trading a stock. It is the marginal investor who determines a stock's price.

The **marginal investor** will want to buy Stock X if its expected rate of return is more than 16 percent, will want to sell it if the expected rate of return is less than 16 percent, and will be indifferent, hence will hold but not buy or sell, if the expected rate of return is exactly 16 percent. Now suppose the investor's portfolio contains Stock X, and he or she analyzes the stock's prospects and concludes that its earnings, dividends, and price can be expected to grow at a constant rate of 5 percent per year. The last dividend was $D_0 = \$2.8571$, so the next expected dividend is

$$D_1 = \$2.8571(1.05) = \$3.$$

Our marginal investor observes that the present price of the stock, P_0, is $30. Should he or she purchase more of Stock X, sell the stock, or maintain the present position?

The investor can calculate Stock X's *expected rate of return* as follows:

$$\hat{k}_X = \frac{D_1}{P_0} + g = \frac{\$3}{\$30} + 5\% = 15\%.$$

This value is plotted on Figure 8-4 as Point X, which is below the SML. Because the expected rate of return is less than the required return, this marginal investor would want to sell the stock, as would most other holders. However, few people would want to buy at the $30 price, so the present owners would be unable to find buyers unless they cut the price of the stock. Thus, the price would decline, and this decline would continue until the stock's price reached $27.27, at which point the market for this security would be in **equilibrium,** defined as the price at which the expected rate of return, 16 percent, is equal to the required rate of return:

Equilibrium
The condition under which the expected return on a security is just equal to its required return, $\hat{k} = k$. Also, $\hat{P} = P_0$, and the price is stable.

$$\hat{k}_X = \frac{\$3}{\$27.27} + 5\% = 11\% + 5\% = 16\% = k_X.$$

FIGURE 8-4   **Expected and Required Returns on Stock X**

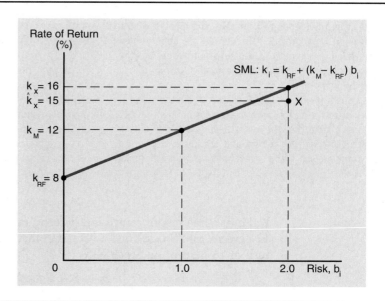

Had the stock initially sold for less than $27.27, say, at $25, events would have been reversed. Investors would have wanted to buy the stock because its expected rate of return would have exceeded its required rate of return, and buy orders would have driven the stock's price up to $27.27.

To summarize, in equilibrium two related conditions must hold:

1. A stock's expected rate of return as seen by the marginal investor must equal its required rate of return: $\hat{k}_i = k_i$.

2. The actual market price of the stock must equal its intrinsic value as estimated by the marginal investor: $P_0 = \hat{P}_0$.

Of course, some individual investors may believe that $\hat{k}_i > k_i$ and $\hat{P}_0 > P_0$, hence they would invest most of their funds in the stock, while other investors may have an opposite view and would sell all of their shares. However, it is the marginal investor who establishes the actual market price, and for this investor, we must have $\hat{k}_i = k_i$ and $P_0 = \hat{P}_0$. If these conditions do not hold, trading will occur until they do hold.

CHANGES IN EQUILIBRIUM STOCK PRICES

Stock prices are not constant—they undergo violent changes at times. For example, on October 19, 1987, the Dow Jones average dropped 508 points, and the average stock lost about 23 percent of its value on that one day. Some individual stocks lost more than 70 percent of their value. More recently, on October 27, 1997, the Dow Jones Industrials fell 554 points, which at the time was a 7.18 percent drop in value. To see how such changes can occur, assume that Stock X is in equilibrium, selling at a price of $27.27 per share. If all expectations were exactly met, during the next year the price would gradually rise to $28.63, or by 5 percent. However, many different events could occur to cause a change in the equilibrium price of the stock. To illustrate, consider again the set of inputs used to develop Stock X's price of $27.27, along with a new set of assumed input variables:

	VARIABLE VALUE	
	ORIGINAL	NEW
Risk-free rate, k_{RF}	8%	7%
Market risk premium, $k_M - k_{RF}$	4%	3%
Stock X's beta coefficient, b_X	2.0	1.0
Stock X's expected growth rate, g_X	5%	6%
D_0	$2.8571	$2.8571
Price of Stock X	$27.27	?

Now give yourself a test: How would the change in each variable, by itself, affect the price, and what is your guess as to the new stock price?

Every change, taken alone, would lead to an *increase* in the price. The first three changes all lower k_X, which declines from 16 to 10 percent:

$$\text{Original } k_x = 8\% + 4\%(2.0) = 16\%.$$

$$\text{New } k_x = 7\% + 3\%(1.0) = 10\%.$$

Using these values, together with the new g value, we find that $\hat{P}_0$ rises from $27.27 to $75.71.[12]

$$\text{Original } \hat{P}_0 = \frac{\$2.8571(1.05)}{0.16 - 0.05} = \frac{\$3}{0.11} = \$27.27.$$

$$\text{New } \hat{P}_0 = \frac{\$2.8571(1.06)}{0.10 - 0.06} = \frac{\$3.0285}{0.04} = \$75.71.$$

At the new price, the expected and required rates of return will be equal:[13]

$$\hat{k}_X = \frac{\$3.0285}{\$75.71} + 6\% = 10\% = k_X.$$

Evidence suggests that stocks, especially those of large companies, adjust rapidly to disequilibrium situations. Consequently, equilibrium ordinarily exists for any given stock, and required and expected returns are generally equal. Stock prices certainly change, sometimes violently and rapidly, but this simply reflects changing conditions and expectations. There are, of course, times when a stock continues to react for several months to favorable or unfavorable developments, but this does not signify a long adjustment period; rather, it simply indicates that as more new pieces of information about the situation become available, the market adjusts to them. The ability of the market to adjust to new information is discussed in the next section.

THE EFFICIENT MARKETS HYPOTHESIS

Efficient Markets Hypothesis (EMH)
The hypothesis that securities are typically in equilibrium—that they are fairly priced in the sense that the price reflects all publicly available information on each security.

A body of theory called the **Efficient Markets Hypothesis (EMH)** holds (1) that stocks are always in equilibrium and (2) that it is impossible for an investor to consistently "beat the market." Essentially, those who believe in the EMH note that there are 100,000 or so full-time, highly trained, professional analysts and traders operating in the market, while there are fewer than 3,000 major stocks. Therefore, if each analyst followed 30 stocks (which is about right, as analysts tend to specialize in the stocks in a specific industry), there would on average be 1,000 analysts following each stock. Further, these analysts work for organizations such as Goldman Sachs, Merrill Lynch, Prudential Insurance, and the like, which have billions of dollars available with which to take advantage of bargains. In addition, as a result of SEC disclosure requirements and electronic information networks, as new information about a stock becomes available, these 1,000 analysts generally receive and evaluate it at about the same time. Therefore, the price of a stock will adjust almost immediately to any new development.

---

[12] A price change of this magnitude is by no means rare. The prices of *many* stocks double or halve during a year. For example, during 2001, Lowe's Companies Inc., which operates a chain of building materials and home improvement superstores in 40 states, increased in value by 108.58 percent. On the other hand, Enron Corporation, once one of the world's largest integrated natural gas and electricity companies, declined by 99.28 percent.

[13] It should be obvious by now that *actual realized* rates of return are not necessarily equal to expected and required returns. Thus, an investor might have *expected* to receive a return of 15 percent if he or she had bought Enron or Lowe's stock in 2001, but, after the fact, the realized return on Lowe's was far above 15 percent, whereas that on Enron was far below.

LEVELS OF MARKET EFFICIENCY

If markets are efficient, stock prices will rapidly reflect all available information. This raises an important question: What types of information are available and, therefore, incorporated into stock prices? Financial theorists have discussed three forms, or levels, of market efficiency.

Weak-Form Efficiency

The *weak form* of the EMH states that all information contained in past price movements is fully reflected in current market prices. If this were true, then information about recent trends in stock prices would be of no use in selecting stocks—the fact that a stock has risen for the past three days, for example, would give us no useful clues as to what it will do today or tomorrow. People who believe that weak-form efficiency exists also believe that "tape watchers" and "chartists" are wasting their time.[14]

For example, after studying the past history of the stock market, a chartist might "discover" the following pattern: If a stock falls three consecutive days, its price typically rises 10 percent the following day. The technician would then conclude that investors could make money by purchasing a stock whose price has fallen three consecutive days.

But if this pattern truly existed, wouldn't other investors also discover it, and if so, why would anyone be willing to sell a stock after it had fallen three consecutive days if he or she knows the stock's price is expected to increase by 10 percent the next day? In other words, if a stock is selling at $40 per share after falling three consecutive days, why would investors sell the stock if they expected it to rise to $44 per share one day later? Those who believe in weak-form efficiency argue that if the stock would really rise to $44 per share tomorrow, its price *today* would actually rise to somewhere near $44 per share immediately, thereby eliminating the trading opportunity. Consequently, weak-form efficiency implies that any information that comes from past stock prices is rapidly incorporated into the current stock price.

Semistrong-Form Efficiency

The *semistrong form* of the EMH states that current market prices reflect all *publicly available* information. Therefore, if semistrong-form efficiency exists, it would do no good to pore over annual reports or other published data because market prices would have adjusted to any good or bad news contained in such reports back when the news came out. With semistrong-form efficiency, investors should expect to earn the returns predicted by the SML, but they should not expect to do any better unless they have good luck or information that is not publicly available. However, insiders (for example, the presidents of companies) who have information that is not publicly available can earn abnormal returns (returns higher than those predicted by the SML) even under semistrong-form efficiency.

Another implication of semistrong-form efficiency is that whenever information is released to the public, stock prices will respond only if the information is different from what had been expected. If, for example, a company announces a 30 percent

---

[14] Tape watchers are people who watch the NYSE tape, while chartists plot past patterns of stock price movements. Both are called "technicians," and both believe that they can tell if something is happening to the stock that will cause its price to move up or down in the near future.

increase in earnings, and if that increase is about what analysts had been expecting, the announcement should have little or no effect on the company's stock price. On the other hand, the stock price would probably fall if analysts had expected earnings to increase by more than 30 percent, but it probably would rise if they had expected a smaller increase.

Strong-Form Efficiency

The *strong form* of the EMH states that current market prices reflect all pertinent information, whether publicly available or privately held. If this form holds, even insiders would find it impossible to earn abnormal returns in the stock market.[15]

Many empirical studies have been conducted to test for the three forms of market efficiency. Most of these studies suggest that the stock market is indeed highly efficient in the weak form and reasonably efficient in the semistrong form, at least for the larger and more widely followed stocks. However, the strong-form EMH does not hold, so abnormal profits can be made by those who possess inside information.

IMPLICATIONS OF MARKET EFFICIENCY

If the EMH is correct, it would be a waste of time for most of us to seek bargains by analyzing stocks. That follows because, if stock prices already reflect all publicly available information and hence are fairly priced, one can "beat the market" only by luck, making it difficult, if not impossible, for anyone to consistently outperform the market averages. To support this viewpoint, efficient market proponents often point out that even the professionals who manage mutual fund portfolios cannot, on average, outperform the overall stock market.[16] Indeed, the relatively poor performance of actively managed mutual funds helps explain the growing popularity of low-cost indexed funds. Rather than spending time and money to find undervalued stocks, index funds try instead only to match overall market returns by buying the basket of stocks that make up a particular index, such as the S&P 500.[17]

---

[15] Over the years, several cases of illegal insider trading have made the news headlines. These cases involved employees of several major investment banking houses and even an employee of the SEC. In the most famous case, Ivan Boesky admitted to making $50 million by purchasing stocks of firms he knew were about to merge. He went to jail, and he had to pay a large fine, but he helped disprove the strong-form EMH.

[16] For a discussion of the recent performance of actively managed funds, see Jonathan Clements, "Resisting the Lure of Managed Funds," *The Wall Street Journal*, February 27, 2001, C1.

[17] We should also note that some Wall Street pros have consistently beaten the market over many years, which is inconsistent with the EMH. An interesting article in the April 3, 1995, issue of *Fortune* (Terence P. Paré, "Yes, You Can Beat the Market") argued strongly against the EMH. Paré suggested that each stock has a fundamental value, but when good or bad news about it is announced, most investors fail to interpret this news correctly. As a result, stocks are generally priced above or below their long-term values.

Think of a graph with stock price on the vertical axis and years on the horizontal axis. A stock's fundamental value might be moving up steadily over time as it retains and reinvests earnings. However, its actual price might fluctuate about the intrinsic value line, overreacting to good or bad news and indicating departures from equilibrium. Successful value investors, according to the article, use fundamental analysis to identify stocks' intrinsic values, and then they buy stocks that are undervalued and sell those that are overvalued.

Paré's argument implies that the market is systematically out of equilibrium and that investors can act on this knowledge to beat the market. That position may turn out to be correct, but it may also be that the superior performance Paré noted simply demonstrates that some people are better at obtaining and interpreting information than others, or have been lucky in the past.

It is important to understand that even if markets are efficient, this does not mean that investors should assume that since all stocks are fairly priced it is all right to just randomly select stocks for their portfolio. Keep in mind that the principles of diversification, which were mentioned in Chapter 5, still apply. Investors should still make sure that they are holding a diversified portfolio of stocks across various industries if they want to maximize their long-run risk-adjusted returns.

Moreover, it is also important to understand that market efficiency does not imply that all stocks are always priced correctly. With hindsight, we can see that at any point in time some stocks are overvalued while others are undervalued. However, it is hard to know which stocks are in each category. The Efficient Markets Hypothesis implies that no simple trading rules based on publicly available data can be used to consistently beat the market. To beat the market, one must have above-average information, above-average skill in evaluating stocks, or above-average luck.

IS THE STOCK MARKET EFFICIENT?

Over the past 25 years, many empirical studies have been conducted to test the validity of the three forms of market efficiency. Up until about 10 years ago, most of these studies suggested that the stock market was highly efficient in the weak form and reasonably efficient in the semistrong form, at least for the larger and more widely followed stocks. However, most evidence also suggested that the strong form of the EMH did not hold, because those who possessed inside information could and did (illegally) make abnormal profits.

More recently, the empirical support for the EMH has been somewhat diminished. Skeptics point to the recent stock market bubble and suggest that at the height of the boom, the prices of many companies (particularly in the technology sector) vastly exceeded their intrinsic values. These skeptics suggest that investors are not simply machines that rationally process all available information—rather, a variety of psychological and perhaps irrational factors also come into play. Indeed, researchers in the area of **behavioral finance** have begun to incorporate elements of cognitive psychology in an effort to better understand how individuals and entire markets respond to different circumstances.[18]

Behavioral Finance
Incorporates elements of cognitive psychology into finance in an effort to better understand how individuals and entire markets respond to different circumstances.

Keep in mind that the EMH does not assume that all investors are rational. Rather, it assumes that whenever stock prices deviate from their intrinsic values due to the availability of new information, investors will quickly take advantage of these mispricings by buying undervalued stocks and selling overvalued stocks. Thus, investors' actions work to drive prices to their equilibrium level. Critics of the EMH stress, however, that the stock market is inherently risky and that rational investors trading in an irrational market can lose a lot of money even if they are ultimately proven to be correct. For example, a "rational" investor in mid-1999 might have concluded that the Nasdaq was overvalued when it was trading at 3,000. If that investor had acted on that assumption, he or she would have lost a lot of money the following year when the Nasdaq soared to over 5,000 as "irrational exuberance" pushed the

---

[18] Three noteworthy sources for students interested in behavioral finance are Richard H. Thaler, Editor, *Advances in Behavioral Finance* (New York: Russell Sage Foundation, 1993); Andrei Shleifer, *Inefficient Markets: An Introduction to Behavioral Finance* (New York: Oxford University Press, 2000); and Nicholas Barberis and Richard Thaler, "A Survey of Behavioral Finance," a National Bureau of Economic Research working paper, forthcoming in the *Handbook of the Economics of Finance*, edited by George Constantinides, Milt Harris, and Rene Stulz, part of the Handbooks in Economics Series, Elsevier/North-Holland. Students interested in learning more about the Efficient Markets Hypothesis should consult Burton G. Malkiel, *A Random Walk Down Wall Street* (New York: W.W. Norton & Company, 1999).

prices of already overvalued stocks to even higher levels. Ultimately, if our "rational investor" had the courage and patience to hold on, he or she would have been vindicated, because the Nasdaq subsequently fell to about 1,300.

The events of recent years, and the new ideas developed by researchers in behavioral finance, indicate that the stock market is not always efficient. Still, the logic behind the EMH is compelling, and most researchers believe that markets are generally efficient in the long run. Thus, for our purposes, it is generally safe to assume that $\hat{k} = k$, that $\hat{P}_0 = P_0$, and that stocks plot on the SML.

SELF-TEST QUESTIONS

For a stock to be in equilibrium, what two conditions must hold?

If a stock is not in equilibrium, explain how financial markets adjust to bring it into equilibrium.

What is the Efficient Markets Hypothesis (EMH)?

What is the difference among the three forms of the EMH: (1) weak form, (2) semistrong form, and (3) strong form?

What are the implications of the EMH for financial decisions?

ACTUAL STOCK PRICES AND RETURNS

Our discussion thus far has focused on *expected* stock prices and *expected* rates of return. Anyone who has ever invested in the stock market knows that there can be, and there generally are, large differences between *expected* and *realized* prices and returns.

Figure 8-5 shows how the market value of a portfolio of stocks has moved in recent years, and Figure 8-6 shows how total realized returns on the portfolio have varied from year to year. The market trend has been strongly up, but it has gone up in some years and down in others and the stocks of individual companies have likewise gone up and down.[19] We know from theory that expected returns, as estimated by a marginal investor, are always positive, but in some years, as Figure 8-6 shows, actual returns are negative. Of course, even in bad years some individual companies do well, so "the name of the game" in security analysis is to pick the winners. Financial managers attempt to take actions that will put their companies into the winners' column, but they don't always succeed. In subsequent chapters, we will examine the actions that managers can take to increase the odds of their firms doing relatively well in the marketplace.

 global

INVESTING IN INTERNATIONAL STOCKS

As noted in Chapter 5, the U.S. stock market amounts to only 40 percent of the world stock market, and this is prompting many U.S. investors to hold at least some foreign stocks. Analysts have long touted the benefits of investing overseas, arguing that foreign stocks both improve diversification and provide good growth opportunities. For example, after the U.S. stock market rose an average of 17.5 percent a year during the 1980s, many analysts thought that the U.S. market in the 1990s was due for a correction, and they suggested that investors should increase their holdings of foreign stocks.

To the surprise of many, however, U.S. stocks outperformed foreign stocks in the 1990s—they gained about 15 percent a year versus only 3 percent for foreign stocks. Figure 8-7 shows how stocks in different countries performed in 2001. The number to the left below the country's name indicates how stocks in each country performed in terms of its local currency, while the numbers to the right show how the country's stocks performed in terms of the U.S. dollar. For example, in 2001 South African stocks rose by 18.81 percent, but the South African rand declined almost 44 percent versus the U.S. dollar. Therefore, if U.S. investors had bought South African stocks, they would have made 18.81 percent in South African rand terms, but those South African rands would have bought 44 percent fewer U.S. dollars, so the effective return would have been −24.81 percent. So, the results of foreign investments depend in part on what happens to the exchange rate. Indeed, when you invest overseas, you are making two bets: (1) that foreign stocks will increase in their local markets and (2) that the currencies in which you will be paid will rise relative to the dollar.

Although U.S. stocks have generally outperformed foreign stocks in recent years, this by no means suggests that investors should avoid foreign stocks. Foreign investments still improve diversification, and it is inevitable that there will be years when foreign stocks outperform domestic stocks. When this occurs, U.S. investors will be glad they put some of their money in overseas markets.

---

[19] If we constructed graphs like Figures 8-5 and 8-6 for individual stocks rather than for a large portfolio, far greater variability would be shown. Also, if we constructed a graph like Figure 8-6 for bonds, it would have the same general shape, but the bars would be smaller, indicating that gains and losses on bonds are generally smaller than those on stocks. Above-average bond returns occur in years when interest rates decline, and losses occur when interest rates rise sharply.

FIGURE 8-5   S&P 500 Index, 1968–2001

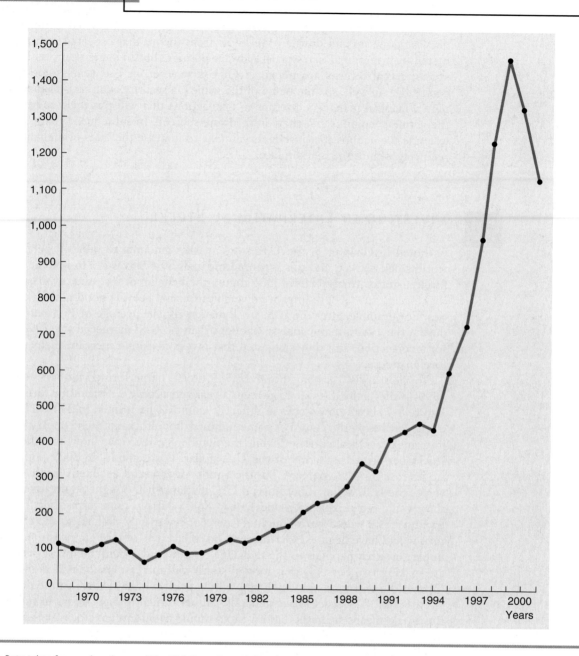

SOURCE: Data taken from various issues of *The Wall Street Journal*, "Stock Market Data Bank" and "Market Boxscore" sections.

STOCK MARKET REPORTING

Figure 8-8, taken from a daily newspaper, is a section of the stock market page for stocks listed on the NYSE. For each stock, the NYSE report provides specific data on the trading that took place the prior day. Similar information is available for stocks listed on the Nasdaq and other exchanges.

FIGURE 8-6

S&P 500 Index, Total Returns: Dividend Yield + Capital Gain or Loss, 1968–2001

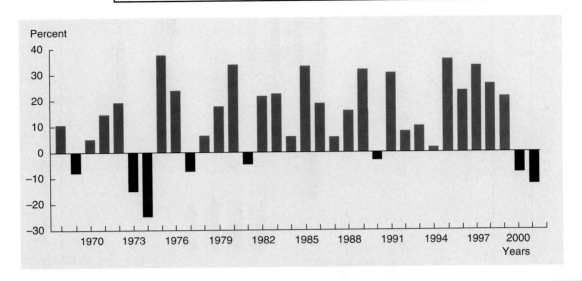

SOURCE: Data taken from various issues of *The Wall Street Journal*, "Investment Scoreboard" section.

Stocks are listed alphabetically, from AAR Industries to Zimmer; the data in Figure 8-8 were taken from the top of the listing. We will examine the data for Abbott Laboratories, AbbotLab, shown toward the bottom of the table. The first column shows the year-to-date percentage change in stock price; Abbot Labs' stock price has declined 39.2 percent over the last year. The next two columns on the left show the highest and lowest prices at which the stock has sold during the past year; Abbott Labs has traded in the range from $35.25 to $58.00 during the preceding 52 weeks. The figure just to the right of the company's ticker symbol is the dividend; Abbott Labs had a current indicated annual dividend rate of $0.94 per share and a dividend yield (which is the current dividend divided by the closing stock price) of 2.8 percent. Next comes the ratio of the stock's price to its last 12 months' earnings (the P/E ratio); Abbot Labs' P/E ratio is 20. The next number is the volume of trading for the day: 8,630,300 shares of Abbott Labs stock were traded on July 10, 2002. Following the volume comes the closing price. On July 10, Abbott Labs' last trade was at $33.90. The last column gives the change from the closing price on the previous day. Abbott Labs' closing price was down $1.51 from the previous day's closing price.

SELF-TEST QUESTIONS

Explain why expected, required, and realized returns are often different.

What are the key benefits of adding foreign stocks to a portfolio?

When a U.S. investor purchases foreign stocks, what two things is he or she hoping will happen?

FIGURE 8-7

2001 Performance of the Dow Jones Global Stock Indexes

SOURCE: Craig Karmin, "World Markets Stumble, Leaving Investors Cautious," *The Wall Street Journal*, January 2, 2002, R21. Reprinted by permission of *The Wall Street Journal*, Copyright © 2002 Dow Jones & Company, Inc. All Rights Reserved Worldwide.

FIGURE 8-8   Stock Market Transactions, July 10, 2002

Wednesday, July 10, 2002

A

YTD % CHG	52-WEEK HI	LO	STOCK (SYM)	DIV	YLD %	PE	VOL 100s	CLOSE	NET CHG
−7.3	17.45	6.96	AAR **AIR**	.10	1.2	dd	2665	8.35	−0.24
8.2	19.75	12.48	ABM Ind **ABM** s	.36	2.1	25	704	16.96	−0.52
5.2	20.44	14.20	ABN Am ADS **ABN**	.80e	4.7	...	2074	17.12	−0.38
−30.8	44.98	18.10♣	ACE Ltd **ACE**	.68f	2.4	dd	19490	27.80	−1.95
−76.0	44.50	3.40♣	AES Cp **AES**	...	...	7	19290	3.92	0.14
−50.9	69.20	11.20	AES Tr x	3.38	19.9	...	1609	17	0.09
20.8	33.15	23	AFLAC **AFL**	.24f	.8	23	17296	29.66	−0.94
20.7	23.70	8.19	AGCO Cp **AG**	.04	.2	50	4740	19.04	−0.08
−5.7	24.50	18.95	AGL Res **ATG**	1.08	5.0	...	1948	21.71	−0.41
9.5	14.50	9.52	AgSvcAm **ASV**	...	...	11	5	12.05	0.02
15.4	52.56	35.02	AIPC **PLB**	...	...	25	2563	48.52	−0.37
1.1	14.85	7.50♣	AK Steel **AKS**	j	...	dd	6485	11.50	−0.19
9.2	31.10	23.08♣	AMB Prop **AMB**	1.64	5.8	22	8894	28.40	...
−11.9	7.50	5.30	AMCOL **ACO**	.08f	1.3	18	44	6.34	−0.21
−0.8	26.98	22.30	AMLI Rsdntl **AML**	1.92	7.7	12	171	25.03	−0.17
−35.7	38.40	14.05	AMR **AMR**	stk	...	dd	10240	14.33	−0.37
−59.2	51.75	12.04	AOL Time **AOL**	...	...	dd	249320	13.11	−0.88

⋮

34.0	28.49	14.45	AaronRent **RNT**	.04	.2	40	188	21.85	0.29
−6.5	14.20	6.10	ABB ADS **ABB**	...	...	...	169	8.80	−0.23
0.6	25.12	23.70	AbbeyNtl **SUA**	1.75	7.0	...	143	24.92	−0.06
1.4	25.90	24.30	AbeyNtl ADS **ANBB** n	1.53e	6.0	...	197	25.55	0.08
1.2	25.80	24.10	AbeyNtl 7 1/4% **SUD**	1.81	7.2	...	48	25.20	−0.05
0.6	25.75	24.12	AbeyNtl nts **SXA** n	1.97	7.8	...	227	25.26	−0.16
−39.2	58	35.25	AbbottLab **ABT**	.94	2.8	20	86303	33.90	−1.51
−5.7	42.75	16.21	Abercrombie A **ANF**	...	...	15	13256	25.01	−1.25
21.2	9.63	6.06	Abitibi g **ABY**	.40g	...	...	2569	8.87	−0.24
22.8	8.65	5.80♣	AcadiaRlty **AKR**	.52	6.7	15	457	7.80	−0.28
−43.4	30.50	11.61	**Accenture ACN** n	...	...	...	75092	15.25	−1.35
−29.3	6.05	3.25♣	AcceptIns **AIF**	...	...	dd	30	3.60	0.01
−23.6	51.99	14.75	**ActionPerf ATN**	...	...	11	8995	23.40	−2.60
13.4	46.15	17.25	Actuant A **ATU**	...	...	21	623	38.09	−0.41
36.0	19.40	10.70	Acuity Br **AYI** n	.45e	2.7	...	397	16.45	−0.65
−4.8	16.95	7.30	Adecco **ADO**	.15e	1.1	...	150	12.85	−0.37
−64.6	36.48	8.30	Administaff **ASF**	...	...	31	1934	9.71	−0.25

NOTES: A "pf" following a stock name tells us that this one is a preferred stock rather than a common stock. A "▲" preceding the first column indicates that the price hit a new 52-week high, whereas a "▼" indicates a new 52-week low. An "x" after the stock's ticker symbol indicates that the stock went ex-dividend that day; this means that someone who buys the stock will not receive the next dividend. An "s" after the stock's ticker symbol indicates that the stock was split within the past 52 weeks. (See the chapter on dividends later in the text for a discussion of stock splits.) An "n" after the stock's ticker symbol indicates that the stock is newly issued within the past 52 weeks. An "f" following the dividend column indicates that the annual dividend was increased on the last declaration date. An "e" following the dividend column indicates that a dividend was declared or paid in the preceding 12 months, but there is no regular dividend rate. A "p" following the dividend column indicates this is an initial dividend and no dividend yield has been calculated. Other dividend indicators are also occasionally used. Finally, a "club" appearing before the company name indicates that *Journal* readers can obtain a copy of the company's annual report.

SOURCE: *The Wall Street Journal*, July 11, 2002; C3. Reprinted by permission of *The Wall Street Journal*, Copyright © 2002 Dow Jones & Company, Inc. All Rights Reserved Worldwide.

PREFERRED STOCK

Preferred stock is a *hybrid*—it is similar to bonds in some respects and to common stock in others. The hybrid nature of preferred stock becomes apparent when we try to classify it in relation to bonds and common stock. Like bonds, preferred stock has

INVESTING IN EMERGING MARKETS

Given the possibilities of better diversification and higher returns, U.S. investors have been putting more and more money into foreign stocks. While most investors limit their foreign holdings to developed countries such as Japan, Germany, Canada, and the United Kingdom, some have broadened their portfolios to include emerging markets such as South Korea, Mexico, Singapore, Taiwan, and Russia.

Emerging markets provide opportunities for larger returns, but they also entail greater risks. For example, Russian stocks rose more than 150 percent in the first half of 1996, as it became apparent that Boris Yeltsin would be reelected president. By contrast, if you had invested in Taiwanese stocks, you would have lost 30 percent in 1995—a year in which most stock markets performed extremely well. More recently, rapidly declining currency values caused many Asian markets to fall more than 30 percent in 1997.

Stocks in emerging markets are intriguing for two reasons. First, developing nations have the greatest potential for growth. Second, while stock returns in developed countries often move in sync with one another, stocks in emerging markets march to their own drummers. Therefore, the correlation between U.S. stocks and those in emerging markets are generally lower than between U.S. stocks and those of other developed countries. Thus, correlation data suggest that emerging markets improve the diversification of U.S. investors' portfolios. (Recall from Chapter 5 that the lower the correlation, the better the diversification.)

On the other hand, stocks in emerging markets are often extremely risky, they are less liquid, they involve higher transaction costs, and most U.S. investors do not have ready access to information on the companies involved. To reduce these problems, mutual fund companies have created country funds, which invest in "baskets of stocks," for many emerging nations. Country funds avoid the problem of picking individual stocks, but as many investors have discovered recently, country funds do little to protect you in situations like the recent decline in Asian stock markets. There the entire market has fallen by more than 10 percent in a single day.

---

a par value and a fixed amount of dividends that must be paid before dividends can be paid on the common stock. However, if the preferred dividend is not earned, the directors can omit (or "pass") it without throwing the company into bankruptcy. So, although preferred stock has a fixed payment like bonds, a failure to make this payment will not lead to bankruptcy.

As noted above, a preferred stock entitles its owners to regular, fixed dividend payments. If the payments last forever, the issue is a perpetuity whose value, V_p, is found as follows:

$$V_p = \frac{D_p}{k_p}. \tag{8-8}$$

V_p is the value of the preferred stock, D_p is the preferred dividend, and k_p is the required rate of return. Allied Food Products has preferred stock outstanding that pays a dividend of $10 per year. If the required rate of return on this preferred stock is 10 percent, then its value is $100, found by solving Equation 8-8 as follows:

$$V_p = \frac{\$10.00}{0.10} = \$100.00.$$

In equilibrium the expected return, $\hat{k}_p$, is equal to the required return, k_p. Thus, if we know the current price of a preferred stock and its dividend, we can solve for the expected rate of return as follows:

$$\hat{k}_p = \frac{D_p}{V_p}. \tag{8-8a}$$

Some preferred stocks have a stated maturity date, say, 50 years. If Allied's preferred matured in 50 years, paid a $10 annual dividend, and had a required return of 8 percent, then we could find its price as follows: Enter N = 50, I = 8, PMT = 10, and FV = 100. Then press PV to find the price, V_p = $124.47. If k = I = 10%, change I = 8 to I = 10, and find V_p = PV = $100. If you know the price of a share of preferred stock, you can solve for I to find the expected rate of return, $\hat{k}_p$.

Most preferred stocks pay dividends quarterly. This is true for Allied Food, so we could find the effective rate of return on its preferred stock (perpetual or maturing) as follows:

$$\text{EFF\%} = \text{EAR}_p = \left(1 + \frac{k_{\text{Nom}}}{m}\right)^m - 1 = \left(1 + \frac{0.10}{4}\right)^4 - 1 = 10.38\%.$$

If an investor wanted to compare the returns on Allied's bonds and its preferred stock, it would be best to convert the nominal rates on each security to effective rates and then compare these "equivalent annual rates."

SELF-TEST QUESTIONS

Explain the following statement: "Preferred stock is a hybrid security."

Is the equation used to value preferred stock more like the one used to evaluate a bond or the one used to evaluate a "normal" common stock?

TYING IT ALL TOGETHER

Corporate decisions should be analyzed in terms of how alternative courses of action are likely to affect a firm's value. However, it is necessary to know how stock prices are established before attempting to measure how a given decision will affect a specific firm's value. This chapter showed how stock values are determined, and also how investors estimate the rates of return they expect to earn. The key concepts covered are summarized below.

- A **proxy** is a document that gives one person the power to act for another, typically the power to vote shares of common stock. A **proxy fight** occurs when an outside group solicits stockholders' proxies in an effort to vote a new management team into office.
- A **takeover** occurs when a person or group succeeds in ousting a firm's management and takes control of the company.
- Stockholders often have the right to purchase any additional shares sold by the firm. This right, called the **preemptive right,** protects the control of the present stockholders and prevents dilution of their stock's value.
- A **closely held corporation** is one that is owned by a few individuals who are typically associated with the firm's management.

- A **publicly owned corporation** is one that is owned by a relatively large number of individuals who are not actively involved in its management.

- Whenever stock in a closely held corporation is offered to the public for the first time, the company is said to be **going public.** The market for stock that is just being offered to the public is called the **initial public offering (IPO) market.**

- The **value of a share of stock** is calculated as the **present value of the stream of dividends** the stock is expected to provide in the future.

- The equation used to find the **value of a constant growth stock** is:

$$\hat{P}_0 = \frac{D_1}{k_s - g}.$$

- The **expected total rate of return** from a stock consists of an **expected dividend yield** plus an **expected capital gains yield.** For a constant growth firm, both the expected dividend yield and the expected capital gains yield are constant.

- The equation for $\hat{k}_s$, the **expected rate of return on a constant growth stock,** can be expressed as follows:

$$\hat{k}_s = \frac{D_1}{P_0} + g.$$

- A **zero growth stock** is one whose future dividends are not expected to grow at all, while a **supernormal growth stock** is one whose earnings and dividends are expected to grow much faster than the economy as a whole over some specified time period and then to grow at the "normal" rate.

- To find the **present value of a supernormal growth stock,** (1) find the dividends expected during the supernormal growth period, (2) find the price of the stock at the end of the supernormal growth period, (3) discount the dividends and the projected price back to the present, and (4) sum these PVs to find the current value of the stock, $\hat{P}_0$.

- The **total company,** or **corporate value, model** is a valuation model used in place of the dividend growth model to determine a firm's value, especially one that does not pay dividends or is privately held. This model discounts a firm's free cash flows at the WACC to determine its value.

- The **marginal investor** is a representative investor whose actions reflect the beliefs of those people who are currently trading a stock. It is the marginal investor who determines a stock's price.

- **Equilibrium** is the condition under which the expected return on a security as seen by the marginal investor is just equal to its required return, $\hat{k} = k$. Also, the stock's intrinsic value must be equal to its market price, $\hat{P}_0 = P_0$, and the market price is stable.

- The **Efficient Markets Hypothesis (EMH)** holds (1) that stocks are always in equilibrium and (2) that it is impossible for an investor who does not have inside information to consistently "beat the market." Therefore, according to the EMH, stocks are always fairly valued ($\hat{P}_0 = P_0$), the required return on a stock is equal to its expected return ($k = \hat{k}$), and all stocks' expected returns plot on the SML.

- **Preferred stock** is a hybrid security having some characteristics of debt and some of equity.
- Most preferred stocks are **perpetuities,** and the value of a share of perpetual preferred stock is found as the dividend divided by the required rate of return:

$$V_p = \frac{D_p}{k_p}.$$

QUESTIONS

8-1 Two investors are evaluating AT&T's stock for possible purchase. They agree on the expected value of D_1 and also on the expected future dividend growth rate. Further, they agree on the riskiness of the stock. However, one investor normally holds stocks for 2 years, while the other normally holds stocks for 10 years. On the basis of the type of analysis done in this chapter, they should both be willing to pay the same price for AT&T's stock. True or false? Explain.

8-2 A bond that pays interest forever and has no maturity date is a perpetual bond. In what respect is a perpetual bond similar to a no-growth common stock, and to a share of preferred stock?

8-3 If you bought a share of common stock, you would typically expect to receive dividends plus capital gains. Would you expect the distribution between dividend yield and capital gains to be influenced by the firm's decision to pay more dividends rather than to retain and reinvest more of its earnings?

8-4 Is it true that the following expression can be used to find the value of a constant growth stock?

$$\hat{P}_0 = \frac{D_0}{k_s + g}.$$

8-5 It is frequently stated that the primary purpose of the preemptive right is to allow individuals to maintain their proportionate share of the ownership and control of a corporation.
  a. How important do you suppose this consideration is for the average stockholder of a firm whose shares are traded on the New York Stock Exchange?
  b. Is the preemptive right likely to be of more importance to stockholders of publicly owned or closely held firms? Explain.

SELF-TEST PROBLEMS (SOLUTIONS APPEAR IN APPENDIX B)

ST-1
Key terms
Define each of the following terms:
  a. Proxy; proxy fight; takeover
  b. Preemptive right
  c. Classified stock; founders' shares
  d. Closely held corporation; publicly owned corporation
  e. Secondary market; primary market
  f. Going public; initial public offering (IPO) market
  g. Intrinsic value ($\hat{P}_0$); market price (P_0)
  h. Required rate of return, k_s; expected rate of return, $\hat{k}_s$; actual, or realized, rate of return, $\bar{k}_s$
  i. Capital gains yield; dividend yield; expected total return; growth rate, g
  j. Zero growth stock
  k. Normal, or constant, growth; supernormal, or nonconstant, growth
  l. Total company (corporate value) model
  m. Terminal (horizon) date; horizon (terminal) value
  n. Marginal investor
  o. Equilibrium
  p. Efficient Markets Hypothesis (EMH); three forms of EMH
  q. Preferred stock

You are considering buying the stocks of two companies that operate in the same industry; they have very similar characteristics except for their dividend payout policies. Both companies are expected to earn $6 per share this year. However, Company D (for "dividend") is expected to pay out all of its earnings as dividends, while Company G (for "growth") is expected to pay out only one-third of its earnings, or $2 per share. D's stock price is $40. G and D are equally risky. Which of the following is most likely to be true?

a. Company G will have a faster growth rate than Company D. Therefore, G's stock price should be greater than $40.

b. Although G's growth rate should exceed D's, D's current dividend exceeds that of G, and this should cause D's price to exceed G's.

c. An investor in Stock D will get his or her money back faster because D pays out more of its earnings as dividends. Thus, in a sense, D is like a short-term bond, and G is like a long-term bond. Therefore, if economic shifts cause k_d and k_s to increase, and if the expected streams of dividends from D and G remain constant, both Stocks D and G will decline, but D's price should decline further.

d. D's expected and required rate of return is $\hat{k}_s = k_s = 15\%$. G's expected return will be higher because of its higher expected growth rate.

e. If we observe that G's price is also $40, the best estimate of G's growth rate is 10 percent.

Ewald Company's current stock price is $36, and its last dividend was $2.40. In view of Ewald's strong financial position and its consequent low risk, its required rate of return is only 12 percent. If dividends are expected to grow at a constant rate, g, in the future, and if k_s is expected to remain at 12 percent, what is Ewald's expected stock price 5 years from now?

Snyder Computer Chips Inc. is experiencing a period of rapid growth. Earnings and dividends are expected to grow at a rate of 15 percent during the next 2 years, at 13 percent in the third year, and at a constant rate of 6 percent thereafter. Snyder's last dividend was $1.15, and the required rate of return on the stock is 12 percent.

a. Calculate the value of the stock today.

b. Calculate $\hat{P}_1$ and $\hat{P}_2$.

c. Calculate the dividend yield and capital gains yield for Years 1, 2, and 3.

STARTER PROBLEMS

Warr Corporation just paid a dividend of $1.50 a share (i.e., $D_0 = \$1.50$). The dividend is expected to grow 5 percent a year for the next 3 years, and then 10 percent a year thereafter. What is the expected dividend per share for each of the next 5 years?

Thomas Brothers is expected to pay a $0.50 per share dividend at the end of the year (i.e., $D_1 = \$0.50$). The dividend is expected to grow at a constant rate of 7 percent a year. The required rate of return on the stock, k_s, is 15 percent. What is the value per share of the company's stock?

Harrison Clothiers' stock currently sells for $20 a share. The stock just paid a dividend of $1.00 a share (i.e., $D_0 = \$1.00$). The dividend is expected to grow at a constant rate of 10 percent a year. What stock price is expected 1 year from now? What is the required rate of return on the company's stock?

Fee Founders has preferred stock outstanding that pays a dividend of $5 at the end of each year. The preferred stock sells for $60 a share. What is the preferred stock's required rate of return?

Hart Enterprises recently paid a dividend, D_0, of $1.25. The company expects to have supernormal growth of 20 percent for 2 years before the dividend is expected to grow at a constant rate of 5 percent. The firm's cost of equity is 10 percent.

a. What year is the terminal, or horizon, date?

b. What is the firm's horizon, or terminal, value?

c. What is the firm's intrinsic value today, $\hat{P}_0$?

Smith Technologies is expected to generate $150 million in free cash flow next year, and it is expected to grow at a constant rate of 5 percent per year. The firm has no debt or preferred stock and has a WACC of 10 percent. If Smith has 50 million shares of stock outstanding, what is the value of the company's stock per share?

EXAM-TYPE PROBLEMS

The problems included in this section are set up in such a way that they could be used as multiple-choice exam problems.

8-7
Corporate value model

Due to the highly specialized nature of the electronic industry, Barrett Industries invests a lot of money in R&D on prospective products. Consequently, it retains all of its earnings and reinvests them into the firm. (In other words, it does not pay any dividends.) At this time, Barrett does not have plans to pay any dividends in the near future. A major pension fund is interested in purchasing Barrett's stock, which is traded on the NYSE. The treasurer of the pension fund has done a great deal of research on the company and realizes that its valuation must be based on the total company model. The pension fund's treasurer has estimated Barrett's free cash flows for the next 4 years as follows: $3 million, $6 million, $10 million, and $15 million. After the fourth year, free cash flow is projected to grow at a constant 7 percent. Barrett's WACC is 12 percent, it has $60 million of total debt and preferred stock, and 10 million shares of common stock.

a. What is the present value of Barrett's free cash flows during the next 4 years?
b. What is the company's terminal value?
c. What is the total value of the firm today?
d. What is Barrett's price per share?

8-8
Corporate value model

Today is December 31, 2002. The following information applies to Vermeil Airlines:

- After-tax, operating income [$EBIT(1 - T)$] for 2003 is expected to be $500 million.
- The company's depreciation expense for 2003 is expected to be $100 million.
- The company's capital expenditures for 2003 are expected to be $200 million.
- No change is expected in the company's net operating working capital.
- The company's free cash flow is expected to grow at a constant rate of 6 percent per year.
- The company's cost of equity is 14 percent.
- The company's WACC is 10 percent.
- The market value of the company's debt is $3 billion.
- The company has 200 million shares of stock outstanding.

Using the free cash flow approach, what should the company's stock price be today?

8-9
Corporate valuation

Dozier Corporation is a fast-growing supplier of office products. Analysts project the following free cash flows (FCFs) during the next 3 years, after which FCF is expected to grow at a constant 7 percent rate. Dozier's WACC is 13 percent.

Time	1	2	3
Free cash flow ($ millions)	−$20	$30	$40

a. What is Dozier's terminal, or horizon, value? (Hint: Find the value of all free cash flows beyond Year 3 discounted back to Year 3.)
b. What is the value of the firm today?
c. Suppose Dozier has $100 million in debt and 10 million shares of stock. What is the price per share?

8-10
Constant growth valuation

You are considering an investment in the common stock of Keller Corp. The stock is expected to pay a dividend of $2 a share at the end of the year ($D_1 = \$2.00$). The stock has a beta equal to 0.9. The risk-free rate is 5.6 percent, and the market risk premium is 6 percent. The stock's dividend is expected to grow at some constant rate g. The stock currently sells for $25 a share. Assuming the market is in equilibrium, what does the market believe will be the stock price at the end of 3 years? (That is, what is $\hat{P}_3$?)

8-11
Preferred stock rate of return

What will be the nominal rate of return on a preferred stock with a $100 par value, a stated dividend of 8 percent of par, and a current market price of (a) $60, (b) $80, (c) $100, and (d) $140?

8-12
Declining growth stock valuation

Martell Mining Company's ore reserves are being depleted, so its sales are falling. Also, its pit is getting deeper each year, so its costs are rising. As a result, the company's earnings and dividends are declining at the constant rate of 5 percent per year. If $D_0 = \$5$ and $k_s = 15\%$, what is the value of Martell Mining's stock?

8-13

Rates of return and equilibrium

The beta coefficient for Stock C is $b_C = 0.4$, whereas that for Stock D is $b_D = -0.5$. (Stock D's beta is negative, indicating that its rate of return rises whenever returns on most other stocks fall. There are very few negative beta stocks, although collection agency stocks are sometimes cited as an example.)

a. If the risk-free rate is 9 percent and the expected rate of return on an average stock is 13 percent, what are the required rates of return on Stocks C and D?

b. For Stock C, suppose the current price, P_0, is $25; the next expected dividend, D_1, is $1.50; and the stock's expected constant growth rate is 4 percent. Is the stock in equilibrium? Explain, and describe what will happen if the stock is not in equilibrium.

8-14

Supernormal growth stock valuation

Microtech Corporation is expanding rapidly, and it currently needs to retain all of its earnings, hence it does not pay any dividends. However, investors expect Microtech to begin paying dividends, with the first dividend of $1.00 coming 3 years from today. The dividend should grow rapidly — at a rate of 50 percent per year — during Years 4 and 5. After Year 5, the company should grow at a constant rate of 8 percent per year. If the required return on the stock is 15 percent, what is the value of the stock today?

8-15

Preferred stock return

Bruner Aeronautics has preferred stock outstanding with a par value of $100. The stock pays a quarterly dividend of $2 and has a current price of $80.

a. What is the nominal rate of return on the preferred stock?

b. What is the effective rate of return?

8-16

Supernormal growth valuation

Mitts Cosmetics Co.'s stock recently paid a $2 dividend. This dividend is expected to grow by 25 percent for the next 3 years, and then grow forever at a constant rate, g. The current stock price is $58.88. At what constant rate is the stock expected to grow following Year if $k_s = 12\%$?

8-17

Constant growth valuation

A stock is expected to pay a dividend of $0.50 at the end of the year (that is, $D_1 = 0.50$). The dividend is expected to grow at a constant rate of 7 percent a year. The stock has a required return of 12 percent. What is the expected price of the stock 4 years from today?

PROBLEMS

8-18

Preferred stock valuation

Ezzell Corporation issued preferred stock with a stated dividend of 10 percent of par. Preferred stock of this type currently yields 8 percent, and the par value is $100. Assume dividends are paid annually.

a. What is the value of Ezzell's preferred stock?

b. Suppose interest rate levels rise to the point where the preferred stock now yields 12 percent. What would be the value of Ezzell's preferred stock?

8-19

Constant growth stock valuation

Your broker offers to sell you some shares of Bahnsen & Co. common stock that paid a dividend of $2 *yesterday*. You expect the dividend to grow at the rate of 5 percent per year for the next 3 years, and, if you buy the stock, you plan to hold it for 3 years and then sell it.

a. Find the expected dividend for each of the next 3 years; that is, calculate D_1, D_2, and D_3. Note that $D_0 = \$2.00$.

b. Given that the appropriate discount rate is 12 percent and that the first of these dividend payments will occur 1 year from now, find the present value of the dividend stream; that is, calculate the PV of D_1, D_2, and D_3, and then sum these PVs.

c. You expect the price of the stock 3 years from now to be $34.73; that is, you expect $\hat{P}_3$ to equal $34.73. Discounted at a 12 percent rate, what is the present value of this expected future stock price? In other words, calculate the PV of $34.73.

d. If you plan to buy the stock, hold it for 3 years, and then sell it for $34.73, what is the most you should pay for it today?

e. Use Equation 8-2 to calculate the present value of this stock. Assume that $g = 5\%$, and it is constant.

f. Is the value of this stock dependent upon how long you plan to hold it? In other words, if your planned holding period were 2 years or 5 years rather than 3 years, would this affect the value of the stock today, $\hat{P}_0$?

8-20

Constant growth stock valuation

Investors require a 15 percent rate of return on Levine Company's stock ($k_s = 15\%$).

a. What will be Levine's stock value if the previous dividend was $D_0 = \$2$ and if investors expect dividends to grow at a constant compound annual rate of (1) -5 percent, (2) 0 percent, (3) 5 percent, and (4) 10 percent?

b. Using data from part a, what is the Gordon (constant growth) model value for Levine's stock if the required rate of return is 15 percent and the expected growth rate is (1) 15 percent or (2) 20 percent? Are these reasonable results? Explain.

c. Is it reasonable to expect that a constant growth stock would have $g > k_s$?

8-21
Stock reporting

Look up the prices of American Telephone & Telegraph's (AT&T) stock in *The Wall Street Journal* (or some other newspaper that provides this information). (Hint: Its stock symbol is T.)

a. What was the stock's price range during the last year?

b. What is AT&T's current dividend? What is its dividend yield?

c. What change occurred in AT&T's stock price the day the newspaper was published?

d. If you had $10,000 and wanted to invest it in AT&T, what return would you expect to get if you bought AT&T's stock? (Hint: Think about capital gains when you answer this question.)

8-22
Supernormal growth stock valuation

It is now January 1, 2003. Wayne-Martin Electric Inc. (WME) has just developed a solar panel capable of generating 200 percent more electricity than any solar panel currently on the market. As a result, WME is expected to experience a 15 percent annual growth rate for the next 5 years. By the end of 5 years, other firms will have developed comparable technology, and WME's growth rate will slow to 5 percent per year indefinitely. Stockholders require a return of 12 percent on WME's stock. The most recent annual dividend (D_0), which was paid yesterday, was $1.75 per share.

a. Calculate WME's expected dividends for 2003, 2004, 2005, 2006, and 2007.

b. Calculate the value of the stock today, $\hat{P}_0$. Proceed by finding the present value of the dividends expected at the end of 2003, 2004, 2005, 2006, and 2007 plus the present value of the stock price that should exist at the end of 2007. The year-end 2007 stock price can be found by using the constant growth equation. Notice that to find the December 31, 2007, price, you use the dividend expected in 2008, which is 5 percent greater than the 2007 dividend.

c. Calculate the expected dividend yield, D_1/P_0, the capital gains yield expected in 2003, and the expected total return (dividend yield plus capital gains yield) for 2003. (Assume that $\hat{P}_0 = P_0$, and recognize that the capital gains yield is equal to the total return minus the dividend yield.) Also calculate these same three yields for 2008.

d. How might an investor's tax situation affect his or her decision to purchase stocks of companies in the early stages of their lives, when they are growing rapidly, versus stocks of older, more mature firms? When does WME's stock become "mature" in this example?

e. Suppose your boss tells you she believes that WME's annual growth rate will be only 12 percent during the next 5 years and that the firm's normal growth rate will be only 4 percent. Without doing any calculations, what general effect would these growth-rate changes have on the price of WME's stock?

f. Suppose your boss also tells you that she regards WME as being quite risky and that she believes the required rate of return should be 14 percent, not 12 percent. Again, without doing any calculations, how would the higher required rate of return affect the price of the stock, its capital gains yield, and its dividend yield? Again, assume that the firm's normal growth rate will be 4 percent.

8-23
Supernormal growth stock valuation

Taussig Technologies Corporation (TTC) has been growing at a rate of 20 percent per year in recent years. This same growth rate is expected to last for another 2 years.

a. If $D_0 = 1.60, $k = 10\%$, and $g_n = 6\%$, what is TTC's stock worth today? What are its expected dividend yield and capital gains yield at this time?

b. Now assume that TTC's period of supernormal growth is to last for 5 years rather than 2 years. How would this affect its price, dividend yield, and capital gains yield? Answer in words only.

c. What will be TTC's dividend yield and capital gains yield once its period of supernormal growth ends? (Hint: These values will be the same regardless of whether you examine the case of 2 or 5 years of supernormal growth; the calculations are very easy.)

d. Of what interest to investors is the changing relationship between dividend yield and capital gains yield over time?

8-24
Equilibrium stock price

The risk-free rate of return, k_{RF}, is 11 percent; the required rate of return on the market, k_M, is 14 percent; and Upton Company's stock has a beta coefficient of 1.5.

a. If the dividend expected during the coming year, D_1, is $2.25, and if $g = $ a constant 5%, at what price should Upton's stock sell?

b. Now, suppose the Federal Reserve Board increases the money supply, causing the risk-free rate to drop to 9 percent and k_M to fall to 12 percent. What would this do to the price of the stock?

c. In addition to the change in part b, suppose investors' risk aversion declines; this fact, combined with the decline in k_{RF}, causes k_M to fall to 11 percent. At what price would Upton's stock sell?

d. Now, suppose Upton has a change in management. The new group institutes policies that increase the expected constant growth rate to 6 percent. Also, the new management stabilizes sales and profits, and thus causes the beta coefficient to decline from 1.5 to 1.3. Assume that k_{RF} and k_M are equal to the values in part c. After all these changes, what is Upton's new equilibrium price? (Note: D_1 is now $2.27.)

8-25
Beta coefficients
Suppose Chance Chemical Company's management conducts a study and concludes that if Chance expanded its consumer products division (which is less risky than its primary business, industrial chemicals), the firm's beta would decline from 1.2 to 0.9. However, consumer products have a somewhat lower profit margin, and this would cause Chance's constant growth rate in earnings and dividends to fall from 7 to 5 percent.

a. Should management make the change? Assume the following: $k_M = 12\%$; $k_{RF} = 9\%$; $D_0 = \$2.00$.

b. Assume all the facts as given above except the change in the beta coefficient. How low would the beta have to fall to cause the expansion to be a good one? (Hint: Set $\hat{P}_0$ under the new policy equal to $\hat{P}_0$ under the old one, and find the new beta that will produce this equality.)

SPREADSHEET PROBLEM

8-26
Supernormal growth and corporate valuation
Rework Problem 8-23, parts a, b, and c, using a spreadsheet model. For part b, calculate the price, dividend yield, and capital gains yield as called for in the problem. After completing parts a through c, answer the following additional question using your spreadsheet model.

d. Suppose an alternative method of valuing TTC's stock has been proposed. It has been suggested that the free cash flow method be used to value the firm's stock. The firm has just introduced a new line of products that have been wildly successful. On the basis of this success and anticipated future success, the projected income statements resulted in the following free cash flow projections:

Year	1	2	3	4	5	6	7	8	9	10
FCF	$5.5	$12.1	$23.8	$44.1	$69.0	$88.8	$107.5	$128.9	$147.1	$161.3

In addition, the firm estimates its overall WACC has fallen to 9 percent. After the 10th year, TTC's financial planners anticipate that free cash flow will grow at a constant rate of 6 percent. TTC's balance sheet also shows that the market value of debt is $1,200 million and that there are 20 million shares of common stock outstanding. Use the free cash flow method to value a share of TTC's stock.

INTEGRATED CASE

MUTUAL OF CHICAGO INSURANCE COMPANY

8-27 Stock Valuation Robert Balik and Carol Kiefer are senior vice-presidents of the Mutual of Chicago Insurance Company. They are co-directors of the company's pension fund management division, with Balik having responsibility for fixed income securities (primarily bonds) and Kiefer being responsible for equity investments. A major new client, the California League of Cities, has requested that Mutual of Chicago present an investment seminar to the mayors of the represented cities, and Balik and Kiefer, who will make the actual presentation, have asked you to help them.

To illustrate the common stock valuation process, Balik and Kiefer have asked you to analyze the Bon Temps Com-

pany, an employment agency that supplies word processor operators and computer programmers to businesses with temporarily heavy workloads. You are to answer the following questions.

a. Describe briefly the legal rights and privileges of common stockholders.

b. (1) Write out a formula that can be used to value any stock, regardless of its dividend pattern.

(2) What is a constant growth stock? How are constant growth stocks valued?

(3) What happens if a company has a constant g that exceeds its k_s? Will many stocks have expected $g > k_s$ in the short run (that is, for the next few years)? In the long run (that is, forever)?

c. Assume that Bon Temps has a beta coefficient of 1.2, that the risk-free rate (the yield on T-bonds) is 7 percent, and that the required rate of return on the market is 12 percent. What is the required rate of return on the firm's stock?

d. Assume that Bon Temps is a constant growth company whose last dividend (D_0, which was paid yesterday) was $2.00 and whose dividend is expected to grow indefinitely at a 6 percent rate.
   (1) What is the firm's expected dividend stream over the next 3 years?
   (2) What is the firm's current stock price?
   (3) What is the stock's expected value 1 year from now?
   (4) What are the expected dividend yield, the capital gains yield, and the total return during the first year?

e. Now assume that the stock is currently selling at $30.29. What is the expected rate of return on the stock?

f. What would the stock price be if its dividends were expected to have zero growth?

g. Now assume that Bon Temps is expected to experience supernormal growth of 30 percent for the next 3 years, then to return to its long-run constant growth rate of 6 percent. What is the stock's value under these conditions? What is its expected dividend yield and capital gains yield in Year 1? Year 4?

h. Suppose Bon Temps is expected to experience zero growth during the first 3 years and then to resume its steady-state growth of 6 percent in the fourth year. What is the stock's value now? What is its expected dividend yield and its capital gains yield in Year 1? Year 4?

i. Finally, assume that Bon Temps' earnings and dividends are expected to decline by a constant 6 percent per year, that is, $g = -6\%$. Why would anyone be willing to buy such a stock, and at what price should it sell? What would be the dividend yield and capital gains yield in each year?

j. Bon Temps embarks on an aggressive expansion that requires additional capital. Management decides to finance the expansion by borrowing $40 million and by halting dividend payments to increase retained earnings. The projected free cash flows for the next 3 years are −$5 million, $10 million, and $20 million. After the third year, free cash flow is projected to grow at a constant 6 percent. The overall cost of capital is 10 percent. What is Bon Temps' total value? If it has 10 million shares of stock and $40 million total debt, what is the price per share?

k. What does market equilibrium mean?

l. If equilibrium does not exist, how will it be established?

m. What is the Efficient Markets Hypothesis, what are its three forms, and what are its implications?

n. Phyfe Company recently issued preferred stock. It pays an annual dividend of $5, and the issue price was $50 per share. What is the expected return to an investor on this preferred stock?

Please go to our web site **http://brigham.swlearning.com** to access the Cyberproblems.

With your Xtra! CD-ROM, access the Thomson Analytics Problems and use the Thomson Analytics Academic online database to work this chapter's problems.

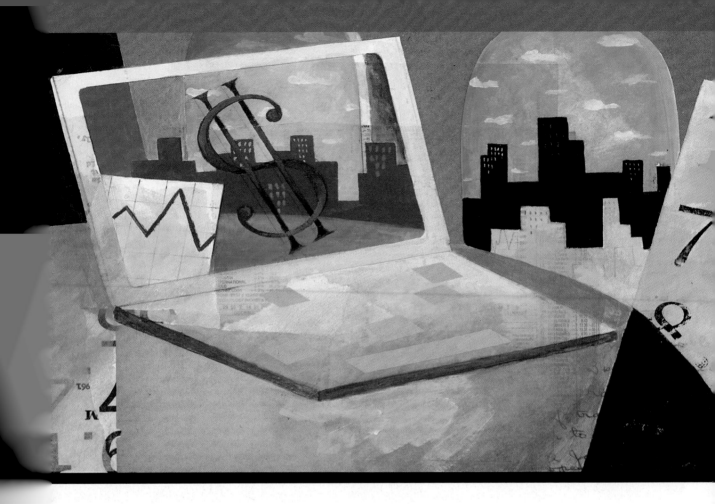

PART 4

INVESTING IN LONG-TERM ASSETS: CAPITAL BUDGETING

THE COST OF
CAPITAL

9

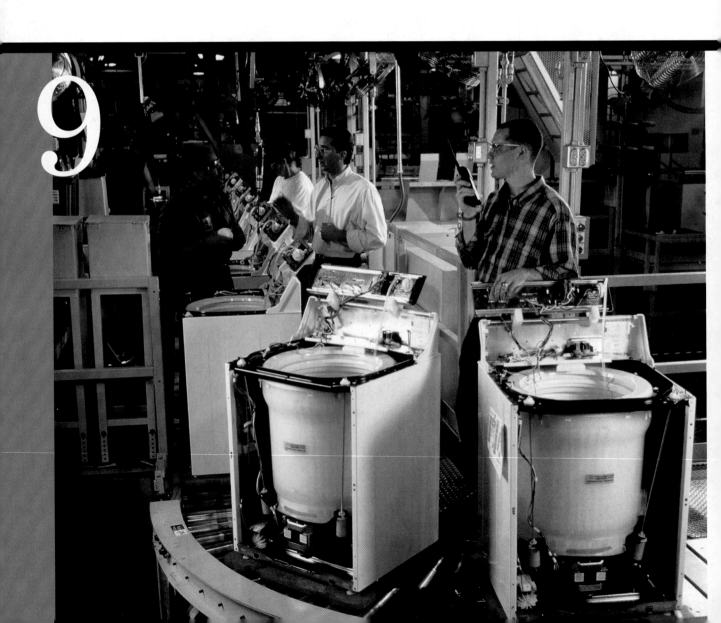

I n Chapter 2 we discussed the concept of EVA — Economic Value Added — which is used by an increasing number of companies to measure corporate performance. Developed by the consulting firm Stern Stewart & Company, EVA is designed to measure a corporation's true profitability, and it is calculated as after-tax operating profits less the annual after-tax cost of all the capital a firm uses.

The idea behind EVA is simple — firms are truly profitable and create value if and only if their income exceeds the cost of all the capital they use to finance operations. The conventional measure of performance, net income, takes into account the cost of debt, which shows up on financial statements as interest expense, but it does not reflect the cost of equity. Therefore, a firm can report positive net income yet still be unprofitable in an economic sense if its net income is less than its cost of equity. EVA corrects this flaw by recognizing that to properly measure performance, it is necessary to account for the cost of equity capital.

A variety of factors influence a firm's cost of capital. Some, such as the level of interest rates, state and federal tax policies, and the regulatory environment, are outside of the firm's control. However, the firm's financing and investment policies, especially the types of capital it uses and the types of investment projects it undertakes, have a profound effect on its cost of capital.

General Electric has long been recognized as one of the world's best-managed companies, and it has rewarded its

CREATING VALUE AT GE

GENERAL ELECTRIC

shareholders with outstanding returns. Given its performance, it is not surprising that GE is always at or near the top of the list of companies in generating EVA. Thus, GE has been able to consistently find projects that earn more than their costs of capital.

Estimating the cost of capital for a company like GE is a fairly straightforward exercise, but it does require judgment. Since GE's capital comes largely from equity, its cost of capital depends to a large extent on the cost of its equity, which is in essence its shareholders' required return. One must recognize that when investors purchase GE stock, they are investing in a company that operates many different divisions throughout the world. Each division has a different level of risk, hence a different cost of capital. GE's appliance division's cost of capital is likely to be different than that of its NBC subsidiary, or than that of its aircraft engine division. Likewise, an overseas project may have different risks and thus a different cost of capital than an otherwise similar domestic project.

As we will see in this chapter, estimating a project's cost of capital is an important process, and one that requires judgment. Companies that manage this process well will probably produce positive economic value for their shareholders.

In the last two chapters, we discussed the values of and required rates of return on stocks and bonds. When companies issue stocks or bonds, they are raising capital for investment in various projects. Capital is a necessary factor of production, and like any other factor, it has a cost. This cost is equal to the marginal investor's required return on the security in question. With this in mind, we now consider the process of estimating the cost of capital.

The firm's primary objective is to maximize shareholder value, and companies can increase shareholder value by investing in projects that earn more than the cost of capital. For this reason, the cost of capital is sometimes referred to as a *hurdle rate*: For a project to be accepted, it must earn more than its hurdle rate.

Although its most important use is in capital budgeting, the cost of capital is also used for at least three other purposes: (1) It is a key input used to calculate a firm's or division's economic value added (EVA). (2) Managers estimate and use the cost of capital when deciding if they should lease or purchase assets. And (3), the cost of capital is important in the regulation of monopoly services provided by electric, gas, and telephone companies. These firms are natural monopolies in the sense that one firm can supply service at a lower cost than could two or more firms. Since it has a monopoly, your electric or telephone company could, if it were unregulated, exploit you. Therefore, regulators (1) determine the cost of the capital investors have provided to the utility and (2) then set rates designed to permit the company to earn its cost of capital, no more and no less.

It should be noted that the cost of capital models and formulas used in this chapter are the same ones we developed in Chapters 7 and 8, where we were concerned with the rates of return investors require on different securities. The same factors that affect investors' required rates of return also determine the cost of capital to a firm, so investors and corporate treasurers often use exactly the same models. ■

THE LOGIC OF THE WEIGHTED AVERAGE COST OF CAPITAL

It is possible to finance a firm entirely with common equity. In that case, the cost of capital used to analyze capital budgeting decisions should be the company's required return on equity. However, most firms raise a substantial portion of their capital as debt, and many also use preferred stock. For these firms, the cost of capital must reflect the average cost of the various sources of funds used, not just the costs of equity.

Assume that Allied Food Products has a 10 percent cost of debt and a 13.4 percent cost of equity. Further, assume that Allied has made the decision to finance next year's projects with debt. The argument is sometimes made that the cost of capital for these projects is 10 percent because only debt will be used to finance them. However, this position is incorrect. If Allied finances a particular set of projects with debt, the firm will be using up some of its capacity for borrowing in the future. As expansion occurs in subsequent years, Allied will at some point find it necessary to raise additional equity to prevent the debt ratio from becoming too large.

To illustrate, suppose Allied borrows heavily at 10 percent during 2003, using up its debt capacity in the process, to finance projects yielding 11.5 percent. In 2004, it has new projects available that yield 13 percent, well above the return on 2003 projects, but it cannot accept them because they would have to be financed with 13.4 percent equity money. *To avoid this problem, Allied should be viewed as an ongoing concern, and the cost of capital used in capital budgeting should be calculated as a weighted average, or composite, of the various types of funds it generally uses, regardless of the specific financing used to fund a particular project.*

SELF-TEST QUESTION

Why should the cost of capital used in capital budgeting be calculated as a weighted average of the various types of funds the firm generally uses, not the cost of the specific financing used to fund a particular project?

BASIC DEFINITIONS

Capital Component
One of the types of capital used by firms to raise money.

The items on the right side of a firm's balance sheet—various types of debt, preferred stock, and common equity—are called **capital components.** Any increase in total assets must be financed by an increase in one or more of these capital components.

The cost of each component is called the *component cost* of that particular type of capital; for example, if Allied can borrow money at 10 percent, its component cost of debt is 10 percent.[1] Throughout this chapter, we concentrate on these three major

---

[1] We will see shortly that there is both a before-tax and an after-tax cost of debt; for now, it is sufficient to know that 10 percent is the before-tax component cost of debt.

capital components: debt, preferred stock, and common equity. The following symbols identify the cost of each:

k_d = interest rate on the firm's new debt = before-tax component cost of debt. For Allied, k_d = 10%.

$k_d(1 - T)$ = after-tax component cost of debt, where T is the firm's marginal tax rate. $k_d(1 - T)$ is the debt cost used to calculate the weighted average cost of capital. For Allied, T = 40%, so $k_d(1 - T)$ = 10%(1 − 0.4) = 10%(0.6) = 6.0%.

k_p = component cost of preferred stock. For Allied, k_p = 10.3%.

k_s = component cost of common equity. It is identical to the k_s developed in Chapters 5 and 8 and defined there as the rate of return investors require on a firm's common stock. Equity capital is raised in two ways: (1) by retaining earnings (internal equity) or (2) by issuing new common stock (external equity). It is generally difficult to estimate k_s, but, as we shall see shortly, a reasonably good estimate for Allied is k_s = 13.4%.

WACC = the weighted average cost of capital. If Allied raises new capital to finance asset expansion, and if it is to keep its capital structure in balance (that is, if it is to keep the same percentage of debt, preferred stock, and common equity funds), then it must raise part of its new funds as debt, part as preferred stock, and part as common equity (with equity coming either from retained earnings or by issuing new common stock).[2] We will calculate WACC for Allied Food Products shortly.

These definitions and concepts are explained in detail in the remainder of the chapter. Later, in the chapter on capital structure and leverage, we extend the analysis to determine the mix of securities that will minimize the firm's cost of capital and thereby maximize its value.

SELF-TEST QUESTION

Identify the firm's three major capital structure components, and give their respective component cost symbols.

COST OF DEBT, $k_d(1 - T)$

After-tax Cost of Debt, $k_d(1 - T)$
The relevant cost of new debt, taking into account the tax deductibility of interest; used to calculate the WACC.

The **after-tax cost of debt, $k_d(1 - T)$,** is used to calculate the weighted average cost of capital, and it is the interest rate on debt, k_d, less the tax savings that result because interest is deductible. This is the same as k_d multiplied by $(1 - T)$, where T is the firm's marginal tax rate.[3]

---

[2] Firms try to keep their debt, preferred stock, and common equity in optimal proportions; we will learn how they establish these "target" proportions in the chapter on capital structure and leverage.

[3] The federal tax rate for most large corporations is 35 percent. However, most corporations are also subject to state income taxes, so the marginal tax rate on most corporate income is about 40 percent. For

(footnote continues)

$$\text{After-tax component cost of debt} = \text{Interest rate} - \text{Tax savings}$$
$$= k_d - k_d T$$
$$= k_d(1 - T). \qquad (9\text{-}1)$$

In effect, the government pays part of the cost of debt because interest is deductible. Therefore, if Allied can borrow at an interest rate of 10 percent, and if it has a marginal federal-plus-state tax rate of 40 percent, then its after-tax cost of debt is 6 percent:

$$k_d(1 - T) = 10\%(1.0 - 0.4)$$
$$= 10\%(0.6)$$
$$= 6.0\%.$$

The reason for using the after-tax cost of debt in calculating the weighted average cost of capital is as follows. The value of the firm's stock, which we want to maximize, depends on *after-tax* cash flows. Because interest is a deductible expense, it produces tax savings that reduce the net cost of debt, making the after-tax cost of debt less than the before-tax cost. We are concerned with after-tax cash flows, and since cash flows and rates of return should be placed on a comparable basis, we adjust the interest rate downward to take account of the preferential tax treatment of debt.[4]

Note that the cost of debt is the interest rate on *new* debt, not that on already outstanding debt; in other words, we are interested in the *marginal* cost of debt. Our primary concern with the cost of capital is to use it for capital budgeting decisions — for example, would a new machine earn a return greater than the cost of the capital needed to acquire the machine? The rate at which the firm has borrowed in the past is irrelevant — we need the cost of *new capital*.

SELF-TEST QUESTIONS

Why is the after-tax cost of debt rather than the before-tax cost used to calculate the weighted average cost of capital?

Is the relevant cost of debt the interest rate on already *outstanding* debt or that on *new* debt? Why?

(Footnote 3 continued)

illustrative purposes, we assume that the effective federal-plus-state tax rate on marginal income is 40 percent. Also, note that the cost of debt is considered in isolation. The effect of debt on the cost of equity, as well as on future increments of debt, is ignored when the weighted cost of a combination of debt and equity is derived in this chapter, but it will be treated in the chapter on capital structure and leverage.

[4] The tax rate is *zero* for a firm with losses. Therefore, for a company that does not pay taxes, the cost of debt is not reduced; that is, in Equation 9-1, the tax rate equals zero, so the after-tax cost of debt is equal to the interest rate.

Strictly speaking, the after-tax cost of debt should reflect the *expected* cost of debt. While Allied's bonds have a promised return of 10 percent, there is some chance of default, so its bondholders' expected return (and consequently Allied's cost) is a bit less than 10 percent. For a relatively strong company such as Allied, this difference is quite small. As we discuss later in the chapter, Allied must also incur flotation costs when it issues debt, but like the difference between the promised and the expected rate of return, flotation costs are generally small. Finally, note that these two factors tend to offset one another — not including the possibility of default leads to an overstatement of the cost of debt, but not including flotation costs leads to an understatement. For all these reasons, k_d is generally a good approximation of the before-tax cost of debt capital.

COST OF PREFERRED STOCK, k~P~

Cost of Preferred Stock, k_p
The rate of return investors require on the firm's preferred stock. k_p is calculated as the preferred dividend, D_p, divided by the current price, P_p.

The component **cost of preferred stock** used to calculate the weighted average cost of capital, $\mathbf{k_p}$, is the preferred dividend, D_p, divided by the current price of the preferred stock, P_p.[5]

$$\text{Component cost of preferred stock} = k_p = \frac{D_p}{P_p}. \qquad (9\text{-}2)$$

For example, Allied has preferred stock that pays a $10 dividend per share and sells for $97.50 per share in the open market. Therefore, Allied's cost of preferred stock is 10.3 percent:

$$k_p = \$10/\$97.50 = 10.3\%.$$

As we can see from Equation 9-2, calculating the cost of preferred stock is generally quite simple. This is particularly true when we consider the traditional, "plain vanilla" form of preferred stock that pays a fixed dividend in perpetuity. We mentioned, however, in Chapter 8 that some preferred stock has a fixed maturity date, and we described how to calculate the expected return on these issues. These expected returns would also represent the cost of preferred stock for these fixed-maturity issues. In some other instances, preferred stock may include an option to convert to common stock. In these cases, calculating the cost of preferred stock becomes considerably more complicated. We will leave these more complicated cases for advanced classes and restrict ourselves to "plain vanilla" preferred issues, such as the ones issued by Allied.

No tax adjustments are made when calculating k_p because preferred dividends, unlike interest on debt, are *not* deductible. Therefore, there are no tax savings associated with the use of preferred stock. However, as we discuss in the accompanying box entitled "Funny-Named Preferred-Like Securities," some companies have tried to come up with ways to issue securities that are similar to preferred stock but that are structured in ways that enable them to deduct the payments made on these securities.

SELF-TEST QUESTION

Is a tax adjustment made to the cost of preferred stock? Why or why not?

COST OF RETAINED EARNINGS, k~s~

The costs of debt and preferred stock are based on the returns investors require on these securities. Similarly, the cost of common equity is based on the rate of return investors require on a company's common stock. Note, though, that new common equity is raised in two ways: (1) by retaining some of the current year's earnings and (2) by issuing new common stock. As we shall see, equity raised by issuing stock has a somewhat higher cost than equity raised as retained earnings due to the flotation

---

[5] To be technically precise, we should make an adjustment for flotation costs, but in Allied's case those costs are not significant.

FUNNY-NAMED PREFERRED-LIKE SECURITIES

Wall Street's "financial engineers" are constantly trying to develop new securities with appeal to issuers and investors. One such new security is a special type of preferred stock created by Goldman Sachs in the mid-1990s. These securities trade under a variety of colorful names, including MIPS (modified income preferred securities), QUIPS (quarterly income preferred securities), and QUIDS (quarterly income debt securities). The corporation that wants to raise capital (the "parent") establishes a trust, which issues fixed-dividend preferred stock. The parent then issues bonds (or debt of some type) to the trust, and the trust pays for the bonds with the cash raised from the sale of preferred. At that point, the parent has the cash it needs, the trust holds debt issued by the parent, and the investing public holds preferred stock issued by the trust. The parent then makes interest payments to the trust, and the trust uses that income to make the preferred dividend payments. Because the parent company has issued debt, its interest payments are tax deductible.

If the dividends could be excluded from taxable income by corporate investors, this preferred would really be a great deal — the issuer could deduct the interest, corporate investors could exclude most of the dividends, and the IRS would be the loser. The corporate parent does get to deduct the interest paid to the trust, but IRS regulations do not allow the dividends on these securities to be excluded.

Because there is only one deduction, why are these new securities attractive? The answer is as follows: (1) Since the parent company gets to take the deduction, its cost of funds from the preferred is $k_p(1-T)$, just as it would be if it used debt. (2) The parent generates a tax savings, and it can thus afford to pay a relatively high rate on trust-related preferred; that is, it can pass on some of its tax savings to investors to induce them to buy the new securities. (3) The primary purchasers of the preferred are low-tax-bracket individuals and tax-exempt institutions such as pension funds. For such purchasers, not being able to exclude the dividend from taxable income is not important. (4) Due to the differential tax rates, the arrangement results in a net tax savings. Competition in capital markets results in a sharing of the savings between investors and corporations.

A recent *SmartMoney Online* article argued that these hybrid securities are a good deal for individual investors for the reasons set forth above and also because they are sold in small increments — often as small as $25. However, these securities are relatively complex, which increases their risk and makes them hard to value. There is also risk to the issuing corporations. The IRS has expressed concerns about these securities, and if at some point the IRS decides to disallow interest paid to the trusts, that will have a profound negative effect on the corporations that have issued them.

SOURCES: Kerry Capell, "High Yields, Low Cost, Funny Names," *BusinessWeek*, September 9, 1996, 122; and Leslie Haggin, "SmartMoney Online: MIPS, QUIDS, and QUIPS," *SmartMoney Interactive*, April 6, 1999.

Cost of Retained Earnings, k_s
The rate of return required by stockholders on a firm's common stock.

k_e
The designation for the cost of common equity raised by issuing new stock, or external equity.

costs involved with new stock issues. We use the symbol $\mathbf{k_s}$ to designate the **cost of retained earnings** and $\mathbf{k_e}$ to designate the cost of common equity raised by issuing new stock, or external equity.[6]

A corporation's management might misguidedly think that retained earnings are "free" because they represent money that is "left over" after paying dividends. While it is true that no direct costs are associated with capital raised as retained earnings, this capital still has a cost. The reason we must assign a cost of capital to retained earnings involves the *opportunity cost principle*. The firm's after-tax earnings belong to its stockholders. Bondholders are compensated by interest payments, and preferred stockholders by preferred dividends. All earnings remaining after interest and preferred dividends belong to the common stockholders, and these earnings serve to compensate stockholders for the use of their capital. Management may either pay out

---

[6] The term *retained earnings* can be interpreted to mean either the balance sheet item "retained earnings," consisting of all the earnings retained in the business throughout its history, or the income statement item "addition to retained earnings." The income statement item is used in this chapter; for our purpose, *retained earnings* refers to that part of the current year's earnings not paid out in dividends, hence available for reinvestment in the business this year.

earnings in the form of dividends or else retain earnings and reinvest them in the business. If management decides to retain earnings, there is an *opportunity cost* involved—stockholders could have received the earnings as dividends and invested this money in other stocks, in bonds, in real estate, or in anything else. *Thus, the firm should earn on its retained earnings at least as much as the stockholders themselves could earn on alternative investments of comparable risk.*

What rate of return can stockholders expect to earn on equivalent-risk investments? First, recall from Chapter 8 that stocks are normally in equilibrium, with expected and required rates of return being equal: $\hat{k}_s = k_s$. Thus, we can assume that Allied's stockholders expect to earn a return of k_s on their money. *Therefore, if the firm cannot invest retained earnings and earn at least k_s, it should pay these funds to its stockholders and let them invest directly in other assets that do provide this return.*[7]

Whereas debt and preferred stocks are contractual obligations that have easily determined costs, it is difficult to measure k_s. However, we can employ the principles developed in Chapters 5 and 8 to produce reasonably good cost of equity estimates. Recall that if a stock is in equilibrium, then its required rate of return, k_s, must be equal to its expected rate of return, $\hat{k}_s$. Further, its *required* return is equal to a risk-free rate, k_{RF}, plus a risk premium, RP, whereas the *expected* return on a constant growth stock is the stock's dividend yield, D_1/P_0, plus its expected growth rate, g:

$$\text{Required rate of return} = \text{Expected rate of return}$$

$$k_s = k_{RF} + RP \quad = \quad D_1/P_0 + g = \hat{k}_s. \tag{9-3}$$

Therefore, we can estimate k_s either as $k_s = k_{RF} + RP$ or as $\hat{k}_s = D_1/P_0 + g$.

THE CAPM APPROACH

One approach to estimating the cost of common equity is to use the Capital Asset Pricing Model (CAPM) as developed in Chapter 5, proceeding as follows:

Step 1: Estimate the risk-free rate, k_{RF}, generally taken to be either the U.S. Treasury bond rate or the short-term (30-day) Treasury bill rate.

Step 2: Estimate the stock's beta coefficient, b_i, and use it as an index of the stock's risk. The i signifies the *i*th company's beta.

Step 3: Estimate the expected rate of return on the market, or on an "average" stock, k_M.

Step 4: Substitute the preceding values into the CAPM equation to estimate the required rate of return on the stock in question:

$$k_s = k_{RF} + (k_M - k_{RF})b_i. \tag{9-4}$$

Equation 9-4 shows that the CAPM estimate of k_s begins with the risk-free rate, k_{RF}, to which is added a risk premium set equal to the risk premium on an average stock, $k_M - k_{RF}$, scaled up or down to reflect the particular stock's risk as measured by its beta coefficient.

---

[7] Dividends and capital gains are taxed differently, with long-term capital gains being taxed at a lower rate than dividends for most stockholders. That makes it beneficial for companies to retain earnings rather than pay them out as dividends, and that, in turn, tends to lower the cost of capital for retained earnings. This point is discussed in detail in the chapter on distributions to shareholders.

To illustrate the CAPM approach, assume that $k_{RF} = 8\%$, $k_M = 13\%$, and $b_i = 0.7$ for a given stock. This stock's k_s is calculated as follows:

$$k_s = 8\% + (13\% - 8\%)(0.7)$$
$$= 8\% + (5\%)(0.7)$$
$$= 8\% + 3.5\%$$
$$= 11.5\%.$$

It should be noted that although the CAPM approach appears to yield an accurate, precise estimate of k_s, there are actually several problems with it. First, as we saw in Chapter 5, if a firm's stockholders are not well diversified, they may be concerned with *stand-alone risk* rather than just market risk. In that case, the firm's true investment risk would not be measured by its beta, and the CAPM procedure would understate the correct value of k_s. Further, even if the CAPM method is valid, it is hard to obtain correct estimates of the inputs required to make it operational because (1) there is controversy about whether to use long-term or short-term Treasury yields for k_{RF}, (2) it is hard to estimate the beta that investors expect the company to have in the future, and (3) it is difficult to estimate the market risk premium.

BOND-YIELD-PLUS-RISK-PREMIUM APPROACH

Analysts who do not have confidence in the CAPM often use a subjective, ad hoc procedure to estimate a firm's cost of common equity: they simply add a judgmental risk premium of 3 to 5 percentage points to the interest rate on the firm's own long-term debt. It is logical to think that firms with risky, low-rated, and consequently high-interest-rate debt will also have risky, high-cost equity, and the procedure of basing the cost of equity on a readily observable debt cost utilizes this logic. For example, if an extremely strong firm had bonds that yielded 8 percent, its cost of equity might be estimated as follows:

$$k_s = \text{Bond yield} + \text{Risk premium} = 8\% + 4\% = 12\%.$$

The bonds of a riskier company might carry a yield of 12 percent, making its estimated cost of equity 16 percent:

$$k_s = 12\% + 4\% = 16\%.$$

Because the 4 percent risk premium is a judgmental estimate, the estimated value of k_s is also judgmental. Empirical work in recent years suggests that the risk premium over a firm's own bond yield has generally ranged from 3 to 5 percentage points, so while this method does not produce a precise cost of equity, it will "get us into the right ballpark."

DIVIDEND-YIELD-PLUS-GROWTH-RATE, OR DISCOUNTED CASH FLOW (DCF), APPROACH

In Chapter 8, we saw that both the price and the expected rate of return on a share of common stock depend, ultimately, on the dividends expected on the stock:

$$P_0 = \frac{D_1}{(1 + k_s)^1} + \frac{D_2}{(1 + k_s)^2} + \cdots$$
$$= \sum_{t=1}^{\infty} \frac{D_t}{(1 + k_s)^t}. \tag{9-5}$$

Here P_0 is the current price of the stock; D_t is the dividend expected to be paid at the end of Year t; and k_s is the required rate of return. If dividends are expected to grow at a constant rate, then, as we saw in Chapter 8, Equation 9-5 reduces to this important formula:

$$P_0 = \frac{D_1}{k_s - g}.$$ (9-6)

We can solve for k_s to obtain the required rate of return on common equity, which, for the marginal investor, is also equal to the expected rate of return:

$$k_s = \hat{k}_s = \frac{D_1}{P_0} + \text{Expected g}.$$ (9-7)

Thus, investors expect to receive a dividend yield, D_1/P_0, plus a capital gain, g, for a total expected return of $\hat{k}_s$, and in equilibrium this expected return is also equal to the required return, k_s. This method of estimating the cost of equity is called the *discounted cash flow, or DCF, method*. Henceforth, we will assume that equilibrium exists, and we will use the terms k_s and $\hat{k}_s$ interchangeably.

It is easy to determine the dividend yield, but it is difficult to establish the proper growth rate. If past growth rates in earnings and dividends have been relatively stable, and if investors appear to be projecting a continuation of past trends, then g may be based on the firm's historic growth rate. *However, if the company's past growth has been abnormally high or low, either because of its own unique situation or because of general economic fluctuations, then investors will not project the past growth rate into the future.* In this case, g must be estimated in some other manner.

Security analysts regularly make earnings and dividend growth forecasts, looking at such factors as projected sales, profit margins, and competitive factors. For example, *Value Line*, which is available in most libraries, provides growth rate forecasts for 1,700 companies, and Merrill Lynch, Salomon Smith Barney, and other organizations make similar forecasts. Therefore, someone making a cost of equity estimate can obtain several analysts' forecasts, average them, use the average as a proxy for the growth expectations of investors in general, and then combine this g with the current dividend yield to estimate $\hat{k}_s$ as follows:

$$\hat{k}_s = \frac{D_1}{P_0} + \text{Growth rate as projected by security analysts}.$$

Again, note that this estimate of $\hat{k}_s$ is based on the assumption that g is expected to remain constant in the future.[8]

Another method for estimating g involves first forecasting the firm's average future dividend payout ratio and its complement, the *retention rate*, and then multiplying the retention rate by the company's expected future rate of return on equity (ROE):

$$g = (\text{Retention rate})(\text{ROE}) = (1.0 - \text{Payout rate})(\text{ROE}).$$ (9-8)

---

[8] Analysts' growth rate forecasts are usually for five years into the future, and the rates provided represent the average growth rate over that five-year horizon. Studies have shown that analysts' forecasts represent the best source of growth rate data for DCF cost of capital estimates. See Robert Harris, "Using Analysts' Growth Rate Forecasts to Estimate Shareholder Required Rates of Return," *Financial Management*, Spring 1986.

Note also that two organizations—IBES and Zacks—collect the forecasts of leading analysts for most larger companies, average these forecasts, and then publish the averages. The IBES and Zacks data are available over the Internet through online computer data services.

Intuitively, firms that are more profitable and retain a larger portion of their earnings for reinvestment in the firm will tend to have higher growth rates than firms that are less profitable and pay out a higher percentage of their earnings as dividends. Security analysts often use Equation 9-8 when they estimate growth rates. For example, suppose a company is expected to have a constant ROE of 13.4 percent, and it is expected to pay out 40 percent of its earnings and to retain 60 percent. In this case, its forecasted growth rate would be g = (0.60)(13.4%) = 8.0%.

To illustrate the DCF approach, suppose Allied's stock sells for $23; its next expected dividend is $1.24; and its expected growth rate is 8 percent. Allied's expected and required rate of return, hence its cost of retained earnings, would then be 13.4 percent:

$$\hat{k}_s = k_s = \frac{\$1.24}{\$23} + 8.0\%$$

$$= 5.4\% + 8.0\%$$

$$= 13.4\%.$$

This 13.4 percent is the minimum rate of return that management must expect to justify retaining earnings and plowing them back in the business rather than paying them out to stockholders as dividends. Put another way, since investors have an *opportunity* to earn 13.4 percent if earnings are paid to them as dividends, then the company's *opportunity cost* of equity from retained earnings is 13.4 percent.

People experienced in estimating equity capital costs recognize that both careful analysis and sound judgment are required. It would be nice to pretend that judgment is unnecessary and to specify an easy, precise way of determining the exact cost of equity capital. Unfortunately, this is not possible — finance is in large part a matter of judgment, and we simply must face that fact.

SELF-TEST QUESTIONS

Why must a cost be assigned to retained earnings?

What three approaches are used to estimate the cost of common equity?

Identify some problems with the CAPM approach.

What is the reasoning behind the bond-yield-plus-risk-premium approach?

Which of the two components of the constant growth DCF formula, the dividend yield or the growth rate, is more difficult to estimate? Why?

COST OF NEW COMMON STOCK, k_e

Companies generally hire an investment banker to assist them when they issue common stock, preferred stock, or bonds. In return for a fee, the investment banker helps the company structure the terms and set a price for the issue, and then sells the issue to investors. The banker's fees are often referred to as *flotation costs*, and the total cost of capital should reflect both the required return paid to investors and the flotation fees paid to the investment banker.

As you can see in the accompanying box, "How Much Does It Cost to Raise External Capital?," flotation costs are often substantial, and they vary depending on the size and risk of the issuing firm and on the type of capital raised. So far, we have ignored flotation costs when estimating the component costs of capital, but some would argue that these costs should be included in a complete analysis of the cost of capital. [The counter-argument is that flotation costs are not high enough to worry about because (1) most equity comes from retained earnings, (2) most debt is raised in private placements and hence involves no flotation costs, and (3) preferred stock is rarely used.] A more complete discussion of flotation cost adjustments can be found in Eugene F. Brigham and Phillip R. Daves, *Intermediate Financial Management*, 7th ed., and other advanced texts, but we describe below two alternative approaches that can be used to account for flotation costs.

The first approach simply adds the estimated dollar amount of flotation costs for each project to the project's up-front cost. The estimated flotation costs are found as the sum of the flotation costs for the debt, preferred, and common stock used to finance the project. Because of the now-higher investment cost, the project's expected rate of return and NPV are decreased. For example, consider a one-year project that has an up-front cost (not including flotation costs) of $100 million. After one year, the project is expected to produce an inflow of $115 million. Therefore, its expected return is $115/$100 − 1 = 0.15 = 15%. However, if the project requires the company to issue new capital with an estimated $2 million of flotation costs, the total up-front cost is $102 million, and the expected rate of return is only $115/$102 − 1 = 0.1275 = 12.75%.

The second approach involves adjusting the cost of capital rather than increasing the project's cost. If the firm plans to continue to use the capital in the future, as is generally true for equity, then this second approach is better. The adjustment process is based on the following logic. If there are flotation costs, the issuing company receives only a portion of the total capital raised from investors, with the remainder going to the underwriter. When calculating the cost of common equity, the DCF approach can be adapted to account for flotation costs. For a constant growth stock, the **cost of new common stock, k_e,** can be expressed as:[9]

Cost of New Common Stock, k_e
The cost of external equity; based on the cost of retained earnings, but increased for flotation costs.

$$\text{Cost of equity from new stock issues} = k_e = \frac{D_1}{P_0(1 - F)} + g. \qquad (9\text{-}9)$$

Here **F** is the percentage **flotation cost** required to sell the new stock, so $P_0(1 - F)$ is the net price per share received by the company.

Flotation Cost, F
The percentage cost of issuing new common stock.

Assuming that Allied has a flotation cost of 10 percent, its cost of new common equity, k_e, is computed as follows:

$$k_e = \frac{\$1.24}{\$23(1 - 0.10)} + 8.0\%$$

$$= \frac{\$1.24}{\$20.70} + 8.0\%$$

$$= 6.0\% + 8.0\% = 14.0\%.$$

---

[9] Equation 9-9 is derived as follows:

Step 1. The old stockholders expect the firm to pay a stream of dividends, D_t, that will be derived from existing assets with a per-share value of P_0. New investors will likewise expect to receive the same stream of dividends, but the funds available to invest in assets will be less than P_0 because of flotation costs. For new investors to receive their expected dividend stream *without impairing*

(footnote continues)

HOW MUCH DOES IT COST TO RAISE EXTERNAL CAPITAL?

A recent study by four professors provides some insights into how much it costs U.S. corporations to raise external capital. Using information from the Securities Data Company, they found the average flotation cost for debt and equity issued in the 1990s as presented below.

The common stock flotation costs are for non-IPOs. Costs associated with IPOs are even higher — flotation costs are about 17 percent of gross proceeds for common equity if the amount raised in the IPO is less than $10 million and about 6 percent if more than $500 million is raised. The data shown below include both utility and nonutility companies. If utilities were excluded, flotation costs would be somewhat higher.

SOURCE: Inmoo Lee, Scott Lochhead, Jay Ritter, and Quanshui Zhao, "The Costs of Raising Capital," *The Journal of Financial Research*, Vol. XIX, No. 1, Spring 1996, 59–74. Reprinted with permission.

AMOUNT OF CAPITAL RAISED (MILLIONS OF DOLLARS)	AVERAGE FLOTATION COST FOR COMMON STOCK (% OF TOTAL CAPITAL RAISED)	AVERAGE FLOTATION COST FOR NEW DEBT (% OF TOTAL CAPITAL RAISED)
2–9.99	13.28	4.39
10–19.99	8.72	2.76
20–39.99	6.93	2.42
40–59.99	5.87	1.32
60–79.99	5.18	2.34
80–99.99	4.73	2.16
100–199.99	4.22	2.31
200–499.99	3.47	2.19
500 and up	3.15	1.64

Investors require a return of $k_s = 13.4\%$ on the stock. However, because of flotation costs the company must earn *more* than 13.4 percent on the net funds obtained by selling stock in order to give investors a 13.4 percent return on the money they put up. Specifically, if the firm earns 14 percent on funds obtained by issuing new stock, then earnings per share will remain at the previously expected level, the firm's expected dividend can be maintained, and, as a result, the price per share will not decline.

(Footnote 9 continued)

the D_t *stream of the old investors*, the new funds obtained from the sale of stock must be invested at a return high enough to provide a dividend stream whose present value is equal to the net price the firm will receive:

$$P_n = P_0(1 - F) = \sum_{t=1}^{\infty} \frac{D_t}{(1 + k_e)^t}. \tag{9-10}$$

Here D_t is the dividend stream to new (and old) stockholders, and k_e is the cost of new outside equity.

Step 2. When growth is constant, Equation 9-10 reduces to

$$P_n = P_0(1 - F) = \frac{D_1}{k_e - g}. \tag{9-10a}$$

Step 3. Equation 9-10a can be rearranged to produce Equation 9-9:

$$k_e = \frac{D_1}{P_0(1 - F)} + g.$$

If the firm earns less than 14 percent, then earnings, dividends, and growth will fall below expectations, causing the stock price to decline. If the firm earns more than 14 percent, the stock price will rise.

Because of flotation costs, dollars raised by selling new stock must "work harder" than dollars raised by retaining earnings. Moreover, since no flotation costs are involved, retained earnings have a lower cost than new stock. Therefore, firms should utilize retained earnings to the extent possible to avoid the costs of issuing new common stock. However, if a firm has more good investment opportunities than can be financed with retained earnings and debt supported by retained earnings, it may find it necessary to issue new common stock. The **retained earnings breakpoint** represents the total amount of financing that can be raised before the firm is forced to sell new common stock. This breakpoint can be calculated as follows:

Retained Earnings Breakpoint
The amount of capital raised beyond which new common stock must be issued.

$$\frac{\text{Retained earnings}}{\text{breakpoint}} = \frac{\text{Addition to retained earnings}}{\text{Equity fraction}}. \tag{9-11}$$

Allied's addition to retained earnings in 2003 is expected to be $68 million, and its capital structure consists of 45 percent debt, 2 percent preferred, and 53 percent equity. Therefore, its retained earnings breakpoint is $68/0.53 = $128 million. If Allied's capital budget called for spending exactly $128 million, then 0.45($128) = $57.6 million would be financed with debt, 0.02($128) = $2.6 million with preferred stock, and 0.53($128) = $67.8 million with equity raised from retained earnings. If Allied's capital budget exceeded the $128 million "breakpoint," the amount of equity required would exceed the amount of available retained earnings, so the company would have to obtain equity by issuing new, high-cost common stock.

It is important to recognize that this breakpoint is only suggestive—it is not written in stone. For example, rather than issuing new common stock, the company could use more debt (hence, less equity), or it could increase its additional retained earnings by reducing its dividend payout ratio. Both actions would increase the retained earnings breakpoint. In any event, firms that have a large number of good investment opportunities generally maximize their retained earnings by paying out a smaller percentage of income as dividends than firms with fewer good investment opportunities. We will discuss dividend policy in more detail in the chapter on distributions to shareholders.

Flotation cost adjustments can also be made for preferred stock and debt. For preferred stock, the flotation-adjusted cost is the preferred dividend, D_p, divided by the net issuing price, P_n, the price the firm receives on preferred after deducting flotation costs. Similarly, if debt is issued to the public and flotation costs are incurred, the after-tax cost is found by calculating the after-tax yield to maturity, where the issue price is the bond's par value less the flotation expense.[10]

---

[10] More specifically, for a newly issued bond at par, the solution value of k_d in this formula is used as the after-tax cost of debt:

$$M(1 - F) = \sum_{t=1}^{N} \frac{\text{INT}(1 - T)}{(1 + k_d)^t} + \frac{M}{(1 + k_d)^N}.$$

Here F is the percentage amount of the bond flotation cost, N is the number of periods to maturity, INT is the dollars of interest per period, T is the corporate tax rate, M is the maturity value of the bond, and k_d is the after-tax cost of debt adjusted to reflect flotation costs. If we assume that the bond in the example calls for annual payments, that it has a 20-year maturity, and that F = 2%, then the flotation-adjusted, after-tax cost of debt is 6.18 percent versus 6 percent before the flotation adjustment. Also see Eugene F. Brigham and Phillip R. Daves, *Intermediate Financial Management*, 7th ed. (Cincinnati, OH: South-Western College Publishing, 2002), Chapter 9.

While flotation costs may seem high, their per-project cost is usually relatively small. For example, if a company issues common stock only once every 10 years, the flotation costs should be spread over all the projects funded during the 10-year period. If flotation costs are charged only during the years in which external capital is raised, a project evaluated during those years would appear worse than the same project analyzed in a year when no external capital is raised. Since flotation costs are not normally very important, unless stated otherwise, we will leave a detailed discussion of flotation costs to advanced finance courses.

SELF-TEST QUESTIONS

Explain briefly the two approaches that can be used to adjust for flotation costs.

Would firms that have many good investment opportunities be likely to have higher or lower dividend payout ratios than firms with few good investment opportunities? Explain.

COMPOSITE, OR WEIGHTED AVERAGE, COST OF CAPITAL, WACC

Target (Optimal) Capital Structure
The percentages of debt, preferred stock, and common equity that will maximize the firm's stock price.

Weighted Average Cost of Capital, WACC
A weighted average of the component costs of debt, preferred stock, and common equity.

As we shall see in the chapter on capital structure and leverage, each firm has an optimal capital structure, defined as that mix of debt, preferred, and common equity that causes its stock price to be maximized. Therefore, a value-maximizing firm will determine its **optimal capital structure,** use it as a **target,** and then raise new capital in a manner designed to keep the actual capital structure on target over time. In this chapter, we assume that the firm has identified its optimal capital structure, that it uses this optimum as the target, and that it finances so as to remain on target. How the target is established will be examined in the capital structure and leverage chapter.

The target proportions of debt, preferred stock, and common equity, along with the costs of those components, are used to calculate the firm's **weighted average cost of capital, WACC.** To illustrate, suppose Allied Food has a target capital structure calling for 45 percent debt, 2 percent preferred stock, and 53 percent common equity (retained earnings plus common stock). Its before-tax cost of debt, k_d, is 10 percent; its after-tax cost of debt = $k_d(1 - T) = 10\%(0.6) = 6.0\%$; its cost of preferred stock, k_p, is 10.3 percent; its cost of common equity, k_s, is 13.4 percent; its marginal tax rate is 40 percent; and all of its new equity will come from retained earnings. We calculate Allied's weighted average cost of capital, WACC, as follows:

$$\text{WACC} = w_d k_d(1 - T) + w_p k_p + w_c k_s \tag{9-12}$$
$$= 0.45(10\%)(0.6) + 0.02(10.3\%) + 0.53(13.4\%)$$
$$= 10.0\%.$$

Here w_d, w_p, and w_c are the weights used for debt, preferred, and common equity, respectively.

WACC ESTIMATES FOR SOME LARGE U.S. CORPORATIONS

As noted in Chapter 2, the New York consulting firm of Stern Stewart & Company regularly estimates EVAs and MVAs for large U.S. corporations. To obtain these estimates, Stern Stewart must calculate a WACC for each company. The table below presents some recent WACC estimates as calculated by Stern Stewart for a sample of corporations, along with their long-term debt-to-total-capital ratios.

These estimates suggest that a typical company has a WACC somewhere in the 7.5 percent to 12.5 percent range and that the WACC varies considerably depending on (1) the company's risk and (2) the amount of debt it uses. Companies in riskier businesses, such as Intel, presumably have higher costs of common equity. Moreover, they tend not to use as much debt. These two factors, in combination, result in higher WACCs than those of companies that operate in more stable businesses, such as BellSouth. We will discuss the effects of capital structure on WACC in more detail in the capital structure and leverage chapter.

Note that riskier companies may also have the potential for producing higher returns, and what really matters to shareholders is whether a company is able to generate returns in excess of its cost of capital, resulting in a positive EVA. Therefore, a high cost of capital is not necessarily bad if it is accompanied by projects with high rates of return.

SOURCE: "The 2000 Stern Stewart Performance 1000," http://www.sternstewart.com/performance/rankings.shtml; and Value Line Investment Survey, February 23, 2001.

COMPANY	WACC	BOOK VALUE DEBT RATIO[a]
General Electric	12.47%	1%
Coca-Cola	12.31	8
Intel	12.19	2
Motorola	11.65	19
Wal-Mart	10.99	36
Walt Disney	9.28	22
AT&T	9.22	20
Exxon Mobil	8.16	10
H.J. Heinz	7.78	55
BellSouth	7.41	39

[a] Long-term debt only.

Every dollar of new capital that Allied obtains consists of 45 cents of debt with an after-tax cost of 6 percent, 2 cents of preferred stock with a cost of 10.3 percent, and 53 cents of common equity (all from additions to retained earnings) with a cost of 13.4 percent. The average cost of each whole dollar, WACC, is 10 percent.

Note that when calculating the firm's target capital structure, total debt includes both long-term debt and bank debt (notes payable). Recall from Chapter 2, that investor-supplied capital does not include other current liabilities such as accounts payable and accruals. Therefore, these other items are not included as part of Allied's capital structure.

As long as Allied keeps its capital structure on target, and as long as its debt has an after-tax cost of 6 percent, its preferred stock costs 10.3 percent, and its common equity costs 13.4 percent, then its weighted average cost of capital will be WACC =

10%.[11] Each dollar the firm raises will consist of some long-term debt, some preferred stock, and some common equity, and the cost of the whole dollar will be 10 percent.[12]

SELF-TEST QUESTIONS

Write out the equation for the weighted average cost of capital, WACC.

Is short-term debt included in the capital structure used to calculate WACC? Why or why not?

Why does the WACC at every amount of capital raised represent the marginal cost of that capital?

FACTORS THAT AFFECT THE COMPOSITE COST OF CAPITAL

The cost of capital is affected by a number of factors. Some are beyond a firm's control, but others are influenced by its financing and investment decisions.

FACTORS THE FIRM CANNOT CONTROL

The two most important factors that are beyond a firm's direct control are the level of interest rates and tax rates.

The Level of Interest Rates

If interest rates in the economy rise, the cost of debt increases because firms will have to pay bondholders more to obtain debt capital. Also, recall from our discussion of the CAPM that higher interest rates increase the costs of common and preferred equity capital. During the last decade, inflation, and consequently, interest rates in the United States declined significantly. This reduced the cost of capital for all firms, en-

---

[11] The 10 percent WACC assumed that Allied's equity capital came exclusively from retained earnings and had a cost of 13.4 percent. If Allied expanded so rapidly and required so much new capital that it had to issue new common stock at a cost of $k_e = 14\%$, then its WACC would rise to 10.3 percent:

$$\text{WACC} = w_d k_d (1 - T) + w_p k_p + w_c k_e$$
$$= 0.45(10\%)(0.6) + 0.02(10.3\%) + 0.53(14.0\%)$$
$$= 10.3\%.$$

The increase in the WACC would occur at the "retained earnings breakpoint" as discussed in the preceding section. However, as we noted, companies can and do change their dividend payout ratios and target capital structures if and when their capital budgets actually approach the breakpoint, so the breakpoint itself is flexible, not set in stone.

[12] As noted in Footnote 11, at times the weighted average cost of capital will not remain constant but will instead increase as the firm raises more and more capital. This situation exists for large, established firms if they require so much capital that they are required to issue new common stock to the public. Note, though, that large firms rarely issue common stock — they typically obtain all the equity they need by retaining earnings. See Brigham and Daves, *Intermediate Financial Management*, 7th ed., Chapter 9.

GLOBAL VARIATIONS IN THE COST OF CAPITAL

For U.S. firms to be competitive with foreign companies, they must have a cost of capital similar to that faced by their international competitors. In the past, many experts argued that U.S. firms were at a disadvantage. In particular, Japanese firms enjoyed a lower cost of capital, which lowered their total costs and thus made it harder for U.S. firms to compete. Recent events, however, have considerably narrowed cost of capital differences between U.S. and Japanese firms. In particular, despite its recent decline, the U.S. stock market has outperformed the Japanese market over the past decade, which has made it possible for U.S. firms to raise equity capital.

As capital markets become increasingly integrated, cross-country differences in the cost of capital are disappearing. Today, most large corporations raise capital throughout the world, hence we are moving toward one global capital market rather than distinct capital markets in each country. Although government policies and market conditions can affect the cost of capital within a given country, this primarily affects smaller firms that do not have access to global capital markets, and even these differences are becoming less important as time goes by. What matters most is the risk of the individual firm, not the market in which it raises capital.

 www Professor Campbell Harvey of Duke University has an interesting web site that looks at country risk, emerging markets, and the global cost of capital. The site can be found at **http://www.duke.edu/~charvey**.

couraging additional investment. Our lower interest rates also enabled U.S. firms to compete more effectively with German and Japanese firms, which in the past had enjoyed lower costs of capital than U.S. firms.

Tax Rates

Tax rates, which are largely beyond the control of an individual firm (although firms can and do lobby for more favorable tax treatment), have an important effect on the cost of capital. Tax rates are used in the calculation of the component cost of debt. In addition, there are other less apparent ways in which tax policy affects the cost of capital. For example, lowering the capital gains tax rate relative to the rate on ordinary income makes stocks more attractive, and that reduces the cost of equity. That would lower the WACC, and, as we will see in the chapter on capital structure and leverage, it would also lead to a change in a firm's optimal capital structure (toward less debt and more equity).

FACTORS THE FIRM CAN CONTROL

A firm can directly affect its cost of capital through its capital structure policy, its dividend policy, and its investment (capital budgeting) policy.

Capital Structure Policy

Until now we have assumed that a firm has a given target capital structure, and we used weights based on that target structure to calculate the WACC. However, a firm can change its capital structure, and such a change can affect its cost of capital. The after-tax cost of debt is lower than the cost of equity. Specifically, if the firm decides to use more debt and less common equity, this change in the weights in the WACC equation will tend to lower the WACC. However, an increase in the use of debt will increase the riskiness of both the debt and the equity, and these increases in component costs will tend to offset the effects of the change in the weights. In the capital structure and leverage chapter, we will discuss this concept in more depth, and we will demonstrate that a firm's optimal capital structure minimizes its cost of capital.

Dividend Policy

As we indicated earlier, firms can obtain new equity either through retained earnings or by issuing new common stock, but because of flotation costs, new common stock is more expensive than retained earnings. For this reason, firms issue new common stock only after they have invested all of their retained earnings. Since retained earnings is income that has not been paid out as dividends, it follows that dividend policy can affect the cost of capital because it affects the level of retained earnings. As we will see in the distributions to shareholders chapter, firms take cost of capital effects into account when they establish their dividend policies.

Investment Policy

When we estimate the cost of capital, we use as the starting point the required rates of return on the firm's outstanding stock and bonds. Those cost rates reflect the riskiness of the firm's existing assets. Therefore, we have implicitly been assuming that new capital will be invested in assets of the same type and with the same degree of risk as is embedded in the existing assets. This assumption is generally correct, as most firms do invest in assets similar to those they currently operate. However, it would be incorrect if the firm dramatically changed its investment policy. For example, if a firm invests in an entirely new line of business, its marginal cost of capital should reflect the riskiness of that new business. To illustrate, ITT Corporation recently sold off its finance company and purchased Caesar's World, a casino gambling firm. This dramatic shift in corporate focus almost certainly affected ITT's cost of capital. Likewise, Disney's purchase of the ABC television network changed the nature and risk of the company in a way that might also influence its cost of capital. The effect of investment decisions on capital costs is discussed in detail in the next section.

SELF-TEST QUESTIONS

What two factors that affect the cost of capital are generally beyond the firm's control?

What policies under the firm's control are likely to affect its cost of capital?

Explain how a change in interest rates would affect each component of the weighted average cost of capital.

ADJUSTING THE COST OF CAPITAL FOR RISK

As noted above, the cost of capital is a key element in the capital budgeting process. As you will see in capital budgeting analysis, which follows this chapter, a project should be accepted if and only if its estimated return exceeds its cost of capital. For this reason, the cost of capital is sometimes referred to as a "hurdle rate" — project returns must "jump the hurdle" to be accepted.

As we saw in Chapter 5, investors require higher returns for riskier investments. Consequently, a company that is raising capital to take on risky projects will have a higher cost of capital than a company that is investing in safer projects. Figure 9-1 illustrates the trade-off between risk and the cost of capital. Firm L is a low-risk business and has a WACC of 8 percent, whereas Firm H is exposed to high risks and has a WACC of 12 percent. Thus, Firm H will accept a typical project only if its expected return is above 12 percent. The corresponding hurdle rate for Firm L's typical project is only 8 percent.

It is important to remember that the cost of capital values at points L and H in Figure 9-1 represent the overall, or composite, WACCs for the two firms, and, thus, only represent the hurdle rate of a "typical" project for each firm. Different projects generally have different risks. Indeed, the hurdle rate for each project should reflect the risk of the project itself, not the risks associated with the firm's average project as reflected in its composite WACC. For example, assume that Firms L and H are both considering Project A. This project has more risk than a typical Firm L project, but less risk than a typical Firm H project. As shown in Figure 9-1, Project A has a 10.5 percent expected return. At first, we might be tempted to conclude that Firm L should accept Project A because its 10.5 percent return is above Firm L's 8 percent WACC, while Firm H should turn down the project because its return is less than H's 12 percent WACC. However, this would be wrong. The relevant hurdle rate is the *project's WACC*, which is 10 percent, as read from the WACC line in Figure 9-1. Since the project's return exceeds its 10 percent cost, *both* firms should accept Project A.

FIGURE 9-1
Risk and the Cost of Capital

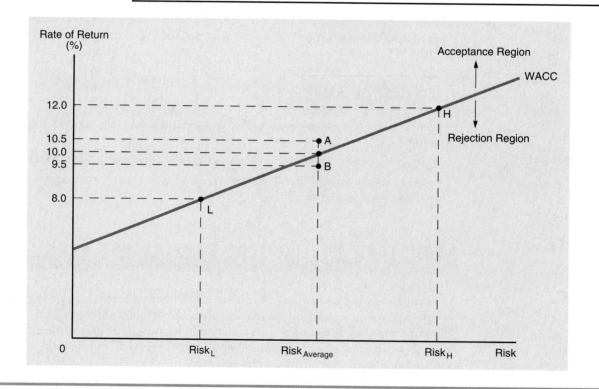

Next, consider Project B. It has the same risk as Project A, but its expected return is 9.5 percent versus its 10 percent hurdle rate. Both firms should reject Project B. However, if they based their decisions on their overall WACCs rather than on the project-specific cost of capital, Firm L would accept Project B because its return is above L's 8 percent WACC. However, if Firm L's managers accept Project B, they would reduce their shareholders' wealth, because the project's return is not high enough to justify its risk. Applying a specific hurdle rate to each project insures that every project is evaluated properly.

Note that these same arguments apply to the cost of capital for a multidivisional firm. Consider Firm A in Figure 9-2. It has two divisions, L and H. Division L has relatively little risk, and if it were operated as a separate firm, its WACC would be 7 percent. Division H has a higher risk, and its divisional cost of capital is 13 percent. If the two divisions were of equal size, Firm A's composite WACC would be 0.50(7%) + 0.50(13%) = 10.0%. However, it would be a mistake to use this 10 percent WACC for either division. To see this point, assume that Division L is considering a relatively low-risk project with an expected return of 9 percent, while Division H is considering a high-risk project with an expected return of 11 percent. As shown in Figure 9-2, Division L's project should be accepted, because its return is above its risk-based cost of capital, whereas Division H's project should be rejected. If the 10 percent corporate WACC were used by each division, the decision would be reversed: Division H would incorrectly accept its project, and Division L would incorrectly reject its project. In general, failing to adjust for differences in risk would lead the firm to accept too many risky projects and reject too many safe ones. Over time, the firm would become more risky, its WACC would increase, and its shareholder value would suffer.

FIGURE 9-2   **Divisional Cost of Capital**

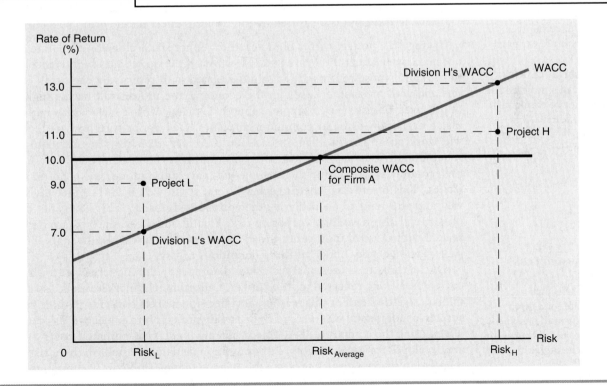

SELF-TEST QUESTIONS

Why is the cost of capital sometimes referred to as a "hurdle rate"?

How should firms evaluate projects with different risks?

Should divisions within the same firm all use the firm's composite WACC when considering capital budgeting projects? Explain.

ESTIMATING PROJECT RISK

Stand-Alone Risk
The risk an asset would have if it were a firm's only asset and if investors owned only one stock. It is measured by the variability of the asset's expected returns.

Corporate, or Within-Firm, Risk
Risk not considering the effects of stockholders' diversification; it is measured by a project's effect on uncertainty about the firm's future earnings.

Market, or Beta, Risk
That part of a project's risk that cannot be eliminated by diversification; it is measured by the project's beta coefficient.

Risk-Adjusted Cost of Capital
The cost of capital appropriate for a given project, given the riskiness of that project. The greater the risk, the higher the cost of capital.

Although it is intuitively clear that riskier projects should be assigned a higher cost of capital, it is often difficult to estimate project risk. First, note that three separate and distinct types of risk can be identified:

1. **Stand-alone risk,** which is the project's risk disregarding the facts (a) that it is but one asset within the firm's portfolio of assets and (b) that the firm is but one stock in a typical investor's portfolio of stocks. Stand-alone risk is measured by the variability of the project's expected returns.

2. **Corporate, or within-firm, risk,** which is the project's risk to the corporation, giving consideration to the fact that the project represents only one of the firm's portfolio of assets, hence that some of its risk effects on the firm's profits will be diversified away. Corporate risk is measured by the project's impact on uncertainty about the firm's future earnings.

3. **Market, or beta, risk,** which is the riskiness of the project as seen by a well-diversified stockholder who recognizes that the project is only one of the firm's assets and that the firm's stock is but one small part of the investor's total portfolio. Market risk is measured by the project's effect on the firm's beta coefficient.

Taking on a project with a high degree of either stand-alone or corporate risk will not necessarily affect the firm's beta. However, if the project has highly uncertain returns, and if those returns are highly correlated with returns on the firm's other assets and with most other assets in the economy, the project will have a high degree of all types of risk. For example, suppose General Motors decides to undertake a major expansion to build commuter airplanes. GM is not sure how its technology will work on a mass production basis, so there are great risks in the venture — its stand-alone risk is high. Management also estimates that the project will do best if the economy is strong, for then people will have more money to spend on the new planes. This means that the project will tend to do well if GM's other divisions do well and will tend to do badly if other divisions do badly. This being the case, the project will also have high corporate risk. Finally, since GM's profits are highly correlated with those of most other firms, the project's beta will also be high. Thus, this project will be risky under all three definitions of risk.

Of the three measures, market risk is theoretically the most relevant measure because it is the one reflected in stock prices. Unfortunately, market risk is also the most difficult to estimate. For this reason, most decision makers consider all three risk measures in a judgmental manner and then classify projects into subjective risk categories. Then, using the composite WACC as a starting point, **risk-adjusted costs of capital** are developed for each category. For example, a firm might establish three risk classes, then assign to average-risk projects the average (composite) cost of capital, to higher-risk projects an above-average cost, and to lower-risk projects a below-average cost. Thus, if a company's composite WACC estimate were 10 percent, its managers might use 10 percent to evaluate average-risk projects, 12 percent for those with high-risk, and 8 percent for low-risk projects. While this approach is better than not making any risk adjustments, these adjustments are subjective and somewhat arbitrary. Unfortunately, there is no perfect way to specify how much higher or lower we should go in setting risk-adjusted costs of capital. However, the CAPM approach often produces reasonable results. For further information on estimating the risk-adjusted cost of capital see Web Appendix 9A, and for more information on measuring market (or beta) risk see Web Appendix 9B.

SELF-TEST QUESTIONS

What are the three types of project risk?

Which type of project risk is theoretically the most relevant? Why?

Explain the classification scheme many firms use when developing *subjective* risk-adjusted costs of capital.

SOME PROBLEM AREAS IN COST OF CAPITAL

A number of difficult issues relating to the cost of capital either have not been mentioned or were glossed over in this chapter. These topics are covered in advanced finance courses, but they deserve some mention now both to alert you to potential dangers and to provide you with a preview of some of the matters dealt with in advanced courses.

1. **Depreciation-generated funds.** The largest single source of capital for many firms is depreciation, yet we have not discussed the cost of funds from this source. In brief, depreciation cash flows can either be reinvested or returned to investors (stockholders *and* creditors). The cost of depreciation-generated funds is approximately equal to the weighted average cost of capital from retained earnings and low-cost debt. See Brigham and Daves, *Intermediate Financial Management*, 7th ed., Chapter 9, for a discussion.

2. **Privately owned firms.** Our discussion of the cost of equity was related to publicly owned corporations, and we have concentrated on the rate of return required by public stockholders. However, there is a serious question about how one should measure the cost of equity for a firm whose stock is not traded. Tax issues are also especially important in these cases. As a general rule, the same principles of cost of capital estimation apply to both privately held and publicly owned firms, but the problems of obtaining input data are somewhat different for each.

3. **Measurement problems.** We cannot overemphasize the practical difficulties encountered when estimating the cost of equity. It is very difficult to obtain good input data for the CAPM, for g in the formula $\hat{k}_s = D_1/P_0 + g$, and for the risk premium in the formula $k_s = $ Bond yield $+$ Risk premium. As a result, we can never be sure just how accurate our estimated cost of capital is.

4. **Costs of capital for projects of differing riskiness.** It is difficult to measure projects' risks, hence to assign risk-adjusted discount rates to capital budgeting projects of differing degrees of riskiness.

5. **Capital structure weights.** In this chapter, we have simply taken as given the target capital structure and have used it to calculate the cost of capital. As we shall see in the capital structure and leverage chapter, establishing the target capital structure is a major task in itself.

Although this listing of problems may appear formidable, the state of the art in cost of capital estimation is really not in bad shape. The procedures outlined in this chapter can be used to obtain cost of capital estimates that are sufficiently accurate for practical purposes, and the problems listed here merely indicate the desirability of refinements. The refinements are not unimportant, but the problems we have identified do not invalidate the usefulness of the procedures outlined in the chapter.

SELF-TEST QUESTION

Identify some problem areas in cost of capital analysis. Do these problems invalidate the cost of capital procedures discussed in the chapter?

TYING IT ALL TOGETHER

We began this chapter by defining three capital components — debt, preferred stock, and common equity — and then estimating each component's cost of capital. After estimating the components' costs, we calculated a weighted average cost of capital (WACC). As we will see in the next chapters, the WACC is a key element in the capital budgeting process. In this chapter we calculated the WACC assuming that the target capital structure is given. In the capital structure and leverage chapter, we will discuss how firms determine their target capital structures and the effects of capital structure on the WACC. The key concepts covered in Chapter 9 are listed below.

- The cost of capital is sometimes referred to as a **hurdle rate.** For a project to increase shareholders' value, it must earn more than its hurdle rate.
- The cost of capital used in capital budgeting is a **weighted average** of the types of capital the firm uses, typically debt, preferred stock, and common equity.
- The **component cost of debt** is the **after-tax** cost of new debt. It is found by multiplying the cost of new debt by $(1 - T)$, where T is the firm's marginal tax rate: $k_d(1 - T)$.
- The **component cost of preferred stock** is calculated as the preferred dividend divided by the current price of the preferred stock: $k_p = D_p/P_p$.
- The **cost of retained earnings, k_s,** is the rate of return stockholders require on the company's common stock. There are two sources of equity capital: (1) internal equity generated through additions to retained earnings and (2) external equity obtained by issuing new shares of common stock.
- To use the **CAPM approach,** one (1) estimates the firm's beta, (2) multiplies this beta by the market risk premium to determine the firm's risk premium, and (3) adds the firm's risk premium to the risk-free rate to obtain the firm's cost of common equity: $k_s = k_{RF} + (k_M - k_{RF})b_i$.

- The **bond-yield-plus-risk-premium approach** calls for adding a risk premium of from 3 to 5 percentage points to the firm's interest rate on long-term debt: $k_s =$ Bond yield $+$ RP.

- To use the **dividend-yield-plus-growth-rate approach,** which is also called the **discounted cash flow (DCF) approach,** one adds the firm's expected growth rate to its expected dividend yield: $\hat{k}_s = D_1/P_0 + g$.

- Two alternative approaches can be used to account for **flotation costs,** the percentage cost of issuing new common stock. The first approach adds the estimated dollar amount of flotation costs for each project to the project's up-front cost — this **lowers the project's expected rate of return.** An alternative approach is to **adjust the cost of equity.** When calculating the **cost of new common stock,** the DCF approach can be adapted to account for flotation costs. For a constant growth stock, this cost can be expressed as: $k_e = D_1/[P_0(1 - F)] + g$. Note that flotation costs cause k_e to be greater than k_s.

- Each firm has an **optimal capital structure,** defined as the mix of debt, preferred stock, and common equity that minimizes its **weighted average cost of capital (WACC):**

$$\text{WACC} = w_d k_d (1 - T) + w_p k_p + w_c k_s.$$

- The **risk-adjusted cost of capital** is the cost of capital appropriate for a given project, given the riskiness of that project. The greater the risk, the higher the cost of capital.

QUESTIONS

9-1   How would each of the following affect a firm's cost of debt, $k_d(1 - T)$; its cost of equity, k_s; and its weighted average cost of capital, WACC? Indicate by a plus $(+)$, a minus $(-)$, or a zero (0) if the factor would raise, lower, or have an indeterminate effect on the item in question. Assume other things are held constant. Be prepared to justify your answer, but recognize that several of the parts probably have no single correct answer; these questions are designed to stimulate thought and discussion.

	EFFECT ON		
	$k_d(1 - T)$	k_s	WACC
a. The corporate tax rate is lowered.	_____	_____	_____
b. The Federal Reserve tightens credit.	_____	_____	_____
c. The firm uses more debt; that is, it increases its debt/assets ratio.	_____	_____	_____
d. The dividend payout ratio is increased.	_____	_____	_____
e. The firm doubles the amount of capital it raises during the year.	_____	_____	_____
f. The firm expands into a risky new area.	_____	_____	_____
g. The firm merges with another firm whose earnings are countercyclical both to those of the first firm and to the stock market.	_____	_____	_____
h. The stock market falls drastically, and the firm's stock falls along with the rest.	_____	_____	_____
i. Investors become more risk averse.	_____	_____	_____
j. The firm is an electric utility with a large investment in nuclear plants. Several states propose a ban on nuclear power generation.	_____	_____	_____

9-2 Distinguish among beta (or market) risk, within-firm (or corporate) risk, and stand-alone risk for a project being considered for inclusion in the capital budget. Of the three measures, which is theoretically the most relevant and why?

9-3 Suppose a firm estimates its cost of capital for the coming year to be 10 percent. What are reasonable costs of capital for evaluating average-risk projects, high-risk projects, and low-risk projects?

9-4 How should a manager determine the capital structure weights that are used to calculate the WACC?

9-5 Assume that there is an increase in the risk-free rate. What impact would this increase have on the cost of debt? What impact would this have on the cost of equity?

9-6 What are the likely effects of a policy in which a company fails to adjust for differences in risk when estimating the cost of capital for their various projects?

SELF-TEST PROBLEMS (SOLUTIONS APPEAR IN APPENDIX B)

ST-1
Key terms

Define each of the following terms:
a. After-tax cost of debt, $k_d(1 - T)$; capital component
b. Cost of preferred stock, k_p
c. Cost of retained earnings, k_s; cost of new common stock, k_e
d. Flotation cost, F; retained earnings breakpoint
e. Target (optimal) capital structure
f. Weighted average cost of capital, WACC
g. Stand-alone risk; corporate (within-firm) risk; market (beta) risk
h. Risk-adjusted cost of capital

ST-2
Marginal cost of capital

Lancaster Engineering Inc. (LEI) has the following capital structure, which it considers to be optimal:

Debt	25%
Preferred stock	15
Common equity	60
	100%

LEI's expected net income this year is $34,285.72, its established dividend payout ratio is 30 percent, its federal-plus-state tax rate is 40 percent, and investors expect earnings and dividends to grow at a constant rate of 9 percent in the future. LEI paid a dividend of $3.60 per share last year, and its stock currently sells at a price of $54 per share.

LEI can obtain new capital in the following ways:
- *Preferred*: New preferred stock with a dividend of $11 can be sold to the public at a price of $95 per share.
- *Debt*: Debt can be sold at an interest rate of 12 percent.

a. Determine the cost of each capital structure component.
b. Calculate the weighted average cost of capital.
c. LEI has the following investment opportunities that are typical average-risk projects for the firm:

PROJECT	COST AT t = 0	RATE OF RETURN
A	$10,000	17.4%
B	20,000	16.0
C	10,000	14.2
D	20,000	13.7
E	10,000	12.0

Which projects should LEI accept? Why?

9-1
Cost of common equity

Percy Motors has a target capital structure of 40 percent debt and 60 percent equity. The yield to maturity on the company's outstanding bonds is 9 percent, and the company's tax rate is 40 percent. Percy's CFO has calculated the company's WACC as 9.96 percent. What is the company's cost of common equity?

9-2
Cost of preferred stock

Tunney Industries can issue perpetual preferred stock at a price of $47.50 a share. The issue is expected to pay a constant annual dividend of $3.80 a share. What is the company's cost of preferred stock, k_p?

9-3
Cost of equity with and without flotation

Javits & Sons' common stock is currently trading at $30 a share. The stock is expected to pay a dividend of $3.00 a share at the end of the year ($D_1 = \$3.00$), and the dividend is expected to grow at a constant rate of 5 percent a year. If the company were to issue external equity, it would incur a 10 percent flotation cost. What are the costs of internal and external equity?

9-4
Project selection

Midwest Water Works estimates that its WACC is 10.5 percent. The company is considering the following seven investment projects:

PROJECT	SIZE	RATE OF RETURN
A	$1 million	12.0%
B	2 million	11.5
C	2 million	11.2
D	2 million	11.0
E	1 million	10.7
F	1 million	10.3
G	1 million	10.2

Assume that each of these projects is just as risky as the firm's existing assets, and the firm may accept all the projects or only some of them. Which set of projects should be accepted?

EXAM-TYPE PROBLEMS

The problems included in this section are set up in such a way that they could be used as multiple-choice exam problems.

9-5
After-tax cost of debt

The Heuser Company's currently outstanding 10 percent coupon bonds have a yield to maturity of 12 percent. Heuser believes it could issue at par new bonds that would provide a similar yield to maturity. If its marginal tax rate is 35 percent, what is Heuser's after-tax cost of debt?

9-6
Cost of preferred stock including flotation

Trivoli Industries plans to issue some $100 par preferred stock with an 11 percent dividend. The stock is selling on the market for $97.00, but Trivoli must pay flotation costs of 5 percent of the market price, so the net price the firm will receive is $92.15 per share. What is Trivoli's cost of preferred stock with flotation considered?

9-7
Cost of common equity with and without flotation

The Evanec Company's next expected dividend, D_1, is $3.18; its growth rate is 6 percent; and the stock now sells for $36. New stock (external equity) can be sold to net the firm $32.40 per share.
a. What is Evanec's cost of retained earnings, k_s?
b. What is Evanec's percentage flotation cost, F?
c. What is Evanec's cost of new common stock, k_e?

9-8
Weighted average cost of capital

The Patrick Company's cost of common equity is 16 percent. Its before-tax cost of debt is 13 percent, and its marginal tax rate is 40 percent. The stock sells at book value. Using the following balance sheet, calculate Patrick's after-tax weighted average cost of capital:

ASSETS		LIABILITIES AND EQUITY	
Cash	$ 120		
Accounts receivable	240		
Inventories	360	Long-term debt	$1,152
Plant and equipment, net	2,160	Equity	1,728
Total assets	$2,880	Total liabilities and equity	$2,880

9-9

WACC and percentage of debt financing

Hook Industries has a capital structure that consists solely of debt and common equity. The company can issue debt at 11 percent. Its stock currently pays a $2 dividend per share ($D_0 = $2), and the stock's price is currently $24.75. The company's dividend is expected to grow at a constant rate of 7 percent per year; its tax rate is 35 percent; and the company estimates that its WACC is 13.95 percent. What percentage of the company's capital structure consists of debt financing?

9-10

Weighted average cost of capital

Midwest Electric Company (MEC) uses only debt and equity. It can borrow unlimited amounts at an interest rate of 10 percent as long as it finances at its target capital structure, which calls for 45 percent debt and 55 percent common equity. Its last dividend was $2, its expected constant growth rate is 4 percent, and its stock sells at a price of $20. MEC's tax rate is 40 percent. Two projects are available: Project A has a rate of return of 13 percent, while Project B has a rate of return of 10 percent. All of the company's potential projects are equally risky and as risky as the firm's other assets.
a. What is MEC's cost of common equity?
b. What is MEC's WACC?
c. Which projects should MEC select?

9-11

Cost of common equity and WACC

Patton Paints Corporation has a target capital structure of 40 percent debt and 60 percent common equity. The company's before-tax cost of debt is 12 percent and its marginal tax rate is 40 percent. The current stock price is $P_0 = $22.50; the last dividend was $D_0 = $2.00; and the dividend is expected to grow at a constant rate of 7 percent. What will be the firm's cost of common equity and its WACC?

9-12

Cost of common equity with flotation

Ballack Co.'s common stock currently sells for $46.75 per share. Assume the stock is in a state of constant growth, has an expected dividend yield of 5 percent, and an expected capital gains yield of 12 percent. The current dividend payout ratio is 25 percent, and the firm's return on equity is 16 percent. The firm requires external funds for a new project and anticipates issuing additional shares of common stock at its current price of $46.75. However, the process of issuing this new equity is expected to result in a flotation expense equivalent to 5 percent of the price of the stock. If the firm goes ahead with its equity issue, what will be the firm's cost for this new common stock?

9-13

WACC and cost of common equity

Kahn Inc. has a target capital structure of 60 percent equity and 40 percent debt to fund its $10 billion in operating assets. Furthermore, Kahn Inc. has a weighted average cost of capital (WACC) of 13 percent, its before-tax cost of debt is 10 percent, and its tax rate is 40 percent. The company's retained earnings are adequate to fund the common equity portion of the capital budget. The firm's expected dividend next year (D_1) is $3 and the current stock price is $35.
a. What is the company's expected growth rate?
b. If the firm's net income is expected to be $1.1 billion, what portion of its net income is the firm expected to pay out as dividends?

9-14

WACC

Klose Outfitters Inc. has determined its optimal capital structure consists of 60 percent equity and 40 percent debt. Klose must raise additional capital to fund its upcoming expansion. The firm has $2 million in retained earnings that has a cost of 12 percent. Its investment bankers have informed the firm that it can issue an additional $6 million of new common stock at a cost of 15 percent. Furthermore, the firm can raise up to $3 million of debt at 10 percent and an additional $4 million at 12 percent. The firm has estimated that the proposed expansion will require an investment of $5.9 million. What is the weighted average cost of capital for the funds Klose will be raising?

9-15

Risk-adjusted discount rate

Ziege Systems is considering the following independent projects for the next year.

PROJECT	REQUIRED INVESTMENT	RATE OF RETURN	RISK
A	$4 million	14.0%	High
B	5 million	11.5	High
C	3 million	9.5	Low
D	2 million	9.0	Average
E	6 million	12.5	High
F	5 million	12.5	Average
G	6 million	7.0	Low
H	3 million	11.5	Low

The company estimates that its WACC is currently 10 percent. The company adjusts for risk by adding 2 percentage points to the WACC for high-risk projects and subtracting 2 percentage points from the WACC for low-risk projects.

a. Which projects should Ziege accept if it faces no capital constraints?

b. If Ziege only has the ability to invest a total of $13 million, which projects should it accept, and what will the firm's capital budget be for next year?

c. Suppose that Ziege can raise additional funds in order to increase its capital budget from the level determined in part b. However, for every $5 million of new capital raised by Ziege, the firm's weighted average cost of capital is expected to increase by 1 percent. If Ziege proceeds to use the same method of risk adjustment, which projects will it accept, and how much in additional funds must be raised to complete its capital budget?

PROBLEMS

9-16
Cost of common equity

The earnings, dividends, and stock price of Carpetto Technologies Inc. are expected to grow at 7 percent per year in the future. Carpetto's common stock sells for $23 per share, its last dividend was $2.00, and the company will pay a dividend of $2.14 at the end of the current year.

a. Using the discounted cash flow approach, what is its cost of common equity?

b. If the firm's beta is 1.6, the risk-free rate is 9 percent, and the average return on the market is 13 percent, what will be the firm's cost of common equity using the CAPM approach?

c. If the firm's bonds earn a return of 12 percent, what will k_s be using the bond-yield-plus-risk-premium approach? (Hint: Use the midpoint of the risk premium range.)

d. On the basis of the results obtained in parts a through c, what would you estimate Carpetto's cost of common equity to be?

9-17
Cost of common equity

The Bouchard Company's EPS was $6.50 in 2002 and $4.42 in 1997. The company pays out 40 percent of its earnings as dividends, and the stock sells for $36.

a. Calculate the past growth rate in earnings. (Hint: This is a 5-year growth period.)

b. Calculate the *next* expected dividend per share, D_1. ($D_0 = 0.4($6.50) = 2.60.) Assume that the past growth rate will continue.

c. What is the cost of retained earnings, k_s, for the Bouchard Company?

9-18
Calculation of g and EPS

Sidman Products' stock is currently selling for $60 a share. The firm is expected to earn $5.40 per share this year and to pay a year-end dividend of $3.60.

a. If investors require a 9 percent return, what rate of growth must be expected for Sidman?

b. If Sidman reinvests retained earnings in projects whose average return is equal to the stock's expected rate of return, what will be next year's EPS? [Hint: $g = (1 - \text{Payout rate})(\text{ROE})$.]

9-19
Weighted average cost of capital

The following tabulation gives earnings per share figures for the Foust Company during the preceding 10 years. The firm's common stock, 7.8 million shares outstanding, is now (1/1/03) selling for $65 per share, and the expected dividend at the end of the current year (2003) is 55 percent of the 2002 EPS. Because investors expect past trends to continue, g may be based on the earnings growth rate. (Note that 9 years of growth are reflected in the data.)

YEAR	EPS	YEAR	EPS
1993	$3.90	1998	$5.73
1994	4.21	1999	6.19
1995	4.55	2000	6.68
1996	4.91	2001	7.22
1997	5.31	2002	7.80

The current interest rate on new debt is 9 percent. The firm's marginal tax rate is 40 percent. Its capital structure, considered to be optimal, is as follows:

Debt	$104,000,000
Common equity	156,000,000
Total liabilities and equity	$260,000,000

a. Calculate Foust's after-tax cost of new debt and common equity. Calculate the cost of equity as $k_s = D_1/P_0 + g$.

b. Find Foust's weighted average cost of capital.

Adams Corporation has four investment projects with the following costs and rates of return:

	COST	RATE OF RETURN
Project 1	$2,000	16.00%
Project 2	3,000	15.00
Project 3	5,000	13.75
Project 4	2,000	12.50

The company estimates that it can issue debt at a before-tax cost of 10 percent, and its tax rate is 30 percent. The company also can issue preferred stock at $49 per share, which pays a constant dividend of $5 per year.

The company's stock currently sells at $36 per share. The year-end dividend, D_1, is expected to be $3.50, and the dividend is expected to grow at a constant rate of 6 percent per year. The company's capital structure consists of 75 percent common stock, 15 percent debt, and 10 percent preferred stock.

a. What is the cost of each of the capital components?
b. What is the WACC?
c. Which projects should the firm select if the projects are all of average risk?

SPREADSHEET PROBLEM

Here is the condensed balance sheet for Skye Computer Company (in thousands of dollars):

	2002
Current assets	$2,000
Net fixed assets	3,000
Total assets	$5,000
Current liabilities	$ 900
Long-term debt	1,200
Preferred stock	250
Common stock	1,300
Retained earnings	1,350
Total common equity	$2,650
Total liabilities and equity	$5,000

Skye Computer's earnings per share last year were $3.20; the stock sells for $55, and last year's dividend was $2.10. A flotation cost of 10 percent would be required to issue new common stock. Skye's preferred stock pays a dividend of $3.30 per share, and new preferred could be sold at a price to net the company $30 per share. Security analysts are projecting that the common dividend will grow at a rate of 9 percent per year. The firm can issue additional long-term debt at an interest rate (or before-tax cost) of 10 percent, and its marginal tax rate is 35 percent. The market risk premium is 5 percent, the risk-free rate is 6 percent, and Skye's beta is 1.516. In its cost of capital calculations, the company considers only long-term capital, hence it disregards current liabilities for this purpose.

a. Calculate the cost of each capital component, that is, the after-tax cost of debt, the cost of preferred stock, the cost of equity from retained earnings, and the cost of newly issued common stock. Use the DCF method to find the cost of common equity.
b. Now calculate the cost of common equity from retained earnings using the CAPM method.
c. What is the cost of new common stock, based on the CAPM? (Hint: Find the difference between k_e and k_s as determined by the DCF method, and add that differential to the CAPM value for k_s.)
d. If Skye Computer continues to use the same capital structure, what is the firm's WACC assuming (1) that it uses only retained earnings for equity and (2) that it expands so rapidly that it must issue new common stock?

COLEMAN TECHNOLOGIES INC.

9-22 **Cost of Capital** Coleman Technologies is considering a major expansion program that has been proposed by the company's information technology group. Before proceeding with the expansion, the company needs to develop an estimate of its cost of capital. Assume that you are an assistant to Jerry Lehman, the financial vice-president. Your first task is to estimate Coleman's cost of capital. Lehman has provided you with the following data, which he believes may be relevant to your task:

(1) The firm's tax rate is 40 percent.
(2) The current price of Coleman's 12 percent coupon, semi-annual payment, noncallable bonds with 15 years remaining to maturity is $1,153.72. Coleman does not use short-term interest-bearing debt on a permanent basis. New bonds would be privately placed with no flotation cost.
(3) The current price of the firm's 10 percent, $100 par value, quarterly dividend, perpetual preferred stock is $111.10.
(4) Coleman's common stock is currently selling at $50 per share. Its last dividend (D_0) was $4.19, and dividends are expected to grow at a constant rate of 5 percent in the foreseeable future. Coleman's beta is 1.2, the yield on T-bonds is 7 percent, and the market risk premium is estimated to be 6 percent. For the bond-yield-plus-risk-premium approach, the firm uses a 4 percentage point risk premium.
(5) Coleman's target capital structure is 30 percent long-term debt, 10 percent preferred stock, and 60 percent common equity.

To structure the task somewhat, Lehman has asked you to answer the following questions.

a. (1) What sources of capital should be included when you estimate Coleman's weighted average cost of capital (WACC)?
 (2) Should the component costs be figured on a before-tax or an after-tax basis?
 (3) Should the costs be historical (embedded) costs or new (marginal) costs?
b. What is the market interest rate on Coleman's debt and its component cost of debt?
c. (1) What is the firm's cost of preferred stock?

(2) Coleman's preferred stock is riskier to investors than its debt, yet the preferred's yield to investors is lower than the yield to maturity on the debt. Does this suggest that you have made a mistake? (Hint: Think about taxes.)
d. (1) Why is there a cost associated with retained earnings?
 (2) What is Coleman's estimated cost of common equity using the CAPM approach?
e. What is the estimated cost of common equity using the discounted cash flow (DCF) approach?
f. What is the bond-yield-plus-risk-premium estimate for Coleman's cost of common equity?
g. What is your final estimate for k_s?
h. Explain in words why new common stock has a higher percentage cost than retained earnings.
i. (1) What are two approaches that can be used to account for flotation costs?
 (2) Coleman estimates that if it issues new common stock, the flotation cost will be 15 percent. Coleman incorporates the flotation costs into the DCF approach. What is the estimated cost of newly issued common stock, taking into account the flotation cost?
j. What is Coleman's overall, or weighted average, cost of capital (WACC). Ignore flotation costs.
k. What factors influence Coleman's composite WACC?
l. Should the company use the composite WACC as the hurdle rate for each of its projects?
m. What are three types of project risk? How is each type of risk used?
n. Coleman is interested in establishing a new division, which will focus primarily on developing new Internet-based projects. In trying to determine the cost of capital for this new division, you discover that stand-alone firms involved in similar projects have on average the following characteristics:

■ Their capital structure is 40 percent debt and 60 percent common equity.
■ Their cost of debt is typically 12 percent.
■ The beta is 1.7.

Given this information, what would your estimate be for the division's cost of capital? Note that Coleman uses the CAPM to calculate the division's cost of capital.

CYBER PROBLEM

Please go to our web site **http://brigham.swlearning.com** to access the Cyberproblems.

With your Xtra! CD-ROM, access the Thomson Analytics Problems and use the Thomson Analytics Academic online database to work this chapter's problems.

THE BASICS OF CAPITAL BUDGETING

10

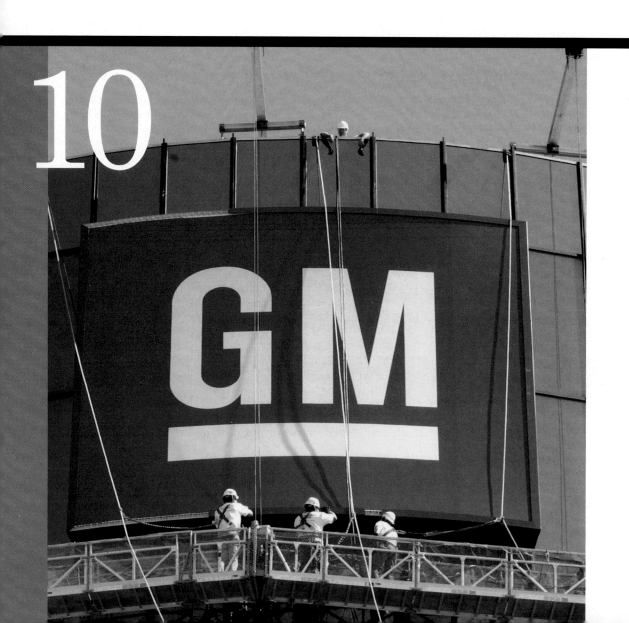

GENERAL MOTORS STRIVES TO FIND THE ROAD TO SUCCESS

GENERAL MOTORS

General Motors has struggled in recent years. Its stock price in mid-2002 was around $50 a share, which was about where it stood six years earlier. GM's earnings per share have plunged from $8.53 a share in 1999 to $1.77 a share in 2001, and the company hasn't increased its dividend since 1997. Moreover, the company continues to be plagued by high costs and a bureaucratic system that has limited its ability to develop innovative products.

Not surprisingly, GM's executives (and shareholders!) are looking for ways to improve the company's financial and operating performance. There are some reasons for optimism. The company's CEO, Rick Wagoner, has taken a number of steps to improve performance. Most notably, Wagoner has brought on two well-respected veterans from the auto industry to turn things around. He hired Bob Lutz, a 70-year-old retired Chrysler executive, to help with product design and John Devine, an ex-Ford executive, to help improve the company's financial performance.

There are signs that the world's largest automotive company is starting to find the road to success. GM's earnings and market share are beginning to turn around, and the company is once again attracting some positive attention on Wall Street. GM's stock, which was trading under $40 a share following the terrorist attacks in September 2001, soared to nearly $70 a share in spring 2002. More recently, however, the sharp decline in the overall stock market has once again pushed GM's stock below $40 a share.

As it tries to turn things around, GM's new leadership team has paid particular attention to the company's capital budgeting practices. Indeed, it is clear that the Wagoner-Lutz-Devine team has taken another look at many of the company's previously planned projects. GM's current capital budget is forecasted to be 10 percent less than the $7.8 billion that was spent in 2001. But it is also clear that GM's leaders are not imposing these cuts across the board. In some areas the company is increasing its investments, while in other areas it is scaling back. For example, the company is backing away from its previous plans to aggressively develop new hybrid vehicles that blend elements of a minivan and a sports utility vehicle.

While it may be too early to tell whether GM's initiatives will ultimately enhance shareholder value, it is clear that the capital investment decisions that the company makes today will have a long-lasting effect on the company's performance. In the years ahead, each of GM's investments will require careful analysis, much of it based on the techniques described in this chapter. With this in mind, as you read this chapter, think about how companies such as GM use capital budgeting analysis to make better investment decisions.

Source: Gregory L. White, "Sharing the Wheel: GM's New Team Undoes Plans Young CEO Once Had Pushed," *The Wall Street Journal*, June 28, 2002, A1.

In the last chapter, we discussed the cost of capital. Now we turn to investment decisions involving fixed assets, or *capital budgeting*. Here the term *capital* refers to long-term assets used in production, while a *budget* is a plan that details projected inflows and outflows during some future period. Thus, the *capital budget* is an outline of planned investments in fixed assets, and **capital budgeting** is the whole process of analyzing projects and deciding which ones to include in the capital budget. ∎

Capital Budgeting
The process of planning expenditures on assets whose cash flows are expected to extend beyond one year.

IMPORTANCE OF CAPITAL BUDGETING

A number of factors combine to make capital budgeting perhaps the most important function financial managers and their staffs must perform. First, since the results of capital budgeting decisions continue for many years, the firm loses some of its flexibility. For example, the purchase of an asset with an economic life of 10 years "locks in" the firm for a 10-year period. Further, because asset expansion is based on expected future sales, a decision to buy an asset that is expected to last 10 years requires a 10-year sales forecast. Finally, a firm's capital budgeting decisions define its strategic direction, because moves into new products, services, or markets must be preceded by capital expenditures.

An erroneous forecast of asset requirements can have serious consequences. If the firm invests too much, it will incur unnecessarily high depreciation and other expenses. On the other hand, if it does not invest enough, two problems may arise. First, its equipment and computer software may not be sufficiently modern to enable it to produce competitively. Second, if it has inadequate capacity, it may lose market share to rival firms, and regaining lost customers requires heavy selling expenses, price reductions, or product improvements, all of which are costly.

Timing is also important—capital assets must be available when they are needed. Edward Ford, executive vice-president of Western Design, a decorative tile company, gave the authors an illustration of the importance of capital budgeting. His firm tried to operate near capacity most of the time. During a four-year period, Western experienced intermittent spurts in the demand for its products, which forced it to turn away orders. After these sharp increases in demand, Western would add capacity by renting an additional building, then purchasing and installing the appropriate equipment. It would take six to eight months to get the additional capacity ready, but by then demand had dried up—other firms with available capacity had already taken an increased share of the market. Once Western began to properly forecast demand and plan its capacity requirements a year or so in advance, it was able to maintain and even increase its market share.

Effective capital budgeting can improve both the timing and the quality of asset acquisitions. If a firm forecasts its needs for capital assets in advance, it can purchase and install the assets before they are needed. Unfortunately, many firms do not order capital goods until existing assets are approaching full-capacity usage. If sales increase because of an increase in general market demand, all firms in the industry will tend to order capital goods at about the same time. This results in backlogs, long waiting times for machinery, a deterioration in the quality of the capital equipment, and an increase in costs. The firm that foresees its needs and purchases capital assets during slack periods can avoid these problems. Note, though, that if a firm forecasts an increase in demand and then expands to meet the anticipated demand, but sales do not increase, it will be saddled with excess capacity and high costs, which can lead to losses or even bankruptcy. Thus, an accurate sales forecast is critical.

Capital budgeting typically involves substantial expenditures, and before a firm can spend a large amount of money, it must have the funds lined up—large amounts of money are not available automatically. Therefore, a firm contemplating a major capital expenditure program should plan its financing far enough in advance to be sure funds are available.

SELF-TEST QUESTIONS

Why are capital budgeting decisions so important?

Why is the sales forecast a key element in a capital budgeting decision?

GENERATING IDEAS FOR CAPITAL PROJECTS

The same general concepts that are used in security valuation are also involved in capital budgeting. However, whereas a set of stocks and bonds exists in the securities market, and investors select from this set, *capital budgeting projects are created by the firm*. For example, a sales representative may report that customers are asking for a particular product that the company does not now produce. The sales manager then discusses the idea with the marketing research group to determine the size of the market for the proposed product. If it appears that a significant market does exist, cost accountants and engineers will be asked to estimate production costs. If they conclude that the product can be produced and sold at a sufficient profit, the project will be undertaken.

A firm's growth, and even its ability to remain competitive and to survive, depends on a constant flow of ideas for new products, for ways to make existing products better, and for ways to operate at a lower cost. Accordingly, a well-managed firm will go to great lengths to develop good capital budgeting proposals. For example, the executive vice-president of one very successful corporation indicated that his company takes the following steps to generate projects:

Strategic Business Plan
A long-run plan that outlines in broad terms the firm's basic strategy for the next five to ten years.

> Our R&D department is constantly searching for new products and for ways to improve existing products. In addition, our executive committee, which consists of senior executives in marketing, production, and finance, identifies the products and markets in which our company should compete, and the committee sets long-run targets for each division. These targets, which are spelled out in the corporation's **strategic business plan,** provide a general guide to the operating executives who must meet them. The operating executives then seek new products, set expansion plans for existing products, and look for ways to reduce production and distribution costs. Since bonuses and promotions are based on each unit's ability to meet or exceed its targets, these economic incentives encourage our operating executives to seek out profitable investment opportunities.

While our senior executives are judged and rewarded on the basis of how well their units perform, people further down the line are given bonuses and stock options for suggestions that lead to profitable investments. Additionally, a percentage of our corporate profit is set aside for distribution to nonexecutive employees, and we have an Employees' Stock Ownership Plan (ESOP) to provide further incentives. Our objective is to encourage employees at all levels to keep an eye out for good ideas, including those that lead to capital investments.

If a firm has capable and imaginative executives and employees, and if its incentive system is working properly, many ideas for capital investment will be advanced. Some ideas will be good ones, but others will not. Therefore, procedures must be established for screening projects, the primary topic of this chapter.

SELF-TEST QUESTION

What are some ways firms get ideas for capital projects?

PROJECT CLASSIFICATIONS

Analyzing capital expenditure proposals is not a costless operation—benefits can be gained, but analysis does have a cost. For certain types of projects, a relatively detailed analysis may be warranted; for others, simpler procedures should be used. Accordingly, firms generally categorize projects and then analyze those in each category somewhat differently:

1. **Replacement: maintenance of business.** One category consists of expenditures to replace worn-out or damaged equipment used in the production of profitable products. Replacement projects are necessary if the firm is to continue in business. The only issues here are (a) should this operation be continued and (b) should we continue to use the same production processes? The answers are usually yes, so maintenance decisions are normally made without going through an elaborate decision process.

2. **Replacement: cost reduction.** This category includes expenditures to replace serviceable but obsolete equipment. The purpose here is to lower the costs of labor, materials, and other inputs such as electricity. These decisions are discretionary, and a fairly detailed analysis is generally required.

3. **Expansion of existing products or markets.** Expenditures to increase output of existing products, or to expand retail outlets or distribution facilities in markets now being served, are included here. These decisions are more complex because they require an explicit forecast of growth in demand. Mistakes are more likely, so a more detailed analysis is required. Also, the go/no-go decision is generally made at a higher level within the firm.

4. **Expansion into new products or markets.** These are investments to produce a new product or to expand into a geographic area not currently being served. These projects involve strategic decisions that could change the fundamental nature of the business, and they normally require the expenditure of large sums

of money with delayed paybacks. Invariably, a detailed analysis is required, and the final decision is generally made at the very top—by the board of directors as a part of the firm's strategic plan.

5. **Safety and/or environmental projects.** Expenditures necessary to comply with government orders, labor agreements, or insurance policy terms fall into this category. These expenditures are called *mandatory investments*, and they often involve *nonrevenue-producing projects*. How they are handled depends on their size, with small ones being treated much like the Category 1 projects described above.

6. **Other.** This catch-all includes office buildings, parking lots, executive aircraft, and so on. How they are handled varies among companies.

In general, relatively simple calculations, and only a few supporting documents, are required for replacement decisions, especially maintenance-type investments in profitable plants. A more detailed analysis is required for cost-reduction replacements, for expansion of existing product lines, and especially for investments in new products or areas. Also, within each category projects are broken down by their dollar costs: Larger investments require increasingly detailed analysis and approval at a higher level within the firm. Thus, whereas a plant manager may be authorized to approve maintenance expenditures up to $10,000 on the basis of a relatively unsophisticated analysis, the full board of directors may have to approve decisions that involve either amounts over $1 million or expansions into new products or markets. Statistical data are generally lacking for new-product decisions, so here judgments, as opposed to detailed cost data, are especially important.

Note that the term "assets" encompasses more than buildings and equipment. Computer software that a firm develops to help it buy supplies and materials more efficiently, or to communicate with customers, is also an asset. So is a customer base like that of AOL developed by sending out millions of free CDs to potential customers. And so is the design of a new computer chip, airplane, or movie. All of these are "intangible" as opposed to "tangible" assets, but decisions to invest in them are analyzed in the same way as decisions related to tangible assets. Keep this in mind as you go through the remainder of the chapter.

SELF-TEST QUESTION

Identify the major project classification categories, and explain how they are used.

SIMILARITIES BETWEEN CAPITAL BUDGETING AND SECURITY VALUATION

Once a potential capital budgeting project has been identified, its evaluation involves the same steps that are used in security analysis:

1. First, the cost of the project must be determined. This is similar to finding the price that must be paid for a stock or bond.

2. Next, management estimates the expected cash flows from the project, including the salvage value of the asset at the end of its expected life. This is similar

to estimating the future dividend or interest payment stream on a stock or bond, along with the stock's expected sales price or the bond's maturity value.

3. Third, the riskiness of the projected cash flows must be estimated. This requires information about the probability distribution (riskiness) of the cash flows.

4. Given the project's riskiness, management determines the cost of capital at which the cash flows should be discounted.

5. Next, the expected cash inflows are put on a present value basis to obtain an estimate of the asset's value. This is equivalent to finding the present value of a stock's expected future dividends.

6. Finally, the present value of the expected cash inflows is compared with the required outlay. If the PV of the cash flows exceeds the cost, the project should be accepted. Otherwise, it should be rejected. (Alternatively, if the expected rate of return on the project exceeds its cost of capital, the project is accepted.)

If an individual investor identifies and invests in a stock or bond whose market price is less than its true value, the investor's wealth will increase. Similarly, if a firm identifies (or creates) an investment opportunity with a present value greater than its cost, the value of the firm will increase. Thus, there is a direct link between capital budgeting and stock values: The more effective the firm's capital budgeting procedures, the higher its stock price.

SELF-TEST QUESTION

List the six steps in the capital budgeting process, and compare them with the steps in security valuation.

CAPITAL BUDGETING DECISION RULES

Five key methods are used to rank projects and to decide whether or not they should be accepted for inclusion in the capital budget: (1) payback, (2) discounted payback, (3) net present value (NPV), (4) internal rate of return (IRR), and (5) modified internal rate of return (MIRR). We will explain how each ranking criterion is calculated, and then we will evaluate how well each performs in terms of identifying those projects that will maximize the firm's stock price.

We use the cash flow data shown in Figure 10-1 for Projects S and L to illustrate each method. Also, we assume that the projects are equally risky. Note that the cash flows, CF_t, are expected values, and that they have been adjusted to reflect taxes, depreciation, and salvage values. Further, since many projects require an investment in both fixed assets and working capital, the investment outlays shown as CF_0 include any necessary changes in net operating working capital.[1] Finally, we assume that all cash flows occur at the end of the designated year. Incidentally, the S stands for *short*

---

[1] The most difficult part of the capital budgeting process is estimating the relevant cash flows. For simplicity, the net cash flows are treated as a given in this chapter, which allows us to focus on the capital

(footnote continues)

FIGURE 10-1   Net Cash Flows for Projects S and L

YEAR (t)	EXPECTED AFTER-TAX NET CASH FLOWS, CF_t	
	PROJECT S	PROJECT L
0^a	($1,000)	($1,000)
1	500	100
2	400	300
3	300	400
4	100	600

```
                 0      1      2      3      4
Project S:       |------|------|------|------|
              -1,000   500    400    300    100

                 0      1      2      3      4
Project L:       |------|------|------|------|
              -1,000   100    300    400    600
```

$^a CF_0$ represents the net investment outlay, or initial cost.

and the L for *long*: Project S is a short-term project in the sense that its cash inflows come in sooner than L's.

PAYBACK PERIOD

Payback Period
The length of time required for an investment's net revenues to cover its cost.

The **payback period,** defined as the expected number of years required to recover the original investment, was the first formal method used to evaluate capital budgeting projects. The payback calculation is diagrammed in Figure 10-2 and it is explained below for Project S.

1. Enter $CF_0 = -1000$ in your calculator. (You do not need to use the cash flow register; just have your display show $-1,000$.)
2. Now add $CF_1 = 500$ to find the cumulative cash flow at the end of Year 1. The result is -500.
3. Now add $CF_2 = 400$ to find the cumulative cash flow at the end of Year 2. This is -100.
4. Now add $CF_3 = 300$ to find the cumulative cash flow at the end of Year 3. This is $+200$.
5. We see that by the end of Year 3 the cumulative inflows have more than recovered the initial outflow. Thus, the payback occurred during the third year.

(Footnote 1 continued)
budgeting decision rules. However, in Chapter 11 we will discuss cash flow estimation in detail. Also, note that *working capital* is defined as the firm's current assets, and that *net operating working capital* is current assets minus non-interest-bearing liabilities.

| FIGURE 10-2 | Payback Period for Projects S and L |

If the $300 of inflows come in evenly during Year 3, then the exact payback period can be found as follows:

$$\text{Payback}_S = \text{Year before full recovery} + \frac{\text{Unrecovered cost at start of year}}{\text{Cash flow during year}}$$

$$= 2 + \frac{\$100}{\$300} = 2.33 \text{ years.}$$

Applying the same procedure to Project L, we find $\text{Payback}_L = 3.33$ years.

The shorter the payback period, the better. Therefore, if the firm required a payback of three years or less, Project S would be accepted but Project L would be rejected. If the projects were **mutually exclusive,** S would be ranked over L because S has the shorter payback. *Mutually exclusive* means that if one project is taken on, the other must be rejected. For example, the installation of a conveyor-belt system in a warehouse and the purchase of a fleet of forklifts for the same warehouse would be mutually exclusive projects—accepting one implies rejection of the other. **Independent projects** are projects whose cash flows are independent of one another.

Some firms use a variant of the regular payback, the **discounted payback period,** which is similar to the regular payback period except that the expected cash flows are discounted by the project's cost of capital. Thus, the discounted payback period is defined as the number of years required to recover the investment from *discounted* net cash flows. Figure 10-3 contains the discounted net cash flows for Projects S and L, assuming both projects have a cost of capital of 10 percent. To construct Figure 10-3, each cash inflow is divided by $(1 + k)^t = (1.10)^t$, where t is the year in which the cash flow occurs and k is the project's cost of capital. After three years, Project S will have generated $1,011 in discounted cash inflows. Since the cost is $1,000, the discounted payback is just under three years, or, to be precise, $2 + (\$214/\$225) = 2.95$ years. Project L's discounted payback is 3.88 years.

$$\text{Discounted payback}_S = 2.0 + \$214/\$225 = 2.95 \text{ years.}$$

$$\text{Discounted payback}_L = 3.0 + \$360/\$410 = 3.88 \text{ years.}$$

For Projects S and L, the rankings are the same regardless of which payback method is used; that is, Project S is preferred to Project L, and Project S would still be selected if the firm were to require a discounted payback of three years or less. Often, however, the regular and the discounted paybacks produce conflicting rankings.

Note that the payback is a type of "breakeven" calculation in the sense that if cash flows come in at the expected rate until the payback year, then the project will break

Mutually Exclusive Projects
A set of projects where only one can be accepted.

Independent Projects
Projects whose cash flows are not affected by the acceptance or nonacceptance of other projects.

Discounted Payback Period
The length of time required for an investment's cash flows, discounted at the investment's cost of capital, to cover its cost.

FIGURE 10-3

Projects S and L: Discounted Payback Period

	0	1	2	3	4
Project S:					
Net cash flow	−1,000	500	400	300	100
Discounted NCF (at 10%)	−1,000	455	331	225	68
Cumulative discounted NCF	−1,000	−545	−214	11	79

	0	1	2	3	4
Project L:					
Net cash flow	−1,000	100	300	400	600
Discounted NCF (at 10%)	−1,000	91	248	301	410
Cumulative discounted NCF	−1,000	−909	−661	−360	50

even. However, the regular payback does not consider the cost of capital—no cost for the debt or equity used to undertake the project is reflected in the cash flows or the calculation. The discounted payback does consider capital costs—it shows the breakeven year after covering debt and equity costs.

An important drawback of both the payback and discounted payback methods is that they ignore cash flows that are paid or received after the payback period. For example, consider two projects, X and Y, each of which requires an up-front cash outflow of $3,000, so $CF_0 = -\$3,000$. Assume that both projects have a cost of capital of 10 percent. Project X is expected to produce cash inflows of $1,000 each of the next four years, while Project Y will produce no cash flows the first four years but then generate a cash inflow of $1,000,000 five years from now. Common sense suggests that Project Y creates more value for the firm's shareholders, yet its payback and discounted payback make it look worse than Project X. Consequently, both payback methods have serious deficiencies. Therefore, we will not dwell on the finer points of payback analysis.[2]

Although the payback method has some serious faults as a ranking criterion, it does provide information on how long funds will be tied up in a project. Thus, the shorter the payback period, other things held constant, the greater the project's *liquidity*. Also, since cash flows expected in the distant future are generally riskier than near-term cash flows, the payback is often used as an indicator of a project's *riskiness*.

Net Present Value (NPV) Method
A method of ranking investment proposals using the NPV, which is equal to the present value of future net cash flows, discounted at the cost of capital.

NET PRESENT VALUE (NPV)

As the flaws in the payback were recognized, people began to search for ways to improve the effectiveness of project evaluations. One such method is the **net present**

---

[2] Another capital budgeting technique that was once used widely is the *accounting rate of return (ARR)*, which examines a project's contribution to the firm's net income. Although some companies still calculate an ARR, it really has no redeeming features, so we will not discuss it in this text. See Eugene F. Brigham and Phillip R. Daves, *Intermediate Financial Management*, 7th ed. (Cincinnati, OH: South-Western College Publishing, 2002), Chapter 11. Yet another technique that we omit here is the *profitability index*, or *benefit/cost ratio*. Brigham and Daves also discuss this method.

Discounted Cash Flow (DCF) Techniques
Methods for ranking investment proposals that employ time value of money concepts.

value (NPV) method, which relies on **discounted cash flow (DCF) techniques.** To implement this approach, we proceed as follows:

1. Find the present value of each cash flow, including both inflows and outflows, discounted at the project's cost of capital.
2. Sum these discounted cash flows; this sum is defined as the project's NPV.
3. If the NPV is positive, the project should be accepted, while if the NPV is negative, it should be rejected. If two projects with positive NPVs are mutually exclusive, the one with the higher NPV should be chosen.

The equation for the NPV is as follows:

$$\text{NPV} = \text{CF}_0 + \frac{\text{CF}_1}{(1+k)^1} + \frac{\text{CF}_2}{(1+k)^2} + \cdots + \frac{\text{CF}_n}{(1+k)^n}$$

$$= \sum_{t=0}^{n} \frac{\text{CF}_t}{(1+k)^t}. \tag{10-1}$$

Here CF_t is the expected net cash flow at Period t, k is the project's cost of capital, and n is its life. Cash outflows (expenditures such as the cost of buying equipment or building factories) are treated as *negative* cash flows. In evaluating Projects S and L, only CF_0 is negative, but for many large projects such as the Alaska Pipeline, an electric generating plant, or IBM's laptop computer project, outflows occur for several years before operations begin and cash flows turn positive.

At a 10 percent cost of capital, Project S's NPV is $78.82:

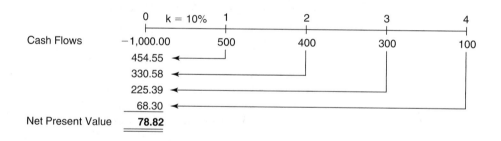

By a similar process, we find $\text{NPV}_L = \$49.18$. On this basis, both projects should be accepted if they are independent, but S should be chosen if they are mutually exclusive.

It is not hard to calculate the NPV as was done in the time line by using Equation 10-1 and a regular calculator. However, it is more efficient to use a financial calculator. Different calculators are set up somewhat differently, but they all have a section of memory called the "cash flow register" that is used for uneven cash flows such as those in Projects S and L (as opposed to equal annuity cash flows). A solution process for Equation 10-1 is literally programmed into financial calculators, and all you have to do is enter the cash flows (being sure to observe the signs), along with the value of k = I. At that point, you have (in your calculator) this equation:

$$\text{NPV}_S = -1,000 + \frac{500}{(1.10)^1} + \frac{400}{(1.10)^2} + \frac{300}{(1.10)^3} + \frac{100}{(1.10)^4}.$$

Notice that the equation has one unknown, NPV. Now, all you need to do is to ask the calculator to solve the equation for you, which you do by pressing the NPV button (and, on some calculators, the "compute" button). The answer, 78.82, will appear on the screen.[3]

Most projects last for more than four years, and, as you will see in Chapter 11, most projects require many calculations to develop the estimated cash flows. Therefore, financial analysts generally use spreadsheets when dealing with capital budgeting projects. See the model for this chapter, 10MODEL.xls.

RATIONALE FOR THE NPV METHOD

The rationale for the NPV method is straightforward. An NPV of zero signifies that the project's cash flows are exactly sufficient to repay the invested capital and to provide the required rate of return on that capital. If a project has a positive NPV, then it is generating more cash than is needed to service its debt and to provide the required return to shareholders, and this excess cash accrues solely to the firm's stockholders. Therefore, if a firm takes on a project with a positive NPV, the position of the stockholders is improved. In our example, shareholders' wealth would increase by $78.82 if the firm takes on Project S, but by only $49.18 if it takes on Project L.

---

[3] The *Technology Supplement* that accompanies this text explains this and other commonly used calculator applications. For those who do not have the *Supplement*, the steps for two popular calculators, the HP-10BII and the HP-17B, are shown below. If you have another type of financial calculator, see its manual or the *Supplement*.

HP-10BII:
1. Clear the memory.
2. Enter CF$_0$ as follows: 1000 +/− CFj.
3. Enter CF$_1$ as follows: 500 CFj.
4. Repeat the process to enter the other cash flows. Note that CF 0, CF 1, and so forth, flash on the screen as you press the CFj button. If you hold the button down, CF 0 and so forth, will remain on the screen until you release it.
5. Once the CFs have been entered, enter k = I = 10%: 10 I/YR.
6. Now that all of the inputs have been entered, you can press ▮ NPV to get the answer, NPV = $78.82.
7. If a cash flow is repeated for several years, you can avoid having to enter the CFs for each year. For example, if the $500 cash flow for Year 1 had also been the CF for Years 2 through 10, making 10 of these $500 cash flows, then after entering 500 CFj the first time, you could enter 10 ▮ Nj. This would automatically enter 10 CFs of 500.

HP-17B:
1. Go to the cash flow (CFLO) menu, clear if FLOW(0) = ? does not appear on the screen.
2. Enter CF$_0$ as follows: 1000 +/− INPUT.
3. Enter CF$_1$ as follows : 500 INPUT.
4. Now, the calculator will ask you if the 500 is for Period 1 only or if it is also used for several following periods. Since it is only used for Period 1, press INPUT to answer "1." Alternatively, you could press EXIT and then #T? to turn off the prompt for the remainder of the problem. For some problems, you will want to use the repeat feature.
5. Enter the remaining CFs, being sure to turn off the prompt or else to specify "1" for each entry.
6. Once the CFs have all been entered, press EXIT and then CALC.
7. Now enter k = I = 10% as follows: 10 I%.
8. Now press NPV to get the answer, NPV = $78.82.

Viewed in this manner, it is easy to see why S is preferred to L, and it is also easy to see the logic of the NPV approach.[4]

There is also a direct relationship between NPV and EVA (economic value added)—NPV is equal to the present value of the project's future EVAs. Therefore, accepting positive NPV projects should result in a positive EVA and a positive MVA (market value added, or the excess of the firm's market value over its book value). So, a reward system that compensates managers for producing positive EVA will lead to the use of NPV for making capital budgeting decisions.

INTERNAL RATE OF RETURN (IRR)

Internal Rate of Return (IRR) Method
A method of ranking investment proposals using the rate of return on an investment, calculated by finding the discount rate that equates the present value of future cash inflows to the project's cost.

IRR
The discount rate that forces the PV of a project's inflows to equal the PV of its costs.

In Chapter 7 we presented procedures for finding the yield to maturity, or rate of return, on a bond—if you invest in a bond, hold it to maturity, and receive all of the promised cash flows, you will earn the YTM on the money you invested. Exactly the same concepts are employed in capital budgeting when the **internal rate of return (IRR) method** is used. The **IRR** is defined as the discount rate that equates the present value of a project's expected cash inflows to the present value of the project's costs:

$$PV(\text{Inflows}) = PV(\text{Investment costs}),$$

or, equivalently, the rate that forces the NPV to equal zero:

$$CF_0 + \frac{CF_1}{(1 + IRR)^1} + \frac{CF_2}{(1 + IRR)^2} + \cdots + \frac{CF_n}{(1 + IRR)^n} = 0$$

$$NPV = \sum_{t=0}^{n} \frac{CF_t}{(1 + IRR)^t} = 0. \qquad (10\text{-}2)$$

For our Project S, here is the time line setup:

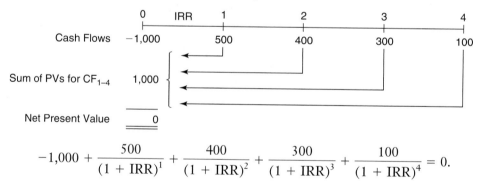

$$-1{,}000 + \frac{500}{(1 + IRR)^1} + \frac{400}{(1 + IRR)^2} + \frac{300}{(1 + IRR)^3} + \frac{100}{(1 + IRR)^4} = 0.$$

Thus, we have an equation with one unknown, IRR, and we need to solve for IRR.

Without a calculator, you must solve Equation 10-2 by trial-and-error—try some discount rate and see if the equation solves to zero, and if it does not, try a different discount rate, and continue until you find the rate that forces the equation to equal zero. The discount rate that causes the equation (and the NPV) to equal zero is de-

---

[4] This description of the process is somewhat oversimplified. Both analysts and investors anticipate that firms will identify and accept positive NPV projects, and current stock prices reflect these expectations. Thus, stock prices react to announcements of new capital projects only to the extent that such projects were not already expected. In this sense, we may think of a firm's value as consisting of two parts: (1) the value of its existing assets and (2) the value of its "growth opportunities," or projects with positive NPVs.

fined as the IRR. For a realistic project with a fairly long life, the trial-and-error approach is a tedious, time-consuming task.

Fortunately, it is easy to find IRRs with a financial calculator. You follow procedures almost identical to those used to find the NPV. First, you enter the cash flows as shown on the preceding time line into the calculator's cash flow register. In effect, you have entered the cash flows into the equation shown below the time line. Note that we have one unknown, IRR, which is the discount rate that forces the equation to equal zero. The calculator has been programmed to solve for the IRR, and you activate this program by pressing the button labeled "IRR." Then the calculator solves for IRR and displays it on the screen. Here are the IRRs for Projects S and L as found with a financial calculator.[5]

$$IRR_S = 14.5\%.$$

$$IRR_L = 11.8\%.$$

Hurdle Rate
The discount rate (cost of capital) that the IRR must exceed if a project is to be accepted.

If both projects have a cost of capital, or **hurdle rate,** of 10 percent, then the internal rate of return rule indicates that if the projects are independent, both should be accepted—they are both expected to earn more than the cost of the capital needed to finance them. If they are mutually exclusive, S ranks higher and should be accepted, while L should be rejected. If the cost of capital is above 14.5 percent, both projects should be rejected.

Notice that the internal rate of return formula, Equation 10-2, is simply the NPV formula, Equation 10-1, solved for the particular discount rate that forces the NPV to equal zero. Thus, the same basic equation is used for both methods, but in the NPV method the discount rate, k, is specified and the NPV is found, whereas in the IRR method the NPV is specified to equal zero, and the interest rate that forces this equality (the IRR) is calculated.

Mathematically, the NPV and IRR methods will always lead to the same accept/reject decisions for independent projects. This occurs because if NPV is positive, IRR must exceed k. However, NPV and IRR can give conflicting rankings for mutually exclusive projects. This point will be discussed in more detail in a later section.

RATIONALE FOR THE **IRR** METHOD

Why is the particular discount rate that equates a project's cost with the present value of its receipts (the IRR) so special? The reason is based on this logic: (1) The IRR on a project is its expected rate of return. (2) If the internal rate of return exceeds the cost of the funds used to finance the project, a surplus remains after paying for the capital, and this surplus accrues to the firm's stockholders. (3) Therefore, taking on a project whose IRR exceeds its cost of capital increases shareholders' wealth. On the other hand, if the internal rate of return is less than the cost of capital, then taking on the project imposes a cost on current stockholders. It is this "breakeven" characteristic that makes the IRR useful in evaluating capital projects.

---

[5] To find the IRR with an HP-10BII or HP-17B, repeat the steps given in Footnote 3. Then, with an HP-10BII, press ▮ IRR/YR, and, after a pause, 14.49, Project S's IRR, will appear. With the HP-17B, simply press IRR% to get the IRR. With both calculators, you would generally want to get both the NPV and the IRR after entering the input data, before clearing the cash flow register. The *Technology Supplement* explains how to find IRR with several other calculators.

What four capital budgeting ranking methods were discussed in this section? Describe each method, and give the rationale for its use.

What two methods always lead to the same accept/reject decision for independent projects?

What two pieces of information does the payback period convey that are not conveyed by the other methods?

COMPARISON OF THE NPV AND IRR METHODS

In many respects the NPV method is better than IRR, so it is tempting to explain NPV only, to state that it should be used to select projects, and to go on to the next topic. However, the IRR method is familiar to many corporate executives, it is widely entrenched in industry, and it does have some virtues. Therefore, it is important for you to understand the IRR method but also to be able to explain why, at times, a project with a lower IRR may be preferable to a mutually exclusive alternative with a higher IRR.

NPV PROFILES

Net Present Value Profile
A graph showing the relationship between a project's NPV and the firm's cost of capital.

A graph that plots a project's NPV against cost of capital rates is defined as the project's **net present value profile;** profiles for Projects L and S are shown in Figure 10-4. To construct NPV profiles, first note that at a zero cost of capital, the NPV is simply the total of the project's undiscounted cash flows. Thus, at a zero cost of capital $NPV_S = \$300$, and $NPV_L = \$400$. These values are plotted as the vertical axis intercepts in Figure 10-4. Next, we calculate the projects' NPVs at three costs of capital, 5, 10, and 15 percent, and plot these values. The four points plotted on our graph for each project are shown at the bottom of the figure.[6]

Recall that the IRR is defined as the discount rate at which a project's NPV equals zero. Therefore, *the point where its net present value profile crosses the horizontal axis indicates a project's internal rate of return.* Since we calculated IRR_S and IRR_L in an earlier section, we can confirm the validity of the graph.

When we connect the data points, we have the net present value profile.[7] NPV profiles can be very useful in project analysis, and we will use them often in the remainder of the chapter.

---

[6] To calculate the points with a financial calculator, enter the cash flows in the cash flow register, enter I = 0, and press the NPV button to find the NPV at a zero cost of capital. Then enter I = 5 to override the zero, and press NPV to get the NPV at 5 percent. Repeat these steps for 10 and 15 percent. We did the calculations and made the graph with our *Excel* model. See 10MODEL.xls.

[7] Notice that the NPV profiles are curved—they are *not* straight lines. NPV approaches the t = 0 cash flow (the cost of the project) as the cost of capital increases without limit. The reason is that, at an infinitely high cost of capital, the PV of the inflows would be zero, so NPV at (k = ∞) is simply CF_0, which in our example is −$1,000. We should also note that under certain conditions the NPV profiles can cross the horizontal axis several times, or never cross it. This point is discussed later in the chapter.

FIGURE 10-4

Net Present Value Profiles: NPVs of Projects S and L at Different Costs of Capital

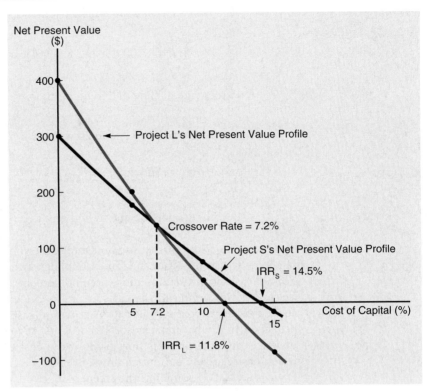

COST OF CAPITAL	NPV_S	NPV_L
0%	$300.00	$400.00
5	180.42	206.50
10	78.82	49.18
15	(8.33)	(80.14)

NPV RANKINGS DEPEND ON THE COST OF CAPITAL

Crossover Rate

The cost of capital at which the NPV profiles of two projects cross and, thus, at which the projects' NPVs are equal.

Figure 10-4 shows that the NPV profiles of both Project L and Project S decline as the cost of capital increases. But notice in the figure that Project L has the higher NPV at a low cost of capital, while Project S has the higher NPV if the cost of capital is greater than the 7.2 percent **crossover rate.** Notice also that Project L's NPV is "more sensitive" to changes in the cost of capital than is NPV_S; that is, Project L's net present value profile has the steeper slope, indicating that a given change in k has a larger effect on NPV_L than on NPV_S.

To see why L has the greater sensitivity, recall first that the cash flows from S are received faster than those from L. In a payback sense, S is a short-term project, while L is a long-term project. Next, recall the equation for the NPV:

$$NPV = \frac{CF_0}{(1 + k)^0} + \frac{CF_1}{(1 + k)^1} + \cdots + \frac{CF_n}{(1 + k)^n}.$$

The impact of an increase in the cost of capital is much greater on distant than on near-term cash flows. To illustrate, consider the following:

$$\text{PV of \$100 due in 1 year @k} = 5\%: \frac{\$100}{(1.05)^1} = \$95.24.$$

$$\text{PV of \$100 due in 1 year @ k} = 10\%: \frac{\$100}{(1.10)^1} = \$90.91.$$

$$\text{Percentage decline due to higher k} = \frac{\$95.24 - \$90.91}{\$95.24} = 4.5\%.$$

$$\text{PV of \$100 due in 20 years @ k} = 5\%: \frac{\$100}{(1.05)^{20}} = \$37.69.$$

$$\text{PV of \$100 due in 20 years @ k} = 10\%: \frac{\$100}{(1.10)^{20}} = \$14.86.$$

$$\text{Percentage decline due to higher k} = \frac{\$37.69 - \$14.86}{\$37.69} = 60.6\%.$$

Thus, a doubling of the discount rate causes only a 4.5 percent decline in the PV of a Year 1 cash flow, but the same doubling of the discount rate causes the PV of a Year 20 cash flow to fall by more than 60 percent. Therefore, if a project has most of its cash flows coming in the early years, its NPV will not decline very much if the cost of capital increases, but a project whose cash flows come later will be severely penalized by high capital costs. Accordingly, Project L, which has its largest cash flows in the later years, is hurt badly if the cost of capital is high, while Project S, which has relatively rapid cash flows, is affected less by high capital costs. Therefore, Project L's NPV profile has the steeper slope.

INDEPENDENT PROJECTS

If an *independent* project is being evaluated, then the NPV and IRR criteria always lead to the same accept/reject decision: if NPV says accept, IRR also says accept. To see why this is so, assume that Projects L and S are independent, and then look back at Figure 10-4 and notice (1) that the IRR criterion for acceptance for either project is that the project's cost of capital is less than (or to the left of) the IRR and (2) that whenever a project's cost of capital is less than its IRR, its NPV is positive. Thus, at any cost of capital less than 11.8 percent, Project L will be acceptable by both the NPV and the IRR criteria, while both methods reject the project if the cost of capital is greater than 11.8 percent. Project S—and all other independent projects under consideration—could be analyzed similarly, and it will always turn out that if the IRR method says accept, then so will the NPV method.

MUTUALLY EXCLUSIVE PROJECTS[8]

Now assume that Projects S and L are *mutually exclusive* rather than independent. That is, we can choose either Project S or Project L, or we can reject both, but we cannot accept both projects. Notice in Figure 10-4 that as long as the cost of capital is

---

[8] This section is relatively technical, but it can be omitted without loss of continuity.

greater than the crossover rate of 7.2 percent, then (1) NPV_S is larger than NPV_L and (2) IRR_S exceeds IRR_L. Therefore, if k is *greater* than the crossover rate of 7.2 percent, the two methods both lead to the selection of Project S. However, if the cost of capital is *less than* the crossover rate, the NPV method ranks Project L higher, but the IRR method indicates that Project S is better. *Thus, a conflict exists if the cost of capital is less than the crossover rate.* NPV says choose mutually exclusive L, while IRR says take S. Which answer is correct? Logic suggests that the NPV method is better, because it selects the project that adds the most to shareholder wealth.[9]

There are two basic conditions that can cause NPV profiles to cross, and thus conflicts to arise between NPV and IRR: (1) when *project size (or scale) differences* exist, meaning that the cost of one project is larger than that of the other, or (2) when *timing differences* exist, meaning that the timing of cash flows from the two projects differs such that most of the cash flows from one project come in the early years while most of the cash flows from the other project come in the later years, as occurred with our Projects L and S.[10]

When either size or timing differences occur, the firm will have different amounts of funds to invest in the various years, depending on which of the two mutually exclusive projects it chooses. For example, if one project costs more than the other, then the firm will have more money at t = 0 to invest elsewhere if it selects the smaller project. Similarly, for projects of equal size, the one with the larger early cash inflows—in our example, Project S—provides more funds for reinvestment in the early years. Given this situation, the rate of return at which differential cash flows can be invested is a critical issue.

The key to resolving conflicts between mutually exclusive projects is this: How useful is it to generate cash flows sooner rather than later? The value of early cash flows depends on the return we can earn on those cash flows, that is, the rate at which we can reinvest them. *The NPV method implicitly assumes that the rate at which cash flows can be reinvested is the cost of capital, whereas the IRR method assumes that the firm can reinvest at the IRR.* These assumptions are inherent in the mathematics of the discounting process. The cash flows may actually be withdrawn as dividends by the stockholders and spent on beer and pizza, but the NPV method still assumes that cash flows can be reinvested at the cost of capital, while the IRR method assumes reinvestment at the project's IRR.

Reinvestment Rate Assumption

The assumption that cash flows from a project can be reinvested (1) at the cost of capital, if using the NPV method, or (2) at the internal rate of return, if using the IRR method.

Which is the better assumption—that cash flows can be reinvested at the cost of capital, or that they can be reinvested at the project's IRR? It can be demonstrated that the best assumption is that projects' cash flows are reinvested at the cost of capital.[11] Therefore, we conclude that *the best* **reinvestment rate assumption** *is the cost of capital, which is consistent with the NPV method.* This, in turn, leads us to prefer the

---

[9] The crossover rate is easy to calculate. Simply go back to Figure 10-1, where we set forth the two projects' cash flows, and calculate the difference in those flows in each year. The differences are $CF_S - CF_L = \$0, +\$400, +\$100, -\$100,$ and $-\$500$, respectively. Enter these values in the cash flow register of a financial calculator, press the IRR button, and the crossover rate, $7.17\% \approx 7.2\%$, appears. Be sure to enter $CF_0 = 0$ or else you will not get the correct answer.

[10] Of course, it is possible for mutually exclusive projects to differ with respect to both scale and timing. Also, if mutually exclusive projects have different lives (as opposed to different cash flow patterns over a common life), this introduces further complications, and for meaningful comparisons, some mutually exclusive projects must be evaluated over a common life. For a discussion of comparing projects with unequal lives refer to Eugene F. Brigham and Joel F. Houston, *Fundamentals of Financial Management*, 10th ed. (Cincinnati, OH: South-Western College Publishing, 2003), Chapter 12 or Web Appendix 11D on the *Concise* web site.

[11] Again, see Brigham and Daves, *Intermediate Financial Management*, 7th ed., Chapter 11, for a discussion of this point.

NPV method, at least for a firm willing and able to obtain capital at a cost reasonably close to its current cost of capital.

We should reiterate that, when projects are independent, the NPV and IRR methods both lead to exactly the same accept/reject decision. However, *when evaluating mutually exclusive projects, especially those that differ in scale and/or timing, the NPV method should be used.*

MULTIPLE IRRs[12]

There is one other situation in which the IRR approach may not be usable—this is when projects with nonnormal cash flows are involved. A project has *normal* cash flows if it has one or more cash outflows (costs) followed by a series of cash inflows. If, however, a project calls for a large cash outflow sometime during or at the end of its life, then the project has *nonnormal* cash flows. Projects with nonnormal cash flows can present unique difficulties when they are evaluated by the IRR method, with the most common problem being the existence of **multiple IRRs.**

Multiple IRRs
The situation where a project has two or more IRRs.

When one solves Equation 10-2 to find the IRR for a project with nonnormal cash flows,

$$\sum_{t=0}^{n} \frac{CF_t}{(1 + IRR)^t} = 0, \tag{10-2}$$

it is possible to obtain more than one solution value for IRR, which means that multiple IRRs occur. Notice that Equation 10-2 is a polynomial of degree n, so it has n different roots, or solutions. All except one of the roots are imaginary numbers when investments have normal cash flows (one or more cash outflows followed by cash inflows), so in the normal case, only one value of IRR appears. However, the possibility of multiple real roots, hence multiple IRRs, arises when the project has nonnormal cash flows (negative net cash flows occur during some year after the project has been placed in operation).

To illustrate this problem, suppose a firm is considering the expenditure of $1.6 million to develop a strip mine (Project M). The mine will produce a cash flow of $10 million at the end of Year 1. Then, at the end of Year 2, $10 million must be expended to restore the land to its original condition. Therefore, the project's expected net cash flows are as follows (in millions of dollars):

	EXPECTED NET CASH FLOWS	
YEAR 0	END OF YEAR 1	END OF YEAR 2
−$1.6	+$10	−$10

These values can be substituted into Equation 10-2 to derive the IRR for the investment:

$$NPV = \frac{-\$1.6 \text{ million}}{(1 + IRR)^0} + \frac{\$10 \text{ million}}{(1 + IRR)^1} + \frac{-\$10 \text{ million}}{(1 + IRR)^2} = 0.$$

---

[12] This section is relatively technical, but it can be omitted without loss of continuity.

When solved, we find that NPV = 0 when IRR = 25% and also when IRR = 400%.[13] Therefore, the IRR of the investment is both 25 and 400 percent. This relationship is depicted graphically in Figure 10-5.[14] Note that no dilemma would arise if the NPV method were used; we would simply use Equation 10-1, find the NPV, and use this to evaluate the project. If Project M's cost of capital were 10 percent, then its NPV would be −$0.77 million, and the project should be rejected. If k were between 25 and 400 percent, the NPV would be positive.

One of the authors encountered another example of multiple internal rates of return when a major California bank *borrowed* funds from an insurance company and then used these funds (plus an initial investment of its own) to buy a number of jet engines, which it then leased to a major airline. The bank expected to receive positive net cash flows (lease payments plus tax savings minus interest on the insurance company loan) for a

---

[13] If you attempted to find the IRR of Project M with many financial calculators, you would get an error message. This same message would be given for all projects with multiple IRRs. However, you can still find Project M's IRRs by first calculating NPVs using several different values for k and then plotting the NPV profile. The intersections with the X-axis give a rough idea of the IRR values. Finally, you can use trial-and-error to find the exact values of k that force NPV = 0.

Note, too, that some calculators, including the HP-10BII and 17B, can find the IRR. At the error message, key in a guess, store it, and repress the IRR key. With the HP-10BII, type 10 ■ STO ■ IRR, and the answer, 25.00, appears. If you enter as your guess a cost of capital less than the one at which NPV in Figure 10-5 is maximized (about 100%), the lower IRR, 25%, is displayed. If you guess a high rate, say, 150, the higher IRR is shown.

[14] Does Figure 10-5 suggest that the firm should try to *raise* its cost of capital to about 100 percent in order to maximize the NPV of the project? Certainly not. The firm should seek to *minimize* its cost of capital; this will cause its stock price to be maximized. Actions taken to raise the cost of capital might make this particular project look good, but those actions would be terribly harmful to the firm's more numerous projects with normal cash flows. Only if the firm's cost of capital is high in spite of efforts to keep it down will the illustrative project have a positive NPV.

FIGURE 10-5 | **NPV Profile for Project M**

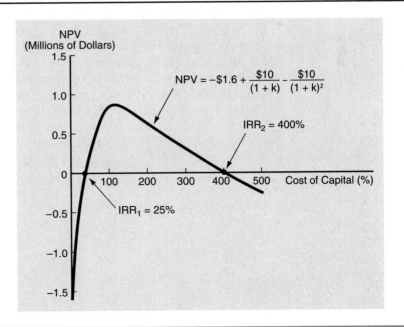

$$NPV = -\$1.6 + \frac{\$10}{(1 + k)} - \frac{\$10}{(1 + k)^2}$$

$IRR_2 = 400\%$

$IRR_1 = 25\%$

number of years, then several large negative cash flows as it repaid the insurance company loan, and, finally, a large inflow from the sale of the engines when the lease expired.

The bank discovered two IRRs and wondered which was correct. It could not ignore the IRR and use the NPV method since the lease was already on the books, and the bank's senior loan committee, as well as Federal Reserve bank examiners, wanted to know the return on the lease. The bank's solution called for calculating and then using the "modified internal rate of return" as discussed in the next section.

The examples just presented illustrate one problem, multiple IRRs, that can arise when the IRR criterion is used with a project that has nonnormal cash flows. Use of the IRR method on projects having nonnormal cash flows could produce other problems such as no IRR or an IRR that leads to an incorrect accept/reject decision. In all such cases, the NPV criterion could be easily applied, and this method leads to conceptually correct capital budgeting decisions.

SELF-TEST QUESTIONS

Describe how NPV profiles are constructed.

What is the crossover rate, and how does it affect the choice between mutually exclusive projects?

What two basic conditions can lead to conflicts between the NPV and IRR methods?

Why is the "reinvestment rate" considered to be the underlying cause of conflicts between the NPV and IRR methods?

If a conflict exists, should the capital budgeting decision be made on the basis of the NPV or the IRR ranking? Why?

Explain the difference between normal and nonnormal cash flows.

What is the "multiple IRR problem," and what condition is necessary for it to occur?

MODIFIED INTERNAL RATE OF RETURN (MIRR)[15]

Modified IRR (MIRR)
The discount rate at which the present value of a project's cost is equal to the present value of its terminal value, where the terminal value is found as the sum of the future values of the cash inflows, compounded at the firm's cost of capital.

In spite of a strong academic preference for NPV, surveys indicate that executives prefer IRR over NPV. Apparently, managers find it intuitively more appealing to evaluate investments in terms of percentage rates of return than dollars of NPV. Given this fact, can we devise a percentage evaluator that is better than the regular IRR? The answer is yes—we can modify the IRR and make it a better indicator of relative profitability, hence better for use in capital budgeting. The new measure is called the **modified IRR**, or **MIRR**, and it is defined as follows:

$$\text{PV costs} = \text{PV terminal value}$$

$$\sum_{t=0}^{n} \frac{COF_t}{(1+k)^t} = \frac{\sum_{t=0}^{n} CIF_t (1+k)^{n-t}}{(1+MIRR)^n}$$

$$\text{PV costs} = \frac{TV}{(1+MIRR)^n}. \tag{10-2a}$$

---

[15] Again, this section is relatively technical, but it can be omitted without loss of continuity.

Here COF refers to cash outflows (negative numbers), or the cost of the project, and CIF refers to cash inflows (positive numbers). The left term is simply the PV of the investment outlays when discounted at the cost of capital, and the numerator of the right term is the compounded value of the inflows, assuming that the cash inflows are reinvested at the cost of capital. The compounded value of the cash inflows is also called the *terminal value*, or *TV*. The discount rate that forces the PV of the TV to equal the PV of the costs is defined as the MIRR.[16]

If the investment costs are all incurred at t = 0, and if the first operating inflow occurs at t = 1, as is true for the illustrative Project S and L that we first presented in Figure 10-1, then this equation may be used:

$$\text{Cost} = \frac{\text{TV}}{(1 + \text{MIRR})^n} = \frac{\displaystyle\sum_{t=1}^{n} \text{CIF}_t(1 + k)^{n-t}}{(1 + \text{MIRR})^n}. \tag{10-2b}$$

We can illustrate the calculation with Project S:

Using the cash flows as set out on the time line, first find the terminal value by compounding each cash inflow at the 10 percent cost of capital. Then enter N = 4, PV = −1000, PMT = 0, FV = 1579.5, and then press the I button to find MIRR$_S$ = 12.1%. Similarly, we find MIRR$_L$ = 11.3%.[17]

The modified IRR has a significant advantage over the regular IRR. MIRR assumes that cash flows from all projects are reinvested at the cost of capital, while the regular IRR assumes that the cash flows from each project are reinvested at the project's own IRR. Since reinvestment at the cost of capital is generally more correct, the modified IRR is a better indicator of a project's true profitability. The MIRR also solves the multiple IRR problem. To illustrate, with k = 10%, Project M (the strip mine project) has MIRR = 5.6% versus its 10 percent cost of capital, so it should be

---

[16] There are several alternative definitions for the MIRR. The differences primarily relate to whether negative cash flows that occur after positive cash flows begin should be compounded and treated as part of the TV or discounted and treated as a cost. A related issue is whether negative and positive flows in a given year should be netted or treated separately. For a complete discussion, see William R. McDaniel, Daniel E. McCarty, and Kenneth A. Jessell, "Discounted Cash Flow with Explicit Reinvestment Rates: Tutorial and Extension," *The Financial Review*, August 1988, 369–385, and David M. Shull, "Interpreting Rates of Return: A Modified Rate of Return Approach," *Financial Practice and Education*, Fall 1993, 67–71.

[17] With some calculators, including the HP-17B, you could enter the cash inflows in the cash flow register (being sure to enter CF$_0$ = 0), enter I = 10, and then press the NFV key to find TV$_S$ = 1,579.50. The HP-10BII does not have an NFV key, but you can still use the cash flow register to find TV. Enter the cash inflows in the cash flow register (with CF$_0$ = 0), then enter I = 10, then press ■ NPV to find the PV of the inflows, which is 1,078.82. Now, with the regular time value keys, enter N = 4, I = 10, PV = −1078.82, PMT = 0, and press FV to find TV$_S$ = 1,579.50. Similar procedures can be used with other financial calculators.

rejected. This is consistent with the decision based on the NPV method, because at k = 10%, NPV = −$0.77 million.

Is MIRR as good as NPV for choosing between mutually exclusive projects? If two projects are of equal size and have the same life, then NPV and MIRR will always lead to the same decision. Thus, for any set of projects like our Projects S and L, if $NPV_S > NPV_L$, then $MIRR_S > MIRR_L$, and the kinds of conflicts we encountered between NPV and the regular IRR will not occur. Also, if the projects are of equal size, but differ in lives, the MIRR will always lead to the same decision as the NPV if the MIRRs are both calculated using as the terminal year the life of the longer project. (Just fill in zeros for the shorter project's missing cash flows.) However, if the projects differ in size, then conflicts can still occur. For example, if we were choosing between a large project and a small mutually exclusive one, then we might find $NPV_L > NPV_S$, but $MIRR_S > MIRR_L$.

Our conclusion is that the MIRR is superior to the regular IRR as an indicator of a project's "true" rate of return, or "expected long-term rate of return," but the NPV method is still the best way to choose among competing projects because it provides the best indication of how much each project will increase the value of the firm.

SELF-TEST QUESTIONS

Describe how the modified IRR (MIRR) is calculated.

What is the primary difference between the MIRR and the regular IRR?

What advantages does the MIRR have over the regular IRR for making capital budgeting decisions?

What condition can cause the MIRR and NPV methods to produce conflicting rankings?

CONCLUSIONS ON CAPITAL BUDGETING METHODS

We have discussed five capital budgeting decision methods, comparing the methods with one another, and highlighting their relative strengths and weaknesses. In the process, we probably created the impression that "sophisticated" firms should use only one method in the decision process, NPV. However, virtually all capital budgeting decisions are analyzed by computer, so it is easy to calculate and list all the decision measures: payback and discounted payback, NPV, IRR, and modified IRR (MIRR). In making the accept/reject decision, most large, sophisticated firms such as IBM, GE, and Royal Dutch Petroleum calculate and consider all of the measures, because each one provides decision makers with a somewhat different piece of relevant information.

Payback and discounted payback provide an indication of both the *risk* and the *liquidity* of a project—a long payback means (1) that the investment dollars will be locked up for many years, hence the project is relatively illiquid, and (2) that the project's cash flows must be forecasted far out into the future, hence the project is probably quite risky. A good analogy for this is the bond valuation process. An investor should never compare the yields to maturity on two bonds without also considering their terms to maturity, because a bond's riskiness is significantly influenced by its maturity.

NPV is important because it gives a direct measure of the dollar benefit of the project to shareholders, so we regard NPV as the best single measure of *profitability*. IRR also measures profitability, but here it is expressed as a percentage rate of return, which many decision makers prefer. Further, IRR contains information concerning a project's "safety margin." To illustrate, consider the following two projects: Project S (for small) costs $10,000 and is expected to return $16,500 at the end of one year, while Project L (for large) costs $100,000 and has an expected payoff of $115,500 after one year. At a 10 percent cost of capital, both projects have an NPV of $5,000, so by the NPV rule we should be indifferent between them. However, Project S has a much larger margin for error. Even if its realized cash inflow were 39 percent below the $16,500 forecast, the firm would still recover its $10,000 investment. On the other hand, if Project L's inflows fell by only 13.5 percent from the forecasted $115,500, the firm would not recover its investment. Further, if no inflows were generated at all, the firm would lose only $10,000 with Project S, but $100,000 if it took on Project L.

The NPV provides no information about either of these factors—the "safety margin" inherent in the cash flow forecasts or the amount of capital at risk. However, the IRR does provide "safety margin" information—Project S's IRR is a whopping 65.0 percent, while Project L's IRR is only 15.5 percent. As a result, the realized return could fall substantially for Project S, and it would still make money. Finally, the modified IRR has all the virtues of the IRR, but (1) it incorporates a better reinvestment rate assumption, and (2) it avoids the multiple rate of return problem.

In summary, the different measures provide different types of information to decision makers. Since it is easy to calculate all of them, all should be considered in the decision process. For most decisions, the greatest weight should be given to the NPV, but it would be foolish to ignore the information provided by any of the methods.

SELF-TEST QUESTIONS

Describe the advantages and disadvantages of the five capital budgeting methods discussed in this chapter.

Should capital budgeting decisions be made solely on the basis of a project's NPV?

THE POST-AUDIT

Post-Audit
A comparison of actual versus expected results for a given capital project.

An important aspect of the capital budgeting process is the **post-audit,** which involves (1) comparing actual results with those predicted by the project's sponsors and (2) explaining why any differences occurred. For example, many firms require that the operating divisions send a monthly report for the first six months after a project goes into operation, and a quarterly report thereafter, until the project's results are up to expectations. From then on, reports on the operation are reviewed on a regular basis like those of other operations.

The post-audit has two main purposes:

1. **Improve forecasts.** When decision makers are forced to compare their projections to actual outcomes, there is a tendency for estimates to improve. Conscious or unconscious biases are observed and eliminated; new forecasting methods are sought as the need for them becomes apparent; and people simply tend to do everything better, including forecasting, if they know that their actions are being monitored.

TECHNIQUES FIRMS USE TO EVALUATE CORPORATE PROJECTS

Professors John Graham and Campbell Harvey of Duke University recently surveyed 392 chief financial officers (CFOs) about their companies' corporate practices. Of those firms, 26 percent had sales less than $100 million, 32 percent had sales between $100 million and $1 billion, and 42 percent exceeded $1 billion.

The CFOs were asked to indicate how frequently they use different approaches for estimating the cost of equity: 73.5 percent use the Capital Asset Pricing Model (CAPM), 34.3 percent use a multi-beta version of the CAPM, and 15.7 percent use the dividend discount model. The CFOs also use a variety of risk adjustment techniques, but most still choose to use a single hurdle rate to evaluate all corporate projects.

The CFOs were also asked about the capital budgeting techniques they use. Most use NPV (74.9 percent) and IRR (75.7 percent) to evaluate projects, but many (56.7 percent) also use the payback approach. These results confirm that most firms use more than one approach to evaluate projects.

The survey also found important differences between the practices of small firms (less than $1 billion in sales) and large firms (more than $1 billion in sales). Consistent with earlier studies, Graham and Harvey found that small firms are more likely to rely on the payback approach, while large firms are more likely to rely on NPV and/or IRR.

SOURCE: John R. Graham and Campbell R. Harvey, "The Theory and Practice of Corporate Finance: Evidence from the Field," *Journal of Financial Economics,* Vol. 60, No. 2–3, May/June 2001, 187–243.

2. **Improve operations.** Businesses are run by people, and people can perform at higher or lower levels of efficiency. When a divisional team has made a forecast about an investment, its members are, in a sense, putting their reputations on the line. If costs are above predicted levels, sales below expectations, and so on, executives in production, sales, and other areas will strive to improve operations and to bring results into line with forecasts. In a discussion related to this point, one executive made this statement: "You academicians worry only about making good decisions. In business, we also worry about making decisions good."

The post-audit is not a simple process—a number of factors can cause complications. First, we must recognize that each element of the cash flow forecast is subject to uncertainty, so a percentage of all projects undertaken by any reasonably aggressive firm will necessarily go awry. This fact must be considered when appraising the performances of the operating executives who submit capital expenditure requests. Second, projects sometimes fail to meet expectations for reasons beyond the control of the operating executives and for reasons that no one could realistically be expected to anticipate. For example, the 2000 runup in oil prices adversely affected many projects. Third, it is often difficult to separate the operating results of one investment from those of a larger system. Although some projects stand alone and permit ready identification of costs and revenues, the cost savings that result from a new computer, for example, may be very hard to measure. Fourth, it is often hard to hand out blame or praise because the executives who were responsible for launching a given investment have moved on by the time the results are known.

Because of these difficulties, some firms tend to play down the importance of the post-audit. However, observations of both businesses and governmental units suggest that the best-run and most successful organizations are the ones that put the greatest emphasis on post-audits. Accordingly, we regard the post-audit as being one of the most important elements in a good capital budgeting system.

What is done in the post-audit?

Identify several purposes of the post-audit.

What are some factors that can cause complications in the post-audit?

USING CAPITAL BUDGETING TECHNIQUES IN OTHER CONTEXTS

The techniques developed in this chapter can help managers make a number of different types of decisions. One example is the use of these techniques when evaluating corporate mergers. Companies frequently decide to acquire other firms to obtain low-cost production facilities, to increase capacity, or to expand into new markets, and the analysis related to such mergers is conceptually similar to that related to regular capital budgeting. Thus, when AT&T decided to go into the cellular telephone business, it had the choice of building facilities from the ground up or acquiring an existing business. AT&T chose to acquire McCaw Cellular. In the analysis related to the merger, AT&T's managers used the techniques employed in regular capital budgeting analysis.

Managers also use capital budgeting techniques when deciding whether to downsize personnel or to sell off particular assets or divisions. Like capital budgeting, such an analysis requires an assessment of how the action will affect the firm's cash flows. In a downsizing, companies typically spend money (that is, invest) in severance payments to employees who are no longer needed, but the companies then receive benefits in the form of lower future wage costs. When assets are sold, the pattern of cash flows is reversed from those in a typical capital budgeting decision—positive cash flows are realized at the outset, but the firm is sacrificing future cash flows that it would have received if it had continued to use the asset. So, when deciding whether it makes sense to shed assets, managers compare the cash received with the present value of the lost outflows. If the net present value is positive, the asset sale would increase shareholder value.

Most decisions should be based on whether they contribute to shareholder value, and that, in turn, can be determined by estimating the net present value of a set of cash flows. However, as you will see in the next chapter, the hardest part is coming up with reasonable estimates of those cash flows.

Give some examples of other decisions that can be analyzed with the capital budgeting techniques developed in this chapter.

TYING IT ALL TOGETHER

This chapter has described five techniques (payback, discounted payback, NPV, IRR, and MIRR) that are used in capital budgeting analysis. Each approach provides the firm with a different piece of information, so in this age of computers, managers often look at a number of measures when evaluating corporate projects. However, NPV is the best single measure, and its use has been increasing over time.

We simplified things in this chapter. You were given a set of cash flows and a cost of capital, and you were then asked to evaluate the projects. The hard part, however, is estimating a project's cash flows and its risk, which affects its cost of capital. We will address these issues in the next chapter. Before proceeding, though, the key concepts covered are listed below.

- **Capital budgeting** is the process of analyzing potential fixed asset investments. Capital budgeting decisions are probably the most important ones financial managers must make.

- The **payback period** is defined as the number of years required to recover a project's cost. The regular payback method ignores cash flows beyond the payback period, and it does not consider the time value of money. The payback does, however, provide an indication of a project's risk and liquidity, because it shows how long the invested capital will be "at risk."

- The **discounted payback method** is similar to the regular payback method except that it discounts cash flows at the project's cost of capital. It considers the time value of money, but it ignores cash flows beyond the payback period.

- The **net present value (NPV) method** discounts all cash flows at the project's cost of capital and then sums those cash flows. The project is accepted if the NPV is positive.

- The **internal rate of return (IRR)** is defined as the discount rate that forces a project's NPV to equal zero. The project is accepted if the IRR is greater than the cost of capital.

- The NPV and IRR methods make the same accept/reject decisions for **independent projects,** but if projects are **mutually exclusive,** then ranking conflicts can arise. If conflicts arise, the NPV method should be used. The NPV and IRR methods are both superior to the payback, but NPV is superior to IRR.

- The NPV method assumes that cash flows will be reinvested at the firm's cost of capital, while the IRR method assumes reinvestment at the project's IRR. **Reinvestment at the cost of capital is generally a better assumption** because it is closer to reality.

- The **modified IRR (MIRR) method** corrects some of the problems with the regular IRR. MIRR involves finding the **terminal value (TV)** of the cash inflows, compounded at the firm's cost of capital, and then determining the discount rate that forces the present value of the TV to equal the present value of the outflows.

- The **post-audit** is a key element of capital budgeting. By comparing actual results with predicted results and then determining why differences occurred, decision makers can improve both their operations and their forecasts of projects' outcomes.

QUESTIONS

10-1 How is a project classification scheme (for example, replacement, expansion into new markets, and so forth) used in the capital budgeting process?

10-2 Explain why the NPV of a relatively long-term project, defined as one for which a high percentage of its cash flows are expected in the distant future, is more sensitive to changes in the cost of capital than is the NPV of a short-term project.

10-3 Explain why, if two mutually exclusive projects are being compared, the short-term project might have the higher ranking under the NPV criterion if the cost of capital is high, but the long-term project might be deemed better if the cost of capital is low. Would changes in the cost of capital ever cause a change in the IRR ranking of two such projects?

10-4 In what sense is a reinvestment rate assumption embodied in the NPV, IRR, and MIRR methods? What is the assumed reinvestment rate of each method?

10-5 "If a firm has no mutually exclusive projects, only independent ones, and it also has both a constant cost of capital and projects with normal cash flows in the sense that each project has one or more outflows followed by a stream of inflows, then the NPV and IRR methods will always lead to identical capital budgeting decisions." Discuss this statement. What does it imply about using the IRR method in lieu of the NPV method? If each of the assumptions made in the question were changed (one by one), how would these changes affect your answer?

10-6 Are there conditions under which a firm might be better off if it were to choose a machine with a rapid payback rather than one with a larger NPV?

10-7 A firm has $100 million available for capital expenditures. It is considering investing in one of two projects; each has a cost of $100 million. Project A has an IRR of 20 percent and an NPV of $9 million. It will be terminated at the end of 1 year at a profit of $20 million, resulting in an immediate increase in earnings per share (EPS). Project B, which cannot be postponed, has an IRR of 30 percent and an NPV of $50 million. However, the firm's short-run EPS will be reduced if it accepts Project B, because no revenues will be generated for several years.
   a. Should the short-run effects on EPS influence the choice between the two projects?
   b. How might situations like the one described here influence a firm's decision to use payback as a part of the capital budgeting process?

10-8 What does it mean for projects to be mutually exclusive? How should managers rank mutually exclusive projects?

10-9 Project X is very risky and has an NPV of $3 million. Project Y is very safe and has an NPV of $2.5 million. Assume that the two projects are mutually exclusive and that each of the net present value calculations takes into account the risk of the respective projects. Should the company accept Project X or Project Y? Explain.

SELF-TEST PROBLEMS (SOLUTIONS APPEAR IN APPENDIX B)

ST-1
Key terms
Define each of the following terms:
   a. Capital budget; capital budgeting; strategic business plan
   b. Regular payback period; discounted payback period
   c. Independent projects; mutually exclusive projects
   d. DCF techniques; net present value (NPV) method
   e. Internal rate of return (IRR) method; IRR
   f. Modified internal rate of return (MIRR) method
   g. NPV profile; crossover rate
   h. Nonnormal cash flow projects; normal cash flow projects; multiple IRRs
   i. Hurdle rate
   j. Reinvestment rate assumption
   k. Post-audit

ST-2
Project analysis
You are a financial analyst for Damon Electronics Company. The director of capital budgeting has asked you to analyze two proposed capital investments, Projects X and Y. Each project has a cost of $10,000, and the cost of capital for each project is 12 percent. The projects' expected net cash flows are as follows:

EXPECTED NET CASH FLOWS

YEAR	PROJECT X	PROJECT Y
0	($10,000)	($10,000)
1	6,500	3,500
2	3,000	3,500
3	3,000	3,500
4	1,000	3,500

   a. Calculate each project's payback period, net present value (NPV), internal rate of return (IRR), and modified internal rate of return (MIRR).
   b. Which project or projects should be accepted if they are independent?

c. Which project should be accepted if they are mutually exclusive?

d. How might a change in the cost of capital produce a conflict between the NPV and IRR rankings of these two projects? Would this conflict exist if k were 5 percent? (Hint: Plot the NPV profiles.)

e. Why does the conflict exist?

STARTER PROBLEMS

10-1
Payback period
Project K has a cost of $52,125, its expected net cash inflows are $12,000 per year for 8 years, and its cost of capital is 12 percent. What is the project's payback period (to the closest year)? (Hint: Begin by constructing a time line.)

10-2
NPV
Refer to Problem 10-1. What is the project's NPV?

10-3
IRR
Refer to Problem 10-1. What is the project's IRR?

10-4
Discounted payback period
Refer to Problem 10-1. What is the project's discounted payback period?

10-5
MIRR
Refer to Problem 10-1. What is the project's MIRR?

10-6
NPV
Your division is considering two investment projects, each of which requires an up-front expenditure of $15 million. You estimate that the investments will produce the following net cash flows:

YEAR	PROJECT A	PROJECT B
1	$ 5,000,000	$20,000,000
2	10,000,000	10,000,000
3	20,000,000	6,000,000

What are the two projects' net present values, assuming the cost of capital is 10 percent? 5 percent? 15 percent?

EXAM-TYPE PROBLEMS

The problems included in this section are set up in such a way that they could be used as multiple-choice exam problems.

10-7
NPVs, IRRs, and MIRRs for independent projects
Edelman Engineering is considering including two pieces of equipment, a truck and an overhead pulley system, in this year's capital budget. The projects are independent. The cash outlay for the truck is $17,100, and that for the pulley system is $22,430. The firm's cost of capital is 14 percent. After-tax cash flows, including depreciation, are as follows:

YEAR	TRUCK	PULLEY
1	$5,100	$7,500
2	5,100	7,500
3	5,100	7,500
4	5,100	7,500
5	5,100	7,500

Calculate the IRR, the NPV, and the MIRR for each project, and indicate the correct accept/reject decision for each.

10-8
Capital budgeting methods
Project S costs $15,000 and is expected to produce cash flows of $4,500 per year for 5 years. Project L costs $37,500 and is expected to produce cash flows of $11,100 per year for 5 years. Calculate the two projects' NPVs, IRRs, and MIRRs, assuming a cost of capital of 14 percent. Which project would be selected, assuming they are mutually exclusive, using each ranking method? Which should actually be selected?

10-9
Present value of costs
The Costa Rican Coffee Company is evaluating the within-plant distribution system for its new roasting, grinding, and packing plant. The two alternatives are (1) a conveyor system with

a high initial cost but low annual operating costs and (2) several forklift trucks, which cost less but have considerably higher operating costs. The decision to construct the plant has already been made, and the choice here will have no effect on the overall revenues of the project. The cost of capital for the plant is 9 percent, and the projects' expected net costs are listed below:

EXPECTED NET CASH COSTS

YEAR	CONVEYOR	FORKLIFT
0	($300,000)	($120,000)
1	(66,000)	(96,000)
2	(66,000)	(96,000)
3	(66,000)	(96,000)
4	(66,000)	(96,000)
5	(66,000)	(96,000)

a. What is the IRR of each alternative?
b. What is the present value of costs of each alternative? Which method should be chosen?

10-10
MIRR and NPV
Your company is considering two mutually exclusive projects, X and Y, whose costs and cash flows are shown below:

YEAR	X	Y
0	($1,000)	($1,000)
1	100	1,000
2	300	100
3	400	50
4	700	50

The projects are equally risky, and their cost of capital is 12 percent. You must make a recommendation, and you must base it on the modified IRR (MIRR). What is the MIRR of the better project?

10-11
NPV and IRR
A company is analyzing two mutually exclusive projects, S and L, whose cash flows are shown below:

```
        0      1      2      3      4
        ├──────┼──────┼──────┼──────┤
S    -1,000   900    250    10     10
L    -1,000    0     250    400    800
```

The company's cost of capital is 10 percent, and it can get an unlimited amount of capital at that cost. What is the *regular IRR* (not MIRR) of the *better* project? (Hint: Note that the better project may or may not be the one with the higher IRR.)

10-12
MIRR
Project X has a cost of $1,000, and it is expected to produce a uniform cash flow stream for 10 years, i.e., the CFs are the same in Years 1 through 10, and it has a regular IRR of 12 percent. The cost of capital for the project is 10 percent. What is the project's modified IRR (MIRR)?

10-13
NPV and IRR
After discovering a new gold vein in the Colorado mountains, CTC Mining Corporation must decide whether to mine the deposit. The most cost-effective method of mining gold is sulfuric acid extraction, a process that results in environmental damage. To go ahead with the extraction, CTC must spend $900,000 for new mining equipment and pay $165,000 for its installation. The gold mined will net the firm an estimated $350,000 each year over the 5-year life of the vein. CTC's cost of capital is 14 percent. For the purposes of this problem, assume that the cash inflows occur at the end of the year.
a. What is the NPV and IRR of this project?
b. Should this project be undertaken, ignoring environmental concerns?
c. How should environmental effects be considered when evaluating this, or any other, project? How might these effects change your decision in part b?

10-14
NPV and IRR
John's Publishing Company, a new service that writes term papers for college students, provides 11-page term papers from a list of more than 500 topics. Each paper will cost $7.50 and is written by a graduate in the topic area. John's will pay $20,000 for the rights to all of the

manuscripts. In addition, each author will receive $0.50 in royalties for every paper sold. Marketing expenses are estimated to be a total of $20,000 divided equally between Years 1 and 2, and John's cost of capital is 11 percent. Sales are expected as follows:

YEAR	VOLUME
1	10,000
2	7,000
3	3,000

a. What is the payback period for this investment? Its NPV? Its IRR?
b. What are the ethical implications of this investment?

10-15
NPV and IRR

Sharon Evans, who graduated from the local university 3 years ago with a degree in marketing, is manager of Ann Naylor's store in the Southwest Mall. Sharon's store has 5 years remaining on its lease. Rent is $2,000 per month, 60 payments remain, and the next payment is due in 1 month. The mall's owner plans to sell the property in a year and wants rents at that time to be high so the property will appear more valuable. Therefore, Sharon has been offered a "great deal" (owner's words) on a new 5-year lease. The new lease calls for zero rent for 9 months, then payments of $2,600 per month for the next 51 months. The lease cannot be broken, and Ann Naylor Corporation's cost of capital is 12 percent (or 1 percent per month). Sharon must make a decision. A good one could help her career and move her up in management, but a bad one could hurt her prospects for promotion.
a. Should Sharon accept the new lease? (Hint: Be sure to use 1 percent per month.)
b. Suppose Sharon decided to bargain with the mall's owner over the new lease payment. What new lease payment would make Sharon indifferent between the new and the old leases? (Hint: Find FV of the first 9 payments at t = 9, then treat this as the PV of a 51-period annuity whose payments represent the incremental rent during Months 10 to 60.)
c. Sharon is not sure of the 12 percent cost of capital—it could be higher or lower. At what *nominal cost* of capital would Sharon be indifferent between the two leases? (Hint: Calculate the differences between the two payment streams, and find the IRR of this difference stream.)

10-16
Capital budgeting criteria

A firm with a WACC of 10 percent is considering the following mutually exclusive projects:

YEAR	PROJECT A	PROJECT B
0	($400)	($600)
1	55	300
2	55	300
3	55	50
4	225	50
5	225	50

a. According to the payback criterion, which project should be accepted?
b. According to the discounted payback criterion, which project should be accepted?
c. According to the NPV criterion, which project should be accepted?
d. According to the IRR criterion, which project should be accepted?
e. According to the MIRR criterion, which project should be accepted?

10-17
NPV and IRR

Justin is evaluating a project that is expected to produce cash flows of $7,500 each year for the next 10 years and $10,000 each year for the following 10 years. The IRR of this 20-year project is 10.98 percent. If the firm's WACC is 9 percent, what is the project's NPV?

10-18
MIRR

A project has the following cash flows:

YEAR	CASH FLOW
0	($500)
1	202
2	(X)
3	196
4	350
5	451

Notice this project requires two cash outflows at Years 0 and 2, and produces positive cash inflows in the remaining periods. The project's appropriate WACC is 10 percent, and its modified internal rate of return (MIRR) is 14.14 percent. What is the value of the project's cash outflow in Year 2?

PROBLEMS

10-19
NPV and IRR

Cummings Products Company is considering two mutually exclusive investments. The projects' expected net cash flows are as follows:

	EXPECTED NET CASH FLOWS	
YEAR	PROJECT A	PROJECT B
0	($300)	($405)
1	(387)	134
2	(193)	134
3	(100)	134
4	600	134
5	600	134
6	850	134
7	(180)	0

a. If you were told that each project's cost of capital was 12 percent, which project should be selected? If the cost of capital was 18 percent, what would be the proper choice?
b. Construct NPV profiles for Projects A and B.
c. What is each project's IRR?
d. What is the crossover rate, and what is its significance?
e. What is each project's MIRR at a cost of capital of 12 percent? At k = 18%? (Hint: Consider Period 7 as the end of Project B's life.)

10-20
Timing differences

The Northwest Territories Oil Exploration Company is considering two mutually exclusive plans for extracting oil on property for which it has mineral rights. Both plans call for the expenditure of $12,000,000 to drill development wells. Under Plan A, all the oil will be extracted in 1 year, producing a cash flow at t = 1 of $14,400,000. Under Plan B, cash flows will be $2,100,000 per year for 20 years.
a. Construct NPV profiles for Plans A and B, identify each project's IRR, and indicate the approximate crossover rate.
b. Suppose a company has a cost of capital of 12 percent, and it can get unlimited capital at that cost. Is it logical to assume that it would take on all available independent projects (of average risk) with returns greater than 12 percent? Further, if all available projects with returns greater than 12 percent have been taken on, would this mean that cash flows from past investments would have an opportunity cost of only 12 percent, because all the firm could do with these cash flows would be to replace money that has a cost of 12 percent? Finally, does this imply that the cost of capital is the correct rate to assume for the reinvestment of a project's cash flows?

10-21
Scale differences

The Parrish Publishing Company is considering two mutually exclusive expansion plans. Plan A calls for the expenditure of $40 million on a large-scale, integrated plant that will provide an expected cash flow stream of $6.4 million per year for 20 years. Plan B calls for the expenditure of $12 million to build a somewhat less efficient, more labor-intensive plant that has an expected cash flow stream of $2.72 million per year for 20 years. Parrish's cost of capital is 10 percent.
a. Calculate each project's NPV and IRR.
b. Graph the NPV profiles for Plan A and Plan B. From the NPV profiles constructed, approximate the crossover rate.
c. Give a logical explanation, based on reinvestment rates and opportunity costs, as to why the NPV method is better than the IRR method when the firm's cost of capital is constant at some value such as 10 percent.

10-22
Multiple rates of return

The Black Hills Uranium Company is deciding whether or not it should open a strip mine, the net cost of which is $2 million. Net cash inflows are expected to be $13 million, all coming at the end of Year 1. The land must be returned to its natural state at a cost of $12 million, payable at the end of Year 2.

a. Plot the project's NPV profile. (Hint: Calculate NPV at k = 0%, 10%, 80%, and 450%, and possibly at other k values.)

b. Should the project be accepted if k = 10%? If k = 20%? Explain your reasoning.

c. Can you think of some other capital budgeting situations in which negative cash flows during or at the end of the project's life might lead to multiple IRRs?

d. What is the project's MIRR at k = 10%? At k = 20%? With this project, does the MIRR method lead to the same accept/reject decision as the NPV method? Does the MIRR method *always* lead to the same accept/reject decision as the NPV method? (Hint: Consider mutually exclusive projects that differ in size.)

10-23
Payback, NPV, and MIRR

Your division is considering two investment projects, each of which requires an up-front expenditure of $25 million. You estimate that the cost of capital is 10 percent and that the investments will produce the following after-tax cash flows (in millions of dollars):

YEAR	PROJECT A	PROJECT B
1	$ 5	$20
2	10	10
3	15	8
4	20	6

a. What is the regular payback period for each of the projects?

b. What is the discounted payback period for each of the projects?

c. If the two projects are independent and the cost of capital is 10 percent, which project or projects should the firm undertake?

d. If the two projects are mutually exclusive and the cost of capital is 5 percent, which project should the firm undertake?

e. If the two projects are mutually exclusive and the cost of capital is 15 percent, which project should the firm undertake?

f. What is the crossover rate?

g. If the cost of capital is 10 percent, what is the modified IRR (MIRR) of each project?

SPREADSHEET PROBLEM

10-24
Capital budgeting tools

Rework Problem 10-19, parts a through e, using a spreadsheet model. Then, answer the following related questions:

f. What is the regular payback period for these two projects?

g. At a cost of capital of 12 percent, what is the discounted payback period for these two projects?

INTEGRATED CASE

ALLIED COMPONENTS COMPANY

10-25 Basics of Capital Budgeting Assume that you recently went to work for Allied Components Company, a supplier of auto repair parts used in the after-market with products from DaimlerChrysler, Ford, and other auto makers.

Your boss, the chief financial officer (CFO), has just handed you the estimated cash flows for two proposed projects. Project L involves adding a new item to the firm's ignition system line; it would take some time to build up the market for this product, so the cash inflows would increase over time. Project S involves an add-on to an existing line, and its cash flows would decrease over time. Both projects have 3-year lives, because Allied is planning to introduce entirely new models after 3 years.

Here are the projects' net cash flows (in thousands of dollars):

EXPECTED NET CASH FLOW

YEAR	PROJECT L	PROJECT S
0	($100)	($100)
1	10	70
2	60	50
3	80	20

Depreciation, salvage values, net operating working capital requirements, and tax effects are all included in these cash flows.

The CFO also made subjective risk assessments of each project, and he concluded that both projects have risk characteristics that are similar to the firm's average project. Allied's weighted average cost of capital is 10 percent. You must now determine whether one or both of the projects should be accepted.

a. What is capital budgeting? Are there any similarities between a firm's capital budgeting decisions and an individual's investment decisions?
b. What is the difference between independent and mutually exclusive projects? Between projects with normal and nonnormal cash flows?
c. (1) What is the payback period? Find the paybacks for Projects L and S.
   (2) What is the rationale for the payback method? According to the payback criterion, which project or projects should be accepted if the firm's maximum acceptable payback is 2 years, and if Projects L and S are independent? If they are mutually exclusive?
   (3) What is the difference between the regular and discounted payback periods?
   (4) What is the main disadvantage of discounted payback? Is the payback method of any real usefulness in capital budgeting decisions?
d. (1) Define the term *net present value (NPV)*. What is each project's NPV?
   (2) What is the rationale behind the NPV method? According to NPV, which project or projects should be accepted if they are independent? Mutually exclusive?

(3) Would the NPVs change if the cost of capital changed?
e. (1) Define the term *internal rate of return (IRR)*. What is each project's IRR?
   (2) How is the IRR on a project related to the YTM on a bond?
   (3) What is the logic behind the IRR method? According to IRR, which projects should be accepted if they are independent? Mutually exclusive?
   (4) Would the projects' IRRs change if the cost of capital changed?
f. (1) Draw NPV profiles for Projects L and S. At what discount rate do the profiles cross?
   (2) Look at your NPV profile graph without referring to the actual NPVs and IRRs. Which project or projects should be accepted if they are independent? Mutually exclusive? Explain. Are your answers correct at any cost of capital less than 23.6 percent?
g. (1) What is the underlying cause of ranking conflicts between NPV and IRR?
   (2) What is the "reinvestment rate assumption," and how does it affect the NPV versus IRR conflict?
   (3) Which method is the best? Why?
h. (1) Define the term *modified IRR (MIRR)*. Find the MIRRs for Projects L and S.
   (2) What are the MIRR's advantages and disadvantages vis-à-vis the NPV?
i. As a separate project (Project P), the firm is considering sponsoring a pavilion at the upcoming World's Fair. The pavilion would cost $800,000, and it is expected to result in $5 million of incremental cash inflows during its 1 year of operation. However, it would then take another year, and $5 million of costs, to demolish the site and return it to its original condition. Thus, Project P's expected net cash flows look like this (in millions of dollars):

YEAR	NET CASH FLOWS
0	($0.8)
1	5.0
2	(5.0)

The project is estimated to be of average risk, so its cost of capital is 10 percent.
(1) What is Project P's NPV? What is its IRR? Its MIRR?
(2) Draw Project P's NPV profile. Does Project P have normal or nonnormal cash flows? Should this project be accepted?

CYBER PROBLEM

Please go to our web site **http://brigham.swlearning.com** to access the Cyberproblems.

CASH FLOW ESTIMATION AND RISK ANALYSIS

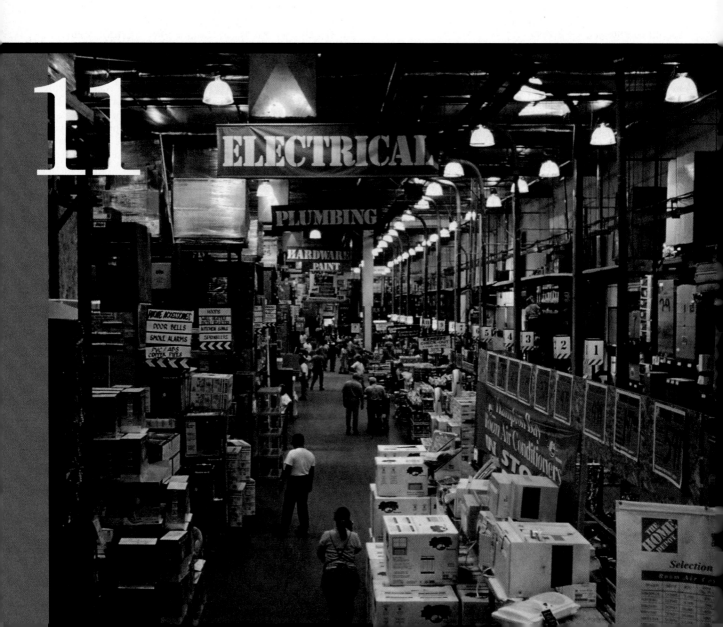

HOME DEPOT

ome Depot Inc. has grown phenomenally over the past decade, and it shows no signs of slowing down. At the beginning of 1990, it had 118 stores, and its annuals sales were $2.8 billion. By early 2002, it had more than 1,400 stores, and its annual sales were in excess of $50 billion. Despite concerns of a slowing economy, the company expects to open another 200 stores in the upcoming fiscal year.

Home Depot recently estimated that it costs, on average, $16 million to purchase land, construct a new store, and stock it with inventory. (The inventory costs about $5 million, but about $2 million of this is financed through accounts payable.) Each new store thus represents a major capital expenditure, so the company must use capital budgeting techniques to determine if a potential store's expected cash flows are sufficient to cover its costs.

Home Depot uses information from its existing stores to forecast new stores' expected cash flows. Thus far, its forecasts have been outstanding, but there are always risks that must be considered. First, store sales might be less than projected if the economy weakens. Second, some of Home Depot's customers might in the future bypass it altogether and buy directly from manufacturers through the Internet. Third, new stores could "cannibalize," that is, take sales away from, ex-

isting stores. This last point was made in the July 16, 1999, issue of *Value Line*:

> The retailer has picked the "low-hanging fruit;" it has already entered the most attractive markets. To avoid "cannibalization"—which occurs when duplicative stores are located too closely together—the company is developing complementary formats. For example, Home Depot is beginning to roll out its *Expo Design Center* chain, which offers one-stop sales and service for kitchen and bath and other remodeling and renovation work . . .

The decision to expand requires a detailed assessment of the forecasted cash flows, including the risk that the forecasted level of sales might not be realized. In this chapter, we describe techniques for estimating a project's cash flows and their associated risk. Companies such as Home Depot use these techniques on a regular basis to evaluate capital budgeting decisions.

The basic principles of capital budgeting were covered in Chapter 10. Given a project's expected cash flows, it is easy to calculate its payback, discounted payback, NPV, IRR, and MIRR. Unfortunately, cash flows are rarely just given—rather, managers must estimate them based on information collected from sources both inside and outside the company. Moreover, uncertainty surrounds the cash flow estimates, and some projects are riskier than others. In this chapter, we first develop procedures for estimating cash flows associated with capital budgeting projects. Then, we discuss techniques used to measure and take account of project risk. ■

ESTIMATING CASH FLOWS

The most important, but also the most difficult, step in capital budgeting is estimating projects' cash flows—the investment outlays and the annual net cash inflows after a project goes into operation. Many variables are involved, and many individuals and departments participate in the process. For example, the forecasts of unit sales and sales prices are normally made by the marketing group, based on their knowledge of price elasticity, advertising effects, the state of the economy, competitors' reactions, and trends in consumers' tastes. Similarly, the capital outlays associated with a new product are generally obtained from the engineering and product development staffs, while operating costs are estimated by cost accountants, production experts, personnel specialists, purchasing agents and so forth.

It is difficult to accurately forecast the costs and revenues associated with a large, complex project, so forecast errors can be quite large. For example, when several major oil companies decided to build the Alaska Pipeline, the original cost estimates were in the neighborhood of $700 million, but the final cost was closer to $7 billion. Similar (or even worse) miscalculations are common in forecasts of product design costs, such as the costs to develop a new personal computer. Further, as difficult as plant and equipment costs are to estimate, sales revenues and operating costs over the project's life are even more uncertain. For example, several years ago, Federal Express developed an electronic delivery service system (ZapMail). It used the correct capital budgeting technique, NPV, but it incorrectly estimated the project's cash flows: Projected revenues were too high, projected costs were too low, and virtually no one was willing to pay the price required to cover the project's costs. As a result, cash flows failed to meet the forecasted levels, and Federal Express ended up losing about $200 million on the venture. This example demonstrates a basic truth—if cash flow estimates are not reasonably accurate, any analytical technique, no matter how sophisticated, can lead to poor decisions. Because of its financial strength, Federal Express was able to absorb losses on the project, but the ZapMail venture could have forced a weaker firm into bankruptcy.

The financial staff's role in the forecasting process includes (1) obtaining information from various departments such as engineering and marketing, (2) ensuring that everyone involved with the forecast uses a consistent set of economic assumptions, and (3) making sure that no biases are inherent in the forecasts. This last point is extremely important, because managers often become emotionally involved with pet projects and also develop empire-building complexes, both of which lead to cash flow forecasting biases that make bad projects look good—on paper.

It is almost impossible to overstate the problems one can encounter in cash flow forecasts. It is also difficult to overstate the importance of these forecasts. Still, observing the principles discussed in the next several sections will help minimize forecasting errors.

SELF-TEST QUESTIONS

What is the most important step in a capital budgeting analysis?

What departments are involved in estimating a project's cash flows?

What is the financial staff's role in the forecasting process for capital projects?

IDENTIFYING THE RELEVANT CASH FLOWS

Relevant Cash Flows
The specific cash flows that should be considered in a capital budgeting decision.

The starting point in any capital budgeting analysis is identifying the **relevant cash flows,** defined as the specific set of cash flows that should be considered in the decision at hand. Analysts often make errors in estimating cash flows, but two cardinal rules can help you avoid mistakes: (1) Capital budgeting decisions must be based on *cash flows*, not accounting income. (2) Only *incremental cash flows* are relevant.

Recall from Chapter 2 that *free cash flow* is the cash flow available for distribution to investors. In a nutshell, the relevant cash flow for a project is the *additional* free cash flow that the company expects if it implements the project, that is, the cash flow above and beyond what the company could expect if it doesn't implement the project. The following sections discuss the relevant cash flows in more detail.

PROJECT CASH FLOW VERSUS ACCOUNTING INCOME

Recall that free cash flow is calculated as follows:

$$\text{Free cash flow} = \frac{\text{After-tax}}{\text{operating income}} + \text{Depreciation} - \frac{\text{Capital}}{\text{expenditures}} - \frac{\text{Change in net}}{\text{operating working capital}}$$

$$= \text{EBIT}(1 - \text{T}) + \text{Depreciation} - \frac{\text{Capital}}{\text{expenditures}} - \left[\begin{array}{c} \Delta \text{ Current assets} - \\ \Delta \text{ Spontaneous liabilities} \end{array} \right].$$

Just as a firm's value depends on its free cash flows, the value of a project depends on its free cash flows. We illustrate the estimation of project cash flow later in the chapter with a comprehensive example, but it is important for you to understand that project cash flow differs from accounting income.

Costs of Fixed Assets

Most projects require assets, and asset purchases represent *negative* cash flows. Even though the acquisition of assets results in a cash outflow, accountants do not show the purchase of fixed assets as a deduction from accounting income. Instead, they deduct a depreciation expense each year throughout the life of the asset.

Note that the full costs of fixed assets include any shipping and installation costs. When a firm acquires fixed assets, it often must incur substantial costs for shipping and installing the equipment. These charges are added to the price of the equipment when the project's cost is being determined. Then, the full cost of the equipment, including shipping and installation costs, is used as the *depreciable basis* when depreciation charges are being calculated. For example, if a company bought a computer with an invoice price of $100,000 and paid another $10,000 for shipping and installation, then the full cost of the computer (and its depreciable basis) would be $110,000. Note too that fixed assets can often be sold at the end of a project's life. If this is the case, then the after-tax cash proceeds represent a positive cash flow. We will illustrate both depreciation and cash flow from asset sales later in the chapter.

Noncash Charges

In calculating net income, accountants usually subtract depreciation from revenues. So, while accountants do not subtract the purchase price of fixed assets when calculating accounting income, they do subtract a charge each year for depreciation. Depreciation shelters income from taxation, and this has an impact on cash flow, but depreciation itself is not a cash flow. Therefore, depreciation must be added to net income when estimating a project's cash flow.

Changes in Net Operating Working Capital

Normally, additional inventories are required to support a new operation, and expanded sales tie additional funds up in accounts receivable. However, payables and accruals increase spontaneously as a result of the expansion, and this reduces the cash needed to finance inventories and receivables. The difference between the required increase in current assets and the spontaneous increase in current liabilities is the **change in net operating working capital.** If this change is positive, as it generally is for expansion projects, then additional financing, over and above the cost of the fixed assets, will be needed.

Change in Net Operating Working Capital
The increased current assets resulting from a new project minus the spontaneous increase in accounts payable and accruals.

Toward the end of a project's life, inventories will be used but not replaced, and receivables will be collected without corresponding replacements. As these changes occur, the firm will receive cash inflows. As a result, the investment in operating working capital will be returned by the end of the project's life.

Interest Expenses Are Not Included in Project Cash Flows

Recall from Chapter 10 that we discount a project's cash flows by its cost of capital, and that the cost of capital is a weighted average of the costs of debt, preferred stock, and common equity (WACC), adjusted for the project's risk. Moreover, the WACC is the rate of return necessary to satisfy all of the firm's investors—debtholders and stockholders. The discounting process *reduces* the cash flows to account for the project's capital costs. If interest charges were first deducted and then the resulting cash flows were discounted, this would double count the cost of debt. *Therefore, you should not subtract interest expenses when finding a project's cash flows.*

Note that this differs from the procedures used to calculate accounting income. Accountants measure the profit available for stockholders, so interest expenses are subtracted. However, project cash flow is the cash flow available for all investors, bondholders as well as stockholders, so interest expenses are not subtracted. All this is analogous to the procedures used in the corporate valuation model of Chapter 8, where the company's free cash flows are discounted at the WACC.[1]

INCREMENTAL CASH FLOWS

Incremental Cash Flow
The net cash flow attributable to an investment project.

In evaluating a project, we focus on those cash flows that occur if and only if we accept the project. These cash flows, called **incremental cash flows,** represent the change in the firm's total cash flow that occurs as a direct result of accepting the project. Three special problems in determining incremental cash flows are discussed next.

Sunk Costs

Sunk Cost
A cash outlay that has already been incurred and that cannot be recovered regardless of whether the project is accepted or rejected.

A **sunk cost** is an outlay that has already occurred, hence is not affected by the decision under consideration. Since sunk costs are not incremental costs, they should not be included in the analysis. To illustrate, in 2002, Northeast BankCorp was considering the establishment of a branch office in a newly developed section of Boston. To help with its evaluation, Northeast had, back in 2001, hired a consulting firm to perform a site analysis; the cost was $100,000, and this amount was expensed for tax purposes in 2001. Is this 2001 expenditure a relevant cost with respect to the 2002 capital budgeting decision? The answer is no—the $100,000 is a *sunk cost,* and it will not affect Northeast's future cash flows regardless of whether or not the new branch is built. It often turns out that a particular project has a negative NPV when all the associated costs, including sunk costs, are considered. However, on an incremental basis, the project may be a good one because the *incremental cash flows* are large enough to produce a positive NPV on the *incremental investment.*

Opportunity Costs

Opportunity Cost
The return on the best *alternative* use of an asset, or the highest return that will *not* be earned if funds are invested in a particular project.

A second potential problem relates to **opportunity costs,** which are cash flows that could be generated from an asset the firm already owns provided it is not used for the project in question. To illustrate, Northeast BankCorp already owns a piece of land that is suitable for the branch location. When evaluating the prospective

---

[1] An alternative approach to capital budgeting is to estimate the cash flows that are available for equity holders. Although this produces the same NPV as our approach, we do not recommend it because to apply it correctly requires that we determine the amount of debt and equity for every year of the project's life.

branch, should the cost of the land be disregarded because no additional cash outlay would be required? The answer is no, because there is an *opportunity cost* inherent in the use of the property. In this case, the land could be sold to yield $150,000 after taxes. Use of the site for the branch would require foregoing this inflow, so the $150,000 must be charged as an opportunity cost against the project. Note that the proper land cost in this example is the $150,000 market-determined value, irrespective of whether Northeast originally paid $50,000 or $500,000 for the property. (What Northeast paid would, of course, have an effect on taxes, hence on the after-tax opportunity cost.)

Effects on Other Parts of the Firm: Externalities

Externalities
Effects of a project on cash flows in other parts of the firm.

The third potential problem involves the effects of a project on other parts of the firm, which economists call **externalities.** For example, some of Northeast's customers who would use the new branch are already banking with Northeast's downtown office. The loans and deposits, hence profits, generated by these customers would not be new to the bank; rather, they would represent a transfer from the main office to the branch. Thus, the net income produced by these customers should not be treated as incremental income in the capital budgeting decision. On the other hand, having a suburban branch would help the bank attract new business to its downtown office, because some people like to be able to bank both close to home and close to work. In this case, the additional income that would actually flow to the downtown office should be attributed to the branch. Although they are often difficult to quantify, *externalities* (which can be either positive or negative) should be considered.

Cannibalization
Occurs when the introduction of a new product causes sales of existing products to decline.

When a new project takes sales from an existing product, this is often called **cannibalization.** Naturally, firms do not like to cannibalize their existing products, but it often turns out that if they do not, someone else will. To illustrate, IBM for years refused to provide full support for its PC division because it did not want to steal sales from its highly profitable mainframe business. That turned out to be a huge strategic error, because it allowed Intel, Microsoft, Compaq, and others to become dominant forces in the computer industry. Therefore, when considering externalities, the full implications of the proposed new project should be taken into account.

TIMING OF CASH FLOW

We must account properly for the timing of cash flows. Accounting income statements are for periods such as years or months, so they do not reflect exactly when during the period cash revenues or expenses occur. Because of the time value of money, capital budgeting cash flows should in theory be analyzed exactly as they occur. Of course, there must be a compromise between accuracy and feasibility. A time line with daily cash flows would in theory be most accurate, but daily cash flow estimates would be costly to construct, unwieldy to use, and probably no more accurate than annual cash flow estimates because we simply cannot forecast well enough to warrant this degree of detail. Therefore, in most cases, we simply assume that all cash flows occur at the end of every year. However, for some projects, it may be useful to assume that cash flows occur at mid-year, or even quarterly or monthly.

Why should companies use project cash flow rather than accounting income when finding the NPV of a project?

How do shipping and installation costs affect the costs of fixed assets and the depreciable basis?

What is the most common noncash charge that must be added back when finding project cash flows?

What is net operating working capital, and how does it affect projects' costs in capital budgeting?

How does the company get back the dollars it invests in net operating working capital?

Explain the following terms: incremental cash flow, sunk cost, opportunity cost, externality, and cannibalization.

Give an example of a "good" externality, that is, one that makes a project look better.

EVALUATING CAPITAL BUDGETING PROJECTS

Up until this point, we have discussed several important aspects of cash flow analysis, but we have not seen how they affect capital budgeting decisions. Conceptually, these decisions are straightforward: A potential project creates value for the firm's shareholders if and only if the net present value of the incremental cash flows from the project is positive. In practice, however, estimating these cash flows can be difficult.

New Expansion Project
A project that is intended to increase sales.

Replacement Project
A project that replaces an existing asset with a new asset.

Incremental cash flows are affected by whether the project is a new expansion project or a replacement project. A **new expansion project** is defined as one where the firm invests in new assets to increase sales. Here the incremental cash flows are simply the project's cash inflows and outflows. In effect, the company is comparing what its value looks like with and without the proposed project. By contrast, a **replacement project** occurs when the firm replaces an existing asset with a new one. In this case, the incremental cash flows are the firm's *additional* inflows and outflows that result from investing in the new asset. In a replacement analysis, the company is comparing its value if it acquires the new asset to its value if it continues to use the existing asset.[2]

Despite these differences, the basic principles for evaluating expansion and replacement projects are the same. In each case, the cash flows typically include the following items:

1. *Initial investment outlay*. The initial investment includes the up-front cost of fixed assets associated with the project plus any increases in net operating working capital.

2. *Operating cash flows over the project's life*. These are the incremental cash inflows over the projects's economic life. Annual operating cash flows equal after-tax

---

[2] For more discussion on replacement analysis decisions refer to Web Appendix 11B on the *Fundamentals* web site, **http://brigham.swlearning.com**.

operating income plus depreciation. Recall (a) that depreciation is added back because it is a noncash expense and (b) that financing costs (including interest expense) are not included because they are accounted for in the discounting process.

3. *Terminal year cash flows.* At the end of a project's life, some extra cash flows are frequently received. These include the salvage value of the fixed assets, adjusted for taxes if assets are not sold at their book value, plus the return of the net operating working capital.

For each year of the project's life, the *net cash flow* is determined as the sum of the cash flows from each of the three categories. These annual net cash flows are then plotted on a time line and used to calculate the project's NPV and IRR.

We will illustrate the principles of capital budgeting analysis by examining a new project being considered by Brandt-Quigley Corporation (BQC), a large Atlanta-based technology company. BQC's research and development department has been applying its expertise in microprocessor technology to develop a small computer designed to control home appliances. Once programmed, the computer will automatically control the heating and air-conditioning systems, security system, hot water heater, and even small appliances such as a coffee maker. By increasing a home's energy efficiency, the computer can cut costs enough to pay for itself within a few years. Developments have now reached the stage where a decision must be made about whether or not to go forward with full-scale production.

BQC's marketing vice-president believes that annual sales would be 20,000 units if the units were priced at $3,000 each, so annual sales are estimated at $60 million. The engineering department has reported that the firm would need additional manufacturing capability, and BQC currently has an option to purchase an existing building, at a cost of $12 million, which would meet this need. The building would be bought and paid for on December 31, 2003, and for depreciation purposes it would fall into the MACRS 39-year class.

The necessary equipment would be purchased and installed late in 2003, and it would also be paid for on December 31, 2003. The equipment would fall into the MACRS 5-year class, and it would cost $8 million, including transportation and installation. Moreover, the project would also require an initial investment of $6 million in net operating working capital, which would also be made on December 31, 2003.

The project's estimated economic life is four years. At the end of that time, the building is expected to have a market value of $7.5 million and a book value of $10.908 million, whereas the equipment would have a market value of $2 million and a book value of $1.36 million.

The production department has estimated that variable manufacturing costs would be $2,100 per unit, and that fixed overhead costs, excluding depreciation, would be $8 million a year. Depreciation expenses would be determined in accordance with the MACRS rates (which are discussed in Web Appendix 11A).

BQC's marginal federal-plus-state tax rate is 40 percent; its cost of capital is 12 percent; and, for capital budgeting purposes, the company's policy is to assume that operating cash flows occur at the end of each year. Because the plant would begin operations on January 1, 2004, the first operating cash flows would occur on December 31, 2004.

Several other points should be noted: (1) BQC is a relatively large corporation, with sales of more than $4 billion, and it takes on many investments each year. Thus, if the computer control project does not work out, it will not bankrupt the company—management can afford to take a chance on the computer control project. (2) If the project is accepted, the company will be contractually obligated to operate it for its full four-year life. Management must make this commitment to its component suppliers. (3) Returns on this project would be positively correlated with returns on BQC's other projects and also with the stock market—the project should do well if other parts of the firm and the general economy are strong.

Assume that you are one of the company's financial analysts, and you must conduct the capital budgeting analysis. For now, assume that the project has the same risk as an average project, and use the corporate weighted average cost of capital, 12 percent.

ANALYSIS OF THE CASH FLOWS

Capital projects can be analyzed using a calculator, paper, and a pencil, or with a spreadsheet program such as *Excel*. Either way, you must set the analysis up as shown in Table 11-1 and go through the steps outlined in Parts 1 through 5 of the table. For exam purposes, you will probably have to work problems with a calculator. However, for reasons that will become obvious as you go through the chapter, in practice spreadsheets are virtually always used. Still, the steps involved in a capital budgeting analysis are the same regardless of whether you use a calculator or a computer to "get the answer."

Table 11-1, which is a printout from the CD-ROM file 11MODEL.xls, is divided into five parts: (1) Input Data, (2) Depreciation Schedule, (3) Net Salvage Values, (4) Projected Net Cash Flows, and (5) Key Output. There are also two extensions, Parts 6 and 7, that deal with risk analysis, which we will discuss later in the chapter when we cover sensitivity and scenario analyses. Note also that the table shows row

TABLE 11-1

Analysis of a New (Expansion) Project
Parts 1 and 2

	A	B	C	D	E	F	G	H	I
29	Table 11-1. Analysis of a New (Expansion) Project								
30									
31	Part 1. Input Data (in thousands of dollars)								
32						Key Output: NPV	=		$5,166
33	Building cost (= Depreciable basis)			$12,000					
34	Equipment cost (= Depreciable basis)			$8,000		Market value of building in 2007			$7,500
35	Net Operating WC			$6,000		Market value of equip. in 2007			$2,000
36	First year sales (in units)			20,000		Tax rate			40%
37	Growth rate in units sold			0.0%		WACC			12%
38	Sales price per unit			$3.00		Inflation: growth in sales price			0.0%
39	Variable cost per unit			$2.10		Inflation: growth in VC per unit			0.0%
40	Fixed costs			$8,000		Inflation: growth in fixed costs			0.0%
41									
42	Part 2. Depreciation Schedule [a]				Years				Cumulative
43					1	2	3	4	Deprn
44	Building Deprn Rate				1.3%	2.6%	2.6%	2.6%	
45	Building Deprn				$156	$312	$312	$312	$1,092
46	Ending Book Val: Cost - Cum. Deprn				11,844	11,532	11,220	$10,908	
47									
48	Equipment Deprn Rate				20.0%	32.0%	19.0%	12.0%	
49	Equipment Deprn				$1,600	$2,560	$1,520	$960	$6,640
50	Ending Book Val: Cost - Cum. Deprn				6,400	3,840	2,320	$1,360	
51									
52	[a] The indicated percentages are multiplied by the depreciable basis ($12,000 for the building and $8,000 for the equipment)								
53	to determine the depreciation expense for the year. See Web Appendix 11A for a review of MACRS depreciation rates.								

TABLE 11-1

Analysis of a New (Expansion) Project
Part 3

	A	B	C	D	E	F	G	H	I
55	Part 3 of Table 11-1. Net Salvage Values in 2007								
56					Building	Equipment	Total		
57	Estimated Market Value in 2007				$7,500	$2,000			
58	Book Value in 2007[b]				10,908	1,360			
59	Expected Gain or Loss[c]				-3,408	640			
60	Taxes paid or tax credit				-1,363	256			
61	Net cash flow from salvage[d]				$8,863	$1,744	$10,607		
62									
63	[b] Book value equals depreciable basis (initial cost in this case) minus accumulated MACRS depreciation. For the								
64	building, accumulated depreciation equals $1,092, so book value equals $12,000 - $1,092 = $10,908. For the equipment,								
65	accumulated depreciation equals $6,640, so book value equals $8,000 - $6,640 = $1,360.								
66									
67	[c] Building: $7,500 market value - $10,908 book value = -$3,408, a loss. This represents a shortfall in depreciation								
68	taken versus "true" depreciation, and it is treated as an operating expense for 2007. Equipment: $2,000 market value -								
69	$1,360 book value = $640 profit. Here the depreciation charge exceeds the "true" depreciation, and the difference is called								
70	"depreciation recapture". It is taxed as ordinary income in 2007.								
71									
72	[d] Net cash flow from salvage equals salvage (market) value minus taxes. For the building, the loss results in a tax credit, so								
73	net salvage value = $7,500 - (-$1,363) = $8,863.								

and column indicators, so cells in the table have designations such as "Cell D33," which is the location of the cost of the building, found in Part 1, Input Data. If we deleted the row and column indicators, the table would look exactly like the setup for pencil-and-paper calculations.[3] Note also that the first row shown is Row 29; the first 28 rows contain information about the model that we omitted from the text.

Part 1, the Input Data section, provides the basic data used in the analysis. The inputs are really "assumptions"—thus, in the analysis we *assume* that 20,000 units can be sold at a price of $3 per unit.[4] Some of the inputs are known with near certainty—for example, the 40 percent tax rate is not likely to change. Others are more speculative—units sold and the variable cost percentage are in this category. Obviously, if sales or costs are different from the assumed levels, then profits and cash flows, hence NPV and IRR, will differ from their projected levels. Later in the chapter, we discuss how changes in the inputs affect the results.

Part 2, which calculates depreciation over the project's four-year life, is divided into two sections, one for the building and one for the equipment. The first row in each section gives the yearly depreciation rates. The second row in each section gives the dollars of depreciation, found as the rate times the asset's depreciable basis, which, in this example, is the initial cost. The third row shows the book value at the end of Year 4, found by subtracting the accumulated depreciation from the depreciable basis.

Part 3 estimates the cash flows the firm will realize when it disposes of the assets. The first row shows the salvage value, which is the sales price the company expects to receive when it sells the assets four years hence. The second row shows the book

---

[3] We first set up Table 11-1 as a "regular" table and did all the calculations with a calculator. We then typed all the labels into a spreadsheet and used the spreadsheet to do the calculations. The "answers" derived were identical. We show the spreadsheet version in Table 11-1, but the only visible difference is that it shows row and column indicators. If you have access to a computer, you might want to look at the model, which is on a file named 11MODEL.xls on the CD-ROM that accompanies this book.

[4] Recall that the sales price is actually $3,000, but for convenience we show all dollars in thousands.

TABLE 11-1

Analysis of a New (Expansion) Project
Part 4

	A	B	C	D	E	F	G	H	I
75	Part 4 of Table 11-1. Projected Net Cash						Years		
76	Flows (Time line of annual cash flows)				0	1	2	3	4
77					2003	2004	2005	2006	2007
78	*Investment Outlays at Time Zero*								
79	Building				($12,000)				
80	Equipment				(8,000)				
81	Increase in Net Operating WC				(6,000)				
82									
83	*Operating Cash Flows over the Project's Life*								
84	Units sold					20,000	20,000	20,000	20,000
85	Sales price					$3.00	$3.00	$3.00	$3.00
86									
87	Sales revenue					$60,000	$60,000	$60,000	$60,000
88	Variable costs					42,000	42,000	42,000	42,000
89	Fixed operating costs					8,000	8,000	8,000	8,000
90	Depreciation (building)					156	312	312	312
91	Depreciation (equipment)					1,600	2,560	1,520	960
92	Oper. income before taxes (EBIT)					8,244	7,128	8,168	8,728
93	Taxes on operating income (40%)					3,298	2,851	3,267	3,491
94	Net Operating Profit After Taxes (NOPAT)					4,946	4,277	4,901	5,237
95	Add back depreciation					1,756	2,872	1,832	1,272
96	Operating cash flow					$6,702	$7,149	$6,733	$6,509
97	*Terminal Year Cash Flows*								
98	Return of net operating working capital[e]								$6,000
99	Net salvage value								10,607
100	Total termination cash flows								$16,607
101									
102	Net Cash Flow (Time line of cash flows)				($26,000)	$6,702	$7,149	$6,733	$23,116
103									
104	[e] Net operating working capital will be recovered at the end of the project's operating life, in 2007, as inventories								
105	are sold off and receivables are collected.								

values at the end of Year 4; these values were calculated in Part 2. The third row shows the expected gain or loss, defined as the difference between the sales price and the book value. As explained in notes c and d to Table 11-1 gains and losses are treated as ordinary income, not capital gains or losses.[5] Therefore, gains result in tax liabilities, and losses produce tax credits, that are equal to the gain or loss times the 40 percent tax rate. Taxes paid and tax credits are shown on the fourth row. The fifth row shows the after-tax cash flow the company expects when it disposes of the asset, found as the expected sales price minus the tax liability or plus the credit. Thus, the firm expects to net $8,863 from the sale of the building and $1,744 from the equipment, for a total of $10,607.

Next, in Part 4, we use the information developed in Parts 1, 2, and 3 to find the projected cash flows over the project's life. Five periods are shown, from Year 0

---

[5] Note again that if an asset is sold for exactly its book value, there will be no gain or loss, hence no tax liability or credit. However, if an asset is sold for other than its book value, a gain or loss will be created. For example, BQC's building will have a book value of $10,908, but the company only expects to realize $7,500 when it is sold. This would result in a loss of $3,408. This indicates that the building should have been depreciated at a faster rate—only if depreciation had been $3,408 larger would the book and market values have been equal. So, the Tax Code stipulates that losses on the sale of operating assets can be used to reduce ordinary income, just as depreciation reduces income. On the other hand, if an asset is sold for more than its book value, as is the case for the equipment, then this signifies that the depreciation rates were too high, so the gain is called "depreciation recapture" by the IRS and is taxed as ordinary income.

TABLE 11-1

Analysis of a New (Expansion) Project
Part 5

	A	B	C	D	E	F	G	H	I
107	Part 5 of Table 11-1. Key Output and Appraisal of the Proposed Project								
108									
109	Net Present Value (at 12%)			$5,166					
110	IRR			19.33%					
111	MIRR			17.19%					
112							Years		
					0	1	2	3	4
113	Cumulative cash flow for payback				(26,000)	(19,298)	(12,149)	(5,416)	17,700
114	Cum. CF > 0, hence Payback Year:				FALSE	FALSE	FALSE	FALSE	3.23
115	Payback found with Excel function			3.23	See note below for an explanation of the Excel calculation.				
116	Check: Payback = 3 + 5,416/23,116			3.23	Manual calculation for the base case.				
117									
118	The Excel payback calculation is based on the logical IF function. Returns FALSE if the cumulative CF is								
119	negative or the actual payback if the cumulative CF is positive. Then, we use the MIN (minimum) function to find								
120	first year when payback is positive. The MIN function procedure is necessary for projects with longer lives,								
121	because then values, not the word FALSE, would appear in a number of cells. The MIN function picks the smallest								
122	number which is the payback.								
123									
124	Based on the firm's 12% weighted average cost of capital, this project has a NPV of $5,166. Since the NPV is								
125	positive, we tentatively conclude that the project should be accepted. The IRR and MIRR confirm this decision								
126	because both exceed the cost of capital. Note, though, that no risk analysis has been conducted. It is possible that								
127	the firm's managers, after appraising the project's risk, might conclude that its projected return is insufficient to								
128	compensate for its risk, and reject it.								

(2003) to Year 4 (2007). The cash outlays required at Year 0 are the negative numbers in the first column, and their sum, −$26,000, is shown at the bottom. Then, in the next four columns, we calculate the operating cash flows. We begin with sales revenues, found as the product of units sold and the sales price.[6] Next, we subtract variable costs, which were assumed to be $2.10 per unit. We then deduct fixed operating costs and depreciation to obtain taxable operating income, or EBIT. When taxes (at a 40 percent rate) are subtracted, we are left with net operating profit after taxes, or NOPAT. Note, though, that we are seeking cash flows, not accounting income. Sales are presumably for cash (or else receivables are collected promptly), and both taxes and all costs other than depreciation must be paid in cash. Therefore, each item in the "Operating Cash Flow" section of Part 4 represents cash *except depreciation*, which is a noncash charge. Thus, depreciation must be added back to obtain the project's cash flows from operations. The result is the row of operating cash flows shown toward the bottom of Part 4, on Row 96.

When the project's life ends, the company will receive the "Terminal Year Cash Flows" as shown in the column for Year 4 in the lower part of the table, on rows 98, 99, and 100. First, note that BQC invested $6,000 in net operating working capital—inventories plus accounts receivable—at Year 0. As operations wind down in Year 4, inventories will be sold and not replaced, and this will provide cash. Similarly, accounts receivable will be collected and not replaced, and this too will provide cash.

---

[6] Notice that in Part 1, Input Data, we show a growth rate in unit sales, and inflation rates for the sales price, variable costs, and fixed costs. BQC anticipates that unit sales, the sales price, and costs will be stable over the project's life; hence, these variables are all set at zero. However, nonzero values can be inserted in the input section to determine the effects of growth and inflation. Incidentally, the inflation figures are all specific for this particular project— they do not reflect inflation as measured by the CPI. The expected CPI inflation is reflected in the WACC, and it is not expected to change over the forecast period.

The end result is that the firm will recover its $6 million investment in net operating working capital during the last year of the project's life. In addition, when the company disposes of the building and equipment at the end of Year 4, it will receive cash as estimated in Part 3 of the table. Thus, the total terminal year cash flow amounts to $16,607 as shown on Row 100. When we sum the columns in Part 4, we obtain the net cash flows shown on Row 102. Those cash flows constitute a *cash flow time line*, and they are then evaluated in Part 5.

MAKING THE DECISION

Part 5 of the table shows the standard evaluation criteria—NPV, IRR, MIRR, and payback—based on the cash flows shown on Row 102. The NPV is positive, the IRR and MIRR both exceed the 12 percent cost of capital, and the payback indicates that the project will return the invested funds in 3.23 years. Therefore, on the basis of the analysis thus far, it appears that the project should be accepted. Note, though, that we have been assuming that the project is about as risky as the company's average project. If the project were judged to be riskier than average, it would be necessary to increase the cost of capital, which might cause the NPV to become negative and the IRR and MIRR to drop below the then-higher WACC. Therefore, we cannot make a final "go, no-go" decision until we evaluate the project's risk, the topic of the next section.

SELF-TEST QUESTIONS

What three types of cash flows must be considered when evaluating a proposed project?

Define the following terms: new expansion project and replacement project.

INTRODUCTION TO PROJECT RISK ANALYSIS

Up to now we have simply assumed that projects will produce a given set of cash flows, and we then analyzed those cash flows to decide whether to accept or reject the project. Obviously, though, cash flows are not known with certainty. We now turn to risk in capital budgeting, examining the techniques firms use to determine a project's risk and then to decide whether its profit potential is worth the risk.

Recall from Chapter 9 that there are three distinct types of risk: stand-alone risk, corporate risk, and market risk. Given that the firm's primary objective is to maximize stockholder value, what ultimately matters is the risk that a project imposes on stockholders. Because stockholders are generally diversified, market risk is theoretically the most relevant measure of risk. Corporate risk is also important for these three reasons:

1. Undiversified stockholders, including the owners of small businesses, are more concerned about corporate risk than about market risk.
2. Empirical studies of the determinants of required rates of return (k) generally find that both market and corporate risk affect stock prices. This suggests that

investors, even those who are well diversified, consider factors other than market risk when they establish required returns.

3. The firm's stability is important to its managers, workers, customers, suppliers, and creditors, as well as to the community in which it operates. Firms that are in serious danger of bankruptcy, or even of suffering low profits and reduced output, have difficulty attracting and retaining good managers and workers. Also, both suppliers and customers are reluctant to depend on weak firms, and such firms have difficulty borrowing money at reasonable interest rates. These factors tend to reduce risky firms' profitability and hence their stock prices, and this makes corporate risk significant.

For these three reasons, corporate risk is important even if a firm's stockholders are well diversified.

SELF-TEST QUESTIONS

What are the three types of project risk?

Why are (1) market and (2) corporate risk both important?

TECHNIQUES FOR MEASURING STAND-ALONE RISK

Why should a project's stand-alone risk be important to anyone? In theory, this type of risk should be of little or no concern. However, it is actually of great importance for two reasons:

1. It is easier to estimate a project's stand-alone risk than its corporate risk, and it is far easier to measure stand-alone risk than market risk.

2. In the vast majority of cases, all three types of risk are highly correlated—if the general economy does well, so will the firm, and if the firm does well, so will most of its projects. Because of this high correlation, stand-alone risk is generally a good proxy for hard-to-measure corporate and market risk.

The starting point for analyzing a project's stand-alone risk involves determining the uncertainty inherent in its cash flows. To illustrate what is involved, consider again Brandt-Quigley Corporation's appliance control computer project that we discussed above. Many of the key inputs shown in Part 1 of Table 11-1 are subject to uncertainty. For example, sales were projected at 20,000 units to be sold at a net price of $3,000 per unit. However, actual unit sales will almost certainly be somewhat higher or lower than 20,000, and the sales price will probably turn out to be different from the projected $3,000 per unit. *In effect, the sales quantity and price estimates are really expected values based on probability distributions, as are many of the other values that were shown in Part 1 of Table 11-1.* The distributions could be relatively "tight," reflecting small standard deviations and low risk, or they could be "flat," denoting a great deal of uncertainty about the actual value of the variable in question and thus a high degree of stand-alone risk.

The nature of the individual cash flow distributions, and their correlations with one another, determine the nature of the NPV probability distribution and, thus, the project's stand-alone risk. In the following sections, we discuss three techniques for assessing a project's stand-alone risk: (1) sensitivity analysis, (2) scenario analysis, and (3) Monte Carlo simulation.

SENSITIVITY ANALYSIS

Intuitively, we know that many of the variables that determine a project's cash flows could turn out to be different from the values used in the analysis. We also know that a change in a key input variable, such as units sold, will cause the NPV to change. **Sensitivity analysis** is a technique that indicates how much NPV will change in response to a given change in an input variable, other things held constant.

Sensitivity analysis begins with a *base-case* situation, which is developed using the *expected* values for each input. To illustrate, consider the data given back in Table 11-1, in which projected income statements for Brandt-Quigley's computer project were shown. The values used to develop the table, including unit sales, sales price, fixed costs, and variable costs, are the most likely, or base-case, values, and the resulting $5.166 million NPV shown in Table 11-1 is called the **base-case NPV.** Now we ask a series of "what if" questions: "What if unit sales fall 15 percent below the most likely level?" "What if the sales price per unit falls?" "What if variable costs are $2.50 per unit rather than the expected $2.10?" Sensitivity analysis is designed to provide the decision maker with answers to questions such as these.

In a sensitivity analysis, each variable is changed by several percentage points above and below the expected value, holding all other variables constant. Then a new NPV is calculated using each of these values. Finally, the set of NPVs is plotted to show how sensitive NPV is to changes in each variable. Figure 11-1 shows the computer project's sensitivity graphs for six of the input variables. The table below the graph gives the NPVs that were used to construct the graph. The slopes of the lines in the graph show how sensitive NPV is to changes in each of the inputs: *the steeper the slope, the more sensitive the NPV is to a change in the variable*. From the figure and the table, we see that the project's NPV is very sensitive to changes in the sales price and variable costs, fairly sensitive to changes in the growth rate and units sold, and not very sensitive to changes in fixed costs and the cost of capital.

If we were comparing two projects, the one with the steeper sensitivity lines would be riskier, because for that project a relatively small error in estimating a variable such as unit sales would produce a large error in the project's expected NPV. Thus, sensitivity analysis can provide useful insights into the riskiness of a project.

Before we move on, we should note that spreadsheet computer programs such as *Excel* are ideally suited for performing sensitivity analysis. We used the model developed in Table 11-1 to conduct the analyses represented in Figure 11-1; it generated the NPVs and then drew the graphs. To conduct such an analysis by hand would be extremely time consuming.

SCENARIO ANALYSIS

Although sensitivity analysis is probably the most widely used risk analysis technique, it does have limitations. For example, we saw earlier that the computer project's NPV is highly sensitive to changes in the sales price and the variable cost per unit. Those sensitivities suggest that the project is risky. Suppose, however, that Home Depot or Circuit City was anxious to get the new computer product and would sign a contract

FIGURE 11-1 Evaluating Risk: Sensitivity Analysis (Dollars in Thousands)

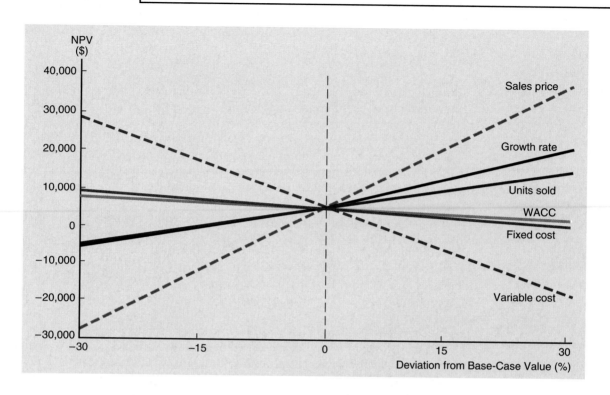

DEVIATION FROM BASE CASE	NPV AT DIFFERENT DEVIATIONS FROM BASE					
	SALES PRICE	VARIABLE COST/UNIT	GROWTH RATE	YEAR 1 UNITS SOLD	FIXED COST	WACC
−30%	($27,637)	$28,129	($ 5,847)	($ 4,675)	$9,540	$8,294
−15	(11,236)	16,647	(907)	246	7,353	6,674
0	5,166	5,166	5,166	5,166	5,166	5,166
15	21,568	(6,315)	12,512	10,087	2,979	3,761
30	37,970	(17,796)	21,269	15,007	792	2,450
Range	$65,607	$45,925	$27,116	$19,682	$8,748	$5,844

Scenario Analysis
A risk analysis technique in which "bad" and "good" sets of financial circumstances are compared with a most likely, or base-case, situation.

to purchase 20,000 units per year for four years at $3,000 per unit. Moreover, suppose Intel would agree to provide the principal component at a price that would ensure that the variable cost per unit would not exceed $2,100. Under these conditions, there would be a zero probability of high or low sales prices and input costs, so the project would not be at all risky in spite of its sensitivity to those variables.

We see, then, that we need to extend sensitivity analysis to deal with the *probability distributions* of the inputs. In addition, it would be useful to vary more than one variable at a time so that we could see the combined effects of changes in the variables. **Scenario analysis** provides these extensions—it brings in the probabilities of changes in the key variables, and it allows us to change more than one variable at a time. In a scenario analysis, the financial analyst begins with the **base case**, or most likely set of values for the input variables. Then, he or she asks marketing, engineering, and other operating managers to specify a **worst-case scenario** (low unit sales, low sales price, high variable costs, and so on) and a **best-case scenario.** Often, the best case and worst case are defined as having a 25 percent probability of conditions being that good or bad, with a 50 percent probability that the base-case conditions will occur. Obviously, conditions could actually take on other values, but parameters such as these are useful to get people focused on the central issues in risk analysis.

The best-case, base-case, and worst-case values for BQC's computer project are shown in Table 11-2 along with plots of the data. If the product is highly successful, then the combination of a high sales price, low production costs, high first year sales, and a strong growth rate in future sales will result in a very high NPV, $144 million. However, if things turn out badly, then the NPV would be −$38.3 million. The graphs show the very wide range of possibilities, indicating that this is indeed a very risky project. If the bad conditions materialize, this will not bankrupt the company—this is just one project for a large company. Still, losing $38 million would certainly not help the stock price.

The project is clearly risky, and that suggests that its cost of capital is higher than the firm's WACC of 12 percent, which is applicable to an average-risk project. BQC generally adds 3 percentage points to the corporate WACC when it evaluates projects deemed to be risky, so it recalculated the NPV using a 15 percent cost of capital. That lowered the base-case NPV to $2,877,000 from $5,166,000. Thus, the project is still acceptable by the NPV criterion.

Scenario analysis provides useful information about a project's stand-alone risk. However, it is limited in that it considers only a few discrete outcomes (NPVs), even though there are an infinite number of possibilities. We briefly describe a more complete method of assessing a project's stand-alone risk in the next section.

MONTE CARLO SIMULATION

Monte Carlo simulation, so named because this type of analysis grew out of work on the mathematics of casino gambling, ties together sensitivities and input variable probability distributions. While Monte Carlo simulation is considerably more complex than scenario analysis, simulation software packages make this process manageable. Many of these packages are included as add-ons to spreadsheet programs such as *Excel*.

In a simulation analysis, the computer begins by picking at random a value for each variable—sales in units, the sales price, the variable cost per unit, and so on. Then those values are combined, and the project's NPV is calculated and stored in the computer's memory. Next, a second set of input values is selected at random, and a second NPV is calculated. This process is repeated perhaps 1,000 times, generating 1,000 NPVs. The mean and standard deviation of the set of NPVs is determined. The mean, or average value, is used as a measure of the project's expected profitability, and the standard deviation (or coefficient of variation) is used as a measure of the project's risk.

Monte Carlo simulation is useful, but it is a relatively complex procedure. Therefore, a detailed discussion is best left for advanced finance courses.

TABLE 11-2	Scenario Analysis (Dollars in Thousands)					
SCENARIO	PROBABILITY	SALES PRICE	UNIT SALES	VARIABLE COSTS	GROWTH RATE	NPV
Best case	25%	$3.90	26,000	$1.47	30%	$144,024
Base case	50	3.00	20,000	2.10	0	5,166
Worst case	25	2.10	14,000	2.73	−30	(38,315)

Expected NPV = Sum, probability times NPV $29,010

Standard deviation (calculated in *Excel* model) $68,735

Coefficient of variation = Standard deviation/Expected NPV   2.37

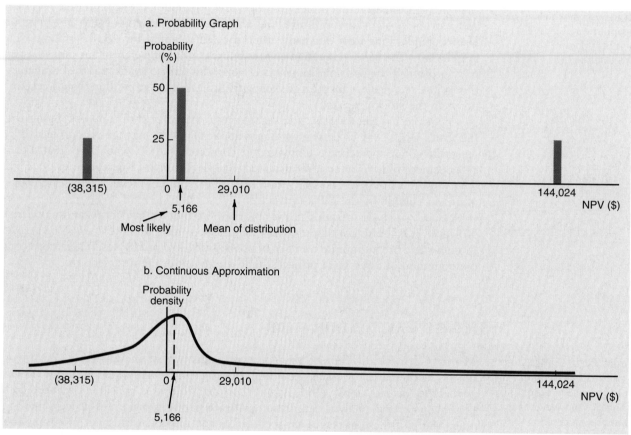

NOTE: The scenario analysis calculations were performed in the *Excel* model, 11MODEL.xls.

SELF-TEST QUESTIONS

List two reasons why, in practice, a project's stand-alone risk is important.

Differentiate between sensitivity and scenario analyses. What advantage does scenario analysis have over sensitivity analysis?

What is Monte Carlo simulation?

CAPITAL BUDGETING PRACTICES IN THE ASIA/PACIFIC REGION

A recent survey of executives in Australia, Hong Kong, Indonesia, Malaysia, the Philippines, and Singapore asked several questions about their companies' capital budgeting practices. The study yielded some interesting results, which are summarized here.

TECHNIQUES FOR EVALUATING CORPORATE PROJECTS

Consistent with evidence on U.S. companies, most companies in this region evaluate projects using IRR, NPV, and payback. IRR use ranged from 86 percent (in Hong Kong) to 96 percent (in Australia) of the companies. NPV use ranged from 81 percent (in the Philippines) to 96 percent (in Australia). Payback use ranged from 81 percent (in Indonesia) to 100 percent (in Hong Kong and the Philippines).

TECHNIQUES FOR ESTIMATING THE COST OF EQUITY CAPITAL

Recall from Chapter 9 that three basic approaches can be used to estimate the cost of equity: CAPM, dividend yield plus growth rate (DCF), and cost of debt plus a risk premium. The use of these methods varied considerably from country to country (see Table A).

We noted in Chapter 10 that the CAPM is used most often by U.S. firms. (See the Industry Practice box in Chapter 10 entitled, "Techniques Firms Use to Evaluate Corporate Projects" on page 412). Except for Australia, this is not the case for Asian/Pacific firms, who instead more often use the other two approaches.

TECHNIQUES FOR ASSESSING RISK

Finally, firms in these six countries rely heavily on scenario and sensitivity analyses to assess project risk. They also use decision trees (which we discuss later) and Monte Carlo simulation, but less frequently than the other techniques (see Table B).

SOURCE: Adapted from George W. Kester et al., "Capital Budgeting Practices in the Asia-Pacific Region: Australia, Hong Kong, Indonesia, Malaysia, Philippines, and Singapore," *Financial Practice and Education*, Vol. 9, No. 1, Spring/Summer 1999, 25–33.

TABLE A

METHOD	AUSTRALIA	HONG KONG	INDONESIA	MALAYSIA	PHILIPPINES	SINGAPORE
CAPM	72.7%	26.9%	0.0%	6.2%	24.1%	17.0%
Dividend yield plus growth rate	16.4	53.8	33.3	50.0	34.5	42.6
Cost of debt plus risk premium	10.9	23.1	53.4	37.5	58.6	42.6

TABLE B

RISK ASSESSMENT TECHNIQUE	AUSTRALIA	HONG KONG	INDONESIA	MALAYSIA	PHILIPPINES	SINGAPORE
Scenario analysis	96%	100%	94%	80%	97%	90%
Sensitivity analysis	100	100	88	83	94	79
Decision tree analysis	44	58	50	37	33	46
Monte Carlo simulation	38	35	25	9	24	35

PROJECT RISK CONCLUSIONS

We have discussed the three types of risk normally considered in capital budgeting analysis—stand-alone risk, within-firm (or corporate) risk, and market risk—and we have discussed ways of assessing each. However, two important questions remain: (1) Should firms be concerned with stand-alone or corporate risk in their capital budgeting decisions, and (2) what do we do when the stand-alone, within-firm, and market risk assessments lead to different conclusions?

These questions have no easy answers. From a theoretical standpoint, well-diversified investors should be concerned only with market risk, and managers should be concerned only with stock price maximization, and these two factors should lead to the conclusion that market (beta) risk ought to be given virtually all the weight in capital budgeting decisions. However, if investors are not well diversified, if the CAPM does not operate exactly as theory says it should, or if measurement problems keep managers from having confidence in the CAPM approach in capital budgeting, it may be appropriate to give stand-alone and corporate risk more weight than financial theory suggests. Note also that the CAPM ignores bankruptcy costs, even though such costs can be substantial, and the probability of bankruptcy depends on a firm's corporate risk, not on its beta risk. Therefore, even well-diversified investors should want a firm's management to give at least some consideration to a project's corporate risk instead of concentrating entirely on market risk.

Although it would be nice to reconcile these problems and to measure project risk on some absolute scale, the best we can do in practice is to estimate project risk in a somewhat nebulous, relative sense. For example, we can generally say with a fair degree of confidence that a particular project has more or less stand-alone risk than the firm's average project. Then, assuming that stand-alone and corporate risk are highly correlated (which is typical), the project's stand-alone risk will be a good measure of its corporate risk. Finally, assuming that market risk and corporate risk are highly correlated (as is true for most companies), a project with more corporate risk than average will also have more market risk, and vice versa for projects with low corporate risk.

SELF-TEST QUESTIONS

In theory, should a firm be concerned with stand-alone and corporate risk? Should the firm be concerned with these risks in practice?

If a project's stand-alone, corporate, and market risk are highly correlated, would this make the task of measuring risk easier or harder? Explain.

INCORPORATING PROJECT RISK AND CAPITAL STRUCTURE INTO CAPITAL BUDGETING

Capital budgeting can affect a firm's market risk, its corporate risk, or both, but it is extremely difficult to quantify either type of risk. Although it may be possible to reach the general conclusion that one project is riskier than another, it is difficult to develop a really good *quantitative measure* of project risk. This makes it difficult to incorporate differential risk into capital budgeting decisions.

Two methods are used to incorporate project risk into capital budgeting. One is called the *certainty equivalent* approach. Here all cash flows that are not known with certainty are scaled down, and the riskier the flow, the lower its certainty equivalent value. The other method, and the one we focus on, is the **risk-adjusted discount rate** approach, under which differential project risk is dealt with by changing the discount rate. Average-risk projects are discounted at the firm's average cost of capital, higher-risk projects are discounted at a higher cost of capital, and lower-risk projects are discounted at a rate below the firm's average cost of capital. Unfortunately, there is no good way of specifying exactly *how much* higher or lower these discount rates should be. Given the present state of the art, risk adjustments are necessarily judgmental and somewhat arbitrary.

As a final consideration, capital structure must also be taken into account if a firm finances different assets in different ways. For example, one division might have a lot of real estate that is well suited as collateral for loans, whereas some other division might have most of its capital tied up in specialized machinery, which is not good collateral. As a result, the division with the real estate might have a higher *debt capacity* than the division with the machinery, hence an optimal capital structure that contains a higher percentage of debt. In this case, the financial staff might calculate the cost of capital differently for the two divisions.[7]

SELF-TEST QUESTION

How are risk-adjusted discount rates used to incorporate project risk into the capital budgeting decision process?

---

[7] We will say more about the optimal capital structure and debt capacity in Chapter 13.

TYING IT ALL TOGETHER

Throughout the book, we have indicated that the value of any asset depends on the amount, timing, and riskiness of the cash flows it produces. In this chapter, we developed a framework for analyzing a project's cash flows and risk. Given a set of inputs, we can use the techniques described back in Chapter 10 to evaluate whether projects should be accepted or rejected. In the next chapter, we discuss some interesting extensions to the basic model. Before proceeding, however, you should review the key concepts listed below.

- The most important (and most difficult) step in analyzing a capital budgeting project is **estimating the incremental after-tax cash flows** the project will produce.
- **Project cash flow** is different from accounting income. Project cash flow reflects: (1) **cash outlays for fixed assets,** (2) the **tax shield provided by depreciation,** and (3) cash flows due to **changes in net operating working capital.** Project cash flow does not include **interest payments.**
- In determining incremental cash flows, **opportunity costs** (the cash flows forgone by using an asset) must be included, but **sunk costs** (cash outlays that have

been made and that cannot be recouped) are not included. Any **externalities** (effects of a project on other parts of the firm) should also be reflected in the analysis.

■ **Cannibalization** occurs when a new project leads to a reduction in sales of an existing product.

■ Capital projects often require an additional investment in **net operating working capital (NOWC).** An increase in NOWC must be included in the Year 0 initial cash outlay, and then shown as a cash inflow in the final year of the project.

■ The incremental cash flows from a typical project can be classified into three categories: (1) **initial investment outlay,** (2) **operating cash flows over the project's life,** and (3) **terminal year cash flows.**

■ Since stockholders are generally diversified, **market risk** is theoretically the most relevant measure of risk. Market, or beta, risk is important because beta affects the cost of capital, which, in turn, affects stock prices.

■ **Corporate risk** is important because it influences the firm's ability to use low-cost debt, to maintain smooth operations over time, and to avoid crises that might consume management's energy and disrupt its employees, customers, suppliers, and community.

■ **Sensitivity analysis** is a technique that shows how much a project's NPV will change in response to a given change in an input variable such as sales, other things held constant.

■ **Scenario analysis** is a risk analysis technique in which the best- and worst-case NPVs are compared with the project's expected NPV.

■ **Monte Carlo simulation** is a risk analysis technique that uses a computer to simulate future events and thus to estimate the profitability and riskiness of a project.

■ The **risk-adjusted discount rate** is the rate used to evaluate a particular project. It is based on the corporate WACC, which is increased for projects that are riskier than the firm's average project but decreased for less risky projects.

QUESTIONS

11-1 Operating cash flows rather than accounting profits are listed in Table 11-1. What is the basis for this emphasis on cash flows as opposed to net income?

11-2 Explain why sunk costs should not be included in a capital budgeting analysis, but opportunity costs and externalities should be included.

11-3 Explain how net operating working capital is recovered at the end of a project's life, and why it is included in a capital budgeting analysis.

11-4 Define (a) simulation analysis, (b) scenario analysis, and (c) sensitivity analysis. If AT&T were considering two investments, one calling for the expenditure of $200 million to develop a satellite communications system and the other involving the expenditure of $12,000 for a new truck, on which one would the company be more likely to use simulation analysis?

SELF-TEST PROBLEMS (SOLUTIONS APPEAR IN APPENDIX B)

ST-1
Key terms
Define each of the following terms:
a. Relevant cash flow
b. Incremental cash flow; sunk cost; opportunity cost; externalities; cannibalization
c. Change in net operating working capital; new expansion project
d. Replacement project
e. Sensitivity analysis
f. Base-case NPV

g. Scenario analysis
h. Worst-case scenario; best-case scenario; base case
i. Monte Carlo simulation
j. Risk-adjusted discount rate

ST-2
New project analysis

You have been asked by the president of Ellis Construction Company, headquartered in Toledo, to evaluate the proposed acquisition of a new earthmover. The mover's basic price is $50,000, and it will cost another $10,000 to modify it for special use by Ellis Construction. Assume that the mover falls into the MACRS 3-year class; the applicable depreciation rates are 33 percent, 45 percent, 15 percent, and 7 percent. It will be sold after 3 years for $20,000, and it will require an increase in net operating working capital (spare parts inventory) of $2,000. The earthmover purchase will have no effect on revenues, but it is expected to save Ellis $20,000 per year in before-tax operating costs, mainly labor. Ellis's marginal federal-plus-state tax rate is 40 percent.

a. What is the company's net investment if it acquires the earthmover? (That is, what are the Year 0 cash flows?)
b. What are the operating cash flows in Years 1, 2, and 3?
c. What is the terminal cash flow?
d. If the project's cost of capital is 10 percent, should the earthmover be purchased?
e. Suppose that the firm's management is unsure about the savings in before-tax operating costs and the earthmover's salvage value.
   (1) What is the earthmover's net present value if the savings in before-tax operating costs increase by 15 percent above the firm's original expectations? Would this change the firm's decision to acquire the earthmover from the decision made in part d?
   (2) What is the earthmover's net present value if the earthmover's salvage value increases by 10 percent above the firm's original expectations? Assume no other change in data from the original problem. Would this change the firm's decision to acquire the earthmover from the decision made in part d?
f. Suppose the firm's capital budgeting manager suggests that the firm do a scenario analysis for this project because of the sensitivities of both the equipment's cost savings and its salvage value. After an extensive analysis, he comes up with the following probabilities and values for the scenario analysis:

SCENARIO	PROBABILITY	BEFORE-TAX SAVINGS	SALVAGE VALUE
Worst case	30%	$15,000	$18,000
Base case	40	20,000	20,000
Best case	30	25,000	24,000

What are the project's expected net present value (NPV), the standard deviation of the NPV, and the coefficient of variation of the NPV?

ST-3
Corporate risk analysis

The staff of Heymann Manufacturing has estimated the following net cash flows and probabilities for a new manufacturing process:

	NET CASH FLOWS		
YEAR	P = 0.2	P = 0.6	P = 0.2
0	($100,000)	($100,000)	($100,000)
1	20,000	30,000	40,000
2	20,000	30,000	40,000
3	20,000	30,000	40,000
4	20,000	30,000	40,000
5	20,000	30,000	40,000
5*	0	20,000	30,000

Line 0 gives the cost of the process, Lines 1 through 5 give operating cash flows, and Line 5* contains the estimated salvage values. Heymann's cost of capital for an average-risk project is 10 percent.

a. Assume that the project has average risk. Find the project's expected NPV. (Hint: Use expected values for the net cash flow in each year.)

b. Find the best-case and worst-case NPVs. What is the probability of occurrence of the worst case if the cash flows are perfectly dependent (perfectly positively correlated) over time? If they are independent over time?

c. Assume that all the cash flows are perfectly positively correlated, that is, there are only three possible cash flow streams over time: (1) the worst case, (2) the most likely, or base, case, and (3) the best case, with probabilities of 0.2, 0.6, and 0.2, respectively. These cases are represented by each of the columns in the table. Find the expected NPV, its standard deviation, and its coefficient of variation.

d. The coefficient of variation of Heymann's average project is in the range 0.8 to 1.0. If the coefficient of variation of a project being evaluated is greater than 1.0, 2 percentage points are added to the firm's cost of capital. Similarly, if the coefficient of variation is less than 0.8, 1 percentage point is deducted from the cost of capital. What is the project's cost of capital? Should Heymann accept or reject the project?

STARTER PROBLEMS

11-1
Investment outlay

Truman Industries is considering an expansion project. The necessary equipment could be purchased for $9 million, and the project would also require an initial $3 million investment in net operating working capital. The company's tax rate is 40 percent. What is the project's initial investment outlay?

11-2
Operating cash flow

Eisenhower Communications is trying to estimate the first-year operating cash flow (at $t = 1$) for a proposed project. The financial staff has collected the following information:

Projected sales	$10 million
Operating costs (excluding depreciation)	7 million
Depreciation	2 million
Interest expense	2 million

The company faces a 40 percent tax rate. What is the project's operating cash flow for the first year ($t = 1$)?

11-3
Net salvage value

Kennedy Air Lines is now in the terminal year of a project. The equipment originally cost $20 million, of which 80 percent has been depreciated. Kennedy can sell the used equipment today to another airline for $5 million, and its tax rate is 40 percent. What is the equipment's after-tax net salvage value?

EXAM-TYPE PROBLEMS

The problems included in this section are set up in such a way that they could be used as multiple-choice exam problems.

11-4
Scenario analysis

Huang Industries is considering a proposed project for its capital budget. The company estimates that the project's NPV is $12 million. This estimate assumes that the economy and market conditions will be average over the next few years. The company's CFO, however, forecasts that there is only a 50 percent chance that the economy will be average. Recognizing this uncertainty, she has also performed the following scenario analysis:

ECONOMIC SCENARIO	PROBABILITY OF OUTCOME	NPV
Recession	0.05	($70 million)
Below average	0.20	(25 million)
Average	0.50	12 million
Above average	0.20	20 million
Boom	0.05	30 million

What are the project's expected NPV, its standard deviation, and its coefficient of variation?

11-5
New project analysis

Holmes Manufacturing Company is considering the purchase of a new machine for $250,000 that will reduce manufacturing costs by $90,000 annually. Holmes will use the 3-year MACRS accelerated method to depreciate the machine, and it expects to sell the machine at the end of its 5-year operating life for $23,000. The applicable depreciation rates are 33 percent, 45 percent, 15 percent, and 7 percent. The firm will need to increase net operating working capital by $25,000 when the machine is installed, but required operating working capital will return to the original level when the machine is sold after 5 years. Holmes' marginal tax rate is 40 percent, and it uses a 10 percent cost of capital to evaluate projects of this nature.

a. What is the project's NPV?

b. Assume the firm is unsure about the savings to operating costs that will occur with the new machine's acquisition. Management believes these savings may deviate from their base-case value ($90,000) by as much as plus or minus 20 percent. What is the NPV of the project under both situations?

c. Suppose the firm's chief financial officer suggests that the firm do a scenario analysis for this project because of concerns raised about data assumptions, particularly the operating cost savings, the new machine's salvage value, and the net operating working capital (NOWC) requirement. After an extensive analysis, she arrives with the following probabilities and values for the scenario analysis:

SCENARIO	PROBABILITY	COST SAVINGS	SALVAGE VALUE	NOWC
Worst case	0.35	$ 72,000	$18,000	$30,000
Base case	0.35	90,000	23,000	25,000
Best case	0.30	108,000	28,000	20,000

What are the project's expected net present value, its standard deviation, and its coefficient of variation?

11-6
Depreciation methods

Kristin is evaluating a capital budgeting project for her company that is expected to last for 4 years. The project begins with the purchase of an $800,000 investment in equipment. She is unsure what method of depreciation to use in her analysis, straight-line depreciation or the 3-year MACRS accelerated method. Straight-line depreciation results in the cost of the equipment depreciated evenly over its life. The 3-year MACRS depreciation rates are 33 percent, 45 percent, 15 percent, and 7 percent. Kristin's company has a WACC of 10 percent and a tax rate of 40 percent.

a. Under each scenario, what would the depreciation expense be for each year?

b. Which depreciation method results in a higher net present value for the project, and by how much?

PROBLEMS

11-7
New project analysis

You have been asked by the president of your company to evaluate the proposed acquisition of a spectrometer for the firm's R&D department. The equipment's base price is $140,000, and it would cost another $30,000 to modify it for special use by your firm. The spectrometer, which falls into the MACRS 3-year class, would be sold after 3 years for $60,000. The applicable depreciation rates are 33 percent, 45 percent, 15 percent, and 7 percent. Use of the equipment would require an increase in net operating working capital (spare parts inventory) of $8,000. The spectrometer would have no effect on revenues, but it is expected to save the firm $50,000 per year in before-tax operating costs, mainly labor. The firm's marginal federal-plus-state tax rate is 40 percent.

a. What is the net cost of the spectrometer? (That is, what is the Year 0 net cash flow?)

b. What are the net operating cash flows in Years 1, 2, and 3?

c. What is the terminal cash flow?

d. If the project's cost of capital is 12 percent, should the spectrometer be purchased?

11-8
New project analysis

The Harris Company is evaluating the proposed acquisition of a new milling machine. The machine's base price is $108,000, and it would cost another $12,500 to modify it for special use by your firm. The machine falls into the MACRS 3-year class, and it would be sold after 3 years for $65,000. The applicable depreciation rates are 33 percent, 45 percent, 15 percent, and 7 percent. The machine would require an increase in net operating working capital (inventory) of $5,500. The milling machine would have no effect on revenues, but it is expected to save the firm $44,000 per year in before-tax operating costs, mainly labor. Harris's marginal tax rate is 35 percent.

a. What is the net cost of the machine for capital budgeting purposes? (That is, what is the Year 0 net cash flow?)

b. What are the net operating cash flows in Years 1, 2, and 3?

c. What is the terminal cash flow?

d. If the project's cost of capital is 12 percent, should the machine be purchased?

11-9
Risky cash flows

The Butler-Perkins Company (BPC) must decide between two mutually exclusive investment projects. Each project costs $6,750 and has an expected life of 3 years. Annual net cash flows from each project begin 1 year after the initial investment is made and have the following probability distributions:

PROJECT A		PROJECT B	
PROBABILITY	NET CASH FLOWS	PROBABILITY	NET CASH FLOWS
0.2	$6,000	0.2	$ 0
0.6	6,750	0.6	6,750
0.2	7,500	0.2	18,000

BPC has decided to evaluate the riskier project at a 12 percent rate and the less risky project at a 10 percent rate.

a. What is the expected value of the annual net cash flows from each project? What is the coefficient of variation (CV)? (Hint: $\sigma_B = \$5,798$ and $CV_B = 0.76$.)

b. What is the risk-adjusted NPV of each project?

c. If it were known that Project B's cash flows were negatively correlated with other cash flows of the firm whereas Project A's cash flows were positively correlated, how would this knowledge affect the decision? If Project B's cash flows were negatively correlated with gross domestic product (GDP), would that influence your assessment of its risk?

11-10
Scenario analysis

Your firm, Agrico Products, is considering the purchase of a tractor that will have a net cost of $36,000, will increase pre-tax operating cash flows before taking account of depreciation effects by $12,000 per year, and will be depreciated on a straight-line basis to zero over 5 years at the rate of $7,200 per year, beginning the first year. (Annual cash flows will be $12,000, before taxes, plus the tax savings that result from $7,200 of depreciation.) The board of directors is having a heated debate about whether the tractor will actually last 5 years. Specifically, Elizabeth Brannigan insists that she knows of some tractors that have lasted only 4 years. Philip Glasgo agrees with Brannigan, but he argues that most tractors do give 5 years of service. Laura Evans says she has known some to last for as long as 8 years.

Given this discussion, the board asks you to prepare a scenario analysis to ascertain the importance of the uncertainty about the tractor's life. Assume a 40 percent marginal federal-plus-state tax rate, a zero salvage value, and a cost of capital of 10 percent. (Hint: Here straight-line depreciation is based on the MACRS class life of the tractor and is not affected by the actual life. Also, ignore the half-year convention for this problem.)

SPREADSHEET PROBLEM

11-11
Issues in capital budgeting

Webmasters.com has developed a powerful new server that would be used for corporations' Internet activities. It would cost $10 million to buy the equipment necessary to manufacture the server, and $3 million of net operating working capital would be required. The servers would sell for $24,000 per unit, and Webmasters believes that variable costs would amount to $17,500 per unit. The company's fixed costs would also rise by $1 million per year. It would take 1 year to buy the required equipment and set up operations, and the server project would have a life of 4 years. Conditions are expected to remain stable during each year of the operating life; that is, unit sales, sales price, and costs would be unchanged. If the project is undertaken, it must be continued for the entire 4 years. Also, the project's returns are expected to be highly correlated with returns on the firm's other assets. The firm believes it could sell 1,000 units.

The equipment would be depreciated over a 5-year period, using the following MACRS rates: 20 percent, 32 percent, 19 percent, 12 percent, 11 percent, and 6 percent. The estimated market value of the equipment at the end of the project's 4-year life is $500,000. Webmasters' federal-plus-state tax rate is 40 percent. Its cost of capital is 10 percent for average-risk projects, defined as projects with a coefficient of variation of NPV between 0.8 and 1.2. Low-risk projects are evaluated with a WACC of 8 percent, and high-risk projects are evaluated at 13 percent.

a. Develop a spreadsheet model and use it to find the project's NPV, IRR, and payback. (Hint: You might want to modify the model on file 11MODEL.xls rather then create an entirely new model.)

b. Now conduct a sensitivity analysis to determine the sensitivity of NPV to changes in the sales price, variable cost per unit, and number of units sold. Set these variables' values at 10 percent and 20 percent above and below their base-case values. Include a graph in your analysis.

c. Now conduct a scenario analysis. Assume that there is a 25 percent probability that "best-case" conditions, with each of the variables discussed in part b being 20 percent better than its base-case value, will occur. There is a 25 percent probability of "worst-case" conditions, with the variables 20 percent worse than base, and a 50 percent probability of base-case conditions.

d. If the project appears to be more or less risky than an average project, find its risk-adjusted NPV, IRR, and payback.

e. On the basis of information in the problem, would you recommend that the project be accepted?

INTEGRATED CASE

ALLIED FOOD PRODUCTS

11-12 Capital Budgeting and Cash Flow Estimation   After seeing Snapple's success with noncola soft drinks and learning of Coke's and Pepsi's interest, Allied Food Products has decided to consider an expansion of its own in the fruit juice business. The product being considered is fresh lemon juice. Assume that you were recently hired as assistant to the director of capital budgeting, and you must evaluate the new project.

The lemon juice would be produced in an unused building adjacent to Allied's Fort Myers plant; Allied owns the building, which is fully depreciated. The required equipment would cost $200,000, plus an additional $40,000 for shipping and installation. In addition, inventories would rise by $25,000, while accounts payable would go up by $5,000. All of these costs would be incurred at t = 0. By a special ruling, the machinery could be depreciated under the MACRS system as 3-year property. The applicable depreciation rates are 33%, 45%, 15%, and 7%.

The project is expected to operate for 4 years, at which time it will be terminated. The cash inflows are assumed to begin 1 year after the project is undertaken, or at t = 1, and to continue out to t = 4. At the end of the project's life (t = 4), the equipment is expected to have a salvage value of $25,000.

Unit sales are expected to total 100,000 cans per year, and the expected sales price is $2.00 per can. Cash operating costs for the project (total operating costs less depreciation) are expected to total 60 percent of dollar sales. Allied's tax rate is 40 percent, and its weighted average cost of capital is 10 percent. Tentatively, the lemon juice project is assumed to be of equal risk to Allied's other assets.

You have been asked to evaluate the projects and to make a recommendation as to whether it should be accepted or rejected. To guide you in your analysis, your boss gave you the following set of questions.

a. Draw a time line that shows when the net cash inflows and outflows will occur, and explain how the time line can be used to help structure the analysis.

b. Allied has a standard form that is used in the capital budgeting process; see Table IC11-1. Part of the table has been completed, but you must replace the blanks with the missing numbers. Complete the table in the following steps:

(1) Fill in the blanks under Year 0 for the initial investment outlay.

(2) Complete the table for unit sales, sales price, total revenues, and operating costs excluding depreciation.

(3) Complete the depreciation data.

(4) Now complete the table down to operating income after taxes, and then down to net cash flows.

(5) Now fill in the blanks under Year 4 for the terminal cash flows, and complete the net cash flow line. Discuss net operating working capital. What would have happened if the machinery were sold for less than its book value?

c. (1) Allied uses debt in its capital structure, so some of the money used to finance the project will be debt. Given this fact, should the projected cash flows be revised to show projected interest charges? Explain.

(2) Suppose you learned that Allied had spent $50,000 to renovate the building last year, expensing these costs. Should this cost be reflected in the analysis? Explain.

(3) Now suppose you learned that Allied could lease its building to another party and earn $25,000 per year. Should that fact be reflected in the analysis? If so, how?

(4) Now assume that the lemon juice project would take away profitable sales from Allied's fresh orange juice business. Should that fact be reflected in your analysis? If so, how?

d. Disregard all the assumptions made in part c, and assume there was no alternative use for the building over the next 4 years. Now calculate the project's NPV, IRR, MIRR, and regular payback. Do these indicators suggest that the project should be accepted?

e. If this project had been a replacement rather than an expansion project, how would the analysis have changed? Think about the changes that would have to occur in the cash flow table.

f. Assume that inflation is expected to average 5 percent over the next 4 years; that this expectation is reflected in the WACC; and that inflation will increase variable costs and revenues by the same percentage, 5 percent. Does it appear that inflation has been dealt with properly in the analysis? If not, what should be done, and how would the required adjustment affect the decision? You can modify the numbers in the table to quantify your results.

END OF YEAR:	0	1	2	3	4
I. INVESTMENT OUTLAY					
Equipment cost					
Installation					
Increase in inventory					
Increase in accounts payable	——				
Total net investment	====				
II. OPERATING CASH FLOWS					
Unit sales (thousands)			100		
Price/unit		$ 2.00	$2.00	——	——
Total revenues		——	——	——	$200.0
Operating costs excluding depreciation			$120.0		
Depreciation				36.0	16.8
Total costs		$199.2	$228.0	——	——
Operating income before taxes				$44.0	
Taxes on operating income		0.3	——		25.3
Operating income after taxes		ⅼ		$26.4	
Depreciation		79.2		36.0	
Operating cash flow	$0.0	$79.7			$54.7
III. TERMINAL YEAR CASH FLOWS					
Return of net operating working capital					
Salvage value					
Tax on salvage value					
Total termination cash flows					—— ====
IV. NET CASH FLOWS					
Net cash flow	($260.0)	——	——	——	$89.7
V. RESULTS					
NPV =					
IRR =					
MIRR =					
Payback =					

Although inflation was considered in the initial analysis, the riskiness of the project was not considered. The expected cash flows, considering inflation (in thousands of dollars), are given in Table IC11-2. Allied's overall cost of capital (WACC) is 10 percent.

You have been asked to answer the following questions.

g. (1) What are the three levels, or types, of project risk that are normally considered?
 (2) Which type is most relevant?
 (3) Which type is easiest to measure?
 (4) Are the three types of risk generally highly correlated?

h. (1) What is sensitivity analysis?
 (2) Discuss how one would perform a sensitivity analysis on the unit sales, salvage value, and cost of capital for the project. Assume that each of these variables devi-ates from its base-case, or expected, value by plus and minus 10, 20, and 30 percent. Explain how you would calculate the NPV, IRR, MIRR, and payback for each case.
 (3) What is the primary weakness of sensitivity analysis? What are its primary advantages?

i. Assume that you are confident about the estimates of all the variables that affect the cash flows except unit sales. If product acceptance is poor, sales would be only 75,000 units a year, while a strong consumer response would produce sales of 125,000 units. In either case, cash costs would still amount to 60 percent of revenues. You believe that there is a 25 percent chance of poor acceptance, a 25 percent chance of excellent acceptance, and a 50 percent chance of average acceptance (the base case).

Allied's Lemon Juice Project Considering Inflation (in Thousands)

			YEAR		
	0	**1**	**2**	**3**	**4**
Investment in:					
Fixed assets	($240)				
Net operating working capital	(20)				
Unit sales (thousands)		100	100	100	100
Sales price (dollars)		$2.100	$2.205	$2.315	$2.431
Total revenues		$210.0	$220.5	$231.5	$243.1
Cash operating costs (60%)		126.0	132.3	138.9	145.9
Depreciation		79.2	108.0	36.0	16.8
Operating income before taxes		$ 4.8	($ 19.8)	$ 56.6	$ 80.4
Taxes on operating income (40%)		1.9	(7.9)	22.6	32.1
Operating income after taxes		$ 2.9	($ 11.9)	$ 34.0	$ 48.3
Plus depreciation		79.2	108.0	36.0	16.8
Operating cash flow		$ 82.1	$ 96.1	$ 70.0	$ 65.1
Salvage value					25.0
Tax on SV (40%)					(10.0)
Recovery of NOWC					20.0
Net cash flow	($260)	$ 82.1	$ 96.1	$ 70.0	$100.1
Cumulative cash flows for payback:	(260.0)	(177.9)	(81.8)	(11.8)	88.3
Compounded inflows for MIRR:		109.2	116.3	77.0	100.1
Terminal value of inflows:					402.6

NPV at 10% cost of capital = $15.0
IRR   =   12.6%
MIRR   =   11.6%

(1) What is the worst-case NPV? The best-case NPV?
(2) Use the worst-, most likely (or base), and best-case NPVs, with their probabilities of occurrence, to find the project's expected NPV, standard deviation, and coefficient of variation.

j. (1) Assume that Allied's average project has a coefficient of variation (CV) in the range of 1.25 to 1.75. Would the lemon juice project be classified as high risk, average risk, or low risk? What type of risk is being measured here?
(2) Based on common sense, how highly correlated do you think the project would be with the firm's other assets? (Give a correlation coefficient or range of coefficients, based on your judgment.)

(3) How would this correlation coefficient and the previously calculated σ combine to affect the project's contribution to corporate, or within-firm, risk? Explain.

k. (1) Based on your judgment, what do you think the project's correlation coefficient would be with respect to the general economy and thus with returns on "the market"?
(2) How would correlation with the economy affect the project's market risk?

l. (1) Allied typically adds or subtracts 3 percentage points to the overall cost of capital to adjust for risk. Should the lemon juice project be accepted?
(2) What subjective risk factors should be considered before the final decision is made?

CYBER PROBLEM

Please go to our web site **http://brigham.swlearning.com** to access the Cyberproblems.

OTHER TOPICS
IN CAPITAL
BUDGETING

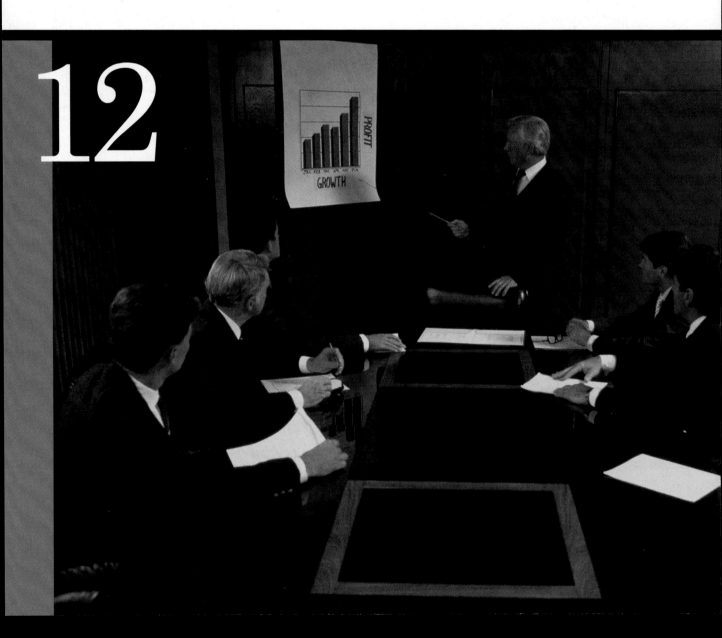

12

KEEPING YOUR OPTIONS OPEN

The last two chapters described the basic procedures used in capital budgeting, whose cornerstone is net present value analysis. NPV is particularly appealing because it provides a single, convenient measure of projects' overall value.

However, many practitioners argue that basic NPV analysis is frequently shortsighted because it assumes that a project's expected cash flows are locked in once it has been accepted, whereas in reality managers are often able to react to changing circumstances, thereby altering the cash flow stream. Consequently, when considering a potential project, managers should recognize that a variety of scenarios can unfold during the life of the project, and that their decisions over time will influence its cash flows and ultimate value.

In this chapter, we describe a technique, *real option analysis,* that has been developed to deal with this situation. It starts from the premise that many projects include embedded options, or choices, that influence the project's true value. For example, a firm using real option analysis might accept a project that has a negative NPV as calculated on the basis of its own cash flows because management recognizes that the proj-

ect, while unprofitable, may create the opportunity to develop other highly profitable projects in the future. In other circumstances, real option analysis might suggest delaying a positive NPV project because the firm has the option to pursue the project at a later date, when better estimates of the cash flows and risk will be available.

A recent article in *Journal of Applied Corporate Finance* surveyed leading corporate managers regarding their use and understanding of real option analysis. The article illustrated some interesting uses of real options and described how companies such as Intel, Texaco, and Genentech use real option analysis in their decision-making process. While some types of real options are quite complex and go beyond the scope of this book, the basic principles can be decribed in simple terms. After reading this chapter, you should see the implications that real option analysis has for corporate decision making.

Source: Alex Triantis and Adam Borison, "Real Options: State of the Practice," *Journal of Applied Corporate Finance,* Summer 2001, Vol. 14, No. 2, 8–24.

Chapters 10 and 11 covered the basic principles of capital budgeting. Now, in Chapter 12, we examine three important extensions to basic capital budgeting. First, we consider mutually exclusive projects with unequal lives. Up until now, we have treated projects as "one-shot" occurrences. However, some projects can be repeated over time. Therefore, when choosing between mutually exclusive projects, we must first determine if they can be repeated, and if so, we must take this into account when we estimate the projects' profitability.

Second, we build upon the focus of the vignette that opened this chapter, the concept of real options. Here we present some examples that demonstrate the profound effects real options can have on capital budgeting decisions. Finally, we conclude our discussion of capital budgeting by outlining the factors that determine a company's optimal capital budget. ■

COMPARING PROJECTS WITH UNEQUAL LIVES

If a company is choosing between two mutually exclusive alternatives with significantly different lives, an adjustment may be necessary.[1] For example, suppose BQC is planning to modernize its distribution center, and it is considering either a conveyor system (Project C) or some forklift trucks (Project F) for moving goods. Figure 12-1 shows both the expected net cash flows and the NPVs for these two mutually exclusive alternatives. We see that Project C, when discounted at a 12 percent cost of capital, has the higher NPV and thus appears to be the better project.

Replacement Chain (Common Life) Approach
A method of comparing projects of unequal lives that assumes that each project can be repeated as many times as necessary to reach a common life span; the NPVs over this life span are then compared, and the project with the higher common life NPV is chosen.

Although the analysis in Figure 12-1 suggests that Project C should be selected, this analysis is incomplete, and the decision to choose Project C is actually incorrect. If we choose Project F, we will have an opportunity to make a similar investment in three years, and if cost and revenue conditions remain at the Figure 12-1 levels, this second investment will also be profitable. However, if we choose Project C, we will not have this second investment opportunity. Therefore, to make a proper comparison of Projects C and F, we could apply the **replacement chain (common life) approach.** This involves finding the NPV of Project F over a six-year period, and then comparing this extended NPV with the NPV of Project C over the same six years.

The NPV for Project C as calculated in Figure 12-1 is already over the six-year common life. For Project F, however, we must add in a second project to extend the

---

[1] The Equivalent Annual Annuity (EAA) method is another approach for dealing with unequal lives. For a discussion of this method, refer to *Concise Fundamentals*, 4th edition, Web Appendix 11D.

FIGURE 12-1

Expected Net Cash Flows for Projects C and F

Project C:

NPV$_C$ at 12.0% = $6,491; IRR = 17.5%.

Project F:

NPV$_F$ at 12.0% = $5,155; IRR = 25.2%.

overall life of the combined projects to six years. Here we assume (1) that Project F's cost and annual cash inflows will not change if the project is repeated in three years and (2) that BQC's cost of capital will remain at 12 percent:

NPV @ 12% = $8,824; IRR = 25.2%.

The NPV of this extended Project F is $8,824, and its IRR is 25.2 percent. (The IRR of two Project Fs is the same as the IRR for one Project F.) Since F's $8,824 extended NPV is greater than the $6,491 NPV of Project C, Project F should be selected.

When should we worry about unequal life analysis? As a general rule, the unequal life issue (1) does not arise for independent projects but (2) can arise if mutually exclusive projects with significantly different lives are being compared. However, even for mutually exclusive projects, it is not always appropriate to extend the analysis to a common life. This should only be done if there is a high probability that the projects will actually be repeated at the end of their initial lives.

We should note several potentially serious weaknesses inherent in this type of analysis: (1) If inflation is expected, then replacement equipment will have a higher price. Moreover, both sales prices and operating costs will probably change. Thus, the static conditions built into the analysis would be invalid. (2) Replacements that occur down the road will probably employ new technology, which in turn might change the cash flows. This factor can be built into the replacement chain analysis. (3) It is difficult enough to estimate the lives of most projects, so estimating the lives of a series of projects is often just a speculation.

In view of these problems, no experienced financial analyst would be too concerned about comparing mutually exclusive projects with lives of, say, eight years and ten years. Given all the uncertainties in the estimation process, such projects would, for all practical purposes, be assumed to have the same life. Still, it is important to recognize that a problem exists if mutually exclusive projects have substantially different lives. When we encounter such problems in practice, we use a computer spreadsheet and build expected inflation and/or possible efficiency gains directly into the cash flow estimates, and then use the replacement chain approach.

> **SELF-TEST QUESTIONS**
>
> Briefly describe the replacement chain (common life) approach.
>
> Why is it not always necessary to adjust project cash flow analyses for unequal lives?

INTRODUCTION TO REAL OPTIONS

Traditional discounted cash flow (DCF) analysis—where an asset's cash flows are estimated and then discounted to obtain the asset's NPV—has been the cornerstone for valuing all types of assets since the 1950s. Accordingly, most of our discussion of capital budgeting has been focused on DCF valuation techniques. However, in recent years a growing number of academics and practitioners have demonstrated that DCF valuation techniques do not always tell the complete story about a project's value and that rote use of DCF can, at times, lead to incorrect capital budgeting decisions.[2]

Option

The right but not the obligation to take some action in the future.

DCF techniques were originally developed to value securities such as stocks and bonds. These securities are passive investments—once they have been purchased, most investors have no influence over the cash flows the assets produce. However, real assets are *not* passive investments—managerial actions can influence their results. Furthermore, investing in a new project often brings with it a potential increase in the firm's future opportunities. Opportunities are, in effect, **options**— the right but not the obligation to take some action in the future. As we discuss in Chapter 18, options are valuable, so any project that expands the firm's set of opportunities has positive **option value.** Similarly, any project that reduces the set of future opportunities has negative option value. A project's impact on the firm's opportunities, or its option value, may not be captured by conventional NPV analysis. Therefore, option value should be considered separately.

Option Value

Value that is not accounted for in a conventional NPV analysis. Positive option value expands the firm's opportunities.

According to traditional capital budgeting theory, a project's NPV is the present value of its expected future cash flows, discounted at a rate that reflects the riskiness of the expected future cash flows. If the NPV is positive, then the project should be accepted. Note, however, that traditional capital budgeting theory says nothing about actions that can be taken after the project has been accepted and placed in operation that might cause the cash flows to change. In other words, traditional capital budgeting theory assumes that a project is like a roulette wheel. A gambler can choose whether or not to spin the wheel, but once the wheel has been spun, there is noth-

---

[2] For an excellent general discussion of the problems inherent in discounted cash flow valuation techniques as applied to capital budgeting, see Avinash K. Dixit and Robert S. Pindyck, "The Options Approach to Capital Investment," *Harvard Business Review*, May–June 1995, 105–115. For more information on the option value inherent in investment timing decisions, see Stephen A. Ross, "Uses, Abuses, and Alternatives to the Net-Present-Value Rule," *Financial Management*, Autumn 1995, 96–101. Also, the Summer 2001 issue of the *Journal of Applied Corporate Finance* contains several interesting articles on the use of option concepts in capital budgeting.

ing he or she can do to influence the outcome. Once the game begins, the outcome depends purely on chance, with no skill involved.

Contrast roulette with other games, such as draw poker. Chance plays a role in poker, and it continues to play a role after the initial deal because players receive additional cards throughout the game. Most important though, poker players are able to respond to their opponents' actions, so skillful players usually win.

Capital budgeting decisions have more in common with poker than roulette because (1) chance plays a continuing role throughout the life of the project and (2) managers can respond to changing market conditions and to competitors' actions. Opportunities to respond to changing circumstances are called **managerial options** because they give managers the option to influence the outcome of a project. They are also called **strategic options** because they are often associated with large, strategic projects rather than routine maintenance projects. Finally, they are called **real options** and are differentiated from financial options because they involve real, rather than financial, assets.

Note the unequal life analysis we covered in the first section of this chapter dealt with a type of real option. If the firm invests in the shorter-life asset, then it will have the opportunity to repeat the investment at some future date. If the product or service the asset provides is still valuable, then the investment will be repeated. If the product or service is no longer needed, the investment will not be made. Thus, the shorter investment contains an "embedded option" to make another investment in the future.

When we consider replacement chain analysis as a real option, we see that the shorter-term project is really less risky than the longer-term project, because the second investment can be made or not made depending on what is happening in the future. Note too that a typical corporation considers many projects each year, and each project may contain one or more different types of embedded real options. Examples include abandonment/shutdown options, investment timing options, growth/expansion options, and flexibility options. We discuss these options in the following sections.

Managerial Options
Opportunities to respond to changing circumstances, giving managers the opportunity to influence a project's outcome. Also called strategic, or real, options.

Strategic Options
Associated with large, strategic projects. Also called managerial, or real, options.

Real Options
Involve real, rather than financial, assets. Also called managerial, or strategic, options. They exist when managers can influence the size and riskiness of a project's cash flows by taking different actions during or at the end of a project's life.

> **SELF-TEST QUESTIONS**
>
> Explain the similarities and differences between capital budgeting projects and such games of chance as roulette and poker.
>
> What are real options?

ABANDONMENT/SHUTDOWN OPTIONS

Abandonment Option
The option of abandoning a project if operating cash flows turn out to be lower than expected. This option can both raise expected profitability and lower project risk.

When we evaluate projects, we generally assume that the firm will operate assets for their full physical lives. However, this is not always the best course of action. If the firm has the **option to abandon** (or shut down) a project before the end of its potential life, this can lower the project's risk and increase its expected profitability.

We can use BQC's computer control project as discussed in Chapter 11 to illustrate the effects of abandonment. Recall that due to labor contracts and other constraints, the project could not be terminated before the end of its four-year life.

Decision Tree

A diagram that shows all possible outcomes that result from a decision. Each possible outcome is shown as a "branch" on the tree. Decision trees are especially useful to analyze the effects of real options in investment decisions.

Under that constraint, we showed the best-case, most-likely-case, and worst-case scenarios. The Chapter 11 analysis is reproduced in the **decision tree** given in Situation 1 of Table 12-1, "Firm Cannot Abandon." In Column B on the far left, which is Time 0, we see that the firm must invest $26 million. We also see the probabilities for each scenario. Columns C through F show the annual cash flows under each scenario, and in Column G we show the probabilities of each scenario. Column H shows the NPV under each scenario when the cash flows are discounted at the 12 percent cost of capital. The products of the probabilities times the branch NPVs are shown

TABLE 12-1	Decision Trees without and with the Abandonment Option (Dollars in Thousands)

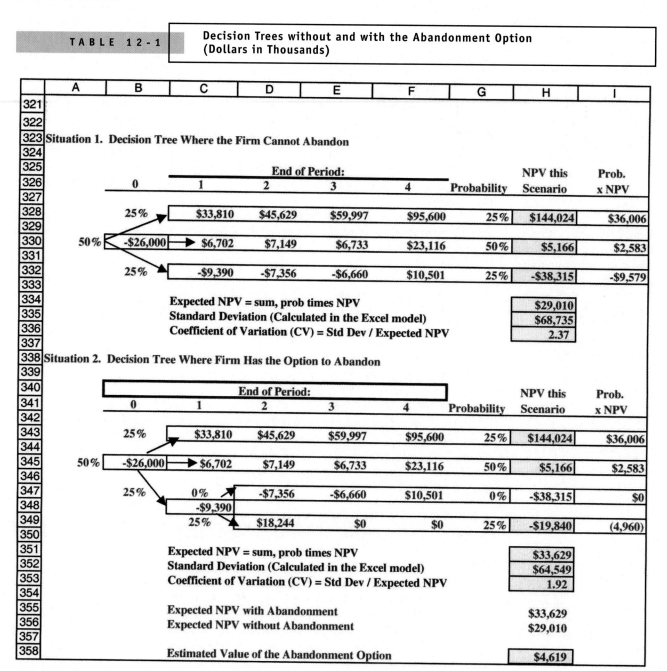

	A	B	C	D	E	F	G	H	I
321									
322									
323	Situation 1. Decision Tree Where the Firm Cannot Abandon								
324									
325				End of Period:				NPV this	Prob.
326		0	1	2	3	4	Probability	Scenario	x NPV
327									
328		25%	$33,810	$45,629	$59,997	$95,600	25%	$144,024	$36,006
329									
330	50%	-$26,000	$6,702	$7,149	$6,733	$23,116	50%	$5,166	$2,583
331									
332		25%	-$9,390	-$7,356	-$6,660	$10,501	25%	-$38,315	-$9,579
333									
334			Expected NPV = sum, prob times NPV					$29,010	
335			Standard Deviation (Calculated in the Excel model)					$68,735	
336			Coefficient of Variation (CV) = Std Dev / Expected NPV					2.37	
337									
338	Situation 2. Decision Tree Where Firm Has the Option to Abandon								
339									
340				End of Period:				NPV this	Prob.
341		0	1	2	3	4	Probability	Scenario	x NPV
342									
343		25%	$33,810	$45,629	$59,997	$95,600	25%	$144,024	$36,006
344									
345	50%	-$26,000	$6,702	$7,149	$6,733	$23,116	50%	$5,166	$2,583
346									
347		25%	0%	-$7,356	-$6,660	$10,501	0%	-$38,315	$0
348			-$9,390						
349			25%	$18,244	$0	$0	25%	-$19,840	(4,960)
350									
351			Expected NPV = sum, prob times NPV					$33,629	
352			Standard Deviation (Calculated in the Excel model)					$64,549	
353			Coefficient of Variation (CV) = Std Dev / Expected NPV					1.92	
354									
355			Expected NPV with Abandonment					$33,629	
356			Expected NPV without Abandonment					$29,010	
357									
358			Estimated Value of the Abandonment Option					$4,619	

in Column I. The sum of these products is the expected NPV, which is a probability-weighted average, and it is $29.01 million. The standard deviation and the coefficient of variation are also provided to give an idea of the project's risk. This project is risky, but given its positive expected NPV, it should probably be accepted. However, if things turn out badly, this would seriously hurt the company.

Now suppose the company could make a second decision, this one at t = 1, to shut down, or "abandon," the project if things turn out badly. To see what would then happen, we add another branch to the tree, as shown in Situation 2 of Table 12-1. Here we assume that the company can abandon the project at the end of Year 1, when additional information about production costs and demand conditions is available. If things are going well, the project will be continued. However, if things are going badly, BQC will sell the related assets at their $18.244 million book value and realize this cash flow at the end of Year 2. (There will be no tax consequences, as a sale at book value produces neither a gain nor a loss.) Thus, the Year 2 cash flow will be a positive $18.244 million rather than a loss of $7.356 million. Of course, if the project is abandoned, the cash flows in Years 3 and 4 will become zero. With these changes, we recalculate the NPV for the bottom (or "Can Abandon") branch. It is still negative, but less negative than in the worst-case scenario before considering abandonment.[3]

The option to abandon raises the expected NPV from $29.01 million to $33.629 million, and it also lowers the standard deviation. Those changes combine to lower the coefficient of variation. The lower risk suggests that we could recalculate the NPV, using a lower WACC. The amount to lower the WACC would be judgmental. Finally, note that the difference between the expected NPV with and without abandonment represents the value of the option to abandon. As shown in the lower part of Table 12-1, the option is worth $4.619 million.

The NPV looks better, but this does not reverse the accept/reject decision. However, it often turns out that if we fail to take account of abandonment, the bad case is so bad that the expected NPV is negative, but when abandonment is considered, the expected NPV becomes positive. Clearly, abandonment must be considered to obtain valid assessments for different projects.

Coca-Cola's failed introduction of "New Coke" several years ago is an example of an abandonment situation. Shortly after its launch, it became apparent that the product would never be the money-maker Coke had anticipated. Note that Coca-Cola faced risks when it embarked on the project: Future operating cash flows and abandonment values might be lower than expected. Coca-Cola benefited by avoiding the "downside" losses that would have occurred due to the lower-than-anticipated operating cash flows by terminating the New Coke project. In general, the opportunity to abandon projects allows companies to limit downside losses.

---

[3] In Situation 2, where the company has the option to abandon if the worst-case scenario occurs, it will abandon the project and that action will minimize its losses. Thus, we show a zero probability of continuing to operate under the worst-case scenario.

Investment Timing Option

An option as to when to begin a project. Often, if a firm can delay a decision, it can increase a project's expected NPV.

A conventional NPV analysis implicitly assumes that projects will either be accepted or rejected, which implies that they will be undertaken now or never. However, in practice companies sometimes have a third choice— delay the decision until later, when more information is available. Such **investment timing options** can dramatically affect a project's estimated profitability and risk.

To illustrate timing options, assume that BQC is considering a project that requires an initial investment of $5 million at the beginning of 2003 (or t = 0). The project will generate positive net cash flows at the end of each of the next four years (t = 1, 2, 3, and 4). However, the size of each yearly cash flow will depend critically on what happens to market conditions in the future. Figure 12-2 provides two decision trees that illustrate the problem at hand. As shown in the top section, Panel A, there is a 50 percent probability that market conditions will be strong, in which case the project will generate cash flows of $2.5 million at the end of each of the next four years. There is also a 50 percent probability that demand for the product will be weak, in which case the annual cash flows will be only $1.5 million.

Note that each branch of the decision tree is equivalent to a time line. Thus, the top line, which describes the payoffs under good conditions, has a cash flow of −$5 million at t = 0 and positive cash flows of $2.5 million for Years 1 through 4. BQC considers the project to have above-average risk, hence it will be evaluated using a 14 percent cost of capital. The NPV, if the market is strong, will turn out to be $2,284,280.76. On the other hand, if product demand is weak, the NPV will turn out to be −$629,431.54, so it will be a money loser.

The expected value for the project is found as a weighted average of the NPVs of the two possible outcomes, with the weights being the probabilities for each outcome. With a 50 percent probability for each branch, the expected value of the project, if it is undertaken today, is $827,425, as shown in the last column of Panel A in Figure 12-2. Since the project has a positive NPV, it appears that the company should proceed with it, even though there is a 50-50 chance that it will actually turn out to be a loser.

However, suppose BQC's managers can wait until next year, when more information will be available about market conditions, before making the decision. The best guess *today* is that the project has a 50-50 chance of generating $2.5 or $1.5 million, hence ending up with a positive or a negative NPV. However, one year from now the company will be better able to estimate whether market conditions will be good or bad. To keep things simple, assume that if the company waits a year, the project's initial investment will still be $5 million, the annual cash flows will still be $2.5 or $1.5 million, but the firm will know for sure whether the market is strong or weak.

Should BQC proceed with the project today, or should it wait a year? In many respects, this decision is similar to choosing among mutually exclusive projects. When comparing two mutually exclusive projects that are both profitable, you should select the one with the higher risk-adjusted net present value. In BQC's case, the mutually exclusive choice is between investing in the project today and waiting a year before deciding whether or not to make the investment. The company should select the strategy with the higher expected net present value.

If the company proceeds today, the project's estimated NPV is $827,425. If it waits a year, there is a 50 percent chance that the annual net cash flows will be $2.5 million, which at a 14 percent cost of capital produces an NPV of $2,284,280.76. However, there is also a 50 percent chance that the annual net cash flows will be only $1.5 million, which translates into an NPV of −$629,431.54.

FIGURE 12-2   A Decision Tree for Analyzing the Timing of an Investment

BQC is considering a proposed expansion project. The project requires an initial investment of $5M, and it has an economic life of four years. The project's yearly cash flows will depend on market conditions. BQC is deciding whether to turn down the project, to proceed with it today, or to wait a year before making the decision. Currently, there is a 50% probability that the market will be good and a 50% probability it will be bad. If the decision is postponed for a year, the market's condition will be known. Given the project's risk, all cash flows are discounted at 14%.

a. PROCEED WITH THE PROJECT TODAY

YEAR	2003	2004	2005	2006	2007	NPV	PROBABILITY OF MARKET CONDITION OCCURRENCE	PRODUCT (NPV × PROBABILITY)
Market is good (50% probability)		+2.5M	+2.5M	+2.5M	+2.5M	$2,284,280.76	0.5	$1,142,140
Initial Investment: −$5M		+1.5M	+1.5M	+1.5M	+1.5M	−629,431.54	0.5	−314,715
Market is bad (50% probability)							Expected NPV =	$ 827,425

b. WAIT A YEAR TO SEE IF THE MARKET IS GOOD OR BAD, THEN INVEST ONLY IF THE MARKET IS GOOD

YEAR	2003	2004	2005	2006	2007	2008	NPV	PROBABILITY OF MARKET CONDITION OCCURRENCE	PRODUCT (NPV × PROBABILITY)
Market is good (50% probability)		−5M	+2.5M	+2.5M	+2.5M	+2.5M	$2,284,280.76	0.5	$1,142,140
Wait: Spend $0		0	0	0	0	0	0	0.5	0
Market is bad (50% probability)								Expected NPV =	$1,142,140

Value of expected NPV in 2003 = $\dfrac{\$1,142,140}{(1.14)}$ = $1,001,877.

Under the "Wait" strategy, BQC would know which market condition existed, and it would make the decision to "Go" if conditions were good and make a "No Go" decision if they were bad. Under the No Go decision, no investment is made, hence the NPV will be zero. Thus, if BQC waits a year, there is a 50 percent probability the project will be undertaken, in which case the NPV will be $2,284,280.76, and there is a 50 percent probability the project will not be undertaken, in which case the NPV will be zero. This is illustrated in Panel B of Figure 12-2. As we see in the last column of Panel B in Figure 12-2, the expected NPV under the Wait option is $1,142,140.

Note, though, that all the cash flows under the Wait case are deferred for one year, hence the Wait case NPV is as of a year from now, in 2004 rather than 2003 as in the "Proceed Immediately" case. Therefore, to make the NPVs comparable, we must discount the Wait NPV back for one year to find the project's *value in today's dollars*. The PV of the Wait NPV, discounted at the 14 percent cost of capital, is shown in the lower right part of the figure to be $1,001,877. Since this number exceeds the NPV based on investing today, the analysis suggests that the company should wait rather than take on the project now.

Note that we used 14 percent as the discount rate for both the Go Now and Wait analyses. Is this reasonable? Definitely not. If we wait, we will have a much better idea of market demand. Indeed, in our simplified example, we have implicitly assumed that there is no uncertainty whatever about the cash flows if we wait a year. Therefore, it would be reasonable to discount the cash flows in Panel B of Figure 12-2 at a rate lower than 14 percent, which was the rate used for high-risk projects. A good case could be made for using 10 percent, the rate for low-risk projects, in the Wait case. Of course, a lower discount rate would cause the Wait NPV to be even higher, thus reinforcing the case for waiting.

If BQC chooses to accept the project today, it is effectively giving up the option to pursue the project next year. In such cases, decision makers should insist on an NPV that is both positive and also large enough to offset the value of the lost option. For this reason, some companies deliberately set hurdle rates that are above the calculated cost of capital when evaluating projects that contain timing options.

When making Go Now versus Wait decisions, financial managers need to consider several other factors. First, if a firm such as BQC decides to wait, it may lose any strategic advantages associated with being the first competitor to enter a new line of business, and this could alter the cash flows. On the other hand, as we saw in the above example, waiting may enable the company to avoid a costly mistake. In general, the more uncertainty there is about future market conditions, the more attractive it becomes to wait, but this risk reduction may be offset by the loss of the "first mover advantage."

SELF-TEST QUESTIONS

Briefly illustrate an investment timing option.

How is an investment timing option similar to choosing among mutually exclusive projects?

Why do some companies deliberately set hurdle rates above the calculated cost of capital when evaluating projects with timing options?

Explain why the following statement is true: "In general, the more uncertainty there is about future market conditions, the more attractive it may be to wait."

Growth Option
If an investment creates the opportunity to make other potentially profitable investments that would not otherwise be possible, then the investment is said to contain a growth option.

GROWTH OPTIONS

We can illustrate **growth options** with another BQC project, Project Z, which requires an initial investment of $3 million at the beginning of 2003 (or t = 0). This project is expected to generate net cash flows of $1 million at the end of each of the next three years (t = 1, 2, and 3). Given that the uncertainties regarding the project's cash flow is the same as for the firm's average project, BQC's management estimates that the project's cost of capital is 12 percent. Since the project's total cash flows never exceed its up-front cost, and considering the time value of money, it has an NPV of −$598,169. On the basis of this quick assessment, BQC's controller recommended that it be rejected. However, the treasurer argued that it should be accepted, because implementing Project Z would provide technical expertise that might lead to profitable future projects.

Conceding this possibility, the controller then estimated the potential profitability of these future projects. He concluded that there was a 25 percent chance that Project Z would create an opportunity with an estimated NPV of $8 million three years from now. In other words, if this opportunity arose, BQC could make an additional investment at t = 3, and that investment would have an NPV of $8 million. At the same time, he estimated that there was a 75 percent chance that the future opportunity would have an NPV of *minus* $8 million.

Looking at these numbers, the controller still argued that Project Z should be rejected. After all, it appeared to be a negative NPV project with an option to invest in another negative NPV project three years from now. However, BQC's treasurer, Ellen Warnes, argued that this logic was flawed. Warnes pointed out that BQC would not invest any money at t = 3 if the new project had a negative NPV. Therefore, she argued that there was a 25 percent probability that the NPV of the project would be $8 million and a 75 percent chance that BQC would not make any additional investments, in which case the NPV would be zero. Thus, Warnes concluded that the estimated cash flow from the subsequent project would be 0.25 × $8,000,000 + 0.75 × $0 = $2 million at t = 3.

Consequently, BQC's finance staff reestimated the cash flows (in millions of dollars) from Project Z as follows:

The cash flow at t = 3 consisted of $1 million from the original project plus the expected $2 million NPV from the future project. Assuming a 12 percent cost of capital, Project Z then had an estimated NPV of $825,392, well above the original estimate of a loss. Therefore, BQC's management accepted Project Z.

Our conclusion is that the true value of a project that includes an embedded option may exceed the project's NPV as calculated in the conventional manner. In many cases, these growth options can have a significant impact on corporate value. For example, a recent study suggests that growth options generated roughly half of Anheuser-Busch's corporate value in the late 1990s. Therefore, it is critically important that managers identify any such options and include them in the analysis. Decision trees similar to the ones shown in this chapter provide one method of dealing formally with embedded options. Also, option pricing models, which we discuss in Chapter 18, can be used in certain situations. A great deal of work is going on in this area, and we expect to see more widespread use of option analysis as a supplement to discounted cash flow analysis in capital budgeting in the future. For now, you should recognize that as a result of embedded options some projects have more or less value than is indicated by their NPVs, and this value should, at a minimum, be subjectively considered when making capital budgeting decisions.[4]

SELF-TEST QUESTIONS

How might the failure to recognize a growth option lead to the underestimation of a project's NPV?

Would the failure to recognize growth options make the capital budget too large or too small? Would your answers be the same for abandonment options?

FLEXIBILITY OPTIONS

Flexibility Option
The option to modify operations depending on how conditions develop during a project's life, especially the type output produced or the inputs used.

Many projects offer **flexibility options** that permit the firm to alter operations depending on how conditions change during the life of the project. Typically, either inputs or outputs, or both, can be changed. BMW's Spartanburg, South Carolina, auto assembly plant provides a good example of output flexibility. BMW needed the plant to produce sports coupes. If it built the plant configured optimally to produce these vehicles, the construction cost would be minimized. However, the company thought that later on it might want to switch production to some other vehicle type, and that would be difficult if the plant was designed just for coupes. Therefore, BMW decided to spend additional funds to construct a more flexible plant, one that could produce different types of vehicles should demand patterns shift. Sure enough, things did change. Demand for coupes dropped a bit, and that for sports utility vehicles soared. But BMW was ready, and the Spartanburg plant is now spewing out hot-selling SUVs. The plant's cash flows are much higher than they would have been without the flexibility option that BMW "bought" by paying more to build a more flexible plant.

Electric power companies provide a good example of input flexibility. Utilities can build plants that generate electricity by burning coal, oil, or natural gas. The prices of those fuels change over time depending on such things as actions in Iraq or Iran, changing environmental policies, and weather conditions. Some years ago, virtually all power plants were designed to burn one type of fuel, as this resulted in the lowest construction cost. However, as fuel cost volatility increased, power companies began to build higher-cost but more flexible plants, especially ones that could switch from oil to gas and back again, depending on relative fuel prices.

In both the BMW and power plant situations, decision trees were quite useful. One branch indicated the cash flows expected from a low-cost, inflexible plant, and other branches were set up for higher-cost but more flexible operations. Probabilities were assigned to different conditions, and expected NPVs for the different branches were calculated and used to help make the final decision.

---

[4] For an excellent discussion on real options see Tom Arnold and Richard L. Shockley, Jr., "Value Creation at Anheuser-Busch: A Real Options Example," *Journal of Applied Corporate Finance*, Summer 2001, Vol. 14, No. 2, 52-61.

Decision trees and the analysis of embedded options go hand-in-glove. Setting up a decision tree forces an analyst to consider various types of embedded options, options that they might have neglected had they not gone through the decision tree exercise. And, as we have seen, a failure to consider all relevant options can lead to serious mistakes in the capital budgeting process.

SELF-TEST QUESTIONS

What is an "input flexibility option" and an "output flexibility option?"

How do flexibility options affect projects' calculated NPVs versus conventionally calculated NPVs?

THE OPTIMAL CAPITAL BUDGET

So far we have described various factors that managers consider when they evaluate individual projects. For planning purposes, managers also need to forecast the total amount of investment in order to determine how much capital must be raised. While every firm goes through this process in its own unique way, there are some commonly used procedures for estimating the optimal capital budget. We use Citrus Grove Corporation, a producer of fruit juices, to illustrate how this process works in practice.

Step 1. The financial vice-president obtains an estimate of her firm's overall composite WACC. As we discussed in Chapter 9, this composite WACC is based on market conditions, the firm's capital structure, and the riskiness of its assets. Citrus Grove's projects are roughly similar from year to year in terms of their risks.

Step 2. The corporate WACC is scaled up or down for each of the firm's divisions to reflect the division's capital structure and risk characteristics. Citrus Grove, for example, assigns a factor of 0.9 to its stable low-risk fresh citrus juice division, but a factor of 1.1 to its more exotic fruit juice group. Therefore, if the corporate cost of capital is determined to be 10.50 percent, the cost for the citrus juice division is $0.9(10.50\%) = 9.45\%$, while that for the exotic juice division is $1.1(10.50\%) = 11.55\%$.

Step 3. Financial managers within each of the firm's divisions estimate the relevant cash flows and risks of each of their potential projects. The estimated cash flows should explicitly consider any real options embedded in the projects, which includes any opportunities to repeat the project at a later date. Then, within each division, projects are classified into one of three groups—high risk, average risk, and low risk—and the same 0.9 and 1.1 factors are used to adjust the divisional cost of capital estimates. (A factor of 1 would be used for an average-risk project.) For example, a low-risk project in the citrus juice division would be assigned a cost of capital of $0.9(9.45\%) = 8.51\%$, while a high-risk project in the exotic juice division would have a cost of $1.1(11.55\%) = 12.71\%$.

Step 4. Each project's NPV is then determined, using its risk-adjusted cost of capital. The optimal capital budget consists of all independent projects with positive NPVs plus those mutually exclusive projects with the highest positive NPVs.

In estimating its optimal capital budget, we assumed that Citrus Grove will be able to obtain financing for all of its profitable projects. This assumption is reasonable for large, mature firms with good track records. However, smaller firms, new firms, and firms with dubious track records may have difficulties raising capital, even for projects that the firm concludes have positive NPVs. In such circumstances, the size of the firm's capital budget may be constrained. This circumstance is called **capital rationing.** In such situations capital is scarce, and it should be used in the most efficient way possible. Procedures are available for allocating capital so as to maximize the firm's aggregate NPV subject to the constraint that the capital rationing ceiling is not exceeded. However, due to its complexity, the details of this process are best left for advanced finance courses.

The four steps outlined above also assume that the accepted projects have, on average, about the same debt-carrying capacity as the firm's existing assets. If this is not true, the corporate WACC determined in Step 1 will not be correct, and it will have to be adjusted.

The procedures discussed in this section cannot be implemented with much precision, but they do force the firm to think carefully about each division's relative risk, about the risk of each project within the divisions, and about the relationship between the total amount of capital raised and the cost of that capital. Further, the process forces the firm to adjust its capital budget to reflect capital market conditions. If the costs of debt and equity rise, this fact will be reflected in the cost of capital used to evaluate projects, and projects that would be marginally acceptable when capital costs were low would (correctly) be ruled unacceptable when capital costs become high.

Capital Rationing
A situation in which a constraint is placed on the total size of the firm's capital budget.

SELF-TEST QUESTIONS

Explain how a financial manager might estimate his or her firm's optimal capital budget.

In estimating the optimal capital budget, what assumption is typically made concerning the amount of capital that can be raised?

What is capital rationing?

TYING IT ALL TOGETHER

The last four chapters have focused on capital budgeting. In Chapter 9, we showed how companies estimate the cost of capital. Then, given a set of cash flows and an estimated cost of capital, we described in Chapter 10 several approaches used to evaluate projects. We demonstrated that net present value (NPV) analysis is conceptually the best approach for evaluating projects. Next, Chapter 11 described techniques for estimating a project's cash flows and risk. Finally, in this chapter we discussed some topics that go beyond the simple capital budgeting framework, including the following:

- If mutually exclusive projects have **unequal lives,** it may be necessary to adjust the analysis to put the projects on an equal life basis.

- The **replacement chain (common life) approach** is used to adjust for unequal lives. Here we assume that each project can be repeated as many times as necessary to reach a common life. The NPVs over this common life are then compared, and the project with the higher common life NPV is chosen.

- Investing in a new project often brings with it a potential increase in the firm's future opportunities. Opportunities are, in effect, **options**—the right but not the obligation to take some future action.

- A project may have an **option value** that is not accounted for in a conventional NPV analysis. Any project that expands the firm's set of opportunities has positive option value.

- Opportunities to respond to changing circumstances are called **managerial options** because they give managers the option to influence the outcome of a project. They are also called **strategic options** because they are often associated with large, strategic projects rather than routine maintenance projects. Finally, they are also called **real options** because they involve "real," rather than "financial," assets.

- **Real options** exist when managers can influence the size and riskiness of a project's cash flows by taking different actions during or at the end of the project's life.

- Many projects include a variety of **embedded options** that can dramatically affect the true NPV. Examples of embedded options include (1) the option to abandon or shut down the project, (2) the option to accelerate or delay a project, (3) "growth options" that might enable a firm to pursue other profitable future projects, and (4) "flexibility" options that allow a firm to modify its operations over time.

- The **abandonment option** is the ability to abandon a project if the operating cash flows and/or abandonment value turn out to be lower than expected. It reduces the riskiness of a project and increases its value.

- An **investment timing option** involves not only the decision of *whether* to proceed with a project but also the decision of *when* to proceed with it. This opportunity to affect a project's timing can dramatically change its estimated value.

- Projects whose capital outlays are made in stages over several years are often evaluated using **decision trees.** Decision trees are also useful for identifying real options, which, in turn, may materially affect a project's true NPV.

- If an investment creates the opportunity to make other potentially profitable investments that would not otherwise be possible, then the investment is said to contain a **growth option.**

- A **flexibility option** is the option to modify operations depending on how conditions develop during a project's life, especially the type of output produced or the inputs used.

- For planning purposes, managers need to forecast the total dollar amount that will be required to fund the acceptable projects, or the **total capital budget** for the planning period. They need this information to determine how much capital will have to be raised.

- **Capital rationing** occurs when management places a constraint on the size of the firm's capital budget during a particular period.

QUESTIONS

12-1 Suppose a firm is considering two mutually exclusive projects. One has a life of 6 years and the other a life of 10 years. Would the failure to employ some type of replacement chain analysis bias an NPV analysis against one of the projects? Explain.

12-2 What factors should a company consider when it decides whether to invest in a project today or to wait until more information becomes available?

12-3 In general, do timing options make it more or less likely that a project will be accepted today?

12-4 If a company has an option to abandon a project, would this tend to make the company more or less likely to accept the project today?

SELF-TEST PROBLEMS (SOLUTIONS APPEAR IN APPENDIX B)

ST-1
Key terms
Define each of the following terms:
a. Replacement chain (common life) approach
b. Options; option value; managerial options
c. Strategic options; real options; embedded option
d. Investment timing option; abandonment option
e. Decision trees
f. Growth option; flexibility option
g. Capital rationing

ST-2
Projects with unequal lives
Wisconsin Dairy Co. is currently making its capital budgeting decisions for the upcoming year. Among the projects they are considering are two machines: Machine W and Machine WW. Machine W costs $500,000 but will produce expected after-tax cash inflows of $300,000 at the end of each of the next 2 years. Machine WW also costs $500,000 but will produce expected after-tax cash inflows of $165,000 at the end of each of the next 4 years. Both projects have a 10 percent cost of capital.
a. Assume that these are independent projects that are not repeatable. Which project or projects should the company accept?
b. Assume that these are mutually exclusive projects that are not repeatable. Which project should the company accept?
c. Assume that these are mutually exclusive projects that can be repeated indefinitely over time with the same expected cash flows. Which project should the company accept?
d. Can replacement chain analysis be used if project cash flows are different each time the project is repeated?

STARTER PROBLEMS

12-1
Unequal lives
Haley's Graphic Designs Inc. is considering two alternative, mutually exclusive projects. Both projects require an initial investment of $10,000 and are typical, average-risk projects for the firm. Project A has an expected life of 2 years with after-tax cash inflows of $6,000 and $8,000 at the end of Years 1 and 2, respectively. Project B has an expected life of 4 years with after-tax cash inflows of $4,000 at the end of each of the next 4 years. The firm's cost of capital is 10 percent.
a. If the projects cannot be repeated, which project will be selected, and what is its net present value?
b. If the projects can be repeated and there are no anticipated changes in the cash flows, which project will be selected, and what is its net present value?

12-2
Optimal capital budget

Hampton Manufacturing estimates that its WACC is 12 percent if equity comes from retained earnings. However, if the company issues new stock to raise new equity, it estimates that its WACC will rise to 12.5 percent. The company believes that it will exhaust its retained earnings at $3,250,000 of capital due to the number of highly profitable projects available to the firm and its limited earnings. The company is considering the following seven investment projects:

PROJECT	SIZE	IRR
A	$ 750,000	14.0%
B	1,250,000	13.5
C	1,250,000	13.2
D	1,250,000	13.0
E	750,000	12.7
F	750,000	12.3
G	750,000	12.2

Assume that each of these projects is independent and that each is just as risky as the firm's existing assets. Which set of projects should be accepted, and what is the firm's optimal capital budget?

12-3
Optimal capital budget

Refer to Problem 12-2. Now assume that Projects C and D are mutually exclusive. Project D has an NPV of $400,000, whereas Project C has an NPV of $350,000. Which set of projects should be accepted, and what is the firm's optimal capital budget?

12-4
Risk-adjusted optimal capital budget

Refer to Problem 12-2. Assume again that each of the projects is independent but that management decides to incorporate project risk differentials. Management judges Projects B, C, D, and E to have average risk, Project A to have high risk, and Projects F and G to have low risk. The company adds 2 percentage points to the cost of capital of those projects that are significantly more risky than average, and it subtracts 2 percentage points from the cost of capital for those that are substantially less risky than average. Which set of projects should be accepted, and what is the firm's optimal capital budget?

EXAM-TYPE PROBLEMS

The problems included in this section are set up in such a way that they could be used as multiple-choice exam problems.

12-5
Unequal lives

Cotner Clothes Inc. is considering the replacement of its old, fully depreciated knitting machine. Two new models are available: (a) Machine 190-3, which has a cost of $190,000, a 3-year expected life, and after-tax cash flows (labor savings and depreciation) of $87,000 per year; and (b) Machine 360-6, which has a cost of $360,000, a 6-year life, and after-tax cash flows of $98,300 per year. Assume both projects can be repeated. Knitting machine prices are not expected to rise, because inflation will be offset by cheaper components (microprocessors) used in the machines. Assume that Cotner's cost of capital is 14 percent. Should the firm replace its old knitting machine, and, if so, which new machine should it use?

12-6
Unequal lives

Zappe Airlines is considering two alternative planes. Plane A has an expected life of 5 years, will cost $100 million, and will produce net cash flows of $30 million per year. Plane B has a life of 10 years, will cost $132 million, and will produce net cash flows of $25 million per year. Zappe plans to serve the route for 10 years. Inflation in operating costs, airplane costs, and fares is expected to be zero, and the company's cost of capital is 12 percent. By how much would the value of the company increase if it accepted the better project (plane)?

12-7
Unequal lives

The Fernandez Company has the opportunity to invest in one of two mutually exclusive machines that will produce a product it will need for the foreseeable future. Machine A costs $10 million but realizes after-tax inflows of $4 million per year for 4 years. After 4 years, the machine must be replaced. Machine B costs $15 million and realizes after-tax inflows of $3.5 million per year for 8 years, after which it must be replaced. Assume that machine prices are not expected to rise because inflation will be offset by cheaper components used in the machines. If the cost of capital is 10 percent, which machine should the company use?

12-8
Investment timing option

Twain Hotels is interested in developing a new hotel in Tokyo. The company estimates that the hotel would require an initial investment of $20 million. Twain expects that the hotel will produce positive cash flows of $3 million a year at the end of each of the next 20 years. The project's cost of capital is 12 percent.

a. What is the project's net present value?

b. While Twain expects the cash flows to be $3 million a year, it recognizes that the cash flows could, in fact, be much higher or lower, depending on whether the Japanese government imposes a large hotel tax. One year from now, Twain will know whether the tax will be imposed. There is a 25 percent chance that the tax will be imposed, in which case the yearly cash flows will be only $2.4 million. At the same time, there is a 75 percent chance that the tax will not be imposed, in which case the yearly cash flows will be $3.2 million. Twain is deciding whether to proceed with the hotel today or to wait 1 year to find out whether the tax will be imposed. If Twain waits a year, the initial investment will remain at $20 million. Assume that all cash flows are discounted at 12 percent. Should Twain proceed with the project today or should it wait a year before deciding?

PROBLEMS

12-9
Abandonment value

The Scampini Supplies Company recently purchased a new delivery truck. The new truck costs $22,500, and it is expected to generate net after-tax operating cash flows, including depreciation, of $6,250 per year. The truck has a 5-year expected life. The expected year-end abandonment values (salvage values after tax adjustments) for the truck are given below. The company's cost of capital is 10 percent.

YEAR	ANNUAL OPERATING CASH FLOW	ABANDONMENT VALUE
0	($22,500)	—
1	6,250	$17,500
2	6,250	14,000
3	6,250	11,000
4	6,250	5,000
5	6,250	0

a. Should the firm operate the truck until the end of its 5-year physical life; if not, what is its optimal economic life?

b. Would the introduction of abandonment values, in addition to operating cash flows, ever *reduce* the expected NPV and/or IRR of a project?

12-10
Investment timing option

The Bush Oil Company is deciding whether to drill for oil on a tract of land that the company owns. The company estimates that the project would cost $8 million today. Bush estimates that once drilled, the oil will generate positive net cash flows of $4 million a year at the end of each of the next 4 years. While the company is fairly confident about its cash flow forecast, it recognizes that if it waits 2 years, it would have more information about the local geology as well as the price of oil. Bush estimates that if it waits 2 years, the project would cost $9 million. Moreover, if it waits 2 years, there is a 90 percent chance that the net cash flows would be $4.2 million a year for 4 years, and there is a 10 percent chance that the cash flows will be $2.2 million a year for 4 years. Assume that all cash flows are discounted at 10 percent.

a. If the company chooses to drill today, what is the project's net present value?

b. Would it make sense to wait 2 years before deciding whether to drill?

12-11
Real options

Nevada Enterprises is considering buying a vacant lot that sells for $1.2 million. If the property is purchased, the company's plan is to spend another $5 million today (t = 0) to build a hotel on the property. The after-tax cash flows from the hotel will depend critically on whether the state imposes a tourism tax in this year's legislative session. If the tax is imposed, the hotel is expected to produce after-tax cash inflows of $600,000 at the end of each of the next 15 years. If the tax is not imposed, the hotel is expected to produce after-tax cash inflows of $1,200,000 at the end of each of the next 15 years. The project has a 12 percent cost of capital. Assume at the outset that the company does not have the option to delay the project.

a. What is the project's expected NPV if the tax is imposed?
b. What is the project's expected NPV if the tax is not imposed?
c. Given that there is a 50 percent chance that the tax will be imposed, what is the project's expected NPV if they proceed with it today?
d. While the company does not have an option to delay construction, it does have the option to abandon the project 1 year from now if the tax is imposed. If it abandons the project, it would sell the complete property 1 year from now at an expected price of $6 million. Once the project is abandoned the company would no longer receive any cash inflows from it. Assuming that all cash flows are discounted at 12 percent, would the existence of this abandonment option affect the company's decision to proceed with the project today?
e. Finally, assume that there is no option to abandon or delay the project, but that the company has an option to purchase an adjacent property in 1 year at a price of $1.5 million. If the tourism tax is imposed, the net present value of developing this property (as of $t = 1$) is only $300,000 (so it wouldn't make sense to purchase the property for $1.5 million). However, if the tax is not imposed, the net present value of the future opportunities from developing the property would be $4 million (as of $t = 1$). Thus, under this scenario it would make sense to purchase the property for $1.5 million. Assume that these cash flows are discounted at 12 percent, and the probability that the tax will be imposed is still 50 percent. How much would the company pay today for the option to purchase this property 1 year from now for $1.5 million?

SPREADSHEET PROBLEM

12-12
Real option analysis

Bankers' Services Inc. (BSI) is considering a project that has a cost of $10 million and an expected life of 3 years. There is a 30 percent probability of good conditions, in which case the project will provide a cash flow of $9 million at the end of each year for 3 years. There is a 40 percent probability of medium conditions, in which case the annual cash flows will be $4 million, and there is a 30 percent probability of bad conditions and a cash flow of −$1 million per year. BSI can, if it chooses, close down the project at the end of any year and sell the related assets for 90 percent of the book value. The asset sale price will be received at the end of the year the project is shut down. The related assets will be depreciated by the straight-line method over 3 years, and the value at the end of Year 3 is zero. (Don't worry about IRS regulations for this problem.) BSI uses a 12 percent cost of capital to evaluate projects like this.

a. Find the project's expected NPV and the coefficient of variation with and without the abandonment option.
b. How sensitive is the NPV to changes in the company's WACC? To the percentage of book value at which the asset can be sold?
c. Now assume that the project cannot be shut down. However, expertise gained by taking it on will lead to an opportunity at the end of Year 3 to undertake a venture that would have the same cost as the original project, and the new project's cash flows would follow whichever branch resulted for the original project. In other words, there would be a second $10 million cost at the end of Year 3, and then cash flows of either $9 million, $4 million, or −$1 million for the following 3 years. This new project could also not be abandoned if it is undertaken. How does this new information affect the original project's expected NPV? Carry out sensitivity analyses on NPV of changes in WACC and percentage of book value at which the asset could be sold. At what WACC would the project break even in the sense that NPV = $0?
d. Now suppose the original (no abandonment) project could be delayed a year. All the cash flows would remain unchanged, but information obtained during that year would tell the company exactly which set of demand conditions existed. How does this option to delay the project affect its NPV?

21ST CENTURY EDUCATIONAL PRODUCTS

12-13 Other Topics in Capital Budgeting 21st Century Educational Products (21st Century) is a rapidly growing software company, and consistent with its growth, it has a relatively large capital budget. While most of the company's projects are fairly easy to evaluate, a handful of projects involve more complex evaluations.

John Keller, a senior member of the company's finance staff, coordinates the evaluation of these more complex projects. His group brings their recommendations directly to the company's CFO and CEO, Kristin Riley and Bob Stevens, respectively.

a. Right now, Keller's group is looking at a variety of interesting projects. For example, the group has been asked to choose between the following two mutually exclusive projects:

EXPECTED NET CASH FLOWS

YEAR	PROJECT S	PROJECT L
0	($100,000)	($100,000)
1	59,000	33,500
2	59,000	33,500
3	—	33,500
4	—	33,500

Both projects may be repeated and both are of average risk, so they should be evaluated at the firm's cost of capital, 10 percent. Which one should be chosen?

b. In recent months, Keller's group has begun to focus on real option analysis.
   (1) What is real option analysis?
   (2) What are some examples of projects with embedded real options?

c. Taking real options into account, one of Keller's colleagues, Barbara Hudson, has suggested that instead of investing in Project L today, it might make sense to wait a year because 21st Century would learn a lot more about market conditions and would be better able to forecast the project's cash flows. Right now, 21st Century forecasts that Project L will generate expected yearly net cash flows of $33,500. However, if the company waits a year, it will learn more about market conditions. There is a 50 percent chance that the market will be strong and a 50 percent chance it will be weak. If the market is strong, the yearly cash flows will be $43,500. If the market is weak, the yearly cash flows will be only $23,500. If 21st Century chooses to wait a year, the initial investment will remain $100,000. Assume that all cash flows are discounted at 10 percent. Should 21st Century invest in Project L today, or should it wait a year before deciding whether to invest in the project?

d. Now let's assume that there is more uncertainty about the future cash flows. More specifically, assume that the yearly cash flows are now $53,500 if the market is strong and $13,500 if the market is weak. Assume that the upfront cost is still $100,000 and that the cost of capital is still 10 percent. Will this increased uncertainty make the firm more or less willing to invest in the project today?

e. 21st Century is considering another project, Project Y. Project Y has an up-front cost of $200,000 and an economic life of 3 years. If the company develops the project, its after-tax operating costs will be $100,000 a year; however, the project is expected to produce after-tax cash inflows of $180,000 a year. Thus, the project's estimated cash flows are as follows:

YEAR	CASH OUTFLOWS	CASH INFLOWS	NET CASH FLOWS
0	−$200,000	$ 0	−$200,000
1	−100,000	180,000	80,000
2	−100,000	180,000	80,000
3	−100,000	180,000	80,000

   (1) The project has an estimated cost of capital of 10 percent. What is the project's NPV?
   (2) While the project's operating costs are fairly certain at $100,000 per year, the estimated cash inflows depend critically on whether 21st Century's largest customer uses the product. Keller estimates that there is a 60 percent chance the customer will use the product, in which case the project will produce after-tax cash inflows of $250,000. Thus, its net cash flows would be $150,000 per year. However, there is a 40 percent chance the customer will not use the product, in which case the project will produce after-tax cash inflows of only $75,000. Thus, its net cash flows would be −$25,000. Write out the estimated cash flows, and calculate the project's NPV under each of the two scenarios.
   (3) While 21st Century does not have the option to delay the project, it will know 1 year from now if the key customer has selected the product. If the customer chooses not to adopt the product, 21st Century has the option to abandon the project. If it abandons the project, it will not receive any cash flows after Year 1, and it will not incur any operating costs after Year 1.

Thus, if the company chooses to abandon the project, its estimated cash flows are as follows:

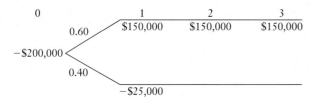

Again, assuming a cost of capital of 10 percent, what is the project's expected NPV if it abandons the project? Should 21st Century invest in Project Y today, realizing it has the option to abandon the project at t = 1?

(4) Up until now we have assumed that the abandonment option has not affected the project's cost of capital. Is this assumption reasonable? How might the abandonment option affect the cost of capital?

f. Finally, 21st Century is also considering Project Z. Project Z has an up-front cost of $500,000, and it is expected to produce after-tax cash inflows of $100,000 at the end of each of the next 5 years (t = 1, 2, 3, 4, and 5). Because Project Z has a cost of capital of 12 percent, it clearly has a negative NPV. However, Keller and his group recognize that if 21st Century goes ahead with Project Z today, there is a 10 percent chance that this will lead to subsequent opportunities that have a net present value at t = 5 equal to $3,000,000. At the same time, there is a 90 percent chance that the subsequent opportunities will have a negative net present value (−$1,000,000) at t = 5. On the basis of their knowledge of real options, Keller and his group understand that the company will choose to develop these subsequent opportunities only if they appear to be profitable at t = 5. Given this information, should 21st Century invest in Project Z today?

CYBER PROBLEM

Please go to our web site **http://brigham.swlearning.com** to access the Cyberproblems.

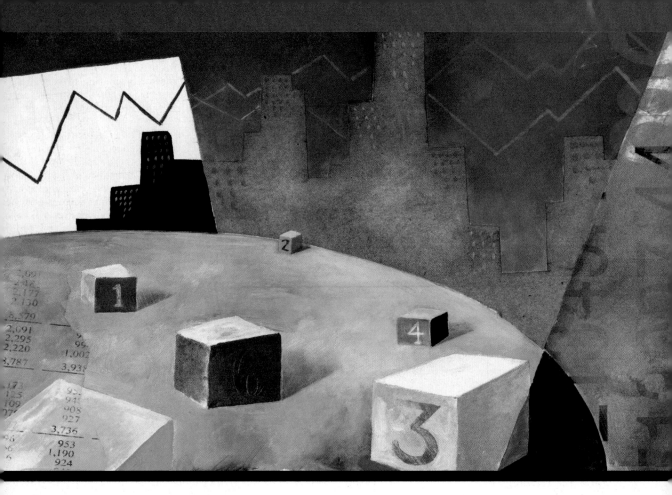

PART 5

CAPITAL STRUCTURE AND DIVIDEND POLICY

CAPITAL STRUCTURE AND LEVERAGE

DEBT: ROCKET BOOSTER
OR ANCHOR?

KELLOGG CO.

When a firm expands, it needs capital, and that capital can come from debt or equity. Debt has two important advantages. First, interest paid is tax deductible, which lowers debt's effective cost. Second, debtholders get a fixed return, so stockholders do not have to share their profits if the business is extremely successful.

However, debt also has disadvantages. First, the higher the debt ratio, the riskier the company, hence the higher its cost of both debt and equity. Second, if a company falls on hard times and operating income is not sufficient to cover interest charges, its stockholders will have to make up the shortfall, and if they cannot, bankruptcy will result. Good times may be just around the corner, but too much debt can keep the company from getting there and thus can wipe out the stockholders.

Companies with volatile earnings and operating cash flows therefore limit their use of debt. On the other hand, companies with less business risk and more stable operating cash flows can take on more debt. Kellogg Co., the world's largest cereal manufacturer, is a good example of a company that uses a lot of debt financing. Indeed, in May 2002, Kellogg was financed with 86 percent debt and 14 percent equity.

At first glance, an 86 percent debt ratio seems extraordinarily high. In the past, there have been numerous examples of high debt pushing otherwise well-regarded companies into bankruptcy. No doubt aware of these concerns, Kellogg's management is surely keeping an eye on its debt ratio. Commenting on Kellogg's capital structure, a recent *Value Line* report suggested that the company was "producing strong cash flow, which will help reduce the recent surge in long-term debt."

At the same time, Kellogg's high debt ratio is perhaps not too bad, given the stability of its business. After all, the consumption of Frosted Flakes and Pop Tarts has historically remained stable even during economic downturns. Moreover, if we examine Kellogg's capital structure in more detail, it soon becomes apparent that there is more here than meets the eye. According to its balance sheet, Kellogg has about $6 billion of total debt versus stockholders' equity of about $1 billion. But in May 2002, the market capitalization of Kellogg's equity (which is simply the stock price times the number of shares outstanding) was approximately $15 billion. From a market value perspective, Kellogg's capital structure ($6 billion of debt and $15 billion of equity) is much more conservative, which helps explain why the company has a relatively strong BBB-level bond rating.

Kellogg and other companies can finance with either debt or equity. Is one better than the other? If so, should firms be financed either with all debt or all equity? If the best solution is some mix of debt and equity, what is the optimal mix? In this chapter, we discuss the key facets of the debt-versus-equity, or capital structure, decision. As you read the chapter, think about these concepts and consider how they can aid managers as they make capital structure decisions.

Two video clips of Steve Walsh, Assistant Treasurer at JCPenney, talking about capital structure are available at **http://fisher.osu.edu/fin/clips.htm**. The first clip on capital structure discusses the cost of capital and debt, while the second clip discusses optimal capital structure at JCPenney relative to the capital structure theory of Modigliani/Miller.

In Chapter 9, when we calculated the weighted average cost of capital for use in capital budgeting, we assumed that the firm had a specific target capital structure. However, the optimal capital structure may change over time, changes in capital structure affect the riskiness and cost of each type of capital, and all this can change the weighted average cost of capital. Moreover, a change in the cost of capital can affect capital budgeting decisions and, ultimately, the firm's stock price.

Many factors influence the capital structure decision, and, as you will see, determining the optimal capital structure is not an exact science. Therefore, even firms in the same industry often have dramatically different capital structures. In this chapter we first consider the effect of capital structure on risk, and then we use these insights to help answer the question of how firms should determine the mix of debt and equity used to finance their operations. ■

THE TARGET CAPITAL STRUCTURE

Target Capital Structure
The mix of debt, preferred stock, and common equity with which the firm plans to raise capital.

Firms should first analyze a number of factors, then establish a **target capital structure.** This target may change over time as conditions change, but at any given moment, management should have a specific capital structure in mind. If the actual debt ratio is below the target level, expansion capital should generally be raised by issuing debt, whereas if the debt ratio is above the target, equity should generally be issued.

Capital structure policy involves a trade-off between risk and return:

- Using more debt raises the risk borne by stockholders.
- However, using more debt generally leads to a higher expected rate of return on equity.

Higher risk tends to lower a stock's price, but a higher expected rate of return raises it. *Therefore, the optimal capital structure must strike a balance between risk and return so as to maximize the firm's stock price.*

Four primary factors influence capital structure decisions.

1. *Business risk*, or the riskiness inherent in the firm's operations if it used no debt. The greater the firm's business risk, the lower its optimal debt ratio.
2. The firm's *tax position*. A major reason for using debt is that interest is tax deductible, which lowers the effective cost of debt. However, if most of a firm's income is already sheltered from taxes by depreciation tax shields, by interest

on currently outstanding debt, or by tax loss carry-forwards, its tax rate will be low, so additional debt will not be as advantageous as it would be to a firm with a higher effective tax rate.

3. *Financial flexibility*, or the ability to raise capital on reasonable terms under adverse conditions. Corporate treasurers know that a steady supply of capital is necessary for stable operations, which is vital for long-run success. They also know that when money is tight in the economy, or when a firm is experiencing operating difficulties, suppliers of capital prefer to provide funds to companies with strong balance sheets. Therefore, both the potential future need for funds and the consequences of a funds shortage influence the target capital structure—the greater the probable future need for capital, and the worse the consequences of a capital shortage, the stronger the balance sheet should be.

4. *Managerial conservatism or aggressiveness*. Some managers are more aggressive than others, hence some firms are more inclined to use debt in an effort to boost profits. This factor does not affect the true optimal, or value-maximizing, capital structure, but it does influence the manager-determined target capital structure.

These four points largely determine the target capital structure, but operating conditions can cause the actual capital structure to vary from the target. For example, a company may have a target debt ratio of 50 percent, but unforeseen circumstances may force it to write down its common equity, which in turn would raise its debt ratio above the target level. Presumably, this company would take steps in the future to return its capital structure to its target level.

SELF-TEST QUESTIONS

What four factors affect the target capital structure?

In what sense does capital structure policy involve a trade-off between risk and return?

BUSINESS AND FINANCIAL RISK

In Chapter 5, when we examined risk from the viewpoint of a stock investor, we distinguished between *market risk*, which is measured by the firm's beta coefficient, and *stand-alone risk*, which includes both market risk and an element of risk that can be eliminated by diversification. Now we introduce two new dimensions of risk: (1) *business risk*, or the riskiness of the firm's stock if it uses no debt, and (2) *financial risk*, which is the additional risk placed on the common stockholders as a result of the firm's decision to use debt.[1]

Conceptually, the firm has a certain amount of risk inherent in its operations: this is its business risk. If it uses debt, then, in effect, it partitions its investors into two groups and concentrates most of its business risk on one class of investors—the

---

[1] Preferred stock also adds to financial risk. To simplify matters, we concentrate on debt and common equity in this chapter.

common stockholders. However, the common stockholders will demand compensation for assuming more risk and thus require a higher rate of return. In this section, we examine business and financial risk within a stand-alone risk framework, which ignores the benefits of stockholder diversification.

BUSINESS RISK

Business Risk
The riskiness inherent in the firm's operations if it uses no debt.

Business risk in a stand-alone sense is a function of the uncertainty inherent in projections of a firm's return on invested capital (ROIC), defined as follows:

$$ROIC = \frac{NOPAT}{Capital} = \frac{\begin{array}{c}\text{Net income to}\\\text{common stockholders}\end{array} + \begin{array}{c}\text{After-tax}\\\text{interest payments}\end{array}}{Capital}.$$

Here NOPAT is net operating profit after taxes and capital is the sum of the firm's debt and common equity. (We ignore preferred stock in this section.) If a firm uses no debt, then its interest payments will be zero, its capital will be all equity, and its ROIC will equal its return on equity, ROE:

$$ROIC \text{ (zero debt)} = ROE = \frac{\text{Net income to common stockholders}}{\text{Common equity}}.$$

Therefore, the business risk of a *leverage-free* firm can be measured by the standard deviation of its ROE, σ_{ROE}.

To illustrate, consider Bigbee Electronics Company, a *debt-free (unlevered)* firm. Figure 13-1 gives some clues about the company's business risk. The top graph shows the trend in ROE from 1992 through 2002; this graph gives both security analysts and Bigbee's management an idea of the degree to which ROE has varied in the past and might vary in the future.

The lower graph shows the beginning-of-year subjectively estimated probability distribution of Bigbee's ROE for 2002, based on the trend line in the top section of Figure 13-1. As both graphs indicate, Bigbee's actual ROE in 2002 was only 8 percent, well below the expected value of 12 percent—2002 was a bad year.

Bigbee's past fluctuations in ROE were caused by many factors—booms and recessions in the national economy, successful new products introduced both by Bigbee and by its competitors, labor strikes, a fire in Bigbee's main plant, and so on. Similar events will doubtless occur in the future, and when they do, the realized ROE will be higher or lower than the projected level. Further, there is always the possibility that a long-term disaster will strike, permanently depressing the company's earning power; for example, a competitor might introduce a new product that would permanently lower Bigbee's earnings. This uncertainty regarding Bigbee's future ROE, *assuming the firm uses no debt financing*, is defined as the company's *business risk*. Because Bigbee uses no debt, stockholders bear all of the company's business risk.

Business risk varies not only from industry to industry but also among firms in a given industry. Further, business risk can change over time. For example, the electric utilities were regarded for years as having little business risk, but a combination of events in recent years altered the utilities' situation, producing sharp declines in their ROEs and greatly increasing the industry's business risk. Now, food processors and grocery retailers frequently are given as examples of industries with low business risk,

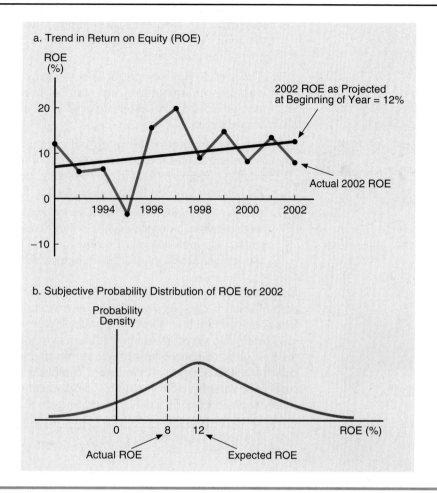

a. Trend in Return on Equity (ROE)

b. Subjective Probability Distribution of ROE for 2002

while cyclical manufacturing industries such as autos and steel, as well as many small startup companies, are regarded as having especially high business risk.[2]

Business risk depends on a number of factors, the more important of which are listed below:

1. *Demand variability.* The more stable the demand for a firm's products, other things held constant, the lower its business risk.

2. *Sales price variability.* Firms whose products are sold in highly volatile markets are exposed to more business risk than similar firms whose output prices are more stable.

---

[2] We have avoided any discussion of market versus company-specific risk in this section. We note now (1) that any action that increases business risk in the stand-alone risk sense will generally also increase a firm's beta coefficient and (2) that a part of business risk as we define it will generally be company-specific, hence subject to elimination by diversification by the firm's stockholders.

3. *Input cost variability*. Firms whose input costs are highly uncertain are exposed to a high degree of business risk.

4. *Ability to adjust output prices for changes in input costs*. Some firms are better able than others to raise their own output prices when input costs rise. The greater the ability to adjust output prices to reflect cost conditions, the lower the degree of business risk.

5. *Ability to develop new products in a timely, cost-effective manner*. Firms in such high-tech industries as drugs and computers depend on a constant stream of new products. The faster its products become obsolete, the greater a firm's business risk.

6. *Foreign risk exposure*. Firms that generate a high percentage of their earnings overseas are subject to earnings declines due to exchange rate fluctuations. Also, if a firm operates in a politically unstable area, it may be subject to political risks. See Chapter 19 for a further discussion.

7. *The extent to which costs are fixed: operating leverage*. If a high percentage of costs are fixed, hence do not decline when demand falls, then the firm is exposed to a relatively high degree of business risk. This factor is called *operating leverage*, and it is discussed at length in the next section.

Each of these factors is determined partly by the firm's industry characteristics, but each of them is also controllable to some extent by management. For example, most firms can, through their marketing policies, take actions to stabilize both unit sales and sales prices. However, this stabilization may require spending a great deal on advertising and/or price concessions to get commitments from customers to purchase fixed quantities at fixed prices in the future. Similarly, firms such as Bigbee Electronics can reduce the volatility of future input costs by negotiating long-term labor and materials supply contracts, but they may have to pay prices above the current spot price to obtain these contracts. Many firms are also using hedging techniques to reduce business risk, as we discuss in Chapter 18.

OPERATING LEVERAGE

As noted above, business risk depends in part on the extent to which a firm builds fixed costs into its operations—if fixed costs are high, even a small decline in sales can lead to a large decline in ROE. So, other things held constant, the higher a firm's fixed costs, the greater its business risk. Higher fixed costs are generally associated with more highly automated, capital intensive firms and industries. However, businesses that employ highly skilled workers who must be retained and paid even during recessions also have relatively high fixed costs, as do firms with high product development costs, because the amortization of development costs is an element of fixed costs.

Operating Leverage
The extent to which fixed costs are used in a firm's operations.

If a high percentage of total costs are fixed, then the firm is said to have a high degree of **operating leverage.** In physics, leverage implies the use of a lever to raise a heavy object with a small force. In politics, if people have leverage, their smallest word or action can accomplish a lot. *In business terminology, a high degree of operating leverage, other factors held constant, implies that a relatively small change in sales results in a large change in ROE.*

Figure 13-2 illustrates the concept of operating leverage by comparing the results that Bigbee could expect if it used different degrees of operating leverage. Plan A calls for a relatively small amount of fixed costs, $20,000. Here the firm would not

FIGURE 13-2   Illustration of Operating Leverage

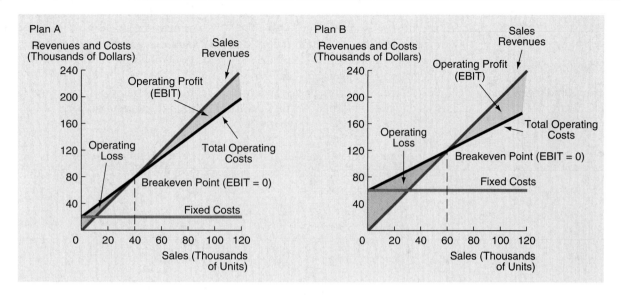

	PLAN A	PLAN B
Price	$2.00	$2.00
Variable costs	$1.50	$1.00
Fixed costs	$20,000	$60,000
Assets	$200,000	$200,000
Tax rate	40%	40%

				PLAN A				PLAN B		
DEMAND	PROBABILITY	UNITS SOLD	DOLLAR SALES	OPERATING COSTS	OPERATING PROFITS (EBIT)	NET INCOME	ROE	OPERATING COSTS	OPERATING PROFITS (EBIT)	NET INCOME	ROE
Terrible	0.05	0	$ 0	$ 20,000	($20,000)	($12,000)	−6.00%	$ 60,000	($ 60,000)	($36,000)	−18.00%
Poor	0.20	40,000	80,000	80,000	0	0	0.00	100,000	(20,000)	(12,000)	−6.00
Normal	0.50	100,000	200,000	170,000	30,000	18,000	9.00	160,000	40,000	24,000	12.00
Good	0.20	160,000	320,000	260,000	60,000	36,000	18.00	220,000	100,000	60,000	30.00
Wonderful	0.05	200,000	400,000	320,000	80,000	48,000	24.00	260,000	140,000	84,000	42.00
Expected value:		100,000	$200,000	$170,000	$30,000	$18,000	9.00%	$160,000	$ 40,000	$24,000	12.00%
Standard deviation:					$24,698		7.41%		$ 49,396		14.82%
Coefficient of variation:					0.82		0.82		1.23		1.23

NOTES: a. Operating costs = Variable costs + Fixed costs.

    b. The federal-plus-state tax rate is 40 percent, so NI = EBIT(1 − Tax rate) = EBIT(0.6).

    c. ROE = NI/Equity. The firm has no debt, so Assets = Equity = $200,000.

    d. The breakeven sales level for Plan B is not shown in the table, but it is 60,000 units or $120,000.

    e. The expected values, standard deviations, and coefficients of variation were found using the procedures discussed in Chapter 5.

have much automated equipment, so its depreciation, maintenance, property taxes, and so on would be low. However, the total operating costs line has a relatively steep slope, indicating that variable costs per unit are higher than they would be if the firm used more operating leverage. Plan B calls for a higher level of fixed costs, $60,000. Here the firm uses automated equipment (with which one operator can turn out a few or many units at the same labor cost) to a much larger extent. The breakeven point is higher under Plan B—breakeven occurs at 60,000 units under Plan B versus only 40,000 units under Plan A.

Operating Breakeven
The output quantity at which EBIT = 0.

We can calculate the breakeven quantity by recognizing that **operating breakeven** occurs when ROE = 0, hence when earnings before interest and taxes (EBIT) = 0:[3]

$$EBIT = PQ - VQ - F = 0. \tag{13-1}$$

Here P is average sales price per unit of output, Q is units of output, V is variable cost per unit, and F is fixed operating costs. If we solve for the breakeven quantity, Q_{BE}, we get this expression:

$$Q_{BE} = \frac{F}{P - V}. \tag{13-1a}$$

Thus for Plan A,

$$Q_{BE} = \frac{\$20,000}{\$2.00 - \$1.50} = 40,000 \text{ units,}$$

and for Plan B,

$$Q_{BE} = \frac{\$60,000}{\$2.00 - \$1.00} = 60,000 \text{ units.}$$

How does operating leverage affect business risk? *Other things held constant, the higher a firm's operating leverage, the higher its business risk.* This point is demonstrated in Figure 13-3, where we develop probability distributions for ROE under Plans A and B.

The top section of Figure 13-3 graphs the probability distribution of sales that was presented in tabular form in Figure 13-2. The sales probability distribution depends on how demand for the product varies, not on whether the product is manufactured by Plan A or by Plan B. Therefore, the same sales probability distribution applies to both production plans; this distribution has expected sales of $200,000, and it ranges from zero to about $400,000, with a standard deviation of $\sigma_{Sales} = \$98,793$.

We use the sales probability distribution, together with the operating costs at each sales level, to develop graphs of the ROE probability distributions under Plans A and B. These are shown in the bottom section of Figure 13-3. Plan B has a higher expected ROE, but this plan also entails a much higher probability of losses. Clearly, Plan B, the one with more fixed costs and a higher degree of operating leverage, is riskier. *In general, holding other factors constant, the higher the degree of operating leverage, the greater the firm's business risk.* In the discussion that follows, we assume that Bigbee has decided to go ahead with Plan B because they believe that the higher expected return is sufficient to compensate for the higher risk.

---

[3] This definition of breakeven does not include any fixed financial costs because Bigbee is an unlevered firm. If there were fixed financial costs, the firm would suffer an accounting loss at the operating breakeven point. We will introduce financial costs shortly.

FIGURE 13-3   Analysis of Business Risk

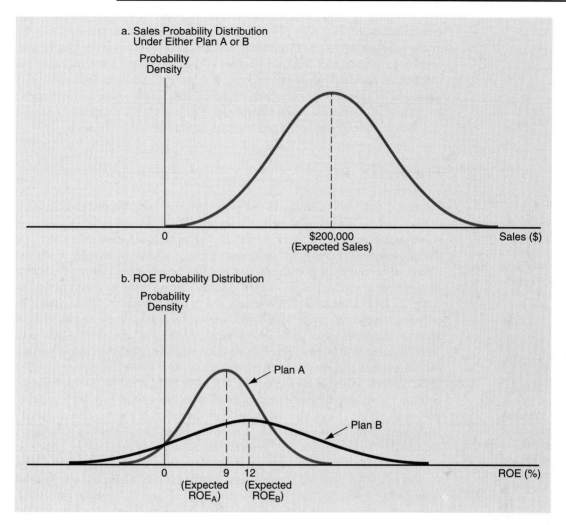

a. Sales Probability Distribution
Under Either Plan A or B

b. ROE Probability Distribution

NOTE: We are using continuous distributions to approximate the discrete distributions contained in Figure 13-2.

To what extent can firms control their operating leverage? To a large extent, operating leverage is determined by technology. Electric utilities, telephone companies, airlines, steel mills, and chemical companies simply *must* have large investments in fixed assets; this results in high fixed costs and operating leverage. Similarly, drug, auto, computer, and other companies must spend heavily to develop new products, and product-development costs increase operating leverage. Grocery stores, on the other hand, generally have significantly lower fixed costs, hence lower operating leverage. Still, although industry factors do exert a major influence, all firms have some control over their operating leverage. For example, an electric utility can expand its generating capacity by building either a gas-fired or a coal-fired plant. The coal plant would require a larger investment and would have higher fixed costs, but its variable operating costs would be relatively low. The gas-fired plant, on the other hand, would require a smaller investment and would have lower fixed costs, but the variable costs (for gas) would be high. Thus, by its capital budgeting decisions, a utility (or any other company) can influence its operating leverage, hence its business risk.

The concept of operating leverage was originally developed for use in capital budgeting. Mutually exclusive projects that involve alternative methods for producing a given product often have different degrees of operating leverage, hence different breakeven points and different degrees of risk. Bigbee Electronics and many other companies regularly undertake a type of breakeven analysis (the sensitivity analysis discussed in Chapter 11) for each proposed project as a part of their regular capital budgeting process. Still, once a corporation's operating leverage has been established, this factor exerts a major influence on its capital structure decision.

FINANCIAL RISK

Financial Risk
An increase in stockholders' risk, over and above the firm's basic business risk, resulting from the use of financial leverage.

Financial risk is the additional risk placed on the common stockholders as a result of the decision to finance with debt. Conceptually, stockholders face a certain amount of risk that is inherent in a firm's operations—this is its business risk, which is defined as the uncertainty inherent in projections of future operating income. If a firm uses debt (financial leverage), this concentrates the business risk on common stockholders. To illustrate, suppose 10 people decide to form a corporation to manufacture disk drives. There is a certain amount of business risk in the operation. If the firm is capitalized only with common equity, and if each person buys 10 percent of the stock, then each investor shares equally in the business risk. However, suppose the firm is capitalized with 50 percent debt and 50 percent equity, with five of the investors putting up their capital as debt and the other five putting up their money as equity. In this case, the five investors who put up the equity will have to bear all of the business risk, so the common stock will be twice as risky as it would have been had the firm been financed only with equity. Thus, the use of debt, or **financial leverage,** concentrates the firm's business risk on its stockholders. This concentration of business risk occurs because debtholders, who receive fixed interest payments, bear none of the business risk.

Financial Leverage
The extent to which fixed-income securities (debt and preferred stock) are used in a firm's capital structure.

To illustrate the concentration of business risk, we can extend the Bigbee Electronics example. To date, the company has never used debt, but the treasurer is now considering a possible change in the capital structure. Changes in the use of debt will cause changes in earnings per share (EPS) as well as changes in risk—both of which will affect the company's stock price. To understand the relationship between financial leverage and EPS, first consider Table 13-1, which shows how Bigbee's cost of debt would vary if it used different percentages of debt. The higher the percentage of debt, the riskier the debt, hence the higher the interest rate lenders will charge.

For now, assume that only two financing choices are being considered—remaining at 100 percent equity, or shifting to 50 percent debt and 50 percent equity. We also assume that with no debt Bigbee has 10,000 shares of common stock outstanding and, if it changes its capital structure, common stock can be repurchased at the $20 current stock price. Now consider Table 13-2, which shows how the financing choice will affect Bigbee's profitability and risk.

First focus on Section I of Table 13-2, which assumes that Bigbee uses no debt. Since debt is zero, interest is also zero, hence pre-tax income is equal to EBIT. Taxes at 40 percent are deducted to obtain net income, which is then divided by the $200,000 of equity to calculate ROE. Note that Bigbee receives a tax credit if the demand is either terrible or poor (which are the two scenarios where net income is negative). Here we assume that Bigbee's losses can be carried back to offset income earned in the

AMOUNT BORROWED[a]	DEBT/ASSETS RATIO	INTEREST RATE, k_d, ON ALL DEBT
$20,000	10%	8.0%
40,000	20	8.3
60,000	30	9.0
80,000	40	10.0
100,000	50	12.0
120,000	60	15.0

[a] We assume that the firm must borrow in increments of $20,000. We also assume that Bigbee is unable to borrow more than $120,000, which is 60 percent of its $200,000 of assets, because of restrictions in its corporate charter.

prior year. The ROE at each sales level is then multiplied by the probability of that sales level to calculate the 12 percent expected ROE. Note that this 12 percent is the same as we found in Figure 13-2 for Plan B.

Section I of Table 13-2 also calculates Bigbee's earnings per share (EPS) for each scenario under the assumption that the company continues to use no debt. Net income is divided by the 10,000 common shares outstanding to obtain EPS. If the demand is terrible, the EPS will be −$3.60, but if demand is wonderful, the EPS will rise to $8.40. The EPS at each sales level is then multiplied by the probability of that sales level to calculate the expected EPS, which is $2.40 if Bigbee uses no debt. We also calculate the standard deviation of EPS and the coefficient of variation as indicators of the firm's risk at a zero debt ratio: $\sigma_{EPS} = \$2.96$, and $CV_{EPS} = 1.23$.[4]

Now let's look at the situation if Bigbee decides to use 50 percent debt financing, shown in Section II of Table 13-2, with the debt costing 12 percent. Demand will not be affected, nor will operating costs, hence the EBIT columns are the same for the zero debt and 50 percent debt cases. However, the company will now have $100,000 of debt with a cost of 12 percent, hence its interest expense will be $12,000. This interest must be paid regardless of the state of the economy—if it is not paid, the company will be forced into bankruptcy, and stockholders will probably be wiped out. Therefore, we show a $12,000 cost in Column 4 as a fixed number for all demand conditions. Column 5 shows pre-tax income, Column 6 the applicable taxes, and Column 7 the resulting net income. When the net income figures are divided by the equity investment—which will now be only $100,000 because $100,000 of the $200,000 total requirement was obtained as debt—we find the ROEs under each demand state. If demand is terrible and sales are zero, then a very large loss will be incurred, and the ROE will be −43.2 percent. However, if demand is wonderful, then ROE will be 76.8 percent. The probability-weighted average is the expected ROE, which is 16.8 percent if the company uses 50 percent debt.

---

[4] See Chapter 5 for a review of procedures for calculating the standard deviation and coefficient of variation. Recall that the advantage of the coefficient of variation is that it permits better comparisons when the expected values of EPS vary, as they do here for the two capital structures.

TABLE 13-2

Effects of Financial Leverage: Bigbee Electronics Financed with Zero Debt or 50 Percent Debt

SECTION I. ZERO DEBT

Debt ratio	0%
Assets	$200,000
Debt	0
Equity	$200,000
Shares outstanding	10,000

DEMAND FOR PRODUCT (1)	PROBABILITY (2)	EBIT (3)	INTEREST (4)	PRE-TAX INCOME (5)	TAXES (40%) (6)	NET INCOME (7)	ROE (8)	EPS[a] (9)
Terrible	0.05	($ 60,000)	$0	($ 60,000)	($24,000)	($36,000)	−18.00%	($3.60)
Poor	0.20	(20,000)	0	(20,000)	(8,000)	(12,000)	−6.00	(1.20)
Normal	0.50	40,000	0	40,000	16,000	24,000	12.00	2.40
Good	0.20	100,000	0	100,000	40,000	60,000	30.00	6.00
Wonderful	0.05	140,000	0	140,000	56,000	84,000	42.00	8.40
Expected value:		$ 40,000	$0	$ 40,000	$16,000	$24,000	12.00%	$2.40
Standard deviation:							14.82%	$2.96
Coefficient of variation:							1.23	1.23

Assumptions: 1. In terms of its operating leverage, Bigbee has chosen Plan B. The probability distribution and EBIT are obtained from Figure 13-2.
2. Sales and operating costs, hence EBIT, are not affected by the financing decision. Therefore, EBIT under both financing plans is identical, and it is taken from the EBIT column for Plan B in Figure 13-2.
3. All losses can be carried back to offset income in the prior year.

[a] The EPS figures can also be obtained using the following formula, in which the numerator amounts to an income statement at a given sales level laid out horizontally:

$$EPS = \frac{(Sales - Fixed\ costs - Variable\ costs - Interest)(1 - Tax\ rate)}{Shares\ outstanding} = \frac{(EBIT - I)(1 - T)}{Shares\ outstanding}.$$

(note continues)

Typically, financing with debt increases the expected rate of return for an investment, but debt also increases the riskiness of the investment to the owners of the firm, its common stockholders. This situation holds with our example—financial leverage raises the expected ROE from 12 percent to 16.8 percent, but it also increases the riskiness of the investment as measured by the coefficient of variation from 1.23 to 1.76.

Figure 13-4 graphs the data in Table 13-2. It shows in another way that using financial leverage increases the expected ROE, but that leverage also flattens out the probability distribution and increases the probability of a large loss, thus increasing the risk borne by stockholders.

We can also calculate Bigbee's EPS if it is financed with 50 percent debt. Once again EPS is calculated as net income divided by shares outstanding. With debt = 0, there would be 10,000 shares outstanding. However, if half of the equity were replaced by debt (debt = $100,000), there would be only 5,000 shares outstanding, and we must use this fact to determine the EPS figures that would result at each of the

TABLE 13-2	Continued

Section II. 50% Debt

Debt ratio	50.00%
Assets	$200,000
Debt	$100,000
Interest rate	12.00%
Equity	$100,000
Shares outstanding	5,000

DEMAND FOR PRODUCT (1)	PROBABILITY (2)	EBIT (3)	INTEREST (4)	PRE-TAX INCOME (5)	TAXES (40%) (6)	NET INCOME (7)	ROE (8)	EPS[a] (9)
Terrible	0.05	($ 60,000)	$12,000	($ 72,000)	($28,800)	($43,200)	−43.20%	($8.64)
Poor	0.20	(20,000)	12,000	(32,000)	(12,800)	(19,200)	−19.20	(3.84)
Normal	0.50	40,000	12,000	28,000	11,200	16,800	16.80	3.36
Good	0.20	100,000	12,000	88,000	35,200	52,800	52.80	10.56
Wonderful	0.05	140,000	12,000	128,000	51,200	76,800	76.80	15.36
Expected value:		$ 40,000	$12,000	$ 28,000	$11,200	$16,800	16.80%	$3.36
Standard deviation:							29.64%	$5.93
Coefficient of variation:							1.76	1.76

For example, with zero debt and sales = $200,000, EPS is $2.40:

$$EPS_{D/A=0} = \frac{(\$200{,}000 - \$60{,}000 - \$100{,}000 - 0)(0.6)}{10{,}000} = \$2.40.$$

With 50 percent debt and sales = $200,000, EPS is $3.36:

$$EPS_{D/A=0.5} = \frac{(\$200{,}000 - \$60{,}000 - \$100{,}000 - \$12{,}000)(0.6)}{5{,}000} = \$3.36.$$

Refer to the tabular data given in Figure 13-2 to arrive at sales, fixed costs, and variable costs that are used in the equations above.

possible demand levels.[5] With a debt/assets ratio of 50 percent, the EPS figure would be −$8.64 if sales were terrible; it would rise to $3.36 if sales were normal; and it would soar to $15.36 if sales were wonderful.

The EPS distributions under the two financial structures are graphed in Figure 13-5, where we use continuous distributions rather than the discrete distributions contained in Table 13-2. Although expected EPS would be much higher if financial leverage were employed, the graph makes it clear that the risk of low, or even negative, EPS would also be higher if debt were used.

Another view of the relationships among expected EPS, risk, and financial leverage is presented in Figure 13-6. The tabular data in the lower section were calculated

[5] We assume in this example that the firm could change its capital structure by repurchasing common stock at its book value of $100,000/5,000 shares = $20 per share. However, the firm may actually have to pay a higher price to repurchase its stock on the open market. If Bigbee had to pay $22 per share, then it could repurchase only $100,000/$22 = 4,545 shares, and, in this case, expected EPS would be only $16,800/(10,000 − 4,545) = $16,800/5,455 = $3.08 rather than $3.36.

FIGURE 13-4

ROE Probability Distributions for Bigbee Electronics, with and without Leverage

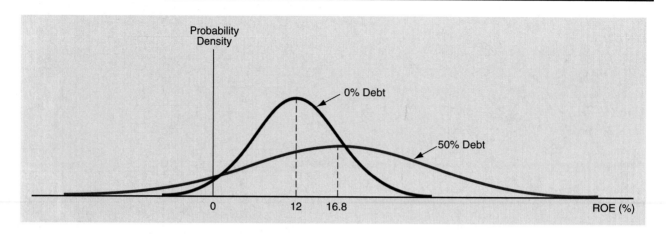

in the manner set forth in Table 13-2, and the graphs plot these data. Here we see that expected EPS rises until the firm is financed with 50 percent debt. Interest charges rise, but this effect is more than offset by the declining number of shares outstanding as debt is substituted for equity. However, EPS peaks at a debt ratio of 50 percent, beyond which interest rates rise so rapidly that EPS falls in spite of the falling number of shares outstanding.

The right panel of Figure 13-6 shows that risk, as measured by the coefficient of variation of EPS, rises continuously, and at an increasing rate, as debt is substituted for equity.

FIGURE 13-5

Probability Distributions of EPS with Different Amounts of Financial Leverage

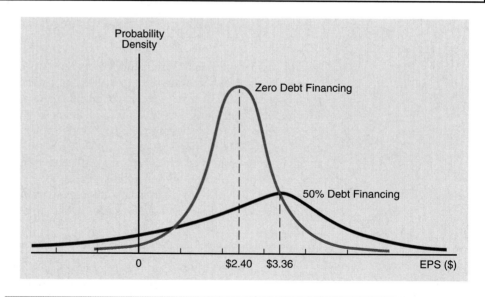

FIGURE 13-6 Relationships among Expected EPS, Risk, and Financial Leverage

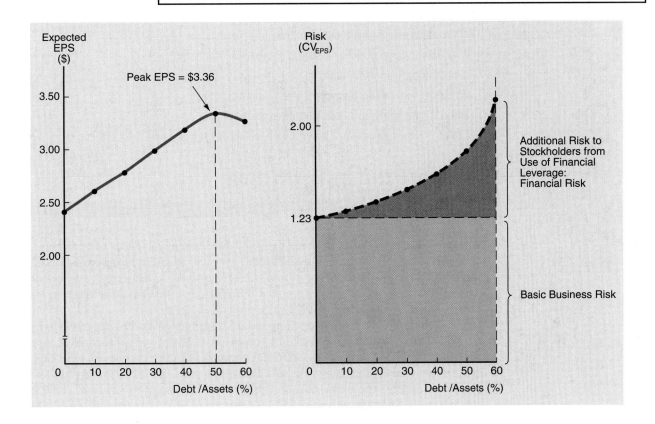

DEBT/ASSETS RATIO	EXPECTED EPS	STANDARD DEVIATION OF EPS	COEFFICIENT OF VARIATION
0%[a]	$2.40[a]	$2.96[a]	1.23[a]
10	2.56	3.29	1.29
20	2.75	3.70	1.35
30	2.97	4.23	1.43
40	3.20	4.94	1.54
50[a]	3.36[a]	5.93[a]	1.76[a]
60	3.30	7.41	2.25

[a] Values for D/A = 0 and D/A = 50 percent are taken from Table 13-2. Values at other D/A ratios were calculated similarly.

We see, then, that using leverage has both good and bad effects: higher leverage increases expected earnings per share (in this example, until the D/A ratio equals 50 percent), but it also increases risk. Clearly, Bigbee's debt ratio should not exceed 50 percent, but where, in the range of 0 to 50 percent, should it be set? This issue is discussed in the following sections.

What is business risk, and how can it be measured?

What are some determinants of business risk?

Why does business risk vary from industry to industry?

What is operating leverage?

How does operating leverage affect business risk?

What is financial risk, and how does it arise?

Explain this statement: "Using leverage has both good and bad effects."

DETERMINING THE OPTIMAL CAPITAL STRUCTURE

As we saw in Figure 13-6, Bigbee's expected EPS is maximized at a debt/assets ratio of 50 percent. Does that mean that Bigbee's optimal capital structure calls for 50 percent debt? The answer is a resounding no—*the optimal capital structure is the one that maximizes the price of the firm's stock, and this generally calls for a debt ratio that is lower than the one that maximizes expected EPS.*

Recall from Chapter 8 that stock prices are positively related to expected dividends but negatively related to the required return on equity. Firms with higher earnings are able to pay higher dividends, so to the extent that higher debt levels raise expected earnings per share, leverage works to increase the stock price. However, higher debt levels also increase the firm's risk, and that raises the cost of equity and works to reduce the stock price. So, even though increasing the debt ratio from 40 to 50 percent raises EPS, the higher EPS is more than offset by the corresponding increase in risk.

WACC AND CAPITAL STRUCTURE CHANGES

Managers should choose the capital structure that maximizes the firm's stock price. However, it is difficult to estimate how a given change in the capital structure will affect the stock price. As it turns out, however, the capital structure that maximizes the stock price is also the one that minimizes the WACC. Because it is usually easier to predict how a capital structure change will affect the WACC than the stock price, many managers use the predicted changes in the WACC to guide their capital structure decisions.

Recall from Chapter 9 that when there is no preferred stock in a firm's capital structure, the WACC is defined as follows:

$$\text{WACC} = w_d(k_d)(1 - T) + w_c(k_s)$$
$$= (D/A)(k_d)(1 - T) + (E/A)(k_s).$$

In this expression, D/A and E/A represent the debt and equity ratios, and they sum to 1.0.

Note that in Table 13-3 an increase in the debt/assets ratio raises the costs of both debt and equity. [The cost of debt, k_d, is taken from Table 13-1, but multiplied by $(1 - T)$ to put it on an after-tax basis.] Bondholders recognize that if a firm has a higher debt ratio, this increases the risk of financial distress, and more risk leads to higher interest rates.

DEBT/ ASSETS (1)	DEBT/ EQUITY[a] (2)	A–T k_d (3)	EXPECTED EPS (AND DPS)[b] (4)	ESTIMATED BETA[c] (5)	$k_s = [k_{RF} + (k_M - k_{RF})b]$[d] (6)	ESTIMATED PRICE[e] (7)	RESULTING P/E RATIO (8)	WEIGHTED AVERAGE COST OF CAPITAL, WACC[f] (9)
0%	0.00%	4.8%	$2.40	1.50	12.0%	$20.00	8.33×	12.00%
10	11.11	4.8	2.56	1.60	12.4	20.65	8.06	11.64
20	25.00	5.0	2.75	1.73	12.9	21.33	7.75	11.32
30	42.86	5.4	2.97	1.89	13.5	21.90	7.38	11.10
40	**66.67**	**6.0**	**3.20**	**2.10**	**14.4**	**22.22**	**6.94**	**11.04**
50	100.00	7.2	3.36	2.40	15.6	21.54	6.41	11.40
60	150.00	9.0	3.30	2.85	17.4	18.97	5.75	12.36

[a] $D/E = \dfrac{D/A}{1 - D/A}$.

[b] Bigbee pays all of its earnings out as dividends, so EPS = DPS.

[c] The firm's unlevered beta, b_U, is 1.5. The remaining betas were calculated using the Hamada Equation, given the unlevered beta, tax rate, and D/E ratio as inputs.

[d] We assume that $k_{RF} = 6\%$ and $k_M = 10\%$. Therefore, at debt/assets equal to zero, $k_s = 6\% + (10\% - 6\%)1.5 = 6\% + 6\% = 12\%$. Other values of k_s are calculated similarly.

[e] Since all earnings are paid out as dividends, no retained earnings will be plowed back into the business, and growth in EPS and DPS will be zero. Hence, the zero growth stock price model developed in Chapter 8 can be used to estimate the price of Bigbee's stock. For example, at Debt/Assets = 0,

$$P_0 = \frac{DPS}{k_s} = \frac{\$2.40}{0.12} = \$20.$$

Other prices were calculated similarly.

[f] Column 9 is found by use of the weighted average cost of capital (WACC) equation developed in Chapter 9:

$$WACC = w_d k_d (1 - T) + w_c k_s$$
$$= (D/A)(k_d)(1 - T) + (1 - D/A)k_s.$$

For example, at D/A = 40%,

$$WACC = 0.4(10\%)(0.6) + 0.6(14.4\%) = 11.04\%.$$

We use book weights here, but market value weights would be theoretically better. See Eugene F. Brigham and Phillip R. Daves, *Intermediate Financial Management*, 7th ed. (Cincinnati, OH: South-Western College Publishing, 2002), Chapter 9, for a discussion of this point.

In practice, financial managers use forecasting techniques to determine how changes in the debt ratio will affect the current ratio, times-interest-earned ratio, and EBITDA coverage ratio. They then discuss their pro forma financial statements with bankers and bond rating agencies, who ask probing questions and may make their own adjustments to the firm's forecasts. The bankers and rating agencies then compare the firm's ratios with those of other firms in its industry, and end up with a rating and corresponding interest rate. Moreover, if the company plans to issue bonds to the public, the SEC requires that it inform investors what the coverages will be after the new bonds have been sold. Recognizing all this, sophisticated financial managers use their forecasted ratios to predict how bankers and other lenders will judge their firms' risks and thus determine their cost of debt. Thus, they can judge quite accurately the effects of capital structure on the cost of debt.

THE HAMADA EQUATION

An increase in the debt ratio also increases the risk faced by shareholders, and this has an effect on the cost of equity, k_s. This relationship is harder to quantify, but it can be done. To begin, recall from Chapter 5 that a stock's beta is the relevant measure of risk for diversified investors. Moreover, it has been demonstrated, both theoretically and empirically, that beta increases with financial leverage. Indeed, Robert Hamada developed the following equation to specify the effect of financial leverage on beta:[6]

$$b = b_U[1 + (1 - T)(D/E)]. \qquad (13\text{-}2)$$

The Hamada equation shows how increases in the debt/equity ratio increase beta. Here b_U is the firm's unlevered beta coefficient, that is, the beta it would have if it has no debt. In that case, beta would depend entirely upon business risk and thus be a measure of the firm's "basic business risk." D/E is the measure of financial leverage used in the Hamada equation.[7]

Note that beta is the only variable under management's control in the cost of equity equation, $k_s = k_{RF} + (k_M - k_{RF})b_i$. Both k_{RF} and k_M are determined by market forces that are beyond the firm's control. However, b_i is determined (1) by the firm's operating decisions as discussed earlier in the chapter, which affect b_U, and (2) by its capital structure decisions as reflected in its D/A (or D/E) ratio.

Unlevered Beta, b_U
The firm's beta coefficient if it has no debt.

As a starting point, a firm can take its current beta, tax rate, and debt/equity ratio and calculate its **unlevered beta, b_U,** by simply transforming Equation 13-2 as follows:

$$b_U = b/[1 + (1 - T)(D/E)]. \qquad (13\text{-}2a)$$

Then, once b_U is determined, the Hamada equation can be used to estimate how changes in the debt/equity ratio would affect the leveraged beta, b_i, and thus the cost of equity, k_s.

We can illustrate the procedure with Bigbee Electronics. First, we assume that the risk-free rate of return, k_{RF}, is 6 percent, and that the required return on an average stock, k_M, is 10 percent. Next, we need the unlevered beta, b_U. Because Bigbee has

---

[6] See Robert S. Hamada, "Portfolio Analysis, Market Equilibrium, and Corporation Finance," *Journal of Finance*, March 1969, 13–31. Note that Thomas Conine and Maurry Tamarkin have extended Hamada's work to include risky debt. See "Divisional Cost of Capital Estimation: Adjusting for Leverage," *Financial Management*, Spring 1985, 54–58. See also Eugene F. Brigham and Phillip R. Daves, *Intermediate Financial Management*, 7th ed. (Cincinnati, OH: South-Western College Publishing, 2002), Chapter 15, for a more detailed discussion of the Hamada equation.

[7] Recall from Chapter 3 that the debt/equity ratio, D/E, is directly related to the D/A ratio:

$$\frac{D}{E} = \frac{D/A}{1 - D/A}.$$

For example, if the firm has $40 of debt and $60 of equity, then D/A = 0.4, E/A = 0.6, and

$$\frac{D}{E} = \frac{0.4}{1 - 0.4} = 0.4/0.6 = 0.6667.$$

Thus any D/A ratio can be directly translated into a D/E ratio. Note also that Hamada's equation assumes that assets are reported at market values rather than accounting book values. This point is discussed at length in Brigham and Daves, *Intermediate Financial Management*, where the feedbacks among capital structure, stock prices, and capital costs are developed.

no debt, its D/E = 0. Therefore, its current beta of 1.5 is also its unlevered beta; hence $b_U = 1.5$. Now, with b_U, k_{RF}, and k_M specified, we can use the CAPM to estimate how much Bigbee's market beta would rise if it began to use financial leverage, hence what its cost of equity would be at different capital structures. These beta estimates are shown in Column 5 of Table 13-3.

Currently, based on Plan B and no debt, Bigbee has a beta of b = 1.5. Further, the risk-free rate is $k_{RF} = 6\%$ and the market risk premium is $k_M - k_{RF} = 10\% - 6\% = 4\%$. Therefore, Bigbee's current cost of equity is 12 percent as shown in Column 6:

$$k_s = k_{RF} + \text{Risk premium}$$
$$= 6\% + (4\%)(1.5)$$
$$= 6\% + 6\% = 12\%.$$

The first 6 percent is the risk-free rate, the second the risk premium. Because Bigbee currently uses no debt, it has no financial risk. Therefore, the 6 percent risk premium reflects only its business risk.

If Bigbee changes its capital structure by adding debt, this would increase the risk stockholders bear. That, in turn, would result in an additional risk premium. Conceptually, this situation would exist:

$$k_s = k_{RF} + \text{Premium for business risk} + \text{Premium for financial risk.}$$

Figure 13-7 (using data calculated in Column 6 of Table 13-3) graphs Bigbee's required return on equity at different debt ratios. As the figure shows, k_s consists of the 6 percent risk-free rate, a constant 6 percent premium for business risk, and a premium for financial risk that starts at zero but rises at an increasing rate as the debt ratio increases.

THE OPTIMAL CAPITAL STRUCTURE

Column 9 of Table 13-3 shows Bigbee's weighted average cost of capital, WACC, at different capital structures. Currently, it has no debt, so its capital structure is 100 percent equity, and at this point WACC = k_s = 12%. As Bigbee begins to use lower-cost debt, the WACC declines. However, as the debt ratio increases, the costs of both debt and equity rise, at first slowly but then at a faster and faster rate. Eventually, the increasing costs of the two components offset the fact that more low-cost debt is being used. At 40 percent debt, the WACC hits a minimum of 11.04 percent, and after that it rises with further increases in the debt ratio.

Note too that even though the component cost of equity is generally higher than that of debt, using only lower-cost debt would not maximize value because of the feedback effects of debt on the costs of debt and equity. If Bigbee were to issue more than 40 percent debt, it would then be relying more on the cheaper source of capital, but this lower cost would be more than offset by the fact that using more debt would raise the costs of both debt and equity. These thoughts were echoed in a recent Annual Report of the Georgia-Pacific Corporation:

> On a market-value basis, our debt-to-capital ratio was 47 percent. By employing this capital structure, we believe that our weighted average cost of capital is nearly optimized—at approximately 10 percent. Although reducing debt significantly would somewhat reduce the marginal cost of debt, significant debt reduction would likely increase our weighted average cost of capital by raising the proportion of higher-cost equity.

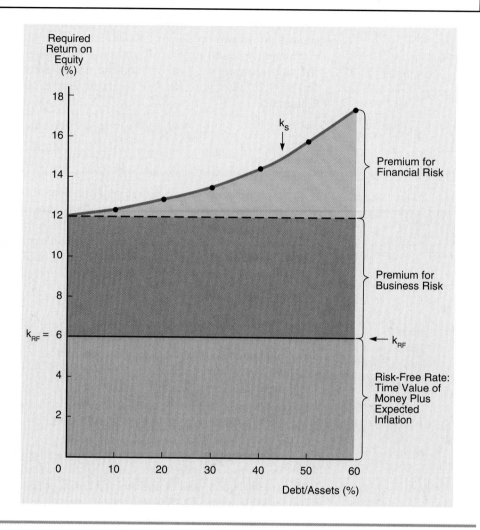

Finally, recall that the capital structure that minimizes the WACC is also the capital structure that maximizes the firm's stock price. In principle, we could use the stock valuation techniques described in Chapter 8 to predict how changes in capital structure would affect the stock price. This exercise is difficult, especially for firms that do not pay a dividend or whose cash flows are not constant over time. However, Bigbee pays out all of its earnings as dividends, so it plows none of its earnings back into the business and its growth in earnings and dividends per share are zero. Thus, in Bigbee's case we can use the zero growth stock price model developed in Chapter 8 to estimate the stock price at each different capital structure. These estimates are shown in Column 7 of Table 13-3. Here we see that the expected stock price first rises with financial leverage, hits a peak of $22.22 at a debt ratio of 40 percent, and then begins to decline. *Thus, Bigbee's optimal capital structure occurs at a debt ratio of 40 percent, and that debt ratio both maximizes its stock price and minimizes its WACC.*

The EPS, cost of capital, and stock price data shown in Table 13-3 are plotted in Figure 13-8. As the graph shows, the debt/assets ratio that maximizes Bigbee's expected EPS is 50 percent. However, the expected stock price is maximized, and the cost of capital is minimized, at a 40 percent debt ratio. *Thus, Bigbee's optimal capital structure calls for 40 percent debt and 60 percent equity.* Management should set its target capital structure at these ratios, and if the existing ratios are off target, it should move toward the target when new security offerings are made.

FIGURE 13-8	Effects of Capital Structure on EPS, Cost of Capital, and Stock Price

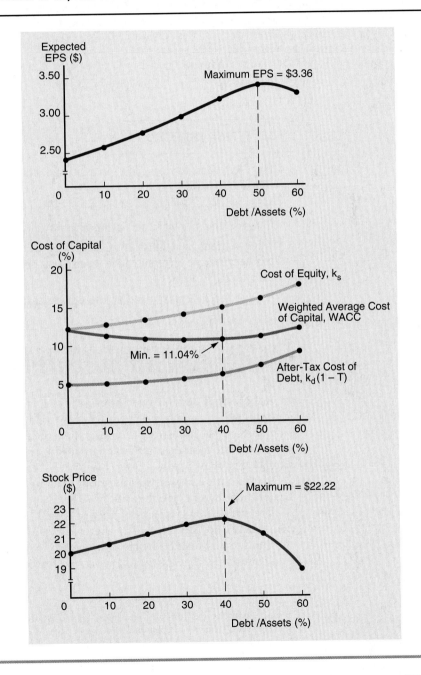

YOGI BERRA ON THE M&M PROPOSITION

When a waitress asked Yogi Berra (Baseball Hall of Fame catcher for the New York Yankees) whether he wanted his pizza cut into four pieces or eight, Yogi replied: "Better make it four. I don't think I can eat eight."[a]

Yogi's quip helps convey the basic insight of Modigliani and Miller. The firm's choice of leverage "slices" the distribution of future cash flows in a way that is like slicing a pizza. M&M recognize that if you fix a company's investment activities, it's like fixing the size of the pizza; no information costs means that everyone sees the same pizza; no taxes means the IRS gets none of the pie; and no "contracting" costs means nothing sticks to the knife.

So, just as the substance of Yogi's meal is unaffected by whether the pizza is sliced into four pieces or eight, the economic substance of the firm is unaffected by whether the liability side of the balance sheet is sliced to include more or less debt under the M&M assumptions.

[a] Lee Green, *Sportswit* (New York: Fawcett Crest, 1984), 228.

SOURCE: "Yogi Berra on the M&M Proposition," *Journal of Applied Corporate Finance*, Vol. 7, No. 4, Winter 1995, 6. Used by permission.

SELF-TEST QUESTIONS

What happens to the costs of debt and equity when the debt/assets ratio increases? Explain.

Using the Hamada equation, show the effect of financial leverage on beta.

Give the equation for calculating a firm's unlevered beta.

Using a graph and illustrative data, identify the premiums for financial risk and business risk at different debt levels. Do these premiums vary depending on the debt level? Explain.

Is expected EPS maximized at the optimal capital structure?

CAPITAL STRUCTURE THEORY

In the previous section, we showed how a firm might estimate its optimal capital structure. For a number of reasons, we would expect capital structures to vary considerably across industries. For example, pharmaceutical companies generally have very different capital structures than airline companies. Moreover, capital structures vary among firms within a given industry. What factors can explain these differences? In an attempt to answer this question, academics and practitioners developed a number of theories, and the theories have been subjected to empirical tests.

Modern capital structure theory began in 1958, when Professors Franco Modigliani and Merton Miller (hereafter MM) published what has been called the most influential finance article ever written.[8] MM proved, under a very restrictive set of assumptions, that a firm's value is unaffected by its capital structure. Put another

---

[8] Franco Modigliani and Merton H. Miller, "The Cost of Capital, Corporation Finance, and the Theory of Investment," *American Economic Review*, June 1958. Modigliani and Miller both won Nobel Prizes for their work.

way, MM's results suggest that it does not matter how a firm finances its operations, hence capital structure is irrelevant. However, MM's study was based on some unrealistic assumptions, including the following:

1. There are no brokerage costs.
2. There are no taxes.
3. There are no bankruptcy costs.
4. Investors can borrow at the same rate as corporations.
5. All investors have the same information as management about the firm's future investment opportunities.
6. EBIT is not affected by the use of debt.

Despite the fact that some of these assumptions are obviously unrealistic, MM's irrelevance result is extremely important. By indicating the conditions under which capital structure is irrelevant, MM also provided us with clues about what is required for capital structure to be relevant and hence to affect a firm's value. MM's work marked the beginning of modern capital structure research, and subsequent research has focused on relaxing the MM assumptions in order to develop a more realistic theory of capital structure. Research in this area is quite extensive, but the highlights are summarized in the following sections.

THE EFFECT OF TAXES

MM published a follow-up paper in 1963 in which they relaxed the assumption that there are no corporate taxes.[9] The Tax Code allows corporations to deduct interest payments as an expense, but dividend payments to stockholders are not deductible. This differential treatment encourages corporations to use debt in their capital structures. Indeed, MM demonstrated that if all their other assumptions hold, this differential treatment leads to a situation that calls for 100 percent debt financing.

However, this conclusion was modified several years later by Merton Miller (this time without Modigliani) when he brought in the effects of personal taxes.[10] He noted that all of the income from bonds is generally interest, which is taxed as personal income at rates going up to 38.6 percent, while income from stocks generally comes partly from capital gains. Further, long-term capital gains are generally taxed at a rate of 20 percent, and this tax is deferred until the stock is sold and the gain realized. If a stock is held until the owner dies, no capital gains tax whatever must be paid. So, on balance, returns on common stocks are taxed at lower effective rates than returns on debt.

Because of the tax situation, Miller argued that investors are willing to accept relatively low before-tax returns on stock relative to the before-tax returns on bonds. (The situation here is similar to that with tax-exempt municipal bonds as discussed in Chapter 7 and preferred stocks held by corporate investors as discussed in Chapter 8.) For example, an investor might require a return of 10 percent on Bigbee's bonds, and if stock income were taxed at the same rate as bond income, the required rate of return on Bigbee's stock might be 16 percent because of the stock's greater

---

[9] Franco Modigliani and Merton H. Miller, "Corporate Income Taxes and the Cost of Capital: A Correction," *American Economic Review*, Vol. 53, June 1963, 433–443.

[10] Merton H. Miller, "Debt and Taxes," *Journal of Finance*, Vol. 32, May 1977, 261–275.

risk. However, in view of the favorable treatment of income on the stock, investors might be willing to accept a before-tax return of only 14 percent on the stock.

Thus, as Miller pointed out, (1) the *deductibility of interest* favors the use of debt financing, but (2) the *more favorable tax treatment of income from stocks* lowers the required rate of return on stock and thus favors the use of equity financing. It is difficult to say what the net effect of these two factors is. Most observers believe that interest deductibility has the stronger effect, hence that our tax system still favors the corporate use of debt. However, that effect is certainly reduced by the lower long-term capital gains tax rate. More recently, John Graham has estimated the overall tax benefits of debt financing. His estimates suggest that the tax benefits associated with debt financing equal about 7 percent of the average firm's value. Graham's analysis also leads him to conclude that some very conservative firms may be overly reluctant to use debt financing.[11]

One can observe changes in corporate financing patterns following major changes in tax rates. For example, in 1993 the top personal tax rate on interest and dividends was raised sharply, but the capital gains tax rate was not increased. This could be expected to result in greater reliance on equity financing, especially through retained earnings, and that has indeed been the case. The lowering of the long-term capital gains tax rate in 1997 has continued this trend.

THE EFFECT OF POTENTIAL BANKRUPTCY

MM's irrelevance results also depend on the assumption that firms do not go bankrupt, hence that there are no bankruptcy costs. However, in practice bankruptcy exists, and it can be quite costly. Firms in bankruptcy have very high legal and accounting expenses, and they also have a hard time retaining customers, suppliers, and employees. Moreover, bankruptcy often forces a firm to liquidate or sell assets for less than they would be worth if the firm were to continue operating. For example, if a steel manufacturer goes out of business, it might be hard to find buyers for the company's blast furnaces, even though they were quite expensive. Assets such as plant and equipment are often illiquid because they are configured to a company's individual needs and also because they are difficult to disassemble and move.

Note, too, that the *threat of bankruptcy*, not just bankruptcy per se, brings about these problems. Key employees jump ship, suppliers refuse to grant credit, customers seek more stable suppliers, and lenders demand higher interest rates and impose more restrictive loan covenants if potential bankruptcy looms.

Bankruptcy-related problems are more likely to arise when a firm includes more debt in its capital structure. Therefore, bankruptcy costs discourage firms from pushing their use of debt to excessive levels.

Bankruptcy-related costs have two components: (1) the probability of their occurrence and (2) the costs they would produce given that financial distress has arisen. Firms whose earnings are more volatile, all else equal, face a greater chance of bankruptcy and, therefore, should use less debt than more stable firms. This is consistent with our earlier point that firms with high operating leverage, and thus greater business risk, should limit their use of financial leverage. Likewise, firms that would face high costs in the event of financial distress should rely less heavily on debt. For

---

[11] John R. Graham, "How Big Are the Tax Benefits of Debt?" *Journal of Finance*, Vol. 55, 2000, 1901–1941; and "Estimating the Tax Benefits of Debt," *Journal of Applied Corporate Finance*, Vol. 14, No. 1, Spring 2001, 42–54.

example, firms whose assets are illiquid and thus would have to be sold at "fire sale" prices should limit their use of debt financing.

TRADE-OFF THEORY

The preceding arguments led to the development of what is called "the trade-off theory of leverage," in which firms trade off the benefits of debt financing (favorable corporate tax treatment) against the higher interest rates and bankruptcy costs. A summary of the trade-off theory is expressed graphically in Figure 13-9. Here are some observations about the figure:

1. The fact that interest is a deductible expense makes debt less expensive than common or preferred stock. In effect, the government pays part of the cost of debt capital, or, to put it another way, debt provides *tax shelter benefits*. As a result, using debt causes more of the firm's operating income (EBIT) to flow through to investors. Therefore, the more debt a company uses, the higher its value and stock price. Under the assumptions of the Modigliani-Miller with-taxes paper, a firm's stock price will be maximized if it uses virtually 100 percent debt, and the line labeled "MM Result Incorporating the Effects of Corporate Taxation" in Figure 13-9 expresses the relationship between stock prices and debt under their assumptions.

2. In the real world, firms rarely use 100 percent debt. The primary reason is that firms limit their use of debt to hold down bankruptcy-related costs.

FIGURE 13-9   **Effect of Leverage on the Value of Bigbee's Stock**

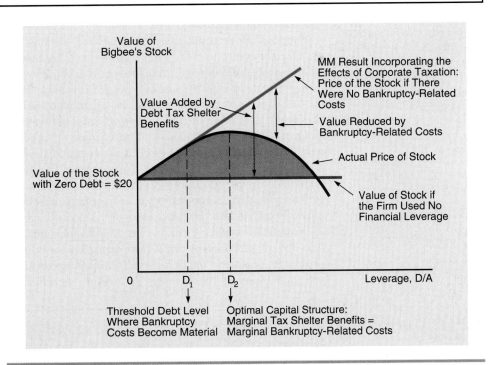

3. There is some threshold level of debt, labeled D_1 in Figure 13-9, below which the probability of bankruptcy is so low as to be immaterial. Beyond D_1, however, bankruptcy-related costs become increasingly important, and they reduce the tax benefits of debt at an increasing rate. In the range from D_1 to D_2, bankruptcy-related costs reduce but do not completely offset the tax benefits of debt, so the firm's stock price rises (but at a decreasing rate) as its debt ratio increases. However, beyond D_2, bankruptcy-related costs exceed the tax benefits, so from this point on increasing the debt ratio lowers the value of the stock. Therefore, D_2 is the optimal capital structure. Of course, D_1 and D_2 vary from firm to firm, depending on their business risk and bankruptcy costs.

4. While theoretical and empirical work supports the general shape of the curves in Figures 13-8 and 13-9, these graphs must be taken as approximations, not as precisely defined functions. The numbers in Figure 13-8 are shown out to two decimal places, but that is merely for illustrative purposes—the numbers are not nearly that accurate in view of the fact that the data on which the graph is based are judgmental estimates.

5. Another disturbing aspect of capital structure theory as expressed in Figure 13-9 is the fact that many large, successful firms, such as Intel and Microsoft, use far less debt than the theory suggests. This point led to the development of signaling theory, which is discussed below.

SIGNALING THEORY

MM assumed that investors have the same information about a firm's prospects as its managers—this is called **symmetric information.** However, in fact managers often have better information than outside investors. This is called **asymmetric information,** and it has an important effect on the optimal capital structure. To see why, consider two situations, one in which the company's managers know that its prospects are extremely favorable (Firm F) and one in which the managers know that the future looks unfavorable (Firm U).

Suppose, for example, that Firm F's R&D labs have just discovered a nonpatentable cure for the common cold. They want to keep the new product a secret as long as possible to delay competitors' entry into the market. New plants must be built to make the new product, so capital must be raised. How should Firm F's management raise the needed capital? If the firm sells stock, then, when profits from the new product start flowing in, the price of the stock would rise sharply, and the purchasers of the new stock would make a bonanza. The current stockholders (including the managers) would also do well, but not as well as they would have done if the company had not sold stock before the price increased, because then they would not have had to share the benefits of the new product with the new stockholders. *Therefore, one would expect a firm with very favorable prospects to try to avoid selling stock and, rather, to raise any required new capital by other means, including using debt beyond the normal target capital structure.*[12]

Now let's consider Firm U. Suppose its managers have information that new orders are off sharply because a competitor has installed new technology that has improved its products' quality. Firm U must upgrade its own facilities, at a high cost, just to maintain its current sales. As a result, its return on investment will fall (but not

---

[12] It would be illegal for Firm F's managers to personally purchase more shares on the basis of their inside knowledge of the new product. They could be sent to jail if they did.

by as much as if it took no action, which would lead to a 100 percent loss through bankruptcy). How should Firm U raise the needed capital? Here the situation is just the reverse of that facing Firm F, which did not want to sell stock so as to avoid having to share the benefits of future developments. *A firm with unfavorable prospects would want to sell stock, which would mean bringing in new investors to share the losses.*[13]

The conclusion from all this is that firms with extremely bright prospects prefer not to finance through new stock offerings, whereas firms with poor prospects do like to finance with outside equity. How should you, as an investor, react to this conclusion? You ought to say, "If I see that a company plans to issue new stock, this should worry me because I know that management would not want to issue stock if future prospects looked good. However, management would want to issue stock if things looked bad. Therefore, I should lower my estimate of the firm's value, other things held constant, if it plans to issue new stock."

If you gave the above answer, your views are consistent with those of sophisticated portfolio managers of institutions such as Morgan Guaranty Trust, Prudential Insurance, and so forth. *In a nutshell, the announcement of a stock offering is generally taken as a* **signal** *that the firm's prospects as seen by its management are not bright.* This, in turn, suggests that when a firm announces a new stock offering, more often than not, the price of its stock will decline. Empirical studies have shown that this situation does indeed exist.[14]

What are the implications of all this for capital structure decisions? Since issuing stock emits a negative signal and thus tends to depress the stock price, even if the company's prospects are bright, a firm should, in normal times, maintain a **reserve borrowing capacity** that can be used in the event that some especially good investment opportunity comes along. *This means that firms should, in normal times, use more equity and less debt than is suggested by the tax benefit/bankruptcy cost trade-off model expressed in Figure 13-9.*

USING DEBT FINANCING TO CONSTRAIN MANAGERS

In Chapter 1 we stated that agency problems may arise if managers and shareholders have different objectives. Such conflicts are particularly likely when the firm's managers have too much cash at their disposal. Managers often use such cash to finance their pet projects or for perquisites such as nicer offices, corporate jets, and sky boxes at sports arenas, all of which may do little to maximize stock prices.[15] By contrast, managers with limited "free cash flow" are less able to make wasteful expenditures.

Firms can reduce excess cash flow in a variety of ways. One way is to funnel some of it back to shareholders through higher dividends or stock repurchases. Another alternative is to shift the capital structure toward more debt in the hope that higher debt service requirements will force managers to become more disciplined. If debt is not serviced as required, the firm will be forced into bankruptcy, in which case its managers would likely lose their jobs. Therefore, a manager is less likely to buy an expensive new corporate jet if the firm has large debt service requirements that could cost the manager his or her job.

Signal
An action taken by a firm's management that provides clues to investors about how management views the firm's prospects.

Reserve Borrowing Capacity
The ability to borrow money at a reasonable cost when good investment opportunities arise. Firms often use less debt than specified by the MM optimal capital structure in "normal" times to ensure that they can obtain debt capital later if they need to.

---

[13] Of course, Firm U would have to make certain disclosures when it offered new shares to the public, but it might be able to meet the legal requirements without fully disclosing management's worst fears.

[14] Paul Asquith and David W. Mullins, Jr., "The Impact of Initiating Dividend Payments on Shareholders' Wealth," *Journal of Business*, January 1983, 77–96.

[15] If you don't believe corporate managers can waste money, read Bryan Burrough, *Barbarians at the Gate* (New York: Harper & Row, 1990), the story of the takeover of RJR-Nabisco.

A leveraged buyout (LBO) is one way to reduce excess cash flow. In an LBO debt is used to finance the purchase of a company's shares, after which the firm "goes private." Many leveraged buyouts, which were especially common during the late 1980s, were designed specifically to reduce corporate waste. As noted, high debt payments force managers to conserve cash by eliminating unnecessary expenditures.

Of course, increasing debt and reducing free cash flow has its downside: It increases the risk of bankruptcy. A former professor (who is now a member of the Federal Reserve Board of Governors) has argued that adding debt to a firm's capital structure is like putting a dagger into the steering wheel of a car.[16] The dagger—which points toward your stomach—motivates you to drive more carefully, but you may get stabbed if someone runs into you, even if you are being careful. The analogy applies to corporations in the following sense: Higher debt forces managers to be more careful with shareholders' money, but even well-run firms could face bankruptcy (get stabbed) if some event beyond their control such as a war, an earthquake, a strike, or a recession occurs. To complete the analogy, the capital structure decision comes down to deciding how big a dagger stockholders should use to keep managers in line.

If you find our discussion of capital structure theory imprecise and somewhat confusing, you are not alone. In truth, no one knows how to identify precisely a firm's optimal capital structure, or how to measure the effects of capital structure on stock prices and the cost of capital. In practice, capital structure decisions must be made using a combination of judgment and numerical analysis. Still, an understanding of the theoretical issues presented here can help you make better judgments on capital structure issues.[17]

SELF-TEST QUESTIONS

Why does M&M's theory with taxes lead to 100 percent debt?

How would an increase in corporate taxes affect firms' capital structure decisions? What about personal taxes?

Explain how "asymmetric information" and "signals" affect capital structure decisions.

What is meant by *reserve borrowing capacity*, and why is it important to firms?

How can the use of debt serve to discipline managers?

CHECKLIST FOR CAPITAL STRUCTURE DECISIONS

In addition to the types of analysis discussed above, firms generally consider the following factors when making capital structure decisions:

1. *Sales stability*. A firm whose sales are relatively stable can safely take on more debt and incur higher fixed charges than a company with unstable sales. Util-

---

[16] Ben Bernake, "Is There Too Much Corporate Debt?" Federal Reserve Bank of Philadelphia *Business Review*, September/October 1989, 3–13.

[17] One of the authors can report firsthand the usefulness of financial theory in the actual establishment of corporate capital structures. In recent years, he has served as a consultant to several of the regional telephone companies established as a result of the breakup of AT&T, as well as to several large electric utilities. On the

(footnote continues)

ity companies, because of their stable demand, have historically been able to use more financial leverage than industrial firms.

2. *Asset structure.* Firms whose assets are suitable as security for loans tend to use debt rather heavily. General-purpose assets that can be used by many businesses make good collateral, whereas special-purpose assets do not. Thus, real estate companies are usually highly leveraged, whereas companies involved in technological research are not.

3. *Operating leverage.* Other things the same, a firm with less operating leverage is better able to employ financial leverage because it will have less business risk.

4. *Growth rate.* Other things the same, faster-growing firms must rely more heavily on external capital. Further, the flotation costs involved in selling common stock exceed those incurred when selling debt, which encourages rapidly growing firms to rely more heavily on debt. At the same time, however, these firms often face greater uncertainty, which tends to reduce their willingness to use debt.

5. *Profitability.* One often observes that firms with very high rates of return on investment use relatively little debt. Although there is no theoretical justification for this fact, one practical explanation is that very profitable firms such as Intel, Microsoft, and Coca-Cola simply do not need to do much debt financing. Their high rates of return enable them to do most of their financing with internally generated funds.

6. *Taxes.* Interest is a deductible expense, and deductions are most valuable to firms with high tax rates. Therefore, the higher a firm's tax rate, the greater the advantage of debt.

7. *Control.* The effect of debt versus stock on a management's control position can influence capital structure. If management currently has voting control (over 50 percent of the stock) but is not in a position to buy any more stock, it may choose debt for new financings. On the other hand, management may decide to use equity if the firm's financial situation is so weak that the use of debt might subject it to serious risk of default, because if the firm goes into default, the managers will almost surely lose their jobs. However, if too little debt is used, management runs the risk of a takeover. Thus, control considerations could lead to the use of *either* debt or equity, because the type of capital that best protects management will vary from situation to situation. In any event, if management is at all insecure, it will consider the control situation.

8. *Management attitudes.* Since no one can prove that one capital structure will lead to higher stock prices than another, management can exercise its own judgment about the proper capital structure. Some managements tend to be more conservative than others, and thus use less debt than the average firm in their industry, whereas aggressive managements use more debt in the quest for higher profits.

9. *Lender and rating agency attitudes.* Regardless of managers' own analyses of the proper leverage factors for their firms, lenders' and rating agencies' attitudes frequently influence financial structure decisions. In the majority of cases, the corporation discusses its capital structure with lenders and rating agencies and gives much weight to their advice. For example, one large utility was recently told by Moody's and Standard & Poor's that its bonds would be downgraded if

---

(Footnote 17 continued)

basis of finance theory and computer models that simulated results under a range of conditions, the companies were able to specify "optimal capital structure ranges" with at least a reasonable degree of confidence. Without finance theory, setting a target capital structure would have amounted to little more than throwing darts.

it issued more bonds. This influenced its decision to finance its expansion with common equity.

10. *Market conditions.* Conditions in the stock and bond markets undergo both long- and short-run changes that can have an important bearing on a firm's optimal capital structure. For example, during a recent credit crunch, the junk bond market dried up, and there was simply no market at a "reasonable" interest rate for any new long-term bonds rated below triple B. Therefore, low-rated companies in need of capital were forced to go to the stock market or to the short-term debt market, regardless of their target capital structures. When conditions eased, however, these companies sold bonds to get their capital structures back on target.

11. *The firm's internal condition.* A firm's own internal condition can also have a bearing on its target capital structure. For example, suppose a firm has just successfully completed an R&D program, and it forecasts higher earnings in the immediate future. However, the new earnings are not yet anticipated by investors, hence are not reflected in the stock price. This company would not want to issue stock—it would prefer to finance with debt until the higher earnings materialize and are reflected in the stock price. Then it could sell an issue of common stock, retire the debt, and return to its target capital structure. This point was discussed earlier in connection with asymmetric information and signaling.

12. *Financial flexibility.* An astute corporate treasurer made this statement to the authors:

> Our company can earn a lot more money from good capital budgeting and operating decisions than from good financing decisions. Indeed, we are not sure exactly how financing decisions affect our stock price, but we know for sure that having to turn down a promising venture because funds are not available will reduce our long-run profitability. For this reason, my primary goal as treasurer is to always be in a position to raise the capital needed to support operations.
>
> We also know that when times are good, we can raise capital with either stocks or bonds, but when times are bad, suppliers of capital are much more willing to make funds available if we give them a secured position, and this means debt. Further, when we sell a new issue of stock, this sends a negative "signal" to investors, so stock sales by a mature company such as ours are not desirable.

Putting all these thoughts together gives rise to the goal of *maintaining financial flexibility*, which, from an operational viewpoint, means *maintaining adequate reserve borrowing capacity*. Determining an "adequate" reserve borrowing capacity is judgmental, but it clearly depends on the factors discussed in the chapter, including the firm's forecasted need for funds, predicted capital market conditions, management's confidence in its forecasts, and the consequences of a capital shortage.

SELF-TEST QUESTIONS

How does sales stability affect the target capital structure?

How do the types of assets used affect a firm's capital structure?

How do taxes affect the target capital structure?

How do lender and rating agency attitudes affect capital structure?

How does the firm's internal condition affect its actual capital structure?

What is "financial flexibility," and is it increased or decreased by a high debt ratio?

VARIATIONS IN CAPITAL STRUCTURES

As might be expected, wide variations in the use of financial leverage occur both across industries and among the individual firms in each industry. Table 13-4 illustrates differences for selected industries; the ranking is in descending order of the ratio of common equity to total capital, as shown in Column 1.[18]

Pharmaceutical and computer companies do not use much debt (their ratios of common equity to total capital are high) because the uncertainties inherent in industries that are cyclical, oriented toward research, or subject to huge product liability suits render the heavy use of debt unwise. Utility companies, on the other hand, use debt relatively heavily. The utilities have traditionally used large amounts of debt, particularly long-term debt, because their fixed assets make good security for mortgage bonds, and also because their relatively stable sales make it safe for them to carry more debt than would be true for firms with more business risk.

Particular attention should be given to the times-interest-earned (TIE) ratio because it gives an indication of how safe the debt is and how vulnerable the company is to financial distress. TIE ratios depend on three factors: (1) the percentage of debt,

---

[18] Information on capital structures and financial strength is available from a multitude of sources. We used the *Dow Jones News Retrieval* system to develop Table 13-4, but published sources include *The Value Line Investment Survey*, *Robert Morris Association Annual Studies*, and *Dun & Bradstreet Key Business Ratios*.

TABLE 13-4

Capital Structure Percentages, 2002: Six Industries Ranked by Common Equity Ratios[a]

INDUSTRY	COMMON EQUITY RATIO[b] (1)	LONG-TERM DEBT RATIO (2)	TIMES-INTEREST-EARNED RATIO (3)	RETURN ON EQUITY (4)
Pharmaceuticals	78.74%	21.26%	17.4×	30.7%
Computers	69.93	30.07	13.2	7.6
Steel	65.79	34.21	1.0	0.3
Aerospace	57.80	42.20	3.9	8.8
Railroads	51.81	48.19	2.8	8.8
Utilities	38.37	61.63	3.8	14.0

NOTES:

[a] Capital structure ratios are calculated as a percentage of total capital, where total capital is defined as long-term debt plus equity, with both measured at book value.

[b] These ratios are based on accounting (or book) values. Stated on a market-value basis, the equity percentages would rise because most stocks sell at prices that are much higher than their book values.

SOURCE: *Dow Jones News Retrieval*, 2002. Data collected through July 24, 2002.

(2) the interest rate on the debt, and (3) the company's profitability. Generally, the least leveraged industries, such as the pharmaceutical industry, have the highest coverage ratios, whereas the utility industry, which finances heavily with debt, has a low average coverage ratio.

Wide variations also exist among firms within given industries. For example, although the average ratio of common equity to total capital in 2002 for the pharmaceutical industry was about 79 percent, Eli Lilly & Co. had a ratio of only 69.4 percent. Thus, factors unique to individual firms, including managerial attitudes, play an important role in setting target capital structures.

SELF-TEST QUESTION

Why do wide variations in the use of financial leverage occur both across industries and among individual firms in each industry?

TYING IT ALL TOGETHER

In Chapter 9, we took the firm's financing choice as given and then calculated the cost of capital based on that capital structure. Then, in Chapters 10, 11, and 12, we described capital budgeting techniques, which use the firm's cost of capital as input. Capital budgeting decisions determine the types of projects that the firm accepts, which affect the nature of the firm's assets and its business risk. In this chapter we reverse the process, taking the firm's assets and business risk as given and then seeking to determine the best way to finance those assets. More specifically, in this chapter we examined the effects of financial leverage on stock prices, earnings per share, and the cost of capital. The key concepts covered are listed below.

- A firm's **optimal capital structure** is that mix of debt and equity that maximizes the stock price. At any point in time, management has a specific **target capital structure** in mind, presumably the optimal one, although this target may change over time.

- Several factors influence a firm's capital structure. These include the firm's (1) **business risk,** (2) **tax position,** (3) need for **financial flexibility,** and (4) **managerial conservatism or aggressiveness.**

- **Business risk** is the riskiness inherent in the firm's operations if it uses no debt. A firm will have little business risk if the demand for its products is stable, if the prices of its inputs and products remain relatively constant, if it can adjust its prices freely if costs increase, and if a high percentage of its costs are variable and hence will decrease if sales decrease. Other things the same, the lower a firm's business risk, the higher its optimal debt ratio.

- **Financial leverage** is the extent to which fixed-income securities (debt and preferred stock) are used in a firm's capital structure. **Financial risk** is the added risk borne by stockholders as a result of financial leverage.

- **Operating leverage** is the extent to which fixed costs are used in a firm's operations. In business terminology, a high degree of operating leverage, other factors held constant, implies that a relatively small change in sales results in a large change in ROE.

- Robert Hamada used the underlying assumptions of the CAPM, along with the Modigliani and Miller model, to develop the **Hamada equation,** which shows the effect of financial leverage on beta as follows:

$$b = b_U [1 + (1 - T)(D/E)].$$

Firms can take their current beta, tax rate, and debt/equity ratio to arrive at their **unlevered beta,** b_U, as follows:

$$b_U = b/[1 + (1 - T)(D/E)].$$

- **Modigliani and Miller** and their followers developed a **trade-off theory of capital structure.** They showed that debt is useful because interest is **tax deductible,** but also that debt brings with it costs associated with actual or potential bankruptcy. Under MM's theory, the optimal capital structure strikes a balance between the tax benefits of debt and the costs associated with bankruptcy.

- An alternative (or, really, complementary) theory of capital structure relates to the **signals** given to investors by a firm's decision to use debt versus stock to raise new capital. A stock issue sets off a negative signal, while using debt is a positive, or at least a neutral, signal. As a result, companies try to avoid having to issue stock by maintaining a **reserve borrowing capacity,** and this means using less debt in "normal" times than the MM trade-off theory would suggest.

- A firm's owners may have it use a relatively large amount of debt to constrain the managers. A **high debt ratio raises the threat of bankruptcy,** which carries a cost but which also forces managers to be more careful and less wasteful with shareholders' money. Many of the corporate takeovers and leveraged buyouts in recent years were designed to improve efficiency by reducing the free cash flow available to managers.

Although it is theoretically possible to determine a firm's optimal capital structure, as a practical matter we cannot estimate it with precision. Accordingly, financial executives generally treat the optimal capital structure as a range—for example, 40 to 50 percent debt—rather than as a precise point, such as 45 percent. The concepts discussed in this chapter help managers understand the factors they should consider when they set the target capital structure ranges for their firms.

QUESTIONS

13-1 Explain why the following statement is true: "Other things the same, firms with relatively stable sales are able to carry relatively high debt ratios."

13-2 Why do public utilities pursue a different financial policy than retail firms?

13-3 Why is EBIT generally considered to be independent of financial leverage? Why might EBIT actually be influenced by financial leverage at high debt levels?

13-4 If a firm went from zero debt to successively higher levels of debt, why would you expect its stock price to first rise, then hit a peak, and then begin to decline?

13-5 Why is the debt level that maximizes a firm's expected EPS generally higher than the one that maximizes its stock price?

13-6 When the Bell System was originally broken up, the old AT&T was split into a new AT&T plus seven regional telephone companies. The specific reason for forcing the breakup was to increase the degree of competition in the telephone industry. AT&T had a monopoly on local service, long distance, and the manufacture of all the equipment used by telephone companies, and the breakup was expected to open most of these markets to competition. In the court order that set the terms of the breakup, the capital structures of the surviving companies were specified, and much attention was given to the increased competition telephone companies could expect in the future. Do you think the optimal capital structure after the breakup should be the same as the pre-breakup optimal capital structure? Explain your position.

13-7 Assume that you are advising the management of a firm that is about to double its assets to serve its rapidly growing market. It must choose between a highly automated production process and a less automated one, and it must also choose a capital structure for financing the expansion. Should the asset investment and financing decisions be jointly determined, or should each decision be made separately? How would these decisions affect one another? How could the leverage concept be used to help management analyze the situation?

13-8 Your firm's R&D department has been working on a new process that, if it works, can produce oil from coal at a cost of about $5 per barrel versus a current market price of $30 per barrel. The company needs $10 million of external funds at this time to complete the research. The results of the research will be known in about a year, and there is about a 50–50 chance of success. If the research is successful, your company will need to raise a substantial amount of new money to put the idea into production. Your economists forecast that although the economy will be depressed next year, interest rates will be high because of international monetary problems. You must recommend how the currently needed $10 million should be raised—as debt or as equity. How would the potential impact of your project influence your decision?

13-9 Explain how profits or losses will be magnified for a firm with high operating leverage as opposed to a firm with lower operating leverage.

13-10 What data are necessary to construct a breakeven analysis?

13-11 What would be the effect of each of the following on a firm's breakeven point?
a. An increase in the sales price with no change in unit costs.
b. A change from straight-line depreciation to the MACRS method with no change in the beginning amount of fixed assets.
c. A reduction in variable labor costs; other things are held constant.

13-12 If Congress considers a change in the Tax Code that will increase personal tax rates but reduce corporate tax rates, what effect would this Tax Code change have on the average company's capital structure decision?

13-13 Which of the following are likely to encourage a firm to increase the amount of debt in its capital structure?

a. The corporate tax rate increases.
b. The personal tax rate increases.
c. The firm's assets become less liquid.
d. Changes in the bankruptcy code make bankruptcy less costly.
e. The firm's earnings become more volatile.

SELF-TEST PROBLEMS (SOLUTIONS APPEAR IN APPENDIX B)

ST-1
Key terms

Define each of the following terms:

a. Target capital structure
b. Business risk; financial risk
c. Financial leverage; operating leverage; operating breakeven
d. Hamada equation; unlevered beta; signal
e. Symmetric information; asymmetric information
f. Trade-off theory; signaling theory
g. Reserve borrowing capacity

ST-2
Financial leverage

Gentry Motors Inc., a producer of turbine generators, is in this situation: EBIT = $4 million; tax rate = T = 35%; debt outstanding = D = $2 million; k_d = 10%; k_s = 15%; shares of stock outstanding = N_0 = 600,000; and book value per share = $10. Since Gentry's product market is stable and the company expects no growth, all earnings are paid out as dividends. The debt consists of perpetual bonds.

a. What are Gentry's earnings per share (EPS) and its price per share (P_0)?
b. What is Gentry's weighted average cost of capital (WACC)?
c. Gentry can increase its debt by $8 million, to a total of $10 million, using the new debt to buy back and retire some of its shares at the current price. Its interest rate on debt will be 12 percent (it will have to call and refund the old debt), and its cost of equity will rise from 15 percent to 17 percent. EBIT will remain constant. Should Gentry change its capital structure?
d. If Gentry did not have to refund the $2 million of old debt, how would this affect things? Assume that the new and the still outstanding debt are equally risky, with k_d = 12%, but that the coupon rate on the old debt is 10 percent.
e. What is Gentry's TIE coverage ratio under the original situation and under the conditions in Part c of this question?

ST-3
Operating leverage and breakeven analysis

Olinde Electronics Inc. produces stereo components that sell for P = $100. Olinde's fixed costs are $200,000; 5,000 components are produced and sold each year; EBIT is currently $50,000; and Olinde's assets (all equity financed) are $500,000. Olinde estimates that it can change its production process, adding $400,000 to investment and $50,000 to fixed operating costs. This change will (1) reduce variable costs per unit by $10 and (2) increase output by 2,000 units, but (3) the sales price on all units will have to be lowered to $95 to permit sales of the additional output. Olinde has tax loss carry-forwards that cause its tax rate to be zero. Olinde uses no debt, and its average cost of capital is 10 percent.

a. Should Olinde make the change?
b. Would Olinde's breakeven point increase or decrease if it made the change?
c. Suppose Olinde were unable to raise additional equity financing and had to borrow the $400,000 to make the investment at an interest rate of 10 percent. Use the Du Pont equation to find the expected ROA of the investment. Should Olinde make the change if debt financing must be used?

STARTER PROBLEMS

13-1
Breakeven quantity

A company estimates that its fixed operating costs are $500,000, and its variable costs are $3.00 per unit sold. Each unit produced sells for $4.00. What is the company's breakeven point? In other words, how many units must it sell before its operating income becomes positive?

13-2
Optimal capital structure

Jackson Trucking Company is trying to determine its optimal capital structure. The company's CFO believes the optimal debt ratio is somewhere between 20 percent and 50 percent. Her staff has compiled the following projections for the company's EPS and stock price for various debt levels:

DEBT RATIO	PROJECTED EPS	PROJECTED STOCK PRICE
20%	$3.20	$35.00
30	3.45	36.50
40	3.75	36.25
50	3.50	35.50

Assuming that the firm uses only debt and common equity, what is Jackson's optimal capital structure? At what debt ratio is the company's WACC minimized?

13-3
Unlevered beta

Harley Motors has $10 million in assets, which is financed with $2 million of debt and $8 million in equity. If Harley's beta is currently 1.2 and its tax rate is 40 percent, what is its unlevered beta, b_U?

EXAM-TYPE PROBLEMS

The problems included in this section are set up in such a way that they could be used as multiple-choice exam problems.

13-4
Breakeven analysis

The Weaver Watch Company manufactures ladies' watches that are sold through discount houses. Each watch is sold for $25; the fixed costs are $140,000 for 30,000 watches or less; variable costs are $15 per watch.
a. What is the firm's gain or loss at sales of 8,000 watches? Of 18,000 watches?
b. What is the breakeven point? Illustrate by means of a chart.
c. What happens to the breakeven point if the selling price rises to $31? What is the significance of the change to the financial manager?
d. What happens to the breakeven point if the selling price rises to $31 but variable costs rise to $23 a unit?

13-5
Financial leverage effects

A company currently has assets of $5 million. The firm is 100 percent equity financed. The company currently has net income of $1 million, and it pays out 40 percent of its net income as dividends. Both net income and dividends are expected to grow at a constant rate of 5 percent per year. There are 200,000 shares of stock outstanding, and it is estimated that the current cost of capital is 13.40 percent.

The company is considering a recapitalization where it will issue $1 million in debt and use the proceeds to repurchase stock. Investment bankers have estimated that if the company goes through with the recapitalization, its before-tax cost of debt will be 11 percent, and the cost of equity will rise to 14.5 percent. The company has a 40 percent federal-plus-state tax rate.
a. What is the current share price of the stock (before the recapitalization)?
b. Assuming that the company maintains the same payout ratio, what will be its stock price following the recapitalization?

13-6
Financial leverage effects

The firms HL and LL are identical except for their leverage ratios and interest rates on debt. Each has $20 million in assets, earned $4 million before interest and taxes in 2002, and has a 40 percent federal-plus-state tax rate. Firm HL, however, has a leverage ratio (D/TA) of 50 percent and pays 12 percent interest on its debt, whereas LL has a 30 percent leverage ratio and pays only 10 percent interest on debt.
a. Calculate the rate of return on equity (net income/equity) for each firm.
b. Observing that HL has a higher return on equity, LL's treasurer decides to raise the leverage ratio from 30 to 60 percent, which will increase LL's interest rate on all debt to 15 percent. Calculate the new rate of return on equity for LL.

13-7
Financial leverage effects

The Neal Company wishes to calculate next year's return on equity under different leverage ratios. Neal's total assets are $14 million, and its federal-plus-state tax rate is 40 percent. The company is able to estimate next year's earnings before interest and taxes for three possible states of the world: $4.2 million with a 0.2 probability, $2.8 million with a 0.5 probability, and $700,000 with a 0.3 probability. Calculate Neal's expected return on equity, standard deviation, and coefficient of variation for each of the following leverage ratios, and evaluate the results:

LEVERAGE (DEBT/TOTAL ASSETS)	INTEREST RATE
0%	—
10	9%
50	11
60	14

13-8
Hamada equation

Cyclone Software Co. is trying to estimate its optimal capital structure. Cyclone's current capital structure consists of 25 percent debt and 75 percent equity; however, management believes the firm should use more debt. The risk-free rate, k_{RF}, is 5 percent, the market risk premium, $k_M - k_{RF}$, is 6 percent, and the firm's tax rate is 40 percent. Currently, Cyclone's cost of equity is 14 percent, which is determined on the basis of the CAPM. What would be Cyclone's estimated cost of equity if it were to change its capital structure from its present capital structure to 50 percent debt and 50 percent equity?

13-9
Recapitalization

Currently, Bloom Flowers Inc. has a capital structure consisting of 20 percent debt and 80 percent equity. Bloom's debt currently has an 8 percent yield to maturity. The risk-freee rate (k_{RF}) is 5 percent, and the market risk premium ($k_M - k_{RF}$) is 6 percent. Using the CAPM, Bloom estimates that its cost of equity is currently 12.5 percent. The company has a 40 percent tax rate.
a. What is Bloom's current WACC?
b. What is the current beta on Bloom's common stock?
c. What would Bloom's beta be if the company had no debt in its capital structure? (That is, what is Bloom's unlevered beta, b_U?)

Bloom's financial staff is considering changing its capital structure to 40 percent debt and 60 percent equity. If the company went ahead with the proposed change, the yield to maturity on the company's bonds would rise to 9.5 percent. The proposed change will have no effect on the company's tax rate.
d. What would be the company's new cost of equity if it adopted the proposed change in capital structure?
e. What would be the company's new WACC if it adopted the proposed change in capital structure?
f. Based on your answer to part e, would you advise Bloom to adopt the proposed change in capital structure? Explain.

PROBLEMS

13-10
Risk analysis

a. Given the following information, calculate the expected value for Firm C's EPS. $E(EPS_A) = \$5.10$, and $\sigma_A = \$3.61$; $E(EPS_B) = \$4.20$, and $\sigma_B = \$2.96$; and $\sigma_C = \$4.11$.

	PROBABILITY				
	0.1	0.2	0.4	0.2	0.1
Firm A: EPS_A	($1.50)	$1.80	$5.10	$8.40	$11.70
Firm B: EPS_B	(1.20)	1.50	4.20	6.90	9.60
Firm C: EPS_C	(2.40)	1.35	5.10	8.85	12.60

b. Discuss the relative riskiness of the three firms' (A, B, and C) earnings.

13-11
Leverage

Wingler Communications Corporation (WCC) supplies headphones to airlines for use with movie and stereo programs. The headphones, which use the latest in electronic components, sell for $28.80 per set, and this year's sales are expected to be 450,000 units. Variable production costs for the expected sales under present production methods are estimated at $10,200,000, and fixed production (operating) costs at present are $1,560,000. WCC has $4,800,000 of debt outstanding at an interest rate of 8 percent. There are 240,000 shares of common stock outstanding, and there is no preferred stock. The dividend payout ratio is 70 percent, and WCC is in the 40 percent federal-plus-state tax bracket.

The company is considering investing $7,200,000 in new equipment. Sales would not increase, but variable costs per unit would decline by 20 percent. Also, fixed operating costs would increase from $1,560,000 to $1,800,000. WCC could raise the required capital by borrowing $7,200,000 at 10 percent or by selling 240,000 additional shares at $30 per share.

a. What would be WCC's EPS (1) under the old production process, (2) under the new process if it uses debt, and (3) under the new process if it uses common stock?

b. At what unit sales level would WCC have the same EPS, assuming it undertakes the investment and finances it with debt or with stock? (Hint: V = variable cost per unit = $8,160,000/450,000, and EPS = [(PQ − VQ − F − I)(1 − T)]/N. Set EPS_{Stock} = EPS_{Debt} and solve for Q.)

c. At what unit sales level would EPS = 0 under the three production/financing setups—that is, under the old plan, the new plan with debt financing, and the new plan with stock financing? (Hint: Note that V_{Old} = $10,200,000/450,000, and use the hints for part b, setting the EPS equation equal to zero.)

d. On the basis of the analysis in parts a through c, and given that operating leverage is lower under the new setup, which plan is the riskiest, which has the highest expected EPS, and which would you recommend? Assume here that there is a fairly high probability of sales falling as low as 250,000 units, and determine EPS_{Debt} and EPS_{Stock} at that sales level to help assess the riskiness of the two financing plans.

13-12
Financing alternatives

The Severn Company plans to raise a net amount of $270 million to finance new equipment and working capital in early 2003. Two alternatives are being considered: Common stock may be sold to net $60 per share, or bonds yielding 12 percent may be issued. The balance sheet and income statement of the Severn Company prior to financing are as follows:

The Severn Company: Balance Sheet as of December 31, 2002
(Millions of Dollars)

Current assets	$ 900.00	Accounts payable	$ 172.50
Net fixed assets	450.00	Notes payable to bank	255.00
		Other current liabilities	225.00
		Total current liabilities	$ 652.50
		Long-term debt (10%)	300.00
		Common stock, $3 par	60.00
		Retained earnings	337.50
Total assets	$1,350.00	Total liabilities and equity	$1,350.00

The Severn Company: Income Statement for Year Ended December 31, 2002
(Millions of Dollars)

Sales	$2,475.00
Operating costs	2,227.50
Earnings before interest and taxes (10%)	$ 247.50
Interest on short-term debt	15.00
Interest on long-term debt	30.00
Earnings before taxes	$ 202.50
Federal-plus-state taxes (40%)	81.00
Net income	$ 121.50

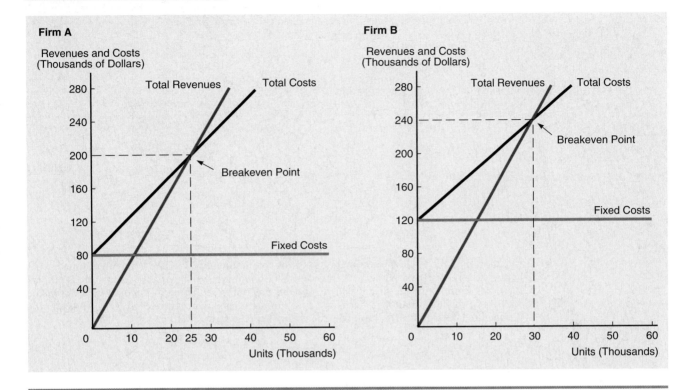

Firm A

Revenues and Costs
(Thousands of Dollars)

Total Revenues   Total Costs

280

240

200 — — — — — Breakeven Point

160

120

Fixed Costs

80

40

0   10   20 25 30   40   50   60

Units (Thousands)

Firm B

Revenues and Costs
(Thousands of Dollars)

Total Revenues   Total Costs

280

240 — — — — — Breakeven Point

200

160

Fixed Costs

120

80

40

0   10   20   30   40   50   60

Units (Thousands)

The probability distribution for annual sales is as follows:

PROBABILITY	ANNUAL SALES (MILLIONS OF DOLLARS)
0.30	$2,250
0.40	2,700
0.30	3,150

Assuming that EBIT is equal to 10 percent of sales, calculate earnings per share under both the debt financing and the stock financing alternatives at each possible level of sales. Then calculate expected earnings per share and σ_{EPS} under both debt and stock financing alternatives. Also, calculate the debt ratio and the times-interest-earned (TIE) ratio at the expected sales level under each alternative. The old debt will remain outstanding. Which financing method do you recommend?

13-13

Breakeven and operating leverage

a. Given the graphs shown at the top of this page, calculate the total fixed costs, variable costs per unit, and sales price for Firm A. Firm B's fixed costs are $120,000, its variable costs per unit are $4, and its sales price is $8 per unit.

b. Which firm has the higher operating leverage at any given level of sales? Explain.

c. At what *sales level*, in units, do both firms earn the same operating profit?

Elliott Athletics is trying to determine its optimal capital structure, which now consists of only debt and common equity. The firm does not currently use preferred stock in its capital structure, and it does not plan to do so in the future. To estimate how much its debt would cost at different debt levels, the company's treasury staff has consulted with investment bankers and, on the basis of those discussions, has created the following table:

DEBT-TO-ASSETS RATIO (w_d)	EQUITY-TO-ASSETS RATIO (w_c)	DEBT-TO-EQUITY RATIO (D/E)	BOND RATING	BEFORE-TAX COST OF DEBT (k_d)
0.0	1.0	0.00	A	7.0%
0.2	0.8	0.25	BBB	8.0
0.4	0.6	0.67	BB	10.0
0.6	0.4	1.50	C	12.0
0.8	0.2	4.00	D	15.0

Elliott uses the CAPM to estimate its cost of common equity, k_s. The company estimates that the risk-free rate is 5 percent, the market risk premium is 6 percent, and its tax rate is 40 percent. Elliott estimates that if it had no debt, its "unlevered" beta, b_U, would be 1.2. On the basis of this information, what is the firm's optimal capital structure, and what would be the weighted average cost of capital at the optimal capital structure?

SPREADSHEET PROBLEM

Rework Problem 13-14 using a spreadsheet model. After completing the problem as it appears, answer the following related questions.
a. Plot a graph of the after-tax cost of debt, the cost of equity, and the WACC versus (1) the debt/assets ratio and (2) the debt/equity ratio.
b. Would the optimal capital structure change if the unlevered beta changed? To answer this question, do a sensitivity analysis of WACC on b_U for different levels of b_U.

INTEGRATED CASE

CAMPUS DELI INC.

13-16 Optimal capital structure Assume that you have just been hired as business manager of Campus Deli (CD), which is located adjacent to the campus. Sales were $1,100,000 last year; variable costs were 60 percent of sales; and fixed costs were $40,000. Therefore, EBIT totaled

$400,000. Because the university's enrollment is capped, EBIT is expected to be constant over time. Since no expansion capital is required, CD pays out all earnings as dividends. Assets are $2 million, and 80,000 shares are outstanding. The management group owns about 50 percent of the stock, which is traded in the over-the-counter market.

CD currently has no debt—it is an all-equity firm—and its 80,000 shares outstanding sell at a price of $25 per share, which is also the book value. The firm's federal-plus-state tax rate is 40 percent. On the basis of statements made in your finance text, you believe that CD's shareholders would be better off if some debt financing were used. When you suggested this to your new boss, she encouraged you to pursue the idea, but to provide support for the suggestion.

In today's market, the risk-free rate, k_{RF}, is 6 percent and the market risk premium, $k_M - k_{RF}$, is 6 percent. CD's unlevered beta, b_U, is 1.0. Since CD currently has no debt, its cost of equity (and WACC) is 12 percent.

If the firm were recapitalized, debt would be issued, and the borrowed funds would be used to repurchase stock. Stockholders, in turn, would use funds provided by the repurchase to buy equities in other fast-food companies similar to CD. You plan to complete your report by asking and then answering the following questions.

a. (1) What is business risk? What factors influence a firm's business risk?

(2) What is operating leverage, and how does it affect a firm's business risk?

b. (1) What is meant by the terms "financial leverage" and "financial risk"?

(2) How does financial risk differ from business risk?

c. Now, to develop an example that can be presented to CD's management as an illustration, consider two hypothetical firms, Firm U, with zero debt financing, and Firm L, with $10,000 of 12 percent debt. Both firms have $20,000 in total assets and a 40 percent federal-plus-state tax rate, and they have the following EBIT probability distribution for next year:

PROBABILITY	EBIT
0.25	$2,000
0.50	3,000
0.25	4,000

TABLE IC 13 - 1	Income Statements and Ratios

	FIRM U			FIRM L		
Assets	$20,000	$20,000	$20,000	$20,000	$20,000	$20,000
Equity	$20,000	$20,000	$20,000	$10,000	$10,000	$10,000
Probability	0.25	0.50	0.25	0.25	0.50	0.25
Sales	$ 6,000	$ 9,000	$12,000	$ 6,000	$ 9,000	$12,000
Operating costs	4,000	6,000	8,000	4,000	6,000	8,000
Earnings before interest and taxes	$ 2,000	$ 3,000	$ 4,000	$ 2,000	$ 3,000	$ 4,000
Interest (12%)	0	0	0	1,200		1,200
Earnings before taxes	$ 2,000	$ 3,000	$ 4,000	$ 800	$	$ 2,800
Taxes (40%)	800	1,200	1,600	320		1,120
Net income	$ 1,200	$ 1,800	$ 2,400	$ 480	$	$ 1,680
Basic earning power (BEP = EBIT/Assets)	10.0%	15.0%	20.0%	10.0%	%	20.0%
ROE	6.0%	9.0%	12.0%	4.8%	%	16.8%
TIE	∞	∞	∞	1.7×	×	3.3×
Expected basic earning power		15.0%			%	
Expected ROE		9.0%			10.8%	
Expected TIE		∞			2.5×	
σ_{BEP}		3.5%			%	
σ_{ROE}		2.1%			4.2%	
σ_{TIE}		0			0.6×	

(1) Complete the partial income statements and the firms' ratios in Table IC13-1.

(2) Be prepared to discuss each entry in the table and to explain how this example illustrates the impact of financial leverage on expected rate of return and risk.

d. After speaking with a local investment banker, you obtain the following estimates of the cost of debt at different debt levels (in thousands of dollars):

AMOUNT BORROWED	DEBT/ASSETS RATIO	DEBT/EQUITY RATIO	BOND RATING	k_d
$ 0	0	0	—	—
250	0.125	0.1429	AA	8.0%
500	0.250	0.3333	A	9.0
750	0.375	0.6000	BBB	11.5
1,000	0.500	1.0000	BB	14.0

Now consider the optimal capital structure for CD.

(1) To begin, define the terms "optimal capital structure" and "target capital structure."

(2) Why does CD's bond rating and cost of debt depend on the amount of money borrowed?

(3) Assume that shares could be repurchased at the current market price of $25 per share. Calculate CD's ex-

pected EPS and TIE at debt levels of $0, $250,000, $500,000, $750,000, and $1,000,000. How many shares would remain after recapitalization under each scenario?

(4) Using the Hamada equation, what is the cost of equity if CD recapitalizes with $250,000 of debt? $500,000? $750,000? $1,000,000?

(5) Considering only the levels of debt discussed, what is the capital structure that minimizes CD's WACC?

(6) What would be the new stock price if CD recapitalizes with $250,000 of debt? $500,000? $750,000? $1,000,000? Recall that the payout ratio is 100 percent, so g = 0.

(7) Is EPS maximized at the debt level that maximizes share price? Why or why not?

(8) Considering only the levels of debt discussed, what is CD's optimal capital structure?

(9) What is the WACC at the optimal capital structure?

e. Suppose you discovered that CD had more business risk than you originally estimated. Describe how this would affect the analysis. What if the firm had less business risk than originally estimated?

f. What are some factors a manager should consider when establishing his or her firm's target capital structure?

g. Put labels on Figure IC13-1, and then discuss the graph as you might use it to explain to your boss why CD might want to use some debt.

h. How does the existence of asymmetric information and signaling affect capital structure?

FIGURE IC13-1   **Relationship between Capital Structure and Stock Price**

Please go to our web site **http://brigham.swlearning.com** to access the Cyberproblems.

With your Xtra! CD-ROM, access the Thomson Analytics Problems and use the Thomson Analytics Academic online database to work this chapter's problems.

DISTRIBUTIONS TO SHAREHOLDERS: DIVIDENDS AND SHARE REPURCHASES

14

Profitable companies regularly face three important questions. (1) How much of its free cash flow should it pass on to shareholders? (2) Should it provide this cash to stockholders by raising the dividend or by repurchasing stock? (3) Should it maintain a stable, consistent payment policy, or should it let the payments vary as conditions change?

In this chapter we will discuss many of the issues that affect a firm's cash distribution policy. As we will see, most firms establish a policy that considers their forecasted cash flows and forecasted capital expenditures, and then try to stick to it. The policy can be changed, but this can cause problems because such changes inconvenience shareholders, send unintended signals, and convey the impression of dividend instability, all of which have negative implications for stock prices. Still, economic circumstances do change, and occasionally such changes require firms to change their dividend policies.

One of the most striking examples of a dividend policy change occurred in May 1994, when FPL Group, a utility holding company whose primary subsidiary is Florida Power & Light, announced a cut in its quarterly dividend from $0.62 per share to $0.42. At the same time, FPL stated that it would buy back 10 million of its common shares over the next three years to bolster its stock price.[1] Here is the text of the letter sent to its stockholders in which FPL announced these changes:

Dear Shareholder,

Over the past several years, we have been working hard to enhance shareholder value by aligning our strategy with a rapidly changing business environment. . . . The Energy Policy Act of 1992 has brought permanent changes to the electric industry. Although we have taken effective and sometimes painful steps to prepare for these changes, one

FPL GROUP

critical problem remains. Our dividend payout ratio of 90 percent—the percentage of our earnings paid to shareholders as dividends—is far too high for a growth company. It is well above the industry average, and it has limited the growth in the price of our stock.

To meet the challenges of this competitive marketplace and to ensure the financial strength and flexibility necessary for success, the Board of Directors has announced a change in our financial strategy that includes the following milestones:

- A new dividend policy that provides for paying out 60 to 65 percent of prior years' earnings. This means a reduction in the quarterly dividend from 62 to 42 cents per share beginning with the next payment.
- The authorization to repurchase 10 million shares of common stock over the next three years, including at least 4 million shares in the next year.
- An earlier dividend evaluation beginning in February 1995 to more closely link dividend rates to annual earnings.

We believe this financial strategy will enhance long-term share value and will facilitate both earnings per share and dividend growth to about 5 percent per year over the next several years.

Adding to shareholder wealth in this manner should be increasingly significant given recent changes in the tax law,

---

[1] For a complete discussion of the FPL decision, see Dennis Soter, Eugene Brigham, and Paul Evanson, "The Dividend Cut Heard 'Round the World: The Case of FPL," *Journal of Applied Corporate Finance*, Spring 1996, 4–15. Also, note that stock repurchases are discussed in a later section of this chapter.

which have made capital gains more attractive than dividend income.

. . . We take this action from a position of strength. We are not being forced into a defensive position by expectations of poor financial performance. Rather, it is a strategic decision to align our dividend policy and your total return as a shareholder with the growth characteristics of our company.

We appreciate your understanding and support, and we will continue to provide updates on our progress in forthcoming shareholder reports.

Several analysts called the FPL decision a watershed event for the electric utility industry. FPL saw that its circumstances were changing — its core electric business was moving from a regulated monopoly environment to one of increasing competition, and the new environment required a stronger balance sheet and more financial flexibility than was consistent with a 90 percent payout policy.

What did the market think about FPL's dividend policy change? The company's stock price fell by 14 percent the day the announcement was made. In the past, hundreds of dividend cuts followed by sharply lower earnings had conditioned investors to expect the worst when a company reduces its dividend — this is the signaling effect, which is discussed later in the chapter. However, over the next few months, as they understood FPL's actions better, analysts began to praise the decision and to recommend the stock. As a result, FPL's stock outperformed the average utility and soon exceeded the pre-announcement price.

PUTTING THINGS IN PERSPECTIVE

 An excellent source of recent dividend news releases for major corporations is available at the web site of Corporate Financials Online at **http://www.cfonews. com/.** By clicking the down arrow of the "News Category" box to the left of the screen, students may select "Dividends" to receive a list of companies with dividend news. Click on any company, and you will see its latest dividend news.

Successful companies earn income. That income can then be reinvested in operating assets, used to acquire securities, used to retire debt, or distributed to stockholders. If the decision is made to distribute income to stockholders, three key issues arise: (1) How much should be distributed? (2) Should the distribution be as cash dividends, or should the cash be passed on to shareholders by buying back some of the stock they hold? (3) How stable should the distribution be; that is, should the funds paid out from year to year be stable and dependable, which stockholders would probably prefer, or be allowed to vary with the firms' cash flows and investment requirements, which would probably be better from the firm's standpoint? These three issues are the primary focus of this chapter, but we also consider two related issues, stock dividends and stock splits. ∎

DIVIDENDS VERSUS CAPITAL GAINS: WHAT DO INVESTORS PREFER?

Target Payout Ratio
The percentage of net income paid out as cash dividends as desired by the firm.

When deciding how much cash to distribute to stockholders, financial managers must keep in mind that the firm's objective is to maximize shareholder value. Consequently, the **target payout ratio**—defined as the percentage of net income to be paid out as cash dividends—should be based in large part on investors' preferences for dividends versus capital gains: do investors prefer (1) to have the firm distribute income as cash dividends or (2) to have it either repurchase stock or else plow the earnings back into the business, both of which should result in capital gains? This preference can be considered in terms of the constant growth stock valuation model:

$$\hat{P}_0 = \frac{D_1}{k_s - g}.$$

If the company increases the payout ratio, this raises D_1. This increase in the numerator, taken alone, would cause the stock price to rise. However, if D_1 is raised, then less money will be available for reinvestment, that will cause the expected growth rate to decline, and that will tend to lower the stock's price. Thus, any change in payout policy will have two opposing effects. Therefore, the firm's **optimal dividend policy** must strike a balance between current dividends and future growth so as to maximize the stock price.

In this section we examine three theories of investor preference: (1) the dividend irrelevance theory, (2) the "bird-in-the-hand" theory, and (3) the tax preference theory, and Web Appendix 14A provides a numerical illustration that explains the three dividend theories.

Optimal Dividend Policy
The dividend policy that strikes a balance between current dividends and future growth and maximizes the firm's stock price.

DIVIDEND IRRELEVANCE THEORY

It has been argued that dividend policy has no effect on either the price of a firm's stock or its cost of capital. If dividend policy has no significant effects, then it would be *irrelevant*. The principal proponents of the **dividend irrelevance theory** are Merton Miller and Franco Modigliani (MM).[2] They argued that the firm's value is determined only by its basic earning power and its business risk. In other words, MM argued that the value of the firm depends only on the income produced by its assets, not on how this income is split between dividends and retained earnings.

To understand MM's argument that dividend policy is irrelevant, recognize that any shareholder can in theory construct his or her own dividend policy. For example, if a firm does not pay dividends, a shareholder who wants a 5 percent dividend can "create" it by selling 5 percent of his or her stock. Conversely, if a company pays a higher dividend than an investor desires, the investor can use the unwanted dividends to buy additional shares of the company's stock. If investors could buy and sell shares and thus create their own dividend policy without incurring costs, then the firm's dividend policy would truly be irrelevant. Note, though, that investors who want additional dividends must incur brokerage costs to sell shares, and investors who do not want dividends must first pay taxes on the unwanted dividends and then incur brokerage costs to purchase shares with the after-tax dividends. Since taxes and brokerage costs certainly exist, dividend policy may well be relevant.

In developing their dividend theory, MM made a number of assumptions, especially the absence of taxes and brokerage costs. Obviously, taxes and brokerage costs do exist, so the MM irrelevance theory may not be true. However, MM argued (correctly) that all economic theories are based on simplifying assumptions, and that the validity of a theory must be judged by empirical tests, not by the realism of its assumptions. We will discuss empirical tests of MM's dividend irrelevance theory shortly.

Dividend Irrelevance Theory
The theory that a firm's dividend policy has no effect on either its value or its cost of capital.

---

[2] Merton H. Miller and Franco Modigliani, "Dividend Policy, Growth, and the Valuation of Shares," *Journal of Business*, October 1961, 411–433.

BIRD-IN-THE-HAND THEORY

The principal conclusion of MM's dividend irrelevance theory is that dividend policy does not affect the required rate of return on equity, k_s. This conclusion has been hotly debated in academic circles. In particular, Myron Gordon and John Lintner argued that k_s decreases as the dividend payout is increased because investors are less certain of receiving the capital gains that are supposed to result from retaining earnings than they are of receiving dividend payments.[3] Gordon and Lintner said, in effect, that investors value a dollar of expected dividends more highly than a dollar of expected capital gains because the dividend yield component, D_1/P_0, is less risky than the g component in the total expected return equation, $k_s = D_1/P_0 + g$.

MM disagreed. They argued that k_s is independent of dividend policy, which implies that investors are indifferent between D_1/P_0 and g and, hence, between dividends and capital gains. MM called the Gordon-Lintner argument the **bird-in-the-hand** fallacy because, in MM's view, most investors plan to reinvest their dividends in the stock of the same or similar firms, and, in any event, the riskiness of the firm's cash flows to investors in the long run is determined by the riskiness of operating cash flows, not by dividend payout policy.

Bird-in-the-Hand Theory
MM's name for the theory that a firm's value will be maximized by setting a high dividend payout ratio.

TAX PREFERENCE THEORY

There are three tax-related reasons for thinking that investors might prefer a low dividend payout to a high payout: (1) Long-term capital gains are generally taxed at a rate of 20 percent, whereas dividend income is taxed at effective rates that go up to 38.6 percent. Therefore, wealthy investors (who own most of the stock and receive most of the dividends) might prefer to have companies retain and plow earnings back into the business. Earnings growth would presumably lead to stock price increases, and thus lower-taxed capital gains would be substituted for higher-taxed dividends. (2) Taxes are not paid on the gain until a stock is sold. Due to time value effects, a dollar of taxes paid in the future has a lower effective cost than a dollar paid today. (3) If a stock is held by someone until he or she dies, no capital gains tax is due at all—the beneficiaries who receive the stock can use the stock's value on the death day as their cost basis and thus completely escape the capital gains tax.

Because of these tax advantages, investors may prefer to have companies retain most of their earnings. If so, investors would be willing to pay more for low-payout companies than for otherwise similar high-payout companies.

WHICH THEORY IS BEST?

These three theories offer contradictory advice to corporate managers, so which, if any, should we believe? The most logical way to proceed is to test the theories empirically. However, there are severe problems with all the empirical tests that have been conducted.

First, some investors clearly prefer dividends, hence could be described as bird-in-the-hand advocates. They like companies that pay high dividends, so if a company

---

[3] Myron J. Gordon, "Optimal Investment and Financing Policy," *Journal of Finance*, May 1963, 264–272; and John Lintner, "Dividends, Earnings, Leverage, Stock Prices, and the Supply of Capital to Corporations," *Review of Economics and Statistics*, August 1962, 243–269.

raises its dividend, they would buy more of its stock, raise its price, and thus lower its cost of equity. However, other investors have no need for current cash dividends and are in high tax brackets, so they prefer lower dividend payouts. Finally, some investors are probably truly indifferent—to them, the advantages and disadvantages of dividends are equally balanced, so their stock buying preferences would not change if companies paid out more or less of their earnings.

Now consider the effects of this situation on empirical tests of investor preferences. What we would like to do is find a set of companies that differ only with respect to their dividend policies and then to test to see if the companies with higher payouts were more or less valuable than those with lower payouts. For example, suppose Companies H (for high) and L (for low) had similar sales, assets, capital structures, and so forth, but H paid out most of its earnings while L had a low payout ratio. Now if H's stock commanded a higher price, its P/E ratio would be higher and its cost of equity would be lower than L's, which would indicate that investors subscribed to the bird-in-the hand theory. The reverse would hold if investors favored L. If we could find a large sample of companies like H and L, then we could conduct a statistical test to determine which theory is more correct.

However, there are obvious problems with such an empirical test. First, it is impossible to find even two companies, let alone a statistically valid sample, that differ only with regard to dividend policy. Second, since we want to know the effects of dividend policy on the cost of equity, we would need an accurate measure of each company's cost of equity, but we know that error-free equity cost estimates do not exist. And third, even if we could solve the first two problems, it might turn out that bird-in-the-hand and tax-preference investors were evenly balanced, causing the aggregate results to indicate that MM's indifference theory is correct, whereas in actuality there are no indifferent investors.

As a result of these problems, empirical tests designed to help managers establish an optimal, value-maximizing dividend policy have not produced useful results. Even so, a consideration of dividend theory does make a few things clear. First, since some investors prefer more dividends while others prefer less, it makes sense for different companies to follow different dividend policies and thus to provide different investors with what they want. In other words, some companies should pay more dividends and others less. This type of differentiation will lead to higher stock prices and lower equity costs in the aggregate. Second, as we will see later in the chapter, some companies are indeed more logical candidates for high-payout policies and others for low payouts. Third, as we will also discuss later, investors like to know what a company's payout policy is, and they prefer companies whose dividend policies are relatively stable. Finally, investors' preferences change over time, as do companies' fundamental positions, so, while stable dividends are desirable, dividend policy should not be set in stone—as conditions change, it may become desirable to change the dividend policy.

We can look at 2002 to illustrate this last point. During the stock market boom of the 1990s, investor preferences shifted away from dividends and toward retained earnings and capital gains. With stock prices increasing at 20 percent or so per year, investors didn't care much about a 3 percent or so dividend yield. In that environment, lower payout ratios increased growth expectations, and stock prices generally benefited. However, times change. First, air started leaking from the stock market bubble in 2000, and double-digit gains became double-digit losses. Simultaneously, investor expectations for returns declined from the vicinity of 15 percent to about 8 percent, and a 3 percent dividend yield is a lot more important when the total expected return is 8 percent than when it's 15 percent. Also, the accounting scandals

DIVIDEND YIELDS AROUND THE WORLD

Dividend yields vary considerably in different stock markets throughout the world. In 1999 in the United States, dividend yields averaged 1.6 percent for the large blue chip stocks in the Dow Jones Industrials, 1.2 percent for a broader sample of stocks in the S&P 500, and 0.3 percent for stocks in the high-tech-dominated Nasdaq. Outside the United States, average dividend yields ranged from 5.7 percent in New Zealand to 0.7 percent in Taiwan. The accompanying table summarizes the dividend picture in 1999.

WORLD STOCK MARKET (INDEX)	DIVIDEND YIELD
New Zealand	5.7%
Australia	3.1
Britain FTSE 100	2.4
Hong Kong	2.4
France	2.1
Germany	2.1
Belgium	2.0
Singapore	1.7
United States (Dow Jones Industrials)	1.6
Canada (TSE 300)	1.5
United States (S&P 500)	1.2
Mexico	1.1
Japan Nikkei	0.7
Taiwan	0.7
United States (Nasdaq)	0.3

SOURCE: Adapted from Alexandra Eadie, "On the Grid Looking for Dividend Yield Around the World," *The Globe and Mail*, June 23, 1999, B16. Eadie's source was Bloomberg Financial Services.

that were revealed beginning in 2001 caused investors to question reported earnings. Moreover, they realized that while companies such as Enron and WorldCom can cook their books and report phony earnings, dividends must be paid in cash, so companies that pay substantial dividends generally have "real" as opposed to phony earnings. As a result of these two factors, in 2002 many investors were seeking companies with high-dividend payouts, and the result was a shift toward the bird-in-the-hand position.[4]

---

[4] To illustrate, an article in *The Wall Street Journal* on August 2, 2002, quoted the manager of a large equity mutual fund as saying that he was looking for stocks that provide shareholders with cash from dividends and stock repurchases. This manager also regards these cash outlays as "signals of a company's cash flow strength, value, and willingness to reward shareholders for their investment." FPL, the company highlighted in the chapter-opening vignette, is given as an example of a company that meets these criteria. Others share this view, as demonstrated by the fact that such stocks have outperformed the broad averages over the last year.

SELF-TEST QUESTIONS

Explain the differences among the dividend irrelevance theory, the bird-in-the-hand theory, and the tax preference theory.

What did Modigliani and Miller assume about taxes and brokerage costs when they developed their dividend irrelevance theory?

How did the bird-in-the-hand theory get its name?

In what sense does MM's theory represent a middle-ground position between the other two theories?

What have been the results of empirical tests of the dividend theories?

OTHER DIVIDEND POLICY ISSUES

Before we discuss how dividend policy is set in practice, we must examine two other theoretical issues that could affect our views toward dividend policy: (1) the *information content*, or *signaling*, *hypothesis* and (2) the *clientele effect*.

INFORMATION CONTENT, OR SIGNALING, HYPOTHESIS

When MM set forth their dividend irrelevance theory, they assumed that everyone—investors and managers alike—has identical information regarding the firm's future earnings and dividends. In reality, however, different investors have different views on both the level of future dividend payments and the uncertainty inherent in those payments, and managers have better information about future prospects than public stockholders.

It has been observed that an increase in the dividend is often accompanied by an increase in the price of a stock, while a dividend cut generally leads to a stock price decline. This could indicate that investors, in the aggregate, prefer dividends to capital gains. However, MM argued differently. They noted the well-established fact that corporations are reluctant to cut dividends, hence do not raise dividends unless they anticipate higher earnings in the future. Thus, MM argued that a higher-than-expected dividend increase is a "signal" to investors that the firm's management forecasts good future earnings.[5] Conversely, a dividend reduction, or a smaller-than-expected increase, is a signal that management is forecasting poor earnings in the future. Thus, MM argued that investors' reactions to changes in dividend policy do not necessarily show that investors prefer dividends to retained earnings. Rather, they argue that price changes following dividend actions simply indicate that there is an important **information, or signaling, content** in dividend announcements.

Information Content (Signaling) Hypothesis
The theory that investors regard dividend changes as signals of management's earnings forecasts.

[5] Stephen Ross has suggested that managers can use capital structure as well as dividends to give signals concerning firm's future prospects. For example, a firm with good earnings prospects can carry more debt than a similar firm with poor earnings prospects. This theory, called *incentive signaling*, rests on the premise that signals with cash-based variables (either debt interest or dividends) cannot be mimicked by unsuccessful firms because such firms do not have the future cash-generating power to maintain the announced interest or dividend payment. Thus, investors are more likely to believe a glowing verbal report when it is accompanied by a dividend increase or a debt-financed expansion program. See Stephen A. Ross, "The Determination of Financial Structure: The Incentive-Signaling Approach," *The Bell Journal of Economics*, Spring 1977, 23–40.

Like most other aspects of dividend policy, empirical studies of signaling have had mixed results. There is clearly some information content in dividend announcements. However, it is difficult to tell whether the stock price changes that follow increases or decreases in dividends reflect only signaling effects or both signaling and dividend preference. Still, signaling effects should definitely be considered when a firm is contemplating a change in dividend policy.

CLIENTELE EFFECT

As we indicated earlier, different groups, or *clienteles*, of stockholders prefer different dividend payout policies. For example, retired individuals and university endowment funds generally prefer cash income, so they may want the firm to pay out a high percentage of its earnings. Such investors (and pension funds) are often in low or even zero tax brackets, so taxes are of no concern. On the other hand, stockholders in their peak earning years might prefer reinvestment, because they have less need for current investment income and would simply reinvest dividends received, after first paying income taxes on those dividends.

If a firm retains and reinvests income rather than paying dividends, those stockholders who need current income would be disadvantaged. The value of their stock might increase, but they would be forced to go to the trouble and expense of selling off some of their shares to obtain cash. Also, some institutional investors (or trustees for individuals) would be legally precluded from selling stock and then "spending capital." On the other hand, stockholders who are saving rather than spending dividends might favor the low dividend policy, for the less the firm pays out in dividends, the less these stockholders will have to pay in current taxes, and the less trouble and expense they will have to go through to reinvest their after-tax dividends. Therefore, investors who want current investment income should own shares in high dividend payout firms, while investors with no need for current investment income should own shares in low dividend payout firms. For example, investors seeking high cash income might invest in electric utilities, which averaged a 73 percent payout from 1998 through 2002, while those favoring growth could invest in the semiconductor industry, which paid out only 10 percent during the same time period.

To the extent that stockholders can switch firms, a firm can change from one dividend payout policy to another and then let stockholders who do not like the new policy sell to other investors who do. However, frequent switching would be inefficient because of (1) brokerage costs, (2) the likelihood that stockholders who are selling will have to pay capital gains taxes, and (3) a possible shortage of investors who like the firm's newly adopted dividend policy. Thus, management should be hesitant to change its dividend policy, because a change might cause current shareholders to sell their stock, forcing the stock price down. Such a price decline might be temporary, but it might also be permanent—if few new investors are attracted by the new dividend policy, then the stock price would remain depressed. Of course, the new policy might attract an even larger clientele than the firm had before, in which case the stock price would rise.

Evidence from several studies suggests that there is in fact a **clientele effect.**[6] MM and others have argued that one clientele is as good as another, so the existence

Clientele Effect
The tendency of a firm to attract a set of investors who like its dividend policy.

---

[6] For example, see R. Richardson Pettit, "Taxes, Transactions Costs and the Clientele Effect of Dividends," *The Journal of Financial Economics*, December 1977, 419–436.

of a clientele effect does not necessarily imply that one dividend policy is better than any other. MM may be wrong, though, and neither they nor anyone else can prove that the aggregate makeup of investors permits firms to disregard clientele effects. This issue, like most others in the dividend arena, is still up in the air.

SELF-TEST QUESTION

Define (1) information content and (2) the clientele effect, and explain how they affect dividend policy.

DIVIDEND STABILITY

As we noted at the beginning of the chapter, the stability of dividends is also important. Profits and cash flows vary over time, as do investment opportunities. Taken alone, this suggests that corporations should vary their dividends over time, increasing them when cash flows are large and the need for funds is low and lowering them when cash is in short supply relative to investment opportunities. However, many stockholders rely on dividends to meet expenses, and they would be seriously inconvenienced if the dividend stream were unstable. Further, reducing dividends to make funds available for capital investment could send incorrect signals to investors, who might push down the stock price because they interpreted the dividend cut to mean that the company's future earnings prospects have been diminished. Thus, maximizing its stock price requires a firm to balance its internal needs for funds against the needs and desires of its stockholders.

How should this balance be struck; that is, how stable and dependable should a firm attempt to make its dividends? It is impossible to give a definitive answer to this question, but the following points are relevant:

1. Virtually every publicly owned company makes a five- to ten-year financial forecast of earnings and dividends. Such forecasts are never made public—they are used for internal planning purposes only. However, security analysts construct similar forecasts and do make them available to investors; see *Value Line* for an example. Further, virtually every internal five- to ten-year corporate forecast we have seen for a "normal" company projects a trend of higher earnings and dividends. Both managers and investors know that economic conditions may cause actual results to differ from forecasted results, but "normal" companies expect to grow.

2. Years ago, when inflation was not persistent, the term "stable dividend policy" meant a policy of paying the same dollar dividend year after year. AT&T was a prime example of a company with a stable dividend policy—it paid $9 per year ($2.25 per quarter) for 25 straight years. Today, though, most companies and stockholders expect earnings to grow over time as a result of retained earnings and inflation. Further, dividends are normally expected to grow more or less in line with earnings. Thus, today a "stable dividend policy" generally means increasing the dividend at a reasonably steady rate.

   Dividend stability has two components: (1) How dependable is the growth rate, and (2) can we count on at least receiving the current dividend in the future? The most stable policy, from an investor's standpoint, is that of a firm whose dividend growth rate is predictable—such a company's total return (dividend yield plus capital gains yield) would be relatively stable over the long run, and its stock would be a good hedge against inflation. The second most stable policy is where stockholders can be reasonably sure that the current dividend will not be reduced—it may not grow at a steady rate, but management will probably be able to avoid cutting the dividend. The least stable situation is where earnings and cash flows are so volatile that investors cannot count on the company to maintain the current dividend over a typical business cycle.

3. Most observers believe that dividend stability is desirable. Assuming this position is correct, investors prefer stocks that pay more predictable dividends to stocks that pay the same average amount of dividends but in a more erratic manner. This means that the cost of equity will be minimized, and the stock price maximized, if a firm stabilizes its dividends as much as possible.

SELF-TEST QUESTIONS

What does the term "stable dividend policy" mean?

What are the two components of dividend stability?

ESTABLISHING THE DIVIDEND POLICY IN PRACTICE

In the preceding sections we saw that investors may or may not prefer dividends to capital gains, but that they do prefer predictable to unpredictable dividends. Given this situation, how should a firm determine the specific percentage of earnings that it will pay out as dividends? While policies undoubtedly vary from firm to firm, we describe in this section the steps that a typical firm takes when it establishes its target payout ratio.

SETTING THE TARGET PAYOUT RATIO: THE RESIDUAL DIVIDEND MODEL[7]

When deciding how much cash to distribute to stockholders, two points should be kept in mind: (1) The overriding objective is to maximize shareholder value, and (2) the firm's cash flows really belong to its shareholders, so management should refrain from retaining income unless they can reinvest it to produce returns higher than shareholders could themselves earn by investing the cash in investments of equal risk. On the other hand, recall from Chapter 9 that internal equity (retained earnings) is cheaper than external equity (new common stock). This encourages firms

---

[7] The term "payout ratio" can be interpreted in two ways: (1) the conventional way, where the payout ratio means the percentage of net income to common paid out as cash dividends, or (2) the percentage of net income distributed to stockholders as dividends and through share repurchases. In this section, we assume that no repurchases occur. Increasingly, though, firms are using the residual model to determine "distributions to shareholders" and then making a separate decision as to the form of that distribution. Further, an increasing percentage of the distribution is in the form of share repurchases.

to retain earnings because they add to the equity base, increase debt capacity, and thus reduce the likelihood that the firm will have to issue common stock at a later date to fund future investment projects.

When establishing a dividend policy, one size does not fit all. Some firms produce a lot of cash but have limited investment opportunities—this is true for firms in profitable but mature industries where few opportunities for growth exist. Such firms typically distribute a large percentage of their cash to shareholders, thereby attracting investment clienteles that prefer high dividends. Other firms generate little or no excess cash but have many good investment opportunities—this is often true of new firms in rapidly growing industries. Such firms generally distribute little or no cash but enjoy rising earnings and stock prices, thereby attracting investors who prefer capital gains.

Over the past few decades, there has been an increasing number of young, high-growth firms trading on the stock exchanges. A recent study by Eugene Fama and Kenneth French shows that the proportion of firms paying dividends has fallen sharply over this time period. In 1978, 66.5 percent of firms on the major stock exchanges paid dividends. By 1999, this proportion had fallen to 20.8 percent. Fama and French's analysis suggests that part of this decline is due to the changing composition of firms on the exchanges. Their analysis also indicates that this decline is due to the fact that firms of all types have become less likely to pay dividends.[8]

As Table 14-1 suggests, dividend payouts and dividend yields for large corporations vary considerably. Generally, firms in stable, cash-producing industries such as utilities, financial services, and tobacco pay relatively high dividends, whereas companies in rapidly growing industries such as computer and cable TV tend to pay lower dividends.

For a given firm, the optimal payout ratio is a function of four factors: (1) investor's preferences for dividends versus capital gains, (2) the firm's investment opportunities, (3) its target capital structure, and (4) the availability and cost of external capital. The last three elements are combined in what we call the **residual dividend model.** Under this model a firm follows these four steps when establishing its target payout ratio: (1) It determines the optimal capital budget; (2) it determines the amount of equity needed to finance that budget, given its target capital structure; (3) it uses retained earnings to meet equity requirements to the extent possible; and (4) it pays dividends only if more earnings are available than are needed to support the optimal capital budget. The word *residual* implies "leftover," and the residual policy implies that dividends are paid out of "leftover" earnings.

If a firm rigidly follows the residual dividend policy, then dividends paid in any given year can be expressed as follows:

$$\text{Dividends} = \text{Net income} - \text{Retained earnings required to help finance new investments}$$

$$= \text{Net income} - [(\text{Target equity ratio})(\text{Total capital budget})].$$

For example, suppose the target equity ratio is 60 percent and the firm plans to spend $50 million on capital projects. In that case, it would need $50(0.6) = $30 million of common equity. Then, if its net income were $100 million, its dividends would be $100 − $30 = $70 million. So, if the company had $100 million of earnings and a

Residual Dividend Model
A model in which the dividend paid is set equal to net income minus the amount of retained earnings necessary to finance the firm's optimal capital budget.

[8] Eugene F. Fama and Kenneth R. French, "Disappearing Dividends: Changing Firm Characteristics or Lower Propensity to Pay?" *Journal of Applied Corporate Finance*, Vol. 14, No. 1, Spring 2001, 67–79; and "Disappearing Dividends: Changing Firm Characteristics or Lower Propensity to Pay?" *Journal of Financial Economics*, Vol. 60, April 2001, 3–43. The last citation is a longer and more technical version of the first paper cited.

TABLE 14-1   Dividend Payouts

COMPANY	INDUSTRY	DIVIDEND PAYOUT	DIVIDEND YIELD
I. COMPANIES THAT PAY HIGH DIVIDENDS			
Laclede Gas	Natural gas distribution	97.77%	6.02%
Empire District Electric	Electric utility	93.58	6.46
R. J. Reynolds Tobacco	Tobacco	91.48	6.65
Alliance Capital Management	Financial services	88.93	5.33
Lance Inc.	Food processor	84.54	4.92
Standard Register	Office equipment	69.23	4.83
II. COMPANIES THAT PAY LITTLE OR NO DIVIDENDS			
Wal-Mart Stores	Retail	17.00%	0.51%
Marriott International	Hotel and gaming	11.48	0.54
Texas Instruments	Semiconductor	6.49	0.25
Delta Air Lines	Airline	2.79	0.23
Dell Computer	Computers	0	0
Genentech	Biotechnology	0	0

SOURCE: Adapted from *Value Line Investment Survey*, CD-ROM, March 2002.

capital budget of $50 million, it would use $30 million of the retained earnings plus $50 − $30 = $20 million of new debt to finance the capital budget, and this would keep its capital structure on target. Note that the amount of equity needed to finance new investments might exceed the net income; in our example, this would happen if the capital budget were $200 million. In that case, no dividends would be paid, and the company would have to issue new common stock in order to maintain its target capital structure.

Most firms have a target capital structure that calls for at least some debt, so new financing is done partly with debt and partly with equity. As long as the firm finances with the optimal mix of debt and equity, and provided it uses only internally generated equity (retained earnings), then the marginal cost of each new dollar of capital will be minimized. Internally generated equity is available for financing a certain amount of new investment, but beyond that amount, the firm must turn to more expensive new common stock. At the point where new stock must be sold, the cost of equity, and consequently the marginal cost of capital, rises.

To illustrate these points, consider the case of Texas and Western (T&W) Transport Company. T&W's overall composite cost of capital is 10 percent. However, this cost assumes that all new equity comes from retained earnings. If the company must issue new stock, its cost of capital will be higher. T&W has $60 million in net income and a target capital structure of 60 percent equity and 40 percent debt. Provided that it does not pay any cash dividends, T&W could make net investments (investments in addition to asset replacements from depreciation) of $100 million, consisting of $60 million from retained earnings plus $40 million of new debt supported by the retained earnings, at a 10 percent marginal cost of capital. If the capital budget exceeded $100 million, the required equity component would exceed net income, which is of course the maximum amount of retained earnings. In this case, T&W would have to issue new common stock, thereby pushing its cost of capital above 10 percent.[9]

At the beginning of its planning period, T&W's financial staff considers all proposed projects for the upcoming period. Independent projects are accepted if their estimated returns exceed the risk-adjusted cost of capital. In choosing among mutually exclusive projects, T&W chooses the project with the highest positive NPV. The capital budget represents the amount of capital that is required to finance all accepted projects. If T&W follows a strict residual dividend policy, we can see from Table 14-2 that the estimated capital budget will have a profound effect on its dividend payout ratio.

If T&W forecasts poor investment opportunities, its estimated capital budget will be only $40 million. To maintain the target capital structure, 40 percent of this capital ($16 million) must be raised as debt, and 60 percent ($24 million) must be equity. If it followed a strict residual policy, T&W would retain $24 million to help finance new investments, then pay out the remaining $36 million as dividends. Under this scenario, the company's dividend payout ratio would be $36 million/$60 million = 0.6 = 60%.

By contrast, if the company's investment opportunities were average, its optimal capital budget would rise to $70 million. Here it would require $42 million of retained earnings, so dividends would be $60 − $42 = $18 million, for a payout of $18/$60 = 30%. Finally, if investment opportunities are good, the capital budget would be $150 million, which would require 0.6($150) = $90 million of equity. T&W would retain all of its net income ($60 million), thus pay no dividends. Moreover, since the required equity exceeds the retained earnings, the company would have to issue new common stock in order to maintain the target capital structure.

Since investment opportunities and earnings will surely vary from year to year, strict adherence to the residual dividend policy would result in unstable dividends. One year the firm might pay zero dividends because it needed the money to finance good investment opportunities, but the next year it might pay a large dividend because

---

[9] If T&W does not retain all of its earnings, its cost of capital will rise above 10 percent before its capital budget reaches $100 million. For example, if T&W chose to retain $36 million, its cost of capital would increase once the capital budget exceeded $36/0.6 = $60 million. To see this point, note that a capital budget of $60 million would require $36 million of equity—if the capital budget rose above $60 million, the company's required equity capital would exceed its retained earnings, thereby requiring it to issue new common stock.

TABLE 14-2	T&W's Dividend Payout Ratio with $60 Million of Net Income When Faced with Different Investment Opportunities (Dollars in Millions)

| | INVESTMENT OPPORTUNITIES | | |
	POOR	AVERAGE	GOOD
Capital budget	$40	$70	$150
Net income	$60	$60	60
Required equity (0.6 × Capital budget)	24	42	90
Dividends paid (NI − Required equity)	$36	$18	−$30[a]
Dividend payout ratio (Dividend/NI)	60%	30%	0%

[a] With a $150 million capital budget, T&W would retain all of its earnings and also issue $30 million of new stock.

investment opportunities were poor and it therefore did not need to retain much. Similarly, fluctuating earnings could also lead to variable dividends, even if investment opportunities were stable. Therefore, following the residual dividend policy would almost certainly lead to fluctuating, unstable dividends. Thus, following the residual dividend policy would be optimal only if investors were not bothered by fluctuating dividends. However, since investors prefer stable, dependable dividends, k_s would be higher, and the stock price lower, if the firm followed the residual model in a strict sense rather than attempting to stabilize its dividends over time. Therefore, firms should

1. Estimate the firm's earnings and investment opportunities, on average, over the next five or so years.
2. Use this forecasted information to find the residual model payout ratio and dollars of dividends during the planning period.
3. Then set a *target payout ratio* on the basis of the projected data.

Thus, firms should use the residual policy to help set their long-run target payout ratios, but not as a guide to the payout in any one year.

Companies do use the residual dividend model as discussed above to help understand the determinants of an optimal dividend policy, but they typically use a computerized financial forecasting model when setting the target payout ratio. Most larger corporations forecast their financial statements over the next five to ten years. Information on projected capital expenditures and working capital requirements is entered into the model, along with sales forecasts, profit margins, depreciation, and the other elements required to forecast cash flows. The target capital structure is also specified, and the model shows the amount of debt and equity that will be required to meet the capital budgeting requirements while maintaining the target capital structure.

Then, dividend payments are introduced. Naturally, the higher the payout ratio, the greater the required external equity. Most companies use the model to find a dividend pattern over the forecast period (generally five years) that will provide sufficient equity to support the capital budget without having to sell new common stock or move the capital structure ratios outside the optimal range. The end result might include a statement, in a memo from the financial vice-president to the chairman of the board, such as the following:

We forecasted the total market demand for our products, what our share of the market is likely to be, and our required investments in capital assets and working capital. Using this information, we developed projected balance sheets and income statements for the period 2003–2007.

Our 2002 dividends totaled $50 million, or $2 per share. On the basis of projected earnings, cash flows, and capital requirements, we can increase the dividend by 8 percent per year. This is consistent with a payout ratio of 42 percent, on average, over the forecast period. Any faster dividend growth rate (or higher payout) would require us to sell common stock, cut the capital budget, or raise the debt ratio. Any slower growth rate would lead to increases in the common equity ratio. Therefore, I recommend that the Board increase the dividend for 2003 by 8 percent, to $2.16, and that it plan for similar increases in the future.

Events over the next five years will undoubtedly lead to differences between our forecasts and actual results. If and when such events occur, we will want to reexamine our position. However, I am confident that we can meet any random cash shortfalls by increasing our borrowings—we have unused debt capacity that gives us flexibility in this regard.

We ran the corporate model under several recession scenarios. If the economy really crashes, our earnings will not cover the dividend. However, in all "reasonable" scenarios our cash flows do cover the dividend. I know the Board does not want to push the dividend up to a level where we would have to cut it under bad economic conditions. Our model runs indicate, though, that the $2.16 dividend can be maintained under any reasonable set of forecasts. Only if we increased the dividend to over $3 would we be seriously exposed to the danger of having to cut the dividend.

I might also note that *Value Line* and most other analysts' reports are forecasting that our dividends will grow in the 6 percent to 8 percent range. Thus, if we go to $2.16, we will be at the high end of the range, which should give our stock a boost. With takeover rumors so widespread, getting the stock up a bit would make us all breathe a little easier.

Finally, we considered distributing cash to shareholders through a stock repurchase program. Here we would reduce the dividend payout ratio and use the funds so generated to buy our stock on the open market. Such a program has several advantages, but it would also have drawbacks. I do not recommend that we institute a stock repurchase program at this time. However, if our free cash flows exceed our forecasts, I would recommend that we use these surpluses to buy back stock. Also, I plan to continue looking into a regular repurchase program, and I may recommend such a program in the future.

This company has very stable operations, so it can plan its dividends with a fairly high degree of confidence. Other companies, especially those in cyclical industries, have difficulty maintaining in bad times a dividend that is really too low in good times. Such companies set a very low "regular" dividend and then supplement it with an "extra" dividend when times are good. General Motors, Ford, and other auto companies have followed the **low-regular-dividend-plus-extras** policy in the past. Each company announced a low regular dividend that it was sure could be maintained "through hell or high water," and stockholders could count on receiving that dividend under all conditions. Then, when times were good and profits and cash flows were high, the companies paid a clearly designated extra dividend. Investors recognized that the extras might not be maintained in the future, so they did not interpret them as a signal that the companies' earnings were going up permanently, nor did they take the elimination of the extra as a negative signal. In recent years, however, the auto companies and many other companies have replaced the "extras" in their low-regular-dividend-plus-extras policy with stock repurchases.

Low-Regular-Dividend-plus-Extras
The policy of announcing a low, regular dividend that can be maintained no matter what, and then when times are good paying a designated "extra" dividend.

EARNINGS, CASH FLOWS, AND DIVIDENDS

We normally think of earnings as being the primary determinant of dividends, but in reality cash flows are more important. This situation is revealed in Figure 14-1, which gives data for Chevron-Texaco Corporation from 1979 through 2001. Chevron's dividends increased steadily from 1979 to 1981; during that period both earnings and cash flows were rising, as was the price of oil. After 1981, oil prices declined sharply, pulling earnings down. Cash flows, though, remained well above the dividend requirement.

Chevron acquired Gulf Oil in 1984, and it issued more than $10 billion of debt to finance the acquisition. Interest on the debt hurt earnings immediately after the merger, as did certain write-offs connected with the merger. Further, Chevron's management wanted to pay off new debt as fast as possible. All of this influenced the company's decision to hold the dividend constant from 1982 through 1987. Earnings

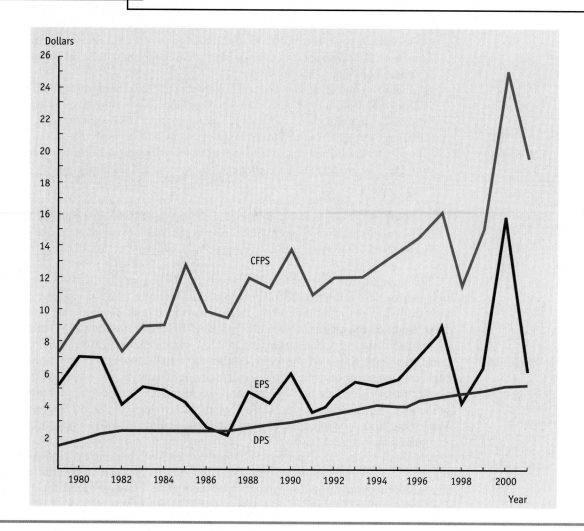

improved dramatically in 1988, and the dividend has increased more or less steadily since then. Note that the dividend was increased in 1991 in spite of the weak earnings and cash flow resulting from the Persian Gulf War. More recently, in October 2001, Chevron merged with Texaco. Earnings in 2001 declined due to the decline in crude oil and natural gas prices. Duplicative costs due to the merger are still being eliminated, and improving oil and gas prices should help improve the firm's 2002 earnings.

Now look at Columns 4 and 6, which show payout ratios based on earnings and on cash flows. The earnings payout is quite volatile—dividends ranged from 26 percent to 120 percent of earnings. The cash flow payout, on the other hand, is much more stable—it ranged from 19 percent to 44 percent. Further, the correlation between dividends and cash flows was 0.82 versus 0.50 between dividends and earnings. Thus, dividends clearly depend more on cash flows, which reflect the company's *ability* to pay dividends, than on current earnings, which are heavily influenced by accounting practices and which do not necessarily reflect the ability to pay dividends.

FIGURE 14-1   Continued

YEAR (1)	DIVIDENDS PER SHARE (2)	EARNINGS PER SHARE (3)	EARNINGS PAYOUT (4)	CASH FLOW PER SHARE (5)	CASH FLOW PAYOUT (6)
1979	$1.45	$5.22	28%	$ 7.29	20%
1980	1.80	7.02	26	9.26	19
1981	2.20	6.96	32	9.61	23
1982	2.40	4.03	60	7.35	33
1983	2.40	5.15	47	8.93	27
1984	2.40	4.94	49	9.00	27
1985	2.40	4.19	57	12.76	19
1986	2.40	2.63	91	9.86	24
1987	2.40	2.13	113	9.47	25
1988	2.55	4.86	52	11.97	21
1989	2.80	4.16	67	11.33	25
1990	2.95	6.02	49	13.75	21
1991	3.25	3.69	88	11.28	29
1992	3.30	4.70	70	12.88	26
1993	3.50	5.60	63	13.12	27
1994	3.70	5.20	71	12.66	29
1995	3.85	6.02	64	13.36	29
1996	4.16	8.12	51	14.90	28
1997	4.56	9.66	47	16.70	27
1998	4.88	4.08	120	11.20	44
1999	4.96	6.28	79	15.04	33
2000	5.20	15.94	33	25.04	21
2001	5.30	6.18	86	19.52	27

NOTE: For consistency, data have not been adjusted for a two-for-one split in 1994.

SOURCE: Adapted from *Value Line Investment Survey*, various issues.

PAYMENT PROCEDURES

Dividends are normally paid quarterly, and, if conditions permit, the dividend is increased once each year. For example, Katz Corporation paid $0.50 per quarter in 2002, or at an annual rate of $2.00. In common financial parlance, we say that in 2002 Katz's *regular quarterly dividend* was $0.50, and its *annual dividend* was $2.00. In late 2002, Katz's board of directors met, reviewed projections for 2003, and decided to keep the 2003 dividend at $2.00. The directors announced the $2 rate, so stockholders could count on receiving it unless the company experienced unanticipated operating problems.

The actual payment procedure is as follows:

Declaration Date
The date on which a firm's directors issue a statement declaring a dividend.

1. **Declaration date.** On the **declaration date**—say, on November 8—the directors meet and declare the regular dividend, issuing a statement similar to the

following: "On November 8, 2002, the directors of Katz Corporation met and declared the regular quarterly dividend of 50 cents per share, payable to holders of record on December 6, payment to be made on January 2, 2003." For accounting purposes, the declared dividend becomes an actual liability on the declaration date. If a balance sheet were constructed, the amount ($0.50) × (Number of shares outstanding) would appear as a current liability, and retained earnings would be reduced by a like amount.

Holder-of-Record Date
If the company lists the stockholder as an owner on this date, then the stockholder receives the dividend.

2. **Holder-of-record date.** At the close of business on the **holder-of-record date,** December 6, the company closes its stock transfer books and makes up a list of shareholders as of that date. If Katz Corporation is notified of the sales before 5 P.M. on December 6, then the new owner receives the dividend. However, if notification is received on or after December 7, the previous owner gets the dividend check.

3. **Ex-dividend date.** Suppose Jean Buyer buys 100 shares of stock from John Seller on December 3. Will the company be notified of the transfer in time to list Buyer as the new owner and thus pay the dividend to her? To avoid conflict, the securities industry has set up a convention under which the right to the dividend remains with the stock until two business days prior to the holder-of-record date; on the second day before that date, the right to the dividend no longer goes with the shares. The date when the right to the dividend leaves the stock is called the **ex-dividend date.** In this case, the ex-dividend date is two days prior to December 6, or December 4:

Ex-Dividend Date
The date on which the right to the current dividend no longer accompanies a stock; it is usually two business days prior to the holder-of-record date.

Dividend goes with stock: December 3
Ex-dividend date: December 4
                          December 5
Holder-of-record date: December 6

Therefore, if Buyer is to receive the dividend, she must buy the stock on or before December 3. If she buys it on December 4 or later, Seller will receive the dividend because he will be the official holder of record.

Katz's dividend amounts to $0.50, so the ex-dividend date is important. Barring fluctuations in the stock market, one would normally expect the price of a stock to drop by approximately the amount of the dividend on the ex-dividend date. Thus, if Katz closed at $30.50 on December 3, it would probably open at about $30 on December 4.[10]

Payment Date
The date on which a firm actually mails dividend checks.

4. **Payment date.** The company actually mails the checks to the holders of record on January 2, the **payment date.**

---

[10] Tax effects cause the price decline on average to be less than the full amount of the dividend. Suppose you were an investor in the 40 percent federal-plus-state tax bracket. If you bought Katz's stock on December 3, you would receive the dividend, but you would almost immediately pay 40 percent of it out in taxes. Thus, you would want to wait until December 4, to buy the stock if you thought you could get it for $0.50 less per share. Your reaction, and that of others, would influence stock prices around dividend payment dates. Here is what would happen:

1. Other things held constant, a stock's price should rise during the quarter, with the daily price increase (for Katz) equal to $0.50/90 = $0.005556. Therefore, if the price started at $30 just after its last ex-dividend date, it would rise to $30.50 on December 3.

2. In the absence of taxes, the stock's price would fall to $30 on December 4 and then start up as the next dividend accrual period began. Thus, over time, if everything else were held constant, the stock's price would follow a sawtooth pattern if it were plotted on a graph.

(footnote continues)

Explain the logic of the residual dividend model, the steps a firm would take to implement it, and why it is more likely to be used to establish a long-run payout target than to set the actual year-by-year payout ratio.

How do firms use planning models to help set dividend policy?

Which are more critical to the dividend decision, earnings or cash flow? Explain.

Explain the procedures used to actually pay the dividend.

Why is the ex-dividend date important to investors?

DIVIDEND REINVESTMENT PLANS

Dividend Reinvestment Plan (DRIP)
A plan that enables a stockholder to automatically reinvest dividends received back into the stock of the paying firm.

During the 1970s, most large companies instituted **dividend reinvestment plans (DRIPs),** whereby stockholders can automatically reinvest their dividends in the stock of the paying corporation.[11] Today most larger companies offer DRIPs, and although participation rates vary considerably, about 25 percent of the average firm's shareholders are enrolled. There are two types of DRIPs: (1) plans that involve only "old stock" that is already outstanding and (2) plans that involve newly issued stock. In either case, the stockholder must pay taxes on the amount of the dividends, even though stock rather than cash is received.

Under both types of DRIPs, stockholders choose between continuing to receive dividend checks or having the company use the dividends to buy more stock in the corporation. Under the "old stock" type of plan, if a stockholder elects reinvestment, a bank, acting as trustee, takes the total funds available for reinvestment, purchases the corporation's stock on the open market, and allocates the shares purchased to the participating stockholders' accounts on a pro rata basis. The transactions costs of buying shares (brokerage costs) are low because of volume purchases, so these plans benefit small stockholders who do not need cash dividends for current consumption.

The "new stock" type of DRIP invests the dividends in newly issued stock, hence these plans raise new capital for the firm. AT&T, Xerox, Union Carbide, and many other companies have had new stock plans in effect in recent years, using them to raise substantial amounts of new equity capital. No fees are charged to stockholders, and many companies offer stock at a discount of 3 percent to 5 percent below the actual market price. The companies offer discounts as a trade-off against flotation costs that would be incurred if new stock had been issued through investment bankers rather than through the dividend reinvestment plans.

(Footnote 10 continued)

3. Because of taxes, the stock's price would neither rise by the full amount of the dividend nor fall by the full dividend amount when it goes ex-dividend.

4. The amount of the rise and subsequent fall would depend on the average investor's marginal tax rate.

See Edwin J. Elton and Martin J. Gruber, "Marginal Stockholder Tax Rates and the Clientele Effect," *Review of Economics and Statistics*, February 1970, 68–74, for an interesting discussion of all this.

[11] See Richard H. Pettway and R. Phil Malone, "Automatic Dividend Reinvestment Plans," *Financial Management*, Winter 1973, 11–18, for an old but still excellent discussion of the subject.

One interesting aspect of DRIPs is that they are forcing corporations to reexamine their basic dividend policies. A high participation rate in a DRIP suggests that stockholders might be better off if the firm simply reduced cash dividends, which would save stockholders some personal income taxes. Quite a few firms are surveying their stockholders to learn more about their preferences and to find out how they would react to a change in dividend policy. A more rational approach to basic dividend policy decisions may emerge from this research.

Note that companies start or stop using new stock DRIPs depending on their need for equity capital. Thus, both Union Carbide and AT&T recently stopped offering a new stock DRIP with a 5 percent discount because their needs for equity capital declined. However, about the same time Xerox began such a plan.

Some companies have expanded their DRIPs by moving to "open enrollment," whereby anyone can purchase the firm's stock directly and thus bypass brokers' commissions. Exxon Mobil not only allows investors to buy their initial shares at no fee but also lets them pick up additional shares through automatic bank account withdrawals. Several plans, including Exxon Mobil's, offer dividend reinvestment for individual retirement accounts, and some, such as U.S. West, allow participants to invest weekly or monthly rather than on the quarterly dividend schedule. In all of these plans, and many others, stockholders can invest more than the dividends they are foregoing—they simply send a check to the company and buy shares without a brokerage commission. According to First Chicago Trust, which handles the paperwork for 13 million shareholder DRIP accounts, at least half of all DRIPs will offer open enrollment, extra purchases, and other expanded services within the next few years.

> ### SELF-TEST QUESTIONS
>
> What are dividend reinvestment plans?
>
> What are their advantages and disadvantages from both the stockholders' and the firm's perspectives?

SUMMARY OF FACTORS INFLUENCING DIVIDEND POLICY

In earlier sections, we described both the major theories of investor preference and some issues concerning the effects of dividend policy on the value of a firm. We also discussed the residual dividend model for setting a firm's long-run target payout ratio. In this section, we discuss several other factors that affect the dividend decision. These factors may be grouped into four broad categories: (1) constraints on dividend payments, (2) investment opportunities, (3) availability and cost of alternative sources of capital, and (4) effects of dividend policy on k_s. Each of these categories has several subparts, which we discuss in the following paragraphs.

CONSTRAINTS

1. **Bond indentures.** Debt contracts often limit dividend payments to earnings generated after the loan was granted. Also, debt contracts often stipulate that

no dividends can be paid unless the current ratio, times-interest-earned ratio, and other safety ratios exceed stated minimums.

2. **Preferred stock restrictions.** Typically, common dividends cannot be paid if the company has omitted its preferred dividend. The preferred arrearages must be satisfied before common dividends can be resumed.

3. **Impairment of capital rule.** Dividend payments cannot exceed the balance sheet item "retained earnings." This legal restriction, known as the *impairment of capital rule*, is designed to protect creditors. Without the rule, a company that is in trouble might distribute most of its assets to stockholders and leave its debtholders out in the cold. (*Liquidating dividends* can be paid out of capital, but they must be indicated as such, and they must not reduce capital below the limits stated in debt contracts.)

4. **Availability of cash.** Cash dividends can be paid only with cash. Thus, a shortage of cash in the bank can restrict dividend payments. However, the ability to borrow can offset this factor.

5. **Penalty tax on improperly accumulated earnings.** To prevent wealthy individuals from using corporations to avoid personal taxes, the Tax Code provides for a special surtax on improperly accumulated income. Thus, if the IRS can demonstrate that a firm's dividend payout ratio is being deliberately held down to help its stockholders avoid personal taxes, the firm is subject to heavy penalties. This factor is generally relevant only to privately owned firms.

INVESTMENT OPPORTUNITIES

1. **Number of profitable investment opportunities.** If a firm typically has a large number of profitable investment opportunities, this will tend to produce a low target payout ratio, and vice versa if the firm's profitable investment opportunities are few in number.

2. **Possibility of accelerating or delaying projects.** The ability to accelerate or postpone projects will permit a firm to adhere more closely to a stable dividend policy.

ALTERNATIVE SOURCES OF CAPITAL

1. **Cost of selling new stock.** If a firm needs to finance a given level of investment, it can obtain equity by retaining earnings or by issuing new common stock. If flotation costs (including any negative signaling effects of a stock offering) are high, k_e will be well above k_s, making it better to set a low payout ratio and to finance through retention rather than through sale of new common stock. On the other hand, a high dividend payout ratio is more feasible for a firm whose flotation costs are low. Flotation costs differ among firms — for example, the flotation percentage is generally higher for small firms, so they tend to set low payout ratios.

2. **Ability to substitute debt for equity.** A firm can finance a given level of investment with either debt or equity. As noted above, low stock flotation costs permit a more flexible dividend policy because equity can be raised either by retaining earnings or by selling new stock. A similar situation holds for debt

policy: If the firm can adjust its debt ratio without raising costs sharply, it can pay the expected dividend, even if earnings fluctuate, by increasing its debt ratio.

3. **Control.** If management is concerned about maintaining control, it may be reluctant to sell new stock, hence the company may retain more earnings than it otherwise would. However, if stockholders want higher dividends and a proxy fight looms, then the dividend will be increased.

EFFECTS OF DIVIDEND POLICY ON k_s

The effects of dividend policy on k_s may be considered in terms of four factors: (1) stockholders' desire for current versus future income, (2) perceived riskiness of dividends versus capital gains, (3) the tax advantage of capital gains over dividends, and (4) the information content of dividends (signaling). Since we discussed each of these factors in detail earlier, we need only note here that the importance of each factor in terms of its effect on k_s varies from firm to firm depending on the makeup of its current and possible future stockholders.

It should be apparent from our discussion that dividend policy decisions are truly exercises in informed judgment, not decisions that can be quantified precisely. Even so, to make rational dividend decisions, financial managers must take account of all the points discussed in the preceding sections.

SELF-TEST QUESTIONS

Identify the four broad sets of factors that affect dividend policy.

What constraints affect dividend policy?

How do investment opportunities affect dividend policy?

How does the availability and cost of outside capital affect dividend policy?

OVERVIEW OF THE DIVIDEND POLICY DECISION

In many ways, our discussion of dividend policy parallels our discussion of capital structure: We presented the relevant theories and issues, and we listed some additional factors that influence dividend policy, but we did not come up with any hard-and-fast guidelines that managers can follow. It should be apparent from our discussion that dividend policy decisions are exercises in informed judgment, not decisions that can be based on a precise mathematical model.

In practice, dividend policy is not an independent decision—the dividend decision is made jointly with capital structure and capital budgeting decisions. The underlying reason for this joint decision process is asymmetric information, which influences managerial actions in two ways:

1. In general, managers do not want to issue new common stock. First, new common stock involves issuance costs—commissions, fees, and so on—and those

costs can be avoided by using retained earnings to finance the firm's equity needs. Also, as we discussed in Chapter 13, asymmetric information causes investors to view new common stock issues as negative signals and thus lowers expectations regarding the firm's future prospects. The end result is that the announcement of a new stock issue usually leads to a decrease in the stock price. Considering the total costs involved, including both issuance and asymmetric information costs, managers strongly prefer to use retained earnings as their primary source of new equity.

2. Dividend changes provide signals about managers' beliefs as to their firms' future prospects. Thus, dividend reductions, or worse yet, omissions, generally have a significant negative effect on a firm's stock price. Since managers recognize this, they try to set dollar dividends low enough so that there is only a remote chance that the dividend will have to be reduced in the future. Of course, unexpectedly large dividend increases can be used to provide positive signals.

The effects of asymmetric information suggest that, to the extent possible, managers should avoid both new common stock sales and dividend cuts, because both actions tend to lower stock prices. Thus, in setting dividend policy, managers should begin by considering the firm's future investment opportunities relative to its projected internal sources of funds. The firm's target capital structure also plays a part, but because the optimal capital structure is a *range*, firms can vary their actual capital structures somewhat from year to year. Since it is best to avoid issuing new common stock, the target long-term payout ratio should be designed to permit the firm to meet all of its equity capital requirements with retained earnings. In effect, managers should use the residual dividend model to set dividends, but in a long-term framework. Finally, the current dollar dividend should be set so that there is an extremely low probability that the dividend, once set, will ever have to be lowered or omitted.

Of course, the dividend decision is made during the planning process, so there is uncertainty about future investment opportunities and operating cash flows. Thus, the actual payout ratio in any year will probably be above or below the firm's long-range target. However, the dollar dividend should be maintained, or increased as planned, unless the firm's financial condition deteriorates to the point where the planned policy simply cannot be maintained. A steady or increasing stream of dividends over the long run signals that the firm's financial condition is under control. Further, investor uncertainty is decreased by stable dividends, so a steady dividend stream reduces the negative effect of a new stock issue, should one become absolutely necessary.

In general, firms with superior investment opportunities should set lower payouts, hence retain more earnings, than firms with poor investment opportunities. The degree of uncertainty also influences the decision. If there is a great deal of uncertainty in the forecasts of free cash flows, which are defined here as the firm's operating cash flows minus mandatory equity investments, then it is best to be conservative and to set a lower current dollar dividend. Also, firms with postponable investment opportunities can afford to set a higher dollar dividend, because in times of stress investments can be postponed for a year or two, thus increasing the cash available for dividends. Finally, firms whose cost of capital is largely unaffected by changes in the debt ratio can also afford to set a higher payout ratio, because they can, in times of stress, more easily issue additional debt to maintain the capital budgeting program without having to cut dividends or issue stock.

Firms have only one opportunity to set the dividend payment from scratch. Therefore, today's dividend decisions are constrained by policies that were set in the past, hence setting a policy for the next five years necessarily begins with a review of the current situation.

Although we have outlined a rational process for managers to use when setting their firms' dividend policies, dividend policy still remains one of the most judgmental decisions that firms must make. For this reason, dividend policy is always set by the board of directors—the financial staff analyzes the situation and makes a recommendation, but the board makes the final decision.

SELF-TEST QUESTION

Describe the dividend policy decision process. Be sure to discuss all the factors that influence the decision.

STOCK DIVIDENDS AND STOCK SPLITS

www Up-to-date information about changes in stock splits and stock repurchases is now just a few clicks away. A good place to get started is The Online Investor at **http://www. investhelp.com**. The Online Investor's home page includes recent stock repurchase and stock split announcements at "Buybacks" and "Splits Center."

Stock dividends and stock splits are related to the firm's cash dividend policy. The rationale for stock dividends and splits can best be explained through an example. We will use Porter Electronic Controls Inc., a $700 million electronic components manufacturer, for this purpose. Since its inception, Porter's markets have been expanding, and the company has enjoyed growth in sales and earnings. Some of its earnings have been paid out in dividends, but some are also retained each year, causing its earnings per share and stock price to grow. The company began its life with only a few thousand shares outstanding, and, after some years of growth, each of Porter's shares had a very high EPS and DPS. When a "normal" P/E ratio was applied, the derived market price was so high that few people could afford to buy a "round lot" of 100 shares. This limited the demand for the stock and thus kept the total market value of the firm below what it would have been if more shares, at a lower price, had been outstanding. To correct this situation, Porter "split its stock," as described in the next section.

STOCK SPLITS

Stock Split
An action taken by a firm to increase the number of shares outstanding, such as doubling the number of shares outstanding by giving each stockholder two new shares for each one formerly held.

Although there is little empirical evidence to support the contention, there is nevertheless a widespread belief in financial circles that an *optimal price range* exists for stocks. "Optimal" means that if the price is within this range, the price/earnings ratio, hence the firm's value, will be maximized. Many observers, including Porter's management, believe that the best range for most stocks is from $20 to $80 per share. Accordingly, if the price of Porter's stock rose to $80, management would probably declare a two-for-one **stock split,** thus doubling the number of shares outstanding, halving the earnings and dividends per share, and thereby lowering the stock price. Each stockholder would have more shares, but each share would be worth less. If the post-split price were $40, Porter's stockholders would be exactly as well off as they were before the split. However, if the stock price were to stabilize above $40, stockholders would be better off. Stock splits can be of any size—for example, the stock could be split two-for-one, three-for-one, one-and-a-half-for-one, or in any other way.[12]

STOCK DIVIDENDS

Stock Dividend
A dividend paid in the form of additional shares of stock rather than in cash.

Stock dividends are similar to stock splits in that they "divide the pie into smaller slices" without affecting the fundamental position of the current stockholders. On a 5 percent stock dividend, the holder of 100 shares would receive an additional 5 shares (without cost); on a 20 percent stock dividend, the same holder would receive 20 new shares; and so on. Again, the total number of shares is increased, so earnings, dividends, and price per share all decline.

If a firm wants to reduce the price of its stock, should it use a stock split or a stock dividend? Stock splits are generally used after a sharp price run-up to produce a large price reduction. Stock dividends used on a regular annual basis will keep the stock price more or less constrained. For example, if a firm's earnings and dividends were growing at about 10 percent per year, its stock price would tend to go up at about that same rate, and it would soon be outside the desired trading range. A 10 percent annual stock dividend would maintain the stock price within the optimal trading range. Note, though, that small stock dividends create bookkeeping problems and unnecessary expenses, so firms today use stock splits far more often than stock dividends.[13]

EFFECT ON STOCK PRICES

If a company splits its stock or declares a stock dividend, will this increase the market value of its stock? Several empirical studies have sought to answer this question. Here is a summary of their findings.[14]

1. On average, the price of a company's stock rises shortly after it announces a stock split or dividend.

2. However, these price increases are more the result of the fact that investors take stock splits/dividends as signals of higher future earnings and dividends

---

[12] *Reverse splits*, which reduce the shares outstanding, can even be used. For example, a company whose stock sells for $5 might employ a one-for-five reverse split, exchanging one new share for five old ones and raising the value of the shares to about $25, which is within the optimal price range. LTV Corporation did this after several years of losses had driven its stock price below the optimal range.

[13] Accountants treat stock splits and stock dividends somewhat differently. For example, in a two-for-one stock split, the number of shares outstanding is doubled and the par value is halved, and that is about all there is to it. With a stock dividend, a bookkeeping entry is made transferring "retained earnings" to "common stock." For example, if a firm had 1,000,000 shares outstanding, if the stock price was $10, and if it wanted to pay a 10 percent stock dividend, then (1) each stockholder would be given one new share of stock for each 10 shares held, and (2) the accounting entries would involve showing 100,000 more shares outstanding and transferring 100,000($10) = $1,000,000 from "retained earnings" to "common stock." The retained earnings transfer limits the size of stock dividends, but that is not important because companies can always split their stock in any way they choose.

[14] See Eugene F. Fama, Lawrence Fisher, Michael C. Jensen, and Richard Roll, "The Adjustment of Stock Prices to New Information," *International Economic Review*, February 1969, 1–21; Mark S. Grinblatt, Ronald M. Masulis, and Sheridan Titman, "The Valuation Effects of Stock Splits and Stock Dividends," *Journal of Financial Economics*, December 1984, 461–490; C. Austin Barker, "Evaluation of Stock Dividends," *Harvard Business Review*, July–August 1958, 99–114; and Thomas E. Copeland, "Liquidity Changes Following Stock Splits," *Journal of Finance*, March 1979, 115–141.

than of a desire for stock dividends/splits per se. Since only companies whose managements think things look good tend to split their stocks, the announcement of a stock split is taken as a signal that earnings and cash dividends are likely to rise. Thus, the price increases associated with stock splits/dividends are probably the result of signals of favorable prospects for earnings and dividends, not a desire for stock splits/dividends per se.

3. If a company announces a stock split or dividend, its price will tend to rise. However, if during the next few months it does not announce an increase in earnings and dividends, then its stock price will drop back to the earlier level.

4. As we noted earlier, brokerage commissions are generally higher in percentage terms on lower-priced stocks. This means that it is more expensive to trade low-priced than high-priced stocks, and this, in turn, means that stock splits may reduce the liquidity of a company's shares. This particular piece of evidence suggests that stock splits/dividends might actually be harmful, although a lower price does mean that more investors can afford to trade in round lots (100 shares), which carry lower commissions than do odd lots (less than 100 shares).

What do we conclude from all this? From a pure economic standpoint, stock dividends and splits are just additional pieces of paper. However, they provide management with a relatively low-cost way of signaling that the firm's prospects look good. Further, we should note that since few large, publicly owned stocks sell at prices above several hundred dollars, we simply do not know what the effect would be if Microsoft, Xerox, Hewlett-Packard, and other highly successful firms had never split their stocks, and consequently sold at prices in the thousands or even tens of thousands of dollars. All in all, it probably makes sense to employ stock dividends/splits when a firm's prospects are favorable, especially if the price of its stock has gone beyond the normal trading range.[15]

SELF-TEST QUESTIONS

What are stock dividends and stock splits?

How do stock dividends and splits affect stock prices?

In what situations should managers consider the use of stock dividends?

In what situations should they consider the use of stock splits?

STOCK REPURCHASES

Several years ago, a *Fortune* article entitled "Beating the Market by Buying Back Stock" discussed the fact that during a one-year period, more than 600 major corporations repurchased significant amounts of their own stock. It also gave illustrations

---

[15] It is interesting to note that Berkshire Hathaway, which is controlled by billionaire Warren Buffett, one of the most successful financiers of the twentieth century, has never had a stock split, and its stock sold on the NYSE for $63,650 per share in July 2002. But, in response to investment trusts that were being formed to sell fractional units of the stock, and thus, in effect, split it, Buffett himself created a new class of Berkshire Hathaway stock (Class B) worth about $\frac{1}{30}$ of a Class A (regular) share.

STOCK REPURCHASES: AN EASY WAY TO BOOST STOCK PRICES?

Looking for a way to boost your company's stock price? Why not buy back some of your company's shares? That reflects the thinking of an increasing number of financial managers.

The buyback rage is in some ways surprising. Given the performance of the stock market in the 1990s, it has become quite expensive to buy back shares. Nevertheless, the market's response to a buyback announcement is usually positive. For example, in mid-1996 Reebok announced that it would buy back one-third of its outstanding shares, and on the announcement day, the stock price rose 10 percent. Reebok's experience is not unique. A recent study found (1) that the average company's stock rose 3.5 percent the day a buyback was announced and (2) that companies that repurchase shares outperform the market over a four-year period following the announcement.[a]

Why are buybacks so popular with investors? The general view is that financial managers are signaling to the investment community a belief that the stock is undervalued, hence that the company thinks its own stock is an attractive investment. In this respect, stock repurchases have the opposite effect of stock issuances, which are thought to signal that the firm's stock is overvalued. Buybacks also help assure investors that the company is not wasting its shareholders' money by investing in sub-par investments. Michael O'Neill, the CFO of BankAmerica, puts it this way: "We look very hard internally, but if we don't have a profitable use for capital, we think we should return it to shareholders."

Despite all the recent hoopla surrounding buybacks, many analysts stress that in some instances repurchases have a downside: If a firm's stock is actually overvalued, buying back shares at the inflated price will harm the remaining stockholders. In this regard, buybacks should not be viewed as a gimmick to boost stock prices in the short run, but should be used only if they are part of a well-thought-out strategy for investment and for distributing cash to stockholders. Indeed, buybacks do not always succeed— Disney, for example, announced a buyback in April 1996, and its stock price fell more than 10 percent in the next six months.

[a] David Ikenberry, Josef Lakonishok, and Theo Vermaelen, "Market Under-Reaction to Open Market Share Repurchases," *Journal of Financial Economics*, 1995, Vol. 39, 181–208.

SOURCE: Adapted from "Buybacks Make News, But Do They Make Sense?" *BusinessWeek*, August 12, 1996, 76.

---

of some specific companies' repurchase programs and the effects of these programs on stock prices. The article's conclusion was that "buybacks have made a mint for shareholders who stay with the companies carrying them out."

In addition, we noted earlier that several years ago FPL cut its dividends but simultaneously instituted a program to repurchase shares of its stock. Thus, it substituted share repurchases for cash dividends as a way to distribute funds to stockholders. FPL is not alone— in recent years Philip Morris, GE, Disney, Citigroup, Merck, and more than 800 other companies took similar actions, and the dollars used to repurchase shares approximately matched the amount paid out as dividends.

Why are stock repurchase programs becoming so popular? The short answer is that they enhance shareholder value: A more complete answer is given in the remainder of this section, where we explain what a **stock repurchase** is, how it is carried out, and how the financial manager should analyze a possible repurchase program.

Stock Repurchase
A transaction in which a firm buys back shares of its own stock, thereby decreasing shares outstanding, increasing EPS, and, often, increasing the stock price.

There are three principal types of repurchases: (1) situations where the firm has cash available for distribution to its stockholders, and it distributes this cash by repurchasing shares rather than by paying cash dividends; (2) situations where the firm concludes that its capital structure is too heavily weighted with equity, and then it sells debt and uses the proceeds to buy back its stock; and (3) situations where a firm has issued options to employees and then uses open market repurchases to obtain stock for use when the options are exercised.

Stock that has been repurchased by a firm is called *treasury stock*. If some of the outstanding stock is repurchased, fewer shares will remain outstanding. Assuming that the repurchase does not adversely affect the firm's future earnings, the earnings

BUYBACKS HAVE LOWERED DIVIDEND YIELDS

Dividend payouts and yields have fallen sharply over the past two decades. In 1980, the average large company paid out 55 percent of its earnings as dividends, and its dividend yield exceeded 5 percent. Today, the average payout is less than 40 percent, and the yield has dipped below 1.5 percent.

A number of theories have been offered to explain these results. First, declining dividend yields imply that stock prices have increased faster than dividends paid. Some analysts point to the low yields as evidence that the stock market is overvalued. Second, lower interest rates led to a decline in required stock returns. This increased stock prices, which, in turn, resulted in lower dividend yields. Third, over the past two decades the composition of the stock market has changed dramatically. In 1980, the market was dominated by oil, industrial, utility, and retail companies that paid high dividends. Today the market includes many high-tech companies that pay little or no dividends.

In addition, dividend yields have fallen because more and more companies now recognize the tax and other advantages of stock repurchases over dividends as a way of distributing cash to shareholders. Indeed, stock repurchases have tripled in recent years, and in each year since 1997 stock repurchases have exceeded cash dividends paid.

The popularity of stock repurchases led Federal Reserve Board economists Nellie Liang and Steve Sharpe to redefine a stock's "total yield." First, they developed a "net repurchases yield," calculated as the dollars per share spent on repurchases minus the cost of shares used to cover the exercise of stock options, divided by the stock price. Then, the stock's "total yield" is found as the sum of the traditional dividend yield plus the net repurchases yield.

Liang and Sharpe's estimated yields for the largest 144 companies in the S&P 500 during 1994–1998 are reported in the accompanying table. These data confirm the declining importance of dividends and the increasing importance of stock repurchases. They also indicate that total yields have been trending downward. Even after including stock repurchases, total yields are still only half of what the dividend yield alone was in 1980. Thus, no matter how you slice it, payouts to shareholders have declined. This is, of course, consistent with lower interest rates and a declining cost of equity capital.

SOURCE: Gene Epstein, "Soaring Buybacks Make Dividend Yield a Misleading Measure of a Stock's Value," *Barron's Online*, November 1, 1999.

YIELDS	1994	1995	1996	1997	1998
Dividend yield	2.76%	2.41%	2.06%	1.73%	1.41%
Repurchase yield	1.19	1.34	1.56	1.98	1.49
Total yield	3.95%	3.75%	3.62%	3.71%	2.90%
Percent of repurchases	30%	36%	43%	53%	51%

per share on the remaining shares will increase, resulting in a higher market price per share. As a result, capital gains will have been substituted for dividends.

THE EFFECTS OF STOCK REPURCHASES

Many companies have been repurchasing their stock in recent years. Until the 1980s, most repurchases amounted to a few million dollars, but in 1985, Phillips Petroleum announced plans for the largest repurchase on record— 81 million of its shares with a market value of $4.1 billion. Other large repurchases have been made by IBM, Coca-Cola, Teledyne, Atlantic Richfield, Goodyear, and Xerox. Indeed, since 1985, more shares have been repurchased than issued.

The effects of a repurchase can be illustrated with data on American Development Corporation (ADC). The company expects to earn $4.4 million in 2003, and 50 percent of this amount, or $2.2 million, has been allocated for distribution to common shareholders. There are 1.1 million shares outstanding, and the market price is $20 a share. ADC believes that it can either use the $2.2 million to repurchase 100,000 of its shares through a tender offer at $22 a share or else pay a cash dividend of $2 a share.[16]

The effect of the repurchase on the EPS and market price per share of the remaining stock can be analyzed in the following way:

1. Current EPS $= \dfrac{\text{Total earnings}}{\text{Number of shares}} = \dfrac{\$4.4 \text{ million}}{1.1 \text{ million}} = \$4$ per share.

2. P/E ratio $= \dfrac{\$20}{\$4} = 5\times$.

3. EPS after repurchasing 100,000 shares $= \dfrac{\$4.4 \text{ million}}{1 \text{ million}} = \$4.40$ per share.

4. Expected market price after repurchase = (P/E)(EPS) = (5)($4.40)

$$= \$22 \text{ per share.}$$

It should be noted from this example that investors would receive before-tax benefits of $2 per share in any case, either in the form of a $2 cash dividend or a $2 increase in the stock price. This result would occur because we assumed, first, that shares could be repurchased at exactly $22 a share and, second, that the P/E ratio would remain constant. If shares could be bought for less than $22, the operation would be even better for *remaining* stockholders, but the reverse would hold if ADC had to pay more than $22 a share. Furthermore, the P/E ratio might change as a result of the repurchase operation, rising if investors viewed it favorably and falling if they viewed it unfavorably. Some factors that might affect P/E ratios are considered next.

ADVANTAGES OF REPURCHASES

The advantages of repurchases are as follows:

1. Repurchase announcements are viewed as positive signals by investors because the repurchase is often motivated by management's belief that the firm's shares are undervalued.

---

[16] Stock repurchases are generally made in one of three ways: (1) A publicly owned firm can simply buy its own stock through a broker on the open market. (2) It can make a *tender offer*, under which it permits stockholders to send in (that is, "tender") their shares to the firm in exchange for a specified price per share. In this case, it generally indicates that it will buy up to a specified number of shares within a particular time period (usually about two weeks); if more shares are tendered than the company wishes to purchase, purchases are made on a pro rata basis. (3) The firm can purchase a block of shares from one large holder on a negotiated basis. If a negotiated purchase is employed, care must be taken to ensure that this one stockholder does not receive preferential treatment over other stockholders or that any preference given can be justified by "sound business reasons." A number of years ago, Texaco's management was sued by stockholders who were unhappy over the company's repurchase of about $600 million of stock from the Bass Brothers' interests at a substantial premium over the market price. The suit charged that Texaco's management, afraid the Bass Brothers would attempt a takeover, used the buyback to get them off its back. Such payments have been dubbed "greenmail."

2. The stockholders have a choice when the firm distributes cash by repurchasing stock—they can sell or not sell. With a cash dividend, on the other hand, stockholders must accept a dividend payment and pay the tax. Thus, those stockholders who need cash can sell back some of their shares, while those who do not want additional cash can simply retain their stock. From a tax standpoint, a repurchase permits both types of stockholders to get what they want.

3. A third advantage is that a repurchase can remove a large block of stock that is "overhanging" the market and keeping the price per share down.

4. Dividends are "sticky" in the short run because managements are reluctant to raise the dividend if the increase cannot be maintained in the future—managements dislike cutting cash dividends because of the negative signal a cut gives. Hence, if the excess cash flow is thought to be only temporary, management may prefer to make the distribution in the form of a share repurchase rather than to declare an increased cash dividend that cannot be maintained.

5. Companies can use the residual model to set a *target cash distribution* level, then divide the distribution into a *dividend component* and a *repurchase component*. The dividend payout ratio will be relatively low, but the dividend itself will be relatively secure, and it will grow as a result of the declining number of shares outstanding. The company has more flexibility in adjusting the total distribution than it would if the entire distribution were in the form of cash dividends, because repurchases can be varied from year to year without giving off adverse signals. This procedure, which is what FPL employed, has much to recommend it, and it is a primary reason for the dramatic increase in the volume of share repurchases.

6. Repurchases can be used to produce large-scale changes in capital structure. For example, a number of years ago Consolidated Edison decided to repurchase $400 million of its common stock in order to increase its debt ratio. The repurchase was necessary because even if the company financed its capital budget only with debt, it would still have taken years to get the debt ratio up to the target level. Con Ed used the repurchase to produce a rapid change in its capital structure.

7. Companies that use stock options as an important component of employee compensation can repurchase shares and then use those shares when employees exercise their options. This avoids the issuance of new shares and a resulting dilution of earnings. Microsoft and other high-tech companies have used this procedure in recent years.

DISADVANTAGES OF REPURCHASES

Disadvantages of repurchases include the following:

1. Stockholders may not be indifferent between dividends and capital gains, and the price of the stock might benefit more from cash dividends than from repurchases. Cash dividends are generally dependable, but repurchases are not. Further, if many firms announced regular, dependable repurchase programs, the improper accumulation tax might become a threat.

2. The *selling* stockholders may not be fully aware of all the implications of a repurchase, or they may not have all the pertinent information about the corporation's present and future activities. However, firms generally announce

repurchase programs before embarking on them to avoid potential stockholder suits.

3. The corporation may pay too high a price for the repurchased stock, to the disadvantage of remaining stockholders. If its shares are not actively traded, and if the firm seeks to acquire a relatively large amount of its stock, then the price may be bid above its equilibrium level and then fall after the firm ceases its repurchase operations.

CONCLUSIONS ON STOCK REPURCHASES

When all the pros and cons on stock repurchases have been totaled, where do we stand? Our conclusions may be summarized as follows:

1. Because of the lower capital gains tax rate and the deferred tax on capital gains, repurchases have a significant tax advantage over dividends as a way to distribute income to stockholders. This advantage is reinforced by the fact that repurchases provide cash to stockholders who want cash but allow those who do not need current cash to delay its receipt. On the other hand, dividends are more dependable and are thus better suited for those who need a steady source of income.

2. Because of signaling effects, companies should not vary their dividends—that would lower investors' confidence in the company and adversely affect its cost of equity and its stock price. However, cash flows vary over time, as do investment opportunities, so the "proper" dividend in the residual model sense varies. To get around this problem, a company can set its dividend at a level low enough to keep dividend payments from constraining operations and then use repurchases on a more or less regular basis to distribute excess cash. Such a procedure would provide regular, dependable dividends plus additional cash flow to those stockholders who want it.

3. Repurchases are also useful when a firm wants to make a large shift in its capital structure within a short period of time, wants to distribute cash from a one-time event such as the sale of a division, or wants to obtain shares for use in an employee stock option plan.

In an earlier edition of this book, we argued that companies ought to be doing more repurchasing and paying out less cash as dividends than they were. Increases in the size and frequency of repurchases in recent years suggest that companies have reached this same conclusion.

SELF-TEST QUESTIONS

Explain how repurchases can (1) help stockholders hold down taxes and (2) help firms change their capital structures.

What is treasury stock?

What are three procedures a firm can use to repurchase its stock?

What are some advantages and disadvantages of stock repurchases?

How can stock repurchases help a company operate in accordance with the residual dividend model?

Once a company becomes profitable, it must decide what to do with the cash it generates. It may choose to retain cash and use it to purchase additional assets or to reduce outstanding debt. Alternatively, it may choose to return cash to shareholders. Keep in mind that every dollar that management chooses to retain is a dollar that shareholders could have received and invested elsewhere. Therefore, managers should retain earnings if and only if they can invest the money within the firm and earn more than stockholders could earn outside the firm. Consequently, high-growth companies with many good projects will tend to retain a high percentage of earnings, whereas mature companies with lots of cash but limited investment opportunities will have generous cash distributions.

This basic tendency has a major influence on firms' long-run distribution policies. However, as we saw in this chapter, in any given year several important situations could complicate the long-run policy. Companies with excess cash have to decide whether to pay dividends or repurchase stock. In addition, due to the importance of signaling and the clientele effect, companies generally find it desirable to maintain a stable, consistent dividend policy over time. The key concepts covered in this chapter are listed below.

- **Dividend policy** involves three issues: (1) What fraction of earnings should be distributed? (2) Should the distribution be in the form of cash dividends or stock repurchases? (3) Should the firm maintain a steady, stable dividend growth rate?

- The **optimal dividend policy** strikes a balance between current dividends and future growth so as to maximize the firm's stock price.

- Miller and Modigliani developed the **dividend irrelevance theory,** which holds that a firm's dividend policy has no effect on either the value of its stock or its cost of capital.

- The **bird-in-the-hand theory** holds that the firm's value will be maximized by a high dividend payout ratio, because investors regard cash dividends as being less risky than potential capital gains.

- The **tax preference theory** states that because long-term capital gains are subject to less onerous taxes than dividends, investors prefer to have companies retain earnings rather than pay them out as dividends.

- **Empirical tests** of the three theories **have been inconclusive.** Therefore, academicians cannot tell corporate managers how a given change in dividend policy will affect stock prices and capital costs.

- Dividend policy should take account of the **information content of dividends (signaling)** and the **clientele effect.** The information content, or signaling, effect relates to the fact that investors regard an unexpected dividend change as a signal of management's forecast of future earnings. The clientele effect suggests that a firm will attract investors who like the firm's dividend payout policy. Both factors should be considered by firms that are considering a change in dividend policy.

- In practice, most firms try to follow a policy of paying a **steadily increasing dividend.** This policy provides investors with stable, dependable income, and departures from it give investors signals about management's expectations for future earnings.

- Most firms use the **residual dividend model** to set the long-run target payout ratio at a level that will permit the firm to satisfy its equity requirements with retained earnings.

- A **dividend reinvestment plan (DRIP)** allows stockholders to have the company automatically use dividends to purchase additional shares of stock. DRIPs are popular because they allow stockholders to acquire additional shares without incurring brokerage fees.

- **Legal constraints, investment opportunities, availability and cost of funds from other sources,** and **taxes** are also considered when firms establish dividend policies.

- A **stock split** increases the number of shares outstanding. Normally, splits reduce the price per share in proportion to the increase in shares because splits merely "divide the pie into smaller slices." However, firms generally split their stocks only if (1) the price is quite high and (2) management thinks the future is bright. Therefore, stock splits are often taken as positive signals and thus boost stock prices.

- A **stock dividend** is a dividend paid in additional shares of stock rather than in cash. Both stock dividends and splits are used to keep stock prices within an "optimal" trading range.

- Under a **stock repurchase plan,** a firm buys back some of its outstanding stock, thereby decreasing the number of shares, which should increase both EPS and the stock price. Repurchases are useful for making major changes in capital structure, as well as for distributing excess cash.

QUESTIONS

14-1 How would each of the following changes tend to affect aggregate (that is, the average for all corporations) payout ratios, other things held constant? Explain your answers.
a. An increase in the personal income tax rate.
b. A liberalization of depreciation for federal income tax purposes—that is, faster tax write-offs.
c. A rise in interest rates.
d. An increase in corporate profits.
e. A decline in investment opportunities.
f. Permission for corporations to deduct dividends for tax purposes as they now do interest charges.
g. A change in the Tax Code so that both realized and unrealized capital gains in any year were taxed at the same rate as dividends.

14-2 Discuss the pros and cons of having the directors formally announce what a firm's dividend policy will be in the future.

14-3 Most firms would like to have their stock selling at a high P/E ratio, and they would also like to have extensive public ownership (many different shareholders). Explain how stock dividends or stock splits may help achieve these goals.

14-4 What is the difference between a stock dividend and a stock split? As a stockholder, would you prefer to see your company declare a 100 percent stock dividend or a two-for-one split? Assume that either action is feasible.

14-5 "The cost of retained earnings is less than the cost of new outside equity capital. Consequently, it is totally irrational for a firm to sell a new issue of stock and to pay dividends during the same year." Discuss this statement.

14-6 Would it ever be rational for a firm to borrow money in order to pay dividends? Explain.

14-7 "Executive salaries have been shown to be more closely correlated to the size of the firm than to its profitability. If a firm's board of directors is controlled by management instead of by outside directors, this might result in the firm's retaining more earnings than can be justified from the stockholders' point of view." Discuss the statement, being sure (a) to discuss the interrelationships among cost of capital, investment opportunities, and new investment and (b) to explain the implied relationship between dividend policy and stock prices.

14-8 Modigliani and Miller (MM) on the one hand and Gordon and Lintner (GL) on the other have expressed strong views regarding the effect of dividend policy on a firm's cost of capital and value.
   a. In essence, what are the MM and GL views regarding the effect of dividend policy on the cost of capital and stock prices?
   b. How does the tax preference theory differ from the views of MM and GL?
   c. According to the text, which of the theories, if any, has received statistical confirmation from empirical tests?
   d. How could MM use the *information content*, or *signaling*, *hypothesis* to counter their opponents' arguments? If you were debating MM, how would you counter them?
   e. How could MM use the *clientele effect* concept to counter their opponents' arguments? If you were debating MM, how would you counter them?

14-9 More NYSE companies had stock dividends and stock splits during 1983 and 1984 than ever before. What events in these years could have made stock splits and stock dividends so popular? Explain the rationale that a financial vice-president might give his or her board of directors to support a stock split/dividend recommendation.

14-10 One position expressed in the financial literature is that firms set their dividends as a residual after using income to support new investment.
   a. Explain what a residual dividend policy implies, illustrating your answer with a table showing how different investment opportunities could lead to different dividend payout ratios.
   b. Think back to Chapter 13, where we considered the relationship between capital structure and the cost of capital. If the WACC-versus-debt-ratio plot were shaped like a sharp V, would this have a different implication for the importance of setting dividends according to the residual policy than if the plot were shaped like a shallow bowl (or a flattened U)?

14-11 Indicate whether the following statements are true or false. If the statement is false, explain why.
   a. If a firm repurchases its stock in the open market, the shareholders who tender the stock are subject to capital gains taxes.
   b. If you own 100 shares in a company's stock and the company's stock splits two for one, you will own 200 shares in the company following the split.
   c. Some dividend reinvestment plans increase the amount of equity capital available to the firm.
   d. The Tax Code encourages companies to pay a large percentage of their net income in the form of dividends.
   e. If your company has established a clientele of investors who prefer large dividends, the company is unlikely to adopt a residual dividend policy.
   f. If a firm follows a residual dividend policy, holding all else constant, its dividend payout will tend to rise whenever the firm's investment opportunities improve.

SELF-TEST PROBLEMS (SOLUTIONS APPEAR IN APPENDIX B)

ST-1
Key terms
Define each of the following terms:
   a. Optimal dividend policy
   b. Dividend irrelevance theory; bird-in-the-hand theory; tax preference theory
   c. Information content, or signaling, hypothesis; clientele effect
   d. Residual dividend model
   e. Extra dividend
   f. Declaration date; holder-of-record date; ex-dividend date; payment date

g. Dividend reinvestment plan (DRIP)
h. Stock split; stock dividend
i. Stock repurchase

ST-2
Alternative dividend policies

Components Manufacturing Corporation (CMC) has an all-common-equity capital structure. It has 200,000 shares of $2 par value common stock outstanding. When CMC's founder, who was also its research director and most successful inventor, retired unexpectedly to the South Pacific in late 2002, CMC was left suddenly and permanently with materially lower growth expectations and relatively few attractive new investment opportunities. Unfortunately, there was no way to replace the founder's contributions to the firm. Previously, CMC found it necessary to plow back most of its earnings to finance growth, which averaged 12 percent per year. Future growth at a 5 percent rate is considered realistic, but that level would call for an increase in the dividend payout. Further, it now appears that new investment projects with at least the 14 percent rate of return required by CMC's stockholders (k_s = 14%) would amount to only $800,000 for 2003 in comparison to a projected $2,000,000 of net income. If the existing 20 percent dividend payout were continued, retained earnings would be $1.6 million in 2003, but, as noted, investments that yield the 14 percent cost of capital would amount to only $800,000.

The one encouraging point is that the high earnings from existing assets are expected to continue, and net income of $2 million is still expected for 2003. Given the dramatically changed circumstances, CMC's management is reviewing the firm's dividend policy.

a. Assuming that the acceptable 2003 investment projects would be financed entirely by earnings retained during the year, calculate DPS in 2003, assuming that CMC uses the residual dividend model.
b. What payout ratio does your answer to part a imply for 2003?
c. If a 60 percent payout ratio is maintained for the foreseeable future, what is your estimate of the present market price of the common stock? How does this compare with the market price that should have prevailed under the assumptions existing just before the news about the founder's retirement? If the two values of P_0 are different, comment on why.
d. What would happen to the price of the stock if the old 20 percent payout were continued? Assume that if this payout is maintained, the average rate of return on the retained earnings will fall to 7.5 percent and the new growth rate will be

$$g = (1.0 - \text{Payout ratio})(\text{ROE})$$
$$= (1.0 - 0.2)(7.5\%)$$
$$= (0.8)(7.5\%) = 6.0\%.$$

STARTER PROBLEMS

14-1
Residual dividend model

Axel Telecommunications has a target capital structure that consists of 70 percent debt and 30 percent equity. The company anticipates that its capital budget for the upcoming year will be $3,000,000. If Axel reports net income of $2,000,000 and it follows a residual dividend payout policy, what will be its dividend payout ratio?

14-2
Stock split

Gamma Medical's stock trades at $90 a share. The company is contemplating a 3-for-2 stock split. Assuming that the stock split will have no effect on the market value of its equity, what will be the company's stock price following the stock split?

14-3
Stock repurchases

Beta Industries has net income of $2,000,000 and it has 1,000,000 shares of common stock outstanding. The company's stock currently trades at $32 a share. Beta is considering a plan in which it will use available cash to repurchase 20 percent of its shares in the open market. The repurchase is expected to have no effect on either net income or the company's P/E ratio. What will be its stock price following the stock repurchase?

EXAM-TYPE PROBLEMS

The problems included in this section are set up in such a way that they could be used as multiple-choice exam problems.

14-4
External equity financing

Northern Pacific Heating and Cooling Inc. has a 6-month backlog of orders for its patented solar heating system. To meet this demand, management plans to expand production capacity by

40 percent with a $10 million investment in plant and machinery. The firm wants to maintain a 40 percent debt-to-total-assets ratio in its capital structure; it also wants to maintain its past dividend policy of distributing 45 percent of last year's net income. In 2002, net income was $5 million. How much external equity must Northern Pacific seek at the beginning of 2003 to expand capacity as desired? Assume the firm uses only debt and common equity in its capital structure.

14-5
Stock split

After a 5-for-1 stock split, the Strasburg Company paid a dividend of $0.75 per new share, which represents a 9 percent increase over last year's pre-split dividend. What was last year's dividend per share?

14-6
Residual dividend model

The Welch Company is considering three independent projects, each of which requires a $5 million investment. The estimated internal rate of return (IRR) and cost of capital for these projects is presented below:

Project H (High risk):   Cost of capital = 16%; IRR = 20%.

Project M (Medium risk):   Cost of capital = 12%; IRR = 10%.

Project L (Low risk):   Cost of capital = 8%; IRR = 9%.

Note that the projects' costs of capital vary because the projects have different levels of risk. The company's optimal capital structure calls for 50 percent debt and 50 percent common equity. Welch expects to have net income of $7,287,500. If Welch bases its dividends on the residual model, what will be its payout ratio?

14-7
Alternative dividend policies

Rubenstein Bros. Clothing is expecting to pay an annual dividend per share of $0.75 out of annual earnings per share of $2.25. Currently, Rubenstein Bros.' stock is selling for $15 per share. Adhering to the company's target capital structure, the firm has $10 million in assets, of which 40 percent is funded by debt. Assume that the firm's book value of equity equals its market value. In past years, the firm has earned a return on equity (ROE) of 18 percent, which is expected to continue this year and into the foreseeable future.

a. Based upon the above information, what long-run growth rate can the firm be expected to maintain? (Hint: g = Retention rate × ROE.)
b. What is the stock's required return?
c. If the firm were to change its dividend policy and pay an annual dividend of $1.50 per share, financial analysts predict that the change in policy will have no effect upon the firm's stock price or ROE. Therefore, what must the firm's new expected long-run growth rate and required return be?
d. Suppose instead that the firm has decided to proceed with its original plan of disbursing $0.75 per share to shareholders, but the firm intends to do so in the form of a stock dividend rather than a cash dividend. The firm will allot new shares based on the current stock price of $15. In other words, for every $15 in dividends due to shareholders, a share of stock will be issued. How large will the stock dividend be relative to the firm's current market capitalization? (Hint: Remember market capitalization = P_0 × number of shares outstanding.)
e. If the plan in part d is implemented, how many new shares of stock will be issued, and by how much will the company's earnings per share be diluted?

PROBLEMS

14-8
Dividends

Bowles Sporting Inc. is prepared to report the following income statement (shown in thousands of dollars) for the year 2003.

Sales	$15,200
Operating costs including depreciation	11,900
EBIT	$ 3,300
Interest	300
EBT	$ 3,000
Taxes (40%)	1,200
Net income	$ 1,800

Prior to reporting this income statement, the company wants to determine its annual dividend. The company has 500,000 shares of stock outstanding and its stock trades at $48 per share.

a. The company had a 40 percent dividend payout ratio in 2002. If Bowles wants to maintain this payout ratio in 2003, what will be its per-share dividend in 2003?

b. If the company maintains this 40 percent payout ratio, what will be the current dividend yield on the company's stock?

c. The company reported net income of $1.5 million in 2002. Assume that the number of shares outstanding has remained constant. What was the company's per-share dividend in 2002?

d. As an alternative to maintaining the same dividend payout ratio, Bowles is considering maintaining the same per-share dividend in 2003 that it paid in 2002. If it chooses this policy, what will be the company's dividend payout ratio in 2003?

e. Assume that the company is interested in dramatically expanding its operations and that this expansion will require significant amounts of capital. The company would like to avoid transactions costs involved in issuing new equity. Given this scenario, would it make more sense for the company to maintain a constant dividend payout ratio or to maintain the same per-share dividend?

14-9
Alternative dividend policies

In 2002 the Keenan Company paid dividends totaling $3,600,000 on net income of $10.8 million. 2002 was a normal year, and for the past 10 years, earnings have grown at a constant rate of 10 percent. However, in 2003, earnings are expected to jump to $14.4 million, and the firm expects to have profitable investment opportunities of $8.4 million. It is predicted that Keenan will not be able to maintain the 2003 level of earnings growth—the high 2003 earnings level is attributable to an exceptionally profitable new product line introduced that year—and the company will return to its previous 10 percent growth rate. Keenan's target capital structure is 40 percent debt and 60 percent equity.

a. Calculate Keenan's total dividends for 2003 if it follows each of the following policies:
   (1) Its 2003 dividend payment is set to force dividends to grow at the long-run growth rate in earnings.
   (2) It continues the 2002 dividend payout ratio.
   (3) It uses a pure residual dividend policy (40 percent of the $8.4 million investment is financed with debt and 60 percent with common equity).
   (4) It employs a regular-dividend-plus-extras policy, with the regular dividend being based on the long-run growth rate and the extra dividend being set according to the residual policy.

b. Which of the preceding policies would you recommend? Restrict your choices to the ones listed, but justify your answer.

c. Assume that investors expect Keenan to pay total dividends of $9,000,000 in 2003 and to have the dividend grow at 10 percent after 2003. The stock's total market value is $180 million. What is the company's cost of equity?

d. What is Keenan's long-run average return on equity? [Hint: g = Retention rate $\times$ ROE = $(1.0 - \text{Payout rate})(\text{ROE})$.]

e. Does a 2003 dividend of $9,000,000 seem reasonable in view of your answers to parts c and d? If not, should the dividend be higher or lower?

14-10
Residual dividend model

Buena Terra Corporation is reviewing its capital budget for the upcoming year. It has paid a $3.00 dividend per share (DPS) for the past several years, and its shareholders expect the dividend to remain constant for the next several years. The company's target capital structure is 60 percent equity and 40 percent debt; it has 1,000,000 shares of common equity outstanding; and its net income is $8 million. The company forecasts that it would require $10 million to fund all of its profitable (i.e., positive NPV) projects for the upcoming year.

a. If Buena Terra follows the residual dividend model, how much retained earnings will it need to fund its capital budget?

b. If Buena Terra follows the residual dividend model, what will be the company's dividend per share and payout ratio for the upcoming year?

c. If Buena Terra maintains its current $3.00 DPS for next year, how much retained earnings will be available for the firm's capital budget?

d. Can the company maintain its current capital structure, maintain the $3.00 DPS, and maintain a $10 million capital budget without having to raise new common stock?

e. Suppose that Buena Terra's management is firmly opposed to cutting the dividend, that is, it wishes to maintain the $3.00 dividend for the next year. Also, assume that the company was committed to funding all profitable projects and was willing to issue more debt (along with the available retained earnings) to help finance the company's capital budget. Assume that the resulting change in capital structure has a minimal impact on the company's composite cost of capital, so that the capital budget remains at $10 million. What portion of this year's capital budget would have to be financed with debt?

f. Suppose once again that Buena Terra's management wants to maintain the $3.00 DPS. In addition, the company wants to maintain its target capital structure (60 percent equity, 40 percent debt) and maintain its $10 million capital budget. What is the minimum dollar amount of new common stock that the company would have to issue in order to meet each of its objectives?

g. Now consider the case where Buena Terra's management wants to maintain the $3.00 DPS and its target capital structure, but it wants to avoid issuing new common stock. The company is willing to cut its capital budget in order to meet its other objectives. Assuming that the company's projects are divisible, what will be the company's capital budget for the next year?

h. What actions can a firm that follows the residual dividend policy take when its forecasted retained earnings are less than the retained earnings required to fund its capital budget?

SPREADSHEET PROBLEM

14-11
Residual dividend model

Rework Problem 14-10 parts a through g using a spreadsheet model.

INTEGRATED CASE

SOUTHEASTERN STEEL COMPANY

14-12 Dividend Policy Southeastern Steel Company (SSC) was formed 5 years ago to exploit a new continuous-casting process. SSC's founders, Donald Brown and Margo Valencia, had been employed in the research department of a major integrated-steel company, but when that company decided against using the new process (which Brown and Valencia had developed), they decided to strike out on their own. One advantage of the new process was that it required relatively little capital in comparison with the typical steel company, so Brown and Valencia have been able to avoid issuing new stock, and thus they own all of the shares. However, SSC has now reached the stage in which outside equity capital is necessary if the firm is to achieve its growth targets yet still maintain its target capital structure of 60 percent equity and 40 percent debt. Therefore, Brown and Valencia have decided to take the company public. Until now, Brown and Valencia have paid themselves reasonable salaries but routinely reinvested all after-tax earnings in the firm, so dividend policy has not been an issue. However, before talking with potential outside investors, they must decide on a dividend policy.

Assume that you were recently hired by Arthur Adamson & Company (AA), a national consulting firm, which has been asked to help SSC prepare for its public offering. Martha Millon, the senior AA consultant in your group, has asked you to make a presentation to Brown and Valencia in which you review the theory of dividend policy and discuss the following questions.

a. (1) What is meant by the term "dividend policy"?

   (2) The terms "irrelevance," "bird-in-the-hand," and "tax preference" have been used to describe three major theories regarding the way dividend policy affects a firm's value. Explain what these terms mean, and briefly describe each theory.

   (3) What do the three theories indicate regarding the actions management should take with respect to dividend policy?

   (4) What results have empirical studies of the dividend theories produced? How does all this affect what we can tell managers about dividend policy?

b. Discuss (1) the information content, or signaling, hypothesis, (2) the clientele effect, and (3) their effects on dividend policy.

c. (1) Assume that SSC has an $800,000 capital budget planned for the coming year. You have determined that its present capital structure (60 percent equity and 40 percent debt) is optimal, and its net income is forecasted at $600,000. Use the residual dividend model approach to determine SSC's total dollar dividend and payout ratio. In the process, explain what the residual dividend model is. Then, explain what would happen if net income were forecasted at $400,000, or at $800,000.

(2) In general terms, how would a change in investment opportunities affect the payout ratio under the residual payment policy?

(3) What are the advantages and disadvantages of the residual policy? (Hint: Don't neglect signaling and clientele effects.)

d. What is a dividend reinvestment plan (DRIP), and how does it work?

e. Describe the series of steps that most firms take in setting dividend policy in practice.

f. What are stock repurchases? Discuss the advantages and disadvantages of a firm's repurchasing its own shares.

g. What are stock dividends and stock splits? What are the advantages and disadvantages of stock dividends and stock splits?

CYBER PROBLEM

Please go to our web site **http://brigham.swlearning.com** to access the Cyberproblems.

THOMSON ™ **ANALYTICS**

With your Xtra! CD-ROM, access the Thomson Analytics Problems and use the Thomson Analytics Academic online database to work this chapter's problems.

PART 6

WORKING CAPITAL MANAGEMENT

MANAGING CURRENT ASSETS

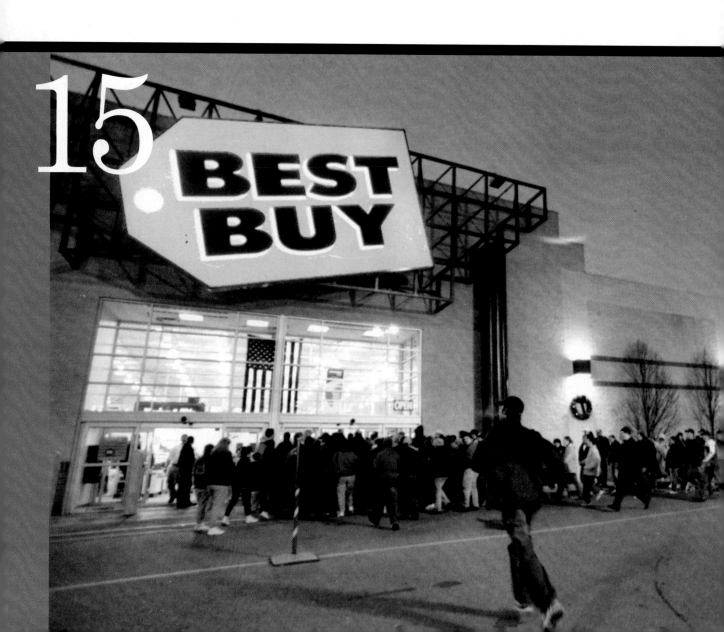

15

Best Buy Company, North America's largest consumer electronics retailer, operates over 500 Best Buy stores and 1,300 Musicland outlets. Its 2002 sales are expected to top $23 billion, it is expected to earn about $690 million, and its stock in mid-2002 sold for $50, up from $1.50 five years ago. This success stems from its sound financial and operating practices, especially its skill in managing its working capital, which is the focus of this chapter.

Working capital management deals with the management of current assets—cash, accounts receivable, and inventory—and procedures financing these assets. Since Best Buy sells largely through the use of credit cards, receivables are not much of a problem, and it has no problem raising the cash needed to support operations. Therefore, the most important element in Best Buy's working capital policy is its inventory management. To maintain sales, the company must ensure that its stores are always stocked with the particular set of goods that customers need. However, inventory is costly to store, and electronics products can lose value through obsolescence if they are not sold promptly. Therefore, to keep its costs down the company is always looking for ways to streamline its inventory and to maximize its inventory turnover ratio. Thus, in its 2001 annual report Best Buy noted with pride that its inventory turnover ratio was the highest in its industry. Later, in a conference call with investors, the CFO noted that although the firm was increasing inventory levels so it wouldn't run out of inventory at a time when it was expanding and remodeling many of its stores, its sales were expected to keep pace with the inventory expansion and thus keep its turnover ratio from declining.

Dramatic improvements in computer technology, along with improvements in the Internet, have transformed the way Best Buy manages its working capital. It employs technology to collect real-time information from each store regarding which products are selling best and the store's current inventory levels, and it uses this information to place orders automatically and then ship goods to stores as the goods are needed. In this way the company is able to minimize costs while still making sure that it has the right amount and mix of inventory to maximize sales.

Sound working capital management is necessary if a company is to compete successfully in today's information age. After reading this chapter, you should have a good understanding of how companies make sound working capital decisions.

About 60 percent of a typical financial manager's time is devoted to working capital management, and many students' first jobs will involve working capital. This is particularly true in smaller businesses, where most new jobs in the United States are being created.

Working capital policy involves two basic questions: (1) What is the appropriate amount of current assets for the firm to carry, both in total and for each specific account, and (2) how should current assets be financed? This chapter addresses current asset holdings, and Chapter 16 addresses their financing.

As you will see in the next two chapters, sound working capital management goes beyond finance. Indeed, most of the ideas for improving working capital management often stem from other disciplines. For example, experts in business logistics, operations management, and information technology often work with the marketing group to develop a better way to deliver the firm's products. Where finance comes into play is in evaluating the profitability of alternative systems, which are generally costly to install. For example, let's say that a firm's information technology and marketing groups decide that they want to (1) develop new software and (2) purchase computer terminals that will be installed in their customers' premises. Customers will then keep track of their own inventories and automatically order new supplies when inventory levels hit specified targets. The system will improve inventory management for both the manufacturer and its customers and also help "lock in" good customers.

Significant costs will be incurred to develop and install the new system, but if it is adopted, the company can meet its customers' needs better, and with smaller inventory, and also increase sales. In many respects, this scenario looks like a typical capital budgeting project— it has an up-front cost followed by a series of positive cash flows. The finance group can use the capital budgeting techniques described in Chapters 10, 11 and 12 to evaluate whether the new system is worth the cost and also whether it should be developed in-house or purchased from an outside source. As with other chapters in this text, the textbook's CD-ROM contains an *Excel* file, 15MODEL.xls, that will guide you through the chapter's calculations. ■

We begin our discussion of working capital policy by reviewing some basic definitions and concepts:

Working Capital

A firm's investment in short-term assets—cash, marketable securities, inventory, and accounts receivable.

Net Working Capital

Current assets minus current liabilities.

Net Operating Working Capital

Current assets minus non-interest-bearing current liabilities.

1. **Working capital,** sometimes called *gross working capital*, simply refers to current assets used in operations.
2. **Net working capital** is defined as current assets minus current liabilities.
3. **Net operating working capital** is defined as current assets minus non-interest-bearing current liabilities. More specifically, net operating working capital is often expressed as cash and marketable securities, accounts receivable, and inventories, less accounts payable and accrued liabilities.[1]
4. The *current ratio*, which was discussed in Chapter 3, is calculated by dividing current assets by current liabilities, and it is intended to measure liquidity. However, a high current ratio does not ensure that a firm will have the cash required to meet its needs. If inventories cannot be sold, or if receivables cannot be collected in a timely manner, then the apparent safety reflected in a high current ratio could be illusory.
5. The *quick ratio*, or *acid test*, also attempts to measure liquidity, and it is found by subtracting inventories from current assets and then dividing by current liabilities. The quick ratio removes inventories from current assets because they are the least liquid of current assets. Therefore, the quick ratio is an "acid test" of a company's ability to meet its current obligations.
6. The best and most comprehensive picture of a firm's liquidity position is shown by its *cash budget*. This statement, which forecasts cash inflows and outflows, focuses on what really counts, namely, the firm's ability to generate sufficient cash inflows to meet its required cash outflows. We will discuss cash budgeting in detail later in the chapter.

Working Capital Policy

Basic policy decisions regarding (1) target levels for each category of current assets and (2) how current assets will be financed.

7. **Working capital policy** refers to the firm's policies regarding (1) target levels for each category of current assets and (2) how current assets will be financed.
8. *Working capital management* involves both setting working capital policy and carrying out that policy in day-to-day operations.

The term *working capital* originated with the old Yankee peddler, who would load up his wagon with goods and then go off on his route to peddle his wares. The merchandise was called working capital because it was what he actually sold, or "turned over," to produce his profits. The wagon and horse were his fixed assets. He generally owned the horse and wagon, so they were financed with "equity" capital, but he borrowed the funds to buy the merchandise. These borrowings were called *working capital loans*, and they had to be repaid after each trip to demonstrate to the bank that the credit was sound. If the peddler was able to repay the loan, then the bank would make another loan, and banks that followed this procedure were said to be employing "sound banking practices."

---

[1] This definition assumes that cash and marketable securities on the balance sheet are at their normal long-run target levels and that the company is not holding any excess cash. Excess holdings of cash and marketable securities are generally not included as part of net operating working capital.

Why is the quick ratio also called an acid test?

How did the term "working capital" originate?

Differentiate between net working capital and net operating working capital.

THE CASH CONVERSION CYCLE

As we noted above, the concept of working capital management originated with the old Yankee peddler, who would borrow to buy inventory, sell the inventory to pay off the bank loan, and then repeat the cycle. That concept has been applied to more complex businesses, where it is used to analyze the effectiveness of a firm's working capital management.

Firms typically follow a cycle in which they purchase inventory, sell goods on credit, and then collect accounts receivable. This cycle is referred to as the *cash conversion cycle*, and it is discussed in detail in the next section. Sound working capital policy is designed to minimize the time between cash expenditures on materials and the collection of cash on sales.

AN ILLUSTRATION

We can illustrate the process with data from Real Time Computer Corporation (RTC), which in early 2002 introduced a new minicomputer that can perform one billion instructions per second and that will sell for $250,000. RTC expects to sell 40 computers in its first year of production. The effects of this new product on RTC's working capital position were analyzed in terms of the following five steps:

1. RTC will order and then receive the materials it needs to produce the 40 computers it expects to sell. Because RTC and most other firms purchase materials on credit, this transaction will create an account payable. However, the purchase will have no immediate cash flow effect.

2. Labor will be used to convert the materials into finished computers. However, wages will not be fully paid at the time the work is done, so, like accounts payable, accrued wages will also build up.

3. The finished computers will be sold, but on credit. Therefore, sales will create receivables, not immediate cash inflows.

4. At some point before cash comes in, RTC must pay off its accounts payable and accrued wages. This outflow must be financed.

5. The cycle will be completed when RTC's receivables have been collected. At that time, the company can pay off the credit that was used to finance production, and it can then repeat the cycle.

Cash Conversion Cycle Model

Focuses on the length of time between when the company makes payments and when it receives cash inflows.

The **cash conversion cycle model**, which focuses on the length of time between when the company makes payments and when it receives cash inflows, formalizes the steps outlined above.[2] The following terms are used in the model:

1. **Inventory conversion period**, which is the average time required to convert materials into finished goods and then to sell those goods. Note that the inventory conversion period is calculated by dividing inventory by sales per day. For example, if average inventories are $2 million and sales are $10 million, then the inventory conversion period is 73 days:

Inventory Conversion Period

The average time required to convert materials into finished goods and then to sell those goods.

$$\text{Inventory conversion period} = \frac{\text{Inventory}}{\text{Sales per day}} \tag{15-1}$$

$$= \frac{\$2,000,000}{\$10,000,000/365}$$

$$= 73 \text{ days.}$$

Thus, it takes an average of 73 days to convert materials into finished goods and then to sell those goods.[3]

Receivables Collection Period

The average length of time required to convert the firm's receivables into cash, that is, to collect cash following a sale.

2. **Receivables collection period**, which is the average length of time required to convert the firm's receivables into cash, that is, to collect cash following a sale. The receivables collection period is also called the *days sales outstanding (DSO)*, and it is calculated by dividing accounts receivable by the average credit sales per day. If receivables are $657,534 and sales are $10 million, the receivables collection period is

$$\frac{\text{Receivables}}{\text{collection period}} = \text{DSO} = \frac{\text{Receivables}}{\text{Sales}/365} \tag{15-2}$$

$$= \frac{\$657,534}{\$10,000,000/365} = 24 \text{ days.}$$

Thus, it takes 24 days after a sale to convert the receivables into cash.

Payables Deferral Period

The average length of time between the purchase of materials and labor and the payment of cash for them.

3. **Payables deferral period**, which is the average length of time between the purchase of materials and labor and the payment of cash for them. For example, if the firm on average has 30 days to pay for labor and materials, if its cost of goods sold are $8 million per year, and if its accounts payable average $657,534, then its payables deferral period can be calculated as follows:

$$\frac{\text{Payables}}{\text{deferral}} = \frac{\text{Payables}}{\text{Purchases per day}}$$
$$\text{period}$$

$$= \frac{\text{Payables}}{\text{Cost of goods sold}/365} \tag{15-3}$$

---

[2] See Verlyn D. Richards and Eugene J. Laughlin, "A Cash Conversion Cycle Approach to Liquidity Analysis," *Financial Management*, Spring 1980, 32–38.

[3] Some analysts define the inventory conversion period as inventory divided by daily cost of goods sold. However, many published sources use the formula we show in Equation 15-1. In addition, some analysts use a 360-day year; however, unless stated otherwise, we will base all our calculations on a 365-day year.

$$= \frac{\$657{,}534}{\$8{,}000{,}000/365}$$

$$= 30 \text{ days}.$$

The calculated figure is consistent with the stated 30-day payment period.[4]

Cash Conversion Cycle
The average length of time a dollar is tied up in current assets.

4. **Cash conversion cycle,** which nets out the three periods just defined and which therefore equals the length of time between the firm's actual cash expenditures to pay for productive resources (materials and labor) and its own cash receipts from the sale of products (that is, the length of time between paying for labor and materials and collecting on receivables). The cash conversion cycle thus equals the average length of time a dollar is tied up in current assets.

We can now use these definitions to analyze the cash conversion cycle. First, the concept is diagrammed in Figure 15-1. Each component is given a number, and the cash conversion cycle can be expressed by this equation:

$$\underset{\substack{\text{Inventory} \\ \text{conversion} \\ \text{period}}}{(1)} + \underset{\substack{\text{Receivables} \\ \text{collection} \\ \text{period}}}{(2)} - \underset{\substack{\text{Payables} \\ \text{deferral} \\ \text{period}}}{(3)} = \underset{\substack{\text{Cash} \\ \text{conversion} \\ \text{cycle}}}{(4)}. \qquad (15\text{-}4)$$

To illustrate, suppose it takes Real Time an average of 73 days to convert raw materials to computers and then to sell them, and another 24 days to collect on receivables. However, 30 days normally elapse between receipt of raw materials and payment for them. In this case, the cash conversion cycle would be 67 days:

Days in Cash Conversion Cycle = 73 days + 24 days − 30 days = 67 days.

To look at it another way,

Cash inflow delay − Payment delay = Net delay

(73 days + 24 days) −   30 days   = 67 days.

---

[4] Some sources define the payables deferral period as payables divided by daily sales.

FIGURE 15-1 **The Cash Conversion Cycle Model**

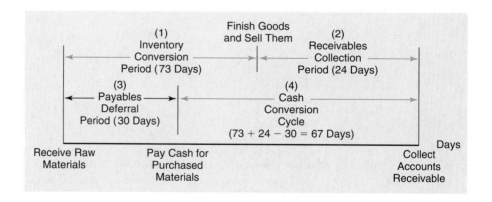

SHORTENING THE CASH CONVERSION CYCLE

Given these data, RTC knows when it starts producing a computer that it will have to finance the manufacturing costs for a 67-day period. The firm's goal should be to shorten its cash conversion cycle as much as possible without hurting operations. This would improve profits, because the longer the cash conversion cycle, the greater the need for external financing, and that financing has a cost.

The cash conversion cycle can be shortened (1) by reducing the inventory conversion period by processing and selling goods more quickly, (2) by reducing the receivables collection period by speeding up collections, or (3) by lengthening the payables deferral period by slowing down the firm's own payments. To the extent that these actions can be taken *without increasing costs or depressing sales*, they should be carried out.

BENEFITS

We can illustrate the benefits of shortening the cash conversion cycle by looking again at Real Time Computer Corporation. Suppose RTC must spend approximately $197,250 on materials and labor to produce one computer, and it takes about nine days to produce a computer. Thus, it must invest $197,250/9 = $21,917 for each day's production. This investment must be financed for 67 days—the length of the cash conversion cycle—so the company's working capital financing needs will be 67 × $21,917 = $1,468,439. If RTC could reduce the cash conversion cycle to 57 days, say, by deferring payment of its accounts payable an additional 10 days, or by speeding up either the production process or the collection of its receivables, it could reduce its working capital financing requirements by $219,170.

Recall that free cash flow (FCF) is equal to NOPAT minus net investment in operating capital. Therefore, if working capital decreases, FCF increases by that same amount. RTC's reduction in its cash conversion cycle would lead to an increase in FCF of $219,170. Notice also that reducing the cash conversion cycle reduces the ratio of net operating working capital to sales (NOWC/Sales). If sales stay at the same level, then the reduction in working capital is simply a one-time cash inflow. However, if sales are expected to grow, and if the NOWC/Sales ratio remains at its new level, then less working capital will be required to support the additional sales, leading to an increase in projected FCF for each future year.

The combination of the one-time cash inflow and the long-term improvement in working capital can add substantial value to companies. Two professors, Hyun-Han Shin and Luc Soenen, studied more than 2,900 companies during a recent 20-year period and found a strong relationship between a company's cash conversion cycle and its performance.[5] In particular, their results show that for the average company a 10-day improvement in the cash conversion cycle was associated with an increase in pre-tax operating profit from 12.76 to 13.02 percent. They also demonstrated that companies with a cash conversion cycle 10 days shorter than average also had an annual stock return that was 1.7 percentage points higher than that of an average company, even after adjusting for differences in risk. Given results like these, it's no wonder firms now place so much emphasis on working capital management!

---

[5] See Hyun-Han Shin and Luc Soenen, "Efficiency of Working Capital Management and Corporate Profitability," *Financial Practice and Education*, Fall/Winter 1998, 37–45.

NEGATIVE WORKING CAPITAL IS A POSITIVE REALITY FOR SOME FIRMS

Many companies have set the ambitious goal of operating with zero net working capital. This may seem impossible, but a few firms have done even better—they have been able to operate with *negative* net working capital!

A typical company orders components and raw materials from its suppliers and then pays cash for these components after some period of time (the payables deferral period). Then, these components and raw materials are transformed into a finished product that the company sells to its customers, who pay for their purchases some time after the purchase. Looking at a typical company's cash conversion cycle, there is generally a sizable lag between the time it has to pay its suppliers and the time it receives cash from its customers.

However, some companies, including Dell Computer Corporation and Amazon.com, have been able to operate with a *negative* cash conversion cycle. When a customer orders a computer from Dell's web site or a book from Amazon's site, he or she provides his or her credit card number, which enables Dell and Amazon to receive next-day cash from the sale. Thus, cash is received before the product is shipped, and it is often received before Dell and Amazon have paid their own suppliers. Thus, those companies are able to use other people's money to run much of their day-to-day business.

Because of their negative cash conversion cycles, for these companies working capital is an important source of cash. Recall that a company's free cash flow (FCF) in a given year can be expressed as follows:

$$FCF = EBIT(1 - T) + Depreciation - \begin{array}{c} Capital \\ expenditures \end{array}$$

$$- \text{ Changes in net operating working capital.}$$

To grow, most companies need cash for both capital expenditures and working capital. However, if a company has a negative cash conversion cycle, growth in sales causes more cash to come in than go out, which means that working capital is *providing* cash rather than *using* it.

In Chapter 8 we demonstrated that a company's overall value is the present value of its free cash flows. Analysts recognize this point when they value Dell and Amazon—these firms generate positive cash flows from their working capital management, which helps increase their stock market valuations.

SELF-TEST QUESTIONS

Define the following terms: inventory conversion period, receivables collection period, and payables deferral period. Give the equation for each term.

What is the cash conversion cycle? What is its equation?

What should the firm's goal be regarding the cash conversion cycle? Explain your answer.

What are some actions the firm can take to shorten its cash conversion cycle?

THE CONCEPT OF ZERO WORKING CAPITAL

At first glance, it might seem that working capital management is not as important as capital budgeting, dividend policy, and other decisions that determine a firm's long-term direction. However, in today's world of intense global competition, working capital management is receiving increasing attention from managers striving for peak efficiency. In fact, the goal of many leading companies today—including American Standard, Campbell Soup, General Electric, Quaker Oats, and Whirlpool—is *zero working capital*. Proponents of the zero working capital concept claim that a movement toward this goal not only generates cash but also speeds up production and helps businesses make more timely deliveries and operate more efficiently. The concept has its own definition of working capital: Inventories + Receivables − Payables. The rationale here is (1) that inventories and receivables are the keys to making sales, but (2) that inventories can be financed by suppliers through accounts payable.

On average, companies use 20 cents of working capital for each dollar of sales. So, on average, working capital is turned over five times per year. Reducing working capital and thus increasing turnover has two major financial benefits. First, every dollar freed up by reducing inventories or receivables, or by increasing payables, results in a one-time contribution to cash flow. Second, a movement toward zero working capital permanently raises a company's earnings. Like all capital, funds invested in working capital cost money, so reducing those funds yields permanent savings in capital costs. In addition to the financial benefits, reducing working capital forces a company to produce and deliver faster than its competitors, which helps it gain new business and charge premium prices for providing good service. As inventories disappear, warehouses can be sold off, both labor and handling equipment needs are reduced, and obsolete and/or out-of-style goods are minimized.

To illustrate the benefits of striving for zero working capital, in just one year Campbell Soup pared its working capital by $80 million. It used the cash to develop new products and to buy companies in Britain, Australia, and other countries. Equally important, the company expects to increase annual profits by $50 million over the next few years by lowering overtime labor and storage costs.

The most important factor in moving toward zero working capital is increased speed. If the production process is fast enough, companies can produce items as they are ordered rather than having to forecast demand and build up large inventories that are managed by bureaucracies. The best companies are able to start production after an order is received yet still meet customer delivery requirements. This system is known as *demand flow*, or *demand-based management*, and it builds on the just-in-time method of inventory control that we will discuss later in this chapter. However, demand flow management is broader than just-in-time, because it requires that all elements of a production system operate quickly and efficiently.

Achieving zero working capital requires that every order and part move at maximum speed, which generally means replacing paper with electronic data. Then, orders streak from the processing department to the plant, flexible production lines produce each product every day, and finished goods flow directly from the production line onto waiting trucks or rail cars. Instead of cluttering plants or warehouses with inventories, products move directly into the pipeline. As efficiency rises, working capital dwindles.

Clearly, it is not possible for most firms to achieve zero working capital and infinitely efficient production. Still, a focus on minimizing receivables and inventories while maximizing payables will help a firm lower its investment in working capital and achieve financial and production economies.

American Standard provides a detailed discussion of how they are applying demand flow production concepts to reengineered manufacturing and office processes in an attempt to achieve zero working capital. The site can be accessed at **http://www.teamflow.com** by clicking on American Standard Inc. under "What Are People Saying About Team Flow?"

SELF-TEST QUESTION

What is the basic idea of zero working capital, and how is working capital defined in this concept?

ALTERNATIVE CURRENT ASSET INVESTMENT POLICIES

The cash conversion cycle highlights the strengths and weaknesses of the company's working capital policy, which depend critically on current asset management and the financing of current assets. In the remaining part of this chapter, we consider each of these items in more detail. We begin by describing alternative current asset investment policies, after which we consider a more detailed analysis of the various components of working capital. In the next chapter we will discuss different strategies for financing current assets.

Figure 15-2 shows three alternative policies regarding the total amount of current assets carried. Essentially, these policies differ with regard to the amount of current assets carried to support any given level of sales, hence in the turnover of those assets.

FIGURE 15-2   **Alternative Current Asset Investment Policies (Millions of Dollars)**

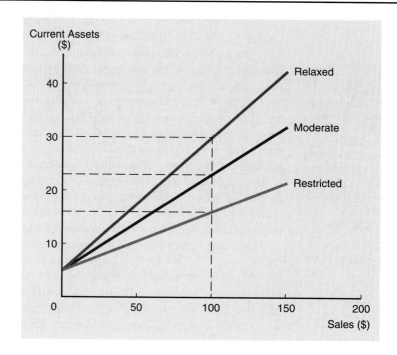

POLICY	CURRENT ASSETS TO SUPPORT SALES OF $100	TURNOVER OF CURRENT ASSETS
Relaxed	$30	3.3×
Moderate	23	4.3×
Restricted	16	6.3×

NOTE: The sales/current assets relationship is shown here as being linear, but the relationship is often curvilinear.

The line with the steepest slope represents a **relaxed current asset investment** (or "fat cat") **policy,** where relatively large amounts of cash, marketable securities, and inventories are carried, and where sales are stimulated by the use of a credit policy that provides liberal financing to customers and a corresponding high level of receivables. Conversely, with the **restricted current asset investment** (or "lean-and-mean") **policy,** the holdings of cash, securities, inventories, and receivables are minimized. Under the restricted policy, current assets are turned over more frequently, so each dollar of current assets is forced to "work harder." The **moderate current asset investment policy** is between the two extremes.

Under conditions of certainty—when sales, costs, lead times, payment periods, and so on, are known for sure—all firms would hold only minimal levels of current assets. Any larger amounts would increase the need for external funding without a corresponding increase in profits, while any smaller holdings would involve late payments to suppliers along with lost sales due to inventory shortages and an overly restrictive credit policy.

However, the picture changes when uncertainty is introduced. Here the firm requires some minimum amount of cash and inventories based on expected payments, expected sales, expected order lead times, and so on, plus additional holdings, or *safety stocks*, which enable it to deal with departures from the expected values. Similarly, accounts receivable levels are determined by credit terms, and the tougher the credit terms, the lower the receivables for any given level of sales. With a restricted current asset investment policy, the firm would hold minimal safety stocks of cash and inventories, and it would have a tight credit policy even though this meant running the risk of losing sales. A restricted, lean-and-mean current asset investment policy generally provides the highest expected return on this investment, but it entails the greatest risk, while the reverse is true under a relaxed policy. The moderate policy falls in between the two extremes in terms of expected risk and return.

Changing technology can lead to dramatic changes in the optimal current asset investment policy. For example, if new technology makes it possible for a manufacturer to speed up the production of a given product from 10 days to five days, then its work-in-progress inventory can be cut in half. Similarly, retailers such as Wal-Mart or Home Depot have installed systems under which bar codes on all merchandise are read at the cash register. The information on the sale is electronically transmitted to a computer that maintains a record of the inventory of each item, and the computer automatically transmits orders to suppliers' computers when stocks fall to prescribed levels. With such a system, inventories will be held at optimal levels; orders will reflect exactly what styles, colors, and sizes consumers are buying; and the firm's profits will be maximized.

MANAGING THE COMPONENTS OF WORKING CAPITAL

Working capital consists of four main components: cash, marketable securities, inventory, and accounts receivable. The remainder of this chapter will focus on the issues involved with managing each of these components. As you will see, a common thread underlies all current asset management. For each type of asset, firms face a fundamental trade-off: Current assets (that is, working capital) are necessary to conduct business, and the greater the holdings of current assets, the smaller the danger of running out, hence the lower the firm's operating risk. However, holding working capital is costly—if inventories are too large, then the firm will have assets that earn a zero or even negative return if storage and spoilage costs are high. And, of course, firms must acquire capital to buy assets such as inventory, this capital has a cost, and this increases the downward drag from excessive inventories (or receivables or even

FREE CASH FLOW, EVA, AND WORKING CAPITAL

Recall from Chapter 2 that a company's value depends on its free cash flow (FCF), defined as follows:

FCF = Net operating profit after taxes − Net investment in operating capital

  = NOPAT − Net investment in operating capital

  = [EBIT × (1 − T)] − [Capital this year − Capital last year].

If a company can reduce its inventories, its cash holdings, or its receivables, then its net investment in operating capital will decline. If these actions don't harm operating profit, then FCF will increase, which will lead to a higher stock price.

Economic Value Added (EVA) provides another useful way of thinking about working capital, particularly if a manager's compensation is linked to EVA. Recall from Chapter 2 that EVA is defined as follows:

$$EVA = NOPAT − (WACC × Total operating capital).$$

A reduction in working capital decreases total operating capital, which increases EVA. Many firms report that when division managers and other operating people begin to think in these terms, they often find ways to reduce working capital, especially if their compensation depends on their divisions' EVAs.

We can also think of working capital management in terms of ROE and the Du Pont equation:

$$ROE = \frac{Profit}{margin} × \frac{Total\ assets}{turnover} × \frac{Leverage}{factor}$$

$$= \frac{Net\ income}{Sales} × \frac{Sales}{Total\ assets} × \frac{Assets}{Equity}.$$

If working capital and hence total assets can be reduced without seriously affecting the profit margin, this will increase the total assets turnover and, consequently, ROE.

cash). So, there is pressure to hold the amount of working capital to the minimum consistent with running the business without interruption.

SELF-TEST QUESTIONS

Identify and explain three alternative current asset investment policies.

What are the principal components of working capital?

What are the reasons for not wanting to hold too little working capital? For not wanting to hold too much?

What is the fundamental trade-off that managers face when managing working capital?

CASH MANAGEMENT

Approximately 1.5 percent of the average industrial firm's assets are held in the form of cash, which is defined as demand deposits plus currency. Cash is often called a "nonearning asset." It is needed to pay for labor and raw materials, to buy fixed assets, to pay taxes, to service debt, to pay dividends, and so on. However, cash itself (and also most commercial checking accounts) earns no interest. Thus, the goal of the cash manager is to minimize the amount of cash the firm must hold for use in conducting its normal business activities, yet, at the same time, to have sufficient cash (1) to take trade discounts, (2) to maintain its credit rating, and (3) to meet unexpected cash needs. We begin our analysis with a discussion of the reasons for holding cash.

REASONS FOR HOLDING CASH

Firms hold cash for two primary reasons:

Transactions Balance
A cash balance associated with payments and collections; the balance necessary for day-to-day operations.

1. *Transactions.* Cash balances are necessary in business operations. Payments must be made in cash, and receipts are deposited in the cash account. Cash balances associated with routine payments and collections are known as **transactions balances.**

2. *Compensation to banks for providing loans and services.* A bank makes money by lending out funds that have been deposited with it, so the larger its deposits, the better the bank's profit position. If a bank is providing services to a customer, it may require the customer to leave a minimum balance on deposit to help offset the costs of providing the services. Also, banks may require borrowers to hold deposits at the bank. Both types of deposits are defined as **compensating balances.**[6]

Compensating Balance
A bank balance that a firm must maintain to compensate the bank for services rendered or for granting a loan.

Two other reasons for holding cash have been noted in the finance and economics literature: for *precaution* and for *speculation.* Cash inflows and outflows are unpredictable, with the degree of predictability varying among firms and industries. Therefore, firms need to hold some cash in reserve for random, unforeseen fluctuations in inflows and outflows. These "safety stocks" are called **precautionary balances,** and the less predictable the firm's cash flows, the larger such balances should be. However, if the firm has easy access to borrowed funds—that is, if it can borrow on short notice—its need for precautionary balances is reduced. Also, as we note later in this chapter, firms that would otherwise need large precautionary balances tend to hold highly liquid marketable securities rather than cash per se. Marketable securities serve many of the purposes of cash, but they provide greater interest income than bank deposits.

Precautionary Balance
A cash balance held in reserve for random, unforeseen fluctuations in cash inflows and outflows.

Some cash balances may be held to enable the firm to take advantage of bargain purchases that might arise; these funds are called **speculative balances.** However, firms today are more likely to rely on reserve borrowing capacity and/or marketable securities portfolios than on cash per se for speculative purposes.

Speculative Balance
A cash balance that is held to enable the firm to take advantage of any bargain purchases that might arise.

The cash accounts of most firms can be thought of as consisting of transactions, compensating, precautionary, and speculative balances. However, we cannot calculate the amount needed for each purpose, sum them, and produce a total desired cash balance, because the same money often serves more than one purpose. For instance, precautionary and speculative balances can also be used to satisfy compensating balance requirements. Firms do, however, consider all four factors when establishing their target cash positions.

ADVANTAGES OF HOLDING ADEQUATE CASH AND NEAR-CASH ASSETS

In addition to the four motives just discussed, sound working capital management requires that an ample supply of cash and near-cash assets be maintained for several specific reasons:

Trade Discount
A price reduction that suppliers offer customers for early payment of bills.

1. It is essential that the firm have sufficient cash and near-cash assets to take **trade discounts.** Suppliers frequently offer customers discounts for early pay-

---

[6] In a 1979 survey, 84.7 percent of responding companies reported that they were required to maintain compensating balances to help pay for bank services. Only 13.3 percent reported paying direct fees for bank services. By 1996 those findings were reversed: only 28 percent paid for bank services with compensating balances, while 83 percent paid direct fees. So, while use of compensating balances to pay for services has declined, it is still a reason some companies hold so much cash.

ment of bills. As we will see in the next chapter, the cost of not taking discounts is very high, so firms should have enough cash to permit payment of bills in time to take discounts.

2. Adequate holdings of cash and near-cash assets can help the firm maintain its credit rating by keeping its current and acid test ratios in line with those of other firms in its industry. A strong credit rating enables the firm both to purchase goods from suppliers on favorable terms and to maintain an ample line of low-cost credit with its bank.

3. Cash and near-cash assets are useful for taking advantage of favorable business opportunities, such as special offers from suppliers or the chance to acquire another firm.

4. The firm should have sufficient cash and near-cash assets to meet such emergencies as strikes, fires, or competitors' marketing campaigns, and to weather seasonal and cyclical downturns.

SELF-TEST QUESTIONS

Why is cash management important?

What are the two primary motives for holding cash?

What are the two secondary motives for holding cash as noted in the finance and economics literature?

THE CASH BUDGET[7]

Cash Budget
A table showing cash flows (receipts, disbursements, and cash balances) for a firm over a specified period.

The firm estimates its needs for cash as a part of its general budgeting, or forecasting, process. First, it forecasts sales, its fixed asset and inventory requirements, and the times when payments must be made. This information is combined with projections about when accounts receivable will be collected, tax payment dates, dividend and interest payment dates, and so on. All of this information is summarized in the **cash budget,** which shows the firm's projected cash inflows and outflows over some specified period. Generally, firms use a monthly cash budget forecasted over the next year, plus a more detailed daily or weekly cash budget for the coming month. The monthly cash budgets are used for planning purposes, and the daily or weekly budgets for actual cash control.

The cash budget provides more detailed information concerning a firm's future cash flows than do the forecasted financial statements, which we will discuss in Chapter 17. Allied's projected 2003 sales are $3,300 million. Will Allied have to worry about cash shortages during 2003? To answer this question, we must construct Allied's cash budget for 2003.

To simplify the example, we will only consider Allied's cash budget for the last half of 2003. Further, we will not list every cash flow but rather focus on the operating cash flows. Allied's sales peak is in September, shortly after the majority of its raw

---

[7] We used an *Excel* spreadsheet to generate the cash budget shown in Table 15-1. It would be worthwhile to go through the model, 15MODEL.xls, which is on the CD-ROM that accompanies this text. This will give you a good example of how spreadsheets can be applied to solve practical problems.

food inputs have been harvested. All sales are made on terms of 2/10, net 40, meaning that a 2 percent discount is allowed if payment is made within 10 days, and, if the discount is not taken, the full amount is due in 40 days. However, like most companies, Allied finds that some of its customers delay payment up to 90 days. Experience has shown that payment on 20 percent of Allied's dollar sales is made during the month in which the sale is made — these are the discount sales. On 70 percent of sales, payment is made during the month immediately following the month of sale, and on 10 percent of sales payment is made in the second month following the month of sale.

The costs to Allied of foodstuffs, spices, preservatives, and packaging materials average 70 percent of the sales prices of the finished products. These purchases are generally made one month before the firm expects to sell the finished products, but Allied's purchase terms with its suppliers allow it to delay payments for 30 days. Accordingly, if July sales are forecasted at $300 million, then purchases during June will amount to $210 million, and this amount will actually be paid in July.

Such other cash expenditures as wages and lease payments are also built into the cash budget, and Allied must make estimated tax payments of $30 million on September 15 and $20 million on December 15. Also, a $100 million payment for a new plant must be made in October. Assuming that Allied's **target cash balance** is $10 million, and that it projects $15 million to be on hand on July 1, 2003, what will its monthly cash surpluses or shortfalls be for the period from July to December?

The monthly cash flows are shown in Table 15-1. Section I of the table provides a worksheet for calculating both collections on sales and payments on purchases. Line 1 gives the sales forecast for the period from May through December. (May and June sales are necessary to determine collections for July and August.) Next, Lines 2 through 5 show cash collections. Line 2 shows that 20 percent of the sales during any given month are collected during that month. Customers who pay in the first month, however, take the discount, so the cash collected in the month of sale is reduced by 2 percent; for example, collections during July for the $300 million of sales in that month will be 20 percent times sales times 1.0 minus the 2 percent discount = $(0.20)($300)(0.98) \approx 59 million. Line 3 shows the collections on the previous month's sales, or 70 percent of sales in the preceding month; for example, in July, 70 percent of the $250 million June sales, or $175 million, will be collected. Line 4 gives collections from sales two months earlier, or 10 percent of sales in that month; for example, the July collections for May sales are $(0.10)($200) = 20 million. The collections during each month are summed and shown on Line 5; thus, the July collections represent 20 percent of July sales (minus the discount) plus 70 percent of June sales plus 10 percent of May sales, or $254 million in total.

Next, payments for purchases of raw materials are shown. July sales are forecasted at $300 million, so Allied will purchase $210 million of materials in June (Line 6) and pay for these purchases in July (Line 7). Similarly, Allied will purchase $280 million of materials in July to meet August's forecasted sales of $400 million.

With Section I completed, Section II can be constructed. Cash from collections is shown on Line 8. Lines 9 through 14 list payments made during each month, and these payments are summed on Line 15. The difference between cash receipts and cash payments (Line 8 minus Line 15) is the net cash gain or loss during the month. For July there is a net cash loss of $11 million, as shown on Line 16.

In Section III, we first determine the cash balance Allied would have at the start of each month, assuming no borrowing is done. This is shown on Line 17. Allied will have $15 million on hand on July 1. The beginning cash balance (Line 17) is then added to the net cash gain or loss during the month (Line 16) to obtain the cumulative

Target Cash Balance
The desired cash balance that a firm plans to maintain in order to conduct business.

	MAY	JUN	JUL	AUG	SEP	OCT	NOV	DEC
I. COLLECTIONS AND PURCHASES WORKSHEET								
(1) Sales (gross)[a]	$200	$250	$300	$400	$500	$350	$250	$200
Collections								
(2) During month of sale: (0.2)(0.98)(month's sales)			59	78	98	69	49	39
(3) During first month after sale: 0.7(previous month's sales)			175	210	280	350	245	175
(4) During second month after sale: 0.1(sales 2 months ago)			20	25	30	40	50	35
(5) Total collections (Lines 2 + 3 + 4)			$254	$313	$408	$459	$344	$249
Purchases								
(6) 0.7(next month's sales)		$210	$280	$350	$245	$175	$140	
(7) Payments (prior month's purchases)			$210	$280	$350	$245	$175	$140
II. CASH GAIN OR LOSS FOR MONTH								
(8) Collections (from Section I)			$254	$313	$408	$459	$344	$249
(9) Payments for purchases (from Section I)			$210	$280	$350	$245	$175	$140
(10) Wages and salaries			30	40	50	40	30	30
(11) Lease payments			15	15	15	15	15	15
(12) Other expenses			10	15	20	15	10	10
(13) Taxes					30			20
(14) Payment for plant construction						100		
(15) Total payments			$265	$350	$465	$415	$230	$215
(16) Net cash gain (loss) during month (Line 8 − Line 15)			($ 11)	($ 37)	($ 57)	$ 44	$114	$ 34
III. LOAN REQUIREMENT OR CASH SURPLUS								
(17) Cash at start of month if no borrowing is done[b]			$ 15	$ 4	($ 33)	($ 90)	($ 46)	$ 68
(18) Cumulative cash: cash at start if no borrowing + gain or − loss (Line 16 + Line 17)			$ 4	($ 33)	($ 90)	($ 46)	$ 68	$102
(19) Target cash balance			10	10	10	10	10	10
(20) Cumulative surplus cash or loan outstanding to maintain $10 target cash balance (Line 18 − Line 19)[c]			($ 6)	($ 43)	($100)	($ 56)	$ 58	$ 92

[a] Although the budget period is July through December, sales and purchases data for May and June are needed to determine collections and payments during July and August.

[b] The amount shown on Line 17 for July, the $15 balance (in millions), is on hand initially. The values shown for each of the following months on Line 17 are equal to the cumulative cash as shown on Line 18 for the preceding month; for example, the $4 shown on Line 17 for August is taken from Line 18 in the July column.

[c] When the target cash balance of $10 (Line 19) is deducted from the cumulative cash balance (Line 18), a resulting negative figure on Line 20 (shown in parentheses) represents a required loan, whereas a positive figure represents surplus cash. Loans are required from July through October, and surpluses are expected during November and December. Note also that firms can borrow or pay off loans on a daily basis, so the $6 borrowed during July would be done on a daily basis, as needed, and during October the $100 loan that existed at the beginning of the month would be reduced daily to the $56 ending balance, which, in turn, would be completely paid off during November.

cash that would be on hand if no financing were done (Line 18). At the end of July, Allied forecasts a cumulative cash balance of $4 million in the absence of borrowing.

The target cash balance, $10 million, is then subtracted from the cumulative cash balance to determine the firm's borrowing requirements, shown in parentheses, or its surplus cash. Because Allied expects to have cumulative cash, as shown on Line 18, of only $4 million in July, it will have to borrow $6 million to bring the cash account up to the target balance of $10 million. Assuming that this amount is indeed borrowed, loans outstanding will total $6 million at the end of July. (Allied did not have any loans outstanding on July 1.) The cash surplus or required loan balance is given on Line 20; a positive value indicates a cash surplus, whereas a negative value indicates a loan requirement. Note that the surplus cash or loan requirement shown on Line 20 is a *cumulative amount*. Allied must borrow $6 million in July. Then, it has an additional cash shortfall during August of $37 million as reported on Line 16, so its total loan requirement at the end of August is $6 + $37 = $43 million, as reported on Line 20. Allied's arrangement with the bank permits it to increase its outstanding loans on a daily basis, up to a prearranged maximum, just as you could increase the amount you owe on a credit card. Allied will use any surplus funds it generates to pay off its loans, and because the loan can be paid down at any time, on a daily basis, the firm will never have both a cash surplus and an outstanding loan balance.

This same procedure is used in the following months. Sales will peak in September, accompanied by increased payments for purchases, wages, and other items. Receipts from sales will also go up, but the firm will still be left with a $57 million net cash outflow during the month. The total loan requirement at the end of September will hit a peak of $100 million, the cumulative cash plus the target cash balance. The $100 million can also be found as the $43 million needed at the end of August plus the $57 million cash deficit for September.

Sales, purchases, and payments for past purchases will fall sharply in October, but collections will be the highest of any month because they will reflect the high September sales. As a result, Allied will enjoy a healthy $44 million net cash gain during October. This net gain can be used to pay off borrowings, so loans outstanding will decline by $44 million, to $56 million.

Allied will have an even larger cash surplus in November, which will permit it to pay off all of its loans. In fact, the company is expected to have $58 million in surplus cash by the month's end, and another cash surplus in December will swell the excess cash to $92 million. With such a large amount of unneeded funds, Allied's treasurer will certainly want to invest in interest-bearing securities or to put the funds to use in some other way.

Here are some additional points about cash budgets:

1. For simplicity, our illustrative budget for Allied omitted many important cash flows that are anticipated for 2003, such as dividends and proceeds from stock and bond sales. Some of these are projected to occur in the first half of the year, but those that are projected for the July–December period could easily be added to the table. The final cash budget should contain all projected cash inflows and outflows, and it should be consistent with the forecasted financial statements.

2. Our cash budget does not reflect interest on loans or income from investing surplus cash. This refinement could easily be added.

3. If cash inflows and outflows are not uniform during the month, we could seriously understate the firm's peak financing requirements. The data in Table 15-1 show the situation expected on the last day of each month, but on any given day during the month, it could be quite different. For example, if all payments

had to be made on the fifth of each month, but collections came in uniformly throughout the month, the firm would need to borrow much larger amounts than those shown in Table 15-1. In this case, we would prepare a cash budget that determined requirements on a daily basis.

4. Since depreciation is a noncash charge, it does not appear on the cash budget other than through its effect on taxable income, hence on taxes paid.

5. Since the cash budget represents a forecast, all the values in the table are expected values. If actual sales, purchases, and so on, are different from the forecasted levels, then the projected cash deficits and surpluses will also be incorrect. Thus, Allied might end up needing to borrow larger amounts than are indicated on Line 20, so it should arrange a line of credit in excess of that amount. For example, if Allied's monthly sales turn out to be only 80 percent of their forecasted levels, its maximum cumulative borrowing requirement will turn out to be $126 million rather than $100 million, a 26 percent increase from the expected figure.

6. Spreadsheet programs are particularly well suited for constructing and analyzing cash budgets, especially with respect to the sensitivity of cash flows to changes in sales levels, collection periods, and the like. We could change any assumption, say, the projected monthly sales or the lag before customers pay, and the cash budget would automatically and instantly be recalculated. This would show us exactly how the firm's borrowing requirements would change if conditions changed. Also, with a spreadsheet model, it is easy to add features like interest paid on loans, interest earned on marketable securities, and so on. See 15MODEL.xls for the spreadsheet model we used to generate the cash budget for this chapter.

7. Finally, we should note that the target cash balance probably will be adjusted over time, rising and falling with seasonal patterns and with long-term changes in the scale of the firm's operations. Thus, Allied will probably plan to maintain larger cash balances during August and September than at other times, and as the company grows, so will its required cash balance. Also, the firm might even set the target cash balance at zero—this could be done if it carried a portfolio of marketable securities that could be sold to replenish the cash account, or if it had an arrangement with its bank that permitted it to borrow any funds needed on a daily basis. In that event, the cash budget would simply stop with Line 18, and the amounts on that line would represent projected loans outstanding or surplus cash. Note, though, that most firms would find it difficult to operate with a zero-balance bank account, just as you would, and the costs of such an operation would in most instances offset the costs associated with maintaining a positive cash balance. Therefore, most firms do set a positive target cash balance.

SELF-TEST QUESTIONS

What is the purpose of a cash budget?

What are the three major sections of a cash budget?

Suppose a firm's cash flows do not occur uniformly throughout the month. What effect would this have on the accuracy of the forecasted borrowing requirements?

How could uncertainty be handled in a cash budget?

Does depreciation appear in a cash budget? Explain.

CASH MANAGEMENT TECHNIQUES

Cash management has changed significantly over the last 20 years for two reasons. First, from the early 1970s to the mid-1980s, there was an upward trend in interest rates that increased the opportunity cost of holding cash. This encouraged financial managers to search for more efficient ways of managing cash. Second, technological developments, particularly computerized electronic funds transfer mechanisms, changed the way cash is managed.

Most cash management activities are performed jointly by the firm and its banks. Effective cash management encompasses proper management of cash inflows and outflows, which entails (1) synchronizing cash flows, (2) using float, (3) accelerating collections, (4) getting available funds to where they are needed, and (5) controlling disbursements. Most business is conducted by large firms, many of which operate regionally, nationally, or even globally. They collect cash from many sources and make payments from a number of different cities or even countries. For example, companies such as IBM, General Motors, and Hewlett-Packard have manufacturing plants all around the world, even more sales offices, and bank accounts in virtually every city where they do business. Their collection points follow sales patterns. Some disbursements are made from local offices, but most are made in the cities where manufacturing occurs, or else from the home office. Thus, a major corporation might have hundreds or even thousands of bank accounts, and since there is no reason to think that inflows and outflows will balance in each account, a system must be in place to transfer funds from where they come in to where they are needed, to arrange loans to cover net corporate shortfalls, and to invest net corporate surpluses without delay. We discuss the most commonly used techniques for accomplishing these tasks in the following sections.

CASH FLOW SYNCHRONIZATION

If you as an individual were to receive income once a year, you would probably put it in the bank, draw down your account periodically, and have an average balance during the year equal to about half your annual income. If you received income monthly instead of once a year, you would operate similarly, but now your average balance would be much smaller. If you could arrange to receive income daily and to pay rent, tuition, and other charges on a daily basis, and if you were confident of your forecasted inflows and outflows, then you could hold a very small average cash balance.

Exactly the same situation holds for businesses — by improving their forecasts and by arranging things so that cash receipts coincide with cash requirements, firms can reduce their transactions balances to a minimum. Recognizing all this, utility companies, oil companies, credit card companies, and so on, arrange to bill customers, and to pay their own bills, on regular "billing cycles" throughout the month. This **synchronization of cash flows** provides cash when it is needed and thus enables firms to reduce cash balances, decrease bank loans, lower interest expenses, and boost profits.

Synchronized Cash Flows
A situation in which inflows coincide with outflows, thereby permitting a firm to hold low transactions balances.

SPEED UP THE CHECK-CLEARING PROCESS

When a customer writes and mails a check, this *does not* mean that the funds are immediately available to the receiving firm. Most of us have been told by someone that "the check is in the mail," and we have also deposited a check in our account and then been told that we cannot write our own checks against this deposit until the **check-clearing** process has been completed. Our bank must first make sure that the check we deposited is good and the funds are available before it will give us cash.

In practice, it may take a long time for a firm to process incoming checks and obtain the use of the money. A check must first be delivered through the mail and then be cleared through the banking system before the money can be put to use. Checks received from customers in distant cities are especially subject to delays because of mail time and also because more parties are involved. For example, assume that we receive a check and deposit it in our bank. Our bank must send the check to the bank on which it was drawn. Only when this latter bank transfers funds to our bank are the funds available for us to use. Checks are generally cleared through the Federal Reserve System or through a clearinghouse set up by the banks in a particular city. Of course, if the check is deposited in the same bank on which it was drawn, that bank merely transfers funds by bookkeeping entries from one depositor to another. The length of time required for checks to clear is thus a function of the distance between the payer's and the payee's banks. In the case of private clearinghouses, it can range from one to three days. Checks are generally cleared through the Federal Reserve System in about two days, but mail delays can slow down things on each end of the Fed's involvement in the process.

USING FLOAT

Float is defined as the difference between the balance shown in a firm's (or individual's) checkbook and the balance on the bank's records. Suppose a firm writes, on average, checks in the amount of $5,000 each day, and it takes six days for these checks to clear and to be deducted from the firm's bank account. This will cause the firm's own checkbook to show a balance $30,000 smaller than the balance on the bank's records; this difference is called **disbursement float.** Now suppose the firm also receives checks in the amount of $5,000 daily, but it loses four days while they are being deposited and cleared. This will result in $20,000 of **collections float.** In total, the firm's **net float** — the difference between the $30,000 positive disbursement float and the $20,000 negative collections float — will be $10,000.

If the firm's own collection and clearing process is more efficient than that of the recipients of its checks — which is generally true of larger, more efficient firms — then the firm could actually show a *negative* balance on its own books but have a *positive* balance on its bank records. Some firms indicate that they *never* have positive book cash balances. One large manufacturer of construction equipment stated that while its account, according to its bank's records, shows an average cash balance of about $20 million, its *book* cash balance is *minus* $20 million — it has $40 million of net float. Obviously, the firm must be able to forecast its disbursements and collections accurately in order to make such heavy use of float.

Delays that cause float arise because it takes time for checks (1) to travel through the mail (mail float), (2) to be processed by the receiving firm (processing float), and (3) to clear through the banking system (clearing, or availability, float). Basically, the size of a firm's net float is a function of its ability to speed up collections on checks received and to slow down collections on checks written. Efficient firms go to great lengths to speed up the processing of incoming checks, thus putting the funds to work faster, and they try to stretch their own payments out as long as possible.

Check Clearing
The process of converting a check that has been written and mailed into cash in the payee's account.

Disbursement Float
The value of the checks that we have written but that are still being processed and thus have not been deducted from our account balance by the bank.

Collections Float
The amount of checks that we have received but that have not yet been credited to our account.

Net Float
The difference between our checkbook balance and the balance shown on the bank's books.

ACCELERATION OF RECEIPTS

Financial managers have searched for ways to collect receivables faster since credit transactions began. Although cash collection is the financial manager's responsibility, the speed with which checks are cleared depends on the banking system. Several techniques are now used both to speed collections and to get funds where they are needed. Included are (1) lockbox plans established close to customers and (2) requiring large customers to pay by wire or automatic debit.

Lockboxes

Lockbox Plan
A procedure used to speed up collections and reduce float through the use of post office boxes in payers' local areas.

A **lockbox plan** is one of the oldest cash management tools. In a lockbox system, incoming checks are sent to post office boxes rather than to corporate headquarters. For example, a firm headquartered in New York City might have its West Coast customers send their payments to a box in San Francisco, its customers in the Southwest send their checks to Dallas, and so on, rather than having all checks sent to New York City. Several times a day a local bank will collect the contents of the lockbox and deposit the checks into the company's local account. The bank then provides the firm with a daily record of the receipts collected, usually via an electronic data transmission system in a format that permits online updating of the firm's accounts receivable records.

A lockbox system reduces the time required for a firm to receive incoming checks, to deposit them, and to get them cleared through the banking system so the funds are available for use. Lockbox services can often increase the availability of funds by two to five days over the "regular" system.

Payment by Wire or Automatic Debit

Firms are increasingly demanding payments of larger bills by wire, or even by automatic electronic debits, whereby funds are automatically deducted from one account and added to another. This is, of course, the ultimate in a speeded-up collection process, and computer technology is making such a process increasingly feasible and efficient.

SELF-TEST QUESTIONS

What is float? How do firms use float to increase cash management efficiency?

What are some methods firms can use to accelerate receipts?

MARKETABLE SECURITIES

Marketable Securities
Securities that can be sold on short notice.

Realistically, the management of cash and marketable securities cannot be separated— management of one implies management of the other. In the first part of the chapter, we focused on cash management. Now, we turn to **marketable securities.**

In many cases, companies hold marketable securities for the same reasons they hold cash. Although these securities are not the same as cash, in most cases they can be converted to cash on very short notice (often just a few minutes) with a single telephone call. Moreover, while cash and most commercial checking accounts yield nothing, marketable securities provide at least a modest return. For this reason, many firms hold at least some marketable securities in lieu of larger cash balances, liquidating part of the portfolio to increase the cash account when cash outflows exceed inflows. In such situations, the marketable securities could be used as a substitute for transactions balances, for precautionary balances, for speculative balances, or for all three. In most cases, the securities are held primarily for precautionary purposes—most firms prefer to rely on bank credit to make temporary transactions or to meet speculative needs, but they may still hold some liquid assets to guard against a possible shortage of bank credit.

Although setting the target cash balance is, to a large extent, judgmental, analytical rules can be applied to help formulate better judgments. For example, years ago William Baumol recognized that the trade-off between cash and marketable securities is similar to the one firms face when setting the optimal level of inventory.[8] Baumol applied the EOQ inventory model to determine the optimal level of cash balances.[9] He suggested that cash holdings should be higher if costs are high and the time to liquidate marketable securities is long, but that those cash holdings should be lower if interest rates are high. His logic was that if it is expensive and time consuming to convert securities to cash, and if securities do not earn much because interest rates are low, then it does not pay to hold securities as opposed to cash. It does pay to hold securities if interest rates are high and the securities can be converted to cash quickly and cheaply.

To summarize, there are both benefits and costs associated with holding cash and marketable securities. The benefits are twofold: (1) the firm reduces transactions costs because it won't have to issue securities or borrow as frequently to raise cash; and (2) it will have ready cash to take advantage of bargain purchases or growth opportunities. The primary disadvantage is that the after-tax return on cash and short-term securities is very low. Thus, firms face a trade-off between benefits and costs.

Recent research supports this trade-off hypothesis as an explanation for firm's cash holdings.[10] Firms with high growth opportunities suffer the most if they don't have ready cash to quickly take advantage of an opportunity, and the data show that these firms do hold relatively high levels of cash and marketable securities. Firms with volatile cash flows are the ones most likely to run low on cash, so they are the ones that hold the highest levels of cash. In contrast, cash holdings are less important to large firms with high credit ratings, because they have quick and inexpensive access to capital markets. As expected, such firms hold relatively low levels of cash. Of course, there will always be outliers, but volatile firms with good growth opportunities are still the ones with the highest cash balances, on average.

---

[8] William J. Baumol, "The Transactions Demand for Cash: An Inventory Theoretic Approach," *Quarterly Journal of Economics*, November 1952, 545–556.

[9] A more complete description of the Economic Ordering Quantity (EOQ) model can be found in Eugene F. Brigham and Phillip R. Daves, *Intermediate Financial Management*, 7th ed. (Cincinnati, OH: South-Western College Publishing, 2002), Chapter 22.

[10] See Tim Opler, Lee Pinkowitz, René Stulz, and Rohan Williamson, "The Determinants and Implications of Corporate Cash Holdings," *Journal of Financial Economics*, Vol. 52, 1999, 3–46.

INVENTORY

Inventories, which may be classified as (1) *supplies*, (2) *raw materials*, (3) *work-in-process*, and (4) *finished goods*, are an essential part of virtually all business operations. As is the case with accounts receivable, inventory levels depend heavily upon sales. However, whereas receivables build up *after* sales have been made, inventory must be acquired *ahead* of sales. This is a critical difference, and the necessity of forecasting sales before establishing target inventory levels makes inventory management a difficult task. Also, since errors in the establishment of inventory levels quickly lead either to lost sales or to excessive carrying costs, inventory management is as important as it is difficult.

Inventory management techniques are covered in depth in production management courses. Still, since financial managers have a responsibility both for raising the capital needed to carry inventory and for the firm's overall profitability, we need to cover the financial aspects of inventory management here. Two examples will make clear the types of issues involved in inventory management, and the financial problems poor inventory control can cause.

RETAIL CLOTHING STORE

Chicago Discount Clothing (CDC) must order swimsuits for summer sales in January, and it must take delivery by April to be sure of having enough suits to meet the heavy May–June demand. Bathing suits come in many styles, colors, and sizes, and if CDC stocks incorrectly, either in total or in terms of the style-color-size distribution, then the store will have trouble. It will lose potential sales if it stocks too few suits, and it will be forced to lower prices and take losses if it stocks too many or the wrong types.

The effects of inventory changes on the balance sheet are important. For simplicity, assume that CDC has a $10,000 base stock of inventory which is financed by common stock. Its balance sheet is as follows:

Inventory (base stock)	$10,000	Common stock	$10,000
Total assets	$10,000	Total claims	$10,000

Now it anticipates that it will sell $5,000 of swimsuits (at cost) this summer. Dollar sales will actually be greater than $5,000, since CDC makes about $200 in profits for every $1,000 of inventory sold. CDC finances its seasonal inventory with bank loans, so its pre-summer balance sheet would look like this:

Inventory (seasonal)	$ 5,000	Notes payable to bank	$ 5,000
Inventory (base stock)	10,000	Common stock	10,000
Total assets	$15,000	Total claims	$15,000

If everything works out as planned, sales will be made, inventory will be converted to cash, the bank loan will be retired, and the company will earn a profit. The balance sheet, after a successful season, might look like this:

Cash	$ 1,000	Notes payable to bank	$ 0
Inventory (seasonal)	0	Common stock	10,000
Inventory (base stock)	10,000	Retained earnings	1,000
Total assets	$11,000	Total claims	$11,000

The company is now in a highly liquid position and is ready to begin a new season.

But suppose the season had not gone well, and CDC had only sold $1,000 of its inventory. As fall approached, the balance sheet would look like this:

Cash	$ 200	Notes payable to bank	$ 4,000
Inventory (seasonal)	4,000	Common stock	10,000
Inventory (base stock)	10,000	Retained earnings	200
Total assets	$14,200	Total claims	$14,200

Now suppose the bank insists on repayment of the $4,000 outstanding on the loan, and it wants cash, not swimsuits. But if the swimsuits did not sell well in the summer, how will out-of-style suits sell in the fall? Assume that CDC is forced to mark the suits down to half their cost (not half the selling price) in order to sell them to raise cash to repay the bank loan. Here is the result:

Cash	$ 2,200	Notes payable to bank	$ 4,000
Inventory (base stock)	10,000	Common stock	10,000
		Retained earnings	(1,800)
Total assets	$12,200	Total claims	$12,200

At this point, CDC is in serious trouble. It does not have the cash to pay off the loan, and the firm's shareholders have lost $1,800 of their equity. If the bank will not extend the loan, and if other sources of cash are not available, CDC will have to mark down its base stock prices in an effort to stimulate sales, and if this does not work, CDC could be forced into bankruptcy. Clearly, poor inventory decisions can spell trouble.

APPLIANCE MANUFACTURER

Now consider a different situation, that of Housepro Corporation, an appliance manufacturer. Here is its inventory position, in millions of dollars:

Raw materials	$ 200
Work-in-process	200
Finished goods	600
Total inventory	$1,000

Suppose Housepro anticipates that the economy is about to get much stronger and that the demand for appliances will rise sharply. If it is to share in the expected boom, Housepro will have to increase production. This means it will have to increase inventory, and, since the inventory buildup must precede sales, additional financing will be required—some liability account, perhaps notes payable, will have to be increased in order to finance the inventory buildup.

Proper inventory management requires close coordination among the sales, purchasing, production, and finance departments. The sales/marketing department is generally the first to spot changes in demand. These changes must be worked into the company's purchasing and manufacturing schedules, and the financial manager must arrange any financing needed to support the inventory buildup. Lack of coordination among departments, poor sales forecasts, or both, can lead to disaster.

SELF-TEST QUESTIONS

Why is good inventory management essential to a firm's success?

What departments should be involved in inventory decisions?

INVENTORY COSTS

The twin goals of inventory management are (1) to ensure that the inventories needed to sustain operations are available, but (2) to hold the costs of ordering and carrying inventories to the lowest possible level. Table 15-2 gives a listing of the typical costs associated with inventory, divided into three categories: carrying costs, ordering and receiving costs, and the costs that are incurred if the firm runs short of inventory.

Inventory is costly to store; therefore, there is always pressure to reduce inventory as part of firms' overall cost-containment strategies. An article in *Fortune* highlights the fact that an increasing number of corporations are taking drastic steps to control inventory costs.[11] For example, Trane Corporation, which makes air conditioners, recently adopted just-in-time inventory procedures described in the next section.

In the past, Trane produced parts on a steady basis, stored them as inventory, and had them ready whenever the company received an order for a batch of air conditioners. However, the company reached the point where its inventory covered an area equal to three football fields, and it still sometimes took as long as 15 days to fill an order. To make matters worse, occasionally some of the necessary components simply could not be located, while in other instances the components were located but found to have been damaged from long storage.

Then Trane adopted a new inventory policy—it began producing components only after an order is received, and then sending the parts directly from the machines that make them to the final assembly line. The net effect: Inventories fell nearly 40 percent even as sales increased by 30 percent.

However, as Table 15-2 indicates, there are costs associated with holding too little inventory, and these costs can be severe. Generally, if a business carries small inventories, it must reorder frequently. This increases ordering costs. Even more important,

---

[11] Shawn Tully, "Raiding a Company's Hidden Cash," *Fortune*, August 22, 1994, 82–87.

TABLE 15-2

	APPROXIMATE ANNUAL COST AS A PERCENTAGE OF INVENTORY VALUE
I. CARRYING COSTS	
Cost of capital tied up	12.0%
Storage and handling costs	0.5
Insurance	0.5
Property taxes	1.0
Depreciation and obsolescence	12.0
Total	26.0%
II. ORDERING, SHIPPING, AND RECEIVING COSTS	
Cost of placing orders, including production and set-up costs	Varies
Shipping and handling costs	2.5%
III. COSTS OF RUNNING SHORT	
Loss of sales	Varies
Loss of customer goodwill	Varies
Disruption of production schedules	Varies

Costs Associated with Inventory

NOTE: These costs vary from firm to firm, from item to item, and also over time. The figures shown are U.S. Department of Commerce estimates for an average manufacturing firm. Where costs vary so widely that no meaningful numbers can be assigned, the term "Varies" is reported.

firms can miss out on profitable sales, and also suffer a loss of goodwill that can lead to lower future sales. So, it is important to have enough inventory on hand to meet customer demands.

Suppose Palm Inc. has developed a new line of handheld computing devices. How much inventory should it produce and have on hand when the marketing campaign is launched? If it fails to produce enough inventory, retailers and customers are likely to be frustrated because they cannot immediately purchase the highly advertised product. Rather than wait, many customers will purchase a handheld device elsewhere. On the other hand, if Palm has too much inventory, it will incur unnecessarily high carrying costs. In addition, handhelds become obsolete quickly, so if inventory levels are high but sales are mediocre, the company may have to discount the devices to sell them. Apart from reducing the profit margin on this year's line of handhelds, these discounts may push down handheld prices in general, thereby reducing profit margins on the company's other products as well.

SELF-TEST QUESTIONS

What are the three categories of inventory costs?

What are some components of inventory carrying costs?

What are some components of inventory ordering costs?

SUPPLY CHAIN MANAGEMENT

Herman Miller Inc. manufactures a wide variety of office furniture, and a typical order from a single customer might require work at five different plants. Each plant uses components from different suppliers, and each plant works on orders for many customers. Imagine all the coordination that is required. The sales force generates the order, the purchasing department orders components from suppliers, and the suppliers must order materials from their own suppliers. Then, the suppliers ship the components to Herman Miller, the factory builds the product, the different products are gathered together to complete the order, and then the order is shipped to the customer. If one part of that process malfunctions, then the order will be delayed, inventory will pile up, extra costs to expedite the order will be incurred, and the customer's goodwill will be damaged, which will hurt future sales growth.

To prevent such consequences, many companies are turning to a process called supply chain management (SCM). The key element in SCM is sharing information all the way from the point-of-sale at the product's retailer to the suppliers, and even back to the suppliers' suppliers. SCM requires special software, but even more important, it requires cooperation between the different companies and departments in the supply chain. This new culture of open communication is often difficult for many companies—they are reluctant to divulge operating information. For example, EMC Corp., a manufacturer of data storage systems, has become deeply involved in the design processes and financial controls of its key suppliers. Many of EMC's suppliers were initially wary of these new relationships. However, SCM has been a win-win situation, with increases in value for EMC and its suppliers.

The same is true at many other companies. After implementing SCM, Herman Miller was able to reduce its days of inventory on hand by a week, and to cut two weeks off of delivery times to customers. Herman Miller was also able to operate its plants at a 20 percent higher volume without additional capital expenditures. Heineken USA can now get beer from its breweries to its customers' shelves in less than six weeks, compared with 10 to 12 weeks before implementing SCM. As these and other companies have found, SCM increases free cash flows and that leads to higher stock prices.

SOURCES: Elaine L. Appleton, "Supply Chain Brain," *CFO*, July 1997, 51–54; and Kris Frieswick, "Up Close and Virtual," *CFO*, April 1998, 87–91.

INVENTORY CONTROL SYSTEMS

Red-Line Method
An inventory control procedure in which a red line is drawn around the inside of an inventory-stocked bin to indicate the reorder point level.

Two-Bin Method
An inventory control procedure in which an order is placed when one of two inventory-stocked bins is empty.

Computerized Inventory Control System
A system of inventory control in which a computer is used to determine reorder points and to adjust inventory balances.

Inventory management requires the establishment of an *inventory control system*. Inventory control systems run the gamut from very simple to extremely complex, depending on the size of the firm and the nature of its inventory. For example, one simple control procedure is the **red-line method** — inventory items are stocked in a bin, a red line is drawn around the inside of the bin at the level of the reorder point, and the inventory clerk places an order when the red line shows. The **two-bin method** has inventory items stocked in two bins. When the working bin is empty, an order is placed and inventory is drawn from the second bin. These procedures work well for parts such as bolts in a manufacturing process, or for many items in retail businesses.

COMPUTERIZED SYSTEMS

Most companies today employ **computerized inventory control systems.** The computer starts with an inventory count in memory. As withdrawals are made, they are recorded by the computer, and the inventory balance is revised. When the reorder point is reached, the computer automatically places an order, and when the order is received, the recorded balance is increased. As we noted earlier, retailers such as Wal-Mart have carried this system quite far — each item has a bar code, and, as an item is checked out, the code is read, a signal is sent to the computer, and the inventory balance is adjusted at the same time the price is fed into the cash register tape. When the balance drops to the reorder point, an order is placed. In Wal-Mart's case, the order goes directly from its computers to those of its suppliers.

A good inventory control system is dynamic, not static. A company such as Wal-Mart or General Motors stocks hundreds of thousands of different items. The sales (or use) of individual items can rise or fall quite separately from rising or falling overall corporate sales. As the usage rate for an individual item begins to rise or fall, the inventory manager must adjust its balance to avoid running short or ending up with obsolete items. If the change in the usage rate appears to be permanent, the safety stock level should be reconsidered, and the computer model used in the control process should be reprogrammed.

JUST-IN-TIME SYSTEMS

Just-in-Time (JIT) System
A system of inventory control in which a manufacturer coordinates production with suppliers so that raw materials or components arrive just as they are needed in the production process.

An approach to inventory control called the **just-in-time (JIT) system** was developed by Japanese firms but has gained popularity throughout the world. Toyota was one of the first companies to aggressively employ a just-in-time system. Their setup was designed to link the company's factories with its suppliers. Delivery of components is tied to the speed of the assembly line, and parts are generally delivered no more than a few hours before they are used. The just-in-time system reduces the need for Toyota and other manufacturers to carry large inventories, but it requires a great deal of coordination between the manufacturer and its suppliers, both in the timing of deliveries and the quality of the parts. It also requires that component parts be perfect; otherwise, a few bad parts could stop the entire production line. Therefore, JIT inventory management has been developed in conjunction with total quality management (TQM).

Not surprisingly, U.S. automobile manufacturers were among the first domestic firms to move toward just-in-time systems. Smaller firms are also adopting just-in-time systems. In fact, some production experts say that small companies are better positioned than large ones to use just-in-time methods, because it is easier to redefine job functions and to educate people in small firms. One small-firm example is Fireplace Manufacturers Inc., a manufacturer of prefabricated fireplaces. The company was having cash flow problems, and it was carrying $1.1 million in inventory to support annual sales of about $8 million. The company went to a just-in-time system, trimmed its raw material and work-in-process inventory to $750,000, and freed up $350,000 of cash, even as sales doubled.

The close coordination required between the parties using JIT procedures has led to an overall reduction of inventory throughout the production-distribution system, and to a general improvement in economic efficiency. This point is made by companies such as Wal-Mart and Toyota, and it is borne out by economic statistics, which show that inventory as a percentage of sales has been declining since the use of just-in-time procedures began.

OUT-SOURCING

Out-Sourcing
The practice of purchasing components rather than making them in-house.

Another important development related to inventory is **out-sourcing,** which is the practice of purchasing components rather than making them in-house. Thus, if GM arranged to buy radiators, axles, and other parts from suppliers rather than making them itself, it would be increasing its use of out-sourcing. Out-sourcing is often combined with just-in-time systems to reduce inventory levels. However, perhaps the major reason for out-sourcing has nothing to do with inventory policy — a bureaucratic, unionized company like GM can often buy parts from a smaller, nonunionized supplier at a lower cost than if it made them itself.

THE RELATIONSHIP BETWEEN PRODUCTION SCHEDULING AND INVENTORY LEVELS

A final point relating to inventory levels is *the relationship between production scheduling and inventory levels*. A firm such as a greeting card manufacturer has highly seasonal sales. Such a firm could produce on a steady, year-round basis, or it could let production rise and fall with sales. If it established a level production schedule, its inventory would rise sharply during periods when sales were low and then decline during peak sales periods, but the average inventory held would be substantially higher than if production rose and fell with sales.

Our discussions of just-in-time systems, out-sourcing, and production scheduling all point out the necessity of coordinating inventory policy with manufacturing/ procurement policies. Companies try to minimize *total production and distribution costs*, and inventory costs are just one part of total costs. Still, they are an important cost, and financial managers should be aware of the determinants of inventory costs and how they can be minimized.

SELF-TEST QUESTIONS

Describe some inventory control systems that are used in practice.

What are just-in-time systems? What are their advantages? Why is quality especially important if a JIT system is used?

What is out-sourcing?

Describe the relationship between production scheduling and inventory levels.

RECEIVABLES MANAGEMENT

Account Receivable
A balance due from a customer.

Firms would, in general, rather sell for cash than on credit, but competitive pressures force most firms to offer credit. Thus, goods are shipped, inventories are reduced, and an **account receivable** is created.[12] Eventually, the customer will pay the account, at which time (1) the firm will receive cash and (2) its receivables will decline. Carrying receivables has both direct and indirect costs, but it also has an important benefit—increased sales.

---

[12] Whenever goods are sold on credit, two accounts are created—an asset item entitled *accounts receivable* appears on the books of the selling firm, and a liability item called *accounts payable* appears on the books of the purchaser. At this point, we are analyzing the transaction from the viewpoint of the seller, so we are concentrating on the variables under its control, in this case, the receivables. We will examine the transaction from the viewpoint of the purchaser in Chapter 16, where we discuss accounts payable as a source of funds and consider their cost relative to the cost of funds obtained from other sources.

Receivables management begins with the decision of whether or not to grant credit. In this section, we discuss the manner in which receivables build up, and we also discuss several alternative ways to monitor receivables. A monitoring system is important, because without it receivables will build up to excessive levels, cash flows will decline, and bad debts will offset the profits on sales. Corrective action is often needed, and the only way to know whether the situation is getting out of hand is with a good receivables control system.

THE ACCUMULATION OF RECEIVABLES

The total amount of accounts receivable outstanding at any given time is determined by two factors: (1) the volume of credit sales and (2) the average length of time between sales and collections. For example, suppose Boston Lumber Company (BLC), a wholesale distributor of lumber products, opens a warehouse on January 1 and, starting the first day, makes sales of $1,000 each day. For simplicity, we assume that all sales are on credit, and customers are given 10 days to pay. At the end of the first day, accounts receivable will be $1,000; they will rise to $2,000 by the end of the second day; and by January 10, they will have risen to 10($1,000) = $10,000. On January 11, another $1,000 will be added to receivables, but payments for sales made on January 1 will reduce receivables by $1,000, so total accounts receivable will remain constant at $10,000. In general, once the firm's operations have stabilized, this situation will exist:

$$
\begin{array}{cccc}
\text{Accounts} \\ \text{receivable} & = & \dfrac{\text{Credit sales}}{\text{per day}} & \times & \begin{array}{c}\text{Length of}\\ \text{collection period}\end{array} & \qquad (15\text{-}5) \\[2ex]
& = & \$1,000 & \times & 10 \text{ days} & = \$10,000.
\end{array}
$$

If either credit sales or the collection period changes, such changes will be reflected in accounts receivable.

Notice that the $10,000 investment in receivables must be financed. To illustrate, suppose that when the warehouse opened on January 1, BLC's shareholders had put up $800 as common stock and used this money to buy the goods sold the first day. The $800 of inventory will be sold for $1,000, so BLC's gross profit on the $800 investment is $200, or 25 percent. In this situation, the beginning balance sheet would be as follows.[13]

Inventories	$800	Common stock	$800
Total assets	$800	Total liabilities and equity	$800

At the end of the day, the balance sheet would look like this:

Accounts receivable	$1,000	Common stock	$ 800
Inventories	0	Retained earnings	200
Total assets	$1,000	Total liabilities and equity	$1,000

To remain in business, BLC must replenish inventories. To do so requires that $800 of goods be purchased, and this requires $800 in cash. Assuming that BLC borrows

---

[13] Note that the firm would need other assets such as cash, fixed assets, and a permanent stock of inventory. Also, overhead costs and taxes would have to be deducted, so retained earnings would be less than the figures shown here. We abstract from these details here so that we may focus on receivables.

the $800 from the bank, the balance sheet at the start of the second day will be as follows:

Accounts receivable	$1,000	Notes payable to bank	$ 800
Inventories	800	Common stock	800
		Retained earnings	200
Total assets	$1,800	Total liabilities and equity	$1,800

At the end of the second day, the inventories will have been converted to receivables, and the firm will have to borrow another $800 to restock for the third day.

This process will continue, provided the bank is willing to lend the necessary funds, until the beginning of the 11th day, when the balance sheet reads as follows:

Accounts receivable	$10,000	Notes payable to bank	$ 8,000
Inventories	800	Common stock	800
		Retained earnings	2,000
Total assets	$10,800	Total liabilities and equity	$10,800

From this point on, $1,000 of receivables will be collected every day, and $800 of these funds can be used to purchase new inventories.

This example makes it clear (1) that accounts receivable depend jointly on the level of credit sales and the collection period, (2) that any increase in receivables must be financed in some manner, but (3) that the entire amount of receivables does not have to be financed because the profit portion ($200 of each $1,000 of sales) does not represent a cash outflow. In our example, we assumed bank financing, but, as we demonstrate in Chapter 16, there are many alternative ways to finance current assets.

MONITORING THE RECEIVABLES POSITION

Investors—both stockholders and bank loan officers—should pay close attention to accounts receivable management, for, as we shall see, one can be misled by reported financial statements and later suffer serious losses on an investment.

When a credit sale is made, the following events occur: (1) Inventories are reduced by the cost of goods sold, (2) accounts receivable are increased by the sales price, and (3) the difference is profit, which is added to retained earnings. If the sale is for cash, then the cash from the sale has actually been received by the firm, but if the sale is on credit, the firm will not receive the cash from the sale unless and until the account is collected. Firms have been known to encourage "sales" to very weak customers in order to report high profits. This could boost the firm's stock price, at least until credit losses begin to lower earnings, at which time the stock price will fall. Analyses along the lines suggested in the following sections will detect any such questionable practice, as well as any unconscious deterioration in the quality of accounts receivable. Such early detection could help both investors and bankers avoid losses.[14]

---

[14] Accountants are increasingly interested in these matters. Investors have sued several of the major accounting firms for substantial damages when (1) profits were overstated and (2) it could be shown that the auditors should have conducted an analysis along the lines described here and then reported the results to stockholders in their audit opinion.

Days Sales Outstanding (DSO)

Suppose Super Sets Inc., a television manufacturer, sells 200,000 television sets a year at a price of $198 each. Further, assume that all sales are on credit with the following terms: if payment is made within 10 days, customers will receive a 2 percent discount; otherwise the full amount is due within 30 days. Finally, assume that 70 percent of the customers take discounts and pay on Day 10, while the other 30 percent pay on Day 30.

Days Sales Outstanding (DSO)
The average length of time required to collect credit sales.

Super Sets's **days sales outstanding (DSO),** sometimes called the *average collection period (ACP)*, is 16 days:

$$DSO = ACP = 0.7(10 \text{ days}) + 0.3(30 \text{ days}) = 16 \text{ days}.$$

Super Sets's *average daily sales (ADS)* is $108,493:

$$ADS = \frac{\text{Annual sales}}{365} = \frac{(\text{Units sold})(\text{Sales price})}{365} \qquad (15\text{-}6)$$

$$= \frac{200,000(\$198)}{365} = \frac{\$39,600,000}{365} = \$108,493.$$

Super Sets's accounts receivable, assuming a constant, uniform rate of sales throughout the year, will at any point in time be $1,735,888:

$$\text{Receivables} = (ADS)(DSO) \qquad (15\text{-}7)$$

$$= (\$108,493)(16) = \$1,735,888.$$

Note also that its DSO, or average collection period, is a measure of the average length of time it takes Super Sets's customers to pay off their credit purchases, and the DSO is often compared with an industry average DSO. For example, if all television manufacturers sell on the same credit terms, and if the industry average DSO is 25 days versus Super Sets's 16 days, then Super Sets either has a higher percentage of discount customers or else its credit department is exceptionally good at ensuring prompt payment.

Finally, note that if you know both the annual sales and the receivables balance, you can calculate DSO as follows:

$$DSO = \frac{\text{Receivables}}{\text{Sales per day}} = \frac{\$1,735,888}{\$108,493} = 16 \text{ days}.$$

The DSO can also be compared with the firm's own credit terms. For example, suppose Super Sets's DSO had been averaging 35 days. With a 35-day DSO, some customers would obviously be taking more than 30 days to pay their bills. In fact, if many customers were paying within 10 days to take advantage of the discount, the others must, on average, be taking much longer than 35 days. One way to check this possibility is to use an aging schedule as described in the next section.

Aging Schedules

Aging Schedule
A report showing how long accounts receivable have been outstanding.

An **aging schedule** breaks down a firm's receivables by age of account. Table 15-3 contains the December 31, 2002, aging schedules of two television manufacturers, Super Sets and Wonder Vision. Both firms offer the same credit terms, and both show the same total receivables. However, Super Sets's aging schedule indicates that all of its customers pay on time—70 percent pay on Day 10 while 30 percent pay on Day 30. Wonder Vision's schedule, which is more typical, shows that many of its customers are not abiding by its credit terms—some 27 percent of its receivables are

TABLE 15-3

Aging Schedules

AGE OF ACCOUNT (DAYS)	SUPER SETS		WONDER VISION	
	VALUE OF ACCOUNT	PERCENTAGE OF TOTAL VALUE	VALUE OF ACCOUNT	PERCENTAGE OF TOTAL VALUE
0–10	$1,215,122	70%	$ 815,867	47%
11–30	520,766	30	451,331	26
31–45	0	0	260,383	15
46–60	0	0	173,589	10
Over 60	0	0	34,718	2
Total receivables	$1,735,888	100%	$1,735,888	100%

more than 30 days past due, even though Wonder Vision's credit terms call for full payment by Day 30.

Aging schedules cannot be constructed from the type of summary data reported in financial statements; they must be developed from the firm's accounts receivable ledger. However, well-run firms have computerized their accounts receivable records, so it is easy to determine the age of each invoice, to sort electronically by age categories, and thus to generate an aging schedule.

Management should constantly monitor both the DSO and the aging schedule to detect trends, to see how the firm's collection experience compares with its credit terms, and to see how effectively the credit department is operating in comparison with other firms in the industry. If the DSO starts to lengthen, or if the aging schedule begins to show an increasing percentage of past-due accounts, then the firm's credit policy may need to be tightened.

Although a change in the DSO or the aging schedule should signal the firm to investigate its credit policy, a deterioration in either of these measures does not necessarily indicate that the firm's credit policy has weakened. In fact, if a firm experiences sharp seasonal variations, or if it is growing rapidly, then both the aging schedule and the DSO may be distorted. To see this point, note that the DSO is calculated as follows:

$$DSO = \frac{\text{Accounts receivable}}{\text{Sales}/365}.$$

Since receivables at a given point in time reflect sales in the last month or so, but sales as shown in the denominator of the equation are for the last 12 months, a seasonal increase in sales will increase the numerator more than the denominator, hence will raise the DSO. This will occur even if the customers are still paying exactly as before. Similar problems arise with the aging schedule if sales fluctuate widely. Therefore, a change in either the DSO or the aging schedule should be taken as a signal to investigate further, but not necessarily as a sign that the firm's credit policy has weakened. Still, days sales outstanding and the aging schedule are useful tools for reviewing the credit department's performance.[15]

---

[15] See Brigham and Daves, *Intermediate Financial Management*, 7th ed., Chapter 22, for a more complete discussion of the problems with the DSO and aging schedule and ways to correct for them.

CREDIT POLICY

Credit Policy
A set of decisions that include a firm's credit period, credit standards, collection procedures, and discounts offered.

The success or failure of a business depends primarily on the demand for its products—as a rule, the higher its sales, the larger its profits and the higher its stock price. Sales, in turn, depend on a number of factors, some exogenous but others under the firm's control. The major controllable determinants of demand are sales prices, product quality, advertising, and the firm's **credit policy.** Credit policy, in turn, consists of these four variables:

1. *Credit period*, which is the length of time buyers are given to pay for their purchases.
2. *Discounts* given for early payment, including the discount percentage and how rapidly payment must be made to qualify for the discount.
3. *Credit standards*, which refer to the required financial strength of acceptable credit customers.
4. *Collection policy*, which is measured by its toughness or laxity in attempting to collect on slow-paying accounts.

The credit manager is responsible for administering the firm's credit policy. However, because of the pervasive importance of credit, the credit policy itself is normally established by the executive committee, which usually consists of the president plus the vice-presidents of finance, marketing, and production.

Credit Terms
A statement of the credit period and any discounts offered — for example, 2/10, net 30.

SETTING THE CREDIT PERIOD AND STANDARDS

Credit Period
The length of time for which credit is granted.

A firm's regular **credit terms,** which include the **credit period** and *discount*, might call for sales on a 2/10, net 30 basis to all "acceptable" customers. Here customers who pay within 10 days would be given a 2 percent discount, and others would be required to pay within 30 days. Its *credit standards* would be applied to determine which customers qualify for the regular credit terms, and the amount of credit available to each customer.

CREDIT STANDARDS

Credit Standards
Standards that stipulate the required financial strength that an applicant must demonstrate to be granted credit.

Credit standards refer to the financial strength and creditworthiness a customer must exhibit in order to qualify for credit. If a customer does not qualify for the regular credit terms, it can still purchase from the firm, but under more restrictive terms. For example, a firm's "regular" credit terms might call for payment after 30 days, and these terms might be extended to all qualified customers. The firm's credit standards would be applied to determine which customers qualified for the regular credit terms, and how much credit each should receive. The major factors considered when setting credit standards relate to the likelihood that a given customer will pay slowly or perhaps end up as a bad debt loss.

Setting credit standards requires a measurement of *credit quality*, which is defined in terms of the probability of a customer's default. The probability estimate for a given customer is, for the most part, a subjective judgment. Nevertheless, credit evaluation is a well-established practice, and a good credit manager can make reasonably accurate judgments of the probability of default by different classes of customers.

Managing a credit department requires fast, accurate, and up-to-date information. To help get such information, the National Association of Credit Management (a group with 43,000 member firms) persuaded TRW, a large credit-reporting agency, to develop a computer-based telecommunications network for the collection, storage, retrieval, and distribution of credit information. A typical business credit report would include the following pieces of information:

1. A summary balance sheet and income statement.
2. A number of key ratios, with trend information.
3. Information obtained from the firm's suppliers telling whether it pays promptly or slowly, and whether it has recently failed to make any payments.
4. A verbal description of the physical condition of the firm's operations.
5. A verbal description of the backgrounds of the firm's owners, including any previous bankruptcies, lawsuits, divorce settlement problems, and the like.
6. A summary rating, ranging from A for the best credit risks down to F for those that are deemed likely to default.

Although a great deal of credit information is available, it must still be processed in a judgmental manner. Computerized information systems can assist in making better credit decisions, but, in the final analysis, most credit decisions are really exercises in informed judgment.[16]

---

[16] Credit analysts use procedures ranging from highly sophisticated, computerized "credit-scoring" systems, which actually calculate the statistical probability that a given customer will default, to informal procedures, which involve going through a checklist of factors that should be considered when processing a credit application. The credit-scoring systems use various financial ratios such as the current ratio and the debt ratio (for businesses) and income, years with the same employer, and the like (for individuals) to determine the statistical probability of default. Credit is then granted to those with low default probabilities. The informal procedures often involve examining the "5 C's of Credit": character, capacity, capital, collateral, and conditions. Character is obvious; capacity is a subjective estimate of ability to repay; capital means how much net worth the borrower has; collateral means assets pledged to secure the loan; and conditions refers to business conditions, which affect ability to repay.

What are credit terms?

What is credit quality, and how is it assessed?

SETTING THE COLLECTION POLICY

Collection Policy
The procedures that a firm follows to collect accounts receivable.

Collection policy refers to the procedures the firm follows to collect past-due accounts. For example, a letter might be sent to customers when a bill is 10 days past due; a more severe letter, followed by a telephone call, would be sent if payment is not received within 30 days; and the account would be turned over to a collection agency after 90 days.

The collection process can be expensive in terms of both out-of-pocket expenditures and lost goodwill—customers dislike being turned over to a collection agency. However, at least some firmness is needed to prevent an undue lengthening of the collection period and to minimize outright losses. A balance must be struck between the costs and benefits of different collection policies.

Changes in collection policy influence sales, the collection period, and the bad debt loss percentage. All of this should be taken into account when setting the credit policy.

How does collection policy influence sales, the collection period, and the bad debt loss percentage?

CASH DISCOUNTS

Cash Discount
A reduction in the price of goods given to encourage early payment.

The last element in the credit policy decision, the use of **cash discounts** for early payment, is analyzed by balancing the costs and benefits of different cash discounts. For example, a firm might decide to change its credit terms from "net 30," which means that customers must pay within 30 days, to "2/10, net 30," where a 2 percent discount is given if payment is made in ten days. This change should produce two benefits: (1) It should attract new customers who consider the discount to be a price reduction, and (2) the discount should cause a reduction in the days sales outstanding, because some existing customers will pay more promptly in order to get the discount. Offsetting these benefits is the dollar cost of the discounts. The optimal discount percentage is established at the point where the marginal costs and benefits are exactly offsetting.

Seasonal Dating
Terms used to induce customers to buy early by not requiring payment until the purchaser's selling season, regardless of when the goods are shipped.

If sales are seasonal, a firm may use **seasonal dating** on discounts. For example, Slimware Inc., a swimsuit manufacturer, sells on terms of 2/10, net 30, May 1 dating. This means that the effective invoice date is May 1, even if the sale was made back in January. The discount may be taken up to May 10; otherwise, the full amount must be paid on May 30. Slimware produces throughout the year, but retail sales of bathing suits are concentrated in the spring and early summer. By offering seasonal dating, the company induces some of its customers to stock up early, saving Slimware some storage costs and also "nailing down sales."

How can cash discounts be used to influence sales volume and the DSO?

What is seasonal dating?

OTHER FACTORS INFLUENCING CREDIT POLICY

In addition to the factors discussed in previous sections, two other points should be made regarding credit policy.

PROFIT POTENTIAL

We have emphasized the costs of granting credit. *However, if it is possible to sell on credit and also to impose a carrying charge on the receivables that are outstanding, then credit sales can actually be more profitable than cash sales.* This is especially true for consumer durables (autos, appliances, and so on), but it is also true for certain types of industrial equipment. Thus, GM's General Motors Acceptance Corporation (GMAC) unit, which finances automobiles, is highly profitable, as is Sears' credit subsidiary.[17] Some encyclopedia companies even lose money on cash sales but more than make up these losses from the carrying charges on their credit sales. Obviously, such companies would rather sell on credit than for cash!

The carrying charges on outstanding credit are generally about 18 percent on a nominal basis: 1.5 percent per month, so $1.5\% \times 12 = 18\%$. This is equivalent to an effective annual rate of $(1.015)^{12} - 1.0 = 19.6\%$. Having receivables outstanding that earn more than 18 percent is highly profitable unless there are too many bad debt losses.

LEGAL CONSIDERATIONS

It is illegal, under the Robinson-Patman Act, for a firm to charge prices that discriminate between customers unless these differential prices are cost-justified. The same holds true for credit — it is illegal to offer more favorable credit terms to one customer or class of customers than to another, unless the differences are cost-justified.

How do profit potential and legal considerations affect a firm's credit policy?

---

[17] Companies that do a large volume of sales financing typically set up subsidiary companies called *captive finance companies* to do the actual financing. Thus, General Motors, DaimlerChrysler, and Ford all have captive finance companies, as do Sears, IBM, and General Electric.

TYING IT ALL TOGETHER

This chapter discussed the management of current assets, particularly cash, marketable securities, inventory, and receivables. While there are unique factors relating to each component of working capital, two important themes run through the chapter.

First, current assets are necessary, but there are costs associated with holding them. Therefore, if a company can manage its current assets more efficiently and thereby operate with a smaller investment in working capital, this will increase its profitability. At the same time, though, a company will have problems if it reduces its cash, inventory, and receivables too much. Thus, the optimal current asset management policy is one that carefully trades off the costs and benefits of holding working capital.

Second, changing technology has enabled companies to streamline their working capital, which has improved their cash flow and profitability. Indeed, companies today that fail to manage their working capital efficiently are finding themselves at a greater and greater competitive disadvantage. The key concepts in this chapter are listed below.

- **Working capital** refers to current assets, and **net working capital** is defined as current assets minus current liabilities. **Working capital policy** refers to decisions relating to current assets and their financing.

- Under a **relaxed current asset policy,** a firm would hold relatively large amounts of each type of current asset. Under a **restricted current asset policy,** the firm would hold minimal amounts of these items.

- The **cash conversion cycle** equals the length of time between the firm's actual cash expenditures to pay for productive resources (materials and labor) and its own cash receipts from the sale of products (that is, the length of time between paying for labor and materials and collecting on receivables).

$$\begin{array}{c} \text{Cash} \\ \text{conversion} \\ \text{cycle} \end{array} = \begin{array}{c} \text{Inventory} \\ \text{conversion} \\ \text{period} \end{array} + \begin{array}{c} \text{Receivables} \\ \text{collection} \\ \text{period} \end{array} - \begin{array}{c} \text{Payables} \\ \text{deferral} \\ \text{period} \end{array}.$$

- **Zero working capital** has its own definition of working capital: Inventories + Receivables − Payables. The rationale is that inventories and receivables are the keys to making sales, and that inventories can be financed by suppliers through accounts payable.

- The **transactions balance** is the cash necessary to conduct day-to-day business, whereas the **precautionary balance** is a cash reserve held to meet random, unforeseen needs. A **compensating balance** is a minimum checking account balance that a bank requires as compensation either for services provided or as part of a loan agreement. Firms also hold **speculative balances,** which allow them to take advantage of bargain purchases. Note, though, that borrowing capacity and marketable security holdings both reduce the need for precautionary and speculative balances.

- A **cash budget** is a schedule showing projected cash inflows and outflows over some period. The cash budget is used to predict cash surpluses and deficits, and it is the primary cash management planning tool.

- **Disbursement float** is the amount of funds associated with checks written by a firm that are still in process and hence have not yet been deducted from the firm's bank account.

- **Collections float** is the amount of funds associated with checks written to a firm that have not been cleared, hence are not yet available for the firm's use.

- **Net float** is the difference between disbursement float and collections float, and it also is equal to the difference between the balance in the firm's own checkbook and the balance on the bank's records. The larger the net float, the smaller the cash balance the firm must maintain, so net float is good.

- Firms can reduce their cash balances by holding **marketable securities,** which can be sold on short notice at close to their quoted prices. They serve both as a substitute for cash and as a temporary investment for funds that will be needed in the near future.

- The twin goals of **inventory management** are (1) to ensure that the inventories needed to sustain operations are available, but (2) to hold the costs of ordering and carrying inventories to the lowest possible level.

- Firms use inventory control systems such as the **red-line method** and the **two-bin method,** as well as **computerized inventory control systems,** to help them keep track of actual inventory levels and to ensure that inventory levels are adjusted as sales change. **Just-in-time (JIT) systems** are used to hold down inventory costs and, simultaneously, to improve the production process. **Outsourcing** is the practice of purchasing components rather than making them in-house.

- When a firm sells goods to a customer on credit, an **account receivable** is created.

- A firm can use an **aging schedule** and the **days sales outstanding (DSO)** to help keep track of its receivables position and to help avoid an increase in bad debts.

Working capital policy involves two basic issues. The first, determining the appropriate level for each type of current asset, was addressed in this chapter. The second, how current assets should be financed, will be addressed in Chapter 16.

QUESTIONS

15-1 Assuming the firm's sales volume remained constant, would you expect it to have a higher cash balance during a tight-money period or during an easy-money period? Why?

15-2 What are the two principal reasons for holding cash? Can a firm estimate its target cash balance by summing the cash held to satisfy each of the two?

15-3 Explain how each of the following factors would probably affect a firm's target cash balance if all other factors were held constant.
  a. The firm institutes a new billing procedure that better synchronizes its cash inflows and outflows.
  b. The firm develops a new sales forecasting technique that improves its forecasts.
  c. The firm reduces its portfolio of U.S. Treasury bills.
  d. The firm arranges to use an overdraft system for its checking account.
  e. The firm borrows a large amount of money from its bank and also begins to write far more checks than it did in the past.
  f. Interest rates on Treasury bills rise from 5 percent to 10 percent.

15-4 Why would a lockbox plan make more sense for a firm that makes sales all over the United States than for a firm with the same volume of business but concentrated in its home city?

15-5 Is it true that when one firm sells to another on credit, the seller records the transaction as an account receivable while the buyer records it as an account payable and that, disregarding discounts, the receivable typically exceeds the payable by the amount of profit on the sale?

15-6 What are the four elements of a firm's credit policy? To what extent can firms set their own credit policies as opposed to having to accept policies that are dictated by "the competition"?

15-7 Suppose that a firm makes a purchase and receives the shipment on February 1. The terms of trade as stated on the invoice read "2/10, net 40, May 1 dating." What is the latest date on which payment can be made and the discount still be taken? What is the date on which payment must be made if the discount is not taken?

15-8 a. What is the days sales outstanding (DSO) for a firm whose sales are $2,920,000 per year and whose accounts receivable are $312,000?

b. Is it true that if this firm sells on terms of 3/10, net 40, its customers probably all pay on time?

15-9 Is it true that if a firm calculates its days sales outstanding, it has no need for an aging schedule?

15-10 Firm A had no credit losses last year, but 1 percent of Firm B's accounts receivable proved to be uncollectible and resulted in losses. Should Firm B fire its credit manager and hire A's?

15-11 Indicate by a (+), (−), or (0) whether each of the following events would probably cause accounts receivable (A/R), sales, and profits to increase, decrease, or be affected in an indeterminant manner:

	A/R	SALES	PROFITS
The firm tightens its credit standards.	_____	_____	_____
The terms of trade are changed from 2/10, net 30, to 3/10, net 30.	_____	_____	_____
The terms are changed from 2/10, net 30, to 3/10, net 40.	_____	_____	_____
The credit manager gets tough with past-due accounts.	_____	_____	_____

15-12 A firm can reduce its investment in inventory by having its suppliers hold raw materials inventory and its customers hold finished goods inventory. Explain actions a firm can take which would result in larger inventory for its suppliers and customers and smaller inventory for itself. What are the limitations of such actions?

SELF-TEST PROBLEMS (SOLUTIONS APPEAR IN APPENDIX B)

ST-1
Key terms
Define each of the following terms:
a. Working capital; net working capital; working capital policy
b. Relaxed current asset investment policy; restricted current asset investment policy; moderate current asset investment policy
c. Cash conversion cycle model; inventory conversion period; receivables collection period
d. Payables deferral period; cash conversion cycle; zero working capital
e. Transactions balance; compensating balance; precautionary balance; speculative balance
f. Cash budget; target cash balance
g. Trade discounts
h. Synchronized cash flows
i. Check clearing; net float; disbursement float; collections float
j. Lockbox plan
k. Marketable securities
l. Red-line method; two-bin method; computerized inventory control system
m. Just-in-time system; out-sourcing
n. Account receivable; days sales outstanding
o. Aging schedule
p. Credit policy; credit period; credit standards; collection policy; credit terms
q. Cash discounts
r. Seasonal dating

ST-2
Working capital policy
The Calgary Company is attempting to establish a current assets policy. Fixed assets are $600,000, and the firm plans to maintain a 50 percent debt-to-assets ratio. The interest rate is 10 percent on all debt. Three alternative current asset policies are under consideration: 40, 50, and 60 percent of projected sales. The company expects to earn 15 percent before interest and taxes on sales of $3 million. Calgary's effective federal-plus-state tax rate is 40 percent. What is the expected return on equity under each alternative?

ST-3
Float
The Upton Company is setting up a new checking account with Howe National Bank. Upton plans to issue checks in the amount of $1 million each day and to deduct them from its own records at the close of business on the day they are written. On average, the bank will receive

and clear the checks at 5 P.M. the third day after they are written; for example, a check written on Monday will be cleared on Thursday afternoon. The firm's agreement with the bank requires it to maintain a $500,000 average compensating balance; this is $250,000 greater than the cash balance the firm would otherwise have on deposit. It makes a $500,000 deposit at the time it opens the account.

a. Assuming that the firm makes deposits at 4 P.M. each day (and the bank includes them in that day's transactions), how much must it deposit daily in order to maintain a sufficient balance once it reaches a steady state? Indicate the required deposit on Day 1, Day 2, Day 3, if any, and each day thereafter, assuming that the company will write checks for $1 million on Day 1 and each day thereafter.

b. How many days of float does Upton have?

c. What ending daily balance should the firm try to maintain (1) on the bank's records and (2) on its own records?

STARTER PROBLEMS

15-1
Net float
On a typical day, Troan Corporation writes $10,000 in checks. It generally takes 4 days for those checks to clear. Each day the firm typically receives $10,000 in checks that take 3 days to clear. What is the firm's average net float?

15-2
Cash management
Williams & Sons last year reported sales of $10 million and an inventory turnover ratio of 2. The company is now adopting a just-in-time inventory system. If the new system is able to reduce the firm's inventory level and increase the firm's inventory turnover ratio to 5, while maintaining the same level of sales, how much cash will be freed up?

15-3
Receivables investment
Medwig Corporation has a DSO of 17 days. The company averages $3,500 in credit sales each day. What is the company's average accounts receivable?

EXAM-TYPE PROBLEMS

The problems included in this section are set up in such a way that they could be used as multiple-choice exam problems.

15-4
Lockbox system
I. Malitz and Associates Inc. operates a mail-order firm doing business on the West Coast. Malitz receives an average of $325,000 in payments per day. On average, it takes 4 days from the time customers mail checks until Malitz receives and processes them. Malitz is considering the use of a lockbox system to reduce collection and processing float. The system will cost $6,500 per month and will consist of 10 local depository banks and a concentration bank located in San Francisco. Under this system, customers' checks should be received at the lockbox locations 1 day after they are mailed, and daily totals will be transferred to San Francisco using wire transfers costing $9.75 each. Assume that Malitz has an opportunity cost of 10 percent and that there are 52 × 5 = 260 working days, hence 260 transfers from each lockbox location, in a year.

a. What is the total annual cost of operating the lockbox system?

b. What is the benefit of the lockbox system to Malitz?

c. Should Malitz initiate the system?

15-5
Receivables investment
McDowell Industries sells on terms of 3/10, net 30. Total sales for the year are $912,500. Forty percent of the customers pay on the 10th day and take discounts; the other 60 percent pay, on average, 40 days after their purchases.

a. What is the days sales outstanding?

b. What is the average amount of receivables?

c. What would happen to average receivables if McDowell toughened up on its collection policy with the result that all nondiscount customers paid on the 30th day?

15-6
Cash conversion cycle
Parlow Packing currently has $35,750 in cash, $47,000 in accounts receivable, $66,000 in inventories, $13,000 in accrued liabilities, and $72,000 in accounts payable on its balance sheet. The firm's production manager has determined that the cost of goods sold accounts for 80 percent of the sales revenue it produces. Furthermore, the firm has determined that the length of the firm's cash conversion cycle is 16.79 days.

a. What is Parlow Packing's annual sales?

b. The firm's production manager has determined that through negotiation with its suppliers, the firm could reduce the ratio of the costs of goods sold to sales down to 70 percent, and thus reduce its cash conversion cycle time. However, the firm would then take this opportunity to use cash to reduce its accounts payable. The firm realizes that reducing accounts payable increases the cash conversion cycle time, but it is more concerned with pleasing its creditors, who are unhappy with the firm's liquidity position. None of these changes is expected to have any impact upon sales. If the firm reduces accounts payable enough to improve the current ratio to 2.0, what would be the length of the firm's cash conversion cycle?

PROBLEMS

15-7
Working capital investment

The Prestopino Corporation is a leading U.S. producer of automobile batteries. Prestopino turns out 1,500 batteries a day at a cost of $6 per battery for materials and labor. It takes the firm 22 days to convert raw materials into a battery. Prestopino allows its customers 40 days in which to pay for the batteries, and the firm generally pays its suppliers in 30 days.

a. What is the length of Prestopino's cash conversion cycle?

b. At a steady state in which Prestopino produces 1,500 batteries a day, what amount of working capital must it finance?

c. By what amount could Prestopino reduce its working capital financing needs if it was able to stretch its payables deferral period to 35 days?

d. Prestopino's management is trying to analyze the effect of a proposed new production process on the working capital investment. The new production process would allow Prestopino to decrease its inventory conversion period to 20 days and to increase its daily production to 1,800 batteries. However, the new process would cause the cost of materials and labor to increase to $7. Assuming the change does not affect the receivables collection period (40 days) or the payables deferral period (30 days), what will be the length of the cash conversion cycle and the working capital financing requirement if the new production process is implemented?

15-8
Cash conversion cycle

The Zocco Corporation has an inventory conversion period of 75 days, a receivables collection period of 38 days, and a payables deferral period of 30 days.

a. What is the length of the firm's cash conversion cycle?

b. If Zocco's annual sales are $3,421,875 and all sales are on credit, what is the firm's investment in accounts receivable?

c. How many times per year does Zocco turn over its inventory?

15-9
Working capital cash flow cycle

The Christie Corporation is trying to determine the effect of its inventory turnover ratio and days sales outstanding (DSO) on its cash flow cycle. Christie's 2002 sales (all on credit) were $150,000, and it earned a net profit of 6 percent, or $9,000. It turned over its inventory 6 times during the year, and its DSO was 36.5 days. The firm had fixed assets totaling $35,000. Christie's payables deferral period is 40 days.

a. Calculate Christie's cash conversion cycle.

b. Assuming Christie holds negligible amounts of cash and marketable securities, calculate its total assets turnover and ROA.

c. Suppose Christie's managers believe that the inventory turnover can be raised to 7.3 times. What would Christie's cash conversion cycle, total assets turnover, and ROA have been if the inventory turnover had been 7.3 for 2002?

15-10
Working capital policy

The Rentz Corporation is attempting to determine the optimal level of current assets for the coming year. Management expects sales to increase to approximately $2 million as a result of an asset expansion presently being undertaken. Fixed assets total $1 million, and the firm wishes to maintain a 60 percent debt ratio. Rentz's interest cost is currently 8 percent on both short-term and longer-term debt (which the firm uses in its permanent structure). Three alternatives regarding the projected current asset level are available to the firm: (1) a tight policy requiring current assets of only 45 percent of projected sales, (2) a moderate policy of 50 percent of sales in current assets, and (3) a relaxed policy requiring current assets of 60 percent of sales. The firm expects to generate earnings before interest and taxes at a rate of 12 percent on total sales.

a. What is the expected return on equity under each current asset level? (Assume a 40 percent effective federal-plus-state tax rate.)

b. In this problem, we have assumed that the level of expected sales is independent of current asset policy. Is this a valid assumption?

c. How would the overall riskiness of the firm vary under each policy?

15-11
Net float

The Stendardi-Stephens Company (SSC) is setting up a new checking account with National Bank. SSC plans to issue checks in the amount of $1.6 million each day and to deduct them from its own records at the close of business on the day they are written. On average, the bank will receive and clear (that is, deduct from the firm's bank balance) the checks at 5 P.M. the fourth day after they are written; for example, a check written on Monday will be cleared on Friday afternoon. The firm's agreement with the bank requires it to maintain a $1.2 million average compensating balance; this is $400,000 greater than the cash balance the firm would otherwise have on deposit. It makes a $1.2 million deposit at the time it opens the account.

a. Assuming that the firm makes deposits at 4 P.M. each day (and the bank includes them in that day's transactions), how much must it deposit daily in order to maintain a sufficient balance once it reaches a steady state? Indicate the required deposit on Day 1, Day 2, Day 3, Day 4, if any, and each day thereafter, assuming that the company will write checks for $1.6 million on Day 1 and each day thereafter.

b. How many days of float does SSC carry?

c. What ending daily balance should the firm try to maintain (1) on the bank's records and (2) on its own records?

d. Explain how net float can help increase the value of the firm's common stock.

15-12
Lockbox system

The Hardin-Gehr Corporation (HGC) began operations 5 years ago as a small firm serving customers in the Detroit area. However, its reputation and market area grew quickly, so that today HGC has customers throughout the entire United States. Despite its broad customer base, HGC has maintained its headquarters in Detroit and keeps its central billing system there. HGC's management is considering an alternative collection procedure to reduce its mail time and processing float. On average, it takes 5 days from the time customers mail payments until HGC is able to receive, process, and deposit them. HGC would like to set up a lockbox collection system, which it estimates would reduce the time lag from customer mailing to deposit by 3 days — bringing it down to 2 days. HGC receives an average of $1,400,000 in payments per day.

a. How many days of collection float now exist (HGC's customers' disbursement float), and what would it be under the lockbox system? What reduction in cash balances could HGC achieve by initiating the lockbox system?

b. If HGC has an opportunity cost of 10 percent, how much is the lockbox system worth on an annual basis?

c. What is the maximum monthly charge HGC should pay for the lockbox system?

15-13
Cash budgeting

Helen Bowers, owner of Helen's Fashion Designs, is planning to request a line of credit from her bank. She has estimated the following sales forecasts for the firm for parts of 2003 and 2004:

May 2003	$180,000
June	180,000
July	360,000
August	540,000
September	720,000
October	360,000
November	360,000
December	90,000
January 2004	180,000

Collection estimates obtained from the credit and collection department are as follows: collections within the month of sale, 10 percent; collections the month following the sale, 75 percent; collections the second month following the sale, 15 percent. Payments for labor and raw materials are typically made during the month following the one in which these costs have been incurred. Total labor and raw materials costs are estimated for each month as follows:

May 2003	$ 90,000
June	90,000
July	126,000
August	882,000
September	306,000
October	234,000
November	162,000
December	90,000

General and administrative salaries will amount to approximately $27,000 a month; lease payments under long-term lease contracts will be $9,000 a month; depreciation charges will be $36,000 a month; miscellaneous expenses will be $2,700 a month; income tax payments of $63,000 will be due in both September and December; and a progress payment of $180,000 on a new design studio must be paid in October. Cash on hand on July 1 will amount to $132,000, and a minimum cash balance of $90,000 will be maintained throughout the cash budget period.

a. Prepare a monthly cash budget for the last 6 months of 2003.
b. Prepare an estimate of the required financing (or excess funds) — that is, the amount of money Bowers will need to borrow (or will have available to invest) — for each month during that period.
c. Assume that receipts from sales come in uniformly during the month (that is, cash receipts come in at the rate of 1/30 each day), but all outflows are paid on the 5th of the month. Will this have an effect on the cash budget — in other words, would the cash budget you have prepared be valid under these assumptions? If not, what can be done to make a valid estimate of peak financing requirements? No calculations are required, although calculations can be used to illustrate the effects.
d. Bowers produces on a seasonal basis, just ahead of sales. Without making any calculations, discuss how the company's current ratio and debt ratio would vary during the year assuming all financial requirements were met by short-term bank loans. Could changes in these ratios affect the firm's ability to obtain bank credit?

SPREADSHEET PROBLEM

15-14
Cash budgeting

Rework Problem 15-13 using a spreadsheet model. After completing parts a through d, answer the following related question.
e. If its customers began to pay late, this would slow down collections and thus increase the required loan amount. Also, if sales dropped off, this would have an effect on the required loan. Do a sensitivity analysis that shows the effects of these two factors on the maximum loan requirement.

INTEGRATED CASE

SKI EQUIPMENT INC.

15-15 Managing Current Assets Dan Barnes, financial manager of Ski Equipment Inc. (SKI), is excited, but apprehensive. The company's founder recently sold his 51 percent controlling block of stock to Kent Koren, who is a big fan of EVA (Economic Value Added). EVA is found by taking the after-tax operating profit and then subtracting the dollar cost of all the capital the firm uses:

$$EVA = EBIT(1 - T) - \text{Capital costs}$$
$$= EBIT(1 - T) - WACC(\text{Capital employed}).$$

If EVA is positive, then the firm is creating value. On the other hand, if EVA is negative, the firm is not covering its cost of capital, and stockholders' value is being eroded. Koren rewards managers handsomely if they create value, but those whose operations produce negative EVAs are soon looking for work. Koren frequently points out that if a company can generate its current level of sales with less assets, it would need less capital. That would, other things held constant, lower capital costs and increase its EVA.

Shortly after he took control of SKI, Kent Koren met with SKI's senior executives to tell them of his plans for the company. First, he presented some EVA data that convinced everyone that SKI had not been creating value in recent years. He then stated, in no uncertain terms, that this situation must change. He noted that SKI's designs of skis, boots, and clothing are acclaimed throughout the industry, but something is seriously amiss elsewhere in the company. Costs are too high, prices are too low, or the company employs too much capital, and he wants SKI's managers to correct the problem or else.

Barnes has long felt that SKI's working capital situation should be studied — the company may have the optimal amounts of cash, securities, receivables, and inventories, but it may also have too much or too little of these items. In the past, the production manager resisted Barnes' efforts to question his holdings of raw materials inventories, the marketing manager resisted questions about finished goods, the sales staff resisted questions about credit policy (which affects accounts receivable), and the treasurer did not want to talk about her cash and securities balances. Koren's speech made it clear that such resistance would no longer be tolerated.

Barnes also knows that decisions about working capital cannot be made in a vacuum. For example, if inventories could be lowered without adversely affecting operations, then less capital would be required, the dollar cost of capital would decline, and EVA would increase. However, lower raw materials inventories might lead to production slowdowns and higher costs, while lower finished goods inventories might lead to the loss of profitable sales. So, before inventories are changed, it will be necessary to study operating as well as financial effects. The situation is the same with regard to cash and receivables.

a. Barnes plans to use the ratios in Table IC15-1 as the starting point for discussions with SKI's operating executives. He wants everyone to think about the pros and cons of changing each type of current asset and how changes would interact to affect profits and EVA. Based on the Table IC15-1 data, does SKI seem to be following a relaxed, moderate, or restricted working capital policy?

b. How can one distinguish between a relaxed but rational working capital policy and a situation where a firm simply has a lot of current assets because it is inefficient? Does SKI's working capital policy seem appropriate?

c. Assume that SKI's payables deferral period is 30 days. Now, calculate the firm's cash conversion cycle.

d. What might SKI do to reduce its cash and securities without harming operations?

e. What is "float," and how is it affected by the firm's cash manager (treasurer)?

In an attempt to better understand SKI's cash position, Barnes developed a cash budget. Data for the first 2 months of the year are shown in Table IC15-2. (Note that Barnes' preliminary cash budget does not account for interest income or interest expense.) He has the figures for the other months, but they are not shown in Table IC15-2.

f. Should depreciation expense be explicitly included in the cash budget? Why or why not?

g. In his preliminary cash budget, Barnes has assumed that all sales are collected and, thus, that SKI has no bad debts. Is this realistic? If not, how would bad debts be dealt with in a cash budgeting sense? (Hint: Bad debts will affect collections but not purchases.)

h. Barnes' cash budget for the entire year, although not given here, is based heavily on his forecast for monthly sales. Sales are expected to be extremely low between May and September but then increase dramatically in the fall and winter. November is typically the firm's best month, when SKI ships equipment to retailers for the holiday season. Interestingly, Barnes' forecasted cash budget indicates that the company's cash holdings will

TABLE IC15-1	Selected Ratios: SKI and Industry Average		
		SKI	**INDUSTRY**
Current		1.75	2.25
Debt/assets		58.76%	50.00%
Turnover of cash and securities		16.67	22.22
Days sales outstanding (365-day basis)		45.63	32.00
Inventory turnover		4.82	7.00
Fixed assets turnover		11.35	12.00
Total assets turnover		2.08	3.00
Profit margin on sales		2.07%	3.50%
Return on equity (ROE)		10.45%	21.00%

	NOV	DEC	JAN	FEB	MAR	APR
I. COLLECTIONS AND PURCHASES WORKSHEET						
(1) Sales (gross)	$71,218	$68,212	$65,213	$52,475	$42,909	$30,524
Collections						
(2) During month of sale (0.2)(0.98)(month's sales)			12,781.75	10,285.10		
(3) During first month after sale (0.7)(previous month's sales)			47,748.40	45,649.10		
(4) During second month after sale (0.1)(sales 2 months ago)			7,121.80	6,821.20		
(5) Total collections (Lines 2 + 3 + 4)			$67,651.95	$62,755.40		
Purchases						
(6) (0.85)(forecasted sales 2 months from now)		$44,603.75	$36,472.65	$25,945.40		
(7) Payments (1-month lag)			44,603.75	36,472.65		
II. CASH GAIN OR LOSS FOR MONTH						
(8) Collections (from Section I)			$67,651.95	$62,755.40		
(9) Payments for purchases (from Section I)			44,603.75	36,472.65		
(10) Wages and salaries			6,690.56	5,470.90		
(11) Rent			2,500.00	2,500.00		
(12) Taxes						
(13) Total payments			$53,794.31	$44,443.55		
(14) Net cash gain (loss) during month (Line 8 − Line 13)			$13,857.64	$18,311.85		
III. CASH SURPLUS OR LOAN REQUIREMENT						
(15) Cash at beginning of month if no borrowing is done			$3,000.00	$16,857.64		
(16) Cumulative cash (cash at start, + gain or − loss = Line 14 + Line 15)			16,857.64	35,169.49		
(17) Target cash balance			1,500.00	1,500.00		
(18) Cumulative surplus cash or loans outstanding to maintain $1,500 target cash balance (Line 16 − Line 17)			$15,357.64	$33,669.49		

exceed the targeted cash balance every month except for October and November, when shipments will be high but collections will not be coming in until later. Based on the ratios in Table IC15-1, does it appear that SKI's target cash balance is appropriate? In addition to possibly lowering the target cash balance, what actions might SKI take to better improve its cash management policies, and how might that affect its EVA?

i. What reasons might SKI have for maintaining a relatively high amount of cash?

j. What are the three categories of inventory costs? If the company takes steps to reduce its inventory, what effect would this have on the various costs of holding inventory?

k. Is there any reason to think that SKI may be holding too much inventory? If so, how would that affect EVA and ROE?

l. If the company reduces its inventory without adversely affecting sales, what effect should this have on the company's cash position (1) in the short run and (2) in the long run? Explain in terms of the cash budget and the balance sheet.

m. Barnes knows that SKI sells on the same credit terms as other firms in its industry. Use the ratios presented in Table IC15-1 to explain whether SKI's customers pay more or less promptly than those of its competitors. If there are differences, does that suggest that SKI should tighten or loosen its credit policy? What four variables make up a firm's credit policy, and in what direction should each be changed by SKI?

n. Does SKI face any risks if it tightens its credit policy?

o. If the company reduces its DSO without seriously affecting sales, what effect would this have on its cash position (1) in the short run and (2) in the long run? Answer in terms of the cash budget and the balance sheet. What effect should this have on EVA in the long run?

CYBER PROBLEM

Please go to our web site **http://brigham.swlearning.com** to access the Cyberproblems.

FINANCING CURRENT ASSETS

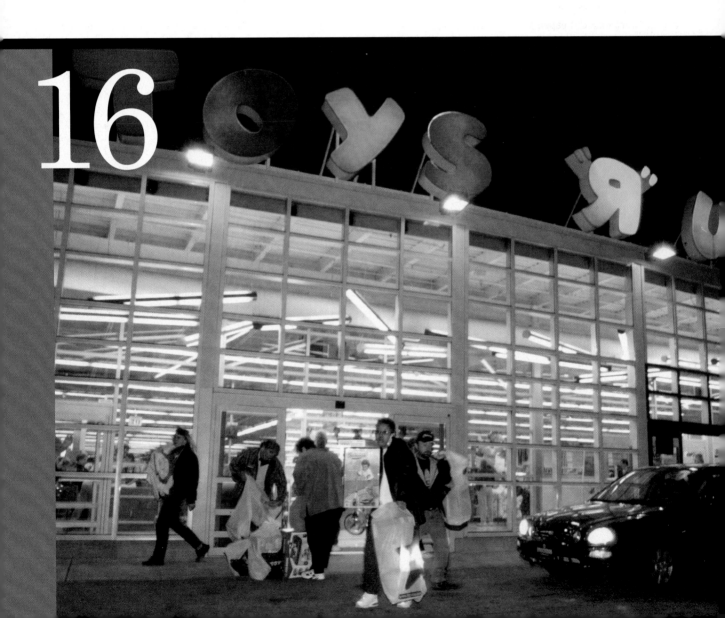

16

SOUND WORKING CAPITAL POLICY REQUIRES APPROPRIATE FINANCING

TOYS "Я" US

The last chapter discussed steps firms can take to improve their working capital management, thus reducing current assets as a percentage of sales through the use of new technology and improved management techniques. Still, most companies must hold large amounts of current assets, and this investment must be financed in some manner. This involves "working capital financing policy," the focus of the current chapter.

Most firms use several types of short-term debt to finance their working capital requirements. Included are bank loans, trade credit, commercial paper, and accrued liabilities. However, the structure of its current liabilities depends on the nature of a firm's business. For example, the sales of Toys "Я" Us are seasonal—nearly half of all sales occur in the final three months of the year. To meet holiday demands, Toys "Я" Us must dramatically increase its inventories during the summer and early fall. This inventory buildup must be financed until after Christmas, when collections bring in cash and debts can be reduced. The company finances the buildup with trade credit, loans from U.S. and foreign banks, commercial paper, and the sale of marketable securities built up during the slack season.

Short-term credit is generally cheaper than long-term capital, but it is a riskier, less dependable source of financing. Interest rates can increase dramatically, and changes in a company's financial position can affect both the cost and availability of short-term credit.

After you have completed this chapter, you will have a better understanding of the ways corporations finance their current assets, and of the costs associated with each type of financing.

In the last chapter, we discussed the first step in working capital management—determining the optimal level for each type of current asset. Now we turn to the second step—financing those assets. We begin with a discussion of alternative financing policies. Some companies use current liabilities as a major source of financing for current assets, while others rely more heavily on long-term debt and equity. In this chapter we consider the advantages and disadvantages of each policy. In addition, we describe the various sources of short-term financing—accrued liabilities, accounts payable, bank loans, and commercial paper. We also show how to estimate the cost of each source, and we discuss how companies choose their banking relationships. ■

ALTERNATIVE CURRENT ASSET FINANCING POLICIES

Most businesses experience seasonal and/or cyclical fluctuations. For example, construction firms have peaks in the spring and summer, retailers peak around Christmas, and the manufacturers who supply both construction companies and retailers follow similar patterns. Similarly, virtually all businesses must build up current assets when the economy is strong, but they then sell off inventories and reduce receivables when the economy slacks off. Still, current assets rarely drop to zero—companies have some **permanent current assets,** which are the current assets on hand at the low point of the cycle. Then, as sales increase during the upswing, current assets must be increased, and these additional current assets are defined as **temporary current assets.** The manner in which the permanent and temporary current assets are financed is called the firm's *current asset financing policy.*

Permanent Current Assets
Current assets that a firm must carry even at the trough of its cycles.

Temporary Current Assets
Current assets that fluctuate with seasonal or cyclical variations in sales.

Maturity Matching, or "Self-Liquidating," Approach
A financing policy that matches asset and liability maturities. This is a moderate policy.

MATURITY MATCHING, OR "SELF-LIQUIDATING," APPROACH

The **maturity matching, or "self-liquidating," approach** calls for matching asset and liability maturities as shown in Panel a of Figure 16-1. This strategy minimizes the risk that the firm will be unable to pay off its maturing obligations. To illustrate, suppose a company borrows on a one-year basis and uses the funds obtained to build and equip a plant. Cash flows from the plant (profits plus depreciation) would not be sufficient to pay off the loan at the end of only one year, so the loan would have to be renewed. If for some reason the lender refused to renew the loan, then the company would have problems. Had the plant been financed with long-term debt, however,

FIGURE 16-1   Alternative Current Asset Financing Policies

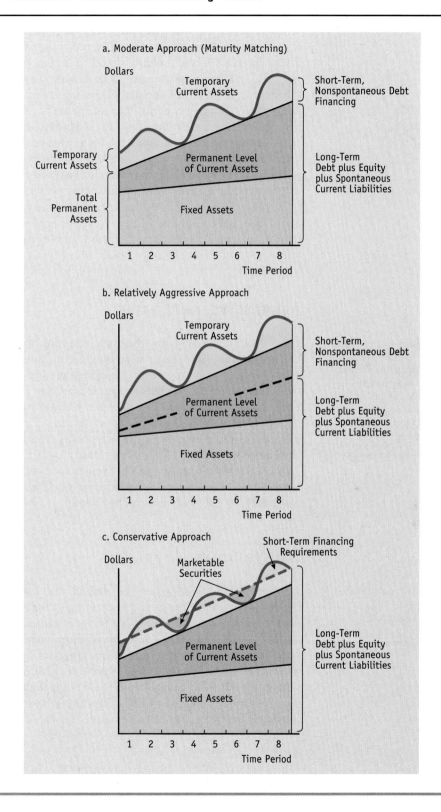

a. Moderate Approach (Maturity Matching)

Dollars

Temporary Current Assets

Short-Term, Nonspontaneous Debt Financing

Temporary Current Assets

Permanent Level of Current Assets

Long-Term Debt plus Equity plus Spontaneous Current Liabilities

Total Permanent Assets

Fixed Assets

1 2 3 4 5 6 7 8

Time Period

b. Relatively Aggressive Approach

Dollars

Temporary Current Assets

Short-Term, Nonspontaneous Debt Financing

Permanent Level of Current Assets

Long-Term Debt plus Equity plus Spontaneous Current Liabilities

Fixed Assets

1 2 3 4 5 6 7 8

Time Period

c. Conservative Approach

Short-Term Financing Requirements

Dollars

Marketable Securities

Permanent Level of Current Assets

Long-Term Debt plus Equity plus Spontaneous Current Liabilities

Fixed Assets

1 2 3 4 5 6 7 8

Time Period

the required loan payments would have been better matched with cash flows from profits and depreciation, and the problem of renewal would not have arisen.

At the limit, a firm could attempt to match exactly the maturity structure of its assets and liabilities. Inventory expected to be sold in 30 days could be financed with a 30-day bank loan; a machine expected to last for 5 years could be financed with a 5-year loan; a 20-year building could be financed with a 20-year mortgage bond; and so forth. Actually, of course, two factors prevent this exact maturity matching: (1) there is uncertainty about the lives of assets, and (2) some common equity must be used, and common equity has no maturity. To illustrate the uncertainty factor, a firm might finance inventories with a 30-day loan, expecting to sell the inventories and then use the cash to retire the loan. But if sales were slow, the cash would not be forthcoming, and the use of short-term credit could end up causing a problem. Still, if a firm makes an attempt to match asset and liability maturities, we would define this as a moderate current asset financing policy.

In practice, firms don't finance each specific asset with a type of capital that has a maturity equal to the asset's life. However, academic studies do show that most firms tend to finance short-term assets from short-term sources and long-term assets from long-term sources.[1]

AGGRESSIVE APPROACH

Students can access various types of historical interest rates, including fixed and variable rates, at the St. Louis Federal Reserve's FRED site. The address is **http://research. stlouisfed.org/fred/**.

Panel b of Figure 16-1 illustrates the situation for a relatively aggressive firm that finances all of its fixed assets with long-term capital and part of its permanent current assets with short-term, nonspontaneous credit. Note that we used the term "relatively" in the title for Panel b because there can be different *degrees* of aggressiveness. For example, the dashed line in Panel b could have been drawn *below* the line designating fixed assets, indicating that all of the permanent current assets and part of the fixed assets were financed with short-term credit; this would be a highly aggressive, extremely nonconservative position, and the firm would be very much subject to dangers from rising interest rates as well as to loan renewal problems. However, short-term debt is often cheaper than long-term debt, and some firms are willing to sacrifice safety for the chance of higher profits.

CONSERVATIVE APPROACH

Panel c of Figure 16-1 has the dashed line *above* the line designating permanent current assets, indicating that long-term capital is being used to finance all permanent asset requirements and also to meet some of the seasonal needs. In this situation, the firm uses a small amount of short-term, nonspontaneous credit to meet its peak requirements, but it also meets a part of its seasonal needs by "storing liquidity" in the form of marketable securities. The humps above the dashed line represent short-term financing, while the troughs below the dashed line represent short-term security holdings. Panel c represents a very safe, conservative current asset financing policy.

---

[1] For example, see William Beranek, Christopher Cornwell, Sunho Choi, "External Financing, Liquidity, and Capital Expenditures," *Journal of Financial Research*, Vol. 18, No. 2, 207–222.

ADVANTAGES AND DISADVANTAGES OF SHORT-TERM FINANCING

The three possible financing policies described above were distinguished by the relative amounts of short-term debt used under each policy. The aggressive policy called for the greatest use of short-term debt, while the conservative policy called for the least. Maturity matching fell in between. Although short-term credit is generally riskier than long-term credit, using short-term funds does have some significant advantages. The pros and cons of short-term financing are considered in this section.

SPEED

A short-term loan can be obtained much faster than long-term credit. Lenders will insist on a more thorough financial examination before extending long-term credit, and the loan agreement will have to be spelled out in considerable detail because a lot can happen during the life of a 10- to 20-year loan. Therefore, if funds are needed in a hurry, the firm should look to the short-term markets.

FLEXIBILITY

If its needs for funds are seasonal or cyclical, a firm may not want to commit itself to long-term debt for three reasons: (1) Flotation costs are higher for long-term debt than for short-term credit. (2) Although long-term debt can be repaid early, provided the loan agreement includes a prepayment provision, prepayment penalties can be expensive. Accordingly, if a firm thinks its need for funds will diminish in the near future, it should choose short-term debt. (3) Long-term loan agreements always contain provisions, or covenants, which constrain the firm's future actions. Short-term credit agreements are generally less restrictive.

COST OF LONG-TERM VERSUS SHORT-TERM DEBT

The yield curve is normally upward sloping, indicating that interest rates are generally lower on short-term debt. Thus, under normal conditions, interest costs at the time the funds are obtained will be lower if the firm borrows on a short-term rather than a long-term basis.

RISKS OF LONG-TERM VERSUS SHORT-TERM DEBT

Even though short-term rates are often lower than long-term rates, short-term credit is riskier for two reasons: (1) If a firm borrows on a long-term basis, its interest costs will be relatively stable over time, but if it uses short-term credit, its interest expense will fluctuate widely, at times going quite high. For example, the rate banks charge large corporations for short-term debt more than tripled over a two-year period in the 1980s, rising from 6.25 to 21 percent. Many firms that had borrowed heavily on a short-term basis simply could not meet their rising interest costs, and as a result, bankruptcies hit record levels during that period. (2) If a firm borrows heavily on a short-term basis, a temporary recession may render it unable to repay this debt. If the borrower is in a weak financial position, the lender may not extend the loan, which could force the firm into bankruptcy. Braniff Airlines, which failed during a credit crunch in the 1980s, is an example.

Another good example of the riskiness of short-term debt is provided by Transamerica Corporation, a major financial services company. Transamerica's former chairman, Mr. Beckett, described how his company was moving to reduce its dependency on short-term loans whose costs vary with short-term interest rates. According to Beckett, Transamerica had reduced its variable-rate (short-term) loans by about $450 million over a two-year period. "We aren't going to go through the enormous increase in debt expense again that had such a serious impact on earnings," he said. The company's earnings fell sharply because money rates rose to record highs. "We were almost entirely in variable-rate debt," he said, but currently "about 65 percent is fixed rate and 35 percent variable. We've come a long way, and we'll keep plugging away at it." Transamerica's earnings were badly depressed by the increase in short-term rates, but other companies were even less fortunate—they simply could not pay the rising interest charges, and this forced them into bankruptcy.

SELF-TEST QUESTION

What are the advantages and disadvantages of short-term debt over long-term debt?

SOURCES OF SHORT-TERM FINANCING

Statements about the flexibility, cost, and riskiness of short-term versus long-term debt depend, to a large extent, on the type of short-term credit that is actually used. There are numerous sources of short-term funds, and in the following sections we describe four major types: (1) accrued liabilities, (2) accounts payable (trade credit), (3) bank loans, and (4) commercial paper.

ACCRUED LIABILITIES

Firms generally pay employees on a weekly, biweekly, or monthly basis, so the balance sheet will typically show some accrued wages. Similarly, the firm's own estimated income taxes, Social Security and income taxes withheld from employee payrolls, and sales taxes collected are generally paid on a weekly, monthly, or quarterly basis, hence the balance sheet will typically show some accrued taxes along with accrued wages.

Accrued Liabilities
Continually recurring short-term liabilities, especially accrued wages and accrued taxes.

These **accrued liabilities** increase automatically, or spontaneously, as a firm's operations expand. Further, this type of debt is "free" in the sense that no explicit interest is paid on funds raised through accrued liabilities. However, a firm cannot ordinarily control its accrued liabilities: The timing of wage payments is set by economic forces and industry custom, while tax payment dates are established by law. Thus, firms use all the accrued liabilities they can, but they have little control over the levels of these accounts.

SELF-TEST QUESTIONS

What types of short-term credit are classified as accrued liabilities?

What is the cost of accrued liabilities?

How much control do financial managers have over the dollar amount of accrued liabilities?

ACCOUNTS PAYABLE (TRADE CREDIT)

Trade Credit
Debt arising from credit sales and recorded as an account receivable by the seller and as an account payable by the buyer.

Firms generally make purchases from other firms on credit, recording the debt as an *account payable*. Accounts payable, or **trade credit,** is the largest single category of short-term debt, representing about 40 percent of the current liabilities of the average nonfinancial corporation. The percentage is somewhat larger for smaller firms: Because small companies often do not qualify for financing from other sources, they rely especially heavily on trade credit.[2]

Trade credit is a "spontaneous" source of financing in the sense that it arises from ordinary business transactions. For example, suppose a firm makes average purchases of $2,000 a day on terms of net 30, meaning that it must pay for goods 30 days after the invoice date. On average, it will owe 30 times $2,000, or $60,000, to its suppliers. If its sales, and consequently its purchases, were to double, then its accounts payable would also double, to $120,000. So, simply by growing, the firm would spontaneously generate an additional $60,000 of financing. Similarly, if the terms under which it bought were extended from 30 to 40 days, its accounts payable would expand from $60,000 to $80,000. Thus, lengthening the credit period, as well as expanding sales and purchases, generates additional financing.

THE COST OF TRADE CREDIT

Firms that sell on credit have a *credit policy* that includes certain *terms of credit*. For example, Microchip Electronics sells on terms of 2/10, net 30, meaning that it gives its customers a 2 percent discount if they pay within 10 days of the invoice date, but the full invoice amount is due and payable within 30 days if the discount is not taken.

Note that the true price of Microchip's products is the net price, or 0.98 times the list price, because any customer can purchase an item at that price as long as the

---

[2] In a credit sale, the seller records the transaction as a receivable, the buyer as a payable. We examined accounts receivable as an asset in Chapter 15. Our focus in this chapter is on accounts payable, a liability item. We might also note that if a firm's accounts payable exceed its receivables, it is said to be *receiving net trade credit*, whereas if its receivables exceed its payables, it is *extending net trade credit*. Smaller firms frequently receive net credit; larger firms generally extend it.

customer pays within 10 days. Now consider Personal Computer Company (PCC), which buys its memory chips from Microchip. One commonly used memory chip is listed at $100, so the "true" price to PCC is $98. Now if PCC wants an additional 20 days of credit beyond the 10-day discount period, it must incur a finance charge of $2 per chip for that credit. Thus, the $100 list price consists of two components:

$$\text{List price} = \$98 \text{ true price} + \$2 \text{ finance charge.}$$

The question PCC must ask before it turns down the discount to obtain the additional 20 days of credit from Microchip is this: Could we obtain credit under better terms from some other lender, say, a bank? In other words, could 20 days of credit be obtained for less than $2 per chip?

PCC buys an average of $11,923,333 of memory chips from Microchip each year at the net, or true, price. This amounts to $11,923,333/365 = $32,666.67 per day. For simplicity, assume that Microchip is PCC's only supplier. If PCC decides not to take the additional trade credit—that is, if it pays on the 10th day and takes the discount—its payables will average 10($32,666.67) = $326,667. Thus, PCC will be receiving $326,667 of credit from Microchip.

Now suppose PCC decides to take the additional 20 days credit and thus must pay the finance charge. Since PCC will now pay on the 30th day, its accounts payable will increase to 30($32,666.67) = $980,000.[3] Microchip will now be supplying PCC with an additional $980,000 − $326,667 = $653,333 of credit, which PCC could use to build up its cash account, to pay off debt, to expand inventories, or even to extend credit to its own customers, hence increasing its own accounts receivable.

The additional trade credit offered by Microchip has a cost—PCC must pay a finance charge equal to the 2 percent discount it is forgoing. PCC buys $11,923,333 of chips at the true price, and the added finance charges increase the total cost to $11,923,333/0.98 = $12,166,666 million. Therefore, the annual financing cost is $12,166,666 − $11,923,333 = $243,333. Dividing the $243,333 financing cost by the $653,333 of additional credit, we find the nominal annual cost rate of the additional trade credit to be 37.2 percent:

$$\text{Nominal annual cost} = \frac{\$243,333}{\$653,333} = 37.2\%.$$

If PCC can borrow from its bank (or from other sources) at an interest rate less than 37.2 percent, it should take discounts and forgo the additional trade credit.

The following equation can be used to calculate the nominal cost, on an annual basis, of not taking discounts, illustrated with terms of 2/10, net 30:

$$\begin{matrix} \text{Nominal} \\ \text{annual} \\ \text{cost} \end{matrix} = \frac{\text{Discount percent}}{100 - \begin{matrix}\text{Discount} \\ \text{percent}\end{matrix}} \times \frac{365 \text{ days}}{\begin{matrix}\text{Days credit is} \\ \text{outstanding}\end{matrix} - \begin{matrix}\text{Discount} \\ \text{period}\end{matrix}} \qquad (16\text{-}1)$$

$$= \frac{2}{98} \times \frac{365}{20} = 2.04\% \times 18.25 = 37.2\%.$$

---

[3] A question arises here: Should accounts payable reflect gross purchases or purchases net of discounts? Generally accepted accounting principles permit either treatment if the difference is not material, but if the discount is material, then the transaction must be recorded net of discounts, or at "true" prices. Then, the higher payment that results from not taking discounts is reported as an additional expense called "discounts lost." *Thus, we show accounts payable net of discounts even if the company does not expect to take discounts.*

The numerator of the first term, Discount percent, is the cost per dollar of credit, while the denominator in this term, $100 -$ Discount percent, represents the funds made available by not taking the discount. Thus, the first term, 2.04%, is the cost per period for the trade credit. The denominator of the second term is the number of days of extra credit obtained by not taking the discount, so the entire second term shows how many times each year the cost is incurred, 18.25 times in this example.

The nominal annual cost formula does not take account of compounding, and in effective annual interest terms, the cost of trade credit is even higher. The discount amounts to interest, and with terms of 2/10, net 30, the firm gains use of the funds for $30 - 10 = 20$ days, so there are $365/20 = 18.25$ "interest periods" per year. Remember that the first term in Equation 16-1, (Discount percent)/(100 $-$ Discount percent) $= 0.02/0.98 = 0.0204$, is the periodic interest rate. This rate is paid 18.25 times each year, so the effective annual cost of trade credit is

$$\text{Effective annual rate} = (1.0204)^{18.25} - 1.0 = 1.4459 - 1.0 = 44.6\%.$$

Thus, the 37.2 percent nominal cost calculated with Equation 16-1 understates the true cost.

Note, however, that the cost of trade credit can be reduced by paying late. Thus, if PCC could get away with paying in 60 days rather than in the specified 30 days, then the effective credit period would become $60 - 10 = 50$ days, the number of times the discount would be lost would fall to $365/50 = 7.3$, and the nominal cost would drop from 37.2 percent to $2.04\% \times 7.3 = 14.9\%$. The effective annual rate would drop from 44.6 to 15.9 percent:

$$\text{Effective annual rate} = (1.0204)^{7.3} - 1.0 = 1.1589 - 1.0 = 15.9\%.$$

Stretching Accounts Payable
The practice of deliberately paying late.

In periods of excess capacity, firms may be able to get away with deliberately paying late, or **stretching accounts payable.** However, they will also suffer a variety of problems associated with being branded a "slow payer." These problems are discussed later in the chapter.

The costs of the additional trade credit from forgoing discounts under some other purchase terms are shown below:

| | COST OF ADDITIONAL CREDIT IF THE CASH DISCOUNT IS NOT TAKEN | |
CREDIT TERMS	NOMINAL COST	EFFECTIVE COST
1/10, net 20	36.9%	44.3%
1/10, net 30	18.4	20.1
2/10, net 20	74.5	109.0
3/15, net 45	37.6	44.9

As these figures show, the cost of not taking discounts can be substantial. Incidentally, throughout the chapter, we assume that payments are made either on the *last day* for taking discounts or on the *last day* of the credit period, unless otherwise noted. It would be foolish to pay, say, on the 5th day or on the 20th day if the credit terms were 2/10, net 30.[4]

EFFECTS OF TRADE CREDIT ON THE FINANCIAL STATEMENTS

A firm's policy with regard to taking or not taking discounts can have a significant effect on its financial statements. To illustrate, assume that PCC is just beginning its operations. On the first day, it makes net purchases of $32,666.67. This amount is recorded on its balance sheet under accounts payable.[5] The second day it buys another $32,666.67. The first day's purchases are not yet paid for, so at the end of the second day, accounts payable total $65,333.34. Accounts payable increase by another $32,666.67 on the third day, for a total of $98,000, and after ten days, accounts payable are up to $326,667.

If PCC takes discounts, then on the 11th day it will have to pay for the $32,666.67 of purchases made on the first day, which will reduce accounts payable. However, it will buy another $32,666.67, which will increase payables. Thus, after the 10th day of operations, PCC's balance sheet will level off, showing a balance of $326,667 in accounts payable, assuming the company pays on the 10th day and takes discounts.

Now suppose PCC decides not to take discounts. In this case, on the 11th day it will add another $32,666.67 to payables, but it will not pay for the purchases made on the 1st day. Thus, the balance sheet figure for accounts payable will rise to 11($32,666.67) = $359,333.37. This buildup will continue through the 30th day, at which point payables will total 30($32,666.67) = $980,000. On the 31st day, PCC will buy another $32,666.67 of goods, which will increase accounts payable, but it will also pay for the purchases made the 1st day, which will reduce payables. Thus, its accounts payable will stabilize at $980,000 after 30 days if it does not take discounts.

The top section of Table 16-1 shows PCC's balance sheet, after it reaches a steady state, under the two trade credit policies. Total assets are unchanged by this policy decision, and we also assume that the accrued liabilities and common equity accounts are unchanged. The differences show up in accounts payable and notes payable; when PCC elects to take discounts and thus gives up some of the trade credit it otherwise could have obtained, it will have to raise $653,333 from some other source. It could have sold more common stock, or it could have used long-term bonds, but it chose to use bank credit, which has a 10 percent cost and is reflected in the notes payable account.

---

[4] A financial calculator can also be used to determine the cost of trade credit. If the terms of credit are 2/10, net 30, this implies that for every $100 of goods purchased at the full list price, the customer has the choice of paying the full amount in 30 days or else paying $98 in 10 days. If a customer decides not to take the discount, then it is in effect borrowing $98, the amount it would otherwise have to pay, from Day 11 to Day 30, or for 20 days. It will then have to pay $100, which is the $98 loan plus a $2 financing charge, at the end of the 20-day loan period. To calculate the interest rate, enter N = 1, PV = 98, PMT = 0, FV = −100, and then press I to obtain 2.04 percent. This is the rate for 20 days. To calculate the effective annual interest rate on a 365-day basis, enter N = 20/365 = 0.05479, PV = 98, PMT = 0, FV = −100, and then press I to obtain 44.6 percent. The 20/365 = 0.05479 is the fraction of a year the "loan" is outstanding, and the 44.6 percent is the annualized cost of not taking discounts.

[5] Inventories also increase by $32,666.67, but we are not now concerned with inventories. Again, note that both inventories and payables are recorded net of discounts regardless of whether discounts are taken.

	TAKE DISCOUNTS; BORROW FROM BANK (1)	DO NOT TAKE DISCOUNTS; USE MAXIMUM TRADE CREDIT (2)	DIFFERENCE (1) − (2)
I. BALANCE SHEETS			
Cash	$ 500,000	$ 500,000	$ 0
Receivables	1,000,000	1,000,000	0
Inventories	2,000,000	2,000,000	0
Fixed assets	2,980,000	2,980,000	0
Total assets	$ 6,480,000	$ 6,480,000	$ 0
Accounts payable	$ 326,667	$ 980,000	$−653,333
Notes payable (10%)	653,333	0	+653,333
Accrued liabilities	500,000	500,000	0
Common equity	5,000,000	5,000,000	0
Total claims	$ 6,480,000	$ 6,480,000	$ 0
II. INCOME STATEMENTS			
Sales	$15,000,000	$15,000,000	$ 0
Less: Purchases	11,923,333	11,923,333	0
Labor	2,000,000	2,000,000	0
Interest	65,333	0	+65,333
Discounts lost	0	243,333	−243,333
Earnings before taxes (EBT)	$ 1,011,334	$ 833,334	$+178,000
Taxes (40%)	404,534	333,334	−71,200
Net income	$ 606,800	$ 500,000	$+106,800

The bottom section of Table 16-1 shows PCC's income statement under the two policies. If the company does not take discounts, then its interest expense will be zero, but it will have a $243,333 expense for discounts lost. On the other hand, if it does take discounts, it will incur an interest expense of $65,333, but it will avoid the cost of discounts lost. Since discounts lost exceed the interest expense, the take-discounts policy results in a higher net income and, thus, in a higher stock price.

Free Trade Credit
Credit received during the discount period.

Costly Trade Credit
Credit taken in excess of free trade credit, whose cost is equal to the discount lost.

COMPONENTS OF TRADE CREDIT: FREE VERSUS COSTLY

On the basis of the preceding discussion, trade credit can be divided into two components: (1) **free trade credit,** which involves credit received during the discount period and which for PCC amounts to 10 days' net purchases, or $326,667, and (2) **costly trade credit,** which involves credit in excess of the free trade credit and whose cost is an implicit one based on the forgone discounts.[6] PCC could obtain $653,333, or 20 days' net purchases, of nonfree trade credit at a nominal cost of 37.2 percent. *Firms should always use the free component, but they should use the costly component only after analyzing the cost of this capital to make sure that it is less than the cost of funds that could be obtained from other sources.* Under the terms of trade found in most industries, the costly component is relatively expensive, so stronger firms will avoid using it.

We noted earlier that firms sometimes can and do deviate from the stated credit terms, thus altering the percentage cost figures cited earlier. For example, a California manufacturing firm that buys on terms of 2/10, net 30, makes a practice of paying in 15 days (rather than 10), but it still takes discounts. Its treasurer simply waits until 15 days after receipt of the goods to pay, then writes a check for the invoiced amount less the 2 percent discount. The company's suppliers want its business, so they tolerate this practice. Similarly, a Wisconsin firm that also buys on terms of 2/10, net 30, does not take discounts, but it pays in 60 rather than in 30 days, thus "stretching" its trade credit. As we saw earlier, both practices reduce the calculated cost of trade credit. Neither of these firms is "loved" by its suppliers, and neither could continue these practices in times when suppliers were operating at full capacity and had order backlogs, but these practices can and do reduce the costs of trade credit during times when suppliers have excess capacity.

SELF-TEST QUESTIONS

What is trade credit?

What is the difference between free trade credit and costly trade credit?

What is the formula for finding the nominal annual cost of trade credit? What is the formula for the effective annual cost of trade credit?

How does the cost of costly trade credit generally compare with the cost of short-term bank loans?

SHORT-TERM BANK LOANS

Commercial banks, whose loans generally appear on balance sheets as notes payable, are second in importance to trade credit as a source of short-term financing for nonfinancial corporations.[7] The banks' influence is actually greater than it appears from the dollar amounts because banks provide *nonspontaneous* funds. As a firm's financing needs increase, it requests additional funds from its bank. If the request is denied, the firm may be forced to abandon attractive growth opportunities. The key features of bank loans are discussed in the following paragraphs.

---

[6] There is some question as to whether any credit is really "free," because the supplier will have a cost of carrying receivables which must be passed on to the customer in the form of higher prices. Still, if suppliers sell on standard terms such as 2/10, net 30, and if the base price cannot be negotiated downward for early payment, then for all intents and purposes, the ten days of trade credit is indeed "free."

[7] Although commercial banks remain the primary source of short-term loans, other sources are available. For example, GE Capital Corporation (GECC) had several billion dollars in commercial loans outstanding. Firms such as GECC, which was initially established to finance consumers' purchases of GE's durable goods, often find business loans to be more profitable than consumer loans.

MATURITY

Although banks do make longer-term loans, *the bulk of their lending is on a short-term basis*—about two-thirds of all bank loans mature in a year or less. Bank loans to businesses are frequently written as 90-day notes, so the loan must be repaid or renewed at the end of 90 days. Of course, if a borrower's financial position has deteriorated, the bank may refuse to renew the loan. This can mean serious trouble for the borrower.

PROMISSORY NOTE

Promissory Note
A document specifying the terms and conditions of a loan, including the amount, interest rate, and repayment schedule.

When a bank loan is approved, the agreement is executed by signing a **promissory note.** The note specifies (1) the amount borrowed; (2) the interest rate; (3) the repayment schedule, which can call for either a lump sum or a series of installments; (4) any collateral that might have to be put up as security for the loan; and (5) any other terms and conditions to which the bank and the borrower have agreed. When the note is signed, the bank credits the borrower's checking account with the funds, so on the borrower's balance sheet both cash and notes payable increase.

COMPENSATING BALANCES

Compensating Balance
A minimum checking account balance that a firm must maintain with a commercial bank, generally equal to 10 to 20 percent of the amount of loans outstanding.

Banks sometimes require borrowers to maintain an average demand deposit (checking account) balance equal to from 10 to 20 percent of the face amount of the loan. This is called a **compensating balance,** and such balances raise the effective interest rate on the loans. For example, if a firm needs $80,000 to pay off outstanding obligations, but if it must maintain a 20 percent compensating balance, then it must borrow $100,000 to obtain a usable $80,000. If the stated annual interest rate is 8 percent, the effective cost is actually 10 percent: $8,000 interest divided by $80,000 of usable funds equals 10 percent.[8]

As we noted in the last chapter, recent surveys indicate that compensating balances are much less common now than 20 years ago. In fact, compensating balances are now illegal in many states. Despite this trend, some small banks in states where compensating balances are legal still require their customers to maintain compensating balances.

INFORMAL LINE OF CREDIT

Line of Credit
An informal arrangement in which a bank agrees to lend up to a specified maximum amount of funds during a designated period.

A **line of credit** is an informal agreement between a bank and a borrower indicating the maximum credit the bank will extend to the borrower. For example, on December 31, a bank loan officer might indicate to a financial manager that the bank regards the firm as being "good" for up to $80,000 during the forthcoming year, provided the borrower's financial condition does not deteriorate. If on January 10 the financial manager signs a promissory note for $15,000 for 90 days, this would be called "taking

---

[8] Note, however, that the compensating balance may be set as a minimum monthly *average*, and if the firm would maintain this average anyway, the compensating balance requirement would not raise the effective interest rate. Also, note that these *loan* compensating balances are added to any compensating balances that the firm's bank may require for *services performed*, such as clearing checks.

down" $15,000 of the total line of credit. This amount would be credited to the firm's checking account at the bank, and before repayment of the $15,000, the firm could borrow additional amounts up to a total of $80,000 outstanding at any one time.

REVOLVING CREDIT AGREEMENT

Revolving Credit Agreement
A formal, committed line of credit extended by a bank or other lending institution.

A **revolving credit agreement** is a formal line of credit often used by large firms. To illustrate, in 2002 Texas Petroleum Company negotiated a revolving credit agreement for $100 million with a group of banks. The banks were formally committed for four years to lend the firm up to $100 million if the funds were needed. Texas Petroleum, in turn, paid an annual commitment fee of ¼ of 1 percent on the unused balance of the commitment to compensate the banks for making the commitment. Thus, if Texas Petroleum did not take down any of the $100 million commitment during a year, it would still be required to pay a $250,000 annual fee, normally in monthly installments of $20,833.33. If it borrowed $50 million on the first day of the agreement, the unused portion of the line of credit would fall to $50 million, and the annual fee would fall to $125,000. Of course, interest would also have to be paid on the money Texas Petroleum actually borrowed. As a general rule, the interest rate on "revolvers" is pegged to the prime rate, the T-bill rate, or some other market rate, so the cost of the loan varies over time as interest rates change.[9] Texas Petroleum's rate was set at prime plus 0.5 percentage point.

Note that a revolving credit agreement is very similar to an informal line of credit, but with an important difference: The bank has a *legal obligation* to honor a revolving credit agreement, and it receives a commitment fee. Neither the legal obligation nor the fee exists under the informal line of credit.

Often a line of credit will have a *clean-up clause* that requires the borrower to reduce the loan balance to zero at least once a year. Keep in mind that a line of credit typically is designed to help finance negative operating cash flows that are incurred as a natural part of a company's business cycle, not as a source of permanent capital. For example, the total annual operating cash flow of Toys "Я" Us is normally positive, even though its operating cash flow is negative during the fall as it builds up inventory for the Christmas season. However, Toys "Я" Us has large positive cash flows in December through February, as it collects on Christmas sales. Their bankers would expect Toys "Я" Us to use those positive cash flows to pay off balances that had been drawn against their credit lines. Otherwise, Toys "Я" Us would be using its credit lines as a permanent source of financing.

> ### SELF-TEST QUESTION
>
> Explain how a firm that expects to need funds during the coming year might make sure the needed funds will be available.

---

[9] Each bank sets its own prime rate, but, because of competitive forces, most banks' prime rates are identical. Further, most banks follow the rate set by the large New York City banks.

In recent years many banks have been lending to the very strongest companies at rates below the prime rate. As we discuss later in this chapter, larger firms have ready access to the commercial paper market, and if banks want to do business with these larger companies, they must match, or at least come close to, the commercial paper rate.

THE COST OF BANK LOANS

The cost of bank loans varies for different types of borrowers at any given point in time and for all borrowers over time. Interest rates are higher for riskier borrowers, and rates are also higher on smaller loans because of the fixed costs involved in making and servicing loans. If a firm can qualify as a "prime credit" because of its size and financial strength, it can borrow at the **prime rate,** which at one time was the lowest rate banks charged. Rates on other loans are generally scaled up from the prime rate, but loans to very large, strong customers are made at rates below prime. Thus, loans to smaller, riskier borrowers are generally stated to carry an interest rate of "prime *plus* some number of percentage points," but loans to larger, less risky borrowers may have a rate stated as "prime *minus* some percentage points."

Prime Rate
A published interest rate charged by commercial banks to large, strong borrowers.

Bank rates vary widely over time depending on economic conditions and Federal Reserve policy. When the economy is weak, then (1) loan demand is usually slack, (2) inflation is low, and (3) the Fed also makes plenty of money available to the system. As a result, rates on all types of loans are relatively low. Conversely, when the economy is booming, loan demand is typically strong, the Fed restricts the money supply, and the result is high interest rates. As an indication of the kinds of fluctuations that can occur, the prime rate during 1980 rose from 11 percent to 21 percent in just four months, and it rose from 6 to 9 percent during 1994. The prime rate is currently (August 2002) 4.75 percent. Interest rates on other bank loans also vary, generally moving with the prime rate.

The terms on a short-term bank loan to a business are spelled out in the promissory note. Here are the key elements contained in most promissory notes:

1. **Interest only versus amortized.** Loans are either *interest-only*, meaning that only interest is paid during the life of the loan, and the principal is repaid when the loan matures, or *amortized*, meaning that some of the principal is repaid on each payment date. Amortized loans are called *installment loans*.

2. **Collateral.** If a short-term loan is secured by some specific collateral, generally accounts receivable or inventories, this fact is indicated in the note. If the collateral is to be kept on the premises of the borrower, then a form called a *UCC-1* (Uniform Commercial Code-1) is filed with the secretary of the state in which the collateral resides, along with a *Security Agreement* (also part of the Uniform Commercial Code) that describes the nature of the agreement. These filings prevent the borrower from using the same collateral to secure loans from different lenders, and they spell out conditions under which the lender can seize the collateral.

3. **Loan guarantees.** If the borrower is a small corporation, its bank will probably insist that the larger stockholders *personally guarantee* the loan. Banks have often seen a troubled company's owner divert assets from the company to some other entity he or she owned, so banks protect themselves by insisting on personal guarantees. However, stockholder guarantees are virtually impossible to get in the case of larger corporations that have many stockholders. Also, guarantees are unnecessary for proprietorships or partnerships because here the owners are already personally liable for the business's debts.

4. **Nominal, or stated, interest rate.** The interest rate can be either *fixed* or *floating*. If it floats, it is generally indexed to the bank's prime rate, to the T-bill rate, or to the London Inter-Bank Offer Rate (LIBOR). Most loans of any size

($25,000 and up) have floating rates if their maturities are greater than 90 days. The note will also indicate whether the bank uses a *360- or 365-day year* for purposes of calculating interest.

5. **Frequency of interest payments.** If the note is on an interest-only basis, it will indicate *how frequently interest must be paid.* Interest is typically calculated on a daily basis but paid monthly.

6. **Maturity.** Long-term loans always have specific maturity dates. A short-term loan may or may not have a specified maturity. For example, a loan may mature in 30 days, 90 days, 6 months, or 1 year, or it may call for "payment on demand," in which case the loan can remain outstanding as long as the borrower wants to continue using the funds and the bank agrees. Banks virtually never call demand notes unless the borrower's creditworthiness deteriorates, so some "short-term loans" remain outstanding for years, with the interest rate floating with rates in the economy.

7. **Discount interest.** Most loans call for interest to be paid after it has been earned, but *discount loans* require that interest be paid in advance. If the loan is on a discount basis, the borrower actually receives less than the face amount of the loan, and this increases the loan's effective cost. We discuss discount loans in a later section.

8. **Add-on basis installment loans.** Auto loans and other types of consumer installment loans are generally set up on an "add-on basis," which means that interest charges over the life of the loan are calculated and then added to the face amount of the loan. Thus, the borrower signs a note for the funds received plus the interest. The add-on feature also raises the effective cost of a loan, as we demonstrate in a later section.

9. **Other cost elements.** As noted above, some loans require compensating balances, and revolving credit agreements often require commitment fees. Both of these conditions will be spelled out in the loan agreement, and both raise the effective cost of a loan above its stated nominal rate.

REGULAR, OR SIMPLE, INTEREST

Regular, or Simple, Interest
The situation when interest is not compounded, that is, interest is not earned on interest.

In this and the following sections, we explain how to calculate the effective cost of different bank loans. For illustrative purposes, we assume a loan of $10,000 at a nominal interest rate of 12 percent, with a 365-day year.

For business loans, the most common procedure is called **regular,** or **simple, interest,** based on an interest-only loan. We begin by dividing the nominal interest rate, 12 percent in this case, by 365 (or 360 in some cases) to get the rate per day:

$$\text{Interest rate per day} = \frac{\text{Nominal rate}}{\text{Days in year}} \qquad (16\text{-}2)$$

$$= 0.12/365 = 0.00032876712.$$

This rate is then multiplied by the actual number of days during the specific payment period, and then times the amount of the loan. For example, if the loan is interest-only, with monthly payments, then the interest payment for January would be $101.92:

$$\text{Interest charge for period} = (\text{Days in period})(\text{Rate per day})(\text{Amount of loan}) \qquad (16\text{-}3)$$

$$= (31 \text{ days})(0.00032876712)(\$10,000) = \$101.92.$$

If interest were payable quarterly, and if there were 91 days in the particular quarter, then the interest payment would be $299.18. The annual interest would be 365 × 0.00032876712 × $10,000 = $1,200.00. Note that if the bank had based the interest calculation on a 360-day year, as most banks do, the interest charges would have been slightly higher, and the annual charge would have been $1,216.67. Obviously, banks use a 360-day year to boost their earnings.

The effective interest rate on a loan depends on how frequently interest must be paid—the more frequently, the higher the effective rate. We demonstrate this point with two time lines, one for interest paid once a year and one for quarterly payments:

Interest paid annually:

The borrower gets $10,000 at t = 0 and pays $11,200 at t = 1. With a financial calculator, enter N = 1, PV = 10000, PMT = 0, and FV = −11200, and then press I to get the effective cost of the loan, 12 percent.

Interest paid quarterly:

Note that the third quarter has 92 days. We enter the data in the cash flow register of a financial calculator (being sure to use the +/− key to enter −299.18), and we find the periodic rate to be 2.9999 percent. The effective annual rate is 12.55 percent:

$$\text{Effective annual rate, quarterly} = (1 + 0.029999)^4 - 1 = 12.55\%.$$

Had the loan called for interest to be paid monthly, the effective rate would have been 12.68 percent, and if interest had been paid daily, the rate would have been 12.75 percent. These rates would be higher if the bank used a 360-day year.

In these examples, we assumed that the loan matured in one year but that interest was paid at various times during the year. The rates we calculated would have been exactly the same as the ones above even if the loan had matured on each interest payment date. In other words, the effective rate on a monthly payment loan would be 12.68 percent regardless of whether it matured after one month, six months, one year, or ten years, providing the stated rate remains at 12 percent.

DISCOUNT INTEREST

Discount Interest
Interest that is calculated on the face amount of a loan but is paid in advance.

In a **discount interest** loan, the bank deducts the interest in advance (*discounts the loan*). Thus, the borrower receives less than the face value of the loan. On a one-year, $10,000 loan with a 12 percent (nominal) rate, discount basis, the interest is

$10,000(0.12) = \$1,200$. Therefore, the borrower obtains the use of only $10,000 - \$1,200 = \$8,800$. If the loan were for less than a year, the interest charge (the discount) would be lower; in our example, it would be $600 if the loan were for six months, hence the amount received would be $9,400.

The effective rate on a discount loan is always higher than the rate on an otherwise similar simple interest loan. To illustrate, consider the situation for a discounted 12 percent loan for one year:

Discount interest, paid annually:

With a financial calculator, enter N = 1, PV = 8800, PMT = 0, and FV = −10000, and then press I to get the effective cost of the loan, 13.64 percent.[10]

If a discount loan matures in less than a year, say, after one quarter, we have this situation:

Discount interest, one quarter:

Enter N = 1, PV = 9700, PMT = 0, and FV = −10000, and then press I to find the periodic rate, 3.092784 percent per quarter, which corresponds to an effective annual rate of 12.96 percent. Thus, shortening the period of a discount loan lowers the effective rate of interest. This occurs because there is a delay in paying interest relative to a longer-term discount loan ($300 paid each quarter rather than $1,200 paid up front).

---

[10] Note that the firm actually receives less than the face amount of the loan:

$$\text{Funds received} = \text{Face amount of loan} (1.0 - \text{Nominal interest rate}).$$

We can solve for the face amount as follows:

$$\text{Face amount of loan} = \frac{\text{Funds received}}{1.0 - \text{Nominal rate(decimal)}}.$$

Therefore, if the borrowing firm actually requires $10,000 of cash, it must borrow $11,363.64:

$$\text{Face value} = \frac{\$10,000}{1.0 - 0.12} = \frac{\$10,000}{0.88} = \$11,363.64.$$

Now, the borrower will receive $11,363.64 − 0.12($11,363.64) = $10,000. Increasing the face value of the loan does not change the effective rate of 13.64 percent on the $10,000 of usable funds.

EFFECTS OF COMPENSATING BALANCES

If the bank requires a compensating balance, and if the amount of the required balance exceeds the amount the firm would normally hold on deposit, then the excess must be deducted at $t = 0$ and then added back when the loan matures. This has the effect of raising the effective rate on the loan. To illustrate, here is the setup for a one-year discount loan, with a 20 percent compensating balance that the firm would not otherwise hold on deposit:

Discount interest, paid annually, with 20 percent compensating balance:

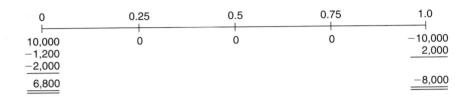

Note that the bank initially gives, and the borrower gets, $10,000 at time 0. However, the bank takes out the $1,200 of interest in advance, and the company must leave $2,000 in the bank as a compensating balance, hence the borrower's effective net cash flow at $t = 0$ is $6,800. At $t = 1$, the borrower must repay the $10,000, but $2,000 is already in the bank (the compensating balance), so the company must repay a net amount of $8,000.

With a financial calculator, enter N = 1, PV = 6800, PMT = 0, and FV = −8000, and then press I to get the effective cost of the discount loan with a compensating balance, 17.65 percent.

INSTALLMENT LOANS: ADD-ON INTEREST

Add-On Interest
Interest that is calculated and added to funds received to determine the face amount of an installment loan.

Lenders typically charge **add-on interest** on automobile and other types of installment loans. The term "add-on" means that the interest is calculated and then added to the amount received to determine the loan's face value. To illustrate, suppose you borrow $10,000 on an add-on basis at a nominal rate of 12 percent to buy a car, with the loan to be repaid in 12 monthly installments. At a 12 percent add-on rate, you will pay a total interest charge of $10,000(0.12) = $1,200. However, since the loan is paid off in monthly installments, you have the use of the full $10,000 for only the first month, and the outstanding balance declines until, during the last month, only $1/12$ of the original loan will still be outstanding. Thus, you are paying $1,200 for the use of only about half the loan's face amount, as the average usable funds is only about $5,000. Therefore, we can calculate the approximate annual rate as follows:

$$\text{Approximate annual rate}_{\text{Add-on}} = \frac{\text{Interest paid}}{(\text{Amount received})/2} \quad (16\text{-}4)$$

$$= \frac{\$1,200}{\$10,000/2} = 24.0\%.$$

To determine the effective rate of an add-on loan, we proceed as follows:

1. The total amount to be repaid is $10,000 of principal, plus $1,200 of interest, or $11,200.
2. The monthly payment is $11,200/12 = $933.33.
3. You are, in effect, paying off a 12-period annuity of $933.33 in order to receive $10,000 today, so $10,000 is the present value of the annuity. Here is the time line:

4. With a financial calculator, enter N = 12, PV = 10000, PMT = −933.33, FV = 0, and then press I to obtain 1.7880 percent. However, this is a monthly rate.
5. The effective annual rate is found as follows:[11]

$$\text{Effective annual rate}_{\text{Add-on}} = (1 + k_d)^n - 1.0$$
$$= (1.01788)^{12} - 1.0$$
$$= 1.2370 - 1.0 = 23.7\%.$$

Annual Percentage Rate (APR)
A rate reported by banks and other lenders on loans when the effective rate exceeds the nominal rate of interest.

The **annual percentage rate (APR),** which by law the bank is required to state in bold print on all "consumer loan" agreements, would be 21.46 percent:

$$\text{APR rate} = (\text{Periods per year})(\text{Rate per period})$$
$$= 12(1.7880\%) = 21.46\%.$$

Prior to the passage of the truth in lending laws in the 1970s, most banks would have called this a 12 percent loan, period. The truth in lending laws apply primarily to consumer as opposed to business loans.

SELF-TEST QUESTIONS

What are some different ways banks can calculate interest on loans?

What is a compensating balance? What effect does a compensating balance requirement have on the effective interest rate on a loan?

CHOOSING A BANK

Individuals whose only contact with their bank is through the use of its checking services generally choose a bank for the convenience of its location and the competitive cost of its services. However, a business that borrows from banks must look

---

[11] Note that if an installment loan is paid off ahead of schedule, additional complications arise. For the classic discussion of this point, see Dick Bonker, "The Rule of 78," *Journal of Finance*, June 1976, 877–888.

at other criteria, and a potential borrower seeking a banking relationship should recognize that important differences exist among banks. Some of these differences are considered next.

WILLINGNESS TO ASSUME RISKS

Banks have different basic policies toward risk. Some are inclined to follow relatively conservative lending practices, while others engage in what are properly termed "creative banking practices." These policies reflect partly the personalities of bank officers and partly the characteristics of the bank's deposit liabilities. Thus, a bank with fluctuating deposit liabilities in a static community will tend to be a conservative lender, while a bank whose deposits are growing with little interruption may follow more liberal credit policies. Similarly, a large bank with broad diversification over geographic regions and across industries can obtain the benefit of combining and averaging risks. Thus, marginal credit risks that might be unacceptable to a small or specialized bank can be pooled by a branch banking system to reduce the overall risk of a group of marginal accounts.[12]

ADVICE AND COUNSEL

Some bank loan officers are active in providing counsel and in stimulating development loans to firms in their early and formative years. Certain banks have specialized departments that make loans to firms expected to grow and thus to become more important customers. The personnel of these departments can provide valuable counseling to customers: The bankers' experience with other firms in growth situations may enable them to spot, and then to warn their customers about, developing problems.

LOYALTY TO CUSTOMERS

Banks differ in their support of borrowers in bad times. This characteristic is referred to as the degree of *loyalty* of the bank. Some banks may put great pressure on a business to liquidate its loans when the firm's outlook becomes clouded, whereas others will stand by the firm and work diligently to help it get back on its feet. An especially dramatic illustration of this point was Bank of America's bailout of Memorex Corporation. The bank could have forced Memorex into bankruptcy, but instead it loaned the company additional capital and helped it survive a bad period. Memorex's stock price subsequently rose from $1.50 to $68, so Bank of America's help was indeed beneficial.

---

[12] Bank deposits are insured by a federal agency, and banks are required to pay premiums to cover the cost of this insurance. Logically, riskier banks should pay higher premiums, but to date political forces have limited the use of risk-based insurance premiums. As an alternative, banks with riskier loan portfolios are required to have more equity capital per dollar of deposits than less risky banks. The savings and loan industry, until the 1980s, had federal insurance, no differential capital requirements, and lax regulations. As a result, some S&L operators wrote very high interest rate, but very risky, loans using low-cost, insured deposits. If the loans paid off, the S&L owners would get rich. If they went into default, the taxpayers would have to pay off the deposits. Those government policies ended up costing taxpayers more than $100 billion.

SPECIALIZATION

Banks differ greatly in their degrees of loan specialization. Larger banks have separate departments that specialize in different kinds of loans—for example, real estate loans, farm loans, and commercial loans. Within these broad categories, there may be a specialization by line of business, such as steel, machinery, cattle, or textiles. The strengths of banks are also likely to reflect the nature of the business and the economic environment in which they operate. For example, some California banks have become specialists in lending to electronics companies, while many Midwestern banks are agricultural specialists. A sound firm can obtain more creative cooperation and more active support by going to a bank that has experience and familiarity with its particular type of business. Therefore, a bank that is excellent for one firm may be unsatisfactory for another.

MAXIMUM LOAN SIZE

The size of a bank can be an important factor. Since the maximum loan a bank can make to any one customer is limited to 15 percent of the bank's capital accounts (capital stock plus retained earnings), it is generally not appropriate for large firms to develop borrowing relationships with small banks.

MERCHANT BANKING

The term "merchant bank" was originally applied to banks that not only made loans but also provided customers with equity capital and financial advice. Prior to 1933, U.S. commercial banks performed all types of merchant banking functions. However, about one-third of the U.S. banks failed during the Great Depression, in part because of these activities, so in 1933 the Glass-Steagall Act was passed in an effort to reduce banks' exposure to risk. In recent years, commercial banks have been attempting to get back into merchant banking, in part because their foreign competitors offer such services, and U.S. banks compete with foreign banks for multinational corporations' business. Currently, the larger banks, often through subsidiaries, are being permitted to get back into merchant banking, at least to a limited extent. This trend will probably continue, and if it does, corporations will need to consider a bank's ability to provide a full range of commercial and merchant banking services when choosing a bank.

OTHER SERVICES

Banks can also provide cash management services, assist with electronic funds transfers, help firms obtain foreign exchange, and the like, and the availability of such services should be taken into account when selecting a bank. Also, if the firm is a small business whose manager owns most of its stock, the bank's willingness and ability to provide trust and estate services should also be considered.

SELF-TEST QUESTION

What are some factors that should be considered when choosing a bank?

COMMERCIAL PAPER

Commercial Paper
Unsecured, short-term promissory notes of large firms, usually issued in denominations of $100,000 or more and having an interest rate somewhat below the prime rate.

Commercial paper is a type of unsecured promissory note issued by large, strong firms and sold primarily to other business firms, to insurance companies, to pension funds, to money market mutual funds, and to banks. At year-end 2001, there was approximately $1,438.8 billion of commercial paper outstanding, versus about $1,026.1 billion of bank loans. Much of this commercial paper outstanding is issued by financial institutions.

MATURITY AND COST

Maturities of commercial paper generally vary from one day to nine months, with an average of about five months.[13] The interest rate on commercial paper fluctuates with supply and demand conditions—it is determined in the marketplace, varying daily as conditions change. Recently, commercial paper rates have ranged from $1\frac{1}{2}$ to 3 percentage points below the stated prime rate, and about $\frac{1}{8}$ to $\frac{1}{2}$ of a percentage point above the T-bill rate. For example, on August 2, 2002, the average rate on three-month commercial paper was 1.71 percent, the stated prime rate was 4.75 percent, and the three-month T-bill rate was 1.68 percent.

USE OF COMMERCIAL PAPER

The use of commercial paper is restricted to a comparatively small number of very large concerns that are exceptionally good credit risks. Dealers prefer to handle the paper of firms whose net worth is $100 million or more and whose annual borrowing exceeds $10 million. One potential problem with commercial paper is that a debtor who is in temporary financial difficulty may receive little help because commercial paper dealings are generally less personal than are bank relationships. Thus, banks are generally more able and willing to help a good customer weather a temporary storm than is a commercial paper dealer. On the other hand, using commercial paper permits a corporation to tap a wide range of credit sources, including financial institutions outside its own area and industrial corporations across the country, and this can reduce interest costs.

SELF-TEST QUESTIONS

What is commercial paper?

What types of companies can use commercial paper to meet their short-term financing needs?

How does the cost of commercial paper compare with the cost of short-term bank loans? With the cost of Treasury bills?

---

[13] The maximum maturity without SEC registration is 270 days. Also, commercial paper can only be sold to "sophisticated" investors; otherwise, SEC registration would be required even for maturities of 270 days or less.

USE OF SECURITY IN SHORT-TERM FINANCING

Secured Loan
A loan backed by collateral, often inventories or receivables.

Thus far, we have not addressed the question of whether or not short-term loans should be secured. Commercial paper is never secured, but other types of loans can be secured if this is deemed necessary or desirable. Other things held constant, it is better to borrow on an unsecured basis, since the bookkeeping costs of **secured loans** are often high. However, firms often find that they can borrow only if they put up some type of collateral to protect the lender, or that by using security they can borrow at a much lower rate.

Several different kinds of collateral can be employed, including marketable stocks or bonds, land or buildings, equipment, inventory, and accounts receivable. Marketable securities make excellent collateral, but few firms that need loans also hold portfolios of stocks and bonds. Similarly, real property (land and buildings) and equipment are good forms of collateral, but they are generally used as security for long-term loans rather than for working capital loans. Therefore, most secured short-term business borrowing involves the use of accounts receivable and inventories as collateral.

To understand the use of security, consider the case of a Chicago hardware dealer who wanted to modernize and expand his store. He requested a $200,000 bank loan. After examining his business's financial statements, the bank indicated that it would lend him a maximum of $100,000 and that the interest rate would be 10 percent, discount interest, for an effective rate of 9.1 percent. The owner had a substantial personal portfolio of stocks, and he offered to put up $300,000 of high-quality stocks to support the $200,000 loan. The bank then granted the full $200,000 loan, and at the prime rate of 4.75 percent, simple interest. The store owner might also have used his inventories or receivables as security for the loan, but processing costs would have been high.[14]

> ### SELF-TEST QUESTIONS
>
> What is a secured loan?
>
> What are some types of current assets that are pledged as security for short-term loans?

---

[14] The term "asset-based financing" is often used as a synonym for "secured financing." In recent years, accounts receivable have been used as security for long-term bonds, and this permits corporations to borrow from lenders such as pension funds rather than being restricted to banks and other traditional short-term lenders.

TYING IT ALL TOGETHER

This chapter examined different policies for financing current assets. In particular, we looked at the factors that affect the use of current liabilities versus long-term capital and the specific types of current liabilities. Some companies have very few current liabilities, while others rely heavily on short-term credit to finance current assets. In some cases, companies even use short-term debt to finance a portion of their long-term assets.

In addition to examining various financing policies, we also considered the costs and features of the different types of short-term credit. The key concepts covered are listed below.

- **Permanent current assets** are those current assets that the firm holds even during slack times, whereas **temporary current assets** are the additional current assets that are needed during seasonal or cyclical peaks. The methods used to finance permanent and temporary current assets define the firm's **current asset financing policy.**

- A **moderate** approach to current asset financing involves matching, to the extent possible, the maturities of assets and liabilities, so that temporary current assets are financed with short-term nonspontaneous debt, and permanent current assets and fixed assets are financed with long-term debt or equity, plus spontaneous debt. Under an **aggressive** approach, some permanent current assets, and perhaps even some fixed assets, are financed with short-term debt. A **conservative** approach would be to use long-term capital to finance all permanent assets and some of the temporary current assets.

- **Short-term credit** is defined as any liability originally scheduled for payment within one year. The four major sources of short-term credit are (1) accrued liabilities, (2) accounts payable, (3) loans from commercial banks and finance companies, and (4) commercial paper.

- **Accrued liabilities,** which are continually recurring short-term liabilities, represent free, spontaneous credit.

- **Accounts payable,** or **trade credit,** is the largest category of short-term debt. Trade credit arises spontaneously as a result of credit purchases. Firms should use all the **free trade credit** they can obtain, but they should use **costly trade credit** only if it is less expensive than other forms of short-term debt. Suppliers often offer discounts to customers who pay within a stated discount period. The following equation may be used to calculate the nominal cost, on an annual basis, of not taking discounts:

$$\frac{\text{Nominal}}{\text{annual cost}} = \frac{\text{Discount percent}}{100 - \dfrac{\text{Discount}}{\text{percent}}} \times \frac{365}{\dfrac{\text{Days credit is}}{\text{outstanding}} - \dfrac{\text{Discount}}{\text{period}}}.$$

- **Bank loans** are an important source of short-term credit. Interest on bank loans may be quoted as **simple interest, discount interest,** or **add-on interest.** The effective rate on a bank loan always exceeds the quoted nominal rate except for a simple interest loan where the interest is paid once a year.

- When a bank loan is approved, a **promissory note** is signed. It specifies: (1) the amount borrowed, (2) the percentage interest rate, (3) the repayment schedule, (4) the collateral, and (5) any other conditions to which the parties have agreed.

- A **line of credit** is an informal agreement between the bank and the borrower indicating the maximum amount of credit the bank will extend to the borrower.

- A **revolving credit agreement** is a formal line of credit often used by large firms; it involves a **commitment fee.**

- The **annual percentage rate (APR)** is a rate reported by banks and other lenders on loans when the effective rate exceeds the nominal rate of interest.

- **Commercial paper** is unsecured short-term debt issued by large, financially strong corporations. Although the cost of commercial paper is lower than the cost of bank loans, it can be used only by large firms with exceptionally strong credit ratings.

- Sometimes a borrower will find that it is necessary to borrow on a **secured basis,** in which case the borrower pledges assets such as real estate, securities, equipment, inventories, or accounts receivable as collateral for the loan.

QUESTIONS

16-1 How does the seasonal nature of a firm's sales influence its decision regarding the amount of short-term credit to use in its financial structure?

16-2 What are the advantages of matching the maturities of assets and liabilities? What are the disadvantages?

16-3 From the standpoint of the borrower, is long-term or short-term credit riskier? Explain. Would it ever make sense to borrow on a short-term basis if short-term rates were above long-term rates?

16-4 If long-term credit exposes a borrower to less risk, why would people or firms ever borrow on a short-term basis?

16-5 "Firms can control their accrued liabilities within fairly wide limits; depending on the cost of accrued liabilities, financing from this source will be increased or decreased." Discuss.

16-6 Is it true that both trade credit and accrued liabilities represent a spontaneous source of capital for financing growth? Explain.

16-7 Is it true that most firms are able to obtain some free trade credit and that additional trade credit is often available, but at a cost? Explain.

16-8 The availability of bank credit is often more important to a small firm than to a large one. Why?

16-9 What kinds of firms use commercial paper? Could Mama and Papa Gus's Corner Grocery borrow using this form of credit?

16-10 Given that commercial paper interest rates are generally lower than bank loan rates to a given borrower, why might firms which are capable of selling commercial paper also use bank credit?

16-11 Suppose a firm can obtain funds by borrowing at the prime rate or by selling commercial paper.
a. If the prime rate is 4.75 percent, what is a reasonable estimate for the cost of commercial paper?
b. If a substantial cost differential exists, why might a firm like this one actually borrow some of its funds in each market?

SELF-TEST PROBLEMS   (SOLUTIONS APPEAR IN APPENDIX B)

ST-1
Key terms

Define each of the following terms:
a. Permanent current assets; temporary current assets
b. Moderate current asset financing policy; aggressive current asset financing policy; conservative current asset financing policy
c. Maturity matching, or "self-liquidating," approach
d. Accrued liabilities
e. Trade credit; stretching accounts payable; free trade credit; costly trade credit
f. Promissory note; line of credit; revolving credit agreement
g. Prime rate; annual percentage rate
h. Simple interest; discount interest; add-on interest
i. Compensating balance (CB)
j. Commercial paper
k. Secured loan

Vanderheiden Press Inc. and the Herrenhouse Publishing Company had the following balance sheets as of December 31, 2002 (thousands of dollars):

	VANDERHEIDEN PRESS	HERRENHOUSE PUBLISHING
Current assets	$100,000	$ 80,000
Fixed assets (net)	100,000	120,000
Total assets	$200,000	$200,000
Current liabilities	$ 20,000	$ 80,000
Long-term debt	80,000	20,000
Common stock	50,000	50,000
Retained earnings	50,000	50,000
Total liabilities and equity	$200,000	$200,000

Earnings before interest and taxes for both firms are $30 million, and the effective federal-plus-state tax rate is 40 percent.

a. What is the return on equity for each firm if the interest rate on current liabilities is 10 percent and the rate on long-term debt is 13 percent?

b. Assume that the short-term rate rises to 20 percent. While the rate on new long-term debt rises to 16 percent, the rate on existing long-term debt remains unchanged. What would be the return on equity for Vanderheiden Press and Herrenhouse Publishing under these conditions?

c. Which company is in a riskier position? Why?

STARTER PROBLEMS

What is the nominal and effective cost of trade credit (on a 365-day basis) under the credit terms of 3/15, net 30?

A large retailer obtains merchandise under the credit terms of 1/15, net 45, but routinely takes 60 days to pay its bills. Given that the retailer is an important customer, suppliers allow the firm to stretch its credit terms. What is the retailer's effective cost of trade credit (on a 365-day basis)?

A chain of appliance stores, APP Corporation, purchases inventory with a net price of $500,000 each day. The company purchases the inventory under the credit terms of 2/15, net 40. APP always takes the discount, but takes the full 15 days to pay its bills. What is the average accounts payable for APP?

On March 1, Minnerly Motors obtained a business loan from a local bank. The loan is a $25,000 interest-only loan with a nominal rate of 11 percent. Interest is calculated on a simple interest basis with a 365-day year. What is Minnerly's interest charge for the first month (assuming 31 days in the month)?

Mary Jones recently obtained an automobile loan from a local bank. The loan is for $15,000 with a nominal interest rate of 11 percent. However, this is an installment loan, so the bank also charges add-on interest. Mary must make monthly payments on the loan, and the loan is to be repaid in 1 year. What is the effective annual rate on the loan (assuming a 365-day year)?

EXAM-TYPE PROBLEMS

The problems included in this section are set up in such a way that they could be used as multiple-choice exam problems.

Calculate the nominal annual cost of nonfree trade credit under each of the following terms. Assume payment is made either on the due date or on the discount date.

a. 1/15, net 20.

b. 2/10, net 60.

c. 3/10, net 45.

d. 2/10, net 45.

e. 2/15, net 40.

16-7
Cost of trade credit

a. If a firm buys under terms of 3/15, net 45, but actually pays on the 20th day and *still takes the discount*, what is the nominal cost of its nonfree trade credit?

b. Does it receive more or less credit than it would if it paid within 15 days?

16-8
Cost of bank loans

Del Hawley, owner of Hawley's Hardware, is negotiating with First City Bank for a $50,000, 1-year loan. First City has offered Hawley the following alternatives. Calculate the effective annual interest rate for each alternative. Which alternative has the lowest effective annual interest rate?

a. A 12 percent annual rate on a simple interest loan, with no compensating balance required and interest due at the end of the year.

b. A 9 percent annual rate on a simple interest loan, with a 20 percent compensating balance required and interest again due at the end of the year.

c. An 8.75 percent annual rate on a discounted loan, with a 15 percent compensating balance.

d. Interest is figured as 8 percent of the $50,000 amount, *payable at the end of the year*, but the $50,000 is repayable in monthly installments during the year.

16-9
Effective cost of short-term credit

The D. J. Masson Corporation needs to raise $500,000 for 1 year to supply working capital to a new store. Masson buys from its suppliers on terms of 3/10, net 90, and it currently pays on the 10th day and takes discounts, but it could forgo discounts, pay on the 90th day, and get the needed $500,000 in the form of costly trade credit. Alternatively, Masson could borrow from its bank on a 12 percent discount interest rate basis. What is the effective annual interest rate of the lower-cost source?

16-10
Effective cost of short-term credit

Yonge Corporation must arrange financing for its working capital requirements for the coming year. Yonge can (a) borrow from its bank on a simple interest basis (interest payable at the end of the loan) for 1 year at a 12 percent nominal rate; (b) borrow on a 3-month, but renewable, loan at an 11.5 percent nominal rate; (c) borrow on an installment loan basis at a 6 percent add-on rate with 12 end-of-month payments; or (d) obtain the needed funds by no longer taking discounts and thus increasing its accounts payable. Yonge buys on terms of 1/15, net 60. What is the effective annual cost (*not* the nominal cost) of the *least expensive* type of credit, assuming 365 days per year?

PROBLEMS

16-11
Cash discounts

Suppose a firm makes purchases of $3.65 million per year under terms of 2/10, net 30, and takes discounts.

a. What is the average amount of accounts payable net of discounts? (Assume that the $3.65 million of purchases is net of discounts—that is, gross purchases are $3,724,490, discounts are $74,490, and net purchases are $3.65 million. Also, use 365 days in a year.)

b. Is there a cost of the trade credit the firm uses?

c. If the firm did not take discounts but it did pay on the due date, what would be its average payables and the cost of this nonfree trade credit?

d. What would its cost of not taking discounts be if it could stretch its payments to 40 days?

16-12
Trade credit versus bank credit

The Thompson Corporation projects an increase in sales from $1.5 million to $2 million, but it needs an additional $300,000 of current assets to support this expansion. The money can be obtained from the bank at an interest rate of 13 percent, discount interest; no compensating balance is required. Alternatively, Thompson can finance the expansion by no longer taking discounts, thus increasing accounts payable. Thompson purchases under terms of 2/10, net 30, but it can delay payment for an additional 35 days—paying in 65 days and thus becoming 35 days past due—without a penalty because of its suppliers' current excess capacity problems.

a. Based strictly on effective, or equivalent, annual interest rate comparisons, how should Thompson finance its expansion?

b. What additional qualitative factors should Thompson consider before reaching a decision?

16-13
Bank financing

The Raattama Corporation had sales of $3.5 million last year, and it earned a 5 percent return, after taxes, on sales. Recently, the company has fallen behind in its accounts payable. Although its terms of purchase are net 30 days, its accounts payable represent 60 days' purchases. The company's treasurer is seeking to increase bank borrowings in order to become current in meeting its trade obligations (that is, to have 30 days' payables outstanding). The company's balance sheet is as follows (thousands of dollars):

Cash	$ 100	Accounts payable	$ 600
Accounts receivable	300	Bank loans	700
Inventory	1,400	Accrued liabilities	200
Current assets	$1,800	Current liabilities	$1,500
Land and buildings	600	Mortgage on real estate	700
Equipment	600	Common stock, $0.10 par	300
		Retained earnings	500
Total assets	$3,000	Total liabilities and equity	$3,000

a. How much bank financing is needed to eliminate the past-due accounts payable?
b. Would you as a bank loan officer make the loan? Why or why not?

16-14
Cost of bank loans
Gifts Galore Inc. borrowed $1.5 million from National City Bank. The loan was made at a simple annual interest rate of 9 percent a year for 3 months. A 20 percent compensating balance requirement raised the effective interest rate.
a. The nominal interest rate on the loan was 11.25 percent. What is the true effective rate?
b. What would be the effective cost of the loan if the note required discount interest?
c. What would be the nominal annual interest rate on the loan if National City Bank required Gifts Galore to repay the loan and interest in 3 equal monthly installments?

16-15
Short-term financing analysis
Malone Feed and Supply Company buys on terms of 1/10, net 30, but it has not been taking discounts and has actually been paying in 60 rather than 30 days. Malone's balance sheet follows (thousands of dollars):

Cash	$ 50	Accounts payable	$ 500
Accounts receivable	450	Notes payable	50
Inventory	750	Accrued liabilities	50
Current assets	$1,250	Current liabilities	$ 600
		Long-term debt	150
Fixed assets	750	Common equity	1,250
Total assets	$2,000	Total liabilities and equity	$2,000

Now, Malone's suppliers are threatening to stop shipments unless the company begins making prompt payments (that is, paying in 30 days or less). The firm is going to have to reduce its $500,000 of accounts payable, either to an amount that is equal to 30 days' purchases (if it does not take discounts) or to 10 days' purchases (if it decides to take discounts). Management has decided to obtain the needed funds by borrowing on an additional 1-year note payable (call this a current liability) from its bank at a rate of 15 percent, discount interest, with a 20 percent compensating balance required. The $50,000 of cash Malone currently has is needed for transactions, so it cannot be used as part of the compensating balance. So, the issue now facing the company is this: How much trade credit should it use, and how large a loan should it obtain from its bank? For parts a through d, assume that accounts payable are recorded at full cost, not net of discounts. For part e, assume that accounts payable are recorded net of discounts.
a. How large would the accounts payable balance be if Malone takes discounts? If it does not take discounts and pays in 30 days?
b. How large must the bank loan be if Malone takes discounts? If Malone doesn't take discounts?

c. What are the nominal and the effective costs of nonfree trade credit? What is the effective cost of the bank loan? Based on these costs, what should Malone do?

d. Assume that Malone forgoes the discount and borrows the amount needed to become current on its payables. Construct a pro forma balance sheet based on this decision. (Hint: You will need to include an account entitled "prepaid interest" under current assets.)

e. Now assume that the $500,000 shown on the balance sheet is recorded net of discounts. How much would Malone have to pay its suppliers to reduce its accounts payable to $250,000? If Malone's tax rate is 40 percent, what is the impact on its net income due to the lost discount when it reduces its accounts payable to $250,000? How much would Malone have to borrow? (Hint: Malone will receive a tax deduction due to the lost discount, which will affect the amount it must borrow.) Construct a pro forma balance sheet based on this scenario. (Hint: You will need to include an account entitled "prepaid interest" under current assets and adjust retained earnings by the after-tax amount of the lost discounts.)

16-16
Alternative financing arrangements

Suncoast Boats Inc. estimates that because of the seasonal nature of its business, it will require an additional $2 million of cash for the month of July. Suncoast Boats has the following 4 options available for raising the needed funds:

(1) Establish a 1-year line of credit for $2 million with a commercial bank. The commitment fee will be 0.5 percent per year on the unused portion, and the interest charge on the used funds will be 11 percent per annum. Assume that the funds are needed only in July, and that there are 30 days in July and 365 days in the year.

(2) Forgo the trade discount of 2/10, net 40, on $2 million of purchases during July.

(3) Issue $2 million of 30-day commercial paper at a 9.5 percent per annum interest rate. The total transactions fee, including the cost of a backup credit line, on using commercial paper is 0.5 percent of the amount of the issue.

(4) Issue $2 million of 60-day commercial paper at a 9 percent per annum interest rate, plus a transactions fee of 0.5 percent. Since the funds are required for only 30 days, the excess funds ($2 million) can be invested in 9.4 percent per annum marketable securities for the month of August. The total transactions cost of purchasing and selling the marketable securities is 0.4 percent of the amount of the issue.

a. What is the dollar cost of each financing arrangement?

b. Is the source with the lowest expected cost necessarily the one to select? Why or why not?

SPREADSHEET PROBLEM

16-17
Short-term financing analysis

Rework Problem 16-15 using a spreadsheet model. After completing parts a through e, answer the following related question.

f. Do a sensitivity analysis that shows how the size of the bank loan would vary with changes in the interest rate and the compensating balance percentage, using interest rates in the range of 5 to 25 percent and compensating balances in the range of 0 to 30 percent.

INTEGRATED CASE

BATS AND BALLS INC.

16-18 Working Capital Financing Policy Bats and Balls (B&B) Inc., a baseball equipment manufacturer, is a small company with seasonal sales. Each year before the baseball season, B&B purchases inventory that is financed through a combination of trade credit and short-term bank loans. At the end of the season, B&B uses sales revenues to repay its short-term obligations. The company is always looking for ways to become more profitable, and senior management has asked one of its employees, Ann Taylor, to review the company's current asset financing policies. Putting together

her report, Ann is trying to answer each of the following questions:

a. B&B tries to match the maturity of its assets and liabilities. Describe how B&B could adopt either a more aggressive or more conservative financing policy.

b. What are the advantages and disadvantages of using short-term credit as a source of financing?

c. Is it likely that B&B could make significantly greater use of accrued liabilities?

d. Assume that B&B buys on terms of 1/10, net 30, but that it can get away with paying on the 40th day if it chooses not to take discounts. Also, assume that it purchases

$3 million of components per year, net of discounts. How much free trade credit can the company get, how much costly trade credit can it get, and what is the percentage cost of the costly credit? Should B&B take discounts?

e. Would it be feasible for B&B to finance with commercial paper?

f. Suppose B&B decided to raise an additional $100,000 as a 1-year loan from its bank, for which it was quoted a rate of 8 percent. What is the effective annual cost rate assuming (1) simple interest, (2) discount interest, (3) dis-count interest with a 10 percent compensating balance, and (4) add-on interest on a 12-month installment loan? For the first three of these assumptions, would it matter if the loan were for 90 days, but renewable, rather than for a year?

g. How large would the loan actually be in each of the cases in part f?

h. What are the pros and cons of borrowing on a secured versus an unsecured basis? If inventories or receivables are to be used as collateral, how would the loan be handled?

CYBER PROBLEM

Please go to our web site **http://brigham.swlearning.com** to access the Cyberproblems.

PART 7

SPECIAL TOPICS IN FINANCIAL MANAGEMENT

FINANCIAL PLANNING AND FORECASTING

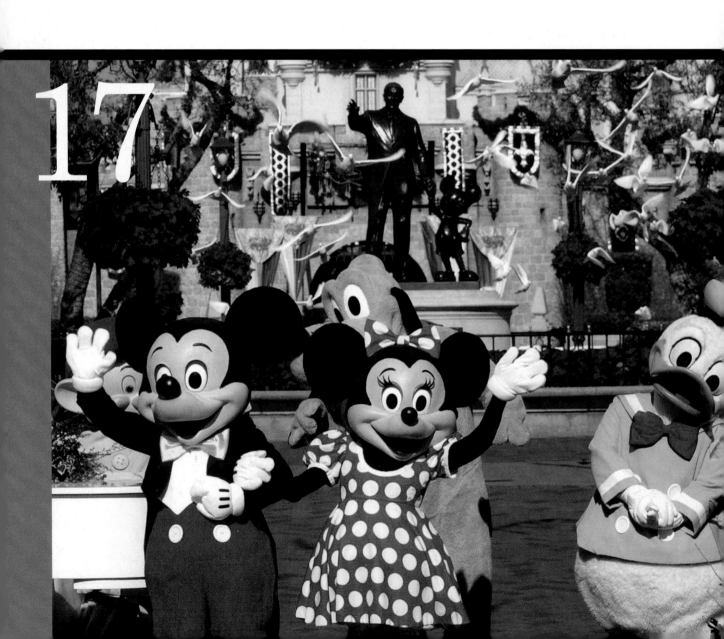

17

FORECASTING DISNEY'S FUTURE

WALT DISNEY CO.

In early 1998, corporations were reporting earnings for 1997. Simultaneously, security analysts were issuing their forecasts of earnings for 1998. Stock prices were extremely volatile moving up with a good earnings surprise — that is, where reported EPS was higher than analysts had been expecting — and down with unpleasant surprises. Corporate executives know that these reactions will occur, so they generally try to give analysts early warnings when unpleasant surprises are likely to occur. The logic is that unpleasant surprises increase uncertainty about the future, so a stock will react less negatively to low earnings if the drop is anticipated than if it is a complete surprise.

Corporate finance staffs also review their own internal plans and forecasts during the first part of the year. Firms' formal plans are generally completed in the fall and then go into effect at the start of the year, so early in the year information starts coming in that indicates how the year is shaping up.

For executives at Walt Disney Co., 1998 was a particularly difficult year. After several years of outstanding performance, Disney's earnings fell, causing a sharp drop in its stock price. Trying to address investors' concerns, Disney's Chairman and Chief Executive, Michael Eisner, began his annual letter to shareholders with the following words:

To Disney Owners and Fellow Cast Members:

I am looking out the window and can see the seasons change (yes, the seasons do change in Los Angeles — the eucalyptus leaves droop more and the sprinklers go on less often). I am reminded that our rhythms are set by the seasons and that any number of human endeavors are ruled by the calendar. Such as this annual report. Every 12 months we compile it, and every 12 months I sit down to write you this letter.

There's just one problem with this annual exercise: It implies that businesses can be run in neat 12-month chunks of time. Unfortunately, the business cycle has its own seasons, which are not ruled by the orderly and predictable orbit of the earth around the sun. Indeed, at Disney we live by a 60-month calendar. We set our goals over rolling five-year timelines. In this context, each year is more like a season. Some are sunny and some are overcast, but each is merely a period of passage and not a destination. Our five-year calendars force us to think long-term. They make us devise strategies that add value, not squeeze profits.

Eisner went on to tell shareholders that the company's long-run forecast remained promising. After acknowledging that Disney had problems in its entertainment and broadcasting divisions, he went on to state that the company was taking steps to cut costs and to improve operations. Eisner also stated that Disney's earnings had been hampered because it had begun a series of expensive new projects, including Disney's Animal Kingdom, its Cruise Line, the launching of *ESPN Magazine*, and the renovation of Anaheim Stadium. However, he argued that they were laying the groundwork for future profitability.

Now, toward the end of 2002, it has been nearly five years since Eisner wrote this letter. During these five years Disney has had its share of ups and downs, but its stock is now lower than it was in 1998. In his most recent letter to shareholders, Eisner spoke candidly about Disney's continued challenges. In particular, Eisner mentioned how the terrorist attacks in September 2001 caused people to cancel their travel plans, which hurt Disney's theme park attendance. He also stated that Disney has been hurt by the sluggish economy, which has reduced both theme park attendance and advertising revenue for its ABC network. Despite these concerns, Disney is still a valuable company, and Eisner remains optimistic that its fortunes will soon improve.

In spite of Eisner's assurances, many analysts are still lukewarm about Disney's future prospects. Many others, though, are betting that the company's stock will rebound. Unfortunately, no crystal ball exists for predicting the future. Instead, both corporate insiders and investors must base decisions on their own financial forecasts. While forecasting is necessarily somewhat subjective, we discuss in this chapter some basic principles that will improve financial forecasts. By the time you finish the chapter, you will have a good idea about how to forecast future results for Disney or any other company.

Source: Walt Disney Co.'s 1998, 1999, and 2001 Annual Reports.

PUTTING THINGS IN PERSPECTIVE

In the last several chapters we have discussed several of the key elements of Corporate Finance. These topics have included the cost of capital, capital budgeting, capital structure, dividend policy, and working capital management. Corporate managers make decisions in these key areas within the context of their companies' overall strategic plans.

When making these important decisions, corporate managers rely heavily on both current and projected financial statements. In Chapters 2 and 3 we reviewed financial statements and showed how managers and investors analyze them to evaluate a firm's past performance. While this is clearly important, it is even more important to look ahead and to anticipate what is likely to happen in the future. So, both managers and investors need to understand how to forecast future results.

Pro Forma (Projected) Financial Statements
Financial statements that forecast the company's financial position and performance over a period of years.

Managers make **pro forma,** or **projected, financial statements** and then use them in four ways: (1) By looking at projected statements, they can assess whether the firm's anticipated performance is in line with the firm's own general targets and with investors' expectations. (2) Pro forma statements can be used to estimate the effect of proposed operating changes. Therefore, financial managers spend a lot of time doing "what if" analyses. (3) Managers use pro forma statements to anticipate the firm's future financing needs. (4) Projected financial statements are used to estimate future free cash flows, which determine the company's overall value. Thus, managers forecast free cash flows under different operating plans, forecast their capital requirements, and then choose the plan that maximizes shareholder value.

We should also point out that security analysts make the same types of projections when they forecast companies' future earnings and cash flows. We showed in Chapter 8 that these estimated cash flows are used to determine the intrinsic value of a company's stock. When making their forecasts, security analysts recognize that they know less than the company's managers, who run the firm on a day-to-day basis and who ultimately make the decisions that determine the firm's future. However, the perceptions of analysts and the investors they influence have an important impact on the company's stock price. For this reason, companies often provide guidance that analysts use when making their forecasts. While this guidance is generally quite useful, good analysts always check things out on their own to make sure that they aren't being misled.

With these issues in mind, we explain in this chapter how to create and use pro forma financial statements to forecast the firm's financial requirements and operating results. To put these statements in the proper perspective, we begin with a discussion of strategic plans. ■

STRATEGIC PLANS

Our primary objective in this book is to explain what managers can do to make their companies more valuable. Managers must understand how investors determine the value of stocks and bonds if they are to identify, evaluate, and implement projects that meet or exceed investor expectations. However, value creation is impossible unless the company has a well-articulated plan. As Yogi Berra once said, "You've got to be careful if you don't know where you're going, because you might not get there."

CORPORATE PURPOSE

Mission Statement
A condensed version of a firm's strategic plan.

Companies begin with a **mission statement,** which is in many ways a condensed version of their strategic plan. Both mission statements and strategic plans usually begin with a statement of the overall *corporate purpose.* PepsiCo is very clear about its corporate purpose. The first sentence of its mission statement notes that its overall mission is to "increase the value of our shareholders' investment." Pepsi then goes on to note the company's commitment to its customers and to the environment. Likewise, in a recent mission statement, Coca-Cola stressed that its mission was to ". . . maximize shareholder value over time." On its current website, Coca-Cola presents "The Coca-Cola Promise," which states that the company "exists to benefit everyone who is touched by our business." Coke concludes by stating that its ultimate objective is to "provide consistently attractive returns to our business." On its web site, Disney talks about its broader objectives, but concludes by talking about the need to take actions that improve long-term shareholder value. Finally, Starbucks makes no explicit mention of maximizing shareholder wealth in its mission statement, but in its six guiding principles it notes that "profitability is essential to our future success."

The four mission statements just discussed demonstrate the various objectives that companies strive to attain. It is increasingly common for U.S. companies to state that their key corporate purpose is to maximize stockholder value, but this has not always been the case. For example, Varian Associates Inc., a New York Stock Exchange company with sales of almost $2 billion, was, in 1990, regarded as one of the most technologically advanced electronics companies. However, Varian's management was more concerned with developing new technology than with marketing it, and its stock price was lower than it had been 10 years earlier. Some of the larger stockholders were intensely unhappy with the state of affairs, and management was faced with the threat of a proxy fight or forced merger. Then management announced a change in policy and stated that it would, in the future, emphasize both technological excellence *and* profitability, rather than focusing primarily on technology. The company then split itself into three separate companies, each focused on its own technology and value, and a share of stock that was worth $6.75 in 1990 is now worth $330!

 A corporate focus on creating wealth for the company's owners is not yet as common abroad as it is in the United States. For example, Veba AG, one of Germany's largest companies, created a stir in 1996 when it stated in its annual report that "Our commitment is to create value for you, our shareholders." This was quite different from the usual German model, in which companies have representatives from labor on their boards of directors and which explicitly state their commitments to a variety of stakeholders. As the trend in international investing continues, more and more non-U.S. companies are adopting a corporate purpose that stresses the importance of maximizing shareholder value.

CORPORATE SCOPE

Its *corporate scope* defines a firm's lines of business and geographic area of operations. As one of its recent mission statements indicates, Coke generally limits its products to soft drinks, but on a global geographic scale. Pepsi-Cola recently followed Coke's lead—it restricted its scope by spinning off its food service businesses.

Several recent studies have found that the market tends to value focused firms more highly than it does diversified firms.[1] Nokia is an example of a company that has taken steps in recent years to sharpen its corporate focus. While most investors think of Nokia as a company that specializes in the wireless phone market, it has actually been around for more than 135 years, and until recently, Nokia was involved in a wide range of different industries. However, over the past decade, the Finnish conglomerate has sold off many of its less productive divisions. Despite a significant decline in its stock price over the past two years, Nokia's stock has still risen nearly 500 percent since early 1996, and the company currently has a $75 billion market capitalization.

It is important to recognize that when it comes to corporate scope, one size doesn't fit all. For example, General Electric has investments in a large number of different areas, yet it is widely recognized as one of the best-managed and highly valued industrial companies in the world.

---

[1] See, for example, Philip G. Berger and Eli Ofek, "Diversification's Effect on Firm Value," *Journal of Financial Economics*, Vol. 37, No. 1, 39–66 (1995); and Larry Lang and René Stulz, "Tobin's Q, Corporate Diversification, and Firm Performance," *Journal of Political Economy*, Vol. 102, Issue 6, 1248–1280 (1994).

CORPORATE OBJECTIVES

The corporate purpose states the general philosophy of the business, but it does not provide managers with operational objectives. The *statement of corporate objectives* sets forth specific goals to guide management. Most organizations have both qualitative and quantitative objectives. For example, one of Coca-Cola's recent mission statements lists six corporate objectives, including becoming "the best marketers in the world" and "leading as a model corporate citizen." However, these statements are qualitative, hence hard to measure, so the objectives need to be restated in quantitative terms, such as attaining a 50 percent market share, a 20 percent ROE, a 10 percent earnings growth rate, or a $100 million economic value added (EVA). Coca-Cola doesn't list its quantitative objectives in its mission statement, but it has them in its detailed strategic plan. Moreover, executive bonuses are based on achieving the quantitative objectives.

CORPORATE STRATEGIES

Once a firm has defined its purpose, scope, and objectives, it must develop a strategy for achieving its goals. *Corporate strategies* are broad approaches rather than detailed plans. For example, one airline may have a strategy of offering no-frills service between a limited number of cities, while another's strategy may be to offer "staterooms in the sky." Broadly speaking, a company's strategy often has several dimensions including whether (1) to invest overseas, (2) to invest in new lines of business and new technologies, and/or (3) to focus on a broad or narrow portion of the customer market. In any event, strategies should be both attainable and compatible with the firm's purpose, scope, and objectives.

SELF-TEST QUESTIONS

What are pro forma financial statements?

What are four ways that pro forma financial statements are used by managers?

Briefly describe the nature and use of the following corporate planning terms: (1) corporate purpose, (2) corporate scope, (3) corporate objectives, and (4) corporate strategies.

OPERATING PLANS

Operating plans provide detailed implementation guidance, based on the corporate strategy, to help meet the corporate objectives. These plans can be developed for any time horizon, but like Disney, most companies use a five-year horizon. A five-year plan is most detailed for the first year, with each succeeding year's plan becoming less specific. The plan explains in considerable detail who is responsible for each particular function, when specific tasks are to be accomplished, sales and profit targets, and the like.

TABLE 17-1	Allied Food Products: Annual Planning Schedule

MONTHS	ACTION
April–May	Planning department analyzes general economic and industry factors. Marketing department prepares sales forecast for each product group.
June–July	Engineering department prepares cost estimates for new processing/distribution facilities and plant modernization programs.
August–September	Financial analysts evaluate proposed capital expenditures, divisional operating plans, and proposed sources and uses of funds.
October–November	Five-year plan is finalized by planning department, reviewed by divisional officers, and put into "semifinal" form.
December	Five-year plan is approved by the executive committee and then submitted to the board of directors for final approval.

Table 17-1 summarizes the annual planning schedule of Allied Food Products. This schedule illustrates the fact that for larger companies, the planning process is essentially continuous. Next, Table 17-2 outlines the key elements of Allied's five-year plan. A full outline would require several pages, but Table 17-2 does provide insights into the format and content of a five-year plan. It should be noted that large, multidivisional companies such as General Electric break down their operating plans by divisions. Thus, each division has its own goals, mission, and plan for meeting its objectives, and these plans are then consolidated to form the corporate plan.[2]

SELF-TEST QUESTIONS

What is the purpose of a firm's operating plan?

What is the most common time horizon for operating plans?

Briefly describe the contents of a typical operating plan.

THE FINANCIAL PLAN

The financial planning process can be broken down into six steps:

1. Project financial statements and use these projections to analyze the effects of the operating plan on projected profits and various financial ratios. The projections can also be used to monitor operations after the plan has been finalized and put into effect. Rapid awareness of deviations from the plan is essential in a good control system, which, in turn, is essential to corporate success in a changing world.

---

[2] For more on the corporate planning process, see Benton E. Gup, *Guide to Strategic Planning* (New York: McGraw-Hill, 1980).

TABLE 17-2   **Allied Food Products: Five-Year Operating Plan Outline**

Part 1. Corporate purpose
Part 2. Corporate scope
Part 3. Corporate objectives
Part 4. Projected business environment
Part 5. Corporate strategies
Part 6. Summary of projected business results
Part 7. Product line plans and policies

a. Marketing

b. Processing/distribution

c. Finance

1. Working capital

(a) Overall working capital policy

(b) Cash and marketable securities

(c) Inventory management

(d) Credit policy and receivables management

2. Dividend policy

3. Capital structure policy

4. Financial forecast

(a) Capital budget

(b) Cash budget

(c) Pro forma financial statements

(d) External financing requirements

(e) Financial condition analysis

5. Accounting plan

6. Control plan

d. Administrative and personnel

e. Research and development

f. New products

2. Determine the funds needed to support the five-year plan. This includes funds for plant and equipment as well as for inventories and receivables, for R&D programs, and for major advertising campaigns.

3. Forecast funds availability over the next five years. This involves estimating the funds to be generated internally as well as those to be obtained from external sources. Any constraints on operating plans imposed by financial restrictions must be incorporated into the plan; constraints include restrictions on the debt ratio, the current ratio, and the coverage ratios.

4. Establish and maintain a system of controls to govern the allocation and use of funds within the firm. In essence, this involves making sure that the basic plan is carried out properly.

5. Develop procedures for adjusting the basic plan if the economic forecasts upon which the plan was based do not materialize. For example, if the economy turns out to be stronger than was forecasted, then these new conditions must be recognized and reflected in higher production schedules, larger marketing quotas, and the like, and as rapidly as possible. Thus, Step 5 is really a "feedback loop" that triggers modifications to the financial plan.

6. Establish a performance-based management compensation system. It is critically important that such a system rewards managers for doing what stockholders want them to do—maximize share prices.

In the remainder of this chapter, we discuss how firms use computerized financial planning models to implement the three key components of the financial plan: (1) the sales forecast, (2) pro forma financial statements, and (3) the external financing plan.

SELF-TEST QUESTION

What are the six steps of the financial planning process?

COMPUTERIZED FINANCIAL PLANNING MODELS

Although financial forecasting as described in this chapter can be done with a calculator, virtually all corporate forecasts are made using computerized forecasting models. Most forecasting models are based on a spreadsheet program such as *Microsoft Excel*. Spreadsheets have two major advantages over pencil-and-paper calculations. First, it is much faster to construct a spreadsheet model than to make a "by-hand" forecast if the forecast period extends beyond a year or two. Second, and more important, with a spreadsheet model you can change inputs and instantaneously recompute the projected financial statements and ratios, thus making it easy for managers to determine the effects of changes in variables such as unit sales, labor costs, and sales prices.

In this chapter, we developed forecasted financial statements for Allied Food Products with an *Excel* model. The model is provided on the CD-ROM for the book, under the filename 17MODEL.xls. You do not have to understand the model to understand the chapter, but working through the model will give you a better feel for the forecasting process.[3]

SELF-TEST QUESTION

What are the two major advantages of spreadsheet models over pencil-and-paper calculations?

---

[3] There are small rounding differences between "by-hand" answers and those obtained using the spreadsheet. The spreadsheet carries calculations out to more decimal places and thus is somewhat more accurate than "by-hand" calculations.

Sales Forecast
A forecast of a firm's unit and dollar sales for some future period; it is generally based on recent sales trends plus forecasts of the economic prospects for the nation, region, industry, and so forth.

The **sales forecast** generally starts with a review of sales during the past five to ten years, expressed in a graph such as that in Figure 17-1. The first part of the graph shows five years of historical sales for Allied. The graph could have contained 10 years of sales data, but Allied focuses on sales figures for the latest five years because the firm's studies have shown that its future growth is more closely related to recent events than to the distant past.

Allied had its ups and downs during the period from 1998 to 2002. In 2000, poor weather in California's fruit-producing regions resulted in low production, which caused 2000 sales to fall below the 1999 level. Then, a bumper crop in 2001 pushed sales up by 15 percent, an unusually high growth rate for a mature food processor. Based on a regression analysis, Allied's forecasters determined that the average annual growth rate in sales over the past five years was 9.1 percent. On the basis of this historical sales trend, on planned new-product introductions, and on Allied's forecast for the economy, the firm's planning committee projects a 10 percent sales growth rate

| FIGURE 17-1 | **Allied Food Products: 2003 Sales Projection (Millions of Dollars)** |

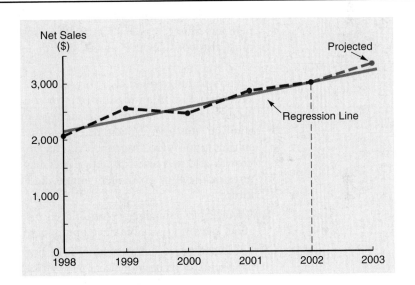

YEAR	SALES
1998	$2,058
1999	2,534
2000	2,472
2001	2,850
2002	3,000
2003	3,300 (Projected)

during 2003, to sales of $3,300 million. Here are some of the factors Allied considered in developing its sales forecast:

1. Allied Food Products is divided into three divisions: canned foods, frozen foods, and packaged foods such as dried fruits. Sales growth is seldom the same for each of the divisions, so to begin the forecasting process, divisional projections are made on the basis of historical growth, and then the divisional forecasts are combined to produce a "first approximation" corporate sales forecast.

2. Next, the level of economic activity in each of the company's marketing areas is forecasted—for example, how strong will the economies be in each of Allied's six domestic and two foreign distribution territories, and what population changes are forecasted in each area?

3. Allied's planning committee also looks at the firm's probable market share in each distribution territory. Consideration is given to such factors as the firm's production and distribution capacity, its competitors' capacities, new-product introductions that are planned by Allied or its competitors, and potential changes in shelf-space allocations, which are vital for food sales. Pricing strategies are also considered—for example, does the company have plans to raise prices to boost margins, or to lower prices to increase market share and take advantage of economies of scale? Obviously, such factors could greatly affect future sales.

4. Allied's foreign sales present unique forecasting problems. In particular, its planners must consider how exchange rate fluctuations would affect sales. Allied must also consider the effects of trade agreements, governmental policies, and the like.

5. Allied's planners must also consider the effects of inflation on prices. Over the next five years, the inflation rate for food products is expected to average 3 to 4 percent, and Allied plans to increase prices, on average, by a like amount. In addition, the firm expects to expand its market share in certain products, resulting in a 4 percent growth rate in unit sales. The combination of unit sales growth and increases in sales prices has resulted in historical revenue growth rates in the 8 to 10 percent range, and this same situation is expected in the future.

6. Advertising campaigns, promotional discounts, credit terms, and the like also affect sales, so probable developments for these items are also factored in.

7. Forecasts are made for each division, both in the aggregate and on an individual product basis. The individual product sales forecasts are summed, and this sum is compared with the aggregated division forecasts. Differences are reconciled, and the end result is a sales forecast for the company as a whole but with breakdowns by the three divisions and by individual products.

If the sales forecast is off, the consequences can be serious. First, if the market expands *more* than Allied has geared up for, the company will not be able to meet demand. Its customers will end up buying competitors' products, and Allied will lose market share. On the other hand, if its projections are overly optimistic, Allied could end up with too much plant, equipment, and inventory. This would mean low turnover ratios, high costs for depreciation and storage, and write-offs of spoiled inventory. All of this would result in low profits, a low rate of return on equity, and a depressed stock price. If Allied had financed an unnecessary expansion with debt, high interest charges would compound its problems. Thus, an accurate sales forecast is critical to the firm's well-being.[4]

> **SELF-TEST QUESTIONS**

> List some factors that should be considered when developing a sales forecast.

> Explain why an accurate sales forecast is critical to profitability.

FINANCIAL STATEMENT FORECASTING: THE PERCENT OF SALES METHOD

Percent of Sales Method
A method of forecasting future financial statements that expresses each account as a percentage of sales. These percentages can be constant, or they can change over time.

Once sales have been forecasted, we must forecast future balance sheets and income statements. The most commonly used technique is the **percent of sales method,** which begins with the sales forecast, expressed as an annual growth rate in dollar sales revenues. Although we showed only one year in our earlier example, Allied's managers actually forecasted sales for eight years, with these results:

YEAR	2003	2004	2005	2006	2007	2008	2009	2010
Growth rate in sales	10%	10%	10%	10%	9%	8%	7%	7%

This eight-year period is called the *explicit forecast period*, with the eighth year being the *forecast horizon.*

The initially forecasted growth rate is 10 percent, but high growth attracts competitors, and eventually the market becomes saturated. Therefore, population growth and inflation determine the *long-term sales growth rate* for most companies. Reasonable values for the long-term sales growth rate are from 5 to 7 percent for companies in mature industries. Table 17-3 shows the average growth rate in sales for a typical company in a mature industry, H. J. Heinz, over the time period 1986–2001. During this period, Heinz's sales grew at an average annual rate of slightly more than 5 percent a year. Heinz's annual earnings over the same time period averaged about 7 percent a year, which indicates that Heinz did a good job of controlling its costs. More generally, Figure 17-2 shows how profits grew for an average U.S. firm, along with the growth in GDP, from 1970 through 2001. Corporate profits are less stable than GDP, but the average firm's growth rate tends to parallel the growth rate in the overall economy.

With these patterns in mind, Allied's managers believe that a long-run sales growth rate of 7 percent is reasonable. Its managers also believe that competition will drive their growth rate down to this level within seven or eight years, so they have chosen an eight-year forecast period.

---

[4] A sales forecast is actually the *expected value of a probability distribution,* so there are many possible levels of sales. Because any sales forecast is subject to uncertainty, financial planners are just as interested in the degree of uncertainty inherent in the sales forecast, as measured by the standard deviation, as in the expected level of sales.

TABLE 17-3   Heinz's Average Annual Growth Rates in Sales and Earnings

YEAR	SALES	ANNUAL GROWTH RATE IN SALES (%)	NET INCOME (EARNINGS)	ANNUAL GROWTH RATE IN NET INCOME (%)
1986	$4,638.76	N/A	$316.45	N/A
1987	5,245.05	13.07	371.36	17.35
1988	5,800.87	10.60	427.84	15.21
1989	6,084.48	4.89	482.96	12.88
1990	6,646.68	9.24	552.59	14.42
1991	6,581.42	−0.98	468.74	−15.17
1992	7,104.46	7.95	629.56	34.31
1993	7,045.34	−0.83	526.72	−16.33
1994	8,085.08	14.76	581.16	10.34
1995	9,111.79	12.70	645.05	10.99
1996	9,355.75	2.68	646.24	0.18
1997	9,209.06	−1.57	781.35	20.91
1998	9,301.47	1.00	861.91	10.31
1999	9,409.34	1.16	893.97	3.72
2000	9,432.12	0.24	889.82	−0.46
2001	9,800.00	3.90	840.00	−5.60
Arithmetic average annual growth rates		5.25		7.54
Geometric average annual growth rates		5.11		6.72

NOTE: The arithmetic average is simply the mean of the annual observations. The geometric average takes into account the effects of compounding, and is therefore better for predicting future results. Web Appendix 17A, "Arithmetic vs. Geometric Averages," provides a more complete discussion of the difference between arithmetic and geometric growth rates.

SOURCE: Adapted from *Value Line Investment Survey*, May 10, 2002.

Companies often have what is called a *competitive advantage period*, during which they can grow at rates higher than the long-term growth rate. For companies with proprietary technology or strong brand identities, such as Microsoft or Coca-Cola, the competitive advantage period might be as long as 20 years. For companies that produce commodities or that are in highly competitive industries, the competitive advantage period might be as short as two or three years, or even be nonexistent.

To summarize, most financial plans have a forecast period of at least 5 years, with 5 to 15 years, depending on the expected length of the competitive advantage period, being most common.

As a starting point, many items on the income statement and balance sheet are often assumed to increase proportionally with sales. As sales increase, items that are tied to sales also increase, and the values of those items for a particular year are estimated as percentages of the forecasted sales for that year. The remaining items on

FIGURE 17-2

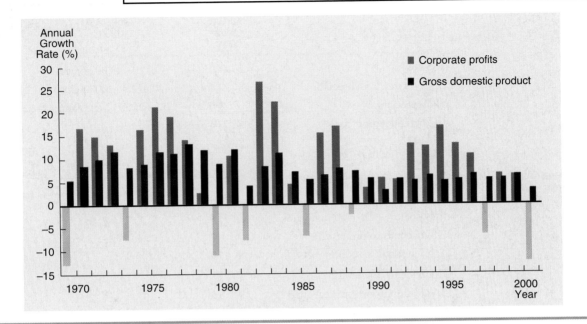

SOURCE: Adapted from Bureau of Economic Analysis, National Income and Product Accounts Tables.

the forecasted statements—items that are not tied directly to sales—are set at "reasonable" levels.

Note that if the forecasted percentage of sales for each item is the same as the percentage for the prior year, then each item will grow at the same rate as sales. Under these assumptions, many of the key ratios will remain constant. For example, if inventories and sales both increase by 10 percent, the inventory turnover ratio will remain the same.

While the financial statement forecasting method often begins by assuming that many key items will grow at the same rate as projected sales, it is important to recognize that this method can be easily adjusted to allow different income statement and balance sheet items to grow at different rates. This process is particularly straightforward whenever a spreadsheet is used to develop the forecast. With this understanding in mind, we explain in the following section how to use this method to forecast Allied's financial statements.

STEP 1. FORECASTED INCOME STATEMENT

First, we forecast the income statement for the coming year. This statement is needed to estimate both income and the addition to retained earnings. Table 17-4 shows the forecast for 2003. Sales are forecasted to grow by 10 percent. The forecast of sales for 2003, shown in Row 1 of Column 3, is calculated by multiplying the 2002

TABLE 17-4

Allied Food Products: Actual 2002 and Projected 2003 Income Statements (Millions of Dollars)

	ACTUAL 2002[a] (1)	FORECAST BASIS (2)	2003 FORECAST (3)
1. Sales	$3,000	1.1×2002 Sales =	$3,300
2. Costs except depreciation	2,616	0.872×2003 Sales =	2,878
3. Depreciation	100	0.1×2003 Net plant =	110
4. Total operating costs	$2,716		$2,988
5. EBIT	$ 284		$ 312
6. Interest	88	$\longrightarrow$	88[b]
7. Earnings before taxes (EBT)	$ 196		$ 224
8. Taxes (40%)	78		89
9. NI before preferred dividends	$ 118		$ 135
10. Dividends to preferred	4	$\longrightarrow$	4[b]
11. NI available to common	$ 114		$ 131
12. Dividends to common	$ 58		$ 63[c]
13. Addition to retained earnings	$ 56		$ 68

[a] To reduce clutter, the income statement as shown previously in Chapter 2 is rounded to whole numbers.

[b] Indicates a 2002 amount carried over for the 2003 forecast. Indicated in Column 2 by an arrow.

[c] See the text for explanation of dividends.

sales, shown in Column 1, by (1 + growth rate) = 1.1. The result is a 2003 sales forecast of $3,300 million.

The percent of sales method assumes initially that all costs except depreciation are a specified percentage of sales. For 2002, Allied's ratio of costs to sales is 87.2 percent ($2,616/$3,000 = 0.872). Thus, for each dollar of sales in 2002, Allied incurred 87.2 cents of costs. Initially, the company's managers assume that the cost structure will remain unchanged in 2003. Later in the chapter we explore the impact of an improvement in the cost structure, but for now we assume that costs will equal 87.2 percent of sales. See Column 3, Row 2.

Allied's managers assume that depreciation will be a fixed percentage of net plant and equipment. For 2002, the ratio of depreciation to net plant and equipment is 10 percent ($100/$1,000 = 0.10), and Allied's managers believe that this is a good estimate of future depreciation. As we discuss in the next section, the forecasted net plant and equipment for 2003 is $1,100. Therefore, the forecasted depreciation for 2003 is 0.10($1,100) = $110.

Total operating costs, shown in Row 4, are the sum of costs and depreciation. EBIT is found by subtraction, while the interest charges in Column 3 are simply carried over from Column 1.

Earnings before taxes (EBT) is then calculated, as is net income before preferred dividends. Preferred dividends are carried over from the 2002 column, and they will remain constant unless Allied decides to issue additional preferred stock. Net income available to common is then calculated, after which the 2003 dividends are forecasted as follows. The 2002 dividend per share is $1.15, and this dividend is expected to increase by about 8 percent, to $1.25. Since there are 50 million shares outstanding, the projected dividends are $1.25(50) = $62.5 million, rounded to $63 million.

To complete the forecasted income statement, the $63 million of projected dividends are subtracted from the $131 million projected net income, and the result is the first-pass projection of the addition to retained earnings, $131 − $63 = $68 million.

STEP 2. FORECAST THE BALANCE SHEET

The assets shown on Allied's balance sheet must increase if sales are to increase. For example, companies such as Allied write and deposit checks every day. Because they don't know exactly when all of these checks will clear, they can't predict exactly what the balance in their checking accounts will be on any given day. Therefore, they must maintain a balance of cash and marketable securities to avoid overdrawing their accounts. We assume that the cash required to support the company's operations is proportional to its sales. (Cash management was discussed in great detail in Chapter 15.) Allied's 2002 ratio of cash to sales was approximately 0.33 percent ($10/$3,000 = 0.003333), and its managers believe this ratio will remain constant in 2003. Therefore, the forecasted cash balance for 2003, shown in Column 3 of Table 17-5, is 0.003333($3,300) = $11 million.

Unless a company changes its credit policy or has a change in its types of customers, accounts receivable will increase proportionately with sales. Allied's 2002 ratio of accounts receivable to sales was $375/$3,000 = 0.125 = 12.5%. Later, we examine the effect of a change in credit policy, but for now we assume a constant credit policy and customer base. Therefore, the forecasted accounts receivable for 2003 is 0.125($3,300) = $412.5 million, rounded to $412 million as shown in Column 3 of Table 17-5.

As sales increase, companies generally need more inventory. For Allied, the 2002 ratio of inventory to sales is $615/$3,000 = 20.5%. Assuming no change in Allied's inventory management, the forecasted inventory for 2003 is 0.205($3,300) = $676.5 million, rounded to $677 million as shown in Column 3 of Table 17-5.

It might be reasonable to assume that cash, accounts receivable, and inventory grow proportionally with sales, but will the amount of net plant and equipment go up and down as sales go up and down? The correct answer could be yes or no. When companies acquire plant and equipment, they often install greater capacity than they currently need, due to economies of scale. For example, it was economically better for GM to build the Saturn automobile plant with a capacity of about 320,000 cars per year than to build the plant with a capacity of only 50,000 cars per year and then add capacity each year. Saturn's sales were far below 320,000 units for the first few years of production, so it was possible to increase sales during those years without also increasing plant and equipment. Even if a factory is at its maximum rated capacity, most companies can produce additional units by reducing the amount of downtime due to scheduled maintenance, by running machinery at a higher than optimal speed, or by running a second (or third) shift. Therefore, there is not necessarily a close relationship between sales and net plant and equipment in the short term.

However, for some companies there is a fixed relationship between sales and plant and equipment, even in the short term. For example, new stores in many retail chains achieve the same sales during their first year as the chain's existing stores. The only way these retailers can grow is by adding new stores, which results in a strong proportional relationship between fixed assets and sales.

TABLE 17-5

Allied Food Products: Actual 2002 and Projected 2003 Balance Sheets (Millions of Dollars)

	ACTUAL 2002 (1)	FORECAST BASIS (2)	2003 FORECAST		
			FIRST PASS (3)	AFN[a] (4)	SECOND PASS (5)
Cash and marketable securities	$ 10	0.33% × 2003 Sales =	$ 11	⟶	$ 11
Accounts receivable	375	12.5% × 2003 Sales =	412	⟶	412
Inventories	615	20.5% × 2003 Sales =	677	⟶	677
Total current assets	$1,000		$1,100		$1,100
Net plant and equipment	1,000	33.33% × 2003 Sales =	1,100	⟶	1,100
Total assets	$2,000		$2,200		$2,200
Accounts payable	$ 60	2% × 2003 Sales =	$ 66	⟶	$ 66
Notes payable	110	⟶	110[b]	+28	138
Accrued liabilities	140	4.67% × 2003 Sales =	154	⟶	154
Total current liabilities	$ 310		$ 330		$ 358
Long-term bonds	754	⟶	754[b]	+28	782
Total debt	$1,064		$1,084		$1,140
Preferred stock	40	⟶	40[b]	⟶	40
Common stock	130	⟶	130[b]	+56	186
Retained earnings	766	+68[c]	834	⟶	834
Total common equity	$ 896		$ 964		$1,020
Total liabilities and equity	$2,000		$2,088	+112	$2,200
Additional funds needed (AFN)			$ 112		

[a] AFN stands for "Additional Funds Needed." This figure is determined at the bottom of Column 3. Then, Column 4 shows how the required $112 of AFN will be raised.

[b] Indicates a 2002 amount carried over as the first-pass forecast. Arrows also indicate items whose values are carried over from one pass to another.

[c] From Line 13 in Column 3 of Table 17-4.

In the long run, there is a relatively close relationship between sales and fixed assets for all companies: No company can continue to increase sales unless it eventually adds capacity. Therefore, as a first approximation it is reasonable to assume that the long-term ratio of net plant and equipment to sales will be constant.

For the first years of a forecast, managers generally use the actual planned dollars of investment in plant and equipment. If those estimates are not available, it is reasonable to assume an approximately constant ratio of net plant and equipment to sales. For Allied, the ratio of net plant and equipment to sales for 2002 is $1,000/$3,000 = 33.33%. Allied's net plant and equipment have grown fairly steadily in the past, and its managers expect steady future growth. Therefore, they forecast net plant and equipment for 2003 to be 0.3333($3,300) = $1,100 million.

Once the individual asset accounts have been forecasted, they can be summed to complete the asset section of the balance sheet. For Allied, the total current assets forecasted for 2003 are $11 + $412 + $677 = $1,100 million, and fixed assets add another $1,100 million. Therefore, as Table 17-5 shows, Allied will need total assets of $2,200 million to support $3,300 million of sales in 2003.

Spontaneously
Generated Funds
Funds that are obtained
automatically from routine
business transactions.

If Allied's assets are to increase, its liabilities and equity must also increase—the additional assets must be financed. Some items on the liability side can be expected to increase spontaneously with sales, producing what are called **spontaneously generated funds.** For example, as sales increase, so will Allied's purchases of raw materials, and those larger purchases will spontaneously lead to a higher level of accounts payable. For Allied, the 2002 ratio of accounts payable to sales is $60/$3,000 = 0.02 = 2%. Allied's managers assume that their payables policy will not change, so the forecasted accounts payable for 2003 is 0.02($3,300) = $66 million.

More sales will require more labor, and higher sales should also result in higher taxable income and thus taxes. Therefore, accrued wages and taxes will both increase. For Allied, the 2002 ratio of accrued liabilities to sales is $140/$3,000 = 0.0467 = 4.67%. If this ratio does not change, then the forecasted level of accrued liabilities for 2003 will be 0.0467 ($3,300) = $154 million.

Retained earnings will also increase, but not at the same rate as sales: The new balance for retained earnings will be the old level plus the addition to retained earnings, which we calculated in Step 1. Also, notes payable, long-term bonds, preferred stock, and common stock will not rise spontaneously with sales—rather, the projected levels of these accounts will depend on financing decisions, as we discuss later.

In summary, (1) higher sales must be supported by additional assets, (2) some of the asset increases can be financed by spontaneous increases in accounts payable and accrued liabilities, and by retained earnings, but (3) any shortfall must be financed from external sources, using some combination of debt, preferred stock, and common stock.

The spontaneously increasing liabilities (accounts payable and accrued liabilities) are forecasted and shown in Column 3 of Table 17-5, the first-pass forecast. Then, those liability and equity accounts whose values reflect conscious management decisions—notes payable, long-term bonds, preferred stock, and common stock—are initially set at their 2002 levels. Thus, 2003 notes payable are initially set at $110 million, the long-term bond account is forecasted at $754 million, and so on. The 2003 value for the retained earnings (RE) account is obtained by adding the projected addition to retained earnings as developed in the 2003 income statement (see Table 17-4) to the 2002 ending balance:

$$2003 \text{ RE} = 2002 \text{ RE} + 2003 \text{ forecasted addition to RE}$$
$$= \$766 + \$68 = \$834 \text{ million.}$$

The forecast of total assets as shown in Column 3 (first-pass forecast) of Table 17-5 is $2,200 million, which indicates that Allied must add $200 million of new assets in 2003 to support the higher sales level. However, the forecasted liability and equity accounts as shown in the lower portion of Column 3 rise by only $88 million, to $2,088 million. Since the balance sheet must balance, Allied must raise an additional $2,200 − $2,088 = $112 million, which we define as **Additional Funds Needed (AFN).** The AFN will be raised by some combination of borrowing from the bank as notes payable, issuing long-term bonds, and selling new common stock.

Additional Funds Needed
(AFN)
Funds that a firm must raise
externally through
borrowing or by selling new
common or preferred stock.

STEP 3. RAISING THE ADDITIONAL FUNDS NEEDED

Allied's financial staff will raise the needed funds based on several factors, including the firm's target capital structure, the effect of short-term borrowing on the current ratio, conditions in the debt and equity markets, and restrictions imposed by existing debt agreements. The financial staff, after considering all of the relevant factors, decided on the following financing mix to raise the needed $112 million:

| | AMOUNT OF NEW CAPITAL | | |
	PERCENT	DOLLARS (MILLIONS)	INTEREST RATE
Notes payable	25%	$ 28	8%
Long-term bonds	25	28	10
Common stock	50	56	—
	100%	$112	

These amounts, which are shown in Column 4 of Table 17-5, are added to the initially forecasted account totals as shown in Column 3 to generate the second-pass balance sheet. Thus, in Column 5 the notes payable account increases to $110 + $28 = $138 million, long-term bonds rise to $754 + $28 = $782 million, and common stock increases to $130 + $56 = $186 million. Then, the balance sheet is in balance.

A COMPLICATION: FINANCIAL FEEDBACKS

Our projected financial statements are incomplete in one sense—they do not reflect the fact that interest must be paid on the debt used to help finance the AFN, and that dividends will be paid on the shares issued to raise the common stock portion of the AFN. Those payments would lower net income and retained earnings shown in the projected statements. One could take account of these *financing feedback effects* by adding columns to Tables 17-4 and 17-5 and then making further adjustments. The adjustments are not difficult, but they do involve a good bit of arithmetic. In view of the fact that all of the data are based on forecasts, and since the adjustments add substantially to the work but relatively little to the accuracy of the forecasts, we leave them to later finance courses.[5]

ANALYSIS OF THE FORECAST

The 2003 forecast as developed above is only the first part of Allied's total forecasting process. We must go on to analyze the projected statements to determine whether the forecast meets the firm's financial targets as set forth in the five-year financial plan. If the statements do not meet the targets, then elements of the forecast must be changed.

Table 17-6 shows Allied's actual ratios for 2002, its projected 2003 ratios, and the latest industry average ratios. (The table also shows a "Revised Forecast for 2003" column, which we will discuss later. Disregard the revised data for now.) The firm's financial condition at the close of 2002 was weak, with many ratios well below the industry averages. For example, Allied's current ratio, based on Column 1 of Table 17-5, was only 3.2 versus 4.2 for an average food processor.

The "Inputs" section shown on the top three rows of the table provides data on three of the model's key drivers: (1) costs (excluding depreciation) as a percentage of sales, (2) accounts receivable as a percentage of sales, and (3) inventories as a percent-

---

[5] For a thorough discussion of financing feedbacks, see Eugene F. Brigham and Phillip R. Daves, *Intermediate Financial Management*, 7th ed. (Forth Worth, TX: South-Western Publishers, 2002), Chapter 8.

TABLE 17-6   Model Inputs, AFN, and Key Ratios

	ACTUAL 2002 (1)	PRELIMINARY FORECAST FOR 2003 (2)	REVISED FORECAST FOR 2003 (3)[a]	INDUSTRY AVERAGE 2002 (4)
MODEL INPUTS				
Costs (excluding depreciation) as a percentage of sales	87.2%	87.2%	86.0%	87.1%
Accounts receivable as a percentage of sales	12.5	12.5	11.8	10.0
Inventories as a percentage of sales	20.5	20.5	16.7	11.1
MODEL OUTPUTS				
NOPAT (net operating profit after taxes)	$ 170.3	$ 187.3	$ 211.2	
Net operating working capital	800.0	880.0	731.5	
Total operating capital	1,800.0	1,980.0	1,831.5	
Free cash flow (FCF)	(109.7)	7.3	179.7	
AFN		112	(60)	
KEY RATIOS				
Current ratio	3.2×	3.1×	3.5×	4.2×
Inventory turnover	4.9	4.9	6.0	9.0
Days sales outstanding (365-day basis)	45.6 days	45.6 days	43.1 days	36.0 days
Total assets turnover	1.5×	1.5×	1.6×	1.8×
Debt ratio	53.2%	51.8%	49.9%	40.0%
Profit margin	3.8	4.0	4.7	5.0
Return on assets	5.7	5.9	7.5	9.0
Return on equity	12.7	12.8	15.6	15.0
Return on invested capital (NOPAT/Total operating capital)	9.5	9.5	11.5	11.4

[a] The "Revised" data show ratios after policy changes related to asset levels, as discussed later, have been incorporated into the forecast. All of the surplus AFN is used to pay off notes payable.

age of sales. The preliminary forecast in Column 2 assumes these variables remain constant. While Allied's cost-to-sales ratio is only slightly worse than the industry average, its ratios of accounts receivable to sales and inventories to sales are significantly higher than those of its competitors. Its investment in inventories and receivables is too high, causing its returns on assets, equity, and invested capital as shown in the lower part of the table to be too low. Therefore, Allied should make operational changes designed to reduce its current assets.

The "Key Ratios" section of Table 17-6 for the forecast period provides more details regarding the firm's weaknesses. Allied's asset management ratios are much worse than the industry averages. For example, its total assets turnover ratio is 1.5 versus an industry average of 1.8. Its poor asset management ratios drag down the return on invested capital (9.5 percent for Allied versus 11.4 percent for the industry average). Furthermore, Allied must carry more than the average amount of debt to support its excessive assets, and the extra interest expense reduces its profit margin to 4.0 percent versus 5.0 percent for the industry. Much of the debt is short term, and this results in a current ratio of 3.1 versus the 4.2 industry average. These problems will persist unless management takes action to improve things.

After reviewing its preliminary forecast, management decided to take three steps to improve its financial condition: (1) It decided to lay off some workers and close certain operations. It forecasted that these steps would lower operating costs (excluding depreciation) from the current 87.2 to 86 percent of sales as shown in Column 3 of Table 17-6. (2) By screening credit customers more closely and by being more aggressive in collecting past-due accounts, the company believes it can reduce the ratio of accounts receivable-to-sales from 12.5 to 11.8 percent. (3) Finally, management thinks it can reduce the inventories-to-sales ratio from 20.5 to 16.7 percent through the use of tighter inventory controls.[6]

These projected operational changes were then used to create a revised set of forecasted statements for 2003. We do not show the new financial statements, but the revised ratios are shown in the third column of Table 17-6. You can see the details in the chapter spreadsheet model, 17MODEL.xls. Here are the highlights of the revised forecast:

1. The reduction in operating costs improved the 2003 NOPAT, or net operating profit after taxes, by $23.9 million. Even more impressive, the improvements in the receivables policy and in inventory management reduced receivables and inventories by $148.5 million. The net result of the increase in NOPAT and the reduction of current assets was a very large increase in free cash flow for 2003, from a previously estimated $7.3 million to $179.7 million. Although we do not show it, the improvements in operations also led to significantly higher free cash flow for each year in the whole forecast period.

2. The profit margin improved to 4.7 percent. However, the firm's profit margin still lagged the industry average because its high debt ratio results in higher-than-average interest payments.

3. The increase in the profit margin resulted in an increase in projected retained earnings. More importantly, by tightening inventory controls and reducing the days sales outstanding, Allied projected a reduction in inventories and receivables. Taken together, these actions resulted in a *negative* AFN of $60 million, which means that Allied would actually generate $60 million more from internal operations during 2003 than it needs for new assets. All of this $60 million of surplus funds would be used to reduce short-term debt, which would lead to a decrease in the forecasted debt ratio from 51.8 to 49.9 percent. The debt ratio would still be well above the industry average, but this is a step in the right direction.

4. The indicated changes would also affect Allied's current ratio, which would improve from 3.1 to 3.5.

5. These actions would also raise the rate of return on assets from 5.9 to 7.5 percent, and they would boost the return on equity from 12.8 to 15.6 percent, which is even higher than the industry average.

Although Allied's managers believe that the revised forecast is achievable, they are not sure of this. Accordingly, they wanted to know how variations in sales would

---

[6] Receivables and inventory management were discussed in detail in Chapter 15.

affect the forecast. Therefore, a spreadsheet model was run using several different sales growth rates, and the results were analyzed to see how the ratios would change under different growth scenarios. To illustrate, if the sales growth rate increased from 10 to 20 percent, the additional funding requirement would change dramatically, from a $60 million *surplus* to an $87 million *shortfall*.

The spreadsheet model was also used to evaluate dividend policy. If Allied decided to reduce its dividend growth rate, then additional funds would be generated, and those funds could be invested in plant, equipment, and inventories; used to reduce debt; or used to repurchase stock.

The model was also used to evaluate financing alternatives. For example, Allied could use the forecasted $60 million of surplus funds to retire long-term bonds rather than to reduce short-term debt. Under this financing alternative, the current ratio would drop from 3.5 to 2.9, but the firm's interest coverage ratio would rise, assuming that the firm's long-term debt carries a higher interest rate than its notes payable.

We see, then, that forecasting is an iterative process, both in the way the financial statements are generated and the way the financial plan is developed. For planning purposes, the financial staff develops a preliminary forecast based on a continuation of past policies and trends. This provides a starting point, or "baseline" forecast. Next, the projections are modified to see what effects alternative operating plans would have on the firm's earnings and financial condition. This results in a revised forecast. Then alternative operating plans are examined under different sales growth scenarios, and the model is used to evaluate both dividend policy and capital structure decisions.

The spreadsheet model can be used to analyze alternative working capital policies—that is, to see the effects of changes in cash management, credit policy, inventory policy, and the use of different types of short-term credit. We will examine Allied's working capital policy within the framework of the company's financial model later, but in the remainder of this chapter, we consider some other aspects of the financial forecasting process.

FORECASTING FREE CASH FLOW

The spreadsheet model can also be used to estimate Allied's free cash flow. Recall from Chapter 2, Equation 2-7, that free cash flow is calculated as follows:

$$\text{FCF} = \text{Operating cash flow} - \text{Gross investment in operating capital.}$$

Alternatively, FCF can be calculated using Equation 2-7a:

$$\text{FCF} = \text{NOPAT} - \text{Net investment in operating capital.}$$

Recall also that free cash flow represents the amount of cash generated in a given year minus the amount of cash needed to finance the additional capital expenditures and operating working capital needed to support the firm's growth.

The detailed spreadsheet model is not provided in the text, but its key outputs were shown in the "Model Outputs" section back in Table 17-6. We see that before the operating changes Allied forecasted a slight increase in NOPAT (net operating profit after taxes), but it projected a very large increase in net operating working capital and in total operating capital. The net result is a very low level of free cash flow, only $7.3 million. Although we do not show projections of the full financial statements for all eight years of the explicit forecast horizon, here are the initially projected free cash flows (FCFs):

YEARS	2003	2004	2005	2006	2007	2008	2009	2010
FCF	7.3	8.4	8.9	9.8	34.6	63.7	96.9	103.7

As we saw in Chapter 8, investors and financial managers use such forecasts to estimate the firm's stock price. Thus, this model helps managers measure the expected changes in the determinants of value under different strategic and operating alternatives.

SELF-TEST QUESTIONS

What is the AFN, and how is the percent of sales method used to estimate it?

Why do accounts payable and accrued liabilities provide "spontaneous funds" to a growing firm?

Would payables and accrued liabilities provide spontaneous funds to a no-growth firm? To one that is declining?

Why do retained earnings not grow at the same rate as sales? In answering this question, think about a firm whose sales are not growing ($g = 0\%$), but that is profitable and does not pay out all of its earnings as dividends.

THE AFN FORMULA

Most firms forecast their capital requirements by constructing pro forma income statements and balance sheets as described above. However, if the ratios are expected to remain constant, then the following formula can be used to forecast financial requirements. Here we apply the formula to Allied based on the 2002 data, not the revised data, as the revised data do not assume constant ratios.

$$\begin{matrix} \text{Additional} & & \text{Required} & & \text{Spontaneous} & & \text{Increase in} \\ \text{funds} & = & \text{increase} & - & \text{increase in} & - & \text{retained} \\ \text{needed} & & \text{in assets} & & \text{liabilities} & & \text{earnings} \end{matrix}$$

$$\text{AFN} = (A^*/S_0)\Delta S - (L^*/S_0)\Delta S - MS_1(RR). \qquad (17\text{-}1)$$

Here

AFN = additional funds needed.

A^* = assets that are tied directly to sales, hence which must increase if sales are to increase. Note that A designates total assets and A^* designates those assets that must increase if sales are to increase. When the firm is operating at full capacity, as is the case here, $A^* = A$. Often, though, A^* and A are not equal, and either the equation must be modified or we must use the projected financial statement method.

S_0 = sales during the last year.

A^*/S_0 = percentage of required assets to sales, which also shows the required dollar increase in assets per \$1 increase in sales. A^*/S_0 = \$2,000/\$3,000 = 0.6667 for Allied. Thus, for every \$1 increase in sales, assets must increase by about 67 cents.

L^* = liabilities that increase spontaneously. L^* is normally much less than total liabilities (L). Spontaneous liabilities include accounts payable and accrued liabilities, but not bank loans and bonds.

L^*/S_0 = liabilities that increase spontaneously as a percentage of sales, or spontaneously generated financing per \$1 increase in sales. L^*/S_0 = (\$60 + \$140)/\$3,000 = 0.0667 for Allied. Thus, every \$1 increase in sales generates about 7 cents of spontaneous financing.

S_1 = total sales projected for next year. Note that S_0 designates last year's sales, and S_1 = \$3,300 million for Allied.

ΔS = change in sales = $S_1 - S_0$ = \$3,300 million − \$3,000 million = \$300 million for Allied.

M = profit margin, or profit per \$1 of sales. M = \$114/\$3,000 = 0.0380 for Allied. So, Allied earns 3.8 cents on each dollar of sales.

RR = retention ratio, which is the percentage of net income that is retained. For Allied, RR = \$56/\$114 = 0.491. RR is also equal to 1 − payout ratio, since the retention ratio and the payout ratio must total to 1.0 = 100%.

Inserting values for Allied into Equation 17-1, we find the additional funds needed to be \$118 million:

$$
\begin{aligned}
\text{AFN} &= \begin{matrix} \text{Required} \\ \text{asset} \\ \text{increase} \end{matrix} - \begin{matrix} \text{Spontaneous} \\ \text{liability} \\ \text{increase} \end{matrix} - \begin{matrix} \text{Increase} \\ \text{in retained} \\ \text{earnings} \end{matrix} \\
&= 0.667\,(\Delta S) - 0.067(\Delta S) - 0.038(S_1)(0.491) \\
&= 0.667(\$300 \text{ million}) - 0.067(\$300 \text{ million}) - 0.038(\$3,300 \text{ million})(0.491) \\
&= \$200 \text{ million} - \$20 \text{ million} - \$62 \text{ million} \\
&= \$118 \text{ million.}
\end{aligned}
$$

To increase sales by \$300 million, the formula suggests that Allied must increase assets by \$200 million. The \$200 million of new assets must be financed in some manner. Of the total, \$20 million will come from a spontaneous increase in liabilities, while another \$62 million will be obtained from retained earnings. The remaining \$118 million must be raised from external sources. This value is an approximation, but it is only slightly different from the initial AFN figure (\$112 million) we developed in Table 17-5.[7]

This equation shows that external financing requirements depend on five key factors:

- *Sales growth* (ΔS). Rapidly growing companies require large increases in assets, other things held constant.
- *Capital intensity* (A^*/S_0). The amount of assets required per dollar of sales, A^*/S_0 in Equation 17-1, is called the **capital intensity ratio.** This ratio has a major effect on capital requirements. Companies with higher assets-to-sales ratios

Capital Intensity Ratio
The amount of assets required per dollar of sales (A^*/S_0).

---

[7] If Table 17-5 had been extended to include financing feedbacks, the forecasted AFN would have been \$119 million, which is very close to the formula AFN.

require more assets for a given increase in sales, hence a greater need for external financing.

■ *Spontaneous liabilities-to-sales ratio (L*/S₀)*. Companies that spontaneously generate a large amount of liabilities from accounts payable and accrued liabilities will have a relatively small need for external financing.

■ *Profit margin (M)*. The higher the profit margin, the larger the net income available to support increases in assets, hence the lower the need for external financing.

■ *Retention ratio (RR)*. Companies that retain more of their earnings as opposed to paying them out as dividends will generate more retained earnings and thus have less need for external financing.

Note that Equation 17-1 provides an accurate forecast only for companies whose ratios are all expected to remain constant. It is useful to obtain a quick "back of the envelope" estimate of external financing requirements for nonconstant ratio companies, but in the planning process one should calculate the actual additional funds needed by the projected financial statement method. The analysis becomes much more complex when we allow for the possibility that the balance sheet ratios may change over time. Web Appendix 17B, "Forecasting Financial Requirements When the Balance Sheet Ratios are Subject to Change," considers these issues in more detail.

SELF-TEST QUESTIONS

If all ratios are expected to remain constant, a formula can be used to forecast AFN. Give the formula and briefly explain it.

How do the following factors affect external capital requirements?

(1) Retention ratio.

(2) Capital intensity.

(3) Profit margin.

(4) Dividend payout ratio.

(5) Sales growth.

OTHER TECHNIQUES FOR FORECASTING FINANCIAL STATEMENTS

If the $A*/S_0$ ratio is not constant, then constant growth forecasting methods as discussed thus far should not be used. Rather, other techniques must be used to forecast asset levels and additional financing requirements. Two of these methods—linear regression and excess capacity adjustments—are discussed in the following sections.

SIMPLE LINEAR REGRESSION

If we assume that the relationship between a certain type of asset and sales is linear, then we can use simple linear regression techniques to estimate the requirements for that type of asset for any given sales increase. For example, Allied's sales, inventories, and receivables during the last five years are shown in the lower section of Figure 17-3, and both current asset items are plotted in the upper section as a scatter diagram versus sales. Estimated regression equations, determined using a financial calculator or a spreadsheet, are also shown with each graph. For example, the estimated relationship between inventories and sales (in millions of dollars) is

$$\text{Inventories} = -\$35.7 + 0.186(\text{Sales}).$$

The plotted points are not very close to the regression line, which indicates that changes in inventory are affected by factors other than changes in sales. In fact, the correlation coefficient between inventories and sales is only 0.71, indicating that there is only a moderate linear relationship between these two variables. Still, the regression relationship is strong enough to provide a reasonable basis for forecasting the target inventory level, as described below.

We can use the regression relationship between inventories and sales to forecast 2003 inventory levels. Since 2003 sales are projected at $3,300 million, 2003 inventories should be $578 million:

$$\text{Inventories} = -\$35.7 + 0.186(\$3,300) = \$578 \text{ million}.$$

This is $99 million less than the preliminary forecast based on the projected financial statement method. The difference occurs because the projected financial statement method assumed that the ratio of inventories to sales would remain constant, when in fact it will probably decline. Note also that although our graphs show linear relationships, we could have easily used a nonlinear regression model had such a relationship been indicated.

FIGURE 17-3   **Allied Food Products: Linear Regression Models (Millions of Dollars)**

YEAR	SALES	INVENTORIES	ACCOUNTS RECEIVABLE
1998	$2,058	$387	$268
1999	2,534	398	297
2000	2,472	409	304
2001	2,850	415	315
2002	3,000	615	375

After analyzing the regression results, Allied's managers decided that a new forecast of AFN should be developed assuming a lower days sales outstanding and a higher inventory turnover ratio. Management recognized that the 2002 levels of these accounts were above the industry averages, hence that the preliminary results projected for 2003 back in Table 17-6 were unnecessarily high. When simple linear regression was used to forecast the receivables and inventories accounts, this caused the 2003 levels to reflect both the average relationships of these accounts to sales over the five-year period and the trend in the variables' values. In contrast, the projected financial statement method we developed earlier assumed that the nonoptimal 2002 relationships would remain constant in 2003 and beyond. These new assumptions were largely responsible for the improved forecasts shown in Column 3 of Table 17-6.

EXCESS CAPACITY ADJUSTMENTS

Consider again the Allied example set forth in Tables 17-4 and 17-5, but now assume that excess capacity exists in fixed assets. Specifically, assume that fixed assets in 2002 were being utilized to only 96 percent of capacity. If fixed assets had been used to full capacity, 2002 sales could have been as high as $3,125 million versus the $3,000 million in actual sales:

$$\begin{array}{l} \text{Full} \\ \text{capacity} \\ \text{sales} \end{array} = \frac{\text{Actual sales}}{\begin{array}{c}\text{Percentage of capacity}\\\text{at which fixed assets}\\\text{were operated}\end{array}} = \frac{\$3{,}000 \text{ million}}{0.96} = \$3{,}125 \text{ million.} \quad \textbf{(17-2)}$$

This suggests that Allied's target fixed assets/sales ratio should be 32 percent rather than 33.3 percent:

$$\text{Target fixed assets/Sales} = \frac{\text{Actual fixed assets}}{\text{Full capacity sales}} \quad \textbf{(17-3)}$$

$$= \frac{\$1{,}000}{\$3{,}125} = 0.32 = 32\%.$$

Therefore, if sales are to increase to $3,300 million, then fixed assets would have to increase to $1,056 million:

$$\begin{array}{l}\text{Required level}\\\text{of fixed assets}\end{array} = (\text{Target fixed assets/Sales})(\text{Projected sales}) \quad \textbf{(17-4)}$$

$$= 0.32(\$3{,}300) = \$1{,}056 \text{ million.}$$

We previously forecasted that Allied would need to increase fixed assets at the same rate as sales, or by 10 percent. That meant an increase from $1,000 million to $1,100 million, or by $100 million. Now we see that the actual required increase is only from $1,000 million to $1,056 million, or by $56 million. Thus, the capacity-adjusted forecast is $100 million − $56 million = $44 million less than the earlier forecast. With a smaller fixed asset requirement, the projected AFN would decline from an estimated $112 million to $112 million − $44 million = $68 million.

Note also that when excess capacity exists, sales can grow to the capacity sales as determined above with no increase whatever in fixed assets, but sales beyond that level will require fixed asset additions as calculated in our example. The same situation could occur with respect to inventories, and the required additions would be determined in exactly the same manner as for fixed assets. Theoretically, the same situation could occur with other types of assets. However, as a practical matter excess capacity normally exists only with respect to fixed assets and inventories.

SELF-TEST QUESTION

If excess capacity exists, how will that affect the AFN?

TYING IT ALL TOGETHER

This chapter described techniques for forecasting financial statements, which is a crucial part of the financial planning process. Both investors and corporations regularly use forecasting techniques to help value a company's stock, to estimate the benefits of potential projects, and to estimate how changes in capital structure, dividend policy, and working capital policy will influence shareholder value. The key concepts covered are listed below.

- To make their firms more valuable, managers must identify, evaluate, and implement projects that meet or exceed investor expectations. However, value creation for a firm is impossible unless a company has a well-articulated **strategic plan.**
- The firm's strategic plan begins with a **mission statement.**
- Key elements of a firm's strategic plan include **corporate purpose, corporate scope, corporate objectives,** and **corporate strategies.**
- **Operating plans** provide detailed implementation guidance to help meet corporate objectives.
- The **financial planning process** can be divided into six steps: (1) project financial statements and analyze them; (2) determine the funds needed to support the 5-year plan; (3) forecast funds availability over the next five years; (4) establish and maintain a system of controls for the allocation and use of funds; (5) develop procedures for adjusting the basic plan if the economic forecasts don't materialize; and (6) establish a performance-based management compensation system.
- Virtually all corporate forecasts are made using **computerized forecasting models** based on spreadsheet programs. Spreadsheets have two major advantages over pencil-and-paper calculations: (1) Spreadsheet models are faster than by-hand calculations and (2) models can be instantaneously recalculated making it easier to determine the effects of changes in variables.
- **Financial forecasting** generally begins with a forecast of the firm's sales, in terms of both units and dollars.
- Either the **projected,** or **pro forma, financial statement method** or the **AFN formula method** can be used to forecast financial requirements. The financial statement method is more reliable, and it also provides ratios that can be used to evaluate alternative business plans.

- A firm can determine its **additional funds needed (AFN)** by estimating the amount of new assets necessary to support the forecasted level of sales and then subtracting from that amount the spontaneous funds that will be generated from operations. The firm can then plan how to raise the AFN most efficiently.

- The **higher a firm's sales growth rate,** the **greater** will be its need for additional financing. In addition, the **greater the firm's capital intensity ratio,** the **greater** the need for external financing. Similarly, the **smaller its retention ratio,** the **greater** its need for additional funds. However, the **higher the profit margin,** the **lower** the need for external financing.

- **Linear regression** and **excess capacity adjustments** can be used to forecast asset requirements in situations in which assets are not expected to grow at the same rate as sales.

The type of forecasting described in this chapter is important for several reasons. First, if the projected operating results are unsatisfactory, management can "go back to the drawing board," reformulate its plans, and develop more reasonable targets for the coming year. Second, it is possible that the funds required to meet the sales forecast simply cannot be obtained. If so, it is obviously better to know this in advance and to scale back the projected level of operations than to suddenly run out of cash and have operations grind to a halt. And third, even if the required funds can be raised, it is desirable to plan for their acquisition well in advance.

QUESTIONS

17-1 Certain liability and net worth items generally increase spontaneously with increases in sales. Put a check ($\checkmark$) by those items that typically increase spontaneously:

Accounts payable	_____
Notes payable to banks	_____
Accrued wages	_____
Accrued taxes	_____
Mortgage bonds	_____
Common stock	_____
Retained earnings	_____

17-2 The following equation can, under certain assumptions, be used to forecast financial requirements:

$$AFN = (A^*/S_0)(\Delta S) - (L^*/S_0)(\Delta S) - MS_1(RR).$$

Under what conditions does the equation give satisfactory predictions, and when should it *not* be used?

17-3 Assume that an average firm in the office supply business has a 6 percent after-tax profit margin, a 40 percent debt/assets ratio, a total assets turnover of 2 times, and a dividend payout ratio of 40 percent. Is it true that if such a firm is to have *any* sales growth ($g > 0$), it will be forced either to borrow or to sell common stock (that is, it will need some nonspontaneous, external capital even if g is very small)?

17-4 Is it true that computerized corporate planning models were a fad during the 1990s but, because of a need for flexibility in corporate planning, they have been dropped by most firms in the millennium?

17-5 Suppose a firm makes the following policy changes. If the change means that external, non-spontaneous financial requirements (AFN) will increase, indicate this by a (+); indicate a decrease by a (−); and indicate indeterminate or no effect by a (0). Think in terms of the immediate, short-run effect on funds requirements.

a. The dividend payout ratio is increased. _____

b. The firm contracts to buy, rather than make, certain components used in its products. _____

c. The firm decides to pay all suppliers on delivery, rather than after a 30-day delay, to take advantage of discounts for rapid payment. _____

d. The firm begins to sell on credit (previously all sales had been on a cash basis). _____

e. The firm's profit margin is eroded by increased competition; sales are steady. _____

f. Advertising expenditures are stepped up. _____

g. A decision is made to substitute long-term mortgage bonds for short-term bank loans. _____

h. The firm begins to pay employees on a weekly basis (previously it had paid employees at the end of each month). _____

SELF-TEST PROBLEMS (SOLUTIONS APPEAR IN APPENDIX B)

ST-1
Key terms

Define each of the following terms:
a. Mission statement
b. Sales forecast
c. Percent of sales method
d. Spontaneously generated funds
e. Pro forma financial statement
f. Additional funds needed (AFN); AFN formula
g. Capital intensity ratio

ST-2
Growth rate

Weatherford Industries Inc. has the following ratios: $A^*/S_0 = 1.6$; $L^*/S_0 = 0.4$; profit margin = 0.10; and retention ratio = 0.55, or 55 percent. Sales last year were $100 million. Assuming that these ratios will remain constant, use the AFN formula to determine the maximum growth rate Weatherford can achieve without having to employ nonspontaneous external funds.

ST-3
Additional funds needed

Suppose Weatherford's financial consultants report (1) that the inventory turnover ratio is sales/inventory = 3 times versus an industry average of 4 times and (2) that Weatherford could reduce inventories and thus raise its turnover to 4 without affecting sales, the profit margin, or the other asset turnover ratios. Under these conditions, use the AFN formula to determine the amount of additional funds Weatherford would require during each of the next 2 years if sales grew at a rate of 20 percent per year.

STARTER PROBLEMS

Carter Corporation's sales are expected to increase from $5 million in 2002 to $6 million in 2003, or by 20 percent. Its assets totaled $3 million at the end of 2002. Carter is at full capacity, so its assets must grow in proportion to projected sales. At the end of 2002, current liabilities are $1 million, consisting of $250,000 of accounts payable, $500,000 of notes payable, and $250,000 of accrued liabilities. The after-tax profit margin is forecasted to be 5 percent, and the forecasted retention ratio is 30 percent. Use this information to answer Problems 17-1, 17-2, and 17-3.

17-1
AFN formula

Use the AFN formula to forecast Carter's additional funds needed for the coming year.

17-2
AFN formula

What would the additional funds needed be if the company's year-end 2002 assets had been $4 million? Assume that all other numbers are the same. Why is this AFN different from the one you found in Problem 17-1? Is the company's "capital intensity" the same or different?

17-3
AFN formula

Return to the assumption that the company had $3 million in assets at the end of 2002, but now assume that the company pays no dividends. Under these assumptions, what would be the additional funds needed for the coming year? Why is this AFN different from the one you found in Problem 17-1?

17-4
Linear regression

Jasper Furnishings has $300 million in sales. The company expects that its sales will increase 12 percent this year. Jasper's CFO uses a simple linear regression to forecast the company's inventory level for a given level of projected sales. On the basis of recent history, the estimated relationship between inventories and sales (in millions of dollars) is

$$\text{Inventories} = \$25 + 0.125(\text{Sales}).$$

Given the estimated sales forecast and the estimated relationship between inventories and sales, what is your forecast of the company's year-end inventory turnover ratio?

17-5
Excess capacity
Walter Industries has $5 billion in sales and $1.7 billion in fixed assets. Currently, the company's fixed assets are operating at 90 percent of capacity.
a. What level of sales could Walter Industries have obtained if it had been operating at full capacity?
b. What is Walter's target fixed assets/sales ratio?
c. If Walter's sales increase 12 percent, how large of an increase in fixed assets would the company need in order to meet its target fixed assets/sales ratio?

17-6
Pro forma income statement
Austin Grocers recently reported the following income statement (in millions of dollars):

Sales	$700
Operating costs	500
EBIT	$200
Interest	40
EBT	$160
Taxes (40%)	64
Net income	$ 96
Dividends	$ 32
Addition to retained earnings	$ 64

This year the company is forecasting a 25 percent increase in sales, and it expects that its year-end operating costs will equal 70 percent of sales. Austin's tax rate, interest expense, and dividend payout ratio are all expected to remain constant.
a. What is Austin's projected 2003 net income?
b. What is the expected growth rate in Austin's dividends?

EXAM-TYPE PROBLEMS

The problems included in this section are set up in such a way that they could be used as multiple-choice exam problems.

17-7
Pro forma income statement
At the end of last year, Roberts Inc. reported the following income statement (in millions of dollars):

Sales	$3,000
Operating costs excluding depreciation	2,450
EBITDA	$ 550
Depreciation	250
EBIT	$ 300
Interest	125
EBT	$ 175
Taxes (40%)	70
Net income	$ 105

Looking ahead to the following year, the company's CFO has assembled the following information:

■ Year-end sales are expected to be 10 percent higher than the $3 billion in sales generated last year.
■ Year-end operating costs excluding depreciation are expected to equal 80 percent of year-end sales.

- Depreciation is expected to increase at the same rate as sales.
- Interest costs are expected to remain unchanged.
- The tax rate is expected to remain at 40 percent.

On the basis of this information, what will be the forecast for Roberts' year-end net income?

17-8
Long-term financing needed

At year-end 2002, total assets for Ambrose Inc. were $1.2 million and accounts payable were $375,000. Sales, which in 2002 were $2.5 million, are expected to increase by 25 percent in 2003. Total assets and accounts payable are proportional to sales, and that relationship will be maintained. Ambrose typically uses no current liabilities other than accounts payable. Common stock amounted to $425,000 in 2002, and retained earnings were $295,000. Ambrose plans to sell new common stock in the amount of $75,000. The firm's profit margin on sales is 6 percent; 60 percent of earnings will be retained.
a. What was Ambrose's total debt in 2002?
b. How much new, long-term debt financing will be needed in 2003? (Hint: AFN − New stock = New long-term debt.)

17-9
Sales increase

Pierce Furnishings generated $2.0 million in sales during 2002, and its year-end total assets were $1.5 million. Also, at year-end 2002, current liabilities were $500,000, consisting of $200,000 of notes payable, $200,000 of accounts payable, and $100,000 of accrued liabilities. Looking ahead to 2003, the company estimates that its assets must increase by 75 cents for every $1 increase in sales. Pierce's profit margin is 5 percent, and its retention ratio is 40 percent. How large a sales increase can the company achieve without having to raise funds externally?

17-10
Linear regression and receivables

Edwards Industries has $320 million in sales. The company expects that its sales will increase 12 percent this year. Edwards' CFO uses a simple linear regression to forecast the company's receivables level for a given level of projected sales. On the basis of recent history, the estimated relationship between receivables and sales (in millions of dollars) is

$$\text{Receivables} = \$9.25 + 0.07(\text{Sales}).$$

Given the estimated sales forecast and the estimated relationship between receivables and sales, what is your forecast of the company's year-end days' sales outstanding (DSO) ratio? Assume that DSO is calculated on the basis of a 365-day year.

17-11
Linear regression and inventories

Charlie's Cycles Inc. has $110 million in sales. The company expects that its sales will increase 5 percent this year. Charlie's CFO uses a simple linear regression to forecast the company's inventory level for a given level of projected sales. On the basis of recent history, the estimated relationship between inventories and sales (in millions of dollars) is

$$\text{Inventories} = \$9 + 0.0875(\text{Sales}).$$

Given the estimated sales forecast and the estimated relationship between inventories and sales, what is your forecast of the company's year-end inventory turnover ratio?

17-12
Excess capacity adjustments

Edney Manufacturing Company has $2 billion in sales and $0.6 billion in fixed assets. Currently, the company's fixed assets are operating at 80 percent of capacity.
a. What level of sales could Edney have obtained if it had been operating at full capacity?
b. What is Edney's target fixed assets/sales ratio?
c. If Edney's sales increase 30 percent, how large of an increase in fixed assets would the company need in order to meet its target fixed assets/sales ratio?

17-13
Pro forma income statement

Kathryn's Cookies Incorporated (KCI) recently reported the following 2002 income statement (in millions of dollars):

Sales	$1,528
Operating costs	933
EBIT	$ 595
Interest	95
EBT	$ 500
Taxes (40%)	200
Net income	$ 300
Dividends (25%)	$ 75
Addition to retained earnings	$ 225

This year the company is forecasting a 20 percent increase in sales, and it expects that its year-end operating costs will equal 60 percent of sales. KCI's tax rate, interest expense, and dividend payout ratio are all expected to remain constant.

a. What is KCI's projected 2003 net income (in millions of dollars)?

b. What is the expected growth rate in KCI's dividends?

PROBLEMS

17-14
Pro forma statements and ratios

Tozer Computers makes bulk purchases of small computers, stocks them in conveniently located warehouses, and ships them to its chain of retail stores. Tozer's balance sheet as of December 31, 2002, is shown here (in millions of dollars):

Cash	$ 3.5	Accounts payable	$ 9.0
Receivables	26.0	Notes payable	18.0
Inventories	58.0	Accrued liabilities	8.5
Total current assets	$ 87.5	Total current liabilities	$ 35.5
Net fixed assets	35.0	Mortgage loan	6.0
		Common stock	15.0
		Retained earnings	66.0
Total assets	$122.5	Total liabilities and equity	$122.5

Sales for 2002 were $350 million, while net income for the year was $10.5 million. Tozer paid dividends of $4.2 million to common stockholders. The firm is operating at full capacity. Assume that all ratios remain constant.

a. If sales are projected to increase by $70 million, or 20 percent, during 2003, use the AFN equation to determine Tozer's projected external capital requirements.

b. Construct Tozer's pro forma balance sheet for December 31, 2003. Assume that all external capital requirements are met by bank loans and are reflected in notes payable.

c. Now calculate the following ratios, based on your projected December 31, 2003, balance sheet. Tozer's 2002 ratios and industry average ratios are shown here for comparison:

	TOZER COMPUTERS		INDUSTRY AVERAGE
	12/31/03	12/31/02	12/31/02
Current ratio	_____	2.5×	3×
Debt/total assets	_____	33.9%	30%
Rate of return on equity	_____	13.0%	12%

d. Now assume that Tozer grows by the same $70 million but that the growth is spread over 5 years—that is, that sales grow by $14 million each year.

(1) Calculate total additional financial requirements over the 5-year period. (Hint: Use 2002 ratios, $\Delta S = \$70$, but *total* sales for the 5-year period.)

(2) Construct a pro forma balance sheet as of December 31, 2007, using notes payable as the balancing item.

(3) Calculate the current ratio, total debt/total assets ratio, and rate of return on equity as of December 31, 2007. [Hint: Be sure to use *total sales*, which amount to $1,960 million, to calculate retained earnings, but 2007 profits to calculate the rate of return on equity—that is, return on equity = (2007 profits)/(12/31/07 equity).]

e. Do the plans outlined in parts b and/or d seem feasible to you? That is, do you think Tozer could borrow the required capital, and would the company be raising the odds on its bankruptcy to an excessive level in the event of some temporary misfortune?

17-15
Excess capacity

Krogh Lumber's 2002 financial statements are shown below.

Krogh Lumber: Balance Sheet as of December 31, 2002 (Thousands of Dollars)

Cash	$ 1,800	Accounts payable	$ 7,200
Receivables	10,800	Notes payable	3,472
Inventories	12,600	Accrued liabilities	2,520
Total current assets	$25,200	Total current liabilities	$13,192
		Mortgage bonds	5,000
		Common stock	2,000
Net fixed assets	21,600	Retained earnings	26,608
Total assets	$46,800	Total liabilities and equity	$46,800

Krogh Lumber: Income Statement for December 31, 2002 (Thousands of Dollars)

Sales	$36,000
Operating costs	30,783
Earnings before interest and taxes	$ 5,217
Interest	1,017
Earnings before taxes	$ 4,200
Taxes (40%)	1,680
Net income	$ 2,520
Dividends (60%)	$ 1,512
Addition to retained earnings	1,008

a. Assume that the company was operating at full capacity in 2002 with regard to all items *except* fixed assets; fixed assets in 2002 were being utilized to only 75 percent of capacity. By what percentage could 2003 sales increase over 2002 sales without the need for an increase in fixed assets?

b. Now suppose 2003 sales increase by 25 percent over 2002 sales. How much additional external capital will be required? Assume that Krogh cannot sell any fixed assets. (Hint: Use the projected financial statement method to develop a pro forma income statement and balance sheet as in Tables 17-4 and 17-5.) Assume that any required financing is borrowed as notes payable. Use a pro forma income statement to determine the addition to retained earnings. (Another hint: Notes payable = $6,021.)

c. Suppose the industry average DSO and inventory turnover ratio are 90 days and 3.33, respectively, and that Krogh Lumber matches these figures in 2003 and then uses the funds released to reduce equity. (It pays a special dividend out of retained earnings.) What would this do to the rate of return on year-end 2003 equity? Use the balance sheet and income statement as developed in part b.

17-16
Additional funds needed

Morrissey Technologies Inc.'s 2002 financial statements are shown below.

Morrisey Technologies Inc.: Balance Sheet as of December 31, 2002

Cash	$ 180,000	Accounts payable	$ 360,000
Receivables	360,000	Notes payable	156,000
Inventories	720,000	Accrued liabilities	180,000
Total current assets	$1,260,000	Total current liabilities	$ 696,000
Fixed assets	1,440,000	Common stock	1,800,000
		Retained earnings	204,000
Total assets	$2,700,000	Total liabilities and equity	$2,700,000

Morrisey Techonologies Inc.: Income Statement for December 31, 2002

Sales	$3,600,000
Operating costs	3,279,720
EBIT	$ 320,280
Interest	20,280
EBT	$ 300,000
Taxes (40%)	120,000
Net Income	$ 180,000

PER SHARE DATA:

Common stock price	$24.00
Earnings per share (EPS)	$ 1.80
Dividends per share (DPS)	$ 1.08

a. Suppose that in 2003 sales increase by 10 percent over 2002 sales and that 2003 DPS will increase to $1.12. Construct the pro forma financial statements using the projected financial statement method. Use AFN to balance the pro forma balance sheet. How much additional capital will be required? Assume the firm operated at full capacity in 2002.

b. If the profit margin were to remain at 5 percent and the dividend payout rate were to remain at 60 percent, at what growth rate in sales would the additional financing requirements be exactly zero? (Hint: Set AFN equal to zero and solve for g.)

17-17
External financing requirements

The 2002 balance sheet and income statement for the Lewis Company are shown below.

Lewis Company: Balance Sheet as of December 31, 2002 (Thousands of Dollars)

Cash	$ 80	Accounts payable	$ 160
Accounts receivable	240	Accrued liabilities	40
Inventories	720	Notes payable	252
Total current assets	$1,040	Total current liabilities	$ 452
Fixed assets	3,200	Long-term debt	1,244
		Total debt	$1,696
		Common stock	1,605
		Retained earnings	939
Total assets	$4,240	Total liabilities and equity	$4,240

Lewis Company: Income Statement for December 31, 2002 (Thousands of Dollars)

Sales	$8,000
Operating costs	7,450
EBIT	$ 550
Interest	150
EBT	$ 400
Taxes (40%)	160
Net income	$ 240

PER SHARE DATA:

Common stock price	$16.96
Earnings per share (EPS)	$ 1.60
Dividends per share (DPS)	$ 1.04

a. The firm operated at full capacity in 2002. It expects sales to increase by 20 percent during 2003 and expects 2003 dividends per share to increase to $1.10. Use the projected financial statement method to determine how much outside financing is required, developing the firm's pro forma balance sheet and income statement, and use AFN as the balancing item.

b. If the firm must maintain a current ratio of 2.3 and a debt ratio of 40 percent, how much financing will be obtained using notes payable, long-term debt, and common stock?

SPREADSHEET PROBLEM

17-18
Forecasting financial statements

Laiho Industries' financial planners must forecast the company's financial results for the coming year. The forecast will be based on the percent of sales method, and any additional funds needed will be obtained by using a mix of notes payable, long-term debt, and common stock. No preferred stock will be issued. Data for the problem, including Laiho Industries' balance sheet and income statement, can be found in the spreadsheet problem for Chapter 2. Use these data to answer the following questions.

a. Laiho Industries has had the following sales since 1997. Assuming the historical trend continues, what will sales be in 2003?

YEAR	SALES
1997	$129,215,000
1998	180,901,000
1999	235,252,000
2000	294,065,000
2001	396,692,000
2002	455,150,000

Base your forecast on a spreadsheet regression analysis of the 1997–2002 sales, and include the summary output of the regression in your answer. By what percentage are sales predicted to increase in 2003 over 2002? Is the sales growth rate increasing or decreasing?

b. Laiho's management believes that the firm will actually experience a 20 percent increase in sales during 2003. Use the Chapter 2 spreadsheet problem to obtain the company's 2002 financial statements, then use those statements to construct 2003 pro forma financial statements. Assume that any additional funds needed (AFN) will be raised as follows: notes payable, 25 percent; long-term debt, 50 percent; and new common stock, 25 percent.

c. Now create a graph that shows the sensitivity of AFN to the sales growth rate. To make this graph, compare the AFN at sales growth rates of 5, 10, 15, 20, 25, and 30 percent.

d. Calculate net operating working capital (NOWC), total operating capital, NOPAT, and operating cash flow (OCF) for 2002 and 2003. Also, calculate the free cash flow (FCF) for 2003.

e. Suppose Laiho's management does not believe that accounts receivable and inventories should remain as a constant percentage of sales. Rather, they think that current assets should be predicted by using a regression analysis of recent levels versus sales. Use the following data on accounts receivable, inventories, and sales to run regressions to estimate the necessary levels of accounts receivable and inventories for 2003.

YEAR	SALES[a]	INVENTORIES[a]	A/R[a]
1997	$129,215	$12,341	$ 24,764
1998	180,901	16,763	39,589
1999	235,252	20,564	53,764
2000	294,065	25,324	64,864
2001	396,692	35,997	98,568
2002	455,150	38,444	103,365

[a] In thousands of dollars.

NEW WORLD CHEMICALS INC.

17-19 Financial Forecasting Sue Wilson, the new financial manager of New World Chemicals (NWC), a California producer of specialized chemicals for use in fruit orchards, must prepare a financial forecast for 2003. NWC's 2002 sales were $2 billion, and the marketing department is forecasting a 25 percent increase for 2003. Wilson thinks the company was operating at full capacity in 2002, but she is not sure about this. The 2002 financial statements, plus some other data, are given in Table IC17-1.

TABLE IC17-1	Financial Statements and Other Data on NWC (Millions of Dollars)

A. 2002 BALANCE SHEET

Cash and securities	$ 20	Accounts payable and accrued		
Accounts receivable	240	liabilities	$ 100	
Inventories	240	Notes payable	100	
Total current assets	$ 500	Total current liabilities	$ 200	
Net fixed assets	500	Long-term debt	100	
		Common stock	500	
		Retained earnings	200	
Total assets	$ 1,000	Total liabilities and equity	$1,000	

B. 2002 INCOME STATEMENT

Sales	$2,000.00
Less: Variable costs	1,200.00
Fixed costs	700.00
Earnings before interest and taxes (EBIT)	$ 100.00
Interest	16.00
Earnings before taxes (EBT)	$ 84.00
Taxes (40%)	33.60
Net income	$ 50.40
Dividends (30%)	$ 15.12
Addition to retained earnings	$ 35.28

C. KEY RATIOS

	NWC	INDUSTRY	COMMENT
Basic earning power	10.00%	20.00%	
Profit margin	2.52	4.00	
Return on equity	7.20	15.60	
Days sales outstanding (365 days)	43.80 days	32.00 days	
Inventory turnover	8.33×	11.00×	
Fixed assets turnover	4.00	5.00	
Total assets turnover	2.00	2.50	
Debt/assets	30.00%	36.00%	
Times interest earned	6.25×	9.40×	
Current ratio	2.50	3.00	
Payout ratio	30.00%	30.00%	

Assume that you were recently hired as Wilson's assistant, and your first major task is to help her develop the forecast. She asked you to begin by answering the following set of questions.

a. Assume (1) that NWC was operating at full capacity in 2002 with respect to all assets, (2) that all assets must grow proportionally with sales, (3) that accounts payable and accrued liabilities will also grow in proportion to sales, and (4) that the 2002 profit margin and dividend payout will be maintained. Under these conditions, what will the company's financial requirements be for the coming year? Use the AFN equation to answer this question.

b. Now estimate the 2003 financial requirements using the projected financial statement approach. Disregard the assumptions in part a, and now assume (1) that each type of asset, as well as payables, accrued liabilities, and fixed and variable costs, grow in proportion to sales; (2) that NWC was operating at full capacity; (3) that the payout ratio is held constant at 30 percent; and (4) that external funds needed are financed 50 percent by notes payable and 50 percent by long-term debt. (No new common stock will be issued.)

c. Why do the two methods produce somewhat different AFN forecasts? Which method provides the more accurate forecast?

d. Calculate NWC's forecasted ratios, and compare them with the company's 2002 ratios and with the industry averages. How does NWC compare with the average firm in its industry, and is the company expected to improve during the coming year?

e. Calculate NWC's free cash flow for 2003.

f. Suppose you now learn that NWC's 2002 receivables and inventories were in line with required levels, given the firm's credit and inventory policies, but that excess capacity existed with regard to fixed assets. Specifically, fixed assets were operated at only 75 percent of capacity.
   (1) What level of sales could have existed in 2002 with the available fixed assets? What would the fixed assets-to-sales ratio have been if NWC had been operating at full capacity?
   (2) How would the existence of excess capacity in fixed assets affect the additional funds needed during 2003?

g. Without actually working out the numbers, how would you expect the ratios to change in the situation where excess capacity in fixed assets exists? Explain your reasoning.

h. On the basis of comparisons between NWC's days sales outstanding (DSO) and inventory turnover ratios with the industry average figures, does it appear that NWC is operating efficiently with respect to its inventories and accounts receivable? If the company were able to bring these ratios into line with the industry averages, what effect would this have on its AFN and its financial ratios?

i. How would changes in these items affect the AFN? (1) The dividend payout ratio, (2) the profit margin, (3) the capital intensity ratio, and (4) if NWC begins buying from its suppliers on terms that permit it to pay after 60 days rather than after 30 days. (Consider each item separately and hold all other things constant.)

CYBER PROBLEM

Please go to our web site **http://brigham.swlearning.com** to access the Cyberproblems.

THOMSON™
ANALYTICS

With your Xtra! CD-ROM, access the Thomson Analytics Problems and use the Thomson Analytics Academic online database to work this chapter's problems.

DERIVATIVES AND RISK MANAGEMENT

18

PROCTER & GAMBLE

Consumer-products giant Procter & Gamble (P&G) has more than 5 billion customers in 130 countries. Its products include such well-known brands as Crest, Tide, Pampers, Folgers, and Charmin. Its products are consumed regularly, and its sales and earnings are fairly immune to changes in the economic cycle, making it a relatively low-risk company. Indeed, *Value Line* estimates that P&G's beta is 0.65, which suggests that its risk is 35 percent below that of an average stock.

Low risk does not mean no risk, and P&G's managers devote considerable time and effort to managing the risks it does face. For example, in a recent annual report management described in detail how the company deals with risks resulting from changes in interest rates, exchange rates, and commodity prices. In each instance, P&G first examines its net exposure to the risk factor, and then it uses derivatives such as options, futures, and swaps to hedge and thus reduce those risks. Here is its statement:

> Derivative positions are monitored using techniques including market value, sensitivity analysis, and value-at-risk modeling. The tests for interest rate and currency rate exposures are based on a Monte Carlo simulation value-at-risk model using a one-year horizon and

a 95 percent confidence level. The model incorporates the impact of correlation and diversification from holding multiple currency and interest rate instruments, and it assumes that financial returns are normally distributed.

It is clear from its annual report that P&G spends a lot of time and energy managing its various risks. However, nothing is completely riskless, and in some instances the steps taken to control risk have actually backfired. Indeed, P&G incurred huge losses in the 1990s on derivative transactions that were supposedly undertaken to reduce risk.

This chapter first discusses the various types of risks that companies face. Then it provides an overview of options, futures, and swaps, and describes how companies use these instruments to help minimize their risks.

Source: Procter & Gamble's 2001 Annual Report, 17.

In this chapter, we discuss risk management, a topic of increasing importance to financial managers. The term *risk management* can mean many things, but in business it involves identifying events that could have adverse financial consequences and then taking actions to prevent and/or minimize the damage caused by these events. Years ago, corporate risk managers dealt primarily with insurance — they made sure the firm was adequately insured against fire, theft, and other casualties, and that it had adequate liability coverage. More recently, the scope of risk management has been broadened to include such things as controlling the costs of key inputs like petroleum by purchasing oil futures, or protecting against changes in interest rates or exchange rates through dealings in the interest rate or foreign exchange markets. In addition, risk managers try to ensure that actions designed to hedge against risk are not actually increasing risks. ■

REASONS TO MANAGE RISK

We know that investors dislike risk. We also know that most investors hold well-diversified portfolios, so at least in theory the only "relevant risk" is systematic risk. Therefore, if you asked corporate executives what type of risk they were concerned about, you might expect the answer to be, "beta." However, this is almost certainly not the answer you would get. The most likely answer, if you asked a CEO to define risk, is something like this: "Risk is the possibility that our future earnings and free cash flows will be significantly lower than we expect." For example, consider Plastics Inc., which manufactures dashboards, interior door panels, and other plastic components used by auto companies. Petroleum is the key feedstock for plastic and thus makes up a large percentage of its costs. Plastics has a three-year contract with an auto company to deliver 500,000 door panels each year, at a price of $20 each. When the company signed this contract, oil sold for $19 per barrel, and oil was expected to stay at that level for the next three years. If oil prices fall, Plastics will have higher than expected profits and free cash flows, but if oil prices rise, profits will fall. Since Plastics' value depends on its profits and free cash flows, a change in the price of oil will cause stockholders to earn either more or less than they anticipated.

Now suppose Plastics announces that it plans to lock in a three-year supply of oil at a guaranteed price of $19 per barrel, and the cost of getting the guarantee is zero. Would that cause its stock price to rise? At first glance, it seems that the answer should be yes, but maybe that's not correct. Recall that the long-run value of a stock depends on the present value of its expected future free cash flows, discounted at the weighted average cost of capital (WACC). Locking in the cost of oil will cause an increase in Plastics' stock price if and only if (1) it causes the expected future free cash flows to increase or (2) it causes the WACC to decline.

Consider first the free cash flows. Before the announcement of guaranteed oil costs, investors had formed an estimate of the expected future free cash flows, based on an expected oil price of $19 per barrel. Therefore, while locking in the cost of oil at $19 per barrel will lower the riskiness of the expected future free cash flows, it will not change the *size* of these cash flows, because investors already expected a price of $19 per barrel.

Now what about the WACC? It will change only if locking in the cost of oil causes a change in the cost of debt or equity, or the target capital structure. Assuming the foreseeable increases in the price of oil were not enough to cause bankruptcy, Plastics' cost of debt should not change, and neither should its target capital structure. Regarding the cost of equity, recall from Chapter 5 that most investors hold well-diversified portfolios, which means that the cost of equity should depend only on systematic risk. Moreover, even though an increase in oil prices would have a negative effect on Plastics' stock price, it would not have a negative effect on all stocks. Indeed, oil producers should have higher than expected returns and stock prices. Assuming that Plastics' investors hold well-diversified portfolios, including stocks of oil-producing companies, there would not appear to be much reason to expect its cost of equity to decrease. The bottom line is this: If Plastics' expected future cash flows and WACC will not change significantly due to an elimination of the risk of oil price increases, then neither should the value of its stock.

We discuss futures contracts and hedging in detail in the next section, but for now let's assume that Plastics has *not* locked in oil prices. Therefore, if oil prices increase, its stock price will fall. However, its stockholders know this, so they can build portfolios that contain oil futures whose values will rise or fall with oil prices and thus offset changes in the price of Plastics' stock. By choosing the correct amount of futures contracts, investors can thus "hedge" their portfolios and completely eliminate the risk due to changes in oil prices. There will be a cost to hedging, but that cost to large, sophisticated investors should be about the same as the cost to Plastics. Since stockholders can hedge away oil price risk themselves, why should they pay a higher price for Plastics' stock just because the company itself hedged away the risk?

Still, a 1995 survey reported that 59 percent of firms with market values greater than $250 million engage in risk management, and that percentage is surely much higher today.[1] Although there is no proof that risk management adds value, here are several good reasons for companies to manage risks:

1. *Debt capacity.* Risk management can reduce the volatility of cash flows, and this decreases the probability of bankruptcy. As we discussed in Chapter 13, firms with lower operating risks can use more debt, and this can lead to higher stock prices due to the interest tax savings.

2. *Maintaining the optimal capital budget over time.* Recall from Chapter 13 that firms are reluctant to raise external equity due to high flotation costs and market pressure. This means that the capital budget must generally be financed with debt plus internally generated funds, mainly retained earnings and depreciation. In years when internal cash flows are low, they may be too small to support the optimal capital budget, causing firms to either slow investment

---

[1] See Gordon M. Bodnar, Gregory S. Hayt, and Richard C. Marston, "1995 Wharton Survey of Derivative Usage by U.S. Non-Financial Firms," *Financial Management*, Winter 1996, 113–133.

below the optimal rate or else incur the high costs associated with external equity. By smoothing out the cash flows, risk management can alleviate this problem.

3. *Financial distress.* Financial distress—which can range from worrying stockholders to higher interest rates on debt to customer defections to bankruptcy—is associated with having cash flows fall below expected levels. Risk management can reduce the likelihood of low cash flows, hence of financial distress.

4. *Comparative advantages in hedging.* Many investors cannot implement a homemade hedging program as efficiently as can a company. First, firms generally have lower transactions costs due to a larger volume of hedging activities. Second, there is the problem of asymmetric information—managers know more about the firm's risk exposure than outside investors, hence managers can create more effective hedges. And third, effective risk management requires specialized skills and knowledge that firms are more likely to have.

5. *Borrowing costs.* As discussed later in the chapter, firms can sometimes reduce input costs, especially the interest rate on debt, through the use of derivative instruments called "swaps." Any such cost reduction adds value to the firm.

6. *Tax effects.* Companies with volatile earnings pay more taxes than more stable companies due to the treatment of tax credits and the rules governing corporate loss carry-forwards and carry-backs. Moreover, if volatile earnings lead to bankruptcy, then tax loss carry-forwards are generally lost. Therefore, our tax system encourages risk management to stabilize earnings.[2]

7. *Compensation systems.* Many compensation systems establish "floors" and "ceilings" on bonuses or else reward managers for meeting targets. To illustrate, suppose a firm's compensation system calls for a manager to receive no bonus if net income is below $1 million, a bonus of $10,000 if income is between $1 million and $2 million, and one of $20,000 if income is $2 million or more. Moreover, the manager will receive an additional $10,000 if actual income is at least 90 percent of the forecasted level, which is $1 million. Now consider the following two situations. First, if income is stable at $2 million each year, the manager gets a $30,000 bonus each year, for a two-year total of $60,000. However, if income is zero the first year and $4 million the second, the manager gets no bonus the first year and $30,000 the second, for a two-year total of $30,000. So, even though the company has the same total income ($4 million) over the two years, the manager's bonus is higher if earnings are stable. So, even if hedging does not add much value for stockholders, it may still be beneficial to managers.

Derivatives
Securities whose values are determined by the market price or interest rate of some other asset.

Since perhaps the most important aspect of risk management involves derivative securities, the next section explains **derivatives,** which are securities whose values are determined by the market price of some other asset. Derivatives include *options*, whose values depend on the price of some underlying asset; *interest rate and exchange rate futures and swaps*, whose values depend on interest rate and exchange rate levels; and *commodity futures*, whose values depend on commodity prices.

---

[2] See Clifford W. Smith and René Stulz, "The Determinants of Firms' Hedging Policies," *The Journal of Financial and Quantitative Analysis*, December 1985, 395–406.

Explain why finance theory, combined with well-diversified investors and "home-made hedging," might suggest that risk management should not add much value to a company.

List and explain some reasons why companies might actually employ risk management techniques.

BACKGROUND ON DERIVATIVES

A historical perspective is useful when studying derivatives. One of the first formal markets for derivatives was the futures market for wheat. Farmers were concerned about the price they would receive for their wheat when they sold it in the fall, and millers were concerned about the price they would have to pay. The risks faced by both parties could be reduced if they could establish a price earlier in the year. Accordingly, mill agents would go out to the wheat belt and make contracts with farmers that called for the farmers to deliver grain at a predetermined price. Both parties benefited from the transaction in the sense that their risks were reduced. The farmers could concentrate on growing their crop without worrying about the price of grain, and the millers could concentrate on their milling operations. Thus, *hedging with futures* lowered aggregate risk in the economy.

 The Chicago Board of Trade has an excellent web site at **http://www.cbot.com**. Make sure to check out the wealth of information on the history and operation of the exchange by clicking on "About CBOT."

These early futures dealings were between two parties who arranged transactions between themselves. Soon, though, middlemen came into the picture, and *trading* in futures was established. The Chicago Board of Trade was an early marketplace for this dealing, and *futures dealers* helped make a market in futures contracts. Thus, farmers could sell futures on the exchange, and millers could buy them there. This improved the efficiency and lowered the cost of hedging operations.

Quickly, a third group—*speculators*—entered the scene. As we will see in the next section, most derivatives, including futures, are highly leveraged, meaning that a small change in the value of the underlying asset will produce a large change in the price of the derivative. This leverage appealed to speculators. At first blush, one might think that the appearance of speculators would increase risk, but this is not true. Speculators add capital and players to the market, and this tends to stabilize the market. Of course, derivatives markets are inherently volatile due to the leverage involved, hence risk to the speculators themselves is high. Still, their bearing that risk makes the derivatives markets more stable for the hedgers.

Natural Hedges
Situations in which aggregate risk can be reduced by derivatives transactions between two parties.

Natural hedges, defined as situations in which aggregate risk can be reduced by derivatives transactions between two parties (called *counterparties*), exist for many commodities, for foreign currencies, for interest rates on securities with different maturities, and even for common stocks where portfolio managers want to "hedge their bets." Natural hedges occur when futures are traded between cotton farmers and cotton mills, copper mines and copper fabricators, importers and foreign manufacturers for currency exchange rates, electric utilities and coal miners, and oil producers and oil users. In all such situations, hedging reduces aggregate risk and thus benefits the economy.

Hedging can also be done in situations where no natural hedge exists. Here one party wants to reduce some type of risk, and another party agrees to sell a contract that

BARINGS AND SUMITOMO SUFFER LARGE LOSSES IN THE DERIVATIVES MARKET

Barings, a conservative English bank with a long, impressive history dating back to its financing of the Louisiana Purchase in the 19th century, collapsed in 1995 when one of its traders lost $1.4 billion in derivatives trades. Nicholas Leeson, a 28-year-old trader in Barings' Singapore office, had speculated in Japanese stock index and interest rate futures without his superiors' knowledge. A lack of internal controls at the bank allowed him to accumulate large losses without being detected. Leeson's losses caught many by surprise, and they provided ammunition to those who argue that trading in derivatives should be more highly regulated if not sharply curtailed.

Most argue that the blame goes beyond Leeson—that both the bank and the exchanges were at fault for failing to provide sufficient oversight. For misreporting his trades, Leeson was sentenced to a 6½-year term in a Singapore prison. What remained of Barings was ultimately sold to a Dutch banking concern.

Many analysts, including those who argued that the Barings episode was just an unsettling but isolated incident, were startled by a similar case a year and a half after the Barings debacle. In June 1996, Japan's Sumitomo Corporation disclosed that its well-respected chief copper trader, Yasuo Hamanaka, had been conducting unauthorized speculative trades for more than a decade. The cumulative loss on these trades was $2.6 billion.

These two events illustrate both the dangers of derivatives and the importance of internal controls. While it is unsettling to learn that the actions of a single, relatively low-level employee can suddenly cripple a giant corporation, these losses should be placed in perspective. The overwhelming majority of firms that use derivatives have been successful in enhancing performance and/or reducing risk. For this reason, most analysts argue that it would be a huge mistake to use the rare instances where fraud occurred to limit a market that has, for the most part, been a resounding success. However, given the volume of business in this market, we can in the future expect to see other problems similar to those encountered by Barings and Sumitomo.

protects the first party from that specific event or situation. Insurance is an obvious example of this type of hedge. Note, though, that with nonsymmetric hedges, risks are generally *transferred* rather than *eliminated*. Even here, though, insurance companies can reduce certain types of risk through diversification.

The derivatives markets have grown more rapidly than any other major market in recent years, for a number of reasons. First, analytical techniques such as the Black-Scholes Option Pricing Model, which is discussed in a later section, have been developed to help establish "fair" prices, and having a better basis for pricing hedges makes the counterparties more comfortable with deals. Second, computers and electronic communications make it much easier for counterparties to deal with one another. Third, globalization has greatly increased the importance of currency markets and the need for reducing the exchange rate risks brought on by global trade. Recent trends and developments are sure to continue if not accelerate, so the use of derivatives for risk management is bound to grow.

Note, though, that derivatives do have a potential downside. These instruments are highly leveraged, so small miscalculations can lead to huge losses. Also, they are complicated, hence not well understood by most people. This makes mistakes more likely than with less complex instruments, and it makes it harder for a firm's top management to exercise proper control over derivatives transactions. One 28-year-old, relatively low-level employee, operating in the Far East, entered into transactions that led to the bankruptcy of Britain's oldest bank (Barings Bank), the institution that held the accounts of the Queen of England. (See the Global Perspectives box entitled, "Barings and Sumitomo Suffer Large Losses in the Derivatives Market.") Just prior to the problems at Barings, Orange County, California, went bankrupt due to its treasurer's speculation in derivatives, and Procter & Gamble got into a nasty fight with Bankers Trust over derivative-related losses. More recently, the high-profile hedge fund, Long Term Capital Management LP, nearly collapsed because of bad bets made in the derivatives market.

The P&G, Orange County, Barings Bank, and Long Term Capital Management affairs make the headlines, causing some people to argue that derivatives should be regulated out of existence to "protect the public." However, derivatives are used far more often to hedge risks than in harmful speculations, but these beneficial transactions never make the headlines. So, while the horror stories point out the need for top managers to exercise control over the personnel who deal with derivatives, they certainly do not justify the elimination of derivatives.

In the balance of this chapter, we discuss how firms can manage risks, and how derivatives are used in risk management.

SELF-TEST QUESTIONS

What is a "natural hedge"? Give some examples of natural hedges.

List three reasons the derivatives markets have grown more rapidly than any other major market in recent years.

OPTIONS

Option
A contract that gives its holder the right to buy (or sell) an asset at a predetermined price within a specified period of time.

An **option** is a contract that gives its holder the right to buy (or sell) an asset at some predetermined price within a specified period of time. Financial managers should understand option theory both for risk management and also because such an understanding will help them structure warrant and convertible financings, a topic we discuss in Chapter 20.

OPTION TYPES AND MARKETS

Strike (Exercise) Price
The price that must be paid for a share of common stock when an option is exercised.

Call Option
An option to buy, or "call," a share of stock at a certain price within a specified period.

Put Option
An option to sell a share of stock at a certain price within a specified period.

There are many types of options and option markets.[3] To illustrate how options work, suppose you owned 100 shares of General Computer Corporation (GCC), which on Friday, August 9, 2002, sold for $53.50 per share. You could sell to someone the right to buy your 100 shares at any time during the next five months at a price of, say, $55 per share. The $55 is called the **strike, or exercise, price.** Such options exist, and they are traded on a number of exchanges, with the Chicago Board Options Exchange (CBOE) being the oldest and the largest. This type of option is defined as a **call option,** because the purchaser has a "call" on 100 shares of stock. The seller of an option is called the option *writer.* An investor who "writes" call options against stock held in his or her portfolio is said to be selling *covered options.* Options sold without the stock to back them up are called *naked options.* When the exercise price exceeds the current stock price, a call option is said to be *out-of-the-money.* When the exercise price is below the current price of the stock, the option is *in-the-money.*

You can also buy an option which gives you the right to *sell* a stock at a specified price within some future period—this is called a **put option.** For example, suppose you think GCC's stock price is likely to decline from its current level of $53.50

---

[3] For an in-depth treatment of options, see Don M. Chance, *An Introduction to Derivatives* (Fort Worth, TX: The Dryden Press, 1995).

sometime during the next five months. Table 18-1 provides data on GCC's options. You could buy a five-month put option (the January put option) for $220.00 ($2.20 × 100) that would give you the right to sell 100 shares (that you would not necessarily own) at a price of $50 per share ($50 is the strike price). Suppose you bought this 100-share contract for $220.00 and then GCC's stock fell to $45. You could buy a share of stock for $45 and exercise your put option by selling the stock for $50. Your profit from exercising the option would be ($50 − $45)(100) = $500. After subtracting the $220.00 you paid for the option, your profit (before taxes and commissions) would be $280.00.

Table 18-1 contains an extract from the Listed Options Quotations Table for Friday, August 9, 2002, as it would appear the next day in a daily newspaper. Sport World's September $55 call option sold for $0.50. Thus, for $0.50(100) = $50 you could buy options that would give you the right to purchase 100 shares of Sport World stock at a price of $55 per share from August until September, or during the next month.[4] If the stock price stayed below $55 during that period, you would lose your $50, but if it rose to $65, your $50 investment would increase in value to ($65 − $55)(100) = $1,000 in less than 30 days. That translates into a very healthy annualized rate of return. Incidentally, if the stock price did go up, you would not actually exercise your options and buy the stock—rather, you would sell the options, which would then have a value of $1,000 versus the $50 you paid, to another option buyer or back to the original seller.

In addition to options on individual stocks, options are also available on several stock indexes such as the NYSE Index and the S&P 100 Index. Index options permit one to hedge (or bet) on a rise or fall in the general market as well as on individual stocks.

Option trading is one of the hottest financial activities in the United States. The leverage involved makes it possible for speculators with just a few dollars to make a

---

[4] Actually, the *expiration date*, which is the last date that the option can be exercised, is the Friday before the third Saturday of the exercise month. Also, note that option contracts are generally written in 100-share multiples.

TABLE 18-1	August 9, 2002, Listed Options Quotations

		CALLS — LAST QUOTE			PUTS — LAST QUOTE		
CLOSING PRICE	STRIKE PRICE	SEPTEMBER	OCTOBER	JANUARY	SEPTEMBER	OCTOBER	JANUARY
GENERAL COMPUTER CORPORATION (GCC)							
53.50	50	4.20	4.70	5.50	0.60	1.40	2.20
53.50	55	1.30	2.10	3.15	2.65	· · ·	4.50
53.50	60	0.35	0.70	1.50	6.55	· · ·	8.00
U.S. MEDICAL							
56.65	55	4.20	5.15	7.00	2.15	3.70	· · ·
SPORT WORLD							
53.10	55	0.50	1.10	· · ·	2.05	· · ·	· · ·

NOTE: · · · means not traded on August 9.

---

fortune almost overnight. Also, investors with sizable portfolios can sell options against their stocks and earn the value of the option (less brokerage commissions), even if the stock's price remains constant. Most importantly, though, options can be used to create *hedges* that protect the value of an individual stock or portfolio. We will discuss hedging strategies in more detail later in the chapter.[5]

Long-Term Equity AnticiPation Securities (LEAPS)

Long-term options that are listed on the exchanges and tied to both individual stocks and to stock indexes.

Conventional options are generally written for six months or less, but a new type of option called a **Long-term Equity AnticiPation Security (LEAPS)** has been trading in recent years. Like conventional options, LEAPS are listed on exchanges and are tied both to individual stocks and to stock indexes. The major difference is that LEAPS are long-term options, having maturities of up to 2½ years. One-year LEAPS cost about twice as much as the matching three-month option, but because of their much longer time to expiration, LEAPS provide buyers with more potential for gains and offer better long-term protection for a portfolio.

Corporations on whose stocks options are written have nothing to do with the option market. Corporations do not raise money in the option market, nor do they have any direct transactions in it. Moreover, option holders do not vote for corporate directors or receive dividends. There have been studies by the SEC and others as to whether option trading stabilizes or destabilizes the stock market, and whether this activity helps or hinders corporations seeking to raise new capital. The studies have not been conclusive, but option trading is here to stay, and many regard it as the most exciting game in town.

FACTORS THAT AFFECT THE VALUE OF A CALL OPTION

A study of Table 18-1 provides some insights into call option valuation. First, we see that there are at least three factors that affect a call option's value: (1) The higher the stock's market price in relation to the strike price, the higher will be the call option price. Thus, Sport World's $55 September call option sells for $0.50, whereas U.S. Medical's $55 September option sells for $4.20. This difference arises because U.S. Medical's current stock price is $56.65 versus only $53.10 for Sport World. (2) The higher the strike price, the lower the call option price. Thus, all of GCC's call options, regardless of exercise month, decline as the strike price increases. (3) The longer the option period, the higher the option price. This occurs because the longer the time before expiration, the greater the chance that the stock price will climb substantially above the exercise price. Thus, option prices increase as the expiration date is lengthened. Other factors that affect option values, especially the volatility of the underlying stock, are discussed in later sections.

EXERCISE VALUE VERSUS OPTION PRICE

How is the actual price of a call option determined in the market? In a later section, we present a widely used model (the Black-Scholes model) for pricing call options,

---

[5] It should be noted that insiders who trade illegally generally buy options rather than stock because the leverage inherent in options increases the profit potential. Note, though, that it is illegal to use insider information for personal gain, and an insider using such information would be taking advantage of the option seller. Insider trading, in addition to being unfair and essentially equivalent to stealing, hurts the economy: Investors lose confidence in the capital markets and raise their required returns because of an increased element of risk, and this raises the cost of capital and thus reduces the level of real investment.

Exercise Value
The value of an option calculated as the current stock price minus the strike, or exercise, price.

but first it is useful to establish some basic concepts. To begin, we define a call option's **exercise value** as follows:

$$\text{Exercise value} = \text{Current price of the stock} - \text{Strike price.}$$

The exercise value is what the option would be worth if you had to exercise it immediately. For example, if a stock sells for $50 and its option has a strike price of $20, then you could buy the stock for $20 by exercising the option. You would own a stock worth $50, but you would only have to pay $20. Therefore, the option would be worth $30 if you had to exercise it immediately. Note that the calculated exercise value of a call option could be negative, but realistically the minimum "true" value of an option is zero, because no one would exercise an out-of-the-money option. Note also that an option's exercise value is only a first approximation value—it merely provides a starting point for finding the actual value of the option.

Now consider Figure 18-1, which presents some data on Space Technology Inc. (STI), a company that recently went public and whose stock price has fluctuated widely during its short history. The third column in the tabular data shows the exercise values for STI's call option when the stock was selling at different prices; the fourth column gives the actual market prices for the option; and the fifth column shows the premium of the actual option price over its exercise value. At any stock price below $20, the exercise value is set at zero, but above $20, each $1 increase in the price of the stock brings with it a $1 increase in the option's exercise value. Note, however, that the actual market price of the option lies above the exercise value at each price of the common stock, although the premium declines as the price of the stock increases. For example, when the stock sold for $20 and the option had a zero exercise value, its actual price, and the premium, was $9. Then, as the price of the stock rose, the *exercise value's increase* matched the stock's increase dollar for dollar, but the *market price* of the option climbed less rapidly, causing the premium to decline. The premium was $9 when the stock sold for $20 a share, but it had declined to $1 by the time the stock price had risen to $73 a share. Beyond that point, the premium virtually disappeared.

Why does this pattern exist? Why should a call option ever sell for more than its exercise value, and why does the premium decline as the price of the stock increases? The answer lies in part in the speculative appeal of options—they enable someone to gain a high degree of personal leverage when buying securities. To illustrate, suppose STI's option sold for exactly its exercise value. Now suppose you were thinking of investing in the company's common stock at a time when it was selling for $21 a share. If you bought a share and the price rose to $42, you would have made a 100 percent capital gain. However, had you bought the option at its exercise value ($1 when the stock was selling for $21), your capital gain would have been $22 − $1 = $21 on a $1 investment, or 2,100 percent! At the same time, your total loss potential with the option would be only $1 versus a potential loss of $21 if you purchased the stock. The huge capital gains potential, combined with the loss limitation, is clearly worth something—the exact amount it is worth to investors is the amount of the premium. Note, however, that buying the option is riskier than buying STI's stock, because there is a higher probability of losing money on the option. If STI's stock price fell to $20, you would have a 4.76 percent loss if you bought the stock (ignoring transaction costs), but you would have a 100 percent loss on the option investment.

Why does the premium decline as the price of the stock rises? Part of the answer is that both the leverage effect and the loss protection feature decline at high stock prices. For example, if you were thinking of buying STI stock when its price was $73 a share, the exercise value of the option would be $53. If the stock price doubled to

FIGURE 18-1   Space Technology Inc.: Option Price and Exercise Value

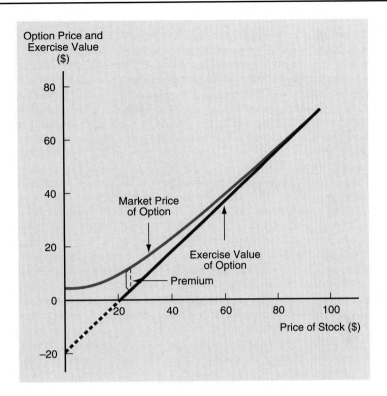

PRICE OF STOCK (1)	STRIKE PRICE (2)	EXERCISE VALUE OF OPTION (1) − (2) = (3)	MARKET PRICE OF OPTION (4)	PREMIUM (4) − (3) = (5)
$20.00	$20.00	$ 0.00	$ 9.00	$9.00
21.00	20.00	1.00	9.75	8.75
22.00	20.00	2.00	10.50	8.50
35.00	20.00	15.00	21.00	6.00
42.00	20.00	22.00	26.00	4.00
50.00	20.00	30.00	32.00	2.00
73.00	20.00	53.00	54.00	1.00
98.00	20.00	78.00	78.50	0.50

$146, you would have a 100 percent gain on the stock. Now note that the exercise value of the option would go from $53 to $126, for a percentage gain of 138 percent versus 2,100 percent in the earlier case. Note also that the potential loss per dollar of potential gain on the option is much greater when the option is selling at high prices. These two factors, the declining leverage impact and the increasing danger of larger losses, help explain why the premium diminishes as the price of the common stock rises.

In addition to the stock price and the exercise price, the price of an option depends on three other factors: (1) the option's term to maturity, (2) the variability of

EXPENSING EXECUTIVE STOCK OPTIONS

In Chapter 1, we noted that many companies give senior managers stock options as part of their compensation packages for two key reasons: (1) Options give managers a strong incentive to increase their companies' stock prices, and (2) options are a substitute for salaries, which reduces cash requirements. However, options are not free to the issuing company—they have a very real cost, because they lead to an increase in the number of shares outstanding, which in turn reduces the company's earnings per share.

Two important differences between option grants and cash compensation have favored the use of options over cash. First, cash for salaries is generally in short supply for young, startup companies, and also for fraudulent companies such as Enron and WorldCom, whereas options can just be created with no cash outlay. Second, cash paid as salaries must be reported as a cost on the income statement, thus lowering reported profits, whereas stock options, even though they may have a true value in the millions, do not have to be reported on the income statement, hence do not reduce reported profits.[a] The first reason—conserving cash—is legitimate, at least for young, cash-strapped companies. The second reason, pumping up reported accounting profits, is much more questionable.

Companies have been reluctant to expense options for two reasons. First, managers generally dislike any action that reduces reported profits because their own salaries, bonuses, and future options are generally based on reported profits. Recent studies indicate that expensing options would reduce the reported profits of an average S&P 500 company by about 15 percent, and for some companies the reduction would be more than 50 percent. Such a hit to earnings could have a negative effect on stock prices, and stockholders would be less inclined to approve the huge option grants that CEOs such as Ken Lay of Enron and Bernie Ebbers of WorldCom received if they were informed of the effects of such grants on net income. So, executives like Lay and Ebbers—and also some honest ones—wanted no part of options expensing.

The second reason for not expensing options is that there is no perfect way to value them. The Black-Scholes model is used most frequently, but it has limitations. In particular, some executive stock options are worth less than the valuations implied by Black-Scholes because grantees must wait several years before they can exercise their options. Accountants, who like precision, used this as an excuse to ignore options and thus curry favor with corporate clients such as Lay, Ebbers, and others.

Despite their reluctance, accountants and corporate managers have come under intense pressure to expense options. This pressure comes from the inherent logic for expensing them and also because of revelations about how they were used to defraud investors and enrich greedy executives. Investors are becoming increasingly reluctant to buy stocks of companies that overstate earnings, and they are telling corporations that it is better to be approximately correct than exactly wrong (i.e., expense options using Black-Scholes to get an approximate valuation rather than don't expense them and get an obviously incorrect result). As a result, a number of leading companies, including Microsoft, Cisco, Citigroup, and GE have announced plans to expense options, and this is increasing the pressure on others to make the change.

---

[a]Options must be reported somewhere in the financial statements, but only as a discussion item, not as a deduction that lowers reported profits.

SOURCE: Anthony Bianco, "The Angry Market," *BusinessWeek*, July 29, 2002, 32–51.

---

the stock price, and (3) the risk-free rate. We will explain precisely how these factors affect call option prices later, but for now, note these points:

1. The longer a call option has to run, the greater its value and the larger its premium. If an option expires at 4 P.M. today, there is not much chance that the stock price will go up very much, so the option must sell at close to its exercise value, and its premium must be small. On the other hand, if the expiration date is a year away, the stock price could rise sharply, pulling the option's value up with it.

2. An option on an extremely volatile stock is worth more than one on a very stable stock. If the stock price rarely moves, then there is only a small chance of a large gain. However, if the stock price is highly volatile, the option could easily become very valuable. At the same time, losses on options are limited—you can make an unlimited amount, but you can only lose what you paid for the

option. Therefore, a large decline in a stock's price does not have a corresponding bad effect on option holders. As a result of the unlimited upside but limited downside, the more volatile a stock, the higher the value of its options.

3. The effect of the risk-free rate on a call option isn't as obvious. The expected growth rate of a firm's stock price increases as interest rates increase, but the present value of future cash flows decreases. The first effect tends to increase the call option's price, while the second tends to decrease it. As it turns out, the first effect dominates the second one, so the price of a call option always increases as the risk-free rate increases. We illustrate this fact later in Table 18-2.

Because of Points 1 and 2, in a graph such as Figure 18-1 the longer an option's life, the higher its market price line would be above the exercise value line. Similarly, the more volatile the price of the underlying stock, the higher is the market price line. We will see precisely how these factors, and also the discount rate, affect option values when we discuss the Black-Scholes option pricing model.

SELF-TEST QUESTIONS

What is an option? A call option? A put option?

Define a call option's exercise value. Why is the actual market price of a call option usually above its exercise value?

What are some factors that affect a call option's value?

INTRODUCTION TO OPTION PRICING MODELS[6]

In the next section, we discuss a widely used but complex option pricing model, the Black-Scholes model. First, though, we go through a simple example to illustrate basic principles. To begin, note that all option pricing models are based on the concept of a **riskless hedge.** Here an investor buys a stock and simultaneously sells a call option on that stock. If the stock's price goes up, the investor will earn a profit on the stock, but the holder of the option will exercise it, and that will cost the investor money. Conversely, if the stock goes down, the investor will lose on his or her investment in the stock, but gain from the option (which will expire worthless if the stock price declines). As we demonstrate, it is possible to set things up such that the investor will end up with a riskless position—regardless of what the stock does, the value of the investor's portfolio will remain constant. Thus, a riskless investment will have been created.

If an investment is riskless, it must, in equilibrium, yield the riskless rate. If it offered a higher rate of return, arbitrageurs would buy it and in the process push the rate of return down, and vice versa if it offered less than the riskless rate.

Given the price of the stock, its potential volatility, the option's exercise price, the life of the option, and the risk-free rate, there is but one price for the option if it is to

Riskless Hedge
A hedge in which an investor buys a stock and simultaneously sells a call option on that stock and ends up with a riskless position.

---

[6] This section and the following one on the Black-Scholes model are relatively technical, and they can be omitted without loss of continuity.

meet the equilibrium condition, namely, that a portfolio that consists of the stock and the call option will earn the riskless rate. We value an illustrative option below, and then we use the Black-Scholes model to value options under more realistic conditions.

1. *Assumptions of the example.* The stock of Western Cellular, a manufacturer of cell phones, sells for $40 per share. Options exist that permit the holder to buy one share of Western at an exercise price of $35. These options will expire at the end of one year, at which time Western's stock will be selling at one of two prices, either $30 or $50. Also, the risk-free rate is 8.0 percent. Based on these assumptions, we must find the value of the options.

2. *Find the range of values at expiration.* When the option expires at the end of the year, Western's stock will sell for either $30 or $50, and here is the situation with regard to the value of the options:

ENDING STOCK PRICE	−	STRIKE PRICE VALUE	=	ENDING OPTION VALUE
$30.00	−	$35.00	=	$ 0.00 (The option will be worthless. It cannot have a negative value.)
50.00	−	35.00	=	15.00
Range $20.00				$15.00

3. *Equalize the range of payoffs for the stock and the option.* As shown above, the ranges of payoffs for the stock and the option are $20 and $15. To construct the riskless portfolio, we need to equalize these ranges. We do so by buying 0.75 share and selling one option (or 75 shares and 100 options) to produce the following situation, where the range for both the stock and the option is $15:

ENDING STOCK PRICE	×	0.75	=	ENDING VALUE OF STOCK	ENDING VALUE OF OPTION
$30.00	×	0.75	=	$22.50	$ 0.00
50.00	×	0.75	=	37.50	15.00
Range $20.00				$15.00	$15.00

4. *Create a riskless hedged investment.* We can now create a riskless investment portfolio by buying 0.75 share of Western's stock and selling one call option. Here is the situation:

ENDING STOCK PRICE	×	0.75	=	ENDING VALUE OF STOCK IN THE PORTFOLIO	+	ENDING VALUE OF OPTION IN THE PORTFOLIO	=	ENDING TOTAL VALUE OF THE PORTFOLIO
$30.00	×	0.75	=	$22.50	+	$ 0.00	=	$22.50
50.00	×	0.75	=	37.50	+	−15.00	=	22.50

The stock in the portfolio will have a value of either $22.50 or $37.50, depending on what happens to the price of the stock. The call option that was sold will have no effect on the value of the portfolio if Western's price falls to $30, because it will then not be exercised — it will expire worthless. However, if the stock price ends at $50, the holder of the option will exercise it, paying the $35 exercise price for stock that would cost $50 on the open market, so in that case, the option would have a cost of $15 to the holder of the portfolio.

Now note that the value of the portfolio is $22.50 regardless of whether Western's stock goes up or down. So, the portfolio is riskless. A hedge has been created that protects against both increases or decreases in the price of the stock.

5. *Pricing the call option.* To this point, we have not mentioned the price of the call option that was sold to create the riskless hedge. How much should it sell for? Obviously, the seller would like to get a high price, but the buyer would want a low price. What is the *fair,* or *equilibrium,* price? To find this price, we proceed as follows:

a. The value of the portfolio will be $22.50 at the end of the year, regardless of what happens to the price of the stock. This $22.50 is riskless.

b. The risk-free rate is 8 percent, so the present value of the riskless $22.50 year-end value is

$$PV = \$22.50/(1.08) = \$20.83.$$

c. Since Western's stock is currently selling for $40, and since the portfolio contains 0.75 share, the cost of the stock in the portfolio is

$$0.75(\$40) = \$30.00.$$

d. If one paid $30 for the stock, and if the present value of the portfolio is $20.83, the option would have to sell for at least $9.17:

$$Price\ of\ option = Cost\ of\ stock - PV\ of\ portfolio$$
$$= \$30 - \$20.83 = \$9.17.$$

If this option sold at a price higher than $9.17, other investors could create riskless portfolios as described above and earn more than the riskless rate. Investors would create such portfolios—and options—until their price fell to $9.17, at which point the market would be in equilibrium. Conversely, if the options sold for less than $9.17, investors would refuse to create them, and the resulting supply shortage would drive the price up to $9.17. Thus, investors (or arbitrageurs) would buy and sell in the market until the options were priced at their equilibrium level.

Clearly, this example is unrealistic—Western's stock price could be almost anything after one year, and you could not purchase 0.75 share of stock (but you could do so in effect by buying 75 shares and selling 100 options). Still, the example does illustrate that investors can, in principle, create riskless portfolios by buying stocks and selling call options against those stocks, and the return on such portfolios should be the risk-free rate. If call options are not priced to reflect this condition, arbitrageurs will actively trade stocks and options until option prices reflect equilibrium conditions. In the next section, we discuss the Black-Scholes Option Pricing Model, which is based on the general premise we developed here—the creation of a riskless portfolio—but which is applicable to "real-world" option pricing because it allows for a complete range of ending stock prices.

SELF-TEST QUESTIONS

Describe how a risk-free portfolio can be created using stocks and options.

How can such a portfolio be used to help estimate a call option's value?

THE BLACK-SCHOLES OPTION PRICING MODEL (OPM)

The *Black-Scholes Option Pricing Model (OPM)*, developed in 1973, helped give rise to the rapid growth in options trading.[7] This model, which has even been programmed into the permanent memories of some hand-held calculators, is widely used by option traders.

OPM ASSUMPTIONS AND EQUATIONS

In deriving their option pricing model, Fischer Black and Myron Scholes made the following assumptions:

1. The stock underlying the call option provides no dividends or other distributions during the life of the option.
2. There are no transaction costs for buying or selling either the stock or the option.
3. The short-term, risk-free interest rate is known and is constant during the life of the option.
4. Any purchaser of a security may borrow any fraction of the purchase price at the short-term, risk-free interest rate.
5. Short selling is permitted, and the short seller will receive immediately the full cash proceeds of today's price for a security sold short.[8]
6. The call option can be exercised only on its expiration date.
7. Trading in all securities takes place continuously, and the stock price moves randomly.

The derivation of the Black-Scholes model rests on the concept of a riskless hedge such as the one we set up in the last section. By buying shares of a stock and simultaneously selling call options on that stock, an investor can create a risk-free investment position, where gains on the stock will exactly offset losses on the option. This riskless hedged position must earn a rate of return equal to the risk-free rate. Otherwise, an arbitrage opportunity would exist, and people trying to take advantage of this opportunity would drive the price of the option to the equilibrium level as specified by the Black-Scholes model.

The Black-Scholes model consists of the following three equations:

$$V = P[N(d_1)] - Xe^{-k_{RF}t}[N(d_2)]. \tag{18-1}$$

$$d_1 = \frac{\ln(P/X) + [k_{RF} + (\sigma^2/2)]t}{\sigma\sqrt{t}}. \tag{18-2}$$

$$d_2 = d_1 - \sigma\sqrt{t}. \tag{18-3}$$

---

[7] See Fischer Black and Myron Scholes, "The Pricing of Options and Corporate Liabilities," *Journal of Political Economy*, May/June 1973, 637–659.

[8] Suppose an investor (or speculator) does not now own any IBM stock. If the investor anticipates a rise in the stock price and consequently buys IBM stock, he or she is said to have *gone long* in IBM. On the other hand, if the investor thinks IBM's stock is likely to fall, he or she could *go short*, or *sell IBM short*. Since the

(footnote continues)

Here

V = current value of the call option.
P = current price of the underlying stock.
$N(d_i)$ = probability that a deviation less than d_i will occur in a standard normal distribution. Thus, $N(d_1)$ and $N(d_2)$ represent areas under a standard normal distribution function.
X = exercise, or strike, price of the option.
$e \approx 2.7183$.
k_{RF} = risk-free interest rate.
t = time until the option expires (the option period).
$\ln(P/X)$ = natural logarithm of P/X.
σ^2 = variance of the rate of return on the stock.

Note that the value of the option is a function of the variables we discussed earlier: (1) P, the stock's price; (2) t, the option's time to expiration; (3) X, the strike price; (4) σ^2, the variance of the underlying stock; and (5) k_{RF}, the risk-free rate. We do not derive the Black-Scholes model — the derivation involves some extremely complicated mathematics that go far beyond the scope of this text. However, it is not difficult to use the model. Under the assumptions set forth previously, if the option price is different from the one found by Equation 18-1, this would provide the opportunity for arbitrage profits, which would force the option price back to the value indicated by the model.[9] As we noted earlier, the Black-Scholes model is widely used by traders, so actual option prices conform reasonably well to values derived from the model.

In essence, the first term of Equation 18-1, $P[N(d_1)]$, can be thought of as the expected present value of the terminal stock price, while the second term, $Xe^{-k_{RF}t}[N(d_2)]$, can be thought of as the present value of the exercise price. However, rather than try to figure out exactly what the equations mean, it is more productive to plug in some numbers to see how changes in the inputs affect the value of an option.

OPM ILLUSTRATION

 Robert's Online Option Pricer can be accessed at **http://www.intrepid.com/~robertl/option-pricer.html**. The site is designed to provide a financial service over the Internet to small investors for option pricing, giving anyone a means to price option trades without having to buy expensive software and hardware.

The current stock price, P, the exercise price, X, and the time to maturity, t, can all be obtained from a newspaper such as *The Wall Street Journal*. The risk-free rate, k_{RF}, is the yield on a Treasury bill with a maturity equal to the option expiration date. The annualized variance of stock returns, σ^2, can be estimated by multiplying the variance of the percentage change in daily stock prices for the past year [that is, the variance of $(P_t - P_{t-1})/P_t$] by 365 days.

Assume that the following information has been obtained:

$P = \$20$.
$X = \$20$.
$t = 3$ months or 0.25 year.
$k_{RF} = 12\% = 0.12$.
$\sigma^2 = 0.16$. Note that $\sigma^2 = 0.16$, then $\sigma = \sqrt{0.16} = 0.4$.

(Footnote 8 continued)

short seller has no IBM stock, he or she would have to borrow the shares sold short from a broker. If the stock price falls, the short seller could, later on, buy shares on the open market and pay back the ones borrowed from the broker. The short seller's profit, before commissions and taxes, would be the difference between the price received from the short sale and the price paid later to purchase the replacement stock.

[9] *Programmed trading*, in which stocks are bought and options are sold, or vice versa, is an example of arbitrage between stocks and options.

Given this information, we can now use the OPM by solving Equations 18-1, 18-2, and 18-3. Since d_1 and d_2 are required inputs for Equation 18-1, we solve Equations 18-2 and 18-3 first:

$$d_1 = \frac{\ln(\$20/\$20) + [0.12 + (0.16/2)](0.25)}{0.40(0.50)}$$

$$= \frac{0 + 0.05}{0.20} = 0.25.$$

$$d_2 = d_1 - 0.4\sqrt{0.25} = 0.25 - 0.20 = 0.05.$$

Note that $N(d_1) = N(0.25)$ and $N(d_2) = N(0.05)$ represent areas under a standard normal distribution function. From Table A-5 in Appendix A at the end of the book, we see that the value $d_1 = 0.25$ implies a probability of $0.0987 + 0.5000 = 0.5987$, so $N(d_1) = 0.5987$. Similarly, $N(d_2) = 0.5199$. We can use those values to solve Equation 18-1:

$$V = \$20\,[N(d_1)] - \$20e^{-(0.12)(0.25)}[N(d_2)]$$

$$= \$20[N(0.25)] - \$20(0.9704)[N(0.05)]$$

$$= \$20(0.5987) - \$19.41(0.5199)$$

$$= \$11.97 - \$10.09 = \$1.88.$$

Thus the value of the option, under the assumed conditions, is $1.88. Suppose the actual option price were $2.25. Arbitrageurs could simultaneously sell the option, buy the underlying stock, and earn a riskless profit. Such trading would occur until the price of the option was driven down to $1.88. The reverse would occur if the option sold for less than $1.88. Thus, investors would be unwilling to pay more than $1.88 for the option, and they could not buy it for less, so $1.88 is the *equilibrium value* of the option.

To see how the five OPM factors affect the value of the option, consider Table 18-2. Here the top row shows the base-case input values that were used above to illustrate the OPM and the resulting option value, V = $1.88. In each of the subsequent rows, the boldfaced factor is increased, while the other four are held constant at their base-case levels. The resulting value of the call option is given in the last column. Now let's consider the effects of the changes:

1. *Current stock price.* If the current stock price, P, increases from $20 to $25, the option value increases from $1.88 to $5.81. Thus, the value of the option in-

TABLE 18-2   **Effects of OPM Factors on the Value of a Call Option**

CASE	INPUT FACTORS					OUTPUT
	P	X	t	k_{RF}	σ^2	V
Base case	$20	$20	0.25	12%	0.16	$1.88
Increase P by $5	**25**	20	0.25	12	0.16	5.81
Increase X by $5	20	**25**	0.25	12	0.16	0.39
Increase t to 6 months	20	20	**0.50**	12	0.16	2.81
Increase k_{RF} to 16%	20	20	0.25	**16**	0.16	1.98
Increase σ^2 to 0.25	20	20	0.25	12	**0.25**	2.27

creases as the stock price increases, but by less than the stock price increase, $3.93 versus $5.00. Note, though, that the percentage increase in the option value, ($5.81 − $1.88)/$1.88 = 209%, far exceeds the percentage increase in the stock price, ($25 − $20)/$20 = 25%.

2. *Exercise price.* If the exercise price, X, increases from $20 to $25, the value of the option declines. Again, the decrease in the option value is less than the exercise price increase, but the percentage change in the option value, ($0.39 − $1.88)/$1.88 = −79%, exceeds the percentage change in the exercise price, ($25 − $20)/$20 = 25%.

3. *Option period.* As the time to expiration increases from t = 3 months (or 0.25 year) to t = 6 months (or 0.50 year), the value of the option increases from $1.88 to $2.81. This occurs because the value of the option depends on the chances for an increase in the price of the underlying stock, and the longer the option has to go, the higher the stock price may climb. Thus, a six-month option is worth more than a three-month option.

4. *Risk-free rate.* As the risk-free rate increases from 12 to 16 percent, the value of the option increases slightly, from $1.88 to $1.98. Equations 18-1, 18-2, and 18-3 suggest that the principal effect of an increase in k_{RF} is to reduce the present value of the exercise price, $Xe^{-k_{RF}t}$, hence to increase the current value of the option.[10] The risk-free rate also plays a role in determining the values of the normal distribution functions $N(d_1)$ and $N(d_2)$, but this effect is of secondary importance. Indeed, option prices in general are not very sensitive to interest rate changes, at least not to changes within the ranges normally encountered.

5. *Variance.* As the variance increases from the base case 0.16 to 0.25, the value of the option increases from $1.88 to $2.27. Therefore, the riskier the underlying security, the more valuable the option. This result is logical. First, if you bought an option to buy a stock that sells at its exercise price, and if $\sigma_2 = 0$, then there would be a zero probability of the stock going up, hence a zero probability of making money on the option. On the other hand, if you bought an option on a high-variance stock, there would be a fairly high probability that the stock would go way up, hence that you would make a large profit on the option. Of course, a high-variance stock could go way down, but as an option holder, your losses would be limited to the price paid for the option—only the right-hand side of the stock's probability distribution counts. Put another way, an increase in the price of the stock helps option holders more than a decrease hurts them, so the greater the variance, the greater is the value of the option. This makes options on risky stocks more valuable than those on safer, low-variance stocks.

Myron Scholes and Robert Merton were awarded the 1997 Nobel Prize in Economics, and Fischer Black would have been a co-recipient had he still been living.[11] Their work provided analytical tools and methodologies that are widely used to solve many types of financial problems, not just option pricing. Indeed, the entire field of

---

[10] At this point, you may be wondering why the first term in Equation 18-1, $P[N(d_1)]$, is not discounted. In fact, it has been, because the current stock price, P, already represents the present value of the expected stock price at expiration. In other words, P is a discounted value, and the discount rate used in the market to determine today's stock price includes the risk-free rate. Thus, Equation 18-1 can be thought of as the present value of the end-of-option-period spread between the stock price and the strike price, adjusted for the probability that the stock price will be higher than the strike price.

[11] See Robert C. Merton, "Theory of Rational Option Pricing," *Bell Journal of Economics and Management Science*, Vol. 4, 1973, 141–183.

modern risk management is based primarily on their contributions. This concludes our discussion of options and option pricing theory. The next section discusses some other types of derivative securities.

SELF-TEST QUESTIONS

What is the purpose of the Black-Scholes Option Pricing Model?

Explain what a "riskless hedge" is and how the riskless hedge concept is used in the Black-Scholes OPM.

Describe the effect of a change in each of the following factors on the value of a call option:

(1) Stock price.

(2) Exercise price.

(3) Option life.

(4) Risk-free rate.

(5) Stock price variance; that is, riskiness of stock.

OTHER TYPES OF DERIVATIVES

Put and call options represent an important class of derivative securities, but there are other types of derivatives, including forward contracts, futures, swaps, structured notes, inverse floaters, and a host of other "exotic" contracts.

FORWARD CONTRACTS VERSUS FUTURES CONTRACTS

Forward Contract
A contract under which one party agrees to buy a commodity at a specific price on a specific future date and the other party agrees to make the sale. Physical delivery occurs.

Forward contracts are agreements where one party agrees to buy a commodity at a specific price on a specific future date and the other party agrees to make the sale. *Goods are actually delivered under forward contracts.* Unless both parties are financially strong, there is a danger that one party will default on the contract, especially if the price of the commodity changes markedly after the agreement is reached.

Futures Contract
Standardized contracts that are traded on exchanges and are "marked to market" daily, but where physical delivery of the underlying asset is virtually never taken.

A **futures contract** is similar to a forward contract, but with three key differences: (1) Futures contracts are "marked to market" on a daily basis, meaning that gains and losses are noted and money must be put up to cover losses. This greatly reduces the risk of default that exists with forward contracts. (2) With futures, physical delivery of the underlying asset is virtually never taken—the two parties simply settle up with cash for the difference between the contracted price and the actual price on the expiration date. (3) Futures contracts are generally standardized instruments that are traded on exchanges, whereas forward contracts are generally tailor-made, are negotiated between two parties, and are not traded after they have been signed.

Futures and forward contracts were originally used for commodities such as wheat, where farmers would sell forward contracts to millers, enabling both parties to lock in prices and thus reduce their risk exposure. Commodities contracts are still important, but today more trading is done in foreign exchange and interest rate futures. To illustrate how foreign exchange contracts are used, suppose GE arranges to buy electric motors from a German manufacturer on terms that call for GE to pay 1 million euros in 180 days. GE would not want to give up the free trade credit, but if the euro appreciated against the dollar during the next six months, the dollar cost of the million euros would rise. GE could hedge the transaction by buying a forward contract under which it agreed to buy the million euros in 180 days at a fixed dollar price. This would lock in the dollar cost of the motors. This transaction would probably be conducted through a money center bank, which would try to find a German company (a "counterparty") that needed dollars in six months. Alternatively, GE could buy a futures contract on an exchange.

Interest rate futures represent another huge and growing market. For example, suppose Simonset Corporation decides to build a new plant at a cost of $20 million. It plans to finance the project with 20-year bonds that would carry an 8 percent interest rate if they were issued today. However, the company will not need the money for about six months. Simonset could go ahead and sell 20-year bonds now, locking in the 8 percent rate, but it would have the money before it was needed, so it would have to invest in short-term securities that would yield less than 8 percent. However, if Simonset waits six months to sell the bond issue, interest rates might be higher than they are today, in which case the value of the plant would be reduced, perhaps to the point of making it unprofitable.

One solution to Simonset's dilemma involves *interest rate futures*, which are based on a hypothetical 20-year Treasury bond with a 6 percent semiannual coupon. If interest rates in the economy go up, the value of the hypothetical T-bond will go down, and vice versa. In our example, Simonset is worried about an increase in interest rates. Should rates rise, the hypothetical Treasury bond's value would decline. Therefore, Simonset could sell T-bond futures for delivery in six months to hedge its position. If interest rates rise, Simonset will have to pay more when it issues its own bonds. However, it will make a profit on its futures position because it will have presold the bonds at a higher price than it will have to pay to cover (repurchase) them. Of course, if interest rates decline, Simonset will lose on its futures position, but this will be offset by the fact that it will get to pay a lower interest rate when it issues its bonds.

Our examples show that forward contracts and futures can be used to hedge, or reduce, risks. It has been estimated that more than 95 percent of all transactions are indeed designed as hedges, with banks and futures dealers serving as middlemen between hedging counterparties. Interest rate and exchange rate futures can, of course, be used for speculative as well as hedging purposes. One can buy a T-bond contract on $100,000 of bonds with only $5,000 down, in which case a small change in interest rates will result in a very large gain or loss. Still, the primary motivation behind the vast majority of these transactions is to hedge risks, not to create them.

SWAPS

Swap
Two parties agree to exchange obligations to make specified payment streams.

A **swap** is just what the name implies—two parties agree to swap something, generally obligations to make specified payment streams. Most swaps today involve either interest payments or currencies. To illustrate an interest rate swap, suppose Company S has a 20-year, $100 million floating rate bond outstanding, while Company F has a $100 million, 20-year, fixed rate issue outstanding. Thus, each company has an obligation to make a stream of interest payments, but one payment stream is fixed while the other will vary as interest rates change in the future.

Now suppose Company S has stable cash flows, and it wants to lock in its cost of debt. Company F has cash flows that fluctuate with the economy, rising when the economy is strong and falling when it is weak. Recognizing that interest rates also move up and down with the economy, Company F has concluded that it would be better off with variable rate debt. If the companies swapped their payment obligations, an *interest rate swap* would occur. Company S would now have to make fixed payments, which is consistent with its stable cash inflows, and Company F would have a floating stream, which for it is less risky.

Note, though, that swaps can involve *side payments*. For example, if interest rates had fallen sharply since Company F issued its bonds, then its old payment obligations would be relatively high, and it would have to make a side payment to get S to agree to the swap. Similarly, if the credit risk of one company was higher than that of the other, the stronger company would be concerned about the ability of its weaker "counterparty" to make the required payments. This too would lead to the need for a side payment.

Currency swaps are similar to interest rate swaps. To illustrate, suppose Company A, an American firm, had issued $100 million of dollar-denominated bonds in the United States to fund an investment in Germany. Meanwhile, Company G, a German firm, had issued $100 million of euro-denominated bonds in Germany to make an investment in the United States. Company A would earn euros but be required to make payments in dollars, and Company G would be in a reverse situation. Thus, both companies would be exposed to exchange rate risk. However, both companies' risks would be eliminated if they swapped payment obligations. As with interest rate swaps, differences in interest rates or credit risks would require side payments.

Originally, swaps were arranged between companies by money center banks, which would match up counterparties. Such matching still occurs, but today most swaps are between companies and banks, with the banks then taking steps to ensure that their own risks are hedged. For example, Citibank might arrange a swap with Company A, which would agree to make specified payments in euros to the bank, and the bank would make the dollar payments Company A would otherwise owe. Citibank would charge a fee for setting up the swap, and these charges would reflect the creditworthiness of Company A. To protect itself against exchange rate movements, the bank would hedge its position, either by lining up a German company that needed to make dollar payments or else by using currency futures.

STRUCTURED NOTES

Structured Note
A debt obligation derived from another debt obligation.

The term **structured note** often means a debt obligation that is derived from some other debt obligation. For example, in the early 1980s, investment bankers began buying large blocks of 30-year, noncallable Treasury bonds and then *stripping* them to create a series of zero coupon bonds. The zero with the shortest maturity was backed by the first interest payment on the T-bond issue, the second shortest zero was backed by the next interest payment, and so forth, on out to a 30-year zero backed by the last interest payment plus the maturity value of the T-bond. Zeros formed by stripping T-bonds were one of the first types of structured notes.

Another important type of structured note is backed by the interest and principal payments on mortgages. In the 1970s, Wall Street firms began to buy large packages of mortgages backed by federal agencies and then place these packages, or "pools," with a trustee. Then bonds called *Collateralized Mortgage Obligations (CMOs)*, backed by the mortgage pool held in trust, were sold to pension funds, individuals for their IRA accounts, and other investors who were willing to invest in CMOs but who would not have purchased individual mortgages. This *securitization* of mortgages made billions of dollars of new capital available to home buyers.

CMOs are more difficult to evaluate than straight bonds for several reasons. First, the underlying mortgages can be prepaid at any time, and when this occurs the prepayment proceeds are used to retire part of the CMO debt itself. Therefore, the holder of a CMO is never sure when his or her bond will be called. This situation is further complicated by the fact that when interest rates decline, this causes bond prices to rise. However, declining rates also lead to mortgage prepayments, which cause the CMOs to be called especially rapidly.

It should also be noted that a variety of structured notes can be created, ranging from notes whose cash flows can be predicted with virtual certainty to other notes whose payment streams are highly uncertain. For example, investment bankers can (and do) create notes called *IOs* (for *Interest Only*), which provide cash flows from the interest component of the mortgage amortization payments, and *POs* (for *Principal Only*), which are paid from the principal repayment stream. In each case, the value of the note is found as the PV of an expected payment stream, but the length and size of the stream are uncertain. Suppose, for example, that you are offered an IO that you expect to provide payments of $100 for ten years (you expect the mortgages to be refinanced after ten years, at which time your payments will cease). Suppose further that you discount the expected payment stream at a rate of 10 percent and determine that the value is $614.46. You have $614.46 to invest, so you buy the IO, expecting to earn 10 percent on your money.

Now suppose interest rates decline. If rates fall, the discount rate would drop, and that would normally imply an increase in the IO's value. However, if rates decline sharply, this would lead to a rash of mortgage refinancings, in which case your payments, which come from interest only, would cease (or be greatly reduced), and the value of your IO would fall sharply. On the other hand, a sharp increase in interest rates would reduce refinancing, lengthen your expected payment stream, and probably increase the value of your IO.

Investment bankers can slice and dice a pool of mortgages into a bewildering array of structured notes, ranging from "plain vanilla" ones with highly predictable cash flows to "exotic" ones (sometimes called "toxic waste") whose risks are almost incalculable but are surely large.

Securitizing mortgages through CMOs serves a useful economic function—it provides an investment outlet for pension funds and others with money to invest, and it makes more money available to homeowners at a reasonable cost. Also, some investors want relatively safe investments, while others are willing to buy more speculative securities for the higher expected returns they provide. Structured notes permit a partitioning of risks to give investors what they want. There are dangers, though. The "toxic waste" is often bought by naive officials managing money for local governments like Orange County, California, when they really ought to be holding only safe securities.

INVERSE FLOATERS

A floating rate note has an interest rate that rises and falls with some interest rate index. For example, the interest rate on a $100,000 note at prime plus 1 percent would be 5.75 percent when the prime rate is 4.75 percent, and the note's rate would move up and down with the prime rate. Since both the cash flows associated with the note and the discount rate used to value it rise and fall together, the market value of the note would be relatively stable.

Inverse Floater
A note in which the interest paid moves counter to market rates.

With an **inverse floater,** the rate paid on the note moves counter to market rates. Thus, if interest rates in the economy rose, the interest rate paid on an inverse floater would fall, lowering its cash interest payments. At the same time, the discount rate used to value the inverse floater's cash flows would rise along with other rates. The combined effect of lower cash flows and a higher discount rate would lead to a very large decline in the value of the inverse floater. Thus, inverse floaters are exceptionally vulnerable to increases in interest rates. Of course, if interest rates fall, the value of an inverse floater will soar.

We have discussed the most important types of derivative securities, but certainly not all types. This discussion should, though, give you a good idea of how and why derivatives are created, and how they can be used and misused.

> ### SELF-TEST QUESTIONS
>
> Briefly describe the following types of derivative securities:
> (1) Futures and forward contracts.
> (2) Swaps.
> (3) Structured notes.
> (4) Inverse floaters.

RISK MANAGEMENT

As businesses become increasingly complex, it is becoming more and more difficult for CEOs and directors to know what problems might lie in wait. Therefore, companies need to have someone systematically look for potential problems and design safeguards to minimize potential damage. With this in mind, most larger firms have designated "risk managers" who report to the chief financial officer, while the CFOs of smaller firms personally assume risk management responsibilities. In any event, **risk management** is becoming increasingly important, and it is something finance students should understand. Therefore, in the remainder of this chapter we discuss the basics of risk management, with particular emphasis on how derivatives can be used to hedge financial risks.

Risk Management
Involves the management of unpredictable events that have adverse consequences for the firm.

FUNDAMENTALS OF RISK MANAGEMENT

It is useful to begin our discussion of risk management by defining some commonly used terms that describe different risks. Some of these risks can be mitigated, or managed, and that is what risk management is all about.

1. *Pure risks* are risks that offer only the prospect of a loss. Examples include the risk that a plant will be destroyed by fire or that a product liability suit will result in a large judgment against the firm.
2. *Speculative risks* are situations that offer the chance of a gain but might result in a loss. Thus, investments in new projects and marketable securities involve speculative risks.

3. *Demand risks* are associated with the demand for a firm's products or services. Because sales are essential to all businesses, demand risk is one of the most significant risks that firms face.

4. *Input risks* are risks associated with input costs, including both labor and materials. Thus, a company that uses copper as a raw material in its manufacturing process faces the risk that the cost of copper will increase and that it will not be able to pass this increase on to its customers.

5. *Financial risks* are risks that result from financial transactions. As we have seen, if a firm plans to issue new bonds, it faces the risk that interest rates will rise before the bonds can be brought to market. Similarly, if the firm enters into contracts with foreign customers or suppliers, it faces the risk that fluctuations in exchange rates will result in unanticipated losses.

6. *Property risks* are associated with destruction of productive assets. Thus, the threat of fire, floods, and riots imposes property risks on a firm.

7. *Personnel risks* are risks that result from employees' actions. Examples include the risks associated with employee fraud or embezzlement, or suits based on charges of age or sex discrimination.

8. *Environmental risks* include risks associated with polluting the environment. Public awareness in recent years, coupled with the huge costs of environmental cleanup, has increased the importance of this risk.

9. *Liability risks* are associated with product, service, or employee actions. Examples include the very large judgments assessed against asbestos manufacturers and some health care providers, as well as costs incurred as a result of improper actions of employees, such as driving corporate vehicles in a reckless manner.

10. *Insurable risks* are risks that can be covered by insurance. In general, property, personnel, environmental, and liability risks can be transferred to insurance companies. Note, though, that the *ability* to insure a risk does not necessarily mean that the risk *should be* insured. Indeed, a major function of risk management involves evaluating all alternatives for managing a particular risk, including self-insurance, and then choosing the optimal alternative.

Note that the risk classifications we used are somewhat arbitrary, and different classifications are commonly used in different industries. However, the list does give an idea of the wide variety of risks to which a firm can be exposed.

AN APPROACH TO RISK MANAGEMENT

Firms often use the following process for managing risks.

1. **Identify the risks faced by the firm.** Here the risk manager identifies the potential risks faced by his or her firm. (See the Industry Practice box entitled, "Microsoft's Goal: Manage Every Risk!")

2. **Measure the potential effect of each risk.** Some risks are so small as to be immaterial, whereas others have the potential for dooming the company. It is useful to segregate risks by potential effect and then to focus on the most serious threats.

3. **Decide how each relevant risk should be handled.** In most situations, risk exposure can be reduced through one of the following techniques:
   a. **Transfer the risk to an insurance company.** Often, it is advantageous to insure against, hence transfer, a risk. However, insurability does not

MICROSOFT'S GOAL: MANAGE EVERY RISK!

Twenty years ago, risk management meant buying insurance against fire, theft, and liability losses. Today, though, due to globalization, volatile markets, and a host of lawyers looking for someone to sue, a multitude of risks can adversely affect companies. Microsoft addressed these risks by creating a virtual consulting practice, called Microsoft Risk Co., to help manage the risks faced by its sales, operations, and product groups.

In an article in *CFO*, Scott Lange, who was head of Microsoft Risk at the time the article appeared, identified these 12 major sources of risk:

1. *Business partners* (interdependency, confidentiality, cultural conflict, contractual risks).
2. *Competition* (market share, price wars, industrial espionage, antitrust allegations, etc.).
3. *Customers* (product liability, credit risk, poor market timing, inadequate customer support).
4. *Distribution systems* (transportation, service availability, cost, dependence on distributors).
5. *Financial* (foreign exchange, portfolio, cash, interest rate, stock market).
6. *Operations* (facilities, contractual risks, natural hazards, internal processes and control).
7. *People* (employees, independent contractors, training, staffing inadequacy).
8. *Political* (civil unrest, war, terrorism, enforcement of intellectual property rights, change in leadership, revised economic policies).
9. *Regulatory and legislative* (antitrust, export licensing, jurisdiction, reporting and compliance, environmental).
10. *Reputations* (corporate image, brands, reputations of key employees).
11. *Strategic* (mergers and acquisitions, joint ventures and alliances, resource allocation and planning, organizational agility).
12. *Technological* (complexity, obsolescence, workforce skillsets).

According to Lange, it is important to resist the idea that risk should be categorized by how the insurance industry views it. Insurance coverage lines are a tiny subset of the risks a modern enterprise faces in the pursuit of its business objectives. He also defined the role of finance in risk management: The role of finance is to put on paper all the risks that can be identified and to try to quantify them. When possible, use a number — one number, perhaps, or a probability distribution. For example, what is the probability of losing $1 million on a product, or $10 million? At Microsoft, the finance department works with the product groups to determine the exposure. "We try to use common sense," Lange says.

In many ways risk management mirrors the quality movement of the 1980s and 1990s. The goal of the quality movement was to take the responsibility for quality out of a separate Quality Control Department and to make all managers and employees responsible for quality. Lange had a similar goal for Microsoft — to have risk management permeate the thinking of all Microsoft managers and employees.

SOURCE: Edward Teach, "Microsoft's Universe of Risk," *CFO*, March 1997, 69–72.

---

necessarily mean that a risk should be covered by insurance. In many instances, it might be better for the company to *self-insure*, which means bearing the risk directly rather than paying another party to bear it.

b. **Transfer the function that produces the risk to a third party.** For example, suppose a furniture manufacturer is concerned about potential liabilities arising from its ownership of a fleet of trucks used to transfer products from its manufacturing plant to various points across the country. One way to eliminate this risk would be to contract with a trucking company to do the shipping, thus passing the risks to a third party.

c. **Purchase derivative contracts to reduce risk.** As we indicated earlier, firms use derivatives to hedge risks. Commodity derivatives can be used to reduce input risks. For example, a cereal company may use corn or wheat futures to hedge against increases in grain prices. Similarly, financial derivatives can be used to reduce risks that arise from changes in interest rates and exchange rates.

d. Reduce the probability of occurrence of an adverse event. The expected loss arising from any risk is a function of both the probability of occurrence and the dollar loss if the adverse event occurs. In some instances, it is possible to reduce the probability that an adverse event will occur. For example, the probability that a fire will occur can be reduced by instituting a fire prevention program, by replacing old electrical wiring, and by using fire-resistant materials in areas with the greatest fire potential.

e. Reduce the magnitude of the loss associated with an adverse event. Continuing with the fire risk example, the dollar cost associated with a fire can be reduced by such actions as installing sprinkler systems, designing facilities with self-contained fire zones, and locating facilities close to a fire station.

f. Totally avoid the activity that gives rise to the risk. For example, a company might discontinue a product or service line because the risks outweigh the rewards, as with the decision by Dow-Corning to discontinue its manufacture of silicon breast implants.

Note that risk management decisions, like all corporate decisions, should be based on a cost/benefit analysis for each feasible alternative. For example, suppose it would cost $50,000 per year to conduct a comprehensive fire safety training program for all personnel in a high-risk plant. Presumably, this program would reduce the expected value of future fire losses. An alternative to the training program would be to place $50,000 annually in a reserve fund set aside to cover future fire losses. Both alternatives involve expected cash flows, and from an economic standpoint the choice should be made on the basis of the lowest present value of future costs. Thus, the same financial management techniques applied to other corporate decisions can also be applied to risk management decisions. Note, though, that if a fire occurs and a life is lost, the trade-off between fire prevention and expected losses may not sit well with a jury. The same thing holds true for product liability, as Ford, GM, and others have learned.

SELF-TEST QUESTIONS

Define the following terms:

(1) Pure risks.

(2) Speculative risks.

(3) Demand risks.

(4) Input risks.

(5) Financial risks.

(6) Property risks.

(7) Personnel risks.

(8) Environmental risks.

(9) Liability risks.

(10) Insurable risks.

(11) Self-insurance.

Should a firm insure itself against all of the insurable risks it faces? Explain.

USING DERIVATIVES TO REDUCE RISKS

Firms are subject to numerous risks related to interest rate, stock price, and exchange rate fluctuations in the financial markets. For an investor, one of the most obvious ways to reduce financial risks is to hold a broadly diversified portfolio of stocks and debt securities, including international securities and debt of varying maturities. However, derivatives can also be used to reduce the risks associated with financial and commodity markets.[12]

HEDGING WITH FUTURES

 Information from the CBOT on the financial market futures they trade is available at **http://www.cbot.com.** The site provides some general information on the various types of financial market instruments that are available and provides information on how to order specific literature or the CBOT's publications catalog.

Commodity Futures
A contract that is used to hedge against price changes for input materials.

Financial Futures
A contract that is used to hedge against fluctuating interest rates, stock prices, and exchange rates.

One of the most useful tools for reducing interest rate, exchange rate, and commodity risk is to hedge in the futures markets. Most financial and real asset transactions occur in what is known as the *spot*, or *cash*, *market*, where the asset is delivered immediately (or within a few days). *Futures*, or *futures contracts*, on the other hand, call for the purchase or sale of an asset at some future date, but at a price which is fixed today.

In 2002, futures contracts were available on more than 30 real and financial assets traded on 14 U.S. exchanges, the largest of which are the Chicago Board of Trade (CBOT) and the Chicago Mercantile Exchange (CME). Futures contracts are divided into two classes, **commodity futures** and **financial futures.** Commodity futures, which cover oil, various grains, oilseeds, livestock, meats, fibers, metals, and wood, were first traded in the United States in the mid-1800s. Financial futures, which were first traded in 1975, include Treasury bills, notes, bonds, certificates of deposit, Eurodollar deposits, foreign currencies, and stock indexes.

To illustrate how futures contracts work, consider the CBOT's contract on Treasury bonds. The basic contract is for $100,000 of a hypothetical 6 percent coupon, semiannual payment Treasury bond with 20 years to maturity. Table 18-3 shows an extract from the Treasury bond futures table that appeared in the August 21, 2002, issue of *The Wall Street Journal.*

---

[12] In Chapter 19, we discuss both the risks involved with holding foreign currencies and procedures for reducing such risks.

TABLE 18-3	Futures Prices

TREASURY BONDS (CBT) — $100,000; PTS. 32NDS OF 100%

						LIFETIME		
DELIVERY MONTH (1)	OPEN (2)	HIGH (3)	LOW (4)	SETTLE (5)	CHANGE (6)	HIGH (7)	LOW (8)	OPEN INTEREST (9)
Sept	109-00	110-04	108-27	110-02	37	112-12	96-07	367,016
Dec	107-30	108-29	107-27	108-28	37	111-04	96-06	96,216

SOURCE: *The Wall Street Journal,* August 21, 2002, C11.

The first column gives the delivery month; the next three columns give the opening, high, and low prices for that contract on that day. The opening price for the September future, 109-00, means 109 plus $0/32$, or 109 percent of par. Column 5 gives the settlement price, which is typically the price at the close of trading. Column 6 reports the change in the settlement price from the preceding day—the September contract rose $37/32$. Columns 7 and 8 give the life-of-contract highs and lows. Finally, Column 9 shows the "open interest," which is the number of contracts outstanding.

To illustrate, we focus on the Treasury bonds for December delivery. The settlement price was 108-28, or 108 plus $28/32$ percent of the $100,000 contract value. Thus, the price at which one could buy $100,000 face value of 6 percent, 20-year Treasury bonds to be delivered in December was 108.875 percent of par, or 1.08875($100,000) = $108,875.00. The contract price increased by $37/32$ of 1 percent of $100,000, or by $1,156.25, from the previous day, so if you had bought the contract yesterday, you would have gained $1,156.25. Over its life, the contract's price has ranged from 96.1875 to 111.125 percent of par, and there were 96,216 contracts outstanding, representing a total value of about $10.476 billion.

Note that the contract increased by $37/32$ of a percent on this particular day. Why would the value of the bond futures contract increase? Since bond prices increase when interest rates fall, we know that interest rates fell on that day. Moreover, we can calculate the implied rates inherent in the futures contracts. (*The Wall Street Journal* formerly provided the implied yields, but now one must calculate them.) Recall that the contract relates to a hypothetical 20-year, semiannual payment, 6 percent coupon bond. The closing price (settlement price) was 108 and $28/32$, or 108.875 percent of par. Using a financial calculator, we can solve for k_d in the following equation:

$$\$1,088.75 = \sum_{t=1}^{40} \frac{\$30}{(1 + k_d/2)^t} + \frac{\$1,000}{(1 + k_d/2)^{40}}.$$

The solution value for the six-month rate is 2.6382, which is equivalent to a nominal annual rate of 5.2764 percent, or approximately 5.28 percent. Since the price of the bond rose by $37/32$ that day, we could find the previous day's closing (settlement) price and its implied interest rate, which would turn out to be 5.37 percent. Therefore, interest rates fell by 9 basis points, which was enough to increase the value of the contract by $1,156.25.

Thus, the futures contract for December delivery of this hypothetical bond sold for $108,875.00 for 100 bonds with a par value of $100,000, which translates to a yield to maturity of about 5.3 percent. This yield reflects investors' beliefs about what the interest rate level will be in December. The spot yield on T-bonds was about 5.1 percent at the time, so the marginal trader in the futures market was predicting about a 20-basis-point increase in yields over the next four months. That prediction could, of course, turn out to be incorrect.

Now suppose that two months later interest rates in the futures market had fallen from the earlier levels, say, from 5.3 to 5.0 percent. Falling interest rates mean rising bond prices, and we could calculate that the December contract would then be worth about $112,551. Thus, the contract's value would have increased by $112,551 − $108,875 = $3,676.

When futures contracts are purchased, the purchaser does not have to put up the full amount of the purchase price; rather, the purchaser is required to post an initial *margin*, which for CBT Treasury bond contracts is $3,000 per $100,000 contract. However, investors are required to maintain a certain value in the margin account, called a *maintenance margin*. If the value of the contract declines, then the owner may be required to add additional funds to the margin account, and the more the contract value falls, the more money must be added. The value of the contract is checked at the end of every working day, and margin account adjustments are made at that time. This is called "marking to market." If an investor purchased our illustrative contract and then sold it later for $112,551, he or she would have made a profit of $3,676 on a $3,000 investment, or a return of about 120 percent in only two months. It is clear, therefore, that futures contracts offer a considerable amount of leverage. Of course, if interest rates had risen, then the value of the contract would have declined, and the investor could easily have lost his or her $3,000, or more. Futures contracts are never settled by delivery of the securities involved. Rather, the transaction is completed by reversing the trade, which amounts to selling the contract back to the original seller.[13] The actual gains and losses on the contract are realized when the futures contract is closed.

Futures contracts and options are similar to one another—so similar that people often confuse the two. Therefore, it is useful to compare the two instruments. A *futures contract* is a definite agreement on the part of one party to buy something on a specific date and at a specific price, and the other party agrees to sell on the same terms. No matter how low or how high the price goes, the two parties must settle the contract at the agreed-upon price. An *option*, on the other hand, gives someone the right to buy (call) or sell (put) an asset, but the holder of the option does not have to complete the transaction. Note also that options exist both for individual stocks and for "bundles" of stocks such as those in the S&P and *Value Line* indexes, but generally not for commodities. Futures, on the other hand, are used for commodities, debt securities, and stock indexes. The two types of instruments can be used for the same purposes. One is not necessarily better or worse than another—they are simply different.

SECURITY PRICE EXPOSURE

Firms are obviously exposed to losses due to changes in security prices when securities are held in investment portfolios, and they are also exposed during times when securities are being issued. In addition, firms are exposed to risk if they use floating rate debt to finance an investment that produces a fixed income stream. Risks such as these can often be mitigated by using derivatives. As we discussed earlier, derivatives are securities whose value stems, or is derived, from the values of other assets. Thus, options and futures contracts are derivatives, because their values depend on the prices of some underlying asset. Now we will explore further the use of two types of derivatives, futures and swaps, to help manage certain types of risk.

Speculation
With futures it involves betting on future price movements.

Futures

Futures are used for both speculation and hedging. **Speculation** involves betting on future price movements, and futures are used because of the leverage inherent in the

---

[13] The buyers and sellers of most financial futures contracts do not actually trade with one another—each trader's contractual obligation is with a futures exchange. This feature helps to guarantee the fiscal integrity of the trade. Incidentally, commodities futures traded on the exchanges are settled in the same way as financial futures, but in the case of commodities much of the contracting is done off the exchange, between farmers and processors, as *forward contracts*, in which case actual deliveries occur.

contract. **Hedging,** on the other hand, is done by a firm or individual to protect against a price change that would otherwise negatively affect profits. For example, rising interest rates and commodity (raw material) prices can hurt profits, as can adverse currency fluctuations. If two parties have mirror-image risks, then they can enter into a transaction that eliminates, as opposed to transfers, risks. This is a "natural hedge." Of course, one party to a futures contract could be a speculator, the other a hedger. Thus, to the extent that speculators broaden the market and make hedging possible, they help decrease risk to those who seek to avoid it.

There are two basic types of hedges: (1) **long hedges,** in which futures contracts are *bought* in anticipation of (or to guard against) price increases, and (2) **short hedges,** where a firm or individual *sells* futures contracts to guard against price declines. Recall that rising interest rates lower bond prices and thus decrease the value of bond futures contracts. Therefore, if a firm or individual needs to guard against an *increase* in interest rates, a futures contract that makes money if rates rise should be used. That means selling, or going short, on a futures contract. To illustrate, assume that in August Carson Foods is considering a plan to issue $10,000,000 of 20-year bonds in December to finance a capital expenditure program. The interest rate would be 7 percent if the bonds were issued today, and at that rate the project would have a positive NPV. However, interest rates may rise over the next four months, and when the issue is actually sold, the interest rate might be substantially above 7 percent, which would make the project a bad investment. Carson can protect itself against a rise in rates by hedging in the futures market.

In this situation, Carson would be hurt by an increase in interest rates, so it would use a short hedge. It would choose a futures contract on that security most similar to the one it plans to issue, long-term bonds. In this case, Carson would probably hedge with Treasury bond futures. Since it plans to issue $10,000,000 of bonds, it would sell $10,000,000/$100,000 = 100 Treasury bond contracts for delivery in December. Carson would have to put up 100($3,000) = $300,000 in margin money and also pay brokerage commissions. For illustrative purposes we use the numbers in Table 18-3. We can see from Table 18-3 that each December contract has a value of 108 plus $^{28}/_{32}$ percent, so the total value of the 100 contracts is 1.08875($100,000)(100) = $10,887,500. Now suppose renewed fears of inflation push the interest rate on Carson's debt up by 100 basis points, to 8 percent, over the next four months. If Carson issued 7 percent coupon bonds, they would bring only $901 per bond, because investors now require an 8 percent return. Thus, Carson would lose $99 per bond times 10,000 bonds, or $990,000, as a result of delaying the financing. However, the increase in interest rates would also bring about a change in the value of Carson's short position in the futures market. Since interest rates have increased, the value of the futures contract would fall, and if the interest rate on the futures contract also increased by the same full percentage point, from 5.3 to 6.3 percent, the contract value would fall to $9,661,534. Carson would then close its position in the futures market by repurchasing for $9,661,534 the contracts which it earlier sold short for $10,887,500, giving it a profit of $1,225,966, less commissions.

Thus, Carson would, if we ignore commissions and the opportunity cost of the margin money, offset the loss on the bond issue. In fact, in our example Carson more than offsets the loss, pocketing an additional $235,966. Of course, if interest rates had fallen, Carson would have lost on its futures position, but this loss would have been offset by the fact that Carson could now sell its bonds with a lower coupon.

If futures contracts existed on Carson's own debt, and interest rates moved identically in the spot and futures markets, then the firm could construct a **perfect hedge,** in which gains on the futures contract would exactly offset losses on the bonds. In reality, it is virtually impossible to construct perfect hedges, because in most cases the underlying asset is not identical to the futures asset, and even when they are, prices (and interest rates) may not move exactly together in the spot and futures markets.

Note too that if Carson had been planning an equity offering, and if its stock tended to move fairly closely with one of the stock indexes, the company could have hedged against falling stock prices by selling short the index future. Even better, if options on Carson's stock were traded in the option market, then it could use options rather than futures to hedge against falling stock prices.

The futures and options markets permit flexibility in the timing of financial transactions, because the firm can be protected, at least partially, against changes that occur between the time a decision is reached and the time when the transaction will be completed. However, this protection has a cost—the firm must pay commissions. Whether or not the protection is worth the cost is a matter of judgment. The decision to hedge also depends on management's risk aversion as well as the company's strength and ability to assume the risk in question. In theory, the reduction in risk resulting from a hedge transaction should have a value exactly equal to the cost of the hedge. Thus, a firm should be indifferent to hedging. However, many firms believe that hedging is worthwhile. Trammell Crow, a large Texas real estate developer, recently used T-bill futures to lock in interest costs on floating rate construction loans, while Dart & Kraft used Eurodollar futures to protect its marketable securities portfolio. Merrill Lynch, Salomon Smith Barney, and the other investment banking houses hedge in the futures and options markets to protect themselves when they are engaged in major underwritings.

Swaps

A *swap* is another method for reducing financial risks. As we noted earlier, a swap is an exchange.[14] In finance, it is an exchange of cash payment obligations, in which each party to the swap prefers the payment type or pattern of the other party. In other words, swaps occur because the counterparties prefer the terms of the other's debt contract, and the swap enables each party to obtain a preferred payment obligation. Generally, one party has a fixed rate obligation and the other a floating rate obligation, or one has an obligation denominated in one currency and the other in another currency.

Major changes have occurred over time in the swaps market. First, standardized contracts have been developed for the most common types of swaps, and this has had two effects: (1) Standardized contracts lower the time and effort involved in arranging swaps, and thus lower transactions costs. (2) The development of standardized contracts has led to a secondary market for swaps, which has increased the liquidity and efficiency of the swaps market. A number of international banks now make markets in swaps and offer quotes on several standard types. Also, as noted above, the banks now take counterparty positions in swaps, so it is not necessary to find another firm with mirror-image needs before a swap transaction can be completed. The bank would

---

[14] For more information on swaps, see Clifford W. Smith, Jr., Charles W. Smithson, and Lee Macdonald Wakeman, "The Evolving Market for Swaps," *Midland Corporate Finance Journal*, Winter 1986, 20–32; and Mary E. Ruth and Steve R. Vinson, "Managing Interest Rate Uncertainty Amidst Change," *Public Utilities Fortnightly*, December 22, 1988, 28–31.

generally find a final counterparty for the swap at a later date, so its positioning helps make the swap market more operationally efficient.[15]

To further illustrate a swap transaction, consider the following situation. An electric utility currently has outstanding a five-year floating rate note tied to the prime rate. The prime rate could rise significantly over the period, so the note carries a high degree of interest rate risk. The utility could, however, enter into a swap with a counterparty, say, Citibank, wherein the utility would pay Citibank a fixed series of interest payments over the five-year period, and Citibank would make the company's required floating rate payments. As a result, the utility would have converted a floating rate loan to a fixed rate loan, and the risk of rising interest rates would have been passed from the utility to Citibank. Such a transaction can lower both parties' risks—because banks' revenues rise as interest rates rise, Citibank's risk would actually be lower if it had floating rate obligations.

Longer-term swaps can also be made. Recently, Citibank entered into a 17-year swap in an electricity cogeneration project financing deal. The project's sponsors were unable to obtain fixed rate financing on reasonable terms, and they were afraid that interest rates would increase and make the project unprofitable. The project's sponsors were, however, able to borrow from local banks on a floating rate basis and then arrange a simultaneous swap with Citibank for a fixed rate obligation.

COMMODITY PRICE EXPOSURE

As we noted earlier, futures markets were established for many commodities long before they began to be used for financial instruments. We can use Porter Electronics, which uses large quantities of copper as well as several precious metals, to illustrate inventory hedging. Suppose that in August 2002, Porter foresaw a need for 100,000 pounds of copper in June 2003 for use in fulfilling a fixed price contract to supply solar power cells to the U.S. government. Porter's managers are concerned that a strike by Chilean copper miners will occur, which could raise the price of copper in world markets and possibly turn the expected profit on the solar cells into a loss.

Porter could, of course, go ahead and buy the copper that it will need to fulfill the contract, but if it does it will incur substantial carrying costs. As an alternative, the company could hedge against increasing copper prices in the futures market. The New York Commodity Exchange trades standard copper futures contracts of 25,000 pounds each. Thus, Porter could buy four contracts (go long) for delivery in June 2003. Assume that these contracts were trading in August for about $1.00 per pound, and that the spot price at that date was about $1.02 per pound. If copper prices do rise appreciably over the next ten months, the value of Porter's long position in copper futures would increase, thus offsetting some of the price increase in the commodity itself. Of course, if copper prices fall, Porter would lose money on its futures contract, but the company would be buying the copper on the spot market at

---

[15] The role of banks in the global swap market is worrisome to the Federal Reserve and other central banks. When banks take positions in swaps, they are themselves exposed to various risks, and if the counterparties cannot meet their obligations, a bank could suddenly become liable for making two sets of payments. Further, swaps are "off balance sheet" transactions, so it is currently impossible to tell just how large the swap market is or who has what obligation. The fear is that if one large multinational bank gets into trouble, the entire worldwide swap market could collapse like a house of cards. See "Swap Fever: Big Money, Big Risks," *Fortune*, June 1, 1992.

a cheaper price, so it would make a higher-than-anticipated profit on its sale of solar cells. Thus, hedging in the copper futures market locks in the cost of raw materials and removes some risk to which the firm would otherwise be exposed.

Eastman Kodak uses silver futures to hedge against short-term increases in the price of silver, which is the primary ingredient in black-and-white film. Many other manufacturers, such as Alcoa with aluminum and Archer Daniels Midland with grains, routinely use the futures markets to reduce the risks associated with input price volatility.

THE USE AND MISUSE OF DERIVATIVES

Most of the news stories about derivatives are related to financial disasters. Much less is heard about the benefits of derivatives. However, because of these benefits, more than 90 percent of large U.S. companies use derivatives on a regular basis. In today's market, sophisticated investors and analysts are demanding that firms use derivatives to hedge certain risks. For example, Compaq Computer was recently sued by a shareholder group for failing to properly hedge its foreign exchange exposure. The shareholders lost the suit, but Compaq got the message and now uses currency futures to hedge its international operations. In another example, Prudential Securities reduced its earnings estimate for Cone Mills, a North Carolina textile company, because Cone did not sufficiently hedge its exposure to changing cotton prices. These examples lead to one conclusion: if a company can safely and inexpensively hedge its risks, it should do so.

There can, however, be a downside to the use of derivatives. Hedging is invariably cited by authorities as a "good" use of derivatives, whereas speculating with derivatives is often cited as a "bad" use. Some people and organizations can afford to bear the risks involved in speculating with derivatives, but others are either not sufficiently knowledgeable about the risks they are taking or else should not be taking those risks in the first place. Most would agree that the typical corporation should use derivatives only to hedge risks, not to speculate in an effort to increase profits. Hedging allows managers to concentrate on running their core businesses without having to worry about interest rate, currency, and commodity price variability. However, problems can arise quickly when hedges are improperly constructed or when a corporate treasurer, eager to report relatively high returns, uses derivatives for speculative purposes.

One interesting example of a derivatives debacle involved Kashima Oil, a Japanese firm that imports oil. It pays with U.S. dollars but then sells oil in the Japanese market for yen. Kashima began by using currency futures to hedge, but then it started to speculate on dollar-yen price movements, hoping to increase profits. When the currency markets moved against Kashima's speculative position, lax accounting rules permitted it to avoid reporting the losses by simply rolling over the contract. By the time Kashima bit the bullet and closed its position, it had lost $1.5 billion. Other companies have experienced similar problems.

Our position is that derivatives can and should be used to hedge against certain risks, but that the leverage inherent in derivatives contracts makes them potentially dangerous instruments. Also, CFOs, CEOs, and board members should be reasonably knowledgeable about the derivatives their firms use, should establish policies regarding when they can and cannot be used, and should establish audit procedures to ensure that the policies are actually carried out. Moreover, a firm's derivatives position should be reported to stockholders, because stockholders have a right to know when situations such as that involving Kashima might arise.

What is a futures contract?

Explain how a company can use the futures market to hedge against rising interest rates.

What is a swap? Describe the mechanics of a fixed rate to floating rate swap.

Explain how a company can use the futures market to hedge against rising raw materials prices.

How should derivatives be used in risk management? What problems can occur?

TYING IT ALL TOGETHER

Companies every day face a variety of risks, for it is hard to succeed without taking some chances. Back in Chapter 5, we discussed the trade-off between risk and return. If some action can lower risk without lowering returns too much, then the action can enhance value. With this in mind, we described in this chapter the various types of risks that companies face, and we discussed the basic principles of corporate risk management. One important tool for managing risk is the derivatives market. Consequently, this chapter has also provided an introduction to derivative securities. The key concepts covered are listed below.

- **Derivatives** are securities whose values are determined by the market price or interest rate of some other security.

- A **hedge** is a transaction that lowers risk. A **natural hedge** is a transaction between two **counterparties** where both parties' risks are reduced.

- **Options** are financial instruments that (1) are created by exchanges rather than firms, (2) are bought and sold primarily by investors, and (3) are of importance to both investors and financial managers.

- The two primary types of options are (1) **call options,** which give the holder the right to purchase a specified asset at a given price (the **exercise,** or **strike, price**) for a given period of time, and (2) **put options,** which give the holder the right to sell an asset at a given price for a given period of time.

- A call option's **exercise value** is defined as the current price of the stock less the strike price.

- The **Black-Scholes Option Pricing Model (OPM)** can be used to estimate the value of a call option.

- A **futures contract** is a standardized contract that is traded on an exchange and is "marked to market" daily, but where physical delivery of the underlying asset usually does not occur.

- Under a **forward contract,** one party agrees to buy a commodity at a specific price and a specific future date and the other party agrees to make the sale. Delivery does occur.

- A **structured note** is a debt obligation derived from another debt obligation.
- A **swap** is an exchange of cash payment obligations. Swaps occur because the parties involved prefer someone else's payment stream.
- **Financial futures** markets permit firms to create **hedge** positions to protect themselves against fluctuating interest rates, stock prices, and exchange rates.
- **Commodity futures** can be used to hedge against input price increases.
- **Long hedges** involve buying futures contracts to guard against price increases.
- **Short hedges** involve selling futures contracts to guard against price declines.
- A **perfect hedge** occurs when the gain or loss on the hedged transaction exactly offsets the loss or gain on the unhedged position.

QUESTIONS

18-1 Why do options typically sell at prices higher than their exercise values?

18-2 Discuss some of the techniques available to reduce risk exposure.

18-3 Explain how the futures markets can be used to reduce interest rate and input price risk.

18-4 How can swaps be used to reduce the risks associated with debt contracts?

18-5 Give two reasons stockholders might be indifferent between owning the stock of a firm with volatile cash flows and that of a firm with stable cash flows.

18-6 List seven reasons risk management might increase the value of a firm.

SELF-TEST PROBLEMS (SOLUTIONS APPEAR IN APPENDIX B)

ST-1
Key terms
Define each of the following terms:
a. Derivative
b. Option; call option; put option
c. Exercise value; strike price
d. Black-Scholes Option Pricing Model; riskless hedge
e. Risk management
f. Futures contract; forward contract
g. Hedging; natural hedge; long hedges; short hedges; perfect hedge
h. Swap; structured note
i. Commodity futures; financial futures
j. Long-term Equity AnticiPation Security (LEAPS)
k. Inverse floater
l. Speculation

ST-2
Black-Scholes model
An analyst is interested in using the Black-Scholes model to value call options on the stock of Ledbetter Inc. The analyst has accumulated the following information:

- The price of the stock is $33.
- The strike price is $33.
- The option matures in 6 months (t = 0.50).
- The standard deviation of the stock's returns is 0.30 and the variance is 0.09.
- The risk-free rate is 10 percent.

Given this information, the analyst is then able to calculate some other necessary components of the Black-Scholes model:

- $d_1 = 0.34177$.
- $d_2 = 0.12964$.

- $N(d_1) = 0.63369$.
- $N(d_2) = 0.55155$.

$N(d_1)$ and $N(d_2)$ represent areas under a standard normal distribution function. Using the Black-Scholes model, what is the value of the call option?

STARTER PROBLEMS

18-1
Options
A call option on the stock of Bedrock Boulders has a market price of $7. The stock sells for $30 a share, and the option has an exercise price of $25 a share.
a. What is the exercise value of the call option?
b. What is the premium on the option?

18-2
Options
Which of the following events are likely to increase the market value of a call option on a common stock? Explain.
a. An increase in the stock's price.
b. An increase in the volatility of the stock price.
c. An increase in the risk-free rate.
d. A decrease in the time until the option expires.

EXAM-TYPE PROBLEMS

The problems included in this section are set up in such a way that they could be used as multiple-choice exam problems.

18-3
Black-Scholes model
Assume you have been given the following information on Purcell Industries:

Current stock price = $15   Exercise price of option = $15
Time to maturity of option = 6 months   Risk-free rate = 10%
Variance of stock price = 0.12 $d_1 = 0.32660$
$d_2 = 0.08165$ $N(d_1) = 0.62795$
$N(d_2) = 0.53252$

Using the Black-Scholes Option Pricing Model, what would be the value of the option?

18-4
Options
The exercise price on one of Flanagan Company's options is $15, its exercise value is $22, and its premium is $5. What are the option's market value and the price of the stock?

18-5
Futures
What is the implied interest rate on a Treasury bond ($100,000) futures contract that settled at 100-16? If interest rates increased by 1 percent, what would be the contract's new value?

PROBLEMS

18-6
Hedging
The Zinn Company plans to issue $20,000,000 of 10-year bonds in December to help finance a new research and development laboratory. It is now August, and the current cost of debt to the high-risk biotech company is 11 percent. However, the firm's financial manager is concerned that interest rates will climb even higher in coming months.
a. Use data in Table 18-3 to create a hedge against rising interest rates.
b. Assume that interest rates in general increase by 200 basis points. How well did your hedge perform?
c. What is a perfect hedge? Are most real-world hedges perfect? Explain.

18-7
Options
Audrey is considering an investment in Morgan Communications, whose stock currently sells for $60. A put option on Morgan's stock, with an exercise price of $55, has a market value of $3.06. Meanwhile, a call option on the stock with the same exercise price and time to maturity

has a market value of $9.29. The market believes that at the expiration of the options the stock price will be either $70 or $50, with equal probability.

a. What is the premium associated with the put option? The call option?

b. If Morgan's stock price increases to $70, what would be the return to an investor who bought a share of the stock? If the investor bought a call option on the stock? If the investor bought a put option on the stock?

c. If Morgan's stock price decreases to $50, what would be the return to an investor who bought a share of the stock? If the investor bought a call option on the stock? If the investor bought a put option on the stock?

d. If Audrey buys 0.6 share of Morgan Communications and sells one call option on the stock, has she created a riskless hedged investment? What is the total value of her portfolio under each scenario?

e. If Audrey buys 0.75 share of Morgan Communications and sells one call option on the stock, has she created a riskless hedged investment? What is the total value of her portfolio under each scenario?

SPREADSHEET PROBLEM

18-8
Black-Scholes model
Rework Problem 18-3 using the spreadsheet model. Then work the next two parts of this problem given below.

a. Construct data tables for the intrinsic value and Black-Scholes exercise value for this option, and graph this relationship. Include possible stock price values ranging up to $30.00.

b. Suppose this call option is purchased today. Draw the profit diagram of this option position at expiration.

INTEGRATED CASE

TROPICAL SWEETS INC.

18-9 Derivatives and Corporate Risk Management Assume that you have just been hired as a financial analyst by Tropical Sweets Inc., a mid-sized California company that specializes in creating exotic candies from tropical fruits such as mangoes, papayas, and dates. The firm's CEO, George Yamaguchi, recently returned from an industry corporate executive conference in San Francisco, and one of the sessions he attended was on the pressing need for smaller companies to institute corporate risk management programs. Since no one at Tropical Sweets is familiar with the basics of derivatives and corporate risk management, Yamaguchi has asked you to prepare a brief report that the firm's executives could use to gain at least a cursory understanding of the topics.

To begin, you gathered some outside materials on derivatives and corporate risk management and used these materials to draft a list of pertinent questions that need to be answered. In fact, one possible approach to the paper is to use a question-and-answer format. Now that the questions have been drafted, you have to develop the answers.

a. Why might stockholders be indifferent to whether or not a firm reduces the volatility of its cash flows?

b. What are seven reasons risk management might increase the value of a corporation?

c. What is an option? What is the single most important characteristic of an option?

d. Options have a unique set of terminology. Define the following terms:
   (1) Call option.
   (2) Put option.
   (3) Exercise price.
   (4) Striking, or strike, price.
   (5) Option price.
   (6) Expiration date.
   (7) Exercise value.
   (8) Covered option.
   (9) Naked option.
   (10) In-the-money call.
   (11) Out-of-the-money call.
   (12) LEAPS.

e. Consider Tropical Sweets' call option with a $25 strike price. The following table contains historical values for this option at different stock prices:

STOCK PRICE	CALL OPTION PRICE
$25	$ 3.00
30	7.50
35	12.00
40	16.50
45	21.00
50	25.50

(1) Create a table that shows (a) stock price, (b) strike price, (c) exercise value, (d) option price, and (e) the premium of option price over exercise value.
(2) What happens to the premium of option price over exercise value as the stock price rises? Why?
f. In 1973, Fischer Black and Myron Scholes developed the Black-Scholes Option Pricing Model (OPM).
(1) What assumptions underlie the OPM?
(2) Write out the three equations that constitute the model.
(3) What is the value of the following call option according to the OPM?

Stock price = $27.00

Exercise price = $25.00

Time to expiration = 6 months

Risk-free rate = 6.0%

Stock return variance = 0.11

g. What effect does each of the following call option parameters have on the value of a call option?
(1) Current stock price.
(2) Exercise price.
(3) Option's term to maturity.

(4) Risk-free rate.
(5) Variability of the stock price.
h. What is corporate risk management? Why is it important to all firms?
i. Risks that firms face can be categorized in many ways. Define the following types of risk:
(1) Speculative risks.
(2) Pure risks.
(3) Demand risks.
(4) Input risks.
(5) Financial risks.
(6) Property risks.
(7) Personnel risks.
(8) Environmental risks.
(9) Liability risks.
(10) Insurable risks.
j. What are the three steps of corporate risk management?
k. What are some actions that companies can take to minimize or reduce risk exposure?
l. What is financial risk exposure? Describe the following concepts and techniques that can be used to reduce financial risks:
(1) Derivatives.
(2) Futures markets.
(3) Hedging.
(4) Swaps.
m. Describe how commodity futures markets can be used to reduce input price risk.

CYBER PROBLEM

Please go to our web site **http://brigham.swlearning.com** to access the Cyberproblems.

MULTINATIONAL FINANCIAL MANAGEMENT*

U.S. FIRMS LOOK OVERSEAS TO ENHANCE SHAREHOLDER VALUE

From the end of World War II until the 1970s, the United States dominated the world economy. However, that situation no longer exists. Raw materials, finished goods, services, and money flow freely across most national boundaries, as do innovative ideas and new technologies. World-class U.S. companies are making breakthroughs in foreign labs, obtaining capital from foreign investors, and putting foreign employees on the fast track to the top. Dozens of top U.S. manufacturers, including Dow Chemical, Colgate-Palmolive, Gillette, Hewlett-Packard, and Xerox, sell more of their products outside the United States than they do at home. Service firms are not far behind, as Citigroup, Merrill Lynch, McDonald's, and AFLAC all receive more than 20 percent of their revenues from foreign sales.

The trend is even more pronounced in profits. In recent years, Coca-Cola and many other companies have made more money in the Pacific Rim and Western Europe than in the United States. However, like other companies, Coke has found that global investing also presents unique challenges and risks. For example, a few years ago, weaknesses in the Asian economy and a contamination scare in Belgium dealt a significant blow to Coke's bottom line.

Successful global companies such as Coca-Cola must conduct business in different economies, and they must be sensitive to the many subtleties of different cultures and political systems. Accordingly, they find it useful to blend into the foreign landscape to help win product acceptance and avoid political problems.

At the same time, foreign-based multinationals are arriving on American shores in ever greater numbers. Sweden's ABB, the Netherlands's Philips, France's Thomson, and Japan's Fujitsu and Honda are all waging campaigns to be identified as American companies that employ Americans, transfer technology to America, and help the U.S. trade balance. Few Americans know or care that Thomson owns the RCA and General Electric names in consumer electronics, or that Philips owns Magnavox.

The emergence of "world companies" raises a host of questions for governments. For example, should domestic firms be favored, or does it make no difference what a company's nationality is as long as it provides domestic jobs? Should a company make an effort to keep jobs in its home country, or should it produce where total production costs are lowest? What nation controls the technology developed by a multinational corporation, particularly if the technology can be used in military applications? Must a multinational company adhere to rules imposed in its home country with respect to its operations outside the home country? And if a U.S. firm such as Xerox produces copiers in Japan and then ships them to the United States, should they be reflected in the trade deficit in the same way as Toshiba copiers imported from Japan? Keep these questions in mind as you read this chapter. When you finish it, you should have a better appreciation of both the problems facing governments and the difficult but profitable opportunities facing managers of multinational companies.

---

* This chapter was coauthored with Professor Roy Crum of the University of Florida and Subu Venkataraman of Morgan Stanley Dean Witter.

723

Managers of multinational companies must deal with a wide range of issues that are not present when a company operates in a single country. In this chapter, we highlight the key differences between multinational and domestic corporations, and we discuss the impact these differences have on the financial management of multinational businesses. ■

MULTINATIONAL OR GLOBAL CORPORATIONS

Multinational, or Global, Corporation
A firm that operates in an integrated fashion in a number of countries.

The term **multinational,** or **global, corporation** is used to describe a firm that operates in an integrated fashion in a number of countries. During the past 20 years, a new and fundamentally different form of international commercial activity has developed, and this has greatly increased worldwide economic and political interdependence. Rather than merely buying resources from and selling goods to foreign nations, multinational firms now make direct investments in fully integrated operations, from extraction of raw materials, through the manufacturing process, to distribution to consumers throughout the world. Today, multinational corporate networks control a large and growing share of the world's technological, marketing, and productive resources.

Companies, both U.S. and foreign, go "global" for six primary reasons:

1. *To broaden their markets.* After a company has saturated its home market, growth opportunities are often better in foreign markets. Thus, such home-grown firms as Coca-Cola and McDonald's are aggressively expanding into overseas markets, and foreign firms such as Sony and Toshiba now dominate the U.S. consumer electronics market. Also, as products become more complex, and development becomes more expensive, it is necessary to sell more units to cover overhead costs, so larger markets are critical. Thus, movie companies have "gone global" to get the volume necessary to support pictures such as *Titanic.*

2. *To seek raw materials.* Many U.S. oil companies, such as Exxon Mobil, have major subsidiaries around the world to ensure access to the basic resources needed to sustain the companies' primary business line.

3. *To seek new technology.* No single nation holds a commanding advantage in all technologies, so companies are scouring the globe for leading scientific and design ideas. For example, Xerox has introduced more than 80 different office copiers in the United States that were engineered and built by its Japanese joint venture, Fuji Xerox. Similarly, versions of the superconcentrated detergent that Procter & Gamble first formulated in Japan in response to a rival's product are now being marketed in Europe and the United States.

4. *To seek production efficiency.* Companies in high-cost countries are shifting production to low-cost regions. For example, GE has production and assembly

plants in Mexico, South Korea, and Singapore, and even Japanese manufacturers are shifting some of their production to lower-cost countries in the Pacific Rim. BMW, in response to high production costs in Germany, has built assembly plants in the United States. The ability to shift production from country to country has important implications for labor costs in all countries. For example, when Xerox threatened to move its copier rebuilding work to Mexico, its union in Rochester agreed to work rule changes and productivity improvements that kept the operation in the United States. Some multinational companies make decisions almost daily on where to shift production. When Dow Chemical saw European demand for a certain solvent declining, the company scaled back production at a German plant and shifted its production to another chemical that had previously been imported from the United States. Relying on complex computer models for making such decisions, Dow runs its plants at peak capacity and thus keeps capital costs down.

5. *To avoid political and regulatory hurdles.* The primary reason Japanese auto companies moved production to the United States was to get around U.S. import quotas. Now Honda, Nissan, Toyota, Mazda, and Mitsubishi are all assembling vehicles in the United States. One of the factors that prompted U.S. pharmaceutical maker SmithKline and Britain's Beecham to merge was that they wanted to avoid licensing and regulatory delays in their largest markets, Western Europe and the United States. Now SmithKline Beecham can identify itself as an inside player in both Europe and the United States. Similarly, when Germany's BASF launched biotechnology research at home, it confronted legal and political challenges from the environmentally conscious Green movement. In response, BASF shifted its cancer and immune system research to two laboratories in Boston suburbs. This location is attractive not only because of its large number of engineers and scientists but also because the Boston area has resolved controversies involving safety, animal rights, and the environment. "We decided it would be better to have the laboratories located where we have fewer insecurities about what will happen in the future," said Rolf-Dieter Acker, BASF's director of biotechnology research.

6. *To diversify.* By establishing worldwide production facilities and markets, firms can cushion the impact of adverse economic trends in any single country. For example, General Motors softened the blow of poor sales in the United States during the 1990–1991 recession with strong sales by its European subsidiaries. In general, geographic diversification works because the economic ups and downs of different countries are not perfectly correlated. Therefore, companies investing overseas benefit from diversification in the same way that individuals benefit from investing in a broad portfolio of stocks.

Over the past 10 to 15 years, there has been an increasing amount of investment in the United States by foreign corporations, and in foreign nations by U.S. corporations. This trend is shown in Figure 19-1, and it is important because of its implications for eroding the traditional doctrine of independence and self-reliance that has been a hallmark of U.S. policy. Just as U.S. corporations with extensive overseas operations are said to use their economic power to exert substantial economic and political influence over host governments in many parts of the world, it is feared that foreign corporations are gaining similar sway over U.S. policy. These developments suggest an increasing degree of mutual influence and interdependence among business enterprises and nations, to which the United States is not immune.

FIGURE 19-1

Direct Investment Positions on a Historical-Cost Basis, 1982–2001

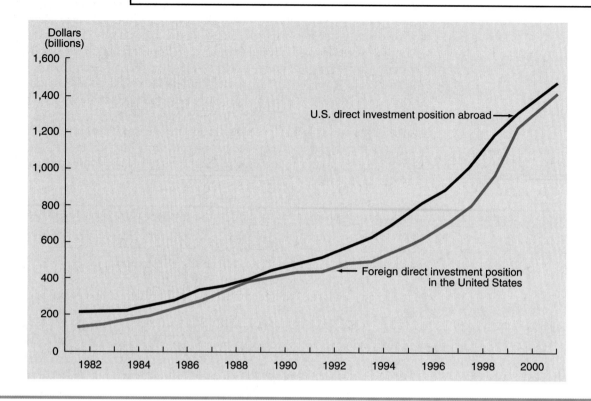

SOURCE: Adapted from Maria Borga and Daniel R. Yorgason, "Direct Investment Positions for 2001: Country and Industry Detail," *Survey of Current Business*, July 2002, 25–35.

SELF-TEST QUESTIONS

What is a multinational corporation?

Why do companies "go global"?

MULTINATIONAL VERSUS DOMESTIC FINANCIAL MANAGEMENT

In theory, the concepts and procedures discussed in the first 18 chapters are valid for both domestic and multinational operations. However, six major factors distinguish financial management in firms operating entirely within a single country from firms that operate globally:

1. *Different currency denominations.* Cash flows in various parts of a multinational corporate system will be denominated in different currencies. Hence, an analysis of exchange rates must be included in all financial analyses.

2. *Economic and legal ramifications.* Each country has its own unique economic and legal systems, and these differences can cause significant problems when a cor-

poration tries to coordinate and control its worldwide operations. For example, differences in tax laws among countries can cause a given economic transaction to have strikingly different after-tax consequences, depending on where the transaction occurs. Similarly, differences in legal systems of host nations, such as the Common Law of Great Britain versus the French Civil Law, complicate matters ranging from the simple recording of business transactions to the role played by the judiciary in resolving conflicts. Such differences can restrict multinational corporations' flexibility in deploying resources, and can even make procedures that are required in one part of the company illegal in another part. These differences also make it difficult for executives trained in one country to move easily to another.

3. *Language differences*. The ability to communicate is critical in all business transactions, and here U.S. citizens are often at a disadvantage because we are generally fluent only in English, while European and Japanese businesspeople are usually fluent in several languages, including English. Thus, they can invade our markets more easily than we can penetrate theirs.

4. *Cultural differences*. Even within geographic regions that are considered relatively homogeneous, different countries have unique cultural heritages that shape values and influence the conduct of business. Multinational corporations find that matters such as defining the appropriate goals of the firm, attitudes toward risk, dealings with employees, and the ability to curtail unprofitable operations vary dramatically from one country to the next.

5. *Role of governments*. Most financial models assume the existence of a competitive marketplace in which the terms of trade are determined by the participants. The government, through its power to establish basic ground rules, is involved in the process, but its role is minimal. Thus, the market provides the primary barometer of success, and it gives the best clues about what must be done to remain competitive. This view of the process is reasonably correct for the United States and Western Europe, but it does not accurately describe the situation in most of the world. Frequently, the terms under which companies compete, the actions that must be taken or avoided, and the terms of trade on various transactions are determined not in the marketplace but by direct negotiation between the host government and the multinational corporation. This is essentially a political process, and it must be treated as such. Thus, our traditional financial models have to be recast to include political and other noneconomic aspects of the decision.

6. *Political risk*. A nation is free to place constraints on the transfer of corporate resources and even to expropriate without compensation assets within their boundaries. This is *political risk*, and it tends to be largely a given rather than a variable that can be changed by negotiation. Political risk varies from country to country, and it must be addressed explicitly in any financial analysis. Another aspect of political risk is terrorism against U.S. firms or executives. For example, U.S. and Japanese executives have been kidnapped and held for ransom in several South American countries.

These six factors complicate financial management, and they increase the risks faced by multinational firms. However, the prospects for high returns, diversification benefits, and other factors make it worthwhile for firms to accept these risks and learn how to manage them.

Identify and briefly discuss six major factors that complicate financial management in multinational firms.

Exchange Rate
The number of units of a given currency that can be purchased for one unit of another currency.

EXCHANGE RATES

An **exchange rate** specifies the number of units of a given currency that can be purchased with one unit of another currency. Exchange rates appear in the financial sections of newspapers each day. Selected rates from *The Wall Street Journal* are given in Table 19-1. The values shown in Column 1 are the number of U.S. dollars required to purchase one unit of foreign currency; this is called a *direct quotation*. Direct quotations have a dollar sign in their quotation. Thus, the direct U.S. dollar quotation for the Swiss franc is $0.6632, because one Swiss franc could be bought for 66.32 cents. The exchange rates given in Column 2 represent the number of units of foreign currency that can be purchased for one U.S. dollar; these are called *indirect quotations*. Indirect quotations often begin with the foreign currency's equivalent to the dollar sign. Thus, the indirect quotation for the Swiss franc is SF1.5078. (The "SF" stands for *Swiss franc*, and it is equivalent to the symbol "$.") Normal practice in the United States is to use indirect quotations (Column 2) for all currencies other

The Bloomberg World Currency Values site provides up-to-the-minute foreign currency values versus the U.S. dollar, as well as a cross-currency table similar to that found in *The Wall Street Journal* for the world's major currencies. The site can be accessed at **http://www.bloomberg.com/ markets/fxc.html.**

TABLE 19-1	**Illustrative Exchange Rates**	

	DIRECT QUOTATION: U.S. DOLLARS REQUIRED TO BUY ONE UNIT OF FOREIGN CURRENCY (1)	**INDIRECT QUOTATION: NUMBER OF UNITS OF FOREIGN CURRENCY PER U.S. DOLLAR (2)**
Brazilian real	$0.3247	3.0800
British pound	1.5398	0.6494
Canadian dollar	0.6308	1.5853
Denmark krone	0.1302	7.6800
Euro	0.9666	1.0346
Hungarian forint	0.003962	252.39
Israeli shekel	0.2129	4.6970
Japanese yen	0.008273	120.87
Mexican peso	0.1027	9.7380
South African rand	0.0943	10.6040
Swedish krona	0.1033	9.6778
Swiss franc	0.6632	1.5078
Venezuelan bolivar	0.000742	1347.50

NOTE: Column 2 equals 1.0 divided by Column 1. However, rounding differences do occur.
SOURCE: Adapted from *The Wall Street Journal*, August 7, 2002, C14.

than British pounds, for which direct quotations are given. Thus, we speak of the pound as "selling at $1.54" but of the Swiss franc as "being at 1.51."

It is also a universal convention on the world's foreign currency exchanges to state all exchange rates except British pounds on a "dollar basis"—that is, as the foreign currency price of one U.S. dollar as reported in Column 2 of Table 19-1. Thus, in all currency trading centers, whether in New York, Frankfurt, London, Tokyo, or anywhere else, the exchange rate for the Swiss franc would be displayed as SF1.5078. This convention eliminates confusion when comparing quotations from one trading center with those from another.

We can use the data in Table 19-1 to show how one works with exchange rates. Suppose a U.S. tourist on holiday flies from New York to London, then to Paris, then on to Zurich, and finally back to New York. When she arrives at London's Heathrow Airport, she goes to the bank to check the foreign exchange listing. The rate she observes for U.S. dollars is $1.5398; this means that £1 will cost her $1.5398. Assume that she exchanges $2,500 for $2,500/$1.5398 = £1,623.59 and enjoys a week's vacation in London, spending £823.59 while there and saving £800.

At the end of the week she travels to Dover to catch the Hovercraft to Calais on the coast of France and realizes that she needs to exchange her 800 remaining British pounds for euros. However, what she sees on the board is the direct quotation between pounds and dollars ($1.5398) and the indirect quotation between euros and dollars (€1.0346). (For our purposes, we assume that the exchange rates in effect at the start of the trip remain in effect throughout our example. This is unrealistic for reasons explained later in this chapter.) The exchange rate between any two currencies is called a *cross rate*. Cross rates are actually calculated on the basis of various currencies relative to the U.S. dollar. For example, the cross rate between British pounds and euros is computed as follows:

$$\text{Cross rate} = \frac{\text{Dollars}}{\text{Pound}} \times \frac{\text{Euros}}{\text{Dollar}} = \frac{\text{Euros}}{\text{Pound}}$$

$$= 1.5398 \text{ dollars per pound} \times 1.0346 \text{ euros per dollar}$$

$$= 1.5931 \text{ euros per pound}.$$

Therefore, for every British pound she would receive 1.5931 euros, so she would receive 1.5931 × 800 = 1,274.46 ≈ 1,274 euros.

When she finishes touring in France and arrives in Switzerland, she again needs to determine a cross rate, this time between euros and Swiss francs. The dollar-basis quotes she sees, as shown in Table 19-1, are €1.0346 per dollar and SF1.5078 per dollar. To find the cross rate, she must divide the two dollar-basis rates:

$$\text{Cross rate} = \frac{\dfrac{\text{Swiss Francs}}{\text{Dollar}}}{\dfrac{\text{Euros}}{\text{Dollar}}} = \frac{\text{Swiss Francs}}{\text{Euro}}$$

$$= \frac{\text{SF1.5078 per \$}}{\text{61.0346 per \$}} = 1.4574 \text{ Swiss francs per euro.}$$

Then, if she had €750 remaining, she could exchange them for 1.4574 × 750 = SF1,093.05, or about 1,093 Swiss francs.

Finally, when her vacation ends and she returns to New York, the quotation she sees is SF1.5078, which tells her that she can buy 1.5078 Swiss francs for a dollar. She now holds 100 Swiss francs, so she wants to know how many U.S. dollars she will receive for her 100 Swiss francs. First, she must find the reciprocal of the quoted indirect rate,

$$\frac{1}{\text{SF1.5078}} = \$0.6632,$$

which is the direct quotation shown in Table 19-1, Column 1. Then she will end up with

$$\$0.6632 \times 100 = \$66.32.$$

In this example, we made three very strong and generally incorrect assumptions. First, we assumed that our traveler had to calculate all the cross rates. For retail transactions, it is customary to display the cross rates directly instead of a series of dollar rates. Second, we assumed that exchange rates remain constant over time. Actually, exchange rates vary every day, often dramatically. We will have more to say about exchange rate fluctuations in the next section. Finally, we assumed that there were no transactions costs involved in exchanging currencies. In reality, small retail exchange transactions such as those in our example usually involve fixed and/or sliding scale fees that can easily consume 5 or more percent of the transaction amount. However, credit card purchases minimize these fees.

Major business publications such as *The Wall Street Journal* regularly report cross rates among key currencies. A set of cross rates is given in Table 19-2. When examining the table, note the following points:

1. Column 1 gives indirect quotes for dollars, that is, units of a foreign currency that can be bought with one U.S. dollar. Examples: $1 will buy 1.0346 euros or 1.5078 Swiss francs. Note the consistency with Table 19-1, Column 2.

2. Other columns show number of units of other currencies that can be bought with one euro, one pound, one Swiss franc, etc. For example, the Yen column shows that 1 yen will buy 0.01312 Canadian dollar, 0.00856 euro, or 0.00827 U.S. dollar.

3. The rows show direct quotes, that is, number of units of the currency of the country listed in the left column required to buy one unit of the currency listed at the top of the corresponding column. The bottom row is particularly interesting, as it shows the direct quotes for the U.S. dollar. This row is consistent

TABLE 19-2	Key Currency Cross Rates						
	DOLLAR	EURO	POUND	SFRANC	PESO	YEN	CDNDLR
Canada	1.5853	1.5324	2.4410	1.0514	0.16280	0.01312	—
Japan	120.87	116.83	186.12	80.163	12.412	—	76.244
Mexico	9.7380	9.4128	14.995	6.4584	—	0.08057	6.1427
Switzerland	1.5078	1.4574	2.3217	—	0.15484	0.01247	0.9511
United Kingdom	0.64940	0.6277	—	0.4307	0.06669	0.00537	0.40966
Euro	1.03460	—	1.5930	0.68613	0.10624	0.00856	0.65259
United States	—	0.9666	1.5398	0.66322	0.10269	0.00827	0.63080

SOURCE: Adapted from "Key Currency Cross Rates," *The Wall Street Journal*, August 7, 2002, C14.

with Column 1 of Table 19-1. Note too that the values on the bottom row are reciprocals of the values in Column 1. Thus, in Column 1 of the United Kingdom row, £0.64940 is equivalent to $1, so the reciprocal, 1/0.64940 = 1.5399 ≈ 1.5398, is shown in the last row (for the United States) under the pound column. In other words, one pound is worth $1.5398.

4. Now notice, by reading down the Euro column, that one euro was worth 1.4574 Swiss francs. This is the same cross rate that we calculated for the U.S. tourist in our example.

The tie-in with the dollar ensures that all currencies are related to one another in a consistent manner. If this consistency did not exist, currency traders could profit by buying undervalued and selling overvalued currencies. This process, known as *arbitrage*, works to bring about an equilibrium wherein the same relationship described earlier would exist. Currency traders are constantly operating in the market, seeking small inconsistencies from which they can profit. The traders' existence enables the rest of us to assume that currency markets are in equilibrium and that, at any point in time cross rates are all internally consistent.

SELF-TEST QUESTIONS

What is an exchange rate?

Explain the difference between direct and indirect quotations.

What is a cross rate?

THE INTERNATIONAL MONETARY SYSTEM

Every nation has a monetary system and a monetary authority. In the United States, the Federal Reserve is our monetary authority, and its task is to hold down inflation while promoting economic growth and raising our national standard of living. Moreover, if countries are to trade with one another, we must have some sort of system designed to facilitate payments between nations.

Floating Exchange Rates
A system under which exchange rates are not fixed by government policy but are allowed to float up or down in accordance with supply and demand.

The United States and other major trading nations currently operate under a system of **floating exchange rates,** whereby currency prices are allowed to seek their own levels without much governmental intervention. However, the central bank of each country does intervene to some extent buying and selling its currency to smooth out exchange rate fluctuations.

Each central bank would like to keep its average exchange rate at a level deemed desirable by its government's economic policy. This is important, because exchange rates have a profound effect on the levels of imports and exports, which influence the level of domestic employment. For example, if a country is having a problem with unemployment, its central bank might try to lower interest rates, which would cause capital to flee the country to find higher rates, which would lead to the sale of the currency, which would cause a *decline* in the value of the currency. This would cause its goods to be cheaper in world markets and thus stimulate exports, production, and domestic employment. Conversely, the central bank of a country that is operating at full capacity and experiencing inflation might try to raise the value of its currency to reduce exports and increase imports. Under the current floating rate system, however, such intervention can affect the situation only temporarily, because market forces will prevail in the long run.

Exchange rate fluctuations can have a profound impact on international monetary transactions. For example, in 1985 it cost Honda Motors 2,380,000 yen to build a particular model in Japan and ship it to the United States. The model carried a U.S. sticker price of $12,000. Since the $12,000 sales price was the equivalent of (238 yen per dollar)($12,000) = 2,856,000 yen, which was 20 percent above the 2,380,000 yen cost, the automaker had built a 20 percent markup into the U.S. sales price. However, three years later the dollar had depreciated to 128 yen. Now if the model still sold for $12,000, the yen return to Honda would be only (128 yen per dollar)($12,000) = 1,536,000 yen, and the automaker would be losing about 35 percent on each auto sold. Therefore, the depreciation of the dollar against the yen turned a healthy profit into a huge loss. In fact, for Honda to maintain its 20 percent markup, the model would have to sell in the United States for 2,856,000 yen/128 yen per dollar = $22,312.50. This situation, which grew even worse, led Honda to build its most popular model, the Accord, in Marysville, Ohio.

The inherent volatility of exchange rates under a floating system increases the uncertainty of the cash flows for a multinational corporation. Because these cash flows are generated in many parts of the world, they are denominated in many different currencies. Since exchange rates can change, the dollar-equivalent value of a company's consolidated cash flows can also fluctuate. For example, Toyota estimates that each one-yen drop in the dollar reduces the company's annual net income by about 10 billion yen. This is known as *exchange rate risk*, and it is a major factor differentiating a global company from a purely domestic one.

Note too that in today's floating-exchange-rate environment, some smaller countries have chosen to peg their currencies to one or more major currencies. Countries with **pegged exchange rates** establish a fixed exchange rate with some major currency, and then the values of the pegged currencies move together over time.

Before closing our discussion of the international monetary system, we should note that not all currencies are **convertible.** A currency is convertible when the nation that issued it allows it to be traded in the currency markets and is willing to redeem it at market rates. This means that, except for limited central bank influence, the issuing government loses control over the value of its currency. However, a lack of convertibility creates major problems for international trade. For example, consider the situation faced by Pepsico when it wanted to open a chain of Pizza Hut restaurants in the former Soviet Union. The Russian ruble is not convertible, so Pepsico could not take the profits from its restaurants out of the Soviet Union in the form of dollars. There was no mechanism to exchange the rubles it earned in Russia for dollars, so the investment in the Soviet Union was essentially worthless to the U.S. parent. However, Pepsico arranged to use the ruble profit from the restaurants to buy Russian vodka, which it then shipped to the United States and sold for dollars. Pepsico managed to work things out, but lack of convertibility significantly inhibits the ability of a country to attract foreign investment.

Pegged Exchange Rate
Occurs when a country establishes a fixed exchange rate with another major currency; consequently, values of pegged currencies move together over time.

Convertible Currency
A currency that may be readily exchanged for other currencies.

SELF-TEST QUESTIONS

What are pegged exchange rates?

What is a convertible currency?

www Updated currency spot and forward rates (from 1 to 12 months) are provided by the Bank of Montreal Treasury Group at **http://www.bmo.com/ economic/regular/fxrates.html.**

Importers, exporters, tourists, and governments buy and sell currencies in the foreign exchange market. For example, when a U.S. trader imports automobiles from Japan, payment will probably be made in Japanese yen. The importer buys yen (through its bank) in the foreign exchange market, much as one buys common stocks on the New York Stock Exchange or pork bellies on the Chicago Mercantile Exchange. However, whereas stock and commodity exchanges have organized trading floors, the foreign exchange market consists of a network of brokers and banks based in New York, London, Tokyo, and other financial centers. Most buy and sell orders are conducted by computer and telephone.[1]

SPOT RATES AND FORWARD RATES

Spot Rate
The effective exchange rate for a foreign currency for delivery on (approximately) the current day.

The exchange rates shown earlier in Tables 19-1 and 19-2 are known as **spot rates,** which means the rate paid for delivery of the currency "on the spot" or, in reality, no more than two days after the day of the trade. For most of the world's major currencies, it is also possible to buy (or sell) currencies for delivery at some agreed-upon future date, usually 30, 90, or 180 days from the day the transaction is negotiated. This rate is known as the **forward exchange rate.**

Forward Exchange Rate
An agreed-upon price at which two currencies will be exchanged at some future date.

For example, suppose a U.S. firm must pay 500 million yen to a Japanese firm in 30 days, and the current spot rate is 120.87 yen per dollar. Unless spot rates change, the U.S. firm will pay the Japanese firm the equivalent of $4.137 million (500 million yen divided by 120.87 yen per dollar) in 30 days. But if the spot rate falls to 100 yen per dollar, for example, the U.S. firm will have to pay the equivalent of $5 million. The treasurer of the U.S. firm can avoid this risk by entering into a 30-day forward exchange contract. This contract promises delivery of yen to the U.S. firm in 30 days at a guaranteed price of 120.67 yen per dollar. No cash changes hands at the time the treasurer signs the forward contract, although the U.S. firm might have to put some collateral down as a guarantee against default. Because the firm can use an interest-bearing instrument for the collateral, though, this requirement is not costly. The counterparty to the forward contract must deliver the yen to the U.S. firm in 30 days, and the U.S. firm is obligated to purchase the 500 million yen at the previously agreed-upon rate of 120.67 yen per dollar. Therefore, the treasurer of the U.S. firm is able to lock in a payment equivalent to $4.144 million, no matter what happens to spot rates. This technique, which is called "hedging," is discussed in more detail in Chapter 18.

Discount on Forward Rate
The situation when the spot rate is less than the forward rate.

Forward rates for 30-, 90-, and 180-day delivery, along with the current spot rates for some commonly traded currencies, are given in Table 19-3. If one can obtain *more* of the foreign currency for a dollar in the forward than in the spot market, the forward currency is less valuable than the spot currency, and the forward currency is said to be selling at a **discount.** Conversely, if one can obtain *less* of the foreign currency for a dollar in the forward than in the spot market, the forward currency is more valuable than the spot currency, and the forward currency is said to be selling

---

[1] For a more detailed explanation of exchange rate determination and operations of the foreign exchange market, see Mark Eaker, Frank Fabozzi, and Dwight Grant, *International Corporate Finance* (Fort Worth, TX: The Dryden Press, 1996).

TABLE 19-3

Selected Spot and Forward Exchange Rates
(Number of Units of Foreign Currency per U.S. Dollar)

	SPOT RATE	FORWARD RATES			FORWARD RATE AT A PREMIUM OR DISCOUNT
		30 DAYS	90 DAYS	180 DAYS	
British pound	0.6494	0.6507	0.6530	0.6566	Discount
Canadian dollar	1.5853	1.5867	1.5897	1.5946	Discount
Japanese yen	120.87	120.67	120.33	119.82	Premium
Swiss franc	1.5078	1.5064	1.5041	1.5008	Premium

NOTES:

a. These are representative quotes as provided by a sample of New York banks. Forward rates for other currencies and for other lengths of time can often be negotiated.

b. When it takes more units of a foreign currency to buy one dollar in the future, the value of the foreign currency is less in the forward market than in the spot market, hence the forward rate is at a *discount* to the spot rate. Likewise, when it takes less units of a foreign currency to buy one dollar in the future, the value of the foreign currency is more in the forward market than in the spot market, hence the forward rate is at a premium to the spot rate.

SOURCE: Adapted from *The Wall Street Journal*, August 7, 2002, C14.

Premium on Forward Rate
The situation when the spot rate is greater than the forward rate.

at a **premium.** Thus, because a dollar would buy *fewer* yen and Swiss francs in the forward than in the spot market, the forward yen and Swiss francs are selling at a premium. On the other hand, a dollar would buy more pounds and Canadian dollars in the forward than in the spot market, so the forward pounds and Canadian dollars are selling at a discount.

SELF-TEST QUESTIONS

Differentiate between spot and forward exchange rates.

Explain what it means for a forward currency to sell at a discount and at a premium.

INTEREST RATE PARITY

Market forces determine whether a currency sells at a forward premium or discount, and the general relationship between spot and forward exchange rates is specified by a concept called "interest rate parity."

Interest Rate Parity
Specifies that investors should expect to earn the same return in all countries after adjusting for risk.

Interest rate parity holds that investors should earn the same return on security investments in all countries after adjusting for risk. It recognizes that when you invest in a country other than your home country, you are affected by two forces—returns on the investment itself and changes in the exchange rate. It follows that your overall return will be higher than the investment's stated return if the currency in which your investment is denominated appreciates relative to your home currency. Likewise, your overall return will be lower if the foreign currency you receive declines in value.

Interest rate parity is expressed as follows:

$$\frac{\text{Forward exchange rate}}{\text{Spot exchange rate}} = \frac{(1 + k_h)}{(1 + k_f)}.$$

Here both the forward and spot rates are expressed in terms of the amount of home currency received per unit of foreign currency, and k_h and k_f are the periodic interest rates in the home country and the foreign country, respectively. If this relationship does not hold, then currency traders will buy and sell currencies—that is, engage in arbitrage—until it does hold.

To illustrate interest rate parity, consider the case of a U.S. investor who can buy default-free 90-day Japanese bonds that promise a 4 percent nominal return. The 90-day interest rate, k_f, is 4%/4 = 1% because 90 days is 1/4 of a 360-day year. Assume also that the spot exchange rate is $0.008273, which means that you can exchange 0.008273 dollar for one yen, or 120.87 yen per dollar. Finally, assume that the 90-day forward exchange rate is $0.008310, which means that you can exchange one yen for 0.008310 dollar, or receive 120.33 yen per dollar exchanged, 90 days from now.

The U.S. investor can receive a 4 percent annualized return denominated in yen, but if he or she ultimately wants to consume goods in the United States, those yen must be converted to dollars. The dollar return on the investment depends, therefore, on what happens to exchange rates over the next three months. However, the investor can lock in the dollar return by selling the foreign currency in the forward market. For example, the investor could simultaneously

- Convert $1,000 to 120,870 yen in the spot market.
- Invest the 120,870 yen in 90-day Japanese bonds that have a 4 percent annualized return or a 1 percent quarterly return, hence will pay (120,870)(1.01) = 122,078.70 yen in 90 days.
- Agree today to exchange these 122,078.70 yen 90 days from now at the 90-day forward exchange rate of 120.33 yen per dollar, or for a total of $1,014.53.

This investment, therefore, has an expected 90-day return of $14.53/$1,000 = 1.45%, which translates into a nominal return of 4(1.45%) = 5.80%. In this case, 4 percent of the expected 5.80 percent return is coming from the bond itself, and 1.80 percent arises because the market believes the yen will strengthen relative to the dollar. Note that by locking in the forward rate today, the investor has eliminated any exchange rate risk. And, since the Japanese bond is assumed to be default-free, the investor is assured of earning a 5.80 percent dollar return.

Interest rate parity implies that an investment in the United States with the same risk as a Japanese bond should have a return of 5.80 percent. Solving for k_h in the parity equation, we indeed find that the predicted interest rate in the United States is 5.80 percent.

Interest rate parity shows why a particular currency might be at a forward premium or discount. Note that a currency is at a forward premium whenever domestic interest rates are higher than foreign interest rates. Discounts prevail if domestic interest rates are lower than foreign interest rates. If these conditions do not hold, then arbitrage will soon force interest rates back to parity.

SELF-TEST QUESTION

Briefly explain interest rate parity, illustrating it with an example.

PURCHASING POWER PARITY

We have discussed exchange rates in some detail, and we have considered the relationship between spot and forward exchange rates. However, we have not yet addressed the fundamental question: What determines the spot level of exchange rates in each country? While exchange rates are influenced by a multitude of factors that are difficult to predict, particularly on a day-to-day basis, over the long run market forces work to ensure that similar goods sell for similar prices in different countries after taking exchange rates into account. This relationship is known as "purchasing power parity."

Purchasing Power Parity (PPP)
The relationship in which the same products cost roughly the same amount in different countries after taking into account the exchange rate.

Purchasing power parity (PPP), sometimes referred to as the *law of one price*, implies that the level of exchange rates adjusts so as to cause identical goods to cost the same amount in different countries. For example, if a pair of tennis shoes costs $150 in the United States and 100 pounds in Britain, PPP implies that the exchange rate be $1.50 per pound. Consumers could purchase the shoes in Britain for 100 pounds, or they could exchange their 100 pounds for $150 and then purchase the same shoes in the United States at the same effective cost, assuming no transaction or transportation costs. Here is the equation for purchasing power parity:

$$P_h = (P_f)(\text{Spot rate}),$$

or

$$\text{Spot rate} = \frac{P_h}{P_f}.$$

Here

P_h = the price of the good in the home country ($150, assuming the United States is the home country).
P_f = the price of the good in the foreign country (100 pounds).

Note that the spot market exchange rate is expressed as the number of units of home currency that can be exchanged for one unit of foreign currency ($1.50 per pound).

PPP assumes that market forces will eliminate situations in which the same product sells at a different price overseas. For example, if the shoes cost $140 in the United States, importers/exporters could purchase them in the United States for $140, sell them for 100 pounds in Britain, exchange the 100 pounds for $150 in the foreign exchange market, and earn a profit of $10 on every pair of shoes. Ultimately, this trading activity would increase the demand for shoes in the United States and thus raise P_h, increase the supply of shoes in Britain and thus reduce P_f, and increase the demand for dollars in the foreign exchange market and thus reduce the spot rate. Each of these actions works to restore PPP.

Note that PPP assumes that there are no transportation or transaction costs, or import restrictions, all of which limit the ability to ship goods between countries. In many cases, these assumptions are incorrect, which explains why PPP is often violated. An additional complication, when empirically testing to see whether PPP holds, is that products in different countries are rarely identical. Frequently, there are real or perceived differences in quality, which can lead to price differences in different countries.

Still, the concepts of interest rate and purchasing power parity are critically important to those engaged in international activities. Companies and investors must anticipate changes in interest rates, inflation, and exchange rates, and they often try to hedge the risks of adverse movements in these factors. The parity relationships are extremely useful when anticipating future conditions.

What is meant by purchasing power parity? Illustrate it.

INFLATION, INTEREST RATES, AND EXCHANGE RATES

Relative inflation rates, or the rates of inflation in foreign countries compared with that in the home country, have many implications for multinational financial decisions. Obviously, relative inflation rates will greatly influence future production costs at home and abroad. Equally important, inflation has a dominant influence on relative interest rates and exchange rates. Both of these factors influence the methods chosen by multinational corporations for financing their foreign investments, and both have an important effect on the profitability of foreign investments.

The currencies of countries with higher inflation rates than that of the United States by definition *depreciate* over time against the dollar. Countries where this has occurred include Mexico and all the South American nations. On the other hand, the currencies of Switzerland and Japan, which have had less inflation than the United States, have *appreciated* against the dollar. *In fact, a foreign currency will, on average, depreciate or appreciate at a percentage rate approximately equal to the amount by which its inflation rate exceeds or is less than our own.*

Relative inflation rates also affect interest rates. The interest rate in any country is largely determined by its inflation rate. Therefore, countries currently experiencing higher rates of inflation than the United States also tend to have higher interest rates. The reverse is true for countries with lower inflation rates.

It is tempting for a multinational corporation to borrow in countries with the lowest interest rates. However, this is not always a good strategy. Suppose, for example, that interest rates in Switzerland are lower than those in the United States because of Switzerland's lower inflation rate. A U.S. multinational firm could therefore save interest by borrowing in Switzerland. However, because of relative inflation rates, the Swiss franc will probably appreciate in the future, causing the dollar cost of annual interest and principal payments on Swiss debt to rise over time. Thus, *the lower interest rate could be more than offset by losses from currency appreciation.* Similarly, multinational corporations should not necessarily avoid borrowing in a country such as Brazil, where interest rates have been very high, because future depreciation of the Brazilian real could make such borrowing relatively inexpensive.

What effects do relative inflation rates have on relative interest rates?

What happens over time to the currencies of countries with higher inflation rates than that of the United States? To those with lower inflation rates?

Why might a multinational corporation decide to borrow in a country such as Brazil, where interest rates are high, rather than in a country like Switzerland, where interest rates are low?

HUNGRY FOR A BIG MAC? GO TO ARGENTINA!

Purchasing power parity (PPP) implies that the same product will sell for the same price in every country after adjusting for current exchange rates. One problem when testing to see if PPP holds is that it assumes that goods consumed in different countries are of the same quality. For example, if you find that a product is more expensive in Switzerland than it is in Canada, one explanation is that PPP fails to hold, but another explanation is that the product sold in Switzerland is of a higher quality and therefore deserves a higher price.

One way to test for PPP is to find goods that have the same quality worldwide. With this in mind, *The Economist* magazine occasionally compares the prices of a well-known good whose quality is the same in nearly 120 different countries: the McDonald's Big Mac hamburger.

The table on the next page provides information collected during 2002. The first column shows the price of a Big Mac in the local currency. Column 2 calculates the price of the Big Mac in terms of the U.S. dollar—this is obtained by dividing the local price by the actual exchange rate at that time. For example, a Big Mac costs 6.30 Swiss francs in Zurich. Given an exchange rate of 1.66 Swiss francs per dollar this implies that the dollar price of a Big Mac is 6.30 Swiss francs/1.66 Swiss francs per dollar ≈ $3.81.

The third column backs out the implied exchange rate that would hold under PPP. This is obtained by dividing the price of the Big Mac in each local currency by its U.S. price. For example, a Big Mac costs 39 rubles in Russia, and $2.49 in the United States. If PPP holds, the exchange rate should be 15.66 ≈ 15.7 rubles per dollar (39 rubles/$2.49).

Comparing the implied exchange rate to the actual exchange rate in Column 4, we see the extent to which the local currency is under- or overvalued relative to the dollar. Given that the actual exchange rate at the time was 31.2 rubles per dollar, this implies that the ruble was 50 percent undervalued.

The evidence suggests that strict PPP does not hold, but recent research suggests that the Big Mac test may shed some insights about where exchange rates are headed. The average price of a Big Mac within the EMU is 2.67 euros. The euro is undervalued by 5 percent. This is considerably less than many market analysts believe. While the EMU has a single currency, the price of a Big Mac within the EMU varies widely—ranging from €2.15 in Greece to €2.95 in France. However, this range has narrowed from a year ago.

Switzerland and England, two European countries that are not part of the EMU, have currencies that appear to be overvalued against the dollar. The Swiss franc is overvalued by 53 percent, while the British pound is overvalued by 16 percent. The British pound is also overvalued by 21 percent against the euro. In contrast, the Australian dollar is the most undervalued rich-world currency—by 35 percent.

According to the Big Mac Index, the U.S. dollar looks more overvalued relative to the other big currencies today than at any other time during the index's 16-year existence. In addition, the currencies of most emerging-market countries look cheap against the dollar. More than half of these emerging-market currencies are undervalued by more than 30 percent. The Big Mac 2002 test suggests that, sooner or later, the U.S. dollar will decline.

One last benefit of the Big Mac test is that it tells us the cheapest places to find a Big Mac. According to the data, if you are looking for a Big Mac, head to Argentina, and avoid Iceland.

SOURCES: Adapted from "Big MacCurrencies," *The Economist*, Vol. 363, April 27, 2002, 76; and Li Lian Ong, "Burgernomics: the Economics of the Big Mac Standard," *Journal of International Money and Finance*, 1997, Vol. 16, No. 6, 867–878.

	BIG MAC PRICES		IMPLIED PPP* OF THE DOLLAR	ACTUAL DOLLAR EXCHANGE RATE 23/04/02	UNDER(−)/OVER(+) VALUATION AGAINST THE DOLLAR, %
	IN LOCAL CURRENCY	IN DOLLARS			
United States[†]	$2.49	2.49	—	—	—
Argentina	Peso 2.50	0.78	1.00	3.13	−68
Australia	A$3.00	1.62	1.20	1.86	−35
Brazil	Real 3.60	1.55	1.45	2.34	−38
Britain	£1.99	2.88	1.25[‡]	1.45[‡]	+16
Canada	C$3.33	2.12	1.34	1.57	−15
Chile	Peso 1,400	2.16	562	655	−14
China	Yuan 10.50	1.27	4.22	8.28	−49
Czech Rep	Koruna 56.28	1.66	22.6	34.0	−33
Denmark	DKr24.75	2.96	9.94	8.38	+19
Euro area	€2.67	2.37	0.93[§]	0.89[§]	−5
Hong Kong	HK$11.20	1.40	4.50	7.80	−42
Hungary	Forint 459	1.69	184	272	−32
Indonesia	Rupiah 16,000	1.71	6,426	9,430	−32
Israel	Shekel 12.00	2.51	4.82	4.79	+1
Japan	¥262	2.01	105	130	−19
Malaysia	M$5.04	1.33	2.02	3.8	−47
Mexico	Peso 21.90	2.37	8.80	9.28	−5
New Zealand	NZ$3.95	1.77	1.59	2.24	−29
Peru	New Sol 8.50	2.48	3.41	3.43	−1
Philippines	Peso 65.00	1.28	26.1	51.0	−49
Poland	Zloty 5.90	1.46	2.37	4.04	−41
Russia	Rouble 39.00	1.25	15.7	31.2	−50
Singapore	S$3.30	1.81	1.33	1.82	−27
South Africa	Rand 9.70	0.87	3.90	10.9	−64
South Korea	Won 3,100	2.36	1,245	1,304	−5
Sweden	SKr26.00	2.52	10.4	10.3	+1
Switzerland	SFr6.30	3.81	2.53	1.66	+53
Taiwan	NT$70.00	2.01	28.1	34.8	−19
Thailand	Baht 55.00	1.27	22.1	43.3	−49
Turkey	Lira 4,000,000	3.06	1,606,426	1,324,500	+21
Venezuela	Bolivar 2,500	2.92	1,004	857	+17

NOTES:

* Purchasing power parity: local price divided by price in the United States.

[†] Average of New York, Chicago, San Francisco, and Atlanta.

[‡] Dollars per pound.

[§] Dollars per euro.

SOURCES: McDonald's; and *The Economist*, Vol. 363, April 27, 2002, 76. Reprinted by permission from *The Economist*.

One way for U.S. citizens to invest in world markets is to buy the stocks of U.S. multinational corporations that invest directly in foreign countries. Another way is to purchase foreign securities—stocks, bonds, or money market instruments issued by foreign companies. Security investments are known as *portfolio investments*, and they are distinguished from *direct investments* in physical assets by U.S. corporations.

From World War II through the 1960s, the U.S. capital markets dominated world markets. Today, however, the value of U.S. securities represents less than one-fourth the value of all securities. Given this situation, it is important for both corporate managers and investors to have an understanding of international markets. Moreover, these markets often offer better opportunities for raising or investing capital than are available domestically.

EURODOLLAR MARKET

Eurodollar
A U.S. dollar deposited in a bank outside the United States.

A **Eurodollar** is a U.S. dollar deposited in a bank outside the United States. (Although they are called Eurodollars because they originated in Europe, Eurodollars are really any dollars deposited in any part of the world other than the United States.) The bank in which the deposit is made may be a non-U.S. bank, such as Barclay's Bank in London; the foreign branch of a U.S. bank, such as Citibank's Paris branch; or even a foreign branch of a third-country bank, such as Barclay's Munich branch. Most Eurodollar deposits are for $500,000 or more, and they have maturities ranging from overnight to about one year.

The major difference between Eurodollar deposits and regular U.S. time deposits is their geographic locations. The two types of deposits do not involve different currencies—in both cases, dollars are on deposit. However, Eurodollars are outside the direct control of the U.S. monetary authorities, so U.S. banking regulations, including reserve requirements and FDIC insurance premiums, do not apply. The absence of these costs means that the interest rate paid on Eurodollar deposits can be higher than domestic U.S. rates on equivalent instruments.

Although the dollar is the leading international currency, British pounds, euros, Swiss francs, Japanese yen, and other currencies are also deposited outside their home countries; these *Eurocurrencies* are handled in exactly the same way as Eurodollars.

Eurodollars are borrowed by U.S. and foreign corporations for various purposes, but especially to pay for goods exported from the United States and to invest in U.S. security markets. Also, U.S. dollars are used as an international currency, or international medium of exchange, and many Eurodollars are used for this purpose. It is interesting to note that Eurodollars were actually "invented" by the Soviets in 1946. International merchants did not trust the Soviets or their rubles, so the Soviets bought some dollars (for gold), deposited them in a Paris bank, and then used these dollars to buy goods in the world markets. Others found it convenient to use dollars this same way, and soon the Eurodollar market was in full swing.

Eurodollars are usually held in interest-bearing accounts. The interest rate paid on these deposits depends (1) on the bank's lending rate, as the interest a bank earns on loans determines its willingness and ability to pay interest on deposits, and (2) on rates of return available on U.S. money market instruments. If money market rates in the United States were above Eurodollar deposit rates, these dollars would be sent back and invested in the United States, whereas if Eurodollar deposit rates were significantly above U.S. rates, which is more often the case, more dollars would be sent out of the United States to become Eurodollars. Given the existence of the Eurodollar market and the electronic flow of dollars to and from the United States, it is easy to see why interest rates in the United States cannot be insulated from those in other parts of the world.

Interest rates on Eurodollar deposits (and loans) are tied to a standard rate known by the acronym *LIBOR*, which stands for *London Interbank Offer Rate*. LIBOR is the rate of interest offered by the largest and strongest London banks on dollar deposits of significant size. In August 2002, LIBOR rates were only slightly above domestic U.S. bank rates on time deposits of the same maturity—1.70 percent for three-month CDs versus 1.7575 percent for LIBOR CDs. The Eurodollar market is essentially a short-term market; most loans and deposits are for less than one year.

INTERNATIONAL BOND MARKETS

Foreign Bond
A bond sold by a foreign borrower but denominated in the currency of the country in which it is sold.

Any bond sold outside the country of the borrower is called an *international bond*. However, there are two important types of international bonds: foreign bonds and Eurobonds. **Foreign bonds** are bonds sold by a foreign borrower but denominated in the currency of the country in which the issue is sold. For instance, Northern Telcom (a Canadian company) may need U.S. dollars to finance the operations of its subsidiaries in the United States. If it decides to raise the needed capital in the United States, the bond will be underwritten by a syndicate of U.S. investment bankers, denominated in U.S. dollars, and sold to U.S. investors in accordance with SEC and applicable state regulations. Except for the foreign origin of the borrower, this bond will be indistinguishable from those issued by equivalent U.S. corporations. Since Northern Telcom is a foreign corporation, however, the bond would be a foreign bond.

Eurobond
A bond sold in a country other than the one in whose currency the bond is denominated.

The term **Eurobond** is used to designate any bond issued in one country but denominated in the currency of some other country. Examples include a Ford Motor Company issue denominated in dollars and sold in Germany, or a British firm's sale of mark-denominated bonds in Switzerland. The institutional arrangements by which Eurobonds are marketed are different than those for most other bond issues, with the most important distinction being a far lower level of required disclosure than is usually found for bonds issued in domestic markets, particularly in the United States. Governments tend to be less strict when regulating securities denominated in foreign currencies, because the bonds' purchasers are generally more "sophisticated." The lower disclosure requirements result in lower total transaction costs for Eurobonds.

Eurobonds appeal to investors for several reasons. Generally, they are issued in bearer form rather than as registered bonds, so the names and nationalities of investors are not recorded. Individuals who desire anonymity, whether for privacy reasons or for tax avoidance, like Eurobonds. Similarly, most governments do not withhold taxes on interest payments associated with Eurobonds. If the investor requires an effective yield of 10 percent, a Eurobond that is exempt from tax withholding would need a coupon rate of 10 percent. Another type of bond—for instance, a domestic issue subject to a 30 percent withholding tax on interest paid to foreigners—would need a coupon rate of 14.3 percent to yield an after-withholding rate of 10 percent. Investors who desire secrecy would not want to file for a refund of the tax, so they would prefer to hold the Eurobond.

Although centered in Europe, Eurobonds are truly international. Their underwriting syndicates include investment bankers from all parts of the world, and the

STOCK MARKET INDICES AROUND THE WORLD

In Chapter 4, we described the major U.S. stock market indices. As discussed below, similar market indices also exist for each major world financial center. The accompanying figure compares four of these indices against the U.S. indices.

HONG KONG

In Hong Kong, the primary stock index is the Hang Seng. Created by HSI Services Limited, the Hang Seng index reflects the performance of the Hong Kong stock market. It is composed of 33 domestic stocks that account for about 70 percent of the market's capitalization. The largest stock in the index is HBSC Holdings, which alone accounts for 21 percent of the index's total market value.

GERMANY

The major indicator of the German stock market, the XETRA DAX, is comprised of 30 German blue chip stocks. These stocks are all listed on the Frankfurt exchange, and they are representative of the industrial structure of the German economy.

GREAT BRITAIN

The FT-SE 100 Index (pronounced "footsie") is the most widely followed indicator of equity investments in Great Britain. It is a value-weighted index composed of the 100 largest companies on the London Stock Exchange whose value is calculated every minute of trading.

JAPAN

In Japan, the principal barometer of stock performance is the Nikkei 225 Index. The index's value, which is calculated every minute throughout daily trading, consists of a collection of highly liquid equity issues thought to be representative of the Japanese economy.

CHILE

The Santiago Stock Exchange has three main share indices: the General Stock Price Index (IGPA), the Selective Stock Price Index (IPSA), and the INTER-10 Index. The IPSA, which reflects the price variations of the most active stocks, is composed of 40 of the most actively traded stocks on the exchange.

INDIA

Of the 22 stock exchanges in India, the Bombay Stock Exchange (BSE) is the largest, with more than 6,000 listed stocks and approximately two-thirds of the country's total trading volume. Established in 1875, the exchange is also the oldest in Asia. Its yardstick is the BSE Sensex, an index of 30 publicly traded Indian stocks that account for one-fifth of the BSE's market capitalization.

SPAIN

In Spain, the IBEX 35 is the official index for measuring equity market performance for continuously traded stocks. This index is composed of the 35 most actively traded securities on the Joint Stock Exchange System (comprising the four Spanish stock exchanges).

---

bonds are sold to investors not only in Europe but also in such faraway places as Bahrain and Singapore. Up until a few years ago, Eurobonds were issued solely by multinational firms, by international financial institutions, or by national governments. Today, however, the Eurobond market is also being tapped by purely domestic U.S. firms, because they often find that by borrowing overseas they can lower their debt costs.

INTERNATIONAL STOCK MARKETS

New issues of stock are sold in international markets for a variety of reasons. For example, a non-U.S. firm might sell an equity issue in the United States because it can tap a much larger source of capital than in its home country. Also, a U.S. firm might tap a foreign market because it wants to create an equity market presence to accompany its operations in that country. Large multinational companies also occasionally

Selected International Stock Indices—Compound Returns from December 1989 through June 2002

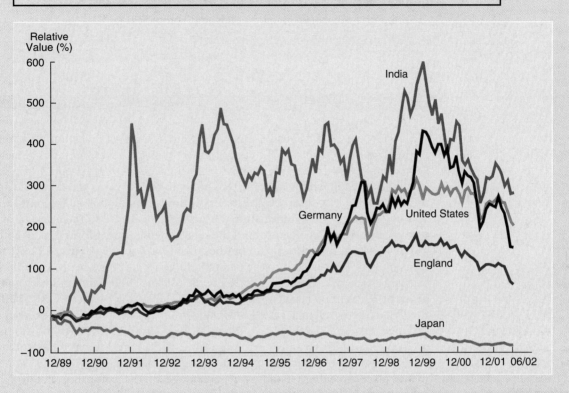

SOURCE: Adapted from Yahoo Finance historical quotes obtained from the web site at **http://finance.yahoo.com**.

issue new stock simultaneously in multiple countries. For example, Alcan Aluminum, a Canadian company, recently issued new stock in Canada, Europe, and the United States simultaneously, using different underwriting syndicates in each market.

In addition to new issues, outstanding stocks of large multinational companies are increasingly being listed on multiple international exchanges. For example, Coca-Cola's stock is traded on six stock exchanges in the United States, four stock exchanges in Switzerland, and the Frankfurt stock exchange in Germany. Some 500 foreign stocks are listed in the United States—an example here is Royal Dutch Petroleum, which is listed on the NYSE. U.S. investors can also invest in foreign companies through *American Depository Receipts (ADRs)*, which are certificates representing ownership of foreign stock held in trust. About 1,700 ADRs are now available in the United States, with most of them traded on the over-the-counter (OTC) market. However, more and more ADRs are being listed on the New York Stock Exchange, including England's British Airways, Japan's Honda Motors, and Italy's Fiat Group.

MULTINATIONAL CAPITAL BUDGETING

Up to now, we have discussed the general environment in which multinational firms operate. In the remainder of the chapter, we will see how international factors affect key corporate decisions. We begin with capital budgeting. Although the same basic principles of capital budgeting analysis apply to both foreign and domestic operations, there are some key differences. First, cash flow estimation is more complex for overseas investments. Most multinational firms set up separate subsidiaries in each foreign country in which they operate, and the relevant cash flows for the parent company are the dividends and royalties paid by the subsidiaries to the parent. Second, these cash flows must be converted into the parent company's currency, hence they are subject to exchange rate risk. For example, General Motors' German subsidiary may make a profit of 100 million euros in 2002, but the value of this profit to GM will depend on the dollar/euro exchange rate: How many *dollars* will 100 million euros buy?

Repatriation of Earnings
The process of sending cash flows from a foreign subsidiary back to the parent company.

Dividends and royalties are normally taxed by both foreign and home-country governments. Furthermore, a foreign government may restrict the amount of the cash that may be **repatriated** to the parent company. For example, some governments place a ceiling, stated as a percentage of the company's net worth, on the amount of cash dividends that a subsidiary can pay to its parent. Such restrictions are normally intended to force multinational firms to reinvest earnings in the foreign country, although restrictions are sometimes imposed to prevent large currency outflows, which might disrupt the exchange rate.

Whatever the host country's motivation for blocking repatriation of profits, the result is that the parent corporation cannot use cash flows blocked in the foreign country to pay dividends to its shareholders or to invest elsewhere in the business. Hence, from the perspective of the parent organization, *the cash flows relevant for foreign investment analysis are the cash flows that the subsidiary is actually expected to send back to the parent.* The present value of those cash flows is found by applying an appropriate discount rate, and this present value is then compared with the parent's required investment to determine the project's NPV.

In addition to the complexities of the cash flow analysis, *the cost of capital may be different for a foreign project than for an equivalent domestic project, because foreign projects may be more or less risky.* A higher risk could arise from two primary sources—(1) exchange rate risk and (2) political risk. A lower risk might result from international diversification.

Exchange Rate Risk
The risk that relates to what the basic cash flows will be worth in the parent company's home currency.

Exchange rate risk relates to the value of the basic cash flows in the parent company's home currency. The foreign currency cash flows to be turned over to the parent must be converted into U.S. dollars by translating them at expected future exchange rates. An analysis should be conducted to ascertain the effects of exchange rate variations, and, on the basis of this analysis, an exchange rate risk premium should be added to the domestic cost of capital to reflect this risk. It is sometimes possible to hedge against exchange rate fluctuations, but it may not be possible to hedge completely, especially on long-term projects. If hedging is used, the costs of doing so must be subtracted from the project's cash flows.

Political Risk
Potential actions by a host government that would reduce the value of a company's investment.

Political risk refers to potential actions by a host government that would reduce the value of a company's investment. It includes at one extreme the expropriation without compensation of the subsidiary's assets, but it also includes less drastic actions that reduce the value of the parent firm's investment in the foreign subsidiary, including higher taxes, tighter repatriation or currency controls, and restrictions on prices charged. The risk of expropriation is small in traditionally friendly and stable countries such as Great Britain or Switzerland. However, in Latin America, Africa, the Far East, and Eastern Europe, the risk may be substantial. Past expropriations include those of ITT and Anaconda Copper in Chile, Gulf Oil in Bolivia, Occidental Petroleum in Libya, and the assets of many companies in Iraq, Iran, and Cuba.

Students can obtain a sample copy of the *International Country Risk Guide* published by The PRS Group, Inc. at **http://www.prsgroup.com**.

Several organizations rate the political risk of countries. For example, The PRS Group, Inc., an independent company based in East Syracuse, New York, publishes the *International Country Risk Guide*, which contains individual ratings for political, financial, and economic risk, along with a composite rating for each country. Table 19-4 contains selected portions of its September 2001 report. The political variable—which is given 50 percent of the weight in the composite rating—includes factors such as government corruption and the gap between economic expectations and reality. The financial rating looks at such things as the likelihood of losses from exchange controls and loan defaults. The economic rating takes into account such factors as inflation and debt-service costs.

The best, or least risky, score is 100 for political factors and 50 each for the financial and economic factors, and the composite risk is a weighted average of the political, financial, and economic factors. The United States is ranked 20th, below countries such as Norway, Switzerland, Singapore, Luxembourg, Finland, Denmark, Netherlands, and Ireland. Zimbabwe, as shown in Table 19-4, is ranked last.

Note that companies can take several steps to reduce the potential loss from expropriation: (1) finance the subsidiary with local capital, (2) structure operations

TABLE 19-4 | **Selected Countries Ranked by Composite Risk**

RANK	COUNTRY	POLITICAL RISK	FINANCIAL RISK	ECONOMIC RISK	COMPOSITE RISK
1	Norway	92.0	47.0	46.5	92.8
1	Switzerland	93.5	47.0	45.0	92.8
12	Canada	91.0	40.0	42.5	86.8
20	United States	89.5	37.5	39.5	83.3
60	Panama	74.5	34.5	36.0	72.5
67	Peru	72.5	37.0	32.5	71.0
72	Venezuela	60.5	42.5	37.5	70.3
75	Israel	64.0	38.5	37.0	69.8
99	Colombia	54.0	39.5	32.5	63.0
140	Zimbabwe	42.0	29.0	13.5	42.3

NOTE: A total of 140 countries are ranked, but only 10 are shown here.
SOURCE: Adapted from *International Country Risk Guide*, September 2001.

so that the subsidiary has value only as a part of the integrated corporate system, and (3) obtain insurance against economic losses from expropriation from a source such as the Overseas Private Investment Corporation (OPIC). In the latter case, insurance premiums would have to be added to the project's cost.

SELF-TEST QUESTIONS

List some key differences in capital budgeting as applied to foreign versus domestic operations.

What are the relevant cash flows for an international investment—the cash flows produced by the subsidiary in the country where it operates or the cash flows in dollars that it sends to its parent company?

Why might the cost of capital for a foreign project differ from that of an equivalent domestic project? Could it be lower?

What adjustments might be made to the domestic cost of capital for a foreign investment due to exchange rate risk and political risk?

INTERNATIONAL CAPITAL STRUCTURES

Companies' capital structures vary among countries. For example, the Organization for Economic Cooperation and Development (OECD) recently reported that, on average, Japanese firms use 85 percent debt to total assets (in book value terms), German firms use 64 percent, and U.S. firms use 55 percent. One problem, however, when interpreting these numbers is that different countries often use very different accounting conventions with regard to (1) reporting assets on a historical- versus a replacement-cost basis, (2) the treatment of leased assets, (3) pension plan funding, and (4) capitalizing versus expensing R&D costs. These differences make it difficult to compare capital structures.

A recent study by Raghuram Rajan and Luigi Zingales of the University of Chicago attempts to control for differences in accounting practices. In their study, Rajan and Zingales used a database that covers fewer firms than the OECD but that provides a more complete breakdown of balance sheet data. They concluded that differences in accounting practices can explain much of the cross-country variation in capital structures.

Rajan and Zingales' results are summarized in Table 19-5. There are a number of different ways to measure capital structure. One measure is the average ratio of total liabilities to total assets—this is similar to the measure used by the OECD, and it is reported in Column 1. Based on this measure, German and Japanese firms appear to be more highly levered than U.S. firms. However, if you look at Column 2, where capital structure is measured by interest-bearing debt to total assets, it appears that German firms use *less* leverage than U.S. and Japanese firms. What explains this difference? Rajan and Zingales argue that much of this difference is explained by the way German firms account for pension liabilities. German firms generally include all pension liabilities (and their offsetting assets) on the balance sheet, whereas firms in other countries (including the United States) generally "net out" pension assets and liabilities on their balance sheets. To see the importance of this difference, consider a firm with $10 million in liabilities (not including pension liabilities) and $20 million in as-

Median Capital Structures among Large Industrialized Countries (Measured in Terms of Book Value)

COUNTRY	TOTAL LIABILITIES TO TOTAL ASSETS (UNADJUSTED FOR ACCOUNTING DIFFERENCES) (1)	DEBT TO TOTAL ASSETS (UNADJUSTED FOR ACCOUNTING DIFFERENCES) (2)	TOTAL LIABILITIES TO TOTAL ASSETS (ADJUSTED FOR ACCOUNTING DIFFERENCES) (3)	DEBT TO TOTAL ASSETS (ADJUSTED FOR ACCOUNTING DIFFERENCES) (4)	TIMES INTEREST EARNED (TIE) RATIO (5)
Canada	56%	32%	48%	32%	1.55×
France	71	25	69	18	2.64
Germany	73	16	50	11	3.20
Italy	70	27	68	21	1.81
Japan	69	35	62	21	2.46
United Kingdom	54	18	47	10	4.79
United States	58	27	52	25	2.41
Mean	64%	26%	57%	20%	2.69×
Standard deviation	8%	7%	10%	8%	1.07×

SOURCE: Raghuram Rajan and Luigi Zingales, "What Do We Know about Capital Structure? Some Evidence from International Data," *Journal of Finance*, Vol. 50, No. 5, December 1995, 1421–1460. Used with permission.

sets (not including pension assets). Assume that the firm has $10 million in pension liabilities that are fully funded by $10 million in pension assets. Therefore, net pension liabilities are zero. If this firm were in the United States, it would report a ratio of total liabilities to total assets equal to 50 percent ($10 million/$20 million). By contrast, if this firm operated in Germany, both its pension assets and liabilities would be reported on the balance sheet. The firm would have $20 million in liabilities and $30 million in assets—or a 67 percent ($20 million/$30 million) ratio of total liabilities to total assets. Total debt is the sum of short-term debt and long-term debt and excludes other liabilities including pension liabilities. Therefore, the measure of total debt to total assets provides a more comparable measure of leverage across different countries.

Rajan and Zingales also make a variety of adjustments that attempt to control for other differences in accounting practices. The effect of these adjustments are reported in Columns 3 and 4. Overall, the evidence suggests that companies in Germany and the United Kingdom tend to have less leverage, whereas firms in Canada appear to have more leverage, relative to firms in the United States, France, Italy, and Japan. This conclusion is supported by data in the final column, which shows the average times-interest-earned ratio for firms in a number of different countries. Recall from Chapter 3 that the times-interest-earned ratio is the ratio of operating income (EBIT) to interest expense. This measure indicates how much cash the firm has available to service its interest expense. In general, firms with more leverage have a lower times-interest-earned ratio. The data indicate that this ratio is highest in the United Kingdom and Germany and lowest in Canada.

SELF-TEST QUESTION

Do international differences in financial leverage exist? Explain.

MULTINATIONAL WORKING CAPITAL MANAGEMENT

CASH MANAGEMENT

The goals of cash management in a multinational corporation are similar to those in a purely domestic corporation: (1) to speed up collections, slow down disbursements, and thus maximize net float; (2) to shift cash as rapidly as possible from those parts of the business where it is not needed to those parts where it is needed; and (3) to maximize the risk-adjusted, after-tax rate of return on temporary cash balances. Multinational companies use the same general procedures for achieving these goals as domestic firms, but because of longer distances and more serious mail delays, such devices as lockbox systems and electronic funds transfers are especially important.

Although multinational and domestic corporations have the same objectives and use similar procedures, multinational corporations face a far more complex task. As noted earlier in our discussion of political risk, foreign governments often place restrictions on transfers of funds out of the country, so although IBM can transfer money from its Salt Lake City office to its New York concentration bank just by pressing a few buttons, a similar transfer from its Buenos Aires office is far more complex. Buenos Aires funds are denominated in australs (Argentina's equivalent of the dollar), so the australs must be converted to dollars before the transfer. If there is a shortage of dollars in Argentina, or if the Argentinean government wants to conserve dollars to purchase strategic materials, then conversion, hence the transfer, may be blocked. Even if no dollar shortage exists in Argentina, the government may still restrict funds outflows if those funds represent profits or depreciation rather than payments for purchased materials or equipment, because many countries, especially those that are less developed, want profits reinvested in the country in order to stimulate economic growth.

Once it has been determined what funds can be transferred, the next task is to get those funds to locations where they will earn the highest returns. Whereas domestic corporations tend to think in terms of domestic securities, multinationals are more likely to be aware of investment opportunities all around the world. Most multinational corporations use one or more global concentration banks, located in money centers such as London, New York, Tokyo, Zurich, or Singapore, and their staffs in those cities, working with international bankers, know of and are able to take advantage of the best rates available anywhere in the world.

CREDIT MANAGEMENT

Like most other aspects of finance, credit management in the multinational corporation is similar to but more complex than that in a purely domestic business. First, granting credit is more risky in an international context because, in addition to the normal risks of default, the multinational corporation must also worry about exchange rate fluctuations between the time a sale is made and the time a receivable is collected. For example, if IBM sold a computer to a Japanese customer for 90 million yen when the exchange rate was 90 yen to the dollar, IBM would receive 90,000,000/90 = $1,000,000 for the computer. However, if it sold the computer on terms of net/6 months, and if the yen fell against the dollar so that one dollar would now buy 112.5 yen, IBM would end up realizing only 90,000,000/112.5 = $800,000 when it collected the receivable. Hedging can reduce this type of risk, but at a cost.

Offering credit is generally more important for multinational corporations than for purely domestic firms for two reasons. First, much U.S. trade is with poorer, less-developed nations, where granting credit is generally a necessary condition for doing business. Second, and in large part as a result of the first point, developed nations whose economic health depends on exports often help their manufacturing firms compete internationally by granting credit to foreign countries. In Japan, for example, the major manufacturing firms have direct ownership ties with large "trading companies" engaged in international trade, as well as with giant commercial banks. In addition, a government agency, the Ministry of International Trade and Industry (MITI), helps Japanese firms identify potential export markets and also helps potential customers arrange credit for purchases from Japanese firms. In effect, the huge Japanese trade surpluses are used to finance Japanese exports, thus helping to perpetuate their favorable trade balance. The United States has attempted to counter with the Export-Import Bank, which is funded by Congress, but the fact that the United States has a large balance of payments deficit is clear evidence that we have been less successful than others in world markets in recent years.

The huge debt that countries such as Korea and Thailand owe U.S. and other international banks is well known, and this situation illustrates how credit policy (by banks in this case) can go astray. The banks face a particularly sticky problem with these loans, because if a sovereign nation defaults, the banks cannot lay claim to the assets of the country as they could if a corporate customer defaulted. Note too that although the banks' loans to foreign governments often get most of the headlines, many U.S. multinational corporations are also in trouble as a result of granting credit to business customers in the same countries where bank loans to governments are on shaky ground.

By pointing out the risks in granting credit internationally, we are not suggesting that such credit is bad. Quite the contrary, for the potential gains from international operations far outweigh the risks, at least for companies (and banks) that have the necessary expertise.

INVENTORY MANAGEMENT

As with most other aspects of finance, inventory management in a multinational setting is similar to but more complex than for a purely domestic firm. First, there is the matter of the physical location of inventories. For example, where should Exxon Mobil keep its stockpiles of crude oil and refined products? It has refineries and marketing centers located worldwide, and one alternative is to keep items concentrated in a few strategic spots from which they can then be shipped as needs arise. Such a strategy might minimize the total amount of inventories needed and thus might minimize the investment in inventories. Note, though, that consideration will have to be given to potential delays in getting goods from central storage locations to user locations all around the world. Both working stocks and safety stocks would have to be maintained at each user location, as well as at the strategic storage centers. Problems like the Iraqi occupation of Kuwait and the subsequent trade embargo, which brought with it the potential for a shutdown of production of about 25 percent of the world's oil supply, complicate matters further.

Exchange rates also influence inventory policy. If a local currency, say, the Danish krone, were expected to rise in value against the dollar, a U.S. company operating in Denmark would want to increase stocks of local products before the rise in the krone, and vice versa if the krone were expected to fall.

Another factor that must be considered is the possibility of import or export quotas or tariffs. For example, Apple Computer Company was buying certain memory chips from Japanese suppliers at a bargain price. Then U.S. chipmakers accused the Japanese of dumping chips in the U.S. market at prices below cost, so they sought to force the Japanese to raise prices.[2] That led Apple to increase its chip inventory. Then computer sales slacked off, and Apple ended up with an oversupply of obsolete computer chips. As a result, Apple's profits were hurt and its stock price fell, demonstrating once more the importance of careful inventory management.

As mentioned earlier, another danger in certain countries is the threat of expropriation. If that threat is large, inventory holdings will be minimized, and goods will be brought in only as needed. Similarly, if the operation involves extraction of raw materials such as oil or bauxite, processing plants may be moved offshore rather than located close to the production site.

Taxes have two effects on multinational inventory management. First, countries often impose property taxes on assets, including inventories, and when this is done, the tax is based on holdings as of a specific date, say, January 1 or March 1. Such rules make it advantageous for a multinational firm (1) to schedule production so that inventories are low on the assessment date, and (2) if assessment dates vary among countries in a region, to hold safety stocks in different countries at different times during the year.

Finally, multinational firms may consider the possibility of at-sea storage. Oil, chemical, grain, and other companies that deal in a bulk commodity that must be stored in some type of tank can often buy tankers at a cost not much greater—or perhaps even less, considering land cost—than land-based facilities. Loaded tankers can then be kept at sea or at anchor in some strategic location. This eliminates the danger of expropriation, minimizes the property tax problem, and maximizes flexibility with regard to shipping to areas where needs are greatest or prices highest.

This discussion has only scratched the surface of inventory management in the multinational corporation—the task is much more complex than for a purely domestic firm. However, the greater the degree of complexity, the greater the rewards from superior performance, so if you want challenge along with potentially high rewards, look to the international arena.

SELF-TEST QUESTIONS

What are some factors that make cash management especially complicated in a multinational corporation?

Why is granting credit especially risky in an international context?

Why is inventory management especially important for a multinational firm?

---

[2] The term "dumping" warrants explanation, because the practice is so potentially important in international markets. Suppose Japanese chipmakers have excess capacity. A particular chip has a variable cost of $25, and its "fully allocated cost," which is the $25 plus total fixed cost per unit of output, is $40. Now suppose the Japanese firm can sell chips in the United States at $35 per unit, but if it charges $40, it will not make any sales because U.S. chipmakers sell for $35.50. If the Japanese firm sells at $35, it will cover variable cost plus make a contribution to fixed overhead, so selling at $35 makes sense. Continuing, if the Japanese firm can sell in Japan at $40, but U.S. firms are excluded from Japanese markets by import duties or other barriers, the Japanese will have a huge advantage over U.S. manufacturers. This practice of selling goods at lower prices in foreign markets than at home is called "dumping." U.S. firms are required by antitrust laws to offer the same price to all customers and, therefore, cannot engage in dumping.

Over the past two decades, the global economy has become increasingly integrated, and more and more companies generate more and more of their profits from overseas operations. In many respects, the concepts developed in the first 18 chapters still apply to multinational firms. However, multinational companies have more opportunities but also face different risks than do companies that operate only in their home market. The chapter discussed many of the key trends affecting the global markets today, and it described the most important differences between multinational and domestic financial management. The key concepts are listed below.

- **International operations** are becoming increasingly important to individual firms and to the national economy. A **multinational,** or **global, corporation** is a firm that operates in an integrated fashion in a number of countries.

- Companies "go global" for six primary reasons: (1) **to expand their markets,** (2) **to obtain raw materials,** (3) **to seek new technology,** (4) **to lower production costs,** (5) **to avoid trade barriers,** and (6) **to diversify.**

- Six major factors distinguish financial management as practiced by domestic firms from that practiced by multinational corporations: (1) **different currency denominations,** (2) **different economic and legal structures,** (3) **languages,** (4) **cultural differences,** (5) **role of governments,** and (6) **political risk.**

- When discussing **exchange rates,** the number of U.S. dollars required to purchase one unit of a foreign currency is called a **direct quotation,** while the number of units of foreign currency that can be purchased for one U.S. dollar is an **indirect quotation.**

- **Exchange rate fluctuations** make it difficult to estimate the dollars that overseas operations will produce.

- The United States and other major trading nations currently operate under a **floating exchange rate system** under which major world currency rates float with market forces, largely unrestricted by governmental intervention. The central bank of each country does operate in the foreign exchange market, buying and selling currencies to smooth out exchange rate fluctuations, but only to a limited extent.

- **Pegged exchange rates** occur when a country establishes a fixed exchange rate with a major currency. Consequently, the values of pegged currencies move together over time.

- A **convertible currency** is one that may be readily exchanged for other currencies.

- **Spot rates** are the rates paid for delivery of currency "on the spot," while the **forward exchange rate** is the rate paid for delivery at some agreed-upon future date, usually 30, 90, or 180 days from the day the transaction is negotiated. The forward rate can be at either a **premium** or a **discount** to the spot rate.

- **Interest rate parity** holds that investors should expect to earn the same return in all countries after adjusting for risk.

- **Purchasing power parity,** sometimes referred to as the *law of one price,* implies that the level of exchange rates adjusts so that identical goods cost the same in different countries.

- **Political risk** is the risk that the foreign government will take some action that will decrease the value of the investment, while **exchange rate risk** is the risk of losses due to fluctuations in the value of the dollar relative to the values of foreign currencies.

- The relevant cash flows in international capital budgeting are the dollars that can be **repatriated** to the parent company.

- **Eurodollars** are U.S. dollars deposited in banks outside the United States. Interest rates on Eurodollars are tied to **LIBOR,** the London Interbank Offer Rate.

- U.S. firms often find that they can raise long-term capital at a lower cost outside the United States by selling bonds in the **international capital markets.** International bonds may be either **foreign bonds,** which are exactly like regular domestic bonds except that the issuer is a foreign company, or **Eurobonds,** which are bonds sold in a foreign country but denominated in the currency of the issuing company's home country.

QUESTIONS

19-1 If the euro depreciates against the U.S. dollar, can a dollar buy more or fewer euros as a result?

19-2 If the United States imports more goods from abroad than it exports, foreigners will tend to have a surplus of U.S. dollars. What will this do to the value of the dollar with respect to foreign currencies? What is the corresponding effect on foreign investments in the United States?

19-3 Why do U.S. corporations build manufacturing plants abroad when they could build them at home?

19-4 Should firms require higher rates of return on foreign projects than on identical projects located at home? Explain.

19-5 What is a Eurodollar? If a French citizen deposits $10,000 in Chase Manhattan Bank in New York, have Eurodollars been created? What if the deposit is made in Barclay's Bank in London? Chase Manhattan's Paris branch? Does the existence of the Eurodollar market make the Federal Reserve's job of controlling U.S. interest rates easier or more difficult? Explain.

19-6 Does interest rate parity imply that interest rates are the same in all countries?

19-7 Why might purchasing power parity fail to hold?

SELF-TEST PROBLEMS (SOLUTIONS APPEAR IN APPENDIX B)

ST-1
Key terms
Define each of the following terms:
a. Multinational corporation
b. Exchange rate; euro
c. Floating exchange rates
d. Exchange rate risk; convertible currency
e. Pegged exchange rates
f. Interest rate parity; purchasing power parity
g. Spot rate; forward exchange rate
h. Discount on forward rate; premium on forward rate
i. Repatriation of earnings; political risk
j. Eurodollar; Eurobond; international bond; foreign bond

ST-2
Cross rates
Suppose the exchange rate between U.S. dollars and EMU euros is Euro 1.1215 = $1.00, and the exchange rate between the U.S. dollar and the Canadian dollar is $1.00 = C$1.5291. What is the cross rate of euros to Canadian dollars?

STARTER PROBLEMS

19-1
Cross rates
A currency trader observes that in the spot exchange market, one U.S. dollar can be exchanged for 4.0828 Israeli shekel or for 111.23 Japanese yen. What is the cross-exchange rate between the yen and the shekel; that is, how many yen would you receive for every shekel exchanged?

19-2
Interest rate parity

Six-month T-bills have a nominal rate of 7 percent, while default-free Japanese bonds that mature in 6 months have a nominal rate of 5.5 percent. In the spot exchange market, one yen equals $0.009.` If interest rate parity holds, what is the 6-month forward exchange rate?

19-3
Purchasing power parity

A television set costs $500 in the United States. The same set costs 725 euros. If purchasing power parity holds, what is the spot exchange rate between the euro and the dollar?

EXAM-TYPE PROBLEMS

The problems included in this section are set up in such a way that they could be used as multiple-choice exam problems.

19-4
Exchange rate

If British pounds sell for $1.50 (U.S.) per pound, what should dollars sell for in pounds per dollar?

19-5
Currency appreciation

Suppose that 1 Danish krone could be purchased in the foreign exchange market for 14 U.S. cents today. If the krone appreciated 10 percent tomorrow against the dollar, how many krones would a dollar buy tomorrow?

19-6
Cross exchange rates

Suppose the exchange rate between the U.S. dollar and the Swedish krona was 10 krona = $1.00, and the exchange rate between the dollar and the British pound was £1 = $1.50. What was the exchange rate between Swedish kronas and pounds?

19-7
Cross exchange rates

Look up the 3 currencies in Problem 19-6 in the foreign exchange section of a current issue of *The Wall Street Journal*. What is the current exchange rate between Swedish kronas and pounds?

19-8
Foreign investment analysis

After all foreign and U.S. taxes, a U.S. corporation expects to receive 3 pounds of dividends per share from a British subsidiary this year. The exchange rate at the end of the year is expected to be $1.60 per pound, and the pound is expected to depreciate 5 percent against the dollar each year for an indefinite period. The dividend (in pounds) is expected to grow at 10 percent a year indefinitely. The parent U.S. corporation owns 10 million shares of the subsidiary. What is the present value in dollars of its equity ownership of the subsidiary? Assume a cost of equity capital of 15 percent for the subsidiary.

19-9
Exchange gains and losses

You are the vice-president of International InfoXchange, headquartered in Chicago, Illinois. All shareholders of the firm live in the United States. Earlier this month, you obtained a loan of 5 million Canadian dollars from a bank in Toronto to finance the construction of a new plant in Montreal. At the time the loan was received, the exchange rate was 75 U.S. cents to the Canadian dollar. By the end of the month, it has unexpectedly dropped to 70 cents. Has your company made a gain or loss as a result, and by how much?

19-10
Foreign capital budgeting

Solitaire Machinery is a Swiss multinational manufacturing company. Currently, Solitaire's financial planners are considering undertaking a 1-year project in the United States. The project's expected dollar-denominated cash flows consist of an initial investment of $1,000 and a cash inflow the following year of $1,200. Solitaire estimates that its risk-adjusted cost of capital is 14 percent. Currently, 1 U.S. dollar will buy 1.62 Swiss francs. In addition, 1-year risk-free securities in the United States are yielding 7.25 percent, while similar securities in Switzerland are yielding 4.5 percent.

a. If this project were instead undertaken by a similar U.S.-based company with the same risk-adjusted cost of capital, what would be the net present value and rate of return generated by this project?
b. What is the expected forward exchange rate 1 year from now?
c. If Solitaire undertakes the project, what is the net present value and rate of return of the project for Solitaire?

PROBLEMS

19-11
Exchange rates

Table 19-1 lists foreign exchange rates for August 7, 2002. On that day, how many dollars would be required to purchase 1,000 units of each of the following: British pounds, Canadian dollars, EMU euros, Japanese yen, Mexican pesos, and Swedish kronas?

19-12
Exchange rates

Look up the 6 currencies in Problem 19-11 in the foreign exchange section of a current issue of *The Wall Street Journal*.
a. What is the current exchange rate for changing dollars into 1,000 units of pounds, Canadian dollars, euros, yen, Mexican pesos, and Swedish kronas?
b. What is the percentage gain or loss between the August 7, 2002, exchange rate and the current exchange rate for each of the currencies in part a?

Early in September 1983, it took 245 Japanese yen to equal $1. Then, 19 years later, in August 2002 that exchange rate had fallen to 121 yen to $1. Assume the price of a Japanese-manufactured automobile was $9,000 in September 1983 and that its price changes were in direct relation to exchange rates.
a. Has the price, in dollars, of the automobile increased or decreased during the 19-year period because of changes in the exchange rate?
b. What would the dollar price of the automobile be in August 2002, again assuming that the car's price changes only with exchange rates?

Chamberlain Canadian Imports has agreed to purchase 15,000 cases of Canadian beer for 4 million Canadian dollars at today's spot rate. The firm's financial manager, James Churchill, has noted the following current spot and forward rates:

	U.S. DOLLAR/CANADIAN DOLLAR	CANADIAN DOLLAR/U.S. DOLLAR
Spot	0.6930	1.4430
30-day forward	0.6935	1.4420
90-day forward	0.6944	1.4401
180-day forward	0.6957	1.4374

On the same day, Churchill agrees to purchase 15,000 more cases of beer in 3 months at the same price of 4 million Canadian dollars.
a. What is the price of the beer, in U.S. dollars, if it is purchased at today's spot rate?
b. What is the cost, in U.S. dollars, of the second 15,000 cases if payment is made in 90 days and the spot rate at that time equals today's 90-day forward rate?
c. If the exchange rate for the Canadian dollar is 1.20 to $1 in 90 days, how much will Churchill have to pay for the beer (in U.S. dollars)?

Assume that interest rate parity holds and that 90-day risk-free securities yield 5 percent in the United States and 5.3 percent in Britain. In the spot market 1 pound equals 1.65 dollars.
a. Is the 90-day forward rate trading at a premium or discount relative to the spot rate?
b. What is the 90-day forward rate?

Assume that interest rate parity holds. In both the spot market and the 90-day forward market 1 Japanese yen equals 0.0086 dollar. And 90-day risk-free securities yield 4.6 percent in Japan. What is the yield on 90-day risk-free securities in the United States?

In the spot market 7.8 Mexican pesos can be exchanged for 1 U.S. dollar. A compact disc costs $15 in the United States. If purchasing power parity (PPP) holds, what should be the price of the same disc in Mexico?

SPREADSHEET PROBLEM

Yohe Telecommunications is a multinational corporation that produces and distributes telecommunications technology. Although its corporate headquarters are located in Maitland, Florida, Yohe usually must buy its raw materials in several different foreign countries using several different foreign currencies. The matter is further complicated because Yohe usually sells its products in other foreign countries. One product in particular, the SY-20 radio transmitter, draws its principal components, Component X, Component Y, and Component Z, from Switzerland, France, and England, respectively. Specifically, Component X costs 165 Swiss francs, Component Y costs 425 French francs, and Component Z costs 105 British pounds. The largest market for the SY-20 is in Japan, where it sells for 38,000 Japanese yen. Naturally, Yohe is intimately concerned with economic conditions that could adversely affect dollar exchange rates. You will find Tables 19-1, 19-2, and 19-3 useful for this problem.
a. How much, in dollars, does it cost for Yohe to produce the SY-20? What is the dollar sale price of the SY-20?
b. What is the dollar profit that Yohe makes on the sale of the SY-20? What is the percentage profit?
c. If the U.S. dollar were to weaken by 10 percent against all foreign currencies, what would be the dollar profit for the SY-20?
d. If the U.S. dollar were to weaken by 10 percent only against the Japanese yen and remained constant relative to all other foreign currencies, what would be the dollar and percentage profits for the SY-20?

e. Using the forward exchange information from Table 19-3, calculate the return on 1-year securities in Switzerland, if the rate of return on 1-year securities in the U.S. is 4.9 percent.

f. Assuming that purchasing power parity (PPP) holds, what would be the sale price of the SY-20 if it were sold in England rather than Japan?

CITRUS PRODUCTS INC.

19-19 **Multinational Financial Management** Citrus Products Inc. is a medium-sized producer of citrus juice drinks with groves in Indian River County, Florida. Until now, the company has confined its operations and sales to the United States, but its CEO, George Gaynor, wants to expand into the Pacific Rim. The first step would be to set up sales subsidiaries in Japan and Australia, then to set up a production plant in Japan, and, finally, to distribute the product throughout the Pacific Rim. The firm's financial manager, Ruth Schmidt, is enthusiastic about the plan, but she is worried about the implications of the foreign expansion on the firm's financial management process. She has asked you, the firm's most recently hired financial analyst, to develop a 1-hour tutorial package that explains the basics of multinational financial management. The tutorial will be presented at the next board of directors meeting. To get you started, Schmidt has supplied you with the following list of questions.

a. What is a multinational corporation? Why do firms expand into other countries?

b. What are the six major factors that distinguish multinational financial management from financial management as practiced by a purely domestic firm?

c. Consider the following illustrative exchange rates.

	U.S. DOLLARS REQUIRED TO BUY ONE UNIT OF FOREIGN CURRENCY
Japanese yen	0.009
Australian dollar	0.650

(1) Are these currency prices direct quotations or indirect quotations?

(2) Calculate the indirect quotations for yen and Australian dollars.

(3) What is a cross rate? Calculate the two cross rates between yen and Australian dollars.

(4) Assume Citrus Products can produce a liter of orange juice and ship it to Japan for $1.75. If the firm wants a 50 percent markup on the product, what should the orange juice sell for in Japan?

(5) Now, assume Citrus Products begins producing the same liter of orange juice in Japan. The product costs 250 yen to produce and ship to Australia, where it can be sold for 6 Australian dollars. What is the U.S. dollar profit on the sale?

(6) What is the exchange rate risk?

d. Briefly describe the current international monetary system.

e. What is a convertible currency? What problems arise when a multinational company operates in a country whose currency is not convertible?

f. What is the difference between spot rates and forward rates? When is the forward rate at a premium to the spot rate? At a discount?

g. What is interest rate parity? Currently, you can exchange 1 yen for 0.0095 U.S. dollar in the 30-day forward market, and the risk-free rate on 30-day securities is 4 percent in both Japan and the United States. Does interest rate parity hold? If not, which securities offer the highest expected return?

h. What is purchasing power parity (PPP)? If grapefruit juice costs $2.00 a liter in the United States and purchasing power parity holds, what should be the price of grapefruit juice in Australia?

i. What impact does relative inflation have on interest rates and exchange rates?

j. Briefly discuss the international capital markets.

k. To what extent do average capital structures vary across different countries?

l. What is the impact of multinational operations on each of the following financial management topics?
   (1) Cash management.
   (2) Capital budgeting decisions.
   (3) Credit management.
   (4) Inventory management.

Please go to our web site **http://brigham.swlearning.com** to access the Cyberproblems.

HYBRID FINANCING: PREFERRED STOCK, LEASING, WARRANTS, AND CONVERTIBLES

20

TAKING A WILD RIDE WITH
AMAZON'S CONVERTIBLE DEBT

The use of convertible securities—generally bonds or preferred stocks that can be exchanged for common stock of the issuing corporation—has soared during the last decade. At the start of 2000, $140 billion of convertible securities were trading in the market.

Why do companies use convertibles so heavily? To answer this question, recognize that convertibles virtually always have coupon rates that are lower than would be required on straight, nonconvertible bonds or preferred stocks. Therefore, if a company raises $100 million by issuing convertible bonds, its interest expense is lower than if it financed with non-convertible debt. But why would investors be willing to buy convertibles, given their lower cash payments? The answer lies in the conversion feature—if the price of the issuer's stock rises, the holder of the convertible can exchange it for stock and realize a capital gain. So, convertibles hold down the cash costs of financing by giving investors an opportunity for capital gains.

A convertible bond's value is tied to the price of the stock into which it is convertible, whereas a nonconvertible bond's price is based on its fixed-income payments. Therefore, convertibles' prices go up and down much more than regular bonds' prices; hence, convertibles are relatively risky. A recent article in *Forbes* reported that if a company's common stock increases in value, the returns on its convertibles also rise, but by only 70 percent of the stock's percentage increase. However, if the stock declines, the convertible will decline by only 50 percent of the stock's decline. Thus, while convertibles are more risky than straight bonds, they are less risky than stock.

To illustrate all this, consider Amazon.com. In January 1999 Amazon issued $1.25 billion of convertible bonds, the largest convertible bond offering in history. Amazon's bonds were issued at a par value of $1,000, and they had a 4.75 percent coupon rate. Because they can be converted to Amazon common stock, changes in the stock price will have a profound effect on the convertibles' value.

During 1999 Amazon's convertibles took their holders on a wild ride. During the first four months Amazon's stock rose about 70 percent, to more than $100 per share, causing its convertibles to rise by 50 percent, to $1,500. During the next four months, the stock lost more than 60 percent of its value. This caused the convertibles' price to drop to $750. Three months later Amazon's stock had rebounded, and its convertibles were once again trading above $1,500, only to decline sharply one month later. By year-end 1999, the convertibles were about back to their $1,000 issue price. Thus, a convertible bondholder holding the bond for the entire year would have ended up close to where he or she had started, with a total return just shy of the 4.75 percent coupon rate.

Since 1999, Amazon and most other "tech" stocks have fallen shaply—Amazon dropped from its 1999 high of more than $100 to a low of $5.51 in 2001, or by about 95 percent. The convertibles also declined, but only to $376, or by about 75 percent, bad but not as bad as the stock. The convertibles held up better for two reasons. First, they paid $47.50 per year interest, whereas the common paid nothing, and second, if Amazon was forced into bankruptcy, which was a real possibility in 2001, the convertibles would have a claim on their $1,000 par value ahead of stockholders' claims. After the 2000 trough, Amazon's fortunes improved. Rumors of impending bankruptcy were dispelled, and the convertibles rose from a low of $376.20 to $720, or by 91 percent, while the stock rose from $5.51 to $20.40, or by 270 percent.

Amazon's experience with convertibles is not unusual. The convertible bonds rose in price with the common, but not as rapidly, and the bonds also declined with the stock, but again the losses were less pronounced. Thus, convertibles offer investors a bit of protection against losses, but also opportunities for capital gains. Not surprisingly, convertibles are used by companies whose futures are highly uncertain to attract investors who are not willing to bear the risks inherent in their common stocks.

When you finish this chapter, you should have a good understanding of what convertibles are, how they are valued, and why a firm might choose to issue a convertible bond rather than either straight debt or common stock.

Source: John Gorham, "Chicken Little Stocks," *Forbes*, December 27, 1999, 200.

PUTTING THINGS IN PERSPECTIVE

In previous chapters we examined common stocks and the various types of long-term debt. In this chapter, we examine four other types of long-term capital: (1) *preferred stock,* which is a hybrid security that represents a cross between debt and common equity; (2) *leasing,* which is used by financial managers as an alternative to borrowing to finance fixed assets; (3) *warrants,* which are derivative securities issued by firms to facilitate the issuance of some other type of security; and (4) *convertibles,* which combine the features of debt (or preferred stock) and warrants. ◼

PREFERRED STOCK

Preferred stock is a hybrid — it is similar to bonds in some respects and to common stock in other ways. Accountants classify preferred stock as equity, hence show it on the balance sheet as an equity account. However, from a finance perspective preferred stock lies somewhere between debt and common equity — it imposes a fixed charge and thus increases the firm's financial leverage, yet omitting the preferred dividend does not force a company into bankruptcy. We first describe the basic features of preferred, after which we discuss other types of preferred stock, and the advantages and disadvantages of preferred stock.

BASIC FEATURES

Preferred stock has a par (or liquidating) value, often either $25 or $100. The dividend is stated as either a percentage of par, as so many dollars per share, or both ways. For example, several years ago Klondike Paper Company sold 150,000 shares of $100 par value perpetual preferred stock for a total of $15 million. This preferred had a stated annual dividend of $12 per share, so the preferred dividend yield was $12/\$100 = 0.12$, or 12 percent, at the time of issue. The dividend was set when the stock was issued; it will not be changed in the future. Therefore, if the required rate of return on preferred, k_p, changes from 12 percent after the issue date — as it did —

then the market price of the preferred stock will go up or down. Currently, k_p for Klondike Paper's preferred is 9 percent, and the price of the preferred has risen from $100 to $12/0.09 = $133.33.

If the preferred dividend is not earned, the company does not have to pay it. However, most preferred issues are **cumulative**, meaning that the cumulative total of all unpaid preferred dividends must be paid before dividends can be paid on the common stock. Unpaid preferred dividends are called **arrearages.** Dividends in arrears do not earn interest; thus, arrearages do not grow in a compound interest sense — they only grow from additional nonpayments of the preferred dividend. Also, many preferred stocks accrue arrearages for only a limited number of years, say, three years, meaning that the cumulative feature ceases after three years. However, the dividends in arrears continue in force until they are paid.

Preferred stock normally has no voting rights. However, most preferred issues stipulate that the preferred stockholders can elect a minority of the directors — say, three out of ten — if the preferred dividend is passed (omitted). Jersey Central Power & Light, one of the companies that owned a share of the Three Mile Island (TMI) nuclear plant, had preferred stock outstanding that could elect a *majority* of the directors if the preferred dividend was passed for four successive quarters. Jersey Central kept paying its preferred dividends even during the dark days following the TMI accident. Had the preferred not been entitled to elect a majority of the directors, the dividend would probably have been passed.

Although nonpayment of preferred dividends will not bankrupt a company, corporations issue preferred with every intention of paying the dividend. Even if passing the dividend does not give the preferred stockholders control of the company, failure to pay a preferred dividend precludes payment of common dividends. In addition, passing the dividend makes it difficult to raise capital by selling bonds, and virtually impossible to sell more preferred or common stock. However, having preferred stock outstanding does give a firm the chance to overcome its difficulties — if bonds had been used instead of preferred stock, Jersey Central would have been in danger of being forced into bankruptcy before it could straighten out its problems. *Thus, from the viewpoint of the issuing corporation, preferred stock is less risky than bonds.*

However, for investors preferred stock is riskier than bonds: (1) Preferred stockholders' claims are subordinated to those of bondholders in the event of liquidation, and (2) bondholders are more likely to continue receiving income during hard times than are preferred stockholders. Accordingly, investors require a higher after-tax rate of return on a given firm's preferred stock than on its bonds. However, since 70 percent of preferred dividends is exempt from corporate taxes, preferred stock is attractive to corporate investors. In recent years, high-grade preferred stock, on average, has sold on a lower pre-tax yield basis than have high-grade bonds. As an example, Duke Energy's preferred stock recently had a market yield of about 6.3 percent, whereas its bonds provided a yield of 7.0 percent, or 0.7 percentage point *more* than its preferred. The tax treatment accounted for this differential; the *after-tax yield* to corporate investors was greater on the preferred stock than on the bonds.[1]

Cumulative
A protective feature on preferred stock that requires preferred dividends previously not paid to be paid before any common dividends can be paid.

Arrearages
Unpaid preferred dividends.

---

[1] The after-tax yield on a 7 percent bond to a corporate investor in the 34 percent marginal tax rate bracket is $7\%(1 - T) = 7\%(0.66) = 4.62\%$. The after-tax yield on a 6.3 percent preferred stock is $6.3\%(1 - \text{Effective T}) = 6.3\%[1 - (0.30)(0.34)] = 6.3\%(0.898) = 5.66\%$. Also, note that tax law prohibits firms from issuing debt and then using the proceeds to purchase another firm's preferred or common stock. If debt is used for stock purchases, then the 70 percent dividend exclusion is voided. This provision is designed to prevent a firm from engaging in "tax arbitrage," using tax-deductible debt to purchase largely tax-exempt preferred stock.

About half of all preferred stock issued in recent years has been convertible into common stock. For example, Lucent Corp. recently issued $1.75 billion of preferred stock with an 8 percent annual dividend rate. Investors in this issue also have the option to convert their preferred stock to common stock at a conversion price of $7.48 a share. Convertibles are discussed at length in a later section.

Some preferred stocks are similar to perpetual bonds in that they have no maturity date, but most new issues now have specified maturities. For example, many preferred shares have a sinking fund provision that calls for the retirement of 2 percent of the issue each year, meaning that the issue will "mature" in a maximum of 50 years. Also, many preferred issues are callable by the issuing corporation, which can also limit the life of the preferred.[2]

Nonconvertible preferred stock is virtually all owned by corporations, which can take advantage of the 70 percent dividend exclusion to obtain a higher after-tax yield on preferred stock than on bonds. Individuals should not own preferred stocks (except convertible preferreds) — they can get higher yields on safer bonds, so it is not logical for them to hold preferreds. As a result of this ownership pattern, the volume of preferred stock financing is geared to the supply of money in the hands of corporate investors. When the supply of such money is plentiful, the prices of preferred stocks are bid up, their yields fall, and investment bankers suggest that companies that need financing consider issuing preferred stock.

For issuers, preferred stock has a tax *disadvantage* relative to debt — interest expense is deductible, but preferred dividends are not. Still, firms with low tax rates may have an incentive to issue preferred stock that can be bought by corporate investors with high tax rates, who can take advantage of the 70 percent dividend exclusion. If a firm has a lower tax rate than potential corporate buyers, the firm might be better off issuing preferred stock than debt. The key here is that the tax advantage to a high-tax-rate corporation is greater than the tax disadvantage to a low-tax-rate issuer. To illustrate, assume that risk differentials between debt and preferred would require an issuer to set the interest rate on new debt at 10 percent and the dividend yield on new preferred at 12 percent in a no-tax world. However, when taxes are considered, a corporate buyer with a high tax rate, say, 40 percent, might be willing to buy the preferred stock if it has an 8 percent before-tax yield. This would produce an $8\%(1 - \text{Effective } T) = 8\%[1 - 0.30(0.40)] = 7.04\%$ after-tax return on the preferred versus $10\%(1 - 0.40) = 6.0\%$ on the debt. If the issuer has a low tax rate, say, 10 percent, its after-tax costs would be $10\%(1 - T) = 10\%(0.90) = 9\%$ on the bonds and 8 percent on the preferred. Thus, the security with lower risk to the issuer, preferred stock, also has a lower cost. Such situations can make preferred stock a logical financing choice.[3]

---

[2] Prior to the late 1970s, virtually all preferred stock was perpetual, and almost no issues had sinking funds or call provisions. Then, insurance company regulators, worried about the unrealized losses the companies had been incurring on preferred holdings as a result of rising interest rates, put into effect some regulatory changes that essentially mandated that insurance companies buy only limited life preferreds. From that time on, virtually no new preferred has been perpetual. This example illustrates the way securities change as a result of changes in the economic environment.

[3] For a more rigorous treatment of the tax hypothesis of preferred stock, see Iraj Fooladi and Gordon S. Roberts, "On Preferred Stock," *Journal of Financial Research*, Winter 1986, 319–324. For an example of an empirical test of the hypothesis, see Arthur L. Houston, Jr., and Carol Olson Houston, "Financing with Preferred Stock," *Financial Management*, Autumn 1990, 42–54.

OTHER TYPES OF PREFERRED STOCK

In addition to the "plain vanilla" variety of preferred stocks, several variations are also used. Two of these, floating rate and market auction preferred, are discussed in the following sections.

Adjustable Rate Preferred Stock

Instead of paying fixed dividends, **adjustable rate preferred stocks (ARPs)** have their dividends tied to the rate on Treasury securities. The ARPs, which are issued mainly by utilities and large commercial banks, were touted as nearly perfect short-term corporate investments since (1) only 30 percent of the dividends are taxable to corporations, and (2) the floating rate feature was supposed to keep the issue trading at near par. The new security proved to be so popular as a short-term investment for firms with idle cash that mutual funds designed just to invest in them sprouted like weeds (shares of the funds, in turn, were purchased by corporations). However, the ARPs still had some price volatility due (1) to changes in the riskiness of the issues (some big banks that had issued ARPs, such as Continental Illinois, ran into serious loan default problems) and (2) to the fact that Treasury yields fluctuated between dividend rate adjustments dates. Thus, the ARPs had too much price instability to be held in the liquid asset portfolios of many corporate investors.

Market Auction Preferred Stock

In 1984, investment bankers introduced **money market,** or **market auction, preferred.** Here the underwriter conducts an auction on the issue every seven weeks (to get the 70 percent exclusion from taxable income, buyers must hold the stock at least 46 days). Holders who want to sell their shares can put them up for auction at par value. Buyers then submit bids in the form of the yields they are willing to accept over the next seven-week period. The yield set on the issue for the coming period is the lowest yield sufficient to sell all the shares being offered at that auction. The buyers pay the sellers the par value; hence, holders are virtually assured that their shares can be sold at par. The issuer then must pay a dividend rate over the next seven-week period as determined by the auction. From the holder's standpoint, market auction preferred is a low-risk, largely tax-exempt, seven-week maturity security that can be sold between auction dates at close to par. However, if there are not enough buyers to match the sellers (in spite of the high yield), then the auction can fail, which has occurred on occasion.

ADVANTAGES AND DISADVANTAGES OF PREFERRED STOCK

There are both advantages and disadvantages to financing with preferred stock. Here are the major advantages from the issuers' standpoint:

1. In contrast to bonds, the obligation to pay preferred dividends is not contractual, and passing a preferred dividend cannot force a firm into bankruptcy.
2. By issuing preferred stock, the firm avoids the dilution of common equity that occurs when common stock is sold.

FUNNY-NAMED PREFERRED-LIKE SECURITIES

Wall Street's "financial engineers" are constantly trying to develop new securities with appeal to issuers and investors. One such new security is a special type of preferred stock created by Goldman Sachs in the mid-1990s. These securities trade under a variety of colorful names, including MIPS (modified income preferred securities), QUIPS (quarterly income preferred securities), and QUIDS (quarterly income debt securities). The corporation that wants to raise capital (the "parent") establishes a trust, which issues fixed-dividend preferred stock. The parent then issues bonds (or debt of some type) to the trust, and the trust pays for the bonds with the cash raised from the sale of preferred. At that point, the parent has the cash it needs, the trust holds debt issued by the parent, and the investing public holds preferred stock issued by the trust. The parent then makes interest payments to the trust, and the trust uses that income to make the preferred dividend payments. Because the parent company has issued debt, its interest payments are tax deductible.

If the dividends could be excluded from taxable income by corporate investors, this preferred would really be a great deal — the issuer could deduct the interest, corporate investors could exclude most of the dividends, and the IRS would be the loser. The corporate parent does get to deduct the interest paid to the trust, but IRS regulations do not allow the dividends on these securities to be excluded.

Because there is only one deduction, why are these new securities attractive? The answer is as follows: (1) Since the par-

ent company gets to take the deduction, its cost of funds from the preferred is $k_p(1 - T)$, just as it would be if it used debt. (2) The parent generates a tax savings, and it can thus afford to pay a relatively high rate on trust-related preferred; that is, it can pass on some of its tax savings to investors to induce them to buy the new securities. (3) The primary purchasers of the preferred are low-tax-bracket individuals and tax-exempt institutions such as pension funds. For such purchasers, not being able to exclude the dividend from taxable income is not important. (4) Due to the differential tax rates, the arrangement results in a net tax savings. Competition in capital markets results in a sharing of the savings between investors and corporations.

A recent *SmartMoney Online* article argued that these hybrid securities are a good deal for individual investors for the reason set forth above and also because they are sold in small increments — often as small as $25. However, these securities are relatively complex, which increases their risk and makes them hard to value. There is also risk to the issuing corporations. The IRS has expressed concerns about these securities, and if at some point the IRS decides to disallow interest paid to the trusts, that will have a profound negative effect on the corporations that have issued them.

SOURCES: Kerry Capell, "High Yields, Low Cost, Funny Names," *BusinessWeek*, September 9, 1996, 122; and Leslie Haggin, "SmartMoney Online: MIPS, QUIDS, and QUIPS," *SmartMoney Interactive*, April 6, 1999.

3. Since preferred stock sometimes has no maturity, and since preferred sinking fund payments, if present, are typically spread over a long period, preferred issues reduce the cash flow drain from repayment of principal that occurs with debt issues.

There are two major disadvantages:

1. Preferred stock dividends are not deductible to the issuer, hence the after-tax cost of preferred is typically higher than the after-tax cost of debt. However, the tax advantage of preferreds to corporate purchasers lowers its pre-tax cost and thus its effective cost.

2. Although preferred dividends can be passed, investors expect them to be paid, and firms intend to pay the dividends if conditions permit. Thus, preferred dividends are considered to be a fixed cost. Therefore, their use, like that of debt, increases financial risk and thus the cost of common equity.

LEASING

Firms generally own fixed assets and report them on their balance sheets, but it is the *use* of buildings and equipment that is important, not their ownership per se. One way of obtaining the use of assets is to buy them, but an alternative is to lease them. Prior to the 1950s, leasing was generally associated with real estate — land and buildings. Today, however, it is possible to lease virtually any kind of fixed asset, and, in 2002, about 30 percent of all new capital equipment acquired by businesses was leased.

TYPES OF LEASES

Leasing takes three different forms: (1) *sale-and-leaseback* arrangements, (2) *operating leases*, and (3) straight *financial*, or *capital, leases*.

Sale and Leaseback

Sale and Leaseback
An arrangement whereby a firm sells land, buildings, or equipment and simultaneously leases the property back for a specified period under specific terms.

Under a **sale and leaseback,** a firm that owns land, buildings, or equipment sells the property and simultaneously executes an agreement to lease the property back for a specified period under specific terms. The purchaser could be an insurance company, a commercial bank, a specialized leasing company, or even an individual investor. The sale-and-leaseback plan is an alternative to taking out a mortgage loan.

Lessee
The party that uses, rather than the one who owns, the leased property.

The firm that is selling the property, or the **lessee,** immediately receives the purchase price put up by the buyer, or the **lessor.**[4] At the same time, the seller-lessee firm retains the use of the property just as if it had borrowed and mortgaged the property to secure the loan. Note that under a mortgage loan arrangement, the financial institution would normally receive a series of equal payments just sufficient to amortize the loan while providing a specified rate of return to the lender on the outstanding balance. Under a sale-and-leaseback arrangement, the lease payments are set up in exactly the same way; the payments are set so as to return the purchase price to the investor-lessor while providing a specified rate of return on the lessor's outstanding investment.

Lessor
The owner of the leased property.

Operating Leases

Operating Lease
A lease under which the lessor maintains and finances the property; also called a *service lease*.

Operating leases, sometimes called *service leases*, provide for both *financing* and *maintenance*. IBM is one of the pioneers of the operating lease contract, and computers and office copying machines, together with automobiles and trucks, are the primary

---

[4] The term *lessee* is pronounced "less-ee," not "lease-ee," and *lessor* is pronounced "less-or."

types of equipment involved. Ordinarily, these leases call for the lessor to maintain and service the leased equipment, and the cost of providing maintenance is built into the lease payments.

Another important characteristic of operating leases is the fact that they are frequently *not fully amortized*; in other words, the payments required under the lease contract are not sufficient to recover the full cost of the equipment. However, the lease contract is written for a period considerably shorter than the expected economic life of the leased equipment, and the lessor expects to recover all investment costs through subsequent renewal payments, through subsequent leases to other lessees, or by selling the leased equipment.

A final feature of operating leases is that they frequently contain a *cancellation clause*, which gives the lessee the right to cancel the lease before the expiration of the basic agreement. This is an important consideration for the lessee, for it means that the equipment can be returned if it is rendered obsolete by technological developments or if it is no longer needed because of a decline in the lessee's business.

Financial, or Capital, Leases

Financial Lease
A lease that does not provide for maintenance services, is not cancelable, and is fully amortized over its life; also called a *capital lease*.

Financial leases, sometimes called *capital leases*, are differentiated from operating leases in three respects: (1) they do *not* provide for maintenance services, (2) they are *not* cancelable, and (3) they *are* fully amortized (that is, the lessor receives rental payments that are equal to the full price of the leased equipment plus a return on the investment). In a typical financial lease arrangement, the firm that will use the equipment (the lessee) selects the specific items it requires and negotiates the price and delivery terms with the manufacturer. The user firm then negotiates terms with a leasing company and, once the lease terms are set, arranges to have the lessor buy the equipment from the manufacturer or the distributor. When the equipment is purchased, the user firm simultaneously executes the lease agreement.

Financial leases are similar to sale-and-leaseback arrangements, the major difference being that the leased equipment is new and the lessor buys it from a manufacturer or a distributor instead of from the user-lessee. A sale and leaseback may thus be thought of as a special type of financial lease, and both sale and leasebacks and financial leases are analyzed in the same manner.[5]

FINANCIAL STATEMENT EFFECTS

Off Balance Sheet Financing
Financing in which the assets and liabilities involved do not appear on the firm's balance sheet.

Lease payments are shown as operating expenses on a firm's income statement, but under certain conditions, neither the leased assets nor the liabilities under the lease contract appears on the firm's balance sheet. For this reason, leasing is often called **off balance sheet financing.** This point is illustrated in Table 20-1 by the balance sheets of two hypothetical firms, B (for Buy) and L (for Lease). Initially, the balance sheets of both firms are identical, and both have debt ratios of 50 percent. Each firm then decides to acquire fixed assets that cost $100. Firm B borrows $100 to make the

---

[5] For a lease transaction to qualify as a lease for *tax purposes*, and thus for the lessee to be able to deduct the lease payments, the life of the lease must not exceed 80 percent of the expected life of the asset, and the lessee cannot be permitted to buy the asset at a nominal value. These conditions are IRS requirements, and they should not be confused with the FASB requirements discussed later in the chapter concerning the capitalization of leases. It is important to consult lawyers and accountants to ascertain whether or not a prospective lease meets current IRS regulations.

TABLE 20-1   Balance Sheet Effects of Leasing

BEFORE ASSET INCREASE				AFTER ASSET INCREASE							
FIRMS B AND L				FIRM B, WHICH BORROWS AND BUYS				FIRM L, WHICH LEASES			
Current assets	$ 50	Debt	$ 50	Current assets	$ 50	Debt	$150	Current assets	$ 50	Debt	$ 50
Fixed assets	50	Equity	50	Fixed assets	150	Equity	50	Fixed assets	50	Equity	50
Total	$100		$100	Total	$200		$200	Total	$100		$100
		Debt ratio: 50%				Debt ratio: 75%				Debt ratio: 50%	

FASB #13

The statement of the Financial Accounting Standards Board that details the conditions and procedures for capitalizing leases.

purchase, so both an asset and a liability are recorded on its balance sheet, and its debt ratio is increased to 75 percent. Firm L leases the equipment, so its balance sheet is unchanged. The lease may call for fixed charges as high as or even higher than those on the loan, and the obligations assumed under the lease may be equally or more dangerous from the standpoint of financial safety, but the firm's debt ratio remains at 50 percent.

To correct this problem, the Financial Accounting Standards Board issued **FASB #13**, which requires that for an unqualified audit report, firms that enter into financial (or capital) leases must restate their balance sheets to report (1) leased assets as fixed assets and (2) the present value of future lease payments as a liability. This process is called *capitalizing the lease*, and its net effect is to cause Firms B and L to have similar balance sheets, both of which will resemble the one shown for Firm B after the asset increase.[6]

The logic behind FASB #13 is as follows. If a firm signs a lease contract, its obligation to make lease payments is just as binding as if it had signed a loan agreement. The failure to make lease payments can bankrupt a firm just as surely as can the failure to make principal and interest payments on a loan. Therefore, for all intents and purposes, a financial lease is identical to a loan.[7] This being the case, when a firm signs a lease agreement, it has, in effect, raised its "true" debt ratio and thereby has changed its "true" capital structure. Accordingly, if the firm had previously established a target capital structure, and if there is no reason to think that the optimal capital structure has changed, then using lease financing requires additional equity just as does debt financing.

---

[6] FASB #13, "Accounting for Leases," November 1976, spells out in detail the conditions under which leases must be capitalized, and the procedures for doing so.

[7] There are, however, certain legal differences between loans and leases. In a bankruptcy liquidation, the lessor is entitled to take possession of the leased asset, and, if the value of the asset is less than the required payments under the lease, the lessor can enter a claim (as a general creditor) for one year's lease payments. In a bankruptcy reorganization, the lessor receives the asset plus three years' lease payments, if needed, to bring the value of the asset up to the remaining investment in the lease. Under a secured loan arrangement, on the other hand, the lender has a security interest in the asset, meaning that if it is sold, the lender will be given the proceeds, and the full unsatisfied portion of the lender's claim will be treated as a general creditor obligation (see Web Appendix 7B). It is not possible to state as a general rule whether a supplier of capital is in a stronger position as a secured creditor or as a lessor. Since one position is usually regarded as being about as good as the other at the time the financial arrangements are being made, a lease is about as risky as a secured term loan from both the lessor-lender's and the lessee-borrower's viewpoints.

If a disclosure of the lease in the Table 20-1 example were not made, then investors could be deceived into thinking that Firm L's financial position is stronger than it actually is. Even if the lease were disclosed in a footnote, investors might not fully recognize its impact and might not see that Firms B and L are in essentially the same financial position. If this were the case, Firm L would have increased its true amount of debt through a lease arrangement, but its required return on debt, k_d, its required return on equity, k_s, and consequently its weighted average cost of capital, would not have increased as much as those of Firm B, which borrowed directly. Thus, investors would be willing to accept a lower return from Firm L because they would mistakenly view it as being in a stronger financial position than Firm B. These benefits of leasing would accrue to stockholders at the expense of new investors, who were, in effect, being deceived by the fact that the firm's balance sheet did not fully reflect its true liability situation. This is why FASB #13 was issued.

A lease must be classified as a capital lease, and hence be capitalized and shown directly on the balance sheet, if any one of the following conditions exists:

1. Under the terms of the lease, ownership of the property is effectively transferred from the lessor to the lessee.

2. The lessee can purchase the property or renew the lease at less than a fair market price when the lease expires.

3. The lease runs for a period equal to or greater than 75 percent of the asset's life. Thus, if an asset has a 10-year life and if the lease is written for more than 7.5 years, the lease must be capitalized.

4. The present value of the lease payments is equal to or greater than 90 percent of the initial value of the asset.[8]

These rules, together with strong footnote disclosures for operating leases, are sufficient to ensure that no one will be fooled by lease financing. Thus, leases are recognized to be essentially the same as debt, and they have the same effects as debt on the firm's required rate of return. Therefore, leasing will not generally permit a firm to use more financial leverage than could be obtained with conventional debt.

EVALUATION BY THE LESSEE

Any prospective lease must be evaluated by both the lessee and the lessor. The lessee must determine whether leasing an asset will be less costly than buying it, and the lessor must decide whether or not the lease will provide a reasonable rate of return. Since our focus in this book is primarily on financial management as opposed to investments, we restrict our analysis to that conducted by the lessee.[9]

For students interested in additional information on leasing, a good place to start is the web site for GE Capital Vendor Financial Services and its Glossary of Leasing Terminology at **http://www.ge.com/capital/vendor/glosterm.html**.

---

[8] The discount rate used to calculate the present value of the lease payments must be the lower of (1) the rate used by the lessor to establish the lease payments or (2) the interest rate which the lessee would have paid for new debt with a maturity equal to that of the lease.

[9] The lessee is typically offered a set of lease terms by the lessor, which is generally a bank, a finance company such as General Electric Capital (the largest U.S. lessor), or some other institutional lender. The lessee can accept or reject the lease, or shop around for a better deal. In this chapter, we take the lease terms as given for purposes of our analysis. See Chapter 18 of Eugene F. Brigham and Phillip R. Daves, *Intermediate Financial Management*, 7th ed. (Cincinnati, OH: South-Western College Publishing, 2002), for a discussion of lease analysis from the lessor's standpoint, including a discussion of how a potential lessee can use such an analysis in bargaining for better terms.

In the typical case, the events leading to a lease arrangement follow the sequence described in the following list. We should note that a great deal of theoretical literature exists about the correct way to evaluate lease-versus-purchase decisions, and some very complex decision models have been developed to aid in the analysis. The analysis given here, however, leads to the correct decision in every case we have ever encountered.

1. The firm decides to acquire a particular building or piece of equipment. This decision is based on regular capital budgeting procedures, and the decision to acquire the asset is a "done deal" before the lease analysis begins. Therefore, in a lease analysis we are concerned simply with whether to finance the machine by a lease or by a loan.

2. Once the firm has decided to acquire the asset, the next question is how to finance it. Well-run businesses do not have excess cash lying around, so new assets must be financed in some manner.

3. Funds to purchase the asset could be obtained by borrowing, by retaining earnings, or by issuing new stock. Alternatively, the asset could be leased. Because of the FASB #13 capitalization/disclosure provision for leases, a lease would have the same capital structure effect as a loan.

As indicated earlier, a lease is comparable to a loan in the sense that the firm is required to make a specified series of payments, and a failure to make these payments can result in bankruptcy. Thus, it is most appropriate to compare the cost of leasing with that of debt financing.[10] The lease-versus-borrow-and-purchase analysis is illustrated with data on the Mitchell Electronics Company. The following conditions are assumed:

1. Mitchell plans to acquire equipment with a five-year life that has a cost of $10,000,000, delivered and installed.

2. Mitchell can borrow the required $10 million, using a 10 percent loan to be amortized over five years. Therefore, the loan will call for payments of $2,637,974.81 per year, found with a financial calculator as follows: input N = 5, I = 10, PV = −10000000, and FV = 0, and then press PMT to find the payment, $2,637,974.81.

3. Alternatively, Mitchell can lease the equipment for five years at a rental charge of $2,800,000 per year, payable at the end of the year. The lessor will own the asset at the expiration of the lease.[11] The lease payment schedule is established by the potential lessor, and Mitchell can accept it, reject it, or negotiate.

4. The equipment will definitely be used for five years, at which time its estimated net salvage value will be $715,000. Mitchell plans to continue using the equipment beyond Year 5, so (1) if it purchases the equipment, the company will

---

[10] The analysis should compare the cost of leasing to the cost of debt financing *regardless* of how the asset is actually financed. The asset may actually be purchased with available cash if it is not leased, but because leasing is a substitute for debt financing, a comparison between the two is still appropriate.

[11] Lease payments can occur at the beginning of the year or at the end of the year. In this example, we assume end-of-year payments, but we demonstrate beginning-of-year payments in Self-Test Problem ST-2.

keep it, and (2) if it leases the equipment, the company will exercise an option to buy it at its estimated salvage value, $715,000.

5. The lease contract stipulates that the lessor will maintain the equipment. However, if Mitchell borrows and buys, it will have to bear the cost of maintenance. This service will be performed by the equipment manufacturer at a fixed contract rate of $500,000 per year, payable at year-end.

6. The equipment falls in the MACRS five-year class life, and Mitchell's effective federal-plus-state tax rate is 40 percent. Also, the depreciable basis is the original cost of $10,000,000. The MACRS depreciation rates are 0.20, 0.32, 0.19, 0.12, 0.11, and 0.06.

NPV Analysis

Table 20-2 shows the cash flows that would be incurred each year under the two financing plans. The table is set up to produce two time lines of cash flows, one for owning as shown on Line 5 and one for leasing as shown on Line 10. All cash flows occur at the end of the year.

The top section of the table (Lines 1 through 6) is devoted to the cost of owning (borrowing and buying). Lines 1 through 4 show the individual cash flow items. Line 5 is a time line that summarizes the annual net cash flows that Mitchell will incur if it finances the equipment with a loan. The present values of these cash flows are summed to find the *present value of the cost of owning*, which is shown on Line 6 in the Year 0 column. (Note that with a financial calculator, we would input the cash flows as shown on Line 5 into the cash flow register, input the interest rate, I = 6, and then press the NPV key to obtain the PV of owning the equipment.)

Section II of the table calculates the present value cost of leasing. The lease payments are $2,800,000 per year; this rate, which in this example (but not in all cases) include maintenance, was established by the prospective lessor and then offered to Mitchell Electronics. If Mitchell accepts the lease, the full $2,800,000 will be a deductible expense, so the tax savings is (Tax rate)(Lease payment) = (0.4)($2,800,000) = $1,120,000. These amounts are shown on Lines 7 and 8.

Line 9 in the lease section shows the $715,000 that Mitchell expects to pay in Year 5 to purchase the equipment. We include this amount as a cost of leasing because Mitchell will almost certainly want to continue the operation and thus will be forced to purchase the equipment from the lessor. If we had assumed that the operation would not be continued, then no entry would have appeared on this line. However, in that case, we would have included the $715,000, minus applicable taxes, as a Year 5 inflow in the cost of owning analysis, because if the asset were purchased originally, it would be sold after five years. Line 10 shows the net cash flows associated with leasing for each year, and Line 11 shows the PV cost of leasing. (As indicated earlier in the cost of owning analysis, using a financial calculator, we would input the cash flows as shown on Line 10 into the cash flow register, input the interest rate, I = 6, and then press the NPV key to obtain the PV cost of leasing the equipment.)

The rate used to discount the cash flows is a critical issue. In Chapter 5, we saw that the riskier a cash flow, the higher the discount rate used to find its present value. This same principle was observed in capital budgeting, and it also applies in lease analysis. Just how risky are the cash flows under consideration here? Most of them are relatively certain, at least when compared with the types of cash flow estimates that were developed in capital budgeting. For example, the maintenance payments are set by contract, as is the lease payment schedule. The depreciation expenses are

TABLE 20-2

Mitchell Electronics Company: NPV Lease Analysis (Thousands of Dollars)

	YEAR					
	0	1	2	3	4	5
I. COST OF OWNING						
1. Net purchase price	($10,000)					
2. Maintenance cost		($ 500)	($ 500)	($ 500)	($ 500)	($ 500)
3. Tax savings from maintenance		200	200	200	200	200
4. Tax savings from depreciation		800	1,280	760	480	440
5. Net cash flow	($10,000)	$ 500	$ 980	$ 460	$ 180	$ 140
6. PV cost of owning at 6%	($ 8,023)					
II. COST OF LEASING						
7. Lease payment		($2,800)	($2,800)	($2,800)	($2,800)	($2,800)
8. Tax savings from lease payment		1,120	1,120	1,120	1,120	1,120
9. Cost to exercise option						(715)
10. Net cash flow	$ 0	($1,680)	($1,680)	($1,680)	($1,680)	($2,395)
11. PV cost of leasing at 6%	($ 7,611)					

III. COST COMPARISON

12. Net Advantage to Leasing = NAL

$$= \text{PV cost of owning} - \text{PV cost of leasing}$$
$$= \$8,023 - \$7,611 = \$412 = \$412,000.$$

NOTE: A line-by-line explanation of the table follows:

1. If Mitchell buys the equipment, it will have to spend $10,000,000 at t = 0.

2. If the equipment is owned, Mitchell must pay $500,000 at the end of each year for maintenance.

3. The $500,000 maintenance expense is tax deductible, so it will produce an annual tax savings of (Tax rate)(Maintenance expense) = 0.4($500,000) = $200,000.

4. If Mitchell buys the equipment, it can depreciate it for tax purposes and thus lower taxable income and taxes. The tax savings in each year is equal to (Tax rate)(Depreciation expense) = 0.4(Depreciation expense). As shown in Web Appendix 11A, the MACRS rates for five-year property are 0.20, 0.32, 0.19, 0.12, and 0.11 in Years 1–5, respectively. To illustrate the calculation of the depreciation tax savings, consider Year 2. The depreciation expense is 0.32($10,000,000) = $3,200,000, and the tax savings is 0.4($3,200,000) = $1,280,000.

5. The net cash flows associated with owning are found by summing Lines 1 through 4.

6. The PV (in thousands) of the Line 5 cash flows, when discounted at 6 percent, is −$8,023.

7. The annual end-of-year lease payment is $2,800,000.

8. Since the lease payment is tax deductible, a tax savings of (Tax rate)(Lease payment) = 0.4($2,800,000) = $1,120,000 results.

9. Because Mitchell plans to continue to use the equipment after the lease expires, it must exercise the purchase option for $715,000 at the end of Year 5 if it leases.

10. The net cash flows associated with leasing are found by summing Lines 7 through 9.

11. The PV (in thousands) of the Line 10 cash flows, when discounted at 6 percent, is −$7,611.

12. The net advantage to leasing is merely the difference between the PV cost of owning (in thousands) and the PV cost of leasing (in thousands) = $8,023 − $7,611 = $412. Since the NAL is positive, leasing is favored over borrowing and buying.

also established by law and are not subject to change. The tax savings are somewhat uncertain because tax rates may change, although tax rates do not change very often. The residual value is the least certain of the cash flows, but even here the $715,000 cost is set, and Mitchell's management is fairly confident that it will want to acquire the property.

Since the cash flows under both the lease and the borrow-and-purchase alternatives are all reasonably certain, they should be discounted at a relatively low rate. Most analysts recommend that the company's cost of debt be used, and this rate seems reasonable in our example. Further, since all the cash flows are on an after-tax basis, *the after-tax cost of debt, which is 6 percent, should be used.* Accordingly, in Table 20-2, we used a 6 percent discount rate to obtain the present values of the costs of owning and leasing. The financing method that results in the smaller present value of costs is the one that should be selected. The example shown in Table 20-2 indicates that leasing has a net advantage over buying: the present value of the cost of leasing is $412,000 less than that of buying. Therefore, it is to Mitchell's advantage to lease.

FACTORS THAT AFFECT LEASING DECISIONS

The basic method of analysis set forth in Table 20-2 is sufficient to handle most situations. However, two factors warrant additional comments.

Estimated Residual Value

Residual Value
The value of leased property at the end of the lease term.

It is important to note that the lessor will own the property upon the expiration of the lease. The estimated end-of-lease value of the property is called the **residual value.** Superficially, it would appear that if residual values are expected to be large, owning would have an advantage over leasing. However, if expected residual values are large — as they may be under inflation for certain types of equipment as well as if real property is involved — then competition among leasing companies will force leasing rates down to the point where potential residual values will be fully recognized in the lease contract rates. Thus, the existence of large residual values on equipment is not likely to bias the decision against leasing.

Increase Credit Availability

As noted earlier, leasing is sometimes said to have an advantage for firms that are seeking the maximum degree of financial leverage. First, it is sometimes argued that a firm can obtain more money, and for a longer period, under a lease arrangement than under a loan secured by the asset. Second, because some leases do not appear on the balance sheet, lease financing has been said to give the firm a stronger appearance in a *superficial* credit analysis, thus permitting it to use more leverage than it could if it did not lease. There may be some truth to these claims for smaller firms. However, now that larger firms are required to capitalize major leases and to report them on their balance sheets, this point is of questionable validity.

SELF-TEST QUESTIONS

Define each of these terms: (1) sale-and-leaseback arrangements, (2) operating leases, and (3) financial, or capital, leases.

What is off balance sheet financing, what is FASB #13, and how are the two related?

List the sequence of events, for the lessee, leading to a lease arrangement.

Why is it appropriate to compare the cost of lease financing with that of debt financing? Why does the comparison *not* depend on how the asset will actually be financed if it is not leased?

Warrant
A long-term option to buy a stated number of shares of common stock at a specified price.

A **warrant** is a certificate issued by a company that gives the holder the right to buy a stated number of shares of the company's stock at a specified price for some specified length of time. Generally, warrants are distributed with debt, and they are used to induce investors to buy long-term debt with a lower coupon rate than would otherwise be required. For example, when Infomatics Corporation, a rapidly growing high-tech company, wanted to sell $50 million of 20-year bonds in 2002, the company's investment bankers informed the financial vice-president that the bonds would be difficult to sell, and that a coupon rate of 10 percent would be required. However, as an alternative the bankers suggested that investors might be willing to buy the bonds with a coupon rate of only 8 percent if the company would offer 20 warrants with each $1,000 bond, each warrant entitling the holder to buy one share of common stock at an *exercise price* of $22 per share. The stock was selling for $20 per share at the time, and the warrants would expire in the year 2012 if they had not been exercised previously.

Why would investors be willing to buy Infomatics' bonds at a yield of only 8 percent in a 10 percent market just because warrants were also offered as part of the package? It is because the warrants are long-term *call options* that have value because holders can buy the firm's common stock at the exercise price regardless of how high the market price climbs. This option offsets the low interest rate on the bonds and makes the package of low-yield bonds plus warrants attractive to investors. (See Chapter 18 for a more complete discussion of options.)

INITIAL MARKET PRICE OF A BOND WITH WARRANTS

The Infomatics bonds, if they had been issued as straight debt, would have carried a 10 percent interest rate. However, with warrants attached, the bonds were sold to yield 8 percent. Someone buying the bonds at their $1,000 initial offering price would thus be receiving a package consisting of an 8 percent, 20-year bond plus 20 warrants. Since the going interest rate on bonds as risky as those of Infomatics was 10 percent, we can find the straight-debt value of the bonds, assuming an annual coupon for ease of illustration, as follows:

Using a financial calculator, input N = 20, I = 10, PMT = 80, and FV = 1000. Then, press the PV key to obtain the bond's value, $829.73, or approximately $830. Thus, a person buying the bonds in the initial underwriting would pay $1,000 and receive in exchange a straight bond worth about $830 plus 20 warrants presumably worth about $1,000 − $830 = $170:

$$\begin{matrix} \text{Price paid for} \\ \text{bond with warrants} \end{matrix} = \begin{matrix} \text{Straight-debt} \\ \text{value of bond} \end{matrix} + \begin{matrix} \text{Value of} \\ \text{warrants} \end{matrix} \qquad \text{(20-1)}$$
$$\$1,000 \quad = \quad \$830 \quad + \quad \$170.$$

Since investors receive 20 warrants with each bond, each warrant has an implied value of $170/20 = $8.50.

The key issue in setting the terms of a bond-with-warrants is valuing the warrants. The straight-debt value can be estimated quite accurately, as was done above.

However, it is more difficult to estimate the value of the warrants. The Black-Scholes Option Pricing Model (OPM), which we discussed in Chapter 18, can be used to find the value of a call option. There is a temptation to use this model to find the value of a warrant, since call options are similar to warrants in many respects: Both give the investor the right to buy a share of stock at a fixed exercise price on or before the expiration date. However, there is a major difference between call options and warrants. When call options are exercised, the stock provided to the optionholder comes from the secondary market, but when warrants are exercised, the stock provided to the warrant holders are newly issued shares. This means that the exercise of warrants dilutes the value of the original equity, which could cause the value of the original warrant to differ from the value of a similar call option. Therefore, investment bankers cannot use the Black-Scholes model to determine the value of warrants.

It is extremely important to assign the correct value to the warrants. If, when the issue is originally priced, the value assigned to the warrants is greater than their true market value, then the coupon rate on the bonds will be set too low, and it will be impossible to sell the bond-with-warrants package at its par value. In this case, Infomatics will not be able to raise the full $50 million that it needs to fund its growth.

Conversely, if the value of the warrants is underestimated, then the coupon rate will be set too high. This means that the true value of the bonds with warrants will be greater than the issue price. Suppose this happens, and the true value of the bonds with warrants is $60 million. Investors will eagerly buy all of the bonds with warrants at the issue price, and Infomatics will receive the full $50 million that it needs. But this is not good news for the existing shareholders.

To see this, think of the total value of Infomatics as being analogous to a pie. The size of the pie is equal to the present value of all the future cash flows expected to be generated by Infomatics' operations and investments. Pieces of the pie belong to different groups of investors, such as debtholders and holders of bonds with warrants. Shareholders come last and get the remaining piece of the pie, after the other investors have received their fair share.

At the time of the bond offering, Infomatics had 10 million shares of common stock outstanding and no other debt or preferred stock. The stock price was $20 per share, so the total market value of Infomatics was 10 million × $20 = $200 million. The offering itself will raise $50 million in cash, which will subsequently be invested in projects. Therefore, immediately after the offering the total value of Infomatics is $250 million ($200 million in stock plus $50 million in cash).[12] If investors in the bonds with warrants pay only $50 million for a piece of pie that is worth $60 million, then the piece of pie remaining for the original shareholders is only worth $190 million ($250 million − $60 million). The result is a $10 million transfer of wealth from the original shareholders to the investors in the bonds with warrants. Therefore, it is extremely important for Infomatics to correctly estimate the value of the warrants at the time the bonds with warrants are issued.

USE OF WARRANTS IN FINANCING

Warrants generally are used by small, rapidly growing firms as "sweeteners" when they sell debt or preferred stock. Such firms frequently are regarded by investors as

---

[12] We assume that the average expected net present value of these projects is zero. If the NPV of the projects is greater than zero, then the total value of Infomatics will be greater than $250 million. In this case, there will be little change in the price of the bonds, since bondholders receive the fixed coupon payment

(footnote continues)

being highly risky, so their bonds can be sold only at extremely high coupon rates and with very restrictive indenture provisions. To avoid this, firms such as Infomatics often offer warrants along with the bonds. However, some years ago, AT&T raised $1.57 billion by selling bonds with warrants. This was the largest financing of any type ever undertaken by a business firm, and it marked the first use ever of warrants by a large, strong corporation.[13]

Getting warrants along with bonds enables investors to share in the company's growth, assuming it does in fact grow and prosper. Therefore, investors are willing to accept a lower interest rate and less restrictive indenture provisions. A bond with warrants has some characteristics of debt and some characteristics of equity. It is a hybrid security that provides the financial manager with an opportunity to expand the firm's mix of securities and thus to appeal to a broader group of investors.

Virtually all warrants today are **detachable.** Thus, after a bond with attached warrants is sold, the warrants can be detached and traded separately from the bond. Further, even after the warrants have been exercised, the bond (with its low coupon rate) remains outstanding.

The exercise price on warrants is generally set some 20 to 30 percent above the market price of the stock on the date the bond is issued. If the firm grows and prospers, and if its stock price rises above the exercise price at which shares may be purchased, warrant holders could exercise their warrants and buy stock at the stated price. However, without some incentive, warrants would never be exercised prior to maturity—their value in the open market would be greater than their value if exercised, so holders would sell warrants rather than exercise them. There are three conditions that encourage holders to exercise their warrants: (1) Warrant holders will surely exercise and buy stock if the warrants are about to expire and the market price of the stock is above the exercise price. (2) Warrant holders will exercise voluntarily if the company raises the dividend on the common stock by a sufficient amount. No dividend is earned on the warrant, so it provides no current income. However, if the common stock pays a high dividend, it provides an attractive dividend yield but limits price growth. This induces warrant holders to exercise their option to buy the stock. (3) Warrants sometimes have **stepped-up exercise prices,** which prod owners into exercising them. For example, Williamson Scientific Company has warrants outstanding with an exercise price of $25 until December 31, 2006, at which time the exercise price rises to $30. If the price of the common stock is over $25 just before December 31, 2006, many warrant holders will exercise their options before the stepped-up price takes effect and the value of the warrants falls.

Detachable Warrant
A warrant that can be detached from a bond and traded independently of it.

Stepped-Up Exercise Price
An exercise price that is specified to rise if a warrant is exercised after a designated date.

(Footnote 12 continued)

no matter how well the company does. However, the stock price and the value of the warrants will increase, since the total value of the company has increased without a commensurate increase in the value committed to the bondholders. The reverse would occur if the expected NPV of the projects is less than zero.

[13] It is interesting to note that before the AT&T issue, the New York Stock Exchange's stated policy was that warrants could not be listed because they were "speculative" instruments rather than "investment" securities. When AT&T issued warrants, however, the Exchange changed its policy, agreeing to list warrants that met certain requirements. Many other warrants have since been listed.

It is also interesting to note that, prior to the sale, AT&T's treasury staff, working with Morgan Stanley analysts, estimated the value of the warrants as a part of the underwriting decision. The package was supposed to sell for a total price in the neighborhood of $1,000. The bond value could be determined accurately, so the trick was to estimate the equilibrium value of the warrant under different possible exercise prices and years to expiration, and then to use an exercise price and life that would cause Bond value + Warrant value ≈ $1,000. Using a warrant pricing model, the AT&T/Morgan Stanley analysts set terms that caused the warrant to sell on the open market at a price that was only 35¢ off from the estimated price.

Another desirable feature of warrants is that they generally bring in funds only if funds are needed. If the company grows, it will probably need new equity capital. At the same time, growth will cause the price of the stock to rise and the warrants to be exercised, hence the firm will obtain additional cash. If the company is not successful, and it cannot profitably employ additional money, the price of its stock will probably not rise sufficiently to induce exercise of the warrants.

WEALTH EFFECTS AND DILUTION DUE TO WARRANTS

Assume that the value of Infomatics' operations and investments, which is $250 million immediately after issuing the bonds with warrants, is expected to grow, and does grow, at 9 percent per year. When the warrants are due to expire in ten years, the total value of Infomatics will be $250(1.09)^{10} = 591.841 million. How is this value allocated among the original stockholders, the bondholders, and the warrant holders?

The bonds will have ten years remaining until maturity, with a fixed coupon payment of $80. If the expected market interest rate is still 10 percent, then:

Using a financial calculator, input N = 10, I = 10, PMT = 80, and FV = 1000. Press the PV key to obtain the bond's value, $877.11. The total value of all of the bonds is 50,000($877.11) = $43.856 million.

The value remaining for the original stockholders and the warrant holders is equal to the remaining value of the firm, after deducting the value due to the bondholders. This remaining value is $591.841 − $43.856 = $547.985 million. If there had been no warrants, then the original stockholders would have been entitled to all of this remaining value. Recall that there are 10 million shares of stock, so the price per share would be $547.985/10 = $54.80. Suppose the company has a basic earning power of 13.5 percent (recall that BEP = EBIT/Total Assets) and total assets of $591.841 million.[14] This means that EBIT is 0.135($591.841) = $79.899 million; interest payments are $4 million ($80 coupon payment per bond × 50,000 bonds); and earnings before taxes are $79.899 − $4 = $75.899 million. With a tax rate of 40 percent, after-tax earnings are equal to $75.899(1 − 0.4) = $45.539 million, and earnings per share are $45.539/10 = $4.55. Therefore, if Infomatics had no warrants, the stock price would be $54.80 per share, and the earnings per share would be $4.55.

But Infomatics *does* have warrants, and with the stock price over $50 the warrant holders surely will choose to exercise their warrants. Infomatics will receive $22 million when the 1 million warrants are exercised at a price of $22 per warrant. This makes the total value $613.841 million (the $591.841 million total value of the firm plus the $22 million raised by the exercise of the warrants). The total value remaining for stockholders is now $569.985 million ($613.841 million less the $43.856 mil-

---

[14] In this case, the total market value equals the book value of assets, but the same calculations would follow even if market and book values were not equal.

lion allocated to bondholders). There are now 11 million shares of stock (the original 10 million plus the new 1 million due to the exercise of the warrants), so the stock price is $569.985/11 = $51.82 per share. Note that this is lower than the $54.80 price per share that Infomatics would have had if there had been no warrants. In other words, the warrants have diluted the value of the stock.

A similar dilution occurs with earnings per share. After exercise, the asset base would increase from $591.841 million to $613.841 million, with the additional $22 million coming from the purchase of 1 million shares of stock at $22 per share. If the new funds have the same basic earning power as the existing funds, then the new EBIT would be 0.135($613.841) = $82.869 million. Interest payments would still be $4 million, so earnings before taxes would be $82.869 − $4 = $78.869 million, and after-tax earnings will be $78.869(1 − 0.4) = $47.321 million. With 10 + 1 = 11 million shares now outstanding, EPS would be $47.321/11 = $4.30, down from $4.55. Therefore, exercising the warrants would dilute EPS.

Has this wealth transfer harmed the original shareholders? The answer is yes and no. Yes, because the original shareholders clearly are worse off than they would have been if there had been no warrants. However, if there had been no warrants attached to the bonds, then the bonds would have had a 10 percent coupon rate instead of the 8 percent coupon rate. Also, if the value of the company had not increased as expected, then it might not have been profitable for the warrant holders to exercise their warrants. In other words, the original shareholders were willing to trade off the potential dilution for the lower coupon rate. In this example, the original stockholders and the investors in the bonds with warrants got what they expected. Therefore, the answer is no, the wealth transfer at the time of exercise did not harm the original shareholders, because they expected an eventual transfer and were fairly compensated by the lower coupon payments.

Note too that investors would recognize the situation, so the actual wealth transfer would occur gradually over time, not in a fell swoop when the warrants were exercised. First, EPS would have been reported on a diluted basis over the years, and on that basis, there would be no decline whatever in EPS. (We discuss this in a later section of this chapter.) Also, investors would know what was happening, so the stock price, over time, would reflect the likely future dilution, so it too would be stable when the warrants were exercised. So, whereas our calculations show the effects of the warrants, those effects would actually be reflected in EPS and the stock price on a gradual basis over time.

THE COMPONENT COST OF BONDS WITH WARRANTS

When Infomatics issued its debt with warrants, the firm received $50 million, or $1,000 for each bond. Simultaneously, the company assumed an obligation to pay $80 interest for 20 years plus $1,000 at the end of 20 years. The pre-tax cost of the money would have been 10 percent if no warrants had been attached, but each Infomatics bond had 20 warrants, each of which entitles its holder to buy one share of Infomatics stock for $22. What is the percentage cost of the $50 million? As we shall see, the cost is well above the 8 percent coupon rate on the bonds.

As we demonstrated earlier, when the warrants expire ten years from now, the expected stock price is $51.82. The company would then have to issue one share of stock worth $51.82 for each warrant exercised and, in return, Infomatics would receive the exercise price, $22. Thus, a purchaser of the bonds, if he or she holds the complete package, would realize a profit in Year 10 of $51.82 − $22 = $29.82 for each common share issued. Since each bond has 20 warrants attached, and each warrant entitles the holder to buy one share of common stock, investors would have a gain of 20($29.82) = $596.40 per bond at the end of Year 10. Here is a time line of the cash flow stream to an investor:

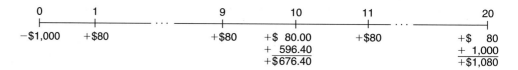

The IRR of this stream is 10.7 percent, which is the investor's overall pre-tax rate of return on the issue. This return is 70 basis points higher than the return on straight debt. This reflects the fact that the issue is riskier to investors than a straight-debt issue because some of the return is expected to come in the form of stock price appreciation, and that part of the return is relatively risky.

The expected rate of return to investors is the before-tax cost to the company—this was true of common stocks, straight bonds, and preferred stocks, and it is also true of bonds sold with warrants.

PROBLEMS WITH WARRANT ISSUES

Although warrants are bought by investors with the expectation of receiving a total return commensurate with the overall riskiness of the package of securities being purchased, things do not always work out as expected. For example, in 1989 Sony paid $3.4 billion for Columbia Pictures, a U.S. movie studio. To help finance the deal, in 1990 Sony sold $470 million of four-year bonds with warrants at an incredibly low 0.3 percent coupon interest rate. The rate was so low because the warrants, which also had a maturity of four years, allowed investors to purchase Sony stock at 7,670 yen per share, only 2.5 percent above the share price at the time the bonds with warrants were issued.

Investors snapped up the issue, and many of the warrants were "peeled off" and sold separately on the open market. The warrant buyers obviously believed that Sony's stock would climb well above the exercise price. From Sony's point of view, the bond-with-warrants package provided a very low-cost "bridge loan" (the bonds) that would be replaced with equity financing when the warrants were exercised, presumably in four years when the bonds became due. This very low cost capital encouraged Japanese firms to acquire foreign companies and to invest huge amounts in new plant and equipment.

However, the willingness of investors to buy Japanese warrants suffered a severe blow when the Japanese stock market fell by 40 percent. By 1994, when the warrants expired, Sony's stock sold for only 5,950 yen versus the 7,670-yen exercise price, so the warrants were not exercised. Thus, Sony's planned infusion of equity capital never materialized, and it had to refinance the four-year bond issue at much higher rates.

Both Sony and its investors lost on the deal. The investors lost because they did not get the return they expected on the issue. Sony lost because it had to alter its financing plans due to the fact that the warrants were not exercised. In spite of presumably good planning by both the company and investors, this bond-with-warrants issue, and many like it, did not work out as anticipated.

What is a warrant?

Describe how a new bond issue with warrants is valued.

How are warrants used in corporate financing?

The use of warrants lowers the coupon rate on the corresponding debt issue. Does this mean that the component cost of a debt-plus-warrants package is less than the cost of straight debt? Explain.

CONVERTIBLES

Convertible Security
A security, usually a bond or preferred stock, that is exchangeable at the option of the holder for the common stock of the issuing firm.

Convertible securities are bonds or preferred stocks that, under specified terms and conditions, can be exchanged for (that is, converted into) common stock at the option of the holder. Unlike the exercise of warrants, which brings in additional funds to the firm, conversion does not provide capital: debt (or preferred stock) is simply replaced on the balance sheet by common stock. Of course, reducing the debt or preferred stock will improve the firm's financial strength and make it easier to raise additional capital, but that requires a separate action.

CONVERSION RATIO AND CONVERSION PRICE

Conversion Ratio, CR
The number of shares of common stock that are obtained by converting a convertible bond or share of convertible preferred stock.

Conversion Price, P_c
The effective price paid for common stock obtained by converting a convertible security.

One of the most important provisions of a convertible security is the **conversion ratio, CR,** defined as the number of shares of stock a bondholder will receive upon conversion. Related to the conversion ratio is the **conversion price, P_c,** which is the effective price investors pay for the common stock when conversion occurs. The relationship between the conversion ratio and the conversion price can be illustrated by the Silicon Valley Software Company's convertible debentures issued at their $1,000 par value in August 2002. At any time prior to maturity on August 15, 2022, a debenture holder can exchange a bond for 20 shares of common stock; therefore, the conversion ratio, CR, is 20. The bond cost purchasers $1,000, the par value, when it was issued. Dividing the $1,000 par value by the 20 shares received gives a conversion price of $50 a share:

$$\text{Conversion price} = P_c = \frac{\text{Par value of bond given up}}{\text{Shares received}} \qquad (20\text{-}2)$$

$$= \frac{\$1,000}{CR} = \frac{\$1,000}{20} = \$50.$$

Conversely, by solving for CR, we obtain the conversion ratio:

$$\text{Conversion ratio} = CR = \frac{\$1,000}{P_c} \qquad (20\text{-}3)$$

$$= \frac{\$1,000}{\$50} = 20 \text{ shares}.$$

Once CR is set, the value of P_c is established, and vice versa.

BERKSHIRE HATHAWAY ISSUES THE FIRST CONVERTIBLE SECURITY WITH A NEGATIVE COUPON

Warren Buffett's investment firm, Berkshire Hathaway, has attained legendary status because of the large returns it has provided its investors over a sustained period of time. Berkshire Hathaway is also one of only eight firms to enjoy a AAA rating from both Moody's and S&P.

Over the years, Buffett has never been afraid to challenge conventional wisdom. His willingness to go against the grain was once again confirmed when Berkshire Hathaway recently issued a new security entitled SQUARZ. These securities consist of a 3 percent coupon bond coupled with a warrant to buy 0.1116 share of Berkshire Hathaway's Class A stock. These securities were made available in a private placement to large institutional investors.

What makes these SQUARZ so different is the provision that requires buyers to make annual "installment payments" on the warrants. These annual payments amount to 3.75 percent of the par value, which exceeds the 3 percent coupon on the bond. Therefore, the net effect is a security with a negative coupon. Note, though, that investors will still come out ahead if Berkshire Hathaway stock performs well.

The security also has some interesting tax implications. Its advantages were summarized in a *Washington Post* article (that was recently referred to in a May 29, 2002, Fool on the Hill column on the popular Motley Fool web site):

"As with any corporate debt service, Berkshire Hathaway gets a tax deduction for the 3 percent interest it pays to bondholders. The 3.75 percent income the company collects, however, is not taxable," said Robert Willens, a managing director of Lehman Brothers and the firm's expert on taxes. And there could be an even bigger tax advantage, theorizes Willens, who stresses that he has not seen the documents involved but is evaluating the deal based on his long experience on tax issues.

It looks as if the bonds fall into a special category of "contingent payment debt instruments," because in addition to the regular 3 percent interest they collect, bondholders can make money by using the warrants to buy Berkshire Hathaway stock. When "contingent" interest costs are involved, the issuer gets to claim much bigger deductions. Instead of deducting 3 percent interest, Berkshire Hathaway might be able to deduct 6 or 7 percent.

Interested students may want to take a closer look at this column—it also describes a number of other theories that have been offered for why Buffett chose to issue these securities.

SOURCE: Whitney Tilson, "Berkshire's Unusual Security," from The Motley Fool's Fool on the Hill column, **http://www.fool.com** web site, May 29, 2002.

Like a warrant's exercise price, the conversion price is typically set at from 20 to 30 percent above the prevailing market price of the common stock at the time the convertible issue is sold. Exactly how the conversion price is established can best be understood after examining some of the reasons firms use convertibles.

Generally, the conversion price and conversion ratio are fixed for the life of the bond, although sometimes a stepped-up conversion price is used. For example, the 2002 convertible debentures for Breedon Industries are convertible into 12.5 shares until 2012; into 11.76 shares from 2012 until 2022; and into 11.11 shares from 2022 until maturity in 2032. The conversion price thus starts at $80, rises to $85, and then goes to $90. Breedon's convertibles, like most, have a ten-year call-protection period.

Another factor that may cause a change in the conversion price and ratio is a standard feature of almost all convertibles—the clause protecting the convertible against dilution from stock splits, stock dividends, and the sale of common stock at prices below the conversion price. The typical provision states that if common stock is sold at a price below the conversion price, then the conversion price must be lowered (and the conversion ratio raised) to the price at which the new stock was issued. Also, if the stock is split, or if a stock dividend is declared, the conversion price must be lowered by the percentage amount of the stock dividend or split. For example, if

Breedon Industries were to have a two-for-one stock split during the first ten years of its convertible's life, the conversion ratio would automatically be adjusted from 12.5 to 25, and the conversion price lowered from $80 to $40. If this protection were not contained in the contract, a company could completely thwart conversion by the use of stock splits and stock dividends. Warrants are similarly protected against dilution.

The standard protection against dilution from selling new stock at prices below the conversion price can, however, get a company into trouble. For example, assume that Breedon's stock was selling for $65 per share at the time the convertible was issued. Further, suppose the market went sour, and Breedon's stock price dropped to $50 per share. If Breedon needed new equity to support operations, a new common stock sale would require the company to lower the conversion price on the convertible debentures from $80 to $50. That would raise the value of the convertibles and, in effect, transfer wealth from current shareholders to the convertible holders. This transfer would, de facto, amount to an additional flotation cost on the new common stock issue. Potential problems such as this must be kept in mind by firms considering the use of convertibles or bonds with warrants.

THE COMPONENT COST OF CONVERTIBLES

In the spring of 2002, Silicon Valley Software was evaluating the use of the convertible bond issue described earlier. The issue would consist of 20-year convertible bonds that would sell at a price of $1,000 per bond; this $1,000 would also be the bond's par (and maturity) value. The bonds would pay a 10 percent annual coupon interest rate, or $100 per year. Each bond would be convertible into 20 shares of stock, so the conversion price would be $1,000/20 = $50. The stock was expected to pay a dividend of $2.80 during the coming year, and it sold at $35 per share. Further, the stock price was expected to grow at a constant rate of 8 percent per year. Therefore, $k_s = \hat{k}_s = D_1/P_0 + g = \$2.80/\$35 + 8\% = 8\% + 8\% = 16\%$. If the bonds were not made convertible, they would have to offer a yield of 13 percent, given their riskiness and the general level of interest rates. The convertible bonds would not be callable for ten years, after which they could be called at a price of $1,050, with this price declining by $5 per year thereafter. If, after ten years, the conversion value exceeds the call price by at least 20 percent, management would probably call the bonds.

Figure 20-1 shows the expectations of both an average investor and the company.[15]

1. The horizontal line at M = $1,000 represents the par (and maturity) value. Also, $1,000 is the price at which the bond is initially offered to the public.

2. The bond is protected against call for ten years. It is initially callable at a price of $1,050, and the call price declines thereafter by $5 per year. Thus, the call price is represented by the solid section of the line V_0M''.

3. Since the convertible has a 10 percent coupon rate, and since the yield on a nonconvertible bond of similar risk was stated to be 13 percent, the expected

---

[15] For a more complete discussion of how the terms of a convertible offering are determined, see M. Wayne Marr and G. Rodney Thompson, "The Pricing of New Convertible Bond Issues," *Financial Management*, Summer 1984, 31–37.

FIGURE 20-1

Silicon Valley Software: Convertible Bond Model

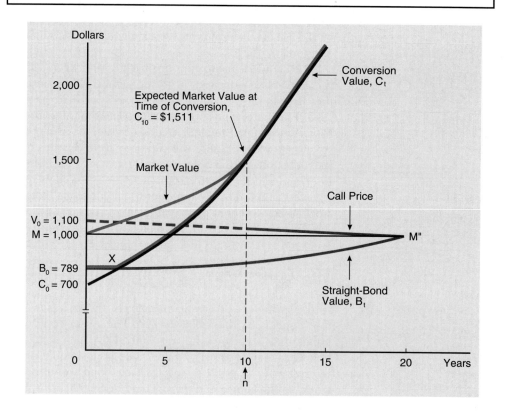

YEAR	PURE-BOND VALUE, B_t	CONVERSION VALUE, C_t	MATURITY VALUE, M	MARKET VALUE	FLOOR VALUE	PREMIUM
0	$ 789	$ 700	$1,000	$1,000	$ 789	$211
1	792	756	$1,000	1,023	792	231
2	795	816	$1,000	1,071	816	255
3	798	882	$1,000	1,147	882	265
4	802	952	$1,000	1,192	952	240
5	806	1,029	$1,000	1,241	1,029	212
6	811	1,111	$1,000	1,293	1,111	182
7	816	1,200	$1,000	1,344	1,200	144
8	822	1,296	$1,000	1,398	1,296	102
9	829	1,399	$1,000	1,453	1,399	54
10	837	1,511	$1,000	1,511	1,511	0
11	846	1,632	$1,000	1,632	1,632	0
.	.	.	.	.	.	.
.	.	.	.	.	.	.
.	.	.	.	.	.	.
20	1,000	3,263	$1,000	3,263	3,263	0

"straight-bond" value of the convertible, B_t, must be less than par. At the time of issue, assuming an annual coupon, B_0 is $789:

$$\text{Pure-debt value at time of issue} = B_0 = \sum_{t=1}^{N} \frac{\text{Coupon interest}}{(1 + k_d)^t} + \frac{\text{Maturity value}}{(1 + k_d)^N} \qquad (20\text{-}4)$$

$$= \sum_{t=1}^{20} \frac{\$100}{(1.13)^t} + \frac{\$1,000}{(1.13)^{20}} = \$789.$$

Note, however, that the bond's straight-debt value must be $1,000 just prior to maturity, so the straight-debt value rises over time. B_t follows the line B_0M'' in the graph.

Conversion Value, C_t
The value of common stock obtained by converting a convertible security.

4. The bond's initial **conversion value, C_t**, or the value of the stock the investor would receive if the bonds were converted at $t = 0$, is $700: the bond's conversion value is $P_t(CR)$, so at $t = 0$, conversion value $= P_0(CR) = \$35(20 \text{ shares}) = \$700$. Since the stock price is expected to grow at an 8 percent rate, the conversion value should rise over time. For example, in Year 5 it should be $P_5(CR) = \$35(1.08)^5(20) = \$1,029$. The expected conversion value over time is given by the line C_t in Figure 20-1.

5. The actual market price of the bond can never fall below the higher of its straight-debt value or its conversion value. If the market price dropped below the straight-bond value, those who wanted bonds would recognize the bargain and buy the convertible as a bond. Similarly, if the market price dropped below the conversion value, people would buy the convertibles, exercise them to get stock, and then sell the stock at a profit. Therefore, the higher of the bond value and conversion value curves in the graph represents a *floor price* for the bond. In Figure 20-1, the floor price is represented by the thicker shaded line B_0XC_t.

6. The bond's market value will typically exceed its floor value. It will exceed the straight-bond value because the option to convert is worth something — a 10 percent bond with conversion possibilities is worth more than a 10 percent bond without this option. The convertible's price will also exceed its conversion value because holding the convertible is equivalent to holding a call option, and, prior to expiration, the option's true value is higher than its expiration (or conversion) value. Without using a sophisticated pricing model, we cannot say exactly where the market value line will lie, but as a rule it will be at or above the floor set by the straight-bond and conversion value lines.

7. At some point, the market value line will touch the conversion value line. This convergence will occur for two reasons. First, the stock should pay higher and higher dividends as the years go by, but the interest payments on the convertible are fixed. For example, Silicon's convertibles would pay $100 in interest annually, while the dividends on the 20 shares received upon conversion would initially be 20($2.80) = \$56. However, at an 8 percent growth rate, the dividends after ten years would be up to $120.90, while the interest would still be $100. Thus, at some point, rising dividends could be expected to push against the fixed interest payments, causing the premium to disappear and investors to convert voluntarily. Second, once the bond becomes callable, its market value cannot exceed the higher of the conversion value and the call price without exposing investors to the danger of a call. For example, suppose that ten years after issue (when the bonds were callable), the market value of

the bond was $1,600, the conversion value was $1,500, and the call price was $1,050. If the company called the bonds the day after you bought ten bonds for $16,000, you would be forced to convert into stock worth only $15,000, so you would suffer a loss of $100 per bond, or $1,000, in one day. Recognizing this danger, you and other investors would simply not pay a premium over the higher of the call price or the conversion value once the bond becomes callable. Therefore, in Figure 20-1, we assume that the market value line hits the conversion value line in Year 10, when the bond becomes callable.

8. Let n represent the year when investors expect conversion to occur, either voluntarily because of rising dividends or because the company calls the convertibles to strengthen its balance sheet by substituting equity for debt. In our example, we assume that n = 10, the first call date.

9. Since n = 10, the expected market value at Year 10 is $35(1.08)^{10}(20) = $1,511. An investor can find the expected rate of return on the convertible bond, k_c, by finding the IRR of the following cash flow stream:

The solution is k_c = IRR = 12.8 percent.

10. The return on a convertible is expected to come partly from interest income and partly from capital gains; in this case, the total expected return is 12.8 percent, with 10 percent representing interest income and 2.8 percent representing the expected capital gain. The interest component is relatively assured, while the capital gain component is more risky. Therefore, a convertible's expected return is more risky than that of a straight bond. This leads us to conclude that k_c should be larger than the cost of straight debt, k_d. Thus, it would seem that the expected rate of return on Silicon's convertibles, k_c, should lie between its cost of straight debt, k_d = 13%, and its cost of common stock, k_s = 16%.

11. Investment bankers use the type of model described here, plus a knowledge of the market, to set the terms on convertibles (the conversion ratio, coupon interest rate, and years of call protection) such that the security will just "clear the market" at its $1,000 offering price. In our example, the required conditions do not hold—the calculated rate of return on the convertible is only 12.8 percent, which is less than the 13 percent cost of straight debt. Therefore, the terms on the bond must be made more attractive to investors. Silicon Valley Software would have to increase the coupon interest rate on the convertible above 10 percent, raise the conversion ratio above 20 (and thereby lower the conversion price from $50 to a level closer to the current $35 market price of the stock), lengthen the call-protected period, or use a combination of these three such that the expected rate of return on the convertible ends up between 13 and 16 percent.[16]

---

[16] In this discussion, we ignore the tax advantages to investors associated with capital gains. In some situations, tax effects could result in k_c being less than k_d.

USE OF CONVERTIBLES IN FINANCING

Convertibles have two important advantages from the issuer's standpoint: (1) Convertibles, like bonds with warrants, offer a company the chance to sell debt with a low interest rate in exchange for a chance to participate in the company's success if it does well. (2) In a sense, convertibles provide a way to sell common stock at prices higher than those currently prevailing. Some companies actually want to sell common stock, not debt, but feel that the price of their stock is temporarily depressed. Management may know, for example, that earnings are depressed because of startup costs associated with a new project, but they expect earnings to rise sharply during the next year or so, pulling the price of the stock up with them. Thus, if the company sold stock now, it would be giving up more shares than necessary to raise a given amount of capital. However, if it set the conversion price 20 to 30 percent above the present market price of the stock, then 20 to 30 percent fewer shares would be given up when the bonds were converted than if stock were sold directly at the current time. Note, however, that management is counting on the stock's price to rise above the conversion price to make the bonds attractive in conversion. If earnings do not rise and pull the stock price up, hence conversion does not occur, then the company will be saddled with debt in the face of low earnings, which could be disastrous.

How can the company be sure that conversion will occur if the price of the stock rises above the conversion price? Typically, convertibles contain a call provision that enables the issuing firm to force holders to convert. Suppose the conversion price is $50, the conversion ratio is 20, the market price of the common stock has risen to $60, and the call price on a convertible bond is $1,050. If the company calls the bond, bondholders can either convert into common stock with a market value of 20($60) = $1,200 or allow the company to redeem the bond for $1,050. Naturally, bondholders prefer $1,200 to $1,050, so conversion would occur. The call provision gives the company a way to force conversion, provided the market price of the stock is greater than the conversion price. Note, however, that most convertibles have a fairly long period of call protection — ten years is typical. Therefore, if the company wants to be able to force conversion fairly early, then it will have to set a short call-protection period. This will, in turn, require that it set a higher coupon rate or a lower conversion price.

From the standpoint of the issuer, convertibles have three important disadvantages: (1) Although the use of a convertible bond may give the company the opportunity to sell stock at a price higher than the price at which it could be sold currently, if the stock greatly increases in price, the firm would probably find that it would have been better off if it had used straight debt in spite of its higher cost and then later sold common stock and refunded the debt. (2) Convertibles typically have a low coupon interest rate, and the advantage of this low-cost debt will be lost when conversion occurs. (3) If the company truly wants to raise equity capital, and if the price of the stock does not rise sufficiently after the bond is issued, then the company will be stuck with debt.

CONVERTIBLES AND AGENCY COSTS

One of the potential agency problems between bondholders and stockholders discussed in Chapter 1 is asset substitution. Stockholders have an "option-related" incentive to take on projects with high upside potential even though they increase the riskiness of the firm. When such an action is taken, there is potential for a wealth transfer between bondholders and stockholders. However, when convertible debt is issued, actions that increase the riskiness of the company may also increase the value of the convertible debt. Thus, some of the gains to shareholders from taking on high-risk projects have to be shared with convertible bondholders. This sharing of benefits lowers agency costs. The same general logic applies to convertible preferred and to warrants.

SELF-TEST QUESTIONS

What is a conversion ratio? A conversion price? A straight-bond value?

What is meant by a convertible's floor value?

What are the advantages and disadvantages of convertibles to issuers? To investors?

How do convertibles reduce agency costs?

A FINAL COMPARISON OF WARRANTS AND CONVERTIBLES

Convertible debt can be thought of as straight debt with nondetachable warrants. Thus, at first blush, it might appear that debt with warrants and convertible debt are more or less interchangeable. However, a closer look reveals one major and several minor differences between these two securities.[17] First, as we discussed previously, the exercise of warrants brings in new equity capital, while the conversion of convertibles results only in an accounting transfer.

A second difference involves flexibility. Most convertible issues contain a call provision that allows the issuer either to refund the debt or to force conversion, depending on the relationship between the conversion value and call price. However, most warrants are not callable, so firms generally must wait until maturity for the warrants to generate new equity capital. Generally, maturities also differ between warrants and convertibles. Warrants typically have much shorter maturities than convertibles, and warrants typically expire before their accompanying debt matures. Further, warrants provide for fewer future common shares than do convertibles because with convertibles all of the debt is converted to common whereas debt remains outstanding when warrants are exercised. Together, these facts suggest that debt-plus-warrant issuers are actually more interested in selling debt than in selling equity.

In general, firms that issue debt with warrants are smaller and riskier than those that issue convertibles. One possible rationale for the use of option securities, especially the use of debt with warrants by small firms, is the difficulty investors have assessing the risk of small companies. If a startup with a new, untested product seeks debt financing, it is very difficult for potential lenders to judge the riskiness of the venture, hence it is difficult to set a fair interest rate. Under these circumstances, many potential investors will be reluctant to invest, making it necessary to set very

---

[17] For a more detailed comparison of warrants and convertibles, see Michael S. Long and Stephen F. Sefcik, "Participation Financing: A Comparison of the Characteristics of Convertible Debt and Straight Bonds Issued in Conjunction with Warrants," *Financial Management*, Autumn 1990, 23–34.

high interest rates to attract debt capital. By issuing debt with warrants, investors obtain a package that offers upside potential to offset the risks of loss.

Finally, there is a significant difference in issuance costs between debt with warrants and convertible debt. Bonds with warrants typically require issuance costs that are about 1.2 percentage points more than the flotation costs for convertibles. In general, bond-with-warrant financings have underwriting fees that closely reflect the weighted average of the fees associated with debt and equity issues, while underwriting costs for convertibles are substantially lower.

SELF-TEST QUESTIONS

What are some differences between debt-with-warrant financing and convertible debt?

Explain how bonds with warrants might help small, risky firms sell debt securities.

REPORTING EARNINGS WHEN WARRANTS OR CONVERTIBLES ARE OUTSTANDING

If warrants or convertibles are outstanding, a firm could theoretically report earnings per share in one of three ways:

1. *Basic EPS*, where earnings available to common stockholders are divided by the average number of shares actually outstanding during the period.

2. *Primary EPS*, where earnings available are divided by the average number of shares that would have been outstanding if warrants and convertibles "likely to be converted in the near future" had actually been exercised or converted. In calculating primary EPS, earnings are first adjusted by "backing out" the interest on the convertibles, after which the adjusted earnings are divided by the adjusted number of shares. Accountants have a formula that basically compares the conversion or exercise price with the actual market value of the stock to determine the likelihood of conversion when deciding on the need to use this adjustment procedure.

3. *Diluted EPS*, which is similar to primary EPS except that *all* warrants and convertibles are assumed to be exercised or converted, regardless of the likelihood of exercise or conversion.

Under SEC rules, firms are required to report both basic and diluted EPS. For firms with large amounts of option securities outstanding, there can be a substantial difference between the basic and diluted EPS figures. For financial statement purposes, firms reported diluted EPS until 1997, when the Financial Accounting Standards Board (FASB) changed to basic EPS. According to FASB, the change was made to give investors a simpler picture of a company's underlying performance. Also, the change makes it easier for investors to compare the performance of U.S. firms with their foreign counterparts, which tend to use basic EPS.

SELF-TEST QUESTIONS

What are the three possible methods for reporting EPS when warrants and convertibles are outstanding?

Which methods are most used in practice?

Why should investors be concerned about a firm's outstanding warrants and convertibles?

TYING IT ALL TOGETHER

While common stock and long-term debt provide most of the capital used by corporations, companies also use several forms of "hybrid securities." The hybrids include preferred stock, leasing, convertibles, and warrants, and they generally have some characteristics of debt and some of equity. We discussed the pros and cons of the hybrids from the standpoints of both issuers and investors, how to determine when to use them, and the factors that affect their values. The basic rationale for these securities, and the procedures used to evaluate them, are based on concepts developed in earlier chapters. The key concepts covered are listed below.

- **Preferred** stock is a hybrid—it is similar to bonds in some respects and to common stock in other ways.

- **Adjustable rate preferred stocks (ARPs)** are those whose dividends are tied to the rate on Treasury securities. **Market auction (money market) preferred** is a low-risk, largely tax-exempt, seven-week maturity security that can be sold between auction dates at close to par.

- **Leasing** is a means of obtaining the use of an asset without purchasing that asset. The three most important forms of leasing are (1) **sale-and-leaseback** arrangements, under which a firm sells an asset to another party and leases it back for a specified period under specific terms; (2) **operating leases,** under which the lessor both maintains and finances the asset; and (3) **financial leases,** under which the asset is fully amortized over the life of the lease, the lessor does not normally provide maintenance, and the lease is not cancelable.

- The **decision to lease or to buy an asset** is made by comparing the financing costs of the two alternatives and choosing the method with the lower PV cost. All cash flows should be discounted at the **after-tax cost of debt,** because the relevant cash flows are relatively certain and are on an after-tax basis.

- A **warrant** is a long-term call option issued along with a bond. Warrants are generally detachable from the bond, and they trade separately in the market. When warrants are exercised, the firm receives additional equity capital, and the original bonds remain outstanding.

- A **convertible** security is a bond or preferred stock that can be exchanged for common stock at the option of the holder. When a security is converted, debt or preferred stock is replaced with common stock, and no money changes hands.

- Warrant and convertible issues are generally structured so that the exercise or **conversion price** is 20 to 30 percent above the stock's price at time of issue.
- Although both warrants and convertibles are option securities, there are several differences between the two, including **separability, impact when exercised, callability, maturity,** and **flotation costs.**
- Warrants and convertibles are **"sweeteners"** used to make the underlying debt or preferred stock issue more attractive to investors. Although the coupon rate or dividend yield is lower when options are part of the issue, the overall cost of the issue is higher than the cost of straight debt or preferred, because option-related securities are riskier.

QUESTIONS

20-1 For purposes of measuring a firm's leverage, should preferred stock be classified as debt or equity? Does it matter if the classification is being made (a) by the firm's management, (b) by creditors, or (c) by equity investors?

20-2 You are told that one corporation just issued $100 million of preferred stock and another purchased $100 million of preferred stock as an investment. You are also told that one firm has an effective tax rate of 20 percent, whereas the other is in the 35 percent bracket. Which firm is more likely to have bought the preferred? Explain.

20-3 One often finds that a company's bonds have a higher yield than its preferred stock, even though the bonds are considered to be less risky than the preferred to an investor. What causes this yield differential?

20-4 Why would a company choose to issue floating rate as opposed to fixed rate preferred stock?

20-5 Distinguish between operating leases and financial leases. Would a firm be more likely to finance a fleet of trucks or a manufacturing plant with an operating lease?

20-6 One alleged advantage of leasing voiced in the past was that it kept liabilities off the balance sheet, thus making it possible for a firm to obtain more leverage than it otherwise could have. This raised the question of whether or not both the lease obligation and the asset involved should be capitalized and shown on the balance sheet. Discuss the pros and cons of capitalizing leases and related assets.

20-7 Suppose there were no IRS restrictions on what constitutes a valid lease. Explain in a manner that a legislator might understand why some restrictions should be imposed.

20-8 Suppose Congress changed the tax laws in a way that (1) permitted equipment to be depreciated over a shorter period, (2) lowered corporate tax rates, and (3) reinstated the investment tax credit. Discuss how each of these changes would affect the relative use of leasing versus conventional debt in the U.S. economy.

20-9 What effect does the expected growth rate of a firm's stock price (subsequent to issue) have on its ability to raise additional funds through (a) convertibles and (b) warrants?

20-10 a. How would a firm's decision to pay out a higher percentage of its earnings as dividends affect each of the following?
  (1) The value of its long-term warrants.
  (2) The likelihood that its convertible bonds will be converted.
  (3) The likelihood that its warrants will be exercised.
  b. If you owned the warrants or convertibles of a company, would you be pleased or displeased if it raised its payout rate from 20 percent to 80 percent? Why?

20-11 Evaluate the following statement: "Issuing convertible securities represents a means by which a firm can sell common stock at a price above the existing market price."

20-12 Suppose a company simultaneously issues $50 million of convertible bonds with a coupon rate of 9 percent and $50 million of pure bonds with a coupon rate of 12 percent. Both bonds have the same maturity. Does the fact that the convertible issue has the lower coupon rate suggest that it is less risky than the pure bond? Would you regard the cost of capital as being lower on the convertible than on the pure bond? Explain. (Hint: Although it might appear at first glance that the convertible's cost of capital is lower, this is not necessarily the case because the interest rate on the convertible understates its cost. Think about this.)

ST-1
Key terms

Define each of the following terms:
a. Cumulative dividends; adjustable rate preferred stock
b. Arrearages; market auction preferred
c. Lessee; lessor
d. Sale and leaseback; operating lease; financial lease
e. Off balance sheet financing; FASB #13
f. Residual value
g. Warrant; detachable warrant; stepped-up exercise price
h. Convertible security; conversion ratio, CR; conversion price, P_c; conversion value, C_t
i. Basic EPS; primary EPS; diluted EPS

ST-2
Lease analysis

The Olsen Company has decided to acquire a new truck. One alternative is to lease the truck on a 4-year contract for a lease payment of $10,000 per year, with payments to be made at the *beginning* of each year. The lease would include maintenance. Alternatively, Olsen could purchase the truck outright for $40,000, financing with a bank loan for the net purchase price, amortized over a 4-year period at an interest rate of 10 percent per year, payments to be made at the *end* of each year. Under the borrow-to-purchase arrangement, Olsen would have to maintain the truck at a cost of $1,000 per year, payable at year-end. The truck falls into the MACRS 3-year class. The applicable MACRS depreciation rates are 0.33, 0.45, 0.15, and 0.07. It has a salvage value of $10,000, which is the expected market value after 4 years, at which time Olsen plans to replace the truck irrespective of whether it leases or buys. Olsen has a federal-plus-state tax rate of 40 percent.
a. What is Olsen's PV cost of leasing?
b. What is Olsen's PV cost of owning? Should the truck be leased or purchased?
c. The appropriate discount rate for use in Olsen's analysis is the firm's after-tax cost of debt. Why?
d. The salvage value is the least certain cash flow in the analysis. How might Olsen incorporate the higher riskiness of this cash flow into the analysis?

STARTER PROBLEMS

20-1
Leasing

Connors Construction needs a piece of equipment that can either be leased or purchased. The equipment costs $100. One option is to borrow $100 from the local bank and use the money to buy the equipment. The other option is to lease the equipment. If Connors chooses to lease the equipment, it *would not* capitalize the lease on the balance sheet. Below is the company's balance sheet *prior* to the purchase or leasing of the equipment:

Current assets	$300	Debt	$400
Fixed assets	500	Equity	400
Total assets	$800	Total liabilities and equity	$800

What would be the company's debt ratio if it chose to purchase the equipment? What would be the company's debt ratio if it chose to lease the equipment? Would the company's financial risk be different depending on whether the equipment was leased or purchased?

20-2
Warrants

Gregg Company recently issued two types of bonds. The first issue consisted of 20-year straight (no warrants attached) bonds with an 8 percent annual coupon. The second issue consisted of 20-year bonds with a 6 percent annual coupon with warrants attached. Both bonds were issued at par ($1,000). What is the value of the warrants that were attached to the second issue?

20-3
Convertibles

Petersen Securities recently issued convertible bonds with a $1,000 par value. The bonds have a conversion price of $40 a share. What is the bonds' conversion ratio, CR?

EXAM-TYPE PROBLEMS

The problems included in this section are set up in such a way that they could be used as multiple-choice exam problems.

20-4
Lease versus buy

Morris-Meyer Mining Company must install $1.5 million of new machinery in its Nevada mine. It can obtain a bank loan for 100 percent of the required amount. Alternatively, a Nevada investment banking firm that represents a group of investors believes that it can arrange for a lease financing plan. Assume that the following facts apply:

(1) The equipment falls in the MACRS 3-year class. The applicable MACRS rates are 0.33, 0.45, 0.15, and 0.07.
(2) Estimated maintenance expenses are $75,000 per year.
(3) Morris-Meyer's federal-plus-state tax rate is 40 percent.
(4) If the money is borrowed, the bank loan will be at a rate of 15 percent, amortized in 4 equal installments to be paid at the end of each year.
(5) The tentative lease terms call for end-of-year payments of $400,000 per year for 4 years.
(6) Under the proposed lease terms, the lessee must pay for insurance, property taxes, and maintenance.
(7) Morris-Meyer must use the equipment if it is to continue in business, so it will almost certainly want to acquire the property at the end of the lease. If it does, then under the lease terms, it can purchase the machinery at its fair market value at that time. The best estimate of this market value is the $250,000 salvage value, but it could be much higher or lower under certain circumstances.

To assist management in making the proper lease-versus-buy decision, you are asked to answer the following questions.

a. Assuming that the lease can be arranged, should Morris-Meyer lease, or should it borrow and buy the equipment? Explain.
b. Consider the $250,000 estimated salvage value. Is it appropriate to discount it at the same rate as the other cash flows? What about the other cash flows — are they all equally risky? (Hint: Riskier cash flows are normally discounted at higher rates, but when the cash flows are *costs* rather than *inflows*, the normal procedure must be reversed.)

20-5
Warrants

Pogue Industries Inc. has warrants outstanding that permit its holders to purchase 1 share of stock per warrant at a price of $21. (Refer to Chapter 18 for parts a, b, and c.)

a. Calculate the exercise value of Pogue's warrants if the common stock sells at each of the following prices: $18, $21, $25, and $70.
b. At what approximate price do you think the warrants would actually sell under each condition indicated in part a? What premium is implied in your price? Your answer will be a guess, but your prices and premiums should bear reasonable relationships to each other.
c. How would each of the following factors affect your estimates of the warrants' prices and premiums in part b?
  (1) The life of the warrant is lengthened.
  (2) The expected variability (σ_p) in the stock's price decreases.
  (3) The expected growth rate in the stock's EPS increases.
  (4) The company announces the following change in dividend policy: whereas it formerly paid no dividends, henceforth it will pay out *all* earnings as dividends.
d. Assume Pogue's stock now sells for $18 per share. The company wants to sell some 20-year, annual interest, $1,000 par value bonds. Each bond will have 50 warrants, each exercisable into 1 share of stock at an exercise price of $21. Pogue's pure bonds yield 10 percent. Regardless of your answer to part b, assume that the warrants will have a market value of $1.50 when the stock sells at $18. What annual coupon interest rate and annual dollar coupon must the company set on the bonds with warrants if they are to clear the market? Round to the nearest dollar or percentage point.

PROBLEMS

20-6
Balance sheet effects of leasing

Two textile companies, McDaniel-Edwards Manufacturing and Jordan-Hocking Mills, began operations with identical balance sheets. A year later, both required additional manufacturing capacity at a cost of $200,000. McDaniel-Edwards obtained a 5-year, $200,000 loan at an 8 percent interest rate from its bank. Jordan-Hocking, on the other hand, decided to lease the required $200,000 capacity from National Leasing for 5 years; an 8 percent return was built into the lease. The balance sheet for each company, before the asset increases, is as follows:

		Debt	$200,000
		Equity	200,000
Total assets	$400,000	Total liabilities and equity	$400,000

a. Show the balance sheet of each firm after the asset increase, and calculate each firm's new debt ratio. (Assume Jordan-Hocking's lease is kept off the balance sheet.)

b. Show how Jordan-Hocking's balance sheet would have looked immediately after the financing if it had capitalized the lease.

c. Would the rate of return (1) on assets and (2) on equity be affected by the choice of financing? How?

20-7
Lease analysis

As part of its overall plant modernization and cost reduction program, the management of Tanner-Woods Textile Mills has decided to install a new automated weaving loom. In the capital budgeting analysis of this equipment, the IRR of the project was found to be 20 percent versus a project required return of 12 percent.

The loom has an invoice price of $250,000, including delivery and installation charges. The funds needed could be borrowed from the bank through a 4-year amortized loan at a 10 percent interest rate, with payments to be made at the end of each year. In the event that the loom is purchased, the manufacturer will contract to maintain and service it for a fee of $20,000 per year paid at the end of each year. The loom falls in the MACRS 5-year class, and Tanner-Woods's marginal federal-plus-state tax rate is 40 percent. The applicable MACRS rates are 0.20, 0.32, 0.19, 0.12, 0.11, and 0.06.

United Automation Inc., maker of the loom, has offered to lease the loom to Tanner-Woods for $70,000 upon delivery and installation (at t = 0) plus 4 additional annual lease payments of $70,000 to be made at the end of Years 1 through 4. (Note that there are 5 lease payments in total.) The lease agreement includes maintenance and servicing. Actually, the loom has an expected life of 8 years, at which time its expected salvage value is zero; however, after 4 years, its market value is expected to equal its book value of $42,500. Tanner-Woods plans to build an entirely new plant in 4 years, so it has no interest in either leasing or owning the proposed loom for more than that period.

a. Should the loom be leased or purchased?

b. The salvage value is clearly the most uncertain cash flow in the analysis. Assume that the appropriate salvage value pre-tax discount rate is 15 percent. What would be the effect of a salvage value risk adjustment on the decision?

c. The original analysis assumed that Tanner-Woods would not need the loom after 4 years. Now assume that the firm will continue to use it after the lease expires. Thus, if it leased, Tanner-Woods would have to buy the asset after 4 years at the then existing market value, which is assumed to equal the book value. What effect would this requirement have on the basic analysis? (No numerical analysis is required; just verbalize.)

20-8
Convertibles

The Hadaway Company was planning to finance an expansion in the summer of 2002. The principal executives of the company agreed that an industrial company like theirs should finance growth by means of common stock rather than by debt. However, they believed that the price of the company's common stock did not reflect its true worth, so they decided to sell a convertible security. They considered a convertible debenture but feared the burden of fixed interest charges if the common stock did not rise enough to make conversion attractive. They decided on an issue of convertible preferred stock, which would pay a dividend of $1.05 per share.

The common stock was selling for $21 a share at the time. Management projected earnings for 2002 at $1.50 a share and expected a future growth rate of 10 percent a year in 2003 and beyond. It was agreed by the investment bankers and management that the common stock would continue to sell at 14 times earnings, the current price/earnings ratio.

a. What conversion price should be set by the issuer? The conversion rate will be 1.0; that is, each share of convertible preferred can be converted into 1 share of common. Therefore, the convertible's par value (as well as the issue price) will be equal to the conversion price, which, in turn, will be determined as a percentage over the current market price of the common. Your answer will be a guess, but make it a reasonable one.

b. Should the preferred stock include a call provision? Why or why not?

20-9
Financing alternatives

The Howe Computer Company has grown rapidly during the past 5 years. Recently, its commercial bank urged the company to consider increasing its permanent financing. Its bank loan under a line of credit has risen to $150,000, carrying a 10 percent interest rate, and Howe has been 30 to 60 days late in paying trade creditors.

Discussions with an investment banker have resulted in the decision to raise $250,000 at this time. Investment bankers have assured Howe that the following alternatives are feasible (flotation costs will be ignored):

■ *Alternative 1:* Sell common stock at $10 per share.

- *Alternative 2:* Sell convertible bonds at a 10 percent coupon, convertible into 80 shares of common stock for each $1,000 bond (that is, the conversion price is $12.50 per share).
- *Alternative 3:* Sell debentures with a 10 percent coupon; each $1,000 bond will have 80 warrants to buy 1 share of common stock at $12.50.

Keith Howe, the president, owns 80 percent of Howe's common stock and wishes to maintain control of the company; 50,000 shares are outstanding. The following are summaries of Howe's latest financial statements:

BALANCE SHEET

		Current liabilities	$200,000
		Common stock, $1 par	50,000
		Retained earnings	25,000
Total assets	$275,000	Total liabilities and equity	$275,000

INCOME STATEMENT

Sales	$550,000
All costs except interest	495,000
EBIT	$ 55,000
Interest	15,000
EBT	$ 40,000
Taxes (40%)	16,000
Net income	$ 24,000
Shares outstanding	50,000
Earnings per share	$0.48
Price/earnings ratio	18×
Market price of stock	$8.64

a. Show the new balance sheet under each alternative. For Alternatives 2 and 3, show the balance sheet after conversion of the debentures or exercise of the warrants. Assume that $150,000 of the funds raised will be used to pay off the bank loan and the rest to increase total assets.
b. Show Keith Howe's control position under each alternative, assuming that he does not purchase additional shares.
c. What is the effect on earnings per share of each alternative if it is assumed that earnings before interest and taxes will be 20 percent of total assets?
d. What will be the debt ratio under each alternative?
e. Which of the three alternatives would you recommend to Keith Howe, and why?

20-10
Convertibles
O'Brien Computers Inc. needs to raise $35 million to begin producing a new microcomputer. O'Brien's straight, nonconvertible debentures currently yield 12 percent. Its stock sells for $38 per share, the last dividend was $2.46, and the expected growth rate is a constant 8 percent. Investment bankers have tentatively proposed that O'Brien raise the $35 million by issuing convertible debentures. These convertibles would have a $1,000 par value, carry an annual coupon rate of 10 percent, have a 20-year maturity, and be convertible into 20 shares of stock. The bonds would be noncallable for 5 years, after which they would be callable at a price of $1,075; this call price would decline by $5 per year in Year 6 and each year thereafter. Management has called convertibles in the past (and presumably will call them again in the future), once they were eligible for call, as soon as their conversion value was about 20 percent above their par value (not their call price).
a. Draw an accurate graph similar to Figure 20-1 representing the expectations set forth in the problem.
b. Suppose the previously outlined projects work out on schedule for 2 years, but then O'Brien begins to experience extremely strong competition from Japanese firms. As a result, O'Brien's expected growth rate drops from 8 percent to zero. Assume that the dividend at the time of the drop is $2.87. The company's credit strength is not impaired, and its

value of k_s is also unchanged. What would happen (1) to the stock price and (2) to the convertible bond's price? Be as precise as you can.

20-11
Warrants
Storm Software wants to issue $100 million in new capital to fund new opportunities. If Storm were to raise the $100 million of new capital in a straight-debt 20-year bond offering, Storm would have to offer an annual coupon rate of 12 percent. However, Storm's advisors have suggested a 20-year bond offering with warrants. According to the advisors, Storm could issue 9 percent annual coupon-bearing debt with 20 warrants per $1,000 face value bond. Storm has 10 million shares of stock outstanding at a current price of $25. The warrants can be exercised in 10 years (on December 31, 2012) at an exercise price of $30. Each warrant entitles its holder to buy one share of Storm Software stock. After issuing the bonds with warrants, Storm's operations and investments are expected to grow at a constant rate of 10 percent per year.

a. If investors pay $1,000 for each bond, what is the value of each warrant attached to the bond issue?
b. What is the expected total value of Storm Software in 10 years?
c. If there were no warrants, what would be Storm's price per share in 10 years? What would be the price with the warrants?
d. What is the component cost of these bonds with warrants? What is the premium associated with the warrants?

SPREADSHEET PROBLEM

20-12
Lease analysis
Use the spreadsheet model to rework parts a and b of Problem 20-7. Then, answer the following question.
c. Accepting that the corporate WACC should be used equally to discount all anticipated cash flows, at what cost of capital would the firm be indifferent between leasing or buying?

INTEGRATED CASE

FISH & CHIPS, INC., PART I

20-13 Lease Analysis Martha Millon, financial manager for Fish & Chips Inc., has been asked to perform a lease-versus-buy analysis on a new computer system. The computer costs $1,200,000, and, if it is purchased, Fish & Chips could obtain a term loan for the full amount at a 10 percent cost. The loan would be amortized over the 4-year life of the computer, with payments made at the end of each year. The computer is classified as special purpose, and hence it falls into the MACRS 3-year class. The applicable MACRS rates are 0.33, 0.45, 0.15, and 0.07. If the computer is purchased, a maintenance contract must be obtained at a cost of $25,000, payable at the beginning of each year.

After 4 years, the computer will be sold, and Millon's best estimate of its residual value at that time is $125,000. Because technology is changing rapidly, however, the residual value is very uncertain.

As an alternative, National Leasing is willing to write a 4-year lease on the computer, including maintenance, for payments of $340,000 at the *beginning* of each year. Fish & Chips' marginal federal-plus-state tax rate is 40 percent. Help Millon conduct her analysis by answering the following questions.

a. (1) Why is leasing sometimes referred to as "off balance sheet" financing?
   (2) What is the difference between a capital lease and an operating lease?

(3) What effect does leasing have on a firm's capital structure?

b. (1) What is Fish & Chips' present value cost of owning the computer? (Hint: Set up a table whose bottom line is a "time line" which shows the net cash flows over the period $t = 0$ to $t = 4$, and then find the PV of these net cash flows, or the PV cost of owning.)
   (2) Explain the rationale for the discount rate you used to find the PV.

c. (1) What is Fish & Chips' present value cost of leasing the computer? (Hint: Again, construct a time line.)
   (2) What is the net advantage to leasing? Does your analysis indicate that the firm should buy or lease the computer? Explain.

d. Now assume that Millon believes the computer's residual value could be as low as $0 or as high as $250,000, but she stands by $125,000 as her expected value. She concludes that the residual value is riskier than the other cash flows in the analysis, and she wants to incorporate this differential risk into her analysis. Describe how this could be accomplished. What effect would it have on the lease decision?

e. Millon knows that her firm has been considering moving its headquarters to a new location for some time, and she is concerned that these plans may come to fruition prior to the expiration of the lease. If the move occurs, the company would obtain completely new computers, and hence Millon would like to include a cancellation clause in the lease contract. What effect would a cancellation clause have on the riskiness of the lease?

FISH & CHIPS INC., PART II

20-14 **Preferred Stock, Warrants, and Convertibles** Martha Millon, financial manager of Fish & Chips Inc., is facing a dilemma. The firm was founded 5 years ago to develop a new fast-food concept, and although Fish & Chips has done well, the firm's founder and chairman believes that an industry shake-out is imminent. To survive, the firm must capture market share now, and this requires a large infusion of new capital.

Because the stock price may rise rapidly, Millon does not want to issue new common stock. On the other hand, interest rates are currently very high by historical standards, and, with the firm's B rating, the interest payments on a new debt issue would be too much to handle if sales took a downturn. Thus, Millon has narrowed her choice to bonds with warrants or convertible bonds. She has asked you to help in the decision process by answering the following questions.

a. How does preferred stock differ from common equity and debt?

b. What is floating rate preferred?

c. How can a knowledge of call options help one understand warrants and convertibles?

d. One of Millon's alternatives is to issue a bond with warrants attached. Fish & Chips' current stock price is $10, and its cost of 20-year, annual coupon debt without warrants is estimated by its investment bankers to be 12 percent. The bankers suggest attaching 50 warrants to each bond, with each warrant having an exercise price of $12.50. It is estimated that each warrant, when detached and traded separately, will have a value of $1.50.

  (1) What coupon rate should be set on the bond with warrants if the total package is to sell for $1,000?

  (2) Suppose the bonds are issued and the warrants immediately trade for $2.50 each. What does this imply about the terms of the issue? Did the company "win" or "lose"?

  (3) When would you expect the warrants to be exercised?

  (4) Will the warrants bring in additional capital when exercised? If so, how much and what type of capital?

  (5) Because warrants lower the cost of the accompanying debt, shouldn't all debt be issued with warrants? What is the expected cost of the bond with warrants if the warrants are expected to be exercised in 5 years, when Fish & Chips' stock price is expected to be $17.50? How would you expect the cost of the bond with warrants to compare with the cost of straight debt? With the cost of common stock?

e. As an alternative to the bond with warrants, Millon is considering convertible bonds. The firm's investment bankers estimate that Fish & Chips could sell a 20-year, 10 percent annual coupon, callable convertible bond for its $1,000 par value, whereas a straight-debt issue would require a 12 percent coupon. Fish & Chips' current stock price is $10, its last dividend was $0.74, and the dividend is expected to grow at a constant rate of 8 percent. The convertible could be converted into 80 shares of Fish & Chips stock at the owner's option.

  (1) What conversion price, P_c, is implied in the convertible's terms?

  (2) What is the straight-debt value of the convertible? What is the implied value of the convertibility feature?

  (3) What is the formula for the bond's conversion value in any year? Its value at Year 0? At Year 10?

  (4) What is meant by the term "floor value" of a convertible? What is the convertible's expected floor value in Year 0? In Year 10?

  (5) Assume that Fish & Chips intends to force conversion by calling the bond when its conversion value is 20 percent above its par value, or at 1.2($1,000) = $1,200. When is the issue expected to be called? Answer to the closest year.

  (6) What is the expected cost of the convertible to Fish & Chips? Does this cost appear consistent with the riskiness of the issue? Assume conversion in Year 5 at a conversion value of $1,200.

f. Millon believes that the costs of both the bond with warrants and the convertible bond are essentially equal, so her decision must be based on other factors. What are some of the factors that she should consider in making her decision?

CYBER PROBLEM

Please go to our web site **http://brigham.swlearning.com** to access the Cyberproblems.

MERGERS AND
ACQUISITIONS

21

AOL AND TIME WARNER MERGER STUNS THE FINANCIAL MARKETS

I n early January 10, 2000, the wire services reported the proposed blockbuster merger between America Online (AOL) and Time Warner. The announcement stunned the financial markets, and it sent shockwaves throughout the investment community.

In January 2000, when Jerry Levin of Time Warner and Steve Case of AOL sealed the agreement that created AOL Time Warner, they described it as a "merger of equals." However, AOL really acquired Time Warner. AOL's shareholders received 55 percent of the combined company's stock, its nominees dominated the new board, and its name came first. Moreover, not long after the merger, Levin was out and Case had been named Chairman and CEO.

Before the announcement, AOL's stock had a market value of $160 billion on revenues of only $4.8 billion, whereas Time Warner's stock was valued at $90 billion versus $26.8 billion of revenues. Clearly, AOL's much higher valuation reflected the market's belief (or hope) that its growth prospects were considerably greater than those of Time Warner. Note, though, that AOL's valuation also reflected the price bubble that drove up most tech stocks, and Internet stocks in particular.

The combined companies' premerger valuation was $160 + $90 = $250 billion. AOL contributed 64 percent ($160/$250) of that total, and Time Warner contributed just 36 percent. However, AOL's shareholders received only 55 percent of the new company's stock. This disparity led many to conclude that AOL paid too much for Time Warner. Indeed, in the days immediately following the announcement, Time Warner's stock rose by 35 percent while AOL's fell by more than 10 percent. Still, some astute analysts argued that AOL's stock was overvalued prior to the merger, and that its managers had great foresight when they used their overvalued stock to buy a blue chip company that had assets, earnings, and cash flow.

The stated reason for the merger was that tremendous synergies would be gained by combining the two companies. AOL had more than 30 million subscribers, and it was the

AOL TIME WARNER

dominant Internet service provider. Time Warner had an impressive cable franchise, with the potential for bringing high-speed broadband Internet access to many millions of households, plus such valuable content providers as Warner Brothers Studios, Warner Music, CNN, HBO, *Time, People, Sports Illustrated*, and *Fortune*. The plan was to use the cable system to sell Time Warner's content to AOL's subscribers. Thus, the two companies were supposed to combine and then to feed off of one another, generating billions of dollars of additional revenues, profits, and cash flow, in the process. Of course, that would lead to a higher stock price.

However, things didn't work out as planned. AOL Time Warner's stock sold for $95 per share just after the merger, but by 2002 it had fallen by 91 percent, to $8.70. Of course, the S&P 500 also declined during that period, but not nearly as sharply. Very clearly, the AOL Time Warner merger was a failure, especially from Time Warner's stockholders' perspective. Without the merger, Time Warner's stock would probably have tracked the general stock market and thus lost 25 to 30 percent of its value. AOL, on the other hand, would probably have experienced the fate of other Internet stocks as the air went out of their bubble, and thus it probably would have dropped by more than 90 percent.

Despite its problems, the combined company still brings together some interesting elements, and the current management continues to talk about a bright future. Perhaps that dream will someday be fulfilled, but to date the problems of coordinating the company's many diverse elements have prevailed. Over time, we will see if these problems persist, or if they were just part of the inevitable growing pains that accompany many large mergers.

Most corporate growth occurs by *internal expansion*, which takes place when a firm's existing divisions grow through normal capital budgeting activities. However, the most dramatic examples of growth, and often the largest increases in firms' stock prices, result from *mergers,* the first topic covered in this chapter. *Leveraged buyouts,* or *LBOs,* occur when a firm's stock is acquired by a small group of investors rather than by another operating company. Since LBOs are similar to mergers in many respects, they are also covered in this chapter. Conditions change over time, causing firms to sell off, or *divest,* major divisions to other firms that can better utilize the divested assets. We also discuss divestitures in the chapter. We leave the discussion of the *holding company* form of organization, wherein one corporation owns the stock of one or more other companies, for Web Appendix 21A. ■

RATIONALE FOR MERGERS

Merger
The combination of two firms to form a single firm.

Many reasons have been proposed by financial managers and theorists to account for the high level of U.S. merger activity. The primary motives behind corporate **mergers** are presented in this section.[1]

SYNERGY

Synergy
The condition wherein the whole is greater than the sum of its parts; in a synergistic merger, the postmerger value exceeds the sum of the separate companies' premerger values.

The primary motivation for most mergers is to increase the value of the combined enterprise. If Companies A and B merge to form Company C, and if C's value exceeds that of A and B taken separately, then **synergy** is said to exist. Such a merger should be beneficial to both A's and B's stockholders.[2] Synergistic effects can arise from four sources: (1) *operating economies*, which result from economies of scale in management, marketing, production, or distribution; (2) *financial economies*, including lower transaction costs and better coverage by security analysts; (3) *differential efficiency*, which implies that the management of one firm is more efficient and that the weaker firm's assets will be more productive after the merger; and (4) *increased market power* due to reduced competition. Operating and financial economies are socially

---

[1] As we use the term, *merger* means any combination that forms one economic unit from two or more previous ones. For legal purposes, there are distinctions among the various ways these combinations can occur, but our focus is on the fundamental economic and financial aspects of mergers.

[2] If synergy exists, then the whole is greater than the sum of the parts. Synergy is also called the "2 plus 2 equals 5 effect." The distribution of the synergistic gain between A's and B's stockholders is determined by negotiation. This point is discussed later in the chapter.

desirable, as are mergers that increase managerial efficiency, but mergers that reduce competition are socially undesirable and illegal.[3]

TAX CONSIDERATIONS

Tax considerations have stimulated a number of mergers. For example, a profitable firm in the highest tax bracket could acquire a firm with large accumulated tax losses. These losses could then be turned into immediate tax savings rather than carried forward and used in the future.[4] Also, mergers can serve as a way of minimizing taxes when disposing of excess cash. For example, if a firm has a shortage of internal investment opportunities compared with its free cash flow, it could (1) pay an extra dividend, (2) invest in marketable securities, (3) repurchase its own stock, or (4) purchase another firm. If it pays an extra dividend, its stockholders would have to pay immediate taxes on the distribution. Marketable securities often provide a good temporary parking place for money, but they generally earn a rate of return less than that required by stockholders. A stock repurchase might result in a capital gain for the remaining stockholders. However, using surplus cash to acquire another firm would avoid all these problems, and this has motivated a number of mergers.

PURCHASE OF ASSETS BELOW THEIR REPLACEMENT COST

Sometimes a firm will be touted as an acquisition candidate because the cost of replacing its assets is considerably higher than its market value. For example, in the early 1980s oil companies could acquire reserves cheaper by buying other oil companies than by doing exploratory drilling. Thus, Chevron acquired Gulf Oil to augment its reserves. Similarly, in the 1980s several steel company executives stated that it was cheaper to buy an existing steel company than to construct a new mill. For example, LTV (the fourth largest steel company) acquired Republic Steel (the sixth largest) to create the second largest firm in the industry.

DIVERSIFICATION

Managers often cite diversification as a reason for mergers. They contend that diversification helps stabilize a firm's earnings and thus benefits its owners. Stabilization of earnings is certainly beneficial to employees, suppliers, and customers, but its value is less certain from the standpoint of stockholders. Why should Firm A acquire Firm B to stabilize earnings when stockholders can simply buy the stock of both firms? Indeed, research of U.S. firms suggests that in most cases diversification does not increase the firm's value. To the contrary, many studies find that diversified firms are worth significantly less than the sum of their individual parts.[5]

---

[3] In the 1880s and 1890s, many mergers occurred in the United States, and some of them were obviously directed toward gaining market power rather than increasing efficiency. As a result, Congress passed a series of acts designed to ensure that mergers are not used as a method of reducing competition. The principal acts include the Sherman Act (1890), the Clayton Act (1914), and the Celler Act (1950). These acts make it illegal for firms to combine if the combination tends to lessen competition. The acts are enforced by the antitrust division of the Justice Department and by the Federal Trade Commission.

[4] Mergers undertaken only to use accumulated tax losses would probably be challenged by the IRS. In recent years Congress has made it increasingly difficult for firms to pass along tax savings after mergers.

[5] See, for example, Philip Berger and Eli Ofek, "Diversification's Effect on Firm Value," *Journal of Financial Economics*, Vol. 37, 1995, 37–65; and Larry Lang and René Stulz, "Tobin's Q, Corporate Diversification, and Firm Performance," *Journal of Political Economy*, Vol. 102, 1994, 1248–1280.

Of course, if you were the owner-manager of a closely held firm, it might be nearly impossible to sell part of your stock to diversify. Also, selling your stock would probably lead to a large capital gains tax. So, a diversification merger might be the best way to achieve personal diversification.

MANAGERS' PERSONAL INCENTIVES

Financial economists like to think that business decisions are based only on economic considerations, especially maximization of firms' values. However, many business decisions are based more on managers' personal motivations than on economic analyses. Business leaders like power, and more power is attached to running a larger corporation than a smaller one. Obviously, no executive would admit that his or her ego was the primary reason behind a merger, but egos do play a prominent role in many mergers.

It has also been observed that executive salaries are highly correlated with company size—the bigger the company, the higher the salaries of its top officers. This too could play a role in corporate acquisition programs.

Personal considerations deter as well as motivate mergers. After most takeovers, some managers of the acquired companies lose their jobs, or at least their autonomy. Therefore, managers who own less than 51 percent of their firms' stock look to devices that will lessen the chances of a takeover. Mergers can serve as such a device. For example, a few years ago Paramount made a bid to acquire Time Inc. Time's managers received a lot of criticism when they rejected Paramount's bid and chose instead to enter into a heavily debt-financed merger with Warner Brothers that enabled them to retain power. Such **defensive mergers** are hard to defend on economic grounds. The managers involved invariably argue that synergy, not a desire to protect their own jobs, motivated the acquisition, but observers suspect that many mergers were designed more to benefit managers than stockholders.

Defensive Merger
A merger designed to make a company less vulnerable to a takeover.

BREAKUP VALUE

Breakup Value
A firm's value if its assets are sold off in pieces.

Firms can be valued by book value, economic value, or replacement value. Recently, takeover specialists have begun to recognize **breakup value** as another basis for valuation. Analysts estimate a company's breakup value, which is the value of the individual parts of the firm if they were sold off separately. If this value is higher than the firm's current market value, then a takeover specialist could acquire the firm at or even above its current market value, sell it off in pieces, and earn a substantial profit.

SELF-TEST QUESTIONS

Define synergy. Is synergy a valid rationale for mergers? Describe several situations that might produce synergistic gains.

Give two examples of how tax considerations can motivate mergers.

Suppose your firm could purchase another firm for only half of its replacement value. Would that be a sufficient justification for the acquisition?

Discuss the pros and cons of diversification as a rationale for mergers.

What is breakup value?

TYPES OF MERGERS

Horizontal Merger
A combination of two firms that produce the same type of good or service.

Vertical Merger
A merger between a firm and one of its suppliers or customers.

Congeneric Merger
A merger of firms in the same general industry, but for which no customer or supplier relationship exists.

Conglomerate Merger
A merger of companies in totally different industries.

Economists classify mergers into four types: (1) horizontal, (2) vertical, (3) congeneric, and (4) conglomerate. A **horizontal merger** occurs when one firm combines with another in its same line of business—the NationsBank/BankAmerica merger is an example. An example of a **vertical merger** would be a steel producer's acquisition of one of its own suppliers, such as an iron or coal mining firm, or an oil producer's acquisition of a petrochemical firm that uses oil as a raw material. *Congeneric* means "allied in nature or action," hence a **congeneric merger** involves related enterprises but not producers of the same product (horizontal) or firms in a producer-supplier relationship (vertical). The Citicorp/Travelers merger is an example. A **conglomerate merger** occurs when unrelated enterprises combine, as illustrated by Mobil Oil's acquisition of Montgomery Ward.

Operating economies (and also anticompetitive effects) are at least partially dependent on the type of merger involved. Vertical and horizontal mergers generally provide the greatest synergistic operating benefits, but they are also the ones most likely to be attacked by the Department of Justice as anticompetitive. In any event, it is useful to think of these economic classifications when analyzing prospective mergers.

> ### SELF-TEST QUESTION
>
> What are the four economic types of mergers?

LEVEL OF MERGER ACTIVITY

Five major "merger waves" have occurred in the United States. The first was in the late 1800s, when consolidations occurred in the oil, steel, tobacco, and other basic industries. The second was in the 1920s, when the stock market boom helped financial promoters consolidate firms in a number of industries, including utilities, communications, and autos. The third was in the 1960s, when conglomerate mergers were the rage. The fourth occurred in the 1980s, when LBO firms and others began using junk bonds to finance all manner of acquisitions. The fifth, which involves strategic alliances designed to enable firms to compete better in the global economy, is in progress today.

As can be seen from Table 21-1, some huge mergers have occurred in recent years.[6] The table lists some of the largest mergers and acquisitions that have occurred in recent years. For example, in recent years there have been a number of high-profile global mergers including the mergers of Daimler-Benz and Chrysler, Deutschebank and Bankers Trust, and British Petroleum and Amoco. In general, recent mergers have been significantly different from those of the 1980s. Most 1980s mergers were financial transactions in which buyers sought companies that were selling at less than

---

[6] For detailed reviews of the 1980s merger wave, see Andrei Shleifer and Robert W. Vishny, "The Takeover Wave of the 1980s," *Journal of Applied Corporate Finance*, Fall 1991, 49–56; Edmund Faltermayer, "The Deal Decade: Verdict on the '80s," *Fortune*, August 26, 1991, 58–70; and "The Best and Worst Deals of the '80s: What We Learned from All Those Mergers, Acquisitions, and Takeovers," *BusinessWeek*, January 15, 1990, 52–57.

TABLE 21-1   A Sample of Large Mergers Announced in Recent Years

BUYER	TARGET	ANNOUNCEMENT DATE	VALUE (BILLIONS, U.S.$)
America Online	Time Warner	January 10, 2000	$160.0
Vodafone AirTouch	Mannesmann	November 14, 1999	148.6
Pfizer	Warner-Lambert	November 4, 1999	90.0
Exxon	Mobil	December 1, 1998	85.2
Bell Atlantic	GTE	July 28, 1998	85.0
SBC Communications	Ameritech	May 11, 1998	80.6
Vodafone	AirTouch	January 18, 1999	74.4
British Petroleum	Amoco	August 11, 1998	61.7
AT&T	MediaOne Group	May 6, 1999	61.0
Pfizer	Pharmacia Corporation	July 15, 2002	60.0
Comcast	AT&T Broadband	July 8, 2001	47.0
Hewlett-Packard	Compaq	September 4, 2001	25.3

SOURCES: Adapted from recent "Year-End Review" articles from *The Wall Street Journal*.

their true values as a result of incompetent or sluggish management. If a target company could be managed better, if redundant assets could be sold, and if operating and administrative costs could be cut, profits and stock prices would rise. On the other hand, most of the mergers have been strategic in nature—companies are merging to gain economies of scale or scope and thus be better able to compete in the world economy. Indeed, many recent mergers have involved companies in the financial, defense, media, computer, telecommunications, and health care industries, all of which are experiencing structural changes and intense competition.

Recently, there has also been an increase in cross-border mergers. Many of these mergers have been motivated by large shifts in the value of the world's leading currencies. For example, in the early 1990s, the dollar was weak relative to the yen and the mark. The decline in the dollar made it easier for Japanese and German acquirers to buy U.S. corporations.

> **SELF-TEST QUESTIONS**
>
> What five major "merger waves" have occurred in the United States?
> What are some reasons for the current wave?

HOSTILE VERSUS FRIENDLY TAKEOVERS

In the vast majority of merger situations, one firm (generally the larger of the two) simply decides to buy another company, negotiates a price with the management of the target firm, and then acquires the target company. Occasionally, the acquired firm will initiate the action, but it is much more common for a firm to seek acquisitions than to seek to be acquired.[7] Following convention, we call a company that seeks to acquire another firm the **acquiring company** and the one that it seeks to acquire the **target company.**

Acquiring Company
A company that seeks to acquire another firm.

Target Company
A firm that another company seeks to acquire.

Once an acquiring company has identified a possible target, it must (1) establish a suitable price, or range of prices, and (2) tentatively set the terms of payment—will it offer cash, its own common stock, bonds, or some combination? Next, the acquiring firm's managers must decide how to approach the target company's managers. If the acquiring firm has reason to believe that the target's management will approve the merger, then it will simply propose a merger and try to work out some suitable terms. If an agreement is reached, then the two management groups will issue statements to their stockholders indicating that they approve the merger, and the target firm's management will recommend to its stockholders that they agree to the merger. Generally, the stockholders are asked to *tender* (or send in) their shares to a designated financial institution, along with a signed power of attorney that transfers ownership of the shares to the acquiring firm. The target firm's stockholders then receive the specified payment, either common stock of the acquiring company (in which case the target company's stockholders become stockholders of the acquiring company), cash, bonds, or some mix of cash and securities. This is a **friendly merger.**

Friendly Merger
A merger whose terms are approved by the managements of both companies.

Hostile Merger
A merger in which the target firm's management resists acquisition.

Often, however, the target company's management resists the merger. Perhaps they feel that the price offered is too low, or perhaps they simply want to keep their jobs. In either case, the acquiring firm's offer is said to be *hostile* rather than friendly, and the acquiring firm must make a direct appeal to the target firm's stockholders. In a **hostile merger,** the acquiring company will again make a **tender offer,** and again it will ask the stockholders of the target firm to tender their shares in exchange for the offered price. This time, though, the target firm's managers will urge stockholders not to tender their shares, generally stating that the price offered (cash, bonds, or stocks in the acquiring firm) is too low.

Tender Offer
The offer of one firm to buy the stock of another by going directly to the stockholders, frequently (but not always) over the opposition of the target company's management.

While most mergers are friendly, recently there have been a number of interesting cases in which high-profile firms have attempted hostile takeovers. For example, Warner-Lambert tried to fight off a hostile bid by Pfizer; however, the merger was completed in 2000. Looking overseas, Olivetti recently successfully conducted a hostile takeover of Telecom Italia, and in another telecommunications merger Britain's Vodafone AirTouch made a hostile bid for its German rival, Mannesmann AG, which was successful.

SELF-TEST QUESTION

What's the difference between a hostile and a friendly merger?

MERGER REGULATION

Proxy Fight
An attempt to gain control of a firm by soliciting stockholders to vote for a new management team.

Prior to the mid-1960s, friendly acquisitions generally took place as simple exchange-of-stock mergers, and a **proxy fight** was the primary weapon used in hostile control battles. However, in the mid-1960s corporate raiders began to operate

---

[7] However, if a firm is in financial difficulty, if its managers are elderly and do not think that suitable replacements are on hand, or if it needs the support (often the capital) of a larger company, then it may seek to be acquired. Thus, when a number of Texas, Ohio, and Maryland financial institutions were in trouble in the 1980s, they lobbied to get their state legislatures to pass laws that would make it easier for them to be acquired. Out-of-state banks then moved in to help salvage the situation and minimize depositor losses.

differently. First, it took a long time to mount a proxy fight—raiders had to first request a list of the target company's stockholders, be refused, and then get a court order forcing management to turn over the list. During that time, the target's management could think through and then implement a strategy to fend off the raider. As a result, management won most proxy fights.

Then raiders began saying to themselves, "If we could bring the decision to a head quickly, before management can take countermeasures, that would greatly increase our probability of success." That led the raiders to turn from proxy fights to tender offers, which had a much shorter response time. For example, the stockholders of a company whose stock was selling for $20 might be offered $27 per share and be given two weeks to accept. The raider, meanwhile, would have accumulated a substantial block of the shares in open market purchases, and additional shares might have been purchased by institutional friends of the raider who promised to tender their shares in exchange for the tip that a raid was to occur.

Faced with a well-planned raid, managements were generally overwhelmed. The stock might actually be worth more than the offered price, but management simply did not have time to get this message across to stockholders or to find a competing bidder. This situation seemed unfair, so Congress passed the Williams Act in 1968. This law had two main objectives: (1) to regulate the way acquiring firms can structure takeover offers and (2) to force acquiring firms to disclose more information about their offers. Basically, Congress wanted to put target managements in a better position to defend against hostile offers. Additionally, Congress believed that shareholders needed easier access to information about tender offers—including information on any securities that might be offered in lieu of cash—in order to make rational tender-versus-don't-tender decisions.

The Williams Act placed the following four restrictions on acquiring firms: (1) Acquirers must disclose their current holdings and future intentions within 10 days of amassing at least 5 percent of a company's stock. (2) Acquirers must disclose the source of the funds to be used in the acquisition. (3) The target firm's shareholders must be allowed at least 20 days to tender their shares; that is, the offer must be "open" for at least 20 days. (4) If the acquiring firm increases the offer price during the 20-day open period, all shareholders who tendered prior to the new offer must receive the higher price. In total, these restrictions were intended to reduce the acquiring firm's ability to surprise management and to stampede target shareholders into accepting an inadequate offer. Prior to the Williams Act, offers were generally made on a first-come, first-served basis, and they were often accompanied by an implicit threat to lower the bid price after 50 percent of the shares were in hand. The legislation also gave the target more time to mount a defense, and it gave rival bidders and white knights a chance to enter the fray and thus help a target's stockholders obtain a better price.

Many states have also passed laws designed to protect firms in their states from hostile takeovers. At first, these laws focused on disclosure requirements, but by the late 1970s several states had enacted takeover statutes so restrictive that they virtually precluded hostile takeovers. In 1979, MITE Corporation, a Delaware firm, made a hostile tender offer for Chicago Rivet and Machine Co., a publicly held Illinois corporation. Chicago Rivet sought protection under the Illinois Business Takeover Act. The constitutionality of the Illinois act was contested, and the U.S. Supreme Court found the law unconstitutional. The court ruled that the market for securities is a national market, and even though the issuing firm was incorporated in Illinois, the state of Illinois could not regulate interstate securities transactions.

The Illinois decision effectively eliminated the first generation of state merger regulations. However, the states kept trying to protect their state-headquartered companies, and in 1987 the U.S. Supreme Court upheld an Indiana law that radically changed the rules of the takeover game. Specifically, the Indiana law first defined "control shares" as enough shares to give an investor 20 percent of the vote. It went on to state that when an investor buys control shares, those shares can be voted only after approval by a majority of "disinterested shareholders," defined as those who are neither officers nor inside directors of the company, nor associates of the raider. The law also gives the buyer of control shares the right to insist that a shareholders' meeting be called within 50 days to decide whether the shares may be voted. The Indiana law dealt a major blow to raiders, mainly because it slows down the action. Delaware (the state in which most large companies are incorporated) later passed a similar bill, as did New York and a number of other important states.

The new state laws also have some features that protect target stockholders from their own managers. Included are limits on the use of golden parachutes, onerous debt-financing plans, and some types of takeover defenses. Since these laws do not regulate tender offers per se, but rather govern the practices of firms in the state, they have withstood all legal challenges to date. But when companies such as IBM offer 100 percent premiums for companies such as Lotus, it is hard for any defense to hold them off.

SELF-TEST QUESTIONS

Is there a need to regulate mergers? Explain.

Do the states play a role in merger regulation, or is it all done at the national level?

MERGER ANALYSIS

In theory, merger analysis is quite simple. The acquiring firm simply performs an analysis to value the target company and then determines whether the target can be bought at that value or, preferably, for less than the estimated value. The target company, on the other hand, should accept the offer if the price exceeds either its value if it continued to operate independently or the price it can get from some other bidder. Theory aside, however, some difficult issues are involved. In this section, we first discuss valuing the target firm, which is the initial step in a merger analysis. Then we discuss setting the bid price and postmerger control. In the next section, we discuss structuring the takeover bid.

VALUING THE TARGET FIRM

Several methodologies are used to value target firms, but we will confine our discussion to the two most common: (1) the discounted cash flow approach and (2) the market multiple method. However, regardless of the valuation methodology, it is crucial to recognize two facts. First, the target company typically will not continue to operate as a separate entity, but will become part of the acquiring firm's portfolio of assets. Therefore, changes in operations will affect the value of the business and must be considered in the analysis. Second, the goal of merger valuation is to value the target firm's equity, because a firm is acquired from its owners, not from its creditors. Thus, although we use the phrase "valuing the firm," our focus is on the value of the equity rather than on total value.

Discounted Cash Flow Analysis

The discounted cash flow (DCF) approach to valuing a business involves the application of capital budgeting procedures to an entire firm rather than to a single project. To apply this method, two key items are needed: (1) pro forma statements that forecast the incremental free cash flows expected to result from the merger and (2) a discount rate, or cost of capital, to apply to these projected cash flows.

Pro Forma Cash Flow Statements   Obtaining accurate postmerger cash flow forecasts is by far the most important task in the DCF approach. In a pure **financial merger,** in which no synergies are expected, the incremental postmerger cash flows are simply the expected cash flows of the target firm. In an **operating merger,** where the two firms' operations are to be integrated, forecasting future cash flows is more difficult.

Table 21-2 shows the projected cash flow statements for Apex Corporation, which is being considered as a target by Hightech, a large conglomerate. The projected data are for the postmerger period, and all synergistic effects have been included. Apex currently uses 50 percent debt, and if it were acquired, Hightech would keep the debt ratio at 50 percent. Both Hightech and Apex have a 40 percent marginal federal-plus-state tax rate.

Lines 1 through 4 of the table show the operating information that Hightech expects for the Apex subsidiary if the merger takes place, and Line 5 contains the earnings before interest and taxes (EBIT) for each year. Unlike a typical capital budgeting analysis, a merger analysis usually *does* incorporate interest expense into the cash flow forecast, as shown on Line 6. This is done for three reasons: (1) acquiring firms often assume the debt of the target firm, so old debt at different coupon rates is often part of the deal; (2) the acquisition is often financed partially by debt; and (3) if the subsidiary is to grow in the future, new debt will have to be issued over time to support the expansion. Thus, debt associated with a merger is typically more complex than the single issue of new debt associated with a normal capital project, and the easiest way to properly account for the complexities of merger debt is to specifically include each year's expected interest expense in the cash flow forecast. Therefore, we are using what is called the **equity residual method** to value the target firm. Here the estimated net cash flows are a residual that belongs solely to the acquiring firm's shareholders. Therefore, they should be discounted at the cost of equity. This is in contrast to the corporate value model of Chapter 8, where the free cash flows (which belong to all investors, not just shareholders) are discounted at the WACC. Both methods lead to the same estimate of equity value.

Line 7 contains the earnings before taxes (EBT), and Line 8 gives taxes based on Hightech's 40 percent marginal rate. Line 9 lists each year's net income, and depreciation is added back on Line 10 to obtain each year's cash flow as shown on Line 11. Since some of Apex's assets will wear out or become obsolete, and since Hightech plans to expand the Apex subsidiary should the acquisition occur, some equity funds must be retained and reinvested in the business. These retentions, which are not available for transfer to the parent, are shown on Line 12. Finally, we have projected only five years of cash flows, but Hightech would likely operate the Apex subsidiary for many years—in theory, forever. Therefore, we applied the constant growth model

Financial Merger
A merger in which the firms involved will not be operated as a single unit and from which no operating economies are expected.

Operating Merger
A merger in which operations of the firms involved are integrated in hope of achieving synergistic benefits.

Equity Residual Method
A method used to value a target firm using net cash flows that are a residual and belong solely to the acquiring firm's shareholders.

TABLE 21-2

Projected Postmerger Cash Flow Statements for the Apex Subsidiary as of December 31 (Millions of Dollars)

	2003	2004	2005	2006	2007
1. Net sales	$105.0	$126.0	$151.0	$174.0	$191.0
2. Cost of goods sold	75.0	89.0	106.0	122.0	132.0
3. Selling and administrative expenses	10.0	12.0	13.0	15.0	16.0
4. Depreciation	8.0	8.0	9.0	9.0	10.0
5. EBIT	$ 12.0	$ 17.0	$ 23.0	$ 28.0	$ 33.0
6. Interest[a]	8.0	9.0	10.0	11.0	11.0
7. EBT	$ 4.0	$ 8.0	$ 13.0	$ 17.0	$ 22.0
8. Taxes (40%)[b]	1.6	3.2	5.2	6.8	8.8
9. Net income	$ 2.4	$ 4.8	$ 7.8	$ 10.2	$ 13.2
10. Plus depreciation	8.0	8.0	9.0	9.0	10.0
11. Cash flow	$ 10.4	$ 12.8	$ 16.8	$ 19.2	$ 23.2
12. Less retentions needed for growth[c]	4.0	4.0	7.0	9.0	12.0
13. Plus terminal value[d]					150.2
14. Net cash flow to Hightech[e]	$ 6.4	$ 8.8	$ 9.8	$ 10.2	$161.4

[a] Interest payments are estimates based on Apex's existing debt, plus additional debt required to finance growth.

[b] Hightech will file a consolidated tax return after the merger. Thus, the taxes shown here are the full corporate taxes attributable to Apex's operations: there will be no additional taxes on any cash flows passed from Apex to Hightech.

[c] Some of the cash flows generated by the Apex subsidiary after the merger must be retained to finance asset replacements and growth, while some will be transferred to Hightech to pay dividends on its stock or for redeployment within the corporation. These retentions are net of any additional debt used to help finance growth.

[d]Apex's available cash flows are expected to grow at a constant 10 percent rate after 2007. The value of all post-2007 cash flows as of December 31, 2007, is estimated by use of the constant growth model to be $150.2 million:

$$V_{2007} = \frac{CF_{2008}}{k_s - g} = \frac{(\$23.2 - \$12.0)(1.10)}{0.182 - 0.10} = \$150.2 \text{ million.}$$

In the next section, we discuss the estimated 18.2 percent cost of equity. The $150.2 million is the PV at the end of 2007 of the stream of cash flows for Year 2008 and thereafter.

[e] These are the net cash flows projected to be available to Hightech by virtue of the acquisition. The cash flows could be used for dividend payments to Hightech's stockholders, to finance asset expansion in Hightech's other divisions and subsidiaries, and so on.

to the 2007 cash flow to estimate the value of all cash flows beyond 2007. (See Note d to Table 21-2.) This "terminal value" represents Apex's projected value at the end of 2007, and it is shown on Line 13.

The net cash flows shown on Line 14 would be available to Hightech's stockholders, and they are the basis of the valuation.[8] Of course, the postmerger cash flows are extremely difficult to estimate, and in a complete merger valuation, just as in a complete capital budgeting analysis, sensitivity, scenario, and simulation analyses should

---

[8] We purposely kept the cash flows relatively simple to help focus on key issues. In an actual merger valuation, the cash flows would be much more complex, normally including such items as additional capital furnished by the acquiring firm, tax loss carry-forwards, tax effects of plant and equipment valuation adjustments, and cash flows from the sale of some of the subsidiary's assets.

be conducted. Indeed, in a friendly merger the acquiring firm would send a team consisting of literally dozens of accountants, engineers, and so forth, to the target firm's headquarters. They would go over its books, estimate required maintenance expenditures, set values on assets such as real estate and petroleum reserves, and the like. Such an investigation, which is called *due diligence*, is an essential part of any merger analysis.

Estimating the Discount Rate   The bottom-line net cash flows shown on Line 14 are after interest and taxes, hence they represent equity. Therefore, they should be discounted at the cost of equity rather than at the overall cost of capital. Further, the discount rate used should reflect the riskiness of the cash flows in the table. The most appropriate discount rate is Apex's cost of equity, not that of either Hightech or the consolidated postmerger firm.

Although we will not illustrate it here, Hightech could perform a risk analysis on the Table 21-2 cash flows just as it does on any set of capital budgeting flows. Sensitivity analysis, scenario analysis, and/or Monte Carlo simulation could be used to give Hightech's management a feel for the risks involved with the acquisition. Apex is a publicly traded company, so we can assess directly its market risk. Apex's market-determined premerger beta was 1.63. Because the merger would not change Apex's capital structure or tax rate, its postmerger beta would remain at 1.63. However, if Apex's capital structure had changed, then the Hamada equation (which was discussed in Chapter 13) could have been used to determine the firm's new beta corresponding to its changed capital structure.

We use the Security Market Line to estimate Apex's postmerger cost of equity. If the risk-free rate is 10 percent and the market risk premium is 5 percent, then Apex's cost of equity, k_s, after the merger with Hightech, would be about 18.2 percent.[9]

$$k_s = k_{RF} + (RP_M)b = 10\% + (5\%)1.63 = 18.15\% \approx 18.2\%.$$

Valuing the Cash Flows   The current value of Apex's stock to Hightech is the present value of the cash flows expected from Apex, discounted at 18.2 percent (in millions of dollars):

$$V_{2002} = \frac{\$6.4}{(1.182)^1} + \frac{\$8.8}{(1.182)^2} + \frac{\$9.8}{(1.182)^3} + \frac{\$10.2}{(1.182)^4} + \frac{\$161.4}{(1.182)^5} \approx \$92.8.$$

Thus, the value of Apex's stock to Hightech is $92.8 million.

Note that in a merger analysis, the value of the target consists of the target's premerger value plus any value created by operating or financial synergies. In this example, we held the target's capital structure and tax rate constant. Therefore, the only synergies were operating synergies, and these effects were incorporated into the

---

[9] In this example, we used the Capital Asset Pricing Model to estimate Apex's cost of equity, and thus we assumed that investors require a premium for market risk only. We could have also conducted a corporate risk analysis, in which the relevant risk would be the contribution of Apex's cash flows to the total risk of the postmerger firm.

In actual merger situations among large firms, companies almost always hire an investment banker to help develop valuation estimates. For example, when General Electric acquired Utah International, GE hired Morgan Stanley to determine Utah's value. We discussed the valuation process with the Morgan Stanley analyst in charge of the appraisal, and he confirmed that they applied all of the standard procedures discussed in this chapter. Note, though, that merger analysis, like the analysis of any other complex issue, requires judgment, and people's judgments differ as to how much weight to give to different methods in any given situation.

forecasted cash flows. If there had been financial synergies, the analysis would have to be modified to reflect this added value. For example, if Apex had been operating with only 30 percent debt, and if Hightech could lower Apex's overall cost of capital by increasing the debt ratio to 50 percent, then Apex's merger value would have exceeded the $92.8 million calculated above.

Market Multiple Analysis

Market Multiple Analysis
A method of valuing a target company that applies a market-determined multiple to net income, earnings per share, sales, book value, and so forth.

The second method of valuing a target company is **market multiple analysis,** which applies a market-determined multiple to net income, earnings per share, sales, book value, or, for businesses such as cable TV or cellular telephone systems, the number of subscribers. While the DCF method applies valuation concepts in a precise manner, focusing on expected cash flows, market multiple analysis is more judgmental. To illustrate the concept, note that Apex's forecasted net income is $2.4 million in 2003, and it rises to $13.2 million in 2007, for an average of $7.7 million over the five-year forecast period. The average P/E ratio for publicly traded companies similar to Apex is 12.

 A video clip entitled "T. Boone Pickens on White Knights," which discusses mergers and takeovers, is available at Ohio State University's web site at **http://www.cob.ohio-state. edu/~fin/clips.htm**. The clip requires a QuickTime video player for either Windows or Macintosh machines (which you download for free over the Internet at **http://www.apple.com/ quicktime/**). One caveat is that the video clip is in excess of 5 MB in size and should therefore only be accessed with a rapid Internet connection.

To estimate Apex's value using the market P/E multiple approach, simply multiply its $7.7 million average net income by the market multiple of 12 to obtain the value of $7.7(12) = $92.4 million. This is the equity, or ownership, value of the firm. Note that we used the average net income over the coming five years to value Apex. The market P/E multiple of 12 is based on the current year's income of comparable companies, but Apex's current income does not reflect synergistic effects or managerial changes that will be made. By averaging future net income, we are attempting to capture the value added by Hightech to Apex's operations.

Note that measures other than net income can be used in the market multiple approach. For example, another commonly used measure is *earnings before interest, taxes, depreciation, and amortization (EBITDA)*. The procedure would be identical to that just described, except that the market multiple would be price divided by EBITDA rather than earnings per share, and this multiple would be multiplied by Apex's EBITDA.

As noted above, in some businesses such as cable TV and cellular telephone, an important element in the valuation process is the number of customers a company has. The acquirer has an idea of the cost required to obtain a new customer and the average cash flow per customer. For example, telephone companies have been paying about $2,000 per customer for cellular operators. Managed care companies such as HMOs have applied similar logic in acquisitions, basing their valuations on the number of people insured.

SETTING THE BID PRICE

Using the DCF valuation results, $92.8 million is the most Hightech could pay for Apex—if it pays more, then Hightech's own value will be diluted. On the other hand, if Hightech can get Apex for less than $92.8 million, Hightech's stockholders will gain value. Therefore, Hightech will bid something less than $92.8 million when it makes an offer for Apex.

Figure 21-1 graphs the merger situation. The $92.8 million is shown as a point on the horizontal axis, and it is the maximum price that Hightech can afford to pay. If Hightech pays less, say, $82.8 million, then its stockholders will gain $10 million from the merger, while if it pays more, its stockholders will lose. What we have, then,

FIGURE 21-1

A View of Merger Analysis (Millions of Dollars)

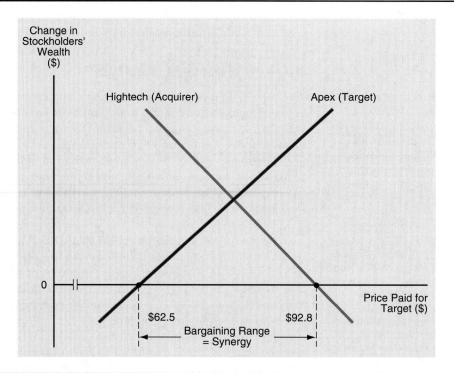

is a 45-degree line that cuts the X axis at $92.8 million, and that line shows how much Hightech's stockholders can expect to gain or lose at different acquisition prices.

Now consider the target company, Apex. It has 10 million shares of stock that sell for $6.25, so its value as an independent operating company is presumably $62.5 million. [In making this statement, we assume (1) that the company is being operated as well as possible by its present management, and (2) that the $6.25 market price per share does not include a "speculative merger premium" in addition to the PV of its operating cash flows.] If Apex is acquired at a price greater than $62.5 million, its stockholders will gain value, while they will lose value at any lower price. Thus, we can draw another 45-degree line, this one with an upward slope, to show how the merger price affects Apex's stockholders.

The difference between $62.5 and $92.8 million, or $30.3 million, represents synergistic benefits expected from the merger. Here are some points to note:

1. If there were no synergistic benefits, the maximum bid would be equal to the current value of the target company. The greater the synergistic gains, the greater the gap between the target's current price and the maximum the acquiring company could pay.

2. The greater the synergistic gains, the more likely a merger is to be consummated.

3. The issue of how to divide the synergistic benefits is critically important. Obviously, both parties will want to get as much as possible. In our example, if

Apex's management knew the maximum price that Hightech could pay, it would argue for a price close to $92.8 million. Hightech, on the other hand, would try to get Apex at a price as close to $62.5 million as possible.

4. Where, within the $62.5 to $92.8 million range, will the actual price be set? The answer depends on a number of factors, including whether Hightech offers to pay with cash or securities, the negotiating skills of the two management teams, and, most importantly, the bargaining positions of the two parties as determined by fundamental economic conditions. To illustrate the latter point, suppose there are many companies similar to Apex that Hightech could acquire, but no company other than Hightech that could gain synergies by acquiring Apex. In this case, Hightech would probably make a relatively low, take-it-or-leave-it offer, and Apex would probably take it because some gain is better than none. On the other hand, if Apex has some unique technology or other asset that many companies want, then once Hightech announces its offer, others will probably make competing bids, and the final price will probably be close to or even above $92.8 million. A price above $92.8 million would presumably be paid by some other company that had a better synergistic fit or, perhaps, whose management was more optimistic about Apex's cash flow potential. In Figure 21-1, this situation would be represented by a line parallel to that for Hightech but shifted to the right of the Hightech line.

5. Hightech would, of course, want to keep its maximum bid secret, and it would plan its bidding strategy carefully and consistently with the situation. If it thought that other bidders would emerge, or that Apex's management might resist in order to preserve their jobs, it might make a high "preemptive" bid in hopes of scaring off competing bids and/or management resistance. On the other hand, it might make a low-ball bid in hopes of "stealing" the company.

We will have more to say about these points in the sections that follow, and you should keep Figure 21-1 in mind as you go through the rest of the chapter.

POSTMERGER CONTROL

The employment/control situation is often of vital interest in a merger analysis. First, consider the situation in which a small, owner-managed firm sells out to a larger concern. The owner-manager may be anxious to retain a high-status position, and he or she may also have developed a camaraderie with the employees and thus be concerned about their retention after the merger. If so, these points would be stressed during the merger negotiations.[10] When a publicly owned firm that is not owned by

---

[10] The acquiring firm may also be concerned about this point, especially if the target firm's management is quite good. Indeed, a condition of the merger may be that the management team agree to stay on for a period such as five years after the merger. In this case, the price paid may be contingent on the acquired firm's performance subsequent to the merger. For example, when International Holdings acquired Walker Products, the price paid was an immediate 100,000 shares of International Holdings stock worth $63 per share plus an additional 30,000 shares each year for the next three years, provided Walker Products earned at least $1 million during each of these years. Since Walker's managers owned the stock and would receive the bonus, they had a strong incentive to stay on and help the firm meet its targets.

Finally, if the managers of the target company are highly competent but do not wish to remain on after the merger, the acquiring firm may build into the merger contract a noncompete agreement with the old management. Typically, the acquired firm's principal officers must agree not to affiliate with a new business that is competitive with the one they sold for a specified period, say, five years. Such agreements are especially important with service-oriented businesses.

WHEN YOU MERGE YOU COMBINE MORE THAN JUST FINANCIAL STATEMENTS

When corporations merge, they combine more than just their financial statements. Mergers bring together two organizations with different histories and corporate cultures. Deals that look good on paper can fail if the individuals involved are unwilling or unable to work together to generate the potential synergies. Consequently, when analyzing a potential merger, it is important to determine whether the two companies are compatible.

Many deals fall apart because, during the "due diligence" phase, synergistic benefits are revealed to be less than was originally anticipated, so there is little economic rationale for the merger. Other negotiations break off because the two parties cannot agree on the price to be paid for the acquired firm's stock. In addition, merger talks often collapse because of "social issues." These social issues include both the "chemistry" of the companies and their personnel and such basic issues as these: What will be the name of the combined company? Where will headquarters be located? And, most important: Who will run the combined company? Robert Kindler, a partner at Cravath, Swaine & Moore, a prominent New York law firm that spe-

cializes in mergers, summarizes the importance of these issues as follows: "Even transactions that make absolute economic sense don't happen unless the social issues work."

Investment bankers, lawyers, and other professionals state that mergers tend to be most successful if there is a clear and well-arranged plan spelling out who will run the company. This issue is straightforward if one firm is clearly dominant and is acquiring the other. However, in cases where there is "a merger of equals," senior personnel issues often become sticky. This situation is made considerably easier if one of the chief executives is at or near the retirement age.

Some analysts believe that social issues often play too large a role, derailing mergers that should take place. In other cases where a merger occurs, concerns about social issues preclude managers from undertaking the necessary changes — like laying off redundant staff—for the deal to benefit shareholders.

SOURCE: "In Many Merger Deals, Ego and Pride Play Big Roles in Which Way Talks Go," *The Wall Street Journal,* August 22, 1996, C1. Reprinted by permission of *The Wall Street Journal,* Copyright © 2002 Dow Jones & Company, Inc. All Rights Reserved Worldwide.

its managers is merged into another company, the acquired firm's managers will be worried about their postmerger positions. If the acquiring firm agrees to retain the old management, then management may be willing to support the merger and to recommend its acceptance to the stockholders. If the old management is to be removed, then it will probably resist the merger.[11]

SELF-TEST QUESTIONS

What is the difference between an operating merger and a financial merger?

Describe the way postmerger cash flows are estimated in a DCF analysis.

What is the basis for the discount rate in a DCF analysis? Describe how this rate might be estimated.

Describe the market multiple approach.

What are some factors that acquiring firms consider when they set a bid price?

How do control issues affect mergers?

---

[11] Managements of firms that are thought to be attractive merger candidates often arrange *golden parachutes* for themselves. Golden parachutes are extremely lucrative retirement plans that take effect if a merger is consummated. Thus, when Bendix was acquired by Allied, Bill Agee, Bendix's chairman, "pulled the ripcord of his golden parachute" and walked away with $4 million. If a golden parachute is large enough, it can also function as a poison pill—for example, where the president of a firm worth $10 million would have to be paid $8 million if the firm is acquired, this will prevent a takeover. Stockholders are increasingly resisting such arrangements, but some still exist.

In a merger, the acquiring firm can either buy the target's assets or buy shares of stock directly from the target's shareholders. If the offer is for the target's assets, the target's board of directors will make a recommendation to the shareholders, who will vote either to accept or reject the offer. If they accept the offer, the payment goes directly to the target corporation, which pays off any debt not assumed by the acquiring firm, pays any corporate taxes that are due, and then distributes the remainder of the payment to the shareholders, often in the form of a liquidating dividend. In this situation, the target firm is usually dissolved and no longer continues to exist as a separate legal entity, although its assets and work force may continue to function as a division or a wholly owned subsidiary of the acquiring firm. The acquisition of assets is a very common form of a takeover for small and medium-sized firms, especially those that are not publicly traded. A major advantage of this method relative to the acquisition of the target's stock is that the acquiring firm simply acquires assets and is not saddled with any hidden liabilities. In contrast, if the acquiring firm buys the target's stock, then it is responsible for any legal contingencies against the target, even for those that might have occurred prior to the takeover.

An offer for a target's stock rather than its assets can be made either directly to the shareholders, as is typical in a hostile takeover, or indirectly through the board of directors, who in a friendly deal make a recommendation to the shareholders to accept the offer. In a successful offer, the acquiring firm will end up owning a controlling interest, or perhaps even all of the target's stock. Sometimes the target retains its identity as a separate legal entity and is operated as a subsidiary of the acquiring firm, and sometimes its corporate status is dissolved and it is operated as one of the acquiring firm's divisions.

The payment offered by the acquiring firm can be in the form of cash, stock of the acquiring firm, debt of the acquiring firm, or some combination. The structure of the bid affects (1) the capital structure of the postmerger firm, (2) the tax treatment of both the acquiring firm and the target's stockholders, (3) the ability of the target firm's stockholders to benefit from future merger-related gains, and (4) the types of federal and state regulations to which the acquiring firm will be subjected. In this section, we discuss how acquiring firms structure their offers.

The tax consequences of the merger depend on whether it is classified as a *taxable offer* or a *nontaxable offer*.[12] In general, a nontaxable offer is one in which the form of payment is predominately stock, although the application of this simple principle is much more complicated in practice. The Internal Revenue Code views a mostly stock merger as an exchange rather than a sale, making it a nontaxable event. However, if the offer includes a significant amount of cash or bonds, then the IRS views it as a sale, and it is a taxable transaction, just like any other sale.

In a nontaxable deal, target shareholders who receive shares of the acquiring company's stock do not have to pay any taxes at the time of the merger. When they eventually sell their stock in the acquiring company, they must pay a tax on the gain. The amount of the gain is the sales price of their stock in the acquiring company

---

[12] For more details, see J. Fred Weston, Juan A. Siu, and Brian A. Johnson, *Takeovers, Restructuring, & Corporate Governance* (Upper Saddle River, NJ: Prentice-Hall, 2001), especially Chapter 4. Also see Kenneth E. Anderson, Thomas R. Pope, and John L. Kramer, eds., *Prentice Hall's Federal Taxation: Corporations, Partnerships, Estates, and Trusts*, 2001 edition (Upper Saddle River, NJ: Prentice-Hall, 2001), especially Chapter 7.

minus the price at which they purchased their original stock in the target company.[13] In a taxable offer, the gain between the offer price and the original purchase price of the target stock is taxed in the year of the merger.[14]

All other things equal, stockholders prefer nontaxable offers, since they may then postpone taxes on their gains. Furthermore, if the target firm's stockholders receive stock, they will benefit from any synergistic gains produced by the merger. Most target shareholders are thus willing to give up their stock for a lower price in a nontaxable offer than in a taxable one. As a result, one might expect nontaxable bids to dominate. However, this is not the case—roughly half of all mergers have been taxable. The reason for this is explained in the following paragraphs.

The form of the payment also has tax consequences for the acquiring and target firms. To illustrate, consider the following situation. The target firm has assets with a book value of $100 million, but these assets have an appraised value of $150 million. The offer by the acquiring firm is worth $225 million. If it is a nontaxable offer, then after the merger the acquiring firm simply adds the $100 million book value of the target's assets to its own assets and continues to depreciate them according to their previous depreciation schedules. To keep the example simple, we assume the target has no debt.

The situation is more complicated for a taxable offer, and the treatment is different depending on whether the offer is for the target's assets or for its stock. If the acquiring firm offers $225 million for the target's assets, then the target firm must pay a tax on the gain of $225 − $100 = $125 million. Assuming a corporate tax rate of 40 percent, this tax is 0.40($125) = $50 million. This leaves the target with $225 − $50 = $175 million to distribute to its shareholders upon liquidation. Adding insult to injury, the target's shareholders must also pay individual taxes on any of their own gains.[15] This is truly a taxable transaction, with taxes assessed at both the corporate and individual levels! In contrast to the tax disadvantages for the target and its shareholders, the acquiring firm receives two major tax advantages. First, it records the acquired assets at their appraised value and depreciates them accordingly. Thus, it will depreciate $150 million of assets in this taxable transaction versus only $100 million in a nontaxable transaction. Second, it will create $75 million in a new asset account called "goodwill," which is the difference between the purchase price of $225 million and the appraised value of $150 million. Tax laws that took effect in 1993 permit companies to amortize this goodwill over 15 years using the straight-line method and deduct the amortization from taxable income. The net effect is that the full purchase price of $225 million can be depreciated or amortized in a taxable merger versus only the original book value of $100 million in a nontaxable transaction.

Now suppose the acquiring firm offers $225 million for the target's stock in a taxable offer. After completing the merger, the acquiring firm must choose between two alternative tax treatments. Under the first alternative, it will record the assets at their book value of $100 million and continue depreciating them using their current schedules. This treatment does not create any goodwill. Under the second alternative, it will record the assets at their appraised value of $150 million and create $75 million

---

[13] This is a capital gain if it has been at least one year since they purchased their original stock in the target.

[14] Even in nontaxable deals, taxes must be paid in the year of the merger by any stockholders who receive cash.

[15] Our example assumes that the target is a publicly owned firm, which means that it must be a "C corporation" for tax purposes. However, if it is privately held, it might be an "S corporation," in which case only the stockholders would be taxed. This helps smaller firms use mergers as an exit strategy.

of goodwill. As described earlier for the asset purchase, this allows the acquiring firm to effectively depreciate the entire purchase price of $225 million for tax purposes. However, there will also be an immediate tax liability on the $125 million gain, just as when the firm purchased assets. Therefore, many companies choose not to mark up the assets.

If you think this is complicated, you are right! At this point you should know enough to talk with specialized accountants and lawyers, or be ready to delve into tax accounting texts, but merger taxation is too complex a subject to be covered thoroughly in a general finance textbook.

Securities laws also have an effect on the construction of the offer. The SEC has oversight over the issuance of new securities, including stock or debt issued in connection with a merger. Therefore, whenever a corporation bids for control of another firm through the exchange of equity or debt, the entire process must take place under the scrutiny of the Securities and Exchange Commission. The time required for such reviews allows target management to implement defensive tactics and other firms to make competing offers, and as a result, nearly all hostile tender offers are for cash rather than securities.

SELF-TEST QUESTIONS

What are some alternative ways of structuring takeover bids?

How do taxes influence the payment structure?

How do securities laws affect the payment structure?

FINANCIAL REPORTING FOR MERGERS

Although a detailed discussion of accounting is best left to accounting courses, the accounting implications of mergers cannot be ignored. Until recently, there were two possible ways to account for mergers: (1) as a pooling of interests or (2) as a purchase. However, beginning in 2002, managers were no longer permitted to use the pooling of interests method. Many corporate managers and their investment bankers argued vehemently against this change in policy because the accounting treatment has a significant effect on the postmerger reported earnings, and reported earnings influence stock prices. To better understand why these accounting issues have been so controversial, it is useful to quickly review the differences between the two methods.

POOLING OF INTERESTS ACCOUNTING

Pooling of Interests
A merger among equals, hence the consolidated balance sheet is constructed by simply adding together the balance sheets of the merged companies.

A **pooling of interests** is, in theory, a merger among equals, and hence the consolidated balance sheet is constructed by simply adding together the balance sheets of the merged companies. The top section of Table 21-3 shows the essential elements of the consolidated balance sheet after Firms A and B have merged under a pooling of interests. This final balance sheet holds regardless of how many shares Firm A (the survivor) gave up to acquire Firm B. (In a pooling, shares, not cash, must be exchanged.)

TABLE 21-3   Accounting for Mergers: A Acquires B

POOLING OF INTERESTS

	FIRM A	FIRM B	POSTMERGER: FIRM A
Current assets	$ 50	$25	$ 75
Fixed assets	50	25	75
Total assets	$100	$50	$150
Debt	$ 40	$20	$ 60
Common equity	60	30	90
Total claims	$100	$50	$150

PURCHASE ACCOUNTING

			POSTMERGER: FIRM A		
	FIRM A (1)	FIRM B (2)	$20 PAID[a] (3)	$30 PAID[a] (4)	$50 PAID[a] (5)
Current assets	$ 50	$25	$ 75	$ 75	$ 80[c]
Fixed assets	50	25	65[b]	75	80[c]
Goodwill[d]	0	0	0	0	10[d]
Total assets	$100	$50	$140	$150	$170
Debt	$ 40	$20	$ 60	$ 60	$ 60
Equity	60	30	80[e]	90	110[f]
Total claims	$100	$50	$140	$150	$170

[a] The price paid is the *net asset value,* that is, total assets minus debt.

[b] Here we assume that Firm B's fixed assets are written down from $25 to $15 before constructing the consolidated balance sheet.

[c] Here we assume that Firm B's current and fixed assets are both increased to $30.

[d] *Goodwill* refers to the excess paid for a firm above the appraised value of the physical assets and intangible assets purchased.

[e] Firm B's common equity is reduced by $10 prior to consolidation to reflect the fixed asset write-off.

[f] Firm B's equity is increased to $50 to reflect the above-book purchase price.

PURCHASE ACCOUNTING

The lower section of Table 21-3, which uses the same data as for the pooled companies, illustrates purchase accounting. Here Firm A is assumed to have "bought" Firm B in much the same way it would buy any capital asset, paying for it with cash, debt, or stock of the acquiring company. If the price paid is exactly equal to the acquired firm's *net asset value*, which is defined as its total assets minus its liabilities, then the consolidated balance sheet will be identical to that under pooling. Otherwise, there is an important difference. If the price paid exceeds the net asset value, then asset values will be increased to reflect the price actually paid, whereas if the price paid is less than the net asset value, then assets must be written down when preparing the consolidated balance sheet.

Note that Firm B's net asset value is $30, which is also its reported common equity value. This $30 book value could be equal to the market value (which is determined by the firm's earning power), but book value could also be more or less than the market value. Three situations are considered in the lower section of Table 21-3. First, in Column 3 we assume that Firm A gives cash or stock worth $20 for Firm B. Thus, B's assets as reported on its balance sheet were overvalued, and A pays less than B's net asset value. The overvaluation could be in either fixed or current assets; an appraisal would be made but we assume that it is fixed assets that are overvalued. Accordingly, we reduce B's fixed assets and also its common equity by $10 before constructing the consolidated balance sheet shown in Column 3. Next, in Column 4, we assume that A pays exactly the net asset value for B. In this case, pooling and purchase accounting would produce identical balance sheets.

Finally, in Column 5 we assume that A pays more than the net asset value for B: $50 is paid for $30 of net assets. This excess is assumed to be partly attributable to undervalued assets (land, buildings, machinery, and inventories), so to reflect this undervaluation, current and fixed assets are each increased by $5. In addition, we assume that $10 of the $20 excess of market value over book value is due to a superior sales organization, or some other intangible factor, and we post this excess as **goodwill.** B's common equity is increased by $20, the sum of the increases in current and fixed assets plus goodwill, and this markup is also reflected in A's postmerger equity account.[16]

Goodwill
Refers to the excess paid for a firm above the appraised value of the physical and intangible assets purchased.

INCOME STATEMENT EFFECTS

Significant differences can also arise in reported profits under the two accounting methods. If asset values are increased, as they often are under a purchase, this must be reflected in higher depreciation charges (and also in a higher cost of goods sold if inventories are written up). This, in turn, will further reduce reported profits. Also, goodwill represents the excess paid for a firm over its adjusted net asset value. This excess is presumably paid because of the acquired firm's superior earning power.

Prior to the recent accounting change, the goodwill associated with a purchase had to be written off, or "amortized" (for financial statement purposes in accordance with GAAP), over a time period that corresponded to the expected life of the superior earning power, but in no case more than 40 years. In many instances these goodwill charges were quite large, and they depressed earnings for a number of years. This explains why most managers preferred pooling to purchase accounting, and why they objected so strongly to the recent guidelines that forbid pooling accounting.

However, as part of a compromise designed to soften the blow of banning pooling, companies no longer have to amortize goodwill as before. Instead, under the new guidelines, each year the company must conduct an "impairment" test, and goodwill must be written down only if the test indicates that there has been an "impairment" of value, that is, if the superior earning power the acquired assets were supposed to provide are in fact providing less earning power than had been expected. This new change will obviously benefit companies that have completed successful mergers, but in cases where shareholder value has fallen after a merger, companies

---

[16] This example assumes that additional debt was not issued to help finance the acquisition. If the acquisition were totally debt financed, the postmerger balance sheet would show increases in the debt account rather than increases in the equity account. If it were financed by a mix of debt and equity, both accounts would be changed.

will be forced to write off part of their goodwill. For example, some analysts believe that this impairment test will force AOL Time Warner to write off tens of billions of dollars of goodwill because the merger has failed to produce the expected benefits.

SELF-TEST QUESTIONS

What is the difference between pooling of interests and purchase accounting for mergers?

What is goodwill? What impact does goodwill have on the firm's balance sheet?

For financial reporting purposes, how does the treatment of goodwill on the income statement differ between the new standard for purchase accounting and the old one?

ANALYSIS FOR A "TRUE CONSOLIDATION"

Most of our analysis in the preceding sections assumed that one firm plans to acquire another. However, in many situations it is hard to identify an "acquirer" and a "target"—the merger appears to be a true "merger of equals," as was the case with the Citicorp/Travelers and NationsBank/BankAmerica mergers. In such cases, how is the analysis handled? Here are the steps one would go through:

1. Develop pro forma financial statements for the consolidated corporation. What are the projected sales, costs, interest charges, taxes, net income, and free cash flows, assuming the two firms merge? How will the consolidated balance sheets look? Synergies are generally expected to be important, so they must be worked into the pro forma income statements. If antitrust considerations require the disposal of certain assets (say, some branches if two banks with overlapping service areas merge), that must be reflected in the projected statements. The key set of figures is the projected consolidated free cash flows available to stockholders.

2. Estimate the new company's cost of equity, and use that rate to discount the equity flows of the consolidated company. This is the value of the equity of the consolidated company.

3. Decide how to allocate the new company's stock between the two sets of old stockholders. Normally, one would expect the consolidated value to exceed the sum of the pre-announcement values of the two companies because of synergy. For example, Company A might have had a premerger equity value of $10 billion, found as (Number of shares)(Price per share), and Company B might have had a premerger value of $15 billion. If the postmerger value of new Company AB is estimated to be $30 billion, then that value must be allocated. Company A's stockholders will have to receive enough shares to cause its stockholders to have a projected value of at least $10 billion, and Company B's stockholders will have to receive at least $15 billion. But how will the remaining $5 billion of synergistic-induced value be divided?

This is a key issue, and one that the two management groups will negotiate long and hard over. There is no rule, or formula, that can be applied, but one basis for the allocation is the relative pre-announcement values of the two companies. For example, in our hypothetical merger of A and B to form AB, the companies might agree to give $10/$25 = 40% of the new stock to A's stockholders and 60% to B's stockholders. Unless a case could be made for giving a higher percentage of the shares to one of the companies because it was responsible for more of the synergistic value, then the premerger value proportions would seem to be a "fair" solution. In any event, the premerger proportions will probably be given the greatest weight in reaching the final decision.

It should also be noted that control of the consolidated company is always an issue in mergers such as the Citicorp/Travelers and NationsBank/BankAmerica deals. Generally, the companies hold a press conference and announce that the CEO of one firm will be chairman of the new company, that the other CEO will be president, that the new board will consist of directors from both old boards, and that power will be shared. With huge mergers such as those we have been seeing lately, there is plenty of power to be shared.

SELF-TEST QUESTIONS

How does merger analysis differ in the case of a large company acquiring a smaller one versus a "true merger of equals"?

Do you think the same guidelines for allocating synergistic gains would be used in both types of mergers?

THE ROLE OF INVESTMENT BANKERS

Investment bankers are involved with mergers in a number of ways: (1) they help arrange mergers, (2) they help target companies develop and implement defensive tactics, (3) they help value target companies, (4) they help finance mergers, and (5) they invest in the stocks of potential merger candidates. These merger-related activities have been quite profitable. For example, the investment bankers and lawyers who arranged the Campeau-Federated merger earned fees of about $83 million — First Boston and Wasserstein Perella split $29 million from Campeau, and Goldman Sachs, Hellman & Friedman, and Shearson Lehman Hutton divided up $54 million for representing Federated. No wonder investment banking houses are able to make top offers to finance graduates!

ARRANGING MERGERS

The major investment banking firms have merger and acquisition groups that operate within their corporate finance departments. (Corporate finance departments offer advice, as opposed to underwriting or brokerage services, to business firms.) Members of these groups identify firms with excess cash that might want to buy other firms, companies that might be willing to be bought, and firms that might, for a number of reasons, be attractive to others. Also, if an oil company, for instance, decided to expand into coal mining, then it might enlist the aid of an investment banker to help it acquire a coal company. Similarly, dissident stockholders of firms with poor track records might work with investment bankers to oust management by helping to arrange a merger. Investment bankers are reported to have offered packages of financing to corporate raiders, where the package includes both designing the securities to be used in the tender offer, plus lining up people and firms who will buy the target firm's stock now and then tender it once the final offer is made.

Investment bankers have occasionally taken illegal actions in the merger arena. For one thing, they are reported to have *parked stock*—purchasing it for a raider under a guaranteed buy-back agreement—to help the raider de facto accumulate more than 5 percent of the target's stock without disclosing the position. People have gone to jail for this.

DEVELOPING DEFENSIVE TACTICS

Target firms that do not want to be acquired generally enlist the help of an investment banking firm, along with a law firm that specializes in mergers. Defenses include such tactics as (1) changing the bylaws so that only one-third of the directors are elected each year and/or so that a 75 percent approval (a *super-majority*) versus a simple majority is required to approve a merger; (2) trying to convince the target firm's stockholders that the price being offered is too low; (3) raising antitrust issues in the hope that the Justice Department will intervene; (4) repurchasing stock in the open market in an effort to push the price above that being offered by the potential acquirer; (5) getting a **white knight** who is acceptable to the target firm's management to compete with the potential acquirer; (6) getting a **white squire** who is friendly to current management to buy enough of the target firm's shares to block the merger; and (7) taking a poison pill, as described next.

Poison pills—which occasionally really do amount to committing economic suicide to avoid a takeover—are such tactics as borrowing on terms that require immediate repayment of all loans if the firm is acquired, selling off at bargain prices the assets that originally made the firm a desirable target, granting such lucrative **golden parachutes** to their executives that the cash drain from these payments would render the merger infeasible, and planning defensive mergers which would leave the firm with new assets of questionable value and a huge debt load. Currently, the most popular poison pill is for a company to give its stockholders *stock purchase rights* that allow them to buy at half-price the stock of an acquiring firm, should the firm be acquired. The blatant use of poison pills is constrained by directors' awareness that excessive use could trigger personal suits by stockholders against directors who voted for them, and, perhaps in the near future, by laws that would further limit management's use of pills. Still, investment bankers and antitakeover lawyers are busy thinking up new poison pill formulas, and others are just as busy trying to come up with antidotes.[17]

Another takeover defense that is being used is the employee stock ownership plan (ESOP). ESOPs are designed to give lower-level employees an ownership stake in the firm, and current tax laws provide generous incentives for companies to establish such plans and fund them with the firm's common stock. Also, Procter & Gamble recently set up an ESOP that, along with an existing profit-sharing plan, eventually will give employees a 20 percent ownership stake in the company. Since the trustees of ESOPs generally support current management in any takeover attempt, and since up to 85 percent of the votes is often required to complete a merger, an ESOP can provide an effective defense against a hostile tender offer. Procter & Gamble stated that its ESOP was designed primarily to lower its costs by utilizing the plan's tax advantages and to improve employees' retirement security. However, the company also noted that the ESOP would strengthen its defenses against a takeover.

White Knight
A company that is acceptable to the management of a firm under threat of a hostile takeover and that will compete with the potential acquirer.

White Squire
An individual or company who is friendly to current management and will buy enough of the target firm's shares to block a hostile takeover.

Poison Pill
An action that will seriously hurt a company if it is acquired by another.

Golden Parachutes
Large payments made to the managers of a firm if it is acquired.

---

[17] It has become extremely difficult and expensive for companies to buy "directors' insurance," which protects the board from such contingencies as stockholders' suits, and even when insurance is available it often does not pay for losses if the directors have not exercised due caution and judgment. This exposure is making directors extremely leery of actions that might trigger stockholder suits.

ESTABLISHING A FAIR VALUE

If a friendly merger is being worked out between two firms' managements, it is important to document that the agreed-upon price is a fair one; otherwise, the stockholders of either company may sue to block the merger. Therefore, in most large mergers each side will hire an investment banking firm to evaluate the target company and to help establish the fair price. For example, General Electric employed Morgan Stanley to determine a fair price for Utah International, as did Royal Dutch to help establish the price it paid for Shell Oil. Even if the merger is not friendly, investment bankers may still be asked to help establish a price. If a surprise tender offer is to be made, the acquiring firm will want to know the lowest price at which it might be able to acquire the stock, while the target firm may seek help in "proving" that the price being offered is too low.[18]

FINANCING MERGERS

Many mergers are financed with the acquiring company's excess cash. However, if the acquiring company has no excess cash, it will require a source of funds. Perhaps the single most important factor behind the 1980s merger wave was the development of junk bonds for use in financing acquisitions.

Drexel Burnham Lambert was the primary developer of junk bonds, defined as bonds rated below investment grade (BBB/Baa). Prior to Drexel's actions, it was almost impossible to sell low-grade bonds to raise new capital. Drexel then pioneered a procedure under which a target firm's situation would be appraised very closely, and a cash flow projection similar to that in Table 21-2 (but much more detailed) would be developed.

With the cash flows having been forecasted, Drexel's analysts would figure out a debt structure—amount of debt, maturity structure, and interest rate—that could be serviced by the cash flows. With this information, Drexel's junk bond people, operating out of Beverly Hills, would approach financial institutions (savings and loans, insurance companies, pension funds, and mutual funds) with a financing plan, and they would offer a rate of return several percentage points above the rate on more conservative investments. Drexel's early deals worked out well, and the institutions that bought the bonds were quite pleased. These results enabled Drexel to expand its network of investors, which increased its ability to finance larger and larger mergers. T. Boone Pickens, who went after Phillips, Texaco, and several other oil giants, was an early Drexel customer, as was Ted Turner.

To be successful in the mergers and acquisitions (M&A) business, an investment banker must be able to offer a financing package to clients, whether they are acquirers who need capital to take over companies or target companies trying to finance stock repurchase plans or other defenses against takeovers. Drexel was the leading player in the merger financing game during the 1980s, but since Drexel's bankruptcy

---

[18] Such investigations must obviously be done in secret, for if someone knew that Company A was thinking of offering, say, $50 per share for Company T, which was currently selling at $35 per share, then huge profits could be made. One of the biggest scandals to hit Wall Street was the disclosure that Ivan Boesky was buying information from Dennis Levine, a senior member of the investment banking house of Drexel Burnham Lambert, about target companies that Drexel was analyzing for others. Purchases based on such insider information would, of course, raise the prices of the stocks and thus force Drexel's clients to pay more than they otherwise would have had to pay. Levine and Boesky, among others, went to jail for their improper use of insider information.

Merrill Lynch, Morgan Stanley Dean Witter, Salomon Smith Barney, and others are all vying for the title.

ARBITRAGE OPERATIONS

Arbitrage
The simultaneous buying and selling of the same commodity or security in two different markets at different prices, and pocketing a risk-free return.

Arbitrage generally means simultaneously buying and selling the same commodity or security in two different markets at different prices, and pocketing a risk-free return. However, the major brokerage houses, as well as some wealthy private investors, are engaged in a different type of arbitrage called *risk arbitrage*. The *arbitrageurs*, or "arbs," speculate in the stocks of companies that are likely takeover targets. Vast amounts of capital are required to speculate in a large number of securities and thus reduce risk, and also to make money on narrow spreads. However, the large investment bankers have the wherewithal to play the game. To be successful, arbs need to be able to sniff out likely targets, assess the probability of offers reaching fruition, and move in and out of the market quickly and with low transactions costs.

The risk arbitrage business has been rocked by insider trading scandals. Indeed, the most famous arb of all, Ivan Boesky, was caught buying inside information from executives of some leading investment banking houses and law firms. The Boesky affair slowed down risk arbitrage activity.

SELF-TEST QUESTIONS

What are some defensive tactics that firms can use to resist hostile takeovers?

What role did junk bonds play in the merger wave of the 1980s?

What is the difference between pure arbitrage and risk arbitrage?

WHO WINS: THE EMPIRICAL EVIDENCE

All the recent merger activity has raised two questions: (1) Do corporate acquisitions create value, and, (2) if so, how is the value shared between the parties?

Most researchers agree that takeovers increase the wealth of the shareholders of target firms, for otherwise they would not agree to the offer. However, there is a debate as to whether mergers benefit the acquiring firm's shareholders. In particular, managements of acquiring firms may be motivated by factors other than shareholder wealth maximization. For example, they may want to merge merely to increase the size of the corporations they manage, because increased size usually brings larger salaries plus job security, perquisites, power, and prestige.

The validity of the competing views on who gains from corporate acquisitions can be tested by examining the stock price changes that occur around the time of a merger or takeover announcement. Changes in the stock prices of the acquiring and target firms represent market participants' beliefs about the value created by the merger, and about how that value will be divided between the target and acquiring firms' shareholders. So, examining a large sample of stock price movements can shed light on the issue of who gains from mergers.

One cannot simply examine stock prices around merger announcement dates, because other factors influence stock prices. For example, if a merger was announced on a day when the entire market advanced, the fact that the target firm's price rose would not necessarily signify that the merger was expected to create value. Hence, studies examine *abnormal returns* associated with merger announcements, where abnormal returns are defined as that part of a stock price change caused by factors other than changes in the general stock market.

Many studies have examined both acquiring and target firms' stock price responses to mergers and tender offers.[19] Jointly, these studies have covered nearly every acquisition involving publicly traded firms from the early 1960s to the present, and they are remarkably consistent in their results: on average, the stock prices of target firms increase by about 30 percent in hostile tender offers, while in friendly mergers the average increase is about 20 percent. However, for both hostile and friendly deals, the stock prices of acquiring firms, on average, remain constant. Thus, the evidence strongly indicates (1) that acquisitions do create value, but (2) that shareholders of target firms reap virtually all the benefits.

In hindsight, these results are not too surprising. First, target firm's shareholders can always say no, so they are in the driver's seat. Second, takeovers are a competitive game, so if one potential acquiring firm does not offer full value for a potential target, then another firm will generally jump in with a higher bid. Finally, managements of acquiring firms might well be willing to give up all the value created by the merger, because the merger would enhance the acquiring managers' personal positions without harming their shareholders.

It has also been argued that acquisitions may increase shareholder wealth at the expense of bondholders—in particular, concern has been expressed that leveraged buyouts dilute the claims of bondholders. Specific instances can be cited in which bonds were downgraded and bondholders did suffer losses, sometimes quite large ones, as a direct result of an acquisition. However, most studies find no evidence to support the contention that bondholders on average lose in corporate acquisitions.

SELF-TEST QUESTIONS

Explain how researchers can study the effects of mergers on shareholder wealth.

Do mergers create value? If so, who profits from this value?

Do the research results discussed in this section seem logical? Explain.

CORPORATE ALLIANCES

Corporate, or Strategic, Alliance
A cooperative deal that stops short of a merger.

Mergers are one way for two companies to join forces, but many companies are striking cooperative deals, called **corporate,** or **strategic, alliances,** which stop far short of merging. Whereas mergers combine all of the assets of the firms involved, as well as their ownership and managerial expertise, alliances allow firms to create combinations that focus on specific business lines that offer the most potential synergies. These alliances take many forms, from simple marketing agreements to joint ownership of worldwide operations.

---

[19] For an excellent summary of the effects of mergers on value, see Michael C. Jensen and Richard S. Ruback, "The Market for Corporate Control: The Scientific Evidence," *Journal of Financial Economics*, April 1983, 5–50.

Joint Venture
A corporate alliance in which two or more independent companies combine their resources to achieve a specific, limited objective.

One form of corporate alliance is the **joint venture,** in which parts of companies are joined to achieve specific, limited objectives.[20] A joint venture is controlled by a management team consisting of representatives of the two (or more) parent companies. Joint ventures have been used often by U.S., Japanese, and European firms to share technology and/or marketing expertise. For example, Whirlpool announced a joint venture with the Dutch electronics giant Philips to produce appliances under Philips's brand names in five European countries. By joining with their foreign counterparts, U.S. firms are attempting to gain a stronger foothold in Europe. Although alliances are new to some firms, they are established practices to others. For example, Corning Glass now obtains over half of its profits from 23 joint ventures, two-thirds of them with foreign companies representing almost all of Europe, as well as Japan, China, South Korea, and Australia.

SELF-TEST QUESTIONS

What is the difference between a merger and a corporate alliance?

What is a joint venture? Give some reasons why joint ventures may be advantageous to the parties involved.

LEVERAGED BUYOUTS

Leveraged Buyout (LBO)
A situation in which a small group of investors (which usually includes the firm's managers) borrows heavily to buy all the shares of a company.

In a **leveraged buyout (LBO)** a small group of investors, usually including current management, acquires a firm in a transaction financed largely by debt. The debt is serviced with funds generated by the acquired company's operations and, often, by the sale of some of its assets. Sometimes, the acquiring group plans to run the acquired company for a number of years, boost its sales and profits, and then take it public again as a stronger company. In other instances, the LBO firm plans to sell off divisions to other firms that can gain synergies. In either case, the acquiring group expects to make a substantial profit from the LBO, but the inherent risks are great due to the heavy use of financial leverage. To illustrate the profit potential, Kohlberg Kravis Roberts & Company (KKR), a leading LBO specialist firm, averaged a spectacular 50 percent annual return on its LBO investments during the 1980s. However, strong stock prices for target firms have dampened the returns on LBO investments, so recent activity has been slower than in its heyday of the 1980s.

A good example of an LBO was KKR's buyout of RJR Nabisco. RJR, a leading producer of tobacco and food products with brands such as Winston, Camel, Planters, Ritz, Oreo, and Del Monte, was trading at about $55 a share in October 1988. Then, F. Ross Johnson, the company's chairman and CEO, announced a $75-a-share, or $17.6 billion, offer to outside stockholders in a plan to take the firm private. This deal, if completed, would have been the largest business transaction up to that time. After the announcement, RJR's stock price soared to $77.25, which indicated that investors thought the final price would be even higher than Johnson's opening bid. A few days later KKR offered $90 per share, or $20.6 billion, for RJR. The battle between the two bidders raged until late November, when RJR's board accepted KKR's revised bid of cash and securities worth about $106 a share, for a total

---

[20] Cross-licensing, consortia, joint bidding, and franchising are still other ways for firms to combine resources. For more information on joint ventures, see Sanford V. Berg, Jerome Duncan, and Phillip Friedman, *Joint Venture Strategies and Corporate Innovation* (Cambridge, MA: Oelgeschlager, Gunn and Hain, 1982).

value of about $25 billion. Of course, the investment bankers' fees reflected the record size of the deal—the bankers received almost $400 million, with Drexel Burnham Lambert alone getting over $200 million. Johnson lost his job, but he walked away with a multimillion-dollar golden parachute.

KKR wasted no time in restructuring the newly private RJR. In June 1989, RJR sold its five European businesses to France's BSN for $2.5 billion. Then, in September RJR sold the tropical fruit portion of its Del Monte foods unit to Polly Peck, a London-based food company, for $875 million. In the same month, RJR sold the Del Monte canned foods business to an LBO group led by Citicorp Venture Capital for $1.48 billion. Next, in October 1990 RJR sold its Baby Ruth, Butterfinger, and Pearson candy businesses to Nestlé, a Swiss company, for $370 million. In total, RJR sold off more than $5 billion worth of businesses in 1990 to help pay down the tremendous debt taken on in the LBO. In addition to asset sales, in 1991 RJR went public again by issuing more than $1 billion in new common stock, which placed about 25 percent of the firm's common stock in public hands. Also, as the firm's credit rating improved due to the retirement of some of its debt, RJR issued about $1 billion of new debt at significantly lower rates and used the proceeds to retire even more of its high-cost debt.

The RJR Nabisco story is the classic LBO tale—a company is taken private in a highly leveraged deal, the private firm's high-cost junk debt is reduced through asset sales, and finally the company again goes public, which gives the original LBO dealmakers the opportunity to "cash out." This story, however, did not have a fairy-tale ending. When KKR finally sold the last of its RJR shares in early 1995, it made a profit of about $60 million on a $3.1 billion investment, hardly a stellar return. The best a KKR spokesman could say about the deal was that "it preserved investors' equity." The transaction was largely financed by outside investors, with KKR putting up only $126 million of the original investment. Even though the return on their investment was the same as that received by outside investors, KKR earned an additional $500 million in transactions, advisor, management, and directors' fees.

> **SELF-TEST QUESTIONS**
>
> What is an LBO?
>
> Have LBOs been profitable in recent years?
>
> What actions do companies typically take to meet the large debt burdens resulting from LBOs?
>
> How do LBOs typically affect bondholders?

DIVESTITURES

Although corporations do more buying than selling of productive facilities, a good bit of selling does occur. In this section, we briefly discuss the major types of divestitures, after which we present some recent examples and rationales for divestitures.

TYPES OF DIVESTITURES

Divestiture
The sale of some of a company's operating assets.

There are four types of **divestitures:** (1) sale of an operating unit to another firm, (2) setting up the business to be divested as a separate corporation and then "spinning it off" to the divesting firm's stockholders, (3) following the steps for a spin-off but selling only some of the shares, and (4) outright liquidation of assets.

Sale to another firm generally involves the sale of an entire division or unit, usually for cash but sometimes for stock of the acquiring firm. In a **spin-off,** the firm's existing stockholders are given new stock representing separate ownership rights in the division that was divested. The division establishes its own board of directors and officers, and it becomes a separate company. The stockholders end up owning shares of two firms instead of one, but no cash has been transferred. In a **carve-out,** a minority interest in a corporate subsidiary is sold to new shareholders, so the parent gains new equity financing yet retains control. Finally, in a **liquidation** the assets of a division are sold off piecemeal, rather than as an operating entity. To illustrate the different types of divestitures, we present some recent examples in the next section.

Spin-Off

A divestiture in which the stock of a subsidiary is given to the parent company's stockholders.

Carve-Out

A minority interest in a corporate subsidiary is sold to new shareholders, so the parent gains new equity financing yet retains control.

Liquidation

A liquidation occurs when the assets of a division are sold off piecemeal, rather than as an operating entity.

Divestiture Illustrations

1. Pepsi recently spun off its fast-food business, which included Pizza Hut, Taco Bell, and Kentucky Fried Chicken. The spun-off businesses now operate under the name Tricon Global Restaurants. Pepsi originally acquired the chains because it wanted to increase the distribution channels for its soft drinks. Over time, however, Pepsi began to realize that the soft-drink and restaurant businesses were quite different, and synergies between them were less than anticipated. The spin-off is part of Pepsi's attempt to once again focus on its core business. However, Pepsi will try to maintain these distribution channels by signing long-term contracts that ensure that Pepsi products will be sold exclusively in each of the three spun-off chains.

2. United Airlines sold its Hilton International Hotels subsidiary to Ladbroke Group PLC of Britain for $1.1 billion, and also sold its Hertz rental car unit and its Westin hotel group. The sales culminated a disastrous strategic move by United to build a full-service travel empire. The failed strategy resulted in the firing of Richard J. Ferris, the company's chairman. The move into nonairline travel-related businesses had been viewed by many analysts as a mistake, because there were few synergies to be gained. Further, analysts feared that United's managers, preoccupied by running hotels and rental car companies, would not maintain the company's focus in the highly competitive airline industry. The funds raised by the divestitures were paid out to United's shareholders as a special dividend.

3. General Motors (GM) spun off its Electronic Data Systems (EDS) subsidiary. EDS, a computer services company founded in 1962 by Ross Perot, prospered as an independent company until it was acquired by GM in 1984. The rationale for the acquisition was that EDS's expertise would help GM both operate better in the information age and build cars that encompassed leading-edge computer technology. However, the spread of desktop computers and the movement of companies to downsize their internal computer staffs caused EDS's non-GM business to soar. Ownership by GM hampered EDS's ability to strike alliances and, in some cases, to enter into business agreements. The best way for EDS to compete in its industry was as an independent, hence it was spun off.

GOVERNMENTS ARE DIVESTING STATE-OWNED BUSINESSES TO SPUR ECONOMIC EFFICIENCY

In many countries governments have traditionally owned or controlled a number of key businesses. When Margaret Thatcher became prime minister of Britain in 1979, she set out to reverse this trend, and soon her officials were devising methods for the government to divest state-owned enterprises. Thatcher coined the term "privatization" to describe the process of transferring productive operations and assets from the public sector to the private sector.

The privatization momentum picked up in the early and mid-1980s, expanding to other countries including France, Germany, Japan, and Singapore. Privatization accelerated further as the communist countries and authoritarian regimes across Eastern Europe, Asia, and Latin America shifted toward market-based economies.

Telecommunications, electric power, and airlines are examples of industries that have undergone extensive privatization throughout the world. These industries are vitally important to the economic infrastructure of every nation, and for this reason governments have historically been heavily involved in owning and regulating them within their national borders. Generally, the government-owned enterprise was granted monopoly power to supply the service in question and was subsidized in an effort to hold down costs to consumers. However, economists have long argued that government operations are inherently less efficient than are enterprises which are subject to competitive pressures and whose managers are guided by the profit motive. Thus, in recent years there have been numerous privatizations in these important industries, and as governments have sold their interests, competition has led to lower costs and improved service.

In Western Europe, privatizations in the telecommunications industry have been given an extra push by a European Union plan that opened markets to competition. Because most European telecoms were government owned, the resulting privatizations brought to market tens of billions of dollars of telecom stock. Globally, governments have raised hundreds of billions of dollars through privatizations.

The results are not all in, but it is clear that the removal of bureaucrats and politicians from the control of key enterprises often results in increased economic efficiency and a higher standard of living.

---

4. AT&T was broken up in 1983 to settle a Justice Department antitrust suit filed in the 1970s.[21] For almost 100 years AT&T had operated as a holding company that owned Western Electric (its manufacturing subsidiary), Bell Labs (its research arm), a huge long-distance network that was operated as a division of the parent company, and 22 Bell operating companies, such as Pacific Telephone, New York Telephone, Southern Bell, and Southwestern Bell. In 1984, AT&T was reorganized into eight separate companies—a slimmed-down AT&T, which kept Western Electric, Bell Labs, and the long-distance operations, plus seven new regional telephone holding companies that were created from the 22 old operating telephone companies. The stock of the seven new telephone companies was then spun off to the old AT&T's stockholders. A person who held 100 shares of old AT&T stock owned, after the divestiture, 100 shares of the "new" AT&T plus 10 shares of each of the seven new operating companies. These 170 shares were backed by the same assets that had previously backed 100 shares of old AT&T common.

   The AT&T divestiture resulted from a suit by the Justice Department, which wanted to divide the Bell System into a regulated monopoly segment (the seven regional telephone companies) and a manufacturing/long-distance segment that would be exposed to competition. The breakup was designed to strengthen competition and thus speed up technological change in those parts of the telecommunications industry that are not natural monopolies.

---

[21] Another forced divestiture involved Du Pont and General Motors. In 1921, GM was in serious financial trouble, and Du Pont supplied capital in exchange for 23 percent of the stock. In the 1950s, the Justice Department won an antitrust suit that required Du Pont to spin off (to Du Pont's stockholders) its GM stock.

5. After its forced breakup, AT&T lost little time in building itself up. In 1991 it acquired computer maker NCR, and in 1994 it bought McCaw Cellular Communications, a cellular phone operator. Then, in 1995, AT&T made a surprise announcement. Its massive combination of technology assets was not paying off, and AT&T's stock was in the doldrums. Then the company split itself into three parts. The surviving AT&T includes the core $53 billion long-distance and cellular phone businesses. The division that makes the switching equipment used by local and long-distance companies was spun off under the name Lucent Technologies. AT&T also spun off its loss-plagued computer business (the former NCR). AT&T shares took off on the announcement, adding more than $6 to the share price and $11 billion to AT&T's total value—more than enough to make up for the purchase of NCR and the ensuing losses. One reason for the breakup was the fact that AT&T and the local telephone companies were entering one another's markets, and the locals were reluctant to buy equipment from a competitor (AT&T). Therefore, Lucent was losing business to other manufacturers. Also, the breakup permitted the managers of each entity to focus exclusively on the problems and opportunities of their own businesses. Now they can concentrate on those areas where they have the greatest expertise without distraction from events in other business lines.

6. Some years ago, Woolworth liquidated all of its 336 Woolco discount stores. This made the company, which had had sales of $7.2 billion before the liquidation, 30 percent smaller. Woolco had posted operating losses of $19 million the year before the liquidation, and its losses in the latest six months had climbed to an alarming $21 million. Woolworth's CEO, Edward F. Gibbons, was quoted as saying, "How many losses can you take?" Woolco's problems necessitated a write-off of $325 million, but management believed it was better to go ahead and "bite the bullet" rather than let the losing stores bleed the company to death.

7. As a result of some imprudent loans to oil companies and to developing nations, Continental Illinois, one of the largest U.S. bank holding companies at the time, was threatened with bankruptcy. Continental then sold off several profitable divisions, such as its leasing and credit card operations, to raise funds to cover bad-loan losses. In effect, Continental sold assets in order to stay alive. Ultimately, Continental was bailed out by the Federal Deposit Insurance Corporation and the Federal Reserve, which arranged a $7.5 billion rescue package and provided a blanket guarantee for all of Continental's $40 billion of deposits, which kept deposits in excess of $100,000 from fleeing the bank because of their uninsured status.

As the preceding examples illustrate, the reasons for divestitures vary widely. Sometimes the market feels more comfortable when firms "stick to their knitting"; the Pepsi and United Airlines divestitures are examples. Other companies need cash either to finance expansion in their primary business lines or to reduce a large debt burden, and divestitures can be used to raise this cash; Continental Bank illustrates this point. The divestitures also show that running a business is a dynamic process—conditions change, corporate strategies change in response, and as a result firms alter their asset portfolios by acquisitions and/or divestitures. Some divestitures, such as Woolworth's liquidation of its Woolco stores, are to unload losing assets that would otherwise drag the company down. The first AT&T example is one of the many instances in which a divestiture is the result of an antitrust settlement. The AT&T and GM spin-offs illustrate situations in which parts of the business can operate more efficiently alone than together.

TYING IT ALL TOGETHER

This chapter included discussions of mergers, divestitures, and LBOs. The majority of the discussion in this chapter was on mergers. We discussed the rationale for mergers, different types of mergers, the level of merger activity, merger regulation, and merger analysis. We also showed how to use two different approaches to valuing the target firm: discounted cash flow and market multiple analyses. We also explained how the acquiring firm can structure its takeover bid, the accounting treatment of mergers, and investment bankers' roles in arranging and financing mergers. In addition, we discussed two cooperative arrangements that fall short of mergers: corporate, or strategic, alliances and joint ventures. The key concepts covered are listed below.

■ A **merger** occurs when two firms combine to form a single company. The primary motives for mergers are (1) synergy, (2) tax considerations, (3) purchase of assets below their replacement costs, (4) diversification, (5) gaining control over a larger enterprise, and (6) breakup value.

■ Mergers can provide economic benefits through **economies of scale** and through putting assets in the hands of **more efficient managers.** However, mergers also have the potential for reducing competition, and for this reason they are carefully regulated by government agencies.

■ In most mergers, one company (the **acquiring firm**) initiates action to take over another (the **target firm**).

■ A **horizontal merger** occurs when two firms in the same line of business combine.

■ A **vertical merger** combines a firm with one of its customers or suppliers.

■ A **congeneric merger** involves firms in related industries, but where no customer-supplier relationship exists.

■ A **conglomerate merger** occurs when firms in totally different industries combine.

■ In a **friendly merger,** the managements of both firms approve the merger, whereas in a **hostile merger,** the target firm's management opposes it.

■ An **operating merger** is one in which the operations of the two firms are combined. A **financial merger** is one in which the firms continue to operate separately; hence, no operating economies are expected.

■ In a typical **merger analysis,** the key issues to be resolved are (1) the price to be paid for the target firm and (2) the employment/control situation. If the merger is a consolidation of two relatively equal firms, an issue is, "What percentage of the ownership do each merger partner's shareholders receive?"

■ Two methods are commonly used to determine the **value of the target firm:** (1) the **discounted cash flow (DCF)** method and (2) the **market multiple** method.

■ The **purchase method** must be used to account for mergers.

- A **joint venture** is a **corporate alliance** in which two or more companies combine some of their resources to achieve a specific, limited objective.

- A **leveraged buyout (LBO)** is a transaction in which a firm's publicly owned stock is acquired in a mostly debt-financed tender offer, and a privately owned, highly leveraged firm results. Often, the firm's own management initiates the LBO.

- A **divestiture** is the sale of some of a company's operating assets. A divestiture may involve (1) selling an operating unit to another firm, (2) **spinning off** a unit as a separate company, or (3) the outright **liquidation** of a unit's assets.

- The **reasons for divestiture** include to settle antitrust suits, to clarify what a company actually does, to enable management to concentrate on a particular type of activity, and to raise capital needed to strengthen the corporation's core business.

QUESTIONS

21-1   Four economic classifications of mergers are (1) horizontal, (2) vertical, (3) conglomerate, and (4) congeneric. Explain the significance of these terms in merger analysis with regard to (a) the likelihood of governmental intervention and (b) possibilities for operating synergy.

21-2   Firm A wants to acquire Firm B. Firm B's management agrees that the merger is a good idea. Might a tender offer be used?

21-3   Distinguish between operating mergers and financial mergers.

21-4   In the spring of 1984, Disney Productions' stock was selling for about $3.125 per share (all prices have been adjusted for 4:1 splits in 1986 and 1992). Then Saul Steinberg, a New York financier, began acquiring it, and after he had 12 percent, he announced a tender offer for another 37 percent of the stock—which would bring his holdings up to 49 percent—at a price of $4.22 per share. Disney's management then announced plans to buy Gibson Greeting Cards and Arvida Corporation, paying for them with stock. It also lined up bank credit and (according to Steinberg) was prepared to borrow up to $2 billion and use the funds to repurchase shares at a higher price than Steinberg was offering. All of these efforts were designed to keep Steinberg from taking control. In June, Disney's management agreed to pay Steinberg $4.84 per share, which gave him a gain of about $60 million on a 2-month investment of about $26.5 million.

When Disney's buyback of Steinberg's shares was announced, the stock price fell almost instantly from $4.25 to $2.875. Many Disney stockholders were irate, and they sued to block the buyout. Also, the Disney affair added fuel to the fire in a congressional committee that was holding hearings on proposed legislation that would (1) prohibit someone from acquiring more than 10 percent of a firm's stock without making a tender offer for all the remaining shares, (2) prohibit poison pill tactics such as those Disney's management had used to fight off Steinberg, (3) prohibit buybacks such as the deal eventually offered to Steinberg (greenmail) unless there was an approving vote by stockholders, and (4) prohibit (or substantially curtail) the use of golden parachutes (the one thing Disney's management did not try).

Set forth the arguments for and against this type of legislation. What provisions, if any, should it contain? Also, look up Disney's current stock price to see how its stockholders have actually fared. Note that Disney's stock was split 3-for-1 in July 1998.

21-5   Two large, publicly owned firms are contemplating a merger. No operating synergy is expected. However, since returns on the 2 firms are not perfectly positively correlated, the standard deviation of earnings would be reduced for the combined corporation. One group of consultants argues that this risk reduction is sufficient grounds for the merger. Another group thinks this type of risk reduction is irrelevant because stockholders can themselves hold the stock of both companies and thus gain the risk-reduction benefits without all the hassles and expenses of the merger. Whose position is correct?

SELF-TEST PROBLEMS   (SOLUTIONS APPEAR IN APPENDIX B)

ST-1   Define each of the following terms:
Key terms
a. Synergy; merger
b. Horizontal merger; vertical merger; congeneric merger; conglomerate merger
c. Friendly merger; hostile merger; defensive merger; tender offer; target company; breakup value; acquiring company

d. Operating merger; financial merger; equity residual method; market multiple analysis
e. White knight; white squire; poison pill; golden parachute; proxy fight
f. Joint venture; corporate alliance
g. Divestiture; spin-off; leveraged buyout (LBO); carve-out; liquidation
h. Arbitrage
i. Goodwill; pooling of interests versus purchase method

ST-2
Merger value

Pizza Place, a national pizza chain, is considering purchasing a smaller chain, Western Mountain Pizza. Pizza Place's analysts project that the merger will result in incremental net cash flows of $1.5 million in Year 1, $2 million in Year 2, $3 million in Year 3, and $5 million in Year 4. In addition, Western's Year 4 cash flows are expected to grow at a constant rate of 5 percent after Year 4. Assume all cash flows occur at the end of the year. The acquisition would be made immediately, if it were undertaken. Western's postmerger beta is estimated to be 1.5, and its postmerger tax rate would be 40 percent. The risk-free rate is 6 percent, and the market risk premium is 4 percent. What is the value of Western Mountain Pizza to Pizza Place?

STARTER PROBLEMS

The following information is required to work Problems 21-1, 21-2, and 21-3.

Harrison Corporation is interested in acquiring Van Buren Corporation. Assume that the risk-free rate of interest is 5 percent and the market risk premium is 6 percent.

21-1
Valuation

Van Buren currently expects to pay a year-end dividend of $2.00 a share ($D_1 = \$2.00$). Van Buren's dividend is expected to grow at a constant rate of 5 percent a year, and its beta is 0.9. What is the current price of Van Buren's stock?

21-2
Merger valuation

Harrison estimates that if it acquires Van Buren, the year-end dividend will remain at $2.00 a share, but synergies will enable the dividend to grow at a constant rate of 7 percent a year (instead of the current 5 percent). Harrison also plans to increase the debt ratio of what would be its Van Buren subsidiary—the effect of this would be to raise Van Buren's beta to 1.1. What is the per-share value of Van Buren to Harrison Corporation?

21-3
Merger bid

On the basis of your answers to Problems 21-1 and 21-2, if Harrison were to acquire Van Buren, what would be the range of possible prices that it could bid for each share of Van Buren common stock?

EXAM-TYPE PROBLEM

The problem included in this section is set up in such a way that it could be used as a multiple-choice exam problem.

21-4
Merger analysis

Apilado Appliance Corporation is considering a merger with the Vaccaro Vacuum Company. Vaccaro is a publicly traded company, and its current beta is 1.30. Vaccaro has been barely profitable, so it has paid an average of only 20 percent in taxes during the last several years. In addition, it uses little debt, having a debt ratio of just 25 percent.

If the acquisition were made, Apilado would operate Vaccaro as a separate, wholly owned subsidiary. Apilado would pay taxes on a consolidated basis, and the tax rate would therefore increase to 35 percent. Apilado also would increase the debt capitalization in the Vaccaro subsidiary to 40 percent of assets, which would increase its beta to 1.47. Apilado's acquisition department estimates that Vaccaro, if acquired, would produce the following net cash flows to Apilado's shareholders (in millions of dollars):

YEAR	NET CASH FLOWS
1	$1.30
2	1.50
3	1.75
4	2.00
5 and beyond	Constant growth at 6%

These cash flows include all acquisition effects. Apilado's cost of equity is 14 percent, its beta is 1.0, and its cost of debt is 10 percent. The risk-free rate is 8 percent.
a. What discount rate should be used to discount the estimated cash flows? (Hint: Use Apilado's k_s to determine the market risk premium.)

b. What is the dollar value of Vaccaro to Apilado?

c. Vaccaro has 1.2 million common shares outstanding. What is the maximum price per share that Apilado should offer for Vaccaro? If the tender offer is accepted at this price, what will happen to Apilado's stock price?

PROBLEMS

21-5
Capital budgeting analysis

The Stanley Stationery Shoppe wishes to acquire The Carlson Card Gallery for $400,000. Stanley expects the merger to provide incremental earnings of about $64,000 a year for 10 years. Ken Stanley has calculated the marginal cost of capital for this investment to be 10 percent. Conduct a capital budgeting analysis for Stanley to determine whether or not he should purchase The Carlson Card Gallery.

21-6
Merger analysis

TransWorld Communications Inc., a large telecommunications company, is evaluating the possible acquisition of Georgia Cable Company (GCC), a regional cable company. TransWorld's analysts project the following postmerger data for GCC (in thousands of dollars):

		2003	2004	2005	2006
Net sales		$450	$518	$555	$600
Selling and administrative expense		45	53	60	68
Interest		18	21	24	27
Tax rate after merger	35%				
Cost of goods sold as a percent of sales	65%				
Beta after merger	1.50				
Risk-free rate	8%				
Market risk premium	4%				
Terminal growth rate of cash flow available to TransWorld	7%				

If the acquisition is made, it will occur on January 1, 2003. All cash flows shown in the income statements are assumed to occur at the end of the year. GCC currently has a capital structure of 40 percent debt, but TransWorld would increase that to 50 percent if the acquisition were made. GCC, if independent, would pay taxes at 20 percent, but its income would be taxed at 35 percent if it were consolidated. GCC's current market-determined beta is 1.40, and its investment bankers think that its beta would rise to 1.50 if the debt ratio were increased to 50 percent. The cost of goods sold is expected to be 65 percent of sales, but it could vary somewhat. Depreciation-generated funds would be used to replace worn-out equipment, so they would not be available to TransWorld's shareholders. The risk-free rate is 8 percent, and the market risk premium is 4 percent.

a. What is the appropriate discount rate for valuing the acquisition?

b. What is the terminal value? What is the value of GCC to TransWorld?

SPREADSHEET PROBLEM

21-7
Merger analysis

Use the spreadsheet model to rework Problem 21-6, and then answer the following question:

c. Suppose GCC has 120,000 shares outstanding. What is the maximum per-share price TransWorld should offer for GCC?

INTEGRATED CASE

SMITTY'S HOME REPAIR COMPANY

21-8 Merger Analysis Smitty's Home Repair Company, a regional hardware chain that specializes in "do-it-yourself"

materials and equipment rentals, is cash rich because of several consecutive good years. One of the alternative uses for the excess funds is an acquisition. Linda Wade, Smitty's treasurer and your boss, has been asked to place a value on a potential target, Hill's Hardware, a small chain that operates in an adjacent state, and she has enlisted your help.

The table below indicates Wade's estimates of Hill's earnings potential if it came under Smitty's management (in millions of dollars). The interest expense listed here includes the interest (1) on Hill's existing debt, (2) on new debt that Smitty's would issue to help finance the acquisition, and (3) on new debt expected to be issued over time to help finance expansion within the new "H division," the code name given to the target firm. The retentions represent earnings that will be reinvested within the H division to help finance its growth.

Hill's Hardware currently uses 40 percent debt financing, and it pays federal-plus-state taxes at a 30 percent rate. Security analysts estimate Hill's beta to be 1.2. If the acquisition were to take place, Smitty's would increase Hill's debt ratio to 50 percent, which would increase its beta to 1.3. Further, because Smitty's is highly profitable, taxes on the consolidated firm would be 40 percent. Wade realizes that Hill's Hardware also generates depreciation cash flows, but she believes that these funds would have to be reinvested within the division to replace worn-out equipment.

Wade estimates the risk-free rate to be 9 percent and the market risk premium to be 4 percent. She also estimates that net cash flows after 2006 will grow at a constant rate of 6 percent. Smitty's management is new to the merger game, so Wade has been asked to answer some basic questions about mergers as well as to perform the merger analysis. To structure the task, Wade has developed the following questions, which you must answer and then defend to Smitty's board.

a. Several reasons have been proposed to justify mergers. Among the more prominent are (1) tax considerations, (2) risk reduction, (3) control, (4) purchase of assets at below-replacement cost, (5) synergy, and (6) globalization. In general, which of the reasons are economically justifiable? Which are not? Which fit the situation at hand? Explain.

b. Briefly describe the differences between a hostile merger and a friendly merger.

c. Use the data developed in the table to construct the H division's cash flow statements for 2003 through 2006. Why is interest expense deducted in merger cash flow statements, whereas it is not normally deducted in a capital budgeting cash flow analysis? Why are earnings retentions deducted in the cash flow statement?

d. Conceptually, what is the appropriate discount rate to apply to the cash flows developed in part c? What is your actual estimate of this discount rate?

e. What is the estimated terminal value of the acquisition; that is, what is the estimated value of the H division's cash flows beyond 2006? What is Hill's value to Smitty's? Suppose another firm were evaluating Hill's as an acquisition candidate. Would they obtain the same value? Explain.

f. Assume that Hill's has 10 million shares outstanding. These shares are traded relatively infrequently, but the last trade, made several weeks ago, was at a price of $9 per share. Should Smitty's make an offer for Hill's? If so, how much should it offer per share?

g. What merger-related activities are undertaken by investment bankers?

	2003	2004	2005	2006
Net sales	$60.0	$90.0	$112.5	$127.5
Cost of goods sold (60%)	36.0	54.0	67.5	76.5
Selling/administrative expense	4.5	6.0	7.5	9.0
Interest expense	3.0	4.5	4.5	6.0
Necessary retained earnings	0.0	7.5	6.0	4.5

CYBER PROBLEM

Please go to our web site **http://brigham.swlearning.com** to access the Cyberproblems.

THOMSON
ANALYTICS

With your Xtra! CD-ROM, access the Thomson Analytics Problems and use the Thomson Analytics Academic online database to work this chapter's problems.

MATHEMATICAL TABLES

EQUATION:

$$PVIF_{i,n} = \frac{1}{(1 + i)^n}$$

FINANCIAL CALCULATOR KEYS:

n	i		0	1.0
N	I	PV	PMT	FV

TABLE
VALUE

PERIOD	1%	2%	3%	4%	5%	6%	7%	8%	9%	10%
1	.9901	.9804	.9709	.9615	.9524	.9434	.9346	.9259	.9174	.9091
2	.9803	.9612	.9426	.9246	.9070	.8900	.8734	.8573	.8417	.8264
3	.9706	.9423	.9151	.8890	.8638	.8396	.8163	.7938	.7722	.7513
4	.9610	.9238	.8885	.8548	.8227	.7921	.7629	.7350	.7084	.6830
5	.9515	.9057	.8626	.8219	.7835	.7473	.7130	.6806	.6499	.6209
6	.9420	.8880	.8375	.7903	.7462	.7050	.6663	.6302	.5963	.5645
7	.9327	.8706	.8131	.7599	.7107	.6651	.6227	.5835	.5470	.5132
8	.9235	.8535	.7894	.7307	.6768	.6274	.5820	.5403	.5019	.4665
9	.9143	.8368	.7664	.7026	.6446	.5919	.5439	.5002	.4604	.4241
10	.9053	.8203	.7441	.6756	.6139	.5584	.5083	.4632	.4224	.3855
11	.8963	.8043	.7224	.6496	.5847	.5268	.4751	.4289	.3875	.3505
12	.8874	.7885	.7014	.6246	.5568	.4970	.4440	.3971	.3555	.3186
13	.8787	.7730	.6810	.6006	.5303	.4688	.4150	.3677	.3262	.2897
14	.8700	.7579	.6611	.5775	.5051	.4423	.3878	.3405	.2992	.2633
15	.8613	.7430	.6419	.5553	.4810	.4173	.3624	.3152	.2745	.2394
16	.8528	.7284	.6232	.5339	.4581	.3936	.3387	.2919	.2519	.2176
17	.8444	.7142	.6050	.5134	.4363	.3714	.3166	.2703	.2311	.1978
18	.8360	.7002	.5874	.4936	.4155	.3503	.2959	.2502	.2120	.1799
19	.8277	.6864	.5703	.4746	.3957	.3305	.2765	.2317	.1945	.1635
20	.8195	.6730	.5537	.4564	.3769	.3118	.2584	.2145	.1784	.1486
21	.8114	.6598	.5375	.4388	.3589	.2942	.2415	.1987	.1637	.1351
22	.8034	.6468	.5219	.4220	.3418	.2775	.2257	.1839	.1502	.1228
23	.7954	.6342	.5067	.4057	.3256	.2618	.2109	.1703	.1378	.1117
24	.7876	.6217	.4919	.3901	.3101	.2470	.1971	.1577	.1264	.1015
25	.7798	.6095	.4776	.3751	.2953	.2330	.1842	.1460	.1160	.0923
26	.7720	.5976	.4637	.3607	.2812	.2198	.1722	.1352	.1064	.0839
27	.7644	.5859	.4502	.3468	.2678	.2074	.1609	.1252	.0976	.0763
28	.7568	.5744	.4371	.3335	.2551	.1956	.1504	.1159	.0895	.0693
29	.7493	.5631	.4243	.3207	.2429	.1846	.1406	.1073	.0822	.0630
30	.7419	.5521	.4120	.3083	.2314	.1741	.1314	.0994	.0754	.0573
35	.7059	.5000	.3554	.2534	.1813	.1301	.0937	.0676	.0490	.0356
40	.6717	.4529	.3066	.2083	.1420	.0972	.0668	.0460	.0318	.0221
45	.6391	.4102	.2644	.1712	.1113	.0727	.0476	.0313	.0207	.0137
50	.6080	.3715	.2281	.1407	.0872	.0543	.0339	.0213	.0134	.0085
55	.5785	.3365	.1968	.1157	.0683	.0406	.0242	.0145	.0087	.0053

PERIOD	12%	14%	15%	16%	18%	20%	24%	28%	32%	36%
1	.8929	.8772	.8696	.8621	.8475	.8333	.8065	.7813	.7576	.7353
2	.7972	.7695	.7561	.7432	.7182	.6944	.6504	.6104	.5739	.5407
3	.7118	.6750	.6575	.6407	.6086	.5787	.5245	.4768	.4348	.3975
4	.6355	.5921	.5718	.5523	.5158	.4823	.4230	.3725	.3294	.2923
5	.5674	.5194	.4972	.4761	.4371	.4019	.3411	.2910	.2495	.2149
6	.5066	.4556	.4323	.4104	.3704	.3349	.2751	.2274	.1890	.1580
7	.4523	.3996	.3759	.3538	.3139	.2791	.2218	.1776	.1432	.1162
8	.4039	.3506	.3269	.3050	.2660	.2326	.1789	.1388	.1085	.0854
9	.3606	.3075	.2843	.2630	.2255	.1938	.1443	.1084	.0822	.0628
10	.3220	.2697	.2472	.2267	.1911	.1615	.1164	.0847	.0623	.0462
11	.2875	.2366	.2149	.1954	.1619	.1346	.0938	.0662	.0472	.0340
12	.2567	.2076	.1869	.1685	.1372	.1122	.0757	.0517	.0357	.0250
13	.2292	.1821	.1625	.1452	.1163	.0935	.0610	.0404	.0271	.0184
14	.2046	.1597	.1413	.1252	.0985	.0779	.0492	.0316	.0205	.0135
15	.1827	.1401	.1229	.1079	.0835	.0649	.0397	.0247	.0155	.0099
16	.1631	.1229	.1069	.0930	.0708	.0541	.0320	.0193	.0118	.0073
17	.1456	.1078	.0929	.0802	.0600	.0451	.0258	.0150	.0089	.0054
18	.1300	.0946	.0808	.0691	.0508	.0376	.0208	.0118	.0068	.0039
19	.1161	.0829	.0703	.0596	.0431	.0313	.0168	.0092	.0051	.0029
20	.1037	.0728	.0611	.0514	.0365	.0261	.0135	.0072	.0039	.0021
21	.0926	.0638	.0531	.0443	.0309	.0217	.0109	.0056	.0029	.0016
22	.0826	.0560	.0462	.0382	.0262	.0181	.0088	.0044	.0022	.0012
23	.0738	.0491	.0402	.0329	.0222	.0151	.0071	.0034	.0017	.0008
24	.0659	.0431	.0349	.0284	.0188	.0126	.0057	.0027	.0013	.0006
25	.0588	.0378	.0304	.0245	.0160	.0105	.0046	.0021	.0010	.0005
26	.0525	.0331	.0264	.0211	.0135	.0087	.0037	.0016	.0007	.0003
27	.0469	.0291	.0230	.0182	.0115	.0073	.0030	.0013	.0006	.0002
28	.0419	.0255	.0200	.0157	.0097	.0061	.0024	.0010	.0004	.0002
29	.0374	.0224	.0174	.0135	.0082	.0051	.0020	.0008	.0003	.0001
30	.0334	.0196	.0151	.0116	.0070	.0042	.0016	.0006	.0002	.0001
35	.0189	.0102	.0075	.0055	.0030	.0017	.0005	.0002	.0001	*
40	.0107	.0053	.0037	.0026	.0013	.0007	.0002	.0001	*	*
45	.0061	.0027	.0019	.0013	.0006	.0003	.0001	*	*	*
50	.0035	.0014	.0009	.0006	.0003	.0001	*	*	*	*
55	.0020	.0007	.0005	.0003	.0001	*	*	*	*	*

*The factor is zero to four decimal places.

EQUATION:

$$PVIFA_{i,n} = \sum_{t=1}^{n} \frac{1}{(1+i)^t} = \frac{1 - \dfrac{1}{(1+i)^n}}{i} = \frac{1}{i} - \frac{1}{i(1+i)^n}$$

FINANCIAL CALCULATOR KEYS:

n	i		1.0	0
N	**I**	**PV**	**PMT**	**FV**
		TABLE VALUE		

NUMBER OF PERIODS	1%	2%	3%	4%	5%	6%	7%	8%	9%
1	0.9901	0.9804	0.9709	0.9615	0.9524	0.9434	0.9346	0.9259	0.9174
2	1.9704	1.9416	1.9135	1.8861	1.8594	1.8334	1.8080	1.7833	1.7591
3	2.9410	2.8839	2.8286	2.7751	2.7232	2.6730	2.6243	2.5771	2.5313
4	3.9020	3.8077	3.7171	3.6299	3.5460	3.4651	3.3872	3.3121	3.2397
5	4.8534	4.7135	4.5797	4.4518	4.3295	4.2124	4.1002	3.9927	3.8897
6	5.7955	5.6014	5.4172	5.2421	5.0757	4.9173	4.7665	4.6229	4.4859
7	6.7282	6.4720	6.2303	6.0021	5.7864	5.5824	5.3893	5.2064	5.0330
8	7.6517	7.3255	7.0197	6.7327	6.4632	6.2098	5.9713	5.7466	5.5348
9	8.5660	8.1622	7.7861	7.4353	7.1078	6.8017	6.5152	6.2469	5.9952
10	9.4713	8.9826	8.5302	8.1109	7.7217	7.3601	7.0236	6.7101	6.4177
11	10.3676	9.7868	9.2526	8.7605	8.3064	7.8869	7.4987	7.1390	6.8052
12	11.2551	10.5753	9.9540	9.3851	8.8633	8.3838	7.9427	7.5361	7.1607
13	12.1337	11.3484	10.6350	9.9856	9.3936	8.8527	8.3577	7.9038	7.4869
14	13.0037	12.1062	11.2961	10.5631	9.8986	9.2950	8.7455	8.2442	7.7862
15	13.8651	12.8493	11.9379	11.1184	10.3797	9.7122	9.1079	8.5595	8.0607
16	14.7179	13.5777	12.5611	11.6523	10.8378	10.1059	9.4466	8.8514	8.3126
17	15.5623	14.2919	13.1661	12.1657	11.2741	10.4773	9.7632	9.1216	8.5436
18	16.3983	14.9920	13.7535	12.6593	11.6896	10.8276	10.0591	9.3719	8.7556
19	17.2260	15.6785	14.3238	13.1339	12.0853	11.1581	10.3356	9.6036	8.9501
20	18.0456	16.3514	14.8775	13.5903	12.4622	11.4699	10.5940	9.8181	9.1285
21	18.8570	17.0112	15.4150	14.0292	12.8212	11.7641	10.8355	10.0168	9.2922
22	19.6604	17.6580	15.9369	14.4511	13.1630	12.0416	11.0612	10.2007	9.4424
23	20.4558	18.2922	16.4436	14.8568	13.4886	12.3034	11.2722	10.3711	9.5802
24	21.2434	18.9139	16.9355	15.2470	13.7986	12.5504	11.4693	10.5288	9.7066
25	22.0232	19.5235	17.4131	15.6221	14.0939	12.7834	11.6536	10.6748	9.8226
26	22.7952	20.1210	17.8768	15.9828	14.3752	13.0032	11.8258	10.8100	9.9290
27	23.5596	20.7069	18.3270	16.3296	14.6430	13.2105	11.9867	10.9352	10.0266
28	24.3164	21.2813	18.7641	16.6631	14.8981	13.4062	12.1371	11.0511	10.1161
29	25.0658	21.8444	19.1885	16.9837	15.1411	13.5907	12.2777	11.1584	10.1983
30	25.8077	22.3965	19.6004	17.2920	15.3725	13.7648	12.4090	11.2578	10.2737
35	29.4086	24.9986	21.4872	18.6646	16.3742	14.4982	12.9477	11.6546	10.5668
40	32.8347	27.3555	23.1148	19.7928	17.1591	15.0463	13.3317	11.9246	10.7574
45	36.0945	29.4902	24.5187	20.7200	17.7741	15.4558	13.6055	12.1084	10.8812
50	39.1961	31.4236	25.7298	21.4822	18.2559	15.7619	13.8007	12.2335	10.9617
55	42.1472	33.1748	26.7744	22.1086	18.6335	15.9905	13.9399	12.3186	11.0140

NUMBER OF PERIODS	10%	12%	14%	15%	16%	18%	20%	24%	28%	32%
1	0.9091	0.8929	0.8772	0.8696	0.8621	0.8475	0.8333	0.8065	0.7813	0.7576
2	1.7355	1.6901	1.6467	1.6257	1.6052	1.5656	1.5278	1.4568	1.3916	1.3315
3	2.4869	2.4018	2.3216	2.2832	2.2459	2.1743	2.1065	1.9813	1.8684	1.7663
4	3.1699	3.0373	2.9137	2.8550	2.7982	2.6901	2.5887	2.4043	2.2410	2.0957
5	3.7908	3.6048	3.4331	3.3522	3.2743	3.1272	2.9906	2.7454	2.5320	2.3452
6	4.3553	4.1114	3.8887	3.7845	3.6847	3.4976	3.3255	3.0205	2.7594	2.5342
7	4.8684	4.5638	4.2883	4.1604	4.0386	3.8115	3.6046	3.2423	2.9370	2.6775
8	5.3349	4.9676	4.6389	4.4873	4.3436	4.0776	3.8372	3.4212	3.0758	2.7860
9	5.7590	5.3282	4.9464	4.7716	4.6065	4.3030	4.0310	3.5655	3.1842	2.8681
10	6.1446	5.6502	5.2161	5.0188	4.8332	4.4941	4.1925	3.6819	3.2689	2.9304
11	6.4951	5.9377	5.4527	5.2337	5.0286	4.6560	4.3271	3.7757	3.3351	2.9776
12	6.8137	6.1944	5.6603	5.4206	5.1971	4.7932	4.4392	3.8514	3.3868	3.0133
13	7.1034	6.4235	5.8424	5.5831	5.3423	4.9095	4.5327	3.9124	3.4272	3.0404
14	7.3667	6.6282	6.0021	5.7245	5.4675	5.0081	4.6106	3.9616	3.4587	3.0609
15	7.6061	6.8109	6.1422	5.8474	5.5755	5.0916	4.6755	4.0013	3.4834	3.0764
16	7.8237	6.9740	6.2651	5.9542	5.6685	5.1624	4.7296	4.0333	3.5026	3.0882
17	8.0216	7.1196	6.3729	6.0472	5.7487	5.2223	4.7746	4.0591	3.5177	3.0971
18	8.2014	7.2497	6.4674	6.1280	5.8178	5.2732	4.8122	4.0799	3.5294	3.1039
19	8.3649	7.3658	6.5504	6.1982	5.8775	5.3162	4.8435	4.0967	3.5386	3.1090
20	8.5136	7.4694	6.6231	6.2593	5.9288	5.3527	4.8696	4.1103	3.5458	3.1129
21	8.6487	7.5620	6.6870	6.3125	5.9731	5.3837	4.8913	4.1212	3.5514	3.1158
22	8.7715	7.6446	6.7429	6.3587	6.0113	5.4099	4.9094	4.1300	3.5558	3.1180
23	8.8832	7.7184	6.7921	6.3988	6.0442	5.4321	4.9245	4.1371	3.5592	3.1197
24	8.9847	7.7843	6.8351	6.4338	6.0726	5.4509	4.9371	4.1428	3.5619	3.1210
25	9.0770	7.8431	6.8729	6.4641	6.0971	5.4669	4.9476	4.1474	3.5640	3.1220
26	9.1609	7.8957	6.9061	6.4906	6.1182	5.4804	4.9563	4.1511	3.5656	3.1227
27	9.2372	7.9426	6.9352	6.5135	6.1364	5.4919	4.9636	4.1542	3.5669	3.1233
28	9.3066	7.9844	6.9607	6.5335	6.1520	5.5016	4.9697	4.1566	3.5679	3.1237
29	9.3696	8.0218	6.9830	6.5509	6.1656	5.5098	4.9747	4.1585	3.5687	3.1240
30	9.4269	8.0552	7.0027	6.5660	6.1772	5.5168	4.9789	4.1601	3.5693	3.1242
35	9.6442	8.1755	7.0700	6.6166	6.2153	5.5386	4.9915	4.1644	3.5708	3.1248
40	9.7791	8.2438	7.1050	6.6418	6.2335	5.5482	4.9966	4.1659	3.5712	3.1250
45	9.8628	8.2825	7.1232	6.6543	6.2421	5.5523	4.9986	4.1664	3.5714	3.1250
50	9.9148	8.3045	7.1327	6.6605	6.2463	5.5541	4.9995	4.1666	3.5714	3.1250
55	9.9471	8.3170	7.1376	6.6636	6.2482	5.5549	4.9998	4.1666	3.5714	3.1250

TABLE A-3 — Future Value of $1 at the End of n Periods

EQUATION:

$$FVIF_{i,n} = (1 + i)^n$$

FINANCIAL CALCULATOR KEYS:

n	i	1.0	0	
N	I	PV	PMT	FV

TABLE VALUE

PERIOD	1%	2%	3%	4%	5%	6%	7%	8%	9%	10%
1	1.0100	1.0200	1.0300	1.0400	1.0500	1.0600	1.0700	1.0800	1.0900	1.1000
2	1.0201	1.0404	1.0609	1.0816	1.1025	1.1236	1.1449	1.1664	1.1881	1.2100
3	1.0303	1.0612	1.0927	1.1249	1.1576	1.1910	1.2250	1.2597	1.2950	1.3310
4	1.0406	1.0824	1.1255	1.1699	1.2155	1.2625	1.3108	1.3605	1.4116	1.4641
5	1.0510	1.1041	1.1593	1.2167	1.2763	1.3382	1.4026	1.4693	1.5386	1.6105
6	1.0615	1.1262	1.1941	1.2653	1.3401	1.4185	1.5007	1.5869	1.6771	1.7716
7	1.0721	1.1487	1.2299	1.3159	1.4071	1.5036	1.6058	1.7138	1.8280	1.9487
8	1.0829	1.1717	1.2668	1.3686	1.4775	1.5938	1.7182	1.8509	1.9926	2.1436
9	1.0937	1.1951	1.3048	1.4233	1.5513	1.6895	1.8385	1.9990	2.1719	2.3579
10	1.1046	1.2190	1.3439	1.4802	1.6289	1.7908	1.9672	2.1589	2.3674	2.5937
11	1.1157	1.2434	1.3842	1.5395	1.7103	1.8983	2.1049	2.3316	2.5804	2.8531
12	1.1268	1.2682	1.4258	1.6010	1.7959	2.0122	2.2522	2.5182	2.8127	3.1384
13	1.1381	1.2936	1.4685	1.6651	1.8856	2.1329	2.4098	2.7196	3.0658	3.4523
14	1.1495	1.3195	1.5126	1.7317	1.9799	2.2609	2.5785	2.9372	3.3417	3.7975
15	1.1610	1.3459	1.5580	1.8009	2.0789	2.3966	2.7590	3.1722	3.6425	4.1772
16	1.1726	1.3728	1.6047	1.8730	2.1829	2.5404	2.9522	3.4259	3.9703	4.5950
17	1.1843	1.4002	1.6528	1.9479	2.2920	2.6928	3.1588	3.7000	4.3276	5.0545
18	1.1961	1.4282	1.7024	2.0258	2.4066	2.8543	3.3799	3.9960	4.7171	5.5599
19	1.2081	1.4568	1.7535	2.1068	2.5270	3.0256	3.6165	4.3157	5.1417	6.1159
20	1.2202	1.4859	1.8061	2.1911	2.6533	3.2071	3.8697	4.6610	5.6044	6.7275
21	1.2324	1.5157	1.8603	2.2788	2.7860	3.3996	4.1406	5.0338	6.1088	7.4002
22	1.2447	1.5460	1.9161	2.3699	2.9253	3.6035	4.4304	5.4365	6.6586	8.1403
23	1.2572	1.5769	1.9736	2.4647	3.0715	3.8197	4.7405	5.8715	7.2579	8.9543
24	1.2697	1.6084	2.0328	2.5633	3.2251	4.0489	5.0724	6.3412	7.9111	9.8497
25	1.2824	1.6406	2.0938	2.6658	3.3864	4.2919	5.4274	6.8485	8.6231	10.835
26	1.2953	1.6734	2.1566	2.7725	3.5557	4.5494	5.8074	7.3964	9.3992	11.918
27	1.3082	1.7069	2.2213	2.8834	3.7335	4.8223	6.2139	7.9881	10.245	13.110
28	1.3213	1.7410	2.2879	2.9987	3.9201	5.1117	6.6488	8.6271	11.167	14.421
29	1.3345	1.7758	2.3566	3.1187	4.1161	5.4184	7.1143	9.3173	12.172	15.863
30	1.3478	1.8114	2.4273	3.2434	4.3219	5.7435	7.6123	10.063	13.268	17.449
40	1.4889	2.2080	3.2620	4.8010	7.0400	10.286	14.974	21.725	31.409	45.259
50	1.6446	2.6916	4.3839	7.1067	11.467	18.420	29.457	46.902	74.358	117.39
60	1.8167	3.2810	5.8916	10.520	18.679	32.988	57.946	101.26	176.03	304.48

PERIOD	12%	14%	15%	16%	18%	20%	24%	28%	32%	36%
1	1.1200	1.1400	1.1500	1.1600	1.1800	1.2000	1.2400	1.2800	1.3200	1.3600
2	1.2544	1.2996	1.3225	1.3456	1.3924	1.4400	1.5376	1.6384	1.7424	1.8496
3	1.4049	1.4815	1.5209	1.5609	1.6430	1.7280	1.9066	2.0972	2.3000	2.5155
4	1.5735	1.6890	1.7490	1.8106	1.9388	2.0736	2.3642	2.6844	3.0360	3.4210
5	1.7623	1.9254	2.0114	2.1003	2.2878	2.4883	2.9316	3.4360	4.0075	4.6526
6	1.9738	2.1950	2.3131	2.4364	2.6996	2.9860	3.6352	4.3980	5.2899	6.3275
7	2.2107	2.5023	2.6600	2.8262	3.1855	3.5832	4.5077	5.6295	6.9826	8.6054
8	2.4760	2.8526	3.0590	3.2784	3.7589	4.2998	5.5895	7.2058	9.2170	11.703
9	2.7731	3.2519	3.5179	3.8030	4.4355	5.1598	6.9310	9.2234	12.166	15.917
10	3.1058	3.7072	4.0456	4.4114	5.2338	6.1917	8.5944	11.806	16.060	21.647
11	3.4785	4.2262	4.6524	5.1173	6.1759	7.4301	10.657	15.112	21.199	29.439
12	3.8960	4.8179	5.3503	5.9360	7.2876	8.9161	13.215	19.343	27.983	40.037
13	4.3635	5.4924	6.1528	6.8858	8.5994	10.699	16.386	24.759	36.937	54.451
14	4.8871	6.2613	7.0757	7.9875	10.147	12.839	20.319	31.691	48.757	74.053
15	5.4736	7.1379	8.1371	9.2655	11.974	15.407	25.196	40.565	64.359	100.71
16	6.1304	8.1372	9.3576	10.748	14.129	18.488	31.243	51.923	84.954	136.97
17	6.8660	9.2765	10.761	12.468	16.672	22.186	38.741	66.461	112.14	186.28
18	7.6900	10.575	12.375	14.463	19.673	26.623	48.039	85.071	148.02	253.34
19	8.6128	12.056	14.232	16.777	23.214	31.948	59.568	108.89	195.39	344.54
20	9.6463	13.743	16.367	19.461	27.393	38.338	73.864	139.38	257.92	468.57
21	10.804	15.668	18.822	22.574	32.324	46.005	91.592	178.41	340.45	637.26
22	12.100	17.861	21.645	26.186	38.142	55.206	113.57	228.36	449.39	866.67
23	13.552	20.362	24.891	30.376	45.008	66.247	140.83	292.30	593.20	1178.7
24	15.179	23.212	28.625	35.236	53.109	79.497	174.63	374.14	783.02	1603.0
25	17.000	26.462	32.919	40.874	62.669	95.396	216.54	478.90	1033.6	2180.1
26	19.040	30.167	37.857	47.414	73.949	114.48	268.51	613.00	1364.3	2964.9
27	21.325	34.390	43.535	55.000	87.260	137.37	332.95	784.64	1800.9	4032.3
28	23.884	39.204	50.066	63.800	102.97	164.84	412.86	1004.3	2377.2	5483.9
29	26.750	44.693	57.575	74.009	121.50	197.81	511.95	1285.6	3137.9	7458.1
30	29.960	50.950	66.212	85.850	143.37	237.38	634.82	1645.5	4142.1	10143.
40	93.051	188.88	267.86	378.72	750.38	1469.8	5455.9	19427.	66521.	*
50	289.00	700.23	1083.7	1670.7	3927.4	9100.4	46890.	*	*	*
60	897.60	2595.9	4384.0	7370.2	20555.	56348.	*	*	*	*

*FVIF > 99,999.

TABLE A-4 Future Value of an Annuity of $1 per Period for n Periods

EQUATION:

$$FVIFA_{i,n} = \sum_{t=1}^{n} (1 + i)^{n-t} = \frac{(1 + i)^n - 1}{i}$$

FINANCIAL CALCULATOR KEYS:

n	i	0	1.0	
N	**I**	**PV**	**PMT**	**FV**

TABLE VALUE

NUMBER OF PERIODS	1%	2%	3%	4%	5%	6%	7%	8%	9%	10%
1	1.0000	1.0000	1.0000	1.0000	1.0000	1.0000	1.0000	1.0000	1.0000	1.0000
2	2.0100	2.0200	2.0300	2.0400	2.0500	2.0600	2.0700	2.0800	2.0900	2.1000
3	3.0301	3.0604	3.0909	3.1216	3.1525	3.1836	3.2149	3.2464	3.2781	3.3100
4	4.0604	4.1216	4.1836	4.2465	4.3101	4.3746	4.4399	4.5061	4.5731	4.6410
5	5.1010	5.2040	5.3091	5.4163	5.5256	5.6371	5.7507	5.8666	5.9847	6.1051
6	6.1520	6.3081	6.4684	6.6330	6.8019	6.9753	7.1533	7.3359	7.5233	7.7156
7	7.2135	7.4343	7.6625	7.8983	8.1420	8.3938	8.6540	8.9228	9.2004	9.4872
8	8.2857	8.5830	8.8923	9.2142	9.5491	9.8975	10.260	10.637	11.028	11.436
9	9.3685	9.7546	10.159	10.583	11.027	11.491	11.978	12.488	13.021	13.579
10	10.462	10.950	11.464	12.006	12.578	13.181	13.816	14.487	15.193	15.937
11	11.567	12.169	12.808	13.486	14.207	14.972	15.784	16.645	17.560	18.531
12	12.683	13.412	14.192	15.026	15.917	16.870	17.888	18.977	20.141	21.384
13	13.809	14.680	15.618	16.627	17.713	18.882	20.141	21.495	22.953	24.523
14	14.947	15.974	17.086	18.292	19.599	21.015	22.550	24.215	26.019	27.975
15	16.097	17.293	18.599	20.024	21.579	23.276	25.129	27.152	29.361	31.772
16	17.258	18.639	20.157	21.825	23.657	25.673	27.888	30.324	33.003	35.950
17	18.430	20.012	21.762	23.698	25.840	28.213	30.840	33.750	36.974	40.545
18	19.615	21.412	23.414	25.645	28.132	30.906	33.999	37.450	41.301	45.599
19	20.811	22.841	25.117	27.671	30.539	33.760	37.379	41.446	46.018	51.159
20	22.019	24.297	26.870	29.778	33.066	36.786	40.995	45.762	51.160	57.275
21	23.239	25.783	28.676	31.969	35.719	39.993	44.865	50.423	56.765	64.002
22	24.472	27.299	30.537	34.248	38.505	43.392	49.006	55.457	62.873	71.403
23	25.716	28.845	32.453	36.618	41.430	46.996	53.436	60.893	69.532	79.543
24	26.973	30.422	34.426	39.083	44.502	50.816	58.177	66.765	76.790	88.497
25	28.243	32.030	36.459	41.646	47.727	54.865	63.249	73.106	84.701	98.347
26	29.526	33.671	38.553	44.312	51.113	59.156	68.676	79.954	93.324	109.18
27	30.821	35.344	40.710	47.084	54.669	63.706	74.484	87.351	102.72	121.10
28	32.129	37.051	42.931	49.968	58.403	68.528	80.698	95.339	112.97	134.21
29	33.450	38.792	45.219	52.966	62.323	73.640	87.347	103.97	124.14	148.63
30	34.785	40.568	47.575	56.085	66.439	79.058	94.461	113.28	136.31	164.49
40	48.886	60.402	75.401	95.026	120.80	154.76	199.64	259.06	337.88	442.59
50	64.463	84.579	112.80	152.67	209.35	290.34	406.53	573.77	815.08	1163.9
60	81.670	114.05	163.05	237.99	353.58	533.13	813.52	1253.2	1944.8	3034.8

NUMBER OF PERIODS	12%	14%	15%	16%	18%	20%	24%	28%	32%	36%
1	1.0000	1.0000	1.0000	1.0000	1.0000	1.0000	1.0000	1.0000	1.0000	1.0000
2	2.1200	2.1400	2.1500	2.1600	2.1800	2.2000	2.2400	2.2800	2.3200	2.3600
3	3.3744	3.4396	3.4725	3.5056	3.5724	3.6400	3.7776	3.9184	4.0624	4.2096
4	4.7793	4.9211	4.9934	5.0665	5.2154	5.3680	5.6842	6.0156	6.3624	6.7251
5	6.3528	6.6101	6.7424	6.8771	7.1542	7.4416	8.0484	8.6999	9.3983	10.146
6	8.1152	8.5355	8.7537	8.9775	9.4420	9.9299	10.980	12.136	13.406	14.799
7	10.089	10.730	11.067	11.414	12.142	12.916	14.615	16.534	18.696	21.126
8	12.300	13.233	13.727	14.240	15.327	16.499	19.123	22.163	25.678	29.732
9	14.776	16.085	16.786	17.519	19.086	20.799	24.712	29.369	34.895	41.435
10	17.549	19.337	20.304	21.321	23.521	25.959	31.643	38.593	47.062	57.352
11	20.655	23.045	24.349	25.733	28.755	32.150	40.238	50.398	63.122	78.998
12	24.133	27.271	29.002	30.850	34.931	39.581	50.895	65.510	84.320	108.44
13	28.029	32.089	34.352	36.786	42.219	48.497	64.110	84.853	112.30	148.47
14	32.393	37.581	40.505	43.672	50.818	59.196	80.496	109.61	149.24	202.93
15	37.280	43.842	47.580	51.660	60.965	72.035	100.82	141.30	198.00	276.98
16	42.753	50.980	55.717	60.925	72.939	87.442	126.01	181.87	262.36	377.69
17	48.884	59.118	65.075	71.673	87.068	105.93	157.25	233.79	347.31	514.66
18	55.750	68.394	75.836	84.141	103.74	128.12	195.99	300.25	459.45	700.94
19	63.440	78.969	88.212	98.603	123.41	154.74	244.03	385.32	607.47	954.28
20	72.052	91.025	102.44	115.38	146.63	186.69	303.60	494.21	802.86	1298.8
21	81.699	104.77	118.81	134.84	174.02	225.03	377.46	633.59	1060.8	1767.4
22	92.503	120.44	137.63	157.41	206.34	271.03	469.06	812.00	1401.2	2404.7
23	104.60	138.30	159.28	183.60	244.49	326.24	582.63	1040.4	1850.6	3271.3
24	118.16	158.66	184.17	213.98	289.49	392.48	723.46	1332.7	2443.8	4450.0
25	133.33	181.87	212.79	249.21	342.60	471.98	898.09	1706.8	3226.8	6053.0
26	150.33	208.33	245.71	290.09	405.27	567.38	1114.6	2185.7	4260.4	8233.1
27	169.37	238.50	283.57	337.50	479.22	681.85	1383.1	2798.7	5624.8	11198.0
28	190.70	272.89	327.10	392.50	566.48	819.22	1716.1	3583.3	7425.7	15230.3
29	214.58	312.09	377.17	456.30	669.45	984.07	2129.0	4587.7	9802.9	20714.2
30	241.33	356.79	434.75	530.31	790.95	1181.9	2640.9	5873.2	12941.	28172.3
40	767.09	1342.0	1779.1	2360.8	4163.2	7343.9	22729.	69377.	*	*
50	2400.0	4994.5	7217.7	10436.	21813.	45497.	*	*	*	*
60	7471.6	18535.	29220.	46058.	*	*	*	*	*	*

*FVIFA > 99,999.

z	0.00	0.01	0.02	0.03	0.04	0.05	0.06	0.07	0.08	0.09
0.0	.0000	.0040	.0080	.0120	.0160	.0199	.0239	.0279	.0319	.0359
0.1	.0398	.0438	.0478	.0517	.0557	.0596	.0636	.0675	.0714	.0753
0.2	.0793	.0832	.0871	.0910	.0948	.0987	.1026	.1064	.1103	.1141
0.3	.1179	.1217	.1255	.1293	.1331	.1368	.1406	.1443	.1480	.1517
0.4	.1554	.1591	.1628	.1664	.1700	.1736	.1772	.1808	.1844	.1879
0.5	.1915	.1950	.1985	.2019	.2054	.2088	.2123	.2157	.2190	.2224
0.6	.2257	.2291	.2324	.2357	.2389	.2422	.2454	.2486	.2517	.2549
0.7	.2580	.2611	.2642	.2673	.2704	.2734	.2764	.2794	.2823	.2852
0.8	.2881	.2910	.2939	.2967	.2995	.3023	.3051	.3078	.3106	.3133
0.9	.3159	.3186	.3212	.3238	.3264	.3289	.3315	.3340	.3365	.3389
1.0	.3413	.3438	.3461	.3485	.3508	.3531	.3554	.3577	.3599	.3621
1.1	.3643	.3665	.3686	.3708	.3729	.3749	.3770	.3790	.3810	.3830
1.2	.3849	.3869	.3888	.3907	.3925	.3944	.3962	.3980	.3997	.4015
1.3	.4032	.4049	.4066	.4082	.4099	.4115	.4131	.4147	.4162	.4177
1.4	.4192	.4207	.4222	.4236	.4251	.4265	.4279	.4292	.4306	.4319
1.5	.4332	.4345	.4357	.4370	.4382	.4394	.4406	.4418	.4429	.4441
1.6	.4452	.4463	.4474	.4484	.4495	.4505	.4515	.4525	.4535	.4545
1.7	.4554	.4564	.4573	.4582	.4591	.4599	.4608	.4616	.4625	.4633
1.8	.4641	.4649	.4656	.4664	.4671	.4678	.4686	.4693	.4699	.4706
1.9	.4713	.4719	.4726	.4732	.4738	.4744	.4750	.4756	.4761	.4767
2.0	.4773	.4778	.4783	.4788	.4793	.4798	.4803	.4808	.4812	.4817
2.1	.4821	.4826	.4830	.4834	.4838	.4842	.4846	.4850	.4854	.4857
2.2	.4861	.4864	.4868	.4871	.4875	.4878	.4881	.4884	.4887	.4890
2.3	.4893	.4896	.4898	.4901	.4904	.4906	.4909	.4911	.4913	.4916
2.4	.4918	.4920	.4922	.4925	.4927	.4929	.4931	.4932	.4934	.4936
2.5	.4938	.4940	.4941	.4943	.4945	.4946	.4948	.4949	.4951	.4952
2.6	.4953	.4955	.4956	.4957	.4959	.4960	.4961	.4962	.4963	.4964
2.7	.4965	.4966	.4967	.4968	.4969	.4970	.4971	.4972	.4973	.4974
2.8	.4974	.4975	.4976	.4977	.4977	.4978	.4979	.4979	.4980	.4981
2.9	.4981	.4982	.4982	.4982	.4984	.4984	.4985	.4985	.4986	.4986
3.0	.4987	.4987	.4987	.4988	.4988	.4989	.4989	.4989	.4990	.4990

SOLUTIONS TO
SELF-TEST PROBLEMS

Note: Except for Chapter 1, we do not show an answer for ST-1 problems because they are verbal rather than quantitative in nature.

CHAPTER 1

ST-1 Refer to the marginal glossary definitions or relevant chapter sections to check your responses.

CHAPTER 2

ST-2 a.

EBIT	$5,000,000
Interest	1,000,000
EBT	$4,000,000
Taxes (40%)	1,600,000
Net income	$2,400,000

b.
$$\text{NCF} = \text{NI} + \text{DEP and AMORT}$$
$$= \$2,400,000 + \$1,000,000 = \$3,400,000.$$

c.
$$\text{NOPAT} = \text{EBIT}(1 - T)$$
$$= \$5,000,000(0.6)$$
$$= \$3,000,000.$$

d.
$$\text{OCF} = \text{NOPAT} + \text{DEP and AMORT}$$
$$= \text{EBIT}(1 - T) + \text{DEP and AMORT}$$
$$= \$5,000,000(0.6) + \$1,000,000$$
$$= \$4,000,000.$$

e.
$$\text{FCF} = \text{NOPAT} + \text{Net investment in operating capital}$$
$$= \$3,000,000 - (\$25,000,000 - \$24,000,000)$$
$$= \$2,000,000.$$

f.
$$\text{EVA} = \text{EBIT}(1 - T) - (\text{Total operating capital})(\text{After-tax cost of capital})$$
$$= \$5,000,000(0.6) - (\$25,000,000)(0.10)$$
$$= \$3,000,000 - \$2,500,000 = \$500,000.$$

CHAPTER 3

ST-2 Billingsworth paid $2 in dividends and retained $2 per share. Since total retained earnings rose by $12 million, there must be 6 million shares outstanding. With a book value of $40 per share, total common equity must be $40(6 million) = $240 million. Since Billingsworth has $120 million of debt, its debt ratio must be 33.3 percent:

$$\frac{\text{Debt}}{\text{Assets}} = \frac{\text{Debt}}{\text{Debt} + \text{Equity}} = \frac{\$120 \text{ million}}{\$120 \text{ million} + \$240 \text{ milliion}}$$

$$= 0.333 = 33.3\%.$$

ST-3 a. In answering questions such as this, always begin by writing down the relevant definitional equations, then start filling in numbers. Note that the extra zeros indicating millions have been deleted in the calculations below.

(1)
$$\text{DSO} = \frac{\text{Accounts receivable}}{\text{Sales}/365}$$

$$40.55 = \frac{\text{A/R}}{\text{Sales}/365}$$

$$\text{A/R} = 40.55(\$2.7397) = \$111.1 \text{ million.}$$

(2)
$$\text{Current ratio} = \frac{\text{Current assets}}{\text{Current liabilities}} = 3.0$$

$$= \frac{\text{Current assets}}{\$105.5} = 3.0$$

$$\text{Current assets} = 3.0(\$105.5) = \$316.50 \text{ million.}$$

(3)
$$\text{Total assets} = \text{Current assets} + \text{Fixed assets}$$
$$= \$316.5 + \$283.5 = \$600 \text{ million.}$$

(4)
$$\text{ROA} = \text{Profit margin} \times \text{Total assets turnover}$$

$$= \frac{\text{Net income}}{\text{Sales}} \times \frac{\text{Sales}}{\text{Total assets}}$$

$$= \frac{\$50}{\$1,000} \times \frac{\$1,000}{\$600}$$

$$= 0.05 \times 1.667 = 0.083333 = 8.3333\%.$$

(5)
$$\text{ROE} = \text{ROA} \times \frac{\text{Assets}}{\text{Equity}}$$

$$12.0\% = 8.3333\% \times \frac{\$600}{\text{Equity}}$$

$$\text{Equity} = \frac{(8.3333\%)(\$600)}{12.0\%}$$

$$= \$416.67 \text{ million.}$$

(6)
$$\text{Total assets} = \text{Total claims} = \$600 \text{ million}$$
$$\text{Current liabilities} + \text{Long-term debt} + \text{Equity} = \$600 \text{ million}$$
$$\$105.5 + \text{Long-term debt} + \$416.67 = \$600 \text{ million}$$
$$\text{Long-term debt} = \$600 - \$105.5 - \$416.67 = \$77.83 \text{ million.}$$

Note: We could have found equity as follows:

$$\text{ROE} = \frac{\text{Net income}}{\text{Equity}}$$

$$12.0\% = \frac{\$50}{\text{Equity}}$$

$$\text{Equity} = \$50/0.12$$

$$= \$416.67 \text{ million.}$$

Then we could have gone on to find long-term debt.

b. Kaiser's average sales per day were $\$1,000/365 = \$2.74$ million. Its DSO was 40.55, so A/R $= 40.55(\$2.74) = \$111.1$ million. Its new DSO of 30.4 would cause A/R $= 30.4(\$2.74) = \$83.3$ million. The reduction in receivables would be $\$111.1 - \$83.3 = \$27.8$ million, which would equal the amount of cash generated.

(1)

$$\text{New equity} = \text{Old equity} - \text{Stock bought back}$$

$$= \$416.7 - \$27.8$$

$$= \$388.9 \text{ million.}$$

Thus,

$$\text{New ROE} = \frac{\text{Net income}}{\text{New equity}}$$

$$= \frac{\$50}{\$388.9}$$

$$= 12.86\% \text{ (versus old ROE of 12.0\%).}$$

(2)

$$\text{New ROA} = \frac{\text{Net income}}{\text{Total assets} - \text{Reduction in A/R}}$$

$$= \frac{\$50}{\$600 - \$27.8}$$

$$= 8.74\% \text{ (versus old ROA of 8.33\%).}$$

(3) The old debt is the same as the new debt:

$$\text{Debt} = \text{Total claims} - \text{Equity}$$

$$= \$600 - \$416.7 = \$183.3 \text{ million.}$$

$$\text{Old total assets} = \$600 \text{ million.}$$

$$\text{New total assets} = \text{Old total assets} - \text{Reduction in A/R}$$

$$= \$600 - \$27.8$$

$$= \$572.2 \text{ million.}$$

Therefore,

$$\frac{\text{Debt}}{\text{Old total assets}} = \frac{\$183.3}{\$600} = 30.6\%,$$

while

$$\frac{\text{New debt}}{\text{New total assets}} = \frac{\$183.3}{\$572.2} = 32.0\%.$$

CHAPTER 4

ST-2 a. Average $= (4\% + 5\% + 6\% + 7\%)/4 = 22\%/4 = 5.5\%$.

b. $k_{\text{T-bond}} = k^* + IP = 2\% + 5.5\% = 7.5\%$.

c. If the 5-year T-bond rate is 8 percent, the inflation rate is expected to average approximately $8\% - 2\% = 6\%$ during the next 5 years. Thus, the implied Year 5 inflation rate is 8 percent:

$$6\% = (4\% + 5\% + 6\% + 7\% + I_5)/5$$
$$30\% = 22\% + I_5$$
$$I_5 = 8\%.$$

CHAPTER 5

ST-2 a. The average rate of return for each stock is calculated simply by averaging the returns over the 5-year period. The average return for each stock is 18.90 percent, calculated for Stock A as follows:

$$k_{\text{Avg}} = (-10.00\% + 18.50\% + 38.67\% + 14.33\% + 33.00\%)/5$$
$$= 18.90\%.$$

The realized rate of return on a portfolio made up of Stock A and Stock B would be calculated by finding the average return in each year as $k_A(\%$ of Stock A) $+ k_B(\%$ of Stock B) and then averaging these annual returns:

YEAR	PORTFOLIO AB'S RETURN, k_{AB}
1998	(6.50%)
1999	19.90
2000	41.46
2001	9.00
2002	30.65
	$k_{\text{Avg}} = $ 18.90%

b. The standard deviation of returns is estimated, using Equation 5-3a, as follows (see Footnote 5):

$$\text{Estimated } \sigma = S = \sqrt{\frac{\sum_{t=1}^{n} (\bar{k}_t - \bar{k}_{\text{Avg}})^2}{n - 1}}. \qquad \text{(5-3a)}$$

For Stock A, the estimated σ is 19.0 percent:

$$\sigma_A = \sqrt{\frac{(-10.00 - 18.9)^2 + (18.50 - 18.9)^2 + \cdots + (33.00 - 18.9)^2}{5 - 1}}$$
$$= \sqrt{\frac{1{,}445.92}{4}} = 19.0\%.$$

The standard deviation of returns for Stock B and for the portfolio are similarly determined, and they are as follows:

	STOCK A	STOCK B	PORTFOLIO AB
Standard deviation	19.0	19.0	18.6

c. Since the risk reduction from diversification is small (σ_{AB} falls only from 19.0 to 18.6 percent), the most likely value of the correlation coefficient is 0.9. If the correlation coefficient were −0.9, the risk reduction would be much larger. In fact, the correlation coefficient between Stocks A and B is 0.92.

d. If more randomly selected stocks were added to a portfolio, σ_p would decline to somewhere in the vicinity of 20 percent; see Figure 5-8. σ_p would remain constant only if the correlation coefficient were +1.0, which is most unlikely. σ_p would decline to zero only if the correlation coefficient, r, were equal to zero and a large number of stocks were added to the portfolio, or if the proper proportions were held in a two-stock portfolio with r = −1.0.

ST-3 a.
$$b = (0.6)(0.70) + (0.25)(0.90) + (0.1)(1.30) + (0.05)(1.50)$$
$$= 0.42 + 0.225 + 0.13 + 0.075 = 0.85.$$

b.
$$k_{RF} = 6\%; RP_M = 5\%; b = 0.85.$$
$$k = 6\% + (5\%)(0.85)$$
$$= 10.25\%.$$

c.
$$b_N = (0.5)(0.70) + (0.25)(0.90) + (0.1)(1.30) + (0.15)(1.50)$$
$$= 0.35 + 0.225 + 0.13 + 0.225$$
$$= 0.93.$$
$$k = 6\% + (5\%)(0.93)$$
$$= 10.65\%.$$

CHAPTER 6

ST-2 a.

$1,000 is being compounded for 3 years, so your balance on January 1, 2007, is $1,259.71:

$$FV_n = PV(1 + i)^n = \$1,000(1 + 0.08)^3 = \$1,259.71.$$

Alternatively, using a financial calculator, input N = 3, I = 8, PV = −1000, PMT = 0, and FV = ? Solve for FV = $1,259.71.

b.

1/1/03		1/1/04		1/1/05		1/1/06		1/1/07

2%

−1,000   FV = ?

$$FV_n = PV\left(1 + \frac{i_{Nom}}{m}\right)^{mn} = FV_{12} = \$1,000(1.02)^{12} = \$1,268.24.$$

Alternatively, using a financial calculator, input N = 12, I = 2, PV = −1000, PMT = 0, and FV = ? Solve for FV = $1,268.24.

c.

1/1/03	8%	1/1/04	1/1/05	1/1/06	1/1/07
		250	250	250	250
					FV = ?

Using a financial calculator, input N = 4, I = 8, PV = 0, PMT = −250, and FV = ? Solve for FV = $1,126.53.

d.

1/1/03	8%	1/1/04	1/1/05	1/1/06	1/1/07
		?	?	?	?
					FV = 1,259.71

Using a financial calculator, input N = 4, I = 8, PV = 0, FV = 1259.71, and PMT = ? Solve for PMT = $279.56. Therefore, you would have to make 4 payments of $279.56 each to have a balance of $1,259.71 on January 1, 2007.

ST-3 a. Set up a time line like the one in the preceding problem:

Note that your deposit will grow for 3 years at 8 percent. The fact that it is now January 1, 2003, is irrelevant. The deposit on January 1, 2004, is the PV, and the FV is $1,000. Using a financial calculator, input N = 3, I = 8, PMT = 0, FV = 1000, and PV = ? Solve for PV = $793.83.

$$PV = \frac{FV_n}{(1 + i)^n} = \frac{\$1,000}{(1.08)^3} = \$793.83.$$

b.

Here we are dealing with a 4-year annuity whose first payment occurs 1 year from today, on 1/1/04, and whose future value must equal $1,000. You should modify the time line to help visualize the situation. Using a financial calculator, input N = 4, I = 8, PV = 0, FV = 1000, and PMT = ? Solve for PMT = $221.92.

c. This problem can be approached in several ways. Perhaps the simplest is to ask this question: "If I received $750 on 1/1/04 and deposited it to earn 8 percent, would I have the required $1,000 on 1/1/07?" The answer is no.

$$FV_3 = \$750(1.08)(1.08)(1.08) = \$944.78.$$

This indicates that you should let your father make the payments rather than accept the lump sum of $750.

You could also compare the $750 with the PV of the payments as shown below:

Using a financial calculator, input N = 4, I = 8, PMT = −221.92, FV = 0, and PV = ? Solve for PV = $735.03.

This is less than the $750 lump sum offer, so your initial reaction might be to accept the lump sum of $750. However, this would be a mistake. The problem is that when you found the $735.03 PV of the annuity, you were finding the value of the annuity *today*, on

January 1, 2003. You were comparing $735.03 today with the lump sum of $750 1 year from now. This is, of course, invalid. What you should have done was take the $735.03, recognize that this is the PV of an annuity as of January 1, 2003, multiply $735.03 by 1.08 to get $793.83, and compare $793.83 with the lump sum of $750. You would then take your father's offer to make the payments rather than take the lump sum on January 1, 2004.

d.

```
1/1/03  i = ?  1/1/04        1/1/05       1/1/06       1/1/07
  ├──────────────┼─────────────┼─────────────┼─────────────┤
         −750                                      1,000
```

Using a financial calculator, input N = 3, PV = −750, PMT = 0, FV = 1000, and I = ? Solve for I = 10.0642%.

e.

```
1/1/03  i = ?  1/1/04        1/1/05       1/1/06       1/1/07
  ├──────────────┼─────────────┼─────────────┼─────────────┤
              186.29         186.29       186.29       186.29
                                                      FV = 1,000
```

Using a financial calculator, input N = 4, PV = 0, PMT = −186.29, FV = 1000, and I = ? Solve for I = 19.9997%.

You might be able to find a borrower willing to offer you a 20 percent interest rate, but there would be some risk involved — he or she might not actually pay you your $1,000!

f.

```
1/1/03  4%   1/1/04        1/1/05       1/1/06       1/1/07
  ├──────┼──────┼──────┼──────┼──────┼──────┼──────┤
        400    ?      ?      ?      ?      ?      ?
                                            FV = 1,000
```

Find the future value of the original $400 deposit:

$$FV_6 = PV(1.04)^6 = \$400(1.2653) = \$506.13.$$

This means that on January 1, 2007, you need an additional sum of $493.87:

$$\$1,000.00 − \$506.13 = \$493.87.$$

This will be accumulated by making 6 equal payments that earn 8 percent compounded semiannually, or 4 percent each 6 months. Using a financial calculator, input N = 6, I = 4, PV = 0, FV = 493.87, and PMT = ? Solve for PMT = $74.46.

Alternatively, input N = 6, I = 4, PV = −400, FV = 1000, and PMT = ? Solve for PMT = $74.46.

g.
$$\text{Effective annual rate} = \left(1 + \frac{i_{Nom}}{m}\right)^m − 1.0$$

$$= \left(1 + \frac{0.08}{2}\right)^2 − 1 = (1.04)^2 − 1$$

$$= 1.0816 − 1 = 0.0816 = 8.16\%.$$

h. There is a reinvestment rate risk here because we assumed that funds will earn an 8 percent return in the bank. In fact, if interest rates in the economy fall, the bank will lower its deposit rate because it will be earning less when it lends out the funds you deposited with it. If you buy certificates of deposit (CDs) that mature on the date you need the money (1/1/07), you will avoid the reinvestment risk, but that would work only if you were making the deposit today. Other ways of reducing reinvestment rate risk will be discussed later in the text.

ST-4   Bank A's effective annual rate is 8.24 percent:

$$\text{Effective annual rate} = \left(1 + \frac{0.08}{4}\right)^4 - 1.0$$

$$= (1.02)^4 - 1 = 1.0824 - 1$$

$$= 0.0824 = 8.24\%.$$

Now Bank B must have the same effective annual rate:

$$\left(1 + \frac{i}{12}\right)^{12} - 1.0 = 0.0824$$

$$\left(1 + \frac{i}{12}\right)^{12} = 1.0824$$

$$1 + \frac{i}{12} = (1.0824)^{1/12}$$

$$1 + \frac{i}{12} = 1.00662$$

$$\frac{i}{12} = 0.00662$$

$$i = 0.07944 = 7.94\%.$$

Thus, the two banks have different quoted rates — Bank A's quoted rate is 8 percent, while Bank B's quoted rate is 7.94 percent; however, both banks have the same effective annual rate of 8.24 percent. The difference in their quoted rates is due to the difference in compounding frequency.

CHAPTER 7

ST-2   a. Pennington's bonds were sold at par; therefore, the original YTM equaled the coupon rate of 12 percent.

b.
$$V_B = \sum_{t=1}^{50} \frac{\$120/2}{\left(1 + \frac{0.10}{2}\right)^t} + \frac{\$1,000}{\left(1 + \frac{0.10}{2}\right)^{50}}.$$

With a financial calculator, input the following: N = 50, I = 5, PMT = 60, FV = 1000, and PV = ? Solve for PV = $1,182.56.

c.
$$\text{Current yield} = \text{Annual coupon payment/Price}$$

$$= \$120/\$1,182.56$$

$$= 0.1015 = 10.15\%.$$

$$\text{Capital gains yield} = \text{Total yield} - \text{Current yield}$$

$$= 10\% - 10.15\% = -0.15\%.$$

d. With a financial calculator, input the following: N = 13, PV = −916.42, PMT = 60, FV = 1000, and $k_d/2$ = I = ? Calculator solution = $k_d/2$ = 7.00%; therefore, k_d = 14.00%.

e.
$$\text{Current yield} = \$120/\$916.42 = 13.09\%.$$

$$\text{Capital gains yield} = 14\% - 13.09\% = 0.91\%.$$

f. The following time line illustrates the years to maturity of the bond:

```
   1/1/02      7/1/02      1/1/03      7/1/03      1/1/04     12/31/08
   |---+-------|-----------|-----------|-----------|--- ... ---|
       3/1/02
```

Thus, on March 1, 2002, there were 13⅔ periods left before the bond matured. Bond traders actually use the following procedure to determine the price of the bond:

(1) Find the price of the bond on the next coupon date, July 1, 2002. Using a financial calculator, input $N = 13$, $I = 7.75$, $PMT = 60$, $FV = 1000$, and $PV = ?$ Solve for $PV = \$859.76$.

(2) Add the coupon, $60, to the bond price to get the total value, TV, of the bond on the next interest payment date: $TV = \$859.76 + \$60.00 = \$919.76$.

(3) Discount this total value back to the purchase date (March 1, 2002):
Using a financial calculator, input $N = 4/6$, $I = 7.75$, $PMT = 0$, $FV = 919.76$, and $PV = ?$ Solve for $PV = \$875.11$.

(4) Therefore, you would have written a check for $875.11 to complete the transaction. Of this amount, $20 = (⅓)(\$60)$ would represent accrued interest and $855.11 would represent the bond's basic value. This breakdown would affect both your taxes and those of the seller.

(5) This problem could be solved *very* easily using a financial calculator with a bond valuation function, such as the HP-12C or the HP-17B. This is explained in the calculator manual under the heading, "Bond Calculations."

ST-3 a. $100,000,000/10 = \$10,000,000$ per year, or $5 million each 6 months. Since the $5 million will be used to retire bonds immediately, no interest will be earned on it.

b. The debt service requirements will decline. As the amount of bonds outstanding declines, so will the interest requirements (amounts given in millions of dollars):

SEMIANNUAL PAYMENT PERIOD (1)	SINKING FUND PAYMENT (2)	OUTSTANDING BONDS ON WHICH INTEREST IS PAID (3)	INTEREST PAYMENT[a] (4)	TOTAL BOND SERVICE (2) + (4) = (5)
1	$5	$100	$6.0	$11.0
2	5	95	5.7	10.7
3	5	90	5.4	10.4
.	.	.	.	.
.	.	.	.	.
.	.	.	.	.
20	5	5	0.3	5.3

[a] Interest is calculated as $(0.5)(0.12)$(Column 3); for example: interest in Period 2 $= (0.5)(0.12)(\$95) = \$5.7$.

The company's total cash bond service requirement will be $21.7 million per year for the first year. The requirement will decline by $0.12(\$10,000,000) = \$1,200,000$ per year for the remaining years.

c. Here we have a 10-year, 9 percent annuity whose compound value is $100 million, and we are seeking the annual payment, PMT. The solution can be obtained with a financial calculator. Input $N = 10$, $I = 9$, $PV = 0$, and $FV = 100000000$, and press the PMT key to obtain $6,582,009.

d. Annual debt service costs will be $\$100,000,000(0.12) + \$6,582,009 = \$18,582,009$.

e. If interest rates rose, causing the bond's price to fall, the company would use open market purchases. This would reduce its debt service requirements.

CHAPTER 8

ST-2 a. This is not necessarily true. Because G plows back two-thirds of its earnings, its growth rate should exceed that of D, but D pays higher dividends ($6 versus $2). We cannot say which stock should have the higher price.

  b. Again, we just do not know which price would be higher.

  c. This is false. The changes in k_d and k_s would have a greater effect on G; its price would decline more.

  d. The total expected return for D is $\hat{k}_D = D_1/P_0 + g = 15\% + 0\% = 15\%$. The total expected return for G will have D_1/P_0 less than 15 percent and g greater than 0 percent, but $\hat{k}_G$ should be neither greater nor smaller than D's total expected return, 15 percent, because the two stocks are stated to be equally risky.

  e. We have eliminated a, b, c, and d, so e should be correct. On the basis of the available information, D and G should sell at about the same price, $40; thus, $\hat{k}_s = 15\%$ for both D and G. G's current dividend yield is $2/\$40 = 5\%$. Therefore, $g = 15\% - 5\% = 10\%$.

ST-3 The first step is to solve for g, the unknown variable, in the constant growth equation. Since D_1 is unknown but D_0 is known, substitute $D_0(1 + g)$ as follows:

$$\hat{P}_0 = P_0 = \frac{D_1}{k_s - g} = \frac{D_0(1 + g)}{k_s - g}$$

$$\$36 = \frac{\$2.40(1 + g)}{0.12 - g}.$$

Solving for g, we find the growth rate to be 5 percent:

$$\$4.32 - \$36g = \$2.40 + \$2.40g$$
$$\$38.4g = \$1.92$$
$$g = 0.05 = 5\%.$$

The next step is to use the growth rate to project the stock price 5 years hence:

$$\hat{P}_5 = \frac{D_0(1 + g)^6}{k_s - g}$$
$$= \frac{\$2.40(1.05)^6}{0.12 - 0.05}$$
$$= \$45.95.$$

(Alternatively, $\hat{P}_5 = \$36(1.05)^5 = \$45.95$.)

Therefore, Ewald Company's expected stock price 5 years from now, $\hat{P}_5$, is $45.95.

ST-4 a. (1) Calculate the PV of the dividends paid during the supernormal growth period:

$$D_1 = \$1.1500(1.15) = \$1.3225.$$
$$D_2 = \$1.3225(1.15) = \$1.5209.$$
$$D_3 = \$1.5209(1.13) = \$1.7186.$$
$$PV\ D = \frac{\$1.3225}{1.12} + \frac{\$1.5209}{(1.12)^2} + \frac{\$1.7186}{(1.12)^3}$$
$$= \$1.1808 + \$1.2125 + \$1.2233$$
$$= \$3.6166 \approx \$3.62.$$

(2) Find the PV of Snyder's stock price at the end of Year 3:

$$\hat{P}_3 = \frac{D_4}{k_s - g} = \frac{D_3(1 + g)}{k_s - g}$$

$$= \frac{\$1.7186(1.06)}{0.12 - 0.06}$$

$$= \$30.36.$$

$$PV\ \hat{P}_3 = \frac{\$30.36}{(1.12)^3} = \$21.61.$$

(3) Sum the two components to find the value of the stock today:

$$\hat{P}_0 = \$3.62 + \$21.61 = \$25.23.$$

Alternatively, the cash flows can be placed on a time line as follows:

Enter the cash flows into the cash flow register and I = 12, and press the NPV key to obtain $P_0 = \$25.23$.

b.

$$\hat{P}_1 = \frac{\$1.5209}{1.12} + \frac{\$1.7186}{(1.12)^2} + \frac{\$30.36}{(1.12)^2}$$

$$= \$1.3579 + \$1.3701 + \$24.2028$$

$$= \$26.9308 \approx \$26.93.$$

(Calculator solution: $26.93.)

$$\hat{P}_2 = \frac{\$1.7186}{1.12} + \frac{\$30.36}{1.12}$$

$$= \$1.5345 + \$27.1071$$

$$= \$28.6416 \approx \$28.64.$$

(Calculator solution: $28.64.)

c.

YEAR	DIVIDEND YIELD	+	CAPITAL GAINS YIELD	=	TOTAL RETURN
1	$\frac{\$1.3225}{\$25.23} \approx 5.24\%$		$\frac{\$26.93 - \$25.23}{\$25.23} \approx 6.74\%$		$\approx 12\%.$
2	$\frac{\$1.5209}{\$26.93} \approx 5.65\%$		$\frac{\$28.64 - \$26.93}{\$26.93} \approx 6.35\%$		$\approx 12\%.$
3	$\frac{\$1.7186}{\$28.64} \approx 6.00\%$		$\frac{\$30.36 - \$28.64}{\$28.64} \approx 6.00\%$		$\approx 12\%.$

CHAPTER 9

ST-2 a. Component costs are as follows:
Common:

$$k_s = \frac{D_1}{P_0} + g = \frac{D_0(1 + g)}{P_0} + g$$

$$= \frac{\$3.60(1.09)}{\$54} + 0.09$$

$$= 0.0727 + 0.09 \hspace{3cm} = 16.27\%.$$

Preferred:

$$k_p = \frac{\text{Preferred dividend}}{P_p} = \frac{\$11}{\$95} \hspace{2cm} = 11.58\%.$$

Debt at $k_d = 12\%$:

$$k_d(1 - T) = 12\%(0.6) \hspace{3cm} = 7.20\%.$$

b. WACC calculation:

$$\text{WACC} = w_d k_d(1 - T) + w_p k_p + w_c k_s$$
$$\text{WACC} = 0.25(7.2\%) + 0.15(11.58\%) + 0.60(16.27\%) = 13.30\%.$$

c. LEI should accept Projects A, B, C, and D. It should reject Project E because its rate of return does not exceed the marginal cost of funds needed to finance it.

CHAPTER 10

ST-2 a. *Payback:*
To determine the payback, construct the cumulative cash flows for each project:

	CUMULATIVE CASH FLOWS	
YEAR	PROJECT X	PROJECT Y
0	($10,000)	($10,000)
1	(3,500)	(6,500)
2	(500)	(3,000)
3	2,500	500
4	3,500	4,000

$$\text{Payback}_X = 2 + \frac{\$500}{\$3,000} = 2.17 \text{ years.}$$

$$\text{Payback}_Y = 2 + \frac{\$3,000}{\$3,500} = 2.86 \text{ years.}$$

Net present value (NPV):

$$\text{NPV}_X = -\$10,000 + \frac{\$6,500}{(1.12)^1} + \frac{\$3,000}{(1.12)^2} + \frac{\$3,000}{(1.12)^3} + \frac{\$1,000}{(1.12)^4}$$
$$= \$966.01.$$

$$\text{NPV}_Y = -\$10,000 + \frac{\$3,500}{(1.12)^1} + \frac{\$3,500}{(1.12)^2} + \frac{\$3,500}{(1.12)^3} + \frac{\$3,500}{(1.12)^4}$$
$$= \$630.72.$$

Alternatively, using a financial calculator, input the cash flows into the cash flow register, enter I = 12, and then press the NPV key to obtain NPV_X = $966.01 and NPV_Y = $630.72.

Internal rate of return (IRR):
To solve for each project's IRR, find the discount rates that equate each NPV to zero:

$$IRR_X = 18.0\%.$$
$$IRR_Y = 15.0\%.$$

Modified internal rate of return (MIRR):
To obtain each project's MIRR, begin by finding each project's terminal value (TV) of cash inflows:

$$TV_X = \$6,500(1.12)^3 + \$3,000(1.12)^2 + \$3,000(1.12)^1 + \$1,000 = \$17,255.23.$$
$$TV_Y = \$3,500(1.12)^3 + \$3,500(1.12)^2 + \$3,500(1.12)^1 + \$3,500 = \$16,727.65.$$

Now, each project's MIRR is that discount rate that equates the PV of the TV to each project's cost, $10,000:

$$MIRR_X = 14.61\%.$$
$$MIRR_Y = 13.73\%.$$

b. The following table summarizes the project rankings by each method:

	PROJECT THAT RANKS HIGHER
Payback	X
NPV	X
IRR	X
MIRR	X

Note that all methods rank Project X over Project Y. In addition, both projects are acceptable under the NPV, IRR, and MIRR criteria. Thus, both projects should be accepted if they are independent.

c. In this case, we would choose the project with the higher NPV at k = 12%, or Project X.

d. To determine the effects of changing the cost of capital, plot the NPV profiles of each project. The crossover rate occurs at about 6 to 7 percent (6.2%). See the graph on the next page.

If the firm's cost of capital is less than 6.2 percent, a conflict exists because $NPV_Y > NPV_X$, but $IRR_X > IRR_Y$. Therefore, if k were 5 percent, a conflict would exist. Note, however, that when k = 5.0%, $MIRR_X$ = 10.64% and $MIRR_Y$ = 10.83%; hence, the modified IRR ranks the projects correctly, even if k is to the left of the crossover point.

e. The basic cause of the conflict is differing reinvestment rate assumptions between NPV and IRR. NPV assumes that cash flows can be reinvested at the cost of capital, while IRR assumes reinvestment at the (generally) higher IRR. The high reinvestment rate assumption under IRR makes early cash flows especially valuable, and hence short-term projects look better under IRR.

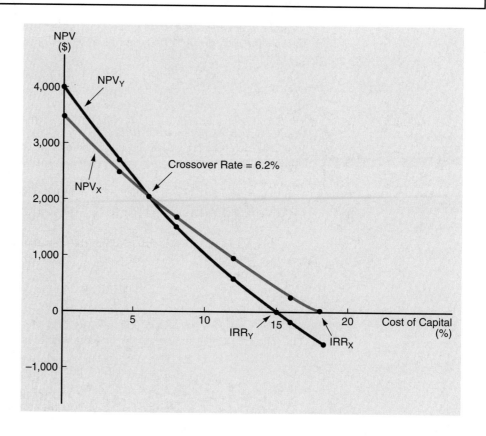

COST OF CAPITAL	NPV$_X$	NPV$_Y$
0%	$3,500	$4,000
4	2,545	2,705
8	1,707	1,592
12	966	631
16	307	(206)
18	5	(585)

CHAPTER 11

ST-2 a. *Estimated investment requirements:*

Price	($50,000)
Modification	(10,000)
Change in net operating working capital	(2,000)
Total investment	($62,000)

b. *Operating cash flows:*

	YEAR 1	YEAR 2	YEAR 3
1. After-tax cost savings[a]	$12,000	$12,000	$12,000
2. Depreciation[b]	19,800	27,000	9,000
3. Depreciation tax savings[c]	7,920	10,800	3,600
Operating cash flow (1 + 3)	$19,920	$22,800	$15,600

[a] $20,000(1 − T).

[b] Depreciable basis = $60,000; the MACRS percentage allowances are 0.33, 0.45, and 0.15 in Years 1, 2, and 3, respectively; hence, depreciation in Year 1 = 0.33($60,000) = $19,800, and so on. There will remain $4,200, or 7 percent, undepreciated after Year 3; it would normally be taken in Year 4.

[c] Depreciation tax savings = T(Depreciation) = 0.4($19,800) = $7,920 in Year 1, and so on.

c. *Terminal cash flow:*

Salvage value	$20,000
Tax on salvage value[a]	(6,320)
Net operating working capital recovery	2,000
Termination cash flow	$15,680

[a] Sales price	$20,000
Less book value	4,200
Taxable income	$15,800
Tax at 40%	$ 6,320

Book value = Depreciable basis − Accumulated depreciation
= $60,000 − $55,800 = $4,200.

d. *Project NPV:*

$$NPV = -\$62,000 + \frac{\$19,920}{(1.10)^1} + \frac{\$22,800}{(1.10)^2} + \frac{\$31,280}{(1.10)^3}$$

$$= -\$1,547.$$

Alternatively, using a financial calculator, input the cash flows into the cash flow register, enter I = 10, and then press the NPV key to obtain NPV = −$1,547. Because the earthmover has a negative NPV, it should not be purchased.

e. (1) *Savings in before-tax operating costs increase 15 percent:*

	YEAR 1	YEAR 2	YEAR 3
1. After-tax cost savings[a]	$13,800	$13,800	$13,800
2. Depreciation	19,800	27,000	9,000
3. Depreciation tax savings	7,920	10,800	3,600
4. Operating cash flow (1 + 3)	$21,720	$24,600	$17,400
Terminal cash flows:			
5. After-tax salvage value			13,680
6. Net operating working capital recovery			2,000
Net cash inflows	$21,720	$24,600	$33,080

[a] $20,000(1.15)(1 − T).

Project NPV:

$$NPV = -\$62,000 + \frac{\$21,720}{(1.10)^1} + \frac{\$24,600}{(1.10)^2} + \frac{\$33,080}{(1.10)^3}$$

$$= \$2,930.$$

Alternatively, using a financial calculator, input the cash flows into the cash flow register, enter I = 10, and then press the NPV key to obtain NPV = $2,930. Because the savings have increased by 15 percent, the decision to purchase the earthmover has changed from that in part d. Since its NPV is positive, the earthmover would now be purchased.

e. (2) *Earthmover's salvage value increases by 10 percent above original expectations.* All other data remain unchanged.

	YEAR 1	YEAR 2	YEAR 3
1. After-tax cost savings	$12,000	$12,000	$12,000
2. Depreciation	19,800	27,000	9,000
3. Depreciation tax savings	7,920	10,800	3,600
4. Operating cash flow (1 + 3)	$19,920	$22,800	$15,600
Terminal cash flows:			
5. Salvage value[a]			22,000
6. Tax on salvage value[b]			(7,120)
7. Net operating working capital recovery			2,000
Net cash inflows	$19,920	$22,800	$32,480

[a] $20,000(1.10).

[b]
Sales price	$22,000
Less book value	4,200
Taxable income	$17,800
Tax at 40%	$ 7,120

Project NPV:

```
  0    10%    1           2           3
  ├──────────┼───────────┼───────────┤
-62,000   19,920      22,800      32,480
```

$$NPV = -\$62,000 + \frac{\$19,920}{(1.10)^1} + \frac{\$22,800}{(1.10)^2} + \frac{\$32,480}{(1.10)^3}$$

$$= -\$645.$$

Alternatively, using a financial calculator, input the cash flows into the cash flow register, enter I = 10, and then press the NPV key to obtain NPV = −$645. Because the earth-mover has a negative NPV, it should not be purchased. Thus, the decision is the same as in part d.

f. *Worst-case scenario:*

	YEAR 1	YEAR 2	YEAR 3
1. After-tax cost savings[a]	$ 9,000	$ 9,000	$ 9,000
2. Depreciation	19,800	27,000	9,000
3. Depreciation tax savings	7,920	10,800	3,600
4. Operating cash flow (1 + 3)	$16,920	$19,800	$12,600
Terminal cash flows:			
5. Salvage value[b]			18,000
6. Tax on salvage value[c]			(5,520)
7. Net operating working capital recovery			2,000
Net cash inflows	$16,920	$19,800	$27,080

[a] $15,000(1 − T).
[b] Given as $18,000.
[c]

Sales price	$18,000
Less book value	4,200
Taxable income	$13,800
Tax at 40%	$ 5,520

Project NPV:

```
  0    10%    1           2           3
  ├──────────┼───────────┼───────────┤
-62,000   16,920      19,800      27,080
```

$$NPV = -\$62,000 + \frac{\$16,920}{(1.10)^1} + \frac{\$19,800}{(1.10)^2} + \frac{\$27,080}{(1.10)^3}$$

$$= -\$9,909.$$

Alternatively, using a financial calculator, input the cash flows into the cash flow register, enter I = 10, and then press the NPV key to obtain NPV = −$9,909.

Base-case scenario: The NPV was calculated in part d as −$1,547.

Best-case scenario:

	YEAR 1	YEAR 2	YEAR 3
1. After-tax cost savings[a]	$15,000	$15,000	$15,000
2. Depreciation	19,800	27,000	9,000
3. Depreciation tax savings	7,920	10,800	3,600
4. Operating cash flow (1 + 3)	$22,920	$25,800	$18,600
Terminal cash flows:			
5. Salvage value[b]			24,000
6. Tax on salvage value[c]			(7,920)
7. Net operating working capital recovery			2,000
Net cash inflows	$22,920	$25,800	$36,680

[a] $25,000(1 − T).
[b] Given as $24,000.
[c]

Sales price	$24,000
Less book value	4,200
Taxable income	$19,800
Tax at 40%	$ 7,920

Project NPV:

$$NPV = -\$62,000 + \frac{\$22,920}{(1.10)^1} + \frac{\$25,800}{(1.10)^2} + \frac{\$36,680}{(1.10)^3}$$

$$= \$7,717.$$

Alternatively, using a financial calculator, input the cash flows into the cash flow register, enter I = 10, and then press the NPV key to obtain NPV = $7,717.

SCENARIO	PROBABILITY	NPV
Worst case	30%	−$9,909
Base case	40	−1,547
Best case	30	7,717
		Expected NPV = −$1,276

$$\sigma_{NPV} = [0.3(-\$9,909 - (-\$1,276)]^2 + 0.4\,[-\$1,547 - (-\$1,276)]^2$$
$$+ 0.3\,[\$7,717 - (-\$1,276)]^2]^{1/2}$$
$$\sigma_{NPV} = [\$22,358,607 + \$29,376 + \$24,262,215]^{1/2}$$
$$\sigma_{NPV} = \$6,830.$$
$$CV_{NPV} = \frac{\$6,830}{-\$1,276} = -5.35.$$

ST-3 a. First, find the expected cash flows:

YEAR				EXPECTED CASH FLOWS
0	0.2(−$100,000)	+ 0.6(−$100,000)	+ 0.2(−$100,000)	= ($100,000)
1	0.2($20,000)	+ 0.6($30,000)	+ 0.2($40,000)	= $30,000
2				$30,000
3				$30,000
4				$30,000
5				$30,000
5*	0.2($0)	+ 0.6($20,000)	+ 0.2($30,000)	= $18,000

```
0   10%  1      2        3        4        5
|--------+------+--------+--------+--------+
-100,000 30,000 30,000   30,000   30,000  48,000
```

Next, determine the NPV based on the expected cash flows:

$$NPV = -\$100,000 + \frac{\$30,000}{(1.10)^1} + \frac{\$30,000}{(1.10)^2} + \frac{\$30,000}{(1.10)^3}$$

$$+ \frac{\$30,000}{(1.10)^4} + \frac{\$48,000}{(1.10)^5} = \$24,900.$$

Alternatively, using a financial calculator, input the cash flows into the cash flow register, enter I = 10, and then press the NPV key to obtain NPV = $24,900.

b. For the worst case, the cash flow values from the cash flow column farthest on the left are used to calculate NPV:

```
0   10%  1      2        3        4        5
|--------+------+--------+--------+--------+
-100,000 20,000 20,000   20,000   20,000  20,000
```

$$NPV = -\$100,000 + \frac{\$20,000}{(1.10)^1} + \frac{\$20,000}{(1.10)^2} + \frac{\$20,000}{(1.10)^3}$$

$$+ \frac{\$20,000}{(1.10)^4} + \frac{\$20,000}{(1.10)^5} = -\$24,184.$$

Similarly, for the best case, use the values from the column farthest on the right. Here the NPV is $70,259.

If the cash flows are perfectly dependent, then the low cash flow in the first year will mean a low cash flow in every year. Thus, the probability of the worst case occurring is the probability of getting the $20,000 net cash flow in Year 1, or 20 percent. If the cash flows are independent, the cash flow in each year can be low, high, or average, and the probability of getting all low cash flows will be

$$0.2(0.2)(0.2)(0.2)(0.2) = 0.2^5 = 0.00032 = 0.032\%.$$

c. The base-case NPV is found using the most likely cash flows and is equal to $26,142. This value differs from the expected NPV of $24,900 because the Year 5 cash flows are not symmetric. Under these conditions, the NPV distribution is as follows:

P	NPV
0.2	($24,184)
0.6	26,142
0.2	70,259

Thus, the expected NPV is 0.2(−$24,184) + 0.6($26,142) + 0.2($70,259) = $24,900. As is generally the case, the expected NPV is the same as the NPV of the expected cash flows found in part a. The standard deviation is $29,904:

$$\sigma^2{}_{NPV} = 0.2(-\$24{,}184 - \$24{,}900)^2 + 0.6(\$26{,}142 - \$24{,}900)^2$$
$$+ 0.2(\$70{,}259 - \$24{,}900)^2$$
$$= \$894{,}261{,}126.$$
$$\sigma_{NPV} = \sqrt{\$894{,}261{,}126} = \$29{,}904.$$

The coefficient of variation, CV, is $29,904/$24,900 = 1.20.

d. Since the project's coefficient of variation is 1.20, the project is riskier than average, and hence the project's risk-adjusted cost of capital is 10% + 2% = 12%. The project now should be evaluated by finding the NPV of the expected cash flows, as in part a, but using a 12 percent discount rate. The risk-adjusted NPV is $18,357, and, therefore, the project should be accepted.

CHAPTER 12

ST-2 a. Machine W:

$$NPV_W = -\$500{,}000 + \frac{\$300{,}000}{(1.10)^1} + \frac{\$300{,}000}{(1.10)^2}$$
$$= \$20{,}661.16.$$

Machine WW:

$$NPV_{WW} = -\$500{,}000 + \frac{\$165{,}000}{(1.10)^1} + \frac{\$165{,}000}{(1.10)^2} + \frac{\$165{,}000}{(1.10)^3} + \frac{\$165{,}000}{(1.10)^4}$$
$$= \$23{,}027.80.$$

Since the projects are independent and both have positive NPVs, both projects should be accepted.

b. Since the projects are mutually exclusive, only one project can be accepted. Therefore, Machine WW has the higher NPV and should be chosen.

c. Machine W's NPV needs to be recalculated under the assumption that it is repeated in Year 2.

Machine W:

$$NPV_W = \$37{,}736.49.$$

$NPV_{WW} = \$23{,}027.80.$ (NPV remains the same since it's calculated over a 4-year life.)

Since the projects are mutually exclusive but repeatable, Machine W should be chosen because its 4-year NPV is higher than Machine WW's.

d. If the two projects can be repeated indefinitely over time but the cash flows are expected to change, then the replacement chain analysis can be used. The analysis would be similar to what was done in part c except that the repeated cash flows would not be identical to the original cash flows.

CHAPTER 13

ST-2 a.

EBIT	$4,000,000
Interest ($2,000,000 × 0.10)	200,000
Earnings before taxes (EBT)	$3,800,000
Taxes (35%)	1,330,000
Net income	$2,470,000

$$EPS = \$2,470,000/600,000 = \$4.12.$$
$$P_0 = \$4.12/0.15 = \$27.47.$$

b.
$$Equity = 600,000 \times \$10 = \$6,000,000.$$
$$Debt = \$2,000,000.$$
$$Total\ capital = \$8,000,000.$$
$$WACC = w_d k_d (1 - T) + w_c k_s$$
$$= (2/8)(10\%)(1 - 0.35) + (6/8)(15\%)$$
$$= 1.63\% + 11.25\%$$
$$= 12.88\%.$$

c.

EBIT	$4,000,000
Interest ($10,000,000 × 0.12)	1,200,000
Earnings before taxes (EBT)	$2,800,000
Taxes (35%)	980,000
Net income	$1,820,000

Shares bought and retired:

$$\Delta N = \Delta Debt/P_0 = \$8,000,000/\$27.47 = 291,227.$$

New outstanding shares:

$$N_1 = N_0 - \Delta N = 600,000 - 291,227 = 308,773.$$

New EPS:

$$EPS = \$1,820,000/308,773 = \$5.89.$$

New price per share:

$$P_0 = \$5.89/0.17 = \$34.65\ versus\ \$27.47.$$

Therefore, Gentry should change its capital structure.

d. In this case, the company's net income would be higher by $(0.12 - 0.10)$ ($2,000,000) $(1 - 0.35) = \$26,000$ because its interest charges would be lower. The new price would be:

$$P_0 = \frac{(\$1,820,000 + \$26,000)/308,773}{0.17} = \$35.18.$$

In the first case, in which debt had to be refunded, the bondholders were compensated for the increased risk of the higher debt position. In the second case, the old bondholders were not compensated; their 10 percent coupon perpetual bonds would now be worth

$$\$100/0.12 = \$833.33,$$

or $1,666,667 in total, down from the old $2 million, or a loss of $333,333. The stockholders would have a gain of

$$(\$35.18 - \$34.65)(308,773) = \$163,650.$$

This gain would, of course, be at the expense of the old bondholders. (There is no reason to think that bondholders' losses would exactly offset stockholders' gains.)

e.
$$\text{TIE} = \frac{\text{EBIT}}{\text{I}}.$$

$$\text{Original TIE} = \frac{\$4,000,000}{\$200,000} = 20 \text{ times.}$$

$$\text{New TIE} = \frac{\$4,000,000}{\$1,200,000} = 3.33 \text{ times.}$$

ST-3   a. (1) Determine the variable cost per unit at present, using the following definitions and equations:

$$Q = \text{units of output (sales)} = 5,000.$$
$$P = \text{average sales price per unit of output} = \$100.$$
$$F = \text{fixed operating costs} = \$200,000.$$
$$V = \text{variable costs per unit.}$$
$$\text{EBIT} = P(Q) - F - V(Q)$$
$$\$50,000 = \$100(5,000) - \$200,000 - V(5,000)$$
$$5,000V = \$250,000$$
$$V = \$50.$$

(2) Determine the new EBIT level if the change is made:

$$\text{New EBIT} = P_2(Q_2) - F_2 - V_2(Q_2)$$
$$= \$95(7,000) - \$250,000 - \$40(7,000)$$
$$= \$135,000.$$

(3) Determine the incremental EBIT:

$$\Delta\text{EBIT} = \$135,000 - \$50,000 = \$85,000.$$

(4) Estimate the approximate rate of return on the new investment:

$$\Delta\text{ROA} = \frac{\Delta\text{EBIT}}{\text{Investment}} = \frac{\$85,000}{\$400,000} = 21.25\%.$$

Since the ROA exceeds Olinde's average cost of capital, this analysis suggests that Olinde should go ahead and make the investment.

b. The change would increase the breakeven point. Still, with a lower sales price, it might be easier to achieve the higher new breakeven volume.

$$\textit{Old: } Q_{BE} = \frac{F}{P - V} = \frac{\$200,000}{\$100 - \$50} = 4,000 \text{ units.}$$

$$\textit{New: } Q_{BE} = \frac{F}{P_2 - V_2} = \frac{\$250,000}{\$95 - \$40} = 4,545 \text{ units.}$$

c. The incremental ROA is:

$$\text{ROA} = \frac{\Delta\text{Profit}}{\Delta\text{Sales}} \times \frac{\Delta\text{Sales}}{\Delta\text{Assets}}.$$

Using debt financing, the incremental profit associated with the investment is equal to the incremental profit found in part a minus the interest expense incurred as a result of the investment:

$$\Delta\text{Profit} = \text{New profit} - \text{Old profit} - \text{Interest}$$
$$= \$135,000 - \$50,000 - 0.10(\$400,000)$$
$$= \$45,000.$$

The incremental sales is calculated as:

$$\Delta \text{Sales} = P_2Q_2 - P_1Q_1$$
$$= \$95(7,000) - \$100(5,000)$$
$$= \$665,000 - \$500,000$$
$$= \$165,000.$$

$$\text{ROA} = \frac{\$45,000}{\$165,000} \times \frac{\$165,000}{\$400,000} = 11.25\%.$$

The return on the new equity investment still exceeds the average cost of capital, so Olinde should make the investment.

CHAPTER 14

ST-2 a.

Projected net income	$2,000,000
Less projected capital investments	800,000
Available residual	$1,200,000
Shares outstanding	200,000

$$\text{DPS} = \$1,200,000/200,000 \text{ shares} = \$6 = D_1.$$

b.
$$\text{EPS} = \$2,000,000/200,000 \text{ shares} = \$10.$$
$$\text{Payout ratio} = \text{DPS/EPS} = \$6/\$10 = 60\%, \text{ or}$$
$$\text{Total dividends/NI} = \$1,200,000/\$2,000,000 = 60\%.$$

c.
$$\text{Currently, } P_0 = \frac{D_1}{k_s - g} = \frac{\$6}{0.14 - 0.05} = \frac{\$6}{0.09} = \$66.67.$$

Under the former circumstances, D_1 would be based on a 20 percent payout on $10 EPS, or $2. With $k_s = 14\%$ and $g = 12\%$, we solve for P_0:

$$P_0 = \frac{D_1}{k_s - g} = \frac{\$2}{0.14 - 0.12} = \frac{\$2}{0.02} = \$100.$$

Although CMC has suffered a severe setback, its existing assets will continue to provide a good income stream. More of these earnings should now be passed on to the shareholders, as the slowed internal growth has reduced the need for funds. However, the net result is a 33 percent decrease in the value of the shares.

d. If the payout ratio were continued at 20 percent, even after internal investment opportunities had declined, the price of the stock would drop to $2/(0.14 − 0.06) = $25 rather than to $66.67. Thus, an increase in the dividend payout is consistent with maximizing shareholder wealth.

Because of the diminishing nature of profitable investment opportunities, the greater the firm's level of investment, the lower the average ROE. Thus, the more money CMC retains and invests, the lower its average ROE will be. We can determine the average ROE under different conditions as follows:

Old situation (with founder active and a 20 percent payout):

$$g = (1.0 - \text{Payout ratio})(\text{Average ROE})$$
$$12\% = (1.0 - 0.2)(\text{Average ROE})$$
$$\text{Average ROE} = 12\%/0.8 = 15\% > k_s = 14\%.$$

Note that the *average* ROE is 15 percent, whereas the *marginal* ROE is presumably equal to 14 percent.

New situation (with founder retired and a 60 percent payout):

$$g = 6\% = (1.0 - 0.6)(ROE)$$
$$ROE = 6\%/0.4 = 15\% > k_s = 14\%.$$

This suggests that the new payout is appropriate and that the firm is taking on investments down to the point at which marginal returns are equal to the cost of capital. Note that if the 20 percent payout was maintained, the *average* ROE would be only 7.5 percent, which would imply a marginal ROE far below the 14 percent cost of capital.

CHAPTER 15

ST-2 The Calgary Company: Alternative Balance Sheets

	RESTRICTED (40%)	MODERATE (50%)	RELAXED (60%)
Current assets	$1,200,000	$1,500,000	$1,800,000
Fixed assets	600,000	600,000	600,000
Total assets	$1,800,000	$2,100,000	$2,400,000
Debt	$ 900,000	$1,050,000	$1,200,000
Equity	900,000	1,050,000	1,200,000
Total liabilities and equity	$1,800,000	$2,100,000	$2,400,000

The Calgary Company: Alternative Income Statements

	RESTRICTED	MODERATE	RELAXED
Sales	$3,000,000	$3,000,000	$3,000,000
EBIT	450,000	450,000	450,000
Interest (10%)	90,000	105,000	120,000
Earnings before taxes	$ 360,000	$ 345,000	$ 330,000
Taxes (40%)	144,000	138,000	132,000
Net income	$ 216,000	$ 207,000	$ 198,000
ROE	24.0%	19.7%	16.5%

ST-3 a. First, determine the balance on the firm's checkbook and the bank's records as follows:

	FIRM'S CHECKBOOK	BANK'S RECORDS
Day 1: Deposit $500,000; write check for $1,000,000	($500,000)	$500,0000
Day 2: Write check for $1,000,000	($1,500,000)	$500,0000
Day 3: Write check for $1,000,000	($2,500,000)	$500,0000
Day 4: Write check for $1,000,000; deposit $1,000,000	($2,500,000)	$500,0000

After Upton has reached a steady state, it must deposit $1,000,000 each day to cover the checks written 3 days earlier.

b. The firms has 3 days of float; not until Day 4 does the firm have to make any additional deposits.

c. As shown above, Upton should try to maintain a balance on the bank's records of $500,000. On its own books it will have a balance of *minus* $2,500,000.

CHAPTER 16

ST-2 a. and b.

Income Statements for Year Ended December 31, 2002 (Thousands of Dollars)

	VANDERHEIDEN PRESS		HERRENHOUSE PUBLISHING	
	a	b	a	b
EBIT	$ 30,000	$ 30,000	$ 30,000	$ 30,000
Interest	12,400	14,400	10,600	18,600
Taxable income	$ 17,600	$ 15,600	$ 19,400	$ 11,400
Taxes (40%)	7,040	6,240	7,760	4,560
Net income	$ 10,560	$ 9,360	$ 11,640	$ 6,840
Equity	$100,000	$100,000	$100,000	$100,000
Return on equity	10.56%	9.36%	11.64%	6.84%

The Vanderheiden Press has a higher ROE when short-term interest rates are high, whereas Herrenhouse Publishing does better when rates are lower.

c. Herrenhouse's position is riskier. First, its profits and return on equity are much more volatile than Vanderheiden's. Second, Herrenhouse must renew its large short-term loan every year, and if the renewal comes up at a time when money is very tight, when its business is depressed, or both, then Herrenhouse could be denied credit, which could put it out of business.

CHAPTER 17

ST-2 To solve this problem, we will define ΔS as the change in sales and g as the growth rate in sales, and then we use the three following equations:

$$\Delta S = S_0 g.$$
$$S_1 = S_0(1 + g).$$
$$AFN = (A^*/S_0)(\Delta S) - (L^*/S_0)(\Delta S) - MS_1(RR).$$

Set AFN = 0, substitute in known values for A^*/S_0, L^*/S_0, M, RR, and S_0, and then solve for g:

$$0 = 1.6(\$100g) - 0.4(\$100g) - 0.10[\$100(1 + g)](0.55)$$
$$0 = \$160g - \$40g - 0.055(\$100 + \$100g)$$
$$0 = \$160g - \$40g - \$5.5 - \$5.5g$$
$$\$114.5g = \$5.5$$
$$g = \$5.5/\$114.5 = 0.048 = 4.8\%$$
$$= \text{Maximum growth rate without external financing.}$$

ST-3 Assets consist of cash, marketable securities, receivables, inventories, and fixed assets. Therefore, we can break the A^*/S_0 ratio into its components—cash/sales, inventories/sales, and so forth. Then,

$$\frac{A^*}{S_0} = \frac{A^* - \text{Inventories}}{S_0} + \frac{\text{Inventories}}{S_0} = 1.6.$$

We know that the inventory turnover ratio is sales/inventories = 3 times, so inventories/sales = $1/3 = 0.3333$. Further, if the inventory turnover ratio can be increased to 4 times, then the inventory/sales ratio will fall to $1/4 = 0.25$, a difference of $0.3333 - 0.2500 = 0.0833$. This, in turn, causes the A^*/S_0 ratio to fall from $A^*/S_0 = 1.6$ to $A^*/S_0 = 1.6 - 0.0833 = 1.5167$.

This change has two effects: First, it changes the AFN equation, and second, it means that Weatherford currently has excessive inventories. Because it is costly to hold excess inventories, Weatherford will want to reduce its inventory holdings by not replacing inventories until the excess amounts have been used. We can account for this by setting up the revised AFN equation (using the new A^*/S_0 ratio), estimating the funds that will be needed next year if no excess inventories are currently on hand, and then subtracting out the excess inventories that are currently on hand:

Present conditions:

$$\frac{\text{Sales}}{\text{Inventories}} = \frac{\$100}{\text{Inventories}} = 3,$$

so

$$\text{Inventories} = \$100/3 = \$33.3 \text{ million at present.}$$

New conditions:

$$\frac{\text{Sales}}{\text{Inventories}} = \frac{\$100}{\text{Inventories}} = 4,$$

so

$$\text{New level of inventories} = \$100/4 = \$25 \text{ million.}$$

Therefore,

$$\text{Excess inventories} = \$33.3 - \$25 = \$8.3 \text{ million.}$$

Forecast of funds needed, first year:

$$\Delta S \text{ in first year} = 0.2(\$100 \text{ million}) = \$20 \text{ million.}$$
$$\text{AFN} = 1.5167(\$20) - 0.4(\$20) - 0.1(0.55)(\$120) - \$8.3$$
$$= \$30.3 - \$8 - \$6.6 - \$8.3$$
$$= \$7.4 \text{ million.}$$

Forecast of funds needed, second year:

$$\Delta S \text{ in first year} = gS_1 = 0.2(\$120 \text{ million}) = \$24 \text{ million.}$$
$$\text{AFN} = 1.5167(\$24) - 0.4(\$24) - 0.1(0.55)(\$144)$$
$$= \$36.4 - \$9.6 - \$7.9$$
$$= \$18.9 \text{ million.}$$

CHAPTER 18

ST-2

$$V = P[N(d_1)] - Xe^{-k_{RF}t}[N(d_2)]$$
$$V = [\$33(0.63369)] - [\$33(0.95123)(0.55155)]$$
$$V = \$20.91 - \$17.31$$
$$V = \$3.60.$$

CHAPTER 19

ST-2

$$\frac{\text{Euros}}{\text{C\$}} = \frac{\text{Euros}}{\text{US\$}} \times \frac{\text{US\$}}{\text{CS}}$$

$$= \frac{1.1215}{\$1} \times \frac{\$1}{1.5291} = \frac{1.1215}{1.5291} = 0.7334 \text{ euro per Canadian dollar.}$$

CHAPTER 20

ST-2 a. *Cost of leasing:*

	BEGINNING OF YEAR			
	0	1	2	3
Lease payment (AT)ᵃ	($ 6,000)	($6,000)	($6,000)	($6,000)
Total PV cost of leasing =	($22,038)			

ᵃ After-tax payment = $10,000(1 − T) = $10,000(0.60) = $6,000.

Using a financial calculator, input the following data after switching your calculator to "BEG" mode: N = 4, I = 6, PMT = 6000, and FV = 0. Then press the PV key to arrive at the answer of ($22,038). Now, switch your calculator back to "END" mode. Note that the interest rate used is the after-tax cost of debt, 10%(1 − T) = 6%.

b. *Cost of owning:*

Depreciable basis = $40,000.

Here are the cash flows under the borrow-and-buy alternative:

	END OF YEAR				
	0	1	2	3	4
1. Depreciation schedule					
(a) Depreciable basis		$40,000	$40,000	$40,000	$40,000
(b) Allowance		0.33	0.45	0.15	0.07
(c) Depreciation		13,200	18,000	6,000	2,800
2. Cash flows					
(d) Net purchase price	($40,000)				
(e) Depreciation tax savings		5,280ᵃ	7,200	2,400	1,120
(f) Maintenance (AT)		(600)	(600)	(600)	(600)
(g) Salvage value (AT)					6,000
(h) Total cash flows	($40,000)	$ 4,680	$ 6,600	$ 1,800	$ 6,520
Total PV cost of owning = ($23,036)					

ᵃ Depreciation(T) = $13,200(0.40) = $5,280.

Input the cash flows for the individual years into the cash flow register and enter I = 6, then press the NPV key to arrive at the answer of ($23,036). Because the present value of the cost of leasing is less than that of owning, the truck should be leased: $23,036 − $22,038 = $998, net advantage to leasing.

c. The discount rate is based on the cost of debt because most cash flows are fixed by contract and, consequently, are relatively certain. Thus, the lease cash flows have about the same risk as the firm's debt. Also, leasing is considered to be a substitute for debt. We use an after-tax cost rate because the cash flows are stated net of taxes.

d. Olsen could increase the discout rate on the salvage value cash flow. This would increase the PV cost of owning and make leasing even more advantageous.

CHAPTER 21

ST-2

$$k_s = 6\% + 4\%(1.5)$$

$$k_s = 12\%.$$

$$*\text{Terminal CF} = \frac{\$5(1.05)}{0.12 - 0.5} = \$75.00$$

To solve this problem, use your financial calculator to enter the following input data: $CF_0 = 0$; $CF_1 = 1.5$; $CF_2 = 2.0$; $CF_3 = 3.0$; $CF_4 = 80$; and I = 12. Then, solve for NPV = $55.91 million.

ANSWERS TO END-OF-CHAPTER PROBLEMS

We present here some intermediate steps and final answers to selected end-of-chapter problems. Please note that your answer may differ slightly from ours due to rounding differences. Also, although we hope not, some of the problems may have more than one correct solution, depending upon what assumptions are made in working the problem. Finally, many of the problems involve some verbal discussion as well as numerical calculations; this verbal material is not presented here.

2-1 $1,000,000.

2-2 $3,600,000.

2-3 $9,000.

2-4 $20,000,000.

2-5 $2,500,000.

2-6 NI = $450,000; NCF = $650,000; OCF = $650,000.

2-7 a.

2-8 a. $2,400,000,000.
b. $4,500,000,000.
c. $5,400,000,000.
d. $1,100,000,000.
e. $400,000,000.

2-9 10,500,000 shares.

2-10 $255,000.

2-11 $89,100,000.

2-12 a. $50,000.
b. $115,000.

2-13 $12,681,482.

2-14 a. $584 million.
b. RE_{01} = $1,302 million.
c. $1,520 million.
d. $15 million.
e. $620 million.

2-15 a. $2,400,000.
b. NI = 0; NCF = $3,000,000.
c. NI = $1,350,000; NCF = $2,100,000.

2-16 $2,500,000.

2-17 a. $90,000,000.
b. $NOWC_{02}$ = $192,000,000.
c. OC_{01} = $460,000,000.
d. FCF = $58,000,000.

3-1 AR = $800,000.

3-2 D/A = 58.33%.

3-3 TATO = 5; EM = 1.5.

3-4 M/B = 4.2667.

3-5 TIE = 2.25.

3-6 $\dfrac{NI}{S}$ = 2%; $\dfrac{D}{A}$ = 40%.

3-7 $262,500.

3-8 TIE = 3.86×.

3-9 2.9867.

3-10 ROE = 23.1%.

3-11 7.2%.

3-12 a.

3-13 a. +5.54%.
b(2). +3.21%.
  (3). +2.50%.

3-14 1.76.

3-15 6.0.

3-16 $142.50.

3-17 $405,682.

3-18 $50.

3-19 $112,500.

3-20 15.31%.

3-21 A/P = $90,000; Inv = $90,000; FA = $138,000.

3-22 a. Current ratio = 1.98×; DSO = 76.3 days; Total assets turnover = 1.7×; Debt ratio = 61.9%.

3-24 a. DSO = 37.4 days; ROE = 13.1%; Debt ratio = 54.8%; P/CF = 2.0×.

4-1 6%; 6.33%.

4-2 1.5%.

4-3 5.5%.

4-4 0.2%.

4-5	8.5%.		**6-1**	$FV_5 = \$16,105.10$.
4-6	6.8%.		**6-2**	$PV = \$1,292.10$.
4-7	a. k_1 in Year 2 = 6%.		**6-3**	$n = 11.01$ years.
	b. $I_1 = 2\%$; $I_2 = 5\%$.		**6-4**	$n = 11$ years.
4-8	k_1 in Year 2 = 9%; $I_2 = 7\%$.		**6-5**	$i = 8.01\%$.
4-9	6.0%.		**6-6**	$FVA_5 = \$1,725.22$.
4-10	1.775%.		**6-7**	$FVA_{5\ Due} = \$1,845.99$.
4-11	2.25%.		**6-8**	$PV = \$923.98$; $FV = \$1,466.24$.
4-12	1.55%.		**6-9**	$PMT = \$444.89$; $EAR = 12.6825\%$.
4-13	0.35%.		**6-10**	a. 14.87%.
4-14	a. $k_1 = 9.20\%$; $k_5 = 7.20\%$.		**6-11**	7.18%.
4-16	a. 8.20%.		**6-12**	9%.
	b. 10.20%.		**6-13**	a. $33,872.11.
	c. $k_5 = 10.70\%$.			b. $26,243.16 and $0.
			6-14	6 years; $1,106.01.
5-1	$\hat{k} = 11.40\%$; $\sigma = 26.69\%$; $CV = 2.34$.		**6-15**	Contract 2; $PV = \$10,717,847.14$.
5-2	$b_p = 1.12$.		**6-16**	$PV_{7\%} = \$1,428.57$; $PV_{14\%} = \$714.29$.
5-3	$k_M = 11\%$; $k = 12.2\%$.		**6-17**	$893.16.
5-4	$k = 10.9\%$.		**6-18**	$984.88 \approx \$985$.
5-5	a. $b = 1$.		**6-19**	57.2%.
	b. $k = 13\%$.		**6-20**	a. $FV = \$1,432.02$.
5-6	a. $\hat{k}_Y = 14\%$.			b. $PMT = \$93.07$.
	b. $\sigma_X = 12.20\%$.		**6-21**	$k_{Nom} = 15.19\%$.
5-7	a. $k_i = 15.5\%$.		**6-22**	$PMT = \$36,949.61$.
	b(1). $k_M = 15\%$; $k_i = 16.5\%$.		**6-23**	a. $18.56 million.
	c(1). $k_i = 18.1\%$.			b. $86.49 million.
5-8	$b_N = 1.16$.			c. $PV = \$17.18$ million; $FV = \$80.08$ million.
5-9	$b_p = 0.7625$; $k_p = 12.1\%$.		**6-24**	a. $666,669.35.
5-10	4.5%.			b. $1,206,663.42.
5-11	a. $CV_X = 3.5$; $CV_Y = 2.0$.		**6-25**	$353,171.50.
	c. $k_X = 10.5\%$; $k_Y = 12\%$.		**6-26**	$17,659.50.
	d. Stock Y.		**6-27**	$35.
	e. $k_P = 10.875\%$.		**6-28**	$84.34.
5-12	$k = 17.05\%$.		**6-29**	a. 31.72 years.
5-13	$k_M - k_{RF} = 4.375\%$.			b. 2.56 years.
5-14	$b = 1.33$.			c. $3,368.
5-15	7.2%.		**6-30**	a. 30-year payment plan; $PV = \$68,249,727$.
5-16	4.5%.			b. 10-year payment plan; $PV = \$63,745,773$.
5-17	$k_P = 11.75\%$.			c. Lump sum; $PV = \$61,000,000$.
5-18	1.7275.		**6-31**	$17,290.89; $19,734.26.
5-19	a. $0.5 million.		**6-32**	a. 47.66 months $\approx$ 48 months.
5-20	a. $k_i = 6\% + (5\%)b_i$.			b. $6.66.
	b. 15%.			c. 11.50 months $\approx$ 12 months.
	c. Indifference rate = 16%.			d. $131.65.
5-21	a. $\bar{k}_A = 11.30\%$.		**6-33**	16.32%.
	c. $\sigma_A = 20.8\%$; $\sigma_P = 20.1\%$.			

6-34   a. $530.
       d. $445.

6-35   a. $895.40.
       b. $1,552.90.
       c. $279.20.
       d. $500.03; $867.14.

6-36   a. ≈10 years.
       c. ≈4 years.

6-37   a. $6,374.97.
       d(1). $7,012.47.

6-38   a. $2,457.83.
       c. $2,000.
       d(1). $2,703.61.

6-39   a. Stream A: $1,251.25.

6-40   b. 7%.
       c. 9%.
       d. 15%.

6-41   a. $881.17.
       b. $895.42.
       c. $903.06.
       d. $908.35.

6-42   a. $279.20.
       b. $276.84.
       c. $443.72.

6-43   a. $5,272.32.
       b. $5,374.07.

6-44   a. 1st City = 7%; 2nd City = 6.14%.

6-45   a. PMT = $6,594.94.

6-46   a. $917.21.
       b. 90.51%.
       c. $118,837.32.
       d. $163,540.19.

6-47   a. Z = 9%; B = 8%.
       b. Z = $558.39; $135.98; 32.2%; B = $1,147.20;
          $147.20; 14.72%.

6-48   a. $61,204.
       b. $11,020.
       c. $6,841.

7-1 $935.82.

7-2   YTM = 6.62%; YTC = 6.49%.

7-3 $1,028.60.

7-4   a. 7.11%.
       b. 7.22%.
       c. $988.46.

7-5   a. V_L at 5 percent = $1,518.98; V_L at 8 percent =
          $1,171.19; V_L at 12 percent = $863.78.

7-6   a. YTM at $829 ≈ 15%.

7-7   15.03%.

7-8   a. 10.37%.
       b. 10.91%.
       c. −0.54%.
       d. 10.15%.

7-9   8.65%.

7-10   10.78%.

7-11   YTC = 6.47%.

7-12   a. 8.35%.
       b. 8.13%.

7-13 $987.87.

7-14 $1,067.95.

7-15   a. 8.875%.
       b. 9.69%.
       c. 0.816%.

7-16 $34.4 million.

7-17   8.88%.

7-19   a. YTM = 8%; YTC = 6.1%.

7-20   10-year, 10% coupon = 6.75%;
       10-year zero = 9.75%;
       5-year zero = 4.76%;
       30-year zero = 32.19%;
       $100 perpetuity = 14.29%.

7-21   a. C_0 = $1,012.79; Z_0 = $693.04;
          C_1 = $1,010.02; Z_1 = $759.57;
          C_2 = $1,006.98; Z_2 = $832.49;
          C_3 = $1,003.65; Z_3 = $912.41;
          C_4 = $1,000.00; Z_4 = $1,000.00.

8-1 D_1 = $1.5750; D_3 = $1.7364; D_5 = $2.1011.

8-2 P_0 = $6.25.

8-3 $\hat{P}_1$ = $22.00; k_s = 15.50%.

8-4 k_p = 8.33%.

8-5   b. $37.80.
       c. $34.09.

8-6 $60.

8-7   a. $24,112,308.
       b. $321,000,000.
       c. $228,113,612.
       d. $16.81.

8-8 $35.00.

8-9   a. $713.33 million.
       b. $527.89 million.
       c. $42.79.

8-10 $\hat{P}_3$ = $27.32.

8-11   a. 13.3%.
       b. 10%.
       c. 8%.
       d. 5.7%.

8-12 $23.75.

8-13   a. $k_C = 10.6\%$; $k_D = 7\%$.

8-14 $P_0 = \$19.89$.

8-15   a. 10%.
       b. 10.38%.

8-16   6.25%.

8-17 $13.11.

8-18   a. $125.
       b. $83.33.

8-19   b. PV = $5.29.
       d. $30.01.

8-20   a(1). $9.50.
       (2). $13.33.
       b(1). Undefined.

8-22   a. Dividend 2005 = $2.66.
       b. $P_0 = \$39.43$.
       c. Dividend yield 2003 = 5.10%; 2008 = 7.00%.

8-23   a. $P_0 = \$54.11$.

8-24   a. $P_0 = \$21.43$.
       b. $P_0 = \$26.47$.
       d. $P_0 = \$40.54$.

8-25   a. New price = $31.34.
       b. beta = 0.49865.

9-1 $k_s = 13\%$.

9-2 $k_p = 8\%$.

9-3 $k_s = 15\%$; $k_e = 16.11\%$.

9-4   Projects A through E should be accepted.

9-5   7.80%.

9-6   11.94%.

9-7   a. $k_s = 14.83\%$.
       b. F = 10%.
       c. $k_e = 15.81\%$.

9-8   WACC = 12.72%.

9-9 $w_d = 20\%$.

9-10   a. $k_s = 14.40\%$.
       b. WACC = 10.62%.
       c. Project A.

9-11 $k_s = 16.51\%$; WACC = 12.79%.

9-12   17.26%.

9-13   a. 9.10%.
       b. 50.39%.

9-14   11.4%.

9-15   a. Projects A, C, E, F, and H should be accepted.
       b. Projects A, F, and H should be accepted; $12 million.
       c. Projects A, C, F, and H should be accepted; $15 million.

9-16   a. 16.3%.
       b. 15.4%.
       c. 16%.

9-17   a. 8%.
       b. $2.81.
       c. 15.81%.

9-18   a. g = 3%.
       b. $EPS_1 = \$5.562$.

9-19   a. $k_d(1 - T) = 5.4\%$; $k_s = 14.6\%$.
       b. WACC = 10.92%.

9-20   a. $k_d = 7\%$; $k_p = 10.20\%$; $k_s = 15.72\%$.
       b. WACC = 13.86%.
       c. Projects 1 and 2 will be accepted.

10-1   4.34 years.

10-2   NPV = $7,486.68.

10-3   IRR = 16%.

10-4   DPP = 6.51 years.

10-5   MIRR = 13.89%.

10-6   5%: $NPV_A = \$16,108,952$; $NPV_B = \$18,300,939$.
       15%: $NPV_A = \$10,059,587$; $NPV_B = \$13,897,838$.

10-7 $NPV_T = \$409$; $IRR_T = 15\%$; $MIRR_T = 14.54\%$;
       Accept; $NPV_P = \$3,318$; $IRR_P = 20\%$; $MIRR_P = 17.19\%$; Accept.

10-8 $NPV_S = \$448.86$; $NPV_L = \$607.20$; $IRR_S = 15.24\%$; $IRR_L = 14.67\%$; $MIRR_S = 14.67\%$; $MIRR_L = 14.37\%$.

10-9   b. $PV_C = -\$556,717$; $PV_F = -\$493,407$; Forklift should be chosen due to lower cost.

10-10 $MIRR_X = 13.59\%$.

10-11 $IRR_L = 11.74\%$.

10-12   MIRR = 10.93%.

10-13   a. NPV = $136,578; IRR = 19.22%.

10-14   a. Payback = 0.33 year;
       NPV = $81,062.35; IRR = 261.90%.

10-15   a. No; $PV_{Old} = -\$89,910.08$;
       $PV_{New} = -\$94,611.45$.
       b. $2,470.80.
       c. 22.94%.

10-16   a. $Payback_A = 4.04$ years; $Payback_B = 2$ years; choose B.
       b. Discounted $payback_A = 4.78$ years; Discounted $payback_B = 4.24$ years; choose B.
       c. $NPV_A = \$30.16$; $NPV_B = \$23.42$; choose A.
       d. $IRR_A = 12.21\%$; $IRR_B = 12.28\%$; choose B.
       e. $MIRR_A = 11.61\%$; $MIRR_B = 10.85\%$; choose A.

10-17 $10,239.20.

10-18 $250.01.

10-19 c. $IRR_A = 18.1\%$; $IRR_B = 24.0\%$.
e. (1). $MIRR_A = 15.10\%$; $MIRR_B = 17.03\%$.
(2). $MIRR_A = 18.05\%$; $MIRR_B = 20.49\%$.

10-20 a. $IRR_A = 20\%$; $IRR_B = 16.7\%$; Crossover rate = $16.07\% \approx 16\%$.

10-21 a. $NPV_A = \$14,486,808$; $NPV_B = \$11,156,893$; $IRR_A = 15.03\%$; $IRR_B = 22.26\%$.

10-22 d. 9.54%; 22.87%.

10-23 a. A = 2.67 years; B = 1.5 years.
b. A = 3.07 years; B = 1.825 years.
d. $NPV_A = \$18,243,813$; choose A.
e. $NPV_B = \$8,643,390$; choose B.
f. 13.53%.
g. $MIRR_A = 21.93\%$; $MIRR_B = 20.96\%$.

11-1 $12,000,000.

11-2 $2,600,000.

11-3 $4,600,000.

11-4 $E(NPV) = \$3,000,000$; $\sigma_{NPV} = \$23.622$ million; CV = 7.874.

11-5 a. NPV = $37,035.13.
b. +20%: $77,975.63;
−20%: NPV = −$3,905.37.
c. $E(NPV) = \$34,800.21$; $\sigma_{NPV} = \$35,967.84$; CV = 1.03.

11-6 b. Accelerated method; $12,781.64.

11-7 a. −$178,000.
b. $52,440; $60,600; $40,200.
c. $48,760.
d. NPV = −$19,549; Do not purchase.

11-8 a. −$126,000.
b. $42,518; $47,579; $34,926.
c. $50,702.
d. NPV = $10,841; Purchase.

11-9 a. Expected $CF_A = \$6,750$; Expected $CF_B = \$7,650$; $CV_A = 0.0703$.
b. $NPV_A = \$10,036$; $NPV_B = \$11,624$.

11-10 $NPV_5 = \$2,212$; $NPV_4 = −\$2,081$; $NPV_8 = \$13,329$.

12-1 a. Project B; $NPV_B = \$2,679.46$.
b. Project A; $NPV_A = \$3,773.65$.

12-2 Accept A, B, C, D, and E; Capital budget = $5,250,000.

12-3 Accept A, B, C, D, and E; Capital budget = $4,000,000.

12-4 Accept B, C, D, E, F, and G; Capital budget = $6,000,000.

12-5 $NPV_{190-3} = \$20,070$; $NPV_{360-6} = \$22,256$.

12-6 $NPV_A = \$12.76$ million.

12-7 Machine A; Extended $NPV_A = \$4.51$ million.

12-8 a. NPV = $2.4083 million.
b. Yes, NPV = $2.6131 million.

12-9 No, $NPV_3 = \$1,307.29$.

12-10 a. NPV = $4.6795 million.
b. No, NPV = $3.2083 million.

12-11 a. NPV = −$2,113,481.31.
b. NPV = $1,973,037.39.
c. E(NPV) = −$70,221.96.
d. E(NPV) = $565,090.13.
e. $1,116,071.43.

13-1 $Q_{BE} = 500,000$.

13-2 30% debt and 70% equity.

13-3 $b_U = 1.0435$.

13-4 a(1). −$60,000.
b. $Q_{BE} = 14,000$.

13-5 a. $P_0 = \$25$.
b. $P_0 = \$25.81$.

13-6 a. $ROE_{LL} = 14.6\%$; $ROE_{HL} = 16.8\%$.
b. $ROE_{LL} = 16.5\%$.

13-7 No leverage: ROE = 10.5%; σ = 5.4%; CV = 0.51; 60% leverage: ROE = 13.7%; σ = 13.5%; CV = 0.99.

13-8 $k_s = 17\%$.

13-9 a. 10.96%.
b. 1.25.
c. 1.086957.
d. 14.13%.
e. 10.64%.

13-11 a. $EPS_{Old} = \$2.04$; New: $EPS_D = \$4.74$; $EPS_S = \$3.27$.
b. 339,750 units.
c. $Q_{New, Debt} = 272,250$ units.

13-12 Debt used: E(EPS) = $5.78; σ_{EPS} = $1.05; E(TIE) = 3.49×.
Stock used: E(EPS) = $5.51; σ_{EPS} = $0.85; E(TIE) = 6.00×.

13-13 a. $FC_A = \$80,000$; $V_A = \$4.80$/unit; $P_A = \$8.00$/unit.

13-14 40% debt and 60% equity; WACC = 11.45%.

14-1 Payout = 55%.

14-2 $P_0 = \$60$.

14-3 $P_0 = \$40$.

14-4 $3,250,000.

14-5 $D_0 = \$3.44$.

14-6 Payout = 31.39%.

14-7	a. 12%.	16-1	k_{Nom} = 75.26%; EAR = 109.84%.

14-7
  a. 12%.
  b. 17%.
  c. 6%; 16%.
  d. 5%.
  e. 24,000 new shares; $0.11 per share.

14-8
  a. $1.44.
  b. 3%.
  c. $1.20.
  d. 33 1/3%.

14-9
  a(1). $3,960,000.
    (2). $4,800,000.
    (3). $9,360,000.
    (4). Regular = $3,960,000; Extra = $5,400,000.
  c. 15%.
  d. 15%.

14-10
  a. $6,000,000.
  b. $2.00; 25%.
  c. $5,000,000.
  e. 50%.
  f. $1,000,000.
  g. $8,333,333.

15-1 $10,000.

15-2 $3,000,000.

15-3 A/R = $59,500.

15-4
  a. $103,350.
  b. $97,500.

15-5
  a. DSO = 28 days.
  b. A/R = $70,000.

15-6
  a. $500,000.
  b. 18.48 days.

15-7
  a. 32 days.
  b. $288,000.
  c. $45,000.
  d(1). 30.
    (2). $378,000.

15-8
  a. 83 days.
  b. $356,250.
  c. 4.87×.

15-9
  a. 69.5 days.
  b(1). 1.875×.
    (2). 11.25%.
  c(1). 46.5 days.
    (2). 2.1262×.
    (3). 12.76%.

15-10
  a. ROE_T = 11.75%; ROE_M = 10.80%; ROE_R = 9.16%.

15-11
  a. $1,600,000.
  c. Bank = $1,200,000; Books = −$5,200,000.

15-12
  b. $420,000.
  c. $35,000.

15-13
  a. Oct. loan = $22,800.

16-1 k_{Nom} = 75.26%; EAR = 109.84%.

16-2 EAR = 8.49%.

16-3 $7,500,000.

16-4 $233.56.

16-5 EAR = 21.60%.

16-6
  b. 14.90%.
  d. 21.28%.

16-7
  a. 45.15%.

16-8
  a. k_d = 12%.
  b. k_d = 11.25%.
  c. k_d = 11.48%.
  d. k_d = 14.47%. Alternative b has lowest interest rate.

16-9 Bank loan = 13.64%.

16-10 d. 8.3723%.

16-11
  a. $100,000.
  c(1). $300,000.
    (2). Nominal cost = 37.24%; Effective cost = 44.59%.

16-13
  a. $300,000.

16-14
  a. 11.73%.
  b. 12.09%.
  c. 18%.

16-15
  a. $83.33; $250.
  b. Discounts: $641.03; No discounts: $384.62.
  c. Trade credit: 18.18%; 19.83%.
    Loan: 23.08%.
  d. Cash = $126.90; NP = $434.60.
  e. $251,515.15; −$1,515.15; $386,946.38.

16-16
  a(1). $27,260.
    (3). $25,616.

17-1 AFN = $410,000.

17-2 AFN = $610,000.

17-3 AFN = $200,000.

17-4 5.01.

17-5
  a. $5,555,555,556.
  b. 30.6%.
  c. $13,600,000.

17-6
  a. $133.50 million.
  b. 39.06%.

17-7 $156 million.

17-8
  a. $480,000.
  b. $18,750.

17-9 ΔS = $68,965.52.

17-10 34.97 ≈ 35 days.

17-11 6.0451.

17-12
  a. $2,500,000,000.
  b. 24%.
  c. $24,000,000.

17-13   a. $383.06.
  b. 27.69%.

17-14   a. $13.44 million.
  b. Notes payable = $13.44 million.
  c. Current ratio = 2.00×; ROE = 14.2%.
  d(1). −14.28 million (surplus).
    (2). Total assets = $147 million; Notes payable = $3.72 million.
    (3). Current ratio = 4.25×; ROE = 10.84%.

17-15   a. 33%.
  b. AFN = $2,549.
  c. ROE = 13.06%.

17-16   a. AFN = $128,783.
  b. 3.45%.

17-17   a. AFN = $667.
  b. Increase in notes payable = $51; Increase in C/S = $368.

18-1   a. $5.00.
  b. $2.00.

18-2   a, b, and c.

18-3 $1.82.

18-4 $27.00; $37.00.

18-5 k_d = 7.95%; $91,227.97.

18-6   b. Futures = +$4,487,701; Bond = −$2,203,701; Net = $2,284,000.

18-7   a. $3.06; $4.29.
  b. 16.67%, 61.46%; −100%.
  c. −16.67%; −100%; 63.40%.
  d. No; $30.00 and $27.00.
  e. Yes; $37.50 and $37.50.

19-1   27.2436 yen per shekel.

19-2   1 yen = $0.00907.

19-3   1 euro = $0.68966 or $1 = 145 euros.

19-4   0.6667 pound per dollar.

19-5   6.49351 krones.

19-6   15 kronas per pound.

19-8 $468,837,209.

19-9   +$250,000.

19-10   a. $52.63; 20%.
  b. 1.5785 SF per U.S. $.
  c. 41.54 Swiss francs; 16.92%.

19-11

| | DOLLARS PER 1,000 UNITS OF: | | | | |
POUNDS	CAN. DOLLARS	EUROS	YEN	PESOS	KRONAS
$1,539.80	$630.80	$966.60	$8.27	$102.70	$103.30

19-13   b. $18,223.

19-14   a. $2,772,003.
  b. $2,777,585.
  c. $3,333,333.

19-15   b. $1.6488.

19-16 $k_{\text{Nom-U.S.}}$ = 4.6%.

19-17   117 pesos.

20-1   55.6%; 50%.

20-2 $196.36.

20-3   CR = 25 shares.

20-4   a. PV cost of leasing = −$954,639; Lease equipment.

20-5   a. EV = −$3; EV = $0; EV = $4; EV = $49.
  d. 9%; $90.

20-6   a. $D/A_{\text{J-H}}$ = 50%; $D/A_{\text{M-E}}$ = 67%.

20-7   a. PV cost of owning = −$185,112; PV cost of leasing = −$187,534; Purchase loom.

20-9   b. Percent ownership: Original = 80%; Plan 1 = 53%; Plans 2 and 3 = 57%.
  c. EPS_0 = $0.48; EPS_1 = $0.60; EPS_2 = $0.64; EPS_3 = $0.86.
  d. D/A_0 = 73%; D/A_1 = 13%; D/A_2 = 13%; D/A_3 = 48%.

20-11   a. $11.20.
  b. $907,809,861.
  c. $82.48; $73.73.
  d. 12.70%; 70 basis points.

21-1 P_0 = $37.04.

21-2 P_0 = $43.48.

21-3 $37.04 to $43.48.

21-4   a. 16.8%.
  b. V = $14.93 million.

21-5   NPV = −$6,747.71; Do not purchase.

21-6   a. 14%.
  b. TV = $1,143.4; V = $877.2.

SELECTED EQUATIONS AND DATA

CHAPTER 2

Net cash flow = Net income − Noncash revenues + Noncash charges.

Net cash flow = Net income + Depreciation and amortization.

$$\begin{matrix} \text{Net operating} \\ \text{working capital} \end{matrix} = \begin{matrix} \text{All current} \\ \text{assets} \end{matrix} - \begin{matrix} \text{All current liabilities that} \\ \text{do not charge interest} \end{matrix}.$$

$$\begin{matrix} \text{Net operating} \\ \text{working} \\ \text{capital} \end{matrix} = \left(\begin{matrix} \text{Cash and} \\ \text{marketable} \\ \text{securities} \end{matrix} + \begin{matrix} \text{Accounts} \\ \text{receivable} \end{matrix} + \text{Inventories} \right) - \left(\begin{matrix} \text{Accounts} \\ \text{payable} \end{matrix} + \text{Accruals} \right).$$

Total operating capital = Net operating working capital + Net fixed assets.

NOPAT = EBIT(1 − Tax rate).

Operating cash flow = NOPAT + Depreciation and amortization.

$$\begin{matrix} \text{Gross investment} \\ \text{in operating capital} \end{matrix} = \begin{matrix} \text{Net} \\ \text{investment} \end{matrix} + \begin{matrix} \text{Depreciation} \\ \text{and amortization} \end{matrix}.$$

Free cash flow = Operating cash flow − Gross investment in operating capital.

Free cash flow = NOPAT − Net investment in operating capital.

MVA = Market value of stock − Equity capital supplied by shareholders
  = [(Shares outstanding)(Stock price)] − Total common equity.

EVA = NOPAT − After-tax dollar cost of operating capital
  = (EBIT)(1 − T) − (Operating capital)(After-tax percentage cost of capital).

CHAPTER 3

$$\text{Current ratio} = \frac{\text{Current assets}}{\text{Current liabilities}}.$$

$$\text{Inventory turnover ratio} = \frac{\text{Sales}}{\text{Inventories}}.$$

$$\text{DSO} = \text{Days sales outstanding} = \frac{\text{Receivables}}{\text{Average sales per day}} = \frac{\text{Receivables}}{\text{Annual sales}/365}.$$

$$\text{Fixed assets turnover ratio} = \frac{\text{Sales}}{\text{Net fixed assets}}.$$

$$\text{Total assets turnover ratio} = \frac{\text{Sales}}{\text{Total assets}}.$$

$$\text{Debt ratio} = \frac{\text{Total debt}}{\text{Total assets}}.$$

$$\text{D/A} = \frac{\text{D/E}}{1 + \text{D/E}}.$$

$$\text{Debt ratio} = 1 - \frac{1}{\text{Equity multiplier}}.$$

$$\text{D/E} = \frac{\text{D/A}}{1 - \text{D/A}}.$$

$$\text{Times-interest-earned (TIE) ratio} = \frac{\text{EBIT}}{\text{Interest charges}}.$$

$$\text{EBITDA coverage ratio} = \frac{\text{EBITDA} + \text{Lease payments}}{\text{Interest} + \text{Principal payments} + \text{Lease payments}}.$$

$$\text{Profit margin on sales} = \frac{\text{Net income available to common stockholders}}{\text{Sales}}.$$

$$\text{Basic earning power ratio} = \frac{\text{EBIT}}{\text{Total assets}}.$$

$$\text{Return on total assets (ROA)} = \frac{\text{Net income available to common stockholders}}{\text{Total assets}}.$$

$$\text{ROA} = \left(\begin{array}{c}\text{Profit} \\ \text{margin}\end{array}\right)(\text{Total assets turnover}).$$

$$\text{Return on common equity (ROE)} = \frac{\text{Net income available to common stockholders}}{\text{Common equity}}.$$

$$\text{ROE} = \text{ROA} \times \text{Equity multiplier}$$

$$= \left(\begin{array}{c}\text{Profit} \\ \text{margin}\end{array}\right)\left(\begin{array}{c}\text{Total assets} \\ \text{turnover}\end{array}\right)\left(\begin{array}{c}\text{Equity} \\ \text{multiplier}\end{array}\right)$$

$$= \left(\frac{\text{Net income}}{\text{Sales}}\right)\left(\frac{\text{Sales}}{\text{Total assets}}\right)\left(\frac{\text{Total assets}}{\text{Common equity}}\right).$$

$$\text{Return on investors' capital} = \frac{\text{Net income} + \text{Interest}}{\text{Debt} + \text{Equity}}.$$

$$\text{Price/earnings (P/E) ratio} = \frac{\text{Price per share}}{\text{Earnings per share}}.$$

$$\text{Price/cash flow ratio} = \frac{\text{Price per share}}{\text{Cash flow per share}}.$$

$$\text{Book value per share} = \frac{\text{Common equity}}{\text{Shares outstanding}}.$$

$$\text{Market/book (M/B) ratio} = \frac{\text{Market price per share}}{\text{Book value per share}}.$$

$$\text{EVA} = \text{Net income} - [(\%\text{ Cost of equity})(\text{Dollars of equity capital})].$$

$$\text{EVA} = (\text{ROE} - \%\text{ Cost of equity})(\text{Dollars of equity capital}).$$

CHAPTER 4

$$k = k^* + IP + DRP + LP + MRP.$$

$$k_{RF} = k^* + IP.$$

$$IP_n = \frac{I_1 + I_2 + \cdots + I_n}{n}.$$

CHAPTER 5

Dollar return = Amount received − Amount invested.

$$\text{Percentage rate of return} = \frac{\text{Amount received} - \text{Amount invested}}{\text{Amount invested}}.$$

$$\text{Expected rate of return} = \hat{k} = \sum_{i=1}^{n} P_i k_i.$$

$$\text{Variance} = \sigma^2 = \sum_{i=1}^{n} (k_i - \hat{k})^2 P_i.$$

$$\text{Standard deviation} = \sigma = \sqrt{\sum_{i=1}^{n} (k_i - \hat{k})^2 P_i}.$$

$$\text{Estimated } \sigma = S = \sqrt{\frac{\sum_{t=1}^{n} (\bar{k}_t - \bar{k}_{Avg})^2}{n - 1}}.$$

$$CV = \frac{\sigma}{\hat{k}}.$$

$$\hat{k}_p = \sum_{i=1}^{n} w_i \hat{k}_i.$$

$$\sigma_p = \sqrt{\sum_{j=1}^{n} (k_{pj} - \hat{k}_p)^2 P_j}.$$

$$b_p = \sum_{i=1}^{n} w_i b_i.$$

$$SML = k_i = k_{RF} + (k_M - k_{RF})b_i.$$

$$RP_i = (k_M - k_{RF})b_i = (RP_M)b_i.$$

CHAPTER 6

$$FV_n = PV(1 + i)^n.$$

$$PV = \frac{FV_n}{(1 + i)^n}.$$

$$FVA_n = PMT \sum_{t=1}^{n} (1 + i)^{n-t}.$$

$$FVA_n(\text{Annuity due}) = FVA_n(1 + i).$$

$$PVA_n = \sum_{t=1}^{n} \frac{PMT}{(1 + i)^t}.$$

$$PVA_n(\text{Annuity due}) = PVA_n(1 + i) = \sum_{t=1}^{n} \frac{PMT}{(1 + i)^{t-1}}.$$

$$PV (\text{Perpetuity}) = \frac{\text{Payment}}{\text{Interest rate}} = \frac{PMT}{i}.$$

$$PV_{\text{Uneven stream}} = \sum_{t=1}^{n} \frac{CF_t}{(1 + i)^t}.$$

$$FV_{\text{Uneven stream}} = \sum_{t=1}^{n} CF_t(1 + i)^{n-t}.$$

$$FV_n = PV\left(1 + \frac{i_{\text{Nom}}}{m}\right)^{mn}.$$

$$\text{Effective annual rate} = \left(1 + \frac{i_{\text{Nom}}}{m}\right)^{m} - 1.0.$$

$$\text{Periodic rate} = i_{\text{Nom}}/m.$$

$$i_{\text{Nom}} = APR = (\text{Periodic rate})(m).$$

CHAPTER 7

$$V_B = \sum_{t=1}^{N} \frac{INT}{(1 + k_d)^t} + \frac{M}{(1 + k_d)^N}.$$

$$V_B = \sum_{t=1}^{2N} \frac{INT/2}{(1 + k_d/2)^t} + \frac{M}{(1 + k_d/2)^{2N}}.$$

$$\text{Price of callable bond} = \sum_{t=1}^{N} \frac{INT}{(1 + k_d)^t} + \frac{\text{Call price}}{(1 + k_d)^N}.$$

$$\text{Current yield} = \frac{\text{Annual interest}}{\text{Bond's current price}}.$$

CHAPTER 8

$$\hat{P}_0 = \text{PV of expected future dividends} = \sum_{t=1}^{\infty} \frac{D_t}{(1 + k_s)^t}.$$

$$\hat{P}_0 = \frac{D_0(1 + g)}{k_s - g} = \frac{D_1}{k_s - g}.$$

$$\hat{k}_s = \frac{D_1}{P_0} + g.$$

For a constant growth stock, $\hat{P}_n = P_0(1 + g)^n$.

$$\text{Horizon value} = \hat{P}_N = \frac{D_{N+1}}{k_s - g}.$$

$$V_{\text{Company}} = \frac{FCF_1}{(1 + WACC)^1} + \frac{FCF_2}{(1 + WACC)^2} + \cdots + \frac{FCF_\infty}{(1 + WACC)^\infty}.$$

$$\text{Terminal value} = V_{\text{Company at } t=N} = \frac{FCF_{N+1}}{WACC - g_{FCF}}.$$

$$FCF = EBIT(1 - T) + \text{Depreciation} - \frac{\text{Capital}}{\text{expenditures}} - \frac{\text{Change in}}{\text{net operating}}.$$
$$\text{working capital}$$

$$V_p = \frac{D_p}{k_p}.$$

$$\hat{k}_p = \frac{D_p}{V_p}.$$

CHAPTER 9

After-tax component cost of debt = $k_d(1 - T)$.

Component cost of preferred stock = $k_p = \dfrac{D_p}{P_p}$.

$k_s = \hat{k}_s = k_{RF} + RP = D_1/P_0 + g$.

$k_s = k_{RF} + (k_M - k_{RF})b_i$.

k_s = Bond yield + Risk premium.

$k_e = \dfrac{D_1}{P_0(1 - F)} + g$.

$M(1 - F) = \displaystyle\sum_{t=1}^{N} \dfrac{INT(1 - T)}{(1 + k_d)^t} + \dfrac{M}{(1 + k_d)^N}$.

g = (Retention rate)(ROE) = (1.0 − Payout rate)(ROE).

$RE_{Breakpoint} = \dfrac{\text{Addition to retained earnings}}{\text{Equity fraction}}$.

WACC = $w_d k_d(1 - T) + w_p k_p + w_c k_s$.

CHAPTER 10

Payback = Year before full recovery + $\dfrac{\text{Unrecovered cost at start of year}}{\text{Cash flow during year}}$.

$NPV = CF_0 + \dfrac{CF_1}{(1 + k)^1} + \dfrac{CF_2}{(1 + k)^2} + \cdots + \dfrac{CF_n}{(1 + k)^n}$

$= \displaystyle\sum_{t=0}^{n} \dfrac{CF_t}{(1 + k)^t}$.

$IRR: CF_0 + \dfrac{CF_1}{(1 + IRR)^1} + \dfrac{CF_2}{(1 + IRR)^2} + \cdots + \dfrac{CF_n}{(1 + IRR)^n} = 0$

$\displaystyle\sum_{t=0}^{n} \dfrac{CF_t}{(1 + IRR)^t} = 0$.

MIRR: PV costs = PV terminal value

$\displaystyle\sum_{t=0}^{n} \dfrac{COF}{(1 + k)^t} = \dfrac{\displaystyle\sum_{t=0}^{n} CIF_t(1 + k)^{n-t}}{(1 + MIRR)^n}$

$PV \text{ costs} = \dfrac{TV}{(1 + MIRR)^n}$.

CHAPTER 13

Return on invested capital = $\dfrac{NOPAT}{Capital}$.

EBIT = $PQ - VQ - F$.

$$Q_{BE} = \frac{F}{P - V}.$$

$$\text{EPS} = \frac{(S - FC - VC - I)(1 - T)}{\text{Shares outstanding}} = \frac{(\text{EBIT} - I)(1 - T)}{\text{Shares outstanding}}.$$

$$b = b_U\,[1 + (1 - T)(D/E)].$$

$$b_U = b/[1 + (1 - T)(D/E)].$$

$$D/E = \frac{D/A}{1 - D/A}.$$

$$k_s = k_{RF} + \text{Premium for business risk} + \text{Premium for financial risk}.$$

CHAPTER 14

$$\text{Dividends} = \text{Net income} - [(\text{Target equity ratio})\,(\text{Total capital budget})].$$

CHAPTER 15

$$\frac{\text{Inventory conversion}}{\text{period}} = \frac{\text{Inventory}}{\text{Sales}/365}.$$

$$\frac{\text{Receivables collection}}{\text{period}} = \text{DSO} = \frac{\text{Receivables}}{\text{Sales}/365}.$$

$$\text{Payables deferral period} = \frac{\text{Payables}}{\text{Cost of goods sold}/365}.$$

$$\frac{\text{Inventory}}{\text{conversion}} + \frac{\text{Receivables}}{\text{collection}} - \frac{\text{Payables}}{\text{deferral}} = \frac{\text{Cash}}{\text{conversion.}}$$
$$\text{period} \qquad \text{period} \qquad \text{period} \qquad \text{cycle}$$

$$\text{A/R} = \frac{\text{Credit sales}}{\text{per day}} \times \frac{\text{Length of}}{\text{collection period}}.$$

$$\text{ADS} = \text{Annual sales}/365 = \frac{(\text{Units sold})(\text{Sales price})}{365}.$$

$$\text{Receivables} = (\text{ADS})(\text{DSO}).$$

CHAPTER 16

$$\text{Nominal annual cost of payables} = \frac{\text{Discount percent}}{100 - \dfrac{\text{Discount}}{\text{percent}}} \times \frac{365}{\dfrac{\text{Days credit is}}{\text{outstanding}} - \dfrac{\text{Discount}}{\text{period}}}.$$

$$\text{Simple interest rate per day} = \frac{\text{Nominal rate}}{\text{Days in year}}.$$

$$\text{Simple interest charge for period} = (\text{Days in period})(\text{Rate per day})(\text{Amount of loan}).$$

$$\text{Face value}_{\text{Discount}} = \frac{\text{Funds received}}{1.0 - \text{Nominal rate (decimal)}}.$$

$$\text{Approximate annual rate}_{\text{Add-on}} = \frac{\text{Interest paid}}{(\text{Amount received})/2}.$$

CHAPTER 17

$$\text{AFN} = (A^*/S_0)\Delta S - (L^*/S_0)\Delta S - MS_1(RR).$$

$$\text{Full capacity sales} = \frac{\text{Actual sales}}{\begin{array}{c}\text{Percentage of capacity at}\\ \text{which fixed assets were operated}\end{array}}.$$

$$\text{Target FA/Sales ratio} = \frac{\text{Actual fixed assets}}{\text{Full capacity sales}}.$$

$$\text{Required level of FA} = (\text{Target FA/Sales ratio})(\text{Projected sales}).$$

CHAPTER 18

$$\text{Exercise value} = \begin{array}{c}\text{Current price}\\ \text{of stock}\end{array} - \text{Strike price}.$$

$$V = P[N(d_1)] - Xe^{-k_{RF}t}[N(d_2)].$$

$$d_1 = \frac{\ln(P/X) + [k_{RF} + (\sigma^2/2)]t}{\sigma\sqrt{t}}.$$

$$d_2 = d_1 - \sigma\sqrt{t}.$$

CHAPTER 19

$$\frac{\text{Forward exchange rate}}{\text{Spot exchange rate}} = \frac{1 + k_h}{1 + k_f}.$$

$$P_h = (P_f)(\text{Spot rate}).$$

$$\text{Spot rate} = \frac{P_h}{P_f}.$$

CHAPTER 20

$$\begin{array}{c}\text{Price paid for}\\ \text{bond with warrants}\end{array} = \begin{array}{c}\text{Straight-debt}\\ \text{value of bond}\end{array} + \begin{array}{c}\text{Value of}\\ \text{warrants}\end{array}.$$

$$\text{Conversion price} = P_c = \frac{\text{Par value of bond given up}}{\text{Shares received}}.$$

$$\text{Conversion ratio} = CR = \frac{\text{Par value of bond given up}}{P_c}.$$

INDEX

FREQUENTLY USED SYMBOLS

APR	Annual percentage rate
A/R	Accounts receivable
b	Beta coefficient, a measure of an asset's riskiness
CAPM	Capital Asset Pricing Model
CF	Cash flow; CF_t is the cash flow in Period t
CR	Conversion ratio
CV	Coefficient of variation
D	Dividend per share of stock (DPS); D_t is the dividend in Period t
DCF	Discounted cash flow
DRP	Default risk premium
DSO	Days sales outstanding
EAR	Effective annual rate, EFF%
EBIT	Earnings before interest and taxes = net operating income
EPS	Earnings per share
EVA	Economic value added
F	(1) Fixed operating costs
	(2) Flotation cost
FV_n	Future value for Year n
FVA_n	Future value of an annuity for n years
g	Growth rate in earnings, dividends, and stock prices
i	Interest rate; also referred to as k
I	Interest rate key on some calculators
INT	Interest payment in dollars
IP	Inflation premium
IRR	Internal rate of return
k	(1) A percentage discount rate, or cost of capital; also referred to as i
	(2) Required rate of return
$\bar{k}$	"k bar," historic, or realized, rate of return
$\hat{k}$	"k hat," an expected rate of return
k*	Real risk-free rate of interest
k_d	Cost of debt
k_e	Cost of new common stock (outside equity)
k_f	Interest rate in foreign country
k_h	Interest rate in home country
k_j	Cost of capital for an individual firm or security
k_M	Cost of capital for "the market," or an "average" stock
k_{Nom}	Nominal rate of interest; also referred to as i_{Nom}
k_p	(1) Cost of preferred stock
	(2) Portfolio's return
k_{RF}	Rate of return on a risk-free security
k_s	(1) Cost of retained earnings
	(2) Required return on a stock
LP	Liquidity premium
M	Maturity value of a bond